Greece

The complete guide, thoroughly up-to-date

Packed with details that will make your trip

The must-see sights, off and on the beaten path

What to see, what to skip

Mix-and-match vacation itineraries

City strolls, countryside adventures

Smart lodging and dining options

Essential local do's and taboos

Transportation tips, distances and directions

Key contacts, savvy travel tips

When to go, what to pack

Clear, accurate, easy-to-use maps

Books to read, videos to watch, background essays

Fodor's Travel Publications, Inc.
New York • Toronto • London • Sydney • Auckland
www.fodors.com

Fodor's Greece

EDITOR: Robert I. C. Fisher

Editorial Contributors: Toula Bogdanos, Stephen Brewer, David Brown, Jeffrey Carson, Melissa Dailey, Daniel Gorney, Kerin Hope, Lea Lane, Diana Farr Lewis, Terrence Moloney, Mark J. Rose, Helayne Schiff, M. T. Schwartzman (Gold Guide editor), B. Samantha Stenzel, Catherine Vanderpool

Editorial Production: Melissa Klurman

Maps: David Linroth, Inc., *cartographer*; Steven Amsterdam and Robert Blake, *map editors*

Design: Fabrizio La Rocca, *creative director*; Guido Caroti, *associate art director*; Jolie Novak, *photo editor*

Production/Manufacturing: Mike Costa

Cover Photograph: Sylvain Grandadam/Tony Stone Images

Copyright

Special Sales

Fodor's Travel Publications are available at special discounts for bulk purchases for sales promotions or premiums. Special editions, including personalized covers, excerpts of existing guides, and corporate imprints, can be created in large quantities for special needs. For more information, contact your local bookseller or write to Special Markets, Fodor's Travel Publications, 201 East 50th Street, New York, NY 10022. Inquiries from Canada should be directed to your local Canadian bookseller or sent to Random House of Canada, Ltd., Marketing Department, 2775 Matheson Boulevard East, Mississauga, Ontario L4W 4P7. Inquiries from the United Kingdom should be sent to Fodor's Travel Publications, 20 Vauxhall Bridge Road, London SW1V 2SA, England.

PRINTED IN THE UNITED STATES OF AMERICA

10 9 8 7 6 5 4 3 2 1

CONTENTS

Maps

ON THE ROAD WITH FODOR'S

WHEN I PLAN A VACATION, the first thing I do is cast around among my friends and colleagues to find someone who's just been where I'm going. That's because there's no substitute for a recommendation from a good friend who knows your tastes, your budget, and your circumstances, someone who's just been there. Unfortunately, such friends are few and far between. So it's nice to know that there's *Fodor's Greece*.

In the first place, this book won't stay home when you hit the road. It will accompany you every step of the way, steering you away from wrong turns and wrong choices and never expecting a thing in return. Most important of all, it's written and assiduously updated by the kind of people you *would* hit up for travel tips if you knew them. They're as choosy as your pickiest friend, except they've probably seen a lot more of Greece. In these pages, they don't send you chasing down every town and sight in the land of Homer but have instead selected the best ones, the ones that are worthy of your time and money. To make it easy for you to put it all together in the time you have, they've created short, medium, and long itineraries and, in cities, neighborhood walks that you can mix and match in a snap. Will this be the vacation of your dreams? We hope so.

About Our Writers

Our success in helping to make your trip the best of all possible vacations is a credit to the hard work of our extraordinary writers.

Journalist **Toula Bogdanos** has savored many an island sunset over ouzo and octopus and can dance a mean tsifteli under duress. She teaches media and cultural studies at Mediterranean College in Athens and reports from Greece's capital for the *New York Times* and other publications.

Stephen Brewer is a New York–based writer who travels to Crete and other Mediterranean shores for various national magazines and guidebooks. He's climbed many a terrifying hairpin bend on the roads between Knossos and Phaestos and has always wondered if the pained expressions of hardy travelers along these roads, fearing their last hour has struck, once inspired Domenikos Theotokopoulos, the famed El Greco, whose birthplace was Crete.

For more than 25 years, native New Yorker **Jeffrey Carson** has lived on Paros, Greece, where he teaches and writes—when not swimming in the dazzling Mediterranean. Most recently, he edited *The Collected Poems of Odysseus Elytis*.

More than occasionally, **Lea Lane** had to resist buying a single rose and bearing it proudly through the streets of Greek villages, an emblem of her pleasure in the moment. She adores the warmth of the gregarious natives and discovered quickly that the word for foreigner and guest (*xenos*) is one and the same for them. Based in the NYC area, Lea contributes to major guidebooks, writes a travel column, and has visited just about 100 countries. She has hopped over to Greece at a moment's notice for 27 years and expects to be discovering new islands there at least 27 more.

Between bouts of learning the classic texts of ancient Greece and the minutiae of modern law, Toronto-based **Terrence Moloney** explored the Greek countryside by foot, bus, train, boat, and even endured the horrors of a Pan-Hellenic odyssey on a not-so-trusty 50cc scooter. He claims degrees in Classics from the University of Toronto and a degree in law from Queen's University, Kingston.

B. Samantha Stenzel is a free-lance travel and food writer who made Athens her home base for 13 years and now divides her time between Chicago and Greece. She heads up her own guided tour company, Mediterranean Odysseys, and often takes small groups on journeys through Greece.

Many thanks to **Eve Tsirigotakis** at the Greek National Tourist Organization in New York City for all of her help.

Connections

We're pleased that the American Society of Travel Agents continues to endorse Fodor's as its guidebook of choice. ASTA is the world's largest and most influential travel trade association, operating in more than 170 countries, with 27,000 members pledged to adhere to a strict code of ethics reflecting the Society's motto, "Integrity in Travel." ASTA shares Fodor's devotion to providing smart, honest travel information and advice to travelers, and we've long recommended that our readers—even those who have guidebooks and traveling friends—consult ASTA member agents for the experience and professionalism they bring to your vacation planning.

On Fodor's Web site (www.fodors.com), check out the new Resource Center, an online companion to the Gold Guide section of this book, complete with useful hot links to related sites. In our forums, you can also get lively advice from other travelers and more great tips from Fodor's experts worldwide.

How to Use This Book

Organization

Up front is the **Gold Guide,** an easy-to-use section arranged alphabetically by topic. Under each listing you'll find tips and information that will help you accomplish what you need to in Greece. You'll also find addresses and telephone numbers of organizations and companies that offer destination-related services and detailed information and publications.

The first chapter in the guide, **Destination: Greece** helps get you in the mood for your trip. New and Noteworthy cues you in on trends and happenings, What's Where gets you oriented, Pleasures and Pastimes describes the activities and sights that make this country so unique, Fodor's Choice showcases our top picks, and Festivals and Seasonal Events alerts you to special events you'll want to seek out.

Exploring chapters in this guide book are arranged geographically. *Fodor's Greece* begins with a chapter on Athens and proceeds to central, southern, and northern Greece, taking in the famous island destinations and Crete. Each chapter covers exploring the sights, then highlights regional topics such as dining and lodging, shop-

ping, outdoor activities and sports, and arts and nightlife.

In the Athens chapter, we first let you in on the big picture, then follow with separate neighborhood sections that suggest—in A Good Walk—a wonderful way to discover each, then list all the neighborhood sights alphabetically in Sights to See. Each regional chapter is divided by geographical area; within each area, towns are covered in logical geographical order—with major cities, such as Corfu town and Thessaloniki handled like Athens, complete with Good Walks and Sights to See—and attractive stretches of road and minor points of interest between them are indicated by the designation *En Route.* And within town sections, all restaurants and lodgings are grouped.

To help you decide what to visit in the time you have, all chapters begin with our recommended itineraries. The **A to Z section** that ends all chapters covers getting there and getting around. It also provides helpful contacts and essential resources. At the end of the book you'll find **Portraits,** with an historical dateline, informative essays about Greek architecture and mythology, a glossary of technical terms, and Greek vocabulary, followed by suggestions for pretrip research, from recommended reading to movies on tape that use Greece as a backdrop.

Icons and Symbols

★	Our special recommendations
✕	Restaurant
🏠	Lodging establishment
✕🏠	Lodging establishment whose restaurant warrants a special trip
🛆	Campgrounds
🐥	Good for kids (rubber duck)
☞	Sends you to another section of the guide for more information
✉	Address
☎	Telephone number
FAX	Fax number
☉	Opening and closing times
💷	Admission prices (those we give apply to adults; substantially reduced fees are almost always available for children, students, and senior citizens)

Tying each chapter together are Fodor's **easy-to-use maps.** Each sight (city, town, or attraction) is marked by a circle with a number—simply connect the dots and you have the ideal city walk or country

drive. Numbers in white and black circles—
③ and ❸, for example—that appear on
the maps, in the margins, and within the
tours correspond to one another, for easy
reference.

Dining and Lodging

The restaurants and lodgings we list are
the cream of the crop in each price range.
Price charts appear in the Pleasures and
Pastimes section that follows each chapter introduction.

Hotel Facilities

We always list the facilities that are available—but we don't specify whether you'll
be charged extra to use them: When pric-
ing accommodations, always ask what's
included. In addition, assume that all
rooms have private baths unless noted
otherwise. In addition, when you book a
room, be sure to mention if you have a dis-
ability or are traveling with children, if you
prefer a private bath or a certain type of
bed, or if you have specific dietary needs
or other concerns.

Assume that hotels operate on the **European Plan** (EP, with no meals) unless we
specify that they include breakfast in their
room rate or if half- or full-board is required. When booking it is always best to
confirm how and if meals are offered by
the hotel within their room rate.

Restaurant Reservations and Dress Codes

Reservations are always a good idea; we
mention them only when they're essential
or are not accepted. Book as far ahead as
you can, and reconfirm as soon as you arrive. Unless otherwise noted, the restaurants listed are open daily for lunch and
dinner. We mention dress only when men
are required to wear a jacket or a jacket
and tie. Look for an overview of local
dining-out specialties and habits in the
Gold Guide and in the Pleasures and Pastimes section that follows each chapter introduction.

Credit Cards

The following abbreviations are used: **AE,**
American Express; **DC,** Diners Club; **MC,**
MasterCard; and **V,** Visa.

Don't Forget to Write

You can use this book in the confidence
that all prices and opening times are based
on information supplied to us at press
time; Fodor's cannot accept responsibility for any errors. Time inevitably brings
changes, so always confirm information
when it matters—especially if you're making a detour to visit a specific place.

Were the restaurants we recommended
as described? Did our hotel picks exceed
your expectations? Did you find a museum
we recommended a waste of time? Keeping a travel guide fresh and up-to-date is
a big job, and we welcome your feed-
back, positive *and* negative. If you have
complaints, we'll look into them and re-
vise our entries when the facts warrant it.
If you've discovered a special place that
we haven't included, we'll pass the information along to our correspondents and
have them check it out. So send us your
thoughts via e-mail at editors@fodors.com
(specifying the name of the book on the
subject line) or on paper in care of the
Greece editor at Fodor's, 201 East 50th
Street, New York, New York 10022. In
the meantime, have a wonderful trip!

Karen Cure
Editorial Director

Black Sea

T U R K E Y

Xanthi
THRACE
Makri

Thassos

Samothrace

Istanbul

Sea of
Marmara

N

Limnos

0   50 miles
0   75 km

Aegean Sea

NORTHERN ISLANDS

Lesbos

T U R K E Y

Chios

Andros   A E G E A N

    I S L A N D S

Tinos

Izmir (Smyrna)

Samos

Ikaria

Siros

Mykonos
Delos

Patmos

Paros
Sifnos

Naxos

Leros
Kalimnos

Bodrum

Kos

C Y C L A D E S   Amorgos

Kos

Ios   Astypalea

Nissyros

Symi

Rhodes

Santorini   Anafi

D O D E C A N E S E

Tilos
Chalki

Rhodes

Sea of Crete

Karpathos

CRETE
Heraklion

Ay.
Nikolaos

Kassos

Mediterranean Sea

Ierapetra

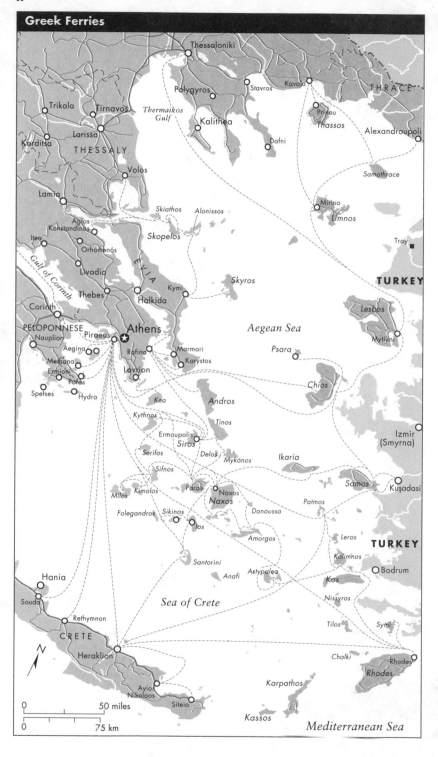

Greek Ferries

SMART TRAVEL TIPS A TO Z

Basic Information on Traveling in Greece, Savvy Tips to Make Your Trip a Breeze, and Companies and Organizations to Contact

ADDRESSES

To make finding your way around as easy as possible, it's wise to learn to recognize letters in the Greek alphabet. Most areas, even Athens, have few signs in English. Sometimes there are several spelling variations in English for the same place: Agios or Ayios, Georgios or Yiorgos. Also, the English version may be quite different from the Greek, or even what locals use informally: Corfu is known as Kerkyra; island capitals are often just called Chora (town) no matter what their formal title; Vasilissis Sofias (Queen Sofia), a main Athens boulevard, now reads Venizelou on maps since royalty was banned, but if you ask for that name, no one will know what you're talking about. A street may change names several times, and a city may have more than one street by the same name, so it's best to know the district you're headed for, or a major landmark nearby, especially if you're taking a taxi.

AIR TRAVEL

BOOKING YOUR FLIGHT

Price is just one factor to consider when booking a flight: Frequency of service and even a carrier's safety record are often just as important. Major airlines offer the greatest number of departures. Smaller airlines—including regional and no-frills airlines—usually have a limited number of flights daily. On the other hand, so-called low-cost airlines usually are cheaper, and their fares impose fewer restrictions, such as advance-purchase requirements. Safety-wise, low-cost carriers as a group have a good history—about equal to that of major carriers.

When you book, **look for nonstop flights** and **remember that "direct" flights stop at least once.** Try to **avoid connecting flights,** which require a change of plane. Two airlines may jointly operate a connecting flight, so ask if your airline operates every segment—you may find that your preferred carrier flies you only part of the way. International flights on a country's flag carrier are almost always nonstop; U.S. airlines often fly direct.

Ask your airline if it offers electronic ticketing, which eliminates all paperwork. There's no ticket to pick up or misplace. You go directly to the gate and give the agent your confirmation number. There's no worry about waiting on line at the airport while precious minutes tick by.

CARRIERS

When flying internationally, you must usually choose between a domestic carrier, the national flag carrier of the country you are visiting, and a foreign carrier from a third country. You may, for example, choose to fly Olympic Airways to Greece. National flag carriers have the greatest number of nonstops. Domestic carriers may have better connections to your home town and serve a greater number of gateway cities. Third-party carriers may have a price advantage.

➤ MAJOR AIRLINES: **Delta** (☎ 800/241–4141). **Northwest** (☎ 800/225–2525). **Olympic Airways** (☎ 212/838–3600; 800/223–1226 outside New York). **United** (☎ 800/241–6522).

European national airlines that fly to Athens from the United States and Canada via their home country's major cities include the following: **Air France** (☎ 800/237–2747). **Alitalia** (☎ 800/223–5730). **Austrian Airlines** (☎ 800/843–0002). **British Airways** (☎ 800/247–9297). **Finnair** (☎ 800/950–5000). **Iberia Airlines** (☎ 800/772–4642). **KLM Royal Dutch Airlines** (☎ 800/777–5553). **LOT Polish Airlines** (☎ 212/869–1074). **Lufthansa** (☎ 800/645–3880).

Sabena Belgian World Airlines (☎ 800/955–2000). **Swissair** (☎ 800/221–4750). **TAP Air Portugal** (☎ 800/221–7370). **Virgin Atlantic** (☎ 800/862–8621). Remember that these are connecting flights that include at least one stop and may require a change of planes.

➤ SMALLER AIRLINES: **Tower Air** (☎ 718/553–8500 or 800/348–6937).

➤ FROM THE U.K.: **Air UK** (☎ 0345/ 666777 or 01293/535353). **British Airways** (☎ 0181/897–4000 or 0345/222–111 outside London). **Easy Jet** (☎ 01582/702900 or 0044/870– 600000). **Olympic Airways** (☎ 0171/ 409–3400).

➤ DOMESTIC AIRLINES: **Olympic Airways** (main Athens ticket offices at ✉ Fillelinon 19, near Syntagma Sq., and Syngrou 96, ☎ 01/966–6666 for reservations; 01/936–3363 through 01/936–3366 for daily arrival and departure information, FAX 01/966– 6111). **Air Greece** (✉ Nikis 20, Athens ☎ 01/325–5011, FAX 01/325–5015); **Cronus Airlines** (✉ Othonos 10, Athens, ☎ 01/331–5515, FAX 01/331– 5505); **LTU International Airways** (✉ Filellinon 14, Athens, ☎ 01/323– 4414; 01/323–0514 booking department, FAX 01/324–1027; 01/322–2789 booking).

CHARTERS

Charters usually have the lowest fares but are the least dependable. Departures are infrequent and seldom on time, flights can be delayed for up to 48 hours or can be canceled for any reason up to 10 days before you're scheduled to leave. Itineraries and prices can change after you've booked your flight.

In the U.S., the Department of Transportation's Aviation Consumer Protection Division has jurisdiction over charters and provides a certain degree of protection. The DOT requires that money paid to charter operators be held in escrow, so if you can't pay with a credit card, **always make your check payable to a charter carrier's escrow account.** The name of the bank should be in the charter contract. If you have any problems with a charter operator, contact the DOT (☞ Airline Complaints, *below*). If

you buy a charter package that includes both air and land arrangements, remember that the escrow requirement applies only to the air component.

CONSOLIDATORS

Consolidators buy tickets for scheduled international flights at reduced rates from the airlines, then sell them at prices that beat the best fare available directly from the airlines, usually without restrictions. Sometimes you can even get your money back if you need to return the ticket. Carefully read the fine print detailing penalties for changes and cancellations, and **confirm your consolidator reservation with the airline.**

➤ CONSOLIDATORS: **Cheap Tickets** (☎ 800/377–1000). **Discount Travel Network** (☎ 800/576–1600). **Unitravel** (☎ 800/325–2222). **Up & Away Travel** (☎ 212/889–2345). **World Travel Network** (☎ 800/409– 6753).

CUTTING COSTS

The least-expensive airfares to Greece are priced for round-trip travel and usually must be purchased in advance. It's smart to **call a number of airlines, and when you are quoted a good price, book it on the spot**—the same fare may not be available the next day. Airlines generally allow you to change your return date for a fee. If you don't use your ticket, you can apply the cost toward the purchase of a new ticket, again for a small charge. However, most low-fare tickets are nonrefundable. To get the lowest airfare, **check different routings.** Compare prices of flights to and from different airports if your destination or home city has more than one gateway. Also price off-peak flights, which may be significantly less expensive.

Travel agents, especially those who specialize in finding the lowest fares (☞ Discounts & Deals, *below*), can be especially helpful when booking a plane ticket. When you're quoted a price, **ask your agent if the price is likely to get any lower.** Good agents know the seasonal fluctuations of airfares and can usually anticipate a sale or fare war. However, waiting can be risky: The fare could go *up* as seats become scarce, and you may wait so long that your preferred flight sells out. A wait-and-see strategy works best if your plans are flexible. If you must arrive and depart on certain dates, don't delay.

DOMESTIC FLIGHTS

The frequency of flights varies according to the time of year, and it is essential to book well in advance for summer or for festivals and holidays, especially on the many three-day weekends. Domestic flights are a good deal for many destinations. In summer 1998 the one-way Athens–Rhodes fare was 28,400 dr.; to Corfu, 24,200 dr.; to Santorini, 25,700 dr.; and to Heraklion, 25,400 dr. This includes the Spata airport tax (6,900 dr. in 1998) tacked onto every flight in order to fund construction of the new Athens airport. Occasionally, there are discounts for early morning flights. Unless the flight is part of an international journey, the baggage allowance is only 33 pounds (15 kilograms) per passenger.

Scheduled (i.e., nonchartered) domestic air travel in Greece is provided predominantly by **Olympic Airways,** which operates out of Athens's West Terminal. There is service from Athens to Alexandroupolis, Ioannina, Kastoria, Kavala, Kozani, Preveza, and Thessaloniki, all on the mainland; Kalamata in the Peloponnese; the Aegean islands: Astypalaia, Karpathos, Kassos, Kythira, Crete (Hania, Heraklion, and Sitia), Chios, Ikaria, Kos, Lesbos (listed as Mytilini in Greek), Limnos, Leros, Milos, Mykonos, Naxos, Paros, Rhodes, Samos, Skiathos, Syros, Skyros, Kastellorizo (only via Rhodes), and Santorini; Corfu (called Kerkyra in Greek), Kefalonia, and Zakynthos in the Ionian Sea. Flights also depart from Thessaloniki for Hania, Chios, Heraklion, Ioannina, Corfu, Limnos, Lesbos, Rhodes, and Samos. Interisland flights, depending on the season, include the following: from Chios to Lesbos, Heraklio, Rhodes, Mykonos (summer only), and Santorini (summer only); from Karpathos to Kassos, Rhodes, and Santorini (winter only); between Kefalonia and Zakynthos in winter; from Lesbos to Chios, Lim-

nos, and Samos (winter); and from Rhodes to Heraklion, Karpathos, Kassos, Kastellorizo, and Mykonos, as well as Kos (summer only). All domestic flights are no-smoking.

If you are traveling to an island that is six or fewer hours away by boat, you may want to forego air travel, as throughout 1998 Olympic Airways passengers suffered numerous delays and cancellations, due to work stoppages over the company's impending privatization.

For those traveling to Thessaloniki, a good alternative is **Cronus Airlines,** which has regular scheduled flights from Athens's East Terminal at cheaper prices than Olympic.

Other airlines flying within Greece include **Air Greece,** which has scheduled flights from Athens to Heraklion, Hania, Rhodes, Thessaloniki, and Samos, as well as between these destinations, and **LTU International Airways,** which in summer operates several flights between points in Greece such as Rhodes and Kos or Athens and Samos.

FLYING TIMES

Flying time to Athens is 8 hours from New York, 10 hours from Chicago, and 14 hours from Los Angeles.

HOW TO COMPLAIN

If your baggage goes astray or your flight goes awry, complain right away. Most carriers require that you **file a claim immediately.**

➤ AIRLINE COMPLAINTS: U.S. Department of Transportation **Aviation Consumer Protection Division** (✉ C-75, Room 4107, Washington, DC 20590, ☎ 202/366–2220). **Federal Aviation Administration Consumer Hotline** (☎ 800/322–7873).

AIRPORTS & TRANSFERS

AIRPORTS

Athens's major gateway is **Ellinikon Airport,** which has two terminals. The West Terminal serves **Olympic Airways** international and domestic flights only; the East Terminal is used by all other international carriers. At the East Terminal, between the arrivals and departures wings, there is a small, white building from which some charters like Hapag-Lloyd leave. There is also a New Charters terminal, known as Terminal B, located just before the East Terminal on the former U.S. military base.

➤ AIRPORT INFORMATION: **Ellinikon Airport** (☎ west terminal, 011–30–01/936–3363 through 011–30–01/936–3366; east terminal, 011–30–1/969–4466 and 011–30–1/969–4467; charters from East Terminal 01/969–4466; New Charters Terminal 01/969–4531 [departures] and 01/997–2581).

TRANSFERS

In Athens express buses connect the two terminals, Syntagma Square, and Omonia Square (Bus 091), running about every half hour around the clock and leaving from the corner of Stadiou and Aiolou streets off Omonia Square and in front of the main post office between Ermou and Mitropoleos streets at Syntagma Square. From Athens, the bus takes about 30 minutes to reach the East Terminal, the first stop, before continuing to the West Terminal, a few minutes away. To Piraeus Bus 019 runs hourly day and night. The fare is 200 dr., 400 dr. after midnight. The Greek National Tourist Organization (GNTO but known as EOT in Greece) dispenses schedules. It's much easier and faster just to queue at the taxi stands in front of each terminal: 1,000 dr. between terminals, 2,200 dr. to the city center, 2,000 dr. to Piraeus; the price goes up by about two-thirds between midnight and 5 AM. In Thessaloniki, municipal bus 078 picks up travelers about every 40 minutes until midnight (120 dr.) for the 30-minute bus ride into town; its final stop is the train station. At other airports throughout Greece, especially on the islands, public transportation from the airport is either infrequent or nonexistent; ask your hotel to make arrangements or take a taxi, keeping in mind that rates are usually set to fixed destinations.

➤ LIMOUSINES: **Yiannis Yiannakopoulos Limousines** (☎ 094/316–798 mobile phone) provides limousine transfers from the airport to city hotels, as does **Royal Prestige Limou-**sine Service (☎ 094/305–000 mobile phone or 01/988–3221; FAX 01/983–0378), for about 14,000 to 15,000 dr.

BOAT TRAVEL

Cruise ships and ferries to and from the Aegean islands leave from Piraeus, 10 km (6 mi) southwest of Athens, although some northern islands, like Thassos and Limnos, are more easily reached from Thessaloniki. The metro (100 dr. and 150 dr., depending on the zones crossed) is the fastest way to get to and from the Athens city center to the port. Ships for the Ionian islands and Italy sail from ports on the west coast, such as Patras and Igoumenitsa. Timetables change frequently, and boats may be delayed by weather conditions, especially when the northwestern winds called meltemi hit in August, so your plans should be flexible. Travel agents in the cities can call the port to check for you; on the islands, each shipping agency posts a board with departure times, or you can call the port authority (limenarchio), where some English is usually spoken. Buy your tickets several days in advance if you are traveling between July 15 and August 30, when most Greeks vacation, or if you're taking a car. Reserve your return journey soon after you arrive.

The other main port in Attica is Rafina, on the eastern coast, where boats to and from Evia and nearby Cyclades (Kea, Andros, Tinos, Mykonos) dock. To get there, take a KTEL bus (☎ 01/821–0872), which leaves every half hour 5:40 AM to 9:30 PM from Aigyptou Square near Pedion Areos park in Athens. The fare is 460 dr. The bus takes about an hour to get to Rafina, where the bus station is slightly up the hill from the port.

If the boat journey will be more than a few hours, take supplies, as food and refreshments on board are quite expensive, and the washrooms always seem to run out of toilet paper. Most of the shops aboard ferries sell Dramamine, as do the kiosks on the harbors.

The Greek National Tourist Organization (EOT) distributes weekly lists for boats leaving Athens, as well as a handy booklet called "Greek Travel

Routes: Domestic Sea Schedules." Or you can call for a recording (☎ 143, data given in Greek) of the day's domestic departures. At 1 PM, a new recording lists boats leaving the following morning. If you speak Greek, you can call (☎ 01/451–1130) to find out what ships sail abroad from Piraeus that day, but it's easier to ask a travel agency. Outside Athens, contact the port authority nearest you or check with the shipping line's local office. Also see Cruise Travel and Yachting, *below.*

➤ INFORMATION: For information on boats departing from Piraeus, Greece's main port, contact a travel agency or the **Piraeus Port Authority** (☎ 01/451–1311 or 01/422–6000). Boats for some of the Cyclades islands closer to Athens (Andros, Tinos, Mykonos) leave from **Rafina** (port authority ☎ 0294/22300).

FERRIES

On the west coast the local ferry between the island of Corfu and Igoumenitsa runs many times daily in each direction. The coastal highway leads directly to Preveza and the ferry across the strait to Action. You then go via Messolonghi to the Rion–Antirion ferry, which crosses to the Peloponnese and the National Road that leads to Athens. Ferries leave frequently from Piraeus (the port of Athens) to the Saronic Gulf islands, the Cyclades, Dodecanese, and Hania and Heraklion on Crete. Shorter crossings to the Cyclades can be made from the other side of Attica; from Rafina to Andros, Tinos, and Mykonos; and from Lavrio to Kea and Kythnos. You can cross to Turkey from the northeastern Aegean islands, from Lesbos to Dikeli, from Chios to Cesme, and from Samos to Kusadasi. Note that British passport holders must have 10 pounds sterling with them to purchase a visa on landing in Turkey and U.S. citizens need $45. U.S. citizens may purchase the visa beforehand, paying drachmas, at the Turkish consulate in Athens.

There are frequent sails between Italy and Greece—at least seven a day in summer from Brindisi, two each from Bari and Ancona, one from Otranto, and four–five a week from Trieste; all go to Corfu and/or Igoumenitsa and Patras (three a week call at Kefalonia). Some of the shipping lines are Adriatic Ferries, Adriatica, Anek Lines, European Seaways, Hellenic Mediterranean Lines, Karageorgis, Marlines, Minoan Lines, Strintzis Lines, and Ventouris Ferries. A few years ago Superfast Ferries were introduced; although about one-third more expensive, they make the trip from Patras to Ancona in just 16 hours, faster than conventional ferries.

British Ferries operates a weekly service from Venice to Athens on their luxury car ferry *Orient Express* from May to October. For info contact the Venice–Simplon Orient Express (☞ Ferry Companies, *below*). Adriatica Lines services routes from Brindisi to Igoumenitsa and Patras; contact the Stena–Sealink Travel Centre. The Minoan Lines car ferries sail from Ancona and Igoumenitsa and Patras; contact P&O European Ferries. Bookings for summer should be made well in advance and reconfirmed shortly before sailing.

➤ FERRY COMPANIES: **Superfast Ferries** (✉ Amalias 30, Athens 10558, ☎ 01/331–2252, ℻ 01/331–0369) sails from Patras to Ancona in about 16 hours, or Bari in 17 hours, and from Igoumenitsa to Bari in 8½ hours. In Patras (✉ Othonos-Amalias 12, 26223, ☎ 061/622–500, ℻ 061/623–574). In Igoumenitsa (✉ Ag. Apostolon at Neo Limani, 46100, ☎ 0665/28150, ℻ 0665/28156). The **Orient Express** (✉ 20 Upper Ground, London SE1 9PD, ☎ 0171/928–6000) sails from Venice to Simplon. Details about the **Adriatica Lines** services from Brindisi to Corfu, Igoumenitsa and Patras can be obtained from the **Stena–Sealink Travel Centre** (✉ Charter House, Park St., Ashford, Kent TN24 8EX, ☎ 01233/647047) opposite Platform 2 in Victoria Station. Adriatica has several office in Greece; its representative in downtown Athens is Argo Travel (✉ Xenofontos 10, 10557, ☎ 01/324–6000, ℻ 01/324–6489). In Piraeus (✉ Akti Miaouli 85, 18538, ☎ 01/429–0487, ℻ 01/452–4860). For information on the **Minoan Lines** car ferries between Ancona and

THE GOLD GUIDE / SMART TRAVEL TIPS

Igoumenitsa (15 hours) and Patras (20 hours), and between Venice, Igoumenitsa, Corfu and Patras, contact **P&O European Ferries** (⊠ Channel House, Channel View Rd., Dover CT17 9TJ, ☎ 01304/203388). In Greece, Minoan has offices in Heraklion, Piraeus, and Athens (⊠ Vas. Konstantinou 2, Athens 11635, ☎ 01/751–2356, ℻ 01/752–0540). Cars cost about 20,000 dr. on a one-way trip in high season, about 12,000 dr. in low season.

For those continuing beyond Greece through the Mediterranean, **Poseidon Lines** runs a twice-weekly car ferry in summer that leaves Piraeus and circuits Rhodes, Limassol in Cyprus, and Haifa in Israel (⊠ Alkyonidon 32, Kavouri 16673, ☎ 01/965–8300, ℻ 01/965–8310). Another ferry that makes roughly the same journey is operated by **Salamis Lines** (⊠ Filellinon 9, Piraeus 18536, ☎ 01/429–4325, ℻ 01/429–4557).

➤ Turkish Consulate: Turkish consulate (⊠ Vas. Pavlou 22, Palio Psychiko, Athens 115452, ☎ 01/671-4828, ℻ 01/687-6430). Visa hours are 8:30-1 pm.

HYDROFOIL

Flying Dolphin hydrofoils carry passengers from Zea in Piraeus to the Saronic Gulf Islands (Aegina, Hydra, Poros, and Spetses), Cycladic islands, and eastern Peloponnesian ports, including Hermioni, Kyparissi, Kythera, Leonidion, Methana, Monemvassia, Nauplion, Neapolis, and Porto Heli. In summer there is additional service. These boats are somewhat pricey, but fast and fun to ride on. Tickets can be purchased through authorized agents.

➤ RESERVATIONS: To make reservations, absolutely necessary in summer, call the **Ceres Group** (⊠ Akti Themistokleous 8, Piraeus 18536, ☎ 01/428-0001 [10 lines], ℻ 01/428-3526.).

BUS TRAVEL

Organized bus tours can be booked together with hotel reservations by your travel agent. Many tour operators have offices in and around Syntagma and Omonia squares in Athens. Bus tours often depart from Syntagma or adjacent streets.

The EOT distributes KTEL regional bus schedules, including prices for each destination and phone numbers for the ticket desk. Make reservations at least one day before your planned trip, earlier for holiday weekends. Board early, because Greeks have a very loose attitude about assigned seating, and ownership is nine-tenths' possession. Although smoking is forbidden on the bus, and the bus takes a break every two hours or so, drivers are exempt from the rule; don't sit near the front seat if smoking bothers you.

In Athens and Thessaloniki avoid riding buses during rush hours. Upon boarding, validate your ticket in the canceling machines, at the front and back of buses (this goes for the yellow trolleys, too). Keep your tickets until you reach your destination, as inspectors who occasionally board are strict about fining offenders. On intracity buses, an inspector boards to check your ticket, so keep it handy. On islands and in smaller towns, you buy tickets from the driver's assistant once seated; try not to pay with anything more than a 1,000-dr. bill to avoid commotion.

The price of public transportation in Greece has risen steeply in the last couple of years, but it is still cheaper than in other western European cities.

Greece has an extensive, inexpensive, and reliable regional bus system (**KTEL**) made up of local operators. Each city has connections to towns and villages in its vicinity; visit the local KTEL office to check routes. Buses from Athens, however, travel throughout the country.

➤ ATHENS PUBLIC TRANSPORTATION: In Athens, the **Organization for Urban Public Transportation** (⊠ Metsovou 15, Athens, ☎ 185 or 01/883–6076), open weekdays 7:30–3 PM, one block north of the National Archaeological Museum, answers questions about city routes and distributes maps.

➤ REGIONAL BUS SERVICE: **Terminal A** (⊠ Kifissou St. 100, ☎ 01/512–4910) is the arrival and departure point for bus lines that serve parts of northern Greece, including Thessaloniki, Epirus, and Macedonia, and the Peloponnese destinations of Epidauros, Mycenae, and Corinth. Each line has its own Athens phone number; the EOT offices distribute a list. **Terminal B** (⊠ Behind Liossion 260, ☎ 01/831–7153 except Saturdays and Sundays, when you need to call the individual counters; EOT distributes phone lists), serving Evia and eastern and central Greece, including Delphi, is in a remote area northwest of Omonia Square. To get into the city center, take Bus 051 from Terminal A (terminus at Zinonos and Menandrou off Omonia Square) or Bus 024 from Terminal B (downtown stop on Amalias in front of the National Gardens).

➤ PRIVATE BUS LINES: The **Tavlaridou travel agency** (⊠ Chalkokondili 32 and Triti Septemvriou, Omonia Sq., Athens, ☎ FAX 01/522–1048) offers more comfortable coach trips (buses have air-conditioning) than KTEL to Thessaloniki daily at 9:30 AM, 1 PM, 4:15 PM, 9 PM and midnight (8,000 dr. one-way, 12,000 dr. round-trip). You make reservations and then pay on departure; the buses leave from Chalkondili 32.

BUSINESS HOURS

BANKS

Banks are normally open Monday–Thursday 8–2, Fridays 8–1:30. In Athens two branches of the **National Bank of Greece** have extended hours: For banking services other than foreign exchange, try the branch on Omonia Square (⊠ Aiolou 86, Omonia Sq., ☎ 01/334–1000), open Monday through Friday 6 PM to 8 PM. For foreign exchange only try the branch on Syntagma Square (⊠ Karageorgi Servias 2, Syntagma Sq., ☎ 01/334–0500), open Monday through Thursday 3:30 to 6:30 PM, Fridays 3 to 6:30 PM, Saturdays 9 AM to 3 PM, and Sundays 9 AM to 1 PM. Hotels also will cash traveler's checks on weekends, and the banks at both airport terminals have longer hours; some at the East Terminal are open all night. Most banks now have ATM machines that accept cards on the Plus system.

CHURCHES & MONASTERIES

There is absolutely no rhyme or reason as to when churches and monasteries are open to the public; in numerous cases monasteries are merely ruins, no longer functioning or looked after. In cities, opening hours are fairly standard, but in rural areas, visitors may need to find the caretaker to unlock the church doors; he or she usually lives nearby. In such cases it is customary to light a candle or buy a postcard in renumeration. The best time to find churches unlocked is during services, especially Sunday mornings; otherwise try from about 8 AM to noon and 5:30 to 7:30 on any day, unless where noted. The hours for monasteries are dependent upon their keepers, but they are generally more likely to be open in the morning to early afternoon; specific hours are noted.

MUSEUMS & HISTORIC SITES

The days and hours for museums and sites vary; they are usually open daily 8–3 except one weekday (usually Monday), although in summer, depending on personnel available that year, the hours are extended to as late as 7 PM; throughout the year arrive at least 30 minutes before closing time to ensure a ticket. Winter hours apply from about October through April. Archaeological sites and museums remain closed on January 1, March 25, the morning of Orthodox Good Friday, Orthodox Easter, May 1, and December 25–26. Sunday visiting hours apply to museums on the following holidays: Epiphany; Ash Monday, Good Saturday, Easter Monday, and Whitsunday (Orthodox dates, which change every year); August 15; and October 28. Museums close early (around 12:30) on January 2, the last Saturday of Carnival, Orthodox Good Thursday, Christmas Eve, and New Year's Eve. Admission to most museums and archaeological sites is free on Sunday November through mid-March. Admission to almost all museums and archaeological sites is free on Sunday from mid-November through March. Entrance is usually free every day for European Union (EU) students, half off for students from other countries, and about a third off for senior citizens.

THE GOLD GUIDE / SMART TRAVEL TIPS

SHOPS

Nominally shops are open Mondays, Wednesdays, and Saturdays 9–3 (8:30–3 in summer); Tuesdays, Thursdays, and Fridays 9–3 (8:30–3 in summer) and 5:30–8:30 (5:30–9 in summer). Supermarkets are open Monday through Friday 8–8, with reduced hours on Saturday. Be warned that shop hours are liable to change at any moment, according to government directives. In tourist areas, shops are allowed to extend their hours; those in Plaka, Athens's popular tourist bazaar, stay open until late into the night.

If it's late in the evening and you need an aspirin, soft drink, cigarettes, newspaper, or a pen, look for the nearest open kiosk, called a *periptero*, which stand on street corners everywhere brimming with all kinds of necessities. Owners stagger their hours, and many towns have at least one kiosk that stays open until all hours, occasionally through the night.

CAMERAS & COMPUTERS

EQUIPMENT PRECAUTIONS

Always **keep your film, tape, or computer disks out of the sun.** Carry an extra supply of batteries, and **be prepared to turn on your camera, camcorder, or laptop** to prove to security personnel that the device is real. Always **ask for hand inspection of film,** which becomes clouded after successive exposure to airport X-ray machines, and **keep videotapes and computer disks away from metal detectors.**

In Greece, non EU-citizens should register laptop computers with customs on entry, then show the stamped passport page with the computer's serial number upon exit to prove they did not buy it in Greece. Although officials may never check you coming or going, it's good to follow procedure to avoid last-minute trouble on departure.

TRAVEL PHOTOGRAPHY

Greece is the perfect f-22 country, and the bright sunlight and endless color and variety of the landscape seem to cry aloud to be photographed or filmed. Note the people of the countryside, while friendly and hospitable, are sometimes camera-shy, and if you want them on film, it is better to play at candid photography than to try to set up a pose.

➤ PHOTO HELP: **Kodak Information Center** (☎ 800/242–2424). *Kodak Guide to Shooting Great Travel Pictures,* available in bookstores or from Fodor's Travel Publications (☎ 800/533–6478; $16.50 plus $4 shipping).

CAR RENTAL

Because driving in Greece can be harrowing, car rental prices are higher than in the U.S., and transporting a car by ferry hikes up the fare substantially, think twice before deciding on car travel. It's much easier to take public transportation or taxis, which are among the cheapest in Europe. The exception is large islands where the distance between towns is greater—and taxi fares higher—then, you may want to rent a car or a moped for the day for concentrated bouts of sightseeing.

Rates in Greece during high season begin at 12,000 dr. a day (first 100 km/60 mi free, then 56 dr. per km/½ mi) to 80,000 dr. a week (unlimited mileage) for an economy car. This does not include tax on car rentals, which is 18%).

➤ MAJOR AGENCIES: **Avis** (☎ 800/ 331–1084, 800/879–2847 in Canada, 008/225–533 in Australia). **Budget** (☎ 800/527–0700, 0800/181181 in the U.K.). **Dollar** (☎ 800/800–4000; 0990/565656 in the U.K., where it is known as Eurodollar). **Europcar** (☎ 800/227–3876; 0345/222525 in the U.K., where it is known as Europcar InterRent). **Hertz** (☎ 800/654–3001, 800/263–0600 in Canada, 0345/ 555888 in the U.K., 03/9222–2523 in Australia, 03/358–6777 in New Zealand).

➤ SMALLER AGENCIES: **Thrifty** (✉ Syngrou 24, Athens, ☎ 01/922–1211 through 01/922–1213 and 01/921– 6000, FAX 01/923–8964). **Fantastico Rent-a-Car** (✉ Mihalakopoulou 62, Ilissia, ☎ 01/778–3771, FAX 01/778– 4860). **Greece Rent A-Car** (✉ Syngrou 7, City Center, Athens, ☎ 01/ 924–9802 or 01/924–9803, FAX 01/

924–9804), which has monthly rates. Also in Athens: **Pappas Rent-A-Car** (✉ Amalias 44, Center, ☎ 01/322–0087 and 01/323–4772, FAX 01/322–6472). The very helpful **Swift Car Rental** (✉ Nikis 21, Center, ☎ 01/324–7855, 01/322–1623, and 01/324–7875, FAX 01/325–0671) will actually drive tourists bewildered by Athens traffic to the city limits.

➤ RENTAL WHOLESALERS: **Europe by Car** (☎ 212/581–3040 or 800/223–1516, FAX 212/246–1458). **DER Travel Services** (✉ 9501 W. Devon Ave., Rosemont, IL 60018, ☎ 800/782–2424, FAX 800/282–7474 for information; 800/860–9944 for brochures). **Kemwel Holiday Autos** (☎ 914/835–5555 or 800/678–0678, FAX 914/835–5126).

INSURANCE

When driving a rented car you are generally responsible for any damage to or loss of the vehicle. Before you rent, **see what coverage you already have** under the terms of your personal auto-insurance policy and credit cards.

Collision policies that car-rental companies sell for European rentals typically do not cover stolen vehicles. Before you buy additional coverage for theft, check with your credit-card company and personal auto insurance—you may already be covered.

Rental agencies offer a full range of insurance: Collision damage waiver costs about 2,000 dr. a day, depending on the deduction; personal insurance 1,000 dr.; and theft 1,000 dr., though some companies include this in the rate.

REQUIREMENTS

In Greece your own driver's license is not acceptable unless you are an EU citizen. An International Driver's Permit is necessary; it's available from the American or Canadian Automobile associations, or, in the United Kingdom, from the Automobile Association or Royal Automobile Club.

SURCHARGES

Before you pick up a car in one city and leave it in another, **ask about drop-off charges or one-way service fees,** which can be substantial. Note, too, that some rental agencies charge

extra if you return the car before the time specified in your contract. To avoid a hefty refueling fee, **fill the tank just before you turn in the car,** but be aware that gas stations near the rental outlet may overcharge.

CAR TRAVEL

Regular registration papers and an international third-party insurance certificate (green card) are required, in addition to a driver's license (EU or international). If you insist on bringing in your own car, contact your local Greek consulate to pick up necessary forms and the latest information. You may import your vehicle duty-free for six months, if you have the car's registration and proof of ownership. Cars with foreign plates are exempt from the alternate-day ban in Athens on driving in the center according to whether the license plate is odd or even. Rental cars, however, must follow the law. Full insurance, including coverage against collision with an uninsured motorist, is recommended. Accidents must be reported (something Greek motorists often fail to do) before the insurance companies consider claims.

The two main highways, both called Ethniki Odos (National Road), leave Athens going north and south. At the city limits, signs in English mark the way to Syntagma and Omonia squares in the center. When you exit Athens, signs are well marked for the highway, usually naming Lamia for the north and Corinth or Patras for the southwest. Gas pumps and service stations are everywhere, and lead-free gas is widely available. Be aware that many stations in cities close after 7 PM.

AUTO CLUBS

➤ IN GREECE: The **Automobile Touring Club of Greece or ELPA** (✉ Athens Tower, 2–4 Messogion St., Athens, ☎ 01/748–8800, FAX 01/778–6642) has a special telephone line (☎ 174) for tourist information that works throughout the country; staff is accommodating. Other branches include Patras (✉ Patroon-Athinon 18, ☎ 061/425–411 or 061/426–416); Heraklion (✉ Knossou Ave. and G. Papandreou 46–50 and Knossou, ☎ 0181/289–440); Thessaloniki (✉ Vas. Olgas 230 and

THE GOLD GUIDE / SMART TRAVEL TIPS

Aegeou, ☎ 031/426–319, 031/426–386, FAX 031/411–0155); and Volos (✉ Iolkou 89, ☎ 0421/47404).

➤ IN AUSTRALIA: **Australian Automobile Association** (AAA, ☎ 06/247–7311).

➤ IN CANADA: **Canadian Automobile Association** (CAA, ☎ 613/247–0117).

➤ IN NEW ZEALAND: **New Zealand Automobile Association** (☎ 09/377–4660).

➤ IN THE U.K.: **Automobile Association** (AA, ☎ 0990/500–600), **Royal Automobile Club** (RAC, ☎ 0990/722–722 for membership, 0345/121–345 for insurance).

➤ IN THE U.S.: **American Automobile Association** (☎ 800/564–6222).

EMERGENCY SERVICES

You must put out a triangular danger sign if you have a breakdown. Roving repair trucks, manned by skilled ELPA mechanics, patrol the major highways (☎ 104 in all of Greece). They assist tourists with breakdowns for free if they belong to AAA or to ELPA; otherwise, there is a charge.

FROM THE U.K.

Driving to Greece from Britain is now possible, though keep in mind that gas may be difficult to find in the former Yugoslavia, especially unleaded. Though it is expensive, you can take a car to Greece (and at the same time greatly reduce your driving and save gasoline and hotel costs) by using the Paris–Milan and Milan–Brindisi car sleeper and then a car ferry to Corfu, Igoumenitsa, or Patras.

IMPORTING YOUR CAR

Contact the **Greek Consulate** for a six-month duty-free license to import your car. When leaving Greece, you must get a customs stamp to take the car out of the country by contacting the **Directorate for the Supervision and Control of Cars, or DIPEA.** There are no extensions; you either must leave the country with the car and return again after six months, under a new six-month permit, or leave the car in Greece for six months (no one can drive it), and then start anew.

➤ CUSTOMS STAMPS: **Directorate for the Supervision and Control of Cars, or DIPEA** (✉ Amvrosiou Frantzi 14, Athens 11473, ☎ 01/922–7315, FAX 01/923–4720).

INSURANCE

In general, auto insurance is not as expensive as in other countries. You must have third-party car insurance to drive in Greece. If possible, get an insurance "green card" valid for Greece from your insurance company before arriving. You can also buy a policy with local companies; keep the papers in a plastic pocket on the inside right front windshield. To get more information, or to locate a local representative for your insurance company, call the **Hellenic Union of Insurance Firms/Motor Insurance Bureau.**

➤ INSURANCE BUREAU: **Hellenic Union of Insurance Firms/Motor Insurance Bureau** (✉ Xenofontos 10, Athens 10557, ☎ 01/323–6733, FAX 01/323–8370).

ROAD CONDITIONS

Driving defensively is the key to safety in Greece. According to a recent survey by Eurostat, the EU statistics agency, Greece is one of the most hazardous European countries for motorists. In the city and on the highways, the streets are riddled with potholes, motorcyclists seem to come out of nowhere, often passing on the right, and cars may even go the wrong way down a one-way street. In the countryside, you must watch for herds of goats and sheep crossing the road, as well as tourists shakily learning the motorbikes they've recently rented.

The many motorcycles and scooters weaving through traffic and the aggressive attitude of fellow motorists can make driving in Greece's large cities unpleasant—and the life of a pedestrian actively dangerous; Greeks often run red lights on side streets or round corners without stopping. In the countryside, off the National Highway (tolls range from 250 dr. to 1,000 dr.), traffic is light, and driving is more enjoyable, but highway route numbers are largely nonexistent. The National Road is very slick when wet—avoid driving in rain and on the days preceding or following major holidays, when traffic is at its worst as urban dwellers leave for their villages. If air pollution has reached dangerous levels in Athens, all cars are banned from the center.

ROAD MAPS

You must put out a triangular danger sign if you have a breakdown. Roving repair trucks, manned by skilled ELPA mechanics, patrol the major highways (☎ 104 in all of Greece). They assist tourists with breakdowns for free if they belong to AAA or to ELPA; otherwise, there is a charge.

RULES OF THE ROAD

International road signs are in use throughout Greece. You drive on the right, pass on the left, and yield right-of-way to all vehicles approaching from the right (except on posted main highways). The speed limits are 120 kph (74 mph) on the National Road, 90 kph (54 mph) outside built-up areas, and 50 kph (31 mph) in cities, unless lower limits are posted. Often, no speed limits are posted, and even when they are, many Greeks don't obey them. In many streets, alternate-side-of-the-street parking rules are in effect. Although it's illegal, sidewalk parking is common. The police have become far more strict, regularly inspecting cars (which must have a fire extinguisher, emergency triangle, and first-aid kit) and introducing alcohol tests. You must always carry a valid driver's license (EU or international), car registration, and insurance contract or green card. The use of seat belts and helmets is compulsory, though Greeks tend to ignore these rules. Police are empowered to impose on-the-spot fines.

CHILDREN & TRAVEL

CHILDREN IN GREECE

Greek parents, who dote on their children to the point of spoiling them, believe this is the natural order of things: you marry, have children, then shower them with attention. They will dote on your children, too, if you take them along. Couples traveling without children, on the other hand, are likely to be interrogated: How many do you have at home? When do

you expect your first child? Despite this fondness for children, organized child-care services are scarce. You'll have to make arrangements for special activities and baby-sitting on an ad hoc basis.

Be sure to plan ahead and **involve your youngsters** as you outline your trip. When packing, include things to keep them busy en route. On sightseeing days try to schedule activities of special interest to your children. If you are renting a car don't forget to **arrange for a car seat** when you reserve.

HOTELS

Most hotels in Greece allow children under a certain age to stay in their parents' room at no extra charge, but others charge them as extra adults; be sure to **ask about the cutoff age for children's discounts.**

➤ BEST CHOICES: The **Athenaeum Inter-Continental** (☎ 800/327–1177 reservations) in Athens lets children up to 17 years stay in parents' rooms for free; they also provide baby-sitting services. Up to two children under 12 stay free with parents at the Holiday Inn in Athens (☎ 800–327–1177 reservations), and the hotel arranges baby-sitting. At the **Best Western** hotels (☎ 800/528–1234 reservations) in Athens, Olympia, Mykonos, Ayios Constantinos, Arachova, and Glyfada, children aged 2–12 stay at a 50% discount with parents; baby-sitting can be organized. The **Hilton** hotel (☎ 800/445–8667 reservations) in Athens allows children under 12 to stay free in parents' room. They also maintain lists of baby-sitters; rates are about 1,000 dr. an hour for one child, 1,500 dr. for two, and after 11 PM, clients pay the sitter's taxi fare home. **Grecotel Rhodos Imperial** (✉ Ixia, Rhodes, ☎ 0241/75000) runs Grecoland, activity programs for children aged from 3 to 5 and 6 to 12 years.

CONSUMER PROTECTION

Whenever possible, **pay with a major credit card** so you can cancel payment or get reimbursed if there's a problem, provided that you can provide documentation. This is the best way to pay, whether you're buying travel

THE GOLD GUIDE / SMART TRAVEL TIPS

arrangements before your trip or shopping at your destination.

➤ LOCAL RESOURCES: In Greece, **INKA, the Consumers Institute,** has set up a nationwide hot line (☎ 1721), open Monday through Friday, 8 AM to 4 PM. Disgruntled consumers may lodge a complaint about everything from overpricing to poor service in taxis, hotels, restaurants, and archaeological sites. According to INKA, most complaints filed by foreign tourists concerned museums and archaeological sites, banking services, road signs, and travel agencies. Complaints were generally related to overpricing, especially at restaurants and nightclubs. INKA, which has branches throughout Greece, offers legal advice and support as well as a complaints and information service.

CRUISE TRAVEL AND YACHTING

CRUISE TRAVEL

Many travelers with limited time find traveling by boat an ideal way to see Greece's mainland ports and islands. It spares you the planning headaches of solitary island-hopping, when you can be stranded en route, waiting several days for the next ferry. The disadvantage: Though cruise ships cover great distances at night, leaving days free for exploring, the usual stop in a port of call is often only a few hours, allowing for only a superficial visit. Often, an island's harbor is some distance from the main town, the more attractive, traditional villages, and the better beaches. Cruises are best for an overview that's useful for planning a return trip to the more appealing stops. Three-day cruises of the Greek islands, for instance, can be combined with a longer land tour. For information on specific lines and ships that offer these sails, consult a travel agent.

➤ CRUISE LINES: Among the major lines sailing to the four most popular islands—Mykonos, Rhodes, Crete, and Santorini (April through October)—are **Golden Sun Cruises** (✉ Akti Miaouli 71, Piraeus 18537, ☎ 01/428–7894, FAX 01/428–7898) and **Royal Olympic Cruises** (✉ One

Rockefeller Plaza, New York, NY 10020, ☎ 212/397–6400; in Greece (✉ Akti Miaouli 87, Piraeus 18538, ☎ 01/429–0700 for reservations, FAX 01/429–0638). Both have downtown Athens representatives. **Minoan Cruises** (✉ 25 Avgoustou 78, Heraklion, Crete 71202, ☎ 081/341–701, FAX 081/341–706) has one-day cruises from Crete to Santorini.

Other major cruise lines that call in the Greek Islands include **Club Med, Costa Cruise Lines, Crystal Cruises, Cunard Line, Holland America Line, Orient Lines, Princess Cruises, Radisson Seven Seas Cruises, Renaissance Cruises, Seabourn Cruise Line, Silversea Cruises, Star Clippers,** and **Windstar Cruises.** These cruises often call at ports outside Greece as well and may begin or end in Italy or Turkey. For more information and exact itineraries contact a cruise-only travel agency.

For a cruise of the islands aboard a small yacht, contact **Club Voyages** (✉ 43 Hooper Ave., Atlantic Highlands, NJ 07716, ☎ 908/291–8228), **Valef Yachts** (✉ Box 391, 7254 Fir Rd., Ambler, PA 19002, ☎ 215/641–1624 or 800/223–3845), or **Zeus Tours and Yacht Cruises** (✉ 566 7th Ave., New York, NY 10018, ☎ 212/221–0006 or 800/447–5667). The refurbished 1931 *Sea Cloud* sailing yacht cruises the Greek islands and Turkey; contact the **Cruise Company of Greenwich** (✉ 31 Brookside Dr., Greenwich, CT 06830; ☎ 800/825–0862) for information. The Greek-based **Viking Star Cruises** (✉ Artemidos 1, Glyfada 16674, ☎ 01/898–0829 or 01/894–9279, FAX 01/894–0952) offers a weeklong cruise from April to October, leaving every Friday to Mykonos, Santorini, Delos, Paros, Naxos, Ios, and Tinos on a 14-cabin yacht. For information on sailing a private yacht through Greek waters, *see* Yachting, *below.*

YACHTING

Life aboard a private yacht or sailboat is quite different from a cruise ship. You can either hire one with a few of your own friends or else, through a travel agency, join a party of people. Once aboard, you can go from island to island, stopping to swim or fish wherever you please—if you don't happen to feel like going ashore one night, you can always stay on board and listen to the nostalgic chants rising in the distance from the inns of the little harbor where your boat has dropped anchor. Yacht-rental agencies and travel agents have boats of all sizes and at all prices—on condition that your budget is not too tight! Zea harbor in Piraeus offers the most modern mooring and wintering facilities. Among the remaining 85 or so yacht supply stations, Vouliag-meni, Rhodes, Patras, Siros, and Thessaloniki are among the largest.

Below we list two associations and a number of leading yachting outfitters. In order to avoid an endless exchange of letters with an agency, it is best to give the following information in your first letter when you inquire to reserve a yacht: desired dates and period of charter and voyage; the number of passengers; and the type of craft you desire—auxiliary sailing yacht, motor yacht, or caïque. Two leading organizations are **Hellenic Professional Yacht Owners Association** (✉ A8-A0 Marina ZEA, Piraeus 18536, ☎ 01/894–6981, FAX 01/894–7467) and **Greek Yacht Brokers and Consultants Association** (✉ 7 Filellinon St., Athens 10557, ☎ 01/322–3221, FAX 01/322–3251). A leading yacht charterer is **Valef Yachts** (✉ 7524 Fir Rd., Ambler, PA 19002, ☎ 215/641–1624, FAX 215/641–1746; in Greece, 22 Akti Themistokleous, Piraeus 18536, ☎ 301/428–1920, FAX 301/413–7805). Two firms that organize highly sophisticated personalized yacht cruises and tours are **Club Voyages** (✉ 43 Hooper Ave., Atlantic Highlands, NJ 07716, ☎ 908/291–8228, FAX 908/291–4277) and **Hellenic Adventures** (✉ 4150 Harriet Ave. S, Minneapolis, MN 55409, ☎ 800/851–6349, FAX 612/827–2444).

Other yacht chartering firms include the following: **Aegean Yachting Center** (✉ 17220 Newhope St., Fountain Valley, CA 92708, ☎ 800/736–5717, FAX 714/641–0303). **Alden Yacht Charters** (✉ 1909 Alden Landing, Portsmouth, RI 02871, ☎ 401/683–1782 or 800/662–2628, FAX 401/683–3668). **G.P.S.C. Charters Club** (✉ 600 St. Andrews Rd., Phila-delphia, PA 19118, ☎ 215/247–3903, FAX 215/247–1505). **Grecian Charters** (862 Guy Lombardo Ave., Freeport, NY 11520, ☎ 516/868–4050, FAX 516/868–4052). **Greek Island Charters, Inc.** (270 N. Canon Dr., Beverly Hills, CA 90210, ☎ 310/278–8427, FAX 310/275–9786). **Greek Islands Cruise Center** (✉ 4141 Heartside Dr., Wilmington, NC 24812, ☎ 910/341–3030, FAX 910/791–9400). **Huntley Yacht Vacations** (✉ 210 Preston Rd., Wernersville, PA 19565, ☎ 610/678–2628 or 800/322–9224, FAX 610/670–1767). **Lynn Jachney Charters** (✉ Box 302, Marblehead, MA 01945, ☎ 617/639–0787 or 800/223–2050, FAX 617/639–0216). **The Moorings** (19345 U.S. 19 N, 4th floor, Clearwater, FL 33764, ☎ 813/530–5424 or 800/535–7289, FAX 813/530–9747). **Ocean Voyages** (✉ 1709 Bridgeway, Sausalito, CA 94965, ☎ 415/332–4681 or 800/299–4444, FAX 415/332–7460). **SailAway Yacht Charters** (✉ 15605 S.W. 92nd Ave., Miami, FL 33157-1972, ☎ 305/253–7245 or 800/724–5292, FAX 305/251–4408). **Zeus Yacht Cruises** (✉ 566 7th Ave., New York, NY 10018, ☎ 800/447–5667).

CUSTOMS & DUTIES

When shopping, **keep receipts** for all of your purchases. Upon reentering the country, **be ready to show customs officials what you've bought.** If you feel a duty is incorrect, appeal the assessment. If you object to the way your clearance was handled, get the inspector's badge number. In either case, first ask to see a supervisor, then write to the appropriate authorities, beginning with the port director at your point of entry.

IN GREECE

You may bring into Greece duty-free: food and beverages up to 22 pounds (10 kilos); 200 cigarettes, 100 cigarillos, or 50 cigars; one liter of alcoholic spirits or two liters of wine; and gift articles up to a total of 51,000 dr. Foreign bank notes amounting to more than $2,500 must be declared for reexport, but there are no restrictions on traveler's checks. Foreign visitors may export no more than 100,000 dr. in Greek currency.

Only one per person of such expensive portable items as cameras, camcorders, tape recorders, and the like is permitted into Greece. Sports equipment, such as bicycles and skis, is also limited to one (pair) per person.

To bring in a dog or a cat, you need a health certificate issued by a veterinary authority and validated by the Greek consulate and the appropriate medical authority (in the U.S., the Department of Agriculture). It must state that your pet doesn't carry any infectious diseases and that it received a rabies inoculation not more than 12 months (for cats, six months) and no fewer than six days before arrival. Dogs must also have a veterinary certificate that indicates they have been wormed against echinococcus.

The export of antiquities from Greece is forbidden. If any such articles are found in a traveler's luggage, they will be confiscated and the individual will be liable for prosecution. Reproductions of ancient works of art, some of very high quality, can be purchased throughout Greece and may be exported freely.

IN AUSTRALIA

Australia residents who are 18 or older may bring back $A400 worth of souvenirs and gifts (including jewelry), 250 cigarettes or 250 grams of tobacco, and 1,125 ml of alcohol (including wine, beer, and spirits). Residents under 18 may bring back $A200 worth of goods.

➤ INFORMATION: **Australian Customs Service** (Regional Director, ✉ Box 8, Sydney, NSW 2001, ☎ 02/9213–2000, FAX 02/9213–4000).

IN CANADA

Canadian residents who have been out of Canada for at least seven days may bring in C$500 worth of goods duty-free. If you've been away less than seven days but more than 48 hours, the duty-free allowance drops to C$200; if your trip lasts 24–48 hours, the allowance is C$50. You may not pool allowances with family members. Goods claimed under the C$500 exemption may follow you by mail; those claimed under the lesser exemptions must accompany you. Alcohol and tobacco products may be included in the seven-day and 48-

hour exemptions but not in the 24-hour exemption. If you meet the age requirements of the province or territory through which you reenter Canada, you may bring in, duty-free, 1.14 liters (40 imperial ounces) of wine or liquor or 24 12-ounce cans or bottles of beer or ale. If you are 16 or older you may bring in, duty-free, 200 cigarettes and 50 cigars.

You may send an unlimited number of gifts worth up to C$60 each duty-free to Canada. Label the package UNSOLICITED GIFT—VALUE UNDER $60. Alcohol and tobacco are excluded.

➤ INFORMATION: **Revenue Canada** (✉ 2265 St. Laurent Blvd. S, Ottawa, Ontario K1G 4K3, ☎ 613/993–0534, 800/461–9999 in Canada).

IN NEW ZEALAND

Although greeted with a "Haere Mai" ("Welcome to New Zealand"), homeward-bound residents with goods to declare must present themselves for inspection. If you're 17 or older, you may bring back $700 worth of souvenirs and gifts. Your duty-free allowance also includes 4.5 liters of wine or beer; one 1,125-ml bottle of spirits; and either 200 cigarettes, 250 grams of tobacco, 50 cigars, or a combo of all three up to 250 grams.

➤ INFORMATION: **New Zealand Customs** (✉ Custom House, 50 Anzac Ave., Box 29, Auckland, New Zealand, ☎ 09/359–6655, ☎ 09/309–2978).

IN THE U.K.

If you are a U.K. resident and your journey was wholly within the European Union (EU), you won't have to pass through customs when you return to the United Kingdom. If you plan to bring back large quantities of alcohol or tobacco, check EU limits beforehand.

➤ INFORMATION: **HM Customs and Excise** (✉ Dorset House, Stamford St., London SE1 9NG, ☎ 0171/202–4227).

IN THE U.S.

U.S. residents may bring home $400 worth of foreign goods duty-free if they've been out of the country for at least 48 hours (and if they haven't used the $400 allowance or any part of it in the past 30 days).

U.S. residents 21 and older may bring back 1 liter of alcohol duty-free. In addition, regardless of your age, you are allowed 200 cigarettes and 100 non-Cuban cigars. Antiques, which the U.S. Customs Service defines as objects more than 100 years old, enter duty-free, as do original works of art done entirely by hand, including paintings, drawings, and sculptures.

You may also send packages home duty-free: up to $200 worth of goods for personal use, with a limit of one parcel per addressee per day (and no alcohol or tobacco products or perfume worth more than $5); label the package PERSONAL USE, and attach a list of its contents and their retail value. Do not label the package UNSOLICITED GIFT, or your duty-free exemption will drop to $100. Mailed items do not affect your duty-free allowance on your return.

➤ INFORMATION: **U.S. Customs Service** (Inquiries, ✉ Box 7407, Washington, DC 20044, ☎ 202/927–6724; complaints, Office of Regulations and Rulings, ✉ 1301 Constitution Ave. NW, Washington, DC 20229; registration of equipment, Resource Management, ✉ 1301 Constitution Ave. NW, Washington DC 20229, ☎ 202/927–0540).

DISABILITIES & ACCESSIBILITY

ACCESS IN GREECE

Visitors will probably find it easier to manage in Greece's more modern resorts and hotels than in rented rooms. Many cruise ships are equipped to accommodate people with disabilities, but access to archaeological sites can present some difficulty, and most two-story museums do not have elevators. Bathrooms, especially in restaurants, may be down a steep flight of stairs in the basement, and the frequently high-curbed and auto-packed sidewalks are difficult to negotiate in larger towns. Call ahead to find out exactly what obstacles you might face and to enlist extra help from staff. Public transportation is generally crowded, and few special provisions are available. The easiest solution is to use

taxis to get between different points, or hire a taxi for the day; most hotels can arrange this. You may encounter stares—until recently Greeks with disabilities were encouraged to stay at home—but people will usually lend a helping hand, since this is a country where hospitality is a time-honored virtue. Athens has a few parking spaces to accommodate people with disabilities, but these are often illegally occupied by other drivers. Traveling with a companion or a group is advisable.

MAKING RESERVATIONS

When discussing accessibility with an operator or reservations agent, **ask hard questions.** Are there any stairs, inside or out? Are there grab bars next to the toilet *and* in the shower/tub? How wide is the door way to the room? To the bathroom? For the most extensive facilities meeting the latest legal specifications, **opt for newer accommodations,** which are more likely to have been designed with access in mind. Older buildings or ships may have more limited facilities. Be sure to **discuss your needs before booking.**

➤ HOTELS: The **Hotel Inter-Continental** (☎ 800/327–1177) in Athens has eight rooms specifically adapted for travelers with disabilities (wider doors, handrails, storage space for wheelchair) and most public areas are accessible. The **Hilton hotel** (☎ 800/445–8667) in Athens has two rooms equipped with extrawide doors and accessible bathrooms, but some public areas, such as the pool, may be difficult to get to by wheelchair. Both the **Holiday Inn** (☎ 800/465—4329) and the **Best Western** (☎ 800/528—1234) hotels in Athens also have one room each for handicapped guests (handrails, less furniture).

TRAVEL AGENCIES & TOUR OPERATORS

As a whole, the travel industry has become more aware of the needs of travelers with disabilities. In the U.S., the Americans with Disabilities Act requires that travel firms serve the needs of all travelers. Note, though, that some agencies and operators specialize in making travel arrangements for individuals and groups with disabilities.

➤ TRAVELERS WITH MOBILITY PROBLEMS: **Access Adventures** (✉ 206 Chestnut Ridge Rd., Rochester, NY 14624, ☎ 716/889–9096), run by a former physical-rehabilitation counselor. **CareVacations** (✉ 5019 49th Ave., Suite 102, Leduc, Alberta T9E 6T5, ☎ 403/986–6404, 800/648–1116 in Canada) has group tours and is especially helpful with cruise vacations. **Flying Wheels Travel** (✉ 143 W. Bridge St., Box 382, Owatonna, MN 55060, ☎ 507/451–5005 or 800/535–6790, FAX 507/451–1685), a travel agency specializing in customized tours and itineraries worldwide. **Hinsdale Travel Service** (✉ 201 E. Ogden Ave., Suite 100, Hinsdale, IL 60521, ☎ 630/325–1335), a travel agency that benefits from the advice of wheelchair traveler Janice Perkins.

DISCOUNTS & DEALS

CLUBS & COUPONS

Many companies sell discounts in the form of travel clubs and coupon books, but these cost money. You must use participating advertisers to get a deal, and only after you recoup the initial membership cost or book price do you begin to save. If you plan to use the club or coupons frequently, you may save considerably. Before signing up, find out what discounts you get for free.

➤ DISCOUNT CLUBS: **Entertainment Travel Editions** (✉ 2125 Butterfield Rd., Troy, MI 48084, ☎ 800/445–4137; $20–$51, depending on destination). **Great American Traveler** (✉ Box 27965, Salt Lake City, UT 84127, ☎ 801/974–3033 or 800/548–2812; $49.95 per year). **Moment's Notice Discount Travel Club** (✉ 7301 New Utrecht Ave., Brooklyn, NY 11204, ☎ 718/234–6295; $25 per year, single or family). **Privilege Card International** (✉ 237 E. Front St., Youngstown, OH 44503, ☎ 330/746–5211 or 800/236–9732; $74.95 per year). **Sears's Mature Outlook** (✉ Box 9390, Des Moines, IA 50306, ☎ 800/336–6330; $19.95 per year). **Travelers Advantage** (✉ CUC Travel Service, 3033 S. Parker

Rd., Suite 1000, Aurora, CO 80014, ☎ 800/548–1116 or 800/648–4037; $59.95 per year, single or family). **Worldwide Discount Travel Club** (✉ 1674 Meridian Ave., Miami Beach, FL 33139, ☎ 305/534–2082; $50 per year family, $40 single).

CREDIT-CARD BENEFITS

When you use your credit card to make travel purchases you may get free travel-accident insurance, collision-damage insurance, and medical or legal assistance, depending on the card and the bank that issued it. American Express, MasterCard, and Visa provide one or more of these services, so **get a copy of your credit card's travel-benefits policy.** If you are a member of an auto club, always **ask hotel and car-rental reservations agents about auto-club discounts.** Some clubs offer additional discounts on tours, cruises, and admission to attractions.

DISCOUNT RESERVATIONS

To save money, **look into discount-reservations services** with toll-free numbers, which use their buying power to get a better price on hotels, airline tickets, even car rentals. When booking a room, always **call the hotel's local toll-free number** (if one is available) rather than the central reservations number—you'll often get a better price. Always ask about special packages or corporate rates.

When shopping for the best deal on hotels and car rentals, **look for guaranteed exchange rates,** which protect you against a falling dollar. With your rate locked in, you won't pay more, even if the price goes up in the local currency.

You may get up to a 15% discount when you book a hotel through a Greek local travel agent rather than reserve directly with the hotel (the agent often has special rates), and prices may be lower than booking through your country's travel agent, who may take a heftier commission. Contact agencies by fax; some even have e-mail addresses, making comparison shopping even easier.

➤ AIRLINE TICKETS: ☎ 800/FLY–4–LESS.

➤ HOTEL ROOMS: **Hotels Plus** (☎ 800/235–0909). **Steigenberger Reservation Service** (☎ 800/223–5652). **Travel Interlink** (☎ 800/888–5898).

PACKAGE DEALS

Packages and guided tours can save you money, but don't confuse the two. When you buy a package, your travel remains independent, just as though you had planned and booked the trip yourself. Fly/drive packages, which combine airfare and car rental, are often a good deal. If you **buy a rail/drive pass,** you'll save on train tickets and car rentals. All Eurail- and Europass holders get a discount on Eurostar fares through the Channel Tunnel. Greek Flexipass options may include sightseeing, hotels, and plane tickets.

ELECTRICITY

To use your U.S.-purchased electric-powered equipment, **bring a converter and adapter.** The electrical current in Greece is 220 volts, 50 cycles alternating current (AC); wall outlets take Continental-type plugs, with two round prongs.

If your appliances are dual-voltage, you'll need only an adapter. Don't use 110-volt outlets, marked FOR SHAVERS ONLY, for high-wattage appliances such as blow-dryers. Most laptops operate equally well on 110 and 220 volts and so require only an adapter.

EMERGENCIES

➤ EMERGENCIES: **Police** (☎ 100), **National Ambulance Service** (EKAV, ☎ 166) (a taxi is faster), **Fire** (☎ 199), **Coast Guard** (☎ 108). The **Tourist Police** (☎ 171 in Athens; 01/171 from outside Athens) or contact the local tourist police in other regions (*see* specific chapters for phone number) can provide general information, help in emergencies, and can mediate in disputes.

➤ POISON CENTER: **Poison center** (☎ 01/779–3777).

GAY & LESBIAN TRAVEL

In Greece, homosexuality has been very much a part of life from antiquity to today. Indeed, many prominent figures of the country's cultural life (both past and present) are openly gay.

Others, such as the late Minister of Culture, Melina Mercouri, have strongly supported gays. One should be aware, however, of the special mentality of the Greek male vis-à-vis homosexuality. Sociological reports indicate a large portion of the population is bisexual, though this does not indicate a conscious recognition of being gay. Greek society remains conservative regarding open declarations of homosexuality by either sex, although homosexual relations for men over 17 have been legal for many decades in Greece. The nearest thing to a gay scene in the Western sense of the word exists in Athens, Thessaloniki, Mykonos, Rhodes, and Ios for men; for women, at Eressos on Lesbos.

➤ LOCAL RESOURCES: *"To Kraximo"* and *"Greek Gay Guide"* (available from kiosks in Omonia Square in Athens and near the Thessaloniki train station) are both published by **Kraximo Publications** (✉ Box 4228, 10210 Athens). The weekly Greek-language entertainment guides "Athinorama" and "Downtown," available at all kiosks, also lists Athens gay bars and dance clubs in its nightlife section.

➤ GAY- AND LESBIAN-FRIENDLY TOUR OPERATORS: **Toto Tours** (✉ 1326 W. Albion Ave., Suite 3W, Chicago, IL 60626, ☎ 773/274–8686 or 800/565–1241, FAX 773/274–8695), for groups.

➤ GAY- AND LESBIAN-FRIENDLY TRAVEL AGENCIES: **Corniche Travel** (✉ 8721 Sunset Blvd., Suite 200, West Hollywood, CA 90069, ☎ 310/854–6000 or 800/429–8747, FAX 310/659–7441). **Islanders Kennedy Travel** (✉ 183 W. 10th St., New York, NY 10014, ☎ 212/242–3222 or 800/988–1181, FAX 212/929–8530). **Now Voyager** (✉ 4406 18th St., San Francisco, CA 94114, ☎ 415/626–1169 or 800/255–6951, FAX 415/626–8626). **Yellowbrick Road** (✉ 1500 W. Balmoral Ave., Chicago, IL 60640, ☎ 773/561–1800 or 800/642–2488, FAX 773/561–4497). **Skylink Travel and Tour** (✉ 3577 Moorland Ave., Santa Rosa, CA 95407, ☎ 707/585–8355 or 800/225–5759, FAX 707/584–5637), serving lesbian travelers.

THE GOLD GUIDE / SMART TRAVEL TIPS

HEALTH

Greece's strong summer sun and low humidity can lead to sunburn or sunstroke if you're not careful. A hat, long-sleeve shirt, and long pants or a sarong are essential for spending a day at the beach or visiting archaeological sites. Sunglasses, a hat, and sunblock are necessities, and insect repellent may keep the occasional horsefly and mosquito at bay. Drink plenty of water. Most beaches present few dangers, but keep a lookout for the occasional jellyfish and, in some areas, sea urchins. Should you step on one, don't break off the embedded spines, which may lead to infection, but remove them with heated olive oil and a needle.

Food is seldom a problem, but the liberal amounts of olive oil used in Greek cooking may be indigestible for some. Tap water in Greece is fine, and bottled spring water is readily available.

For minor ailments, go to the local pharmacy first, where the licensed staff can make recommendations for over-the-counter drugs. Most pharmacies are closed in the evenings and on weekends, but each posts the name of the nearest pharmacy open off-hours. Newspapers also carry a listing of pharmacies open late or, in large cities, all night. For tending to minor ailments, most state hospitals and rural clinics won't charge you, even if you're not an EU citizen, or you'll just pay a minimal fee. In an emergency you can call an ambulance (☎ 166), but waving down a taxi is faster, since cars in big cities give way reluctantly to ambulances. Most hotels will call a doctor for you. In Athens, you can locate a doctor on call 2 PM–7 AM on Sunday and on holidays by dialing 105, but the message is in Greek. For a dentist, check with your hotel, embassy, or the tourist police.

DIVERS' ALERT

Do not fly within 24 hours after scuba diving.

MEDICAL PLANS

No one plans to get sick while traveling, but it happens, so **consider signing up with a medical-assistance company.** Members get doctor referrals, emergency evacuation or repatriation, 24-hour telephone hot lines for medical consultation, cash for emergencies, and other personal and legal assistance. Coverage varies by plan, so **review the benefits of each carefully.**

➤ MEDICAL-ASSISTANCE COMPANIES: **International SOS Assistance** (⌧ 8 Neshaminy Interplex, Suite 207, Trevose, PA 19053, ☎ 215/245–4707 or 800/523–6586, ℻ 215/244–9617; ⌧ 12 Chemin Riantbosson, 1217 Meyrin 1, Geneva, Switzerland, ☎ 4122/785–6464, ℻ 4122/785–6424; ⌧ 10 Anson Rd., 14-07/08 International Plaza, Singapore 079903, ☎ 65/226–3936, ℻ 65/226–3937).

HOLIDAYS

1999: January 1 (New Year's Day); January 6 (Epiphany); February 22 (Clean Monday, first day of Lent); March 25 (Feast of the Annunciation and Independence Day); April 9 (Good Friday); April 11 (Greek Easter Sunday); April 12 (Greek Easter Monday); May 1 (Labor Day and Flower Festival); May 30 (Pentecost); August 15 (Assumption of the Holy Virgin); October 28 (Ochi Day); December 25–26 (Christmas Day and Boxing Day). 2000: Dates are the same as above except March 13 (Clean Monday, first day of Lent); April 28 (Good Friday); April 30 (Greek Easter Sunday); May 1 (Greek Easter Monday); June 18 (Pentecost).

INSURANCE

Travel insurance is the best way to **protect yourself against financial loss.** The most useful plan is a comprehensive policy that includes coverage for trip cancellation and interruption, default, trip delay, and medical expenses (with a waiver for preexisting conditions).

Without insurance, you will lose all or most of your money if you cancel your trip, regardless of the reason. Default insurance covers you if your tour operator, airline, or cruise line goes out of business. Trip-delay covers unforeseen expenses that you may incur due to bad weather or mechanical delays. It's important to compare the fine print regarding trip-delay coverage when comparing policies.

For overseas travel, one of the most important components of travel insurance is its medical coverage. Supplemental health insurance will pick up the cost of your medical bills should you get sick or injured while traveling. U.S. residents should note that Medicare generally does not cover health-care costs outside the United States, nor do many privately issued policies. Residents of the United Kingdom can buy an annual travel-insurance policy valid for most vacations taken during the year in which the coverage is purchased. If you are pregnant or have a preexisting condition, make sure you're covered. British citizens should buy extra medical coverage when traveling overseas, according to the Association of British Insurers. Australian travelers should buy travel insurance, including extra medical coverage, whenever they go abroad, according to the Insurance Council of Australia.

Always **buy travel insurance directly from the insurance company**; if you buy it from a cruise line, airline, or tour operator that goes out of business you probably will not be covered for the agency or operator's default, a major risk. Before you make any purchase, **review your existing health and home-owner's policies** to find out whether they cover expenses incurred while traveling.

➤ TRAVEL INSURERS: In the U.S., **Access America** (✉ 6600 W. Broad St., Richmond, VA 23230, ☎ 804/285–3300 or 800/284–8300). **Travel Guard International** (✉ 1145 Clark St., Stevens Point, WI 54481, ☎ 715/345–0505 or 800/826–1300). In Canada, **Mutual of Omaha** (✉ Travel Division, 500 University Ave., Toronto, Ontario M5G 1V8, ☎ 416/598–4083, 800/268–8825 in Canada).

➤ INSURANCE INFORMATION: In the U.K., **Association of British Insurers** (✉ 51 Gresham St., London EC2V 7HQ, ☎ 0171/600–3333). In Australia, the **Insurance Council of Australia** (☎ 613/9614–1077, FAX 613/9614–7924).

LANGUAGE

Greek is the native language not only of Greece but also of Cyprus, parts of Chicago, and Astoria, New York. Though it's a byword for incomprehensible ("it was all Greek to me," says Casca in Shakespeare's *Julius Caesar*), much of the difficulty lies in its different alphabet. Not all the 24 Greek letters have precise English equivalents, and there is usually more than one way to spell a Greek word in English. For instance, the letter delta sounds like the English letters "dh," and the sound of the letter gamma may be transliterated as a "g," "gh," or "y." Because of this the Greek for Holy Trinity might appear in English as Agia Triada, Aghia Triada, Ayia Triada, or even (if the initial aspiration and the "dh" are used) Hagia Triadha. It seems complicated, but don't let it throw you. With a little time spent learning the alphabet and some basic phrases, you can acquire enough Greek to navigate—i.e., exchange greetings, find a hotel room, and get from one town to another. Many Greeks know some English but will appreciate a two-way effort.

If you only have 15 minutes to learn Greek, memorize the following: *miláte angliká?* (do you speak English?); *den katalavéno* (I don't understand); *parakaló* (please/you're welcome); *signómi* (excuse me); *efharistó* (thank you); *ne* (yes); *óhee* (no); *pósso?* (how much?); *pou eéne ee trápeza?* (where is the bank?), . . . *ee toiléta?* (. . . the toilet?), . . . *to tahidromío?* (. . . the post office?); *kali méra* (good morning), *kali spéra* (good evening), *kali níhta* (good night). Also *see* Greek Vocabulary at the back of this guide.

LODGING

The array of accommodations ranges from luxury island resorts to traditional settlements that incorporate local architecture to inexpensive rented rooms peddled at the harbor. Family-run pensions and guest houses outside Athens and Thessaloniki are usually clean, bright, and recently built; they also let you get better acquainted with the locals. Self-catering apartments are available as well in most resort areas.

Although lodging is less expensive in Greece than in most of the EU and the U.S., the quality tends to be lower.

Sometimes you can reduce the price by eliminating breakfast, by bargaining when it's off-season, or by going through a local travel agency for the larger hotels on major islands and in Athens and Thessaloniki. Many Greeks rent rooms in their houses, which can be less expensive and more homey than a hotel, but you might have to scout around a bit to find them, and it's a good idea to see them first, for quality and location. Also, make sure you feel comfortable with the owners, if you'll be living in close proximity. Owners wait for tourists at the harbor, and signs in English throughout villages indicate rooms available. Accommodations may be hard to find in smaller resort towns during the winter and beginning of spring. Remember that the plumbing in rooms and most low-end hotels (and restaurants, shops, and other public places) is delicate enough to require that toilet paper and other detritus be put in the wastebasket and not flushed.

APARTMENT & VILLA RENTALS

If you want a home base that's roomy enough for a family and comes with cooking facilities, **consider a furnished rental.** These can save you money, especially if you're traveling with a large group of people. Home-exchange directories list rentals (often second homes owned by prospective house swappers), and some services search for a house or apartment for you (even a castle if that's your fancy) and handle the paperwork. Some send an illustrated catalog; others send photographs only of specific properties, sometimes at a charge. Up-front registration fees may apply.

➤ RENTAL AGENTS: Europa-Let/Tropical Inn-Let (⊠ 92 N. Main St., Ashland, OR 97520, ☎ 541/482–5806 or 800/462–4486, FAX 541/482–0660). Property Rentals International (⊠ 1008 Mansfield Crossing Rd., Richmond, VA 23236, ☎ 804/378–6054 or 800/220–3332, FAX 804/379–2073). Rent-a-Home International (⊠ 7200 34th Ave. NW, Seattle, WA 98117, ☎ 206/789–9377 or 800/488–7368, FAX 206/789–9379). Vacation Home Rentals Worldwide (⊠ 235 Kensington Ave., Norwood, NJ 07648, ☎ 201/767–9393 or 800/633–3284,

FAX 201/767–5510). Villas International (605 Market St., San Francisco, CA 94105, ☎ 415/281–0910 or 800/221–2260, FAX 415/281–0919). Hideaways International (⊠ 767 Islington St., Portsmouth, NH 03801, ☎ 603/430–4433 or 800/843–4433, FAX 603/430–4444; membership $99) is a club for travelers who arrange rentals among themselves.

CAMPING

There are numerous campgrounds, most privately owned, throughout Greece. One or more can usually be found close to popular archaeological sites and beach resorts—they aren't intended for those who want to explore the wilds of Greece. Their amenities range from basic to elaborate, and those operated by the EOT are cushier than most.

The EOT distributes information on available campgrounds with site listings; the tourist organization manages campgrounds in Athens (near Voula beach); in the Peloponnese at Killini; in Thrace at Fanari 31 km (18½ mi) from Komotini; in central Greece at Kamena Vourla; and in Macedonia at about nine sites, including Olympos, Bati beach in Kavala, and Thermaikos, 28 km (17 mi) from Thessaloniki. What the Greeks call "freelance" camping is also available (though technically illegal). These informal sites spring up annually, often around an island's nudist beaches. Usually there is some form of running water and a nearby taverna—ask around.

➤ INFORMATION: Greek Camping Association (⊠ Solonos 102, Athens 10680, ☎ FAX 01/362–1560).

HOME EXCHANGES

If you would like to exchange your home for someone else's, **join a home-exchange organization,** which will send you its updated listings of available exchanges for a year and will include your own listing in at least one of them. It's up to you to make specific arrangements.

➤ EXCHANGE CLUBS: HomeLink International (⊠ Box 650, Key West, FL 33041, ☎ 305/294–7766 or 800/638–3841, FAX 305/294–1148; $83 per year).

HOSTELS

No matter what your age, you can **save on lodging costs by staying at hostels.** In some 5,000 locations in more than 70 countries around the world, Hostelling International (HI), the umbrella group for a number of national youth hostel associations, offers single-sex, dorm-style beds and, at many hostels, "couples" rooms and family accommodations. Membership in any HI national hostel association, open to travelers of all ages, allows you to stay in HI-affiliated hostels at member rates (one-year membership is about $25 for adults; hostels run about $10–$25 per night). Members also have priority if the hostel is full; they're eligible for discounts around the world, even on rail and bus travel in some countries.

For the moment, hostels (whether called that or not) are operating in Athens and Thessaloniki on the mainland; Patras and Olympia in the Peloponnese; Santorini; and Heraklion and Rethymnon on Crete.

➤ HOSTEL ORGANIZATIONS: **Hostelling International—American Youth Hostels** (✉ 733 15th St. NW, Suite 840, Washington, DC 20005, ☎ 202/783–6161, FAX 202/783–6171). **Hostelling International—Canada** (✉ 400-205 Catherine St., Ottawa, Ontario K2P 1C3, ☎ 613/237–7884, FAX 613/237–7868). **Youth Hostel Association of England and Wales** (✉ Trevelyan House, 8 St. Stephen's Hill, St. Albans, Hertfordshire AL1 2DY, ☎ 01727/855215 or 01727/845047, FAX 01727/844126); membership in the U.S. $25, in Canada C$26.75, in the U.K. £9.30).

➤ IN GREECE: You can also contact the **Greek Youth Hostel Organization** (✉ Damareos 75, Pangrati, Athens 11633, ☎ 01/751–9530, FAX 01/751–0616), but because of some bureaucracy with the EOT, not all hostels fall under their jurisdiction. The **YWCA in Athens** (✉ Amerikis 11, 10672, ☎ 01/362–4291 through 01/362–4293, FAX 01/362–2400) also takes overnight guests, women only.

HOTELS

The EOT authorizes the construction and classification of hotels through-out Greece. It classifies hotels into six categories: L (stands for De Luxe), and A–E, which govern the rates that can be charged, though don't expect hotels to have the same amenities as their U.S. and northern European counterparts. Ratings are based on considerations such as room size, hotel services, and amenities like furnishing of the room and quality of the lobby. Within each category, quality varies greatly, but prices don't. Still, you may come across an A-category hotel that charges less than a B-class, depending on facilities. The classifications can be misleading—a hotel rated C in one town might qualify as a B in another. For the categories L, A, and B, you can expect something along the lines of a chain motel in the U.S., although the room will probably be somewhat smaller. A room in a C hotel can be perfectly acceptable; with a D the bathroom may or may not be shared. Ask to see the room before checking in. You can sometimes find a bargain if a hotel has just renovated but has not yet been reclassified. The government is discussing switching to a star-rating system like several other European countries, hoping this standardization will encourage hotels to upgrade, as well as make things easier for travel agents.

Official prices are posted in each room, usually on the back of the door or inside the wardrobe. The room charge varies over the course of the year, peaking in the high season when breakfast or half board (at hotel complexes) may also be obligatory.

The EOT distributes lists of hotels for each region, although it will not make recommendations. Annual hotel directories are available at most English-language bookstores in Athens and Thessaloniki and at city kiosks in late spring.

➤ GUIDES: One of the most complete guides is *Hellenic Traveling Pages* (✉ Info Publications, Pironos 51, Athens 16341, ☎ 01/994–0109, FAX 01/993–6564), a monthly publication available at most Greek bookstores; it also lists travel agencies, bus, boat, and airplane routes, and museum hours.

RENTAL ROOMS

Although you will be approached by owners of rental rooms upon your arrival at most islands in summer, you may want to check an annual publication in English, *Holiday Rentals in Greece: Rooms, Apartments and Studios,* which details prices and facilities of rental rooms, with photos of accommodations to help you decide. Information is also often obtainable at the local tourist police or the municipal tourist information offices.

➤ GUIDES: *Holiday Rentals in Greece: Rooms, Apartments and Studio* is published by **Touristiki Ekdotiki** (✉ P. Tsaldari 48, Vironas, Athens 16232, ☎ 01/765–1065, FAX 01/765–6616) and is available at Athens kiosks and English-language bookstores.

TRADITIONAL SETTLEMENTS

In an effort to provide tourist accommodations in traditional settings, the EOT has begun a restoration program, converting older buildings into guest houses. Some of the villages developed so far include Oia on Santorini; Vizitsa and Argalasti on Mt. Pelion; Mesta on Chios and nearby Psara island; Korischades in Evritania; Papingo in Epirus; Vathia in the Mani with its curious tower homes; and Monemvassia in the Southern Peloponnese.

Many of these settlements are detailed and photographed in an EOT handout, "Traditional Settlements," as well as in a guide called *Traditional Inns in Greece: Alternative Forms of Tourism,* in English, published by **Vertical Advertising.**

➤ RESERVATIONS & INFORMATION: For reservations call the **Greek Hotel and Cruise Reservation Center** (☎ 714/641–3502 or 800/736–5717, FAX 714/641–0303). **Vertical Advertising** (✉ Katehaki 61A, Athens 11525, ☎ 01/691–2219, FAX 01/649–6782).

MAIL

In Greece, you must take packages open to the post office for inspection. Bring brown butcher paper, tape, and string along, since the post office does not provide wrapping materials.

POSTAL RATES

At press time (summer 1998), airmail letters and postcards to North America weighing up to 20 grams cost 170 dr., and 260 dr. for 50 grams (140 and 220 dr. to the United Kingdom and Europe). If you are mailing a package, you must bring it open with your wrapping materials to the post office so it can be inspected.

POST OFFICES

Post offices are open weekdays 8–2, although in city centers they may stay open in the evenings and on weekends. The main post offices in Athens (✉ Aiolou 100 and Syntagma Square at Mitropoleos) are open weekdays 7:30 AM–8 PM, Saturdays 7:30–2, and Sundays 9–2. Throughout the country, mailboxes are yellow.

RECEIVING MAIL

Mail service can be quite slow in Greece. There are numerous couriers available for domestic and international destinations, but one of the most reliable is **DHL**, slightly more expensive than other companies but worth it for its prompt door-to-door delivery and extensive network (Fillelinon 28, near Plaka, Athens, ☎ 01/989–0000).

MONEY

COSTS

Although costs have risen astronomically since Greece joined the EU, the country will seem reasonably priced to travelers from the U.S. and Great Britain. Popular tourist resorts (including some of the islands) and the larger cities are markedly more expensive than the countryside. Though the price of eating in a restaurant has increased over the past several years, it often remains a bargain. Hotels are generally moderately priced, and the extra cost of accommodations in a luxury hotel, compared to an average hotel, often seems unwarranted.

Transportation is a good deal in Greece. Bus and train tickets are inexpensive, though renting a car is costly; there are relatively cheap—and slow—ferries to the islands, and express boats and hydrofoils that cost more. If your time is limited, domestic flights are a fair trade-off in cost and time saved, compared with sea and land travel.

Some sample prices: Admission to archaeological sites: 500 dr.–2,000 dr.; authentic Greek sponge: 2,000 dr.; coffee: 600 dr.–900 dr.; beer: at the store (500 ml) 400 dr., in a bar 700 dr.–900 dr.; Coca-Cola: (can) 250 dr., and in a café 500 dr.; spinach pie: 250 dr.; taxi ride: about 2,200 dr. from the airport to downtown Athens; local bus: 100 dr. in one zone; foreign newspaper: 350 dr.–700 dr.

CREDIT & DEBIT CARDS

Should you use a credit card or a debit card when traveling? Both have benefits. A credit card allows you to delay payment and gives you certain rights as a consumer (☞ Consumer Protection, *above*). A debit card, also known as a check card, deducts funds directly from your checking account and helps you stay within your budget. When you want to rent a car, though, you may still need an old-fashioned credit card. Although you can always *pay* for your car with a debit card, some agencies will not allow you to *reserve* a car with a debit card.

Otherwise, the two types of plastic are virtually the same. Both will get you cash advances at ATMs worldwide if your card is properly programmed with your personal identification number (PIN). (For use in Greece, your PIN must be four digits long.) Both offer excellent, wholesale exchange rates. And both protect you against unauthorized use if the card is lost or stolen. Your liability is limited to $50, as long as you report the card missing.

➤ ATM LOCATIONS: **Cirrus** (☎ 800/424–7787). **Plus** (☎ 800/843–7587) for locations in the U.S. and Canada, or visit your local bank.

➤ REPORTING LOST CARDS: To report lost or stolen credit cards, call the following toll-free numbers: **American Express** (☎ 800/327–2177); **Diners Club** (☎ 800/234–6377); **Discover Card** (☎ 800/347–2683); **Master-Card** (☎ 800/307–7309); and **Visa** (☎ 800/847–2911).

CURRENCY

The drachma (dr.) is the Greek unit of currency. Bills are in denominations of 10,000, 5,000, 1,000, 500, 200, and 100 dr. Coins are 100, 50, 20, 10, 5. At press time (summer 1998) the average exchange rate was 301 dr. to the U.S. dollar, 206 dr. to the Canadian dollar, and 502 dr. to the pound sterling.

EXCHANGING MONEY

For the most favorable rates, **change money through banks.** Although fees charged for ATM transactions may be higher abroad than at home, Cirrus and Plus exchange rates are excellent, because they are based on wholesale rates offered only by major banks. You won't do as well at exchange booths in airports or rail and bus stations, in hotels, in restaurants, or in stores, although you may find their hours more convenient. To avoid lines at airport exchange booths, **get a bit of local currency before you leave home.**

➤ EXCHANGE SERVICES: **Chase *Currency to Go*** (☎ 800/935–9935; 935–9935 in NY, NJ, and CT). **International Currency Express** (☎ 888/842–0880 on the East Coast, 888/278–6628 on the West Coast). **Thomas Cook Currency Services** (☎ 800/287–7362 for telephone orders and retail locations).

TRAVELER'S CHECKS

Do you need traveler's checks? It depends on where you're headed. If you're going to rural areas and small towns, go with cash; traveler's checks are best used in cities, though even in Athens, many tavernas don't take traveler's checks. Lost or stolen checks can usually be replaced within 24 hours. To ensure a speedy refund, buy your own traveler's checks—don't let someone else pay for them: irregularities like this can cause delays. The person who bought the checks should make the call to request a refund.

OUTDOOR ACTIVITIES & SPORTS

BICYCLING

Bicycling is impossible on the crowded city streets but can be a pleasure on the islands and the countryside. Resort areas usually have at least one bicycle rental shop but helmets are seldom provided. Greek drivers still aren't used to seeing cyclists on the road, which can make bicycling occasionally nerve-racking, especially on narrow, curvy mountain roads. Most adventure travel agencies, like Trekking Hellas and F-Zein (☞ Hiking & Mountain Biking, *below*), offer mountain biking tours, and depending on the difficulty level, these may be your best bet.

GOLFING

Golfing in Greece is possible, but there aren't many 18-hole courses. Those with complete facilities include the **Glyfada Golf Course** (☎ 01/894–6820, ℻ 01/894–3721) near Athens, the **Afandou Golf** (☎ 0241/51257) on Rhodes, the **Porto Carras Golf Club** (☎ 0375/71381, ext. 6463, ℻ 0375/71502 via Porto Carras Meliton hotel) in Chalkidiki, and the **Corfu Golf Club** (☎ 0661/94220) in the central part of the island (Livadi tou Ropa) near the village Ermones.

HIKING & MOUNTAIN BIKING

The country offers plenty of rugged terrain for serious hiking and mountaineering. The **Greek Federation of Mountaineering Associations** (⊠ Milioni 5, Kolonaki 10673, ☎ 01/364–5904, ℻ 01/364–4687) can supply details of refuges, mountain paths, and contact numbers for local hiking clubs. The closest refuges near Athens, located on Mt. Parnitha, are Flambouri (⊠ ☎ 01/246–4666), run by the **Alpine Club of Aharnon** (⊠ Filadelfias 126, Aharnes, 13671, ☎ 01/246–1528 or 01/246–6666, ℻ 01/246–9777), and the Bafi refuge on the same mountain (⊠ ☎ 01/246–9050), run by the **Alpine Club of Athens** (⊠ Kapnikareas Sq. 2, top floor, Monastiraki, 13671, ☎ 01/321–2355, ℻ 01/246–9777). Both clubs arrange hikes in Attica and throughout the mainland to places like Evritania and Arcadia, as well as adventure camps for children in summer.

Treks throughout Greece are organized by adventure travel agencies, which also offer kayaking, rafting,

mountain biking, and camping trips; try **Trekking Hellas,** in Athens (⊠ Fillelinon 7, 3rd floor, Syntagma, 10557, ☎ 01/331–0323 through 01/331–0326, ℻ 01/324–4548) and in Thessaloniki (⊠ Aristotelous 11, 54624, ☎ 031/242–190 through 031/242–029, ℻ 031/242–029); and **F-Zein** (⊠ Syngrou 132, 5th floor, Athens 17671, ☎ 01/921–6285, ℻ 01/922–9995).

HORSEBACK RIDING

The helpful **Hellenic Equestrian Federation** (⊠ Messinias 55, Goudi, Athens 15341, ☎ 01/652–8139) provides a list of riding clubs throughout the country.

RAFTING & KAYAKING

Alpin Club (⊠ Mihalakopoulou 39, Ilisia, Athens 11528, ☎ 01/721–2773 or 01/729–5426) organizes trips, including transportation, guides, and equipment, to rivers throughout Greece. Trekking Hellas and F-Zein (☞ Hiking & Mountain Biking, *above*) also offer many whitewater expeditions.

ROCK CLIMBING & MOUNTAINEERING

The **Alpine Club of Aharnon** (☞ Hiking & Mountain Biking, *above*) runs rock-climbing seminars throughout Greece, including the monastery-crowned pinnacles of Meteora, as does **Alpamayo Club** (⊠ Panepistimiou 44 in Harilaou Trikoupi arcade, Athens 10679, ☎ 01/362–7032), which also has mountaineering and paragliding classes.

SAILING & WINDSURFING

The **Greek Sailing Federation** (⊠ Leoforos Poseidonos 51, Moschato, Athens 18344, ☎ 01/930–4826 through 01/930–4828) can recommend clubs with equipment and lessons available for both sailing and windsurfing. Those who have a diploma for sailing on the open sea can legally rent a sailboat (without a captain, if two people on board are licensed); rentals range from about 28,000 dr. to 200,000 dr. a day, depending on the size and age of the boat and whether a skipper is included. Contact **Ghiolman Yachts** (⊠ Fillelinon 7, Syntagma, Athens

10557, ☎ 01/322–8530 or 01/323–
0330, FAX 01/322–3251), **Mediterranean Yachts** (✉ Vas. Sofias 11,
Syntagma, Athens 10671, ☎ 01/362–
0000, FAX 01/360–2364), or **Vernicos
Yachts** (✉ Leoforos Poseidonos 11,
Alimos, Athens 17455, ☎ 01/985–
0122 through 01/985–0128,
FAX 01/985–0130).

SCUBA DIVING

Greece, according to the recent EU
Blue Flag survey, has the cleanest
beaches in Europe. With its numerous
islands and long coastline, it offers
tourists everything from glamorous
trendy stretches like Super Paradise in
Mykonos, packed with Bodies Beautiful, to secluded coves like Mikro
Seitani in Samos, reached only after
an hour's hike. Greeks don't really go
swimming until June, but the water is
fine usually by May and stays warm
through September or even mid-
October.

In Athens **EOT outlets** (main info
office, ✉ Amerikis 2, Athens, ☎ 01/
331–0561 or 01/331–0562) can give
you a list of their local beaches, which
have snack bars and beach umbrellas,
chairs, dressing rooms, and sports
equipment for rent, and occasionally
windsurfing and waterskiing lessons.

Scuba diving is heavily restricted to
protect underwater artifacts. It is
forbidden to dive at night or remove
anything from the sea floor. Areas
where limited diving is permitted
include Corfu, Chalkidiki, Mykonos,
and Rhodes. A travel agent can steer
you to a supervised dive trip, or you
can call the **Greek Diving Center**
(✉ Vas. Pavlou 26, Kastella, Piraeus
18533, ☎ 01/412–1708, FAX 01/
411–9207), which offers lessons up
to the instructor's level, rents equipment, and organizes one- to two-day
diving excursions on weekends. The
Aegean Dive Center (✉ Pandoras 42
and Zamanou 53, Glyfada 16674,
☎ 01/894–5409, FAX 01/898–1120)
provides equipment rental and service, diver training including first-aid
courses, dive trips, and an air center.
For those who want an introduction
to the sport, **Scuba Diving Club of
Vouliagmeni** (✉ Leoforos Poseidonos
below Agnadia café-bar, 16671
Ormos Vouliagmeni, near Athens,

☎ 01/696–4609) runs a one-hour
orientation for about 15,000 dr.
called Discover Scuba, where complete beginners can dive with an
instructor. The center also offers
regular diving courses, equipment,
boat rentals with accompaniment for
expeditions, and water sports. Call a
day ahead to arrange matters. Remember that any school dispensing
diplomas should be recognized by the
Greek state.

SKIING & SNOWBOARDING

Ski Centre Parnassos (☎ 0234/22689
or 0234/22695) is one of the country's best resorts, about three hours
north of Athens. The **Hellenic Skiing
Federation** (✉ Karageorgi Servias 7,
8th floor, Syntagma, Athens 10563,
☎ 01/323–0182 or 01/323–4412,
FAX 01/323–0142) can give you a
bilingual brochure with addresses for
other ski centers as well as mountain
refuges. The brochure is also available
from the EOT. The **Alpine Club of
Athens** (✉ Kapnikareas Sq. 2, Center,
☎ 01/321–2355 or 01/321–2429)
organizes mountain skiing classes for
experienced skiers and snowboarding
lessons for kids on Parnassos as well.

SPELUNKING

Tourists with troglodyte tendencies
are welcome to subterranean Greece.
Twelve of the caves have some facilities for tourists and more are being
developed. Spelunkers in search of
wild caves should contact the **Hellenic
Speleological Society** (✉ Mantzarou
8, Athens 10672, ☎ 01/361–7824,
FAX 01/364–3476), open Mondays
and Wednesdays 8 PM to 10 PM.

TENNIS

There are tennis clubs in most large
cities and island resorts. Call the
Hellenic Tennis Federation (✉ Olympic Stadium offices, Kalogreza, ☎ 01/
726–3170) for information on tennis
clubs, from which you can rent courts
by the hour, or check with your hotel
concierge to help you find one that
admits nonmembers.

PACKING

PACKING LIST

It's a good idea to itemize the contents of each bag and keep the list, in
case you need to file an insurance

claim. Be certain to put your home or business address on and inside each piece of luggage, including carry-on bags. It's also a good idea to mark your bags with a bright ribbon, since few Greek airports check passengers' baggage claim checks against luggage upon exit.

Outside Athens, Greek dress tends to be middle of the road—you won't see patched jeans or expensive suits, though locals tend to dress up for nightclubs and bouzoukia. In the summer bring lightweight, casual clothing and good walking shoes. A light sweater or jacket is a must for cool evenings, especially in the mountains. There's no need for rain gear in high summer, but don't forget sunglasses and a sun hat. Be prepared for cooler weather and some rain in spring and fall, and in winter, add a warm coat.

Casual attire is acceptable everywhere except in the most expensive restaurants in large cities, but you should dress conservatively when visiting churches or monasteries. It's not appropriate to show a lot of bare arm and leg; men wearing shorts must cover up as well, as must women in pants, in some stricter monasteries. Monasteries (e.g., in Meteora) and churches will not admit improperly dressed men or women, though they often provide long skirts or some sort of draping at the entrance. In cities, and everywhere in winter, revealing too much skin may lead to unwelcome harassment. Swimsuits are technically required, but most beaches are topless, except those near the harbor or town center. The number of beaches where nude bathing is acceptable is slowly growing. Watch to see what others do, and err on the conservative side.

For dimly lit icons in churches and moonless island walks, a small flashlight comes in handy, as does a jackknife with a corkscrew for picnicking, though they may show up on the airport security scanner and cause you to open your bag. It's a good idea to bring zip-closing plastic bags, mosquito repellent for more verdant areas, moist towelettes, a roll of transparent tape, and a pocket calculator, all indispensable. A pair of opera glasses can greatly enhance the appreciation of an archaeological site or give the tourist a better view of wall paintings in a church, for example.

PASSPORTS & VISAS

When traveling internationally, **carry a passport even if you don't need one** (it's always the best form of I.D.), and make **two photocopies of the data page** (one for someone at home and another for you, carried separately from your passport). If you lose your passport, promptly call the nearest embassy or consulate and the local police.

ENTERING GREECE

All U.S., Canadian, and U.K. citizens, even infants, need only a valid passport to enter Greece for stays of up to 90 days.

PASSPORT OFFICES

The best time to apply for a passport or to renew is during the fall and winter. Before any trip, be sure to check your passport's expiration date and, if necessary, renew it as soon as possible. (Some countries won't allow you to enter on a passport that's due to expire in six months or less.)

➤ AUSTRALIAN CITIZENS: **Australian Passport Office** (☎ 13–1232).

➤ CANADIAN CITIZENS: **Passport Office** (☎ 819/994–3500 or 800/567–6868).

➤ NEW ZEALAND CITIZENS: **New Zealand Passport Office** (☎ 04/494–0700 for information on how to apply, 0800/727–776 for information on applications already submitted).

➤ U.K. CITIZENS: **London Passport Office** (☎ 0990/21010), for fees and documentation requirements and to request an emergency passport.

➤ U.S. CITIZENS: **National Passport Information Center** (☎ 900/225–5674; calls are charged at 35¢ per minute for automated service, $1.05 per minute for operator service).

SAFETY

Greece is still one of the safest countries in Europe; even Athens has a low crime rate, with serious crimes rare,

although the number of bank rob-
beries, burglaries, and pickpocketing
at train and bus stations has gone up
in the last five years. You will often
see people sitting at cafés with their
handbag carelessly dangling over
chairs, or women and elderly people
walking home late at night. If you
take the normal precautions of carrying your money in a security pouch,
and if you avoid isolated places at
night, you should have little problem.
If you feel unsure about the safety of
an area, ask your hotel before setting
out. For example, in the last few
years, crime has gone up around
Omonia Square in Athens, because of
the large transient population that
congregates there.

In general, women traveling alone are
safe in Greece, though Greek men will
try to talk to them, especially if they
look foreign. It's best to do as the
Greek women do, and ignore the
amorous overtures; responding will
only be interpreted as a sign that
you're interested. If you feel threatened, don't hesitate to shout; this will
be enough to scare off most offenders.
Greeks, especially in Athens, where
people are out until all hours, will
usually come to your aid. One way to
avoid unwanted advances is to try to
blend in with the Greeks: Dress as
they do, walk like you know where
you're going, and don't openly carry
a map or a foreign newspaper. If you
are taking a taxi at night, the driver
won't usually pick up a male passenger; if he does, he is obligated to ask
your permission.

SENIOR-CITIZEN TRAVEL

Despite the dearth of facilities at
hotels, museums, and archaeological
sites for those with impaired movement, traveling in Greece can be quite
pleasurable. Elders are treated with
respect: Most Greeks still take care of
their parents at home, and crimes
against the elderly are infrequent.
Most people—even taxi drivers—will
go out of their way to make sure
senior citizens receive good treatment.

To qualify for age-related discounts,
**mention your senior-citizen status up
front** when purchasing tickets—
whether to enter a pay beach, see a
movie, or visit an archaeological site.

Greece does not have senior discounts
for hotels or restaurants. When renting a car, **ask about promotional car-
rental discounts,** which can be
cheaper than senior-citizen rates.

➤ EDUCATIONAL PROGRAMS: **Elderhos-
tel** (✉ 75 Federal St., 3rd floor,
Boston, MA 02110, ☎ 617/426–
8056). **Interhostel** (✉ University of
New Hampshire, 6 Garrison Ave.,
Durham, NH 03824, ☎ 603/862–
1147 or 800/733–9753, ℻ 603/
862–1113). **Folkways Institute** (✉
14600 Southeast Aldridge Rd., Port-
land, OR 97236-6518, ☎ 503/658–
6600 or 800/225–4666, ℻ 503/
658–8672).

SHOPPING

Because of hefty VAT taxes, most
items in Greece, especially electric
appliances and clothing, cost more
than in the U.S. and Canada, though
Greece does have inexpensive shoes,
furs, and leather goods. Good gift
ideas are the natural Kalymnos
sponges; flokati rugs made from
longhaired goat wool; handicrafts
such as embroidery, ceramics, and
kilims; fisherman's caps and hand-
knit sweaters; koboloi (worry beads)
in plastic, wood, and onyx; and blue-
and white amulets that protect
against mati (the evil eye). What is
cheaper in Greece is silver and gold
jewelry, often original and unusual
pieces. In some stores, chains are sold
by the gram. Always bargain in
tourist shops and with street vendors
(except for sponges—prices are set by
the government), and always get a
receipt from shops. In an attempt to
diminish tax fraud, the government
heavily fines buyers who walk out of
a store without proof of purchase.
Most stores will not give you a cash
refund, but they may give you a credit
slip. Traditional sale periods run for
about a month in February and
August, though shop owners have
extended these periods recently to
bolster flagging sales.

A delightful institution in Greece is
the laiki (open-air market), which
offers fresh produce at prices lower
than in produce stores, as well as
items sold by political and economic
refugees, such as linen tablecloths
(sold by the meter), caviar, and

THE GOLD GUIDE / SMART TRAVEL TIPS

Russian lacquered dolls. Every town has a laiki, and big cities like Athens have several a day in different neighborhoods.

STUDENT TRAVEL

For students, Greece is an inexpensive destination. Not only are museums and archaeological sites free for EU members and cheaper for non-EU students (you must have an ISIC card), but student and youth rates are offered on public transportation as well as domestic and EU flights. Many travel agencies catering to students are on Fillelinon and Nikis streets in Athens, off Syntagma Square.

Rented rooms and camping are the most inexpensive lodging—in summer, you can rent roof space if you've brought a sleeping bag. Take advantage of souvlaki stands (the filling fast food of Greece), local tavernas, and the open-air market; convenience stores in tourist areas are wildly overpriced. Finally, watch expenditures in bars—in most, an alcoholic drink costs at least 1,800 dr.

TRAVEL AGENCIES

To save money, **look into deals available through student-oriented travel agencies.** To qualify you'll need a bona fide student I.D. card. Members of international student groups are also eligible.

➤ IN GREECE: A good agency to try, especially if you haven't managed to get your ISIC card and need a student pass for Greece, is **International Student and Youth Travel Service** (✉ Nikis 11, 1st floor, Athens 10557, ☎ 01/323–3767, FAX 01/322–1531).

➤ STUDENT I.D.s & SERVICES: **Council on International Educational Exchange** (CIEE, ✉ 205 E. 42nd St., 14th floor, New York, NY 10017, ☎ 212/822–2600 or 888/268–6245, FAX 212/822–2699), for mail orders only, in the United States. **Travel Cuts** (✉ 187 College St., Toronto, Ontario M5T 1P7, ☎ 416/979–2406 or 800/667–2887) in Canada.

➤ STUDENT TOURS: **Contiki Holidays** (✉ 300 Plaza Alicante, Suite 900, Garden Grove, CA 92840, ☎ 714/740–0808 or 800/266–8454,

FAX 714/740–2034). **AESU Travel** (✉ 2 Hamill Rd., Suite 248, Baltimore, MD 21210-1807, ☎ 410/323–4416 or 800/638–7640, FAX 410/323–4498).

TAXES

Taxes are always included in the stated price, unless otherwise noted.

An 8.2% government tax and 2.4% municipality tax (total 10.6%) is added to hotel bills, though usually the rate quoted to you will include the taxes. Ask.

VALUE-ADDED TAX (VAT)

Value-added tax, 4% for books and about 18% for almost everything else, called FPA (pronounced fee-pee-ah) by Greeks, is included in the cost of most consumer goods and services. As an individual, you may get a VAT refund on products worth 40,000 dr. or more bought in Greece from licensed stores that usually display a Tax-Free Shopping sticker in their window. The shop will complete a Tax-Free check for you, which you must fill out and show at Greek Customs, along with the item to prove you are taking it out of the country. If you're leaving Greece late at night, the Customs desk is immediately after the X-ray machine in the East Terminal; just call from the desk phone available and someone will appear. Customs—at the airport or port—will stamp the paper, which you can then mail back to the shop from the airport. You should have arranged the method of repayment with the shop; it can take up to a year to see your money.

TAXIS

In Greece, as everywhere, unscrupulous taxi drivers will try to take advantage of out-of-towners or foreigners. Rather than memorize all the allowable surcharges, you might ask your hotel concierge or owner before engaging a taxi what the fare to your destination ought to be. You are more likely to be overcharged in Athens and vicinity than elsewhere, especially when traveling to and from airport terminals. It should cost no more than 2,000–2,200 dr. from the airport (depending on the terminal and the traffic) to city center. Make sure that the driver turns on the meter to Tarifa 1, unless it's between midnight and 5 AM, when the price goes up. Remember that an extra 300 dr. is expected when taking a taxi to and from the airport and 150 dr. from (but not to) ports and bus and train stations. There is also a surcharge during holiday periods, about 120 dr. Each item of baggage is likewise charged (55 dr.). At Piraeus port, drivers will often wait until they fill the taxi with passengers going in the same direction, which costs you time and money. It's faster and cheaper to take the nearby metro (100 dr.) into the center or walk out of the port onto a main road and flag down a cab. If you suspect a driver is overcharging, demand to be taken to the police station; this usually brings them around. As a last resort contact the tourist police (☎ 171 in Athens).

When you're taking an early-morning flight, it's a good idea to reserve a radio taxi the night before (600 dr. surcharge, 400 dr. for immediate response). They are usually quite reliable and punctual; if you're not staying in a hotel, the local tourist police can give you some phone numbers for companies.

TELEPHONES

COUNTRY CODES

The country code for Greece is 30. When dialing Greece from the U.S. or Canada, you would first dial 011, then 30 (011-30). From continental Europe or the U.K. you just dial 0030. Each region in Greece has several area codes (01 for Athens, 031 for Thessaloniki, 061 for Patras). When dialing from outside Greece, you drop the "0" in the area code; within Greece you must include the "0." So, for example, if you dial Athens from New York, you direct dial: 011-30-1-XXX-XXXX, but from Thessaloniki, you would have to dial 01-XXX-XXXX.

Throughout this guide, establishments may include several phone numbers rather than a central switchboard. Until recently, getting a second phone line from OTE was an expensive and lengthy process (some areas had to wait up to 10 years), so owners may "rent" lines directly from other peo-

ple. Also, they now use mobile phones, indicated by numbers that begin with the area code 093 or 094.

Doing business over the phone in Greece can be extremely frustrating—the lines always seem to be busy, and English-speaking operators and clerks are few. You may also find people too busy to address your problem—the independent-minded Greeks are not very service-conscious. It is far better to develop a relationship with someone, for example a travel agent, to get information about train schedules and the like, or to go in person and ask for information face-to-face. Though OTE is updating its archaic phone system, it may take you several attempts to get through. Try dialing slowly, and if you get a wrong number, don't assume it's your mistake—the lines frequently get crossed. Don't discuss highly sensitive matters on the phone; party lines are still a social hazard in Greece. Local and international calls are cheaper weekdays 3 PM to 5 PM and 10 PM to 8 AM, on the weekends, from Saturday 3 PM to Monday 8 AM.

DIRECTORY & OPERATOR INFORMATION

There are English-speaking operators on the International Exchange (☎ 161 and 162), and recorded instructions in English, French, and German for making direct international calls on ☎ 169. In most cases, there is a three-minute minimum charge for operator-assisted station-to-station calls, a four-minute minimum for person-to-person connections. For directory information, call 131, but know that often you need to give surname of a shop or restaurant's proprietor to be able to get the phone number; tourist police are more helpful for the numbers of such establishments.

FAXING

If you need to send a fax and can't find a hotel or travel agency to let you use theirs, you may send one from most post offices.

INTERNATIONAL CALLS

AT&T, MCI, and Sprint international access codes make calling the United States relatively convenient, but you may find the local access number blocked in many hotel rooms. First ask the hotel operator to connect you. If the hotel operator balks, ask for an international operator, or dial the international operator yourself. One way to improve your odds of getting connected to your long-distance carrier is to travel with more than one company's calling card (a hotel may block Sprint, for example, but not MCI). If all else fails, call from a pay phone in the hotel lobby.

➤ ACCESS CODES: AT&T Direct (☎ 00/800–1311; 800/435–0812 for other areas;). MCI WorldPhone (☎ 00/800–1211; 800/444–4141 for other areas). **Sprint International Access** (☎ 00/800–1411; 800/877–4646 for other areas;).

➤ LONG-DISTANCE CARRIERS: AT&T (☎ 800/225–5288). MCI (☎ 800/888–8000). Sprint (☎ 800/366–2255).

PUBLIC PHONES

The Greek telephone company, the OTE (pronounced "oh-tay"), has card phones virtually everywhere, though some may not be in working order. Phone cards up to 1,000 units (at 11,300 dr., figure about one unit per local call) used for intercity and overseas calls can be purchased at kiosks, convenience stores, or the local OTE office. If you want more privacy—the card phones tend to be on busy street corners and people waiting to make their own calls may try to hurry you—use a card phone in a hotel lobby or OTE offices, though these tend to have limited hours. You can also use coins by calling from a kiosk phone (a local call is about 20 dr.). If you don't get a dial tone at first, you probably need to ask the kiosk owner to set the meter to zero (Óboreéte na to mitheneéste?). Try to avoid making calls from your hotel, where the surcharge can be quite hefty.

TIPPING

How much to tip in Greece, especially at restaurants, is confusing. By law a 13% service charge is figured into the price of a meal (menus sometimes list entrées with and without service, to let you know their net cost—not to imply you have a choice of how much

to pay), so, technically, you don't have to leave any additional tip, but it is customary to do so. If the service was poor or the waiter rude (very unlikely), you are not obligated to do so, but if the service was good, leave about 10% more. For taxis, round up the fare to the nearest 50 dr.

The appropriate tip for maid service at your hotel will depend, of course, on the quality of the service, the length of your stay, and the quality of the hotel. A service charge is included in the price of the room, but you might consider leaving an additional 200 dr. per person per night, or more for an extended stay. Porters, found only at the more expensive hotels, should get 100 dr.–200 dr. per bag, and hatcheck persons would like the same amount. For rest-room attendants 100 dr. is appropriate. Theater ushers and people dispensing programs at cinemas also get 100 dr. On cruises, cabin and dining-room stewards get about 500 dr. a day; guides receive about the same.

TOUR OPERATORS

Buying a prepackaged tour or independent vacation can make your trip to Greece less expensive and more hassle-free. Because everything is prearranged, you'll spend less time planning.

Operators that handle several hundred thousand travelers per year can use their purchasing power to give you a good price. Their high volume may also indicate financial stability. But some small companies provide more personalized service; because they tend to specialize, they may also be more knowledgeable about a given area.

BOOKING WITH AN AGENT

Travel agents are excellent resources. In fact, large operators accept bookings made only through travel agents. But it's a good idea to **collect brochures from several agencies,** because some agents' suggestions may be influenced by relationships with tour and package firms that reward them for volume sales. If you have a special interest, **find an agent with expertise in that area**; ASTA (☞ Travel Agencies, *below*) has a database of specialists worldwide.

Make sure your travel agent knows the accommodations and other services. Ask about the hotel's location, room size, beds, and whether it has a pool, room service, or programs for children, if you care about these. Has your agent been there in person or sent others you can contact?

Do some homework on your own, too: Local tourism boards can provide information about lesser-known and small-niche operators, some of which may sell only direct.

BUYER BEWARE

Each year consumers are stranded or lose their money when tour operators—even very large ones—with excellent reputations—go out of business. So **check out the operator.** Find out how long the company has been in business, and ask several travel agents about its reputation. If the package or tour you are considering is priced lower than in your wildest dreams, **be skeptical.** Try to **book with a company that has a consumer-protection program.** If the operator has such a program, you'll find information about it in the company's brochure. If the operator you are considering does not offer some kind of consumer protection, then ask for references from satisfied customers.

In the U.S., members of the National Tour Association and United States Tour Operators Association are required to set aside funds to cover your payments and travel arrangements in case the company defaults. It's also a good idea to choose a company that participates in the American Society of Travel Agent's Tour Operator Program (TOP). This gives you a forum if there are any disputes between you and your tour operator; ASTA will act as mediator.

➤ TOUR-OPERATOR RECOMMENDATIONS: **American Society of Travel Agents** (☞ Travel Agencies, *below*). **National Tour Association** (NTA, ✉ 546 E. Main St., Lexington, KY 40508, ☎ 606/226–4444 or 800/755–8687). **United States Tour Operators Association** (USTOA, ✉ 342 Madison Ave., Suite 1522, New York, NY 10173, ☎ 212/599–6599 or 800/468–7862, ℻ 212/599–6744).

COSTS

The more your package or tour includes, the better you can predict the ultimate cost of your vacation. Make sure you know exactly what is covered, and **beware of hidden costs.** Are taxes, tips, and service charges included? Transfers and baggage handling? Entertainment and excursions? These can add up.

Prices for packages and tours are usually quoted per person, based on two sharing a room. If traveling solo, you may be required to pay the full double-occupancy rate. Some operators eliminate this surcharge if you agree to be matched with a roommate of the same sex, even if one is not found by departure time.

GROUP TOURS

Among companies that sell tours to Greece, the following are nationally known, have a proven reputation, and offer plenty of options. The classifications used below represent different price categories, and you'll probably encounter these terms when talking to a travel agent or tour operator. The key difference is usually in accommodations, which run from budget to better, and better-yet to best.

➤ SUPER-DELUXE: **Abercrombie & Kent** (✉ 1520 Kensington Rd., Oak Brook, IL 60521-2141, ☎ 630/954–2944 or 800/323–7308, ℻ 630/954–3324). **Travcoa** (✉ Box 2630, 2350 S.E. Bristol St., Newport Beach, CA 92660, ☎ 714/476–2800 or 800/992–2003, ℻ 714/476–2538).

➤ DELUXE: **Globus** (✉ 5301 S. Federal Circle, Littleton, CO 80123-2980, ☎ 303/797–2800 or 800/221–0090, ℻ 303/347–2080). **Maupintour** (✉ 1515 St. Andrews Dr., Lawrence, KS 66047, ☎ 785/843–1211 or 800/255–4266, ℻ 785/843–8351). **Tauck Tours** (✉ Box 5027, 276 Post Rd. W, Westport, CT 06881-5027, ☎ 203/226–6911 or 800/468–2825, ℻ 203/221–6866).

➤ FIRST-CLASS: **Brendan Tours** (✉ 15137 Califa St., Van Nuys, CA 91411, ☎ 818/785–9696 or 800/

421–8446, FAX 818/902–9876).
Caravan Tours (✉ 401 N. Michigan
Ave., Chicago, IL 60611, ☎ 312/
321–9800 or 800/227–2826, FAX
312/321–9845). **Central Holidays**
(✉ 206 Central Ave., Jersey City, NJ
07307, ☎ 201/798–5777 or 800/
935–5000). **Collette Tours** (✉ 162
Middle St., Pawtucket, RI 02860,
☎ 401/728–3805 or 800/832–4656,
FAX 401/728–1380). **DER Tours**
(✉ 9501 W. Devon St., Rosemont, IL
60018, ☎ 800/937–1235, FAX 847/
692–4141 or 800/282–7474, 800/
860–9944 for brochures). **General
Tours** (✉ 53 Summer St., Keene, NH
03431, ☎ 603/357–5033 or 800/
221–2216, FAX 603/357–4548).
Insight International Tours (✉ 745
Atlantic Ave., No. 720, Boston, MA
02111, ☎ 617/482–2000 or 800/
582–8380, FAX 617/482–2884 or
800/622–5015). **Trafalgar Tours**
(✉ 11 E. 26th St., New York, NY
10010, ☎ 212/689–8977 or 800/
854–0103, FAX 800/457–6644).

➤ BUDGET: **Cosmos** (☞ Globus,
above).

PACKAGES

Like group tours, independent vacation packages are available from
major tour operators and airlines.
The companies listed below offer
vacation packages in a broad price
range.

➤ AIR/HOTEL: **Central Holidays** (☞
Group Tours, *above*). **Delta Vacations**
(☎ 800/872–7786). **DER Tours** (☞
Group Tours, *above*). **General Tours**
(☞ Group Tours, *above*). **TWA
Getaway Vacations** (☎ 800/438–
2929).

➤ FROM THE U.K.: **British Airways
Holidays** (Astral Towers, Betts Way,
London Rd., Crawley, West Sussex
RH10 2XA, ☎ 01293/722–727,
FAX 01293/722–624). **First Choice**
(✉ First Choice House, Peel Cross
Rd., Salford, Manchester M4 2AN,
☎ 0161/745–7000). **Inspirations**
(✉ Caledonian House, Perimeter Rd.
S., Gatwick Airport, Surrey RH6
0LF, ☎ 01293/579579). **Unijet**
(✉ Sandrocks, Rocky Ln., Haywards
Heath, West Sussex RH16 4RH,
☎ 0990/114114).

THEME TRIPS

Travel Contacts (✉ Box 173, Cam-
berley GU15 1YE, England, ☎
01276/677217, FAX 01276/63477)
represents more than 150 tour operators in Europe.

➤ ARCHAEOLOGY: **Archaeological
Tours** (✉ 271 Madison Ave., New
York, NY 10016, ☎ 212/986–3054,
FAX 212/370–1561).

➤ BICYCLING: **Classic Adventures**
(Box 153, Hamlin, NY 14464-0153,
☎ 716/964–8488 or 800/777–8090,
FAX 716/964–7297). **Naturequest**
(✉ 934 Acapulco St., Laguna Beach,
CA 92651, ☎ 714/499–9561 or 800/
369–3033, FAX 714/499–0812).
Uniquely Europe (✉ 2819 1st Ave.,
Ste. 280, Seattle, WA 98121-1113,
☎ 206/441–8682 or 800/426–3615,
FAX 206/441–8862).

➤ HORSEBACK RIDING: **Equitour
Worldwide Riding Holidays** (✉ Box
807, Dubois, WY 82513, ☎ 307/
455–3363 or 800/545–0019,
FAX 307/455–2354).

➤ JUDAISM: **American Jewish Con-
gress** (✉ 15 E. 84th St., New York,
NY 10028, ☎ 212/879–4588 or 800/
221–4694).

➤ KAYAKING: **Mountain Travel-Sobek**
(✉ 6420 Fairmount Ave., El Cerrito,
CA 94530, ☎ 510/527–8100 or 888/
687–6235, FAX 510/525–7710).
Naturequest (☞ Bicycling, *above*).

➤ LEARNING: **Earthwatch** (✉ Box
9104, 680 Mount Auburn St., Water-
town, MA 02272, ☎ 617/926–8200
or 800/776–0188, FAX 617/926–
8532) organizes research expeditions.
IST Cultural Tours (225 W. 34th St.,
New York, NY 10122-0913, ☎ 212/
563–1202 or 800/833–2111, FAX
212/594–6953). **Smithsonian Study
Tours and Seminars** (✉ 1100 Jeffer-
son Dr. SW, Room 3045, MRC 702,
Washington, DC 20560, ☎ 202/357–
4700, FAX 202/633–9250).

➤ SINGLES AND YOUNG ADULTS: **Contiki Holidays** (✉ 300 Plaza Alicante,
No. 900, Garden Grove, CA 92640,
☎ 714/740–0808 or 800/266–8454,
FAX 714/740–0818).

➤ SPAS: **Spa-Finders** (✉ 91 5th Ave.,
No. 301, New York, NY 10003-

3039, ☎ 212/924–6800 or 800/255–7727).

➤ WALKING/HIKING: **Adventure Center** (✉ 1311 63rd St., No. 200, Emeryville, CA 94608, ☎ 510/654–1879 or 800/227–8747, FAX 510/654–4200). **Backroads** (✉ 801 Cedar St., Berkeley, CA 94710-1800, ☎ 510/527–1555 or 800/462–2848, FAX 510-527–1444). **Himalayan Travel** (✉ 110 Prospect St., Stamford, CT 06901, ☎ 203/359–3711 or 800/225–2380, FAX 203/359–3669). **Uniquely Europe** (☞ Bicycling, *above*).

TRAIN TRAVEL

Fares are reasonable, and trains offer a good, though slow, alternative to long drives or bus rides (there are IC express trains from Athens to Thessaloniki and Patras). The main line running north from Athens divides into three lines at Thessaloniki, continuing on to Belgrade, Istanbul, and Bulgaria. The Peloponnese in the south is served by a narrow-gauge line dividing at Corinth into the Mycenae-Argos route and Patras-Olympia-Kalamata. The leisurely Peloponnesian train is a pleasant way to see southern Greece, but the Patras–Athens leg can be crowded during the high season because of tourists arriving in Patras from Italy. The assigned seating of first class may be a good idea at such times. The Greek Railway Organization (OSE) has two stations in Athens, side by side, off Diliyianni Street west of Omonia Square. Trains from northern Greece and abroad use **Stathmos Larissis** (☎ 01/823–7741). Take Trolley 1 from the terminal to Omonia square. Trains from the Peloponnese use **Stathmos Peloponnisou** (☎ 01/513–1601) next door. To Omonia and Syntagma squares, take Bus 057. OSE buses for Albania, Bulgaria, and Turkey also leave from this station (☎ 01/513–5768 or 01/513–5769).

➤ INFORMATION: Contact the **Greek Railway Organization** (OSE) at your local station, or at their main offices in Athens (✉ Karolou St. 1 near Omonia Sq., ☎ 01/522–4302 for Peloponnese, 01/522–2491 for northern Greece destinations; ✉ Sina St. 6, ☎ 01/362–4402 through 01/362–4406; and ✉ Filellinon St. 17

near Syntagma Square, ☎ 01/323–6747 or 01/323–6273). Since the phones at the stations are inevitably busy and the ticket office clerks harried, it's best to call OSE's helpful general information switchboard for timetables and prices (✉ ☎ 01/529–7777), open daily 7 AM–9 PM. You may also call ☎ 145 for a recorded departure timetable, in Greek, of trains within Greece; call ☎ 147 for information on trains to Europe and Russia.

DISCOUNT PASSES

To save money, **look into rail passes.** But be aware that if you don't plan to cover many miles, you may come out ahead by buying individual tickets.

Greece is one of 17 countries in which you can **use Eurailpasses,** which provide unlimited first-class rail travel, in all of the participating countries, for the duration of the pass. If you plan to rack up the miles, get a standard pass. These are available for 15 days ($538), 21 days ($698), one month ($864), two months ($1,224), and three months ($1,512).

If Greece is your only destination in Europe, **consider purchasing a Greece Flexipass Rail 'n Fly.** For $202 you get three days of first-class rail travel within a one-month period two selected Olympic Airways flights.

The **Balkan Flexipass** covers first-class train travel through Greece as well as Bulgaria, Romania, Macedonia, Turkey, and Yugoslavia; there are passes for 5, 10, or 15 travel days in a one-month period for $152, $264, and $317 respectively.

If your plans call for only limited train travel, **look into a Europass,** which costs less money than a Eurailpass. Unlike with Eurailpasses, however, you get a limited number of travel days, in a limited number of countries, during a specified time period. For example, a two-month pass ($326) allows between 5 and 15 days of rail travel but costs $200 less than the least expensive Eurailpass. Keep in mind, however, that the Europass is good only in France, Germany, Italy, Spain, and Switzerland, and the number of countries you can visit is further limited by the type of pass you buy. For example, the basic two-month pass allows you to visit only three of the five participating countries.

In addition to standard Eurailpasses, **ask about special rail-pass plans.** Among these are the Eurail Youthpass (for those under age 26), the Eurail Saverpass (which gives a discount for two or more people traveling together), a Eurail Flexipass (which allows a certain number of travel days within a set period), the Euraildrive Pass and the Europass Drive (which combines travel by train and rental car). Whichever pass you choose, remember that you must **purchase your pass before you leave** for Europe.

Many travelers assume that rail passes guarantee them seats on the trains they wish to ride. Not so. You need to **book seats ahead even if you are using a rail pass;** seat reservations are required on some European trains, particularly high-speed trains, and are a good idea on trains that may be crowded—particularly in summer on popular routes. You will also need a reservation if you purchase sleeping accommodations.

➤ INFORMATION AND PASSES: **Rail Europe** (500 Mamaroneck Ave., Harrison, NY 10528, ☎ 914/682–5172 or 800/438–7245, ℻ 800/432–1329; 2087 Dundas E, Suite 106, Mississauga, Ontario L4X 1M2, ☎ 800/361–7245, ℻ 905/602–4198). **DER Travel Services** (✉ 9501 W. Devon Ave., Rosemont, IL 60018, ☎ 800/782–2424, ℻ 800/282–7474 for information; 800/860–9944 for brochures). **CIT Tours Corp.** (15 W. 44th St., 10th floor, New York, NY 10036, ☎ 212/730–2400 or 800/248–7245 in the U.S., 800/387–0711 or 800/361–7799 in Canada).

FROM THE U.K.

There are two main routes to Greece by train from the United Kingdom: the overland route via Munich, Salzburg, Ljubljana, and Zagreb has resumed operation (about three days); it is more pleasant to travel through Italy, then go by ferry from Brindisi to Patras in the Peloponnese. In high

summer, catch the train from London's Victoria Station to Dover for the crossing to Calais and the connecting service to Paris's Gare du Nord. From there, transfer to the Gare de Lyon for the train that runs via Switzerland to Milan. Switch there and travel through to Brindisi Maritime station, where you connect with the ferry to Patras (about 17 hours), and arrive the following day. From Patras there is bus and train service to Athens (total time London–Athens 2½ days). Given the numerous and inexpensive deals available from summer, and taking in account food costs, it might be cheaper to fly from London.

TIMETABLES

The **Thomas Cook European Timetable** is essential. It is available in U.S. from Forsyth Travel Library (✉ Box 2975, Shawnee Mission, KS 66201–1375, ☎ 800/307–7984) and in the United Kingdom from Thomas Cook, Timetable Publishing Office (✉ Box 36, Thorpe Wood, Peterborough, Cambridgeshire PE3 6SB).

TRANSPORTATION

Try to avoid driving in Greece. In big cities, it's easier and cheaper to take taxis, especially for couples or families. Urban public transportation is also a good alternative, inexpensive, frequent, and operating until at least midnight. To travel throughout Greece's mainland, rely on KTEL buses, which operate an extensive network to even the most remote villages. Trains have fewer stops, are slower (except for the ICs between Athens and Patras or Athens and Thessaloniki), but are slightly cheaper. To get to an island, the ferry is usually the best bet, if the journey is six hours or less. Those pressed for time can take the much more expensive hydrofoils to nearby islands or fly, usually with Olympic, which may mean delays and cancellations. However, a 45-minute flight to Santorini beats the arduous ferry trip (10 to 12 hours), especially in summer around August 15, when every cranny of the decks is jammed with vacationing Greeks. If you do take a long ferry trip, try to book a cabin. For most islands, it's liberating to rent a motorbike for long-distance sightseeing not tied to bus schedules, but be extremely cautious and drive defensively.

TRAVEL AGENCIES

A good travel agent puts your needs first. Look for an agency that has been in business at least five years, emphasizes customer service, and has someone on staff who specializes in your destination. In addition, **make sure the agency belongs to a professional trade organization,** such as ASTA in the United States. If your travel agency is also acting as your tour operator, *see* Buyer Beware in Tour Operators, *above*).

➤ LOCAL AGENT REFERRALS: **American Society of Travel Agents** (ASTA, ☎ 800/965–2782 24-hr hot line, FAX 703/684–8319). **Association of British Travel Agents** (✉ 55–57 Newman St., London W1P 4AH, ☎ 0171/637–2444, FAX 0171/637–0713). **Association of Canadian Travel Agents** (✉ Suite 201, 1729 Bank St., Ottawa, Ontario K1V 7Z5, ☎ 613/521–0474, FAX 613/521–0805). **Australian Federation of Travel Agents** (☎ 02/9264–3299). **Travel Agents' Association of New Zealand** (☎ 04/499–0104).

VISITOR INFORMATION

Contact the **Greek National Tourist Organization** (GNTO, but known as in Greece), which has offices throughout the world.

➤ EOT IN GREECE: EOT main office, near Syntagma Square (✉ Amerikis 2, ☎ 01/331–0561 or 01/331–0562). There are also information booths at the Athens airport (✉ East Terminal, ☎ 01/961–2722 or 01/969–4500), and the Zea Marina, near where the hydrofoils dock (✉ EOT Building, 1st floor, Zea Marina, ☎ 01/452–2591). In Thessaloniki, the EOT runs offices in the city center (✉ Mitropoleos 34 on Platia Aristotelous, ☎ 031/222–935, 031/271–888, and 031/265–574) and the airport (☎ 031/471–170). To locate the EOT office nearest nearest your destination, check with your country's EOT representative.

➤ GREEK NATIONAL TOURIST ORGANIZATION: In the U.S. (✉ 645 5th Ave., New York, NY 10022, ☎ 212/ 421–5777, FAX 212/826–6940; ✉ 611 W. 6th St., Suite 2198, Los Angeles, CA 90017, ☎ 213/626–6696, FAX 213/489–9744; ✉ 168 N. Michigan Ave., Suite 600, Chicago, IL 60601, ☎ 312/782–1084, FAX 312/782–1091). In Canada (✉ 1233 Rue de la Montagne, Suite 101, Montréal, Québec H3G 1Z2, ☎ 514/871–1535, FAX 514/871–1498; ✉ 1300 Bay St., Toronto, Ontario M5R 3K8, ☎ 416/968–2220, FAX 416/968–6533). In the U.K. (✉ 4 Conduit St., London W1R 0DJ, ☎ 0171/734–5997).

WHEN TO GO

The best time to visit Greece is late spring and early fall. In May and June the days are warm, even hot, but dry, and the sea water has been warmed by the sun. The evenings, which seem endless, are pleasant enough to dine alfresco. For sightseeing, exploring the cities or countryside, or hitting the beach, this is the time. Greece is relatively tourist free in the spring, so if you don't like crowds, and the beach and swimming aren't high on your agenda, April and early May are a good time to tour the country. Carnavali, usually in February just before Lent, and Greek Easter, with its religious processions, lambs, and red eggs, are the highlights of the season.

September and October are a good alternative to spring and early summer. Things begin to shut down in November, however, and the winter chill and rains begin. Winter in Greece is deceptive. Any given day may not be very cold. Except in the mountains, snow is uncommon in Athens and to the south. But the cold is persistent, and the level of heating visitors may be accustomed to is not usual in Greece. Over the course of a few days you will feel chilled to the bone. Transportation to the islands is limited in winter, and many hotels outside large cities are closed until the beginning of April. Unless you are going to Greece in pursuit of winter sports, try a different season.

Toward the end of July and through August the temperatures climb, pushing the 100°F (38°C) mark. In the south a dry, hot wind may blow across the Mediterranean from the

THE GOLD GUIDE / SMART TRAVEL TIPS

coast of Africa. The air quality in Athens, which is surrounded on all sides by mountains (except in the direction of the harbor and oil refineries of Piraeus), can be unhealthy on especially hot days, and air-conditioning is far from ubiquitous. Coincident with these unfortunate climatic conditions is the peak of the tourist season. In August you should flee Athens as soon as possible and head off the beaten path.

CLIMATE

Greece enjoys a typical Mediterranean climate: hot, dry summers and cool, wet winters. The average high and low temperatures for Athens and Heraklion (Crete) and average temperatures for Thessaloniki and Northern Greece are presented below. Note that although average temperatures in the north and the south may not be too dissimilar, the temperature on a given day can differ substantially.

Climate in Greece

ATHENS

Jan.	52F	13C	May	77F	25C	Sept.	84F	29C
	43	6		61	16		66	19
Feb.	57F	14C	June	86F	30C	Oct.	75F	24C
	45	7		68	20		59	15
Mar.	61F	16C	July	91F	33C	Nov.	66F	19C
	46	8		73	23		54	12
Apr.	68F	20C	Aug.	91F	33C	Dec.	59F	15C
	52	11		73	23		46	8

HERAKLION

Jan.	61F	16C	May	73F	23C	Sept.	81F	27C
	48	9		59	15		66	19
Feb.	61F	16C	June	81F	27C	Oct.	75F	24C
	48	9		66	19		63	17
Mar.	63F	17C	July	84F	29C	Nov.	70F	21C
	50	10		72	22		57	14
Apr.	68F	20C	Aug.	84F	29C	Dec.	64F	18C
	54	12		72	22		52	11

THESSALONIKI AND NORTHERN GREECE

Jan.	45F	8C	May	74F	24C	Sept.	80F	27C
Feb.	51F	11C	June	86F	30C	Oct.	69F	21C
Mar.	54F	13C	July	90F	32C	Nov.	58F	15C
Apr.	65F	19C	Aug.	90F	32C	Dec.	50F	10C

➤ FORECASTS: **Weather Channel Connection** (☎ 900/932–8437), 95¢ per minute from a Touch-Tone phone.

1 Destination: Greece

FROM ZEUS TO ZORBA

HE WAG WHO CALLED GREECE "a landscape and some old stones" left out one indispensable element: the Greeks. Maybe he wanted to ignore them. But this is impossible. You can't ignore 8 million electric eels even during siesta time when the battery runs down. Yet visitors to Greece, conditioned by museums, textbooks, and college Greek, are astonished to find that the country is populated at all. It is most unexpected to find real people here—like stumbling upon a cocktail party in a mausoleum. To add to the surprise, the Greeks don't have the "proper Greek look." Travelers who were nurtured on the truth and beauty of Keats' Grecian Urn find it surprising to see the natives roaring around in sport cars and talking about the latest nouvelle restaurant. Incongruous as it may seem, in fact, most Greeks have two arms and two legs attached to the torso in the normal places. The torso itself is not swathed in mother's best percale bedsheet, which would be unfashionable in Athens. But, in the end, although their countryside may be bleached and stony, the Greeks themselves—as the lucky visitor will soon learn—provide the vibrant color that has long since vanished from classic monuments once saturated with pigment, blue, gold, and vermilion, under the eye-searing Aegean sun.

Their spirit is a miracle. They are open, generous, and full of a frank, probing curiosity about you, the foreigner. The Greeks do not have a word for standoffishness. Their approach is direct. American? British? Where are you staying? Are you married or single? How much do you make? Thus, with the subtlety of an atomic icebreaker, the Greeks get to know you, and you, perforce, get to know them. "Come back tomorrow night. We're always here at this time" is the gracious invitation that usually terminates the first meeting with your outgoing Greek hosts, usually a meeting set in a café or *kafenion*—that living room–office–club–gambling casino that many Greeks call their real home. On repeat visits, you may be rewarded with native hospitality, the tenor of which recalls Nestor's orders to his servants in re-

gard to departing Telemachus: "After him and force him to come back!" Many and touching are the tales of poverty-stricken villages that have slaughtered a kid or a lamb in honor of visiting tourists, thus conferring on them a truly Olympian status. In such villages there is always at least one English-speaking person for whom it is a matter of national pride and honor to welcome you and, perhaps, insist on lending you his only mule to scale a particular mountain, then offer a tasty dinner meal. This is the typically Greek, deeply moving hospitality that money cannot buy and for which, of course, no money could be offered in payment.

Chances are that your host—no doubt, luxuriantly moustached—will greet you as he counts the beads of what appears to be amber rosaries. They are *koboloi*, or "worry beads," a legacy from the Turks, and Greeks click them on land, on the sea, in the air to ward off that insupportable silence that threatens to reign whenever conversation lags. Shepherds do it, cops do it, merchants in their shops do it. More aesthetic than thumb-twiddling, less expensive than smoking, this obsession indicates a tactile sensuousness, characteristic of a race that has produced the Western world's greatest sculpture.

Although the Greeks are a practical and materialistic people, they know the secret of amusing themselves with little or no money. "They are," said an admiring French traveler, "the enchanters of themselves." The chief enchantments accessible to most tourists, since a language barrier usually keeps them from active participation in Greek political discussions, are singing and dancing. Occasionally at night in the narrow streets of the Plaka, you will hear the timeless strains of a lover's serenade, one of the flowing, melodic Ionian *cantades*, which still have the power to ravish the ear and melt the heart of a dark-eyed beauty. The true place to discover the charm of Greek song and folk dancing is the *taverna*, an institution as old as Greece itself, mother of all the tavernas in the world. The entertainment, often featuring those extraordinary dances, the *zeimbekiko*, performed by men, is sure to be vigorous, colorful, spontaneous, authentic. In the taverna you reach the apogee of Greek hospitality, Greek gaiety, Greek melancholy, Greek humanity.

When does Greece slow down? In Athens, it seems never. But head out to the countryside villages and you'll find another tradition as old as Homer himself, the siesta—the only time Greeks stop talking and really sleep, it seems. Usually after lunch and until 4 PM, barmen drowse over their bars, waiters fall asleep in chairs, and all good Greeks drift off into slumber wherever they are, like the enchanted courtiers of Sleeping Beauty. Then, with a yawn, a sip of coffee, and a large glass of ice water, Greece goes back to the business of the day. But don't get us wrong—even some Athenians slow down for a siesta, and many enjoy another ritual as old as Aristotle—the *peripato,* or evening stroll.

"If you don't sing the praises of your house," says an old Greek proverb, "it will fall down on your head." Greece is an old house with a glorious history. It has survived four centuries of occupation by uninvited Turkish guests, a horrid tenancy by the Nazis, and the difficulties of being divided against itself, but the roof is miraculously intact and the legal tenants have a right to sing its praises. Don't be surprised if your taxi driver from the Athens airport does so—he only wants you to share his admiration for his country. He wants you to love it too. Remember, however, that you are in a taxi, not a chariot. You are not about to step into the Athens of Pericles. Although there are noble temples and ruins that evoke Homer, Sophocles, Plato, and the rest, today's Greeks are not just the cut-rate descendants of a noble people living in the ruined halls of their ancestors—modern Greece is a vital, living, enthralling, unforgettable nation.

WHAT'S WHERE

Athens

Voyagers touch down in Athens, both the stronghold of ancient Greece and the beating aorta of modern Greece. It is, of course, the point to which all roads lead and from which many tours take off. The greatest sight of the glory that was Greece is here: the Parthenon and the other legendary buildings of the Acropolis. Also, other ancient must-dos beckon: the Agora, Monument of Lysikrates, the Odeon of Herod Atticus, and that treasure trove of great art, the National Archaeological Museum. After exploring evocative ancient Athens, you may climb Pnyx hill and view a postsunset sound-and-light spectacle cast upon the sacred vestiges. Then, take the time to explore modern Athens' patchwork of neighborhoods—from quaint Plaka to ritzy Kolonaki—to truly get a sense of the history of this gregarious city, its people, and what lies beyond the ubiquitous modern concrete facades. After immersing yourself in the hectic vibrancy of the metropolis, and making a side trip to the port of Piraeus, you'll fully understand why Athens remains a paradox of the old and new.

Excursions from Athens

Athens lies in a basin defined by three mountain masses: Mt. Hymettos to the east, Mt. Parnis and Mt. Aigaleo to the west, and Mt. Pendeli to the north. East of Mt. Hymettos unfold the gently undulating hills of the Mesogeion. Scattered among and beyond these ranges are engaging sites and villages. Due west is Delphi, where the priestesses of antiquity uttered their enigmatic prophecies. Athenians, Europeans, and far-flung travelers alike are drawn to the quirky Saronic Gulf Islands of Aegina, Poros, Hydra, and Spetses. The famous Marathon and monasteries such as Daphni lay just beyond the forbidding mountains guarding the passes into Athens.

Northern Sporades and Evia

Strung from Mt. Pelion to the center of the Aegean, the Northern Sporades are distinct in character: tourist-addled Skiathos is closest to the mainland; due east is Skopelos, marked with dense pines, scenic villages, and lovely beaches. Farther east is rugged Alonnisos, the least progressed, and a jumping-off point for the uninhabited islands. Wild-nature lovers behold Skyros as the jewel of the isles for its remoteness, myth, and stark beauty. Evia almost touches the mainland, its vast coastline dotted with fishing villages, beaches, and occasional sites.

Epirus and Thessaly

The region consists of two areas: the mountainous province of Epirus, bordered by Albania and the Ionian Sea, with the capital Ioannina to the west. Marking the threshold between Epirus and Thessaly is Metsovo, just beyond the lofty Katara Pass, which threads through the breathtaking Mt. Pindos range. At the western edge is the agricultural Thessalian plain, where the monasteries of Meteora seemingly float in midair, built atop dizzying pinnacles that tower over the town of Kalambaka.

Northern Greece

The region we call northern Greece, comprising Macedonia to the west and Thrace to the east, covers the Balkan frontier from Albania to Bulgaria and also touches Turkey. It is both a meeting point and a crossroads between Europe, the Mediterranean, and Asia—imbued with sights, sounds, and colors of a range of different cultures, their interaction telling of successful commingling and fierce discord.

Corfu

Northwesterly Corfu is an island unto itself with a distinct European feel, its outline aptly mimicking a miniature Italy. Corfu's strategic presence in the northern Ionian Sea at the entrance to the Adriatic shaped its ancient history. Today isolated beaches, stylish restaurants, and tony resorts dot its landscape of serendipitous beauty.

Northern Peloponnese

Greece blessed the Northern Peloponnese—among its jewels Mycenae, Nauplion, and Olympia—with natural beauty and the mysteries of forgotten civilizations. Separated from the north by a narrow isthmus, the Northern Peloponnese comprises the Argive peninsula, jutting into the Aegean, and runs westward past the isthmus and along the Gulf of Corinth to the Adriatic coast.

Southern Peloponnese

The Southern Peloponnese is divided into regions established by the ancients—Messinia in the southwest, Laconia in the southeast, and Arcadia to the north. Massive mountain ranges sweep down the fingers of the peninsula. The beaches are some of the finest and least developed in Greece, some giving way to limestone caves. Tower houses jutting from the craggy landscape are spooky reminders of the clan feuds of centuries past.

The Cyclades

The Cyclades compose a quintessential, pristine Mediterranean archipelago, with ancient sites, droves of vineyards and olive trees, and stark whitewashed cubist houses, all seemingly crystallized in a backdrop of lapis lazuli. The six major stars in this constellation of islands in the central Aegean Sea—Andros, Mykonos, Naxos, Paros, Tinos, and Santorini—are well visited but still cast a magnificent fusion of sunlight, stone, and sparkling aqua sea. Plus, they promise culture and flaunt hedonism: ancient sites, Byzantine castles and museums, lively nightlife, shops, restaurants, and beaches plain and fancy.

Crete

To Greeks, Crete is the Megalonissi, the Great Island, where a sophisticated culture flourished 5,000 years ago, though its location in the eastern Mediterranean 175 km (108½ mi) from Athens did not discourage invasions from the mainland in ancient times. In all of Crete, you'll find the most development on the north shore, and for the most part the southern coast remains blessedly unspoiled. Western Crete is especially rugged, with inland mountains and the rough southern shoreline; Hania and Rethymnon, mysterious old cities that trace their roots to the Arab and Venetian worlds, are found here.

Rhodes and the Dodecanese

The Dodecanese (Twelve Islands) are the easternmost holdings of Greece, wrapped around the shores of Turkey and Asia Minor. Romans, Crusaders, Turks, and Venetians have left their architectural mark here, but most likely to hypnotize the visitor are the landscape—from the rugged mountains of Patmos to the verdant fields of Kos and lush hillsides of Rhodes—and a way of life that, despite invasions of armies and sunseekers—remains essentially and delightfully Greek.

The Northern Islands

Each of these far-flung Aegean islands bordering Asia Minor is distinct: Chios is extraordinary for its architecture; Lesbos, to the north, is dappled with mineral springs and a petrified forest; northernmost is volcanic Limnos; and Samos, land of wine and honey, is farthest south.

PLEASURES AND PASTIMES

Dining: Greece "à la Carte"

In days long gone by, Greek food was patriotically or romantically overpraised by nationals or foreigners. This was because, on the reverse side of the drachma coin, Greek food had been exaggeratedly condemned by travelers who had had bad luck, or had not known what to order. Today, the great news is that the Greek food scene is very much on the up and up. Glossy American publications are dispatching writers to Athens, now home to some of the Europe's most alluring and innovative restaurants, while the traditional dishes of countryside tavernas continue to be the darling of foodies everywhere, as chic new tavernas from London to New York City prove. In these posh eateries, of course, you don't get the full experience—after all, in Greece, it is a habit for customers to go into the kitchen and look into the pots, rather than to choose their food from a *katalogos* (menu). You know what you are getting, and what you can face.

Now, for some ABCs. Breakfast ends at about 10, and lunch is usually between 1:30 and 3:30, after which restaurants close for the afternoon. Dinner starts late; 8 is on the early side. Breakfast in Greece is pretty light. Hotels will ply you with a Nescafé-and-bread Continental breakfast, but you might try a "toast," a sort of dry grilled-cheese sandwich (a "mixed toast" if it has a paper-thin ham slice added), or a sesame-coated bread ring sold by street vendors in the cities. Local bakeries may offer fresh doughnuts in the morning. For lunch, heavyweight meat-and-potato dishes can be had, but you might prefer a real Greek salad (no lettuce, a slice of feta with a pinch of oregano, and ripe tomatoes) or souvlaki or grilled chicken from a taverna.

The hour or so before restaurants open for dinner is a pleasant time to have an *ouzo* (a clear licorice-flavored drink) or glass of wine and try Greek hors d'oeuvres, called *mezedes*. As the sun sets over the Aegean, seek out a seaside *ouzeri*. It's the perfect setting for conversing or post-card writing. Dinner is the main meal of the day, and there's plenty of food. Starters include *taramosalata* (a dip or spread made from fish roe) and *melitzanosalata* (made from smoked eggplant, lemon, oil, and garlic), along with the well-known yogurt, cucumber, and garlic *tzatziki*.

On menus all over Greece you'll run into three categories of staple entrée dishes: there's *magirefta* (food that has been cooked in the oven in advance and left in the pan all day, usually served at room temperature)—like *moussaka* (ground beef or lamb and sliced eggplant topped with gravy and cheese), *pastitsio* (a baked dish of minced lamb and macaroni), or *gemista* (stuffed tomatoes or peppers, which usually has some ground lamb). Then there are *tisoras* (grills), with a subcategory called *stakarvouna* (meaning "of the hour"), food that is cooked on the coals and served immediately—like chops or steak. And last, there is fish, of all kinds, which is outstanding (look for gilt-head bream, or *tsipoura*).

Ouzo and brandy are the national aperitifs of Greece. Served in small glasses and diluted with water (which turns the liqueur milky white), ouzo is usually enjoyed on summer evenings and should be lingered over. Try a tiny sip undiluted first, and ask for mezedes, which might include anything from tomato slices, olives, and cheese to shrimp or sausage. Give the stale crackers that accompany ouzo at outdoor cafés to the sparrows flitting around your feet. In winter, people usually ask for brandy: Botrys and the higher-grade Metaxa are both good, and you might also like the *mavrodaphne* (a heavy dessert wine).

Greek wine is relatively inexpensive. Restaurants and tavernas often sell locally produced *kokkino* (red) and *aspro* (white) table wine from the barrel; many of them, purchased by the half-kilogram or kilogram, are perfectly good wines. For bottled wine, look for Hymettos from Attica, Boutari or Tsantalis from Naousa in Macedonia, Carras Estate from Chalkidiki, and red wines from Nemea in the Peloponnese. There are many others. Enthusiasts should consult Miles Lambert-Gocs's comprehensive *The Wines of Greece* (Faber and Faber, London, 1990) for a history of modern wine making in Greece and for descriptions of regional wines. For additional information on Greek wines and wineries contact the **Federation of Greek Wine and Spirits Indus-**

tries (⌗ 15A Xenofonto, Athens, ☎ 01/ 322–6053) or visit the **Central Union of Vine and Wine Cooperatives of Greece** store (⌗ L. Riancourt St. at Panormou, Athens, ☎ 01/692–3102), open Wednesday– Monday 8–2:30, Tuesdays 5–8.

The origins of *retsina,* the piney, aromatic, resinated wine considered Greece's *vin du pays,* are uncertain. According to ancient authors, resin was one of many ingredients added to wine to prevent it from turning to vinegar, but the substance may initially have been used to seal wine containers. Whatever the original intent, the results can be splendid. Give retsina a chance; don't take one sip, make a face, then declare you don't like it. Perhaps you've read or been told that retsina is an acquired taste. This isn't true: Most people like it immediately. Besides, wouldn't it be fun to drink retsina drawn from the barrel while eating a traditional meal on a late summer's evening in Greece? If retsina out of the barrel isn't available, or if you feel safer with the bottled version, try Achaia Clauss, Thebes, Botrys, Cambas, Kourtakis, Marko, or Pikermi. Have it unchilled with pastitsio, moussaka, or grilled chicken, lamb, or souvlaki.

Oppa!: Folk Music and Dance

The dramatic ups and downs of Greek history and the five centuries of Turkish domination are clearly reflected in the wailing airs of popular folk music. Of national dances, to which this music is the accompaniment, there are two categories: one favored by the inhabitants of Athens, the Piraeus, and the industrial suburbs, and the other, older and more traditional, by the provincial towns and villages. Of the former, the most popular is the *zeimbekiko,* of obvious Anatolian origin. A solo dance for men, it is performed with a pantherlike grace and an air of mystical awe, the dancer, with eyes rivetted to the floor, repeatedly bending down to run his hand piously across the ground. The music, played by *bouzoukia,* large mandolins, is nostalgic and weighted with melancholy. Other dances include the *chassapiko,* the butcher's dance; the *serviko,* probably of Slav origin; and the *tsifteteli,* a sort of, believe it or not, belly dance for men. The zeimbekiko remains the most popular of these. *Bouzouki* solos, which sounds like frenzied cadenzas, demand a high standard of virtuosity. The burden

of their sorrowful refrains invariably deals with death, exile, and the faithlessness of women.

The popular dances of the country are not only older but more indigenous and, like the folklore of the country, rooted in ancient mythology. The vase paintings of the classical age depict a variety of poses and movements that can be recognized in the traditional country dances. These include the Cretan *chaniotiko,* a circular dance originally performed by men preparing for battle; the *sousta,* danced by Achilles round the funeral pyre of Patroclus; and the Epriot dance of the *mirologhia,* a mixture of austerity, poetry, and almost unbearable anguish. The most popular, however, of all Greek dances are the *kalamatianos* and *tsamikos.* The former is performed in a circle, the male leader waving a handkerchief, swirling, bounding, and lunging acrobatically. The latter, more martial in spirit, represents men going to battle, all to the sound of stamping, springing, and twisting cries of *oppa!* No matter which dance you may decide to jump up and perform in, remember that plate-smashing is now verboten in most places. In lieu of flying pottery, however, a more loving tribute is paid—many places have flower vendors, whose beautiful blooms are purchased to be thrown upon the dancers as they perform.

Olympiad: Outdoor Activities and Sports

For the ancients, athletics were a kind of religion of human vigor. They flocked to Olympia, Delphia, and Nemea to honor the exploits of the best athletes. For military reasons athletics was encouraged, and when athletic competition lagged to the point where it threatened to disappear, the Greek cities organized the pan-Hellenic games, the first of which took place at Olympia in 776 BC. With the news that these games—today we known them as the Olympics, of course—are about to return to Athens in 2004, modern Greeks, once content to put on weight and slide into middle age without a fight, are now on the fitness trail. Gymnasiums, aerobics studios, and martial-arts schools can be found in cities and larger towns. Soccer and basketball are kings of the spectator sports in Greece, and the World Cup brings the country to a standstill. Waterskiing, windsurfing, skiing, and mountaineering are gaining in popularity. The country offers plenty of unspoiled, challenging terrain for serious hiking and mountaineering.

Shopping

Many of the goods tourists purchase in Greece are inspired by the country's ancient civilization. Reproductions of early bronzes, Cycladic figurines, and Geometric, Corinthian, and Athenian vase paintings are ubiquitous. Some are poorly made and some feature rude subjects, but others are charming and even of museum quality.

Objects made of the fragrant olive wood—from worry beads to bowls and sculptures—can be very attractive. Wooden bread stamps and hand guards used in harvesting grain are among the more easily found items of Greek folk culture. Old jewelry and textiles, which are getting rather expensive, can still be a good deal and an adventure to track down.

Leather bags and sandals and heavy wool sweaters are popular; some may be good buys, but some may soon fall apart. Take your time and inspect the seams and stitches before buying. Lightweight sundresses may look wonderful on the hanger in a store, but they're often made of flimsy fabrics—beware their transparency in the bright Greek sunlight.

NEW AND NOTEWORTHY

Visitors to **Athens** will immediately note the capital's urgent preparation for the **2004 Olympic Games.** Gaping construction sites line the extension of the subway, to be completed in 2000, and the new airport at Spata will open in 2001, ready to handle 16 million passengers a year (which will eventually increase to 50 million annually). Other construction projects include an Olympic village at the base of Mount Parnitha, a sports complex near the Neo Faliro racetrack, an equestrian center in Tatoi, a sailing center in front of the present-day airport, and a rowing and canoeing basin near Marathon.

Throughout the city, there is also an intensified focus on remodeling city squares, revamping neoclassical mansions, and reasphalting grand boulevards. As part of the campaign to make Athens more livable and environmentally friendly, cars were banned from several streets in the historical center, a popular move that has led to the creation of even more pedestrian zones downtown. Several natural gas buses, free to passengers, will now begin circulating in the historical center, as well as electric cars, some equipped for individuals with special needs. The city will set up information booths detailing local bus lines, taxi drivers will post mandatory fare scales in three languages (complete with suggested prices to landmarks), new signs at Piraeus harbor will indicate ferries' locations and sailing times, and more tourist police will be hired.

Ultimately, Athens officials dream of linking all major ancient sites like the Acropolis, the Temple of Olympian Zeus, and the ancient cemetery of Kerameikos by pedestrian networks to create **a vast archaeological park.** If it comes to fruition—and officials claim 70% of the project will be completed by the time of the Olympic Games—it will recast central Athens as a great open museum, uniting the city's ancient history with modern, everyday life.

Greek hotels nationwide are also gearing up for the increase in tourism. To attract higher-income travelers, the government plans to adopt a **star classification system,** based on those used by other countries like Switzerland, Austria, and Spain. Criteria include a hotel's location, appearance, maintenance, and customer service. The switch is viewed as an opportunity to pressure hotels to upgrade facilities and personnel, should they want a high-star classification; apparently, hotels now labeled "De Luxe" under the old system will not automatically receive five stars. Making good use of grants available under the EU's Delors II structural aid package, many hotel chains upgraded or expanded in 1998, and there are plans for seven new hotels in Athens and the Attica plain alone, as well as more resorts like a 1,000-bed hotel, conference center, and theme park in Loutra Killinis in the Peloponnese.

In the next two years Greece will spend more than 22 billion drachmas upgrading its museums and restoring archaeological sites. Speeding up work on the Acropolis is a priority, but the monastic community of **Mt. Athos** will also undergo one of the biggest transformations in its 1,000-year history. By the end of the century, the Greek government and the EU will carry out restoration work on most of the monasteries, including Xenofon Monastery, which celebrates its millennium in 1999. About 80 of the many smaller monastic conclaves, cells, and hermitages will also benefit from the effort, which includes revamping guest facilities and spaces in which to preserve the monasteries' rare treasures, as well as preserving the Athos peninsula's ecological system, home to more than 1,400 kinds of plants and 105 species of birds. The aim is to ensure that Mount Athos, so long a pristine refuge for monks and increasingly a tourist destination, will not become a paradise lost.

The thousands of visitors who come daily to marvel at the **prehistoric settlement of Akrotiri on Santorini,** for decades covered by an eyesore of a protective shelter, will appreciate the new design under way. Besides a revolutionary shelter that allows for natural light and ventilation—a relief from the asbestos fumes and oppressive heat induced by the current shelter—the design provides for visitor stations and exhibits tracing the ancients' daily lives. There will be three routes through the site: along the perimeter, under the roof for an overview, and through an internal circuit for researchers with permits.

The long-awaited reopening of Athens's Benaki museum and its tremendous collection is now scheduled for the summer of 1999, while in northern Greece, **Kavala's archaeological museum** will take on greater significance when it completes its new wing at the end of 1999. It will be used to exhibit prehistoric and classical finds uncovered over the last 50 years in Macedonia and Thrace. Archaeologists recently discovered a wealth of finds in northern Greece. These include an ancient brothel and bathhouse in Thessaloniki's ancient agora, complete with mosaic floors, ceramics decorated with phallic symbols, and animal bones on the ground floor where guests stopped for a meal before availing themselves of other services upstairs. Archaeologists are now trying to determine if these structures were part of a larger complex that extended to the Egnatia Way, which linked the Roman Empire to its colonies. Near the ancient city of Dion at the foothills of Mount Olympus, researchers unearthed a laurel-wreathed head from a statue of Emperor Trajan, whose likeness appears on copper coins also found at the site. Dion was the Macedonians' favorite military camp. The latest discovery includes inscriptions on tablets from the 4th to the 2nd century BC, which offer important clues about public affairs. One epigraph refers to the treaty signed by Perseus of Macedon with the Boetians, a last attempt by the threatened Macedonian kingdom to rally southern Greece in a united front against Rome.

For those who are more interested in beaches than Boetians, the EU rewarded **Greek beaches** more Blue Flags for cleanliness than any other member country. Nineteen out of 20 Greek coastal sites were described in the EU's latest report released in 1998 as having excellent-quality bathing waters; about 1,700 beaches had been inspected. (On the other hand, the report declared freshwater quality in Greece's lakes and rivers had deteriorated.) In addition, Greece ranked fourth in a survey of forest management released in 1998 by the World Wildlife Fund, which ranked 15 European countries on criteria such as government promotion of forest growth, levels of air pollution, and extension of protected areas. Greece came behind Switzerland, Finland, and Austria.

To prevent further damage from sun, salt, and wind, archaeologists will replace the 2,600-year-old **marble lions of Delos island** with silicon copies. Visited annually by thousands of tourists who sail from nearby Mykonos, uninhabited Delos was one of ancient Greece's most sacred sites, with a renowned Temple of Apollo and the treasury of the Delian League. Still standing on the site are seven of the original 16 lions, a gift from nearby Naxos island; after their removal they will be on display in the island's museum.

Sometime in the year 2000 **Thessaloniki's landmark White Tower** will become the City Museum. Tentative plans indicate the permanent exhibit will map out the city's history from its founding in the 4th century BC to the Asia Minor disaster in 1922. One section will trace Thessaloniki's history through its monuments and architecture; another will highlight its social surroundings, commercial activities, demography, and native customs; and a third section will focus on inhabitants' daily life. Built in the 15th century as part of the city's fortifications, the White Tower was also known as the Tower of Blood in the 19th century when it served as a prison. Until the mid-1990s, it housed works from the Byzantine period, which have since been moved to the city's newly created Museum of Byzantine Civilization nearby.

FODOR'S CHOICE

No two people will agree on what makes a perfect vacation, but it can be fun and helpful to find out what others think. Here are a few choice ideas to enhance your visit to Greece. For more details, refer to the appropriate chapter.

Ancient Sites

★ **Ancient Akrotiri, Santorini.** In the 1860s, in the course of quarrying tephra, or volcanic ash, the remains of an ancient town were discovered, frozen in time by layers of pumice that buried it at the time of the eruption, 3,600 years ago, long before Pompeii's disaster.

★ **Delphi, Central Greece.** One of the most popular sites in Greece, Delphi is preserved just as it was in antiquity. Follow the sacred way taken by ancient pilgrims seeking prophecies and contemplate the remnants of their offerings to the god Apollo.

★ **Mystras, Laconia.** At the sunset of the dying Byzantine Empire a brief burst of renaissance lit up the Eastern Mediterranean, and today the ruins of the sprawling city it left behind engage the visitor as thoroughly as the intellectuals of Mystras enraptured the Greeks.

★ **Parthenon on the Acropolis, Athens.** With its stark beauty, shimmering golden-white on the city's horizon, this architecturally sophisticated temple is a testament to the golden age of Greece.

★ **Temple of Poseidon at Sounion.** The view from the summit is spectacular. Particularly in the slanting light of the late-afternoon sun, the land masses to the west stand out in sharp profile: the bulk of Aegina backed by the mountains of the Peloponnese.

★ **Theater at Epidauros.** The best-preserved ancient Greek theater in the world is still in use. Whether you're there in the day, or there for a summer show, you're sure to be awed by how seriously the Greeks took drama.

★ **Tower of the Winds in Roman Agora, Athens.** The delightful octagonal water clock has been keeping time since the 1st century BC. Also a sundial and weather vane, it was topped by a bronze Triton pointing to expressive reliefs that personify the eight winds.

Hotels

★ **Elounda Mare, near Elounda, Crete.** This hotel, a Relais & Château property on the Mirabello Gulf, has been a longtime favorite. Stunning design, superlative service, private villas and pools, and extensive wine lists are among the luxurious details. $$$$

★ **Atlantis Villas, Santorini.** Each "villa" is actually built inside a cave in Oia's cliff face, one of the most unusual and dramatic places to stay in the world. Balconies have an epic view, 600 ft up, across the magnificent caldera. $$$–$$$$

★ **Epaminondas, Andros.** Cool, handsome interiors, ensconced in marble and traditional details, promote relaxing. Favorite pastimes: taking a midnight dip in the freshwater pool and gazing at Batsi Bay from the huge balconies. $$–$$$

★ **Malvasia, Monemvassia.** A fairy tale–like old tower in a living Byzantine town offers an unparalleled view into a forgotten time while you take in gorgeous surroundings. $$

Museums

★ **Museum, Olympia.** Some of the most impressive pieces of military equipment were uncovered at Olympia, placed there by victorious athletes in honor of the gods who brought them success.

★ **Archaeological Museum, Thessaloniki.** Inside this unassuming structure is a stunning collection of artifacts and treasures attributed to Philip of Macedon, including a brilliant gold funerary box embossed with the 16-point Macedonian sun and a legendary skull.

★ **Goulandris Cycladic and Ancient Art Museum, Athens.** A sure cure for museum burnout, this outstanding collection spans the Cycladic civilization (3000–2000 BC), dominated by the slender marble figurines that millennia later inspired artists like Picasso.

★ **Royal Tombs, Vergina.** The Royal Tombs and their golden contents are gorgeously ensconced in their new home here under a burial mound, adapted and air-conditioned to be one of the world's most striking museums. Only an hour from Thessaloniki, this site is a must for visitors to northern Greece.

Picturesque Villages, Towns, and Neighborhoods

★ **Agiassos, Lesbos.** Nestled at the foot of Mt. Olympus in a remote wooded valley, this special village is marked with gray stone houses, cobblestone lanes, a medieval castle, and shops offering local wood handicrafts.

★ **Anafiotika quarter of Plaka, Athens.** Nestled below the Acropolis on land the Delphic Oracle once declared sacred, this serene "island village," with its tiny churches and bougainvillea-framed houses, is a blissful contrast to the cacophony of the modern city.

★ **Monemvassia.** Part ancient site, part living town, Monemvassia has been called the Greek Gibraltar. Built on a rock jutting out from the southern Peloponnese, its jumble of ruins next to shops and old churches disorients in a delightful way.

★ **Oia, Santorini.** Oia is reputed to be the most beautiful settlement in the Aegean, straddling the wondrous caldera: a crescent of cliffs, striated in black, pink, brown, white, and pale green, rising 1,100 ft. Here you will find the cubical white houses you've dreamed of, and a sunset that is unsurpassed.

★ **Pirgi, Chios.** One of the few villages that once prospered from mastic production, in this case for gum used by the odalisques of Ottoman harems, Pirgi is lined with tiny arched streets with houses adorned with the lavish Italianate *xysta* design, and more than 50 churches.

Restaurants

★ **Bajazzo, Athens.** Splurge with no regrets at what may be Greece's best restaurant, where the chef experiments with wildly imaginative creations for an unforgettable culinary experience. $$$$

★ **Cavo D'Oro, Rethymnon.** Lobster and a panoply of innovative fresh fish are served amid the stylish grace of the high, wood-paneled dining room, once a medieval storeroom, at one of Crete's best restaurants. $$

★ **Chez Cat'rine, Mykonos.** You will savor exquisite French cuisine and formality amid a mélange of Cycladic and château ambience. Just one tantalizing *amuse-gueule* is baby squid stuffed with rice and Greek mountain spices. $$$$

★ **Ta Kioupia, outside Rhodes Town.** The quality and variety of the dishes are as exceptional as the linen-, fine china–, and crystal-appointed tables. Elegance reigns among white stucco, exposed beams, and antique farm tools. $$$

★ **Casa la Monte Tirotaverna, Epirus.** The chef has based the menu around Metsovo's delightful, expensive smoked cheese; generous helpings go in everything from highly recommended baked pasta to the freshly made pizza. $$

Stellar Views

★ **Katara Pass, Metsovo.** Greece's highest mountain pass traverses the border between Thessaly and Epirus; descend through the mountains with the sun, taking in the peaceful ravine below.

★ **Mega Spileo, Zakhlorou.** Ascend the towering pinnacles and precipitous rock walls of the Northern Peloponnese's Vouraikos Gorge in a diminutive train, and stop to take a hike to this 4th-century monastery through evergreen oak, cypress, and fir, with panoramic views.

★ **Molyvos castle on Lesbos at dawn.** The illuminated mountains of Asia Minor seem to shoot brilliant hues into the sky, juxtaposed by a shimmering sea and red-tile rooms below.

★ **Watching the sunset from Mt. Lycabettus, Athens.** On a clear day, the view from the top is the finest in Athens, stretching across the Attica basin, all the way to Piraeus and Aegina and Poros. Watch the sunset and then turn in the other direction to see the moon rise over violet-crowned Mt. Hymettos.

FESTIVALS AND SEASONAL EVENTS

The Greek calendar is filled with religious celebrations, cultural festivals, and civic occasions. Those events with roots in Byzantine Greece are especially intriguing, as they combine religious belief and national pride in a way unfamiliar to most Americans. Shops may close early for local or national celebrations, and hotels may be booked during major events (such as Carnavali at Patras). Verify the dates of events with the Greek National Tourist Organization (GNTO or EOT; ✉ Amerikis 2, Athens, ☎ 01/331–0561 or 01/331–0562). Here is a list of public holidays and major religious observance days:

1999: January 1 (New Year's Day); January 6 (Epiphany); February 22 (Clean Monday, first day of Lent); March 25 (Feast of the Annunciation and Independence Day); April 9 (Good Friday); April 11 (Greek Easter Sunday); April 12 (Greek Easter Monday); May 1 (Labor Day and Flower Festival); May 30 (Pentecost); August 15 (Assumption of the Holy Virgin); October 28 (Ochi Day); December 25–26 (Christmas Day and Boxing Day). **2000:** dates are the same as above except: March 13 (Clean Monday, first day of Lent); April 28 (Good Friday); April 30 (Greek Easter Sunday); May 1 (Greek Easter Monday); June 18 (Pentecost).

WINTER

DEC. 31➤ New Year's Eve is the occasion for carol singing by children and exchanging gifts. On the island of Chios the day is marked by a contest for the best model boat.

JAN. 1➤ The Feast of Saint Basil marks the beginning of the New Year. A special cake, the *Vassilopita*, is baked with a coin in it, which brings good luck to the finder.

JAN. 6➤ Epiphany, the day that marks the baptism of Christ, is celebrated by blessing the waters—marked by an official ceremony at Athens's harbor, Piraeus. Elsewhere, crosses are immersed in seas, lakes, and rivers.

JAN. 8➤ Gynaecocracy, in northeastern Greece, reverses the traditional roles of men and women: In the area around Serres, Kilkis, Xanthi, and Komotini, women spend the day at the cafés while the men do the housekeeping until evening.

FEB. 1–22, 1999; FEB. 22–MAR. 13, 2000➤ Carnavali, like Mardi Gras, celebrates the period before the beginning of Lent. The evenings are marked by parades, music, and dancing, and costumes are required. Carnavali, more correctly known as Apokries, runs three weeks before the begin-

ning of Greek Lent (Clean Monday). So, depending on the date for Orthodox Easter (which changes annually), Apokries usually begins in February. For example, in 1999, Apokries runs for three weeks through February 21, the Sunday before Clean Monday; in 2000, until March 12 (Sunday). Towns and islands known to celebrate Carnavali in style are Patras, Naousa, Veria, Kozani, Zante, Skyros, Xanthi, Mesta and Olimbi on Chios; Galaxidi, Thebes, Poligiros, Thimiana, Lamia, Cefallonia, Messini, Soho, Serres, and Agiassos on Lesbos; Karpathos, Heraklion and Rethymnon on Crete; Amfissa, Efxinoupolis, and Ayia Anna on Evia.

MAR. 25➤ Independence Day commemorates the call for independence in 1821 by Germanos, the Metropolitan of Patras, which began the uprising in the Peloponnese that eventually freed Greece from Ottoman rule. Today it is marked by parades of the armed forces, especially in Athens.

SPRING

APR. 23➤ The **Feast of Saint George** is a day for horse racing at Kaliopi on Limnos and at Pili on Kos.

On Crete, a three-day-long feast begins at Arachova, near Delphi, while at Assi Gonia, near Hania, a sheep-shearing contest follows the religious fiesta. Note that if St. George's Feast Day falls before Orthodox Easter Sunday, it is celebrated instead on Easter Monday; this will be the case in the year 2000 (i.e., May 1). That will be something—Easter Monday, May Day, and the nameday of the thousands of Georges celebrating in Greece!

APR. 9–12, 1999; APRIL 28–MAY 1, 2000➤ **Good Friday, Holy Saturday, and Easter Sunday** are the most sacred days on the Orthodox calendar. The traditional candlelight funeral processions staged throughout the country on Good Friday are very powerful to watch. Not only do they attest to the strength of the participants' faith, but they link modern Greece with its Byzantine roots, and the soldiers carrying the coffins illustrate the ties between church and government. Processions to churches on the night of Holy Saturday are a memorable sight. Following the midnight ceremony of the Resurrection, the congregations head homeward to feast, with the traditional red-dyed eggs and *mayiritsa* soup. More red-dyed eggs and roast lamb highlight the feasting on Easter Sunday. Seeing the rituals of Holy Week makes you understand the depth of meaning that the Easter greeting *Christos aneste,* "Christ is risen," and its response *Alithos aneste,* "He has indeed risen," have for most Greeks.

MAY–SEPT.➤ **Folk dancing** is performed at the amphitheater on Filopappou Hill in Athens.

MAY 21–23➤ The **Anastenaria,** a traditional fire-walking ritual with pagan roots and a Byzantine overlay, is performed in Ayia Eleni near Ayia Serres, and in Langada near Thessaloniki, where villagers dance on live embers while clasping icons of St. Constantine and St. Helen.

SUMMER

JUNE–SEPT.➤ The **Athens Festival** presents ancient dramas, operas, music, and ballet performed by nationally and internationally famous artists, in the 2nd-century Odeon of Herodes Atticus on the south slope of the Acropolis.

JUNE–OCT.➤ **Folk-dancing** performances are held in the theater in the old town of Rhodes on that island.

MID-JUNE–LATE AUG.➤ **Lycabettus Theater** presents a variety of performances in the amphitheater on Lycabettus Hill overlooking Athens.

LATE JUNE–EARLY JULY➤ Coastal towns honor the Greek navy with the celebrations of **Navy Week.** Fishermen at Plomari on Lesbos and Agria near Volos stage festivals, and at Volos the last day of Navy Week is marked by a reenactment of the mythical voyage of the ship *Argo,* with its crew led by Jason in search of the Golden Fleece.

JULY–SEPT. WEEKENDS➤ The **Epidauros Festival,** world renowned for the excellence of the performances, is held in the ancient theater, known for its superb acoustics. Watching a classical comedy or tragedy in this peaceful rural setting sends chills down your spine—twilight falls, the audience quiets, and a play first performed 2,500 years ago begins. The **Dodoni, Philippi,** and **Thassos festivals,** like the better-known one at Epidauros, stage classical dramas in ancient theaters.

AUG.➤ The **Epirotika Festival** in Ioannina, Epirus, celebrates Epirotikan authors and artists with exhibitions, theatrical performances, and concerts. At the **Olympus Festival,** a series of cultural events is held at the village of Litochoro near Olympus, in the well-preserved Frankish castle of Platamona. The **Hippokrateia Festival** on the island of Kos honors the father of medicine, a native son. Events include performances of ancient dramas and music, a flower show, and a costumed reenactment of the first swearing of the Hippocratic oath.

AUG.–SEPT.➤ At the **Aeschilia** festival, ancient dramas are staged at the archaeological site of Eleusis near Athens.

AUTUMN

SEPT.–OCT.➤ Following Thessaloniki's **International Trade Fair** in September come the **Festival of Popular Song,** the **Film Festival,** and the **Demetria Festival,** with theater, concerts, ballet, and opera.

2 Athens

Arriving in a taxi (sorry, no chariots), you may be surprised to find Athenians garbed by Armani and driving motor cycles. Shouldn't they look like truncated statues in the British Museum and have brows habitually crowned with wild olive? Incongruous as it may seem, most natives have two arms attached to the torso in the normal place—and today, many residents are busy dressing up Athens for the 2004 Olympic Games. Long a city of olympic proportions, Athens offers treasures like the Parthenon and myriad other pleasures—the purple glow of sundown on Mt. Hymetus, the candlelight of a Byzantine church, and Zorbaesque nights in timeless tavernas.

By
B. Samantha
Stenzel
and Toula
Bogdanos

Updated
by Toula
Bogdanos

I WOULD URGE THAT YOU FIX YOUR EYES on the greatness of Athens as she really is and fall in love with her. . . ." These are the words (as reported by Thucydides) of Pericles, the mastermind of Greece's golden age, in his oration for the dead of the Peloponnesian war. In 1185, Michael Akominatos, archbishop of the city, wrote otherwise: "You cannot look upon Athens without tears. . . . She has lost the very form, appearance, and character of a city." Today, after another 800 years, the truth falls somewhere in between. Raise your eyes 200 ft above the city to the Parthenon, its honey-color columns of Pentelic marble rising from a massive limestone base, and you behold architectural perfection that has not been surpassed in two and a half thousand years. But this perpetual shrine of classical architecture, symbol of western civilization and political thought, dominates a 20th-century boomtown. Athens is now home to 4.3 million souls, most of whom spend the day discussing the city's faults: the murky pollution cloud known as the *nefos,* the overcrowding, the traffic jams with their hellish din, and the characterless cement apartment blocks. Romantic travelers, nurtured on the truth and beauty of Keats' Grecian Urn, are aghast to find that most of Athens has succumbed to that red tubular glare that owes only its name, neon, meaning new, to the Greeks.

Still, it's no wonder this fascinating and maddening metropolis is the point to which all roads lead and from which most tours take off. To experience Athens fully is to understand the essence of Greece: ancient monuments surviving in a sea of cement, startling beauty amid the squalor, tradition juxtaposed with modernity—a smartly dressed lawyer chatting on her mobile phone as she maneuvers around a priest in flowing robes waiting for the trolley. Locals depend upon humor and flexibility to deal with the chaos; visitors should do the same. The rewards are immense for those who take the time to catch the purple glow of sundown on Mt. Hymettus, light a candle in a Byzantine church amid heavy incense and black-shrouded grandmas while teens outside argue vociferously about soccer, or breathe in the tangy sea air while enjoying a Greek coffee after a night at the coastal clubs.

Although Athens may seem like one huge city, it is really a series of small villages strung together. Most of the major historic sites are within the central area; it is possible to see them on foot. When you (inevitably) wander off your planned route into less touristy areas, take the opportunity to explore. You will often discover pockets of incomparable charm, in refreshing contrast to the dreary repetition of the modern facades. For instance, a visit (if possible by moonlight) to the Plaka, the historic district set on the northern slope of the Acropolis, takes you back to the 19th-century city once beloved by Lord Byron. In this maze of narrow, winding streets and steps, vestiges of the older city are everywhere: small, color-washed houses with upper wooden stories; miniature Byzantine chapels; dank cellars filled with wine vats; occasionally a court or tiny garden, enclosed within high walls and filled with magnolia trees and the flaming trumpet-shape flowers of hibiscus bushes; and narrow crumbling stairways lined with festive tavernas.

Here, in this lovely Athenian neighborhood, you can still delight in the pleasures of strolling. *Peripato,* the Athenians call it, and it's older than Aristotle, whose students learned as they roamed about in his peripatetic school. Today, be sure your wanderings take you to a taverna to observe modern Athens and the Athenians in their element. They are lively and expressive, their hands fiddling with worry beads or gesturing excitedly. While often expansively friendly, they are aggressive and stubborn when feeling threatened, and they're also insatiably curious.

As you take in the city from its ancient treasures—the Acropolis, the Agora, and the Roman theater of Herod Atticus—to the more recent 19th-century pleasures of Anafiotika and Plaka, you'll see that the pickax, pneumatic drill, and cement mixer have done their work: There are countless office buildings, modern apartments, and streets choked with vehicles (an official report once stated that 75% of females had lost their sexual ardor as a result of air pollution in the capital—but failed to tell how it arrived at this depressing conclusion, or why males apparently had been spared). It's true: There is hardly a monument of importance to attest to the city's history between the completion of the temple of Olympian Zeus 18 centuries ago and the present day. That is the tragedy of Athens: the long vacuum in its history, the centuries of decay, neglect, and even oblivion. But if a tragedy, why not also a symptom of the vitality and amazing powers of recovery of the Greeks? Is it not fair to remember that within the last 150 years they have created a modern capital of more than 4 million inhabitants out of a village of 5,000 souls centered on a group of ruined marble columns?

Pleasures and Pastimes

Cafés and Kafenias
On any street corner, at any time of day, you will see Athenians practicing the fine art of "hanging out," sipping their coffees, debating the latest political fiasco, or just watching the world go by. Walking in the city may seem difficult at times because of cars parked on the sidewalk, uneven pavements, and the ongoing subway extension, but there is no shortage of squares, *kafenia* (traditional Greek coffeehouses), trendy cafés, or makeshift arrangements—two tables set up outside a dairy store—where you can sit for hours with an ouzo or the ubiquitous summer refreshment called frappé: instant Nescafé shaken with ice water and served with milk and sugar. The *kafenion*, in fact, is a cross between a living room, an office, a reading room, a club, and a gambling casino (backgammon is the favorite game of chance, played for very low stakes but with a passion that makes the Monte Carlo Casino seem like a bingo game in a church basement). The social life of the average Athenian takes place in the kafenion—this is where the heart is; home is just a place to sleep.

Dining
Recently, awards were handed out to the city's top 10 restaurants by the weekly entertainment guide *Athinorama*; not one winner offered traditional Greek cuisine. Instead, the spotlight went to places offering the food of France, Thailand, Italy, Polynesia, China, and the Pacific Rim. As it turns out, some honorees blended those cuisines with that of Greece, making nouvelle Greek a leading contender in the city's oven-hot dining scene. Today, chic spots like Vitrina and Bajazzo are turning Athens into a place gourmands are traveling to just for the sake of food. Remember, however, that Greece is the land where lunch can be bread and olives. The simple, traditional dishes are still to be had at many restaurants, some featuring the pots du jour on view back in the kitchen. And in a land where the prices are still gentle, Athens has many options for bargain "dining." After all, nothing beats a souvlaki—charcoal-grilled shish kebabs swathed in warmed pita bread—as a take-out snack to enjoy on your stroll through Plaka.

Nightlife
Athens is a sociable, late-night town where people love to see and be seen, and the action goes on until morning: Even at 3 AM central *platias* (squares) and streets are often crowded with revelers. Options range

from *rembetika* (Asia Minor blues from the 1920s) clubs to *bouzoukia* (melancholy folk music) joints to seaside bars blasting rave or rock. First-time visitors must check out a taverna, an institution as old as Greece itself. The entertainment, often featuring those extraordinary dances, the *zeimbekiko*, performed by men, is sure to be vigorous, colorful, spontaneous, and Zorbaesque. Neither the drachma devaluation, frozen wage scales, nor changing bar curfews seems to slow the social pace—clubs and restaurants are usually packed.

EXPLORING ATHENS

Although Athens covers a huge area, the major landmarks of the ancient Greek, Roman, and Byzantine periods are conveniently close to the modern city center. You can easily stroll from the Acropolis to the other sites, taking time to browse in shops and relax in cafés and tavernas along the way. The center of modern Athens is small, stretching from the Acropolis to Mt. Lycabettus, crowned by the small white chapel of Ayios Georgios. The layout is simple: Three parallel streets—Stadiou, Eleftheriou Venizelou (familiarly known as Panepistimiou), and Akadimias—link two main squares, Syntagma (Constitution) and Omonia (Concord). Try to wander off this beaten tourist track: Seeing the Athenian butchers in the Central Market sleeping on their cold marble slabs during the heat of the afternoon siesta may give you more of a feel for the city than seeing scores of toppled columns.

From many quarters of the city one can glimpse "the glory that was Greece" in the form of the Acropolis looming above the horizon, but only by actually climbing that rocky precipice can you feel the impact of the ancient settlement. The Acropolis and Filopappou, two craggy hills sitting side by side; the ancient Agora (marketplace); and Kerameikos, the first cemetery, form the core of ancient and Roman Athens. In the National Archaeological Museum is a vast array of artifacts illustrating the many millennia of Greek civilization; smaller museums such as the Cycladic and the Byzantine illuminate the history of particular regions or periods.

The city's Asian character after the 400-year rule under the Ottoman Empire is still evident in Monastiraki, the bazaar area near the foot of the Acropolis. Strolling through Plaka, a delightful area of tranquil streets lined with renovated mansions, you will get the flavor of the 19th century's gracious lifestyle. The narrow lanes with tiny churches and the whitewashed, bougainvillea-framed houses of Anafiotika, a section of Plaka, are reminiscent of an island village. Formerly run-down old quarters, such as Thission, a popular nightlife area with its string of new bars, and Psirri are now in the process of gentrification, although they still retain much of their original charm, as does the colorful produce and meat market on Athinas. The area around Syntagma Square, the tourist hub, and Omonia Square, the commercial heart of the city about 1 km (½ mi) northwest, is distinctly European, having been designed by the court architects of King Otho, a Bavarian. The most modern neighborhood downtown, ritzy, chic Kolonaki with its smart shops and bistros, is nestled at the foot of Mt. Lycabettus, Athens's highest hill (909 ft). Each of Athens's outlying suburbs has a distinctive character: In the north is wealthy, tree-lined Kifissia, once a summer resort for aristocratic Athenians, and in the south is down-to-earth Piraeus, with its bustling harbors and Saronic Gulf views.

Except for August and major holidays, when Athenians migrate to their ancestral villages outside the city, the streets are crowded. The best times to visit Athens are late fall and spring, when you can avoid the oppressive heat and the hordes of package tourists at major archaeological sites; you can also enjoy the bustling "winter" nightlife in the center, because after June many restaurants and clubs shut down or relocate to the seaside. Holy Week of the Orthodox Easter, usually in April or May, affords visitors the chance to observe Greece's most sacred holiday, including mournful Good Friday processions accompanying Christ's bier, and the candlelit Easter midnight service, complete with fireworks. If you must come in summer, visit the sights in the early morning; then—as the Greeks do—take a nap or eat a leisurely lunch before continuing your explorations after 5 PM, when several museums and sites are still open.

Admission to almost all museums and archaeological sites is free on Sundays from mid-November through March. Entrance is usually free every day for EU students, half off for students from other countries, and about a third off for senior citizens. Archaeological sites and museums remain closed on January 1, March 25, the morning of Orthodox Good Friday, Orthodox Easter, May 1, and December 25–26. Sunday visiting hours apply to museums on the following holidays: Epiphany; Ash Monday, Good Saturday, Easter Monday, and Whitsunday (on the Orthodox dates, which change every year); August 15; and October 28. Museums close early (around 12:30) on January 2, the last Saturday of Carnival, Orthodox Good Thursday, Christmas Eve, and New Year's Eve. In summer, opening hours are extended, depending on available personnel, but throughout the year, arrive at least 30 minutes before official closing times to ensure a ticket. Winter hours usually apply from October to April.

The best time to visit churches is during a service, especially on Sundays (dress conservatively). Otherwise, hours are not set in stone; try from about 8 AM to noon and 5:30 PM to 7:30 PM on any day, unless otherwise noted. For walking in Athens, city streets are considerably less crowded Saturday afternoon through Sunday.

Great Itineraries

IF YOU HAVE 1 DAY

Early in the morning, pay homage to Athens's most impressive legacy, the **Acropolis.** Then descend through **Anafiotika,** the closest thing you'll find to an island village. Explore the 19th-century quarter of **Plaka,** with its neoclassical houses, and stop for lunch at one of its many tavernas. Do a little bargaining with the merchants in the old Turkish bazaar around **Monastiraki Square.** Spend a couple of hours in the afternoon marveling at the stunning collection of antiquities in the **National Archaeological Museum**; then pass by **Syntagma Square** to watch the changing of the costumed Evzone guards in front of the Tomb of the Unknown Soldier. You can then window-shop or people-watch in the tony neighborhood of **Kolonaki.** Nearby, take the funicular up to **Mt. Lycabettus** for the sunset before enjoying a show at the **Roman theater of Herod Atticus,** followed by dinner in the newly revived district of **Psirri.**

IF YOU HAVE 3 DAYS

After a morning tour of the **Acropolis,** with a stop at the **Acropolis Museum** to view sculptures found on the site, pause on your descent at **Areopagus,** the site of the ancient supreme court; the view is excellent. Continue through **Anafiotika** and **Plaka,** making sure to stop at the **Greek Folk Art Museum**; the **Roman Agora,** with its Tower of the Winds, an enchanting water clock from the 1st century BC; and the **Little Mitropolis church** on the outskirts of the quarter. After a late lunch, detour to **Hadrian's Arch** and the **Temple of Olympian Zeus,** Athens's most important Roman monuments. In **Syntagma Square,** watch the changing of the Evzone guards, and then head to **Kolonaki,** followed by an ouzo on the slopes of **Mt. Lycabettus** at I Prasini Tenta, with its splendid panorama of the Acropolis and the sea. Dine in a local taverna, perhaps in a neighborhood near the **Panathenaic Stadium,** which is lit at night. This Roman arena was reconstructed for the first modern Olympics in 1896. On day two, visit the cradle of democracy, the **ancient Agora,** with Greece's best-preserved temple, the Hephaistion. Explore the **Monastiraki area,** including the tiny Byzantine chapel of **Kapnikarea,** which stands in the middle of the street. In Monastiraki you can snack on the city's best souvlaki, then hop the metro to **Piraeus** to explore its neighborhoods and feast on fish in Mikrolimano Harbor. On the third day, start early for the **National Archaeological Museum,** breaking for lunch in one of the city's *mezedopolia* (places that sell mezes). Swing through the city center, past the **Old University complex,** a vestige of King Otho's reign, to the **Cycladic Museum** in Kolonaki, with the curious figurines that inspired artists such as Modigliani and Picasso. Stroll through the **National Gardens,** and have a coffee in the romantic setting of To Kafenedaki café. Complete the evening with a ballet performance or pop music show at **Herod Atticus,** a movie at a *therina* (open-air cinema), or, in winter, a concert at the Megaron Symphony Hall.

IF YOU HAVE 5 DAYS

Spend your first three days as detailed above. On the fourth, see the **Byzantine museum,** which houses Christian art from the 4th to the 19th century, including masterful icons and rooms that are arranged like Greek Orthodox churches; then take a taxi (or Bus 224 followed by a 30-minute walk) to the peaceful Byzantine monastery of **Kaisariani** in the foothills of Mt. Hymettus. Here you can enjoy a picnic lunch with your Acropolis view. In the evening, splurge at Bajazzo, Athens's best haute-cuisine restaurant, and then dance the *tsifteteli* (the Greek version of a belly dance) to Asia Minor blues in a rembetika club, or, if it's summer, visit the coastal stretch toward the airport, where the irrepressible bars stay open until dawn. On the last day, elbow your way through the boisterous **Central Market,** and then cut through the old, fairly intact neighborhood of **Psirri** to **Kerameikos,** Athens's ancient cemetery. After lunch in **Thission,** for a complete change from the urban pace take the metro to the lovely suburb of **Kifissia** and view the grand homes from a horse-drawn carriage, shop, or relax in one of the many cafés. As an alternative, you may want to catch a bus near the Zappion hall entrance of the National Gardens to one of the government-run beaches in Varkiza, Vouliagmeni, or Voula.

The Acropolis, Filopappou, and Environs

Described by the French poet Lamartine as "the most perfect poem in stone," the Acropolis, or "High City," is a true testament to the golden age of Greece. From 461 to 429 BC was the magical period when the intellectual and artistic life of Athens flowered at the height of the Athenian statesman Pericles' influence. Archaeological evidence has shown that the flat-top limestone outcrop, 512 ft high, attracted settlers in as early as Neolithic times because of its defensible position and its natural springs. It is believed to have been continuously inhabited throughout the Bronze Age and since.

Over the years the Acropolis buildings have borne the damages of war as well as unscrupulous transformations into, at various times, a Florentine palace, an Islamic mosque, and a Turkish harem. The hazards of war continued up to 1944, when British paratroopers sited their bazookas between the Parthenon's columns. Since then, a more insidious enemy has arrived—pollution. The site is now undergoing conservation as part of an ambitious 20-year rescue plan launched in 1983 by Greek architects with international support. Despite the restoration works under way, a visit to the Acropolis can evoke the spirit of the ancient heroes and gods who were once worshiped there. See the buildings first and save the museum for last; familiarity with the overall setting will give the statues and friezes more meaning. The "Acropolis" neighborhood includes fine neoclassical buildings lining its main street, Dionyssiou Areopagitou; the centuries-old Odeon of Herod Atticus; the Dionyssos theater; and one of the newest museums in Greece, the Ilias LALAoUNIS Jewelry Museum. Nearby is Filopappou, a pine-clad summit that offers the city's best view of the Acropolis and the tiny, rustic church of Ayios Dimitrios Loumbardiaris.

Numbers in the text correspond to numbers in the margin and on the Exploring Ancient Athens, Exploring Athens, and Exploring Piraeus maps.

A Good Walk

If you see nothing else in Athens, you must visit the **Acropolis** ①. Even jaded Athenians, when overwhelmed by the city, need only lift their eyes to this great monument to feel renewed. Wear a hat for protection from the sun and low-heel, rubber-sole shoes, as the marble on the Acropolis steps and near the other monuments is quite slippery. Take a taxi or Bus 230 to Dionyssiou Areopagitou, which winds around the Acropolis to its entrance at the Beulé Gate. Buildings include the architecturally complex Erechtheion temple, most sacred of the shrines of the Acropolis, and the Parthenon, which dominates the Acropolis and, indeed, the city skyline: it is the most architecturally sophisticated temple of its period. Time and neglect have given its marble pillars their golden-white shine, and the beauty of the building is made all the more stark and striking. Even with summer's hordes wandering around the ruins, you will still feel a sense of wonder.

While on the outcrop, pause at the edge of the southern fortifications, where, on a clear day, you can see the coastline toward Sounion and the Saronic Gulf Islands of Aegina and Salamina. Be sure to leave enough time for the **Acropolis Museum** ②, which houses some superb sculptures from the Acropolis, including most of the caryatids and a large collection of colored *korai* (statues of women dedicated to the goddess Athena). As you exit the gate, detour right to the rock of **Areopagus** ③, the ancient supreme court, from which St. Paul later preached to the Athenians.

Cross Dionyssiou Areopagitou to **Filopappou** ⑤, but before climbing the summit, via the footpaths crisscrossing the hill, stop at tiny **Ayios Dimitrios Loumbardiaris** ④ church, and then for a coffee at the tourist pavilion. Descend Dionyssiou Areopagitou, past the **Odeon of Herod Atticus** ⑥ and the Hellenistic **theater of Dionyssos** ⑦. Nearby is the **Ilias LALAoUNIS Jewelry Museum** ⑧, with more than 3,000 pieces and a workshop where visitors can observe ancient techniques still used today. Off the main boulevard on Makriyianni, for those who have the time and the interest, is the **Center for Acropolis Studies** ⑨, with exhibits on the great monument.

TIMING

Normally, the earlier you start out the better, but a summertime alternative is to visit the Acropolis after 5 PM, when the light is best for taking photographs. Depending on the crowds waiting to get in, the walk takes about four hours, including one actually spent in the Acropolis Museum. Once a month in summer, the site is open from about 9 PM to midnight so you can enjoy the spectacle of the full moon rising and casting long shadows over the Parthenon. The Ilias LALAoUNIS Jewelry Museum is closed Tuesdays, so you may want to take this tour another day.

Sights to See

★ ❶ **Acropolis.** Today's traveler to the Acropolis is, almost perforce, a pilgrim returning to the very source of the highest civilization that the West has produced. Even in its bleached and silent state, the Parthenon—the great Panathenic temple that crowns the Acropolis, the tablelike hill that represented the "upper city" of ancient Athens—has the power to stir the heart as few other ancient relics can. Seeing it bathed in the sunlight of the south, or sublimely swathed in moonglow, to which has been added the incandescent glow of the spirit that seems to emanate from Greek art itself, one marvels at the continuing vitality of this monument of ageless intellect. Well, not completely ageless. Foundations for a grand new temple honoring the city's patron, goddess Athena, were, in fact, laid after the victory at Marathon in 490 BC but were destroyed by Persians in 480–79 BC. After a 30-year building moratorium, ended by the peace treaty at Susa in 448 BC, Pericles undertook the ambitious project of reconstructing it on a monumental scale. This extraordinary Athenian general is an enigmatic figure, considered by some scholars to be the brilliant architect of the destiny of Greece at its height and by others a megalomaniac who bankrupted the coffers of an empire and an elitist who catered to the privileged few at the expense of the masses.

The appearance of the buildings that composed the major portion of the Acropolis remained largely unaltered until AD 52, when the Roman Claudius embellished the entrance to it with a typically flamboyant staircase. In the 2nd century Hadrian had his turn at decorating many of the shrines, and in 529 Justinian closed the philosophical schools in the city, emphasizing the defensive character of the citadel and changing the temples into Christian churches.

Visitors enter through the **Beulé Gate,** a late Roman structure named for the French archaeologist Ernest Beulé, who discovered it in 1852. Made of marble fragments from destroyed monuments, it has an inscription above the lintel dated 320 BC, dedicated by "Nikias son of Nikodemos of Xypete," who had apparently won a musical competition. Before Roman times, the entrance to the Acropolis was a steep processional ramp below the Temple of Athena Nike. This Sacred Way was used every fourth year for the Panathenaic Procession, a spectacle that ended the festival celebrating Athena's remarkable birth (she sprang from the head of her father, Zeus), which included chariot races, athletic and musical competitions, and poetry recitals. Toward the end of July, all strata of Athenian society gathered at the Dipylon Gate of Kerameikos and followed a sacred ship wheeled up to the summit. The ship was anchored at the rocky outcrop below Areopagus, just northwest of the Acropolis.

The **Propylaea** is a typical ancient gate, an imposing structure designed to instill proper reverence in worshipers as they crossed from the temporal world into the spiritual world of the sanctuary, for this was to be the main function of the Acropolis. Conceived by Pericles, it was the masterwork of the architect Mnesicles. It was to have been the grandest secular building in Greece, the same size as the Parthenon. Construction was suspended during the Peloponnesian War, and it was never finished. The Propylaea was used as a garrison during the Turkish period; in 1656, a powder magazine there was struck by lightning, causing much damage; and the Propylaea was again damaged during the Venetian siege under Morosini in 1687.

The Propylaea shows the first use of both Doric and Ionic columns together, a style that can be called Attic. Six of the sturdier fluted Doric columns, made from Pendelic marble, correspond with the gateways of the portal. Processions with priests, chariots, and sacrificial animals entered via a marble ramp in the center (now protected by a wooden stairway), while ordinary visitors on foot entered via the side doors.

The slender Ionic columns (two-thirds the diameter of the Doric) had elegant capitals, some of which have been restored, along with a section of the famed paneled ceiling, originally decorated with gold eight-pointed stars on a blue background. The well-preserved north wing housed the Pinakotheke, or art gallery, specializing in paintings of scenes from Homer's epics and mythological tableaux on wooden plaques. Connected to it was a lounge with 17 couches arranged around the walls so that weary visitors could enjoy a siesta. The south wing was a decorative portico (row of columns). The view from the inner porch of the Propylaea is stunning: The Parthenon is suddenly revealed in its full glory, framed by the columns.

The 2nd-century traveler Pausanias referred to the **Temple of Athena Nike** as the Temple of Nike Apteros, or Wingless Victory, for "in Athens they believe Victory will stay forever because she has no wings." Designed by Kalliktrates, the mini-temple was built in 427–424 BC to celebrate peace with Persia, with four Ionic columns at each portico end. It was from this temple's platform that, according to Pausanias, the distraught King Aegeus flung himself into the sea—no mean achievement considering the 10-km (6-mi) distance—to which he has given his name. His son, Theseus, had forgotten to hoist the white sails proclaiming his slaying of the Minotaur, and on seeing the black sails, the aggrieved father committed the somewhat acrobatic suicide. The bas-reliefs of the Frieze of Victoires on the surrounding parapet must have been of exceptional quality, judging from the "Nike Unfastening Her Sandal" in the Acropolis Museum. Many sections of the frieze, which depicts the Battle of Plataia with Greeks fighting the Persians, were whisked away to the British Museum two centuries ago and replaced with cement copies. In 1998 Greek archaeologists began the arduous task of dismantling the last original but badly weathered sections for conservation. They will laser or microblast the sculpted reliefs to clean them of soot before installing them in the new Acropolis museum to be built nearby.

At the loftiest point of the Acropolis is the **Parthenon,** the architectural masterpiece conceived by Pericles and executed between 447 and 438 BC by the brilliant sculptor Pheidias, who supervised the architects Iktinos and Callicrates in its construction. Although dedicated to the goddess Athena (the name Parthenon comes from the Athena Parthenos, or the virgin Athena) and inaugurated at the Panathenaia Festival of 438 BC, the Parthenon was primarily the treasury of the Delian League. For the populace, the Erechtheion—*not* the Parthenon—remained Athena's sanctified holy place.

Though the structure of the Parthenon is of marble, the inner ceilings and doors were made of wood. The original building was ornate, covered with a tile roof, decorated with statuary and marble friezes, and so brightly painted that the people protested, "We are gilding and adorning our city like a wanton woman" (Plutarch). Pheidias himself may have sculpted some of the exquisite, brightly painted metopes, but most were done by other artists under his guidance. The only ones remaining in situ show scenes of battle: Athenians versus Amazons, and gods and goddesses against giants. One of the most evocative friezes, depicting the procession of the Panathenaia, was 524 ft long, an ex-

Exploring Ancient Athens

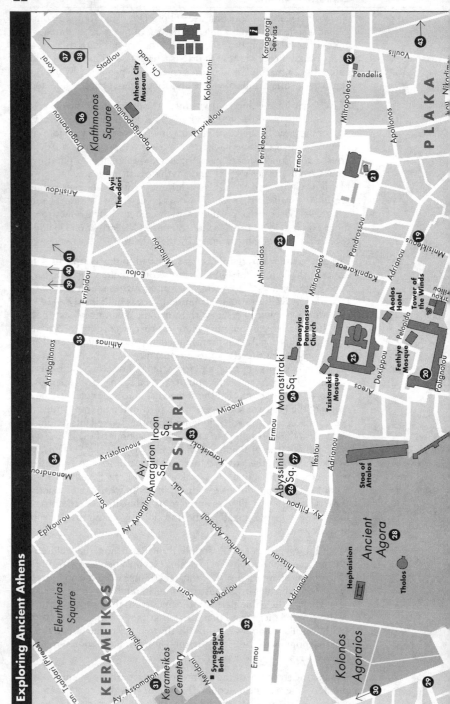

KERAMEIKOS

PSIRRI

PLAKA

Eleutherias Square

Klafthmonos Square

Kerameikos Cemetery

Kolonos Agoraios

Ancient Agora

Stoa of Attalos

Hephaistion

Tholos

Athens City Museum

Ayii Theodori

Synagogue Beth Shalom

Panayia Pantanassa Church

Monastiraki Sq.

Abyssinia Sq.

Tzistarakis Mosque

Fethiye Mosque

Tower of the Winds

Aeolos Hotel

Ayii Anargiron Iroon Sq.

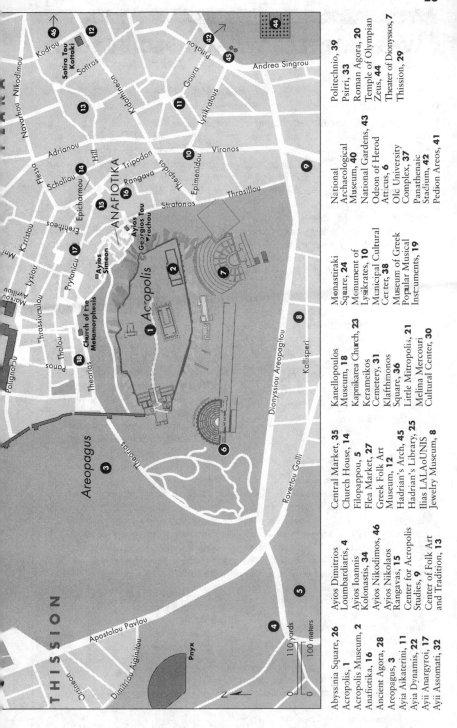

Abyssinia Square, **26**
Acropolis, **1**
Acropolis Museum, **2**
Anafiotika, **16**
Ancient Agora, **28**
Areopagus, **3**
Ayia Aikaterini, **11**
Ayia Dynamis, **22**
Ayii Anargyroi, **17**
Ayii Assomati, **32**

Ayios Dimitrios
Loumbardiaris, **4**
Ayios Ioannis
Kolonastis, **34**
Ayios Nikodimos, **46**
Ayios Nikolaos
Rangavas, **15**
Center for Acropolis
Studies, **9**
Center of Folk Art
and Tradition, **13**

Central Market, **35**
Church House, **14**
Filopappou, **5**
Flea Market, **27**
Greek Folk Art
Museum, **12**
Hadrian's Arch, **45**
Hadrian's Library, **25**
Ilias LALAoUNIS
Jewelry Museum, **8**

Kanellopoulos
Museum, **18**
Kapnikarea Church, **23**
Kerameikos
Cemetery, **31**
Klafthmonos
Square, **36**
Little Mitropoli, **21**
Melina Mercouri
Cultural Center, **30**

Monastiraki
Square, **24**
Monument of
Lysikrates, **10**
Municipal Cultural
Center, **38**
Museum of Greek
Popular Musical
Instruments, **19**

National
Archaeological
Museum, **40**
National Gardens, **43**
Odeon of Herod
Atticus, **6**
Olé University
Complex, **37**
Panathenaic
Stadium, **42**
Pedion Areos, **41**

Politechnio, **39**
Psirri, **33**
Roman Agora, **20**
Temple of Olympian
Zeus, **44**
Theater of Dionyssos, **7**
Thission, **29**

WHEN GREECE WORSHIPED BEAUTY

GREEK ART DID NOT spring in a blinding flash like Athena fully modeled from the brain of Zeus. The earliest ceramic cup in a Greek museum, said by legend to have been molded after the breast of Helen of Troy, is a libel on that siren's reputation: It is coarse, clumsy, and rough. But fast-forward a millennium or so and you arrive at the golden age, when Greek art forevermore set the standard for ideals of beauty, grace, and realism in Western art, when the Parthenon gave proof of an architectural genius unique in history. The time was the 5th century BC, about 2,000 years before the Italian Renaissance. Just as that glorious age flourished, thanks to Italian city-states, so did ancient Greece reach its apogee in its cities. And it was in Athens that Greek citizens realized they could reveal the free blossoming of the human being and respect the individualistic character of men and women through art and architecture. This affirmation was largely the work of one man, Pericles.

To understand this celebrated Athenian general you must understand that amazing conundrum called Athenian democracy. This democracy was really an aristocracy, the watchdog of private property and public order. It financed athletic games and drama festivals; it constructed the Parthenon. Its model was not only *live*, but *live well*. Surrounded by barbarians, the age of Pericles was the more striking for its high level of civilization, its qualities of proportion, reason, clarity, and harmony. This is nowhere more apparent than in Greek art and architecture. Greek artistic genius fed on a physical ideal—spectacularly represented in the culture with its hero worship of athletes—as it did on religion, and religion itself, far from being an abstraction, was an anthropomorphic reflection of a passion for physical beauty.

The inspiration, however, would not have sufficed to ensure the grandeur of Greek art had it not been served by a perfection of technique. Whoever created any object had to know to perfection every element of his model, whether it was a man or woman or god or goddess. Witness the marvels of the sculpture of the age, such as the *Delphi Charioteer*, the Parthenon frieze figures, or the *Venus de Milo*. Basically the cult of the god was the cult of beauty. The women of Sparta, desirous of having handsome children, adorned their bedchambers with statues of male and female beauties. Beauty contests are not an invention of modern times. The Greeks organized them as early as the 7th century BC, until Christianity came to frown on such practices.

In like form, architecture was also the reflection of the personality of this Greek world. Thus, when we note the buildings of the Acropolis, we note the Doric order is all mathematics; the Ionian, all poetry. The first expresses proud reserve, massive strength, and severe simplicity; the second, suppleness, sensitivity, and elegance. No matter what the order, the column was the binding force—the absolute incarnation of reason in form. Study the columns of the Parthenon and you quickly realize that the Greeks did not propose to represent reality with its clutter of details; their aim was to seize the essence of things and let its light shine forth.

But it would be false to conclude, as certain romantic spirits have done, that the Greeks were mere aesthetes, lost in ecstasy before abstract beauty and subordinating their lives to it. Quite the reverse: it was the art of living which, for the Greeks, was the supreme art. A healthy utilitarian inclination combined with their worship of beauty to such an extent that art within their homes was not an idle ornament, but had a functional quality related to everyday life.

traordinary parade of 400 people including maidens, magistrates, horsemen, musicians, and 200 animals. To show ordinary mortals, at a time when almost all sculpture was of mythological or battle scenes, was lively and daring. About 50 of the best-preserved pieces, called the "Parthenon marbles" by Greeks but known as the Elgin Marbles by almost everyone else, are in the British Museum; a few others can be seen in the Acropolis Museum. In the first decade of the 19th century, during the time of the Ottoman Empire, Lord Elgin, British Ambassador in Constantinople, was given permission by the Sultan Selim III to remove stones with inscriptions from the Acropolis; he took this as license to dismantle shiploads of sculptures. It remains a highly controversial issue to this day: On one side, many argue that the marbles would have been destroyed if left on site; on the other side, a spirited campaign spearheaded by the late Mclina Mercouri, the actor turned politician, aims to have them returned to Greece, to be appreciated in their original context.

Pheidias's most awesome contribution to the Parthenon was the 39-ft-high statue of Athena that stood in the inner chamber of the sanctuary. It was made on a wooden frame, with ivory for the flesh and more than a ton of gold for the ankle-length tunic, helmet, spear, and shield. The alleged theft of some of this gold (some say the ivory) was the basis of charges against Pheidias, who is said to have cleared his name by removing it from the statue and having the statue weighed to prove it all was there. After the Christian emperor Thesodosius II closed all pagan sanctuaries in AD 435, the statue seems to have disappeared. The Parthenon was later converted into a church, but the basic structure remained intact until the Venetian siege of Athens in the 17th century, when Morosini's artillery hit a powder magazine, causing a fire that burned for two days. Many of the 46 columns were destroyed, along with the roof and most of the interior.

If the Parthenon is the masterpiece of Doric architecture, the **Erechtheion** is undoubtedly that of the more graceful and feminine Ionic order. A considerably smaller structure than the Parthenon, for sheer elegance and refinement of design and execution, it cannot be matched by any other building of the Greco-Roman world. More than any other ancient monument, this temple has its roots in the legendary origins of Athens. Here it was that the contest between Poseidon and Athena took place for the possession of the city. On this spot, the sea god dramatically plunged his trident into the rock next to the Erechtheion and produced a spring of water; Athena more prudently created an olive tree, the main staple of Greek society. The panel of judges declared her the winner, and the city was named Athena. A gnarled olive tree outside the west wall was planted where Athena's once grew, and marks said to be from Poseidon's trident can be seen on a rock wedged in a hole near the north porch. His gift should not be slighted, for the continual springs of the Acropolis have made habitation possible from earliest times, as well as the watering of the olive trees. Completed in 406 BC, the Erechtheion was actually divided into two Ionic sanctuaries, the eastern one containing an olive-wood statue of Athena Polias, protectress of the city, and the western one dedicated to Poseidon-Erechtheus.

The most endearing feature of the Erechtheion, which has recently undergone extensive repair, is the south portico, facing the Parthenon, known as the **Caryatid Porch**. It is supported on the heads of six strapping but shapely maidens (caryatids) wearing delicately draped Ionian garments, their folds perfectly aligned to resemble flutes on columns (what you see today are copies; except for the caryatid dismantled by Lord Elgin, now in the British Museum, the originals were removed in 1977 to the Acropolis Museum to protect them from erosion caused by air pollution). Taking into account the enormous burden that these impassive maidens are carrying, their uniformly complacent, almost simpering expressions seem a little out of place.

If asked what is the best time to see the Acropolis, one might be hard put to find an answer. Such is the beauty of the monument and the grandeur of the setting that a visit in all weathers and at all hours is rewarding. The moonlight visit—usually scheduled by the authorities during the full moon period—is generally the most romantic. But in winter if there are clouds trailing across the mountains, and shafts of sun sometimes lighting up the marble columns, which glisten with added brilliance after a shower of rain or a thunderstorm, the setting takes on an even more dramatic quality. In summer the heat is blistering at noontime, and the reflection of the light thrown back by the rock and the marble ruins almost blinding, so morning and early afternoon are preferable. But the ideal—indeed, Platonic—time might be the two hours before sunset; it is then that the famous violet light can occasionally be seen spreading from the crest of Mt. Hymettus, gradually embracing the Acropolis in all its radiance, and reminding us that Athens was once called "the violet-crowned" by the ancients. After dark, of course, the Acropolis is now spectacularly floodlit for some of the most effective sound-and-light performances in the world. ✉ *Dionyssiou Areopagitou,* ☎ *01/321–4172.* 💰 *2,000 dr., joint ticket for Acropolis and Acropolis Museum.* ☉ *Weekdays 8–6:30 (winter 8–4:30), weekends 8:30–2:30.*

★ ❷ **Acropolis Museum.** Full of fabled objects of Attic art found on the Acropolis, this museum is unobtrusively snuggled in the southeast corner of the Acropolis site. Among the exhibits are legendary sculptures, plus the votive offerings to Athena. The displays are well executed, but their labeling in English is sketchy. In Room I, the anguished expression of a calf being devoured by a lioness in a porous-stone pediment of the 6th century BC brings to mind Picasso's *Guernica.* Room II contains the charismatic *Calf-Bearer,* or *Moschophoros,* an early Archaic work showing a man named Rhombos carrying on his shoulders a calf intended to be sacrificed. A porous-stone pediment of the Archaic temple of Athena shows Heracles fighting against Triton—on its right side, note the rather scholarly-looking "three-headed demon," bearing traces of the original red-and-black embellishment. The most notable displays of the museum are sculptures from the Archaic and classical periods, pieces of unique appeal, including, in Room IV, the *Horseman* and the compelling *Hound,* both by the sculptor Phaidimos. In Rooms IV and V, take a good look at the exquisite korai, with fascinating details of hair, clothing, and jewelry of the Archaic period. Room V also has striking pedimental figures from the Old Temple of Athena (525 BC), depicting the battle between Athena and the Giants. In Room VI is the 5th-century BC relief *Mourning Athena,* a fine example of the severe style favored in the classical period. In Room VIII, a superbly rendered slab from the eastern side of the Acropolis represents the seated Poseidon, Artemis, and Apollo. Incomparably graceful movement is suggested in *Nike Unfastening Her Sandal,* taken from the parapet of the Temple of Athena Nike. In a dimly lit, air-conditioned glass case in Room IX are the badly damaged original caryatids, salvaged from the Erechtheion. ✉ *Acropolis,* ☎ *01/323–6665.* 💰 *2,000 dr., joint ticket for Acropolis and Acropolis Museum.* ☉ *Mon. 11–6:30 (winter 11–4:30), Tues.–Fri. 8:30–6:30 (winter 8:30–4:30), weekends 8:30–2:30.*

❸ **Areopagus.** From this limestone "Hill of Ares," surefooted visitors have a good view of the Propylaea, the ancient Agora below, and the modern metropolis to the northwest. This was once Athens's supreme judicial court, and legend says that Orestes was tried here for the murder of his mother, Clytemnestra. From the outcrop, St. Paul delivered such a moving sermon on the "Unknown God" that he converted the senator Dionysius, who became the first bishop of Athens. Some of St. Paul's words (Acts 17:22–34) are written in Greek on a bronze plaque at the foot of the hill. ⊠ *Outside the Acropolis's entrance.* ▤ *Free.*

④ Ayios Dimitrios Loumbardiaris. A delightful grove borders this church, which derives its name from *loumbarda* (cannon). Here in 1656 on St. Dimitrios' Day, as is told in a text posted on the church, the congregation was gathered, while on the Acropolis a Turkish garrison commander readied the cannons of the Propylaea to open fire during the final Te Deum. The moment it started, a bolt of lightning struck the cannons, blowing up the Propylaea and killing the commander and many of his men. The stone church contains many icons and has an old-fashioned wood ceiling and roof. ⊠ *Filopappou hill.* ☉ *Daily 7–7.*

NEED A
BREAK?

The little **Tourist Pavilion** (⊠ Filopappou hill, ☎ 01/923–1665) is a blissful oasis far from the bustle of the archaeological sites and the streets. It is beautifully landscaped, shaded by overhanging pines, and the background music is provided by chirping birds. It serves drinks, snacks, and a few hot plates and is open daily from 9 AM to 1 AM.

⑨ Center for Acropolis Studies. The spacious, sunny ground floor is devoted to casts of sculptures of lounging gods and friezes of heroes battling giants or centaurs that were once (or still are) on the Acropolis. The most notable are copies of the much-touted Elgin Marbles, presented as a sorry consolation gift to Greece in 1846 (the British government kept the heartbreakingly beautiful originals). On the first floor an exhibit of models depicts the various incarnations of the Acropolis, and there is one of the new Acropolis museum to be built nearby. Don't miss the terra-cotta antefixes, the ornaments at the termination of the roofing tiles, invented by the classical Greeks. On one the elegant bright-on-dark abstract design is offset by a naughty gorgon with bulging black eyes sticking out his cherry-color tongue. ⊠ *Makriyianni 2–4,* ☎ 01/923–9381. ▤ *Free.* ☉ *Daily 9–2:45.*

⑤ Filopappou. This summit's three hills include **Lofos Mouseion** (Hill of the Muses), whose peak offers the city's best view of the Parthenon, which appears almost at eye level. Here, too, is the **Monument of Filopappus,** a Syrian prince who was such a generous benefactor, the people accepted him as a distinguished Athenian. The marble monument is a tomb decorated by a frieze showing Filopappus driving his chariot. In 294 BC a fort strategic to Athens's defense was built here, overlooking the road to the sea. On the second hill, called **Pnyx** (meaning "crowded"), the general assembly (Ecclesia) met during the time of Pericles. Gathering the quorum of 5,000 citizens necessary to take a vote was not always easy. Archers armed with red paint were sent out to dab it on vote dodgers; the offenders were then fined. Farther north is the **Hill of the Nymphs,** with a 19th-century observatory.

☺ ⑧ Ilias LALAoUNIS Jewelry Museum. Housing the creations of the internationally renowned artist Ilias Lalaounis, this private foundation also operates as a study center. The 45 collections include 3,000 pieces inspired by subjects as diverse as the Treasure of Priam to the wildflowers of Greece; many of the works are eye-catching, especially the massive necklaces evoking the Minoan and Byzantine periods. Besides well-made videos that explain jewelry making (order up No. 11 on goldsmithery through the intercom), craftspeople in the workshop demonstrate ancient and modern techniques, such as chain weaving and hammering for visitors. During the academic year the museum can arrange educational programs in English for groups of children, and it provides child care for visiting parents year-round (call in advance). The founder also has several stores in Athens (☞ Shopping, *below*). ⊠ *Kallisperi 12 at Karyatidon, Acropolis,* ☎ *01/922–1044.* ⚏ *800 dr., free on Wed. after 3* PM. ☽ *Mon. and Thurs.–Sat. 9–4, Wed. 9–9, Sun. 10–4. Closed 1st 2 wks. of Aug.*

❻ Odeon of Herod Atticus. This hauntingly beautiful ancient theater was dedicated by an affluent benefactor and built, Greek-style, into the hillside, but with typically Roman arches in its three-story stage building and barrel-vaulted entrances. The circular orchestra has now become a semicircle, and the long-vanished cedar roof probably covered only the stage and dressing rooms, not the 34 rows of seats. The theater, which holds 5,000, was restored and reopened in 1955 for the Athens Festival and is now open only to ticket holders who are attending the scheduled summer performances, which range from the Royal Ballet to ancient tragedies and Attic comedies usually performed in modern Greek. Contact the Athens Festival box office for ticket information (☞ Nightlife and the Arts, *below*). ⊠ *Dionyssiou Areopagitou near intersection with Propylaion St.,* ☎ *01/323–2771.*

❼ Theater of Dionyssos. It was on this spot in the 6th century BC that the Dionyssia festivals took place; a century later, dramas such as Sophocles' *Oedipus Rex* and Euripides's *Medea* were performed for the entire population of the city. Foundations are visible of a stage dating from about 330 BC, when it was built for 15,000 spectators as well as the assemblies formerly held on Pnyx. In the middle of the orchestra stood the altar to Dionyssos. Most of the upper rows of seats have been destroyed, but the lower levels, with labeled chairs for priests and dignitaries, remain. The fantastic throne in the center was reserved for the priest of Dionyssos: It is adorned by regal lions' paws, and the back is carved with reliefs of satyrs and griffins. On the hillside above the theater stand two columns, vestiges of the little temple erected in the 4th century BC by Thrasyllus the Choragus (the ancient counterpart of a modern impresario). ⊠ *Dionyssiou Areopagitou, across from Mitsaion St.,* ☎ *01/322–4625.* ⚏ *500 dr.* ☽ *Daily 8:30–2:45.*

Plaka and Anafiotika

One of Athens's prettiest neighborhoods, Plaka remains the last corner of 19th-century Athens, with Byzantine accents provided by churches. During the 1950s and '60s, the area became garish with neon as nightclubs moved in and residents moved out, but residents, architects, and academicians joined forces in the early 1980s to transform a decaying neighborhood. Noisy discos and tacky pensions were closed, streets were changed into pedestrian zones, and old buildings were well restored. At night the area is still crowded with merrymakers visiting the old tavernas, which feature traditional music and dancing, many with rooftops facing the Acropolis. If you keep off the main tourist shopping streets of Kidathineon and Adrianou, you will be amazed at how peaceful the area can be, even in the height of the summer. Above Plaka is Anafiotika, built on winding lanes that climb up the slopes of the Acropolis, its upper reaches resembling a tranquil village. In classical times it was abandoned because the Delphic Oracle claimed it as sacred ground. The buildings here were constructed by masons from Anafi island, who came to find work in the rapidly expanding Athens of the 1830s and 1840s. They took over this area, whose rocky terrain was similar to Anafi's, building their homes illegally during the night. Ethiopians who had arrived during the Ottoman period and stayed on after independence lived higher up, in caves, on the northern slopes of the Acropolis.

A Good Walk

After the Acropolis, the historical quarter of Plaka is the next must-see. Take time to explore the side streets graced by old mansions under renovation by the Ministry of Culture. Begin your stroll on Lysikra-tous, across from Hadrian's Arch, which leads northwest to a square with the **Monument of Lysikrates** ⑩, one of the few remaining supports (334 BC) for tripods awarded to the producer of the best play in the ancient Dionyssia festival; off the square on Galanou and Goura is the pretty church of **Ayia Aikaterini** ⑪. Take Herefondos to Plaka's central square, Filomoussou Eterias (or Platia Kidathineon), a great place to people-watch.

Up Kidathineon is the **Greek Folk Art Museum** ⑫, with a rich collection ranging from 1650 to the present, including works by the beloved naïve artist Theophilos. Across from the museum is the 11th- to 12th-century church of **Sotira Tou Kottaki,** set in a tidy garden with a fountain that was the main source of water for the neighborhood until some time after Turkish rule. Around the corner on Hatzimichali Aggelou is the **Center of Folk Art and Tradition** ⑬. Continue west to the end of that street, crossing Adrianou to Hill, then right on Epimarchou and the striking **Church House** ⑭ (on the corner of Scholeiou), once a Turkish police post and the headquarters for Richard Church, who led Greek forces in the War of Independence.

At the top of Epimarchou is **Ayios Nikolaos Rangavas** ⑮, an 11th-century church built with fragments of ancient columns. The church marks the edge of the **Anafiotika quarter** ⑯, a village smack dab in the middle of the metropolis: Its main street, Stratonos, is lined with cottages, occasional murals painted on the stones, and a few little shops. Wind your way through the narrow lanes off Stratonos, visiting the churches **Ayios Georgios tou Vrachou, Ayios Simeon,** and **Metamorphosis Sotiros.** Another interesting church is **Ayii Anargyroi** ⑰, at the top of Erechtheos, an 8th-century chapel that according to legend was built by Empress Irene. From the church, make your way to Theorias, which parallels the ancient *peripatos* (public roadway) that ran around the Acropolis. The collection at the **Kanellopoulos Museum** ⑱ spans Athens's history; nearby on Panos you'll pass the **Athens University Museum (Old University),** the city's first higher-learning institution.

Walk down Panos to the **Roman Agora** ⑳, which includes the **Tower of the Winds** and the **Fethiye Mosque.** For an engaging detour, visit the nearby **Museum of Greek Popular Musical Instruments** ⑲, where recordings will take you back to the age of rembetika. On your way back to Syntagma Square, cut across Mitropolis (Cathedral) Square to the 12th-century Byzantine church known as **Little Mitropolis** ㉑, whose outer walls are covered with reliefs. Closer to Syntagma Square, on the corner of Pendelis and Mitropoleos, is the curious sight of **Ayia Dynamis** ㉒, a chapel peering out from between the cement columns of a Ministry building.

TIMING

Plaka is a delight any time of day, liveliest in the early evening, or Sunday afternoons, when locals congregate at its outdoor cafés. Perhaps the best time to explore Anafiotika is just before sunset, when the haze is reduced and you can catch great views of the city. If you want to visit the museums (usually open until 3 PM) or the churches (open from 8 AM to noon and sometimes from 5 to 7 PM), begin your excursion as early as possible. For planning ahead, note that some of the museums are closed Mondays (Center of Folk Art and Tradition, Children's Museum, the Greek Folk Art Museum, the Roman Agora, Museum of Greek Popular Musical Instruments, and the Kanellopoulos Museum). The walk, with leisurely stops at one or two museums, and time for a coffee break, takes about three hours. During Carnivali in February, costumed Athenians gather in Plaka for a stroll through the quarter, bopping each other with plastic clubs, showering confetti, and spraying foam at passersby: Beware!

Sights to See

★ ☞ ⑯ **Anafiotika.** Set in the shadow of the Acropolis, this is the closest thing to a Cycladic village one will find in Athens. Still populated by many descendants of the Anafi stonemasons who arrived in the 19th century to expand the capital, Anafiotika is an enchanting area of simple stone houses, many nestled right into the bedrock, most little changed over the years, others stunningly restored. Cascades of bougainvillea and pots of geraniums and marigolds enliven the balconies and rooftops, and the prevailing serenity is in blissful contrast to the cacophony of modern Athens. You seldom see the residents—only a line of washing hung out to dry, the lace curtains on the tiny houses, or the curl of smoke from a wood-burning fireplace indicate human presence. Perched on the bedrock of the Acropolis is **Ayios Georgios tou Vrachou** (St. George of the Rock), which marks the southeast edge of the district. One of the most beautiful churches of Athens, it is still in use today. **Ayios Simeon,** a neoclassical church built in 1847 by the settlers, marks the western boundary and contains a copy of a famous miracle-working icon from Anafi, Our Lady of the Reeds. The **Church of the Metamorphosis Sotiros** (Transfiguration), a high-dome 14th-century stone chapel, has a rear grotto carved right into the Acropolis. For those with children, there is a small playground at Stratonos and Vironos. ⊠ *On northeast slope of Acropolis rock.*

⑪ **Ayia Aikaterini.** Built in the late-11th to early 12th centuries and enlarged in 1927, the church took its name in 1769, when it was acquired by the Monastery of Saint Catherine in the Sinai. It is cruciform, with a dome resting on a drum supported by four interior columns; the large courtyard and garden make it popular for baptisms and weddings. ⊠ *Off square on Galanou and Goura,* ☎ *01/322–8974.* ☉ *Weekdays 7 AM–12:30 PM and 5:30–7 (in winter 7:30–12:30 and 5–6:30), weekends 7 AM–12:30 PM and 5–10.*

㉒ **Ayia Dynamis.** The "Divine Power" chapel, named for the Virgin Mary's supposed ability to help childless women conceive and topped by a dainty arch and bell, peeks out between the cement columns of the modern Ministry of Education and Religion. Its romantic history makes it worth mentioning. A Greek named Mastropavlis made cartridges here for the Turkish garrison, which had turned the church into a munitions works. At the same time, he secretly made ammunition for the Greek revolutionaries, which was smuggled to them by a courageous washerwoman. These were the first bullets fired at the Turks on the Acropolis when the War of Independence broke out. ⊠ *On corner of Pendelis and Mitropoleos.*

⑰ **Ayii Anargyroi.** According to legend, the church, also known as Metochion Panagiou Tafou, was built in the late-8th century by the empress Irene, once an Athenian orphan, and sole ruler of Byzantium, after the death of her husband. The Church of the Holy Sepulchre at Jerusalem, needing an outpost in Athens, acquired it in the 1700s and continues to occupy it today. The church has a gingerbread-like exterior, a delightful little garden containing fragments of ancient ruins, and a well that was used as a hiding place in troubled times. ⊠ *Top of stairs where Erechtheos meets Pritaniou.*

⑮ **Ayios Nikolaos Rangavas.** On the southeast side of this 11th-century Byzantine church rebuilt in the 18th century, you can see fragments of ancient columns and capitals incorporated into its walls, an example of the pragmatic recycling of the time. It is above the stairs off Pryitaniou, named after the center of the ancient city where a sacred flame was kept burning. ⊠ *Pritaniou 1, at top of Epimarchou,* ☎ *01/322–8193.*

⑬ **Center of Folk Art and Tradition.** Exhibits in this comfortable family mansion of folklorist Angeliki Hatzimichali include detailed costumes, ceramic plates from Skyros, handwoven fabrics and embroideries, and family portraits. ⊠ *Hatzimichali Aggelou 6,* ☎ *01/324–3972.* ⌨ *Free.* ◷ *Sept.–July, Tues.–Fri. 9–1 and 5–9, weekends 9–1.*

NEED A
BREAK?

Off Plaka's main square, visit the **De Profundis Tea Room** (⊠ Hatzimichali Aggelou 1, ☎ 01/323-1764), in an old mansion, for pastries and a large variety of teas; it is closed from late June through August. **Byzantino** (⊠ Kidathineon 18, ☎ 01/322-9636) is directly on the square—great for people-watching and a good, reasonably priced bite to eat. Go around the corner to **Glikis** (⊠ Aggelou Geronta 2, ☎ 01/332-3925) and its shady courtyard for a Greek coffee or ouzo and a *mikri pikilia* (a small plate of appetizers, including cheese, sausage, olives, and dips).

🖐 ㊽ **Children's Museum.** In the courtyard, you may see children pressing melted chocolate into molds, a group upstairs concocting toys out of recycled materials, and others on the top floor of this neoclassical building learning to blow gigantic soap bubbles. The museum allows visitors up to the age of 12 to play freely and experiment; experienced staff encourage them to interact. Each room is designed around a particular theme: A darkened corner encloses the solar system, another room reveals the world of computers, and a third lets children don hard hats and walk through a mock metro construction site. Throughout the year, parents can sign children up for events like "a night at the museum," when they play, cook, and overnight in the room of their choice. The museum also runs a shop with toys and books. ⊠ *Kidathineon 14,* ☎ *01/331–2995.* ⌨ *Free.* ◷ *Sept.–July, Tues. and Thurs.–Fri. 9:30–1:30, Wed. 9:30–6:30, weekends 10–2.*

⑭ **Church House.** The striking, abandoned tower house with tiny windows, thick stone walls, and a tall chimney still bears traces of its past glory. Probably dating from the 18th century and used as a Turkish police post, it became the fortress of Richard Church, commander-in-chief of the Greek forces during the War of Independence. After the liberation, historian George Finlay, a veteran of the war, and his wife lived here for half a century, while he wrote his many volumes of Greek history, including what is considered the definitive work on the War of Independence. ⊠ *Corner of Epimarchou and Scholeiou.*

⑫ **Greek Folk Art Museum.** Run by the Ministry of Culture, the collection includes examples of folk art from 1650 to the present, with especially interesting embroideries, stone and wood carvings, carnival costumes, and *Karaghiozis* (shadow player figures). Everyday tools—stamps for communion bread, spinning shuttles, raki flasks—attest to the imagination with which Greeks embellished the most utilitarian objects. Don't miss the room of uniquely fanciful landscapes and historical portraits by naive painter Theophilos Hatzimichalis, from Mytilini, one of the most beloved Greek artists. ⊠ *Kidathineon 17,* ☎ *01/322–9031.* ⌨ *500 dr.* ◷ *Tues.–Sun. 10–2.*

⑱ **Kanellopoulos Museum.** The stately Michaleas Mansion built in 1884 now showcases the Kanellopoulos family collection, spanning Athens history from the 3rd century BC to the 19th century, with especially fine Byzantine icons, jewelry, and Mycenaean and Geometric vases and bronzes. Note the painted ceiling gracing the first floor. ⊠ *Theorias and Panos,* ☎ *01/321–2313.* ⊡ *500 dr.* ⊙ *Tues.–Sun. 8–2:30 (8:30–3 in winter).*

NEED A BREAK?	Pause for a cool drink at the **Nefeli Café** (⊠ Panos 24, ☎ 01/321–2475), a large complex with an idyllic outdoor café shaded by smart awnings and draped with grapevines. It's perched just below the Acropolis cliffs, looking down on Ayia Anna church. Or go around the corner to less upscale **Cafe Dioscouri** (⊠ Dioscouron and Mitroou, ☎ 01/321–9607), which lines the pedestrian zone by the same name and has a view of the Hephaistion temple.

★ ㉑ **Little Mitropolis.** This church snuggles up to the pompous **Mitropolis** (⊠ On the northern edge of Plaka), the ornate Cathedral of Athens. Also called Panayia Gorgoepikoos (the Virgin Who Answers Prayers Quickly), the chapel dates to the 12th century, and its most interesting features are its outer walls, covered with reliefs dating from the classical to the Byzantine period. Reliefs of animals and allegorical figures decorate slabs set above the entrance. Most of the paintings inside were destroyed, but the famous 13th- to 14th-century Virgin, said to perform miracles, remains. If you would like to follow Greek custom and light an amber beeswax candle for yourself and someone you love, drop the price of the candle in the slot. ⊠ *Platia Mitropoleos.*

★ ⑩ **Monument of Lysikrates.** This monument was built by a *choregos* (producer) as the support for the tripod he won for sponsoring the best play at the Theater of Dionyssos. It dates to 335 BC–334 BC. Six of the earliest Corinthian columns are arranged in a circle on a square base, topped by a marble dome from which rise acanthus leaves. In the 17th century the monument was incorporated into a Capuchin monastery where Byron stayed while writing part of *Childe Harold.* The monument was once known as the Lantern of Demosthenes because it was incorrectly believed to be where the famous orator practiced speaking with pebbles in his mouth in an effort to overcome his stutter. ⊠ *Lysikratous and Herefondos.*

⑲ **Museum of Greek Popular Musical Instruments.** An amusing crash course in the development of Greek music, especially rembetika, this museum has three floors of instruments. Headphones are available so visitors can appreciate the sounds made by such unusual delights as goatskin bagpipes and the Cretan lyra. The museum is also the Fivos Anoyiannakis Center of Ethnimusicology. ⊠ *Diogenous 1–3,* ☎ *01/325–0198.* ⊡ *Free.* ⊙ *Tues. and Thurs.–Sun. 10–2, Wed. noon–7 (noon–6 in winter).*

⑳ **Roman Agora.** The Roman market served as the city's commercial center during the 1st century BC to the 4th century AD. The large rectangular courtyard had a peristyle that provided shade for the arcades of shops. Its most notable feature is the **Gate of Athena Archegetis**, completed around AD 2; the inscription records that it was erected with funds from Julius Caesar and Augustus. Halfway up one solitary square pillar behind the gate's north side an edict inscribed by Hadrian regulates the sale of oil. On the north side of the Roman Agora stands one of the few remains of the Turkish occupation, the **Fethiye (Victory) Mosque.** The eerily beautiful mosque was built in the late-15th century on the site of a Christian church to celebrate the Turkish conquest of Athens and was dedicated by Mehmet II (the Conqueror). The mosque was converted in the 17th century to a Roman Catholic church and is now used as a storehouse. It's closed to the public. Three steps in the right-hand corner of the porch lead to the base of the minaret, the rest of

★ which no longer exists. The octagonal **Tower of the Winds (Aerides)**

is the most appealing and well preserved of the Roman monuments of Athens, keeping time since the 1st century BC. It was originally a sundial, water clock, and weather vane topped by a bronze Triton with a metal rod in his hand, which followed the direction of the wind. Expressive reliefs around the octagonal tower personify the eight winds, called *I Aerides* (the Windy Ones) by Athenians. Note the north wind, Boreas, blowing on a conch and the beneficent west wind Zephyros scattering flowers. ⊠ *Pelopidas and Adrianou,* ☎ *01/324–5220.* ☜ *500 dr.* ☉ *Tues.–Sun. 8–2:30 (8:30–3 in winter).*

Ancient Agora, Monastiraki, and Thission

The Agora was once the focal point of community life in ancient Athens. It was the place where Socrates met with his students and where merchants squabbled over the price of olive oil. It was here that the Assembly first met, before it moved to the Pnyx, and where locals gathered to talk about current events. The Agora first became important under Solon (6th century BC), founder of Athenian democracy; construction continued for almost a millennium. Today, the site's sprawling confusion of stones, slabs, and foundations is dominated by the best-preserved Doric temple in Greece, the Hephaistion, built during the 5th century BC, and the impressive reconstructed Stoa of Attalos II, which houses the Museum of the Agora Excavations. You can still experience the sights and sounds of the marketplace in Monastiraki, the former Turkish bazaar area, which retains vestiges of Orientalism from the 400-year period when Greece was subject to the Ottoman Empire. On the opposite side of the Agora is another meeting place of sorts: Thission, a former red-light district complete with a hat factory, has in the last few years become one of the most sought-after residential neighborhoods while still being a popular nightspot draw.

A Good Walk

Approach Monastiraki from Ermou: In the middle of the Kapnikareas intersection is striking **Kapnikarea Church** ㉓. Make your way to Pandrossou, a main shopping street that leads to **Monastiraki Square** ㉔, graced by the **Tzistarakis Mosque** and **Panayia Pantassa church,** exemplifying the East-West paradox that characterizes Athens. Unfortunately, as in many other parts of the city, the square is marred by metro construction. Walk up Areos, which during the Ottoman Empire was the Lower Bazaar, roofed and covered with vines. On the corner of Aiolou, you'll pass a nicely restored Othonian building, the former Aeolos Hotel, built in 1837 just after Athens was made capital of Greece. Advertisements boasted that it offered all European conveniences including beds, at a time when guests in public lodging usually brought their blankets and slept on the floor. This area was the edge of the Upper Bazaar. You will arrive at what remains of **Hadrian's Library** ㉕, built in AD 132 and the intellectual center of its time. Return to the square and head west on Ifestou to **Abyssinia Square** ㉖, where junk dealers and antiques merchants gather; it's the perfect place to see a side of the city that is vanishing. It is also the heart of a rambunctious Sunday **flea market** ㉗.

After browsing through the stalls, enter the **ancient Agora** ㉘ at the corner of Kinetou and Adrianou (the latter runs parallel to Ifestou). Be sure to visit the site's **Museum of Agora Excavations,** which offers a fascinating glimpse of everyday life in the ancient city. Exit at the site's opposite end onto Dionyssiou Areopagitou, crossing the boulevard to the **Thission** ㉙ quarter, a lively area with neoclassical homes overlooking trendy cafés. At the **Melina Mercouri Cultural Center** ㉚, exhibits re-create the streets of Athens during different epochs.

Those who want to escape Athens for a while should board the metro at the Thission station (at the end of Dionyssiou Areopagitou) to the northern suburb of **Kifissia,** once a summer resort for wealthy Athenians, evident in its tree-lined boulevards and grand villas.

TIMING

Monastiraki is at its best on Sunday mornings, when the flea market is in full swing. The ancient Agora is closed Mondays; it offers little shade, so in summer it's better to visit the site in early morning or late afternoon. Late-afternoon visits are strongly encouraged, as you can stay to ease into Thission's café scene. Assuming you visit the Agora for about two hours, including a visit to the Museum of Agora Excavations, allow about four hours for the walk. You can spend an entire afternoon or evening in Kifissia. The trip takes about 40 minutes each way; the last train leaves Kifissia for Athens around midnight.

Sights to See

㉖ Abyssinia Square. All day long the square bustles with activity, with shop owners refinishing furniture and rearranging the bric-a-brac in their stalls. Weekend mornings, dealers flock from all over Greece to peddle an incredible array of goods, from old toasters to exquisite icons, while street musicians stroll amid the café tables, jostling their accordions and singing ballads of love and loss. ⊠ *Entrance off Ermou, between Normanou and Kinetou.*

★ ㉘ **Ancient Agora.** This marketplace was the hub of ancient Athenian life. Besides administrative buildings, it was surrounded by the schools, theaters, workshops, houses, stores, and market stalls of a thriving town.

Prominent on the grounds is the **Stoa of Attalos,** a two-story building, now a museum, designed as a retail complex and erected in the 2nd century BC by Attalos, a king of Pergamum. The reconstruction in 1953–56 (funded by private American donors) used Pendelic marble and creamy limestone from the original structure. The colonnade, designed for promenades, is protected from the blistering sun and cooled by breezes. The most notable sculptures, of historical and mythological figures from the 3rd and 4th centuries BC, are at ground level outside the museum. In the exhibition hall, chronological displays of pottery and objects from everyday life (note the child's terra-cotta potty) demonstrate the continual settlement of the area from Neolithic times. There are such toys as knucklebones, and miniature theatrical masks carved from bone (case 50); a *klepsydra* (a terra-cotta water clock designed to measure the time allowed for pleadings in court), and bronze voting discs (cases 26–28); and, in case 38, bits of *ostraka* (pottery shards used in secret ballots to recommend banishment), from which the word "ostracism" comes. Among the famous candidates for a 10-year banishment—considered a fate worse than death—were Themistocles, Kimon, and even Pericles, who had his fair share of enemies.

Take a walk around the site and speculate on the location of Simon the Cobbler's house and shop, which was a meeting place for Socrates and his pupils. The carefully landscaped grounds display a number of plants known in antiquity, such as almond, myrtle, and pomegranate. By standing in the center, you have a glorious view up to the Acropolis, which on a clear day is given a mellow glow by the famous Attic light.

On a mound in the northwest corner of the grounds stands the best-preserved extant Doric temple, the **Hephaistion,** sometimes called the Thission because of its friezes showing the exploits of Theseus. Like the other monuments, it is roped off, but you can walk around it to admire its 34 columns. It was originally dedicated to Hephaistos, god of metalworkers; metal workshops still exist in this area near Ifestou.

The temple was converted to Christian use in the 7th century; the last services held here were a Te Deum in 1834, to celebrate King Otho's arrival, and a centenary Te Deum in 1934.

Behind the temple, paths lead to the northwest slope of the **Kolonos Agoraios,** an area dotted with archaeological ruins half hidden in deep undergrowth, where you can sit on a bench and contemplate the same scene that Englishman Edward Dodwell saw in the early 19th century, when he came to sketch antiquities. ⊠ *Three entrances: from Mona-stiraki on Adrianou; from Thission on Apostolou Pavlou; and descending from Acropolis on Ayios Apostoli,* ☎ *01/321–0185.* ⊟ *1,200 dr.* ⊙ *Tues.–Sun. 8:30–2:45.*

㉗ Flea market. For Athenians, all the world's a stage. Just watching the social interplay between Greeks, complete with wildly gesturing hands and dramatic facial expressions, will provide hours of entertainment. The Sunday morning market is a fitting setting in which to see lively haggling, and a fine destination in itself. Music blares from the carts pushing bootleg cassettes, mingling with the twang of a bouzouki a prospective buyer is strumming. Peddlers shout their wares: Everything's for sale here, from gramophone needles to old matchboxes, from nose rings sold by young nomads to lacquered eggs and cool white linens by the Pontian Greeks from the former USSR. Haggle, no matter how low the price. ⊠ *Along Ifestou, Kynetou, and Adrianou.*

㉕ Hadrian's Library. Built in AD 132, it is closed to the public, but you can easily see the remains of this public building (400 ft by 270 ft). The east wall is supported by six attached Corinthian columns, and Pausanias mentions "one hundred splendid columns of Phrygian marble," which apparently enclosed a cloistered court with a garden and pool. On the east side was the library itself, the intellectual center of its age, decorated with statues and murals under an alabaster and gold ceiling. Other areas were used for lectures and classes. On the west wall are traces of a fresco showing the outline of the Byzantine Ayios Assomati, which stood next to it. ⊠ *Areos and Dexippou.*

㉓ Kapnikarea Church. It's said that the chapel was named for the *kap-nikarious* (tax collectors who during the Byzantine period assessed residents for smoke coming from their chimneys); emanating smoke meant wealth enough to burn possessions. The building is really two adjoining chapels, one a cruciform structure of the 11th century, and the other a handsome building of typical Byzantine raised brickwork, with a dome supported by four Roman columns. The latter was carefully restored by the University of Athens, of which it is now the official church. A prominent modern mosaic of the Virgin and Child adorns the west entrance, and within are colorful frescoes. ⊠ *In middle of intersection at Kapnikareas and Ermou,* ☎ *01/322–4462.* ⊙ *Mon. and Wed. 8–2, Tues. and Thurs.–Fri. 8–2 and 4:30–7:30, Sat. 8–1:30, Sun. 6:30 AM –1:30 PM.*

㉚ Melina Mercouri Cultural Center. Installed in the former Poulopoulos hat factory built in 1886, the center offers a rare glimpse of Athens during the 19th century. Visitors can walk through a reconstructed Athens street whose facades of neoclassical homes evoke the civilized elegance of the past (note the sign on the the the mayor's house, which warns he's only available at the town hall), a pharmacy, printing press, dry goods store, kafenion, and dress shop, all painstakingly fitted out with authentic objects collected by the Greek Literary and Historical Archives. The center will soon unveil its recreation of ancient and Byzantine Athens, and throughout the year it showcases temporary exhibitions, usually featuring contemporary Greek art. ⊠ *Iraklidon 66,* ☎ *01/345–2150*

36

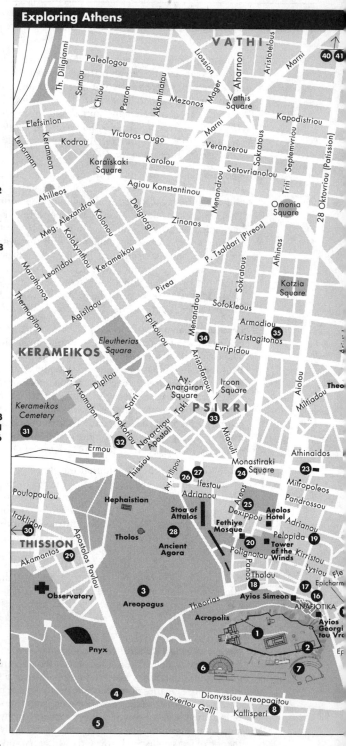

Exploring Athens

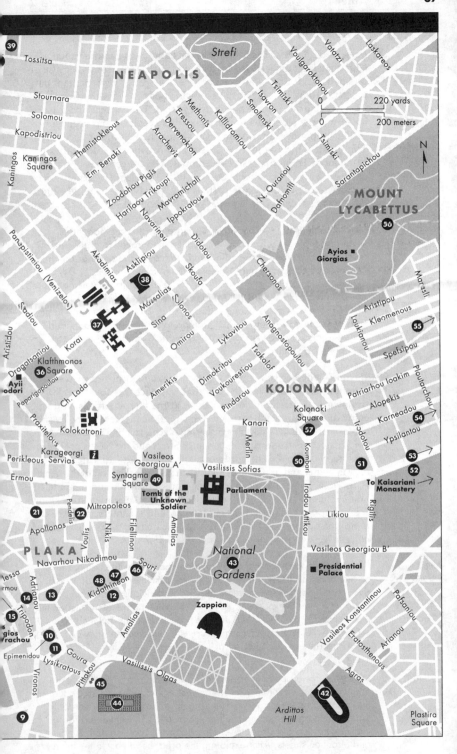

Strefi

NEAPOLIS

Tossitsa

Stournara

Solomou

Kapodistriou

Kaningos
Square

Kaningos

Themistokleous

Em. Benaki

Zoodohou Pigis

Hariloou Trikoupi

Navarinou

Methonis

Eressou

Dervenakion

Arachevis

Kallidromiou

Mavromichali

Ippokratous

Didotou

Tsimiski

Isavron

Smolenski

N. Ouranou

Dafnomili

Voulgaroktonou

Vatatzi

Laskareos

Sarantapichou

Tsimiski

MOUNT
LYCABETTUS

56

Ayios
Giorgias

Marasli

Panepistimiou (Venizelos)

Stadiou

Aristidou

Akadimias

Asklipiou

Skouta

Mavilis

Sina

Omirou

Korai

Dragatsaniou

Klafthmonos
Square

Ayii
odori

Paparigopoulou

Ch. Lada

Praxitelous

Kolokotroni

Karageorgi
Perikleous Servias

Ermou

Pendelis

Apollonos

PLAKA

Navarhou Nikodimou

Iessa

rmou

Adrianou

Tripodon

gios
rachou

Epimenidou

Vironos

Voulis

Nikis

Lysikratous

Pittakou

Goura

38

37

36

Amerikis

Dimokritou

Voukourestiou

Pindarou

Clonos

Lykavitou

Tsakalof

Anagnostopoulou

Chersanos

Aristipou

Kleomenous

Loukianou

Patriarhou Ioakim

Alopekis

Spefsipou

Ixodotou

Karneadou

Ypsilantou

Plouarchou

KOLONAKI

Kanari

Kolonaki
Square

55

54

53

52

57

Merlin

Koumbari

50

51

To Kaisariani
Monastery

Vasileos
Georgiou A'

Syntagma
Square

Tomb of the
Unknown
Soldier

49

Vasilissis Sofias

Parliament

Irodou Attikou

Likiou

Rigillis

Vasileos Georgiou B'

Presidential
Palace

Mitropoleos

Filellinon

Souri

Amalias

National
Gardens

43

Vasileos Konstantinou

Eratosthenous

Pafsaniou

Afianou

21

22

48 47 46

14   13   12

15

10

11

Kidathineon

Amalias

Zappion

44

45

9

Vasilissis Olgas

Agras

42

Arditos
Hill

Plastira
Square

N

0   220 yards
0   200 meters

or 01/362–1601. 🎫 *Free.* ⊙ *Mid-Aug.–mid-July, Tues.–Sat. 9–1 and 5–9, Sun. 9–1.*

㉔ Monastiraki Square. The square takes its name from **Panayia Pantanassa Church,** commonly called Monastiraki (Little Monastery) because of its smallness. It once flourished as an extensive convent, perhaps dating to the 10th century. The nuns took in poor people, who earned their keep weaving the thick textiles known as *abas.* The convent's basic basilica form, now recessed a few steps below street level, has been altered through a poor restoration in 1911, when the bell tower was added. The square's focal point, the **Tzistarakis Mosque** (1759) houses the **Museum of Traditional Greek Ceramics.** The collection is beautifully designed, with the exhibits handsomely lit and labeled. The mihrab (niche facing Mecca) is of delicate pastel stone. *Areos 1,* ☎ *01/324–2066.* 🎫 *Museum 500 dr.* ⊙ *Museum Wed.–Mon. 9–2:30.*

NEED A BREAK?

On Mitropoleos just off Monastiraki Square you'll find a handful of counter-front places selling souvlaki, grilled meat rolled in a pita with onions, *tzatziki* (yogurt-garlic dip), and tomatoes—the best bargain in Athens. Your choices include **Thanassis** (⊠ Mitropoleos 69, ☎ 01/324–4705)—which is always crowded with Greeks—for its juicy meat and crunchy pitas, and **Savvas** (⊠ Mitropoleos 86, ☎ 01/321–3201), which also serves gyros—sandwiches of spicy spit-roasted meat—to patrons who can carry them across the road to a small umbrella-shaded square. Make sure you specify either a souvlaki sandwich, or a "souvlaki plate," an entire meal.

㉙ Thission. Whether you want to enjoy a snack in a turn-of-the-century ouzeri, listen to hard rock in a bar that was once the Royal Stables, or sit down to a late supper after a show at the Herod Atticus, you will enjoy this vibrant neighborhood, which, in the last few years, has become one of Athens's popular gathering places, rivaling upscale Kolonaki Square. The main strip is Akamantos Street and the Nileos pedestrian zone across from the ancient Agora entrance, lined with cafés that are cozy in winter and have outdoor tables in summer. The rest of the neighborhood is quiet, an odd mix of ma-and-pop stores and dilapidated houses that are now slowly being renovated; take a brief stroll along Akamantos (which becomes Galatias) around the intersections of Dimofontos or Aginoros to get a feel for the quarter's past. ⊠ *West of ancient Agora, Apostolou Pavlou, and Akamantos.*

NEED A BREAK?

It's a great concept: an old-style kafenion complete with ouzo, Greek coffee, and *tavli* (backgammon games) for customers, but with 1990s decor, designer lighting, foreign music, and delicious iced cappuccino *freddo.* No wonder most people rolling the dice at **Kafenion Thission** (⊠ Akamantos 2, ☎ 01/347–3133) are not elderly gents but the under-40 set, who, when the weather warms up, spill out onto the sidewalk. At night, the Thission becomes a bar.

OFF THE BEATEN PATH

KIFISSIA – For a peaceful afternoon, hop on the metro heading to this northern suburb, a summer resort for aristocratic Athenians at the turn of the century. The streets north of the Kifissia station, with their verdant landscaping and ostentatious villas, evoke another, gentler era. Especially rewarding are Dragoumi, Tatoi, Rangavi, Pan, Tsaldari, Amalias, and Strofiliou streets. After exploring the area, head east to the main street, Kassaveti, where young people flock to the many cafés. Be sure to stop for a *rizogalo* (rice pudding) at Varsos (⊠ Kassaveti 5, ☎ 01/ 801–2472), a Kifissia institution. If you have children, you may want to stop at **Goulandris Natural History Museum** (⊠ Levidou 13, ☎ 01/

808–6405), admission 800 dr., for its displays of animal and plant life, fossils, and reconstructed prehistoric animals; it's closed mid-July through mid-August. Intersecting Levidi is Kolokotroni, which ends at shady Kefalari Square, where decorated horse-drawn carriages await to take you on a ride through the cool, quiet roads.

Central Athens, Kerameikos, and Psirri

Downtown Athens—an unlikely combination of the squalid and the grand—is not for the fainthearted. The cavernous, chaotic Central Market, which replaced the Bazaar when it burned down in 1885, is just 10 minutes from the elegant, neoclassical Old University complex. But to central Athens all must journey to see one of the must-dos of Greece: the stately National Archaeological Museum, home to one of the most exciting collections of Greek antiquities in the world. Here are the sensational finds made by Heinrich Schliemann, discoverer of Troy and father of modern archeology, in the course of his excavations of the royal tombs on the Homeric site of Mycenae in the 1870s; here, too, are the world-famous bronzes of the Jockey of Artemision and of Poseidon throwing a trident (or is it Zeus hurling a thunderbolt?).

Archaeology buffs will also want to visit Kerameikos, the main cemetery in ancient Athens until Sulla destroyed the city in 86 BC. The name is associated with the modern word "ceramic": In the 12th century BC the district was populated by potters who used the abundant clay from the languid Iridanos River to make funerary urns and grave decorations. It contains the foundations of two ancient monuments: the Dipylon Gate where visitors entered the city, and the Sacred Gate used for both the pilgrimage to the Eleusinian rites and for the Panathenaic procession in which the tunic for the statue of Athena was carted to the Acropolis. The area outside Kerameikos was settled by Turkish gypsies before the War of Independence, and then by Athens's Jewish community. The shops of the leading families ran along Ermou; on Melidoni stands the Synagogue Beth Shalom, where congregants still worship. Nearby Psirri, one of the city's oldest neighborhoods, though still rather ramshackle, is now being renovated, with new bars and restaurants opening monthly.

A Good Walk

Those interested in archaeology should begin at **Kerameikos Cemetery** ㉛, where ancient Athens's famous citizens were buried. Continue east on Ermou to the intersection with Ayion Assomaton, where the 11th-century church of **Ayii Assomati** ㉜ stands. The quirky, run-down neighborhood of **Psirri** ㉝, which affords visitors a different view of the city, starts here. After taking some time to explore its narrow streets, make your way to Evripidou and the oddest church in Athens, **Ayios Ioannis Kolonastis** ㉞, at the intersection with Menandrou.

Continue east on Evripidou, lined with aromatic shops selling herbs, nuts, olive oil soap, and household items, until you reach the **Central Market** ㉟ on the corner of Athinas. Hectic, crowded Athinas stretches from Omonia Square to Monastiraki and is replete with everything from canaries to garlic braids, but it is the 19th-century meat and fish market that is the most entertaining. Evripidou ends at **Klafthmonos Square** ㊱ and what is perhaps the oldest church in Athens, **Ayii Theodori.** Cross Stadiou, walking up the Korai pedestrian zone to the **Old University complex** ㊲ on Panepistimiou. Behind the three grand buildings is the **Municipal Cultural Center** ㊳, which hosts interesting exhibitions and has a theater museum.

Cut through the student neighborhood of Exarchia or take Trolley 2, 4, or 11 from Panepistimiou to the **Politechnio** ㊴, a national symbol of student resistance, and the **National Archaeological Museum** ㊵, one of the most important museums in Greece. Athens's other main square, Omonia, is to the west, but it's not really worth the detour owing to the ongoing metro construction. Its controversial jagged glass sculpture representing a runner has been temporarily placed in front of the Athens Hilton. Two blocks up from the museum at the intersection of 28 Oktovriou (Patission) and Leoforos Alexandras is Athens's largest park, **Pedion Areos** ㊶, which provides visual relief from the urban sprawl.

TIMING

Weekday mornings are the best time to take this approximately five-hour walk: The museums will be open, and the Central Market, which is closed Saturday afternoon and Sundays, bustles with pensioners picking over the produce and Athenians exchanging news with the fishmonger. Those coming from Omonia should walk down Aiolou Street, a pedestrian zone with cafés and old shops as well as an interesting view of the Acropolis. You'll also get a better sense of Psirri as a neighborhood then, although the area is liveliest during Sunday afternoons and evenings, when Athenians tend to congregate in its new bars and mezedopolia. Try to visit the National Archaeological Museum after lunch, when most tour groups have departed. Look at a floor plan to organize your plan of attack; the collection is too huge to cover comfortably in one stretch. If you hang on to your admission ticket, you can take a break at the pleasant although pricey garden café in front of the museum. The National Archaeological Museum and the Kerameikos Cemetery are closed on Mondays; the Vouros-Eftaxias Athens City Museum is closed Saturday through Tuesday—plan accordingly.

Sights to See

㉜ **Ayii Assomati.** Named after the Bodiless Angels, the church dates to the 11th century. It was poorly rebuilt in 1880 but properly restored in 1959. It is in the form of a Greek cross, with a hexagonal dome and impressive exterior stonework. Some fragments of frescoes inside are probably from the 17th century, but art historians dispute the claim that an oil painting to the left of the entrance is by El Greco. ⊠ *At intersection of Ermou and Ayion Assomaton.*

㉞ **Ayios Ioannis Kolonastis.** St. John of the Column is undoubtedly the most peculiar church in Athens. A Corinthian column, probably from a gymnasium dedicated to Apollo, protrudes from the tiled rooftop of the little one-sided basilica built around it in AD 565, and people with a high fever still come here to perform "curative" rituals that include tying a colored thread to the column and saying a special prayer. Mosaic floors that were unearthed here were probably part of an ancient temple to Asklepeios. ⊠ *72 Evripidou (at intersection with Menandrou, behind square).*

㉟ **Central Market.** The market runs along Athinas: On one side are open-air stalls selling fruit and vegetables at the best prices in town, although wily merchants may slip overripe items into your bag. At the corner of Armodiou, shops stock live poultry and rabbits. Across the street, in the huge covered market built in 1870, the surrealistic composition of suspended carcasses and shimmering fish on marble counters emits a pungent odor that is overwhelming on hot days. The shops at the north end of the market, to the right on Sofokleous, offer the best cheese, olives, halvah, bread, and cold cuts, including *pastourma* (Mediterranean pastrami), available in Athens. ⊠ *Athinas.* ☉ *Closed Sat. afternoon and Sun.*

NEED A
BREAK? "If you don't behave, I won't take you to **Krinos**" (✉ Aiolou 87, ☎ 01/
321–6852), mothers in the Central Market used to warn unruly off-
spring. The lure: *loukoumades* (an irresistible, doughnutlike fritter sprin-
kled with cinnamon and drizzled with a honeyed syrup based on a
Smyrna recipe), which the shop has been serving since it opened its
doors in the 1920s. The shop is closed Sundays.

③ **Kerameikos Cemetery.** From the entrance of ancient Athens's cemetery, you can still see remains of the **Makra Teixoi** (Long Walls of Themistocles), which ran to Piraeus, and the largest gate in the ancient world,
the **Dipylon Gate,** where visitors entered Athens. The walls rise to 10
ft, just a fraction of their original height (up to 45 ft). Here was also
the **Sacred Gate,** used by pilgrims headed to the mysterious rites in Eleusis and those who participated in the Panathenaic procession, which
followed the Sacred Way. Between the two gates are the foundations
of the **Pompeion,** from where the Panathenaic procession began. It is
said the courtyard was large enough to fit the ship on which the huge
peplum banner dedicated to Athena was hung. On the **Street of Tombs,**
which branches off the Sacred Way, plots were reserved for affluent
Athenians. A number of the distinctive *stelae* (funerary monuments)
remain, including a replica of the marble relief of Dexilios, a knight
who died in the war against Corinth (394 BC), who is shown on horseback preparing to spear a fallen foe. From the terrace near the tombs,
Pericles gave his celebrated speech honoring those who died in the early
years of the Peloponnesian War, thus persuading many to sign up for
a campaign that ultimately wiped out thousands of Athenians. To the
left of the site's entrance is the **Oberlaender Museum,** whose four
rooms contain sculpture, terra-cotta figures, and some striking red-and-
black-figured pottery. The extensive grounds are marshy in some spots;
in spring, frogs exuberantly croak their mating songs near magnificent
stands of lilies. ✉ *Ermou 148,* ☎ *01/346–3552.* ☞ *Site and museum
500 dr.* ☉ *Tues.–Sun. 8–2:30 (8:30–3 in winter).*

③ **Klafthmonos Square.** Public servants from the surrounding ministries
lamented loudly here after being dismissed; hence, its name, the Square
of Wailing. Behind the square at the corner of Evripidou and Aristidou is **Ayii Theodori,** a lovely mid-11th-century cruciform church, probably the oldest in Athens. The **Vouros-Eftaxias Athens City Museum,**
across from the square, was home to the teenage King Otho and his
bride Amalia for seven years, while the royal palace was being built.
In a subbasement you can see a segment of the ancient city walls. A
Throne Room still exists, and on the ground floor a model of Athens
in 1842 shows how sparsely populated the new capital was. The first
floor displays paintings by European artists who came to Athens, such
as Edward Lear, Gasparini, and Dodwell. ✉ *Off Stadiou, between Paparigoupoulou and Dragatsaniou. Museum:* ✉ *Paparigoupoulou 7,* ☎
01/324–6164. ☞ *500 dr.* ☉ *Wed.–Fri. 9–1:30.*

③ **Municipal Cultural Center.** Following a cholera epidemic in 1835,
Athens's first mayor made a national plea to raise money for the city's
first public hospital—resulting in this handsome building, now used
for lectures and exhibits. In front stands the only known surviving statue
of Pericles, a fine work in Parian marble by Heinrich Faltermeier,
showing Pericles with sturdy legs and the helmet he always wore because his skull was, it's said, slightly deformed—which explains his nick-
name, Onion Head. Almost directly across Akadimias, facing Pericles,
is a much smaller and less-skillful bust of Aspasia, the cultured cour-
tesan who was his beloved companion and mother of his son. On the
lower level is the **Hellenic Theater Museum and Study Center.** (☎ 01/
362–9430), admission 500 dr., which is open weekdays 9–2:30. It fea-

tures dressing rooms and costumes of Greek stage and screen stars plus posters, playbills, and other theatrical memorabilia. ✉ *Akadimias 50,* ☎ *01/362–1601.* 🎟 *Free.* ☺ *Offices weekdays 7:30–3, exhibit halls Tues.–Sat. 9–1 and 5–9.*

The spacious **Athinaiko Kafenio** (✉ Akadimias 50, entrance on Solonos in the rear of the Municipal Cultural Center, ☎ 01/361-9265) beckons, offering good coffees, drinks, and tempting sweets, with both indoor and shady outdoor seating. The area east of the center is packed with student cafés; a popular venue is the cozy **Gallerie Amsterdam** (✉ Sina 21 and Skoufa, ☎ 01/361-9593), whose closely set tables and tiny gallery make it a favorite among couples. The café is closed July through August.

★ **㊵** **National Archaeological Museum.** By far the most important museum in Athens, this collection contains artistic highlights from every period of ancient Greek civilization, from Neolithic to Roman times. Sculpture is on the ground floor, ceramics on the first floor, and ceramics and **frescoes from Santorini** on the upper level of the first floor. These outstanding frescoes, delightful re-creations of daily life in Minoan Santorini, should not be missed. They are scheduled to be returned to Santorini upon completion of its long-awaited museum. In fact, new discoveries are constantly added to the collection, though on occasion they remain only until the construction of a local museum.

By far, the most celebrated finds are in the central **Hall of Mycenaean Antiquities,** Room 4. Here are the stunning gold treasures from Schliemann's excavations of Mycenae in 1876: the funeral mask of a bearded king, once thought to be the image of Agamemnon but now believed to be much older, from about the 15th century BC; a splendid silver bull's-head libation cup; and the 15th-century BC Vaphio Goblets, masterworks in embossed gold. Mycenaeans were famed for their carving in miniature, and an exquisite example is the ivory statuette of two curvaceous mother goddesses with a child nestled on their laps.

Rooms 7–14 contain Geometric and Archaic art (10th–6th centuries BC), and Rooms 11–14 have kouroi and funerary stelae (8th–5th centuries BC), among them the stelae of the warrior Aristion signed by Aristokles, and the unusual *Running Hoplite.* Rooms 15–21 focus on classical art (5th–3rd centuries BC). Be sure to see the bareback *Jockey of Artemision,* a 2nd-century BC Hellenistic bronze salvaged from the sea; from the same excavation, the bronze *Artemision Poseidon* (some say Zeus), poised and ready to fling a trident (or thunderbolt?); and the *Varvakion Athena,* a marble version of the goddess half the size of Pheidias's gigantic gold-and-ivory cult statue that stood in the Parthenon.

Room 28 displays funerary architecture: the spirited 2nd-century relief of a rearing stallion held by a black groom, which exemplifies the transition from classical to Hellenistic style. Room 30 holds the famous humorous marble group of a nude *Aphrodite* getting ready to slap an advancing Pan with a sandal, while Eros floats overhead and grasps one of Pan's horns. ✉ *28 Oktovriou (Patission) 44,* ☎ *01/821–7717.* 🎟 *2,000 dr.* ☺ *Mon. 12:30–7 (10:30–4:45 in winter), Tues.–Fri. 8–7 (8:30–3 in winter), weekends 8:30–3.*

㊲ **Old University complex.** In the sea of concrete that is central Athens, this imposing group of marble buildings conjures up an illusion of Classical antiquity. These three dramatic buildings belonging to the University of Athens were designed by the Hansen Brothers in the period after independence, and are built of white Pendelic marble, with tall columns and decorative friezes. In the center is the **Senate House** of the university; on the right is the **Academy,** flanked by two slim columns topped by statues of Athena and Apollo (this structure was paid for by the Austro-Greek Baron Sina and is a copy of the Parliament in Vienna); and on the left is the **National Library,** containing more than 2 million Greek and foreign-language volumes and now facing the daunting task of modernization. ✉ *Panepistimiou between Ippokratous and Sina,* ☎ *01/361–4301 Senate; 01/360–0207 or 01/360–0209 Academy; 01/361–4413 Library.* ☉ *Senate and Academy weekdays 9–2; library weekdays 9–9. Closed Aug.*

🐣 ④ **Pedion Areos.** An oasis of calm and wispy eucalyptus trees, Athens's largest park is open 24 hours a day. Statues of war heroes from the 1821 revolution dot the many walkways and hidden corners, and during the summer a small theater and cultural center stage performances. The park, once a firing range, was appropriately named for Ares, the god of war. It extends all the way to the **Courts,** where at night several ouzeris are packed with Athenians taking advantage of the cool forest air. There are three **playgrounds:** two near the central entrance and one off Evelpidon. A small train for youngsters traverses the park, though its proprietor doesn't keep fixed hours. ✉ *Main entrance at 28 Oktovriou (Patission) and Leoforos Alexandras,* ☎ *01/821–2239,*

㊴ **Politechnio.** In late 1973 students occupied this University of Athens building to protest the junta. In response to their calls for resistance, many Greeks disobeyed military orders and showed their support by smuggling in supplies. On the night of November 16, snipers were ordered to fire into the courtyards while tanks rammed the gates: No one knows how many students were killed because they were secretly buried in mass graves. The public was outraged, and less than a year later, the junta was toppled. Every year on November 17, students still march from the Politechnio to the embassy of the United States, which supported the dictatorship. It is still the site for frequent student demonstrations, especially since police are legally barred from entering its gates. ✉ *28 Oktovriou (Patission) 42,* ☎ *01/772–4000.* ☉ *Offices weekdays 8–2; grounds always open.*

㉝ **Psirri.** The district has many buildings older than those in picturesque Plaka, though until lately it has been less fashionable. Similar to New York City's TriBeCa, it has been targeted by developers eager to renovate, resulting in a flurry of building, with new restaurants and bars opening rapidly. The streets are quiet, too narrow for most cars. This was the setting for a number of popular Greek novels around the turn of the century and is still predominantly a mercantile area with small workshops supplying leather and glassware to retail shops. Peek over the wrought-iron gates of the old houses on the narrow side streets between Ermou and Kerameikou, a street north of Kerameikos Cemetery, to see the charming courtyards bordered by long, low buildings, whose many small rooms were rented out to different families. On warm nights, many of Psirri's streets are lined with Athenians dining alfresco amid spotlighted buildings and tiny churches. ✉ *Just north of Monastiraki, between Ermou, Athinas, and Evripidou.*

NEED A
BREAK?

Especially late on weekend afternoons, Athenians, be it couples from Kolonaki or elderly women from Patissia, head for Psirri and **Taki 13** (✉ Taki 13, ☎ 01/325–4707) for its unusual mezes and live Greek music, which often sets the crowd to dancing. In spring, the shaded courtyard remains open until late at night. The restaurant is usually closed from the end of July to mid-August.

Syntagma Square, National Gardens, and Kolonaki

Sooner or later, everyone passes through Syntagma Square. Unfortunately, even after several beautification campaigns, the square is rather nondescript, surrounded by fast-food restaurants and metro construction. However, the area has several sights spanning Athens's history, from Emperor Hadrian (Temple of Olympian Zeus) to King Otho's reign after the War of Independence in 1821 (the National Gardens and Parliament). Neighboring Kolonaki—the chic shopping district and one of the most fashionable residential areas—occupies the lower slopes of Mt. Lycabettus. Besides visiting its several museums, you will enjoy window-shopping and people-watching, since cafés are busy from early morning to dawn.

A Good Walk

Begin at the site of the first modern Olympics (1896), the **Panathenaic Stadium** ㊷ on Vasileos Konstantinou. You may want to detour right onto Irodou Attikou, which leads to the **Presidential Palace,** used by Greece's kings after the restoration of 1935 and now by the head of state. Across the street from the stadium are the **National Gardens** ㊸, a pet project of Queen Amalia. Bear right, past the neoclassical **Zappion hall,** where you exit onto Vasilissis Olgas, dominated by the **Temple of Olympian Zeus** ㊹, built by Emperor Hadrian in AD 132, and around the corner on Amalias, **Hadrian's Arch** ㊺, which marks the spot where the ancient city ended and Hadrian's Athens began.

Off Amalias is the large Russian Orthodox church of **Ayios Nikodimos** ㊻ and, nearby, the **Jewish Museum of Greece** ㊼, which details the history of one of Greece's decimated communities. Amalias also passes above **Syntagma Square** ㊾ in front of the **Parliament** and the **Tomb of the Unknown Soldier,** guarded by massive Evzones. Proceed up Vasilissis Sofias (often indicated as Eleftheriou Venizelou on maps) to the **Benaki Museum** ㊿ and the delightful **Goulandris Cycladic and Ancient Art Museum** ㊿①, with nearly 100 exhibits of the Cycladic civilization (3000–2000 BC). A few blocks up Vasilissis Sofias, the **Byzantine Museum** ㊿②, housed in an 1848 mansion built by an eccentric French aristocrat, features a unique collection of icons.

Five minutes east of the museum is the **National Gallery of Art** ㊿③, worth a visit more for its special exhibits than for its uninspiring permanent collection. Turn off Vasilissis Sofias onto Gennadiou, passing the 12th-century **Moni Petraki** ㊿④, to **Gennadius Library** ㊿⑤, containing one of the greatest collections on Greek subjects. Go left on Souidias (which becomes Spefsipou); at Ploutarchou, steps ascend to the funicular to the top of **Mt. Lycabettus** ㊿⑥, which reaches to three times the height of the Acropolis. The view from the top—pollution permitting—is one of the finest in Athens. You can see all the Attica basin, the harbor, and the islands of Aegina and Poros laid out before you. Minibus 060 from Kolonaki Square also drops you at the funicular station. Walk or ride back to **Kolonaki Square** ㊿⑦, which, especially on Saturdays at noon, is crammed with chattering crowds who relax on the café-lined pedestrian zones or shop in the designer boutiques.

TIMING

Because most of the museums close around 3 PM—as do shops on Mondays, Wednesdays, and Saturdays—plan your walk for mid-morning. The walk takes about four hours, but you may want to extend this to visit Mt. Lycabettus in the late afternoon, when the light produces the best view. Kaisariani monastery stays open until about 2:30, but you can hike through its wooded grounds until sunset. Most of the sites are closed one day a week, though all are open Wednesday through Friday; choose your route accordingly.

Sights to See

㊻ Ayios Nikodimos. In 1780 the notoriously brutal Hadji Ali Haseki pulled down this 11th-century chapel of a convent and used the stone to build a defensive wall around Athens. The church was sold to the Russian government, who in 1852–56 modified it into a larger, cruciform building with a distinctive terra-cotta frieze; the separate tower was built to hold a massive bell donated by Tsar Alexander II. Note the displays of ornate Russian embroidery and the bright blues of the Pantocrator (Godhead) overhead. The female chanters of this Russian Orthodox church are renowned. ⊠ *Fillelinon 21,* ☎ *01/323–1090.*

㊿ Benaki Museum. Greece's oldest private museum, established in 1926 by an illustrious Athenian family, the Benaki was one of the first to place emphasis on Greece's later heritage at a time when many archaeologists were destroying Byzantine artifacts to access ancient objects. The museum has been closed several years for renovation but is scheduled to reopen in summer 1999 and is already hosting some temporary exhibitions. Although its massive collection ranges from Geometric vases to an Early Christian collection of Coptic art, from traditional costumes to the archives of well-known Greek photographers Voula Papaioannou and Nelly, it is the Greek collection that will preside in the newly reopened site. The mansion was designed by Anastassios Metaxas, the architect who helped restore the Panathenaic Stadium. Other parts of the collection—Islamic art, Chinese porcelain, 18th- to 20th- century toys—will be displayed in branches throughout the city. Call to confirm hours and ticket prices, unavailable at press time. ⊠ *Koubari 1,* ☎ *01/361–1617.*

★ ㊼ Byzantine Museum. One of the few museums in Europe concentrating exclusively on Byzantine art, this is housed in the porticoed villa of the Duchess of Plaisance, built from 1840 to 1848 by Stamatis Kleanthis. Rooms are arranged to look like Greek churches of different eras—an early Christian basilica, a medieval cross-in-square domed church, a post-Byzantine chapel—and the upper floor contains mostly icons, many quite valuable. Much of the museum is still closed due to construction work being done on the new wings. ⊠ *Vasilissis Sofias 22,* ☎ *01/721–1027 or 01/723–1570.* 🎫 *500 dr. during restoration.* ☉ *Tues.–Sun. 8:30–2:50.*

OFF THE BEATEN PATH	**MONASTERY OF KAISARIANI –** For an exceptional trek outside central Athens, head to the slopes of Mt. Hymettus, where you'll find one of the city's most evocative Byzantine remains. The well-restored 11th-century church, built on the site of a sanctuary of Aphrodite, is surrounded by cells, a bathhouse, and refectory. Most of the vivid frescoes date back to the Ottoman occupation—note the embroidered cloth worn by prophets and angels in the dome's drum, reproductions of Turkish fabrics of the period. The oldest mural is in the side chapel of St. Anthony, a praying Virgin Mary depicted in the provincial style of the 14th century. On the hill above the monastery is a fountain whose waters were prescribed for curing sterility; according to local legend, a dove flew over the waters on Ascension Day. The now destroyed, adjacent Aphrodite temple was the backdrop for the jealous lovers in Ovid's *Ars Amatoria (Art of Love).* Nearby is a ruined basilica and a picnic site with a superb view of the Acropolis and Piraeus. Take a taxi or Bus 224 from in front of the Byzantine Museum for 6 km (4 mi) east of central Athens to the terminal in the working-class suburb of Kaisariani. The monastery is an additional 30-minute walk along the paved road that climbs Mt. Hymettus. ⊠ *The mountain road starting at Ethniki Antistaseos,* ☎ *01/723–6619.* 🎫 *800 dr.* ☉ *Tues.–Sun. 8:30–2:45; grounds daily sunrise– sunset.*

⑤ **Gennadius Library.** Book lovers who ascend the grand staircase into the hallowed aura of the Reading Room may have difficulty tearing themselves away from this superb collection of material on Greek subjects, from first editions of Greek classics to the complete works of Nobel Laureate Odysseas Elytis. Besides the thousands of volumes bequeathed in the 1920s by founder John Gennadius, there are many rare books, some of Lord Byron's memorabilia (including a lock of his hair), the collected letters of Schliemann and Seferis, and watercolors of Greece by Edward Lear. Needless to say, this is not a lending library. The library facade is imposing, a portico of Ionic columns in front of a brilliantly colored facade. ⊠ *Souidias 61,* ☎ *01/721–0536.* ⊘ *Mid-Sept.–mid-Aug., Mon.–Tues. and Fri. 9–5, Wed.–Thurs. 9–8, Sat. 9–2.*

★ ⑤ **Goulandris Cycladic and Ancient Art Museum.** Funded by one of Greece's richest families, this museum has an outstanding collection dating from the Bronze Age, including many of the enigmatic Cycaldic marble figurines, whose slender shapes so fascinated artists like Picasso, Modigliani, and Brancusi. In 1994 a new wing opened in the gorgeous adjacent Stathatos Mansion, where temporary exhibits are now held. ⊠ *Neofitou Douka 4 or Irodotou 1,* ☎ *01/722–8321 through 01/722–8323.* ▥ *800 dr.* ⊘ *Mon. and Wed.–Fri. 10–4, Sat. 10–3.*

④ **Hadrian's Arch.** Presently under scaffolding while archaeologists clean and buttress its crumbling facade, this marble gateway was built in AD 131 with Corinthian details. It was intended both to honor the Hellenophile emperor Hadrian and to separate the ancient and imperial sections of Athens. On the side facing the Acropolis an inscription reads THIS IS ATHENS, THE ANCIENT CITY OF THESEUS, but the side facing the Temple of Olympian Zeus proclaims THIS IS THE CITY OF HADRIAN AND NOT OF THESEUS. ⊠ *Amalias and Dionyssiou Areopagitou.*

④ **Jewish Museum of Greece.** The museum's vivid memorabilia, relocated in 1998 to an elegantly renovated neoclassical building near Plaka, tells the story of the Jews in Greece, from the 6th century BC to the Holocaust, when 87% of the Greek Jews were killed; only about 5,000 remain today. The museum pays tribute to the diversity of the various Jewish communities with a collection organized according to periods and themes. These include the early history of the Romaniotes (Jews who espoused Greek culture and wrote Greek in the Hebrew script), many of whom lived in Halkida, one of Europe's oldest Jewish communities; the arrival of the Ladino-speaking Sephardic Jews after they were expelled from Spain during the Holy Inquisition in the late-15th century; the Jewish calendar and holidays; and religious items used in synagogues as well as in everyday domestic life. One room contains the reconstruction of the interior of the old Romaniote Synagogue of Patras, a community established by Jews from Syria 323 to 281 BC. ⊠ *Nikis 39,* ☎ *01/322–5582.* ▥ *500 dr. (ring bell).* ⊘ *Weekdays 9:30–2:30, Sun. 10–2.*

☝ ⑤ **Kolonaki Square.** Athenians don't actually gather on the square, officially called Filikis Eterias, but along the Tsakalof and Milioni pedestrian-zone cafés, to see and be seen. Glittery models, middle-aged executives, elegant pensioners—all congregate here for a quick coffee before work, after a hard day of shopping, or for foreign newspapers at the all-night kiosk. On the lower side of the square is the **British Council Library** (⊠ Kolonaki Sq. 17, ☎ 01/364–5768), which has some children's videos and and a screening facility. ⊠ *Where Patriarchou Ioakeim and Kanari meet.* ⊘ *Library Mon. and Thurs. 3–8, Tues.–Wed. and Fri. 9:30–2:30 (weekdays 10–1:30 in June–July). Closed 3 wks. in Aug.*

NEED A
BREAK?   Enjoy a cappuccino and an Italian sweet standing at **Da Capo** (⊠
           Tsakalof 1, ☎ 01/360-2497), frequented by young trendsetters, espe-

cially on Saturday afternoons from noon to five. Or you can walk to **Ouzeri Dexameni** (✉ Deinokratous and Xanthippou, Dexameni Sq., ☎ 01/729–2578), a favorite whose tables line either side of a tree-shaded lane, making it an ideal spot for people-watching.

54 **Moni Petraki.** Tucked into a sweet little park at Iassou, this church was built in the 12th century and decorated with paintings by Yiorgios Markos in the 18th century. ✉ *Off Moni Petraki,* ☎ *01/721–2402.* ☉ *Mon.–Sat. 6 AM–noon, Sun. 6 AM–noon and 6:30–9:30 PM (opens 5:30 PM in winter).*

★ **56** **Mt. Lycabettus.** Myth claims that Athens's highest hill came into existence when Athena removed a piece of Mt. Pendeli, intending to boost the height of her temple on the Acropolis. While she was en route, a crone brought her bad tidings, and the flustered goddess dropped the rock in the middle of the city. A steeply inclined *teleferique* (funicular) takes visitors to the summit, crowned by whitewashed **Ayios Georgios** chapel with a bell tower donated by Queen Olga. On the side of the hill, near the I Prasini Tenta café, there is a small shrine to **Ayios Isidoros** built into a cave. It was here that in 1859 students prayed for those fighting against the Austrians, French, and Sardinians with whom King Otho had allied. From Mt. Lycabettus you can watch the sun set and then turn about to watch the moon rise over "violet-crowned" Hymettus as the lights of Athens blink on all over the city. ✉ *Funicular at Aristippou and Ploutarchou (take Bus 060 from Kolonaki Square),* ☎ *01/722–7065.* ☉ *Fri.–Wed. 8:45 AM–12:30 AM (8:45–midnight in winter), Thurs. 10:30 AM–12:30 AM (10:30–midnight in winter).* 🎫 *1,000 dr. round-trip, 500 dr. one-way.*

NEED A BREAK?

The pricey café at the top of Lycabettus may be the most convenient place to stop, but persevere and you'll get a better deal and a more romantic, pine-scented setting at **I Prasini Tenta** (✉ 5 mins down path that leaves from Ayios Giorgios or, if driving, turn left at fork when descending, ☎ 01/361-9447), an outdoor café where you can savor an ouzo and appetizers such as mushrooms stuffed with four cheeses along with your Acropolis view.

53 **National Gallery of Art.** The permanent collections of Greek painting and sculpture of the 19th and 20th centuries, including the work of naive artist Theophilos, have made way for long-running exhibitions, usually major loan shows from around the world. ✉ *Vasileos Konstandinou 50,* ☎ *01/721–1010.* 🎫 *1,000 dr.* ☉ *Mon. and Wed. 9–3 and 6–9, Thurs.–Sat. 9–3, Sun. 10–4.*

OFF THE BEATEN PATH

DESTE FOUNDATION, CENTRE FOR CONTEMPORARY ART – Art collector Dakis Joannou, who owns one of the world's largest collections of modern art, opened this lively complex in 1998 in a renovated paper warehouse. His private holdings range from Duchamp to Warhol to Koons, but the exhibition space is most more often devoted to progressive exhibits such as the recent "Global Vision: New Art from the '90s," designed to develop audiences for contemporary art in Greece and to offer opportunities for up-and-coming artists. The complex eschews the usual formality of museums and instead casually mixes art, entertainment, new media, and shopping. Included are the ground-floor Cosmos bar-restaurant, a video projection room, an art shop, and a Cybercafé. ✉ *Omirou 8, Neo Psychiko,* ☎ 01/672-9460. 🎫 *Free.* ☉ *Weekdays 11 am–midnight, Sat. noon–4 and 9–midnight (11 am–midnight in winter). Closed Sun. and 1st 2 wks. in Aug.*

National Gardens. When you can't take the city noise anymore, step into this oasis completed in 1860 as part of Otho and Amalia's royal holdings. Here old men on the benches argue politics, policemen take their coffee break, and animal lovers feed the stray cats that roam among the more than 500 species of trees and plants, many labeled. At the east end is the neoclassical **Zappion hall,** built in 1888 and used for major political and cultural events: It was here that Greece signed its entrance into what was the EC. Children will enjoy the **playgrounds, duck pond, and small zoo** (⊠ East end of park). The Hellenic Ornithological Society runs an **information kiosk on birds with an activity program for children,** including games to recognize the park's visitors, drawing contests, and the making of swallow's nests to ensure sanctuary for homeless birds (Near zoo, ☎ 01/381–1271 or 01/330–1167); it's open September–July, Saturday–Sunday 11–2:30. Youngsters aged 5–15 may settle into a good book at the **Children's Library** (☎ 01/323–6503), a rustic, vine-covered stone cottage in a tranquil corner of the garden; it is open September–July, Tuesday–Saturday 8:30–2:30. Of its 4,000 books, only 60 are in English and French. It also has games and puzzles (some in English), a chess set, dominoes, crayons, and coloring books. Albums, including a large selection of classical music, can be played on the turntable. ⊠ *East of Amalias, between Vasilissis Olgas and Vasilissis Sofias,* ☎ *01/721–5019.* ☉ *Daily 7 AM–sunset.*

NEED A
BREAK?

Visit the romantic café **Kafenedaki** (⊠ In the National Gardens), sometimes called Kipos, for a cool oasis of wrought-iron chairs and tables nestled under a bower of flowering vines. The café is next to a stone cottage just inside the park's Irodou Attikou entrance (near Lykeiou). The menu is limited to a *poikilia* (variety) of mezes, grilled "toast" (with ham and cheese), ice cream, apple pie, and drinks.

Panathenaic Stadium. Constructed by Lykourgus from 330 to 329 BC and used intermittently for Roman spectacles, the stadium was reseated for the Panathenaic Games of AD 144 by Roman citizen Herod Atticus of Marathon, a magistrate, senator, and wealthy patron of Athens. It later fell into ruin, and its marble was quarried for other buildings. By the mid-18th century, when it was painted by French artist Le Roy, it had become little more than a wheat field with scant remains and was later the midnight site of the secret rites of the witches of Athens. A blinding-white marble reconstruction of the ancient Roman stadium was rebuilt for the first modern Olympics, in April of 1896, and is now used mainly for an occasional concert and the finish of the annual marathon; it seats 80,000 spectators. ⊠ *Vasileos Konstantinou, across from National Gardens.* ☉ *Daily 9–2 but can be viewed in its entirety without entering.*

OFF THE
BEATEN PATH

FIRST CEMETERY OF ATHENS – This is Athens's equivalent of Paris's Père-Lachaise, but it is whitewashed and cheerful rather than gloomy and Gothic. The graves are surrounded by well-tended gardens and decorated with small photographs of the departed, and doves coo perpetually in the stately cypress trees. The main entrance off Anapafseos leads to an open-air museum of mind-boggling funerary architecture, including the imposing temple dedicated to Heinrich Schliemann, which is adorned with scenes from the Trojan War, and the touching marble *Sleeping Maidon* sculpture by Yiannoulis Halepas on the grave of Sophia Afendaki. It was commissioned by her parents in the hope that some day their young daughter would be awakened by a prince's kiss. Perhaps the most popular grave is that of actress and national sweetheart Aliki Vouyiouklaki, bedecked with lit candles, flowers, and fan letters left daily. The film star and politician Melina Mercouri is also buried here, as is the popular, controversial former prime minister Andreas Papandreou, who died in 1996. ⊠ *Anapafseos and Trivonianou, near Panathenaic Stadium,* ☎ *01/923–6118 or 01/923–6720.* ⊙ *Daily 7:30–7 (7:30–5 in winter).*

49 **Syntagma (Constitution) Square.** The traditional heart of the city, Syntagma Square is bordered with hotels and festive cafés, its central expanse of asphalt brightened by orange trees and a fountain. At the top of the square stands **Parliament,** formerly the royal palace, completed
★ in 1838 for the new monarchy. Here you can watch the **changing of the Evzone guard** at the Tomb of the Unknown Soldier—located in front of Parliament on a lower level—which happens every day at different times, except on Sundays, when it is scheduled around 11 AM. On Sundays the honor guard of tall young men don dress costume—a short white *foustanella* (kilt) with 400 neat pleats, one for each year of the Ottoman occupation, and red shoes with pompons—and still manage to look brawny rather than silly. A band accompanies a large troop of them in a memorable ceremony that begins at 10:45 AM from the barracks and ends in front of Parliament. Every day, a group of the Evzones raise the Greek flag on the Acropolis and lower it at closing time. On a wall behind the Tomb of the Unknown Soldier, the bas relief of a dying soldier is modeled after a sculpture on the Temple of Aphaia in Aegina; the text is from the funeral oration said to have been given by Pericles. ⊠ *Where Vasilissis Sofias becomes Panepistimiou.*

NEED A BREAK? Since 1910, **Ariston** (⊠ Voulis 10, ☎ 01/322–7626) has been turning out arguably the city's best *tiropites* (cheese pies) since 1910; these are a little more piquant than usual and have a thicker phyllo. Avoid the tasteless variety often sold on the street and make a pit stop here for the real thing, or try the equally good potato pies; the establishment is open during shopping hours.

44 **Temple of Olympian Zeus.** Begun in the 6th century BC, it was completed in AD 132 by Hadrian, who had also built one huge gold-and-ivory statue of Zeus for the inner chamber and another, only slightly smaller, of himself. Only 15 of the original Corinthian columns remain, but standing next to them inspires a sense of awe at their bulk, which is softened by the graceful carving on the acanthus-leaf capitals. The clearly defined segments of a column blown down in 1852 give you an idea of the method used in its construction. The site is floodlighted in summer, a majestic scene when you round the bend from Syngrou. On the outskirts of the site to the north are remains of houses, the city walls, and a Roman bath. ⊠ *Vasilissis Olgas 1,* ☎ *01/922–6330.* ⊠ *500 dr.* ⊙ *Tues.–Sun. 8:30–3.*

Piraeus

To those who remember the film *Never on Sunday,* the name Piraeus evokes images of earthy waterfront cafés frequented by free-spirited sailors and hookers, though many Athenians regard Piraeus (except for Mikrolimano or Kastella) as merely low class. Neither image is correct: The restoration of older buildings and the addition of shopping centers and cafés have brought about a rejuvenation, both of place and community pride. Piraeus caters more to Greek families and young singles than to the rough-and-tumble crowd, and living in some parts of it carries a certain cachet these days. Also in its favor: The air pollution, noise level, and temperatures are considerably lower than they are in inner Athens.

Today, Piraeus remains the port of Athens, 11 km (7 mi) southwest of the center, and a city in its own right (third-largest after Athens and

Thessaloniki), with a population, including suburbs, of about 500,000. In 1834, after gaining independence from the Turks, the government offered land in Piraeus (at that point a mere wilderness) on favorable terms, and it was resettled by islanders from other parts of Greece. The first factory was founded by Hydriots in 1847, and by the turn of the century there were 76 steam-powered factories. After the 1920s Piraeus developed as an economic center, while Athens maintained the cultural sphere. In the years following 1922, refugees from Asia Minor swelled the population, bringing with them rembetika music.

A Good Walk

The fastest and cheapest way to get to Piraeus from central Athens is to take the electric train (about 20–30 minutes, depending on whether you leave from Omonia, Monastiraki, or Thission station). The metro station is just off Akti Kallimasioti on the main harbor. For those who don't have much time, take Bus 904, 905, or 909 opposite the Piraeus station directly to the Archaeological Museum rather than walking there; get off at the Fillelinon stop. If it's Sunday, detour a few blocks from the metro to the **flea market** ⑤⑧, along Omiridou Skilitsi, and then stop for a coffee in one of the popular spots at the intersection with 34ou Syntagmatos Pezikou where Athenians come Sunday afternoons. If walking, turn left when exiting the metro, following Akti Kallimasioti to Akti Poseidonos. South of here is the Customs House and Port Authority—through which one passes to board boats going to other countries—and a modern exhibition center, where the Poseidonia Shipping Exhibition is held in June in connection with a biannual Nautical Week. Continuing on Akti Poseidonos, turn onto Vasileos Georgiou A', which passes the splendid 800-seat **Municipal Theater** ⑤⑨ near Korai Square. Head south on Iroon Polytechneiou, cutting through Terpsithea Square, and then go east on Harilaou Trikoupi to the remodeled **Archaeological Museum** ⑥⓪, containing such rare finds as the Piraeus Kouros, a cult statue of Apollo from the 6th century BC. The street ends at the harbor of **Pasalimani** ⑥① (Zea Marina). To the west is the coastal road Akti Themistokleous, whose lantern-lined stretch offers good views and reasonably priced seafood restaurants. Incorporated into the foundation of the **Hellenic Maritime Museum** ⑥②, also on the road, are the original Long Walls. To the east is the pretty, crescent-shape harbor of **Mikrolimano** ⑥③, lined with seafood restaurants (you can take a bus from the Fillelinon stop near the Archaeological Museum to Palio Faliro station if you don't want to walk). Mikrolimano had lost favor with some Athenians because the harbor suffers from pollution, but the delightful atmosphere remains intact, the harbor is still crowded with yachts, and young people flock to its cafés on Sundays.

Above Mikrolimano is charming **Kastella** ⑥④, terraces of 19th-century houses tucked up against the sloping hillside—an ideal spot for a walk before dinner on the harbor or a show at its **Veakio Theater.**

TIMING

On a day trip to Piraeus you can see the main sights, explore the neighborhoods around its three harbors, and have a seafood meal before returning to Athens. If you are taking an early morning ferry or seeing a performance at the Veakio Theater, it makes good sense to stay in one of the seaside hotels. Note that the flea market is held only on Sundays, the Archaeological Museum is closed Mondays, the Maritime Museum is closed on Sundays and Mondays, and the Municipal Theater is closed weekends.

Sights to See

★ ⑥⓪　**Archaeological Museum.** Besides an admirable collection of funerary stelae, urns, monuments, and korai, the museum's prize exhibits, found

BLUE GLAMOUR: YACHTING IN GREEK WATERS

BY FAR THE MOST UNIQUE way to see the Greek islands is a yachting vacation. Discovering these 1,425 geological jewels—thickly scattered over the Aegean Sea like stepping stones between East and West—by yacht, boat, or caïque is a once-in-a-lifetime experience. Many yachting expeditions set out or pass through Piraeus harbor—offering the most modern mooring and wintering facilities in the country—to discover magic in the Aegean. Greece's jagged coasts let you explore a world of secluded hamlets, white chapels, and little villages reflected in blue water, as you ride out the sunny breeze that blows over the hills. Not that Zeus should set your schedule (during the idyllic days in mid-winter he forbade the winds to blow), but keep in mind the Aegean can be a great deal rougher than most people think during August, when the *meltemi*, the north wind, is a regular visitor to these waters.

The array of seaside destinations in Greece is spectacular. If you are sailing from directly from Italy or along the Dalmation Coast, Corfu is the first destination, a lush Ionian resort once the favorite of yachtsman King Paul of Greece. From here, yachters sometimes work their way down to Messolonghi, in the Gulf of Patras, where Byron died and the sunsets can be unbelievable. You would be wise to land at Patras, at the entrance of the Gulf of Corinth, for this is one of the main crossroads of travel in Greece. It is here that yacht crews decide to take a short cut through the Corinth Canal to Piraeus or the long way around the Peloponnese. If you choose the short cut, a short bus ride from the harbor of Itea takes you to Delphi, the most venerated sanctuary of ancient Greece. Southward, few people fail to put in at Crete—the island where civilization is counted by the millenium. Sailing in an counterclockwise direction—old sea dogs maintain that this is the best way of covering the Aegean—you can enter the waters of the Dodecanese from the southwest, but this trip across the open sea lacks the surprises you discover traveling from harbor to harbor.

Another Mediterranean delight is Rhodes, with its ancient temples and medieval fortresses *and* wide range of discos. If you are looking for dreaminess, head west across the waters of the Dodecanese to the Cyclades. The island of Milos does not mass-produce Venuses and the volcano on Thira is not in constant eruption, of course, but, even so, the islands here are all winners: Delos, for its archaeological wealth; Mykonos, where the Greek nobs go to outsnob the snobs; Paros, whence the fabled marble came; Tinos, the Greek counterpart of Lourdes; Naxos, whose new wine is harvested in September. Next port of call could be the Northern Islands, including Chios, Lesbos, Sappho, and, on the far, far horizon, Samothrace, famed as the home of the Louvre's *Winged Victory*. Crossing the Gulf of Salonika to reach the Sporades requires good skill, but once you round Cape Sounion—give thanks to Poseidon at his incredible cliff-top temple here—you enter the hospitable waters of the Saronic Gulf. It you head back to anchor in Piraeus, you return to Attic soil, your odyssey now having taken you to the heart of Greek civilization—ancient Athens, Mycenae, and Epidaurus. For practical details about yachting and an extensive list of outfitters, *see* Cruise Travel and Yachting *in* The Gold Guide.

You can "do" Greece in your own yacht according to your taste, pausing at will for scenery, swimming or sightseeing, setting your own schedule and your own itinerary. However, to *enjoy* yachting, remember to "shift gears" mentally from the smooth speed of straight paved highways to the far more leisurely route of bay-indented coasts, lovely isthmuses, and beckoning bays.

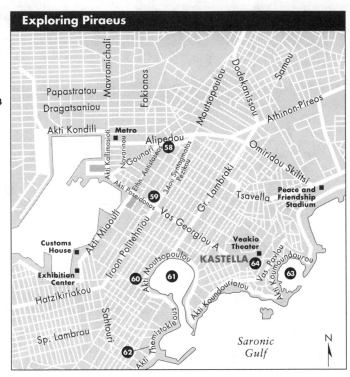

Exploring Piraeus

in a sewage drain in 1959, include the exquisitely made **Piraeus Kouros** (probably a cult statue of Apollo from the 6th century BC, and therefore the oldest known hollow-cast bronze statue); a 4th-century bronze of a pensive Athena, wearing a helmet decorated with griffins and owls; and two bronze versions of Artemis. ⊠ *Harilaou Trikoupi 31,* ☎ *01/ 452–1598.* 🖅 *500 dr.* ☉ *Tues.–Sun. 8–2:30 (8:30–3 in winter).*

⑤⑧ Flea market. In the "Monastiraki" of Piraeus, outdoor stalls overflow on Sundays with household items, electronic goods, and offbeat videocassettes, but there are also several interesting shops and stalls throughout the week selling everything from antique Mytilini mirrors ("antique" at the flea market means from about 1850 on) to Thracian wedding gowns to '50s furniture. The most rewarding stretch is along Omiridou Skilitsi between Ippodamias Square and Pilis Street. On Navarinou, parallel to Akti Kallimasioti, there's another market selling cheese, cold cuts, dried fruit, bread, and nuts. It's good to buy provisions before taking a ferry because the snack bars on board often have just a few items, and at high prices. ⊠ *Omiridou Skilitsi, parallel to metro tracks.* ☉ *Sun. 8–2.*

☙ ⑥② Hellenic Maritime Museum. The 13,000 items on display include scale models and actual sections of triremes and famous boats, Byzantine flags, figureheads, documents, and uniforms. A section of the **Long Walls** is incorporated into the museum's foundation, and other well-preserved segments run along Akti Themistokleous, south of Zea Marina. ⊠ *Akti Themistokleous at Freattida,* ☎ *01/451–6822.* 🖅 *500 dr.* ☉ *Sept.– July, Tues.–Sat. 8:30–2:30.*

⑥④ Kastella. This neighborhood behind Mikrolimano retains the charm of a bygone era, its neoclassical houses skillfully restored. On the hill the **Veakio Theater** (⊠ Idis on Lofos Prof. Ilias, ☎ 01/419–4520) has a cultural festival late June through September, featuring visiting dance troupes, plays, and concerts. ⊠ *Behind Mikrolimano.*

★ ⓾ **Mikrolimano.** The most touristy part of Piraeus, this graceful, small harbor is known to old-timers as **Turkolimano.** Sitting under the awnings by the sea and watching the water and the gaily painted fishing boats is the next best thing to hopping on a ferry boat and going to an island. During high season, it is a good idea to have lunch here, as in the evening most of the many restaurants lining the harbor are packed. The hawkers in front of the restaurants are entertaining but can be aggressive. Don't be afraid to ask to see the prices on the menu or go to look at the fish stored in iced compartments. Be sure to specify how large a portion you want, and ask its price in advance. ⊠ *Akti Koumoudourou.*

⑤⑨ **Municipal Theater.** The 800-seat theater was modeled after the Opéra Comique in Paris and finished in 1895. In the same building is the **Panos Aravantinos Decor Museum,** which displays sketches and models of the artist's theatrical sets. *Theater and museum: Ayios Konstantinou 2, ☎ 01/412–2339. ⊠ Free. ⏱ Sept.–July, Mon.–Wed. 4–8, Thurs.–Fri. 9–2.*

⑥① **Pasalimani (Zea Marina).** The small harbor has a new marina, complete with shops and all yachting facilities, including berths for more than 400 boats. The surrounding area has been rejuvenated, with the addition of many enticing cafés and pubs. There's a Greek National Tourist Organization (GNTO or EOT) office with maps, brochures, and timetables on the west side of the harbor close to the departure point for Saronic Gulf Islands hydrofoils.

DINING

Whether you sample octopus and ouzo near the sea, roasted goat in a turn-of-the-century taverna, or cutting-edge cuisine in Athens's latest restaurants, dining in the city is just as relaxing as it is elsewhere in Greece. Waiters never rush you, reservations are often unnecessary, and no matter how crowded, the establishment can always make room for another table. The best of Athens' restaurants have recently made enormous strides in quality and style, thanks to the new influence on native dishes by foreign cuisines, particularly French, Italian, and Japanese. Indeed, you may have a hard time finding a traditional *taramosalata,* as many chefs are eager to take Aegean-inspired cuisine and tweak it a notch higher. So forgo the ubiquitous moussaka and opt instead for the newer-than-now nouvelle house specialties—for a while, at least. After all, native Greek food can be sensational, as you'll find out if you taste *Iman Bayildi* ("the cleric fainted"—presumably because the eggplant with garlic and tomato was so delicious). Don't hesitate to try the barrel wine, inexpensive and often quite good. If you can't understand the menu, just go to the kitchen and point at what looks most appealing. This is a good idea especially in tavernas, where not everything on the menu may be available at the time you order. In most cases, you don't need to ask—just walk to the kitchen (some places have food displayed in a glass case right at the kitchen's doorway), or point to your eye and then the kitchen; the truly ambitious can say "Bo-RO na dtho tee Eh-hen-teh steen koo-ZI-na?" or "May I see what's in the kitchen?" At some rustic places, like Margaro in the port of Piraeus, you may also wind up in the kitchen for another reason: When its crowded, the staff asks you to prepare your own salad. Most places serve at least until midnight.

CATEGORY	COST*
$$$$	over 13,000 dr.
$$$	9,000 dr.–13,000 dr.
$$	4,500 dr.–9,000 dr.
$	under 4,500 dr.

per person for a three-course meal, including service and tax but excluding drinks

In the last three weeks of August, when the city empties out and most residents head for the seaside, more than 75% of the restaurants and tavernas popular among the locals close, though hotel restaurants, seafood restaurants in Mikrolimano, and tavernas in Plaka usually remain open.

Eating Places

Eating places fall into several categories. **Greek/Mediterranean** and **international restaurants** offer a more sophisticated selection of dishes than do tavernas, as well as trendier or more formal decor. A few years ago the category of "haute cuisine" would not have existed, but Athens now has restaurants of international standard, in both preparation and presentation; we list such special-event places, like Bajazzo and Spondi, under the International heading below. Truly authentic **tavernas** have wicker chairs that inevitably pinch your bottom, checkered tablecloths covered with butcher paper, wobbly tables that need coins under one leg, and wine drawn from the barrel and served in small metal carafes. If a place looks inviting and is filled with Greeks, give it a try. **Mezedopolia,** sometimes called **ouzeri,** are friendly little publike establishments that serve plates of appetizers—basically Levantine tapas—to feast on while sipping ouzo, though many now serve barrel and bottled wine as well. **Greek fast-food** and **seafood** spots offer a change of pace.

What to Wear

As in most other cosmopolitan cities, dress varies from casual to fancy, according to the establishment. Although Athens is informal and none of the restaurants listed here require a jacket or tie, you'll feel more comfortable dressing up a bit in the most expensive places. Conservative casual attire (not shorts) is acceptable at most establishments.

Greek/Mediterranean (Contemporary)

$$$　✕ **Azul.** In this jewel of a restaurant, the space is cramped with just 12 tables, the chairs designer uncomfortable, but the food is heavenly. Start with fresh tagliatelle with shrimp in a bisque sauce, and then move on to the sea bass filled with fragrant herbs, *avgotaracho* (the smoked roe of gray mullet), and sun-dried tomatoes—an unparalleled combination. Other memorable main dishes are chicken stuffed with the uniquely textured Cypriot cheese, *haloumi,* beef fillet with apricots, and sole in caper and lemon sauce. The smart wine list is reasonably priced, with most selections under 6,000 dr. In summer, there are a few additional tables outside on the pedestrian zone, the location for several popular bars. ⊠ *Haritos 43, Kolonaki,* ☎ *01/725–3817. Reservations essential in summer, Fri. and Sat. in winter. AE, DC, V. Closed last 3 wks. in Aug. No lunch.*

$$　✕ **Stous 7 Anemous.** A peculiar ridged ceiling, tiled wooden tables, and seven antique fans for which the restaurant is named ("anemos" means wind): The decor is beautiful but not exactly unified, a bit of postmodern pastiche in Monastiraki. Never mind: The playful food with intense flavors is what's impressive here. Appetizers not to be missed are the fried Dodoni feta wrapped in a sesame-enhanced crust and served with fleshy marinated tomatoes and walnut sauce, and the grilled mixed vegetables and chèvre with a tangy arugula puree. One of the best pasta dishes is plump fusilli with mushrooms (wild, oyster, and button), as-

paragus, and truffles. Main dishes include expertly grilled fish; moist pork fillet with a dense coffee–black currant sauce; chicken with shrimp and pistachios doused with brandy; and salmon, monkfish, and shrimp poached in lettuce leaves and served with a lemon-chive sauce. ⊠ *Astiggos 17 (from Ermou 121), Monastiraki,* ☎ *01/324–0386. Reservations essential on weekends. AE, DC, MC, V. Closed Aug.*

$$ ✕ **Vitrina.** It's obvious this highly stylized restaurant is the creation of
★ a fashion photographer—from the chair backs with attached drawer handles to the row of silver minimalist wall clocks. The specialty here is high-style Aegean-inspired cuisine: One of the best appetizers is lettuce-leaf dolmades stuffed with shrimp and served with saffron-ouzo sauce. The combinations are often bold: crayfish with coffee and coriander or grilled lamb ribs with grapefruit, honey and buttermilk. Try the pork tenderloin in retsina, the rabbit croquettes served with lentils and fried onions, or the shrimp with vodka sauce flecked with avgotaracho, considered a delicacy. Desserts include the "chocolate island," with chocolate cream in a bittersweet chocolate shell and drizzled with white chocolate sauce. Reserve early enough so you can book a table upstairs; downstairs is claustrophobic. In summer, the chef packs up for Santorini, where he runs the equally wonderful restaurant Domata. ⊠ *Navarhou Apostoli 7 (off Ermou), Psirri,* ☎ *01/321–1200 or 01/321 1511. Reservations essential. No credit cards. Closed Mon. and mid-June–Sept. No lunch Tues.–Sat., no dinner Sun.*

Greek/Mediterranean (Traditional)

Also *see* reviews under Mezedopolia and Tavernas, *below.*

$$ ✕ **Ideal.** The original Ideal burned down after almost 70 years, and its Art Deco protégé is in bright contrast, with comfy booths and tasteful decor. The oldest restaurant in the city center, it has a following for its large gamut of traditional Greek dishes cooked with unremitting reliability and its numerous daily specials, depending on what's good at the market. Best bets on the regular menu are the egg-lemon soup, fried mussels with garlic sauce, leek croquettes, grilled Aivaliotika minced beef with sweet peppers and mustard sauce (from Anatolia), and the Smyrnaika *tsoutsoukakia* (spicy meat patties made with ouzo and cumin). Sweet wines, such as mavrodaphne, is available by the glass, making a smooth partner for the strawberry coupe. The service is fast but fastidious. ⊠ *Panepistimiou 46, Omonia,* ☎ *01/330–3000. Reservations essential. AE, DC, MC, V. Closed Sun.*

$$ ✕ **Tade Efi Anna.** One of the city's newer establishments, this bar-restaurant opened in an area that, though close to sights like the ancient Agora and Monastiraki, lacked a decent place to eat. Near the end of the Ermou pedestrian zone, this serves classic Greek cuisine with a modern touch at gratifying prices. Look for the narrow doorway—easy to miss—and proceed upstairs to the simply decorated dining room with splashes of orange and yellow, iron candelabras, plants, and a small bar in the rear. *Melitzanes amigdalou* is an unusual dish of thinly sliced eggplant layered with tomatoes and cheese with a thick topping of crushed almonds, big enough for two, and unadorned except for salt, pepper, and parsley. The rabbit is cooked with cinnamony plums, nicely contrasted with fresh spinach, and the chicken fillet is first wrapped around Gruyère, then baked in a crust of Aigina pistachios. ⊠ *Ermou 72, Monastiraki,* ☎ *01/321–3652. No credit cards. Closed Aug.*

International

$$$$ ✕ **Bajazzo.** If you have only one big splurge in Athens, have it here,
★ one of the finest restaurants in the Mediterranean world, and the only

one in Greece to receive a Michelin star. "Bajazzo" means clown, and the decor is a joyful explosion of trompe-l'oeil birds and mounted puppets; even the waiters—who begin the show by trotting out platters of appetizers, in lieu of a printed menu—wear colorful bow ties. Scents and colors soon engulf you, as chef Klaus Feuerbach experiments with wildly imaginative creations. Starters may include seafood tart spiked with ouzo, or porcini mushrooms and pine nuts layered in crepes and served with basil sauce. Also delectable are the beef fillets with Metaxa sauce grilled in tobacco leaves; simple but flawess pork tenderloin with brie; sole with smoked salmon mousse, mascarpone cheese, and chive sauce; and partridge with quince, apple, and foie gras. Leave room for dessert: various stunning chocolate masterpieces, herbed ice cream (rosemary, tarragon, dill), or the incredibly light *île flottant*. ⊠ *Anapafseos 14, Mets,* ☎ *01/921–3013. Reservations essential. AE, DC, V. Closed Sun. No lunch Mon.–Sat.*

$$$$ ✕ **Vardis.** Compared to Taillevent in Paris, this grand restaurant is worth
★   the ride to the northern and elegant suburb of Kifissia. The award-winning chef executes both classic and modern French dishes with finesse. He demands quality ingredients, transporting rare sweetwater crayfish from Orhomenos and large shrimp (250 grams each) from Thassos island. The clientele may be a little sedate, but the food dazzles. Especially good are the warm foie gras with dried fig puree, the superb crayfish linguine, and the tournedos Rossini served with a demi-glace enriched with foie gras. Few can say no to the irresistible chocolate fondant for dessert. ⊠ *Diligianni 66 in Hotel Pendelikon, Kefalari, Kifissia,* ☎ *01/623–0650. Reservations essential. AE, DC, MC, V. Closed Sun. and Aug. No lunch.*

$$$$ ✕ **White Elephant.** Except for the leopard-print chairs and sculptured candelabra, there's nothing exotic about the discreet decor at this restaurant, but it serves the best Chinese cuisine in the city, as well as Polynesian dishes. The shrimp won ton are exquisitely light, the steamed prawn dumplings plump and juicy; the lettuce wrapped around pork, vegetables, and rice noodles a refreshing accompaniment to the fiery *kamoa moa* soup. Along with mango beef, other entrées to contemplate are the lamb with lemongrass and the tea-smoked duck. ⊠ *Kolokotroni 34, Kefalari Square, Kifissia,* ☎ *01/801–8560. Reservations essential. AE, DC, MC, V. Closed 1 wk. in Aug. No lunch.*

$$$–$$$$ ✕ **Kiku.** For those in need of a sushi fix, this has become an Athenian favorite despite hefty prices. Besides flawless sushi and sashimi, which often utilize local catch like bonito, dorado, sea bass, and cuttlefish, as well as fish flown in from Japan and London, the restaurant offers standards like perfectly fried vegetable and seafood tempura, crunchy yaki soba noodles, and chicken teriyaki. There is a separate menu for Japanese clients that includes gems like melt-in-your-mouth eggplant with miso flavored with sake and poppy seeds, pork *tonkatsu* marinated in mirin and fried in bread crumbs, and a memorable fish-cake soup (*oden moriawase*); ask the server for recommendations. ⊠ *Dimokritou 12, Kolonaki,* ☎ *01/364–7033. Reservations essential in winter. AE, DC, V. Closed Sun. and Aug. No lunch.*

$$$ ✕ **Boschetto.** Set in Evangelismos park, Boschetto pampers diners with
★   a soothing view, an expert maître d', and creative Italian nouvelle cuisine: You may even forget you're in the center of Athens. The specialty here is fresh pasta, such as papardelle with wild mushrooms and quail-Parmesan ragoût, airy capellini with crab and sautéed tomatoes; or ravioli with crayfish, foie gras, and poppy seeds. Favorite entrées include sea bass grilled in a salt crust and beef fillet with black truffles and red wine. End your meal with the bittersweet chocolate mousse or the crème brûlée, followed by the finest espresso in Athens (cigars available). The tables tend to be close together; reserve near the window or in the court-

yard during summer. ✉ *Alsos Evangelismos, near the Hilton,* ☎ *01/721–0893 or 01/722–7324. Reservations essential. AE, V. Closed Sun. and 2 wks. in Aug. No lunch weekends.*

$$$ ✕ **L'Abreuvoir.** A more central alternative to Vardis in Kifissia is this restaurant, which focuses on traditional French dishes and recently made a comeback, much to the delight of its loyal clientele. Located in the chic neighborhood of Kolonaki, it offers all the classics: cheese soufflé, frog legs Provençal, probably the city's best steak tartare, and crêpes suzettes prepared at your table, also available with homemade vanilla ice cream. One delectable house specialty is the foie gras sautéed with Calvados; others include duck with cherry vinegar and sea bass with fennel. In summer, there is outdoor dining in the tree-shaded courtyard. ✉ *Xenokratous 51, Kolonaki,* ☎ *01/722–9106. Reservations essential. AE, DC, MC, V.*

$$$ ✕ **Royal Thai.** Silk-clad waitresses will settle you comfortably amid the
★ Thai antiques, gilded dishes, and soothing decor of the restaurant that successfully introduced the tantalizing flavors of a relatively unknown cuisine to Athens. The knowledgeable staff can explain dishes to the uninitiated, but you won't go wrong if you concentrate on appetizers, the restaurant's forte. Near flawless tidbits include the blue dumplings stuffed with aromatic minced chicken and topped with toasted garlic; *yauvalat* pork spare ribs slow-cooked in a sour plum, chili, and soy sauce; and *tom kha gai* soup, a delicate chicken broth with nuances of coconut milk. If you're ordering a main dish, opt for thinly sliced beef with green curry, first deceptively mild, then deliciously hot. ✉ *Zirini 12, Kifissia,* ☎ *01/623–2322 or 01/623–2323. Reservations essential. AE, DC, V. No lunch in summer, no lunch Mon.–Sat. in winter.*

$$$ ✕ **Spondi.** You may feel like you're dining in a medieval wine cellar—the brick-and-stone room is vaulted and the furniture is massive and wood—but the cuisine is delightfully contemporary, and the menu is always changing. Perfectly balanced is the salad of tiny livers, radicchio, and onion sauce; sweetbreads come in a tart with mushrooms and lentil sauce, modest ingredients transformed in a masterful dish. Savor the lamb with a crust of garlic, parsley, and rosemary or the grilled fresh foie gras with caramelized endive in *mavrodaphne* cheese sauce, together with a red wine chosen by the award-winning sommelier, who has assembled more than 150 labels. After dinner, there is a choice of cigars to accompany your cognac, port, or whiskey. When weather permits, diners sit in the magnificent courtyard. ✉ *Pirronos 5, Pangrati,* ☎ *01/726–4021 or 01/752–0658. Reservations essential. V. No lunch.*

$$ ✕ **Il Tinello.** Walking into this Italian trattoria is like dropping in on a dinner party: a boisterous atmosphere, convivial guests, and a host who tells jokes as he strolls from table to table, taking orders, humming along to the canzione, and occasionally asking a guest to dance. In 1998 the restaurant won an award for its price-quality ratio, so diners shouldn't be put off by its location on the edge of a seaside suburb. Scrumptious dishes include roasted goat cheese with anchovy sauce and parsley; intense risotto with garlic, Parmesan, and porcini mushrooms; and plate-brimming servings of rustic pastas such as ravioli with a hint of chamomile; orecchiette with potatoes, tomatoes, and garden rocket; or fettuccine with almonds and chicken. ✉ *Knossou 54, Alimos,* ☎ *01/982–8462. Reservations essential. No credit cards. Closed Sun.–Mon. and mid-July through Aug. No lunch.*

Mezedopolia

$$ ✕ **Athinaikon.** This renowned establishment moved here after almost 60 years near the law courts, and it is still a favorite of attorneys and local office workers. The decor is no-nonsense ouzeri, with rectangular

marble tables, dark wood, and framed memorabilia. Abide by the classic specialties: grilled octopus, giant beans in a decadent tomato sauce, swordfish souvlaki with bay leaves and a light mustard sauce, and *ameletita* (sautéed testicles). A favorite dish is *patsaggka* (cured, spicy meat called "pastourmas" wrapped in phyllo with cheese and tomato). All go well with the light barrel red. ✉ *Themistokleous 2, Omonia,* ☎ *01/383–8485. No credit cards. Closed Sun. and Aug.*

$$ ✕ **H′ (7th) Monopolio Athinon.** Formerly a state-run monopoly that sold such goods as matches and petroleum, this has the feeling of a '50s *oinomageirio,* or "eating house." The emphasis is on regional Greek cuisine, with a few dishes from Asia Minor, Sicily, and Morocco. It is run by an actor and his mother, who turns out some of the best *pites* (pies) in the city. Try the traditional Cypriot *eliota,* its crisp, sesame-sprinkled pastry a deft contrast to the olive-onion filling, or the Cretan *souhli,* stuffed with meat, tomato, and kefalograviera cheese. Skip the osso buco and opt for the *tsoutsoukakia Smyrnaikia,* spicy patties with a dash of cumin and filled with olives, or "Aggeliki's tigania," bites of pork with mustard and *throubi,* a Sifnos herb resembling oregano. ✉ *Ippothontidon 10 and Keiriadon, Kato Petralona,* ☎ *01/ 345–9172. No credit cards. Closed Mon. and mid-June–Aug.*

$$ ✕ **Kafenio.** A Kolonaki institution, this ouzeri is slightly fancier than the norm, with cloth napkins, candles on the tables, and a handsome dark wood interior. The menu is enormous, with many unusual creations. The tender marinated octopus, fried eggplant, and the onion pie are good choices. ✉ *Loukianou 26, Kolonaki,* ☎ *01/722–9056. No credit cards. Closed Sun. and 3 wks. in Aug.*

$$ ✕ **Ta Tria Tetarta.** There's something dollhouse-like about this tri-level stone-and-wood interior with nooks and crannies, decorated with eye-catching objects like an old narghile. The mezedes served here include spicy feta sprinkled with red pepper and roasted in foil, cheese bread, skewered *seftalies* (a tasty mix of lamb liver bits and onions wrapped in suet), seafood pie, and spinach crepes with tomato, basil, and yogurt. ✉ *Oikonomou 25, Exarchia,* ☎ *01/823–0560. Reservations essential. No credit cards. Closed Aug. No lunch Mon.–Sat.*

$ ✕ **To Ouzadiko.** If you're exploring Kolonaki's boutiques and muse-
★   ums, plan to lunch here for the cozy interior (old posters, abundant wood, small marble tables), the friendly service, and the enticing mezedes. Depending on what the owner bought at market that morning, you may find delicious Thessaloniki mini meat pies called *tsigerosarmadakia;* any variety of croquettes like fluffy cheese balls spiked with red pepper; duckling with rice and chestnuts; eggplants capped (or *kapakiastes*) with feta and tomato; rustic black-eyed peas cooked with sweet greens; and juicy rooster with onions. To Ouzadiko lives up to its name, serving 110 kinds of ouzo and that regional grappa-like liquor, *tsipouro.* ✉ *Karneadou 25–29 in Lemos shopping mall, Kolonaki,* ☎ *01/729–5484. Reservations essential for dinner. No credit cards. Closed Sun. and last 2 wks. in Aug.*

$ ✕ **Zeidoron.** This usually crowded Psirri hangout has decent mezes, but the real draw is its location, the metal tables lining the main pedestrian walkway, great for watching all the world go by or for enjoying the neighborhood's illuminated churches and alleys. Appetizers include spicy grilled feta, green peppers stuffed with cheese, pork in mustard and wine, eggplant baked with tomato and pearl onions, and garbanzo bean croquettes. The wines are overpriced for the food; opt for ouzo instead. ✉ *Taki 10 and Ayion Anargiron, Psirri,* ☎ *01/321-5368. No credit cards. Closed 2 wks. in early Aug.*

Seafood

$$$-$$$$ ✕ **Varoulko.** Acclaimed chef Lefteris Lazarou has joined forces with
★ Fabrizio Buliani and the results are splendid as they try to outdo each
other. Customers wait in line to sample such appetizers as sturgeon-
filed phyllo triangles or carpaccio made from *petrobarbouno* (a kind
of rockfish). Although the restaurant is famous for its creative pre-
sentations of monkfish, there is a mind-boggling array of other seafood
dishes: swordfish with porcini mushrooms, baby squid with pesto; lob-
ster with wild rice, celery, and champagne sauce; and the lowly cab-
bage transformed into dolmades filled with crayfish and leeks. Varoulko
boasts one of the largest wine cellars in Athens. ⊠ *Deligeorgi 14, Pi-
raeus,* ☎ *01/411–2043 or 01/411–1283. Reservations essential. AE,
DC, V. Closed Sun. and Aug. No lunch.*

$$-$$$ ✕ **Kaldera.** Dedicated to specialties not found at most tavernas, this
restaurant brings back fond memories to those who love the Greek is-
lands. Although technically a mezedopolio, it serves very good, reasonably
priced seafood. Amid the blue-and-white Cycladic decor, diners can in-
dulge in such delights as *soupies krasates* from Smyrna—cuttlefish with
pine nuts and raisins; *gavros* (fresh anchovy) marinated in vinegar as
it's done in Salamina; a salad of sun-dried mackerel from Chios; and
steaming hot mussels in mustard sauce from Skopelos. Nonseafood ap-
petizers include a tangy, bright orange cheese dip from Mykonos, *sko-
rdalia* (but here the garlic-mashed potatoes are made with walnuts), squash
croquettes sparked with mint from Ermioni, and saganaki, in this case
with pastourmas and phyllo. If you can manage an entrée, try the
makaronada thalassina (al dente pasta with crab, shrimp, and mussels)
or any of the fresh catch, like sargus, sole, sea bream, and Kaldera's
specialty, monkfish. ⊠ *Leoforos Poseidonos 54, Palio Faliro,* ☎ *01/
982–9647 or 01/983–9636. Reservations essential weekends. AE, DC,
MC, V. Closed a few days around Christmas and Aug. 15.*

$$-$$$ ✕ **Kollias.** The restaurant's terrace, with pots of geranium and jasmine,
★ evokes the Athens of the '60s. Friendly owner Tassos Kollias has a way
with seafood, often creating dishes that range from the humble to the
aristocratic, from marinated gavros to lobster with lemon, balsamic
vinegar, and a shot of honey. He is also known for bringing in the best
quality catch, whether oysters culled by sponge divers from Kalymnos
or cuttlefish from Messolonghi. Order the grilled scorpion fish flavored
with mastic; the flambéed mackerel; or mussels stuffed with rice,
grapes, and pine nuts. Besides piping-hot tomato and other vegetable
croquettes, there are large mixed salads with white beets, arugula, let-
tuce, parsley, caper leaves, endive, and radishes. A fitting end to such
a meal are the warm *loukoumades* (like hot, fried doughnut holes with
syrup), best with the kumquat liqueur. ⊠ *Stratigou Plastira 3, Tabouria,
Piraeus,* ☎ *01/462–9620, 01/461–9150, or 01/093/226–9999 (mo-
bile phone). Reservations essential on weekends. AE, DC, MC, V.
Closed Sun. and Aug. No lunch.*

$$-$$$ ✕ **Thalassinos.** Decidedly different from its Piraeus sister establishment,
Thalassinos in Kolonaki guarantees some of the best seafood to visi-
tors who want to stay in central Athens. Located in a neoclassical house
that has a patina of nostalgia, the place is reminiscent of an old French
restaurant with linen tablecloths, mirrors, a large wooden chest of draw-
ers behind the bar, and frescoes on the ceiling. A fine, rarely found ap-
petizer is the salted eel from Komotini, or the house-made seafood
pastourmas, excellent with a shot of icy tsipouro. Hot entrées include
fresh octopus with a dense tomato–green olive sauce and garlic shrimp
baked amid layers of potato. This is one of the few places in Athens
that serve sea urchin that tastes like it's just been plucked from the sea,
either in the shell, with pasta, or just the eggs in a salad. For those watch-

Athens Dining and Lodging

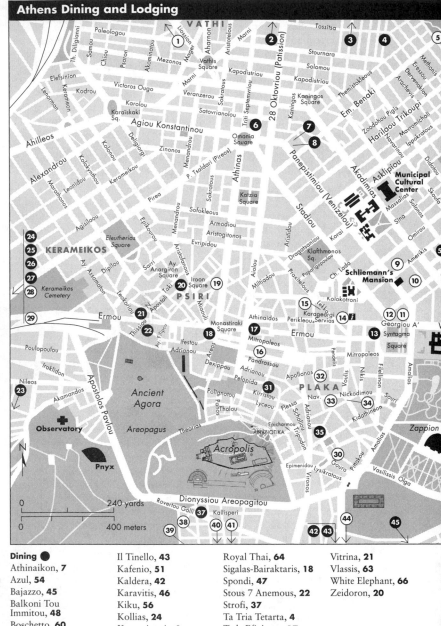

Dining ●

Athinaikon, **7**
Azul, **54**
Bajazzo, **45**
Balkoni Tou Immitou, **48**
Boschetto, **60**
Everest, **55**
Flocafe Espresso Bar, **2**
H' (7th) Monopolio Athinon, **23**
Ideal, **8**

Il Tinello, **43**
Kafenio, **51**
Kaldera, **42**
Karavitis, **46**
Kiku, **56**
Kollias, **24**
Kostoyiannis, **3**
L'Abreuvoir, **59**
Loxandra, **13**
Manessis, **36**
Margaro, **25**
Neon, **6**
O Platanos, **31**

Royal Thai, **64**
Sigalas-Bairaktaris, **18**
Spondi, **47**
Stous 7 Anemous, **22**
Strofi, **37**
Ta Tria Tetarta, **4**
Tade Efi Anna, **17**
Taverna Xynou, **35**
Thalassinos, **57**
To Ouzadiko, **52**
Vardis, **65**
Varoulko, **26**
Vassilenas, **27**

Vitrina, **21**
Vlassis, **63**
White Elephant, **66**
Zeidoron, **20**

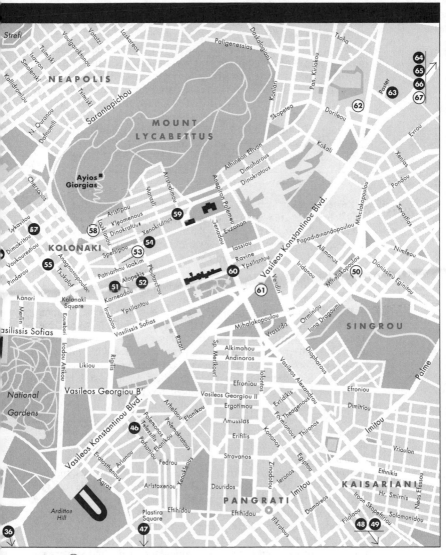

ing their budget, the lunch menu is cheaper, featuring seafood pastas. ⊠ *Tsakalof 36A, Kolonaki,* ☎ *01/361–4695. Reservations essential. AE, DC, V. Closed Sun. and mid-June–Aug.*

$ ✕ **Margaro.** If you are in Piraeus and want to forego the tourists and undeservedly expensive fish places on Mikrolimano, consider this fish taverna in the nearby neighborhood of Hatzyikyriakeio. Located at the gates of the Naval School, it serves just four items, along with excellent barrel wine: fried crayfish, fried red mullet, fried *marida* (a small white fish), and huge Greek salads—which you may be asked to prepare yourself when the staff is overwhelmed by a hungry rush-hour crowd. ⊠ *Hatzikyriakou 126, Piraeus,* ☎ *01/451–4226. No credit cards. Closed Sun. and Aug.*

Tavernas

$$ ✕ **Kostoyiannis.** If you're looking for authenticity, this is the place to go, liveliest late at night after the theatergoers arrive. One of the oldest and most popular tavernas in the area, it has an impressively wide range of Greek dishes—including shrimp salads, stuffed mussels, rabbit *stifado* (a stew of meat, white wine, garlic, cinnamon, and spices), and sautéed sweetbreads. ⊠ *Zaimi 37, Pedion Areos, behind the Archaeological Museum,* ☎ *01/821–2496 or 01/822–0624. No credit cards. Closed Sun. and last wk. of July through 3rd wk. of Aug. No lunch.*

$$ ✕ **Manessis.** One of the best of the old-time haunts, Manessis is a homey garden in summer and several rooms of a little house in winter. New dishes added recently to the menu are *tarama* (fish roe paste) croquettes; giant charcoal-grilled shrimp; green peppers stuffed with *midopilafo* (mussel-studded rice); and a fisherman's salad, composed of black-eyed peas, mussels, and shrimp. Specialties include Zakynthos-style beef with red sauce and Regato cheese, lamb baked in wax paper with garlic and tomato, *gardoumba* (spit-roasted innards and meat), and chicken souvlaki. There are also vegetarian dishes like falafel, hummus, and tabbouleh. Sweets include *ravani,* a semolina cake doused in syrup. ⊠ *Markou Moussourou 3, Mets,* ☎ *01/922–7684. No credit cards. Closed Sun. and a few days in Aug. No lunch.*

$$ ✕ **Strofi.** Just a few blocks from the Odeon of Herod Atticus, this taverna draws theatergoers for its congenial service and dramatic roof garden views of the illuminated Acropolis. Inside the old two-story house, signed glossy photos indicate the many performers who have dined here after a show at the ancient theater. Despite the many tourists, Strofi continues to attract locals who have been coming here for decades. The tzatziki, with its ground cucumber, abundant garlic, and velvety yogurt, goes well with the perfectly fried, thinly sliced zucchini, or the village bread. Another good appetizer is *fava,* a puree of yellow split peas. Reliable entrées include roast lamb with homemade noodles called *hilopites,* rabbit stifado, kid prepared with oil and oregano, and rooster stewed in red wine. ⊠ *Rovertou Galli 25, Makriyianni,* ☎ *01/ 921–4130. DC, MC, V. Closed Sun. and a few days in Aug. No lunch.*

$$ ✕ **Taverna Xynou.** Stepping into the courtyard of this Plaka taverna is like entering a time warp: Athens in the '50s. According to loyal customers, nothing has changed much since then, including the excellence of the food. Start with the classic appetizer of stuffed grape leaves, and then move on to the taverna's forte—cooked dishes such as lamb *yiouvetsi* (meat baked in ceramic dishes with tomato sauce and barley-shaped pasta), livers with sweetbreads in vinegar and oregano, and piquant *tsoutsoukakia* laced with cinnamon. In summer, tables move outside; nightly, a guitar duo drops by to charm the crowd with ballads of yesteryear. ⊠ *Aggelou Geronda 4, Plaka (entrance down the walkway next to Glikis kafenion),* ☎ *01/322–1065. No credit cards. Closed weekends and July. No lunch.*

$$ ✕ **Vlassis.** Relying on traditional recipes from Thrace, Roumeli, Thes-
★ saly, and the islands, the cooks here whip up Greek home cooking in
generous portions that more than make up for the daunting noise
level. The best way to sample as much as possible is to order several
appetizers for a meal (there are more than 20, all reasonably priced).
Essentials include the spicy cheese salad, *lahanodolmades* (cabbage rolls),
pastitsio (baked minced meat and pasta with tiny bits of liver), pork
with quince and red sauce, and the octopus stifado, tender and sweet
with lots of onions. Also good are the kebabs, seftalies, oven-baked
lamb, and *katsiki ladorigani* (goat with oil and oregano). Fresh fish is
also served, and for dessert, the huge slice of *galaktobouriko* (custard
in phyllo) is delicious. ✉ *Paster 8, Mavili Sq.,* ☎ *01/646–3060. Reser-
vations essential. DC, MC, V. Closed Sun. and Aug.–mid-Sept. No lunch.*

$ ✕ **Balkoni Tou Immitou.** This large, unpretentious place on a hill has
a huge balcony, with panoramic views of the Saronic Gulf Islands. It's
known to few tourists, though the waiters speak some English. The
extensive menu covers the standards, plus quail, partridge, and rabbit
stew, and gardoumba, which tastes much better than it looks. ✉
Pavlou Mela 13, Karea (take Bus 203 from Akadimias to Byzantio stop),
☎ *01/764–0240. No credit cards. No lunch Mon.–Sat., no dinner Sun.*

$ ✕ **Karavitis.** In this neighborhood favorite near the Panathenaic Sta-
★ dium, the winter dining room is insulated with huge wine casks, and
in summer there is a garden seating; get there early so you don't end
up at the noisy sidewalk tables. The classic Greek cuisine is well pre-
pared, including pungent tzatziki, *bekri meze* (lamb chunks in zesty
red sauce), and *stamnaki* (beef baked in a clay pot). ✉ *Arktinou 35
and Pausaniou 4, Pangrati,* ☎ *01/721–5155. No credit cards. Closed
a few days around Aug. 15. No lunch.*

$ ✕ **O Platanos.** Set on a picturesque corner, this is one of the oldest tav-
★ ernas in Plaka, and it's a welcome sight compared with the many over-
priced tourist traps in the area. Its shady courtyard is fine for outdoor
dining. Don't miss the oven-baked potatoes, roasted lamb, and the ex-
ceptionally cheap but delicious barrel retsina. Although not much En-
glish is spoken, the staff is extremely friendly; you can always go back
to the kitchen and point to what you want. ✉ *Diogenous 4, Plaka,* ☎
01/322–0666. No credit cards. Closed Sun. and 2 wks. in Aug.

$ ✕ **Sigalas–Bairaktaris.** Run by the Bairaktaris family for more than
a century, this is the best place to eat in Monastiraki Square. After ad-
miring the painted wine barrels and black-and-white snapshots of
Greek film stars, go to the window case to view the day's *magirefta*
(stove-top cooked dish, usually made earlier)—beef *kokkinisto* (stew
with red sauce), tsoutsoukakia spiked with cloves—or sample the gyro
platter. Appetizers include small cheese pies with sesame seeds, tender
mountain greens, and fried zucchini with a garlicky dip. ✉ *Monasti-
raki Sq. 2,* ☎ *01/321–3036. AE, V.*

$ ✕ **Vassilenas.** Longtime residents and frequent visitors rejoice in this
precious vestige of the good old days, a family-run taverna that is prob-
ably as good a bargain now as it was 70 years ago, when it operated
as a grocery store during the day and a diner at night. The decor is
minimal; in warm weather the operation moves to the upper terrace.
Come here ravenously hungry with friends, so you can do justice to
the set menu of 16 dishes (5,000 dr. per person), brought in a steady
stream to your table. Zesty shrimp yiouvetsi and fried monkfish are
two standouts, as is the dessert called *diples* (a deep-fried pastry served
with walnuts and honey syrup). ✉ *Etolikou 72, Ayia Sofia, Piraeus,*
☎ *01/461–2457. No credit cards. Closed Sun. and Aug. No lunch.*

Fast Food

The souvlaki joints in Monastiraki (☞ Exploring Athens, *above*) provide a satisfying and cheap snack. The souvlaki chain **Loxandra** (✉ Ermou 2, Syntagma Sq., ☎ 01/331–2212) has branches throughout the city, including one near the Archaeological Museum (✉ 28 Oktovriou [Patission] 43, ☎ 01/522-4296). Especially good are the chicken Loxandra, a roasted breast served in a homemade pita, and the pita Loxandra with spicy *seftalies,* a kind of Cypriot meatball. Night owls looking for a snack will probably find something to their liking at **Everest** (✉ Tsakalof 14, Kolonaki, ☎ 01/361–3477; ✉ Omonia Sq. 18, ☎ 01/324–2329), with a wide menu, including various *pites* (pies) with meat, spinach, and cheese fillings; pastries; and *tost,* grilled sandwiches you stuff with as many ingredients as you can handle. Order first, and then pay, bringing your receipt to pick up the food.

More upscale though still self-service is the **Flocafe Espresso Bar** chain, which has baguette and croissant sandwiches for the health-conscious, salads, sinful pastries, and a variety of coffees; branches are scattered around the city, including one across the street from the Archaeological Museum (✉ 28 Oktovriou [Patission] 53, ☎ 01/522–6818) and another off Syntagma (✉ Stadiou 5, ☎ 01/324–3028).

Neon (✉ Omonia Sq. and Dorou, ☎ 01/522–3201), a remodeled cafeteria in a landmark 1920s building that's open until at least 2 AM, was so popular that other branches immediately appeared at Tsakalof 6, Kolonaki; Mitropoleos 3, Syntagma Square; and G. Lambrakis 156, Zea Marina. The vast selection ranges from salad-bar fare, pasta, and meat dishes to sandwiches, ice cream, and other desserts, and prices are moderate.

If you *must* placate the children in American terms, there are local **Mc-Donald's, Wendy's,** and **Pizza Huts,** as well as **Goody's,** a Greek chain that serves good, inexpensive burgers.

LODGING

Athens has true luxury hotels and many in the budget range, but a shortage of middle-rank family-style hotels. The Greek word for hotel is *xenodochion,* meaning container for strangers, and occasionally, this is all they are: adequate for a rest and a wash, but not to spend a great deal of time in. The Greeks are an outdoor people and they rarely spend much time at home, let alone in an hotel. Staying in the northern suburb of Kifissia or along the coast is a good way to beat the heat and smog of the city center in summer, although the extra traveling time may be a deterrent.

Greek hotels are classified as De Luxe (L) and A–E, though the government, who awards the ratings (and therefore determines the official price), has announced it will switch to a star system to encourage hotels to upgrade. Within each category quality varies greatly, but prices usually don't. Still, you may come across an A-class hotel that charges less than a B-class, depending on facilities. Paradoxically, you may get up to a 20% discount if you book the hotel through a local travel agent; it's also a good idea to bargain over the rack rates in person at smaller hotels, especially off-season. Some of the older hotels in Plaka and near Omonia are comfortable and clean, their charm inherent in their age. But along with charm may come leaking plumbing and sagging mattresses—take a good look at the room. The thick stone walls of neoclassical buildings keep them cool in the summer, but few of the budget hotels have central heating, and it can be devilishly cold in the winter, especially in the $$ and $$$ categories; also, don't assume all rooms have TVs. All hotels in the $$$ and $$$$ categories have air-conditioning; those in the lower-price categories that have air-conditioning are indicated. A buffet breakfast is often served, which includes cold cuts and cheese, even poached eggs and other meat, but nothing cooked to order. The cost is not included unless noted.

CATEGORY	COST*
$$$$	over 55,000 dr.
$$$	30,000 dr.–55,000 dr.
$$	17,000 dr.–30,000 dr.
$	under 17,000 dr.

All prices are the official rates for a standard double room, including tax and service, in high season.

Athens

$$$$ **Andromeda Athens Hotel.** Set on a quiet street near the U.S. Embassy, this small luxury hotel caters to business travelers, but all guests will relish the meticulous service and sumptuous decor. The spacious rooms have a salmon color scheme with quilted headboards, wall-to-wall carpeting, double-glazed windows, and TV (computers and fax machines are available on request). At press time, the hotel was putting the finishing touches on a building across the street with 12 executive suites (one- and two-room apartments), complete with refrigerator, microwave oven, computer, and pay-TV system. The Michelangelo restaurant features very good Italian cuisine. ⊠ *Timoleondos Vassou 22, Mavili Sq., near the U.S. Embassy, 11521,* ☎ *01/643–7302 through 01/643–7304,* FAX *01/646–6361. 20 rooms, 6 suites, 4 penthouses. Restaurant. AE, DC, MC, V.*

$$$$ **Astir Palace Vouliagmeni.** Sprawling across a pine-studded promontory 25 km (16 mi) south of downtown Athens, with a view of nearby islands, this 80-acre resort offers a haven from the city's heat and commotion—which is yours soon enough to enjoy, thanks to the hotel's shuttle bus which transports guests to the center in the mornings. The soothing, seaside setting makes it difficult to think about going into town. Less expensive than luxury-category establishments in the center, the complex is actually made up of three hotels, all freshly decorated in the last few years. The private beach, sports, lovely landscaping, and sea views are bonuses. Buffet breakfast is included in the price. ⊠ *Apollonos 40, Vouliagmeni, 16671,* ☎ *01/890–2000, 212/682–9191 in the U.S.;* FAX *01/896–2582, 212/682–9254 in the U.S. 456 rooms, 73 bungalows, 30 suites. 5 restaurants, 4 pools. AE, DC, MC, V.*

$$$$ **Athenaeum Inter-Continental.** With its marble atrium lobby, central fountain, and private art collection, this hotel is a cool oasis on busy Syngrou Avenue, the main road from the center to the sea. The rooms are spacious, with sitting areas, marble bathrooms, and thick carpeting; ask for one with an Acropolis view. The Inter-Con is one of the few establishments in Athens with a health club. The hotel has renovated the eighth and ninth floors to create the Club section, which includes private check-in, lounge, and library; complimentary breakfast, coffee, and evening cocktails; and rooms with video, stereo, and CD players, trouser press, and safe. Twice each morning a shuttle takes guests to the airport, and then throughout the day to Syntagma Square, about 10 minutes away. ⊠ *89–93 Syngrou Ave., near Neos Kosmos, 11745,* ☎ *01/920–6000,* FAX *01/924–3000. 548 rooms, 59 suites. 2 restaurants, pool, in-room safes. AE, DC, MC, V.*

$$$$ **Athens Hilton.** A 200-year-old olive tree with a Turkish cannonball lodged in its branches adds an earthy touch to the glamorous entrance, with its multilevel lobby of variegated marble and eye-catching collection

of works by Greek artists. Opened in 1963, this is still one of the top hotels in the city, giving an impression of calm confidence amid the comings and goings of various conventions, banquets, and meetings. The rooms have a subdued color scheme and carpeting, double-glazed windows and thick curtains buffer the street noise, and the balconies face either the Acropolis or Mt. Hymettus. On the top floor, the Galaxy bar with its long terrace and Athens panorama is the ideal place to recoup from a hard day of sightseeing; for livelier nightlife, there is a strip of popular bars behind the Hilton. Syntagma Square is about a 20-minute walk away with many museums en route, but a shuttle transports less energetic guests during the day. ⊠ *Vasilissis Sofias 46, 11528,* ☎ *01/ 725–0201,* FAX *01/725–3110. 454 rooms, 19 suites. 3 restaurants, pool. AE, DC, MC, V.*

$$$$ 🏨 **Grande Bretagne.** Built in 1842, the GB is an Athens landmark, and its guest list testifies to its colorful history, with visitors like Edith Piaf, Jackie Kennedy, various royals, and rock stars. During World War II, the GB served, in turn, as the headquarters for the Greek, German, and British forces; when Churchill was visiting on Christmas Eve 1944, a plot to blow up the hotel from the sewers was foiled. Renovated in 1992, the hotel's marble lobby is graced with plush sofas, Oriental rugs, tapestries, and ornate chandeliers. The most coveted rooms are the Syntagma rooms, with Acropolis views and huge balconies. Lounge areas on each floor have velvet couches, antiques, and etchings; the ceilings are so high that corridors seem like tall tunnels. The hotel has now added a nonsmoking floor and "Smart" rooms, with desk, printer, fax, photocopier, and direct phone line. ⊠ *Vasileos Georgiou A' 1, Syntagma Sq., 10563,* ☎ *01/330–0000, 01/331–5555 through 01/331–5559 for reservations;* FAX *01/322–8034, 01/322–2261 for reservations. 364 rooms, 23 suites. Restaurant. AE, DC, MC, V.*

$$$$ 🏨 **Holiday Inn.** Despite its location—about a 10-minute drive from Syntagma—this has become a favorite with businesspeople, especially after the hotel completed a two-year renovation in 1998, earning it several awards. The light, modern rooms now have voice mail, satellite TV, video, hair dryer, trouser press, fireproof doors, computer hookups dubbed "PC points," and express check-out. The new Executive Rooms on the fifth and sixth floors also include complimentary juice, coffee, and newspaper, private balcony, and twice-daily maid service. A recently installed rooftop health studio includes weight machines, a sauna, and various cardiovascular contraptions like treadmill and stepper; massage is available. The rooftop pool sits alongside a snack bar, which operates as a full-fledged restaurant on summer evenings. ⊠ *Mihalakopoulou 50, Ilisia, 11528,* ☎ *01/724–8322 through 01/724–8329,* FAX *01/724–8187. 189 rooms, 3 suites. Restaurant, pool, massage, exercise room. AE, DC, MC, V.*

$$$$ 🏨 **Ledra Marriott.** As a Marriott, the Ledra's main calling cards are its high-performance staff and its attractive decor. The lobby piano bar sits below a spectacular 1,000-crystal chandelier; Kona Kai, the Polynesian restaurant, is excellent; and the Zephyros Café has a bountiful Sunday brunch. The rooftop pool has a view of the Acropolis that is breathtaking at sunset. The pastel rooms have vast closet space and armchairs, and some have views of the Acropolis. Shuttles run daily to and from Constitution Square. ⊠ *Syngrou 111, near Neos Kosmos, 11745,* ☎ *01/934– 7711,* FAX *01/935–8603. 258 rooms with bath, 1 suite. 3 restaurants, 3 bars, pool, shops, business services, meeting rooms. AE, DC, MC, V.*

$$$$ 🏨 **N. J. V. Athens Plaza.** Sharing an exclusive Syntagma Square address with its more historical neighbor, the Grande Bretagne (☞ *above*), this is a good alternative if the Grande Bretagne is full. In 1998 the hotel was completely renovated by Grecotel, and now its "1913" lobby, named after the year Crete (the proprietors' island) united with Greece, is a

cool mixture of light wood floors, white marble, spiky light fixtures, and burgundy and gray-green upholstery. The spacious rooms, again in gray and burgundy with a painting of the Acropolis (in case you don't have a view), come equipped with minibar, direct-dial phones, a soon-to-be-installed "Interactive Web TV" with Internet facilities and video games, and large marble bathrooms with phone extensions. The few rooms in the back are quieter, but even those in the front are fine, due to double glazing and air-conditioning. Under the family plan, one child under 12 may stay with parents at no extra cost. Named after designers, the individually decorated suites on the eighth and ninth floors have sitting areas, breathtaking Acropolis views, and interiors decked out with designer fabrics and furnishings. The Parliament restaurant specializes in Mediterranean cuisine, and the Explorers Bar is soothing, with dark wood, green tapestry, and leather chairs. At press time, a swimming pool was in the works. ⊠ *Vasileos Georgiou A' and Stadiou, Syntagma Sq., 10564,* ☎ *01/325–5301,* 𝔽𝔸𝕏 *01/323–5856. 182 rooms, 25 suites. Restaurant. AE, DC, MC, V.*

$$$$ 🏨 **St. George Lycabettus.** This hotel, in a great location on the wooded slopes of Mt. Lycabettus in upscale Kolonaki, has a splendid view. Getting there, however, involves a steep, short walk or a ride up (remember: taxis are inexpensive), though the hotel offers minibus service regularly until mid-afternoon. The sumptuous rooms (those facing outward have balconies) and suites include the Maria Christina presidential suite, inaugurated by Princess Michael of Kent. Business guests become members (no fee) of the Privilege Club, with such benefits as children up to 12 years staying free with parents, in-room voice-mail and fax service, guaranteed rooms, upgrades, and extended check-out up to 3 PM. The hotel has a rooftop pool; the soothing, recently renovated Tony's Bar; and its trump card, Le Grand Balcon, a rooftop restaurant with a panoramic view. Buffet breakfast is included in the price. ⊠ *Kleomenous 2, Kolonaki, 10675,* ☎ *01/729–0711 through 01/729–0719,* 𝔽𝔸𝕏 *01/729–0439 or 01/724–7610. 162 rooms, 5 suites. 2 restaurants, pool. AE, DC, MC, V.*

$$$–$$$$ 🏨 **Kefalari Suites.** Escape Athens's bustle among the neoclassical man-
★ sions and tree-lined boulevards of Kifissa at this new hotel with imaginatively themed rooms. Installed in a turn-of-the-century building, the hotel offers suites at a range of prices lower than downtown deluxe lodging—for example, the Deck House (no need to go to sea), the chateau-inspired Malmaison, exotic Aqaba, and the romantic Daphnis and Chloe. Although the neighborhood boasts several fine restaurants, the suites include kitchenettes with utensils and refrigerators. Other amenities include minibars and verandas or balconies; guests share the sundeck with a Jacuzzi. Laptop computers with modem and faxes are available. Continental deluxe breakfast (cheese and cold cuts) is included in the price. ⊠ *Pendelis 1 and Kolokotronis, Kefalari, Kifissia, 14562,* ☎ *01/623–3333,* 𝔽𝔸𝕏 *01/623–3330. 13 suites. Kitchenettes, minibars. AE, DC, MC, V.*

$$$ 🏨 **Electra Palace.** At the edge of Plaka, this hotel has cozy rooms done in warm hues, complete with balconies—for comparatively low prices. It recently replaced all its TVs and introduced a pay movie system. Keep in mind that rooms from the fifth floor up are smaller but have larger balconies; the top floor has wonderful views facing either the Acropolis or Mt. Lycabettus. The staff is helpful, the American breakfast (included in the price) is abundant, and best of all, you can spend hours by the rooftop pool, sipping a cool drink and gazing at the Parthenon. ⊠ *Nikodimou 18, Plaka, 10557,* ☎ *01/324–1401 through 01/324–1410,* 𝔽𝔸𝕏 *01/324–1875. 101 rooms, 5 suites. Restaurant, pool. AE, DC, MC, V.*

$$$ ⊡ **Novotel Athenes.** Though not central and in a decidedly unaesthetic neighborhood, this hotel is just a 10-minute walk to the rail station and the National Archaeological Museum. One of the city's better values, it has an elegant lobby and tranquil rooms with sofas. The underground parking is free for guests, a bonus in this part of town. The rooftop pool is beside the hotel's Greek restaurant, from which, in summer, you can watch the sun set behind the Acropolis. ⊠ *M. Voda 4– 8, Vathis Sq., 10439,* ☎ *01/825–0422 through 01/825–0430,* FAX *01/ 883–7816. 189 rooms, 6 suites. 2 restaurants, pool. AE, DC, MC, V.*

$$ ⊡ **Acropolis View.** Major sights are just a stone's throw away from
★   this hotel tucked into a quiet neighborhood below the Acropolis. About half of the agreeable, air-conditioned rooms have Parthenon views. There is a roof garden, staff members in the homey lobby are efficient, and full breakfast (eggs, ham, cheese, cake) is included in the price. ⊠ *Webster 10, Acropolis, 11742,* ☎ *01/921–7303 through 01/921– 7305,* FAX *01/923–0705. 32 rooms. Air-conditioning. AE, MC, V.*

$$ ⊡ **Astor.** A good choice for those who want to stay near Syntagma Square without breaking the bank, the Astor is convenient, with amenities such as TV and air-conditioning, though it is at the low end of its price range. The rooms, including the bathrooms, were completely renovated in 1998; request one above the sixth floor for a memorable view of the Acropolis, which may also be taken in from the roof-garden restaurant where guests enjoy their (included) buffet breakfast. ⊠ *Karageorgi Servias 16, Syntagma, 10562,* ☎ *01/335–1000,* FAX *01/325–5115. 131 rooms. Restaurant, air-conditioning. AE, DC, V.*

$$ ⊡ **Athenian Inn.** "Your home in Athens" is this hotel's motto, and perhaps the main reason people keep coming back is gracious Epaminondas Artemiou, who's been running the place since 1975. The other advantage of this hotel, with its flowering plants, terra-cotta tile floors, and watercolors of Greek scenes, is its location in the heart of Kolonaki. With such distinguished past visitors as Lawrence Durrell, it has a loyal clientele, so you must book well ahead. The lounge and breakfast room has an open fireplace, and Continental buffet breakfast is included in the price. Guest rooms have carpeting and traditional Greek spreads on the wood-frame beds; most have balconies (those on the fourth to sixth floor are larger), and some look toward Mt. Lycabettus. The street has little traffic, but occasionally loud conversation is heard from the popular Ratka restaurant nearby. ⊠ *Haritos 22, Kolonaki, 10675,* ☎ *01/723–8097, 01/723–9552, or 01/721–8756,* FAX *01/724–2268. 25 rooms, 3 suites. Breakfast room, air-conditioning. AE, DC, V.*

$$ ⊡ **Austria.** This small, unpretentious hotel is on Filopappou Hill, opposite the Acropolis, ideal as a base for wandering around the heart of ancient Athens. Buffet breakfast (included in the price) is not mandatory; without it, deduct 900 dr. per person. ⊠ *Mouson 7, Filopappou, 11742,* ☎ *01/923–5151 or 01/922–0777,* FAX *01/924–7350. 37 rooms. Air-conditioning. AE, DC, MC, V.*

$$ ⊡ **Hotel Achilleas.** Owned by the same family that runs Plaka Hotel (☞ *above*), this modern hotel is just a few minutes from Syntagma but priced at the low end of its category. Completely renovated in 1995, it has plain but spacious, airy rooms with TV and air-conditioning, and on the top floor, two rooms share a bath, convenient for larger parties. Breakfast, including fruit and corn flakes, is served in an interior courtyard filled with jungly plants and cheerful marble-topped blue tables. ⊠ *Lekka 21, Syntagma, 10562,* ☎ *01/322–5826, 01/322–8531, or 01/323–3197,* FAX *01/322–2412. 34 rooms. Air-conditioning, babysitting. AE, DC, MC, V.*

$$ ⊡ **Lycabette.** This convenient hotel near Syntagma has a gregarious atmosphere and pleasant service, but the "pedestrian" street is sometimes filled with motorbikes from those visiting the many surrounding cafés.

The comfortable rooms all have TVs and balconies (those overlooking Akadimias are smaller). The lobby is cheerful, and the optional Continental breakfast is served in a pretty breakfast room. ✉ *Valaoritou 6, Syntagma, 10671,* ☎ *01/363–3514 through 01/363–3517,* FAX *01/363–3518. 39 rooms. Restaurant, air-conditioning. AE, DC, MC, V.*

$$ 🏨 **Plaka Hotel.** Close to many sights and the Monastiraki Square metro, this hotel has a roof garden overlooking the Plaka's rooftops to the Parthenon. Double-glazed windows cut down the noise; the highest floors are the quietest. All rooms, done in blue and white, have TV and are simply furnished; those in back from the fifth floor up have the best Acropolis views. ✉ *which,areas 7 and Mitropoleos, Plaka, 10556,* ☎ *01/322–2096 through 01/322–2098,* FAX *01/322–2412. 67 rooms. Air-conditioning. AE, DC, MC, V.*

$–$$ 🏨 **Acropolis House.** This landmark pension ensconced in a 19th-century home in Plaka is frequented by artists and academics, who appreciate its large rooms, original frescoes, and genteel owners, the Choudalakis family. All rooms have private bathrooms, though about 10 have their bath immediately outside in the hallway. Some rooms have air-conditioning, and a full breakfast is included in the price. ✉ *Kodrou 6–8, Plaka, 10558,* ☎ *01/322–2344 or 01/322–6241,* FAX *01/324–4143. 20 rooms. V.*

$ 🏨 **Adams Hotel.** This quiet pension sits across from Ayia Aikaterini church in Plaka, a favorite with young people for its clean rooms and good value. Most of the rooms have balconies and many, including all on the top floor, enjoy splendid views of the Acropolis. All but nine rooms have air-conditioning, though travelers on a very tight budget might consider the four rooms that have their private bath outside the room (about 4,000 dr. less). The owners, who also run the Meltemi Hotel in Paros, are helpful to first-time visitors to Athens. ✉ *Herefondos 6 at Thalou, Plaka, 10558,* ☎ *01/322–5381 or 01/324–6582,* FAX *01/323–8553. 14 rooms. V.*

$ 🏨 **Aphrodite Hotel.** Halfway between Syntagma and Plaka, this perfectly comfortable hotel has quiet and tidy, if rather spare, rooms. With the facilities of a more costly hotel, a gracious and professional staff, and buffet breakfast included in the price, it offers excellent value. About half the rooms have Acropolis views, and the gleaming white marble lobby ends in a bar, where guests often relax in the evenings. ✉ *Apollonos 21, Syntagma, 10557,* ☎ *01/323–4357,* FAX *01/322–5244. 84 rooms. Bar, air-conditioning. AE, DC, MC, V.*

$ 🏨 **Art Gallery Pension.** This handsome house has an old-fashioned look,
★ with family paintings on the muted white walls, earth-tone spreads on the comfortable beds, hardwood floors, and ceiling fans. Located in a residential area not far from the Acropolis, this friendly place, much prized by visiting students and single travelers, draws a congenial crowd. Many rooms have balconies with views of Filopappou hill or the Acropolis. ✉ *Erechthiou 5, Koukaki, 11742,* ☎ *01/923–8376 or 01/923–1933,* FAX *01/923–3025. 19 rooms, 2 suites. No credit cards. Closed Nov.–Feb.*

$ 🏨 **Attalos Hotel.** The market area, where you'll find the Attalos, is full of life and color by day but fairly quiet at night. The pleasant hotel is well run by its friendly owner, Kostas Zisis, who goes out of his way for guests. The hotel has a rooftop garden, and many rooms have an exceptionally fine view of the Acropolis and Mt. Lycabettus; about 12 have balconies. Try to get a room in the rear, where the street noise is reduced; it's further diminished by double-glazed windows. ✉ *Athinas 29, Monastiraki, 10554,* ☎ *01/321–2801 through 01/321–2803,* FAX *01/324–3124. 80 rooms. Air-conditioning. V.*

$ 🛏 **Marble House.** This popular pension, in a cul-de-sac about a 15-minute walk from the Acropolis, has a steady, satisfied clientele—even in winter, when it offers low monthly and weekly rates. Rooms are clean and quiet, with ceiling fans and basic furniture, and there is a breakfast room. At press time, the owners were installing air-conditioning on the third floor. The international staff is always willing to help out, and the courtyard is a lovely place to relax. Take Trolley 1, 5, or 9 from Syntagma and get off at the Zinni stop. ⊠ *A. Zinni 35, Koukaki, 11741,* ☎ *01/923–4058 or 01/922–6461. 16 rooms, 11 with bath. No credit cards.*

$ 🛏 **Orion and Dryades.** These two hotels in a residential area across from the park on craggy Lofos Strefis are often booked by local fashion agencies, who house their models here. Orion is the humbler and cheaper, with smaller rooms and shared baths for every two rooms; its third-floor roof garden serves as the breakfast area for both hotels. Each hotel has a kitchen guests may use, and most rooms have balconies. For those who don't want to go far for dinner, the park has several inexpensive ouzeris open in summer. ⊠ *Emmanuel Benaki 105, Lofos Strefi, 11473,* ☎ *01/330–2387, 01/330–2388, 01/382–0191, 01/382–7116, or 01/382–7362,* 𝔽𝔸𝕏 *01/380–5193. Orion: 23 rooms share bath; Dryades: 15 rooms. No credit cards.*

$ 🛏 **XEN (YWCA).** This centrally located budget choice for women (from 4,000 dr. for a bed in a triple room with shared bath to 9,500 dr. for a double with private bath) has rooms mostly with shared bathrooms. The marble floors have rugs in winter; sheets and blankets are provided. The rooms are not air-conditioned, but those at the back are cooler and quieter; some have fans. Breakfast and snacks are available in the cafeteria, and there is a TV lounge on the fourth floor. Overnight guests pay an additional membership fee of 600 dr., good for a year. ⊠ *Amerikis 11, Syntagma, 10672,* ☎ *01/362–4291 through 01/362–4293,* 𝔽𝔸𝕏 *01/362–2400. 26 rooms share bath, 4 with private bath. Cafeteria. No credit cards.*

Piraeus

$$ 🛏 **Castella Hotel.** Perched on the hill above picturesque Mikrolimano, this is a fine choice if you have an early boat to catch. Rooms are fairly large; some have a sea view, as does the flower-filled roof garden that overlooks the small harbor and the yacht club. ⊠ *Vasileos Pavlos 75, Kastella, 18533,* ☎ *01/411–4735,* 𝔽𝔸𝕏 *01/417–5716. 32 rooms. Restaurant, air-conditioning. AE, DC, MC, V.*

$ 🛏 **Scorpios.** The view of the Makra Teixoi is the draw at this little hotel in Piraiki, not far from Zea Marina, and close to several seafood ouzeries. At the low end of the moderate range, the rooms are small but attractive, with wood furniture and brown decor. Sixteen rooms have balconies; those in front have fine views of the ancient walls and the Saronic Gulf, including Aegina on a clear day, though those in back are quieter. Ideal for families, the top floor has two large rooms that share a balcony. ⊠ *Akti Themistokleous 156, Piraiki, 18539,* ☎ 𝔽𝔸𝕏 *01/451–2172 or 01/452–4751. 26 rooms. Air-conditioning. AE, MC, V.*

NIGHTLIFE AND THE ARTS

The weekly magazines *DownTown* and *Athinorama* (both in Greek) cover current performances, gallery openings, and films, as do the English-language newspapers, the weekly *Hellenic Times,* the *Athens News* published Tuesday through Sunday, and the English summary of *Kathemerini,* inserted in the *International Herald Tribune,* available Monday through Saturday.

Nightlife

Bars

Bars are the staple of Greek nightlife, with new establishments opening every week. In summer, many of the most popular spots, especially dance clubs, move to the coastal road; check with your hotel first. Most bars stay open at least until 3 AM. Drinks are rather steep (from 1,700 to 2,000 dr.) but generous, and often there is a surcharge on weekend nights at the most popular clubs, which also usually have bouncers, aptly called "face-control" by Greeks. Most clubs and bars do not take credit cards for drinks.

Balthazar (✉ Tsoha 27, Ambelokipi, ☎ 01/644–1215 or 01/645–2278) is a bar-restaurant in a neoclassical house, with a lush garden court yard and subdued music, where Athenians of all ages come to escape the summer heat.

Fairly new but sure to endure, **Banana Moon** (✉ Vas. Olgas 1, Zappio, ☎ 01/321–5414) offers both a lively bar with loud music and a glamour crowd and quieter surrounding tables set among the trees of the National Gardens. In winter the bar moves to a Kolonaki address.

Movie stars, romancing couples, girlfriends, the local Lotto vendor—all show up at **En Delfois** (✉ Skoufa 75 on Delfon pedestrian zone, Kolonaki, ☎ 01/360–8269) for its see-and-be-seen atmosphere in a friendly setting with good snacks, eclectic music played at conversational level, and generous drinks. During the day, it's also a good place to stop for a coffee.

To enjoy Greek *kefi* (high spirits) without the formalities of a big bouzouki club, visit **Karpouzi** (✉ Politechniou and 34ou Syntagmatos Pezikou, Piraeus, ☎ 01/412–6074), especially on a Sunday afternoon, when DJs spin Greek music and the audience inevitably dances on the tabletops.

A relaxed café during the day, **Horostasion** (✉ Skouleniou 10, Klathmonos Sq., ☎ 01/331–4330) morphs into a packed, three-level club with mainstream music and special nights dedicated to everything from hip-hop to drum 'n' bass. The upstairs-downstairs space is comfortable with dark wood, handmade candlesticks, and ceiling-high windows for those who want to check who's walking by on the pedestrian zone outside or gaze upon illuminated Ayii Theodori church. Afterward, just step outside to enjoy a souvlaki from one of the several joints nearby—Greek youngsters have dubbed this evening duo "beat and eat."

Gregarious **Memphis** (✉ Ventiri 5, Ilisia, behind the Hilton, ☎ 01/722–4104) is an Athens classic, where the good-natured crowds listen to rock, including Gothic-theme nights and occasional live music.

All ages will feel comfortable at **Stavlos** (✉ Iraklidon 10, Thission, ☎ 01/345–2502 or 01/346–7206), in what used to be the Royal Stables. Sit in the courtyard or the brick-walled restaurant for a snack like Cretan *kaltsounia* (like a calzone) or dance in the long bar, which usually features rock and Brit or American pop. Stavlos often hosts art exhibits, film screenings, miniconcerts, and other "happenings," as the Greeks call them, on Sundays.

Managing to stay at the forefront of the club scene for several years now, **Zoo** (✉ Mihalakopoulou and Sevasteias, near the Holiday Inn, Ilisia, ☎ 01/778–6672) continues to be popular, especially among the media (the owner is a press photographer), for its free-style beats and zany decor, including gigantic posters, stucco butterflies swarming the ceiling, and plastic lemons.

Bouzoukia

Many tourists think Greek social life centers on large clubs where live bouzouki music is played and patrons get their kicks by smashing up the plates. This practice, called *spasta,* is now prohibited. Instead, plates of flowers are sold for scattering over the performer or your companions when they take to the dance floor. An upscale form of bouzoukia is found from the lower end of Syngrou all the way south to the airport, where top entertainers command top prices. Be aware that the food is overpriced and often second-rate. There is a per-person minimum (usually around 7,000 dr.) or a prix-fixe menu; a bottle of whiskey costs about 30,000 dr., a drink 4,000 dr.

Currently the "in" place with Athenians who want to hear Greece's most famous singers, such as Antonis Vardis and Kaiti Garbi, is **Diogenis Palace** (⊠ Syngrou 259 and Amfitheas, Nea Smyrni, ☏ 01/942–4267 and 01/941–7602), closed Mondays and Tuesdays. Decadence reigns at **Posidonio** (⊠ Poseidonos 18, Elliniko, ☏ 01/894–1033), where Greeks dance the seductive tsifteteli with enthusiasm and order flower vendors to shower gardenias on their favorite singers.

Dance Clubs

Dance clubs come and go every year, and most move around the town, especially in summer when they go seaside. Currently popular among young Athenians, who swarm the dance floors for everything from house to Greek pop tunes, are (more permanent winter addresses listed): **Plus Soda** (⊠ Ermou 161, Thission, ☏ 01/345–6187); **Tango** (⊠ Kifissias 7, Filothei, ☏ 01/685–0740); **Vareladiko** (⊠ Distomo and E. Zanni 1, Piraeus, ☏ 01/422–7500; and **Kingsize** (⊠ Amerikis 3, Syntagma, ☏ 01/364–2160).

The crowd at **Wild Rose** (⊠ Panepistimiou 10 in the arcade, Syntagma, ☏ 01/364–2160; in summer: Kiprou 64, Glyfada, ☏ 01/894–7085) is older, and studded with celebrities and Beautiful People, despite having been around for more than a decade. The music is eclectic (rock, soul, rave, and "future sound").

Jazz and Blues Clubs

The jazz scene has built up momentum in Greece, and several new venues opened in 1998. Tickets to shows can be purchased at the venues or major record stores.

The original and best jazz club in town, sophisticated **Half Note** (⊠ Trivonianou 17, Mets, ☏ 01/921–3310) is the place for serious jazz fans. It's a good idea to reserve a table, especially one near the stage, but latecomers can always stand at the bar in back. Cozy **Parafono** (⊠ Asklippiou 130a, Exarchia, ☏ 01/644–6512) leaves the big names to other clubs and instead taps into the homegrown jazz circuit. At lively **Hi-Hat Cafe** (⊠ Dragoumi 28, Hilton, ☏ 01/721–8171) even the blues are scorching, perhaps a vestige of the club's Latin days—often, several groups are invited to improvise together. The best seats are on the higher level in the back for a good view. Blues have found a home in the basement club **Blues Hall** (⊠ Ardittou 44, Mets, ☏ 01/924–7448), which has room for 400.

Live-Music Bars

Many venues close during August, if not for the entire summer. A small bar with few tables, **Cafe Asante** (⊠ Damareos 78, Pangrati, ☏ 01/726–0102) hosts ethnic music groups (Afro-Cuban, Indian, Peruvian); be sure to order potent *rakomelo* (raki with honey). Named after an important Maya city, with decor to match, **Palenque Club** (⊠ Farantaton 41, Goudi, ☏ 01/748–7548 or 01/771–8090) also features musicians from around the world (Peru, Brazil, even some Greek groups) several times a week. Rock fans should check the listings for **Rodon** (✉ Marni 24, Vathis Sq., ☎ 01/524–7427); blue jeans and anything black are the usual attire. For a less energetic evening, try **Baraki tou Vassili** (✉ Zoodohos Pigis 98, Exarchia, ☎ 01/381–5345), a tiny but congenial place where the owner books all kinds of groups, from flamenco guitarists to jazz trios.

Every July Athens hosts the three-day outdoor **Rockwave Festival,** a dense lineup including such big-name acts as Sonic Youth and Sisters of Mercy in the past. Tickets, which range from 6,000 to 8,000 dr., are cheaper if bought before the day of the show at major record stores.

Plaka Tavernas with Music

Klimataria (✉ Klepsidras 5, ☎ 01/324–1809 or 01/321–1215), a century-old taverna with music, is in an old house without a roof. It features a guitarist and an accordion player who play sing along favorites much appreciated by the largely Greek audience. This slice of old-style Greek entertainment is surprisingly reasonable.

Yeros tou Morea (✉ Mnisikleous 27, ☎ 01/322–1753), a vine-draped outdoor club that has stood for almost 150 years at the top of a steep pedestrian street, features pleasant popular Greek music (guitar, bouzouki, and accordion) and satisfactory food.

Stamatopoulou Palia Plakiotiki Taverna (✉ Lysiou 26, ☎ 01/322–8722 or 01/321–8549) is in a converted 1822 Plaka house. Here you'll find good food and an acoustic band of three guitars and bouzouki playing old Athenian songs. In summer the show moves to a cool garden. Greeks will often get up and dance, beckoning you to join them, so don't be shy.

Rembetika Clubs

The Greek equivalent of the urban blues, rembetika is rooted in the traditions of Asia Minor and was brought to Greece by refugees from Smyrna in the 1920s. It filtered up from the lowest economic levels to become one of the most enduring genres of Greek popular music, still enthralling club goers today. At these thriving clubs, you can catch a glimpse of Greek social life and even join the dances (but remember, it is considered extremely rude to interrupt a solo dance). Most of the clubs are closed in the summer, so call in advance. They have reasonable prices for an evening of live entertainment (drinks range from 1,500 dr. to 2,500 dr., a bottle of whiskey from 17,000 dr. to 23,000 dr.), but the food is often expensive and unexceptional; it's wisest to order a fruit platter or a bottle of wine.

Anifori (✉ Vasileos Georgiou A' 47, Pasalimani, Piraeus, ☎ 01/411–5819) is a friendly club popular with young people that plays both rembetika and *dimotika* (Greek folk music). It is closed Monday through Thursday.

An ambience underscored by old posters and photographs and a dedication to authenticity make **Stathmos** (✉ Mavromateon 22, opposite Pedion Arios park, ☎ 01/883–2393 or 01/822–0883) a good choice for newcomers to the music. Headliners have included rembetika greats like gravel-voiced bouzouki player Bobis Goles and the Athinaiki Compania. It's closed Mondays and Tuesdays.

10 Entoles (✉ Aharnon 257, Ayios Nikolaos, ☎ 01/832–5523), or "10 Commandments," is dark and smoky in the best rembetika tradition, featuring such classic second-generation singers as Dimitris Tsaousakis. The club is closed Tuesdays.

Usually crowded and pleasantly raucous **Boemissia** (✉ Solomou 19, Exarchia, ☎ 01/384–3836 or 01/330–0865) attracts many young people, who quickly start gyrating in various forms of the tsifteteli. Doors are shut on Mondays.

Stoa ton Athanaton (✉ Sofokleous 19, Central Market, ☎ 01/321–4362 or 01/321–0342), or Arcade of the Immortals, has been around since 1930 in a renovated warehouse in the meat market. Not much has changed since then. The music is enhanced by an infectious, devil-may-care mood and the enthusiastic participation of the audience, who come especially for the "best-of-rembetika" afternoons (3:30–7:30 PM). The small dance floor is jammed; the food is delicious and reasonably priced, but liquor is expensive. Reservations are essential for evenings, when the orchestra is led by old-time rembetes Theodoros Polykandriotis and Koulis Skarpelis, who is in his eighties. The club is closed Sundays.

The Arts

Athens Festival and Other Shows

The city's primary artistic event, the **Athens Festival,** in the Odeon of Herod Atticus from the end of May through September, has showcased performers such as Pavarotti and Diana Ross; such dance troupes as the Royal London Ballet and Maurice Béjart; symphony orchestras; and local groups performing ancient Greek drama. It is a delightful setting, with the floodlit Acropolis looming behind the audience and the Roman arches below making a stunning backdrop for the performers. The upper-level seats have no cushions, so come prepared with something to sit on, a light wrap, and low shoes, since the marble steps are steep. For most performances the Gamma zone is the best. Tickets sell out quickly for popular shows; they are available from the **Festival box office** (✉ In the arcade at Stadiou 4, ☎ 01/322–1459), open Monday–Friday 10–4:30, Saturday 10–2. Prices range from 4,000 dr. to as high as 20,000 dr. for the big names.

Other festival events are held at the more intimate **Lycabettus Theater** (✉ At the top of Mt. Lycabettus, ☎ 01/322–1459 Athens Festival; 01/722–7233 theater box office), set on a pinnacle of Mt. Lycabettus, with wooden bleachers and a glorious view. The specialty here is popular concerts, with such performers as B.B. King, Bob Dylan, Smashing Pumpkins, and Paco de Lucia. Since buses travel only as far as the bottom of the hill, and taxi drivers often won't drive to the top, buy a one-way ticket on the funicular and walk about 10 minutes to the theater.

Every evening from April through October, **Sound and Light Spectacles** casts dramatic lighting upon the Acropolis along with a brief recorded history. The English-language version is at 9 PM. Seating is on the **Pnyx hill** opposite the Acropolis, a great place to view the sunset before the show. Tickets are sold at the box office of the Pnyx (✉ West of the Acropolis, Dionyssiou Areopagitou, ☎ 01/922–6210) before shows; tickets cost 1,500 dr. and the box office opens at 8:20 PM.

The **Dora Stratou Troupe,** a young, spirited dance company, performs a fine selection of **Greek folk dances** from all regions, as well as from Cyprus, in eye-catching authentic costumes. Performances are held daily from mid-May through September at 10:15 PM; Wednesdays and Sundays there are additional shows at 8:15 PM at the **Dora Stratou Theater** (✉ Arakinthou and Voutie, near Filopappou, ☎ 01/324–4395 office, 01/921–4650 theater, FAX 01/324–6921). Tickets cost 3,000 dr. and can be purchased at the box office before the show.

Concerts and Operas

Concerts and operas are given September through June at the Megaron by world-class Greek and international artists. Information and tickets are available from the **Megaron Athens Concert Hall** (⊠ Vasilissis Sofias and Kokkali, ☎ 01/728–2333, FAX 01/728–2300), open Monday–Friday 10–4, next to the U.S. Embassy. Prices range from 2,500 dr. to 20,000 dr. Tickets go on sale a few weeks in advance but many events sell out within hours. On the first day of sales, tickets can be purchased by cash or credit card only in person at the Megaron. From the second day on, remaining tickets may be purchased by phone or in person from the **Megaron's downtown box office** (⊠ In the arcade at Stadiou 4).

Film

Films are shown in original-language versions with subtitles (except for major animated films), a definite boon for foreigners. Check the *Athens News* or *Kathemerini* in the *International Herald Tribune* for programs, schedules, and addresses and phone numbers of theaters (including the outdoor theaters, and the Hellenic-American Union and the British Council, both of which screen films free).

Best bets are the **downtown theaters,** which have the most advanced equipment and most comfortable seats (tickets are about 1,800 dr.). Near Syntagma, try **Apollon Renault** (⊠ Stadiou 19, ☎ 01/323–6811) or **Attikon Renault** (⊠ Stadiou 19, ☎ 01/322–8221); close to Omonia Square is **Ideal** (⊠ Panepistimiou 46, ☎ 01/362–6720), which has the plushest seats in Athens and Saturday after-midnight showings. The newly renovated, spacious **Danaos Telestet** (⊠ Kifissias 109, Ambelokipi, ☎ 01/692–2655) is a bit farther out but worth it for its comfortable seats and great sound system.

Unless theaters have air-conditioning, most close June–September, giving way to *therina* (outdoor cinemas), an enchanting, uniquely Greek entertainment that offers instant escapism under a starry sky. A feature of postwar Mediterranean countries that has survived only in Greece, open-air cinemas saw their popularity decline after the advent of television. Recently, there has been a resurgence in their appeal and about 75 now operate in the greater Athens area. They are usually set up in vine-covered empty lots and on rooftops with customers sitting on lawn chairs at small tables, where they enjoy snacks and drinks ordered from the bar. A disadvantage is the mandatory low sound level at the second screening, so audiences have to resort to lip reading, especially a drag at comedies, when the laughter drowns out the lines. Ticket prices range from 1,300 dr. to 1,800 dr. Some of the best theaters include the following: **Cine Paris** (⊠ Kidathineon 22, Plaka, ☎ 01/322–2071), convenient for most tourists since it sits on Plaka's main walkway; **Thissio** (⊠ Apostolou Pavlou 7, ☎ 01/342–0864 or 01/347–0980), where films compete with a view of the Acropolis, often dramatically lit during the sound- and-light shows; **Dexameni** (⊠ Dexameni Sq., Kolonaki, ☎ 01/721–5717), which screens only new films and also offers after-midnight showings; and **Cine Psirri Refresh** (⊠ Sarri 40–44, Psirri, ☎ 01/321–2476 or 01/324–7234), a new favorite in a lovely space, close to Psirri's mezedopolia but far away enough from apartment buildings so the sound isn't lowered during the second show.

Galleries

Galleries that hang some of the more interesting contemporary Athenian work include **Kappatos** (⊠ Ayia Irinis 6, Psirri, ☎ 01/321–7931); **Babel** (⊠ 1 Londou at Zoodohou Pigis, Exarchia, ☎ 01/382–5430); **Ileana Tounda** (⊠ Armatolon and Klefton 48, Ambelokipi, ☎ 01/643–9466); **Nees Morphes** (⊠ Valaoritou 9, Syntagma, ☎ 01/361–6165); **Rebecca Camkhi** (⊠ Sofokleous 23, Central Market area, ☎ 01/321–0448); and **Down Town People** (⊠ Ayion Anargiron 20–22, Psirri, ☎ 01/324–4717).

OUTDOOR ACTIVITIES AND SPORTS

Beaches and Beach Volleyball

Volleyball games open to the public begin in July at Palio Faliro, Skinies, and Palaia Fokaia beaches.

The beaches at **Palio Faliro** and **Piraeus** have signs warning you of the high levels of pollution. Believe them. The **Greek National Tourist Organization** (GNTO or EOT; ☞ Visitor Information *in* Athens A to Z, *below*) can give you a list of their beaches, which have snack bars and beach umbrellas, chairs, dressing rooms, and sports equipment for rent, and occasionally windsurfing and waterskiing lessons. Most are open from 8 AM to 8 PM in summer; tickets run about 600 dr., with reduced rates for children.

The main beaches close to Athens are found at the shoreline in the regions by the same name: **Alimos** (☎ 01/982–7064); **Porto Rafti** (☎ 0299/72–572); **Voula** (1st beach: ☎ 01/895–3296; 2nd beach: ☎ 01/895–9587); **Vouliagmeni** (☎ 01/896–0906); and **Varkiza** (☎ 01/897–2402). **Vouliagmeni Lake** (☎ 01/896–2237), whose spring-fed waters are reputed to have curative powers, is popular with older Greeks. The lake opens at 6:30 AM; tickets are 1,100 dr. A number of pleasant tavernas line the sandy shoreline.

Bird-Watching

The **Hellenic Ornithological Society** arranges two- and three-day trips to important bird habitats, like the Dounavi Delta, the Vikos Gorge, and the Messolonghi wetlands (Em. Benaki 53, Athens, ☎ 01/381–1271).

Golf

Glyfada Golf Course (✉ Glyfada, ☎ 01/894–6820) has 18 holes, locker rooms, a restaurant, and a bar, all open to the public.

Health Clubs

Health clubs abound these days, and you'll have little problem finding one near your hotel. The Athens Hilton, Holiday Inn, and Athenaeum Inter-Continental have excellent facilities with saunas and pools that can be used by the general public for a fee.

Hiking and Mountain Biking

The **Greek Federation of Mountaineering Associations** (✉ Milioni 5, Kolonaki, ☎ 01/364–5904) supplies details on mountain paths and refuges and has contact numbers for local hiking groups. One local hiking group to try is **Alpine Club of Aharnon** (✉ Filadelfias 126, Aharnes, ☎ 01/246–1528 or 01/246–6666), which runs the Flambouri refuge on nearby Parnitha (☎ 01/246–4666). The **Alpine Club of Athens** (✉ Kapnikareas Sq. 2, top floor, Monastiraki, ☎ 01/321–2355 or 01/321–2429) runs the Bafi refuge on Parnitha (☎ 01/246–9050) and arranges hikes throughout the month to places like Evritania and Arcadia, as well as adventure camps for children in summer.

Trips in and around Athens are often offered by specialist travel agencies. Try **Trekking Hellas** (✉ Fillelinon 7, 3rd floor, Syntagma, 10577, ☎ 01/331–0323 through 01/331–0326) for trips. **F-Zein** (✉ Syngrou 132, 5th floor, near Olympic Airways office, ☎ 01/921–6285) offers trips and also organizes kayaking, rafting, mountain biking, and camping expeditions for youngsters.

Sailing and Windsurfing

The **Hellenic Sailing Federation** (✉ Leoforos Posidonios, 51, Moschato, ☎ 01/930–4826 through 01/930–4828) can recommend clubs and places to windsurf, sail, and take lessons.

Many sailing clubs in the area give lessons and information. **Vouliagmenis Sailing Club** (✉ Laimos Vouliagmenis, ☎ 01/896–2142) sails out of Vouliagmenis Bay, 20 km (12½ mi) south out of Athens. **Piraeus Sailing Club** (✉ Mikrolimano, ☎ 01/417–7636) provides lessons. For children's sailing lessons only, contact **Alimos Sailing Club** (✉ Loutra Alimou, off Leoforos Poseidonos, ☎ 01/983–8358). Sailing and windsurfing lessons, plus equipment, are available at the **Varkiza Sailing Club** (✉ Leoforos Poseidonos in Vari Bay, ☎ 01/897–4305).

Those who have a diploma for sailing on the open sea can legally rent a sailboat (without a captain, if two people on board are licensed); rentals range from about 28,000 dr. to 200,000 dr. a day, depending on the size and age of the boat and whether a skipper is included. Contact **Ghiolman Yachts** (Fillelinon 7, Syntagma, ☎ 01/322–8530 or 01/323–0330), **Mediterranean Yachts** (Vas. Sofias 11, Syntagma, ☎ 01/362–0000), or **Vernicos Yachts** (Leoforos Poseidonos 11, Alimos, ☎ 01/985–0122 through 01/985–0128).

Scuba Diving

Scuba diving is heavily restricted, to protect underwater artifacts, although there are about seven designated diving areas near Athens and another 15 within a radius of 100 km (60 mi). It is forbidden to dive at night and to remove anything from the sea floor. A travel agent can direct you to a supervised diving trip or a less populated diving base, or you can call the **Greek Diving Center** (✉ Vasileos Pavlou 26, Kastella, ☎ 01/412–1708), which offers lessons up to the instructor's level, rents equipment, and organizes one- to two-day diving excursions on weekends. The **Aegean Dive Center** (Pandoras 42 and Zamanou 53, Glyfada, ☎ 01/894–5409) provides equipment rental and service, diver training including first-aid courses, dive trips, and an air center. For those who want an introduction to the sport, **Scuba Diving Club of Vouliagmeni** (✉ Leoforos Poseidonos below the Agnadia café-bar, Ormos Vouliagmeni, ☎ 01/896–4609) runs a one-hour orientation for about 15,000 dr. called Discover Scuba, where total beginners can dive with an instructor. The 20-year-old center, which is one of the few directly on the sea (visitors can just show up with a towel), also offers regular diving courses, equipment, boat rentals with guides for expeditions, and water sports. Call a day ahead for reservations. Remember that any school dispensing diplomas must be recognized by the Greek state.

Tennis

The **Hellenic Tennis Federation** (✉ Olympic Stadium offices, Kalogreza, ☎ 01/685–2511 or 01/685–2512) can give you information on the nearest tennis clubs that rent courts by the hour; several are near the EOT beaches.

SHOPPING

The main shopping districts are in the area bounded by Syntagma, Monastiraki, Omonia, and Kolonaki. For serious retail therapy, most natives head to the shopping streets that branch off central Syntagma and Kolonaki squares. Syntagma is the starting point for popular Ermou—now a pedestrian zone lined with hundreds of stores and adorned with the occasional street performer—which leads down to Monastiraki. Streets parallel/perpendicular to Ermou make up this shopping area: Mitropoleos, Voulis, Nikis, Perikleous, Praxitelous among them. Much ritzier is the Kolonaki quarter, with boutiques and designer shops on fashionable streets near the square like Anagnostopoulou, Tsakalof, Skoufa, Solonos, and

Kanari. One of the main hurdles is figuring out when shops in Athens are open—there always seems to be some bill in parliament to change the hours. In general, stores are open Mondays, Wednesdays, and Saturdays 9–3, Tuesdays, Thursdays, and Fridays 9–2 and 5:30–8. In summer they often stay open until 8:30 or 9.

The **souvenir shops** in Plaka are usually open from early morning until the last tourist leaves. **Periptera,** the Greek version of a convenience store, are set up by the government to provide employment for veterans. Many of them have public phones, some metered for long-distance calls. Those in central squares are often open until very late and occasionally are open around the clock.

The **flea market** centered on Pandrossou and Ifestou in Monastiraki operates on Sunday mornings and has practically everything, from secondhand guitars to Russian vodka (☞ Ancient Agora, Monastiraki, and Thission *in* Exploring Athens, *above*). **Ifestou,** where coppersmiths have their shops, is more interesting on a weekday—and you can pick up copper wine jugs, candlesticks, cookware, and more, for next to nothing.

Antiques and Icons

Antiques and older wares are in vogue now, so the prices of these items have naturally soared in price. Shops on Pandrossou sell small antiques and icons, but keep in mind that many of these are fakes, and you must have government permission to export genuine objects from the Greek, Roman, or Byzantine periods.

The **Benaki Museum gift shop** (✉ Koumbari and Vasilissis Sofias, Kolonaki, ☎ 01/362–7367) has excellent copies of Greek icons at fair prices.

Martinos (✉ Pandrossou 50, Monastiraki, ☎ 01/321–2414) should be the destination for serious antiques collectors, including such items as exquisite dowry chests, old swords, and Venetian glass.

Motakis (✉ Abyssinia Sq. 3, in the basement, Monastiraki, ☎ 01/321–9005), run by the same family for more than 90 years, is a *palaiopolio* (junk dealer), and it sells antiques, beautiful old objects, or that fabulous old trident you simply cannot live without.

At **Nasiotis** (✉ Ifestou 24, Monastiraki, ☎ 01/321–2369), with a little perseverance, you can make some interesting finds in this huge basement stacked with books: engravings, old magazines, first editions.

Clothing

Greece is known for its well-made shoes (most shops are clustered around the Ermou pedestrian zone and in Kolonaki), its furs (Mitropoleos near Syntagma), and its durable leather items (Pandrossou in Monastiraki). Fishermen's caps—always a good present—have now surfaced at high prices across the United States (triple the Athens price), as have the natural wool undershirts and hand-knit sweaters worn by fishermen; all can be found in many Plaka shops.

Stavros Melissinos (✉ Pandrossou 89, Monastiraki, ☎ 01/321–9247), a legendary poet and gentle soul, sends many tourists packing with his handmade sandals. The Beatles once visited his shop. He also makes handsome boots.

Voula Mitsakou (✉ Mitropoleos 7, Syntagma, ☎ 01/322–8561) is the best place to shop for furs near Syntagma. Despite the anti-fur campaign, Mitropoleos is lined with shops selling everything from pieced-together stoles to full-length minks, often from the northern city of Kastoria.

Coins and Stamps

Check out **Pylarinos** (✉ Stadiou 6, Syntagma, ☎ 01/321–0834) for unusual Greek coins and stamps as well as catalogs for collectors.

Gold Coin Jewelry (✉ Stadiou 17, Syntagma, ☎ 01/322–9004) is known for its decorative copies of ancient Greek coins.

Engravings, Prints and Postcards

At **Sillektiko** (✉ Ayion Anargiron 1, Iroon Sq., Psirri, ☎ 01/321–5029), a quaint photographic studio dominated by a pre–World War II antique camera, the owner, a former photo journalist, sells collectors' postcards, old photos and magazines, and a large selection of engravings and advertisements from the turn of the century.

Gifts

Athens has great gifts, particularly handmade crafts. Better tourist shops sell copies of traditional Greek jewelry, silver filigree, enamel, Skyrian pottery, onyx ashtrays and dishes, woven bags, attractive rugs (including flokati, or shaggy goat wool rugs, often brightly colored), and little blue-and-white pendants designed as amulets to ward off the *mati* (evil eye).

An inexpensive but unusual gift is a string of *koboloi* (worry beads) in plastic, wood, or stone. You can pick them up very cheaply in Monastiraki or look in antiques shops for more expensive versions, with amber or black onyx beads. Reasonably priced natural sponges from Kalymnos also make good presents. Look for those that are unbleached, since the lighter ones tend to fall apart quickly. They're usually sold in front of the National Bank on Syntagma and in Plaka souvenir shops. The price is set by the government, so don't bother to bargain.

Greeks can spend hours heatedly playing *tavli*, or backgammon. To take home a game set of your own, look closely for the hole-in-the-wall, no-name shop affectionately called **Baba** (✉ Ifestou 30, Monastiraki, ☎ 01/321–9994), which sells boards and pieces in all sizes and designs.

George Goutis (✉ Pandrossou 40, Monastiraki, ☎ 01/321–3212) is one of the more interesting stores on Pandrossou; it has an eclectic jumble of jewelry, costumes, embroidery, and old, handcrafted silver objects.

At **Riza** (✉ Voukourestiou 35 and Skoufa, Kolonaki, ☎ 01/361–1157) you can pick up wonderful lace in romantic designs, often handmade. The shop also carries fabric at good prices, and decorative items like handblown glass bowls and brass candlesticks.

Mati (✉ Voukourestiou 20, Syntagma, ☎ 01/362–6238) has finely designed amulets, for protection against the evil eye and an unusual collection of monastery lamps and candlesticks that make excellent gifts.

Karamichos Mazaraki (✉ Voulis 31–33, Syntagma, ☎ 01/323–9428 or 01/322–4932) offers a large selection of luxurious flokatis (rugs) in a variety of colors and will ship your purchases to your home so you don't have to carry them with you.

Karoukis (✉ Skoufa 25, Kolonaki, ☎ 01/361–1012) carries all kinds of miniatures, and if you browse long enough, the proprietor is likely to brew you a Greek coffee.

Centuries-old **Ilias Kokkonis** (✉ Stoa Arsakeiou 8, Omonia [enter from Panepistimiou or Stadiou St.], ☎ 01/322–1189 or 01/322–6355; ✉ Kifissias 264, Halandri, ☎ 01/689–1491 or 01/683–4708) most certainly stocks any flag you've hankered over—large or small, from any country.

Handicrafts

The **National Welfare Organization** (⊠ Vasilissis Sofias 135, ☏ 01/646–0603; ⊠ Ipatias 6 and Apollonos, Plaka, ☏ 01/321–8272), relying on craftspeople throughout Greece, carries fine examples of folk crafts: stunning handwoven carpets, flat-weave kilims, and tapestries from original designs, as well as hand-embroidered tablecloths and wall decorations. Napkins and place mats, ceramics, and embroidered pillowcases make handsome presents, and the shaggy woolen flokati rugs can be found here, too.

The **Center of Hellenic Tradition** (⊠ Entrance on Mitropoleos 59 or Pandrossou 36, Monastiraki, ☏ 01/321–3023; 01/321–3842 café) is an outlet for quality handicrafts—ceramics, weavings, sheep bells, and old paintings. Afterward, you can take a break from shopping in its wonderful Oraia Ellada café, in clear view of the Parthenon.

At **Amorgos** (⊠ Kodrou 3, Plaka, ☏ 01/324–3836) the owners make hand-carved and hand-painted wood furniture using motifs from regional Greek designs. They also sell needlework, hanging ceiling lamps, shadow puppets, and other decorative accessories, including lamps with shades fashioned from embroidered muslins, or even the client's own needlework.

EOMMEX (⊠ Mitropoleos 9, Syntagma, ☏ 01/323–0408), the Greek cooperative, operates a showroom with beautiful rugs made on wooden frames from more than 30 weavers around the country.

At the gracious **P. Serafetinidis** (⊠ Haritos 29, Kolonaki, ☏ 01/721–4186; ⊠ Parnassou 7, Karitsi Sq., ☏ 01/322–5207), enjoy the stunning colors and patterns of rare rugs and kilims from Persia, the Caucus, and Turkey.

Jewelry

Prices are much lower for gold and silver in Greece than in many Western countries, and jewelry is of high quality. Many shops in Plaka carry original pieces available at a good price if you bargain hard enough (a prerequisite).

For those with more expensive tastes, the Voukourestiou pedestrian mall off Syntagma Square has a number of the city's leading jewelry shops: **PentheRoudakiS** (⊠ No. 19 Voukourestiou, ☏ 01/361–3187) has classic designs. **Xanthopoulos** (⊠ No. 4 Voukourestiou, ☏ 01/322–6856) has traditional gold, silver, and jewels. The baubles at **J. Vourakis & Fils** (⊠ No. 8 Voukourestiou, ☏ 01/323–1258) will put a twinkle in your eye.

Some of the most original work in gold can be had at **Fanourakis** (⊠ Patriarchou Ioakeim 23, Kolonaki, ☏ 01/721–1762; ⊠ Evangelistrias 2, Center, ☏ 01/324–6642), where you'll find contemporary designs by Athenian artists.

LALAoUNIS (⊠ Panepistimiou 6, Syntagma, ☏ 01/362–4354 or 01/361–1371; ⊠ The Athens Tower, Sinopis 2, ☏ 01/770–0000; and ⊠ The Athens Hilton, Vasilissis Sofias 46, ☏ 01/725–0201), the world-famous Greek jeweler, is always experimenting with designs, taking ideas from nature, biology, and ancient Greek pieces.

Zolotas (⊠ Pandrossou 8, Plaka, ☏ 01/323–2413; ⊠ Stadiou 9, Syntagma, ☏ 01/322–1212), LALAoUNIS's main competitor, is noted for its superb museum copies.

Other finely rendered copies of classical jewelry are available at the **Benaki Museum gift shop** (⊠ Koumbari 1 and Vasilissis Sofias, Kolonaki, ☏ 01/362–7367). The **Goulandris Cycladic Museum** (⊠ Neofitou Douka 4, Kolonaki, ☎ 01/724–9706) sells exceptional modern versions of classic jewelry designs as well.

Local Delicacies

Try the central market on Athinas for tasty local foods to bring home: packaged dried figs, packaged pistachios, *pastelli* (sesame seed and honey candy), and olives other than those from Kalamata, which are widely available outside of Greece.

Brothers (Afoi.) Hatzigeorgiou (✉ Evripidou 37, Central Market area, ☎ 01/325–0434). This shop, founded in 1935, is an assault on the senses, with bags of Greek herbs and spices from around the world.

Bachar (✉ Evripidou 31, Central Market area, ☎ 01/321–7225), one of the many spice shops lining Evripidou, carries aromatic and pharmaceutical herbs.

At **Papalexandris** (✉ Sokratous 9, Central Market, ☎ 01/321–1461), the gentlemanly owner will walk you through the array of multihued olives, gathered from throughout Greece and sold by the kilo, along with grapevine leaves, pickled vegetables, and other deli items.

For an inexpensive but unique gift, pick up some freshly ground Greek coffee at **Miseyiannis** (✉ Levendio 7, Kolonaki, ☎ 01/721–0136).

ATHENS A TO Z

Arriving and Departing

By Bus

Travel by bus is inexpensive, usually comfortable, and relatively fast. The journey from Athens to Thessaloniki takes roughly the same time as the train, though the IC express covers the distance 1¼ hours faster. To reach the Peloponnese, however, buses are speedier than trains. Information and timetables are available at tourist information offices. Make reservations at least one day before your planned trip, earlier for holiday weekends.

Terminal A (✉ At Kifissou 100, ☎ 01/512–4910) is the arrival and departure point for bus lines that serve parts of northern Greece, including Thessaloniki, Epirus, and Macedonia, and the Peloponnese destinations of Epidaurus, Mycenae, and Corinth. Each has its own phone number; EOT offices distribute a list. **Terminal B** (☎ 01/831–7153), serving Evia, eastern, and central Greece, including Delphi, is behind Liossion 260, in a remote area northwest of Omonia Square near the Tris Yefiris (Three Bridges) district. Tickets for these buses are sold only at this terminal, so you should call to book seats well in advance during high season or holidays.

From Terminal A, take Bus 051 to Omonia Square; from Terminal B, take Bus 024 downtown. To get to the stations, catch Bus 051 at Zinonos and Menandrou off Omonia Square (for Terminal A) and Bus 024 on Amalias in front of the National Gardens (for Terminal B). International buses drop their passengers off on the street, usually in the Omonia or Syntagma Square areas or at the Peleponnisos train station.

By Car

The main highways going north and south link up in Athens and both are called *Ethniki Odos* (the National Road). At the city limits, signs in English clearly mark the way to both Syntagma Square and Omonia Square in the town center. Leaving Athens, routes to the National Road are well marked; signs usually name Lamia for points north and Corinth or Patras for points southwest. On the road map distributed

by the EOT (☞ *below*), the National Roads are yellow and are marked
by European road numbers, although these are not used on the roads
themselves. Beware: The highways are very slick when wet, and there
are many fatal accidents. Avoid driving in rain and on days preceding
or following major holidays; Greece's car-accident rate, one of the highest in the EU, escalates wildly during the mass migrations to and from
the city. The speed limit is 120 kph (74 mph) on the National Road
(though watch for temporary speed signs where the highway is under
repair), 90 kph (54 mph) outside urban areas. From Athens to Thessaloniki, the distance is 515 km (309 mi); to Kalamata, 257 km (154
mi); to Corinth, 84 km (50 mi); to Lamia, 214 km (128 mi); to Patras,
218 km (131 mi); to Igoumenitsa, 472 km (283 mi).

By Plane

Athens's **Ellinikon Airport** (✉ Vasileos Georgiou B', ☎ 01/936–3363
West Terminal; ☎ 01/969–4466 East Terminal) is between Alimos and
Glyfada on the southwest coast of Attica, about 10 km (6 mi) from
the city center. **Olympic Airways** (✉ Filellinon 15 near Syntagma and
Syngrou 96, ☎ 01/966–6666) has service between Athens and several
cities and islands. Reservations can be made by telephone daily from
7:20 AM to 9:30 PM. All domestic and international Olympic Airways
flights depart from the West Terminal (☎ 01/936–3363 through 01/
936–3366 for arrival and departure information). Other airlines use
the East Terminal (☎ 01/969–4466 or 01/969–4467). In summer
charter flights are available and leave from the charter terminal (☎ 01/
969–4686 through 01/969–4687 American based; 01/997–2686 and
01/997–2581 others).

For travel to and from the airport, yellow-and-blue double-decker express **buses** connect the two airport terminals, Syntagma Square, Omonia Square, and Piraeus. Between the terminals and Athens, express
bus 091 runs about every half hour around the clock. You can catch
the bus to the airport on Syntagma Square in front of McDonald's or
off Omonia Square on Stadiou and Aiolou. From the airport terminals to Karaiskaki Square in Piraeus, express bus 019 runs hourly day
and night. The night express buses for both lines leave at irregular intervals; ask for a schedule from an EOT office (☞ *below*). The fare is
200 dr., 400 dr. after midnight.

It's easier to take a **taxi** from the airport stands: about 2,000 dr. to Piraeus; 1000 dr. between terminals; 2,200 dr. to the center. The price
goes up by about two-thirds between midnight and 5 AM. If you want
to arrive at your hotel in style, **Yiannis Yiannakopoulos Limousines** (☎
094/316–798 mobile phone) will pick you up at the airport and drop
you at your hotel or vice versa, as will **Royal Prestige Limousine Service** (☎ 01/988–3221; 094/305–000 mobile phone, ☎ FAX 01/983–
0378) for about 14,000 dr. to 15,000 dr. one-way; call in advance.

By Ship

Cruise ships and ferries to and from the Aegean islands dock at **Piraeus**
(✉ Port Authority, Akti Miaouli, ☎ 01/422–6000 or 01/451–1311),
the main port, 10 km (6 mi) southwest of Athens. Ships for the Ionian
islands sail from ports nearer to them, such as **Patras** and **Igoumenitsa**.
Connections from Piraeus to the main island groups are good, connections from main islands to smaller ones within a group less so, and
services between islands of different groups or areas—such as Rhodes
and Crete—are less frequent. Travel agents (☞ *below*) and ship offices
in Athens and Piraeus have details. Timetables change very frequently,
and boats may be delayed by weather conditions, so your plans should
be flexible. Buy your tickets two or three days in advance, especially

if you are traveling in summer or taking a car. Reserve your return journey or continuation soon after you arrive.

From Piraeus, the quickest way to get into town center, if you are traveling light, is to walk to the metro station and take an electric train to Omonia Square, a trip of about 25 minutes (100 dr.). Those arriving by hydrofoil at the smaller **Zea Marina Harbor** should take Bus 905 or Trolley 20 to the metro station. Alternatively, you can take a taxi (if you find one), which may take longer owing to traffic and will cost around 1,700 dr. Often, drivers will wait until they fill their taxi with people debarking and headed in the same direction. It's faster to walk to the main street and hail a passing cab.

The other main port is **Rafina** (✉ Port, Port Authority, ☎ 0294/22300), on the eastern coast of Attica, where boats to and from Evia and some of the closer Cyclades dock. Orange KTEL buses (☎ 01/821–0872) make the trip to Athens every half hour from 5:40 AM to 9:30 PM; they leave from the station slightly up the hill from the port and the fare is 460 dr. The trip takes about one hour.

By Train

Greek trains have a well-earned reputation for being slow and for having a limited network. The main line runs north from Athens, dividing into three lines at Thessaloniki. The main line continues on to Belgrade, a second line goes east to the Turkish border and Istanbul, and a third line heads northeast to Bulgaria. The Peloponnese in the south is served by a narrow-gauge line dividing at Corinth into the Mycenae–Argos route and Patras–Olympia–Kalamata.

The **Greek Railway Organization (OSE)** has two stations in Athens, side by side: Trains from the north and international trains arrive at, and depart from, **Stathmos Larissis** (✉ Between Diliyianni and Leoforos Konstantinoupoleos, ☎ 01/823–7741). Take Trolley 1 from the terminal to Omonia Square; trains from the Peloponnese use the quaint **Stathmos Peloponnisou** (✉ Between Diliyianni and Leoforos Konstantinoupoleos, ☎ 01/513–1601) next door. The café continues the station's striking art-nouveau motif, from its burgundy ceiling with ornate moldings and antique crystal–teardrop chandelier to its original bronze gas lamps. Both stations have left-luggage service and snack bar. Since the phones at the stations are inevitably busy and the clerks harried, it's best to call the general information switchboard for timetables and prices (✉ ☎ 01/529–7777); it's open daily 7 AM–9 PM.

OSE buses (☎ 01/513–5768 or 01/513–5769) for Albania, Bulgaria, and Turkey also leave from Stathmos Peloponnisou station. To Omonia and Syntagma squares, take Bus 057.

The **IC express service** from the north is fast and reliable (Thessaloniki–Athens takes six hours). Express service has also begun on the Athens–Patras line (about four hours). On any train, it is best to travel first class, with a reserved seat, as the difference between the first-class and tourist coaches can be vast: Without a seat reservation you could end up standing or crouched among the baggage.

For those already in the center who want to buy tickets ahead of time, it's easier to visit a railway office downtown (✉ Karolou 1, near Omonia Sq., ☎ 01/522–4302 for Peloponnese destinations; ☎ 01/52–4291 for northern Greece; ✉ Filellinon 17, near Syntagma Sq., ☎ 01/323–6747 or 01/323–6273). You may also call ☎ 145 for a recorded departure timetable, in Greek, of trains within Greece; call ☎ 147 for information on trains to Europe and Russia.

Getting Around

Many of the sights you'll want to see, and most of the hotels, cafés, and restaurants, are within a fairly small central area. It's easy to walk everywhere.

The price of public transportation has risen steeply in the last couple of years, but it is still less than that in Western European capitals. Riding during rush hours is definitely not recommended. Upon boarding, validate your ticket in the orange canceling machines at the front and back of buses and trolleys and in the stations of the electric trains. Keep your tickets until you reach your destination, as inspectors occasionally pop up to check that they have been canceled and validated. They are strict about fining offenders, including tourists.

The **Organization for Urban Public Transportation** (⊠ Metsovou 15, ☎ 185 or 01/883–6076), open Monday to Friday 7:30–3, is one block north of the National Archaeological Museum, answers questions about routes (usually only in Greek), and distributes maps with street names in Greek. The EOT (☞ *below*) also distributes information about bus lines.

By Bus and Trolley

Main bus stations are at Akadimias and Sina and at Kaningos Square. Bus and trolley tickets cost 100 dr. No transfers are issued; you validate a new ticket every time you change vehicles. Monthly passes are available for 6,000 dr. Tickets are sold in special booths at bus terminals and at selected *periptera* (street kiosks). Buses run from the center to all suburbs and suburban beaches from 5 AM to midnight, and major routes have infrequent owl service. For suburbs farther north than central Kifissia, you have to change at Kifissia.

KTEL orange buses provide efficient bus service throughout the Attica basin. Most buses to the east Attica coast—including those for **Sounion** (☎ 01/823–0179), fare 1,150 dr. for inland route or 1,200 dr. for coastal road, and **Marathon** (☎ 01/821–0872), fare 700 dr.— leave from the **KTEL terminal** (⊠ Platia Aigyptou at corner of Mavromateon and Leoforos Alexandras).

By Car

Driving in Athens is not recommended unless you have nerves of steel. Red traffic lights are frequently ignored, and it is not unusual to see motorists passing other vehicles on hills and while rounding corners. Driving is on the right, and although the vehicle on the right has the right-of-way, don't expect this or any other driving rule to be obeyed. The speed limit is 50 kph (31 mph) in town. Seat belts are compulsory, as are helmets for motorcyclists, though many natives ignore the laws. In downtown Athens do not drive in the bus lanes marked by a yellow divider.

Unless you are a citizen of an EU country, you must have an international driver's license. The **Automobile and Touring Club of Greece** (ELPA; ⊠ Athens Tower, Messoghion 2–4, 11525, ☎ 01/748–8800, 104 in an emergency, FAX 01/778–6642) no longer issues these, so non-EU members should arrange for a license through their local automobile association. ELPA can help with tourist information for drivers (☎ 174), and they assist tourists with breakdowns free of charge if they belong to AAA or to ELPA; otherwise, there is a charge.

Downtown **parking spaces** are hard to find—you can pay to use one of the few temporary parking areas set up in vacant lots, but you're better off leaving your car in the hotel garage and walking or taking a cab. Gas pumps and service stations are everywhere, and lead-free gas is widely available. Be aware that all-night stations are few and far between.

By Subway

The one partially underground electric train line stretches from Piraeus to Kifissia, northeast of the city's center, with 20 stops in between, including Thission, Monastiraki, Omonia Square, and Platia Victorias (the stop for the National Archaeological Museum). It was constructed in 1868, one of the earliest in Europe, and electrified in 1904. Currently, it is being extended, a project that has been delayed for years but now should be completed by the year 2000. It is limited but functions well and is very safe, even late at night. The trains run 5 AM–midnight and the fare is 100 dr. or 150 dr. depending on the distance. There are no special fares or day tickets for visitors, but a monthly pass that covers bus, trolley, and subway is available for 8,000 dr. Validate your ticket by stamping it in the orange machines at the entrance to the platforms.

By Taxi

Taxi rates are still affordable compared to fares in other European capitals. It seems paradoxical that more than 17,000 taxis are on the streets of Athens, yet during peak hours it's impossible to find an empty one. Taxis with passengers operate unofficially on the jitney system, indicating willingness to pick up others by blinking their headlights or simply slowing down. Would-be passengers shout their destination as the driver cruises past.

Radio taxis can be booked by your hotel (a good idea when taking an early morning flight) with a surcharge of 400 dr. for immediate response and 500–1,000 dr. for an appointment to come later. Some radio-taxi companies are **Athina 1** (☎ 01/921–7942 or 01/922–1755); **Ellas** (☎ 01/645–7000 or 01/801–4000 through 01/801–4004); **Ermis** (☎ 01/411–5200 or 01/411–5660); **Evropi** (☎ 01/502–3783 or 01/502–3583); **Ikaros** (☎ 01/525–2800); **Kosmos** (☎ 01/1300); and **Parthenon** (☎ 01/581–1809, 01/581–4711, and 01/582–1292).

Most taxi drivers are honest and hardworking, but a few con artists infiltrate the ranks at the airports and near popular restaurants and clubs frequented by foreigners. Get an idea from your hotel how much the fare should be, and if there's trouble, ask to go to a police station, although most disagreements don't ever get that far. Make sure the driver turns on the meter and that the rate listed in the lower corner is 1, the normal rate before midnight. Don't be alarmed if your driver picks up other passengers (although protocol indicates he should ask your permission first). Each passenger pays full fare for the distance he or she has traveled.

The fare begins at 200 dr., and even if you join other passengers, you must add this charge to the final amount: Note the fare on the meter when you get in an occupied taxi. The rate is 66 dr. per 1 km (½ mi), 130 dr. between midnight and 5 AM and outside city limits. Surcharges are made for holidays (120 dr.); fares from, not to, the airport (300 dr.); fares from ports, railway stations, and bus terminals (150 dr.); and for each bag weighing more than 10 kilograms (55 dr.). Waiting time is 2,200 dr. per hour.

Taxi drivers know the major central hotels, but if your hotel is less well known, show the driver the address written in Greek and make note of the phone number and if possible a nearby landmark. If all else fails, the driver can call from a periptera. Athens has thousands of short side streets, and few taxi drivers have maps. If your driver gets lost despite all precautions, use the time to practice answering personal questions graciously.

Contacts and Resources

Doctors and Dentists

Most hotels will call a **doctor** for you. You can also call your embassy. For a doctor on call 2 PM–7 AM on Sundays and holidays, call ☎ 105 (in Greek). For a **dentist,** check with your hotel, embassy, or the tourist police.

Embassies

United States (✉ Vasilissis Sofias 91, ☎ 01/721–2951); **Canada** (✉ Gennadiou 4, ☎ 01/727–3400); **United Kingdom** (✉ Ploutarchou 1, ☎ 01/723–6211).

Emergencies and Hospitals

For auto accidents call the **city police** (☎ 100). **Tourist police** (✉ Dimitrakopoulou 77, Koukaki, ☎ 171). **Fire** (☎ 199). **Ambulance** (☎ 166), though a taxi is often faster.

Not all hospitals are open nightly. Call ☎ 106 (in Greek); check the *Athens News* or the *Kathemerini* insert in the *International Herald Tribune*; or ask your hotel to check the Greek papers to find out which emergency hospitals are open.

Asklepion Hospital (✉ Vasileos Pavlou 1, Voula, ☎ 01/895–8301 through 01/895–8306); **KAT Hospital** (✉ Nikis 2, Kifissia, ☎ 01/801–4411; 01/801–4731 for accidents); **Ygeia** (✉ Er. Stavrou 4 and Kifissias, Maroussi, ☎ 01/682–7940). One maternity hospital is **Mitera** (✉ Er. Stavrou 6 and Kifissias, Maroussi, ☎ 01/682–0110). Children go to **Aglaia Kyriakou Hospital** (✉ Levadias 3 and Thivon, Goudi, ☎ 01/777–5610 or 01/778–3212) or **Ayia Sofia Hospital** (✉ Mikras Asias and Thivon, Goudi, ☎ 01/777–1811) Note that children's hospitals answer the phone with "Pedon" and not the specific name of the institution.

English-Language Bookstores and Libraries

The **Booknest** (✉ Folia Tou Bibliou, Panepistimiou 25–29, near Syntagma, ☎ 01/322–9560) has an ample selection of American authors. **Compendium** (✉ Nikis 28 upstairs, near Syntagma, ☎ 01/322–1248) has travel books, books on Greece, one of Athens's few women's-studies sections, and used books. Go to **Eleftheroudakis** (✉ Nikis 4, Syntagma Sq., ☎ 01/322–9388) for fiction, language guides, and coffee-table editions and its newer six-floor store with a great café that provides reading material and serves fresh salads, pastas, and luscious desserts (✉ Panepistimiou 17, ☎ 01/331–4180). There's also **Kauffman** (✉ Stadiou 28, Center, ☎ 01/322–2160), for a limited selection of American fiction. Try **Pantelides** (✉ Amerikis 9-11, Syntagma Sq., ☎ 01/362–3673). Worth a visit is **Reymondos** (✉ Voukourestiou 18, Center, ☎ 01/364–8188).

At the **Hellenic-American Union** (✉ Massalias 22, Exarchia) is the **American Library** (☎ 01/363–8114), although this was still closed for remodeling at press time. The **Greek Library** (☎ 01/362–9886) has a section of books in English on Greek topics. Also try the **British Council Library** (✉ Kolonaki Sq. 17, ☎ 01/364–5768). The **Gennadius Library, American School of Classical Studies** (✉ Soudias 61, Kolonaki, ☎ 01/721–0536) is also interesting, though it is not a lending library. Call first; many libraries close for several weeks in summer.

Guided Tours

EXCURSIONS

Most agencies offer excursions at about the same prices, but **CHAT** (☞ *below*) is reputed to have the best service and guides. Taking a half-day trip to the breathtaking Temple of Poseidon at Sounion avoids the hassle of dealing with the crowded public buses or paying a great deal more for a taxi. The 7,100 dr. cost is well spent. A one-day tour to Delphi with lunch costs 19,500 dr. (17,000 dr. without lunch), but the two-day tour (29,500 dr.) is far preferable. There's also a one-day tour to Nauplion, Mycenae, and Epidauros (19,500 dr. with lunch), and a two-day tour to Mycenae, Nauplion, and Epidaurus (30,400 dr. including half-board). A three-day tour takes in both Delphi and the stunning monasteries of Meteora with half-board in first-class hotels (73,000 dr.). For those who have more time, the four-day tour covers Nauplion, Mycenae, Epidauros, Olympia, and Delphi for 97,000 dr. A full-day cruise from Piraeus, visiting three nearby islands—Aegina, Poros, and Hydra—costs around 18,000 dr. (including buffet lunch on the ship).Athens travel agencies can also arrange a six-day **northern Greece** tour including Delphi, Meteora, and Thessaloniki for 191,500 dr.

ORIENTATION TOURS
Many travel agencies offer four-hour morning bus tours (9,300 dr.), including a guided tour of the Acropolis. Reservations can be made through most hotels or you can contact one of the major travel agencies (☞ *below*).

PERSONAL GUIDES
Major travel agencies can provide English-speaking guides. The **Union of Guides** (✉ Apollonas 9A, ☎ 01/322–9705, FAX 01/323–9200) provides licensed guides for individual or group tours, starting at about 25,000 dr. including taxes for a four-hour tour of the Acropolis and its museum. It is advisable to arrange for a guide through a reliable agency; only hire one licensed by the EOT, which means they have successfully completed a two-year state program.

SPECIAL-INTEREST TOURS
Athens by Night tours, offered by all agencies, are a convenient way to see some of the touristy evening entertainment, especially for single travelers who may not want to venture out alone. For those interested in **folk dancing,** there is a four-hour evening tour (9,000 dr.) from April to October, which includes the Sound and Light Spectacle and a performance of Dora Stratou folk dances. Another evening tour follows the Sound and Light Spectacle with a **dinner show at a Plaka taverna** (12,500 dr.). Any travel agency can arrange these tours, but go first to CHAT Tours (☞ *below*) for reliable and efficient service.

The **Amphitrion Holidays** agency (☞ *below*) specializes in educational and offbeat tours for individuals in Athens and elsewhere, including island-hopping tours and treks in the Pindos mountains.

Cruises to the four most popular islands—Mykonos, Rhodes, Crete, and Santorini—usually operate from April through October. Try **Golden Sun Cruises** (✉ Akti Miaouli 71, Piraeus, ☎ 01/428–7894, FAX 01/428–7898) and **Royal Olympic Cruises** (✉ Akti Miaouli 87, Piraeus, ☎ 01/429–0700 for reservations, FAX 01/429–0638). Most also have downtown Athens representatives.

For hiking tours, the **Greek Federation of Mountaineering Associations** (✉ Milioni 5, Kolonaki, ☎ 01/364–5904) supplies details on mountain paths, refuges, and contact numbers for local clubs.

For horseback riding tours, the helpful **Hellenic Equestrian Federation** (✉ Messinias 55, Goudi, ☎ 01/652–8139) provides a list of Athens's riding clubs.

Late-Night Pharmacies
Call ☎ 107 for a Greek-language recording of pharmacies open on holidays and late at night or check the *Athens News*. Each pharmacy posts

in its window a list of establishments close by that are open during the afternoon break or late at night. A conveniently located pharmacy where English is spoken is **Mantika** (⊠ Stadiou 41, between Syntagma and Omonia Sqs., ☎ 01/331–2060 or 01/331–2062). **Thomas** (⊠ Papadiamantopoulou 6, near the Hilton Hotel and Holiday Inn, Ilissia, ☎ 01/721–6101) is another safe bet for convenience and spoken English.

Travel Agencies

American Express (⊠ Ermou 2, ☎ 01/324–4975, FAX 01/322–7893); **Amphitrion Holidays** (⊠ Syngrou 7, ☎ 01/924–9701, FAX 01/924–9671; ⊠ Deuteras Merachias 3, Piraeus, ☎ 01/411–2045 through 01/411–2049, FAX 01/417–0742); **CHAT Tours** (⊠ Stadiou 4, ☎ 01/322–2886, FAX 01/323–5270); **Key Tours** (⊠ Kallirois 4, ☎ 01/923–3166, FAX 01/923–2008); **Magic Travel Service (Magic Bus)** (⊠ Filellinon 20, ☎ 01/323–7471, FAX 01/322–0219); and **Travel Plan** (⊠ Christou Lada 9, ☎ 01/323–8801 through 01/323–8804, and 01/324–0224/5, FAX 01/322–2152). Near Omonia, try **Condor Travel** (⊠ Stadiou 43, ☎ 01/321–2453 or 01/321–6986, FAX 321–4296) and **Pharos Travel and Tourism** (⊠ 18 Triti Septemvriou, ☎ 01/523–3403 or 01/523–6142, FAX 01/523–6261). In New York **Pharos Travel and Tourism** (⊠ 230 W. 31st St., ☎ 212/736–6070, FAX 212/736–3921) can help you put together an independent tour at competitive prices.

Visitor Information

Greek National Tourist Organization (EOT) offices (⊠ Amerikis 2, near Syntagma Sq., ☎ 01/331–0561 through 01/331–0562; ⊠ East Terminal of Ellinikon Airport, ☎ 01/961–2722 or 01/969–4500; ⊠ EOT Building, 1st floor, near where the hydrofoils dock, Zea Marina, ☎ 01/452–2591).

The **tourist police** (⊠ Dimitrakopoulou 77, ☎ 171) can answer questions in English about transportation, steer you to an open pharmacy or doctor, and locate phone numbers of hotels and restaurants.

3 Excursions from Athens

Attica, the Saronic Gulf Islands, and Delphi

The crumbling 19th-century merchants' mansions of Aegina and Hydra, the white and periwinkle homes in the labyrinthine streets of Poros, and the ghosts of Spetsiot pirates will steal you away to the Saronic Gulf Islands. Or maybe the fame of Marathon, or the rich iconography of Daphni monastery will inspire an excursion over the forbidding mountains guarding the passes into Athens. All who land in Athens are destined sooner or later to make a pilgrimage to Delphi, where the priestesses of antiquity uttered their enigmatic prophecies.

By Catherine
Vanderpool

Updated by
Toula
Bogdanos

IF ANYTHING WAS EVER TRULY "CLASSICAL," it is the landscape of Attica. Atikí is a mountainous country, bounded
on three sides by sea and an indented coastline fringed
with innumerable beaches. On the stony foothills the soil is so poor
that only a few pungently aromatic shrubs grow: thyme, myrtle, and
lentisk. Higher up, the feathery pine of Attica is supplanted by dark
fir trees. But in the Mesogeion, or "inland," are gently undulating hills
and fields laced with vineyards and dotted with olive trees, and the source
of the sweet-smelling thyme, food for the bees whose hives in blue boxes
were once a familiar sight along any country road. Here, too, are the
quarries of Mt. Penteli, from which there has never ceased to be ex-
tracted a special quality of marble that weathers to a warm golden tint.
Over all hangs the purest of lights, sharply delineating the exquisite
configuration of mountains, sea, and plain that is Attica.

It is the proper setting for a region immensely rich in mythological and
historical allusions. In fact, recorded history began here, in the towns
of the Boetian plain, although where legend leaves off and fact begins
is often a matter of conjecture (witness Thebes, home to the luckless
Oedipus). However, historians can be sure that since the first millennium BC, the story of Attica has been almost inextricably bound to that
of Athens, the most powerful of the villages that lay scattered over the
peninsula. By force and persuasion Athens brought these towns together,
creating a unit that by the 5th century BC had become the center of an
empire. The heart of the region was the sacred precinct of Delphi. For
the ancient Greeks, this site was the center of the universe, home to
Apollo and the most sacred oracle, and today it remains a principal
place of pilgrimage for visitors to Greece.

Northeast of Pendeli, between the slopes and the sea, lies the fabled
plain of Marathon, its flat expanse now dotted with small agricultural
communities and seaside resorts, second home to many Athenians. Attica includes such sites as the Temple of Poseidon, spectacularly perched
on Cape Sounion, and, up the coast and around the northern flank of
Pendeli, the enchantingly rural archaeological site at the Amphiareion.
It takes in the Fortress of Phyle, on the slopes of Parnitha; the Sanctuary of Demeter and Kore at Eleusis; and the Monastery of Daphni.

Set in a sun-ridden sea, the Saronic Gulf Islands straddle the gulf between Athens and the Peloponnese. Aegina, Poros, Hydra, and Spetses are especially popular with Athenians, owing to their proximity and,
especially in the case of the latter two, their natural beauty. Aegina,
the closest Saronic island to Piraeus, in ancient times was renowned
for its bronze work and eventually succumbed to the power of Athens
and two millenniums later played a pivotal role in the War of Independence. Tiny Poros, almost grazing the shores of the Peloponnese,
was once the site of an important Temple of Poseidon, now dilapidated.
Extant proof of Hydra's and Spetses's prosperity in the 18th and 19th
centuries are the stately, forbidding mansions built by the fleet-own-
ing shipping magnates; they are now the stomping grounds of wealthy
European vacationers. All in all, many of the region's sights enjoy sin-
gularly memorable settings and make for enchanting destinations.

Pleasures and Pastimes

Dining
The cuisine of Attica resembles that of Athens, central Greece, and the
Peloponnese. Local ingredients predominate, with fresh fish perhaps the
greatest (and most expensive) delicacy. Since much of Attica's vegetation

used to support herds of grazing sheep and the omnivorous goat, the meat of both animals is also a staple in many country tavernas. Although it is becoming increasingly difficult to find the traditional Greek taverna with large stewpots full of the day's hot meal, or big *tapsi* (pans) of *pastitsio* (layers of pasta, meat, and cheese laced with cinnamon) or *papoutsakia* (eggplant slices filled with minced meat), market towns and villages in Attica still harbor the occasional rustic haunt, offering tasty, inexpensive meals. Always ask to see the *kouzina* (kitchen) to look at the day's offerings, or even peer inside the pots. Regional cuisine in Delphi and Arachova relies heavily on meats, including game, while on the Saronic islands and in the coastal town of Galaxidi, fresh fish and seafood courses dominate. Informal dress is appropriate at all but the very fanciest of restaurants, and unless noted, reservations are not necessary.

CATEGORY	COST*
$$$$	over 13,000 dr.
$$$	9,000 dr.–13,000 dr.
$$	4,500 dr.–9,000 dr.
$	under 4,500 dr.

for three-course meal, including VAT and service charge but excluding drinks and tip

Lodging

Many of the hotels in Attica are resorts catering to package tourists or to Athenian families who move to the coast for the summer. In the last two decades, many have been built of reinforced concrete slabs, with spindly metal balconies and diverse facilities, but the decor, which varies little from one to the next, tends to be a modern "Greek island" look: simple pine furnishings, tile floors, and, at most, a colorful bedspread. Be forewarned: Some of the large hotels ask you to take half-board, particularly in high season. If you know your plans ahead of time, you should book through a travel agent, who can negotiate a good price and eliminate the half-board requirement, if you wish. Delphi and Arachova, which have had recent minibooms in hotel construction, have a number of appealing small establishments, with fresh, cheerful rooms and public spaces, but elsewhere, these picturesque, cozy, family-owned country inns and pensions are rare. Note also that many hotels close in late fall and reopen usually around Easter week, except in Delphi and Arachova, where high season (with top prices) is during ski season, though even then weekdays are about half the price of weekends. Accommodations on the islands range from elegant 19th-century mansions, usually labeled as traditional settlements, to spare rental rooms overlooking a noisy waterfront. In the listings, all $$$ and $$$$ hotels have air-conditioning unless otherwise noted.

CATEGORY	COST*
$$$$	over 55,000 dr.
$$$	30,000 dr.–55,000 dr.
$$	17,000 dr.–30,000 dr.
$	under 17,000 dr.

All prices are the official rate for a standard double room, including taxes but excluding breakfast unless so noted, during the summer high season (Arachova and Delphi's high season is winter).

Nightlife

Perhaps it is the daytime heat through so many months of the year; perhaps it is an excess of energy; perhaps it is their intense sociability, unrequited during the workday; but whatever the reason, Greeks love going out at night. Traffic can be as bad at 3 AM as in the morning rush hour. Some nightspots emphasize the show over the cuisine, others do the opposite, and they range from the simplest taverna with a bouzouki trio to fancy nightclubs where Greek youths party beachside until dawn.

For dancing, the discos at most large resort hotels are usually open to outsiders as well as guests, but more popular are the Athens dancing clubs that move to rented space on the coastal road, especially south of the capital from Glyfada to Vouliagmeni, and at eastern beach towns like Porto Rafti and Nea Makri. Clubs and addresses change annually, so ask around or, if you can read Greek, check the weekly entertainment guide *Athinorama,* available at kiosks. Of the islands, Hydra and Spetses offer the most sophisticated bars and discos.

Exploring Attica, the Saronic Gulf Islands, and Delphi

Athens lies in a basin defined by three mountain masses: Mt. Hymettos to the east, Mt. Aigaleos and Mt. Parnis (called Parnitha in Greek) to the west, and Mt. Pendeli to the north. We set out from this region and first head south along the coast down to Cape Sounion and the breathtaking Temple of Poseidon, then back up along the water to storied Marathon and the sylvan glades of Amphiareion. As you travel back to Athens, the tour takes in the great Byzantine monastery of Daphni and the famous sanctuary of Demeter. The second tour explores the lovely Saronic Gulf Islands, beloved by Athenians for their pleasure and proximity. The third tour is a pilgrimage to Delphi, seat of the most important oracle in ancient Greece and of the then known world; it enjoys a classical setting out of a picture.

Numbers in the text correspond to numbers in the margin and on the Attica and the Saronic Gulf Islands and Delphi maps.

Great Itineraries

If you only have a few days to explore the areas around Athens, you'll probably want to stick to the most important site, which is Delphi. In a five- or six-day itinerary you'll be able to see Delphi, some of the major sites around Athens such as Daphni and Sounion, and maybe an island (Aegina is the closest). A 9- or 10-day trip will enable you to see all of the above, a few more sites in Attica, and the farther Saronic Gulf Islands, such as Hydra and Spetses.

IF YOU HAVE 3 DAYS

A three-day trip means concentrating on the essentials so you get the most out of your time. Exploring ⚑ **Delphi** ㉒–㉕ requires at least one full day, so be sure to go early in the morning (it's a three-hour drive or bus ride) or even the night before. A second day could be spent visiting the principal sites of Attica, starting with ⚑ **Sounion** ④, up to ⚑ **Marathon** ⑧, and **Amphiareion** ⑪. A third day offers the chance to visit ⚑ **Aegina** ⑮–⑯, the Saronic Gulf Island closest to Athens.

IF YOU HAVE 6 DAYS

Attica makes the most reasonable start of a six-day tour; begin by going to Poseidon's temple at ⚑ **Sounion** ④, followed by a foray north to **Brauron** ⑦, ⚑ **Marathon** ⑧, and either **Rhamnous** ⑨ or the **Amphiareion** ⑪. A morning seeing the Sanctuary of Demeter at ancient **Eleusis** ⑭ is best succeeded by an afternoon at the Byzantine **Monastery of Daphni** ⑬. Spend your third and fourth days in and around ⚑ **Delphi** ㉒–㉕, where nearby **Osios Loukas** ⑳, with its early Byzantine monastic complex, and ⚑ **Arachova** ㉑, with its sophisticated cafés and bars, offer pleasant digressions from the ancient sites. Finally, a couple of days among the Saronic Gulf Islands will round out your trip. Two days could pass very quickly on ⚑ **Aegina** ⑮–⑯, but you could also see the principal sites (the **Sanctuary of Aphaia** ⑯ being the foremost) in one day, and spend a second on ⚑ **Hydra** ⑱, an island whose shops, nightlife, and pace appeal to an international clientele.

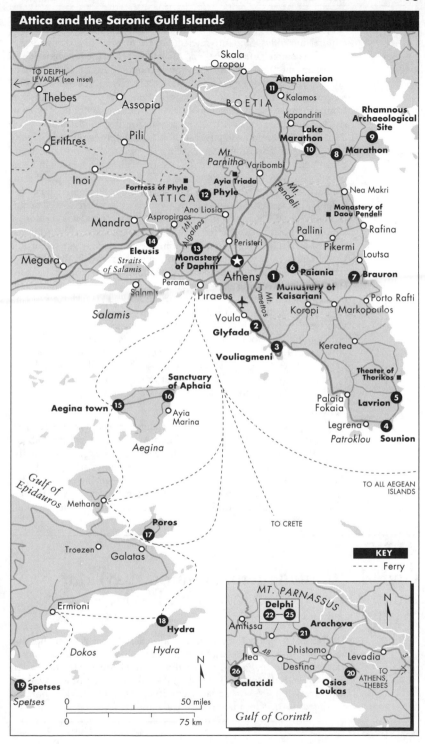

Attica and the Saronic Gulf Islands

TO DELPHI,
LEVADIA (see inset)

Thebes

Assopia

Erithres

Pili

Inoi

Skala
Oropou

BOETIA

Amphiareion
11
Kalamos

Kapandriti

**Lake
Marathon**
10

**Rhamnous
Archaeological
Site**
9

8 **Marathon**

Mandra

Mt.
Parnitha

Varibombi

Fortress of Phyle
Ayia Triada
ATTICA
12 **Phyle**

Ano Liosia

Aspropirgos

Nea Makri

**Monastery of
Daou Pendeli**

Megara

Eleusis
14

13
**Monastery
of Daphni**

Peristeri

Pallini

Rafina

Pikermi

Loutsa

Salnmis

Perama

Athens
1

6 **Paiania**

7 **Brauron**

Straits
of Salamis

Piraeus

**Monastery of
Kaisariani**

Koropi

Porto Rafti

Markopoulos

Salamis

Voula

2
Glyfada

3

Vouliagmeni

Keratea

**Sanctuary
of Aphaia**
16

15
Aegina town

Ayia
Marina

Aegina

Palaia
Fokaia

**Theater of
Thorikos**

Lavrion
5

4 **Sounion**

Legrena

Patroklou

Gulf of
Epidauros

Methana

TO ALL AEGEAN
ISLANDS

TO CRETE

Poros
17

Troezen

Galatas

KEY
----- Ferry

Ermioni

18
Hydra

Dokos

Hydra

19 **Spetses**

Spetses

0   50 miles

0   75 km

MT. PARNASSUS

Delphi
22 — 25

Amfissa

Arachova
21

Itea
48

Dhistomo

Levadia

Desfina

TO
ATHENS,
THEBES

26
Galaxidi

20
**Osios
Loukas**

Gulf of Corinth

A thorough exploration of Attica, the Saronic Gulf Islands, and Delphi requires nine days. Step into ancient Greece on your first day with visits to ☷ **Sounion** ④, **Brauron** ⑦, ☷ **Marathon** ⑧ and the **Amphiareion** ⑪ or perhaps the ancient fortress of **Phyle** ⑫ on Mt. Parnitha. On day two, take a break from ancient Greece and visit the Byzantine **Monastery of Kaisariani** ①, and the Vorres museum at **Paiania** ⑥. Next day, go west from Athens to the **Monastery of Daphni** ⑬ and ancient and vast **Eleusis** ⑭. After three days of Attica start your journey to ☷ **Delphi** ㉒–㉕, deep in the mountains northwest of Attica. **Delphi** is one of Greece's most impressive sites, with an excellent museum, a world-famous archaeological site, and stunning scenery; the region can be seen in a day or two. The nearby mountain village of ☷ **Arachova** ㉑ and the charming harbor town of ☷ **Galaxidi** ㉖ make fabulous alternative bases for **Delphi,** especially for those eager for a taste of modern as well as ancient Greece. While in the vicinity don't forget to visit **Osios Loukas** ⑳, a monastery with priceless frescoes, nestled in a secret valley. Your last three or four days will find you relishing the surprisingly varied Saronic Gulf Islands, each with its own flavor, but all sharing in the common credo that the leisurely life is better than the fast lane. Your island tour can begin at ☷ **Aegina** ⑮–⑯, where you can snack on the island's famous pistachios and visit the **Sanctuary of Aphaia** ⑯. A day on Aegina can only be outdone by a day on ☷ **Hydra** ⑱, to which the European jet set escapes when struck by an urge to lounge in beautiful mansion-hotels and putter about the island's shops, cafés, and nightclubs. Once you've wandered around the car-free streets of Hydra you may not want to go anywhere else, but ☷ **Spetses** ⑲ also doesn't allow cars (motorcycles are permitted), and it has about an equal number of sites scattered along its extensive shoreline and pine-forested hills.

When to Tour

As with elsewhere in Greece, services in these areas are greatly reduced during the winter, except in Delphi and Arachova, which are refuges for skiers who flock to Mt. Parnassus. The islands explode into activity during July and August, so be prepared to go head to head with the crowds and the heat; a better time to visit is May or September through October. In spring an extraordinary variety of wild flowers carpet the arid hillsides of Attica and the Marathonian plain and hills leading to Ramnous.

ATTICA

Glyfada, Vouliagmeni, Sounion, Lavrion, Paiania, Brauron, Marathon, Phyle, Daphni, Eleusis

The bulk of Attica, which stretches southeast into the Aegean, lies east and north of Athens. Separated from Central Greece by mountains—Pateras, Kithairon, Pastra, and Parnitha—and bordered by the sea, Attica was easily defensible. It also had several fertile plains, well watered with rivers and seasonal streams, and its coves and natural harbors encouraged the development of seafaring and trade.

Kaisariani

6 km (4 mi) east of Athens center.

The neighborhood of Kaisariani lies on the slopes of Hymettos, the eastern "wall" of Athens, which yields the sun each morning and catches its last purple shadows at night. Denuded of its pine forests in the destructive years during World War II, the mountain has since been partially reforested.

A glen of pine, cypress, and plane trees fed by a copious flow of water cradles the **Monastery of Kaisariani.** A temple of Aphrodite stood on the hill just above the present-day monastery, which dates to the 11th century. The buildings surround a central court, including, besides the church, a refectory, cells, and a bathhouse, all restored in 1956–57. Most of the frescoes are from the 17th and 18th centuries; the oldest, in the side chapel of St. Anthony, is a Virgin Mary at prayer shown in the style of the 14th century. The now destroyed Aphrodite temple was the backdrop for the jealous lovers in Ovid's *Ars Amatoria* (*Art of Love*). A spring feeds the fountain to the left of the monastery's entrance; the ram's head, whose original is in the Archaeological Museum, was part of a Roman sarcophagus. For a spectacular view of Athens, including the Acropolis and the ships in Piraeus harbor, walk 10 minutes on the dirt path beginning from the monastery gate to a clearing with a picnic bench. ⊠ *Mountain road starting at Ethnikis Antistaseos, 6 km (4 mi) east of Athens center,* ☎ *01/723–6619.* ☞ *800 dr.* ☉ *Tues.–Sun. 8:30–2:45; grounds daily sunrise–sunset.*

The **Moni Asteriou** (⊠ 9 km/5½ mi up the hill from Kaisariani Monastery) also dates to the 11th century. A nearby path descends 1½ km (about 1 mi) to the chapel of **Ayios Ioannis Theologou** above the suburb of Goudi. On this pleasant detour, you will enjoy another view of Athens and a closer look at—and scent of—the tiny aromatic shrubs (sage, mostly) that once lured the bees of Mt. Hymettos, giving that special flavor to its famous honey.

Festivals

From June through July and again in September, the **Krystalleia Festival** offers outdoor evening concerts of pop and classical music in the Megaron Plakentias, the former Rododafni Palace that served as the Duchess de Plaisance's home in Pendeli (⊠ 16 km/10 mi northeast of Athens on Mount Pendeli, near the Athenian suburb of Ayia Paraskevi). It was built for this eccentric lady in 19th-century neo-Gothic style by the architect Stamatis Kleanthis, who also designed the Villa Ilissia, now Athens's Byzantine Museum, for her. The concurrent **Pendelis Festival** (end of July and September) focuses on classical music, often importing international orchestras to take advantage of the Megaron's excellent acoustics. For information on the festivals, contact the Greek National Tourist Organization (GNTO or EOT) in Athens or the Megaron (☎ 01/804–2575). Tickets run from 2,000 dr. to 4,000 dr. and are usually sold at major record stores in downtown Athens.

Glyfada

❷ *17 km (10½ mi) southeast of Athens, 21 km (13 mi) south of Kaisariani.*

This prosperous seaside resort town is best used as a base from which to explore Attica. Glyfada has a few beautiful villas, a fine golf course, several large marinas, and the dubious distinction of offering the highest concentration of shopping centers found in Greece. Its proximity to the airport should please those with early morning flights but distress all others.

Beaches

Attica's southwestern coast is mainly rock, with some short sandy stretches in **Glyfada** and **Voula,** which have been made into public pay beaches by EOT, with snack bars, changing rooms, beach umbrellas, rental water-sports equipment, and sometimes windsurfing and waterskiing lessons. Most are open from 8 AM to 8 PM in summer, unless there is a heat wave, when the government has kept them open to the public, free, until midnight. Tickets run about 600 drs., with reduced rates for children. In recent years, western Attica's beaches have become cleaner, though those on the east side are preferable in this respect. The pay beaches close to Glyfada are those at **Alimos** (☎ 01/982–7064) and **Voula** (☎ 01/895–3296 1st beach; 01/895–9587 2nd beach), which all received Blue Flags for cleanliness from the EU despite their proximity to Athens.

Dining and Lodging

$$$ ✕ **Sphinx.** Successful in Santorini, the owners opened this second Sphinx in 1998 to good reviews—and who can resist dining in this luscious garden or the cozy dining room, complete with glass roof, listening to light jazz. The house features Continental cuisine with an emphatic Italian influence, as you can see in the long list of pastas, including pesto Genovese, spaghetti with lobster, and black fettuccine with cuttlefish. A house specialty is the sliced veal fillet with foie gras and a sauce made from Santorini Vizanto; diners can also choose from a selection of fresh fish and daily specials. Hats off to the chef for the sweets—the restaurant's strong suit—particularly the chocolate soufflé. ⊠ *Kyprou 65A behind the Glyfada public pool,* ☎ *01/894–0050 or 01/898–1295. Reservations essential. AE, DC, MC, V. Closed Sun. and 2 wks. in Aug. No lunch.*

$$ ✕ **Loxandra.** Known for home-style Greek cuisine, Loxandra also provides bouzouki-guitar accompaniment with your meal winter weekends, October through Easter. Enjoy *magirefta* (stove-top or oven-cooked dishes, usually made earlier) in winter such as *yiouvetsi Loxandra* (pork with miniature macaroni), and in summer the many grilled meats *tis oras*, like beef stuffed with graviera cheese and served with mushroom sauce. No matter the season, order the well-made appetizers such as *bourekakia* (cheese fingers in flaky pastry) and the zucchini pie. Sweets lovers will get their fix from *karidopita*, a syrupy walnut cake. ⊠ *Eleftherios Venizelou 15 (near golf course),* ☎ *01/963–1731. DC, V. Closed Mon. and Aug. No lunch July–mid-Sept.*

$$ ✕ **Palai Pote.** This mezedopolio evokes bygone years with its old-fashioned courtyard and rembetika companies, who usually play evenings October through April. Try the *yiaourtada*, lamb baked in the oven with yogurt and grapes; fat sardines wrapped in vine leaves and cooked with onion; and the shrimp lavished with poppy and sesame seeds. Other popular dishes include the spicy lobster claws, and mussels with a fragrant sauce of orange and saffron; a few fresh pastas are also on the menu. ⊠ *Gr. Lambraki 75,* ☎ *01/963–2739. Reservations essential Fri.–Sat. V. Closed Mon. No lunch except Sun. Oct.–Apr. (with music).*

$$$ 🏨 **Hotel Best Western Fenix.** For a good price at the low end of its category, this hotel offers comfortable rooms, modern facilities, and proximity to the airport and the Glyfada golf course. Renovated in 1995, all rooms have new furniture and redone bathrooms, satellite TV with a pay-movie system, and direct-dial phones. In summer, guests can lounge at the poolside bar. Double-glazed windows help reduce the noise (and block stray golf balls?). Continental breakfast is included in the price. ⊠ *Artemisiou 1, 16675; mailing address:* ⊠ *Box 70183, Glyfada 16610;* ☎ *01/898–1255,* FAX *01/894–9122. 133 rooms, 3 suites. Restaurant, pool. AE, DC, MC, V.*

$$ 🏨 **Palace Hotel.** Rooms, baths, and public spaces at the Palace are attractively contemporary, with new tables and chairs, as well as air-conditioning. Room service operates until midnight, the bar is open 24 hours, and the reception staff is friendly and accommodating. Buffet breakfast is included in the price. Just 20 minutes from the center and off on the side of the airport (away from the runways so it doesn't get much airplane noise), this is a good choice for those who want a first-class city hotel out of the city. ⊠ *Vasileos Georgiou B 4, 16675,* ☎ *01/894– 8361, 01/894–6068, or 01/898–0847,* FAX *01/894–9061. 75 rooms. Restaurant, bar, air-conditioning, pool. AE, DC, MC, V.*

Festival

Glyfada hosts a **summer concert festival** featuring ethnic and Greek music at the carved marble open-air theater Aixoni (⊠ Hydras 11, Glyfada) in July. Tickets are available from the box office (☎ 01/898– 2506) or the Glyfada town hall (⊠ Saki Karagiorga 2, Glyfada, ☎ 01/ 898–2182) and cost 3,000 dr.–5,000 dr.

Nightlife

CLUBS

Some popular Athens clubs move from downtown to Glyfada for the summer. For example, in 1998 the popular rock-oriented club **Camel** operated near the golf course, **Savvia** opened at Asteria beach, **Tango** moved to EOT Voula's second beach, and the super disco **Plus Soda** relocated to where the Nea Deilina bouzoukia operate in winter. It's best to ask your hotel for the latest information concerning the hottest spots, locations, and telephone numbers, many of which change season to season.

Outdoor Activities and Sports

GOLF

The **Glyfada Golf Course** (⊠ End of Pronois, at the southeast side of Athens International Airport, ☎ 01/894–6820, FAX 01/894–3721) has on its roster many distinguished politicians, businessmen, and members of the diplomatic community. Visitors need to make reservations for the weekends by Wednesday. The greens are open Tuesdays through Sundays from 7:30 AM to sunset and on Mondays 1 PM (noon in winter) until sunset.

SAILING

Many yacht brokers charter boats and organize underwater "safaris," scuba tours, and "flotilla" cruises in small, rented sailboats around the islands. **Viking Star Cruises** (⊠ Artemidos 1, Glyfada 16674, ☎ 01/898– 0829 or 01/894–9279, FAX 01/894–0952) arranges weeklong cruises from April through October, leaving every Friday for Mykonos, Santorini, Delos, Paros, Naxos, Ios, and Tinos on a 14-cabin yacht. Tourists who have a diploma for the open sea can legally rent a sailboat (without a captain if two people on board are licensed); rentals range from about 28,000 dr. to 200,000 dr. a day, depending on the size and age of the boat and whether a skipper is included. Located in a nearby seaside suburb is **Vernicos Yachts** (⊠ Leoforos Poseidonos 11, Alimos, Athens 17455, ☎ 01/985–0122 through 01/985–0128, FAX 01/985–0130).

Vouliagmeni

❸ *25 km (15½ mi) south of Athens, 8 km (5 mi) southwest of Glyfada.*

Vouliagmeni had little to distinguish itself in the past except being home to many American families when the United States maintained a major base at the airfield; it is now an expensive seaside residential suburb for Athenians, coveted for its large yacht harbor. Its most scenic corner is a green promontory called Laimos (Neck) Vouliagmenis, including an area called Kavouri with several seaside fish tavernas. Much like Glyfada, today it serves the tourist as a base from which to explore Attica.

Beaches

Cleaner than the pay beaches farther north are the EOT-run **beaches** in this area, including **Vouliagmeni** (☎ 01/896–0906) and **Varkiza** (☎ 01/897–2402), which are always popular. They're open 8 AM to 8 PM; tickets are 600 dr., with lower rates for youngsters. Varkiza's bay is popular with windsurfers. The more upscale **Asteras Beach** (☎ 01/890–1774) on the promontory belongs to the Astir Palace Vouliagmenis hotel but is open to the public for a hefty fee (2,000 dr. weekdays, 2,500 dr. weekends), which means its green lawns and sandy stretch are usually less crowded. **Vouliagmeni Lake** (☎ 01/896–2237), whose spring-fed waters are reputed to have curative powers, is popular with older Greeks; the lake opens at 6:30 AM, and tickets are 1,100 dr.

En Route Beyond Vouliagmeni the road threads along a rocky coastline dotted with inlets, where intrepid bathers swim off the rocks, after leaving their cars in the roadside parking areas and scrambling down to the inviting coves below. If you join them, take along your snorkels, fins, and masks so you can enjoy the underwater scenery, but avoid the sea urchins clustered on rocks. The coastal road south of Vouliagmeni is one of the most heavily developed seacoasts in Greece; only the many tavernas, especially in Palaia Fokaia, proclaiming *psaria freska* (fresh fish) remind us of the former fishing villages here. Two of them are reviewed here.

Dining and Lodging

$$–$$$ ✕ **Apaggio.** A top spot in the countryside outside Vouliagmeni (☞ En Route, *above*), this is run by the owner of the well-known Apaggio in Athens. Newly opened, this multilevel seafood restaurant (it holds 500) offers the same high quality and traditional Greek recipes, now with a view of the Saronic Gulf. The menu is always changing, but if you're lucky you can find among the seafood and magirefta dishes like *sinagrida* (dentex) made Rhodes-style (with white sauce and mushrooms); codfish croquettes from Andros; a saganaki crammed with mussels, shrimp, and crayfish; or a fried mix of squid, mussels, and other shellfish. More than 70 Greek labels are featured on the wine list, and you can stop here just for an ouzo, a cocktail, or a coffee, from noon until late at night. ✉ *On coastal road to Sounion, about 17 km (10½ mi) after Vouliagmeni, at 41-km (25½-mi) mark, Lagonissi,* ☎ *0291/26441 and 0291/26261. AE, DC, V. Closed weekdays Oct.–Apr.*

$$ ✕ **I Remvi.** The last of the fish tavernas lining the coastal road in Palaia Fokaia (☞ En Route, *above*), this is the smallest, the cheapest, and the most romantic. "Remvi" means daydreaming, easy to do as you contemplate the small beach and the Mediterranean beyond while waiting for your fish soup, made with the freshest bream, sweet onions, carrots, and potatoes (it takes a little time, but it's worth it). The superfresh fish, even the red mullet, runs about 1,000 dr. a kilo less than at the other tavernas, but you can also order seafood appetizers like crab salad and fried squid (throughout Greece fresh only in spring, otherwise fresh frozen), grilled bread called *lagana* brushed with olive oil and oregano, and potent retsina from the barrel (about 1,000 dr. for a kilo). ✉ *On coastal road 16 km (10 mi) before Sounion, Palaia Fokaia,* ☎ *0291/36236. No credit cards.*

$$ ✕ **Panorama.** For the best food in Vouliagmeni, head to the seaside
★ stretch called Kavouri. Panorama is almost impossible to get into for Sunday lunch because of the crowds of Athenians who come to feast on the large selection of fish and relax on the cool seaside terrace. Besides the fresh catch, especially good are the squid and the *garides yinouvetsi* (shrimp baked in a red sauce with tiny noodles). You can also stuff yourself on a sampling of appetizers, like seafood salad and *mides gemistes,* mussels stuffed with rice. ✉ *Iliou 4, Kavouri,* ☎ *01/895–1298 or 01/965–8401. Reservations essential. V.*

$$$$ 🏨 **Astir Palace Vouliagmeni.** Sprawling across a pine-studded promontory, this 80-acre resort is actually made up of three hotels. All have been freshly decorated in the last few years. The compound is often used for international summits, because of its secluded and prestigious location, and amenities include a private beach, sports, lovely landscaping, and sea views. A shuttle transports guests to downtown Athens in the mornings. Buffet breakfast is included in the price. ⊠ *Apollonos 40, 16671,* ☎ *01/890–2000, 212/682–9191 in the U.S.;* 𝔽𝔸𝕏 *01/896–2582, 212/682–9254 in the U.S. 456 rooms, 73 bungalows, 30 suites. 5 restaurants, 4 pools, beach. AE, DC, MC, V.*

$$$ 🏨 **Armonia.** Just 300 ft from the sea, the Armonia hotel (part of a complex that includes the smaller Paradise hotel) has impeccable rooms, decorated with wood furniture and light brown appointments, all with private terraces, and one-third with sea views. If the sea is unswimmable during your stay, the pool offers an alternative, one that features a snack bar with refreshments and a section for children. Continental breakfast is included in the price. ⊠ *Armonias 1, 16671,* ☎ *01/896–0030, 01/896–0105, 01/896–2656, or 01/896–3184,* 𝔽𝔸𝕏 *01/896–3698. 104 rooms, 25 suites. Restaurant, pool. AE, DC, MC, V.*

Sounion

④ *70 km (43½ mi) southeast of Athens, 50 km (31 mi) southeast of Vouliagmeni.*

Here at the southernmost tip of Attica, the ancients chose to honor the
★ god of the sea by building their enormous **Temple of Poseidon.** No wonder: The site is magnificent—a rugged cliff rises 195 ft high, overlooking an expanse of azure water at the entrance to the Saronic Gulf. The panorama of sea and islands from this airy platform is, particularly at sunset, one of the most spectacular in Attica. The view from the cliff was matched emotion for emotion in antiquity by the sight of the mighty temple from the sea, which brought joy to sailors, knowing upon spotting the massive beacon that they were close to home. Today, Athenians returning from a sea journey exhibit the same gratitude, rushing to the side of the ferry to point out Sounion to their children. Lord Byron once carved his name on one of the 12 remaining Doric columns of the temple, and today, the site is one of the most photographed in Greece. Beyond a seaport with a well-protected harbor, a beach, a hotel, and a few tavernas accommodate visitors and those paying homage to the gods.

Beyond the scanty remains of an ancient *propylon* (gateway) you enter the temple compound. On your left are the remains of the **Temenos** (precinct) **of Poseidon,** on your right a **stoa** and **rooms.** The temple itself (now off-limits to tourists) may have been designed just after the middle of the 5th century BC by the same architect who built the Temple of Hephaistos in the ancient Agora of Athens: The people here were considered Athenian citizens, the sanctuary was Athenian, and Poseidon occupied a position second only to Athena herself. Situated on the highest point of the acropolis, the temple was built on the site of an earlier cult to Poseidon, and two colossal statues of youths, perhaps votives to the god, carved well over a century before the temple's construction, were discovered in early excavations (both are now in the National Archaeological Museum in Athens). The remaining columns, some of which have recently been re-erected, now stand sentinel over the Aegean, visible from miles away. The view from the summit is breathtaking. In the slanting light of the late afternoon sun, the land masses to the west stand out in sharp profile: the bulk of Aegina backed by the mountains of the Peloponnese. To the east, on a clear day, one can spot the Cycladic islands of Kea, Kythnos, and Serifos. On the land side, the slopes of the acropolis retain traces of the fortification walls. ⊠ *From promontory, pass through gate and climb rocky path that follows, roughly, the ancient approach,* ☎ *0292/39363.* ☞ *800 dr.* ⊙ *Daily 10 AM–sunset.*

Beach

If you spend the morning at Sounion and have lunch on the beach below, you may also want to take a swim, although the sandy strip becomes uncomfortably crowded in summer. On your approach to the temple (4 km/2½ mi north of Sounion) there is a decent beach at Legrena, and sometimes a small boat ferries across to the uninhabited isle of Patroklou—look for the sign shortly before the turnoff for Haraka (6 km/4 mi north of Sounion).

Dining and Lodging

$$ ✕ **Akroyiali.** Run by the Trikaliotis family, including Barba (Uncle) Giorgos—well past 80 and keeping an eagle eye on proceedings—this place is full on weekends, when locals stop in for the fresh sargus, saddled bream, pandora, and red mullet, caught by fishing caïques in Lavrion. There are just a few appetizers—taramosalata, tzatziki, octopus, shrimp salad—and a small selection of wine. ⊠ *On beach below Temple of Poseidon,* ☎ *0292/39107. No credit cards. Closed weekdays Oct.– Apr. No dinner weekends in Oct.–Apr.*

$–$$ ✕ **Assimakis.** On the road between Sounion and Lavrion, just a few yards from the sea, this simple restaurant will keep everyone happy with its large selection of reasonably priced fish—pandora, sole, red mullet, white and common bream—and its magirefta, including beef in red sauce, pastitsio, and moussaka. You can also order grilled chops, souvlaki, and chicken. The large, flower-filled veranda has a soothing view overlooking the coast, and for those too weary to continue, the Assimakis family, who live here, also rent a few rooms. ⊠ *4 km (2½ mi) from Sounion at 60-km (37-mi) mark on Sounion-Lavrion coastal road,* ☎ *0292/39442 or 0291/39270. No credit cards.*

$$$ 🏠 **Cape Sounion Beach.** The rooms at this self-contained complex of little bungalows are tasteful, with solid furniture, refrigerator, fan, and attractive Greek-island colors. All have balconies and many have a view over the garden and southeast toward the Temple of Poseidon. The hotel's cove-embraced beach would be idyllic without the din of the nearby road. The obligatory half-board includes American breakfast and à la carte lunch or buffet dinner; nevertheless, room rates remain at the low end of its price category. ⊠ *Poseidonios at 67-km (37-mi) mark, Plakes, 19500,* ☎ *0292/39391 or 0292/39821; winter, in Athens 01/861–7837;* FAX *0292/39038; winter, in Athens 01/861–6473. 188 bungalows. 2 restaurants, 3 bars, pool, 5 tennis courts, exercise room, dance club, beach. AE, DC, MC, V. Closed Nov.–Mar.*

$$ 🏠 **Aegeon Hotel.** This hotel has seen better days but is starting to renovate on a piecemeal, basis and nothing can beat its location—much objected to by environmentalists and archaeologists—on *the* beach below the Temple of Poseidon, at the very harbor where ancient ships once navigated. Even the rooms in back (all have balconies), which look up the slopes flanking the acropolis, have a good view. Rooms now have TVs, and those on the second and third floors enjoy air-conditioning. The restaurant, from where you can enjoy the sunset, serves Continental and Greek cuisine and fresh fish. Be warned: The beach will be crowded in high season, and the heating system may or may not be effective in the winter. ⊠ *Sounion Beach, 19500,* ☎ *0292/39200,* ☎ FAX *0292/39234. 44 rooms, 1 suite. Restaurant, air-conditioning, beach. MC, V.*

Lavrion

❺ *80 km (50 mi) southeast of Athens, 10 km (6 mi) north of Sounion.*

After Sounion roads enter a dreary stretch of country—curiously metallic in color and completely un-Attic in contour and quality. There are reason for this, as Lavrion, a postindustrial town with a few remnants of Belle Epoque architecture, was celebrated in antiquity for its silver mines. Several thousand ancient shafts have been discovered in the area, and without the riches they yielded, Themistocles could not have built the fleet that saved Greece from the Persians, nor Pericles the monuments on the Acropolis. There is a one-room **mineralogical museum,** housed in the remains of an 1875 building, displaying an eclectic collection of jewel-color minerals from the surrounding hillsides, as well as mining tools used by the slaves. ⊠ *Leoforos Kordela next to the school (Lykeiou), Lavrion,* ☎ *0292/26270.* 🎫 *500 dr.* ☉ *Wed. and weekends 10–noon.*

Lodging

$ 🏨 **Belle Epoque Hotel.** Not even the inhabitants of Lavrion know about this small, quite inexpensive in-town hotel set in a renovated Belle Epoque house, a welcome alternative to the area's high-priced resorts. The outside is much more inviting than the inside, whose cell-like rooms are now air-conditioned, but the public areas have been lovingly decorated with the owners' collections of minerals, shells, and bric-a-brac. The hotel includes a small cafeteria serving refreshments, and the owner can whip up breakfast for those too lazy to try their luck on the waterfront. ⊠ *Pleion 23, 19500,* ☎ *0292/27130 or 0291/26564,* FAX *0292/26059. 20 rooms. Cafeteria, air-conditioning. No credit cards.*

En Route The road winds inland, through bare hilly country spoiled by cement-box dwellings, running past **Keratea** and **Markopoulos,** a market center of the Mesogeion, known for its wine and good-quality bread. Continuing through stands of olive trees and vineyards, the road now runs almost due west, with Mt. Hymettos hovering straight ahead.

Paiania

❻ *18 km (11 mi) east of Athens, 34 km (21 mi) northwest of Lavrion.*

Paiania was the birthplace of the famous orator Demosthenes, and although there's not much to see of the ancient town now, most people come to visit the unique **Vorres Museum,** which displays folk art and an intriguing collection of contemporary Greek works in buildings restored in traditional style. Ion Vorres owns, operates, and even lives in the museum. He has salvaged many treasures and incorporated them beautifully—a stack of millstones transformed into sculptures when embedded in a wall; polished marble well-heads emerging from a flower bed; oak tables fashioned from monastery doors; commemorative plates bestowed by returning sea captains on their loved ones; paintings of historic moments like the opening of the Corinth canal. The modern gallery and sculpture courtyard are dedicated to postwar art, including work by Moralis, Tsarouchis, Ghika, Pavlos, and Vassiliou. When he's not busy in his museum, Mr. Vorres wears the hat of mayor. Those without cars can take Bus A5 from Akadimias in Athens; in Ayia Paraskevi transfer to Bus 308 or 310 and get off in Paiania's main square. The museum is about 328 ft farther. ⊠ *Diadochou Konstantinou 1,* ☎ *01/664–2520 or 01/664–4771.* 🎫 *600 dr.* ☉ *Sept.–July, weekends 10–2.*

☾ The **Koutouki cave,** discovered in 1926 by a shepherd who had lost his goat, is just the right depth and darkness to awe young children into silence without frightening them. High on the eastern slopes of Hymettos, connected to Paiania village by a good paved road, the cave has been rigged with paths, lights, and sound to highlight the stalagmites and stalactites—one is named "Statue of Liberty"—the cavernous vaults and narrow corridors, and rainbow-color walls formed at the rate of half an inch a year. There are regularly scheduled 20-minute tours; guides can speak English. ✉ *Above village of Paiania on road to cemetery,* ☎ *01/664–2108.* 🎫 *1,500 dr.* ☉ *Daily 9–4.*

Brauron

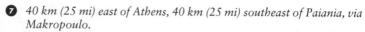

❼ *40 km (25 mi) east of Athens, 40 km (25 mi) southeast of Paiania, via Makropoulo.*

Brauron, where the **Sanctuary of Artemis** rises on the site of an earlier shrine, lies in a waterlogged depression at the foot of a small hill. Found here are a **5th-century** BC **temple** and a horseshoe-shape **stoa**. Here, the virgin huntress was worshiped as the protector of childbirth. Every four years, the Athenians celebrated the Brauronia, an event in which girls between ages 5 and 10 took part in arcane ceremonies, including a dance in which they were dressed as bears. The **museum** next to the site contains statues of these little girls, as well as many votive offerings. The carless should take Bus A5 from Akadimias to its terminus in Ayia Paraskevi, switch to Bus 304, 305, or 316, and ride to the end; the site is 1 km (½ mi) from there. ✉ *At foot of hill near fork in road to northern Loutsa,* ☎ *0299/27020.* 🎫 *500 dr.* ☉ *Museum and site Tues.–Sun. 8–2:30 (in winter, museum Tues.–Fri. 8:30–3, site Thurs.–Sun. 8:30–3).*

Beach

The coast road north from Brauron, which skirts an extensively (and poorly) developed coastline, leads to a pleasant **beach** at Loutsa (✉ 8 km/5 mi north of Brauron), framed by a backdrop of umbrella pines and with shallow waters—perfect for small children, though crowded in the summer.

Dining and Lodging

$$ ✕🏨 **Mare Nostrum Hotel Club.** Visit the antiquities in the morning, go for a swim on the beach midday, and then spend the afternoon getting facials or seaweed treatments. It all makes for an ideal day, here made possible thanks to the addition in 1996 of a thalassotherapy spa. Visit the Olympiades section, which includes sauna, hamam (turkish steam bath), and a fitness room; Nereides, devoted to hydrotherapy with seaweed and mud remedies for ailments such as arthritis and varicose veins; or the Aphrodite, with beauty treatments like Swedish massage, reflexology, shiatsu, and facials. You can also regenerate at the hotel proper, which features myriad sports facilities—from volleyball to minigolf to waterskiing—several eateries, including a taverna and sea-view bar, and rooms with balcony or terrace and air-conditioning. If all this isn't enough, the restless can zip over to the beach town of Loutsa, about 5 km (3 mi) away, for some taverna-and-bar-hopping; KTEL buses pass regularly near the hotel. Buffet breakfast is included in the price, and both half- and full board are available. Room rates don't include spa services, but guests may sign up for various packages, just as tourists passing by may simply use the spa. ✉ *Above Brauron (Vravrona) cove, 19003,* ☎ *0294/48112 or 0294/47712, Athens office 01/362–0619;* 🖷 *0294/47790, Athens office 01/364–1391. 237 rooms, 112 bungalows, 3 suites. 3 restaurants, air-conditioning, pool, miniature golf, 3 tennis courts, exercise room, volleyball, waterskiing. AE, DC, MC, V.*

Marathon

8 *42 km (26 mi) northeast of Athens, 33 km (20½ mi) north of Brauron.*

Today, Athenians enter the fabled plain of Marathon only to enjoy a break from the capital, visiting the freshwater lake created by the dam or sunning at the area's beaches. But when the Athenians hoplites, assisted by the Plataians, entered the plain in 490 BC, it was to crush a numerically superior Persian force. Some 6,400 invaders were killed fleeing to their ships, while the Athenians lost just 192 warriors. This, their proudest victory, became the stuff of Athenian legends; the hero Theseus was said to have appeared himself in aid of the Greeks, along with the god Pan. The Athenian commander Miltiades sent a messenger, Pheidippides, to Athens with glad tidings of the victory; it's said he ran the 42 km (26 mi) without hardly taking a breath, pronounced the good news, then dropped dead of fatigue (more probably of a heart attack), the inspiration for the marathon race in today's Olympics.

At the foot of the 30-ft-high **Marathon Tomb,** built over the graves of the Athenian dead, is a reproduction of the original gravestone, the Soldier of Marathon, which depicts a hoplite; the original is in the National Archaeological Museum in Athens. About 1½ km (1 mi) north is the smaller burial mound of the Plataians and the **Museum of Marathon,** which contains objects from excavations in the area, including a funerary urn for a child, shaped like a cocoon. Excavations continue around a nearby prehistoric cemetery, which will eventually be open to the public. ⊠ *Plataion 114, approximately 6 km (4 mi) south of modern village of Marathon, 2 km (1 mi) from Leoforos Marathonas,* ☎ *0294/55155.* ☜ *500 dr.* ☉ *Tues.–Sun. 8–2:30 (8:30–3 in winter).*

9 Fifteen kilometers (9 miles) north of Marathon, the archaeological site at **Rhamnous,** an isolated, romantic spot on a small promontory, overlooks the sea between continental Greece and the island of Euboia. From at least the Archaic period, Rhamnous was known for the worship of Nemesis, the great leveler, who brought down the proud and punished the arrogant. The site, excavated over many years, preserves traces of temples from the 6th and 5th centuries BC. The smaller temple from the 6th century BC was dedicated to Themis, goddess of Justice; the later temple housed the cult statue of Nemesis, envisioned as a woman, the only cult statue (even fragmentary) left from the High Classical period. Many fragments have turned up, including the head, now in the British Museum. The acropolis stood on the headland, where ruins are visible from a fortress (5th and 4th centuries BC). Recently, excavations helped archaeologists locate the garrison headquarters and determine exactly where the permanent guard was housed. As you wander over this usually serene, and always evocative, site you'll discover at its edge little coves where you can enjoy a swim. For those going by public transportation, take a KTEL bus from Athens toward the Ayia Marina port, get off at the Ayia Marina and Rhamnous crossroads, and follow the signs on the flat road, about 3 km (2 mi). Or take a taxi from Marathon village (1,700 dr.). ⊠ *10 km (6 mi) northeast of Marathon,* ☎ *0294/63477.* ☜ *500 dr.* ☉ *Daily 7–6.*

10 **Lake Marathon** (⊠ 8 km/5 mi west of Marathon), a man-made reservoir formed by the **Marathon Dam,** was built by an American company in 1925–31. Walk or drive across the dam (⊠ 9 km/5½ mi west down a side road from the village of Ayios Stefanos); you may be astonished by the sight of all that landlocked water in Greece.

Beaches

Near Marathon, the best beach is the long, sandy stretch called **Skinies.** Other, less populated beaches (pebble), usually lined with a taverna or two, include **Paralia Varnavas,** reached from Varnavas village, and **Sessi** near Grammatikon village, both only accessible by car. The coves at **Rhamnous** are delightful (about 2,000 ft from the site), but beware of spiny sea urchins when swimming off the rocks.

Dining and Lodging

$–$$ ✕ **Argentina.** While living in South America, owner Nikos Milonas learned how to carve beef, how high to fire up the grill, exactly how to time a perfect medium-rare steak, and the meat-loving population of Greece has been benefiting from his expertise ever since. At his taverna, which on a clear day offers a peek of the sea from its large veranda, young beef brought from Holland is priced by the kilo, grilled, and then served for you to slice off as much as you can handle. The rest of the fare is simple but solid: dense tzatziki that's light on the garlic; well-fried eggplant, pepper, and zucchini slices; mountain greens; and the classic Greek feta-cheese salads, *horiatiki* in summer and grated cabbage-carrot in winter. The service is polite and the prices are low. ✉ *Bitakou 3, Kaletzi about 1½ km (1 mi) after the dam crossing,* ☎ *0294/66476 or 0294/67814. Reservations essential on weekends. AE, V. Closed 3 wks. in Aug. No lunch weekdays.*

$ ✕ **Patitiri Petsa.** Housed in a former wine press, this taverna has been serving the same high-quality dishes for decades, simplicity graced by authenticity. The two dining rooms (one opens to the outdoors in summer) are decorated with the personal effects of owner Isidoros Petsas, as well as farming tools and wine barrels. If you go in winter, sit next to one of the four fireplaces and feast on fantastic ribs, juicy baby lamb, and for the brave, succulent tidbits like charcoal-grilled kidneys and sweetbreads. If it's summer, be sure to try the masterful tomato salad, made from famous Marathon tomatoes picked from the owner's plot. The mountain greens—dandelion, notchweed, whatever is available—taste different every time but are unparalleled as a side dish. Best of all, the owner produces his own wine; it won't hurt to try what he's offering by the barrel. ✉ *3-km (2-mi) mark on Leoforos Marathonas, about 1½ km (¾ mi) after intersection for Marathon Tomb (Timvos),* ☎ *0294/55007. No credit cards. Closed Mon. Oct.–Apr. No lunch weekdays (in Aug. no lunch Mon.–Sat.).*

$$ ☷ **Golden Coast Hotel and Bungalows.** Right on the beach, the Golden
🐣 Coast has the kind of simple, functional, air-conditioned rooms and facilities that are perfect for families; you don't have to go anywhere else during your stay since it has a disco, three bars, a restaurant, grill, and evening programs with skits, games, and Greek dancing. Guests can either stay in the main building or in the bungalows set in a verdant garden. Half-board is available for another 4,500 dr. per person. Although the beach is narrow and rocky—as on most of this coast—children have a choice of two pools, and the adults can take a dip in three others. There's a wide variety of sports available. The restaurant's food is unusually good, and buffet breakfast is included in the price. Golden Coast is joined by a seaside promenade to the nearest beach town, Nea Makri, 2 km (1 mi) on foot, or 4 km (2½) by car, which in summer is jumping with clubs and tavernas. A hotel shuttle takes guests to Nea Makri three times daily and the closest bus stop is 1,500 ft. from the hotel. ✉ *Marathon Beach, 19005,* ☎ *0294/57100, Athens office 01/362–0662;* FAX *0294/ 57300, Athens office 01/364–1391. 240 rooms, 256 bungalows, 45 apartments. Restaurant, 3 bars, air-conditioning, 5 pools, 3 tennis courts, volleyball, minigolf, Ping-Pong, basketball, waterskiing, windsurfing, dance club. AE, DC, MC, V. Closed Nov.–Mar.*

Outdoor Activities and Sports

RUNNING

Every year on November 1 the **International Athens Peace Marathon** is run over the same course taken in 490 BC by the courier Pheidippides, when he carried to Athens the news of victory over the Persians. The 42-km (26-mi) race, open to men and women of all ages, starts in Marathon and finishes at the Olympic Stadium in Athens. There is a $50 entry fee. Apply by mail (⊠ SEGAS, Race Organizers, Syngrou 137, Athens 17121, ☎ 01/935–9302, 01/934–4126, or 01/934–1603, 𝔸𝕏 01/934–2980 or 01/935–8594).

Amphiareion

⓫ *49 km (30½ mi) northeast of Athens; 18 km (11 mi) north of Lake Marathon.*

Cradled in a hidden valley at a bend in the road, the **Sanctuary of Amphiareos** is a quiet, well-watered haven, blessed with dense pines and other foliage. It is startlingly different from the surrounding countryside, where overgrazing, fires, and development have destroyed most of the trees. Amphiareos was the Bronze Age king of Argos, a mortal transformed after death into a healing divinity. In the sanctuary dedicated to his cult are the remains of a miniature **theater**; a 4th-century BC **Doric temple**; the long **stoa**; and **Enkimiterion** (literally, "dormitory"), where patients stayed awaiting their cure. They would sacrifice a ram, then lie down wrapped in its skin, waiting for a dream, which resident priests would interpret for the prescribed cure, usually involving baths in the miraculous waters. It was customary for patients to thank the gods by throwing coins into the water, which priests retrieved to melt into votives they could sell. At the sanctuary's entrance to the left stand many statueless pedestals. Look for the pedestal in the middle (with the date 240 BC) that once supported a likeness of Brutus, whose murder of Julius Caesar scored big points in Greece. The easiest way to get to the site, after driving, is to take a KTEL bus to Skala Oropos and then a taxi (about 800 dr.). The guards can help you call a taxi for a pick-up. ⊠ *Site,* ☎ *0295/62144.* ⬛ *500 dr.* ☉ *Weekdays 8–2:30, weekends 8:30–3.*

Mt. Parnitha

33 km (20½ mi) northwest of Athens but accessible from sites in east Attica, such as Amphiareion, Marathon, and Rhamnous.

The summit of Mt. Parnitha offers a splendid view of the plain of Athens cradled by Mt. Pendeli and Mt. Hymettos. In spring the forest blooms with wildflowers, red poppies, white crocuses, purple irises, and numerous species of orchids. Once the heavily wooded habitat of wolves and bears, the mountain provided fuel for the charcoal burners of Acharnes in the days before oil. There are many lovely nature walks through the Mt. Parnitha massif, reachable from the chapel of Ayia Triada, including two-hour walks to the Cave of Pan or the Skipiza spring. There is a map behind the church.

Phyle

⓬ *31 km (19¼ mi) northwest of Athens.*

Evidence of the modern village Fili's source of wealth, livestock, is everywhere: in the dozens of whole lambs, pigs, and goats strung up in front of butcher shops; in the numerous tavernas lining the main street; in the many window displays of fresh sheep yogurt. Beyond the village, known as Hasia by locals, the road climbs Mt. Parnitha; there is a turnoff for Moni Kleiston.

The Athenians built several fortresses on the ancient road between Mt. Parnitha and Thebes, including the untended 4th-century BC **Fortress**

of Phyle (✉ On a high bluff west of the road to Thebes, 9½ km/6 mi
north of Fili village). The road looping back and around the flank of
Mt. Parnitha climbs slowly through rugged, deserted country along the
ancient road northwest to Thebes. Here, the fortress watched over the
passes between Attica and Boeotia, a dramatically beautiful site, its
rugged rectangular masonry scattered about the site. Fragments of the
wall still stand; it was made of blocks, each up to 9 ft high, and was
reinforced with five towers (two are still visible).

Dining

$ ✕ **To Frourio.** If you visit the Fortress of Phyle on a weekend, be sure
to stop at "The Fort," for great, inexpensive lamb and other grilled
meats, potatoes, and salads. On cold days, you'll wish you had marsh-
mallows for the fireplace; on warm days the outdoor terrace offers an
unforgettable setting. *Note:* When it snows on Parnitha, the road up
to the fortress may be closed, so check with your hotel about weather
conditions on the mountain. The taverna closes early, around 9 or 10
PM. ✉ *Several hundred ft beyond turnoff to ruins, Phyle,* ☎ *no phone.
No credit cards. Closed weekdays.*

Monastery of Daphni

⓭   *11 km (7 mi) west of Athens.*

In turn sacked by Crusaders, inhabited by Cistercian monks, and des-
ecrated by Turks, Daphni remains one of the most splendid Byzantine
monuments in Greece. Dating from the 11th century, the golden age
of Byzantine art, the church contains a series of miraculously preserved
mosaics without parallel in the legacy of Byzantium: powerful portraits
of figures from the Old and New Testaments, images of Christ and his
mother, and, in the golden dome, a stern Pantokrator, "ruler of all."
Daphni means "laurel tree," sacred to Apollo, which reminds us that
his sanctuary once occupied this site. It was destroyed in AD 395 after
the antipagan edicts of the emperor Theodosius, and the Orthodox
monastery was probably established in the 6th century. Reoccupied by
Orthodox monks only in the 16th century, Daphni has since been a
barracks and a lunatic asylum, and it has been restored extensively in
several phases. ✉ *End of Iera Odos (also reached by taking the A16,
B16, and G16 buses from Platia Koumoundourou in Athens), Haidari,*
☎ *01/581–1558.* 🎟 *800 dr.* ☉ *Daily 8:30–2:45.*

Eleusis

⓮   *22 km (13½ mi) west of Athens, 11 km (7 mi) west of the Monastery
of Daphni.*

The growing city of Athens co-opted the land around Eleusis, placing
shipyards in the pristine gulf and steel mills and petrochemical plants
along its shores. It is hard to imagine that there once stretched in every
direction fields of corn and barley sacred to the goddess Demeter,
whose realm was symbolized by the sheaf and sickle. The **sanctuary
of Demeter** now lies in the new town, on the east slope and at the foot
of the acropolis, which is hardly visible amid the modern buildings.
The legend of Demeter and her daughter Persephone explained for the
ancients the cause of the seasons and the origins of agriculture:

It was to Eleusis that Demeter traveled in search of Persephone after
the girl had been kidnapped by Hades, god of the underworld. Zeus
himself interceded to restore her to the distraught Demeter but succeeded only partially, giving mother and daughter just half a year together. Nevertheless, in gratitude to King Keleos of Eleusis, who had

given her refuge in her time of need, Demeter presented his son Triptolemos with wheat seeds, the knowledge of agriculture, and a winged chariot so he could spread them to mankind. Keleos built a megaron (large hall) in her honor, the first Eleusinian sanctuary.

The worship of Demeter took the form of mysterious rites, and both the Lesser and the Greater Eleusinian rituals closely linked Athens with the sanctuary. The procession for the Greater Eleusinia began and ended there, following the route of the Sacred Way. Much of what we see now in the sanctuary is of Roman construction or repair, although physical remains on the site date back to the Mycenaean period. One follows the old Sacred Way to the **Great Propylaea** (Gates) and continues on to the **Precinct of Demeter**, which was strictly off-limits on pain of death to any but the initiated. The **Telesterion**, or Temple of Demeter, now a vast open space surrounded by battered tiers of seats, was the hall of initiation. It had a roof supported by six rows of seven columns, presumably so the mysteries would be obscured, and it could accommodate 3,000 people. The **museum,** just beyond, contains an array of pottery and sculpture, particularly of the Roman period. ⊠ *Iera Odos 1,* ☎ *01/554–6019.* ⊠ *500 dr.* ☉ *Tues.–Sun. 8:30–2:45.*

The Arts

FESTIVAL WITH GREEK DRAMA
From the end of August to mid-September, Eleusis hosts the **Aeschilia** festival, with ancient Greek drama presented on the archaeological site and at an old soap factory on the beach next to the Titanas plant. Performances start at 9 PM and tickets, which cost 2,000 dr. (5,000 dr. for a festival pass), are available at the sites before the show, at major Athens record stores, and at the Elefsina Cultural Center (⊠ Pangalou 52, ☎ 01/554–8997), which can supply more information.

OFF THE
BEATEN PATH

STRAITS OF SALAMIS – It was here that the desperate and wily Athenians aided by Sparta, Corinth, and Aegina destroyed the Persian fleet. In 490 BC, the Persians had returned to exact revenge for their defeat at Marathon in 480 BC, attacking and burning the Acropolis. The Athenians, told by the Delphic oracle to protect themselves with "wooden walls," interpreted this to mean their ships. Evacuating their women and children, they drew up their wooden boats and, by a ruse, lured the Persians into a trap. So sure were the Persians of a devastating victory that Xerxes, the king, had a fine silver throne placed on the hill overlooking the strait, to watch his troops thrash the Greeks. He witnessed instead a disaster that, even more than that at Marathon, put a definitive end to Persian ambitions in the western Aegean. Ferries leave Perama (15 km/9⅓ mi west of Athens) around the clock, crossing the straits (3 km/2 mi) to the island of Salamina, which in 1998 suffered heavily from forest fires. From 5 AM to 6 AM and from 10:30 PM to 1 AM the boat leaves every half hour; from 6 AM to 10:30 PM every 15 minutes, and from 1 AM to 5 AM every hour; tickets cost 120 dr. For more information, call the Perama port authority (☎ 01/441–0441 or 01/441–4676).

THE SARONIC GULF ISLANDS
Aegina, Poros, Hydra, Spetses

The Saronic Gulf Islands are a diverse group: Aegina's pine forests mix with groves of pistachio trees, a product for which Aegina is justly famous. Water taxis buzz to Poros, more like an islet, from the Peloponnese, carrying weary locals eager to relax on its beaches and linger in the island cafés. Hydra and Spetses are farther south and more rewarding:

Both ban automobiles, and though Hydra's restaurants and boutiques cater to the sophisticated European traveler, Spetses's broad forests and scattered resorts lure Greeks.

Aegina

30 km (18½ mi) south of Piraeus.

Aegina has become an inexpensive resort area frequented primarily by Athenians. By the 6th century BC, Aegina, the commercial entrepôt, had become a major art center, known in particular for its bronze foundries, worked by such sculptors as Kallon, Onatas, and Anaxagoras. This powerful island, lying so close off the coast of Attica, could not fail to come into conflict with Athens. As Athens's imperial ambitions grew, Aegina became a thorn in its side. In 458 BC Athens laid siege to the city, eventually conquering the island. In the 19th century, it experienced a remarkable rebirth as an important base in the War of Independence, and it was briefly the capital of the new Greek state.

⑮ The boats and hydrofoils dock at the main town, **Aegina town,** a busy little harbor city on the western side of the island, where a few surviving neoclassical buildings mingle with a modern cement-and-cinder-block sprawl. Idyllic seascapes and a few beautiful gardens make Aegina attractive; its numerous cafés and restaurants lining the harbor face a road along the water teeming with horse-and-carriage traffic, trucks, and taxis. Take a stroll around town before heading to the eastern shore. This side of the island is more fertile and less mountainous than the east side; its gardens and fields are blessed with grapes, olives, figs, almonds, and, above all, the treasured pistachio trees.

As you approach from the sea, your first view of the town of Aegina takes in the sweep of the harbor, punctuated by the tiny white chapel of **Ayios Nikolaos** (⊠ Aegina town harbor). During the negotiations for Greece, Ioannis Kapodistrias, the first president of Greece, conducted meetings in the medieval **Markelon Tower** (⊠ Aegina town center).

Much of the ancient city lies under the modern, with public buildings and sanctuaries built on the promontory just north of the modern town. Still visible on this hill (known as Kolonna, or "column") is a single column of a late-Archaic Temple of Apollo. The small **archaeological museum** on the site has finds from the Temple of Aphaia and excavations throughout the island, including Bronze Age pottery found in the excavations and a Hercules sculpture from the Temple of Apollo. ⊠ *Aegina town, 100 ft from where ferries dock on the harbor (follow signs),* ☎ *0297/22248 or 0297/22637.* 🎫 *500 dr.* ☉ *Tues.–Sun. 8–2:30 (8:30–3 in winter).*

NEED A
BREAK?

A must in Aegina is to have a bite to eat in the *psaragora* (fish market). On narrow Pan Irioti street behind the harbor you'll find ouzieris and tavernas—generally without an official name—try the grilled octopus, monkfish with garlic potatoes, or crisp fried shrimp from **Geladakis** (☎ ☎ 0297/27308), perfect with an afternoon ouzo. You'll know you're in the right place when you see elderly gents worrying their beads while seated beside glistening octopus hung up to dry.

In the midst of a valley filled with gardens of pistachio, almond, and olive trees sits the **Monastery of Ayios Nektarios** (⊠ 6 km/4 mi east of Aegina town), the island's patron saint (canonized in 1961), whose relics lie in a dozen churches throughout Greece. The sprawling remains of the medieval "Old Town," or **Palaiochora** (⊠ 6 km/4 mi east of Aegina town), built in the 9th century by islanders whose seaside town was the constant prey of pirates, are set on the rocky barren hill above the monastery. Capital of the island until 1826, Palaiochora still has more than 20 **churches** in various stages of decay, some still in use, amid the rubble of its houses and streets.

Beaches

Aegina's beaches near town are pleasant enough, though crowded. South of town toward scenic Perdika village there are some good swimming spots at **Aiginitissa** and around **Marathonas.**

Dining and Lodging

$–$$ ✕ **Taverna O Kyriakos.** Serving some of the freshest fish on the island, this inexpensive taverna looks out over the sea. Order the pandora, red mullet, or sargus, expertly grilled. Magirefta such as oven-roasted lamb and *kokkinisto* (chuck roast in tomato sauce) are even cheaper options, and, for meat lovers, there is the gamut from chops to souvlaki. Excellent appetizers include eggplant salad, zucchini pie, and bourekakia, all a heady mix with the sea air and potent barrel retsina. ⊠ *Marathona beach, 5 km (3 mi) from Aegina town,* ☎ *0297/24025. No credit cards. Closed Dec. and weekdays Oct.–Nov. and Feb.–Mar.*

$–$$ ✕ **To Maridaki.** The gracious owner will do his best to make you feel welcome at this crowded waterfront restaurant. In addition to the large selection of fresh fish, the restaurant also serves grilled octopus and grilled meats—souvlaki, beef patties heavy on the onions, pork chops—and of course, magirefta such as pastitsio, pepper stuffed with rice, delicious okra with tomatoes, and moussaka. Be sure to have a nibble of the homemade *tiropites.* ⊠ *Dimokratias St. between Town Hall and Panagitsa church, Paralia Aeginas (Aegina beach),* ☎ *0297/ 25869. V. Closed 2 wks in Feb.*

$ ✕ **En Aigini.** In a newly renovated neoclassical mansion, this is actually three spaces in one: a lovely tree-shaded courtyard that operates as a taverna in summer; the upper floor rec room with billiards, backgammon, TV, and fireplace, where guests can also dine in summer or winter weekends; and a cellar featuring live music in winter. The cook's specialties include the onion, cheese, or leek pies; an unusual dish called *manti tis Rozi,* consisting of minced lamb pies with yogurt and tomato; and *strapazada,* a scrambled-egg dish with tomatoes and paprika. Hungrier diners can order one of the magirefta, like *lahanodolmades* (cabbage rolls), *tzoutzoukakia* (spicy meat patties), stuffed peppers and tomatoes, and beef *kokkinisto* (in a red sauce), or the grilled meats like turkey souvlaki (seldom seen on a Greek menu). ⊠ *Spiro Rodis 44, Aegina town,* ☎ *0297/2922 or 094/596318 (mobile). AE, DC, MC, V. Taverna closed Nov.–Apr. No dinner on upper floor weekdays Nov.–Apr; no lunch.*

$ ▥ **Eginitiko Archontiko (Traditional Settlement).** This jewel of a pension was once the home of the wealthy Bitrou merchant family and their daughter, the legendary Zinovia, who garnered fame for her independent ways and her literary salons, attracting such luminaries as Kazantzakis and the island's own St. Nektarios. Guests can stay in his room with its lovely balcony; it is the only one with the bath outside in the hallway. The great lady died in 1985, but her spirit lives on in the house. Care has been taken to preserve the original painted walls and ceilings in the salon and the suite, and every nook and cranny has been fitted out in period style. The wonderful sunporch has colored glass windows, an ideal place to enjoy breakfast in winter or a drink from the small bar; in summer guests may eat breakfast in the roof garden. There is a small communal kitchen with refrigerator and range. The pension's in-town location, 300 ft from the port and opposite the Markelos Tower, is most convenient. ⊠ *Ayiou Nikolaou and Thomaidou 1, 18010,* ☎ *0297/24968,* ℻ *0297/26716. 12 rooms (1 with private bath in hallway), 1 suite. Air-conditioning. AE, DC, MC, V.*

$ ⊞ **I Pansion tis Renas.** The owner has decorated the eight rooms of this pension with taste and loving care for a homey atmosphere reinforced by the handmade lace curtains, solid wood and marble furniture, and tasteful knickknacks. To make guests feel especially welcome, the gracious Rena Kappou places a rose from her garden in each newcomer's room. All rooms have a refrigerator, ceiling or standing fan, and balcony; those on the upper floor boast sea views. The pension is located at the edge of Aegina town, about a 15-minute walk from the port. Breakfast (cake, homemade sweets, and delicious jams), included in the price, is served family-style in the air-conditioned dining room or in the green courtyard. If you request so in advance, she can also cook dinner for guests, including her specialties, *yiouvetsaki* (meat baked in ceramic dishes with tomato sauce and barley-shaped pasta) and *kasseropita* (a pie made from Kasseri cheese). ⊠ *Parodos Ayias Irinis, Faros, Aegina town 18010,* ☎ *0297/24760,* ☎ ℻ *0297/24244. 8 rooms. AE, MC, V.*

Nightlife

Some popular bars include the classic **Perdikiotika,** set in an 1860 building that was once a combination bank–produce store, with beat sounds, lots of wood, a painted ceiling depicting Hermes, and the original safe; **Tsitras,** which plays rock and occasionally jazz in a British pub atmosphere; and **Avli,** a cozy courtyard that serves as a café-bistro days, a bar at night.

Shopping

CERAMICS

In the region of Polies Elies (Many Olives), Nikos Kottakis and his wife, Triantafillia, run one of the island's most prestigious ceramics workshops. Their handmade work (the art of ceramics has a long tradition on the island) is displayed in Aegina town at the pottery store **Neo Ergastirio Keramikis Tehnis** (⊠ Spirou Rodi 33, ☎ 0297/26484) and the **Kivotos** tourist shop (⊠ Eakou 3, ☎ 0297/28688), which is closer to the harbor. It's worth taking a drive to see their workshop; call for directions (☎ 0297/251152). The studio is located on Leoforos Kipselis, a little after Ayios Trifonas church. You can order all kinds of items to be made, even complete coffee and tea services or dinnerware sets, at reasonable prices.

PISTACHIO STANDS

Aegina's famous pistachios can be bought from stands along the harbor. They make welcome snacks and gifts.

Eastern Aegina

Area approximately 11 km (7 mi) east of Aegina town.

The eastern side of Aegina is rugged and sparsely inhabited, except for a former fishing hamlet now given over to tourism. The small port of **Ayia Marina** (⊠ Below the Sanctuary of Aphaia [☞ *below*], via the small paved road) has many hotels, cafés, restaurants, and a beach, to accommodate visitors.

⑯ The **Sanctuary of Aphaia** perches on a promontory with superb views of Athens and Piraeus across the water. This site has been occupied by many sanctuaries to Aphaia; the ruins visible today are those of the temple built in the early 5th century BC. Aphaia was apparently a pre-Hellenic deity, whose worship eventually converged with that of Athena. The temple, one of the finest extant examples of Archaic architecture, was adorned with an exquisite group of pedimental sculptures that are now in the Munich Glyptothek. From Aegina, catch the bus for Ayia Marina near where the ferries dock; ask the driver to let you off at the temple.

⊠ *13 km (8½ mi) east of Aegina town,* ☎ *0297/32398.* ☜ *800 dr.* ☉ *Weekdays 8–8 (8–5 in winter), weekends 8–2:30 (8:30–3 in winter).*

Beaches

Besides Ayia Marina, which can become very crowded, you can swim at sandy **Tourlo** and **Vayia,** on the northern coast of the island.

Lodging

$$ ⊞ **Hotel Apollo.** To take advantage of the fine location on the beach at Ayia Marina, all (except singles) of the air-conditioned, fairly quiet rooms at this hotel have balconies and sea views. TVs and refrigerators are available for rent. While its 1997 renovation didn't improve its cement-block exterior, the hotel has many amenities ideal for active travelers who don't want to go far, including a large terrace with seawater pool. The hotel is surrounded by greenery, and steps lead down to a rocky beach with a sand floor. Buffet breakfast is included in the price, and the restaurants serve Greek and Continental cuisine. Buses pass regularly for the overdeveloped resort of Ayia Marina, a 10-minute walk from the hotel, and for Aegina; the stop is 750 ft from the hotel. ⊠ *Ayia Marina beach, 18010,* ☎ *0297/32281, and 0297/ 32271 through 0297/32274; winter, in Athens 01/323–4292;* ℻ *0297/ 32688; winter, in Athens 01/322–4136, 107 rooms. Restaurant, air-conditioning, saltwater pool, tennis court, minigolf, table tennis. AE, DC, MC, V. Closed Nov.–Mar.*

Poros

⑰ *21½ km (13½ mi) south of Aegina.*

The island of Poros sits due south of Aegina, separated from the Peloponnese by a narrow strait. **Poros town** (⊠ Draped over the promontory guarding the strait) has a long, attractive waterfront skirting the base of the hill. In antiquity, Poros was the site of an important **Sanctuary of Poseidon,** whose scrappy ruins can be seen at the approximate center of the island. Many of the blocks from the temple were carried off in the 18th century to build the monastery on nearby Hydra, reachable by hydrofoil or ferry.

As you clear the narrow straits of Poros and head east, you will see on your left the 18th-century monastery of **Zoodochos Pighi,** or Life-giving Spring (⊠ On a pine-clad hillside just east of the town of Poros).

Hydra

⑱ *28 km (17½ mi) south of Poros.*

As you round the easternmost finger of the Northern Peloponnese, before you stretches the full length of Hydra, mountainous and barren. Although there are traces of an ancient settlement, the island was sparsely inhabited until the Ottoman period. In the 16th century, its rugged slopes offered a haven for refugees from the Peloponnese during the constant wars between the Ottomans and the Venetians. The settlers turned to the sea and began building boats, and by the early 18th century, their trade routes stretched from the mainland to Asia Minor and even America. By its end, the fleet, profiting from the Napoleonic Wars, had captured much of the lucrative grain trade between the Ukraine and western Europe, earning great fortunes and much notoriety in blockade-running. After the Greek Revolution, Hydra sank into relative obscurity until well past the middle of this century, when it was discovered by outsiders; its noble port and houses have since been rescued and placed on the Council of Europe's list of protected monuments, with strict ordinances regulating construction and renovation. All motor traffic is banned from the island (except for several rather noisy garbage trucks).

As you approach the island, **Hydra town,** invisible at first, gradually reveals itself, with gray and white houses climbing steep slopes surrounding a nearly round harbor, looking much as it did in 1821, when Hydra was crucial in the struggle for independence.

Many of the waterfront houses, built between 1770 and 1821, consist of a rectangular basic unit two to three stories tall, with the upper floor set back to create a terrace, and most have courtyards with large subterranean cisterns. (People claim that the cisterns were also used to hide gold and other treasure in the 18th and 19th centuries, and that eels were introduced in them to keep the water clean and drinkable.)

In the early 19th century, the tremendous surge in disposable wealth enabled shipowners to build the characteristic *archontika* ("great houses"), massive gray-stone mansions facing the harbor, with forbidding, fortresslike exteriors. Good examples include the **Tsamados House,** which now shelters the School of the Merchant Navy (⊠ On the harbor opposite the ferry landing); the **Tombazi House,** an annex of Athens's School of Fine Arts (⊠ Halfway up the west side of the harbor); the **Voulgaris (Merikles-Oikonomou) House** (⊠ On the west harbor); and the **Koundouriotis House** (⊠ Looming on the west headland). The **Monastery of the Panaghia** (⊠ Along the central section of the harbor) was built in the late-18th century partly of stone taken from the Sanctuary of Poseidon on Poros. The monastery's bell tower is a fine example of the early 19th-century marble carving done by a guild of traveling artisans (perhaps from the island of Tinos) who left their mark all over the Aegean in this period.

After exploring Hydra, pack a picnic and set out of town, looking back through the labyrinth of lanes for views of the red roofs set against turquoise waters, perhaps stopping at Kanoni Square, which overlooks the gulf. Take a walk to Hydra's oldest settlement, **Episkopi,** with its scattered ruins; **Profitis Ilias monastery,** renowned for its library; and the nearby convent of **Ayia Efpraxia,** where the nuns sell handwoven fabrics, both about an hour's walk from Hydra town.

Beaches

The only sandy beach near town lies east at Mandraki, the private domain of the Miramare, though the windsurfing center is open to everyone. West of town is **Vlichos bay,** 30 minutes' walk past Kamini, a pretty hamlet with tavernas, a historic bridge, and a rocky beach. You may also hire a water taxi to transport you to a more private beach, such as **Avlaki, Bisti,** or **Limnioniza,** or a nearby **islet,** like Dokos, Kivotos, or Petasi.

Dining and Lodging

$ ✕ **To Geitoniko.** Great home cooking at good prices is the hallmark of this restaurant, where you can dine on a starlit terrace on summer nights. Try the baby beet salad topped with a dollop of garlic potatoes; the magirefta-like octopus *stifado,* a kind of stew; and oven-baked pork stuffed with Parmesan and peppers. Grilled meats and fresh fish are available, and the cook prepares scrumptious desserts: halvah (a sesame confection), baklava, and some Hydriot delicacies like an irresistible almond-honey square. Because there are only 20 tables and one can't make reservations, it's a good idea to go early to beat the crowd; the restaurant starts serving dinner around 9 PM. ⊠ *Spiliou Harami St. opposite Pension Antonis,* ☎ *0298/53615. No credit cards. Closed Nov.–Jan.*

$ ✕ **To Krifo Limani.** Called the "Secret Harbor," this spot still attracts groups of fishermen on their days off, even though Capt. Andreas Voulgaris has retired. He passed on this small taverna to his son Dimitris, who with his fisherman brother, Andreas, and their pal Kostas catch the fish, spear the octopus, and run this busy little place. Sit in the courtyard and order fresh fish, or for a cheaper seafood selection, fried *maridakia* (white bait). Known for its fish soup, the taverna also serves several *magirefta*, like *kotopoulo lemonato* (chicken in lemon-oil sauce) and kokkinisto (lamb or beef), as well as appetizers—zucchini croquettes, homemade dolmades, fried meat balls (*keftedakia*), and dips like taramosalata. Do like the fishermen do and wash it all down with the barrel retsina or rosé. ⊠ *On alley near Bratsera off main road, left side of harbor,* ☎ *0298/52585. No credit cards. Closed Jan.–mid-Feb.*

$ ✕ **To Steki.** Shuck your tourist inhibitions and skip the fixed-price menu at this classic hangout with gray shutters, a veranda, and folk murals of Hydriot life. Instead, order what the locals do, the delicious fish soup, and reliable *magirefta*, such as stuffed peppers, lamb in red sauce or roasted in the oven, and *briam* (a type of ratatouille). Run by the brothers Christos and Argyris (the latter sports what may be the bushiest mustache on the island), the taverna also serves grilled meats—*paidakia*(lamb ribs), beef patties, souvlaki—fresh local fish, and numerous appetizers, like taramosalata, eggplant dip, and octopus *xidato,* marinated in oil and vinegar. Barrel white and rosé and some Greek bottled wines are available. ⊠ *Miaouli St., in "Droom" alley, across from Loulakis store, Aegina town,* ☎ *0298/53517. MC, V.*

$$$ ✕⊞ **Bratsera.** An 1860 sponge factory was transformed into this posh
★ hotel with doors made out of old packing crates still bearing the "Piraeus" stamp. Hints of the former factory are still visible in the Hydriot gray stonework and timber beams incorporated into the lounge and the restaurant, blending harmoniously with the modern furnishings. The service is excellent in the hotel, which is just minutes from the port. The rooms, located in two old buildings and one new one, are all decorated individually, some with four-poster beds, others with cozy lofts, and all with portraits and engravings. The restaurant operates in the oleander- and bougainvillea-graced courtyard, and its kitchen, which specializes in European cuisine, is considered one of the island's best. The courtyard pool makes up for Hydra's dearth of beaches and becomes part of the extended bar with quiet music at night. Buffet breakfast is included in the price. ⊠ *1st street to left as you leave ferry, near Hydra Tours office, 18040,* ☎ *0298/53971 through 0298/53975; 0298/52794 restaurant; winter, in Athens 01/721–8102;* ℻ *0298/53626, winter, in Athens 01/722–1619. 19 rooms, 4 suites. Restaurant, pool. AE, DC, MC, V. Closed Nov.–Clean Mon. weekend, usually mid-Feb.*

$$$ ⊞ **Miramare Beach Bungalows.** This small, simple hotel is perfect for
☾ families with small children, especially because of its children's pool and baby-sitting arrangements. Rooms have direct-dial phone, air-conditioning or a ceiling fan, refrigerator, and individual courtyard with lounge chairs. All open directly onto the little beach, the only stretch of sand in or near the town of Hydra, which offers a beach bar and facilities for waterskiing, canoeing, sailing, paddleboating, and floating in a boat-pulled rubber banana. The town is about a 25-minute walk away, but the hotel's boat service shuttles back and forth to the main harbor. The attached restaurant has expensive Greek and Continental food, which is not particularly good, but at least it's convenient if you are spending the day on the beach. Buffet breakfast is included in the price, which is at the low end of the category, and the hotel often negotiates. Half-board is available for the unadventurous. ⊠ *Miramare Beach near Mandraki, 18040,* ☎ ℻ *0298/52300. 28 bungalows. Restaurant, refrigerators, wading pool, baby-sitting, beach. MC, V. Closed Oct.–Mar.*

$$$ ⊞ **Orloff.** Built in 1798 by Catherine the Great for Count Orloff, who
★ came to Greece with a Russian fleet to try to dislodge the Turks, this

archontiko (settlement) still retains the splendor of the past with the added benefit of modern amenities. The heavy single shutters, which were used to defend against attack, have been preserved, and antiques—walnut furniture, paintings, and lithographs—grace the lace-curtained rooms. No two are alike; those categorized superior rooms have sitting areas and color TVs (about 8,000 dr. more), and all have minibars and views of the town or the pretty courtyard, shaded by a mulberry tree. Included in the price, the breakfast is one of the best in town, with corn flakes, boiled eggs, yogurt bought from a local shepherd, pastries, orange juice, and fruit. ⊠ *Rafalia 9, 18040,* ☎ *0298/ 52564 or 0298/52495; winter, in Athens 01/522–6125;* ℻ *0298/ 53532; winter, in Athens 01/522–7265. 10 rooms. Minibars. AE, V. Closed Nov.–late-Mar.*

$$ 🏠 **Miranda.** Artists and art collectors alike will feel at home in this aesthetically decorated traditional Hydriot home, built in 1821 by a Captain Danavasi and now classified by the Ministry of Culture as a national monument. It contains an interesting collection of 18th- and 19th-century furniture and art—Oriental rugs, wooden chests, nautical engravings—and the ground-floor art gallery hosts local exhibits and international artists in July and August. The suites on the top floor have huge balconies, air-conditioning, sea views, and graceful ceilings done by Venetian painters. The price includes full breakfast, served in the interior courtyard fragrant with lemon blossoms, jasmine, and bougainvillea. ⊠ *Miaouli, 2 blocks inland from center of port, 18040,* ☎ *0298/52230 or 0298/53953; winter, in Athens 01/684–9268;* ℻ *0298/53510. 9 rooms, 3 suites. Air-conditioning. No credit cards. Closed Nov.–Feb.*

$$ 🏠 **Mistral Hotel.** This imposing stone mansion offers cozy rooms in simple, traditional style; five have sea views, while the rest enjoy panoramas of the town. About half have air-conditioning, some have TV or minibar. The Mistral is small and fills up quickly in summer. Breakfast is included and, depending on the staff's mood, may feature a mouthwatering pastry like *galaktobouriko* (custard in phyllo); it is served in the vine-shaded courtyard, which also doubles as a snack bar. ⊠ *1,500 ft from port, 18040,* ☎ *0298/52509 or 0298/53411,* ℻ *0298/53412. 18 rooms, 1 studio. Air-conditioning. AE, V. Closed Nov.–mid-Feb.*

Festivals

For three days in mid-July, the alleys of Hydra resemble Lilliputia, with colorful marionette troupes from all over the world performing for free during **International Puppet Theater Days.** A longtime collaboration between Greek puppeteers Lakis Christidis and Antigoni Paroussi and the founder of Sweden's Marionetteatern, Michael Meschke, the festival has attracted such diverse groups as Compagnie Danaye of Togo, El Khatib from Palestine, and the Brazilian group Amaglama Production. There are also puppet exhibitions and workshops for children. For more information, call the organizers (☎ 0298/53105). The island also celebrates its crucial role in the War of Independence with the **Miaoulia,** which takes place the third week of June; it includes military parades and dancing and culminates in a reenactment of the night Admiral Miaouls loaded a vessel with explosives and sent it upwind to the Turkish fleet. Naturally, the enemy's ship goes down in flames. On **Good Friday** of Orthodox Easter, a mournful procession of parishioners holding candles follows the funeral bier (*Epitaphio*) as it winds its way to Kaminia harbor, where the bier is set afloat, illuminated by several fishing boats; youth dive in to retrieve it. Greek Orthodox Holy Week ends in midnight **Anastasi** liturgies, with the joyful singing of hymns, exploding fireworks, and churches competing to see who can raise the Resurrection cross highest. Contact the Hydra tourist police for more information (☞ Visitor Information *in* Excursions from Athens A to Z, *below*).

Nightlife

CLUBS

Around forever, **Pirate** nevertheless remains popular for its harbor location and long list of celebrity visitors. Another die-hard club, **Cavos** near Kamini, goes wild after midnight, when revelers start to dance on the tables. Less boisterous spots include minuscule **Hydronetta** (think "groovy"), on the coast just past Kanoni, and **Amalour,** behind the port for thirtysomethings. Bars often change names, ownership, and music—if not location—so check with your hotel for what's in season.

Shopping

A number of elegant shops (some of them offshoots of Athens stores) sell fashionable and amusing clothing and jewelry, though you won't save anything by shopping here.

Spetses

19 *24 km (15 mi) southwest of Hydra.*

In the years leading up to the revolution, Hydra's great rival and ally was the island of Spetses. Lying at the entrance to the Argolic Gulf, just off the mainland, Spetses was known even in antiquity for its hospitable soil and verdant, pine-clad slopes. The pine trees on the island today, however, were planted by a Spetsiot philanthropist dedicated to restoring the beauty stripped by the shipbuilding industry. There are far fewer trees than there were in antiquity, but the island is still well watered, and the many prosperous Athenians who have made Spetses their second home compete to have the prettiest gardens and terraces. The island shows evidence of continuous habitation through all of antiquity. From the 16th century, settlers came over from the mainland and, as on Hydra, they soon began to look to the sea, building their own boats. They became master sailors, successful merchants, and later, in the Napoleonic Wars, skilled blockade runners, earning fortunes that they poured into building larger boats and grander houses. With the outbreak of the War of Independence in 1821, the Spetsiots dedicated their best ships and brave men (and women) to the cause.

Ships meet Spetses at **Dapia,** the jetty protecting the modern harbor. Fortified with cannons dating from the War of Independence, it faces the attractive waterfront, full of outdoor cafés and restaurants. The harbormaster's offices, to the right as you face the sea, occupy a building designed in the simple two-story, center-hall architecture typical of the period and this place.

In front of a popular park is **Bouboulina's house,** where guided tours in English on this interesting heroine's life are given. Laskarina Bouboulina was the bravest of all Spetsiot revolutionaries, the daughter of a Hydriot sea captain, and the wife, then widow, of two more sea captains. Left with a considerable inheritance and nine children, she dedicated herself to increasing her already substantial fleet and fortune. On her flagship, the *Agamemnon,* the largest in the Greek fleet, she sailed into war against the Ottomans at the head of the Spetsiot ships. Her fiery temper led to her death in a family feud many years later. ⊠ *Behind Dapia, near the harbor,* ☎ *0298/72416.* ☑ *1,000 dr.* ☺ *45-min tours in English daily 9:45–2:15 and 4:30–8:15 (last tour). Closed Nov.–mid.-Mar.*

Spetses's **museum** found an unlikely home in a fine late-18th-century archontiko built in a style that might be termed Turko-Venetian. It contains articles from the period of Spetses's greatness, including Bouboulina's bones, in a room festooned with the revolutionary flag. ⊠ *Near town center in the Archontiko Hatziyianni-Mexi, 600 ft south of harbor,* ☎ *0298/72994.* 🖃 *500 dr.* ☉ *Tues.–Sun. 8–2:30 (8:30–1 in winter).*

The promontory is the site of the little 19th-century **Church of Ayios Mamas.** On the headland sits the **Monastery of Ayios Nikolaos** (⊠ On the road heading southeast from the Dapia), now the episcopal seat. Its lacy white-marble bell tower recalls that of Hydra's port monastery, and it was here that the islanders first raised their flag of independence.

Spetses has two harbors, with the **Old Harbor** slumbering in obscurity. It is dominated by the gray-stone mansion of the Botassis family, one of the earliest to settle on Spetses. The Old Harbor is perfect for an afternoon or evening stroll, while you might imagine it as it was in its heyday: the walls of the mansions resounding with the noise of shipbuilding and the streets humming with discreet whisperings of revolution and piracy.

Well-to-do Athenians would descend to the 1914 **Posidonion Hotel** (⊠ Immediately west of the Dapia, near the harbor), the scene of glamorous society parties and balls in the era between the two world wars. The hotel's public rooms have retained this marvelous, unusual elegance.

The **Anargyrios and Korgialenios School** (½ km/¼ mi west of the Dapia), established as an English-style boarding school for the children of Greece's Anglophilic upper class, is known as the inspiration for the school in John Fowles's *The Magus.*

You may wish to walk up to **Kastelli,** the original settlement of Spetses, of which little remains but four churches: the **Panaghia** or *Koimisis tis Theotokou* (the Assumption of the Virgin Mary), from the 17th century; **Ayios Vassilis** (Saint Basil); the **Taxiarchoi** (Archangels), early 19th century; and **Ayia Triada** (Holy Trinity), late-18th century. The churches are kept locked, but ask for the property owner or the guardian, who has a key.

Beaches
Spetses's best beaches are on the south side of the island, in **Ayioi Anargyroi** and **Ayia Paraskevi.**

Biking
The lack of cars and the predominantly level roads make Spetses ideal for bicycling. One good trip is along the coastal road that circles the island, going from the main town to Ayia Paraskevi beach. You can also rent a mountain bike to use on the paths that zigzag through the island. Contact **Trek Mountain Bikes,** run by Nikolaos Kondaratos and his British wife, Elizabeth Allen, located on the main road about 750 ft left of the new harbor (☎ 0298/74505). They rent well-maintained bikes and equipment and can dispense advice about where to go, including crossing over to the Peloponnese for a few days.

Dining and Lodging
$–$$ ✕ **Exedra.** Called Sioras or Giorgos by locals (all three names are on the sign), this waterside taverna is in the old harbor where the yachts pull up. House specialties are fish Spetsiota, baked with tomato and wine; a dish called Argo, shrimp and lobster baked with feta; and mussels saganaki; fresh fish is always available. Magirefta include the hard-to-find *gouronopoulo kokkinisto,* boar in red sauce. One can also order grilled meats like souvlaki and even schnitzel. ⊠ *At edge of Palio Limani (go left from new harbor, 10-min walk),* ☎ *0298/73497.* MC. *Closed Nov.–Feb.*

$ ✕ **Lazaros.** One of the last traditional tavernas in town, Lazaros draws a boisterous local crowd to its place, decorated with old family photos and barrels of retsina lining the walls. The small selection of well-cooked dishes includes some daily specials, like goat in lemon sauce, chicken kokkinisto, grilled meats, and, occasionally, fresh fish at good prices. Tasty appetizers include homemade tzatziki, black-eyed bean salad called *mavromatika*, garlic potatoes, and tender, marinated beets. Order the barrel retsina (priced by the kilo). In summer, diners eat outside in a courtyard. ✉ *Botassi St., 900 ft up from Dappia,* ☎ *0298/72600. No credit cards. Closed mid-Nov.–mid-Mar. No lunch.*

$ ✕ **Patralis.** The seaside veranda here is the best place in town to savor
★ seafood mezedes and fresh fish—fried, grilled, or baked. Especially good are the fish soup; the lobster with spaghetti; and a kind of paella stuffed with mussels, shrimp, and crayfish. Fish includes the dorado, red mullet, pandora, common bream, and *skarptharia* (somewhat like sargus). Magirefta include stuffed peppers and tomatoes, oven-baked lamb, and eggplant with minced meat (*papoutsakia,* or "little shoes") or with tomatoes and onion. They make a mean baked apple for dessert, and the service is especially friendly. ✉ *2,500 ft right of new harbor, near Spetses Hotel,* ☎ *0298/72134. MC, V. Closed Nov.–Dec.*

$$$ ✕🏨 **Spetses Hotel.** This self-contained resort has the best of both worlds: privacy and proximity to the delightful town. The rooms are comfortable, with TVs and air-conditioning, and some of them have a sea view. Moreover, the hotel has its own beach, and buffet breakfast is included in the price. ✉ *Spetses beach, 18050,* ☎ *0298/72602 through 0298/72604; winter, in Athens 01/821–3126;* 📠 *0298/72494; winter, in Athens 01/821–0602. 77 rooms. Restaurant, beach. MC, V. Closed Nov.–Mar.*

$$$ 🏨 **Nissia Traditional Residences.** The impressive entrance of this new,
★ deluxe waterfront hotel is like a movie set, its facade the carefully restored Daskalakis factory. Each suite is named after an island and there are rooms for all tastes—romantic, modern, aristocratic—with direct-dial phone, independent heating and air-conditioning, color satellite-TV, private veranda or balcony, and fully equipped kitchen. Even the smallest accommodations seem roomy, and two-thirds have spacious sitting areas with fireplace. Only the studios don't have a sea view, and overlook the garden instead. The splurge-worthy "presidential" suites are in two towers with exceptionally roomy layouts and top-view verandas. Buffet breakfast is bountiful and included in the rates. ✉ *1,500 ft from Dappia, Kounoupitsa, 18050,* ☎ *0298/75000 through 00298/75011, Athens office 01/346–2879 or 01/342–1279;* 📠 *0298/75012, Athens office 01/346–5313. 14 studios, 15 suites. Restaurant, pool. AE, DC, MC, V.*

$$ 🏨 **Hotel Posidonion.** This glorious fin-de-siècle waterfront hotel has a
★ remarkable vantage stretching from Spetses Harbor to the mainland opposite. The Belle Epoque public areas have the grace of an earlier age and an air of grandeur atypical of Greece. The high-ceiling guest rooms are more modest than the public rooms, although the windows in the front rooms frame the wonderful view. Facilities include a bar and breakfast room. ✉ *Dapia waterfront, 18050,* ☎ *0298/72308 or 0298/72006; winter, in Athens 01/361–3751;* 📠 *0298/72208; winter, in Athens 01/360–7964. 50 rooms. Restaurant, bar, breakfast room. AE, DC, V. Closed mid-Oct.–Mar.*

Festival

BATTLE REENACTMENT

Spetses puts on an enormous reenactment of a War of Independence naval battle for one week in early September, complete with costumed fighters and burning ships. Book your hotel well in advance if you wish to see this popular event; check with the Spetses tourist police for more information (☞ Visitor Information *in* Excursions from Athens A to Z, *below*).

Nightlife

CLUBS

Surviving many years and with ever bigger dimensions is **Figaro** (⊠ Palio Limani), which plays mainstream rhythms; on weekends it's packed with writhing bodies, or as the Greeks would say *ginete hamos*; chaos reigns. For the newest "in" bars, ask your hotel or just stroll down to the old harbor, which has the highest concentration of clubs.

DELPHI

Arachova, Delphi, Galaxidi

The sublime ruins of Delphi will invigorate those new to the study of ancient Greece, as well as those who have long awaited a chance to see where the Pythian priestesses uttered their cryptic prophecies. After the Acropolis of Athens, the site of Delphi is the one that is likely to make the most powerful and lasting impression on the traveler in Greece. Its history reaches back at least as far as the Mycenaean period, and in Homer's *Iliad* it is referred to as Pytho. Nearby is Mt. Parnassus, where the formerly quiet mountain village of Arachova is now an odd confluence of traditional Greek mountain village and Athenian cafés, thanks to the proximity of ski lifts. On the coast, Galaxidi now caters to wealthy Athenians who have restored many of the mansions once owned by shipbuilders.

The preferred route to Delphi follows the National Road to the Thebes turnoff, at 74 km (46 mi). Take the secondary road south past Thebes and continue west through the fertile plain, now planted with cotton, to busy Levadia, capital of the nome of Boeotia. Almost halfway between Levadia and Delphi the traveler passes the famous junction of roads, the Triple Way, where the roads from Delphi, Daulis, and Levadia meet. It is here, according to legend, and so described by Sophocles in *Oedipus Rex,* that Oedipus, returning on foot from Delphi, met his father, Laius, King of Thebes. The latter, having struck Oedipus with his whip in order to make room for his chariot to pass, was in turn attacked and accidentally killed by the young man, who did not recognize his father, not having seen his parents since his birth. Journeying to Thebes, Oedipus, of course, then ascended the city throne and unknowingly married his mother, Jocasta, thus fulfilling the prophecy that had caused his parents to abandon him at birth. If you detour in Levadia by following the signs for the *piges,* you will come to the banks of the ancient springs of Lethe and Mnemosyne, or Oblivion and Remembrance (these springs are about a 10-minute walk from the main square); in antiquity the Erkinas (Hercyne) gorge was believed to be the entrance to the underworld. Today, the plane- and maple tree–shaded river is spanned by an old stone arch bridge built in Ottoman times.

Osios Loukas

㉑ *150 km (93 mi) northwest of Athens, 24 km (15 mi) southeast of Arachova.*

The monastic complex Osios Loukas, still inhabited by a number of monks, looms on a prominent rise above a sparsely inhabited, fertile valley and remains one of the finest extant examples of a great Byzantine shrine of the 11th century. Named after a local hermit called Luke—not the Evangelist—this important monastery was founded by the emperor Romanos II in 961, in recognition of the accuracy of Luke's prophecy that Crete would be liberated by an emperor named Romanos. The highlight of the complex is the 11th-century Katholikon, which can be compared to the Church at Daphni in the beauty of its architecture and quality of the mosaics in the narthex and in portions of the domed nave. Particularly impressive are the gaunt saints and warriors in the dome and pendentives and the tomb of Osios Loukas, set in the crypt. ⊠ *On rise above valley,* ☎ *0267/22797.* ▭ *800 dr.* ☉ *May–mid-Sept., daily 8–2 and 4–7; mid-Sept.–Apr., daily 8–5.*

En Route From Dhistomo, 10 km (6 mi) west of Osios Loukas, an alternate, less-traveled route to Delphi climbs over the plain of Desfina and descends sharply to the sea just east of Itea. This route is slightly longer but more pleasant and lets you stop in Itea for a seaside lunch. The conventional route ignores Dhistomo and continues west past the Schiste turnoff, climbing ever higher as it nears Mt. Parnassus.

Arachova

㉑ *24 km (15½ mi) northwest of Osios Loukas, 157 km (97 mi) from Athens.*

Arachova's gray-stone houses with red-tile roofs cling to the steep slopes. Mt. Parnassus, the highest mountain in Greece after Mt. Olympus, has been undergoing development for skiing since 1980 and is now a popular winter resort. The new energy and money the change has brought into the region have been put to good use: The sophisticated newcomers (mostly Athenians) have preserved and restored many otherwise doomed houses, and several good tavernas and cozy hotels now line the cobbled alleyways.

Dining and Lodging

$$ ✗ **Fterolakka.** Cozy up to the fireplace in winter and enjoy the mouth-watering game: local pheasant and quail, wild duck and goose baked in clay pots, *lago stifado* (hare with tiny sweet onions), and wild boar. The restaurant also prepares numerous magirefta, including rooster in wine sauce with fat spaghetti, and lamb or beef kokkinisto. Grilled meats cover everything from a simple souvlaki to the more exotic *kokkoretsi* (lamb innards on a spit, held together by intestines). A local tasty dessert is *strifto,* similar to baklava, with house-made phyllo. ⊠ *Delfon St. at bottom of stairs ascending to Ayios Giorgos church, near Platia Tomarovrissi,* ☎ *0267/32556. AE, MC, V. Closed June–Oct. (open only for tourist groups).*

$ ✗ **Taverna O Platanos.** About a 15-minute walk from Arachova's center, this traditional taverna is a meat lover's dream-come-true, with goodies like *splinandera, gardoumba,* and kokkoretsi, various combinations of lamb organs spit-roasted or oven-baked. Be bold and you will be rewarded. ⊠ *Platia Tropaion, Platanies, near Ayios Giorgos church,* ☎ *0267/31891. V. No lunch Mon.–Thurs. May–Oct.*

$ ✗ **Taverna P. Dasargiris (Barba Yiannis).** The son of the late Barba Yiannis (Uncle John) now runs this busy taverna, the first in Arachova. The gargantuan summer and winter throngs can cause occasional surliness among the staff, but the food is worth your patience. In a town that counted its wealth by the size of its flocks, this taverna fittingly serves standard meat dishes and, above all, lamb. Excellent magirefta include the lamb with oregano and the beef in red sauce, both served with the noodles called *hilopites,* for which the area is known. Sample the fried *formaella* (a mild local sheep's milk cheese); the *hortopites,* pastries filled with mountain greens; grilled beef patties stuffed with formaella, gouda, or kefalograviera cheese; or *splinandera* (a tasty mix of various lamb organs), which Greeks customers swear by. At Easter, the cook makes an unforgettable roast lamb and the famous egg-lemon soup called *magiritsa*. Don't forget to try the homemade *brusco* wine (a dark red), which seemingly cuts right through the cholesterol. ⊠ *Arachova–Delfon 56 Rd.,* ☎ *0267/31291. No credit cards. No lunch May–Oct.*

$$ 🏨 **Arachova Inn.** Opened in 1991 and run by friendly staff, about half of this inn's small, efficient, yellow-and-peach-tone guest rooms have a view of the lower town and valley. All have color TV and direct-dial phone. The sitting rooms and dining area have touches of local handicrafts and rustic wood furnishings. In winter the dining room and the lounge are warmed by fireplaces; buffet breakfast is included. ⊠ *Arachova–Delfon Rd., 32004,* ☎ *0267/31353, 0267/31497, or 0267/ 32195,* 🆎 *0267/31134. 42 rooms. Restaurant. AE, DC, MC, V.*

$$ 🏨 **Hotel Anemolia Best Western.** At this homey hotel on a bluff above
★ the Delphi road at the western edge of Arachova, most of the large guest rooms have a view of the plain of Amphissa from their balconies; on a clear day you may be able to see as far as the Peloponnese. All rooms have TV and some have bathtubs instead of showers; the eight new rooms have fireplaces but no balconies. Enjoy après-ski among the simple furnishings, large lobby fireplace, and country antiques. The only covered swimming pool in Arachova here is usable year-round. Buffet breakfast is included in the price, at the high end of its category. ⊠ *Arachova–Delfon Rd., 32004,* ☎ *0267/31640 through 0267/31644,* ☎ 🆎 *0267/31644. 63 rooms. Restaurant, bar, pool, sauna, exercise room. AE, DC, MC, V.*

$ 🏨 **Apollo Inn.** This fairly new inn makes up for its crammed location in the center of town with neat rooms with wooden furniture and lovely terraces. Buffet breakfast is included in the price. Be careful not to confuse this hotel with the Apollo Hotel at the other end of town, run by the same family but with shared bathrooms. ⊠ *Arachova–Delfon Rd. 106, 32004,* ☎ *0267/31540,* ☎ 🆎 *0267/31057. 19 rooms. AE, MC, V.*

$ 🏨 **Hotel Parnassos.** Offering a rock-bottom solution to the housing problem, this little family-run hotel is comfortable for the budget price. The quiet bedrooms in the old two-story family home are of various sizes, mostly large, with high ceilings and neat, plain furniture. The six rooms in the front have a view of the illuminated clocktower, Mt. Xerovouni, and the valley below. There is a sitting area with fireplace and a loft where guests eat breakfast. ⊠ *Delfon 18 near the traffic bridge, 32004,* ☎ *0267/31307. 9 rooms with shared bath. DC, MC, V.*

Nightlife

On winter weekends Arachova streets are jammed with Athenians who come almost as much for the nightlife as for the skiing. Clubs change frequently; recent popular additions are **Petra,** located on Platia Lekka, with quiet foreign and Greek music, and small rooms with fireplaces and darts; the rowdier **Cinema Snow Me,** a split-level club with young things dancing on the bar and "face control" to keep out the unhip; and lovely **Emboriko** on Delfon Street, for the older crowd, where politicians, journalists, and artists mingle with the anonymous, either in the two quieter sections where you can order a bite or in the action-packed bar. Check with your hotel for the latest in the club scene, which can only get more hectic in the coming years.

Outdoor Activities and Sports

HIKING

The summit of Mt. Parnassus (8,061 ft) is now easily accessible, thanks to roads opened up for the ski areas. The less hardy can drive to within 45 minutes of the summit. You can also drive to the Hellenic Alpine Club's refuge at 6,201 ft to spend the night and then walk to the summit in time to catch the sunrise—the best way to climb Mt. Parnassus!

For information on hiking activities, *see* Hiking *in* Outdoor Activities and Sports, *below.*

SKIING

If you hear that the snow is good on Parnassus, go for it. Ski with the muses, just 40 minutes from Arachova, at the **Ski Center Parnassos** (☎ ☎ 0234/22689 or 0234/22695). **Kelaria** has more challenging runs, but **Fterolakka** has better restaurants and beginners' slopes. Rental equipment is available at both and in Arachova. Contact the EOT for a brochure on skiing in Greece or the **Hellenic Skiing Federation** (✉ Karageorgi Servias 7, 8th floor, Syntagma, Athens 10563, ☎ 01/323–0182 or 01/323–4412, ℻ 01/323–0142). The **Alpine Club of Athens** (Kapnikareas Sq. 2, Athens 10563, ☎ 01/321–2355 or 01/321–4412, ℻ 01/324–4789) organizes mountain-skiing classes for experienced skiers and snowboarding classes for children.

Shopping

Arachova's main street is lined with shops selling rugs and weavings; the town was known even in pre-ski days as a place to shop for handicrafts, honey, and wine.

HANDICRAFTS

The modern mass produced bedspreads and kilim-style carpets sold today in Arachova are colorful and reasonably priced. If you poke into dark corners in the stores, you still might turn up something made of local wool, though anything that claims to be antique bears a higher price.

LOCAL SPECIALTIES

Here you'll also find delicious Parnassus honey; formaella (local, rather sweet) cheese; and *hilopites,* or "thousand pies" (thin homemade noodles cut into thousands of tiny squares, often served with chicken and lamb). Be sure to try the fiery *rakomelo,* a combination of raki and honey, served in most of the bars and cafés.

Delphi

189 km (117½ mi) northwest of Athens, 10 km (6 mi) west of Arachova.

Home to Apollo and to the most famous oracle of antiquity, Delphi enjoys a site of the greatest possible grandeur, whether seen from the ruins of the sanctuary or from one of the town's hotels or terraced village houses. The road from Arachova to Delphi is guarded by great twin cliffs, the **Phaedriades** (the Bright Ones)—at sunset the sides of the cliffs glow red with the reflection of the sun's rays and the whole ravine of the Pleistos and the steep terraced vineyards in the valley leading to the rocky pass of Arahova are bathed in a warm, deep purple light. These cliffs form the eastern gate, so to speak, of the site, whose ancient ruins lie cradled in a theatrical curve between the Phaedriades and Mt. Profitis Ilias to the west. In the gorge below Delphi, the bed of the Pleistos winds between a narrow strip of olive trees flanked by precipitous cliffs, opening out into the Sacred Plain, where the silvery-green sea of olives, possibly the finest grove in all Greece, ends in the calm aquamarine waters of the Bay of Itea. The modern city of Delphi is traversed by a main street, thick with restaurants and souvenir shops, with the entrance to the sanctuary reached easily from almost any point in the central town, in anything from 5 to 10 minutes' walk. When first seen from the road, it would appear that there is hardly anything left to attest to the existence of the religious city. Only the treasury of the Athenians and a few other columns are left standing; but once you are within the precincts, the plan becomes clearer and the layout is revealed in such detail that it is not impossible to conjure up

Delphi

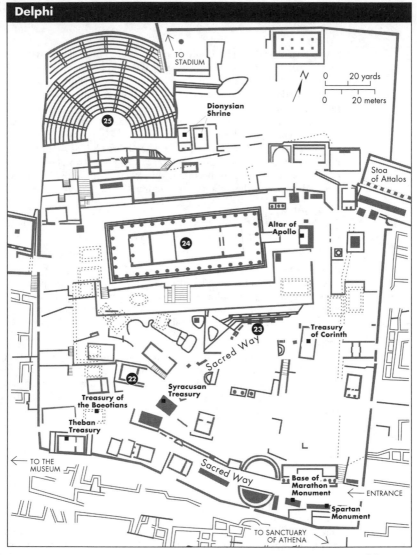

TO
STADIUM

Dionysian
Shrine

Stoa
of Attalos

0   20 yards

0   20 meters

Altar of
Apollo

25

24

23

Treasury
of Corinth

Sacred Way

22

Syracusan
Treasury

Treasury of
the Boeotians

Theban
Treasury

← TO THE
MUSEUM

Sacred Way

Base of
Marathon
Monument

← ENTRANCE

Spartan
Monument

TO SANCTUARY
OF ATHENA

Treasury of the
Athenians, **22**
Stoa of the
Athenians, **23**
Temple of Apollo, **24**
Theater, **25**

a vision of what the scene must have once been when Delphi was the holiest place in all Greece.

At first the settlement probably was sacred to a female deity; toward the end of the Greek Dark Ages (circa 1100 BC–800 BC), the site incorporated the cult of Apollo. According to Plutarch, who was a priest of Apollo at Delphi, the oracle was discovered by chance, when a shepherd noticed that his flock went into a frenzy when it came near a certain chasm in the rock. When he approached, he also came under a spell and began to utter prophecies, as did his fellow villagers. They chose from among their number a woman to sit over the chasm on a three-footed stool and to prophesy.

Traditionally, the Pythia was a woman over 50, who, upon her anointment, gave up normal life and lived thereafter in seclusion. On oracle day, the seventh of the month, the Pythia prepared herself by washing in the Castalian Spring and undergoing a purification involving barley smoke and laurel leaves. If the male priests of Apollo determined the day was propitious for prophesying, she entered the Temple of Apollo to sit on the tripod, where she drank the Castalian water, chewed laurel leaves, and presumably sank into a trance. Questions presented to her received strange and garbled answers, which were then translated into verse by the priests. A number of the lead tablets on which questions were inscribed have been uncovered, but the official answers were inscribed only in the memories of questioners and priests. Those that have survived, from various sources, suggest the equivocal nature of these sibylline emanations: Perhaps the most famous is the answer given to King Croesus of Lydia, who asked if he should attack the Persians. "Croesus, having crossed the Halys River, will destroy a great realm," said the Pythia. Thus encouraged, he crossed it, only to find his *own* empire destroyed.

During the 8th and 7th centuries BC, the oracle's advice played a significant role in the colonization of southern Italy and Sicily (Magna Graecia) by Greece's Amphictyonic League. By 582 BC the Pythian Games had become a quadrennial festival similar to those held at Olympia. Increasingly an international center, Delphi attracted supplicants from beyond the Greek mainland, including such valued clients as King Midas and King Croesus, both hailing from wealthy kingdoms in Asia Minor. During this period of prosperity many cities built treasure houses at Delphi. The sanctuary was threatened during the Persian War but never attacked, and it continued to prosper, in spite of the fact that Athens and Sparta, two of its most powerful patrons, were locked in war.

Delphi came under the influence first of Macedonia and then of the Aetolian League (290 BC–190 BC) before yielding to the Romans in 189 BC. Although the Roman general Sulla plundered Delphi in 86 BC, there were at least 500 bronze statues left to be collected by Nero in AD 66, and the site was still full of fine works of art when Pausanias visited and described it a century later. The emperor Hadrian restored many sanctuaries in Greece, including Delphi's, but within a century or two the oracle was silent. In AD 385, Theodosius abolished the oracle. Only in the late-19th century did French excavators begin to uncover the site of Apollo.

The **Sanctuary of Athena** is just below the Arachova road before you reach the Phaedriades. The most notable among the numerous remains on the terrace is the **Tholos**, or Round Building, a graceful 4th-century BC ruin of Pentelic marble, whose purpose and dedication are unknown. This remains one of the purest and most exquisite monuments of antiquity still to be seen at Delphi. Theodoros, its architect, wrote a treatise on his work: an indication in itself of the exceptional architectural quality of the monument. Beneath the Phaedriades, in the cleft between the rocks a path leads to the **Castalian Fountain,** a spring where visitors bathed to purify themselves before approaching the sanctuary. Access to the fountain is presently restricted because of the danger of falling rocks.

On the main road, beyond the spring, is the modern entrance to the sanctuary. Passing through a **square** surrounded by late-Roman porticoes, the path leads through the main gate onto the **Sacred Way.** On its way up the hill the Sacred Way passes between building foundations and bases for votive dedications, stripped now of ornament and statue, mere scraps of what was one of the richest collections of art and treasures in antiquity. Thanks to the 2nd-century AD writings of Pausanias, archaeologists have identified treasuries built by the Thebans, the Corinthians, the Syracusans, and others—a roster of 6th- and 5th-century BC powers.

㉒ The **Treasury of the Athenians** was built with money from the victory over the Persians at Marathon. Northeast of the treasury are the re-
㉓ mains of the **Stoa of the Athenians,** which housed, among other objects, an immense cable with which the Persian king Xerxes roped together a pontoon bridge for his army to cross the Hellespont from Asia to Europe.

㉔ The **Temple of Apollo** visible today (there were three successive temples built on the site) is from the 4th century BC. Although ancient sources speak of a chasm within, there is no trace of that opening in the earth from which emanated trance-inducing vapors. Above the temple is the
㉕ well-preserved **Theater** (which seated 5,000); it was built in the 4th century BC, restored in about 160 BC, and later was restored again by the Romans. From a sun-warmed seat on the last tier, the visitor may obtain a panoramic bird's-eye view of the sanctuary and the convulsed landscape that encloses it. Also worth the climb is the view from the **Stadium,** still farther up the mountain, at the highest point of the ancient town. Built and restored in various periods and cut partially from the living rock, the stadium underwent a final transformation under Herodes Atticus, the Athenian benefactor of the 2nd century AD. It lies cradled in a grove of pine trees, a quiet refuge removed from the sanctuary below and backed by the sheer, majestic rise of the mountain. ✉ *Delphi site, immediately east of Delphi modern town along road to Arachova,* ☎ *0265/82312.* 🎫 *1,200 dr.* ⊙ *Weekdays 7:30–7:30 (9:30–3:30 in winter), weekends 8:30–3.*

Housed in a modern eyesore of a building, the **Delphi Museum** contains a wonderful collection of art and architectural sculpture, principally from the Sanctuaries of Apollo and Athena Pronoia. Here is one of the greatest ancient statues of all, the bronze *Charioteer,* a delicate, diminutive sculpture whose size is surprising if you are seeing it in person for the first time. Created in about 470 BC to commemorate the victory of a Syracusan prince in the Pythian chariot races, the statue is believed to have stood on a terrace wall above the Temple of Apollo, near which it was found in 1896. It is not established who executed the work, although the donor is supposed to have been a well-known patron of chariot racing, Gelon, the Tyrant of Syracuse. The statue commemorates a victory in the Pythian Games at the beginning of the 5th century BC. Most striking is the severe classical simplicity of the execution, which does not detract from the intensely natural and lifelike aspect of the beautiful young man holding the reins. Note the eyes, inlaid with a white substance resembling enamel, the pupils consisting of two concentric onyx rings of different colors. The sculpture of the feet and of the hair clinging to the nape of the neck is perfect in detail. This is one of the few ancient bronzes to survive pillage and war, and its strength and quality remind us of what we have lost.

Other masterpieces on view are sculpted scenes from the Siphnian Treasury of the Trojan War and of the Olympic gods in battle with the Giants; a statue of Antinoos, Emperor Hadrian's favorite; and the twin statues of Kleobis and Biton, stylized representations of young brothers who were given the gift of eternal sleep by Hera, after they yoked themselves to a chariot to carry their mother to Hera's temple, and of whom it was said, "those whom the gods love die young." Dating to the first half of the 6th century BC, these statues are related to the series of *kouroi* (stylized statues of young men) in the National Museum in Athens. There are also fragments of a silver-plated bull of the 6th century BC, the largest example surviving from antiquity of a statue in precious metal. In the same room are the remarkable remains of a male figure executed in the chryselephantine technique, which used *chrys-* (gold) and *elephantine* (ivory). Finally, in Room 11 note the family monument of nine statues, which reproduces in marble a group originally sculpted in bronze, at least partially by Lysippos, one of the best artists of the 4th century BC. ⊠ *Immediately east of Delphi modern town along road to Arachova,* ☎ *0265/82312.* 🎫 *1,200 dr.* ◉ *Weekdays 7:30–7:30 (9:30–3:30 in winter), weekends 8:30–3.*

Dining and Lodging

$$ ✕ **Iniochos.** This excellent restaurant serving local specialties offers some of Delphi's best eating, with an emphasis on appetizers: zucchini croquettes, roast feta, *bekri meze* (spicy lamb stew). In winter, warm yourself at the fireplace in the dining room; in summer eat on the enormous veranda overlooking Delphi. Try the *hortopites* (vegetable pies), quail filled with cheese, pork with celery, or *kokkora krasato* (wine-stewed rooster), a regional favorite. ⊠ *Vas. Pavlou and Friderikis 19,* ☎ *0265/82710, 0265/82151, 0265/82316, or 0265/82480. Reservations essential. AE, DC, MC, V.*

$ ✕ **Sunflower.** You'll find all the Greek classics here, well prepared and inexpensively priced—dolmades, tzatziki, a rich bean soup called *fassolada*—but the restaurant is known for its savory bourekakia, pastries stuffed with cheese and minced meat. ⊠ *Vas. Pavlou and Friderikis 33,* ☎ *0265/82442. AE, V. Closed weekdays in Nov.*

$$ ✕🖭 **Kastalia.** Simple rooms with paintings of the area offer views over Mt. Parnassus or to the Gulf of Itea. The restaurant serves traditional Greek food, sometimes with a twist; lamb fricassee, for example, has lettuce rather than the typical cabbage. The price includes Continental breakfast, and half-board is available. In a separate new wing called Villa Apollonia, more luxurious, larger rooms have air-conditioning and TVs. ⊠ *Vas. Pavlou and Friderikis 13, 33054,* ☎ *0265/82205 through 0265/82207, reservations 0265/82919 or 0265/82325,* ℻ *0265/82208; Villa Apollonia,* ☎ *0265/82325,* ℻ *0265/82609. Kastalia, 26 rooms; Villa Apollonia 12 rooms. Restaurant, air-conditioning. AE, DC, MC, V.*

$$$ 🖭 **Hotel Vouzas.** The hotel crests the edge of a gorge and has won-★ derful views from every room, and an intimate living room with a fireplace. It is also the closest (about 1,600 ft) to the archaeological site. A fantastic new veranda, where breakfast is served half the year, overlooks the gorge, olive groves, and the Pleistos river. The hotel fills up on winter weekends with Athenians who come to challenge Mt. Parnassus, fortified by the buffet breakfast. Half-board is available. ⊠ *Vas. Pavlou and Friderikis 1, 33054,* ☎ *0265/82232 through 0265/82234,* ℻ *0265/82033. 58 rooms, 1 suite. Restaurant. MC, V.*

$$ ▦ **Apollo.** Owned and operated by a husband-and-wife team ("She's
★   the decorator, I do the public relations," says he), this hotel is lovely.
The *saloni* (living room) here has traditional wall hangings and old prints
among its carefully selected furnishings. The cheerful rooms have light-
wood furniture set off by blue quilts and striped curtains, with pretty
bathroom tiles, hair dryers, TVs, and minibars. Many have wood bal-
conies with black-iron railings, and a full breakfast is included. ⊠ *Vas.
Pavlou and Friderikis 59B, 33054,* ☎ *0265/82580 or 0265/82244,* FAX
*0265/82455. 21 rooms. Air-conditioning, minibars. MC, V. Closed week-
days Jan.–mid-Mar.*

$$ ▦ **Villa Filoxenia-Apollo.** Rustic, charming, and tastefully decorated
by the same people who own the Apollo hotel (☞ *above*), Delphi's newest
addition has amenities like electronic keys and air-conditioning, a
game area, and a lounge with fireplace, despite its price at the low end
of its category. Rooms include TV, minibar, and hair dryer; most have
balconies and a view. Full breakfast is included. ⊠ *Vas. Pavlou and
Friderikis 15, 33054,* ☎ *0265/83114,* FAX *0265/82455. 14 rooms. Air-
conditioning. MC, V. Closed weekdays Jan.–mid-Mar.*

$ ▦ **Acropole.** This friendly, family-run hotel has a garden and a spec-
★   tacular view—bare mountainside and a sea of olive groves—so that
guests feel as though they're completely secluded. The rooms are
freshly furnished with carved Skyrian furniture, traditional linens, and
paintings, strangely enough, of the islands. Ten rooms have air-conditioning; all have satellite TV, direct-dial phones, and hair dryers. ⊠
Filellinon 13, 33054, ☎ *0265/82675,* FAX *0265/83171. 42 rooms. Air-
conditioning. AE, DC, MC, V.*

Festival

Sit in the ancient stadium of Delphi under the stars and watch everything from the National Beijing Opera Theater doing *Bacchae* to *Pour
Antigone* danced by the Centre Choréographique National du Mont-
pellier Languedoc-Roussillion at the **summer arts festival,** organized
by the European Cultural Centre of Delphi in July. The festival is in
conjunction with an annual symposium. All performances, which
begin around 8:30 PM, are open to the public and require a token fee.
For program information, call the center in Athens (☎ 01/331–2781
through 01/331–2785), or the ancient stadium (☎ 0265/82731).

En Route   The road west from Delphi winds down into the Sacred Plain, passing the modern village of Chryssa and leading through olive groves to
the seaside port of Itea, which takes its name from the *ites* (willows)
that used to stretch down to the sea.

Galaxidi

㉖   *17½ km (11 mi) southwest of Itea.*

The harbor town of Galaxidi still has preserved traces of classical masonry but enjoyed its heyday in the 19th century, thanks to shipbuilding and a thriving mercantile economy. After the invention of steamships,
the town faded until its recent discovery by outsiders, who appreciated the sea captains' fine houses and the idyllic atmosphere, reminiscent of an island. Now a historical monument, Galaxidi is undergoing
renovation and restoration. If you are a shore person rather than a mountain person, Galaxidi is a good alternative to Delphi as a base. Stroll
the narrow streets with their elegant stone seafarers' mansions and
squares with geraniums and palm trees, taking a peek into **Ayios Nikolaos**—the cathedral is named after the patron saint of sailors and possesses a beautiful carved 19th-century altar screen. If you walk to the
far side of the sheltered harbor, Galaxidi will appear reflected in the

still waters. After a late-afternoon swim in one of the pebbly coves around the headland to the north, dine along the waterfront.

Dining and Lodging

$–$$ ✕ **Barko tis Maritsas.** This charming restaurant, located in a former captains' *kafenion* (coffeehouse) (1850) and decorated with a nautical theme, serves traditional Greek cuisine, including some local specialties. Interesting are the pies—zucchini pie with dill and spinach pie—as well as the eggplant dip enhanced by grated walnut. There is a large selection of fresh fish and seafood appetizers, but mussels are what Galaxidi is known for—here they're served in a saganaki, steamed, and in a pilaf. Another local dish is *kemelia,* minced meat and rice wrapped in onion. Homemade sweets include the regional *amigdalopasta,* made with almonds and topped with *kaimaki* (vanilla flavored with mastic gum) ice cream. During Carnival, the restaurant hosts a rambunctious *glendi* (celebration), with live music, dancing, and a special custom of throwing flour about the restaurant, not to be missed. ⊠ *Akti Ianthis 34 on the waterfront,* ☎ *0265/41059. Reservations essential Sat. eve. No credit cards.*

$–$$ ✕ **Porto.** This popular restaurant is one of many near the harbor that, unsurprisingly, specialize in fish: porgy, common bream, sargus, sea bass, dentex (when in season), and, of course, mussels, served several ways. You could buck the trend and order the equally good meat dishes like *kotopoulo krasato* (chicken stewed in wine); oven-baked lamb; beef *yiouvetsi,* made with rice-shape noodles; or succulent lamb ribs. ⊠ *Akti Ianthis 53, near start of harbor,* ☎ *0265/41182. No credit cards.*

$ ✕ **O Dervenis.** Galaxidi's tiny main port is lined with restaurants, bars, and cafés, but some of the best food in town can be found a few blocks inland, at O Dervenis. The restaurant has a covered garden for outdoor dining and serves excellent taverna fare. It will be tough choosing an appetizer from the homemade tzatziki, the spinach pie made with feta and kefalograviera; marinated octopus or gavros (resembles a large anchovy); minced meat wrapped in a fresh vine leaf (that only grows a few weeks in summer); and a local specialty, *avgopita* (egg pie). ⊠ *N. Gourgouri St. next to old girls' school,* ☎ *0265/41177. No credit cards.*

$$ ⌂ **Galaxa Hotel.** Opened in 1988 in a 180-year-old blue-and-white captain's house by the nice, professional Emanuel Papilaris, the Galaxa has simple rooms decorated with reproductions of antique ship photos. All have color TV, phone, and air-conditioning; six have a coveted sea view, but if yours hasn't, you have an excuse to sidle up to the terrace garden, which also serves as a bar and breakfast area. A full breakfast is included in the price; juice, eggs, homemade marmalades, and local honey. The owner's wife, Maria, will cook for guests on request: *pites* (savory pies) with homemade phyllo, baked *gavros,* mussels, and other shellfish. Guests may also rent a captained boat that holds about 15 people with a licensed captain for excursions at reasonable prices. ⊠ *Eleftherias 8, near John Kennedy Rd., 33052,* ☎ *0265/ 41620 or 0265/41625,* ℻ *0265/42053. 10 rooms. Air-conditioning. AE, DC, MC, V.*

$ ⌂ **Ganimede.** Owner Brunello Perocco has taken full advantage of the elegant spaces provided by a typical 19th-century Galaxidi captain's house (1881). He combines Italian finesse with Roumeliot sensibility. Here and there stand furnishings from the former residents—a secretariat with white marble, trunks, old closets, and grand mirrors—interspersed with modern artifacts like Arachova weavings and small sculptures and paintings. Each room is decorated differently; all have independent heating and air-conditioning. In winter the sitting room with a blazing fire beckons for breakfast, a space where the owner sometimes hosts art exhibits when the weather warms. In summer, breakfast moves to the lush courtyard and is a legendary feast: bread, cake, cheese scones, Bruno's concoctions like olive cream and garbanzo bean pâté, and his famous marmalades—apricot chutney, plum-fig jam, tangerine with whiskey—all accompanied by the owner's gentle multilingual humor. Book ahead in high season; the few rooms go fast. ⊠ *N. Gourgouris 20, 33052,* ☎ *0265/41328 or 094/834354 (mobile phone),* 𝐅𝐀𝐗 *0265/42160. 8 rooms. Air-conditioning. No credit cards. Closed Nov.–Dec. 20.*

NEED A   For a coffee, drink, or snack, try the **Omilo** (⊠ Old Yacht Club, ☎
BREAK?   0265/42111, 𝐅𝐀𝐗 0265/42298), at the entrance to the main harbor
            and open from early morning to late at night. The chairs and tables on a
            little beach make a simple setting, and one of the best bartenders in
            town provides exceptional service. The view is unforgettable, especially
            at sunset: The Gulf of Itea stretches before you and the peaks of Parnas-
            sus tower in the background, with the little gray houses of Delphi clus-
            tered on its slopes. You can swim off the pebble beach here, and
            midnight dips are encouraged.

EXCURSIONS FROM ATHENS A TO Z

Arriving and Departing

See Athens A to Z *in* Chapter 2.

Getting Around

By Bus

Places close to Athens can be reached with the blue city bus lines (100 dr.): Bus A16 from Platia Eleftherias for **Dafni** and **Elefsina**; Bus 224 from Akadimias station coupled with a 25-minute walk for **Kaisariani**; the A3 from Syntagma Square for **Glyfada, Vouliagmen,** and **Varkiza**; Bus A2 from Syntagma for **Voula.** For the rest of the destinations, if you can't rent a car, the next most efficient mode of travel is the regional KTEL bus system in combination with taxis. The extensive network serves all points in **Attica** from Athens, and local buses connect the smaller towns and villages at least daily. The orange KTEL buses leave hourly from their main station in downtown Athens (⊠ Platia Aigyptou at the corner of Mavromateon and Leoforos Alexandras) for **Sounion** (☎ 01/821–0179); fare is 1,150 dr. inland route through Mesogeion, and 1,200 dr. for coastal road. One can also catch this bus from Klathmonos Square or Fillelinon Street. They also leave regularly for **Marathon** (☎ 01/821–0872), with fare of 700 dr., and every half hour to **Lavrio** (☎ 01/821–3203), with fare of 950 dr. For more distant locales, see the individual site listings; the EOT distributes a list of bus schedules. For **Delphi,** there are six de-partures daily from Terminal B at Liossion 260 in Athens (☎ 01/831–7096), beginning at 7:30 AM. The journey takes about three hours and costs 2,850 dr. From the same station, there are four buses daily mak-ing the four-hour trip to **Galaxidi** (☎ 01/831–7096), starting at 7:30 AM; the fare is 3,450 dr. Buses depart hourly from 5:50 AM to 8:30 PM for Levadia near **Osios Loukas** (☎ 01/831–7173). The journey takes two hours and costs 2,250 dr. To get to Terminal B from downtown Athens, catch Bus 024 on Amalias Street in front of the National Gardens. Tick-ets for these buses are sold only at this terminal, so you should call to book seats well in advance during high season or holidays.

By Car

Points in Attica can be reached from the main Thessaloniki–Athens and Athens–Patras highways, with the National Road (Ethniki Odos) the most popular route. From the Peloponnese, you can drive east via Corinth to Athens, or from Patras, take the Rion–Antirion ferry and the coast road, visiting Delphi first. Most of the roads when you get off the highway are two-lane secondary arteries; a few of them (notably from Athens to Delphi and Itea and to Sounion) have been recently upgraded, are very good, and are often spectacularly scenic. Expect heavy traffic to Delphi in summer and ski season, and to and from Athens on weekends. Cars are not allowed on Hydra and Spetses.

The **Automobile and Touring Club of Greece** (ELPA, ✉ Athens Tower, Messoghion 2–4, 11525, ☎ 01/748–8800; in an emergency, 104; FAX 01/778–6642) can help with tourist information for drivers (☎ 174), and it assists tourists with breakdowns free of charge if they belong to AAA or to ELPA; otherwise, there is a charge.

By Ferry

The islands of Poros and Spetses are so close to the Peloponnese mainland that you can drive there, park, and ferry across the channel in any of a number of caïques (price negotiable), but to get to them from Athens or to visit the other Saronic Gulf Islands, you must take to the sea in a ship.

The **Argosaronikos Lines** (☎ 01/412–6181 or 01/417–6792; or call Piraeus port authority, ☎ 01/422–6000 or 01/451–1311) will take you and your car from the main port in Piraeus to Aegina (1½ hours) and Poros (3 hours, 40 minutes), or you alone to Hydra (4 hours, 10 minutes) and Spetses (5 hours, 25 minutes). The **Consortium Poseidon** also travels to Aegina and Poros (☎ 01/417–5382 or 01/417–1395). You can get a weekly boat schedule from the EOT. There are approximately a half dozen departures per day, and fares range from about 1,400 dr. per person for Aegina to about 3,100 dr. for Spetses. Car rates are usually four times the passenger rate. These ferries are the leisurely—meaning *very* slow—and cheap way to travel. From downtown Athens take the metro station to the port, a trip of about 25 minutes (100 dr.).

Most people now prefer the speedier **Flying Dolphins** (☎ 01/428–0001 through 01/428–0010), hydrofoils (no cars carried) that depart from the Zea Marina, also in Piraeus. There are about a half dozen departures daily, and you should make reservations ahead of time—they fill quickly. The cost ranges from 2,600 dr. for Aegina to 5,950 dr. for Spetses. You can also reserve through a travel agent. From downtown Athens take the metro to the port, then Trolley 20 to Zea Marina. Or you can take a taxi, about 1,700 dr.

Contacts and Resources

Car Rentals

Most international agencies have offices in Athens and desks at the airport.

Avis (✉ Amalias 46–48, ☎ 01/322–4951 through 01/322–4957, FAX 01/322–0216; ✉ West Terminal, ☎ 01/981–4404; ✉ East Terminal, ☎ 01/995–3440; ✉ Athens Hilton, ☎ 01/725–0200; ✉ Akti Miaouli 7 [Piraeus], ☎ 01/428–0218). **Budget** (✉ Syngrou 8, ☎ 01/921–4771 through 01/921–4773, FAX 01/924–1603; central reservations center ☎ 01/922–6666 or 01/342–8536; ✉ West Terminal, ☎ 01/988–3792; ✉ East Terminal, ☎ 01/961–3634). **Europcar** (✉ Syngrou 4, ☎ 01/958–8990 for reservations, FAX 01/959–5382 for reservations; ✉ West Terminal, ☎ 01/982–9565; ✉ East Terminal, ☎ 01/961–3424). **Hertz** (✉ Syngrou 12, ☎ 01/922–0102 through 01/922–0104, FAX 01/922–7921; ✉ Vas. Sofias 71, ☎ 01/724–7071, ☎ FAX 01/722–7391; ✉ West Terminal, ☎ 01/981–3701; ✉ East Terminal, ☎ 01/961–3625).

A good local agency to call is **Swift Car Rental** (⊠ Nikis 21 near Syntagma Sq., ☎ 01/322–1623, 01/324–7875, or 01/324–7855, FAX 01/325–0671), where the manager, Elias Manouas, will take good care of you; he'll even arrange to drive clients awed by Athens traffic to the edge of the city.

Emergencies

Tourist Police: Aegina (☎ 0297/27777); **Attica** (☎ 171); **Delphi** (☎ 0265/82222); **Hydra** (☎ 0298/52205); **Poros** (☎ 0298/22462); **Spetses** (☎ 0298/73100).

Police (☎ 100). **Fire** (☎ 199). **Ambulance**(☎ 166, but hailing a cab may be faster). **Forest Service (fires)** (☎ 191). **Road Assistance** (☎ 104).

Guided Tours

Most agencies offer excursions at about the same prices, but **CHAT** (⊠ Stadiou 4, Syntagma, Athens 10564, ☎ 01/322–2886, FAX 01/323–5270) is reputed to have the best service and guides. Taking a half-day trip to the breathtaking Temple of Poseidon at Sounion avoids the hassle of dealing with the crowded public buses or paying a great deal more for a taxi. The 7,100 dr. cost is well spent. A one-day tour to Delphi with lunch costs 19,500 dr. (17,000 dr. without lunch), but the two-day tour (29,500 dr.) is far preferable. A full-day cruise from Piraeus, visiting three nearby islands—Aegina, Poros, and Hydra—costs around 18,000 dr. (including buffet lunch on the ship).

Moped Rentals

On the islands of Aegina and Spetses, many people rent scooters, mopeds, and bicycles from shops along the harbor, but extreme caution is advised: The equipment may not be in good condition, roads can be narrow and treacherous, and many drivers scorn your safety. Wear a helmet, and drive defensively.

Outdoor Activities and Sports

HIKING

For a booklet on Greece's refuges and information on hiking paths, including the E4 and E6 trails, and local hiking groups, contact the **Greek Federation of Mountaineering Associations** in Athens (⊠ Milioni 5, Kolonaki, 10673, ☎ 01/364–5904, FAX 01/364–4687). Some Attica hiking groups include the **Alpine Club of Aharnon** (⊠ Filadelfias 126, Aharnes, 13671, ☎ 01/246–1528 or 01/246–6666, FAX 01/246–9777), which runs the Flambouri refuge on Parnitha (☎ 01/246–4666), and the **Alpine Club of Athens** (⊠ Kapnikareas Sq. 2, top floor, Monastiraki, 10563, ☎ 01/321–2355 or 01/321–2429, FAX 01/324–4789), which operates the Bafi refuge on Parnitha (☎ 01/246–9050). Hiking trips are offered regularly by specialist travel agencies. Try **Trekking Hellas** (⊠ Fillelinon 7, 3rd floor, Syntagma, Athens 10577, ☎ 01/331–0323 through 01/331–0326, FAX 01/323–4548) or **F-Zein** (⊠ Syngrou 132, 5th floor, Athens 17561, ☎ 01/921–6285, FAX 01/922–9995), which besides hiking expeditions, arranges all kinds of adventure travel, including rafting, mountain climbing and biking, and canyoning.

RUNNING

Athens Open International Peace Marathon (⊠ SEGAS, Race Organizers, Syngrou 137, Athens 17121, ☎ 01/935–9302, FAX 01/934–2980).

TENNIS

Hellenic Tennis Federation (⊠ Ymittou 267, Pangrati, Athens 11631, ☎ 01/726–3170, FAX 01/726–3173).

WINDSURFING

Hellenic Windsurfing Association (⊠ Fillelinon 7, 1st floor, Syntagama, Athens 10557, ☎ 01/323–3696 or 01/323–0068, ℻ 01/322–3251).

Visitor Information

Tourist office: Municipal tourist office **Aegina** (⊠ Town Hall, ☎ 0297/22220); **Arachova** (winter only; ⊠ Arachova–Delfon Rd., ☎ 0267/31692); **Delphi** (⊠ Vas. Pavlou and Friderikis 12, ☎ 0265/82900).

Tourist Police: Aegina (⊠ Leonardou Lada 11, ☎ 0297/22777); **Attica** headquarters (⊠ Dimitrakopoulou 77, Koukaki, Athens, ☎ 171); **Delphi** (⊠ Aggelos Sikelianou 3, ☎ 0265/82220); **Hydra** (⊠ Port, ☎ 0298/52205); **Poros** (⊠ Dimosthenous St. off Platia Iroon, ☎ 0298/22462); **Spetses** (⊠ Near museum on Hatziyianni-Mexi St., ☎ 0298/73744).

Greek National Tourist Organization (GNTO or EOT): Athens (⊠ Amerikis 2, near Syntagma, ☎ 01/331–0561 through 01/331–0562; ⊠ East Terminal of Ellinikon Airport, ☎ 01/961–2722 or 01/969–4500; ⊠ Zea Marina near the hydrofoils, EOT Building, 1st floor, Zea Marina, ☎ 01/452–2591).

4 The Northern Sporades

Skiathos, Skopelos, Alonnisos, Skyros, and Evia

Island-hopping the Northern Sporades, strung from Mt. Pelion to the center of the Aegean, delivers quintessential Greek-island pleasures: boat journeys, pretty harbors, villages spilling down hillsides like giant sugar cubes, Byzantine monasteries, screaming nightlife. Weekenders don't make it far beyond the Skiathos, but the special charm of the Sporades is found on the quieter islands, where the tinkle of goat bells may be the only sound for miles and scarlet poppies line silent paths, cobbled in the last millennium.

By Lea Lane

LIKE EMERALD BEADS SCATTERED ON SAPPHIRE velvet, the verdant Northern Sporades islands of Skiathos, Skopelos, and Alonnisos, and a nearby host of tiny, uninhabited islets—resplendent with pines, fruit trees, and olives, and marked with sloping, slate roofs and wooden balconies—strongly resemble the Pelion peninsula to which they were once attached. Only on Skyros, farther out in the Aegean, will you see a windswept, treeless landscape, or the cubistlike architecture of the Cyclades. Sitting by itself east of Evia, Skyros is neither geographically nor historically related to the other Sporades, though in recent years air shuttles from Athens and hydrofoils skimming between the islands and Evia, and the mainland, have brought these aptly named Sporades ("scattered ones") closer together. Evia itself—Greece's second-largest island (after Crete)—presents a curious mix of mainland and island culture. A kind of Long Island or Cape Cod escape for harried Athenians, it remains a favorite for sun seekers of all nationalities.

The Sporades have changed hands constantly throughout history, and wars, plunder, and earthquakes have eliminated all but the strongest ancient walls. A few castles and monasteries remain, but these islands are now geared more for fun than for sightseeing. Skiathos, closest to the mainland and the first to be discovered, is the most touristy—to the point of overkill—with a diverse social scene, international restaurants, English pubs, and luxury hotels. Less-developed Skopelos has several lovely villages to explore by day—its main town is said to be the most beautiful of the Sporades—though far fewer beaches and nightlife.

Owing to natural disasters, the second half of the 20th century has been hard on Alonnisos, once called Evoinos (Goodwine). In 1950 its grapevines suffered a plague of phylloxera that destroyed most of them virtually overnight and, 15 years later, an earthquake ruined the lovely acropolis. Still, its scenery is so stunning that nature-lovers flock there in increasing numbers and visitors are reclaiming and reinventing the hilltop town. Skyros, late to attract tourists, is the least traveled of the Sporades. Yet those who discover its well-preserved traditions, its arcane rabbit warren of a town, and its expansive beaches are drawn to return year after year.

The once undiscovered Northern Sporades are no longer so—after all, they are so easily reached from Athens and Thessaloniki and each other—yet some parts of all remain idyllic. Quintessential Greek-island delights beckon: sun, seabathing, and surf, with memorable dining under the stars. Almost all restaurants have outside seating, often under leafy trees, where you can watch the passing Greek dramas of daily life: dark-haired lovers arm-in-arm, stealing a kiss; animated conversations between shopkeeper and patron that may last for the entire meal; fishermen cleaning their bright yellow nets and debating and laughing as they work. All in all, the Northern Sporades offer wondrous places to relax and immerse yourself in the blue and green watercolor of it all.

Pleasures and Pastimes

Beaches

The Sporades boast a huge number of beaches, both pebbly and sandy, and with a bit of research and adventuresome spirit you will find one you like—from those crowded with people, water sports, and music to secluded coves accessible only by boat; and of course, nude beaches can be found on each island. Of all the islands, Skiathos is perhaps best for major beaches—the star location remains Koukounaries, whose golden sands are famous throughout Greece.

Dining

By the water or in the heart of a rural village, in a simple taverna or a fancier restaurant, dining in Evia and the Sporades is as much to savor the day as to consume the fresh island food. Greeks here, as on the mainland, love to eat and drink, share and talk. To facilitate these pleasures, tavernas are tucked throughout the islands and pastry shops offer afternoon respite with refreshing frappés, tall glasses of cold, sweetened coffee and milk. If in doubt, eat where the locals do; few tourist hangouts are as good, and prices decrease the farther you get from views or water. Although you may not have many great meals in the Sporades, you'll have a hard time finding a bad one, and the service inevitably will be friendly and caring.

Ask your waiter for suggestions about local specialties—you won't go wrong with the catch of the day on any of the islands. Octopus and juicy prawns, grilled with oil and lemon or baked with cheese and fresh tomatoes, are traditional dishes. Alonnisos and Skyros especially are noted for spiny lobster, which is almost as sweet as the North Atlantic variety. Of course, ordering several *mezedes* (starters) rather than a first and second course is a tasty and popular option. Sadly, only on Skyros will you find barrel wine; the small amount produced elsewhere is savored at home. As in all of Greece, portions are large, and desserts simple—puddings, spoon sweets (such as preserved figs or cherries), and pastries.

CATEGORY	COST (ALL ISLANDS)*
$$$$	over 6,000 dr.
$$$	3,200–6,000 dr.
$$	2,200–3,200 dr.
$	under 2,200 dr.

per person for two appetizers, salad, and main course, including service and tax but excluding drinks

Festivals

The **pre-Lenten Carnival** revelry on Skyros relates to pre-Christian fertility rites and is famous throughout Greece. Young men dressed as old men, maidens, or "Europeans" roam the streets teasing and tormenting onlookers with ribald songs and clanging bells. The "old men" wear elaborate shepherd's outfits, with masks made of baby goat hides and belts dangling with as many as 40 sheep bells. Their costumes and antics are simply extraordinary.

Also on Skyros the August 15 **Panayia** (Festival of the Virgin) is celebrated on the beach at Magazia, where children race on the island's domesticated small ponies, similar to Shetland ponies. The Skopelos Municipality sponsors a Panayia on August 15 and a series of cultural events in late August, with the last day a celebration of the plum harvest (☞ Visitor Information *in* The Northern Sporades A to Z, *below*). The pre-Lenten Carnival traditions of Skopelos, although not as exotic as those of Skyros, parody the expulsion of the once-terrifying Barbary pirates. Skiathos hosts a series of cultural events in the summer, including a dance festival in July. Evia holds a Drama Festival all summer long, in Halkidha. Finally, the islands celebrate **feast days** in honor of their patron saints, with special banquets, carnivals, processions from the church, costumes, folk dancing, fireworks, and revelry late into the night. Skiathos's feast day is July 26, in honor of St. Paraskevi; on Skopelos it is February 25, in honor of St. Riginosi. And if you are lucky enough to happen by a wedding party on any of the islands, you may be invited to join in the fun—eating, dancing, and feeling part of the family in no time.

Hiking

All the islands are wonderful for walking, especially in spring, when Greece's wildflowers are unsurpassed. For those who like isolated beauty and smaller scale, Skyros and Alonnisos are special, with their acropoli and rural vistas, and once out of the main town you are in isolated environs. Some of the islands' monasteries and more remote refuges are only accessible on foot and often are linked together by marked trails. Skopelos has old stone farmhouses set in plum orchards. Evia offers an exhilarating mountain climb up Mt. Ochi. You can buy walkers' maps in souvenir shops and tourist offices in the main towns.

Lodging

Accommodations reflect the pace of tourism and vary greatly in level and number from town to town and island to island. Skopelos has a fair number of hotels, Skiathos and Evia a huge number; there are not many hotels on Alonnisos, and Skyros has even fewer. Most hotels close for winter, as noted in their individual listings; reservations are a good idea, unless you are looking for a private room. The best bet, especially for those on a budget, is to rent a converted room in a private house—look for the Greek National Tourist Organization (GNTO or EOT) license displayed in windows. Owners meet incoming boats to offer rooms; negotiate over the price and ask about the island location. At the height of summer, island-hopping without reservations might be risky, especially on Evia, which fills with weekenders driving across the bridge from the Athens area.

In Skyros most people rent rooms in town or along the beach at Magazia and Molos. Accommodations are basic and television sets are not standard. You must choose between being near the sea or the town's bars and eateries. The average room cost in August is about 8,000 dr. In Skiathos, tourists are increasingly renting private apartments, villas, and minivillas with kitchen facilities. Contact the local island travel agents to discuss the range of possibilities.

The hotels recommended here vary from simple, clean, family-run pensions to large, impersonal, self-contained resorts. You can expect air-conditioning in $$$ and $$$$ hotels, and buffet breakfast is usually included in the rate everywhere. Rates fluctuate considerably from season to season; the August prices listed in the lodging chart below may drop by more than half between October and May. You should always negotiate off-season.

CATEGORY	COST (ALL ISLANDS)*
$$$$	over 25,000 dr.
$$$	17,000–25,000 dr.
$$	11,000–17,000 dr.
$	under 11,000 dr.

for a standard double room for two, including breakfast, service, and tax

Nature Cruises

Alonnisos is the gateway to the National Marine Park, which comprises all the islands in the vicinity, some of which are off-limits to all visitors. Found here is one of the last preserves of the endangered monk seal. Nature-lovers can enjoy excursions such as the caïque cruise, run by a marine biologist, from Skopelos to Psathoura and Kyra Panayia in the National Marine Park. On the other islands, you can hire a caïque and explore the natural beauty of the coastline and islets.

Sailing

With some of the clearest waters in the Aegean and hundreds of protected coves, the Northern Sporades (excluding Skyros) are ideal for yachting, especially the uninhabited islands. Mooring can be arranged at the ports at each island.

Shopping

Evia caters to short-term tourists, with lots of forgettable trinkets, but Alonnisos excepted, all the Sporades have some charming local handicrafts and also sell goods from other islands and the mainland, including attractive pottery, kilims, antiques, and embroideries. Skopelos has galleries selling paintings and photographs; on Skiathos, boutiques display an array of modern jewelry and stylish items. Save money for shopping on Skyros. This isolated island's traditional handcrafted ceramics, carpentry work, rugs, and detailed embroidery are among the finest in Greece.

Exploring the Northern Sporades

Each of the Northern Sporades has a distinct character. Touristed, sophisticated Skiathos is closest to the mainland; it has the liveliest nightlife and a pretty harbor area. Due east is Skopelos, covered with dense, fragrant pines, where you can enjoy scenic villages, hundreds of churches, and lovely beaches. Farther east in the Aegean, and close by, is rugged and rural Alonnisos, the least progressive of the islands, but the most naturally beautiful, with an exceptional old hill town.

Mythic Skyros, southeast of the other islands, has quiet fishing villages and a stunning cubist town that seems to spill down a hill. It is the most remote and quirky of the Sporades, but as a current citadel of Greek defense it also has the bonus of an airport; it is often difficult to get to Skyros from the other Sporades without a mainland stop, but from Athens by air it is a quick daily connection.

Evia—not really part of the Sporades but so near them it seems to be—is even closer to the mainland; you could drive back and forth, as it is connected by a bridge. The island is a vast, elongated strip of coast with plenty of beaches, fishing villages, and touristy towns. Each of these islands is connected by ferry and/or hydrofoil, although some are infrequently scheduled, especially in the off-season. A number of uninhabited islands in the Sporades archipelago can also be visited by boat.

Numbers in the text correspond to numbers in the margin and on the Northern Sporades map.

Great Itineraries

If you are taking it easy, you can generally just jump on a caïque and island-hop as you choose. If time is limited and you want to do something in particular, it is best to plan your schedule in advance. Flying Dolphin hydrofoils and Olympic Airways timetables are available from travel agents; for regular boats, consult the EOT in Athens (☞ Visitor Information *in* The Northern Sporades A to Z, *below*).

You could get around Skiathos, Skopelos, and Alonnisos in three days, but to enjoy the relaxed nature of the islands, stay on one, and take a day trip or two to the others. The trip between these three and Skyros requires advance planning and more time; except for the summer, ferries and Flying Dolphin hydrofoils may run sporadically and can cause havoc with your schedule. Also, make sure that you are arriving and leaving from the correct harbor; some islands, such as Evia and Skopelos, have more than one area from which to leave. Five days can be just enough for touching each island in the summer; off-season you will need more days to adjust for the ferry schedule. Eight days would be

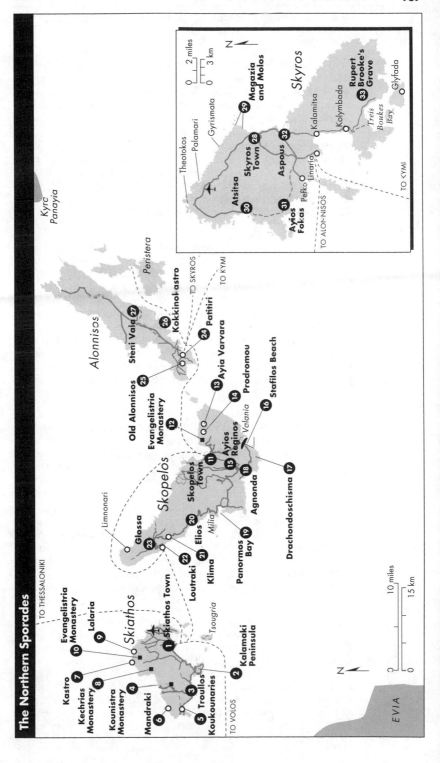

The Northern Sporades

more than enough to see all the islands and still enjoy a delightfully relaxed sojourn.

IF YOU HAVE 3 DAYS

Inveterate island-hoppers might spend one night on each of three islands. Otherwise, choose one and stay there, with day trips to a nearby island or two if you wish. On 🏝 **Skiathos** ①–⑩, by day take in the beautiful but crowded beaches and a museum or perhaps **Evangelistria monastery** ⑩, and at night join the night owls at a taverna or restaurant, and then a bustling nightclub. Day people should stay on 🏝 **Skopelos** ⑪–㉓ to explore the numerous monasteries and churches. If you want to escape civilization as much as possible, head for 🏝 **Alonnisos** ㉔–㉗. Or you could drive to Evia, spend some time there, and then take a ferry from its harbor at Kimi to 🏝 **Skyros** ㉘–㉝ with its slower pace and shopping opportunities. Or leave the car in Evia, ferry over to Skyros, and fly back to Athens from there.

IF YOU HAVE 5 DAYS

Pick and choose. You can rush through every island with a well-thought-out schedule, or be selective and come away with the essence of a few of these distinctive islands. Fly to 🏝 **Skyros** ㉘–㉝ from Athens. Spend a couple of relaxing days and take a day or so to explore Evia. Alternatively, base yourself in the main group of Skiathos, Skopelos, and Alonnisos. If you like it lively, spend a day and a couple of nights on **Skiathos** ①–⑩; then head for 🏝 **Skopelos** ⑪–㉓ and stay there for three nights. You can take a day cruise from Skopelos to see **Alonnisos** ㉔–㉗ and some of the uninhabited islands, with deserted beaches, ancient monasteries, and wildlife reserves. If natural beauty and peaceful surroundings are your thing, split the nights between the latter two islands.

IF YOU HAVE 8 DAYS

This is long enough for a truly relaxed exploration of the Sporades, and you can divide the time depending on your interests and scheduling. Start in Evia and visit **Halkidha** and **Eretria** before heading to **Kimi** for the boat to 🏝 **Skyros** ㉘–㉝. Alternatively, you can fly from Athens direct to Skyros, which, although it is undeveloped and small, has a military airport. Enjoy the handicrafts and dramatically set Skyros town, and plan ahead so that you can catch the sporadic Flying Dolphin to 🏝 **Alonnisos** ㉔–㉗. Spend a night or more there or at least visit it as part of a cruise from **Skopelos** ⑪–㉓. Its natural, unspoiled beauty captivates nature-lovers, and its part-destroyed hilltop village is haunting. Stay awhile on **Skopelos** and perhaps rent a car to explore the inland forests and out-of-the-way churches. If you seek a lively club and social scene, spend your last couple of nights on 🏝 **Skiathos** ①–⑩; from here you might leave time to go on to **Volos** and **Pelion** on the mainland.

When to Tour

Winter is least desirable, as the weather is iffy; most hotels, rooms, and restaurants are closed; and ferry service is minimal. If you do go from November through March, book everything in advance and leave nothing to chance. The same advice applies to July and August, when everything is open but overcrowded, except on Skyros. The *meltemi*, the brisk northerly summer wind of the Aegean, keeps things clearer and cooler than the mainland even on the hottest days. Late spring and early summer are ideal, as most hotels are open, crowds have not arrived, the air is warm, and the roadsides and fields of flowers are incredible; September is also lusciously sensual, and the beach crowds have returned to work.

SKIATHOS

Part sacred, with scores of churches, part profane, the hilly, wooded island of Skiathos is the closest of the Sporades to the Pelion peninsula. It covers an area of only 42 square km (16 square mi), but it boasts some 70 beaches and sandy coves. A jet-set island 25 years ago, today it teems with tourists on package deals, attracted by promises of sun, sea, and parties—and these are delivered. But higher prices and a bit of Mykonos-style attitude can be delivered as well.

In winter most of the island's 5,000 or so inhabitants live in its main town, Skiathos, built after the War of Independence on the site of the colony founded in the 8th century BC by the Euboean city-state of Chalkis. Like Skopelos and Alonnisos, Skiathos was on good terms with the Athenians, prized by the Macedonians, and treated gently by the Romans. Saracen and Slav raids left it virtually deserted during the early Middle Ages, but it started to prosper during the later Byzantine years.

When the Crusaders deposed their fellow Christians from the throne of Constantinople in 1204, Skiathos and the other Sporades became the fief of the Ghisi, knights of Venice. One of their first acts was to fortify the hills behind the islet separating the two bays of Skiathos Harbor. Now connected to the shore, this former islet, the Bourtzi, still has a few stout walls and buttresses shaded by some graceful pine trees.

Skiathos Town

❶ *8 km (5 mi) east of Troullos.*

Though the harbor is picturesque from a distance—especially from a ferry docking at sunset when a purple light casts a soft glow and the lights on the hills behind the quay start twinkling like faint stars—Skiathos town close up has few buildings of any distinction. Many traditional houses were burned by the Germans in 1944, and postwar development has pushed up cement apartments between the pleasantly squat, red-roof older houses. Magenta bougainvillea, sweet jasmine, and the casual charm of brightly painted balconies and shutters camouflage most of the eyesores as you wander through the narrow lanes and climb up the steep steps that serve as streets. Activity centers on the waterfront or on Papadiamantis Street, the main drag: banks, travel agents, telephones, post office, police and tourist police stations, plus myriad cafés, fast-food joints, postcard stands, tacky souvenir shops, tasteful jewelry stores, and rent-a-car and bike establishments. Shops, bars, and restaurants line the cobbled side streets, where you will also spot the occasional modest hotel and rooms-to-rent signs.

A **museum** devoted to Alexandros Papadiamantis (1851–1911), one of Greece's finest writers who wrote about Skiathos in his short stories, stands near the entrance to the street named after him. Three humble rooms with his bed; the low, narrow divan where he died; some photos; and a few personal belongings are all that is exhibited, but the case with his pen, inkwell, and pot of sand for blotting recall times past. For further understanding, try to find a translation of his most famous novel, *The Murderess.* ⊠ *In small platia to right of Papadiamantis at fork in road,* ☎ *0427/23843.* ☒ *250 dr.* ⊘ *Tues.–Sun. 9:30–1 and 4–6.*

The **Bourtzi** is a piney islet that was once a fortress. It divides the harbor and now is a cultural center with numerous activities in the summer. West of the waterfront is the fishing port and the dock where caïques depart for round-the-island trips and the beaches. The sidewalk is filled with cafés and ouzieris catering more to people-watchers than gourmets. At the far end of the port, beginning at the square around the 1846 church of Trion Hierarchon, fancier restaurants spread out under awnings, overlooking the sea. A few good restaurants are hidden on backstreets in this neighborhood, many of them serving foreign foods. The east side of the port, past the Bourtzi, where the larger boats and Flying Dolphins dock, is not as interesting. The little church and clock tower of Ayios Nikolaos watch over it from a hill reached by steps so steep they're almost perpendicular to the earth.

Beaches

Skiathos is known for its beaches, but as has happened so many times before, popularity has a way of spoiling special places. Since the arrival of English expatriates in the early 1960s, the beautiful, piney 14-km (9-mi) stretch of coast running south of town to famed, gold-sand Koukounaries has become almost one continuous ribbon of villas, hotels, and tavernas. This development is a real blight on the landscape. One beach succeeds another, and in summer the asphalted coast road carries a continual stream of cars, buses, motorbikes, and pedestrians buzzing beach to beach, like frenzied bees sampling pollen-laden flowers. To access most beaches, you must take a little, usually unpaved, lane down to the sea. Along this coast, the beaches, **Megali Ammos, Vassilias, Achladia, Tzaneria, Vromolimnos,** and **Platania,** all offer water sports, umbrellas, lounge chairs, and plenty of company.

Dining and Lodging

$$$$ ✕ **The Windmill.** Views from the outdoor platform of this old mill turned elegant restaurant are spectacular, but be prepared to climb up to—and descend from—the top of the hill above Ayios Nikolaos. Here a Scottish couple has created an eclectic, emphatically French menu, with traditional meat-with-sauce dishes, as well as offerings for vegetarians. Diners giddily dip fruit and sweets into the chocolate Cointreau fondue. Follow signs near the clock tower; the restaurant is at the top of the short but steep staircase. ✉ *Skiathos town,* ☎ *0427/21223 or 0427/ 21224,* ℻ *0427/21791. V. Closed mid-Oct.–mid-May. No lunch.*

$$$ ✕ **Asprolithos.** Despite the backstreet location, this fine taverna with
★ a stone fireplace is not a paper-tablecloth, set-your-own-cutlery establishment. The kitchen is surprisingly ambitious and it's easier to list what's *not* on the menu. Interesting dishes include artichokes and prawns with cheese and snapper with wild greens. The wine selection is also extensive. ✉ *Skiathos town,* ☎ *0427/23110. AE, D, MC, V. No lunch.*

$$$ ✕ **Lemon Tree.** At this tiny restaurant with six tables, you'll find not only vegetarian dishes, but also Indian selections—extremely rare in Greece—prepared by a chef from Bradford, capital of England's Asian community. A garden is at the rear—and this one is no lemon. It's just off Odhos Papadhiamndiou in Skiathos town, opposite the National Bank. ✉ *Skiathos town. No credit cards. Closed Nov.–Apr.*

$$–$$$ ✕ **Family.** Not much is homey here, except for the owner's mother's baklava. The tables, on three levels under capacious white awnings, have a superb view of the harbor. Miniature cheese pie and cabbage roll appetizers, among others, are delightful, and the wine list is extensive. It's halfway up the steps to the Ayios Nikolaos clock tower, hidden in the back alleys. ✉ *Ouranitsa St., Skiathos town,* ☎ *0427/ 21439. AE, MC, V. Closed Sept. 26–May 19. No lunch, but will usually serve on request anyway.*

$$ ✕ **Ta Psarädika.** You can't get any closer to the fish market than this next-door neighbor taverna, and the fresh seafood dishes served in summer prove it. Locals love the tripe soup in winter, but you might want to sit at an outside table, sip the local wine, and stay with the mezedes and finny creatures. ✉ *Skiathos town,* ☎ *0427/23412. MC, V.*

AND THE PRETTIEST PLACE IN GREECE IS . . .

IF YOU WANT TO take a quick survey of the leading contenders in Greece's geographical beauty contest, we suggest you read *The Most Beautiful Villages in Greece* (Thames & Hudson, 1998), a spectacular art book written by Mark Ottaway and with photography by Hugh Palmer. Here, in 224 sumptuous pages, are collected the most visually luscious destinations in Greece, from the Maniot towns of the Peloponnese to the flat-roofed white villages of the Cyclades. But to some travelers, one area will always stand out as the Platonic Ideal of Greek country style—the Pelion peninsula, across the water from Skiathos town, on the mainland about 320 Km (200 mi) northeast of Athens. Here, an incredibly charming landscape of stone churches, elegant houses adorned with rose arbors, and storybook town squares lies to seduce all.

While a realm small in size, Pelion looms large in myth and legend. Jason and the Argonauts are said to have embarked from the port of ancient Iolkos, once set opposite modern Volos, located on the northwestern tip of the peninsula, to make good a vague claim to the Golden Fleece. Mt. Pelion, still thickly wooded with pine, cypress, and fruit trees, was the home of the legendary Centaurs, those half-man-half-horse beings notorious for lasciviousness and drunkenness. Here, too, on a cypress-clad hill overlooking Volos, was the site of the wedding banquet of Peleus and Thetis, where the uninvited goddess of discord, Eris, flung a golden apple between Athena and Aphrodite, asking Prince Paris of Troy to decide who was the fairest (and thereby giving Homer one heck of a plot).

Today, the Pelion country is much more serenely peaceful, dotted with no fewer than 24 lovely villages. As you leave Volos (having explored its waterfront esplanade and splendid archaeological museum), you ascend along serpentine roads into the cooler mountains, enjoying great views over Volos Bay. Some roads wind down to beautiful white-sand or round-stone beaches, such as Horefto and Milopotamos. Nestled among the forests are delightful villages, such as Tsangarades, Milies (with the beautifully frescoed Ag Taxiarchis church), and Vyzitsa, while high above Volos is exquisite Portaria, whose *kokkineli* red wine has to be consumed on the spot, as it does not stand up well to transport. Neither visitors nor locals complain of this. Separated by a deep ravine is Makrynitsa, incredibly rich in *couleur locale*. Here, the village square would not be amiss in fairyland: a large, paved terrace, overhanging the town and gulf below, and keeping its intimacy by a backdrop of huge plane trees that shade a small Byzantine church and a lulling fountain.

On the numerous feast days in the Pelion, there is dancing till late at night, and in their natural surroundings the national dances have none of the stiff artificiality they assume in town. Local custom prescribes that every *zembeikiko* dancer should perform for his friend, squatting at the edge of the dance floor and keeping time by clapping his hands. Each dancer rewards the partner with an occasional high kick over his head.

Most of the Pelion villages have archetypal Greek houses whose elegance, replete with bay windows, stained glass, and fine ornamentation, cannot be bettered. To get to Pelion from Skiathos by car, take the three-hour ferry town to Volos; you can also board the hydrofoil and rent a car in Pelion. There is daily train service to Volos from Athens's Stathmos Larissa station (this ride takes six hours). For information on the Pelion region and accommodations in the lovely government-renovated village inns, contact the EOT in Volos (E Riga Fereous Sq., P 0421/23500), open Monday through Friday, 7 AM–2:30 PM.

$$$$ ⊞ **Skiathos Princess.** Covering virtually the whole of Platania Bay below Ayia Paraskevi, this luxury-class hotel has all the expected amenities, but not much in the way of charm. Air-conditioned rooms with patios or balconies are comfortable and private, built in three tiers around a lawn. The carpeted pink rooms have luxurious marble bathrooms. There's also a money-exchange service, a *kafenion* (traditional Greek coffeehouse), and a poolside bar. ✉ *Ayia Paraskevi 37002,* ☎ *0427/49226 or 0427/ 49369,* ℻ *0427/49666.* **Athens:** ✉ *Amalias 42, Athina 10558,* ☎ *01/ 324–2152, 01/324–2153, and 01/324–5963,* ℻ *01/323–3667. 132 rooms, 27 suites. Restaurant, 2 bars, in-room safes, mini-refrigerators, 2 pools, beauty salon, hot tub, sauna, waterskiing, shop, playground, laundry service, meeting rooms. AE, DC, V. Closed Nov.–Apr.*

$$ ⊞ **Bourtzi and Pothos.** To be near the action and have some peace and ★ quiet too, choose either of these hotels (run by the same management). Both are no-frills and spotlessly clean, with rooms that look onto a pleasant green garden and courtyard untouched by the bustle on nearby Papadiamantis. The furniture is simple but functional; the staff, warm and conscientious. Bourtzi is two or three streets farther from the waterfront than Pothos. Both cater to groups but you should be able to find a room with advance booking. ✉ *Skiathos town 37002,* ☎ *0427/22694 or 0427/ 21304,* ℻ *0427/23243. Pothos: 22 rooms with shower; Bourtzi: 23 rooms with shower. Mini-refrigerators. AE, DC, MC, V. Closed Nov.–Apr.*

$ ⊞ **Pension Danaos.** A first choice for budget travelers, this basic hotel is centrally located, and there is even a roof garden. Despite the decent facilities, including TVs, these clean, airy rooms, most with small balconies, are among the cheapest in Skiathos (except during August). The owner often waits at the pier to find guests. ✉ *Skiathos town 37002 (just off Odhos Papadhiandi, 2 blocks inland from the post office),* ☎ *0427/22834. 16 rooms with shower. Refrigerators. No credit cards.*

Nightlife

Skiathos is filled with night owls, and for good reason. Bars for all tastes are on main and side streets, from pubs with draft beer run by Brits to quintessential Greek bouzouki joints in beach tavernas. You can sometimes spot a celeb making the summer scene—such as Jack Nicholson— among the throngs of tanned, hard-drinking northern Europeans on package tours.

MUSIC AND NIGHTCLUBS

Among the perennial favorites are **La Piscine**; it is open all day for swimming and drinking, and its disco has live music from 9:30 to midnight, then a DJ afterward. This entertainment emporium has four bars, video games, outdoor dancing, and an ample swimming pool. For oldies-but-goodies, try the **Kentavros,** a small music bar. For heavy rock, **Café Santan** is the place. **Borzoi,** the oldest club in Skiathos, is decorated like a folk art museum and has a tiny dance floor, too. Popular **Remezzo** (✉ Near the old shipyards) airs a blend of old and new music at the water's edge. And that's just scratching the surface.

Outdoor Activities and Sports

FISHING

The Aegean is a haven for fresh seafood, but overfishing and such scurrilous practices as dynamiting and bottom trawling have greatly diminished the once abundant resources of the Northern Sporades. It is now illegal to fish with scuba equipment. You can hire fishing boats to seek what remains, and what remains tastes wonderful; look for signs on the boats at the ports.

HIKING

Other islands in the Sporades have more expanses of unspoiled walking terrain. In Skiathos, a Dutch couple takes people on nature walks;

check with **Mare Nostrum Travel** (☞ Contacts and Resources *in* The Northern Sporades A to Z, *below*).

SAILING

Nine idyllic islets lush with pines and olive groves surround Skiathios, and two lie across the main harbor, with safe anchorage and a small marina. You can sail over, or hire a caïque, to swim and sun on the isolated beaches. The **Yachting Club** (⌧ Skiathos town, ☎ 094/505426) organizes daily and moonlight cruises, two-day trips to Planitis, and special charters.

SCUBA DIVING

Skiathos is the only island with a scuba diving school, the **Dolphin Diving Center** (⌧ Porto Nostos Beach, ☎ 0427/21599, ℻ 0427/22525). Popular beaches often have diving equipment and instructors on hand.

Shopping

ANTIQUES AND CRAFTS

The **Archipelago** (⌧ Near Papadiamantis museum, ☎ 0427/22163) is the most stunning shop on the island. Browse here among the antiques, pottery, jewelry made from fossils, and embroideries. Archipelago also has a stylish **boutique** (⌧ Waterfront, ☎ 0427/21681). **Galerie Varsakis** (⌧ Trion Hierarchon Sq., ☎ 0427/22255), another fabulous antiques store, has kilims, embroideries, jewelry, and hundreds of other objects, set off by the proprietor's unusual surrealistic paintings.

JEWELRY

Seraïna (⌧ Near Papadiamantis museum, ☎ 0427/22039) has jewelry and unusually eclectic tourist junk. **Simos** (⌧ Waterfront, opposite the excursion caïques, ☎ 0427/22916) has unique silver and gold designs. **G&P Papapanagiotakis** (⌧ Waterfront, opposite the excursion caïques, ☎ 0427/21056) also has fine gold and silver. The jewelry creations at **Pan** (⌧ Waterfront, ☎ 0427/23347) are the most imaginatively displayed.

Kalamaki Peninsula

❷ *6 km (4 mi) south of Skiathos town.*

The less-developed area on the south coast is the Kalamaki peninsula, where the British built their first villas. Some are available for rent in summer, many above tiny, unfrequented coves. Access here is by boat only, and you can usually find your own private beach to get away from the crowds. Motor launches run at regular intervals to the most popular beaches, and you can always hire a boat at the harbor for a private journey.

Lodging

$$$–$$$$ ☷ **Atrium.** Stone and ocher walls, terra-cotta tiles, and sloping roofs fulfill its claim to resemble "a Mt. Athos monastery." There's nothing monastic, however, about its squashy white leather sofas, mellow antiques, cozy nooks for conversation, TV room, backgammon, top-floor pool, and bar. Quiet, air-conditioned rooms with balconies have in-your-face green wood furniture and apricot fabrics. Ask for a room with a sea view, and prepare for the climb up from the beach at Ayia Paraskevi. ⌧ *7 km (4½ mi) west of Platanias town 37002,* ☎ *0427/49345 or 0427/49376,* ℻ *0427/49444. 75 rooms, 6 suites. Restaurant, bar, pool, exercise room, Ping-Pong, shop, billiards. AE, DC, MC, V. Closed mid-Oct.–Apr.*

$$$–$$$$ ☷ **Plaza.** Just 328 ft from Kanapitsa Bay, this ultramodern hotel is set against a green hillside, in staggered wings. Decorated in tones of gray, aqua, and pink, its contemporary accommodations have large beds and generous balconies. A garden softens the stark white facade, honeycombed with arches. There's also a roof garden, money exchange, and pool bar. ⊠ *Kanapitsa 37002,* ☎ *0427/21971 through 0427/21974,* ℻ *0427/22109. Athens: 69 Vassilis Giorgiou, Athina 16675,* ☎ *01/ 967/0393,* ℻ *01/896/2285. 79 rooms, 2 suites. Restaurant, 2 bars, minibars, pool, 2 tennis courts, Ping-Pong, volleyball, windsurfing, waterskiing, shop, billiards, playground. MC, V. Closed Oct.–May.*

Troullos

❸ *8 km (5 mi) west of Skiathos town, 4 km (2½ mi) west of Kalamaki peninsula.*

On the coast road west of Kalamaki peninsula are Troullos and Troullos Bay, a resort for visitors to Koukounaries seeking a relatively isolated beach. The curve of the sand and the islets beyond are appealing.

The dirt road north of Troullos leads to beaches and also branches off
❹ to the small and now deserted **Kounistra Monastery,** 4 km (2½ mi) north of Troullos. It was built in the late-17th century on the spot where an icon of the Virgin miraculously appeared, swinging from a pine tree. The icon spends most of the year in the church of Trion Hierarchon, in town, but on November 20 the townspeople parade it to its former home for the celebration of the Presentation of the Virgin the following day. The interior of the monastery church has been blackened by fire and its 18th-century frescoes are hard to see.

Beaches

❺ Though **Koukounaries** (⊠ 12 km/8 mi west of Skiathos town, and 4 km/2½ mi northwest of Troullos) has been much touted as Greece's best beach, photos displaying it must either have been taken a long time ago or on a brilliant winter's day. All summer it is so packed with umbrellas, beach chairs, and blistering tourists that you can hardly see the sand. The beach can only be reached from its ends, as a lagoon separates it from the hinterland.

Around the island's western tip are more **beaches facing Pelion** (⊠ 13 km/8 mi west of Skiathos town, and 1 km/½ mi west of Koukounaries beach), which looms close by. These are Ayia Eleni and **Krassas,** also known as Big and Little Banana, perhaps because sun worshipers— mainly gay guys on Little—peel their clothes off on these beaches. Toplessness is in vogue just about everywhere, but around here, rocky coves provide some privacy.

You'll find better privacy but less organization at some of the more re-
❻ mote beaches. **Mandraki** (⊠ 5 km/3 mi west of Troullos Bay and 12 km/8 mi west of Skiathos town), for example, is a 25-minute walk. Sometimes called Xerxes' Harbor, this is where the Persian king stopped on his way to ultimate defeat at the battles of Artemisium and Salamis. The reefs opposite are the site of a monument he supposedly erected as a warning to ships, the first such marker known in history.

Megalos Aselinos and Mikros Aselinos beaches (⊠ About 8 km/5 mi west of Skiathos town and 7 km/4½ mi north of Troullos), north of Mandraki beach, can be reached by car or bike. Except for a ramshackle taverna, there is nothing here but broad sands and, at times, local women donning hair rollers.

Dining and Lodging

$$ ✕ **Trouillos.** Swordfish souvlaki is delicious, typical of the simple variety of fish dishes at this friendly taverna, with tables practically up to the water's edge. ⊠ *On the beach, Trouillos,* ☎ *0427/49255. MC, V. Closed Apr.–Oct.*

$$$$ ⊞ **Skiathos Palace.** On the famed beach at Koukounaries, this deluxe resort hotel set amid the pines offers views of, and easy access to, the action. The disco is popular, and all water sports and then some will lure you out of the modern, air-conditioned rooms, which have balconies. ✉ *Koukounaries, 37002,* ☎ *0427/49700–6,* ℻ *0427/49666. 212 rooms, 8 suites. 2 restaurants, 2 bars, pool, tennis court, dance club, meeting room, minibars, parking. AE, MC, V. Closed Nov.–Mar.*

$$–$$$ ⊞ **Troullos Bay.** This homey beachfront hotel invites reading, chatting, and relaxing in bamboo chairs around the lobby's usually unlit fireplace. Bedrooms have wood furniture, striped duvets, tile floors, and colorful prints. Most rooms have balconies and views of the pretty beach. The restaurant, decorated with bamboo and chintz, serves good food and opens onto the lawn near the sand's edge. ✉ *Troullos Bay 37002,* ☎ *0427/49390, 0427/49391, or 0427/21223,* ℻ *0427/49218. 43 rooms with shower, 6 suites. Restaurant, bar. V. Closed Nov.–Apr.*

Outdoor Activities and Sports

HORSEBACK RIDING

Skiathos's **Pinewood Riding Centre** (✉ On the road to Aselinos Beach) conducts lessons, mountain-trail outings, and all-day excursions for beginners and experienced riders.

Kastro

❼ *5 km (3 mi) north of Skiathos town.*

A caïque will bring you to Kastro, perched on a forbidding promontory high above the water and accessible only by steps; you can also take the three-hour walk from Skiathos town (☞ *below*). Skiathians founded this former capital in the 16th century when they fled from the pirates and the turmoil on the coast to the security of this remote cliff—staying until 1829. Its landward side was additionally protected by a moat and drawbridge, and inside the stout walls they erected 300 houses and 22 churches, of which only 2 still remain. The little Church of the Nativity has some fine icons and must have been filled with prayers for deliverance from the sieges that left the Skiathians close to starvation.

❽ Four kilometers (2½ miles) southwest of Kastro is the deserted **Kechrias monastery.** Be warned: The road to Kechrias and the beach below is tough going; stick to a four-wheel-drive vehicle.

Outdoor Activities and Sports

HIKING

Birds, mountain springs, deserted monasteries, churches, wildflowers— if you'd like to find some of these remote pleasures on this active island, and if you like to hike, wear comfortable shoes, leave the boat at Kastro, and walk back to Skiathos. The walk takes about three hours through the orchards, fields, and forests of the interior; the paths are well marked and are downhill most of the way.

Lalaria

❾ *7 km (4 ½ mi) north of Skiathos town.*

Roads are being carved out of the pine forests, but some key spots still can only be reached by caïque. Chief among them is the much-photographed, lovely Lalaria, on the north coast, flanked by a majestic, arched limestone promontory. The polished limestone and marble beach adds extra sparkle to the already shimmering Aegean. In the same area are **Skoteini (Dark) Cave, Galazia (Azure) Cave,** and **Halkini (Copper) Cave.** If caïque-hopping, you'll stop an hour or two here to swim and frolic. Bring along a flashlight to turn the water inside these grottoes an incandescent blue.

⑩ The island's best-known and most beautiful monastery, **Evangelistria,** was dedicated in the late-18th century to the Annunciation of the Virgin by monks from Mt. Athos. It encouraged education and gave a base to the revolutionaries, who pledged an oath to freedom and first hoisted the blue and white flag of Greece here in 1807. Looming above a gorge, and surrounded by pines and cypresses, the monastery's high wall once kept pirates out; today, it encloses a ruined refectory kitchen, the cells, a small museum library, and a magnificent church with three domes. It's about a 10-minute drive from town, or about an hour's walk. ⊠ *5 km (3 mi) north of Skiathos town, 2 km (1 mi) south of Lalaria.* ☉ *Daily 9–5.*

NEED A
BREAK?
A couple of miles south of Evangelistria monastery, the dirt road veers off toward the north and northwest of the island. Follow this route for a quick repast; about 2 km (1 mi) farther on, an enterprising soul has set up a café and snack bar, **Platanos** (⊠ On route south of Evangelistria monastery), where you can stare at the astounding view of the harbor for as long as you like.

SKOPELOS

This triangular island's name means "a sharp rock" or "a reef"—a fitting description for the terrain on its northern shore. It's an hour away from Skiathos by hydrofoil and is the second largest of the Sporades. Most of its 122 sq km (47 sq mi), up to its highest peak on Mt. Delfi, are covered with dense pine forests, olive groves, and orchards. On the south coast, villages overlook the shores, and pines line the pebbly beaches, casting jade shadows on turquoise water. Although this is the most populated island of the Sporades, with two major towns, Skopelos retains a peaceful, quaint atmosphere and absorbs tourists into its life rather than giving itself up to their sun-and-fun needs. It's not surprising that ecologists claim it's the greenest island in the region.

Legend has it that Skopelos was settled by Peparethos and Staphylos, colonists from Minoan Crete, said to be the sons of Dionysos and Ariadne, King Minos's daughter. They brought with them the lore of the grape and the olive. The island was called Peparethos until Hellenistic times, and its most popular beach still bears the name Stafilos. Here, in the 1930s, a tomb believed to be Staphylos's was unearthed, filled with weapons and golden treasures (now in the Volos museum on the Pelion peninsula).

The Byzantines were exiled here, and the Venetians ruled for 300 years, until 1204. In times past, Skopelos was known for its wine, but today its plums and almonds are eaten rather than drunk, and incorporated into the simple cuisine. Many artists and photographers have settled on the island and throughout the summer are part of an extensive cultural program. Little by little, Skopelos is establishing an image as a green and artsy island, still unspoiled by success.

Skopelos Town

⑪ *11 km (7 mi) southeast of Loutraki.*

Pretty Skopelos town, the administrative center of the Sporades, overlooks a bay on the north coast, on a steep hill below scant vestiges of the ancient acropolis and medieval castle. It works hard to remain charming—building permits are difficult to obtain, signs must be in native style, pebbles are embedded into the stones of walkways. Three- and four-story houses rise virtually straight up the hillside, reached by flagstone steps, where women sit chatting and knitting by their doorways. The whitewashed houses look prosperous and well tended, their facades enlivened by brightly painted or brown timber balconies, doors, shutters, flamboyant vines, and potted plants. Interspersed among their red-tile roofs are several with traditional gray fish-scale slate—too heavy and expensive to be built much nowadays.

For a glimpse of the interior of a Skopelan house, visit the **Folk Art Museum,** a 19th-century mansion with period furniture, traditional tools, and an example of an elaborate festive women's costume :silk shirt embroidered with tiny flowers, velvet coat with wide embroidered sleeves, and silk head scarf. Even today, women in the villages will dress up in this way for special occasions. The museum is open July and August. *Hatzistamati, Skopelos town.* ⊠ *Free.* ⊘ *Daily 7 AM–10 PM.*

Off the waterfront, gear your legs for a breath-snatching climb up the almost perpendicular steps in Skopelos town, at the sea wall. You will encounter many **churches** as you go. The uppermost, the 11th-century **Ayios Athanasios,** was built on a 9th-century foundation. At the top you'll be standing within the walls of the 13th-century castle, erected by the Venetian Ghisi lords who held all the Sporades as their fief. It in turn rests upon polygonal masonry of the 5th century BC, as this was the site of one of the island's three ancient acropoli. Once you've admired the view and the stamina of the old women negotiating the steps like mountain goats, wind your way back down the sea-wall steps by any route you choose. Wherever you turn, you'll probably spy a church; Skopelos claims some 360, of which 123 are in the town alone. Unfortunately, most of them seem to be curiously locked, though you'll nevertheless be taken with their exteriors—some incorporating ancient artifacts, Byzantine plates, or early Christian elements—and their slate-capped domes.

A few of Skopelos's 40 monasteries—dazzling white and topped with terra-cotta roofs—are perched on the mountainside opposite, circling in tiers to the shore. Most offer spectacular views of the town; some are deserted, but others are in operation and welcome visitors (dress appropriately: no bare legs or arms; women must wear skirts). You can drive or go by bike, but even with just a good walking guide, you can **⑫** visit them all in a few hours. One is **Evangelistria Monastery** (⊠ On the mountainside opposite Skopelos town, 1½ km/1 mi northeast), founded in 1676 and completely rebuilt in 1712. It contains no frescoes, but it is justly proud of its intricately carved iconostasis and an 11th-century icon of the Virgin with Child, said to be miraculous.

Following the signs east of Skopelos town will bring you first to **Ayia ⑬ Varvara,** empty behind fortresslike walls. The **Metamorphosis tou Sotera,** the oldest monastery on the island (circa 1600), is open only **⑭** on August 6 and is occupied by a sole monk. The **Prodromou** (Forerunner), dedicated to St. John the Baptist, now operates as a convent and is found 2½ km (1½ mi) east of Skopelos town. Besides being of an unusual design, its church contains some outstanding 14th-century triptychs, an enamel tile floor, and an iconostasis spanning four centuries (half carved in the 14th, half in the 18th). The nuns sell their elaborate woven and embroidered handiwork.

⑮ About 2 km (1 mi) south of Skopelos town, the **Ayios Reginos** monastery, the namesake of the island's patron saint, is disappointingly modern

Beaches

Most beaches lie on the sheltered coast, south and west of the main town, and are reached from the road by footpath. The water in this area is calm, and pines grow down to the waterfront. Scattered farms and tavernas, houses with rooms for rent, and one or two pleasant hotels line the road to **Stafilos Beach** (⊠ 8 km/5 mi southeast of Skopelos), the closest to town and the most crowded. Prehistoric walls, a watchtower, and particularly an unplundered grave suggest that this was the site of an important prehistoric settlement. **Valania** (⊠ East of Stafilos Beach), reachable by footpath, takes its name from the *valanium* (Roman bath) that once stood here, which has since disintegrated under the waves. It is a naturist beach today.

Dining and Lodging

$$ ✕ **Alexander.** When you've had enough of the waterfront, follow the signs up from the Emboriki Bank to this little garden restaurant. Here, none of the main dishes are prefab; your order is cooked for you. Especially recommended are *orektika* (appetizers) such as fried eggplant or zucchini, served with *tzatziki* (garlic and yogurt dip) or *tirosalata* (cheese dip). After these you might not have room for the main courses! ⊠ *Odhos Manolaki,* ☎ *0424/22324. MC, V. Closed Nov.–Mar. No lunch.*

$$ ✕ **Perivoli.** Locals come to get away from the crowds and to enjoy the owner's traditional Greek cooking in his candlelit garden. *Dolmades* (stuffed cabbage leaves), *stamna* (lamb stew with cheese in an earthenware pot), and *tsoutzoukakia* (cumin-flavored meatballs in tomato sauce) are some of the treats. Follow the signs up from Platanos (a.k.a. Souvlaki) Square. You may find it crowded. ⊠ *Skopelos town,* ☎ *0424/ 23758. Reservations essential in Aug. No credit cards. Closed Oct. 1– May 31. No lunch.*

$ ✕ **Molos.** The best of the cluster of tavernas near the ferry dock, Molos serves excellent orektika and precooked dishes. Exceptional is the Melintzanes Imam, eggplant in a rich sauce, that might just make you swoon, as did the Turkish Sultan to whom it was first served. It's one of the few places in town open for lunch, especially delightful at an outdoor table. ⊠ *Waterfront,* ☎ *0424/22551. No credit cards. Closed Nov. 1–May 25.*

$ ✕ **Spiros.** Spiros is a favorite waterfront taverna where you can't go wrong—the food is fresh and well prepared. Aside from the usual starters and meat dishes, the specialty here is salads—10 or 12 different ones served every night. Atmosphere is the strong point here, but the service and food make it an excellent value. ⊠ *On waterfront, Skopelos town,* ☎ *0424/23146. No credit cards. Closed Nov.–Mar. No lunch.*

$$$–$$$$ ⌂ **Skopelos Village.** Bungalows on the water each have a balcony or a patch of lawn, kitchen, large bedroom(s), and a living room, and sleep from two to six people. The decor is traditional northern Greek, with a large corner hearth. Children will enjoy the pool and playground, parents the congenial bar and taverna, and the housekeeping service. Don't confuse this place with Sunrise Village next door. It's about a 15-minute walk from the town center. ⊠ *Skopelos town 37003,* ☎ *0424/ 22517,* ⅎ *0424/22958. 36 bungalows with shower. Bar, pool, playground. No credit cards. Closed Nov.–Apr.*

$$$ ⌂ **Alkistis.** Amid a grove of olive trees stand four buildings of cheerful air-conditioned apartments with kitchenettes, housekeeping, and a pool bar. The exteriors are pastel-contemporary, but the lounges and dining terraces are more traditional, though airy and bright. It's 2 km (1 mi) out of town on the road to Stafilos Beach. Geared toward families or couples with cars, it makes an agreeable alternative to a beach or town hotel. ⊠ *Skopelos town 37003,* ☎ *0424/23006 through 0424/23009, 01/682–3129 in Athens;* ⅎ *0424/22116. 25 apartments.*

*Restaurant, 2 bars, pool, wading pool, playground. No credit cards.
Closed mid-Oct.–mid-May.*

$$–$$$ ☒ **Dionysos.** Although it's in town, this hotel is well appointed: from
★   the umbrellas that shade the bamboo chairs on the terrace, to the
lobby with embroidered curtains, to the air-conditioned rooms with
balconies and a view of the hills, to the pool (with a bar, of course).
The rooms, with brown woodwork, slate floors, and rustic-style furniture, are spotless. Intelligent design and traditional decor help it to
blend in with its neighbors. ☒ *Skopelos town 37003,* ☎ *0424/23210
through 0424/23215,* FAX *0424/22954. 52 rooms. Restaurant, 2 bars,
pool. DC, MC, V. Closed Nov.–mid-Apr.*

$–$$ ☒ **Pension Sotos.** This cozy, remodeled family house on the waterfront
is near the action, inexpensive, and extremely casual. Tiny rooms look
onto one of the hotel's two courtyard terraces, where guests can bring
their own food and are welcome to use the kitchen and refrigerator.
It's not very private, but it's fun—one block from the Emboriki Bank,
next to Ecstasy Café. ☒ *Skopelos town 37003,* ☎ *0424/22549,* FAX *0424/
23668. 12 rooms with shower. No credit cards. Closed Oct.–Apr.*

Outdoor Activities and Sports

NATURE CRUISES

A big caïque captained by a marine biologist makes two-day weekend
cruises from Skopelos to Psathoura and Kyra Panayia in the National
Marine Park. Videos, slides, binoculars, snorkeling equipment, underwater cameras, and hydrophones to record dolphin signals make
the trip educational and fun. The trip costs 40,000 dr.; make reservations at Madro Travel (☞ Contacts and Resources *in* The Northern
Sporades A to Z, *below*).

Nightlife

BARS AND DISCOS

Nightlife on Skopelos is more sedate than it is on Skiathos. There is a
smattering of cozy bars playing music of all kinds, and there is at least
one disco, which changes each year (look for advertisements). The Costa
Bar is at the eastern part of the harbor, near the Platanos Jazz Club,
and plays new age in the AM, blues and jazz in the PM. On the beach-
front, Akti Panorama features live music.

BOUZOUKI CLUB

Meintani (☒ Skopelos town), a traditional Greek bouzouki club, stages
performances in a beautifully converted olive oil factory.

OUZIERI

At **Anatoli** (☒ In the Old Kastro), an ouzieri, the proprietor strums his
bouzouki and sings *rembetika* (blues) without benefit of microphone.
Sometimes, other musicians join in, and with enough ouzo, you might
too.

Shopping

The town's tiny shops are tucked into a few streets behind the central
part of the waterfront. Handicrafts include loom-woven textiles made
by nuns. Local honey, prunes, almonds, and candy are especially delicious.

CLOTHING

Phaedra (☎ 0424/23806) specializes in imaginative clothing from
Greece, Italy, and Bali. Try **Riska** (☎ 0424/23339) for children's
clothing.

LOCAL CRAFTS

One of the most alluring shops is **Archipelago** (☎ 0424/23127), a branch
of the Skiathos shop; it has modern ceramics and crafts—even a rain-

bow-hued hammock—as well as antiques. **Armoloi** (☏ 0424/22707), one of the neatest shops, displays an array of ceramics made by local potters, kilims, tapestries, embroideries, and bags crafted from fragments of old Asian rugs and kilims. Also try **Ploumisti** (☏ 0424/22059) for kilims, bags, hand-painted T-shirts, and jewelry. **Kriezy's** (☏ 0424/23186) sells original jewelry and gifts. **To Sinnefo,** off Velizariou, has handmade toys and specializes in marionettes and mobiles. **Mesaio** has rag dolls, pottery, and watercolors. **Armonia** (☏ 0424/22392) has unusual ceramic, stone, and metal items. **Photo Gallerie** has a large collection of cards and photographs from all over the island.

Drachondoschisma

⑰ *Peninsula about 5 km (3 mi) south of Skopelos town.*

The road from Stafilos Beach runs southwest through the rounded Drachondoschisma peninsula, where Reginos dispatched the dragon.

Agnonda

⑱ *5 km (3 mi) south of Skopelos town.*

The tiny port of Agnonda has many tavernas along its pebbled beach. It is named after a local boy named Agnonas who returned here from Olympia in 546 BC wearing the victor's wreath.

Panormos Bay

⑲ *6 km (4 mi) west of Skopelos town, 4 km (2½ mi) northwest of Agnonda.*

Due northwest of Agnonda is Panormos Bay, the smallest of the ancient towns of Peparethos, founded in the 8th century BC by colonists from Chalkis. A few well-concealed walls are visible among the pine woods on the acropolis above the bay. With its long beach and its sheltered inner cove ideal for yachts, this is fast becoming a holiday village, although it retains its quiet charm. Inland, the interior of Skopelos is green and lush, as in much of the Sporades, but not far from Panormos Bay you'll find traditional farmhouses called *kalivia,* set in plum orchards. Some are occupied; others have been turned into overnight stops or are used only for feast-day celebrations. Look for the outdoor ovens, which baked the fresh plums when Skopeles was turning out prunes galore. This rural area is charming, but lack of signposts makes it easy to get lost, so mark your route.

Beaches
Just north of Panormos Bay is pebbly **Milia,** Skopelos's longest beach, considered by many its best. Deserted beaches in the vicinity include Adrina. Dassia, the verdant islet across the bay, was named after a pirate who drowned there—a woman.

Lodging
$$–$$$ 🏨 **Adrina Beach.** Atop a picture-book cove, this terraced hotel boasts uninterrupted views of Panormos Bay from every level. Outside there is multihued bougainvillea; indoors, the blue and white is carried throughout, complemented by terra-cotta floors. Plates adorn the walls, amphorae the corners. The comfy bedrooms have fans but no air-conditioning. The only fly on the baklava might be the stairs between the private beach, pool, taverna area, and your room, and the steep walk back from the little town. ⊠ *Adrina Beach 37003,* ☏ *0424/23373 through 0424/23375, 01/682/6886 in Athens;* FAX *0424/23372. 45 rooms, 10 suites. Restaurant, bar, snack bar, pool, beach, jet-skiing, parasailing, waterskiing, playground. AE, DC, MC, V. Closed Nov.–Apr.*

$$ ▦ **Panormos Beach.** The owner's attention to detail shows in the beau-
★ tifully tended flower garden; the immaculate, air-conditioned rooms
with pine furniture and handwoven linens; the country dining room; and
the entrance case displaying his grandmother's elaborate costume. Don't
miss the Skopelan mezedes prepared by his mother-in-law. This traditional,
exceptionally peaceful hotel is a five-minute walk from the beach. ⊠ *Panor-
mos Beach 37003,* ☎ *0424/22711,* ⅋ *0424/23366. 34 rooms with
shower. Bar, snack bar, playground. No credit cards. Closed Nov.–Apr.*

Elios

⑳   *6 km (4 mi) west of Skopelos town, 4 km (2½ mi) north of Panormos
Bay.*

Residents of Klima who were dislodged in 1965 by the same earth-
quake that devastated Alonnisos now live here in a new development.
The origin of its name is more intriguing than the village: Legend has
it that when Reginos arrived to save the island from the dragon, which
demanded human nourishment, he demanded, "Well, where in *eleos*
(God's mercy) is the beast?"

Lodging

$$ ▦ **Zanétta.** If you want to feel as if you've really escaped from the rat
race, stay awhile in these fully equipped, air-conditioned apartments
surrounded by woods but close to the sea. The well-equipped kitchen
means you can stay put and spend some time exploring the rural interior of this lush island. The hotel is about five minutes from the water.
⊠ *Elios, 37005,* ☎ *0424/33140,* ⅋ *0424/33717. 16 apartments.
Restaurant, pool, kitchenettes, parking. MC, V. Closed Nov.–Apr.*

Klima

㉑   *10 km (6 mi) northwest of Skopelos town, 3 km (2 mi) north of Elios.*

Klima means "ladder," and Kato ("Lower") Klima leads to Ano
("Upper") Klima, clinging to the mountainside. The area is being
slowly restored from the 1965 earthquake, but plenty of ruined houses
are still for sale. If you crave an island retreat, this could be your chance.

Loutraki

㉒   *11 km (7 mi) northwest of Skopelos town, 1 km (½ mi) northwest of
Klima.*

Loutraki is the tiny port village where the ferries and hydrofoils stop,
and it is not very charming. Three hundred yards away are the remains
of the **acropolis of Selinous,** the island's third ancient city. Unfortunately,
everything lies buried except the walls.

Glossa

㉓   *19 km (11¾ mi) northwest of Skopelos town, 1 km (½ mi) north of
Loutraki.*

Delightful Glossa is the island's second-largest settlement, where whitewashed, red-roof houses are clustered on the steep hillside above the
harbor of Loutraki. Venetian towers and traces of Turkish influence
remain; the center is closed to traffic. This is a place to relax, dine, and
enjoy the quieter beaches. Just to the east, check out Ayios Ioannis
monastery, dramatically perched above a pretty beach.

Dining

$ ✕ **Taverna T'Agnanti.** Moussaka and the other classics are good and
inexpensive at this popular taverna. Ask the owners to recommend a

room to rent in this charming town, which doesn't cater to tourists. ⊠ *Above the bus stop, on the left side of Agiou Riginou,* ☎ *0424/33606. No credit cards.*

ALONNISOS

Ah, Alonnisos. Set in the clearest waters of the Aegean, this is the unspoiled Greece tourists long for, and until recently, most of the rugged coast was accessible only by boat. Barter was still the usual method of trade until the late 1960s, when tourism finally catapulted this serene island into the 20th century, sort of. Nature has conspired to keep Alonnisos underpopulated and undeveloped. Although the island was famous for its wine in past centuries, the vines were ruined by disease in the 1950s, and many residents left. Another fiasco was the proposed airport. When rocks made it hard to complete a runway, the project was abandoned, and jets, and big-time package tourism, never got off the ground. As a relative backwater the island may lack chic beaches and groovy nightclubs, but the trade-offs are bigtime: forest walks, boat trips to islands and nature preserves, caves and beaches where jet-skiing and parasailing are unknown. You'll find a few hotels, several rooms to rent, some nice tavernas, and a cheerful laid-back atmosphere. Europeans love it, but most of the tourists and day-trippers are nature-lovers rather than party people. Thank God.

Alonnisos hardly gets more than a line or two in the history books, and because of its different names—Ikos and Liadromia—researchers find it difficult to trace. Peleus, Achilles' father, once lived on the island; Philip of Macedon coveted it; the Venetians erected a fortress here. Its waters cover dozens of fascinating shipwrecks, not to mention a ruined city or two, but little else is known of its past. The center of the island submerged long ago, perhaps in a cataclysmic earthquake, leaving only islets and a rock called Psathoura.

While Skiathos and Skopelos were sending merchant fleets to the Black Sea and Egypt in the 18th and early 19th centuries, sailors from Alonnisos were probably plundering them. When the Sporades and Greece gained independence, the pirates turned to fishing. Today, their heirs are still fishing, farming, and herding sheep. Most of the 3,000 or so inhabitants (half that in winter) live in and around the port of Patitiri, hurriedly developed to house victims of the 1965 earthquake, which devastated the hilltop capital. Many fishing families live in Steni Vala, farther northeast. On a conical hill 600 ft above the port is haunting Old Alonnisos, or Chora. Its tiny houses, deserted after the earthquake, have been lovingly restored by Athenians and Europeans who bought them for next to nothing and thus are somewhat resented by the resettled villagers in the port areas below. Chora comes to life in summer, but for much of the time it seems almost a ghost town, aside from an occasional cat and a few stalwart year-rounders.

Lush with pine, oak, fruit trees, mastic and arbutus bushes, hilly Alonnisos has small, fertile plains; a steep northwestern coastline; and an east coast with pebbled beaches. To explore beyond Patitiri and Old Alonnisos, you can either rent a motorbike or car, or take a caïque, which can also take you to the neighboring islets. The roads to the various beaches along the way have fairly decent dirt surfaces. The road from Patitiri to Steni Vala is now paved; north of Steni Vala are virtually no signs of habitation. The interior of the island is dirt tracks, where hikers, bikers, and shepherds sporadically wend their ways.

Patitiri

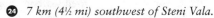 *7 km (4½ mi) southwest of Steni Vala.*

Patitiri ("Winepress") was once a wine-making center, but today it's the island's main port, set in a pretty cove flanked by white, pine-clad cliffs. Along the diminutive waterfront are tavernas and cafés, a couple of hotels, the boat agency, and a gas station. Most of the buildings are modern and drab, built to house and serve the refugees from Old Alonnosis, the half-destroyed old capital up the hill. But the backstreet houses have flower-filled boxes, and the sun twinkling on the blue Aegean keeps things cheery. Nearby, 4 km (2½ mi) north of Patitiri, is Votsi, a tiny harbor set among cliffs—a perfect spot to sit in a taverna, watch the fishing boats come in, and sip ouzo. Swimming off the rocks here is excellent.

Beaches

Find one and claim it. Rocks and coves throughout the coast are quiet havens tucked among cliffs, and you can easily clamber from rocky ledges to the calm and sparkling turquoise water. Most beaches are on the east coast. Going north from Patitiri, unpaved roads will get you to swimming areas with some facilities, including **Hrysi Milia, Kokkinokastro, Tzórtzi, Steni Vala, Kalamakia,** and, farther north, **Aglos Dimitrios,** a nudist beach. At the tip of Alonnisos, the deserted beach at **Gerakas** is good for snorkeling.

OFF THE BEATEN PATH   The islets surrounding Alonnisos, reachable by caïque from Patitiri, are special for many reasons; excursions can be arranged on Skiathos or Skopelos. **Peristera** ("pigeon") is the closest. It has a tiny shepherd population, the ruins of a castle, and a few delightful sandy beaches that the caïques buzz along. Take a chartered caïque ride southeast to **Skantzoura,** which has marble beaches, a monastery, and the submerged ruins of the ancient town of Skandyle. Bring binoculars, and if you're lucky you'll spot an Eleanora falcon, or a rare Aegean seagull with white wings and a black hood. The biggest in the island group is **Kyra Panayia** (Pelagos), which has sometimes been identified as ancient Alonnisos. Here, too, there is a monastery (16th century) and traces of a Neolithic settlement. Its two bays, Planitis and Ayios Petros, are often filled with flotillas—groups of yachts usually chartered by visitors.
Yioura, to the northeast, was once used as place of exile for undesirable politicos. Unusual flora and a rare species of wild goat thrive here, and the most impressive of its caves, crammed with colorful stalagtites and stalagmites, is said to be where Homer's Cyclops lived. Recent excavations show remains from 3000 BC, including pottery and hooks made of bone. This local civilization is not found in any other part of Greece. Excavations were going on at press time—check if the cave is open.
Psathoura, the most northerly of the Sporades, has a big, old lighthouse said to have the brightest beacon in the Aegean, and for good reason. The islet is so low in the water it can hardly be seen until you're on top of it. Near its harbor are the ruins of yet another sunken city—perhaps ancient Ikos?

Dining and Lodging

$$–$$$ ✕ **Argo.** A great place for brunch, this quiet restaurant on a cliff overlooking the rocky east coast has a garden setting and serves good fresh fish, crayfish, and lobster. For dinner it's romantic: enveloped in flowers, tiles, breezes, and, on some nights, moonlight, sparkling silver on the Aegean. ✉ *Next door to Paradise Hotel,* ☎ *0424/65141. No credit cards. Closed Nov.–Apr.*

$$ ✕ **Ta Kamaki.** Locals love this basic ouzieri, renowned for its calamari, baked mussels, and large portions of assorted seafood appetizers. In summer, when the boats leave a daily haul, the fish and shellfish, grilled by owner Spiros, couldn't be fresher. Outdoor tables beckon. ⊠ *Ikion Dolopon,* ☎ *0424/65245. No credit cards. Closed Nov.–Mar. No lunch Mon.*

$ ✕ **Flisvos.** Outdoor tables are across the road under a shady awning, next to the water, and this is an excellent spot to await the boat. The specialty is *tiropitta alonnisou* (a deep-fried cheese pie formed of swirls of pastry). Freshly made pizza and pasta add an Italian accent to the usual taverna food. Don't miss the salad with locally produced olive oil. It's open at 7 AM for breakfast and lunch—a rarity here. ⊠ *Patitiri (on corner of main street and seafront),* ☎ *0424/65307. No credit cards. Closed Oct. 16–Apr. 14.*

$$ ⌕ **Charavagi.** Harbor comings and goings can be enjoyed from the balconies of this simple, clean, conveniently located hotel set in a garden and near swimming areas and tavernas. ⊠ *On the waterfront, Patitiri 37005,* ☎ *0424/65090. 12 rooms. No credit cards. Closed Nov.–Apr.*

$$ ⌕ **Liadromia.** Most rooms in this three-story hotel overlook the port, but there's an even better view from the rooftop terrace bar and breakfast room. Traditional furnishings include dark wood, mustard-and-green striped fabrics, and built-in beds. The halls display family memorabilia and photos of Alonnisos before the quake. Some rooms have refrigerators, and some have double beds—ask. ⊠ *Patitiri 37005,* ☎ *0424/65521,* ℻ *0424/65096. 20 rooms with shower. Bar. MC, V. Closed Nov.–Mar.*

$$ ⌕ **Paradise.** Although the rooms and balconies here are small and rudimentary, the hotel's flower garden is lovely, and just below, among the pines and rocks, guests can swim at any time in secluded coves. Some hang out all day talking to Kostas, the handsome owner, at the bar or shady terrace beside the pool, which doubles as a snack bar and breakfast area. ⊠ *Patitiri 37005,* ☎ *0424/65160 or 0424/65213,* ℻ *0424/65161. 30 rooms with shower. 2 bars, pool. MC, V. Closed Nov.–Apr.*

Nightlife

Surprisingly, the island has lots of little bars and cafés, some with live music. Ask the locals when you get here for whichever is best at the moment. Two clubs, **Hot Stuff** and **Club Enigma,** near the harbor, offer a combination of recorded music and live bouzouki. If you need more music than this, bring a CD player.

Old Alonnisos (Chora)

㉕ *1½ km (1 mi) west of Patitiri.*

Despite its still-ravaged state, in many ways this traditional village, which was once the island capital, is the most spectacular in all the Sporades. The destruction caused by the 1965 earthquake is still being repaired, but it has been repopulated by Europeans who cherish its beauty. The original town dates from the 10th century, when the population sought safety above the sea. Ruins of walls from the 15th-century Byzantine-Venetian fortress still crown the peak, and the little chapel called tou Christou, with a fish-scale roof, is especially charming (you'll need to find the man who keeps the key to let you in; ask a nearby shopkeeper where to find him).

The town seems frozen in time. Indeed, until the earthquake, all goods were hauled up by mule. The narrow cobbled paths of Old Alonnisos are lined with whitewashed stone buildings hung with ornate wooden balconies painted in varied hues and dripping with vines, wildflowers turning cracks into beauty spots, and old pots standing guard by ancient doorways. Each corner offers quirky angles, sharp shadows in the sunshine, and glimpses of blue sea beyond. The scale of the town is intimate and compelling, and if you peek inside the villas' windows as you navigate the mud and stone, you will most often see books and the household items of the contented new residents, mainly German and English, who took the place of the residents after they were moved by the government to safer quarters in the harbor area.

At the top is a 360-degree view of the Aegean, cove beaches set within cliffs, and medieval watchtowers, and on the clearest days you can see as far as Mt. Olympus in northern Greece, 177 km (110 mi) away. A few charming restaurants, a couple of transient boutiques, and a tiny museum, midway in the maze of buildings, make up the tourist attractions. In addition, in a small plaza is a memorial to 11 Greek patriots executed by Germans in World War II.

You might decide to stay in rooms here rather than in the port below, to contemplate it all. If you can't hack the steep 45-minute hike up the ecological trail from Patitiri to Old Alonnisos—through forest, fields of mustard and poppies, lemon orchards, and olive groves—you can forego exercise for ease and take the island's single bus.

Dining

$$–$$$ ✗ **Astrofengia.** In this restored family house you can enjoy a delightful garden and the stunning view (the name means "starlight"). From the varied, innovative menu choose one of the many organic salads, some Cypriot hummus, three-cheese pie, or tagliatelli with a choice of sauces, and tiramisu. It's just before the entrance to Old Alonnisos; take the path to the left as soon as you get off the bus. ⊠ *Old Alonnisos,* ☎ *0424/65182. No credit cards. Closed Oct.–May. No lunch.*

$$ ✗ **Paraport.** With views of the sea and nearby islands on both sides of Alonnisos, the setting is as good as the food. Tables spill out in both directions on the narrow, winding main street just underneath the picturesque ruins of the Kastro. Taverna fare is spicier here on this island than in most of Greece, but for a mild old standby, try the potatoes au gratin. ⊠ *Old Alonnisos,* ☎ *0424/65608. No credit cards. Closed Oct. 1–May 19. No lunch.*

Kokkinokastro

㉖ *4 km (2½ mi) northeast of Patitiri.*

At Kokkinokastro, where the red cliffs and pebble beach contrast with the surrounding pines and water, you can find traces of an acropolis—shards, tombs, walls—as well as a Ghisi fortress. Some experts think Kokkinokastro was also the site of the ancient city of Ikos.

Steni Vala

㉗ *3 km (2 mi) northeast of Kokkinokastro.*

Steni Vala, a tiny fishing village, has little to offer except that it's the headquarters of the International Centre for Research on the Mediterranean Monk Seal, providing useful displays and a video. The islands around Alonnisos are some of the last preserves of this endangered mammal; only about 500 exist throughout the world, about 10% of them here. Scientists are always on the lookout for orphans, and they track the mature seals, too. This is the gateway to the National Marine Park, founded in 1992, which comprises the waters and all the islands in the vicinity, some of which are off-limits to visitors.

A day trip by boat to the National Marine Park is a must for nature-lovers. You'll need to be on a guided tour unless you get a special permit. While watching for the winsome but elusive monk seals, you will also discover a wide variety of rare wildlife, flora, and fauna. Gulls, terns, warblers, falcons, herons, kingfishers, and migrant birds all fill the air throughout different times of the year. Elaborate jellyfish colonies look like iridescent balloons bobbing with the waves, and groups of playful dolphin love to dive in wakes of boats.

Dining

$$ ✕ **Steni Vala.** Whether overlooking the fjordlike harbor from the terrace or in the large dining room, you'll enjoy seafood caught in the waters near here, as well as freshly made Greek specialties, such as cheese pie. This is a great place to eat after a day on the water, or to start, with breakfast. ⊠ *Steini Vala,* ☎ *0424/65545, No credit cards.*

SKYROS

Even among these unique isles, Skyros stands out. Its rugged terrain looks like a Dodecanese island, and its main town, occupied on and off for the last 3,300 years and filled with mythic ghosts, looks Cycladic. It has military bases, and an airport with connections to Athens, yet it remains the most difficult ferry connection in the Sporades. With nothing between it and Lesbos, off the coast of Turkey, its nearest neighbor is the town of Kimi, on the east coast of Evia.

Strangely enough, although the island is adrift in the Aegean, the Skyrians have not had a seafaring tradition, and they have looked to the land for their living. Their isolation has brought about notable cultural differences from the other Greek islands, such as pre-Christian Carnival rituals and a renowned style in home decoration. Here you'll find an almost extinct breed of pony, and exceptional crafts—carpentry, pottery, embroidery—practiced by dedicated artisans. You will not find luxury accommodations or swank restaurants: This idiosyncratic island makes no provisions for mass tourism, but if you've a taste for the offbeat, you'll feel right at home.

Surprisingly beguiling, this southernmost and largest (209 square km/81 square mi) of the Northern Sporades, divides into two almost equal parts, whose names reflect their characters—*Meri* or *Imero* (tame) for the north, and *Vouno* (literally, mountain) for the south, with Mt. Kochilas its highest peak (2,598 ft). The southern half of Skyros (meaning tough, stony) is forbidding, barren, and mountainous, its western coast outlined with coves and deep bays dotted with a series of islets. The heavily populated north, attached by a narrow, flat isthmus, is virtually all farmland and forests.

Until Greece won independence in 1831, the island's population squeezed sardine-fashion into the area under the castle on the inland face of the rock. Not a single house was visible from the sea. Though the islanders could survey any movement in the Aegean for miles, they kept a low profile, living in dread of the pirates based at Treis Boukes bay on Vouno.

In the *Iliad,* legends interweave about Skyros: Before the Trojan War, Theseus, the deposed hero-king of Athens, sought refuge in his ancestral estate on Skyros. King Lykomedes, afraid of the power and prestige of Theseus, took him up to the acropolis one evening, pretending to show him the island, and pushed him over the cliff—an ignominious end. In historical times, Timon of Athens unearthed what he said were Theseus's bones and sword, and placed them in the Theseion — more commonly called the Temple of Hephaistion—in Athens (☞ The Ancient Agora in Exploring Athens *in* Chapter 2), in what must be one of the earliest recorded archaeological investigations.

According to the island's other legend, Skyros was the hiding place of Achilles. The sea-nymph Thetis disguised her son Achilles as a girl and hid him among the daughters of King Lykomedes, hoping to stop Odysseus from luring Achilles off to Troy, where she knew he would be doomed. Odysseus delivered some presents to the palace, among them a sword; when he pretended to attack, Achilles revealed himself by reaching for the sword to help in the defense. Having fallen into Odysseus's trap, Achilles went to Troy, where he could not avoid his fate.

Linaria

40 km (25 mi) northeast of Kimi on Evia.

All boats and hydrofoils dock at the tiny port of Linaria because the northeast coast is either straight, sandy beach or steep cliffs. A bus to Skyros town meets arrivals. To get to the otherwise inaccessible sea caves of Pentekáli and Diatryptí, you can take a caïque from here. This dusty area offers scenes of fishermen tending their bright yellow nets, and not much more.

Skyros Town

10 km (6 mi) north of Linaria.

As you drive south from the airport, past brown, desolate outcroppings with only an occasional goat as a sign of movable life, Skyros town suddenly looms around a bend, looking for all appearances like a breathtaking amalgam of an imaginary painting by Monet, Cézanne, or El Greco: blazing white, cubist, dense and otherworldly; clinging, precariously it seems, to the precipitous rock beneath it, and topped gloriously by a fortress-monastery.

Called *Horio, Hora,* and *Chora* (town) by the locals, Skyros town is home to 90% of the island's 3,000 inhabitants. The impression as you get closer is of stark, simple buildings creeping up the hillside, with a tangle of labyrinthine lanes winding up, down, and around the tiny houses, Byzantine churches, and big squares.

Most commercial activity takes place in or near Agora (Market) Street (familiarly known as Sisifos, as in the myth, because of its frustrating steepness). Found here are the town's pharmacies, travel agencies, shops with wonderful Skyrian pottery, and an extraordinary number of tiny bars and tavernas, but few boutiques and even less kitsch.

The best way to get an idea of the town and its history is to follow the sinuous cobbled lanes past the mansions of the old town to the **Kastro,** the highest point, and the 10th-century fortified **Monastery of St. George,** which stands on the site of the ancient acropolis and Bronze Age settlement. Little remains of the legendary fortress of King Lykomedes, portrayed in Skyros's two most colorful myths (☞ *above*), though lower down on the north and southwest face of the rock are the so-called Pelasgian bastions of immense rectangular fitted blocks, dated to the classical period or later.

A white marble lion, once thought to be left over from the Venetian occupation, is in the wall above the entrance to the monastery. This classical symbol is a reminder of when Skyros was under Athenian dominion and heavily populated with Athenian settlers to keep it that way. This part of the castle was built on ancient foundations (look right) during the early Byzantine era and reinforced in the 14th century by the Venetians. The monastery itself was founded in 962 and radically rebuilt in 1600. Today it is inhabited by a sole monk.

Unfortunately, the once splendid frescoes of the Monastery of St. George are now mostly covered by layers of whitewash, but look for the charming St. George and startled dragon outside to the left of the church door. Within, its ornate iconostasis is considered a masterpiece. The icon of St. George on the right is said to have been brought by the waves of settlers from Constantinople traveling to Skyros during the Iconoclast Controversy of the 9th century. The icon has a black face and is familiarly known as Ayios Georgis o Arapis (the Negro); the Skyrians view him as the patron saint not only of their island but of lovers as well.

Take the vaulted passageway from the monastery courtyard to the ruined church of **Episkopi,** the former seat of the bishop of Skyros, built in 895 on the ruins of a temple of Athena. This was the center of Skyros's religious life from 1453 to 1837. Farther up, the summit is crowned with three tiny cubelike churches with blue and pink interiors, and the ruined Venetian cistern, once used as a dungeon. From here, you have a spectacular view of the town and surrounding hills. The roofs are flat, the older ones covered with a dark gray shale that has splendid insulating properties. The house walls and roofs are interconnected, forming a pattern that from above looks like a magnified form of cuneiform writing. Here and there, the shieldlike roof of a church stands out from the cubist composition of white houses that fills the hillside—with not an inch to spare.

As you stroll down from the ruins and churches of the Kastro, or explore the alleyways off the main drag, try to peek discreetly into the houses. Skyrians are house-proud and often leave their windows and doors open to show off. You'll find walls and conical mantelpieces richly decorated with European- and Asian-style porcelain, copper cooking utensils, wood carvings, and embroideries. Wealthy families originally obtained much of the porcelain from the pirates in exchange for grain and food, and its possession was a measure of social standing. Then enterprising potters started making exact copies, along with the traditional local ware, leading to the unique Skyrian style of pottery. The furniture is equally beautiful. Typical is the miniature carved Skyrian chairs, which can just about accommodate adult posteriors. If peeking into windows isn't your thing, a traditional house with local furnishings is recreated at the **Municipal Museum.** ⊠ *Megálou Stratoú,* ☎ *0222/91256.* ⬚ *500 dr. (free Sun.).* ⊙ *Daily 8–2:30. Closed winter.*

The tiny **archaeological museum** contains finds, mostly from graves, from Neolithic to Roman times. Weapons, pottery, and jewelry are represented. ⊠ *Eternal Poetry Sq. (at far end of Sisifos),* ☎ *0222/91327.* ⬚ *500 dr.* ⊙ *Tues.–Sun. 8:30–3.*

The **Faltaits Historical and Folklore Museum** has a rich collection of Skyrian decorative arts. This house, built after Independence by a wealthy family who later gave it to the town, is far larger than the usual Skyros dwelling, and it is almost overflowing with rare books, costumes, photographs, paintings, local embroideries, and other heirlooms. The embroideries are noted for their flamboyant colors and vivacious renderings of mermaids, hoopoes (the Skyrians' favorite bird), and human figures whose clothes and limbs sprout flowers. ⊠ *Eternal Poetry Sq.,* ☎ *0222/91232.* ⬚ *Free.* ⊙ *Daily 10–1 and 5:30–8.*

You can't miss the **statue dedicated to Rupert Brooke** (⊠ Eternal Poetry Sq.) the English poet we all read about in high school. The Skyrians call this well-known landmark *To Brook,* and every street seems to lead either to it or to the Kastro. He was 28, on his way to the Dardanelles in 1915 to fight in the first world war, but died of septicemia on a French hospital ship just off Skyros. You can visit his grave in the southern part of the island, near where he died (☞ *below*). Brooke was a socialist, but he became something of a paragon for war leaders such as Churchill. The imposing statue, a classical bronze symbolizing poetry, provokes strong emotions among islanders who object to the nudity and have defaced it accordingly.

Beaches

Around the northern tip of the island is a dirt road to **Theotokos** beach. The large Greek air base near the northern tip is off-limits.

Dining and Lodging

$$ ✕ **Christina's Restaurant.** Australian Christina, the charming owner
★ and chef, prepares international and local cuisine with imagination. The menu always includes warm herb bread and a light cheesecake. Try the chicken fricassee and the barrel wine. To find the restaurant, with its romantic walled garden, look for a sign downhill from the taxi stand. (And friendly Christina knows everybody and everything about the island. At press time she was finishing a few lovely rooms with private baths for overnighters, with great breakfasts included.) ⊠ *Market St.,* ☎ *0222/91778. No credit cards. Closed Sun. June 1–Sept. 30 and weekdays Oct. 1–May 31.*

$$ ✕ **Margetis Taverna.** A vest-pocket taverna wedged in among shops on the main drag, it is known locally as the best place for meat and fish on the island. It's popular, so get there early (8–8:30). Though fish and lobster are always pricey, they are worth it here, as is the lamb. Try the good barrel wine, and sit outside under the big tree and watch the folks walk by. ⊠ *Market St.,* ☎ *0222/91311. Reservations not accepted. No credit cards. No lunch.*

$ ✕ **To Glaros.** Stuffed tomatoes, moussaka, vegetable dishes—if simple, good, precooked classics with no frills are your choice, this small taverna is the place for you. It's a fine place for lunch, if you're not relaxing on the beach. ⊠ *Market St., near the central square,* ☎ *0222/ 92363. No credit cards.*

$$ ▥ **Nefili.** You'll feel like you're living in a traditional Skyrian house. This unassuming but superb little hotel has special duplexes that show off the artful nature of these islanders, with a loft king-size bed overlooking a charming main room decorated with handcrafted artifacts and embroidery, a working fireplace, kitchen, and a balcony with view of the town. Everything sparkles, including the new pool. The hotel is located five minutes from town center and the beach. ⊠ *Plageiá area,* ☎ *0222/91964,* FAX *0222/92061. 10 rooms, 9 cottages. Breakfast room, bar, pool. AE, MC, V.*

$$ ▥ **Paliopirgos Hotel.** Five minutes between both the beach at Magazia and the town center, rooms at this intimate hotel are air-conditioned and pristinely decorated, each with a small, well-equipped kitchen area, a single and double bed, and a balcony with a sea view. The rental mopeds are fun for tooling around the island. Maria Makris is the perfect host at breakfast in the roof garden; in the evening, sip a cocktail in the same spot, and watch the sun set and the moon rise. ⊠ *Skyros town 37007,* ☎ *0222/91014 or 0222/92405,* FAX *0222/92185. 9 rooms with shower. 2 bars, air-conditioning. MC.* ☺ *Winter with advance booking.*

Nightlife

BARS

Local bars with loud music are the extent of Skyros nightlife. **Calypso** (⊠ Market St.) is the oldest, opened in 1982. **Rodon** (⊠ Market St.) is popular and open late. **Renaissance** (⊠ Market St.) is another hot spot that blares on until the wee hours.

Shopping

Want to buy something really unusual for a shoe lover? Check out the multithonged trohadia, worn along with pantaloons by Skyrian men as part of their traditional costume. You can find these conversation stoppers at the **Argo Shop** (⊠ Near Plateia Rupert Brooke).

FURNITURE

Skyrian furniture can be shipped anywhere. **Lefteris Avgoklouris** is a carpenter with flair; you may visit his workshop (⊠ About 100 yards from square on right of road heading down the hill, ☎ 0222/91106). Ask around to find other master carpenters and craftspersons for original furniture and other artistic handicrafts.

POTTERY

Skyrian pottery is both utilitarian and decorative. Although you will see it all over town, the best places to shop are all on Market Street. First on the right near the square is **Emmanouil Andreou's** (⊠ Market St., ☎ 0222/91631), with both local and imported ceramics. Also on the right is **Stamatis Ftoulis's** (⊠ Market St., ☎ 0222/91559 or 0222/91887), with a big selection of plates, bowls, cups, and vases. You can watch him and his assistants painting the pottery at his workshop in Magazia. Perhaps the most interesting for reproductions is **Kallio,** G. Nittis's tiny atelier (⊠ On the left behind the pale blue kiosk, just before the turn for *To Brook*, ☎ 0222/92213). He specializes in meticulously exact copies of historic pieces of Anatolian origin and enjoys talking about his research over a glass of ouzo. It is hard to find pottery of this kind and quality outside Turkey.

Magazia and Molos

㉙ *1 km (½ mi) northeast of Skyros town.*

Coastal expansions of the main town, these two resort areas are the place to stay if you love to swim. **Magazia,** where the residents of Horio used to have their storehouses and wine presses, and **Molos,** a bit farther north, where the small fishing fleet anchors, are both growing fast. You can hire a boat, explore the isolated coastline, and stop at sea caves for a swim. Nearby are rooms to rent and tavernas serving the day's catch and local wine. From here, Skyros town is only 15 minutes away, along the steps that lead to Eternal Poetry Square past the archaeological museum.

Beaches

Just north of Molos, past low hills, fertile fields, and the odd farmhouse, a dirt road leads to the beach at **Palamari.** Between Molos and Magazia is a long, sandy beach. A short walk south of Magazia, **Pouria** offers good snorkeling, and nearby on the cape is a small treasure: a sea cave turned into a chapel.

Lodging

$$$ ⊞ **Skyros Palace.** With a big seawater pool and an isolated, adjacent beach, this is a water baby's idea of paradise. Separate low-rise buildings with arched windows and comfortable, traditionally furnished rooms and verandas are evocative of cubist Skyros town. ⊠ *Girismata, just north of Molos, 34007,* ☎ *0222/91994,* ℻ *0222/92070. 80 rooms. Restaurant, bar, cafeteria, saltwater pool, parking. MC, V. Oct.–mid-May.*

$$ ⊞ **Skyron Studios.** Recently renovated and looking fresh and sparkling, these traditional white Skyrian bungalows with verandas are set among the pines overlooking the Aegean. They are fully equipped with kitchens, and can easily accommodate up to four people. ⊠ *Molos, on Vina Beach, 34007,* ☎ ℻ *01/7230957 in Athens. 3 cottages. Parking. No credit cards. Closed Oct.–May.*

Nightlife

DANCE CLUB

For late-night dancing, the best club is **Skiropoulo** (⊠ On the beach just before Magazia). Music is western and (later on) Greek, and its laser lighting system illuminates the rocks of the acropolis after the sun has gone down. It can be reached from Eternal Poetry Square by descending the steps past the archaeological museum.

Atsitsa

30 *13 km (8 mi) west of Skyros town.*

The beaches along the way from Skyros town, Kalogriaand Kyra-Panagria, are sheltered from the strong northern winds called the *meltimi*. Atsitsa, farther along on the northwest coast, has pine forests growing down the the rocky coast. It is home to the chapel of **Ayios Panteleimon** (⊠ On dirt road south).

Skyros Centre was founded in 1978 in this remote area. It was the first and remains the foremost center for holistic vacations. Participants come for a two-week session and can take part in activities as diverse as windsurfing, creative writing with well-known authors, art, tai chi, yoga, massage, dance, drama, and psychotherapy. Courses also take place in Skyros town, where participants live in rooms in villagers' houses. Skyros's courses are highly reputed and have been well reviewed by hardened journalists. For more information, contact the London office well in advance of leaving for Greece. ⊠ *Skyros, 92 Prince of Wales Rd., London NW5 3NE, England,* ☎ *0171/267–4424 or 0171/284–3065; 0222/92279 on Skyros,* FAX *0171/284–3063.*

Outdoor Activities and Sports

HIKING

Experienced hikers can take the 6-km (4-mi) walk around the headland from Atsitsa to Ayios Fokas, but the trek takes skill to negotiate at times and can be hazardous in bad weather.

Ayios Fokas

31 *12 km (7½ mi) west of Skyros town, 5 km (3 mi) south of Atsitsa.*

At Ayios Fokas, you will find three lovely white-pebbled beaches and the fabulous cooking of Kyria Kali, who serves her husband's just-caught fish with her own vegetables, homemade cheese, and bread at her small taverna. This is a real end-of-the-road atmosphere in more ways than one, because if you're coming from Atsitsa, the road south deteriorates into a rutted track, nerve-wracking even for experienced motorbike riders. If you want to stay overnight, Kyria has a couple of rooms, but without electricity or plumbing. We're talking basic.

Beaches

The beaches at **Aherounes** and **Pefko** (⊠ 7½km/5 mi southeast of Ayios Fokas, near Linaria) are most accessible from the Linaria–Horio main road. At Pefko, the dirt road south from Atsitsa becomes smooth and paved again.

Vouno

Access to southern territory starts at Ahilli, 4 km (2½ mi) south of Skyros town. Points south: Kalamitsa 4 km (2½ mi) south of Ahilli; Kolymbada 5 km (3 mi) south of Kalamitsa.

This is the mountainous southern half of Skyros, though a passable
32 dirt road heads south at the eastern end of the isthmus, from **Aspous**

to **Ahilli.** The little **bay of Ahilli** (from where legendary Achilles set sail with Odysseus) is a yacht marina. Some beautiful, practically untouched beaches and sea caves are well worth the trip for hard-core explorers.

Thorny bushes warped into weird shapes, oleander, and rivulets running between sharp rocks are the predominant features here; only goats and rare Skyrian ponies can survive this desolate environment. Many scholars consider the beautifully proportioned, diminutive horses to be the same breed as the horses sculpted on the Parthenon frieze. They are, alas, an endangered species, and only about one hundred survive.

㉝ Pilgrims to **Rupert Brooke's grave** should continue along the wide dirt road through this wilderness down toward the shore. As you reach the valley, you'll catch sight of the grave, set in an olive grove, on your left. He was buried the same night he died on Skyros, and his marble grave was immortalized with his prescient words, "If I should die think only this of me: /That there's some corner of a foreign field/ That is forever England." Restored by the British Royal Navy in 1961, a stout wrought-iron and cement railing surrounds the gravesite. You can arrange for a visit by taxi or caïque in the town.

Beaches

The beach of **Kalamitsa** (⊠ Western coast) is 4 km (2½ mi) along the road south from Ahilli. Three tavernas are at this old harbor.

The inviting, deserted **Kolymbada** beach is 5 km (3 mi) south of Kalamitsa.

EVIA

In any other country, an island as large and beautiful as Evia would be a prime tourist attraction. Yet it is often ignored by travelers to Greece, who tend to think of it not as an island but a suburb, as it is only 80 km (50 mi) north of Athens. Athenian daytrippers and weekenders do crowd in, ironically, to get away from it all. Lying to the south and west of the Sporades, and connected to the almost contiguous mainland by bridge and frequent ferry service, Evia is the second-largest island in the country, after Crete. It has sandy beaches, fertile valleys, wooded mountains, and some pretty villages—just what tourists think of as pleasantly Greek.

In ancient times, Evia (then called Euboea) flourished early, and by the 7th century BC its four city-states—Chalkis (present-day Halkidha), Eretria, Kimi, and Histiaia—had colonies in Asia Minor and Italy, as well as on the Greek mainland. The city-states' glory paled as Athens ascended, but Chalkis—which controlled the narrow Evripos Channel between mainland and island—was seen as a strategic prize by subsequent conquerors, from Philip of Macedon to the Romans, the Crusaders, and the Turks.

Long and narrow, with mountains running north to south, the island has good roads and varied terrain, with steep cliffs in the east and beach resorts in the west. Some towns along the main route are touristed and commercialized while others, off the beaten track, remain peaceful and basically unchanged. A tour of the highlights of Evia could be done in a couple of days, as an easy island getaway from Athens, by ferry, or car. This tour begins in Karystos in the south, one of the ferry and hydrofoil ports, and ends in the north coast, characterized by fishing villages and miniresorts; you may also start where the boats port (in Marmari, Eretria, Kimi, Aedipsos) or you can cross the bridge at Halkidha.

Karystos

90 km (56 mi) southeast of Halkidha.

Set in a valley below Mt. Ohi on the Karystian Bay, Karystos is one of the most popular southeastern resorts in Evia, a one-hour boat ride from the mainland port of Rafina. This neoclassical town was designed in a grid pattern by a Bavarian architect named Bierbach, commissioned by King Otho. Ancient ruins are scattered through the area, and a Byzantine church is worth visiting. Near the harbor are the remains of a 14th-century Venetian castle called the **Bourtzi**, its walls filled with marble quarried near here, confiscated from an earlier temple to Apollo. Four kilometers (2½ miles) away, near the village of Myli, are the russet ruins of a 14th-century Franco-Turkish fortress, built with the colorful stone that gave the town its earlier name, Castel Rosso. An aqueduct behind it once carried spring water by tunnel to the Bourtzi.

To climb the 4,610-ft Mt. Ohi, take the path from Myli in the lush slopes above the town to the bizarre half-hewn marble columns lying like felled logs among the rocks; near the summit is a structure called the Dragon's House, thought to be a temple of Hera. The mountain was a quarry site in the Roman era, and the Dragon's House, which is unlike anything Greek, may have been erected by workers from Asia Minor. On the coast below Karystos are beaches; tucked among them is the lighthouse that marks the Cava d'Oro, the strait between Evia and Andros.

Dining and Lodging

$$ ✕ **Kavo d'Oro.** This gold-star taverna has outdoor dining and local wine to go along with the hearty home-style Greek meals, which feature meat stews, vegetables cooked in olive oil, great stuffed grape leaves, and freshly cooked eggplant. ✉ *Parados Sachtouri,* ☎ 0224/22326. *No credit cards. Closed Oct.–Dec.*

$$$ ⌂ **Apollon Suite Hotel.** Shining white, and modern throughout, this all-suite hotel's accommodations have separate living areas overlooking palm-studded lawns, a terraced pool, and the beach beyond. For families or friends traveling together, it is an especially good value. ✉ *Beachside, Karystos 34001,* ☎ ℻ 0224/22049. *36 suites. Restaurant, pool. MC, V. Closed Nov.–Mar.*

Marmari

80 km (49½ mi) southeast of Halkidha, 10 km (6 mi) northwest of Karystos.

The port of Marmari, rapidly sprouting with hotels and summer homes, is served by Rafina on the mainland. The road north goes inland along the middle of the island, flaunting glimpses of Frankish watchtowers and bisecting tiny villages inhabited by Greeks of Albanian origin. Their ancestors were brought by the Venetians during the 14th century, and later by the Turks, to supplement the declining local population. Many still speak Albanian at home, and their own Greek dialect.

En Route On the drive from Marmari to Eretria you'll pass several interesting towns and sights. **Stira,** set amid streams and forests, has an ancient citadel. **Nea Stira,** on a bay, has beaches with changing facilities and mysterious, huge blocks of stone. In this wooded area, fossils of prehistoric animals have been discovered. **Aliveri,** along with Byzantine churches and an old tower, also has a major power plant belching smoke.

Eretria

15 km (9 mi) southeast of Halkidha, 65 km (40 mi) northwest of Marmari.

In ancient times, this was Evia's second city, after Halkidha—a major maritime power, with a school of philosophy, founded in the 3rd century BC, by one of Plato's pupils. Today, drab, dusty Eretria is regarded just as a place where people board the 30-minute ferry to the mainland. Neither its interesting ruins nor its jewel of a museum is even signposted, but do persevere.

West of the acropolis are the ruins of a temple, a palace, and Eretria's **ancient theater** (⊠ North of the museum). It has two vaulted passageways—one leading to, the other under, the orchestra—no doubt used for deus ex machina solutions and spectral apparitions. You can tour the ruins at any time.

The **museum** (⊠ Odhos Arheou Theatrou), set amid cypress trees, opened in 1991 in collaboration with the Swiss School of Archaeology, which is responsible for digging at Eretria. It has beautifully exhibited finds from the area—including magnificent Black Figure vases, ex-votos galore, and children's toys and jewelry. ⊠ Odos Archaio Theatrou, ☏ 0229/62206. ▤ 500 dr. ☉ Tues.–Sun. 8:30–3.

Ask the guard to take you to the **House of the Mosaics,** five minutes away, to view the 4th-century BC treasures. (Hours are the same as for the museum; ☞ above.)

Kimi

50 km (31 mi) northeast of Halkidha, 40 km (29 mi) northeast of Eretria.

Kimi, the port for Skyros, is a fishing village that sits high on a plateau, overlooking its harbor. It has stone houses; a busy main square; pine, fir, and mulberry trees everywhere; and good beaches (follow the secondary roads).

In a traditional house is a charming little **folk museum,** which has displays of memorabilia, costumes, and historical facts. Probably the dried-fig capital of Greece, Kimi was an important port in the late-19th century and has a good deal of Victoriana and some diaphanous silk garments; it was once known for its silk production. It is also the birthplace of George Papanicolaou, who developed the Pap test technique to detect uterine cancer. ⊠ On road to the port, ☏ 0222/22011. ▤ 400 dr. ☉ Daily 10–1 and 6–8:30.

NEED A
BREAK?
Stop to rest your feet at **To Balkoni** (⊠ Above the port), with its splendid view of the extravagant hillside vegetation and the sleepy, one-street port below.

Dining

$$ ✕ **Lalari.** Set on the waterfront, this taverna is one you can count on for succulent seafood, dressed simply with lemon. Locals recommend the grilled shrimp and octopus, washed down with local wine. Service is caring, outside tables are appealing, and live music adds to the experience. ⊠ At the harborside, Kimi, ☏ 0424/22624. No credit cards. Closed Nov.–Apr.

Halkidha

90 km (56 mi) northeast of Athens.

Halkidha (Chalkis), Evia's largest town, has been linked by a bridge to the mainland since the 5th century BC. It was a major producer of weaponry, and its metalwork can be seen at Olympia, Delphi, and other ancient sites. The current rushing through the 50-yard channel changes direction several times a day, confounding travel plans in past generations and perplexing scientists. Halkidha is still a major commercial center; cement factories blight its southern suburbs. It is a big market town, with a population mix of Orthodox Greeks, Muslims, and Jews working together, reflecting the trade routes of Evia over the centuries. Though the town may have more urban problems than blessings, you can dine royally in its fish tavernas for a pittance.

OFF THE
BEATEN PATH

STENI – If you head 30 km (18½ mi) north from Halkidha's extended suburbs, you'll see signs for Steni, a pretty village with clear mountain springs, halfway up Mt. Dirfis, Evia's highest mountain. At 5,725 ft, it's a challenge to hikers; a boon to botanists because of its many unique species; and to ordinary mortals a place of glorious views. You can drive a good way up it.

En Route On the coast going north from Halkidha to Prokopi, the road runs parallel to a river shaded by enormous plane trees. One of them is so huge it takes 27 men to encircle its trunk.

Prokopi

40 km (25 mi) northwest of Halkidha.

Prokopi is filled with descendants of the Turkish refugees who came here in 1923, bringing with them the relics of St. John the Russian. Every May 27 this otherwise quiet farming town is filled with pilgrims at the **shrine of Ayios Yannis o Rossos.**

Also just outside of Prokopi is **Ahmet Aga,** the vast estate of the Noel-Baker family. The original Noel, a cousin of Lady Byron, bought the property from the Turks in 1830, and it has often been a source of violent resentment in this district inhabited by rather poor, often unemployed Greeks.

Limni

50 km (31 mi) northwest of Halkidha, 10 km (6 mi) west of Prokopi.

The west coast's Limni possesses a tranquil island atmosphere—except for tourists on weekends and in summer season. This ancient fishing village has white houses, lots of flowers, and narrow lanes and it fronts on a stretch of water that is often as smooth as a lake (which its name signifies). It also has a couple of decent hotels, plenty of rooms, three ouzieris, and two good tavernas on the waterfront.

Sightseers can poke around the remains of the Roman baths and the 15th-century convent of **Ayios Nikolaos,** built on the site of a temple of Apollo, where legend has it that Hera and Zeus were married.

Dining
$$ ✕ **To Pyrofani.** Sit outside and enjoy the house specialty, baked shrimp, or any of the other seafood dishes. Service is solicitous, the music sometimes live, and the local wine fun to sip. ⊠ *Next to Ayia Triada, Limni,* ☎ *0227/31640. MC, V.*

Aedipsos

80 km (50 mi) northwest of Halkidha, 30 km (18½ mi) northwest of Limni.

For a therapeutic spa with state-of-the-art facilities, head to the fishing village of Aedipsos, via the corniche road full of spectacular views. Here hot springs have been soothing aches and pains since antiquity, and the likes of Aristotle and Plutarch have sung its praises. Take a whiff of the sulfurous vapors, a peek at the yellow rocks and, if you're stiff from all that driving, take a dip. Hotels here have the bubbling waters piped right into their private rooms. The ferry here goes to Arkitsa, the National Road, and to Athens.

THE NORTHERN SPORADES A TO Z

Arriving and Departing

By Bus and Ferry

For information, it is always best first to contact the EOT (☞ Visitor Information, *below*), where someone will be able to give you the information you need in English. Car ferries vary, but most provide clean and comfortable service and private overnight quarters between destinations.

ALONNISOS, SKIATHOS, AND SKOPELOS

Leaving from Athens's Terminal B, buses for Lamia stop in Ayios Konstandinos (usually just called Ayios), the main port for the Sporades. The bus fare is about 3,000 dr. and the trip takes about 2½ hours. There are at least two or three ferries per day during the summer, fewer in winter: Check with the EOT's Athens office (☞ Visitor Information, *below*). Tickets are available from several travel agents on the dock. From Ayios Konstandinos, the trip costs 3,300 dr. to Skiathos and about 1,000 dr. extra to Skopelos or Alonnisos; the trip takes about 3½ hours to Skiathos, and about an hour between each island. Tickets for the islands can be bought at the **travel agencies** (☞ *below*). (Hydrofoils are twice as expensive but also twice as fast.)

SKYROS AND EVIA

A bus leaves Athens's Terminal B (✉ Behind Liossion 260, ☎ 01/831–7153) daily at 1:30 (Sunday at 2:30) to catch the *Lykomedes* at Kimi on Evia. The bus fare is 3,000 dr. and the trip takes 3½ hours. You can buy boat tickets on the dock when you get off the bus. The boat trip from Kimi takes two hours and costs 1,700 dr. The return boat from Skyros leaves at 8 AM except Sunday (3 PM).

Buses: Athens–Ayios Konstandinos (☎ 01/831–7147); Athens–Skyros (☎ 01/831–7163).

Port Authorities: Alonnisos (☎ 0424/65595); **Ayos Konstandinos** (☎ 0235/31759); **Kimi** (☎ 0222/22606); **Skiathos** (☎ 0427/22017); **Skopelos** (☎ 0424/22180). **Skyros** (☎ 0222/96475).

By Car

SKIATHOS, SKOPELOS, AND ALONNISOS

You must drive to the port of Ayios Konstandinos (Ayios) and from there take the ferry. The drive to Ayios from Athens takes about two hours. Visitors with cars might have to reserve a place on the car ferry a day ahead.

SKYROS AND EVIA

You must drive to the port of Kimi on Evia. From Athens, take the Athens–Lamia National Road to Skala Oropou and make the 30-minute ferry crossing to Eretria on Evia (every half hour in the daytime). No reservations are needed.

Because it is so close to the mainland, you can skip the ferry system and drive directly to Evia over a short land bridge connecting Ayios Minas on the mainland with Halkida. From Athens, about 80 km (50 mi) away, take the National Road 1 to the Schimatari exit, and then follow the signs to Halkida.

By Hydrofoil

The **Flying Dolphins** are about twice as fast as ferries and cost twice as much. They call at ports more frequently, and with careful planning in summer it is possible to use them to travel the entire distance from Evia to Skyros and the other Sporades, continuing on to either Volos or Ayios Konstandinos. Ask any travel agent for a timetable.

From Athens, a **Ceres Lines** bus (Pireas: ☎ 01/428–0001 or 01/428–3555) leaves Syntagma (Constitution) Square to meet Flying Dolphins at Ayios Konstandinos. Ask for information when you book. Fares are as follows: bus from Athens to Ayios Konstandinos, 3,000 dr.; Ayios Konstandinos to Skiathos, Skopelos, and Alonnisos, at least three times per day, 6,000 dr.–9,000 dr.; Kimi to Skyros, the other Sporades and Volos, Tuesday only, 4,600 dr.–19,000 dr.

By Plane

Alonnisos, Skopelos, and Evia have no air service. Skiathos airport (⊠ 5 minutes northeast of Skiathos town, ☎ 0427/22049) handles direct charter flights from many European cities and **Olympic Airways** (☎ 01/936–9111 Athens; 0427/22220 Skiathos) flights (at least daily, more in summer) from Athens's Ellinikon Airport West Terminal (☎ 01/969–9466). The trip takes 40 minutes; the fare is 12,200 dr. In summer there are daily Olympic Airways (☎ Skyros: 0222/91600) flights from Athens to Skyros airport (⊠ 11 km/8 mi northwest of Skyros town, ☎ 0222/91625). The flight takes 50 minutes; the fare is 13,300 dr.

Getting Around

By Boat

SKIATHOS

Small motorboats can be rented at the **Marine Center** (⊠ Near the airport runway, ☎ 0427/22888 or 0427/21178, ᴙᴬᴬ 0427/23262).

ALONNISOS

Boats can also be rented at the **Marine Center** (⊠ Near the Elinoil gas station on the waterfront, ☎ 0424/65206).

By Bus

SKIATHOS

Buses on Skiathos leave Skiathos town to make the beach-run as far as Koukounaries every 30 minutes from early morning till 11:30 PM.

SKOPELOS

Buses on Skopelos run six times a day from Skopelos town to Glossa and Loutraki, stopping at the beaches.

ALONNISOS

Alonnisos has one bus that makes the trip from Patatiri to Alonnisos town (Chora) and back from 9 AM to 2 PM only.

SKYROS

Skyros buses carry ferry passengers between Linaria and Horio, stopping in Molos in summer.

EVIA

All cities are serviced with frequent bus service. For information contact the **KTEL bus station** (☎ 0221/22026).

By Caïque

On all islands, caïques leave from the main port for the most popular beaches, and interisland excursions are made between Skiathos, Skopelos, and Alonnisos. You can also hire a caïque (haggle over the price) to tour around the islands; they are generally the preferred way to get around by day. For popular routes, captains have signs posted showing their destinations and departure times. On Skyros, check with Skyros Travel (☞ Travel Agencies, *below*) for caïque tours. In Alonnisos, day trips are organized to the many smaller islands in the vicinity.

By Ferry or Hydrofoil

Journeys between islands are usually made by ferry or hydrofoil. There are usually several boats per day between Skiathos and Skopelos, and they almost always serve Alonnisos as well. Hydrofoils usually ply between these islands at least three times per day. Between Skyros and the other Sporades there is no regular boat service, but there is a hydrofoil on Tuesdays, and sometimes on other days.

Because schedules are likely to change, check the times listed outside travel agencies.

By Motorbike and Car

The road networks on all four islands are so rudimentary that cars are not really needed, but it's not a bad idea to rent one for a day to get a feel for the island, then use the bus or a motorbike thereafter. Four-wheel drives and other cars can be rented everywhere. If you rent a motorbike, however, be extra cautious: Many of those for hire are in poor condition. The locals are not used to the heavy summer traffic on their narrow roads, and accidents provide the island clinics with 80% of their summer business. Check with the travel agencies (☞ *below*) for information.

By Taxi

All the islands have taxis waiting at the ferry landings. Even Alonnisos has three. They are unmetered, so negotiate your fare in advance.

Contacts and Resources

Emergencies

SKIATHOS
Police (☎ 0427/21111). **Medical center** (☎ 0427/22222).

SKOPELOS
Police: Skopelos town (☎ 0424/22235); Glossa (☎ 0424/33333). **Medical center** (☎ 0424/22222).

ALONNISOS
Police (✉ Patitiri, ☎ 0424/65205). **Medical center** (☎ 0424/65208).

SKYROS
Police (☎ 0222/91274). **Medical center** (☎ 0222/92222).

EVIA
Police (✉ Karystos, ☎ 0224/22262; ✉ Marmari, ☎ 0224/31333; ✉ Eretria, ☎ 0229/61111; ✉ Kimi, ☎ 0222/22555; ✉ Halkidha, ☎ 0221/87000 or 0221/83333; ✉ Prokopi, ☎ 0227/41203; ✉ Limni, ☎ 0227/31209; ✉ Aedipsos, ☎ 0226/22456). **Medical center** (✉ Karystos, ☎ 0224/22207; ✉ Marmari, ☎ 0224/31300; ✉ Eretria, ☎ 0229/62222; ✉ Kimi, Oxylithos, ☎ 0222/46202; ✉ Halkidha, ☎ 0221/21901; ✉ Prokopi, ☎ 0227/41212; ✉ Limni, ☎ 0227/32222; ✉ Aedipsos, ☎ 0226/55311).

Travel Agencies

SKIATHOS
Mare Nostrum Travel (✉ 21 Papadiamantis, 37002, ☎ 0427/21463 or 0427/21464, FAX 0427/21793), aside from handling all your inquiries and issuing boat and plane tickets, is the only American Express representative in the Sporades.

SKOPELOS

Madro Travel (⊠ On the waterfront, ☎ 0424/22145, 0424/22300, 0424/22767, 0424/23060, or 0424/23061, FAX 0424/22941).

ALONNISOS

Alonnisis Travel & Tourism Agency (⊠ Near the waterfront, ☎ 0424/61588 or 0424/65619, FAX 0424/65511). Anything and everything on the island can be arranged here.

SKYROS

Skyros Travel (⊠ Market St., Skyros town 34007, ☎ 0222/91123 or 0222/91600, FAX 0222/92123) has a virtual monopoly on hydrofoil tickets, rooms, excursions, and car rentals.

Visitor Information

Greek National Tourist Organization (GNTO or EOT) office (⊠ Karageorgi Servias 2, in the National Bank Building, Athens, ☎ 01/322–2545). **Travel agents** can be helpful on Alonnisos and Skyros.

SKIATHOS

Tourist police (⊠ At the inland end of Odhos Papadhiamndiou, ☎ 0427/23172).

SKOPELOS

Tourist offices and facilities (⊠ On the waterfront under a row of mulberry trees or on the first street parallel to it). **Skopelos Municipality** (⊠ Chora, ☎ 0424/22205).

5 Epirus and Thessaly

*Ioannina, Metsovo,
and the Meteora Monasteries*

Monasteries-in-air, the seraglio of Ali Pasha, and the Dodona oracle all beckon the inquisitive traveler to remote Epirus and Thessaly. At Meteora, a spiritual center of Orthodox Greece, the quiet contemplation of generations of monks is preserved in wondrously frescoed monasteries hovering on rocky pedestals above the plain. Nearby, spectacular mountain passes reveal shepherd villages with richly costumed women whispering the strange, secret Vlach vernacular. Over in Epirus, discover Ioannina and track the exotic shadows of that larger-than-life Byronic figure Ali Pasha.

BORDERED BY ALBANIA AND THE IONIAN SEA, the province of Epirus is a land of stark mountains, lush forests, swift rivers, and remote villages marked with unique customs, language, and architecture. Epirus means "the solid land," standing in contrast to the neighboring islands of Corfu, Paxi, and Lefkas, strung along the littoral. The abrupt changes from the delicately shaded green of the idyllic olive and orange groves on the coast to the tremendous solidity of the bare mountains have been faithfully depicted by that intrepid Victorian author and artist Edward Lear (of limerick fame)—this was the splendid massive landscape that came to cast its spell over Lord Byron, who traveled here to meet the most extraordinary figure in modern Greek history, Ali Pasha. The tour described below begins in the Epirote capital of Ioannina, which still bears many vestiges of this larger-than-life figure who seems to have stepped from the pages of the *Arabian Nights*.

By Toula
Bogdanos

Updated by
Terrence
Moloney

Sinan Pasha was just the latest tyrant in this region, for millenia a stormy backwater of tribal warfare. Mountainous provinces may often be spared a surfeit of history, but in Greece the last 4,000 years have been so crammed with momentous events that Epirus received its fair share. Going back in time, and an easy trip southwest of Ioannina, you can visit Dodona, the site of the oldest oracle in Greece. The itinerary continues on to the thriving traditional village of Metsovo in the Pindos Mountains and over the Katara Pass on one of the most dramatic roads in Greece. It ends in the fertile province of Thessaly where, on the edge of the plain, the Byzantine-era monasteries of Meteora seem to float in midair, built atop bizarrely shaped pinnacles that tower over the town of Kalambaka.

Viewing these extraordinary rock-pinnacle monasteries—today one of Greece's most famous attractions—it's easy to credit the story about the original ascent being achieved by way of a rope fastened to an eagle's leg, whose nest lay atop one of the rocks. The days of jointed ladders, pulled up in an emergency, are no more, and the nets are strictly limited to hauling up supplies. Occasional romantics, who misguidedly hanker after the good old days when the traveler was pulled up uncomfortably squeezed into an outsize string-bag, are quickly cured of their rash desire by one look at the rusty and rotting windlass, especially if accompanied by the gruesome story that the rope was never changed until it broke. Today, a comfortable road winds ingeniously through the sandstone labyrinth close to the breaktaking cliff, making Meteora a destination for thousands of travelers eager to discover an extinct way of life, whose infinite pain and labor required a religious fervor incomprehensible to later generations.

Pleasures and Pastimes

Dining
The curious diner will muse over Epirus's local specialties. In Ioannina's lakeside restaurants you can sample unusual dishes like those using ingredients culled from lakes: frogs' legs, eel, crayfish, and turtles. Those with a penchant for sweets will savor *bougatsa* (a local sweet custard pastry). For Greeks, Metsovo brings to mind the costly but delectable smoked Metsovone cheese and Katogi wine pressed from French Bordeaux grapes grown locally. Other Metsovo specialties include boiled goat, *trahanas* soup (made from cracked wheat boiled in milk and dried), and sausages stuffed with leeks. In all but the fanciest restaurants, check out what's cooking because the menus change seasonally. Informal dress is usually appropriate.

CATEGORY	COST*
$$$$	over 7,000 dr.
$$$	5,000 dr.–7,000 dr.
$$	2,500 dr.–5,000 dr.
$	under 2,500 dr.

per person for appetizer, main course, and fruit or dessert, including taxes and service charge but no drinks

Lodging

Except for the best hotels, rooms in the region are simply decorated. Though prices don't vary much within each government classification category, quality does. Ask to see the room first, and don't assume anything; if you have special requests, such as a mountain view; a *diplo krevati* (double bed) rather than a *diklino* (twin bed); a balcony; or a bathtub, speak up. Rooms are usually easy to find in Ioannina. Reservations might be necessary for Kalambaka, which is packed with tour groups in late spring and summer, and in Metsovo during ski season or the town's July 26 festival. In these two towns, private rooms are likely to be far cheaper than comparable hotel rooms—look for advertisements as you arrive. Off-season, prices drop drastically from those listed here, and you should always try to negotiate. Hotels in the $$$–$$$$ range are assumed to have air-conditioning and televisions; listings indicate them only when they are present in hotels in the $–$$ range.

CATEGORY	ALL AREAS*
$$$$	over 39,000 dr.
$$$	22,000 dr.–39,000 dr.
$$	13,000 dr.–22,000 dr.
$	under 13,000 dr.

for a standard double room in high season, including taxes but not breakfast, unless indicated

Exploring Epirus and Thessaly

The region consists of two areas: the mountainous province of Epirus, with villages such as Metsovo and its capital, Ioannina, to the west; and the Thessalian plain, an agricultural heartland with Meteora at its edge.

Numbers in the text correspond to numbers in the margin and on the Epirus and Thessaly map.

Great Itineraries

The distance from Ioannina to Meteora is small, but the mountain road that connects the two cannot be negotiated swiftly; a tour of the region should take this into account. If you only have two or three days, visit the Meteora monasteries and head to Metsovo if you have time. Five days will allow you to cover, at a fair pace, all the sites described in this chapter, or to concentrate on a smaller area. Eight days will allow a thorough exploration of the region, leaving the tourist trail to visit remote villages and sights.

IF YOU HAVE 2 DAYS

Base yourself in 🖼 **Kalambaka** ⑥ and spend as long as possible at the monasteries at **Meteora** ⑦. A full day should allow you to visit many of them.

IF YOU HAVE 5 DAYS

Start with 🖼 **Ioannina** ① and visit **Dodona** ③ in the morning to see the ancient oracle of Zeus. See the old town in the afternoon and the nearby island that night. The next morning head to 🖼 **Metsovo** ⑤, stopping at **Perama cave** ④ on the way; spend the day exploring **Metsovo,** and be sure to get a taste of the Metsovone cheese! On the following day

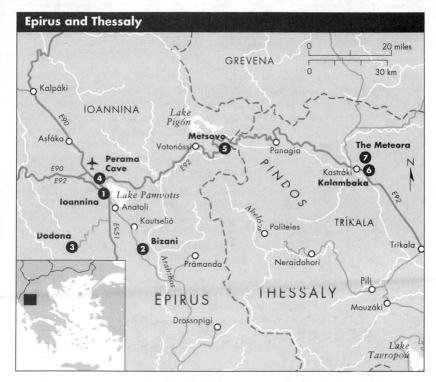

Epirus and Thessaly

move on to ⛫ **Kalambaka** ⑥ to make the trek along the monastery route of **Meteora** ⑦.

IF YOU HAVE 8 DAYS

With eight days you can explore the region at your leisure; if you prefer a speedy pace, you might find yourself with too much time on your hands. Start with ⛫ **Ioannina** ① and end with ⛫ **Kalambaka** ⑥ and the monasteries of **Meteora** ⑦. To get the most out of the experience, hire a car to visit the **Perama cave** ④ and to explore mountain villages surrounding ⛫ **Metsovo** ⑤.

When to Tour

As in all of Greece, places are more likely to be open in the mornings than in the afternoons, and museums and sites are often closed on Mondays. Although Metsovo might be delightful in high summer—the town festival is held July 26—the heat is oppressive elsewhere. The mountain roads to Metsovo are often blocked and impassable in winter; if you get there, however, the ski center will be open. The ancestral home of Baron Michalis Tositsa in Metsovo is closed on Thursdays, so plan accordingly.

The Meteora monasteries are open Wednesdays, Saturdays, and Sundays year-round. They attract considerably fewer visitors in winter, when you might find a sense of spirituality in their windy isolation.

EPIRUS

Ioannina, Dodona, and Metsovo

Ancient Epirus was once a huge country that stretched from modern-day Albania (an area the Greeks still call "Northern Epirus" and where Greek is still spoken) to the Gulf of Arta and modern Preveza. The region is bordered by the Mediterranean Sea to the west, the islands of Lefkadha to the south, and Corfu to the north. Inland it is defined by a tangle of mountain peaks and upland plains, and the climate is markedly Balkan.

Despite the region's natural physical barriers, it has been invaded many times. Its hinterland character has made it the perfect hideout for rebels and has led it to be inhabited by disparate peoples. In ancient times the province was ruled by a king, the last being the famous Pyrrhus (his victories were not worth the cost); the Macedonian, Roman, Byzantine, and Ottoman empires ruled the region in succession (but not always successfully). In modern times, the Italians failed and the Germans succeeded in passing through here.

Epirus became part of Greece in 1913, almost 100 years after Greece's liberation from the Turks, and the cultural influence from its Ottoman occupation is evident. Moreover it boasts a sizable non-Greek population, the Vlachs, said to be descendants of legionnaires from garrisons on the Via Egnatia, one of the Roman Empire's main east–west routes. The Vlachs speak a Romance language (related to Italian and Romanian).

In this section we describe—in geographical succession—the capital of the province, Ioannina, with its rich Ottoman heritage; nearby Dodona, most ancient of Greek oracles; and the traditional Vlach mountain village of Metsovo to the west, perhaps the most accessible of these villages and a good base for exploring.

Ioannina

 305 km (189½ mi) northwest of Athens, 204 km (126¾ mi) west-southwest of Thessaloniki.

On the rocky promontory of Lake Pamvotis lies Ioannina, its fortress punctuated by mosques and minarets whose reflections, along with those of the snowy peaks of the Pindos range, appear in the calm water. Although the city may seem noisy and undistinguished, its old quarter, encircled by the somber castle walls, and its peaceful islet, called Nissa, or "island," where nightingales still sing and fishermen mend their nets, make it an ideal retreat from the bustle of Athens.

Founded by Emperor Justinian in AD 527, Ioannina suffered under many rulers: It was invaded by the Normans in 1082, made a dependence of the Serbian kingdom in 1345, and was conquered by the Turks in 1431. Above all, this was Ali Pasha's city, where, from 1788 to 1821 the cunning despot carved a fiefdom from much of western Greece.

Born in the 1740s in Tepeline, Albania, Ali rose to power by unscrupulous means. He was made pasha of Trikala in 1787 and a year later seized Ioannina, the largest town in Greece. For the next 33 years, Ali pursued his lifelong ambition: to break from the Ottoman Empire and create his own kingdom. He paid only token tribute to the Sultan and allied himself according to his needs with the French, the British, and the Turks. In 1797 he collaborated with Napoléon; the next year he seized Preveza from the French; and by 1817 he was wooing the British and Admiral Nelson, who gave him Parga. His territory extended from the Ionian sea to the Pindos range and from Vaona in the north to Arta in the south.

The most notorious ruler of Epirus, Ali Pasha had a guard of assassins to carry out his plots of murder and brigandage. He combed the countryside looking for attractive concubines, and his harem numbered in the hundreds. He attacked the Turkish Porte (from "Sublime Porte" [or gate] of the Sultan's palace, where justice was administered; by extension, the Ottoman government), and he brutalized his Greek subjects. Perhaps Ali's most infamous crime was the drowning of the beautiful Kyra Frosini, his son's mistress, and 16 other women, by tying them in stone-laden bags and dumping them in the lake. Apparently, he was in love with Frosini, who rejected him, and, spurred on by his jealous daughter-in-law, Ali had Frosini killed on charges of infidelity. He regretted his deed and ordered that 1,000 *kantaria* (250 pounds) of sugar be thrown into the lake to sweeten the water Frosini would drink.

By 1820, the Porte had become fed up with Ali and sent 50,000 men to besiege Ioannina and execute the 80-year-old tyrant. He was killed while hiding in the guest house of an island monastery. His head was cut off and paraded around Epirus, then buried in Constantinople; his other remains are allegedly interred in the citadel in Ioannina. In the end, Ali Pasha's way of rule had caught up with him: As he once boasted, "I sent some heads to Constantinople to amuse the Sultan, and some money to his ministers, for envy never sleeps."

The spacious, well-arranged **archaeological museum** is the best in the area, with finds from several ancient sites. (Your children may prefer to stay in the nearby **playground**.) Of special interest are the artifacts from ancient Dodona, a 200,000-year-old Paleolithic stone tool found near Preveza, and two winsome bronze statuettes of children from the late 4th century BC. The bronze priapic warrior wearing nothing but a waist guard to protect his belly is of the Geometric period (first half of the 8th century BC). Best of all is the collection of inscribed lead tablets (6th–3rd centuries BC) found at the oracle. The questions for the gods are translated for your amusement: "Shall I take another wife?" "Has Pistos stolen the wool from the mattress?" "Will it be all right to buy the small lake by the sanctuary of Demeter?" Read the evolution of the temple of Zeus, especially if you plan to visit the site (☞ Dodona, below). ⊠ *Platia 25 Martiou,* ☎ *0651/33.357 or 0651/25490.* ◻ *500 dr.* ◷ *Tues–Sun. 8:30–3.*

Along with the archaeological museum, Ioannina's other main attraction is the **citadel,** at the lakeside end of Odhos Averoff. The city's once-large Jewish population lived within the walls, alongside Turks and Christians. The Jews were deported by the Nazis during World War II, never to return; there are only about 150 remaining today. Outside the citadel walls, near the lake, a **monument** commemorates the slaughter. The citadel's massive stone walls, which once dropped into the lake on three sides, are more or less intact; Ali Pasha completely rebuilt them in 1815.

Tree-lined **Dionissiou Filosofou Street,** which circles the **castle** along the lake, is ideal for a late-afternoon stroll. A moat, now filled, ran around the southwest landward side, and today the walls divide the old town—with rose-laden whitewashed houses, cobblestone streets, and birdsong—from the new. ⊠ *At lakeside end of Odhos Averoff.*

At the north end of the citadel is the remarkably well preserved **Aslan Mosque,** now the municipal museum, whose collection recalls the three communities that lived together inside the fortress from 1400 to 1900. In revenge for a failed revolt against the Turks in 1611, Aslan Pasha destroyed the Church of Ioannis Prodromos and built this mosque in its place in 1618. Near the entrance are the ruins of the three-dome Turkish library. Make your way past the numerous stacked cannonballs and the many-arched *medresse* (a theological school) with cells for Turkish imams, once part of the Koranic School of Ioannina. In front of the medresse and below the mosque there are other arches with fountains, where believers washed before entering to pray.

In Greece it is rare to glimpse the interior of a mosque. The vestibule has recesses for shoes and, inscribed over the doorway, is the name of Aslan Pasha and THERE IS ONLY ONE GOD, ALLAH, AND HIS PROPHET IS MAHOMET. The mosque retains its original decoration and *mehrab* (altar), which faces Mecca. Around the room are a walnut and mother-of-pearl table from Ali Pasha's period, clothes chests, and a water pipe. The *oulema* (priest) traditionally read the Koran from the seventh step of the pulpit. In the right corner, a small door leads to the minaret, up which the muezzin climbed five times a day to call the faithful to prayer. You can see Arabic graffiti on the columns. The mosque was active until most Turks left in the disastrous 1922 population "exchange" after the war in Asia Minor. ⊠ *North end of citadel,* ☎ *0651/26536.* ⊡ *700 dr.* ☉ *Winter: weekdays 8–3, weekends 9–3, summer: weekdays 8–8, weekends 9–8.*

The **fortress,** called *Its Kale* by the Turks, is where Ali Pasha built his palace. Full-scale excavation and renovation are under way in this area, revealing remains from the Byzantine period; in 1995 the **Byzantine Museum** opened in the fortress. Its small collection of antiquities from all over Epirus is carefully arranged in the front half of the museum; there's much information in English on the walls. The second half of the museum houses an important collection of icons from the 16th and 17th centuries. Nearby is the **Fetiye (Victory) mosque,** which purports to contain Ali Pasha's tomb. ⊠ *Palace grounds, eastern corner of citadel,* ☎ *0651/39692.* ⊡ *500 dr.* ☉ *Tues.–Sun. 8:30–3; palace grounds daily 7 AM–10 PM.*

In the **old bazaar** (⊠ Clustered around the citadel's gates) you may still see some Turkish-era buildings, and a smattering of the copper-, tin-, and silversmiths who fueled the city's economy for centuries.

NEED A
BREAK?
Stop for a drink in the **café** (⊠ Palace grounds) and enjoy a panoramic view of the lake.

The square **Platia Mavili** (⊠ On the waterfront) is lined with smart cafés, which are full of tourists having breakfast or waiting for the next boat to the nearby island; in the evening this is *the* place to hang out—the youth of Ioannina while away the hours here over frappés or long drinks. At sunset, catch the *volta* (ritual promenade) of showing off and gossiping.

As you chug from the shore toward the tiny **island,** or "Nissa," look back at the outline of the citadel and its mosques in a wash of green. The whitewashed lakeside island village, founded in the late-16th century by refugees from the Mani, seems centuries away from Ioannina. Ali Pasha once kept deer here for hunting. With its neat houses and flower-trimmed courtyards, pine-edged paths, runaway chickens, and reed-filled backwater, it's the perfect place to relax, have lunch, and visit some of the monasteries. Restaurants and tavernas abound here, even more than in Ioannina. The emphasis is strongly on fish and other creatures from the lake, although traditional taverna food can also be found.

Lake Pamvotis, now seriously polluted, is fed by streams from the northern Mt. Mitsikeli. Catch the boat below the citadel near Platia Mavili; it leaves every half hour from 8:30 AM to 10:30 PM; the ride takes 10 minutes and costs 200 dr.

The main attraction on Ioannina's island is the **Ali Pasha Museum.** It was in the monks' cells here on January 17, 1822, that Ali Pasha was killed, after holding out for almost two years. In the final battle, Ali ran into an upstairs cell, but the soldiers shot him through its floorboards from below. You'll hear more than one version of his last days, each more romantic than the last. Until recently you could see the original floorboards with the seven bullet holes, but the floor had to be replaced, and now newly drilled, circled holes indicate the position of the originals. The museum has a famous portrait of Ali Pasha sleeping on his wife Vasiliki's lap, the crypt where Vasiliki hid, prints and paintings of that era, an edict signed by Ali Pasha with his ring seal (he couldn't write), and his water pipe standing on the fireplace. ✉ *On island, take left from boat landing and follow signs,* ☎ *0651/81791.* ▣ *100 dr.* ☉ *Any time boats are running.*

Agios Nikolaos ton Filanthropinon has the best frescoes of the island's several monasteries. The monastery was built in the 13th century by an important Byzantine family, the Filanthropinos, and a fresco in the northern exonarthex depicts five of them kneeling before St. Nikolaos (1542). Many of the frescoes are by the Kontari brothers, who later decorated the mighty Varlaam in Meteora. You will note the similarities in the bold coloring, expressiveness, realism, and Italian influence—especially in the bloody scenes of martyrdom. The corner crypts were the meeting places of the secret Greek school during the Ottoman occupation. Instead of returning to the landing when you head back to the main road, follow signs for Filanthropini, which is on a grassy knoll at the other side of the village. Dress appropriately, and carry a flashlight, the better to see the frescoes. The spry caretaker will let you in; if she doesn't see you immediately, hang around conspicuously for a few minutes. ✉ *On island, follow signs.* ▣ *Leave 200 dr. donation.* ☉ *Daily 8–8.*

Dining and Lodging

$–$$ ✗ **Limnopoula.** If you arrive early enough you can take advantage of
★ the swimming pool or have a predinner drink at the lakeside bar. The restaurant has tables inside and outside. The cook prepares standard taverna fare with plenty of traditional Epirote dishes—especially boiled meat—and the cook will prepare just about anything if you call in advance. A local specialty is *saganaki* cocktail (a mix of Roquefort, *kefalograviera*, feta, and Edam cheeses melted in a frying pan and served with pita bread). For dessert try the homemade *tis rinis* (halvah). The restaurant is in lush parkland a short drive from Limnopoula. Take a taxi from Platia Pirrou or from the entrance to the citadel; the ride is about 400 dr. ✉ *Kanari 10, Limnopoula,* ☎ *0651/33288 or 0651/39908. Reservations essential in Aug. AE, DC, MC, V.*

$ ✗ **Ivi.** Not much to look at, Ivi (written HBH in Greek) serves excellent *magirefta*, or precooked dishes, in large portions for lunch; sometimes there's a line outside the door. Especially good are the vegetable dishes, such as leeks sautéed and baked with celery, green beans, or artichokes. Meat dishes include boiled goat, *tas* kebab (with bits of pork in red sauce), and beef with *kritharakia* (ricelike pasta). There's usually a fish entrée such as trout, cod with garlic sauce, or sea bream. Late at night, the cook serves pasta Ioannina style and a tripe soup with the cow's head and feet, said to be good for hangovers. Whatever is left over from lunch is served at dinner, and though it may not look as inviting, remember that magirefta taste just as good after sitting for hours. ✉ *Platia Yoryiou 4,* ☎ *0651/27085. No credit cards. Closed Sun.*

$ ✗ **Propodhes.** Propodhes, near the museum, is said to be the best of the island's numerous eating places. When you ask to see the menu, however, don't be surprised if the owner produces various startled-looking frogs, turtles, fish, and birds from the cages and tanks in front of the restaurant—if you don't want to look your food in the eye, head elsewhere. Sweets include homemade *gliko* (preserves made from quince or cherries soaked in syrup). Try Zitsa, a dry white wine produced from the local Debina grape, with your meal. ✉ *Island, outside entrance to Ali Pasha museum,* ☎ *0651/81214. No credit cards.*

$ ✗ **To Mandeio.** Opposite the entrance to the citadel, this spot is open
★ all day and particularly popular for late meals. The menu has all the
usual taverna favorites: Order appetizers to share such as *koloukithakia*
(fried zucchini), *gigantes* (baked giant beans), saganaki, and *piperato*
(spicy cheese dip). The menu has entries printed in English and Greek;
only the items with prices next to them are available, and they change
with the seasons. ⊠ *Platia Yoryiou 15,* ☎ *0651/25452. No credit cards.*

$$$ ⊞ **Xenia.** The nicest hotel in Ioannina, this was the site of a 1994 sum-
★ mit on Bosnia. Xenia is set back from a central street behind huge oak
trees and a rose-studded gazebo. Its soothing lounge and eating areas,
with mirrored columns and pastel upholstery, are pleasant retreats. The
quiet guest rooms are done in the same gray-white-rose hues and have
either mountain or garden views. The hotel has central heating, but
no air-conditioning, which is rarely necessary. Buffet breakfast is in-
cluded in the price. ⊠ *Dhodhonis 33, 45221,* ☎ *0651/47301, 0651/
47187, or 0651/47188,* 𝔽𝔸𝕏 *0651/47189. 60 rooms. Restaurant, bar,
refrigerators, meeting rooms, parking. AE, DC, MC, V.*

$$–$$$ ⊞ **Castro Hotel.** The Castro Hotel—opened in 1998 and the only hotel
★ within the old town walls—is a brilliant new addition to Ioannina's lodg-
ing scene. Set in a neoclassical mansion, it only has seven rooms, so it
may soon be difficult to make reservations, especially when word gets
out about the well-appointed quarters, the gorgeous wood beams, the
painted wooden ceiling of the second-floor lobby, and the two work-
ing fireplaces. Size keeps other services modest, and the breakfast room
is regrettably small. Nonetheless, the location and charm of this hotel
make it a delight. ⊠ *In the Old Town, just outside the Inner Castro,
45332,* ☎ *0651/22866 or 0651/22780. 7 rooms. Breakfast room. V.*

$$ ⊞ **Palladion.** Don't be put off by the plain exterior; inside, the lobby feels
like a bar on a '30s cruise liner, from the polished wooden phone booths
to the plush red sofas and neon clock. Upstairs there's a cozy lounge with
a fireplace, and the hotel decor is eclectic (from African sculptures to lithos
of abstract art). The bathrooms are small, but about 40 rooms have great
lake views. All have color TVs, though more adventurous visitors should
pop into the outdoor summer cinema next door. Public rooms are air-
conditioned in summer, and all rooms are heated in winter; some have
air-conditioning and about half are supplied with hair dryers. ⊠ *Bot-
sari 1, 45444,* ☎ *0651/25856 through 25859, 0651/34601, or 0651/
34602,* 𝔽𝔸𝕏 *0651/74034. 128 rooms, 120 with bath, 4 suites. Restaurant,
bar, meeting rooms, parking. AE, DC, MC, V.*

$ ⊞ **Pension Dellas.** What makes this place so special is the hospitality
of the owners (Titika and Sotirios Dellas), freshly picked flowers,
maybe a homemade *koulouraki* (cookie) made from their chickens' eggs,
and hand-pressed linens. A delightful change from hotels in town, this
lakeshore pension was originally built for the Dellas children. Rooms
are immaculate, sunny, and quiet, with balconies or access to the courtyard, a congenial meeting place. Most visitors come March through
October since the pension has no central heating, but you'll get a
portable heater and plenty of blankets in winter. Call beforehand and
someone will meet you at the main dock, about five minutes away. ⊠
Island, 45444, ☎ *0651/81494. 8 rooms, 1 with bath. No credit cards.*

Nightlife and the Arts

BARS

There are several excellent bars and clubs in Ioannina, including **Makris**
(☞ *above*).

Right smack in the center of town near Plateia Pirrhou is **Oasis** (☎
0651/92128), which serves as a restaurant-bar-café in one. Seating is
extensive: On one side there's an outdoor patio overlooking the plateia
and, on the other, a patio overlooking the lake and the island. In be-

tween there's the restaurant proper, complete with steaming dishes of food displayed in the front foyer.

FESTIVAL

Ioannina hosts the **Epirotika festival** in July and August, with performances at the Frontzos theater. For information, contact the Ioannina Tourist Office (☞ Visitor Information *in* Epirus and Thessaly A to Z, *below*).

FILM

Several **cinemas** clustered around Platia Pirrhou feature an array of new releases and art-house movies.

Shopping

CRAFTS

Ioannina has long been known throughout Greece for its silver craftsmanship. There are many silver shops on Odhos Averoff, near Platia Yoryious, and a careful eye can discern some prizes amid the tourist drek. In particular, avoid the shinier and brighter items in stores near the entrance to the citadel.

Bizani

② *293 km (182 mi) northwest of Athens, 12 km (7½ mi) south of Ioannina.*

Pavlos Vrellis wax museum, in the village of Bizani, is where you'll see a collection of historical Epirote figures, among them a tableau of Ali Pasha's murder sculpted by a local man. ⊠ *Mouseio Pavlos Vrellis, Bizani,* ☎ *0651/92128.* 🖃 *1,000 dr.* ☉ *Daily 10–4.*

Dodona

③ *308 km (191½ mi) northwest of Athens, 22 km (13½ mi) southwest of Ioannina.*

Said to be the oldest in Greece, the **oracle At Dodona** flourished from at least the 8th century BC until the 4th century AD, when Christianity succeeded the cult of Zeus. Homer, in the *Iliad,* mentions "wintry Dodona," where Zeus's pronouncements, made known through the wind-rustled leaves of a sacred oak, were interpreted by priests "whose feet are unwashed and who sleep on the ground." The oak tree was central to the cult, and its image appears on the region's ancient coins. It was here that Odysseus sought forgiveness for slaughtering his wife's suitors, and it was from this oak that the Argonauts took the sacred branch to mount on their ship's prow. According to one story, Apollo ordered the oracle moved here from Thessaly; Herodotus writes that it was locally believed a dove from Thebes in Egypt landed in the oak and announced, in a human voice, that the oracle of Zeus should be built. The oracle had its ups and downs. Consulted in the heroic age by Heracles, Achilles, and all the best people, it went later into a gentle decline, because of its failure to equal the masterly ambiguity of Delphi. Enduring for a time as the poor man's Delphi, Dodona became again fashionable under the Macedonian dynasty.

As you enter the archaeological site of Dodona you pass the **stadium** on your right, built for the Naïa games and completely overshadowed by the **theater** on your left. One of the largest and best preserved on the Greek mainland, the theater once seated 17,000, and it has been restored for the annual summer festival. Its building in the early 3rd century BC was overseen by King Pyrrhus of Epirus, from whose name comes the phrase "Pyrrhic victory": His armies habitually won battles with great losses. His theater was destroyed, rebuilt under Philip V of Macedon in the late 3rd century, and then converted by the Romans into an arena for gladiatorial games. Its retaining wall, reinforced by bastions, is still standing. East of the theater are the foundations of the **bouleuterion** (headquarters and council house) of the Epirote League, built by King Pyrrhus, and a small rectangular temple dedicated to Aphrodite. The remains of the **acropolis** behind the theater include house foundations and a cistern that supplied water in times of siege.

The remains of the **sanctuary to Zeus Naios** included the Sacred Oak and temples to Zeus, Dione, and Herakles; until the 4th century BC there was no temple. The Sacred Oak was surrounded by abutting cauldrons on bronze tripods. When struck, they reverberated for a long time, and the sound was interpreted by soothsayers. Fragments from as early as the 8th century have been recovered. In the 4th century BC, a small temple was built near the oak, and a century later the temple and oak were enclosed by a stone wall. By King Pyrrhus's time, the wall had acquired Ionic colonnades. After a 219 BC Aetolian attack, a larger Ionic temple was built, and the surrounding wall was enhanced by a monumental entrance. The oak tree currently on the site was planted by archaeologists; the original was probably cut down by Christians in the 4th century AD.

Two buses leave daily from Ioannina's Vyzantinou station. For about 5,000 dr., you can hire a taxi, which will wait an hour at the site. Negotiate with one of the drivers near Ioannina's bell tower or call a radio taxi (☎ 0651/46777, 0651/45777, or 0651/25452). ⊠ *Archaeological site,* ☎ *0651/82287.* ☜ *500 dr.* ☉ *Tues.–Sun. 8:30–3.*

The Arts
For information about the **ancient Greek drama at Dodona** contact the Ioannina Tourist Office (☞ Visitor Information *in* Epirus and Thessaly A to Z, *below*).

Perama Cave

❹ *312 km (194 mi) northwest of Athens, 4 km (2½ mi) northwest of Ioannina.*

Perama cave's passageways, discovered in the early 1940s by locals hiding from the Nazis, extend for more than 1 km (½ mi) under the hills. The high caverns and many-hued limestone stalagmites and stalactites have names such as Statue of Liberty and Sphinx, which you'll learn during the 45-minute guided tour; one begins every 10 minutes; one of the guides will speak English. You can catch Bus 8 from Ioannina's clock tower. ⊠ *Along E 92 east from Ioannina,* ☎ *0651/81521.* ☜ *1,500 dr.* ☉ *Summer 8 AM–sunset.*

Metsovo

❺ *293 km (182 mi) northwest of Athens, 58 km (36 mi) east of Ioannina.*

The traditional village of Metsovo cascades down the mountain below the 6,069-ft Katara Pass, which is the highest in Greece and marks the border between Epirus and Thessaly. Early evening is a wonderful time to arrive. As you descend through the mist, dazzling lights twinkle in the ravine. Stone houses with slate roofs and sharply projecting wooden balconies line steep, serpentine alleys. In the square, especially after the Sunday service, old men—dressed in black flat caps, dark baggy pants, and wooden shoes with pom-poms—sit on a bench, like crows on a tree branch. Should you arrive on a religious feast day, many villagers will be decked out in traditional costume.

Although most villages are fading, Metsovo, designated a traditional settlement by the Greek National Tourist Organization (GNTO or EOT), has become a prosperous community with a growing population. In winter it draws skiers headed for Mt. Karakoli, and in summer it is a favorite destination for tourist groups. Despite the souvenir shops offering "traditional handicrafts" that may sell you imports, the slate roofs that have been replaced with easy-to-maintain tile, and the kitsch that occasionally mars the scene, for the most part Metsovo has preserved its character.

The natives are descendants of nomadic Vlach shepherds, once believed to have migrated from Romania but now thought to be Greeks trained by Romans to guard the Egnatia Highway connecting Constantinople and the Adriatic. The Vlach language is so influenced by Latin that it was used during World War II to communicate with occupying Italian forces, and villagers still speak it among themselves. During winter, while the village lies buried in snow, shepherds move their flocks from the mountains to the lowlands around Trikala, while their wives, aptly nicknamed the "white widows," tend to their heaths in isolation. The shepherds numbers are dwindling, however (they herd about 15,000 sheep today), as many have turned to tourism for their livelihoods.

After Metsovo became an important center of finance, commerce, handicrafts, and sheepherding, the Vlachs began trading farther afield—in Constantinople, Vienna, and Venice. Ali Pasha abolished the privileges in 1795, and in 1854 the town was invaded by Ottoman troops led by Abdi Pasha. In 1912 Metsovo was freed by the Greek army. Many important families lived here, including the Averoffs and Tositsas, who made their fortunes on Egyptian cotton. They contributed to the new Greek state's development and bequeathed large sums to restore Metsovo and finance small industries. Testimony to their largesse is the **Foundation Baron Michalis Tositsa** (⊠ In the square, ☎ 0656/41205), which helped the local weaving industry get a start (one year its stock was used in Yves Saint Laurent's Paris collection) and also financed the nearby **ski resort** (⊠ Just outside the village, ☎ 0656/41206), which has one chairlift, nestled in the slopes of Mt. Karakoli.

For generations, the Tositsa family had been one of the most prominent of Metsovo, and to get a sense of how Metsovites lived (and endured the arduous winters in style), visit the late-Ottoman-period, restored, stone-and-timber **ancestral home of the Barons Tositsa.** Now a museum of popular art, it is devoted to local Epirote crafts. Built in 1661 and renovated in 1954, this typical Metsovo mansion has carved woodwork, sumptuous textiles in rich colors, and Vlach handcrafted furniture. In the stable you'll see the gold-embroidered saddle used for special holidays and, unique to this area, a fanlight in the fireplace, ensuring that the hearth would always be illuminated. The goatskin bag on the wall was used to store cheese. ⊠ *Up stone stairs to right off Tositsa (main road) as you descend to main square,* ☎ *0656/41024 or 0656/41814.* 🖭 *300 dr.* ⊙ *Fri.– Wed. 8:30–1 and 4–6 (3–5 in winter). Guided tours every ½ hr; wait for the guard to open the door.*

NEED A BREAK?	Metsovo is famous throughout Greece for its expensive smoked cheeses. Sample one or two at the **cheese shop** in the main square; the owner is happy to let you taste before you buy.

The 18th-century church of **Agia Paraskevi** (⊠ Main square) has a flamboyantly decorated altar screen that's worth a peek.

At **Averoff Gallery** you may view Evangelos Averoff's personal art collection: paintings of revolutionary scenes and local landscapes, as well as modern art by contemporary Greek artists. One painting known to all Greeks is Nikiforos Litras's *The Burning of the Turkish Flagship by Kanaris,* a scene from a historic battle in Chios. Look on the second staircase for Paris Prekas's *The Mosque of Aslan Pasha in Ioannina* to see what contemporary Ioannina looked like in the Turkish period. ⊠ *Main square,* ☎ *0656/41210.* 🎫 *300 dr.* ⊘ *Wed.–Mon. 10–7 (10–4:30 in winter).*

Visit the **cooperative** (⊠ Metsovo village, ☎ 0656/41235), open daily 6:30–1:30, to see how cheeses are made. The **winery** (⊠ Outside the village, in the Upper Aoos Valley, ☎ 0656/41010) also welcomes visitors.

If you're staying in Metsovo a few days, visit **Politses** (⊠ 4 km/2½ mi northwest of Metsovo, in the valley), a picturesque spot with several springs surrounded by a forest of beech, fir, and pine trees.

The **nearby mountain villages** of **Votonosi,** 5 km (3 mi) west of Metsovo; **Anthohori,** 5 km (3 mi) southwest; and **Chrysovitsa,** 9 km (5½ mi) west, are somewhat less tourist-overrun communities with plenty of local color.

OFF THE BEATEN PATH | **AYIOS NIKOLAOS MONASTERY –** Not to be missed, unless you are pressed for time, is a visit to the restored 14th-century Ayios Nikolaos monastery, about 30 minutes into the valley (with the trip back up about an hour). The *katholikon* (main church) is topped by a barrel vault, and what may have once been the narthex was converted to a *ginaikonitis* (a woman's gallery). Two images of the Pantocrator (Godhead), one in each dome—perhaps duplicated to give the segregated women their own view—stare down on the congregation. You can also see the monks' cells, with insulating walls of mud and straw; the abbot's quarters; and the school where Greek children were taught during the Turkish occupation. In 1960, while on a summer stroll, Evangelos Averoff scraped the blackened walls out of curiosity and discovered brilliant colors underneath. With the help of the foundation, the 16th-century frescoes—depicting scenes from the life of Christ and various martyrdoms—were cleaned and illuminated. The church is still used on religious feast days. The keepers will give you a closely guided tour and explanation of the frescoes. ⊠ *Down into valley via footpath (follow signs near National Bank of Greece; turn left where paving ends).* 🎫 *Leave a 200 dr. donation in the box.* ⊘ *Usually until 7 pm (1 pm in winter).*

Dining and Lodging

$$ ✕ **Casa la Mounte Tirotaverna.** The owner has based his entire menu
★ around Metsovo's delightful, expensive smoked cheese. Strongly recommended is *hilopites* (oven-baked pasta with a little sauce and lots of cheese). Also try the freshly made pizza topped with Metsovo, and for true aficionados, cheese soup—it's truly different. ⊠ *Tositsa, just up from square,* ☎ *0656/42600. No credit cards.*

$$ ✕ **Taverna Metsovitiko Saloni.** The dining room seduces its patrons with a large fireplace, Metsovo costumes on the walls, charming old photos, and carved wooden furniture. Try the various vegetable pies made from corn flour, unusual in Greece, and especially the saganaki made with Metsovo cheese. Savor the large wine selection and a generous choice of desserts, including Metsovitiko baklava, thick sheep yogurt (with pastry, honey, and walnuts), and gliko. ⊠ *Tositsa 10, above post office,* ☎ *0656/42142. No credit cards.*

$ ✕ **Koutouki.** Koutouki ("little box"), aptly named for its diminutive interior, proves to be one of the best—it's popular among locals and is a good value. All the taverna favorites are here, but order something made with the local cheese. Don't miss the strong barrel wine, because, as owner Kostas Todis jokingly points out, high altitudes go hand in hand with *zali* (giddiness). It's open late, until 3 AM. ⊠ *Under post office,* ☎ *0656/41732. No credit cards.*

$$$ ▣ **Apollon.** The Apollon's traditional lobby has a carved pine ceiling,
★ a fireplace, chandeliers, red-and-green woven upholstery, hammered-
copper plates, and a pet bird, whose cheery song brings spring to
mind, no matter what the season. Built in 1986 in typical Metsovo style
with stone and wood, the hotel has cozy, carpeted rooms with pine fur-
niture, televisions, and balconies overlooking the gorge. The best are
those in the *sofrita* (attic) but they're approximately 8,000 dr. extra;
several have hot tubs. ✉ *Near main square, behind Tositsa Founda-
tion, 44200,* ☎ *0656/41844, 0656/42442, or 0656/41833,* ℻ *0656/
42110. 28 rooms, 2 suites, 10 attic-suites. Bar, breakfast room, re-
frigerators, parking. AE, DC, MC, V.*

$$ ▣ **Bitounis.** Owned by the good-natured Bitounis couple, who might
teach you a few words of Vlach, this hotel has a lounge with a fire-
place, wooden ceiling, flagstone floors, and bright hand weavings.
Rooms are plain, with TVs, radios, and phones, and most have fantastic views of the valley. A sign in the breakfast area reads NO PLAY-
ING AFTER MIDNIGHT to ward off late-night backgammon fanatics.
Have the breakfast at least once —local yogurt and butter, jam, hot bread,
eggs, juice, coffee, fruit, and a slab of delicious smoked Metsovo. The
hotel is equipped for travelers with disabilities. ✉ *Tositsa 48, 44200,*
☎ *0656/41217 or 0656/41700,* ℻ *0656/41515. 25 rooms, 6 suites.
Bar, breakfast room, parking. V.*

$$ ▣ **Kassaros Hotel.** Quiet and reasonably priced, this hotel has its own
travel agency, which books flights and arranges group trips to nearby
sights. The lounge has brightly colored hand weavings and a U-shape
couch that runs along three walls. Rooms on the first floor have ubiq-
uitous striped woolen curtains, TVs, and balconies with views of ei-
ther the Pindos or the garden. The newer rooms on the upper floor
have superior furnishings but no balconies. From July to September
and during holidays the Continental breakfast is mandatory. ✉
Tsoumaka 6, 44200 (2-min walk from main square), ☎ *0656/41800,
0656/41346, 0656/41662, 094/383131, and 093/407494,* ℻ *0656/
41262. 31 rooms. Bar, breakfast room, parking. AE, DC, MC, V.*

$ ▣ **Athine Hotel.** For budget-level food and lodging, this hotel is a good
choice. Built in 1925 it was the first hotel in the area, and owner Yian-
nis Bitounis named it after Athens to remind him of a sister who had
gone to that faraway metropolis to marry. The hospitality is superb:
The owners, who now sleep upstairs, gave up their private quarters to
guests. The rooms have no views, but they're comfortable enough, with
carpeting and central heating. At the taverna, the mother prepares tra-
ditional fare and her own specialties—pies, soups, and meats—and there's
usually a roaring fire in winter. ✉ *S. Klidi 2 (below National Bank off
main square), 44200,* ☎ *0656/41332 or 0656/41725. 9 rooms. No credit
cards.*

THESSALY
Kalambaka and the Meteora Monasteries

Though Thessaly is the home of the immortal gods, a Byzantine site
holds pride of place: Meteora, the amazing medieval monasteries on
top of inaccessible rock-needles. Their extraordinary geological setting
stands in vivid contrast to the rest of Thessaly, a huge plain in central
Greece, almost entirely surrounded by mountains: Pindos to the west,
Pelion to the east, Othrys to the south, and the Kamvounian range to
the north. It is one of the country's most fertile areas and has sizable
population centers in Lamia, Larissa, Trikkala, and Volos. Thessaly was
not ceded to Greece until 1878, after five centuries of Ottoman rule;
today, vestiges of this period remain. Archaeology enthusiasts will be

intrigued by its Neolithic sites to the east, Dhimini and Sesklo near Volos. Kalambaka and Meteora are in the northwest corner of the plain, just before the Pindos Mountains. The best time to come here is the spring, especially at the Meteora monasteries, when the mountains are still snow covered and blend harmoniously with the green fields, the red poppies, and the white and pink fruit trees.

Kalambaka

6 *154 km (95½ mi) southwest of Thessaloniki, 71 km (44 mi) east of Metsovo.*

Kalambaka, a drab modern town, seems to promise little as you approach it. Yet it is one of the most popular tourist destinations in Greece, because of the Meteora monastery complex just north of town (☞ *below*). It's quite a contrast to spend the afternoon at Meteora, getting acquainted with the history and architecture of the Greek Orthodox Church, then returning to modern Kalambaka. Invariably, you'll wind up at a rooftop pool and bar to sip ouzo and contemplate the asceticism of the Meteora monks.

Burned by the Germans during World War II, Kalambaka has only one building of interest, the cathedral church of the **Dormition of the Virgin.** Patriarchal documents in the outer narthex indicate that it was built in the first half of the 12th century by Emperor Manuel Comnenos, but some believe it was founded as early as the 7th century, on the site of a temple of Apollo (various classical drums and other fragments are incorporated into the walls, and mosaics can be glimpsed under the present floor). The latter theory explains the church's paleo-Christian features, including its center-aisle *ambo* (great marble pulpit), which is usually to the right of the sanctuary; its rare *synthronon* (four semicircular steps where the priest sat when not officiating) east of the altar; and its Roman-basilica style, originally adapted to Christian use and unusual for the 12th century. The church has vivid 16th-century frescoes, work of the Cretan monk Neophytos, son of the famous hagiographer Theophanes. A large underground crypt was used to house church vessels. The marble baldachin in the sanctuary, decorated with crosses and stylized grapes, probably predates the 11th century. The courtyard outside the church provides welcome respite under the cool shade of a eucalyptus tree. Behind the church you can stroll through a small necropolis: boxes upon boxes of bones that have been disinterred and washed in accordance with Orthodox tradition. ✉ *North end of town, follow signs from Platia Riga Fereou or from central square,* ☏ *0432/24297.* 🎫 *300 dr.* ◷ *Daily 7 AM–10 AM and 3:30–7.*

Dining and Lodging

$$ ✕ **Estiatorio-Meteora.** At this spot, a local favorite since 1925, the Gert-
★ zos family serves food prepared by the family matriarch, Ketty. Expect lots of meaty main courses and some specialties from Asia Minor. For a light lunch, try one of the salads and a tasty local wine. ✉ *Ekonomou 4, main square,* ☏ *0432/22316. No credit cards.*

$$ ✕ **Kipos.** This taverna's eclectic 140-dish menu—traditional Greek with the addition of Mexican and even children's dishes—might make the journey outside town worthwhile. The owners opened Kipos in December 1993, aiming to bring flawless service and quality food to Kalambaka at reasonable prices, they have certainly succeeded. You'll enjoy the garden setting, complete with waterfalls, and the antiques proudly pointed out by the owner. During winter weekends, there is live Greek music. It's open until 1 AM. ✉ *Trikalon Rd., before entrance to Kalambaka,* ☏ *0432/23218. No credit cards.*

$–$$ ✕ **Vachos.** In the nondescript Riga Fereou Square, you could easily pass this taverna without a second glance. Its secret is the flower-filled garden in the back, where you can enjoy a spectacular view of the Meteora rocks, which are floodlit at night (get a seat toward the front). There's a large selection of the usual taverna *orektika* (starters) and meat and fish main dishes. Try the homemade desserts and barrel wine. ⊠ *Platia Riga Fereou,* ☏ *0432/24678. No credit cards. Closed Nov.–Feb.*

$$$ ⊞ **Amalia.** Built in 1991, Amalia's low-lying complex has spacious, handsome public rooms that somehow avoided the generic stamp. Relax in the sitting room, with a fireplace and floral murals, or enjoy the poolside bar, with glistening blue tiles and rustic rafters. Rooms are done in soothing colors and have large beds and prints; some also have TVs and balconies. Buffet breakfast is included in the price. ⊠ *Trikalon 14, Theopetra, Kalambaka 42200,* ☏ *0432/81216,* ℻ *0432/81457. 171 rooms, 2 suites. Restaurant, 2 bars, cafeteria, pool, shops, meeting rooms. AE, DC, MC, V.*

$$$ ⊞ **Motel Divani.** A few minutes from the center of town, this A-class hotel has optimal views of the Meteora rocks from the rooms' balconies (an advantage over the Amalia; ☞ *above*). Its large open spaces, quiet corners, and private garden encourage relaxation. The exterior is plain, as are the rooms, but they're shielded from outside noise. However, readers have written to note the frayed state of furniture throughout the "past-its-prime" complex. The professional reception staff will arrange and negotiate a price for a leisurely taxi ride to the monasteries. Breakfast is included. ⊠ *Trikalon 1, 42200,* ☏ *0432/23330,* ℻ *0432/23638. 165 rooms. Restaurant, 2 bars, pool, shop, meeting rooms, parking. AE, DC, MC, V.*

$$ ⊞ **Hotel Antoniadis.** Recently renovated, the Antoniadis provides reliable, comfortable accommodations. Everything is clean and simple, and very modern. Every room comes with television, air-conditioning, and minibar. ⊠ *Trikalon 148, 42200,* ☏ *0432/24387,* ℻ *0432/24319. 69 rooms. Restaurant, bar, air-conditioning, pool. MC, V.*

$–$$ ⊞ **Hotel Edelweiss.** This hotel, built in 1990, has a bright and clean sparkle. Almost too much so: Every room is spotless and white, but the walls are completely bare and you feel a little like you're in a hospital. The rooms are comfortable enough, with TVs and air-conditioning. They look out over the pool and the towering Meteora rocks beyond. The bar has a lively local crowd, and the hotel runs a Western and Greek popular music club right next door. ⊠ *E. Venizelou 3, 42200,* ☏ *0432/23966, 0432/23884, and 0432/24918,* ℻ *0432/24733. 60 rooms. Restaurant, 2 bars, air-conditioning, pool, dance club, parking. MC, V.*

Nightlife

BARS

Kalambaka doesn't have much in the way of nightlife, but one or two of the **bars** in the central square and along the Trikala Road stay open late.

NIGHTCLUB

For dancing, try the **Hotel Edelweiss club,** right next to the hotel (☞ *above*).

En Route On the road to the Meteora monasteries, which begins just outside of Kalambaka in Kastraki, you'll pass the 12th-century **Chapel of the Virgin** (⊠ At Doupani), where the monks first gathered. About 8 km (5 mi) outside Kastraki on St. George's Day (celebrated on April 23 or on the Tuesday following Easter, whichever comes first) you will spot what looks like a clothesline hung with brightly colored fabrics set high up in a crevice. According to legend, a woodcutter who lost his leg promised to give St. George all his wife's clothing if he was healed—

which he was. On St. George's Day, women offer scarves or other items of clothing and young men scale the rocks to hang them up for the saint.

The Meteora

❼ *178 km (110½ mi) southwest of Thessaloniki, 3 km (2 mi) north of Kalambaka.*

The name Meteora comes from the Greek word *meteorizome* ("to hang in midair"), and the monasteries, perched on a handful of strangely shaped pinnacles that rise 984 ft above the Peneus Valley, seem to do just that. Their lofty aeries imbue them with an otherworldly quality; the azure heavens seem close enough to touch while the valley of worldly distractions remains far below. Looming between the Pindos range and the Thessalian plain, the rocks remain an enigma. Some geologists say a lake that covered the area 30 million years ago swept away the soil and softer stone as it forced its way to the sea. Others believe the Peneus River slowly carved out the towering pillars, now eroded by wind and rain. Legend, of course, has a more colorful story—these rock-needles were meteors hurled by an angry god.

By the 9th century ascetic hermits were inhabiting the rocks' crevices. On Sundays and holidays they gathered at Stagi (present-day Kalambaka) and Doupiani, and they eventually formed religious communities. With Byzantine power on the wane and an increase in religious persecution from invading foreigners, the monks retreated to the inaccessible rocks. In 1336 they were joined by two monks from Mt. Athos, Abbot Gregorios of Magoula and his companion St. Athanasios. The abbot returned to Athos, but he commanded St. Athanasios to build a monastery here. Notwithstanding the legend that says that the saint flew up to the rocks on the back of an eagle, St. Athanasios began the backbreaking task of building the Megalo Meteoro (1356–72) using pulleys and ropes to haul construction material. The monks themselves had to endure a harrowing ride in a swinging net to reach the top.

Despite St. Athanasios's strictness of rule, the monastery attracted many devotees, including, in 1371, John Urosh of Serbia, who relinquished accession to the throne to become a monk, using the name Ioasaph. His royal presence brought contributions to the monasteries, and the congregation grew quickly. By the 16th century, there were at least 20 smaller settlements and 13 monasteries, which were embellished with frescoes and icons by such great artists as Theophanis Strelitzas, a monk from Crete. The larger monasteries prospered on revenues from estates in Thessaly and eastern Europe; during the late-Byzantine period, they served as bastions of Christianity against Turkish domination.

The architecture of the monasteries is conditioned by the restricted space available, with buildings rising from different levels. Some are whitewashed, while others display the pretty Byzantine pattern of stone and brick, the multiple domes of the many churches dominating the wooden galleries and balconies that hang precariously over frightening abysses.

The monastic communities eventually disappeared for several reasons. Some of the wealthy monasteries were plagued by bitter power struggles. Monasticism as a vocation gradually lost its appeal, causing even grand communities to dwindle. Smaller, poorer monasteries could not afford to maintain the old buildings; many of their structures were neglected or abandoned. Today only six monasteries at Meteora are open to the public. After the Greco-Turkish War of 1919–22, the already diminished monastic lands and revenues were appropriated by the state on behalf of refugees from Asia Minor, another blow to the few remaining monasteries.

Visitors are expected to dress decorously: Men must tuck up long hair and wear long pants, women's skirts should fall to the knee, and both sexes should cover their shoulders, if bare. Some monasteries provide appropriate coverings at their entrances. Opening hours vary depending on the season, but information is readily available in Kalambaka from your hotel receptionist. All monasteries can be visited in a single journey from Kalambaka—a 21-km (13-mi) round-trip by car. A bus leaves Kalambaka for Megalo Meteoro five times daily (once daily in winter). Megalo Meteoro and Varlaam are the two most rewarding monasteries to visit. You can hike along the footpaths between monasteries, but you'd better be in good shape, because there are many steps up to most monasteries. Once on the monastery circuit, you'll find just a few overpriced concession stands; if you plan to make a day of it, stock up on picnic goods in town.

The monastery of **Ayios Nikolaos Anapafsas** seems impossibly crammed atop its narrow rock. The katholikon was built in 1388 and was later expanded; the monastery itself dates from the end of the 15th century. Because of the rock's peculiar shape, the katholikon faces north rather than the usual east. Its superb 16th-century frescoes are the work of Theophanis Strelitzas. Though conservative, his frescoes are lively and expressive: Mountains are stylized, and plants and animals are portrayed geometrically. Especially striking are the treatments of the Temptation, the scourging of Christ, and a scene of Adam naming the animals. The serpent is in the form of the legendary basilisk, which could kill with a mere look or a breath. The rock's small area precluded the construction of a cloister, so the monks studied in the larger-than-usual narthex. Visitors are admitted in small groups. ⊠ *Along monastery route, about 3 km (2 mi) outside Kalambaka,* ☎ *0432/22375.* ☜ *500 dr.* ☉ *Daily 9–6.*

The inaccessible **Ayia Moni** monastery has been deserted since an 1858 earthquake. Locals believe the area is haunted owing to its ominous ambience. ⊠ *Along monastery route, across from Agios Nikolaos monastery.*

Because of its breathtaking location, the compact monastery of **Ayia Barbara,** also called Roussanou, is the favorite for picture-taking. Abandoned in the early 1900s, it stood empty until nuns moved in some years ago and began a restoration program. Its founding in 1288 by the monks Nicodemus and Benedict has yet to be confirmed, but it is known that 156 years later the monastery was restored for the first time. The main church, dedicated to the Transfiguration, has well-preserved frescoes dating from the mid-16th century. Most depict gory scenes of martyrdom, but one shows lions licking Daniel's feet during his imprisonment. A smaller church houses the skull of St. Barbara. ⊠ *Along monastery route, across vertiginous bridges from Ayia Moni,* ☎ *0432/ 22649.* ☜ *500 dr.* ☉ *Daily 9–6.*

The highest and most powerful monastery is **Megalo Meteoro,** or the Church of the Metamorphosis (Transfiguration). Founded by St. Athanasios, the monk from Athos, it was built of massive stones on the highest rock, 1,361 ft above the valley. As you walk toward the entrance, you will see the chapel containing the cell where St. Athanasios once lived. This monastery had extensive privileges and held jurisdiction over the others for centuries; an 18th-century engraving in its museum depicts it towering above the other monasteries.

The sanctuary of the present church was the chapel first built by St. Athanasios, later added to by St. Ioasaph. The rest of the church was erected in 1552 with an unusual transept built on a cross-in-square plan with lateral apses topped by lofty domes, as in the Mt. Athos monasteries. To the right of the narthex are the tombs of Ioasaph and Athanasios; a fresco shows the austere saints holding a monastery in their hands. Also of interest are the gilded iconostasis, with plant and animal motifs of exceptionally fine workmanship; the bishop's throne (1617) inlaid with mother-of-pearl and ivory; and the 15th-century icons in the sanctuary. The expressiveness and attention to color and detail of these icons have led art historians to conclude they may also be the work of Theophanis Strelitzas. In the narthex are frescoes of the Martyrdom of the Saints, gruesome scenes of persecution under the Romans. A chamber stacked with skulls and bones of monks is opposite.

The refectory now houses the treasury, with fine miniatures, golden bulls, historic documents, and elaborately carved crucifixes, including one that the monk Daniel labored over for 10 years. The front shows 10 scenes with several figures each, and representations of 24 single figures. Portable icons include the Virgin, by Tzanes, another well-known artist. The adjacent kitchen is blackened by centuries of cooking. ⊠ *Along monastery route, 600 ft west of Megalo Meteoro, past the intersection for Varlaam monastery,* ☏ *0432/22278.* ⌸ *500 dr.* ☾ *Wed.–Mon. 9–1 and 3:20–6 (winter hrs vary).*

The monks from **Varlaam,** which is situated atop a ravine and reached by a climb of 195 steps, were famous for their charity. Originally here were the Church of Three Hierarchs (14th century), and the cells of a hermitage started by St. Varlaam, who arrived shortly after St. Athanasios. Two brothers from the wealthy Aparas family of Ioannina rebuilt the church in 1518, incorporating it into a larger katholikon called Agii Pandes (All Saints). A church document relates how it was completed in 20 days, after the materials had been accumulated atop the rock over a period of 22 years. Its main attraction are the 16th-century frescoes— mostly of ascetic subjects, including scenes from the life of John the Baptist and a disturbing Apocalypse with a yawning hell's mouth— which completely cover the walls, beams, and pillars. The frescoes' realism, the sharp contrasts of light and dark, and the many-figured scenes show an Italian influence, though in the portrayal of single saints they follow the Orthodox tradition (the West had no models to offer). Note the Pantocrator peering down from the dome. These are the work of Frangos Katellanos of Thebes, one of the most important 16th-century hagiographers.

Other buildings include the infirmary, a chapel to Sts. Cosmas and Damien, and the refectory, now a sacristy, which displays the manuscript Gospel Book of the Byzantine emperor Constantine Porphyrogennetus, bearing his signature. There are storerooms with the monks' 2,640-gallon barrel and an ascent tower with a net and a winch. Until the 1920s the only way to reach most of the monasteries was by retractable ladder or net. A bishop of Trikala subsequently decreed that steps be cut to allow access to all the monasteries, and today the ropes are used only for hauling up supplies. ⊠ *Along monastery route, 328 ft southwest of intersection,* ☏ *0432/22277.* ⌸ *500 dr.* ☾ *Sat.–Thurs. 9–1 and 3:20–6 (3–5 in winter).*

The least-visited site, along the eastern route, is **Ayios Stephanos,** which is the oldest monastery. According to an inscription that was once on the lintel, the rock was inhabited before AD 1200 and was the hermitage of Jeremiah. By the beginning of the 14th century, the monks lived a cenobitic (common) life. After the Byzantine emperor Andronicus Paleologos stayed here in 1333 on his way to conquer Thessaly, he made generous gifts to the monks, which funded the building of a church in 1350. About a half century later, the Lord of Hungro-Wallachia donated a piece of the True Cross, relics of John the Baptist, as well as property in Romania; his nephew gave the monastery the head of St. Haralambos, now housed in the katholikon (1798) named after that saint. A permanent bridge has replaced the movable one that once connected the monastery with the hill opposite.

Today Ayios Stephanos is an airy convent, where the nuns spend their time painting Byzantine icons, writing, or studying music; some are involved in the community as doctors and professors. The katholikon has no murals but boasts a fine carved wooden baldachin and an iconostasis depicting the Last Supper. A two-headed eagle, the symbol of the Byzantine Empire, embellishes the floor. You can also visit the **old church of Ayios Stephanos,** with late-15th-century frescoes, as well as a **small museum,** with icons by Tzanes, 17th-century illuminated manuscripts, and an exquisite Epitaphios cloth—used to cover the bier on Good Friday—embroidered with thread and sequins. ⊠ *Along eastern monastery route (from main road at intersection for Kalambaka, bear right at fork),* ☎ *0432/22279.* ⊠ *500 dr.* ⊙ *Tues.– Sun. 9–1 and 3:20–6 (3–5 in winter).*

NEED A BREAK?	Although you may stop anywhere on the circuit, the stretch approaching Ayia Triada from Ayios Stephanos has the best views for a midday **picnic.** Just hike a few yards off the road to a spot overlooking the valley and unpack.

James Bond fans will recognize **Ayia Triada** from the movie *For Your Eyes Only.* Of all the monasteries, it feels the most primitive and remote, and in fact, if pressed for time, you'll want to skip this one. According to local legend, the Monk Dometius was the first to arrive in 1438; the main church, dedicated to the Holy Trinity, was built in 1476, and the narthex and frescoes were added more than 200 years later. Look for the fresco with St. Sisois gazing upon the skeleton of Alexander the Great, meant to remind the viewer that power is fleeting. In the early 1980s thieves stole precious antique icons, which have never been recovered. The iconostasis has one icon (1662) that depicts Christ in local costume; another scene, of three angels, symbolizes the Holy Trinity. The apse's pseudo-trefoil window and the sawtooth decoration around it and beneath other windows lend a measure of grace to the structure. There are also a chapel dedicated to St. John the Baptist, a small folk museum, the monks' cells, a kitchen, a refectory, and cisterns. Ayia Triada is best known for its view, with Ayios Stephanos and Kalambaka in the south and Varlaam and Megalo Meteoro to the west. A footpath near the entrance (red arrows) descends to Kalambaka, about 3 km (2 mi). ⊠ *Along eastern monastery route, 656 ft north of Ayios Stefanos,* ☎ *0432/22220.* ⊠ *500 dr.* ⊙ *Fri.–Wed. 9–12:30 and 3–5.*

EPIRUS AND THESSALY A TO Z

Arriving and Departing

By Bus
The **KTEL bus** system is preferable to the train. Eight or nine buses daily go from Athens's Terminal A (⊠ Kifissou 100, ☎ 01/512–5954) to Ioannina station (⊠ Between Sina and Zosimadou, ☎ 0651/27422); the trip takes about seven hours. Some buses take the longer route east through Kalambaka and Trikala rather than the usual southern route to the Rion–Antirion ferry and the Peloponnese. The 110-dr. ferry ride is not included in the bus ticket.

From Athens's dismal Terminal B (⊠ Near Liossion 260, ☎ 01/831–7153) seven buses leave daily for Trikala (six hours), where you then make the 25-minute connection to Kalambaka. On Sundays there is a reduced schedule for all towns.

For information in English on bus schedules, telephone the EOT in Athens (⊠ Syntagma [Constitution] Square, ☎ 01/322–2545).

By Car

Driving to Kalambaka or Ioannina from Athens takes the greater part of a day. To reach Ioannina, take the National Road west past Corinth in the Peloponnese, to the Rion–Antirion ferry (9 km/5½ mi before Patras), then continue north past Mesolonghi, Agrinion, Amfiloxia, and Arta (447 km/277 mi). For Kalambaka, take the National Road north past Thebes and Lamia to N. Monastirio (about 53 km/33 mi) north of Lamia, where there is a turnoff for Trikala and Kalambaka (a total of 330 km/204 mi). You may then drive on to Metsovo and Ioannina (another 126 km/78 mi).

By Plane

Olympic Airways has one flight daily from Athens to Ioannina, and one flight daily from Thessaloniki. In **Athens** (⊠ Odos Othonos 6, Syntagma Square, ☎ 01/966–6666); **Ioannina** (⊠ Katsadima 1, Platia Pyrrou, ☎ 0651/28526); airport (⊠ 5 km/3 mi outside town, ☎ 0651/28218 or 0651/39131); **Thessaloniki** (☎ 031/473720).

By Train

The cheapest way to get to Kalambaka is by train, though it is not recommended. From Athens you must change trains at Palaiofarsalo, and the trip takes at least eight hours (the IC express cuts the time by an hour but costs 2,000 dr. extra). For more information, contact the **Greek Railway Organization (OSE)**: Athens (⊠ Karolou 1, ☎ 01/524–0601); Kalambaka (☎ 0432/22451).

Getting Around

By Bus

Four buses (KTEL) daily leave Ioannina for Metsovo (1½ hours) and two buses make the full journey to Kalambaka (three hours); frequencies are the same in the opposite direction. One bus daily leaves Ioannina for Dodona, returning in the afternoon. There is a bus to most villages once a day, but getting around is much easier in a rented car.

By Car

A rented car is by far the best way to explore the region, and one is essential to go beyond the main sites. The road from Ioannina to Metsovo to Kalambaka is one of the most scenic in northern Greece, but it traverses the famous Katara Pass, which is curvy and possibly hazardous, especially in winter (snow chains are necessary).

Contacts and Resources

Car Rentals

Ioannina: Budget (☎ 0651/43901, 0651/33382 airport); **European** (☎ 0651/70086).

Emergencies

IOANNINA
Police (☎ 0651/25673 or 0651/26431). **Emergencies** (☎ 100). **Hospital** (☎ 0651/99111 or 0651/99504).

KALAMBAKA
Police (☎ 0432/2210). **Hospital** (☎ 0432/22222).

METSOVO
Police (☎ 0656/41233). **Health center** (☎ 0656/41111).

Guided Tours

In Athens **CHAT Tours** (✉ Stadiou 4, ☎ 01/322–2886) and **Key Tours** (✉ Kallirois 4, ☎ 01/923–3166) offer guided trips to Meteora and northern Greece. A three-day tour to Delphi and Meteora with lodging and half-board costs 66,000 dr.–73,000 dr.

Contact the **Greek Alpine Club** (☎ 0651/22138) for walking-tour information; it's open from 7 PM to 9 PM.

Travel Agencies

In Metsovo, **Kassaros Travel** (✉ Tsourmaka 3, ☎ 0656/41800, 0656/41346, 0656/41662, 093/407494, 094/383131, or 094/397778, FAX 0656/41262) can issue plane tickets, arrange accommodations, and occasionally organize trips to the nearby lake or ski center.

Visitor Information

IOANNINA

Greek National Tourist Organization (GNTO or EOT) (✉ N. Zerva 2, Platia Pyrrou, 45332, ☎ 0651/25086, FAX 0651/72148) is open weekdays 7:30–2:30 and 4–8, weekends 9–2:30. **Ioannina Tourist Office** (☎ 0651/25086).

KALAMBAKA

Tourist Police (✉ Hatzipetrou 10–11, ☎ 0432/22109). In the summertime a tourist information booth is erected in the main square.

6 Northern Greece

Thessaloniki, Chalkidiki, and the Alexander the Great Sites

From the frescoed tomb of Phillip II of Macedon to Zeus's mythical throne atop Mt. Olympus, Northern Greece bestows surprising superlatives. You can observe (and sometimes join) a dig at Greece's most active archaeological site, stroll empty beaches, hike virgin trails through rampant wildflowers, or experience the solitary majesty of Mt. Athos monastery. Thessaloniki was once home to Alexander the Great and the crossroads of the ancient world; today, it is Greece's second city, as it was Byzantium's, brimming with antiquities, street markets, and the shadows of history.

By Lea Lane

THE REGION WE CALL NORTHERN GREECE, comprising Macedonia in the west and Thrace in the east, covers the Balkan frontier from Albania to Bulgaria and also touches Turkey. It is both a meeting point and a crossroads for Europe, the Mediterranean, and Asia and is imbued with the sights, sounds, and colors of cultures that have blended harmoniously and clashed violently throughout history.

This mountainous fist of land with three fingerlike peninsulas jutting into the Aegean has vast, fertile plains overflowing with monuments and artifacts of the powerful and rich civilizations that fought and lived here: marble temples and fortifications built by Athens and Sparta, rough-hewn Macedonian tombs, the arches and rotundas of Imperial Rome, the domes of Byzantium, and the minarets and *hamams* (baths) of the Ottomans.

The area first figured in Greek history when it was colonized by Greek city-states during the 7th century BC. In 512 BC, both Macedonia and Thrace were conquered by Darius I, the Persian, and later his son Xerxes marched through on his ill-fated expedition to Greece. Then came the Macedonians. Within a hundred years, Philip II and his son Alexander the Great had conquered all of Greece except Sparta, and all of Persia as well. After Alexander's death his brother-in-law Cassander established Thessaloniki as the capital (316 BC), naming it for his new bride, Alexander's half-sister. She was the daughter of the much-married Philip, who had named her after his famous *niki* (victory) in Thessaly, where her mother had been one of his prizes.

Profiting from squabbles among Alexander's successors, the Romans took over Macedonia, and by 146 BC, the rest of Greece had become a Roman province. In 42 BC, after the assassination of Julius Caesar, Marc Anthony defeated Brutus and Cassius at the double battles of Philippi in Macedonia. Under the Pax Romana that followed, St. Paul twice traveled through on his way to Corinth, paving the way for the second great flowering of Greek and Macedonian culture—that of the Byzantine Empire.

Byzantium held sway for 1,100 years, the center of Greek civilization shifted from Athens to Constantinople, and Thessaloniki became the second most important city in the empire. It remained that way under the Ottoman Turks, who sacked Constantinople in 1453 and whose dominance over Northern Greece lasted until the 1912–13 Balkan Wars. Macedonia was then united with the rest of Greece, and the 1923 Peace of Lausanne established the present-day borders of Thrace—but two of the bloodiest battles were yet to come. In 1941, Mussolini's troops invaded Northern Greece and were pushed back into Albania, causing the German army to intervene and fight its way through the country from the north. Then, at the end of World War II, the region became the principal arena for the Greek Civil War (1946–49) between the Communists and Royalists.

Today, Northern Greece still feels a bit threatened, as the collapse of Yugoslavia has brought to life age-old ethnic and religious animosities. Because the Serbians are Orthodox Christians, they are natural allies in any confrontations against non-Christians. It has been difficult, therefore, for the Greeks to understand why the rest of the Christian world seems to be against their fellow believers. Northern Greeks are especially resentful of Skopje's insistence on calling itself "Macedonia," with the ancient Greek Macedonian sun as a regional symbol. And rumors remain of international plots to redraw the map of the

Balkans. These things have happened so often through the ages, this generation sees no reason why they won't again.

In spite of continuing tensions, Northern Greece, and especially Thessaloniki, is flourishing. The city is the site of Greece's annual Trade Fair and of the country's largest university; new hotels have been built and older ones upgraded; the highway connecting Macedonia with more remote regions of Thrace has been widened and extended; and Thessaloniki was the proud and successful 1997 Cultural Capital of Europe. To the far northeast, Thrace—with a mountainous terrain, rural villages, and a decidedly Turkish influence—still has a ways to go regarding facilities, transportation scheduling, and tourist amenities. But as for most of Northern Greece, natural and historical attractions, along with the genuine hospitality of the people, make it the country's underrated surprise, filled with delights.

Pleasures and Pastimes

Dining

The cosmopolitan, multiracial character of Thessaloniki—building on its historic Byzantine and Ottoman influences, and its liberal use of fragrant Levantine spices—has created a hearty cuisine of sometimes subtle sophistication. Traditional Thracian and Macedonian cooks adapt to the seasons: In winter, rich game such as boar and venison is served—and in summer, mussels and other seafood from the Aegean, and fruits and vegetables from the fertile plains. Wheat, corn, rye, and barley grown in this breadbasket of Greece yield especially fine baked goods. The relatively cooler climate here is reflected in rich chicken soups, roast chicken, stuffed vegetables, and stewed lamb and pork.

Specialties include *patsas* (a tripe soup), *peinirli* (an open-faced cheese sandwich), and *soutzoukakia* (meatballs in tomato sauce, seasoned with cumin). Along the coast, informal restaurants specialize in barbecued chicken. Meals are complemented by generous amounts of wine, ouzo, and tsipouro, the local version. In most villages, pastry shops offering traditional sweets, and cafés pouring dark, strong coffee, are bustling at all hours. The sensual joy of good food and the ritual of eating out, both so essential to Greek life, involve shared emotions, new friends, and treasured family.

Neighborhoods center on tavernas and casual bars. You are encouraged to go to the kitchen and choose your meals, generally from a dozen or so trays filled to the brim. Even at the best restaurants dress is usually casual, and although at higher-priced establishments reservations are theoretically possible, nothing is guaranteed. Therefore, it is prudent to arrive around 8 PM, earlier than most Greeks like to eat (but note that many places do not open before then).

CATEGORY	COST*
$$$$	over 7,000 dr.
$$$	4,500 dr.–7,000 dr.
$$	2,500 dr.–4,500 dr.
$	under 2,500 dr.

for a three-course meal, including tax and service but excluding drinks

Hiking and Walking

Hundreds of paths—some pioneered by shepherds, some believed to be remnants of underground passageways from World War II—wend through the mountains, peninsulas, and valleys of Northern Greece. Trails are easy to hike and offer chances to chat with villagers, wander through uncrowded ancient sites, and swim in crystal ponds or Aegean coves. The Chalkidiki peninsulas and the island of Thasos offer unspoiled sea and mountain vistas, and the national park area of Mt. Olympus, carpeted in spring with rare wildflowers, seems blessed by Zeus himself.

Lodging

Despite some recent improvements, Thessaloniki's hotels (much like Athens's) are nothing to write home about and are mostly geared to the needs of transient businesspeople, with little emphasis on capturing the spirit-of-place so appealing to tourists. Selection of hotels elsewhere in Northern Greece varies from exclusive seaside resorts in Chalkidiki to modest, family-managed hostel-like housing on the slopes of Mt. Olympus. Throughout the area, hotels are usually small, somewhat spartan affairs whose charm comes mainly from their surroundings. Some establishments, particularly in Chalkidiki, close for the winter (we've noted when it's otherwise); it is best to make arrangements ahead.

CATEGORY	COST*
$$$$	over 30,000 dr.
$$$	15,000 dr.–30,000 dr.
$$	10,000 dr.–15,000 dr.
$	under 10,000 dr.

*All prices are for a standard double room, including tax, service, and breakfast unless noted otherwise.

Monasteries

Monks got to Northern Greece long before tour groups, and the sites they chose for their monasteries are the most beautiful locations throughout the cities and countryside. In this region of extraordinary Byzantine architecture, one of the the most impressive monastic complexes in the world is near the Ayion Oros (Holy Mountain) of Mt. Athos.

Exploring Northern Greece

A delightful geographic mix awaits you: In the mountains, from snow-covered Mt. Olympus to the mineral-rich eastern ranges, forests of pine, spruce, juniper, oak, and chestnut abound, and ski resorts and climbing opportunities beckon. Cosmopolitan Thessaloniki lies in the strategic center of Macedonia, nestled gracefully in the wide but protective arms of the Thermaic Gulf and buttressed on its inland side by a low-lying mountain range around which the Axios River flows south to the Aegean. This is a vast, fertile plain of grain, vegetables, and fruit. In the lowlands of Chalkidiki, parts of Thrace, and the island of Thasos, fruit and olive trees flourish with vineyards and tobacco plantations. In summer the air is redolent of thyme and oregano. White-sand beaches along miles of inleted coastline are lapped by a turquoise sea. You don't have to travel far from Thessaloniki to find these pleasures: The famed three-fingered peninsulas, with their vistas of mountain and sea, and tipped by famed Mt. Athos monastery, are only a few hours away by car on good highways.

Numbers in the text correspond to numbers in the margin and on the Exploring Thessaloniki and Northern Greece maps.

Great Itineraries

Thessaloniki's central location in Macedonia makes it a perfect base for the short itinerary; the ancient sites are within a couple of hours by car or bus. For the longer itineraries, a car rented in Thessaloniki will simplify drives and give you time for serendipitous pleasures. As Kavala has an airport with frequent flights back to Thessaloniki and Athens, and frequent ferry service to Aegean islands, you don't necessarily have to drive back to your western starting point. Make sure you have up-to-date ferry schedules, and take hydrofoils to cut time in half going to and from the island of Thasos.

IF YOU HAVE 3 DAYS

Starting in ▦ **Thessaloniki** ①–⑲, explore both the old and the new city, not missing the **archaeological museum** ②, the Kastro, and the **White Tower** ①. Take a long promenade on the boardwalk to people-watch and join all the Thessalonians for coffee by the sea. Overnight in **Thessaloniki.** Spend your second day visiting the famous Alexander the Great sites: **Pella** ⑳ and **Vergina** ㉑, and then head back to Thessaloniki for nightlife. On the third day, relax, visit a museum or shop in the morning, then have lunch on Mt. Olympus and explore ▦ **Dion,** ㉒ or spend the entire day in the mountain area.

IF YOU HAVE 5 DAYS

Using ▦ **Thessaloniki** ①–⑲ as your base, on the first day visit **Pella** ⑳ and **Vergina** ㉑; then head back to Thessaloniki. On the second day explore the Byzantine face of the city; later venture outside the old walls for dinner. On the third day visit ▦ **Dion** ㉒ and **Mt. Olympus** ㉓, overnighting in Dion or returning to Thessaloniki. On the fourth day drive down the coast of ▦ **Chalkidiki,** stopping first at the **Caves of Petralona** ㉔ and then going for a leisurely swim in the azure waters, and overnight on one of the peninsulas. The next morning, drive back to Thessaloniki and immerse yourself in the museums and nightlife, or go farther east to ▦ **Kavala** ㉙, where you can spend the day exploring the city and environs, including **Phillippi** ㉚. Then overnight in Kavala, or fly back to Thessaloniki or Athens in the evening.

IF YOU HAVE 8 DAYS

Begin in your home base, ▦ **Thessaloniki** ①–⑲, taking a day to explore the city. On the second day head northeast to ▦ **Kavala** ㉙ and **Philippi** ㉚, enjoying the seaside and historic sites, and staying over in Kavala. Or take a late-evening ferry to the island of ▦ **Thasos** ㉛ with its excellent beaches, ruins, traditional villages, and mountain hikes. Spend the third day there, and next morning, return to Thessaloniki by way of Alexander the Great territory, including **Pella** ⑳ and **Vergina** ㉑. After viewing those sights, backtrack to overnight in Thessaloniki for your fourth night. On the fifth day, hike or take a four-wheel drive through the terrain of ▦ **Dion** ㉒ and **Mt. Olympus** ㉓. If you wish, overnight in the village of ▦ **Litochoro** or the nearby village of **Kastoria.** On the sixth day venture off the beaten path northwest to **Lake Prespas** and **Kastoria**; for your sixth overnight, head for the ▦ **peninsula adjacent to Mt. Athos,** or simply head back to the hub of Thessaloniki, which is only a couple of hours away from most of these sights. The next morning drive to **the Chalkidiki area,** and spend the seventh day outdoors, or (if you can) at Mt. Athos. Return that evening to **Thessaloniki** for further delving into museums, historic areas, and shops before departing.

When to Tour

Thessaloniki provides interesting events and cultural activities throughout the year, and all seasons have their special treats. Even winter—less crowded with tourists—offers the savory pleasures of hot coffee, fiery ouzo, and warm Thessalonian friendship. Note, however, that September and October are especially crowded due to festivals and trade fairs, when prices go up and accommodations are almost impossible to find.

Travel throughout the rest of Northern Greece is best from May through October, when all establishments are open. A profusion of red, yellow, and purple wildflowers edges most roads in spring, and the golden harvest season is a mellow time of wheat, wine, and olives. Summer months are most crowded but best for sunning, swimming, and schmoozing with northern Europeans and Greek families on holiday. Get an early start in warmer months, because the days heat up and siesta hours cut them short. Do as the Greeks: Indulge in a rest in the afternoon, so you can enjoy the late hours!

THESSALONIKI

At the crossroads of East and West, where North blends into South, Thessaloniki (accent on the "ni") has seen the rise and fall of all manner of civilizations: Macedonian, Hellenic, Roman, Byzantine, Ottoman, and that of the Jews and of the modern Greeks. Each of its successive conquerors has plundered, razed, and buried much of what went before. Thus, little remains of the Macedonian-Hellenistic civilization that built the city's fortifications. The Romans took most of what was of portable value back to Italy and buried the rest. The Roman temples then became Byzantine churches, and structures were torn down to refortify the walls and build the towers, where both Hellenistic and Roman elements can still be seen. The Ottoman Turks, in turn, transformed the Byzantine churches into mosques and demolished many other buildings for their minarets, hamams, imarets (almshouses), fountains, and private mansions. When the Greeks regained the city, they had their churches reconsecrated and tore down most of the minarets. Then, in 1917, a great fire destroyed much of what was left of the colorful, teeming blend of cultures that the Ottoman reign had packed in: the bazaars, the elegant hotels and banks, the multistoried Turkish town houses, and the distinctive European Christian, Jewish, and Greek quarters.

Thessaloniki today, a vibrant city of close to 1 million people, is largely a result of the spacious, orderly vision of the French architect Ernest Hébrard, who rebuilt the city after the fire. But its more distant past can still be seen and sensed, and a little walking will be well rewarded: parks, squares, old neighborhoods with narrow alleyways and gardens, courtyards draped with laundry, neoclassic mansions, more than 50 churches and 40 monasteries—the mix is exciting, charming, ever-changing, and ongoing. For example, Ladadika, the former warehouse district by the port, was the home of hookers and toughs a decade ago. Today the warehouses have been recycled into a pedestrian zone of restaurants and clubs, and the scene is filled with young and old, strolling by fountains, snapping fingers to the music in the air, and enjoying moussaka and microbrewery beers at tables spilling onto the stone squares.

Unlike Athens, which sprawls among hills and is difficult to get a handle on, Thessaloniki is fairly centralized and easy to get used to; whether it's the upper old town or the modern city along the bay, its charm in part, is its warmth and accessibility. It lends itself to lazy meandering, the exploring of in-town archaeological sites and Byzantine treasures, and café-style people-watching. Ask locals where a pastry shop is and chances are they will not only tell you (especially if you smile with a Greek "thank you," *efcharisto*, and invariably get answered with a delighted *parakalo,* or "you are welcome"), but will lead you there—and then *buy* you the pastry.

Exploring Thessaloniki

We suggest two routes for exploring some highlights. The best tour, however, is simply to wander through the streets responding to whatever you encounter. It is hard to get lost, since the entire city slopes downhill to the bay, where you can always align yourself with the White Tower and the city skyline.

The White Tower, Sintrivaniou Square, and Southern City Environs

Exploring the area from the White Tower west along the gulf to Aristotelous Square reveals icons of the city's history: grand monuments of Emperor Galerius, artifacts from the Neolithic period through the Roman occupation housed in the archaeological museum, prominent churches, as well as the city's most important landmark, the tower itself. The lively shopping streets, bustling markets, and cafés reward with the fascinating, unexpected encounters and sensual treats of a great city.

A GOOD WALK

Begin at the **White Tower** ①; after viewing the Byzantine works, take in the city's expanse from the rooftop. From the White Tower walk east on the seaside promenade Nikis until you see the dramatic bronze **statue of Alexander and his horse, Bucephalus.** Meander for five minutes through the lovely park to the north, with its inviting cafés and children's playground; across the wide promenade cutting through the park is the renowned **archaeological museum** ②, with finds dating from prehistoric Greece to Alexander's Macedonia. The **Byzantine Museum** ③ is just east of the museum, and farther east, at the intersection of Vasilis Olgas and 25 Martiou (25th of March St.), is the **Pinacothiki** (Municipal Gallery). Head across the street toward the city center to the beginning of the city's fanciest shopping street, **Tsimiski.** In the middle of the city block, after the second streetlight, is the beautiful pedestrian **Dimitriou Gounari street** lined with delightful shops and cafés. It crosses Tsimiski and leads you north directly to the **Arch of Galerius** ④. Even if the **Rotunda** ⑤ is closed, try to explore the narrow streets surrounding the area, rich with cluttered junk and antiques shops; on Wednesdays you'll see the eclectic Russian Market. Cross Egnatia again to the south side of the street and continue west to the lovely 14th-century **Church of the Metamorphosis** ⑥. Continuing west on Egnatia, turn right and walk a half block up Ayios Sofias to the oldest Byzantine church in the city, the 5th-century **Panagia Achiropiitos** ⑦. Next head south again on Ayios Sofias for a short downhill walk to reach the 8th-century church of **Ayia Sofia** ⑧.

To explore a more contemporary part of the city center, exit via Ayias Sofia's parklike entrance, cross the street, and walk due west on Ermou. Ermou will carry you directly into **Modiano market** ⑨, the heart of the central marketplace, complete with myriad foods and faces to check out. Take a look at the evocative **Memorial to Grigoris Lambrakis** ⑩ just west of the market. You can quit now or head south to Aristotelous Square, the *kafenia-* (traditional Greek coffeehouses) lined village square of the city center, for a drink and postcard-writing session before a well-deserved Greek siesta.

TIMING

Leave most of a day, depending upon your speed. Plan to spend at least an hour at the archaeological museum. The best time to explore churches is during mass, especially on Sundays. Otherwise, hours are not set in stone; try from about 8 AM to noon and 5:30 to 7:30 on any day, except where noted.

SIGHTS TO SEE

❹ **Arch of Galerius.** The imposing arch, or *kamára,* is one of a number of monuments built by Galerius around AD 305, during his reign as co-emperor of Diocletian's divided Roman Empire (☞ Rotunda *and* Platia Navarino, *below*). It was built to celebrate the victory over Persia in AD 297, and you can still see scenes of those battles on the badly eroded bas-reliefs. Originally, the arch had four pediments and a dome and was intended to span not only the Via Egnatia, the ancient road leading Rome to the rest of its territory, but also a passageway leading north to the Rotunda. Only the large arches remain. ☒ *Egnatia Odos, Sintrivaniou Sq.*

★ ❷ **Archaeological Museum.** This unpretentious, single-story white structure gives no hint from the outside of the treasures within, including a superb collection of artifacts from Neolithic times, with sculptures from the Archaic, classical, and Roman eras and remains from the archaic temple at Thermi. (However, its extraordinary Philip of Macedon finds from the tomb of Vergina have been transferred to the museum there.) Start off in Gallery 4, which traces the ancient city's history from archaeological finds. ☒ *Hanth Sq., opposite the exhibition grounds,* ☎ *031/830538.* ☒ *1,500 dr.* ☉ *Mon. 12:30–7, Tues.–Fri. 8–7, weekends 8:30–3.*

★ ❽ **Ayia Sofia.** Although this is the focal point of the city's Easter and Christmas celebrations, its founding date has experts disagreeing over the centuries. From its architecture it is believed to be late-8th century, a time of transition from the domed basilica toward the cruciform plan. Ecclesiastics think it was built after the first Council of Nicea (325), when Christ was declared a manifestation of Divine Wisdom; other church historians say it was contemporaneous with the magnificent church of Ayia Sofia in Constantinople, on which it was modeled. In any case, its rather drab interior contains two superb mosaics: one of the Ascension, and the other of the Virgin Mary holding Jesus in her arms. This latter mosaic is an interesting example of the conflict in the Orthodox Church (726–843) between the Iconoclasts (icon smashers, which they often literally were) and the Iconodules (icon venerators or "slaves"). At one point in this doctrinal struggle, the Virgin Mary in the mosaic was replaced by a large cross (still partly visible), and only later, after the victory of the Iconodules, was it again replaced with an image of Virgin Mary holding baby Jesus. ☒ *Pavlou Mela, Ayias Sophias Sq.,* ☎ *031/270253.* ☒ *Free.* ☉ *Daily 8–9.*

Ayios Panteleimon. A prime example of Macedonian 14th-century church architecture, the facades of this church reveal the ornamental interplay of brick and stonework and a dome displaying typical, strong upward motion. ☒ *Egnatia Odos.*

❸ **Byzantine Museum.** Inaugurated in 1994, this structure is the most modern museum in Greece and the repository of most of the country's finest Byzantine art: priceless icons, frescoes, sculpted reliefs, jewelry, glasswork, manuscripts, pottery, and coins. Eight rooms hold treasures such as a gold-embroidered epitaph and a silver relic case with engraved scenes from the Bible. Its 1997–98 exhibition in conjunction with the Cultural Capital of Europe celebration displayed the coveted Byzantine collection from Mt. Athos (you may, unfortunately, have to wait another millennium to see it again). Meanwhile, the Byzantine treasures that had been stored in the White Tower have been transferred to their new home here. ☒ *2 Leoforos Stratou,* ☎ *031/868570.* ☒ *2,000 dr.* ☉ *Mon. 3–9, Tues.–Sat. 11–1 and 5–9, Sun. 11–3.*

❻ **Church of the Metamorphosis.** This sunken church is a fine example of 14th-century Macedonian church architecture, with a decorative mix of brick and stonework and the strong upward thrust of the dome. ☒ *Egnatia Odos.*

Egnatia Odos. It was during the Byzantine period that Thessaloniki came into its own as a commercial crossroads, because the Via Egnatia, which already connected the city to Rome (with the help of a short boat trip across the Adriatic), was extended east to Constantinople. Today Egnatia Odos virtually begins along the same path; it is Thessaloniki's main commercial thoroughfare, although not as upscale as the parallel Tsimiski Street, two blocks to the south. ✉ *City points southwest to northeast.*

🔟 **Memorial to Grigoris Lambrakis.** This is especially moving if you have read the novel *Z* by Vassilis Vassilikos or seen the Costas-Gavras film about the leftist member of parliament (played by Yves Montand), whose murder by rightists in 1963 precipitated the events that resulted in the 1967 takeover of the colonels' junta. A dramatic bronze head and arm rising out of the earth marks the site of the murder. ✉ *Just west of Modiano market, on corner of Ermou and Eleftherios Venezelou.*

★ ⑨ **Modiano Market.** This old landmark was overhauled in 1922 by a Jewish architect who gave the covered market its name. It is especially popular with students and artists, and worth a visit—as is the generally cheaper **open-air market** (✉ On the north side of Ermou)—even if you have no intention of buying anything. Both are rich not only with all manner of fish, meats, vegetables, fruits, breads, spices, wines, and household items but with true human characters as well: the whole spectrum of colorful hangers-on who congregate at markets the world over, even strolling gypsy musicians best watched while eating and drinking in the market's ouzieris and tavernas. ✉ *Along city block on south side of Ermou.*

Municipal Gallery (Pinacothiki). Housed in the 1905 Villa Mordoh, amid lush gardens, the art gallery has a collection of more than 800 pieces, including etchings, engravings, sculpture, Byzantine icons, and modern Thessaloniki art from the turn of the century to 1967. ✉ *162 Vasilis Olgas,* ☎ *031/425531,* 🖷 *031/411101.* ⌾ *Free.* ☉ *Tues.–Fri. 9–1 and 5–9, Sat. 5–9, Sun. 9–1.*

⑦ **Panagia Achiropiitos.** This 5th-century Byzantine church is an early example of the basilica form and marvels the eye with arcades, monolithic columns topped by elaborate capitals, and exquisite period mosaics of birds and flowers. Its name means "made without hands," because in the 12th century an icon supposedly appeared there, miraculously. An engraved statement by Sultan Murat states that he had conquered Thessaloniki in the year 1430. ✉ *Ayios Sofias.*

Platia Navarino. This tree- and awning-shaded square proper, its fountain a marvelous bronze of a young boy peeing, is a favorite drinking, eating, and nightlife hub among students. The remaining structures in Galerius's city-center complex include a racetrack (hence the name of Platia Hippodromiou, which covers it today), a palace, and an octagonal structure that may have been his throne room. Parts of these buildings have been excavated and can be seen in sunken areas around the square and the pedestrian street bordering it. ✉ *Directly south of Rotunda and Triumphal Arch.*

★ ⑤ **Rotunda.** Also known as Ayios Giorgios, this brickwork edifice has become a layered monument to the city's rich history. Built in AD 306, it was probably intended as Roman Emperor Galerius's mausoleum. However, when he died in Bulgaria, his successor refused to have the body brought back. Under Theodosius the Great, the Byzantines converted the Rotunda into a church dedicated to St. George (thus, the name), with minimal alterations, except for adding impressive 4th-century AD mosaics of early saints; the Ottomans made it a mosque (whose minaret still stands), and it was last restored after the damage suffered in a 1978 earthquake. Today, it occasionally houses art exhibits and concerts and remains a veritable museum of Christian art. If you have time, explore the narrow **surrounding streets**; on Wednesdays they are flooded with the **Russian Market,** a novel commercial enterprise featuring tchotchkes and the occasional interesting heirloom, antique, or folk art piece hawked by Eastern European refugees, a good many of Greek descent. ⊠ *On D. Gounari St., just off Sintrivaniou Sq.,* ☎ *031/ 213627.* ☉ *Special events.*

★ ❶ **White Tower.** The formidable sea walls and intermittent towers encircling the medieval city were erected under Theodosius the Great, probably in the 15th century on the site of earlier walls. In 1866, with the threat of piracy diminishing and European commerce increasingly imperative, the Ottoman Turks began demolishing them. This tower is the only one along the seafront left standing (the other remaining is its twin, the Trigoniou, in the old city). During the 18th century the tower was an infamous prison and later a place of execution, and became known as the Bloody Tower. But the Turks literally whitewashed it, perhaps in deference to the foreign businessmen whom they hoped to attract, and it has become the city's most famous landmark. These days, the tower that looks like a big chesspiece houses interesting artifacts from the history and cultural life of the city from AD 300 to 1400. ⊠ *Waterfront Promenade, Nikis and Pavlou Melas Sts.,* ☎ *031/267832.* ▦ *800 dr.* ☉ *Mon. 12:30–7, Tues.–Fri. 8–7, weekends 8:30–3.*

Upper City, Panagia Chalkeon, and Aristotelous Square

Upper City (Ano Polis) is called Ta Kastra ("the castles") because of the castle of Eptapyrghion and the many fortified towers that once bristled along the walls. This is the former Turkish quarter, comprising what is left of 19th-century Thessaloniki, and is filled with timber-framed houses with their upper stories overhanging the steep streets. The views of the modern city below and the Thermaic gulf are stunning, but other than Byzantine churches, there are few specific places of historical interest. You'll find it an experience in itself to navigate the steps, past gossipy women, grandfathers playing backgammon in smokey cafés, and giggling children playing tag in tiny courtyards filled with sweet-smelling flowers, stray cats, and flapping laundry.

Unfortunately, getting there can be a chore, as taxi drivers often try to avoid the cramped, congested streets and fear missing a fare back down. Have your hotel find a willing driver, or take a local bus. Buses 22 and 23 leave from the terminal at Platia Eleftherios (⊠ 2 blocks west of Aristotelous Sq.) every 10 to 15 minutes and follow an interesting route through the narrow streets of the Upper City.

A GOOD WALK

Start this excursion with the superb aerial city view from the **Tower of Trigoniou** ⑪; then walk west along the inside of the seaward wall (the wall should be to your right). Walk a few yards past the second *portara* (large open gateway) and to your left you will see the entrance to the grounds of **Moni Vlatádon** ⑫ and its tiny chapel to Sts. Peter and Paul. The **castle of Eptapyrghion** ⑬ is north along Eptapyrghiou. Backtrack to the Tower of Trigoniou and continue west along Eptapyrghiou street to the first wide street on your left, Dimitriou Poliorkitou, and take the broad flight of stairs to the beginning of the **Old Turkish Quarter** toward the sea. Follow Dimitriou Poliorkitou west, bearing left, and take the winding descent to the left and then to the right until you come to the doors of the 5th-century **Osios David** ⑭.

Turn right and continue down the narrow cobblestone street to the first intersection. Below a strange tin "palace" of the self-proclaimed "King of the Greeks," follow Akropoleos to the small Platia Romfei; walk along Eolou to see the beautiful frescoes in the small but exceptional 14th-century **Ayios Nikolaos Orfanos** ⑮.

202

Exploring Thessaloniki

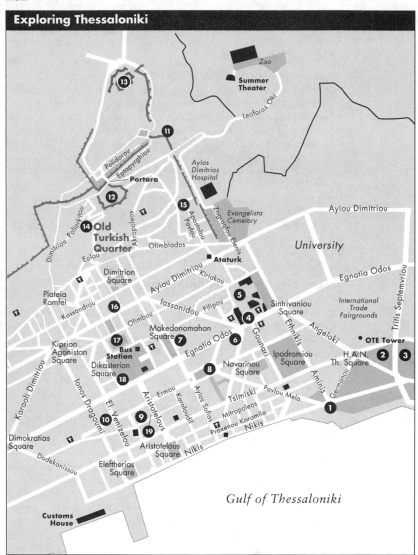

Arch of Galerius, **4**
Archaeological Museum, **2**
Ayia Sofia, **8**
Ayios Dimitrios, **16**
Ayios Nikolaos Orfanos, **15**
Byzantine Museum, **3**
Castle of Eptapyrghion, **13**

Church of the Metamorphosis, **6**
Jewish Community Memorial Museum, **19**
Memorial to Grigoris Lambrakas, **10**
Modiano Market, **9**
Moni Vlatádon, **12**
Osios David, **14**
Panagia Achiropiitos, **7**

Panagia Chalkeon, **18**
Roman Forum, **17**
Rotunda, **5**
Tower of Trigoniou, **11**
White Tower, **1**

Walk downhill on Apostolou Pavlou, the legendary path Apostle Paul took to the Upper City to address the Thessalonians, and cross busy Kassandrou. At Ataturk turn right onto Ayiou Dimitriou, which can be crowded, noisy, and not very attractive, so you may choose to walk along a smaller, more pleasant parallel street. Continue west about six blocks until you reach **Ayios Dimitrios** ⑯ church, named for Thessaloniki's patron saint and where he was martyred. Forge on downhill, one block south from the church, to the very active excavation of the ancient **Roman Forum** ⑰. Walk west on Olimbou and turn left at the second corner onto short, diagonal Tositsa Street, and you will enter the *paliatzidiko* (flea market), the city's primo junk, antiques, and roaming-peddler promenade. From **Panagia Chalkeon** ⑱, on the southwest corner of the immense Dikasterion Square, cross to the lower side of Egnatia Odos; a half block down, take a right on Aristotelous. Along Aristotelous, take a right on Vasiliou Irakleiou, the corner after Ermou, and walk half a block to the **Jewish Community Memorial Museum** ⑲, a moving tribute to the persecution during World War II.

TIMING

This tour should take a few hours, at least. You will want to spend some time at Ayios Dimitrios, possibly to observe a mass (☞ Timing *in* A Good Walk, *above*). Of course, finding yourself gazing endlessly at evocations of the city's rich past, both artistic and historic, plus enjoying attractions such as flea markets—especially if you get caught up in haggling over a Byzantine trinket—can easily mean an exploration of this district can take a whole day.

SIGHTS TO SEE

★ **Ano Polis (Upper City).** The Upper City is also called Ta Kastra ("the castles") because of the castle of Eptapyrghion and the many fortified towers that once bristled along the walls. The area within and just outside the remains of the walls is like a village unto itself, a charming jumble of the rich, the poor, and the renovated. Rustic one-story peasant houses, many still occupied by the families that built them, sit side by side with houses newly built or restored by the wealthier class. And, as the area continues to be upgraded, new tavernas, café-bars, and restaurants spring up to serve the visitors, both Greek and foreign, who flock there for a cool evening out. ⊠ *Elevated northern area of city.*

Ataturk's House. The birthplace of Mustafa Kemal, which also houses the Turkish consulate, is a high point for those interested in the history of the Turkish influence in Thessaloniki. The soldier and statesman who established the Turkish republic, and became its president, Ataturk was born here in 1881. He participated in the city's Young Turk movement, which eventually led to the collapse of the sultanate and the formation of the modern Turkish state. In this modest, wood-frame house you can also explore a museum honoring his early life in Thessaloniki. To get in, ring the bell at the Turkish Consulate down the block, show your passport, and you'll be given an escorted tour. ⊠ *151 Ayiou Dimitriou,* ☎ *031/269964.* ⊠ *Free.* ☉ *Irregular hrs, usually 2–6.*

NEED A BREAK?
Throughout the city, little shops and cellars specialize in a Macedonian treat called a submarine, a spoonful of sweets such as cherries in syrup, dipped in a glass of ice water. In nice weather, sit outside and enjoy the sweet street life as well.

★ ⑯ **Ayios Dimitrios.** This magnificent five-aisle basilica, covered in mosaics, is Greece's largest church and a powerful tribute to the patron saint of Thessaloniki. It was rebuilt and restored from 1926 to 1949 with attention to preserving the details of the original; the marks left by a fire can still be seen throughout. In the time of the emperor Galerius, the young, scholarly Dimitrios was preaching Christianity in the coppersmith district, in contravention of a recent edict. He was arrested and jailed in a room in the old Roman baths, on the site of the present church. While he was incarcerated, Dimitrios gave a Christian blessing to a gladiator friend named Nestor, who was about to fight Galerius's champion, Lyaios. AD In 303, when Nestor fought and killed Lyaios, after having made Dimitrios's blessing public, the enraged Galerius had Nestor executed on the spot and had Dimitrios speared to death in his cell. His Christian brethren were said to have buried him there. A church was built on the ruins of this bath in the 5th century AD but was then destroyed by an earthquake in the 7th century. The church was rebuilt, and gradually the story of Dimitrios and Nestor grew to be considered apocryphal until the great 1917 fire burned down most of the 7th-century church and brought to light its true past. The process of rebuilding uncovered rooms beneath the apse that appear to be those very baths, and the discovery there of a reliquary containing a vial of bloodstained earth leaves little doubt that this is indeed the spot where St. Dimitrios was martyred. You can enter through a small doorway to the right of the altar. The church had been plastered over by the Turks, who had turned it into a mosque, but eight original mosaics remain on either side of this altar. You may work your way through the crypt, containing sculpture from the 3rd to 5th centuries AD and Byzantine artifacts, or peruse the parish women's craft-works cooperative. ⊠ *Ayiou Dimitriou and Ayios Nikolaos at Egnatias St.,* ☏ *031/2213627.* ⊞ *Free.* ⊙ *Mon. 12:30–7; Tues., Thurs., and Sat. 8–10; Fri. 8–11; Sun. 10:30–8.*

⑮ Ayios Nikolaos Orfanos. This small 14th-century church became a dependency of the Vlatadon monastery in the 17th century, and is noted for marvelous frescoes, an intriguing mix of Byzantine architectural styles, and perhaps the most beautiful midnight Easter service in the city. ⊠ *Eolou and Apostolou Pavlou Sts., Upper City.*

⑬ Castle of Eptapyrghion. This Byzantine bastion was used in modern times as a notoriously abysmal prison, closed only in 1988. Plans for its future entail a cultural center. The walls and the area just inside the portara have been restored and made into a park, but that's about it. ⊠ *Eptapyrghiou, Upper City.*

⑲ Jewish Community Memorial Museum. Thessaloniki was the center of culture for Sephardic Jews, who made up a huge percentage of the city from their arrival in 1492 until this century. Tragically, almost 95% of the Jewish community was exterminated during World War II, so this museum is of great interest to those who want to learn not only about Judaism but about this city's cultural loss. The tiny, but very active, Jewish community presents artifacts and a collection of photographs of the city's Jewish heritage and the Holocaust, in modest quarters in the heart of the Modiano Market. A simple, first-floor **synagogue** is also at the site, as moving as the museum by its mere existence. ⊠ *Vasileos Irakleou 26, 2nd floor,* ☏ *031/273767 or 031/223231.* ⊞ *Free.* ⊙ *Call ahead to check on sporadic hours. Closed Sat.*

⑫ Moni Vlatádon (Vlatades Monastery). Shaded with pine and cypress, this structure is cruciform and displays a mixture of architectural additions from Byzantine times to the present. It is known for its Ecumenical Foundation for Patriarchal Studies, the only one in the world. The small central church just right of the apse has a tiny **chapel dedicated to Sts. Peter and Paul,** though it is seldom open. It is believed to have been built on the spot where Paul first preached to the Thessalonians, in AD 49. ⊠ *Eptapyrghiou, Upper City.*

Old Turkish Quarter. During the Ottoman occupation, this area, probably the most picturesque in the city, was considered the best place to live. In addition to the superb views, in summer it catches whatever breeze there is. Until recently the home of some of the poorest families in Thessaloniki, the area is rapidly gentrifying, thanks to EU development funds (which repaired the cobblestones), strict new zoning and building codes, and the zeal of young couples with the money to restore the narrow, charming old houses. ⊠ *Upper City, south of Dimitriou Poliorkitou.*

★ ⑭ **Osios David** (Blessed David). This entrancing little church was supposedly built about AD 500 in honor of Galerius's daughter, who was secretly baptized while her father was away fighting. It was later converted into a mosque, and somewhere along the line it lost its western side—the traditional place of entrance (in order to look east when facing the altar)—so you enter Osios David from the south. No matter; this entirely suits the rather battered magic of this tiny church, which has a kind of street-urchin feel to it. You can still see the radiantly beautiful mosaic in the dome of the apse, which shows a beardless, somewhat Orphic Christ, as he seems to have been described in the vision of Ezekiel. The special magic of this mosaic is that it was forgotten for centuries and then found through a vision, or so the local tale goes. To save it from destruction, the mosaic was hidden under a layer of calfskin during the Iconoclastic ravages of the 8th and 9th centuries. Plastered over by the Turks when the church was converted into a mosque, it seems to have been forgotten until 1921 when an Orthodox monk in Egypt had a vision telling him to go to the church. On the day he arrived, March 25 (the day of Greek Independence from the Turks), an earthquake shattered the plaster and revealed the mosaic to the monk—who promptly died. ⊠ *Dimitriou Poliorkitou, Upper City.*

⑱ **Panagia Chalkeon.** The beautiful "Virgin of the Copper Workers" stands in what is still the traditional copper-working area of Thessaloniki. Completed in 1028, it is one of the oldest churches in the city displaying the domed cruciform style and is filled with ceramic ornaments and glowing mosaics. You may encounter artisans and workers who frequently drop by during the day to light a candle to this patron of physical laborers. The area offers many shops featuring traditional copper crafts at low prices. ⊠ *Southwest corner of Dikasterion Sq.*

⑰ **Roman Forum.** This large open area is undergoing vigorous excavation. Its small amphitheater is often the site of romantic concerts on balmy summer evenings. **Tositsa Street,** one block west, is the best junk, antiques, and roaming- peddler street in the city, where good finds range from brass beds to antique jewelry. The area is flanked by coppersmith shops and the Church of the Panagia Chalkeon, the Virgin of the Coppersmiths, to the southeast. ⊠ *Between Olimbou and Filipou, just south of Ayios Dimitrios.*

⑪ **Tower of Trigoniou.** From here, you can see the city spread out below you in a graceful curve around the bay, from the suburbs in the east to the modern harbor in the west and, on a clear day, even Mt. Olympus, rising near the coastline at the southwest reaches of the bay. There is, however, little of historic interest to see within the walls. ⊠ *Upper City.*

Dining

$$$$ ✕ **Aigli.** Set in a two-dome Turkish hamam with an old outdoor Greek
★ cinema, this is one of Thessaloniki's most authentically Greek restaurants, with lots to do besides eat. Delicately prepared and spiced dishes are evocative of old Levantine Thessaloniki and Constantinople. In the

Thessaloniki Dining and Lodging

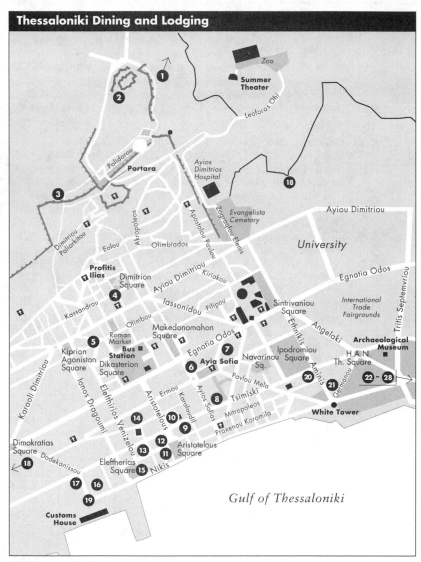

Dining

Aigli, **4**

Aristotelous
Ouzeri, **10**

B&B, **9**

Buenos Serras/
Totti's, **11**

Corner, **6, 17**

Gondola, **23**

Gonia tis Soulis, **27**

Kiopia, **16**

Klimataria, **7**

Krikelas, **20**

Loutros, **15**

Miami, **21**

Mikis, **28**

Panselino, **22**

Petros, **14**

Porto Marina, **24**

Syracuses, **25**

Tiffany's, **8**

To Makedoniko, **3**

To Yenti, **2**

Wolves, **22**

Zythos Dore, **20**

Lodging

Astoria, **17**

Capsis, **18**

Electra Palace, **12**

Makedonia
Palace, **26**

Mediterranean
Palace, **19**

Metropolitan, **30**

Olympia, **5**

Philippion, **1**

Tourist, **13**

evening, Aigli presents entertainment, from Greek and French singers to instrumentalists from Turkey. ⊠ *Corner of Kassandrou and Ayios Nikolaos, just behind Ayios Dimitrios church,* ☎ *031/270715. Reservations not accepted. No credit cards.*

$$$$ ✕ **B & B.** Pampering with formal service among elegant appointments, this restaurant in an apartment is decorous but relaxed, with the kind of old-world European grandeur you might find at the home of a wealthy friend. Dishes are European with a Greek slant; the spinach crepe is delicate, and a rare find in these parts. ⊠ *46 Tsimiski, 2nd floor,* ☎ *031/275731. Reservations essential. AE, MC, V.*

$$$$ ✕ **Krikelas.** The grandmother of upscale tavernas, opened in 1940 and looking every bit its age, with murals in arches and diamond-pattern floors, Krikelas is a standby for old-fashioned cooking. It is famous for its local wines, variety of *mezedes* (appetizers), and venison, boar, and other specialty game dishes. Try the homemade cheese and the mixed grill, and leave room for Asia Minor–influenced sweets such as *dandourma*, a concoction flavored with mastic from the island of Chios and mixed with milk and cherry syrup. ⊠ *32 Ethnikis Antistasis, about 1 km (½ mi) east of the amusement park,* ☎ *031/451690. Reservations not accepted. DC, MC, V.*

$$$$ ✕ **Porto Marina.** One of the best fish tavernas in the region, it offers simple surroundings and friendly service. Come here for fresh seafood, from grilled fish to lobsters, but be prepared for slightly elevated prices. You will find it in the noisy seafood restaurant strip in Nea Krini, slightly out of the city center but worth the trek. ⊠ *79 Plastiras, Kalamaria,* ☎ *031/451333. Reservations essential weekends. AE, DC, MC, V.*

$$$$ ✕ **Syracuses.** Rub elbows with Thessaloniki's beautiful people in this wood-beam villa, and get a feel for the grand beauty of the past, too. From the glassed-in gazebo, you can survey the plantings surrounding the house, or just have a long drink in the lovely front garden. Every dish is good, and their tiramisu is authentic. It's a 10- to 15-minute taxi drive from the city center and worth the trip. ⊠ *Corner of Vasilis Olgas and Vulgari,* ☎ *031/414445. Reservations essential weekends after 10. AE, DC, MC, V.*

$$$ ✕ **Aristotelous Ouzeri.** Behind an iron gate, artists, scholars, and businesspeople pack marble-topped tables at this convivial place and, inevitably, you will have to wait. But once you sample the cuttlefish stuffed with cheese, fried eggplant with garlic, and whitebait, you'll understand why no one is in a hurry to leave. ⊠ *8 Aristotelous, in a hidden alleyway just off the road,* ☎ *031/230762. Reservations not accepted. No credit cards.*

$$$ ✕ **Buenos Serras/Totti's.** This reasonably priced Italian restaurant is clean, quiet, and usually pleasurable. Most evenings feature a piano bar and a good view of people coming and going in the central square of Thessaloniki, which adds spice to the ravioli. You'll see the restaurant's famous sign in the square. ⊠ *West side of Aristotelous Sq., just below Electra Palace,* ☎ *031/223216. Reservations not accepted. No credit cards.*

$$$ ✕ **Kiopia.** Family run, this former warehouse is filled with candlelight, brick, chandeliers, antiques, and charm. Especially good are casseroles such as chicken and mushrooms with fresh vegetables, whether served outdoors across from the splashing fountain or under the indoor Gothic arches. Service is tops—a waiter actually ran out to departing guests to return money left for a tip (don't expect this again!). ⊠ *Pl. Morichovou, in the revived district of Ladadika, 1/2 km (¼ mi) from the train station,* ☎ *031/553239. AE, DC, MC, V.*

$$$ ✕ **Miami.** More reminiscent of a white-and-blue Cycladic beach house than South Florida, this seafood taverna, acquired by the owners of the institution Krikelas (☞ *above*), has been featuring mezedes and tra-

ditional seafood since 1945. The food is good, and the wine list has more than 100 choices, most of them regional. ✉ *18 Thetidos, Nea Krini, about 15 mins from city center,* ☎ *031/447996. Reservations essential weekends after 9. AE, DC, MC, V.*

$$$ ✕ **Panselino** (Full Moon). In a renovated neoclassical mansion, it has the excellent food and charm of Syracuses but will not break the fanny pack. The famous wine cellar alone makes this restaurant worthwhile—you can even sip fine vintages in the *cava* itself. ✉ *133 Vasilis Olgas,* ☎ *031/860978. Reservations essential weekends after 9:30. AE, DC.*

$$ ✕ **Gondola.** This family seaside taverna in the nearby village of Ayia Triada is a good-quality, low-cost option. Grilled octopus is to die for, and fried everything—from smelts to zucchini—is light and delicious. Dress is informal, and the seaside view is nothing less than the Thessaloniki skyline. ✉ *Seafront restaurant strip, Ayia Triada, 40 mins by bus or taxi from city center,* ☎ *0392/51311. Reservations not accepted. No credit cards.*

$$ ✕ **Gonia tis Soulis** (Souli's Corner). Converted from a family home into an intimate restaurant by Souli, who decorated it herself with personal bric-a-brac, this restaurant brims with charm. Live music is played nightly, but Souli provides the best entertainment, moving from table to table welcoming everyone while they savor traditional mezedes and Thessalonian specialties. ✉ *12 Raidestou, just below large church at top of hill at 40 Ekklesias, Upper City,* ☎ *031/201113. Reservations not accepted. No credit cards.*

$$ ✕ **Klimataria.** This *psistaria* (grilled-meat taverna) dishes up typical good meals, supported by Greek salad, fresh bread, and other staples, in a simple atmosphere—at low prices. For an after-dinner treat head across the street to one of the best chocolate shops in Greece, Hadjifotiou (which now has a branch near the Makedonia Palace hotel). ✉ *34 Pavlou Mela, just behind Ayia Sofia church,* ☎ *031/277854. Reservations not accepted. No credit cards.*

$$ ✕ **Loutros.** Hearty Greek stew and grilled fish are popular at this traditional downtown taverna near the flower market. Students rub shoulders at wooden tables with lawyers and out-of-towners till late into the night, all enjoying the rustic atmosphere, fast service, low prices, and good food. Wine is drawn from huge drums, which dominate the decor, and on weekday nights you may hear traditional music. ✉ *15 Komninon St., next to the Bazaar-Hamam,* ☎ *031/228895. Reservations not accepted. No credit cards.*

$$ ✕ **Tiffany's.** Not as swank as its namesake, this downtown favorite among Thessalonians has paneled walls, sconces, long tables, outside dining on a pedestrian walk, and the feel of a Parisian bistro. Its grilled meats and stews are the essence of Northern Greece: simple, tasty, and traditional. ✉ *3 Iktinou,* ☎ *031/274022. Reservations not accepted. No credit cards.*

$$ ✕ **To Yenti.** In the Upper City, with tables under the trees, on the sidewalk, and even spilling onto the street, this charming taverna-ouzeri serves delicious grilled and ready-made favorites. The *keftedes* (fried meatballs) and mezedes are especially good. Arrive early to avoid crowds. ✉ *7 Ioannis Papareka, outside gates of castle of Eptapyrghion,* ☎ *031/ 246495. Reservations not accepted. No credit cards. Closed Sun.*

$$ ✕ **Wolves.** The name has nothing to do with the cuisine or staff attitude but comes from the original owner's allegiance to an English soccer club. (In Greek, it's called *Oi Lykoi.*) Comfortable, with high ceilings and well-spaced tables, it dispenses classics such as moussaka and pastitsio (a casserole of pasta, meat, and cheese with cinnamon). ✉ *6 Vasilis Olgas, near the Makedonia Palace hotel,* ☎ *031/812855. Reservations not accepted. No credit cards. No dinner Sun.*

$$ ✕ **Zythos Dore.** Named after, and on the same spot as, the legendary and now-vanished Café Dore, this spacious bistro has tile floors, towering columns, and the city's best buzz. Greek and international food and bottled or barrel beers and wine from around the world offer something for anyone, from a drink to a bite to a big-deal meal, late into the night. Noisy, crowded, and lots of fun, it also has a great view of the White Tower. ✉ *7 Tsiroyiannis, across a little park near White Tower,* ☎ *031/279010. Reservations not accepted. No credit cards.*

$ ✕ **Corner.** Turn the corner for the best pizzas in town, baked in a wood-burning oven. The ice cream and sweets are also tasty. It's a great favorite with the younger crowd. ✉ *42 Ayios Sofias, 1 block north of White Tower,* ☎ *031/426531. Reservations not accepted. No credit cards.*

$ ✕ **Mikis.** Loved by locals, this plain storefront taverna near the Makedonia Palace serves basics such as moussaka and meatballs. If you choose from a steam table you get to talk to the mustachioed owner, whose brother lives in Astoria, Queens. Eating outside on the commercial street on a warm evening adds to the fun. ✉ *19 Vas Olgas, 2 blocks from the bay,* ☎ *031/819703. Reservations not accepted. No credit cards.*

$ ✕ **Petros.** Gypsy musicians and all kinds of characters from the market pack into this little place where Petros and his son cook tasty mezedes, seafood casseroles, grilled meats, and batter fried cod. ✉ *Inside western entrance of Modiano market. Reservations not accepted. No credit cards. Closed Sun.*

$ ✕ **To Makedoniko.** This basic taverna is a favorite among university students and young professionals—hence it's crowded, but not touristy. Actually built into an arch on the western edge of the old walls of the Upper City, it remains otherwise unadorned. Favorites include mussels in broth and grilled meats. If you're feeling daring, order the local firewater called *tsipouro* (a variety of ouzo). ✉ *32 Giorgiou Papadopoulou,* ☎ *031/627438. Reservations not accepted. No credit cards. Closed Sun.*

Lodging

$$$$ 🏨 **Electra Palace.** On the most interesting seaside square, this curving, ★ arcaded, well-kept hotel is centrally located. Upper, front rooms are the largest, with the best views, but are more susceptible to noise from the streets and from the events—political and musical—that take place on the square. ✉ *9 Aristotelous Sq., 54624,* ☎ *031/232221 through 031/232229,* FAX *031/235947. 65 rooms, 5 suites. 2 restaurants, bar, refrigerators, convention center. AE, MC, V.*

$$$$ 🏨 **Makedonia Palace.** This modernized luxury hotel has a boxlike fa-★ cade but within evokes a real sense of place, with marble mosaics, classical murals, and local artifacts. One of the only buildings rising on the coastline, it offers stunning views of the city sunset over the Aegean (and on a clear day, Mt. Olympus) from most rooms and its rooftop bar and restaurant. The adjacent boardwalk is great for early-morning or late-night runs, walks, and people-watching. A state-of-the-art convention center lures business travelers, but you're almost as apt to see a rock star or the president of Albania. ✉ *2 Alexander the Great Ave., 54640,* ☎ *031/861400,* FAX *031/832291. 272 rooms, 16 suites. 3 restaurants, 2 bars, 3 pools, beauty salon, spa, shop, meeting rooms. AE, DC, MC, V.*

$$$$ 🏨 **Mediterranean Palace.** Built in 1997, this luxury addition to the hotel scene is the closest competitor to the Makedonia Palace (☞ *above*)—but half its size, so you feel you're a more personal atmosphere. High-tech from the get-go, it offers internet service as well as amenities expected from international-level hostelries, such as soundproofed windows. Just opened, it is bright and shining, and the polish extends to exemplary service. ✉ *3 Salaminos and Karatasou Sts., near the As-*

toria, 54626, ☎ FAX 031/552554. 118 rooms. 2 restaurants, bar, lobby lounge, meeting rooms. AE, DC, MC, V.

$$$ ⛨ **Astoria.** Although somewhat out of the way in an uninspiring, traffic-ridden commercial district, this renovated hotel is near the picturesque area of Ladadika, with its restaurants, clubs, and lively nightlife. It is clean, functional, and acceptable, with TVs. One question: Is it named after Astoria, Queens, in NYC? Just about everybody in this city seems to have a relative or friend living there. ⊠ 7 Salaminos, at western end of Tsimiski, 54626, ☎ 031/554902, FAX 031/531564. 84 rooms, 6 suites. Restaurant, bar, minibars, meeting rooms, parking. AE, MC, V.

$$$ ⛨ **Capsis.** An old standby that was recently overhauled, this big, full-facility hotel is now stylish and sophisticated, with inlaid marble halls and comfortable rooms done in soothing tones, providing king-size beds, 24-hour room service, and in-room movies. The view from the popular rooftop restaurant sweeps the city. Beware of long lines when conferences take over, but otherwise this is one of the best-managed venues in the city. ⊠ 18 Monastiiou St., 54629, ☎ 031/521321, FAX 031/510555. 415 rooms, 7 suites. 2 restaurants, 2 bars, minibars, pool, shops, meeting rooms. AE, DC, MC, V.

$$$ ⛨ **Metropolitan.** Locals love this newly renovated hotel near the bayside, within walking distance of major museums and the White Tower. It has been around since the late 1960s, but its major overhaul in 1995 was a great success. The results are well-maintained, basic rooms, with traditional floral drapes and spreads. ⊠ 65 Vasilisis Olgas, at 2 Flemming St., 54629, ☎ FAX 031/824221. 111 rooms, 7 suites. Restaurant, bar, minibars, meeting rooms. AE, DC, MC, V.

$$$ ⛨ **Olympia.** Near the flea market, copper market, Roman Forum, and Ayios Dimitrios, this well-maintained modern hotel on a corner is simple but professionally managed. And location counts. ⊠ 65 Olympou, 54631, ☎ 031/235421, FAX 031/276133. 115 rooms. Restaurant, bar, cafeteria, meeting rooms, free parking. AE, DC, MC, V.

$$$ ⛨ **Philippion.** For those who are driving around, or dislike staying in the city center, this modern and well-appointed hotel sits in the forest of Sheih-Sou on a hilltop overlooking Thessaloniki. The city center is 5 km (3 mi) away, a 15-minute ride on the hotel shuttle-bus, which leaves by prearranged schedule (available at the desk) mornings intermittently until 3 PM. The airport, too, is an easy 15-minute drive away, and the highway to Chalkidiki is readily accessible. ⊠ Box 19002, 56610, ☎ 031/203321, FAX 031/218528. 84 rooms, 4 suites. Restaurant, bar, coffee shop, grill, minibars, 2 nightclubs, business services, meeting rooms, free parking. AE, DC, MC, V.

$$ ⛨ **Tourist.** This extremely modest family-run hotel in a dignified high-ceiling building built around the turn of the century has absolutely no frills: Single rooms, for example, have bathrooms and toilets down the hall. But, for modest budgets, it is one of the best in the city. ⊠ Mitropoleos 21, in city center, 1 block west of Aristotelous Sq., 54624, ☎ 031/276335. 37 rooms, 10 with shared bath. No credit cards.

Nightlife and the Arts

Nightlife

Except for summertime, Thessaloniki's nightlife is one of its true assets. Bars, pubs, breweries, discos, and clubs within the city center—particularly in the area east of Aristotelous Square and in Ladadika, the former warehouse district near the port—fill the streets with an endless barrage of young people in search of fun. In summer, most clubs close, as their clients flock to the beaches of Chalkidiki. There are several discos on the road to the airport, but since they go in and out of fashion, ask at your hotel for the newest and best.

The **Hyatt Regency Casino** (✉ Just outside the airport, ☎ 031/491234, FAX 031/476129) is one of the largest and most elaborate in all of Europe. The entrance fee is 2,000 dr., which includes markers for slot machines; it's open daily 1 PM–8 AM.

CLUBS

The road to the airport is the best area to hear bouzouki and other Greek music, while the city center is filled with clubs and discos. Open year-round, the extraordinary **Mylos** (✉ 25 Andreadou Georgiou, on the southwest edge of the city just off October 28th St., ☎ 031/516945), is a complex of clubs, bars, discos, bars and ouzieri-taverna, art galleries, and a concert stage. This former mill has become perhaps the best venue in all of Greece for jazz, folk, and pop groups, Greek and foreign. Visiting foreign and Greek pop, jazz, and folk artists occasionally appear at the **Palais de Sports** (✉ International Trade Fairgrounds, ☎ 031/516945), and at Mylos.

JAZZ

Jazz gurus perform at local clubs such as **Malt and Jazz, Indrogeios,** the **Mill,** and **Radio City.**

The Arts

As the Cultural Capital of Europe in 1997, Thessaloniki established itself as a venue for world-class touring performances, as well as local artists. Check with your hotel or the Greek National Tourist Organization (GNTO or EOT) for current happenings.

FESTIVALS

No chapter on Northern Greece would be complete without mention of the famous *anastanarides* (fire dancers). Every year on May 21, the feast day of Sts. Constantine and Eleni, groups of religious devotees in the villages of **Langadha** (25 km/15 mi north of Thessaloniki) and **Ayia Eleni** (80 km/50 mi northeast of Thessaloniki) take part in a three-day rite called the *pirovassia* (literally, "fire dancing") in which, unharmed, they dance barefoot over a bed of hot coals while holding the saints' icons. Although assumed to be of pre-Christian origin, the tradition adopted its Christian aspects about 1250 in the eastern Thracian village of Kosti. At this time the villagers are said to have rescued the original icons from a burning church, all unharmed by the blaze. For information, check with the EOT or American Educational Services(☞ Visitor Information *in* Northern Greece A to Z, *below*).

In mid-September the **International Trade Festival** is celebrated at the Fairgrounds just north of the archaeological museum, marked by the modern, pinnacled tower of the Greek Telecommunications Organization (OTE), called the Pirgos Oté.

St. Dimitrios's feast is celebrated on October 26, but its secular adjunct has developed into a series of cultural events that brings an enormous amount of outside commerce. The October **Dimitria festival** exhibits works by artists and musicians from all over the country, including the Greek Film Festival (☞ *below*).

FILM

The city has more than a hundred movie theaters, but most in the city center close in summer. A few outdoor cinemas in the city and suburbs show movies in English with Greek subtitles. You'll be immersed in Greek community life; seeing friends meeting and greeting and neighbors watching from their balconies is part of the fun. Check the local papers and ask at your hotel. In October, there is an annual **Greek Film Festival,** but, as the title implies, movies are all in Greek.

MUSIC

Thessaloniki originated rebetika, the Greek version of the blues. You can hear it in bouzoukia, in and around the city, and the melodies fill the streets outside little clubs into the early hours. International orchestras perform classics throughout the year, and the **Municipal Orchestra of Thessaloniki** plays at its concert hall (⊠ In the university, just opposite the northern entrance of the International Trade Fairgrounds) from fall through spring.

THEATER

In winter, the State Theater of Northern Greece sponsors plays, ballets, and special performances of visiting artists at the **Kratiko Theatro** (State Theater) (⊠ Just opposite the White Tower, ☎ 031/223785). In summer, performances are given at the **Theatro Kypou** (Garden Theater) (⊠ In Municipal Park off Germanou St. between State Theater and archaeological museum) and at **Theatro Dasous** (Forest Theater) (⊠ In the forest east of the Upper City, ☎ 031/218092). All performances are in Greek, although there are occasional visits by English-speaking groups.

Outdoor Activities and Sports

Beaches

Beaches in Thessaloniki and its suburbs are on water too polluted to be recommended, even though you may see locals swimming there.

The nearest safe beaches are in **Perea** and **Ayia Triada,** past the airport, about 15 and 25 km (10 and 15 mi, just over half an hour by bus) away, respectively, from the Thessaloniki city center. At Ayia Triada, on the headland of the bay, the EOT runs a bathing facility at **Akti Thermaikou** (⊠ Ayia Triada, ☎ 0392/51352), with changing cabins, snack bars, tennis courts, and a children's playground.

Participant Sports

HORSEBACK RIDING

Contact **ALMA,** the eco-adventure tourism office, which can help you arrange daily riding or weeklong riding excursions in recommended areas (☞ Contacts and Resources *in* Northern Greece A to Z, *below*). The **Thessaloniki Riding Club** (⊠ Panorama, near Anatolia College, ☎ 031/270676) has riding outside of the city. An alternative is **Cavalier** (⊠ 14th km Georgikis Scholis, ☎ 031/473537).

SAILING

The bay here offers a safe harbor for sailors, with a dramatic backdrop of mountains, the hilltop old city, and the more modern city skyline. Try the **Sailing Club** (⊠ Megalou Alexandrou Ave., ☎ 031/830939) or **Thessaloniki Yacht Club** (⊠ 96 Themistokli Sofouli St., Mikro Emvolo, ☎ 031/414521). Like to row your boat, even in Thessaloniki? You can, from the **Kalamaria Yacht Club** (⊠ Mikro Emvolo, ☎ 031/412068).

SWIMMING

As most lodgings cater to business travelers in this business-oriented city, hotel pools are not a given. Check before booking if it's a priority. An acceptable alternative, aside from Waterland (☞ *below*), is the **National Swimming Pool of Thessaloniki** (☎ 031/203126), where you can splash with the locals.

TENNIS

Courts can be rented at the **Tennis Club** (⊠ 16 Kiprou St., ☎ 031/411569) and **Poseidonio Athletic Center** (⊠ Nea Paralia and 25th of March St., at the eastern end of the seaside promenade, ☎ 031/427414). Outside the city try **Anatolia College** (✉ On the road to Panorama after Pylea village, ☎ 031/323711) and **Akti Thermaikou** (✉ Ayia Triada, ☎ 0392/51352).

Waterland, a water-activity amusement park (✉ Off the highway to Chalkidiki, just past the airport exit, ☎ 0392/72025), has six well-kept courts available at inexpensive prices. It's especially nice for families, as there is something for everyone—wave pools, water slides, children's pools, restaurants, and basketball courts.

Spectator Sports

BASKETBALL
Basketball fans here are as rabid as those in Chicago, since Thessaloniki has three of the best basketball teams in the country: **Aris, Iraklis,** and **PAOK,** all three with Americans and Eastern Europeans on the roster. Aris and POAK play at the Palais de Sport, the domed athletic center within the International Trade Fairgrounds; Iraklis has its own large sports complex north of the university.

SOCCER
Two of the best teams in Greece—again **Aris** and **PAOK**—play their seasons in the spring and fall. The **Aris stadium** is in the suburb of Harilaou (✉ Papanastasiou St., about 1 km/½ mi north of the seafront amusement park, ☎ 031/305402). The **PAOK stadium** is several blocks northeast of the International Trade Fairgrounds (☎ 031/238560).

Shopping

Despite its cosmopolitan polish, Thessaloniki has nowhere near the choice or variety of goods for tourists' tastes as those found in Athens, although interesting items can be picked up in the shops of local craftspeople. Among the best buys are folk arts and crafts, leather, and jewelry. Complicated regulations control the opening and closing hours of shops. The afternoon siesta is still honored, which means that the shops are open from about 9 to 1:30 or 2, and most open again in the evenings, but only on Tuesdays, Thursdays, and Fridays, and never in July. The best shopping streets are Tsimiski, Mitropoleos, and Proxenou Koromila, which run east–west, between Pavlou Mela (the diagonal street connecting Ayios Sofias with the White Tower) and Eleftherios Venizelou.

Antiques
Antiques shops on Mitropoleos Street between Ayios Sofias and the White Tower are perfect for leisurely browsing. One of the best is **Relics** (✉ 6 Giorgio Lassani, east of Mitropoleos cathedral, ☎ 031/226506), which has an interesting selection of non-classical, exportable antiques; look for quality, not bargains. The best places to shop for finds—besides prowling through the **street markets**—are in the narrow streets around the **Rotunda** and the **flea market** on Tositsa Street. The latter offers a marvelous jumble of fascinating, musty old shops, with the wares of itinerant junk collectors spread out on the sidewalks, intermingled with small upscale antiques shops.

Books
Newspapers and magazines are also sold at kiosks at the intersection of Tsimiski and Aristotelou streets, and at another kiosk near the White Tower. Both of the following bookstores are rich with beautifully illustrated children's books on ancient Greek heroes and myths— a thoughtful gift to take home.

The oldest bookshop in the city is **Molchos** (✉ 10 Tsimiski, just west of Elefthirios Venizelou, ☎ 031/275271), which has a wide selection of newspapers and magazines in myriad languages, and specializes in

English and French books. **Ianos** (⊠ 7 Aristotelous St., just north of Electra Palace) is another well-stocked bookstore for foreign travelers.

Greek Souvenirs

The shop **ZM,** or Zeeta Mee (⊠ 1 Proxeno Koromila, ☎ 031/240591), sells a high-class selection of various Greek crafts. In the entrance of **Ayios Dimitrios** you can find an interesting display of Greek handmade crochet and embroidery from the women of the parish, all proceeds of which go to various charities. **La Rose** (⊠ 24 Tsimiski, at the lower end of Tottis Arcade) is an absolutely charming little shop featuring the popular Greek blown blue glass in every form imaginable. They also have an excellent selection of charms for protection from the *mati* (evil eye).

Just south of Egnatia Odos, the narrow streets between Aristotelous and Ayios Sofias are chock-full of local color, and many small craft shops have been opened by the craftspeople themselves. A most unusual one is named after **Haido,** the beautiful woman who creates works of art from tin and clay.

Sweets

It seems that every neighborhood in Thessaloniki can claim the city's best candy shop—and each has a delicious specialty, such as chocolate baklava. The truth is that as you walk through the city, you can usually find the best sweetshops by their seductive aroma. One of the best is **Agapitos** (⊠ North side of Tsimiski between Ayios Sofias and Karolou Dil, ☎ ☎ 031/279107), which aptly means "loved one," owned by the oldest son of a venerable Thessaloniki family.

Toys and Handicrafts

Greek toys are rare, but a wonderful and inexpensive locally produced gift is the playful **Kouvalias** pull toy. They are usually hidden away behind the more glamorous toys, but look for their bright paint and solid-wood construction.

One delightful store is **Skitso** (⊠ 11 Grigori Palama, a short diagonal street between Tsimiski and Platia Navarino, ☎ 031/269822), which sells a cornucopia of toys, ships, puppets, crosses, and other handmade objects. **Rotunda** (⊠ Just behind the Rotunda, off Sintrivaniou Sq.) offers some interesting Greek toys.

CENTRAL MACEDONIA
Pella, Vergina, Dion, Mt. Olympus

Few places in the world have greater ancient sites than Pella, Vergina, and Dion, the three major areas of Central Macedonia, which are connected to Alexander the Great and his father, Philip II, heroes of the ages. Even one would be worth a detour, but they are so close to Thessaloniki that it is easy to see all of them. You can rush and explore all three in a harried day trip from Thessaloniki. Better would be scheduling a relaxed day for each, allowing time for contemplation, or after seeing the first two, spending the night near Dion or Mt. Olympus and visiting both of these the next day.

In the 7th century BC the Dorian Makednoi tribe moved out of the Pindos mountains (between Epirus and Macedonia), settled in the fertile plains below, and established a religious center at the sacred springs of Dion at the foot of Mt. Olympus. Perdiccas, the first king of the Macedonians, held court at a place called Aigai, now known to have been at Vergina, and in the 5th century BC, the king of that time, Archelaos (413–399), moved his capital from Aigai to Pella, which was then on a rise above a lagoon leading to the Thermaic Gulf.

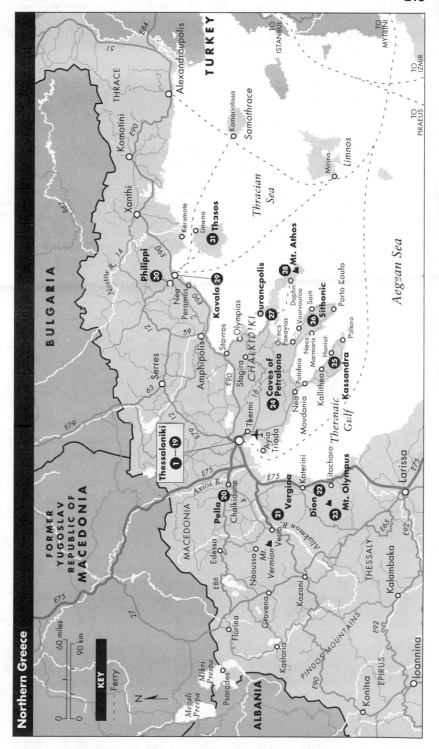

Northern Greece

KEY

Ferry

N

60 miles

90 km

ALBANIA

FORMER YUGOSLAV REPUBLIC OF MACEDONIA

BULGARIA

TURKEY

THRACE

Komotini

Xanthi

Alexandroupolis

Serres

Philippi **30**

Kavala **29**

31 Thasos

Limena

Keramote

Nea Peramos

Samothrace

Kamariotissa

Thracian Sea

Limnos

Mirina

Aegean Sea

Amphipolis

Stavros

Olympias

Stagira

CHALKIDIKI

Thermi

Ouranopolis **27**

28 Mt. Athos

Daphni

Vourvourou

Sarti

26 Sithonic

Porto Koufo

Ormos Panayias

Neos Marmaras

Haniot

Polidoia

Paliero

Thessaloniki **1—19**

Ayia Triada

24 Caves of Petralona

Nea Moudania

Kallithea

25 Kassandra

Thermaic Gulf

Pella **20**

Chalkidone

21 Veria

Vergina

Katerini

Litochoro

22 Dion

23 Mt. Olympus

MACEDONIA

Axios R.

Edessa

Naoussa

Mt. Vermion

Aliakmon R.

Kozani

Grevena

Florina

Kastoria

Mikri Prespa

Metali Prespa

Psarades

PINDOS MOUNTAINS

THESSALY

Kalambaka

Larissa

Konitsa

EPIRUS

Ioannina

TO ISTANBUL

TO IZMIR

TO MYTILINI

TO PIRAEUS

In 359 BC, after a succession of kings and assassinations and near anarchy exacerbated by the raids of barbarian tribes from the north, the 23-year-old Philip II was elected regent. Philip II pulled the kingdom together through diplomacy and by his seven marriages, and then began expanding it, taking in the all-important gold mines of the Pangeon mountains, and founding Philippi there. In 356 BC, on the day that Alexander the Great was born, Philip II was said to have simultaneously taken the strategic port of Potidea in Chalkidiki, received news of his horse's triumph in the Olympic Games, and learned of a general's victory against the Illyrians. That was also the day the temple of Artemis at Ephesus was destroyed by fire, which later prompted people to say that the goddess was away on that day, tending to Alexander's birth. In 336 BC, Philip II was assassinated in Vergina at a wedding party for one of his daughters. (It had been assumed that his tomb there had been looted and lost, until it was discovered in 1977 by the Greek archaeologist Manolis Andronikos.) Alexander, then 20, assumed power, and within two years he had gathered an army to be blessed at Dion, before setting off to conquer the Persians and most of the known world.

Pella

 40 km (25 mi) west of Thessaloniki.

Alexander's birthplace, and the capital of the Macedonian state in the 4th century, Pella is farthest from the sea of these ancient sites. A sign on the right points to the modern-day village, but the archaeological site and its museum are on either side of the main road toward Edessa (its waterfalls invite a possible further trip for nature-lovers). It's best to visit the Pella museum first, to understand what you will see at the site.

The **museum** stands just northwest of the old lagoon; it contains fascinating artifacts of Neolithic, Bronze, and Iron Age settlers, some as old as the 7th century BC, as well as a model of the 4th-century BC dwelling that stood across the road. Note also the unique statuette of a horned Athena, apparently influenced by Minoan Crete, and the statue of Alexander sprouting the horns of Pan. Both the museum and site are best known for their intricate, artful, beautifully preserved floor mosaics, mainly of mythological scenes. ⊠ *Pella, Archaeological Site and Museum,* ☎ *0383/31160 or 0383/31278.* ⌸ *1,000 dr.* ☉ *Weekdays 8–7, weekends 8:30–3.*

In 1914, two years after the departure of the Turks, the people who lived on the land were moved to a village north of here, and excavations of the **ancient site** began. These include portions of the walls; the sanctuaries of Aphrodite, Demeter, and Cybele; the marketplace; cemetery; and several houses. In 1987, on a small rise to the north, the remains of the **palace** came to light, though at present they're of little interest to the general public. It's hoped that the **theater** where Euripides' *The Bacchae* was first performed may also be located here (he is known to have written while in exile at the court).

Four important 4th-century BC **Macedonian tombs** with magnificent frescoes can be seen (⊠ Along the main road, before the turnoff to Naoussa).

OFF THE   **KASTORIA AND LAKES OF PRESPA** – Nestled in the Pindos mountains in
BEATEN PATH   Western Macedonia, 221 km (137 mi) west of Thessaloniki and 168 km
              (104 mi) west of Pella, is the beautiful town of Kastoria, filled with narrow lanes and stately homes. It sits on a promontory projecting into a lake garlanded in poplar and willow trees and mirroring the mountains,

while ducks, swans, and flat-bottom skiffs glide across the surface. In the Byzantine era, the town was famous for its Macedonian school of religious painting; its many fine Byzantine churches are richly decorated with frescoes and icons. The city prospered during the Turkish occupation, and the 18th- and 19th-century three-story mansions reflect those good times. Today, it is known for its embroidery and fur trade, and shops all over the city offer fur-tail key rings, slippers, vests, hats, and mink coats. The place to stay is the Tsamis Hotel, which overlooks a mountain-rimmed lake in an enchanting setting and whose comfortable, traditionally styled lodgings provide a a get-away-from-it-all atmosphere (⊠ 3 km/2 mi along the National Road between Athens and Thessaloniki, ☎ 0467/85334). Two hours by car through the forests and meadows northwest of Kastoria are the serenely lovely lakes of Prespa, along the border Greece shares with Albania and the former Yugoslavia. Separated only by a narrow, thickly reeded strip of land, these peaceful waters are officially designated bird sanctuaries, home to more than 250 species of birds—65 of which are internationally recognized as rare or endangered species. The islet in the smaller lake, Mikri Prespa, is filled with ancient and Byzantine ruins and caves once used as shrines, decorated with religious paintings.

Vergina

㉑ *135 km (84 mi) southwest of Thessaloniki.*

Some of antiquity's greatest treasures await you at the **Royal Tombs** of Vergina, opened to the public only in 1993, 16 years after their discovery. Today, the complex has been made into a new museum, a fitting shrine to the original capital of the kingdom of Macedonia (then known as Aigai). The entrance is appropriately stunning: You walk down a white sandstone ramp into the partially underground structure, roofed over by a large earth-covered dome approximately the size of the original tumulus. Here on display are some of the legendary artifacts from the age of Philip of Macedonia.

For years, both archaeologists and grave robbers had suspected that the large mound that stood on this site might contain something of value, but try as they might, neither of these professional groups was successful in penetrating its secret. In his fascinating book *The Royal Tombs of Vergina*, Professor Andronikos theorizes that one of Alexander's successors, wanting to protect Philip's tomb from robbers, had it covered with broken debris and tombstones to make it appear that the grave had already been plundered, and then built the tumulus so that Philip's tomb would be near the edge rather than the center. But this was speculation after the fact: When Andronikos discovered it, on the last day of excavation in 1977 before closing the site for the winter, he had been trying one of the last approaches, with little hope of finding anything—certainly not the tomb of Philip II, in as pristine condition as the day it was closed.

This was the first intact Macedonian tomb ever found—breathtaking, imposing, exquisite, with a huge frieze of a hunting scene, a masterpiece similar to those of the Italian Renaissance, but a1,000 years older. It, along with a massive yet delicate fresco depicting Pluto's abduction of Persephone (a copy of which is displayed along one wall of the museum), is the only original work of great painting surviving from antiquity. On the left are two tombs and one altar that had been looted and destroyed in varying degrees by the time Andronikos discovered them. Macedonian Tomb III, on the right, found intact in 1978, is believed to be that of the young Prince Alexander IV, Alexander the Great's son, who was at first kept alive by his "protectors" after Alexander's death and then poisoned (along with his mother) when he was 14. To the left of Tomb III is that of Philip II. He was assassinated in the nearby theater, a short drive away; his body was burned, his bones washed in wine, wrapped in royal purple, and put into the magnificent, solid gold casket with the 16-point sun, which is displayed in the museum. His wife, Cleopatra—not the Egyptian queen—was later buried with him.

The tombs alone would be worth a special trip, but the treasure trove of golden objects and unusual artifacts that were buried within them is equally impressive. First housed in the archaeological museum in Thessaloniki, they have been artfully transferred here to their stunning, permanent home. Among them, in practically perfect condition and displayed in dramatic dimmed light, are delicate ivory reliefs, elegantly wrought gold laurel wreaths, and Philip's crown, armor, and shield. Especially interesting are those items that seem most certainly Philip's: a pair of greaves (shin guards), one shorter than the other—Philip was known to have a limp. ⊠ *Archaeological site,* ☎ *031/830538.* ⊡ *1,200 dr.* ◐ *Tues.–Sun. 8:30–3.*

The winding road to the **site of Philip's assassination** goes through rolling countryside west of the village, much of it part of the vast royal **burial grounds of ancient Aigai.** On the way, you pass three more Macedonian tombs of little interest, being rough-hewn stone structures in typical Macedonian style. The palace itself is nothing more than a line of foundation stones that shows the outline of its walls. It was discovered by French archaeologists in 1861 but not thought to have any particular significance; ancient Aigai was then thought to be somewhere near Edessa. In the field just below are the remnants of the **theater,** located by Andronikos in 1982. It was on Philip's way here, for the wedding games that were to follow the marriage of his daughter to the king of Epirus, that he was murdered.

Dining

$$ ✕ **Philippion.** Eat outside under the trees, where a colorful chicken may wander under your table (probably hiding). Inside, under an arched ceiling, you can choose from a tasty lineup of traditional foods, such as moussaka. Vegetables grown in this region are especially delicious, and fresh frozen yogurt is made from local fruits. The charismatic manager, Philippides Manolis, couldn't be friendlier—nor could the chicken. Reservations are not needed, but try to get in ahead of tour buses. ⊠ *Across from the tombs,* ☎ *031/92892. AE, MC, V.*

Dion

㉒   *87 km (54 mi) southwest of Thessaloniki.*

At the foothills of Mt. Olympus lies ancient Dion. Even before Zeus and the Olympian gods, Mt. Olympus was home to the Muses and Orpheus, who entranced the men of the area with his mystical music. The story says that the life-giving force of Dion came from the waters in which the murderers of Orpheus (the women of Mt. Olympus, jealous for attention from their men) washed their hands on the slopes of the sacred mountain to remove the stain of their own sin. The waters entered the earth to cleanse it, and rose again in the holy city of Dion. Today, underground streams from the sacred mountain emerge where ancient Dion was founded, consecrating the ground, as it were, with its bubbling, life-giving springs.

Although a lesser-known ancient site to the non-Greek visitor, Dion is especially exciting because of daily discoveries being made throughout the year. The superb **museum** contains the best finds from the area, which is still under intense excavation. (The friendly excavators may even let you dig around the edges a bit in mock labor and take a photo—if you are careful.) It's best to visit the museum first and view the videotape (in English) prepared by the site's renowned archaeologist, Dimitris Pandermalis, which describes the excavations, the finds, and their significance. (His efforts to keep the artifacts in the place where they were found have won him the unqualified admiration of the villagers and established a new trend for decentralization of archaeological finds throughout Greece.) On the second floor, there is an excellent topographical relief of the area, and in the basement you'll see a wooden model of the ancient city, together with interactive learning centers about the daily life of ancient Greece. ⊠ *Next to archaeological site,* ☎ *0351/53206.* 🎫 *800 dr.* ☼ *Mon. 12:30–7, Tues.–Sun. 8–7.*

The road from the museum divides the diggings at the **archaeological site** into two areas. On the left is the ancient city of Dion itself, with the juxtaposition of public toilets and several superb floor mosaics. On the right side is the **ancient theater** and, a bit farther on, the **Sanctuaries of Asklepios and Demeter** and the **Sanctuary of Isis.** In the latter, a vividly beautiful approximation of how it once looked, copies of the original statues, now in the museum, have been put in place.

Today, a feeling of peace prevails at Dion, at the foot of the mountain of the gods. Visitors are few at this vast, underrated site, and the silence is punctuated now and then by goats, their bells jangling, driven around the toppled columns and mosaic floors by shepherds and their busy dogs. Springs bubble up where excavators dig, and scarlet poppies bloom among the cracks. This is the essence of Greece. ⊠ *Archaeological site,* ☎ *0351/53206.* 🎫 *800 dr.* ☼ *Tues.–Sun. 8:30–3 (Mon. noon–7 in winter).*

Dining and Lodging

$$ ✕ **Dionysos.** A combination tourist shop, café, and restaurant in a setting of varnished modernity, Dionysos has excellent food and good, cheerful service. Try the specialty of the area, roast goat on a spit. Also recommended are the *loukaniko* (sausages); rolled, spiced, and spit-roasted meat; and the *saganaki* (fried feta or kefaloteri). ⊠ *Village center, directly opposite museum,* ☎ *0351/53276. No credit cards.*

$ 🏨 **Dion Resort Hotel.** Proximity to the beach, Mt. Olympus, and the archaeological site is the selling point here. Every room has an excellent view, of either the sea or the peaks. Direct-dial phones are available, and a small selection of water sports is offered. ⊠ *Paralia Dion 60100,* ☎ *0352/61222,* ℻ *0352/61220. 200 rooms. Restaurant, bar, air-conditioning, snack bar, minibars, 2 pools, tennis court. AE, DC, MC, V.*

Mt. Olympus

㉓ *100 km (62 mi) southwest of Thessaloniki, 17 km (10½ mi) southwest of Dion.*

As you drive from the sea to Mt. Olympus, this site appears as a conglomeration of thickly bunched summits and not as a majestic single peak. To understand how the mountain must have impressed the ancient Greeks and caused them to shift their allegiance from the earth-rooted deities of the Mycenaeans to those of the airy heights of Olympus, you need to see the mountain clearly from several different perspectives. From the south, if there is still snow on the range, it appears as a massive, flat-topped acropolis, much like the one in Athens, its vast, snowy crest hovering in the air, seemingly capable of supporting as many gods and temples as the ancients could have imagined. On its northern side, the Olympus range catches clouds in a turbulent, stormy bundle, letting fly about 12 times as many (surely Zeus-inspired) thunder-and-lightning storms as anywhere else in Greece. The third perspective comes from actually climbing the mountain, to the truly awe-inspiring summit at the throne of Zeus.

If you hike up Mt. Olympus (☞ *below*), when you come from Prionia take time to visit the **monastery of Ayios Dionysus** (⊠ In the forest at the bottom of a turnoff to the right just below the refuge). During World War II, the monastery, rightly suspected of harboring resistance fighters, was blown up by the Nazis. It is now slowly being restored by the single monk who lives there and in its unfinished state has a stark and impressive beauty.

Lodging

$$ 🏨 **Aphrodite Hotel.** On the village square, this lodging is acceptable but doesn't live up to its name and lacks Myrto's (☞ *below*) spiffier character. ⊠ *Plateia Kentriki, Litochoro 60200,* ☎ *0352/281–415 or 0352/21868. 24 rooms, 14 with shared bath. No credit cards.*

$$ 🏨 **Hotel Myrto.** White walls and wood decor give this hotel a cheery Alpine flavor, and every room has a lovely view from a balcony. Near the main square, this is the best hotel in Litochoro village, bright and clean, and with a paneled TV lounge and bar. ⊠ *Off the main road, Litochoro 60200,* ☎ *0352/81498. 18 rooms with bath. Bar. No credit cards.*

Outdoor Activities and Sports

HIKING

Mt. Olympus provides the traveler with some of the most beautiful nature trails in Europe. Hundreds of species of wildflowers and herbs bloom in the spring, more than 85 of which are found only on this mountain.

From **Litochoro** you can climb all the way on foot or take a car to the end of the road at Prionia and trek the rest of the way. The climb to Prionia takes about four hours; the ride, on a bumpy gravel road with no guardrails between you and breathtakingly precipitous drops, takes little less than an hour, depending on your nerves. If you can manage to take your eyes off the road, the scenery is magnificent. The hiking refuge **Spilios Agapitos** (Refuge A) (⊠ Two-thirds of the way to the summit, ☎ 0352/81800) is run by Kostas Zolotas, the venerable English-speaking guru of climbers. In the morning, it is just another two hours—some of it a bit hair-raising—to the Throne of Zeus and the summit, at 9,751 ft. The trail is snow-free from about mid-May until late October. For further details, contact ALMA or the Hellenic Alpine Club (☞ Contacts and Resources *in* Northern Greece A to Z, *below*).

EASTERN MACEDONIA
Chalkidiki, Kavala, Philippi, Thasos

Eastern Macedonia, with its curving sand beaches, coves, and Mediterranean landscape, has had a considerably less violent history than the western end of the realm. The birthplace of Aristotle, it was colonized in the 5th century BC by settlers from Athens and Evia and later, in 1922, saw large numbers of Greek refugees from Asia Minor who were resettled in the exchange of populations.

Caves of Petralona

㉔ *50 km (31 mi) southeast of Thessaloniki.*

On the northern edge of the first peninsula of the three-fingered hand of Chalkidiki, past golden fields, pine forests, and rural towns, you can stop at the dramatic Paleolithic caves of Petralona, at the foot of Mt.

Katsika, 750 ft high. With huge stalagtites and stalagmites configured like a fantasy scene from a Disney animation, the caves are easily accessible for those in good shape and good shoes; walkways take you through dramatically lit grottoes, some with life-size figures of cave dwellers squatting before their fires. Traces of fire, dating back more than a million years, are the earliest yet found on earth; the ancient human skeleton, one of the oldest in the world—and definitely the oldest in Europe—was found in the 11th level of the cave. An adjoining museum offers in-depth explanations of the cave and the findings but needs some TLC to improve lighting and displays, which at press time looked a bit like a 1965 high school science fair. Happily, Aris Poulianos, the anthropologist who found the ancient skeleton at Petrolona and named him Archanthropus Europaeus Petraloniensis, is still hardy and loves to talk prehistory. He is charming and modest and will pull up a chair by the site's snack bar, share a soft drink, and practice (good) English with interested visitors. Ask for him after you visit the cave, and a couple of ready questions will make the most of the time. ⊠ 16 km (10 mi) before turnoff for Nea Moudania, ☎ 0396/31300. 🏷 800 dr. ☾ Daily: winter 9–5, summer 9–8.

Kassandra

㉕ 69 km (43 mi) southeast of Thessaloniki, 19 km (11¾ mi) southeast of the Caves of Petralona.

The most westerly of the three peninsulas, Kassandra was named after Cassander, the man who founded Thessaloniki. He also named a city on the peninsula after himself, presently called **Potidaia,** which once was important but gradually faded into insignificance as Thessaloniki became the major port. Potidaia's medieval walls date from 600 BC, when it was founded by Corinth. The small canal that leads to the town was cut across the isthmus in 1937.

Kassandra's white-sand beaches, rocky coves, and hour-or-so proximity to Thessaloniki have made it the most popular—and populous—resort area in Chalkidiki. Pine-forested promontories isolate the resort areas from one another, so it feels less crowded than it actually is. Farming villages with stone houses, fishing hamlets, and Byzantine towers remain, alongside a plethora of fast-food joints, discos, shopping centers, good hotels, and resort complexes. Kallithea has the the ruins of the Temple of Ammon Zeus, an Egyptian-Libyan version of the Greek god, said to have inspired Alexander the Great to set off for the Nile area. Kalandra has a 7th-century church with gorgeous frescoes. For an interesting look at how the life-loving Greeks celebrate their vacations, dip into the energy generated at seaside villages such as **Hanioti** and **Paliouri** near the tip of the peninsula, particularly in the evenings.

Lodging

$$$$ 🏨 **Athos Palace.** Along with its sister hotel, the Pallini Beach (☞ above), this is one of the best in the area. The modern building has well-landscaped grounds, excellent service, views of the sea or the hills from room balconies, lots of activities, and a wonderful beach. ⊠ Kallithea, Kassandra, Chalkidiki 63077, ☎ 0374/22100 through 0374/22109, FAX 0374/23605. 465 rooms, 44 suites, 18 bungalows. 2 restaurants, 2 bars, 2 pools, horseback riding, nightclub, meeting room. AE, DC, MC, V.

$$$$ 🏨 **Pallini Beach.** A big, boxy resort with a domed indoor pool complex (like the Athos Palace next door; ☞ above), this is an excellent hotel, but it also can be noisy and crowded when weekenders and summer vacationers arrive in force. It shares the great beach with its next-door neighbor. All accommodations except bungalows are

air-conditioned. ✉ *Kallithea, Kassandra, Chalkidiki 63077,* ☎ *0374/22480 through 0374/22489,* ☏ *0374/22489. 345 rooms, 98 bungalows. Restaurant, bar, cafeteria, indoor pool, dance club, convention center. AE, DC, MC, V.*

Sithonia

 76 km (47½ mi) southeast of Thessaloniki, 26 km (16 mi) east of Kassandra.

Olive groves, red-roof and half-timbered houses, pine trees turning the blue of the Aegean green at its rugged shoreline—that is Sithonia, the middle peninsula, with perhaps the most beautiful scenery and coastline in all of Chalkidiki. Because it is farther from Thessaloniki than Kassandra, it is far less developed and crowded. Narrow-laned villages are inviting, and a tour around the entire peninsula with leisurely stops for lunch and a swim, round-trip from Thessaloniki, is an easy day trip. Keep in mind that most establishments on the peninsula are open only during the tourist season (May–late October).

The area of **Ormos Panayias** and its adjoining bay of **Vourvourou,** midway on the eastern coast of the peninsula, provides an idyllic setting. Tiny pine-blanketed islands dot the shoreline and harbor, and fishing caïques bob at anchor in charming coves. Many feel that the look is similar to that of the northern California coast. Boats leave at 9:30 AM for a round-trip to Mt. Athos, on the adjoining peninsula, stopping for lunch at Ouranopolis, and get back around 5. This is a convenient way to see the third peninsula without having to drive there.

On the drive south, excellent views of the holy peninsula of Mt. Athos rise across the bay. This is as close as most will come to seeing the great monastery at Mt. Athos. **Sarti,** the next village down from Vourvourou, is the fishing port settled by refugees in the 1922 population exchange with Turkey. Each family built its house according to its own visions, resulting in a glorious lack of uniformity and, sometimes, taste. The beach is long and wide, and it drifts right up to the little flower gardens fronting the houses. Rooms for rent are plentiful; one hotel sits on the southern outskirts of the village.

The secluded bay of **Porto Koufo,** on the southwestern end of the tip of the peninsula, is almost completely encircled by rocky headlands, and the sea is so still here the name translates as "deaf port." It has several tavernas, their relaxing setting warranting an eye-opening drink. North of Porto Koufo are a succession of small, not-yet-overly commercialized beach communities, of which nearby **Toroni,** with a few tavernas and cafés and an excellent beach, is probably the most picturesque. Its ruins of Byzantine fortifications and early Christian basilicas offer a good opportunity to walk and stretch your limbs after a long drive. In the bustling fishing village of **Neos Marmaras,** north of Torini, fishermen haul their catch in front of numerous cafés, tavernas, bars, and restaurants along the seafront. Nightlife is lively, and big resort hotels are being developed to add to the plethora of rooming houses.

Dining and Lodging

$$ ✕ **Pergola.** Two friends from the area have painted this little house purple and orange, and claim their cuisine is "Greek and exotic," but you won't go wrong with traditional fried calamari or roast chicken, accompanied by salad with feta, tomato, and cucumber. You're out of luck if a tour bus has just unloaded, but otherwise it's fun to sit on the porch and talk with the outgoing owners over wine poured from the barrel. ✉ *Sarti, 2 blocks from the seaside on the main road into town,* ☎ *0375/94005. No credit cards.*

$$$$ 🏨 **Grecotel Meliton Beach.** The best in Chalkidiki, this huge new family resort offers every activity and is within a few minutes' drive of 33 beaches, so getting away to a secluded stretch of sand is possible when you tire of group fun. There's a huge array of water sports available. Cheerful accommodations have plenty of space and built-ins. ✉ *Neos Marmaras, near the Marina, part of the Porto Carras complex, 63081,* ☎ FAX *0375/7138. 428 rooms, 18 suites. 3 restaurants, 3 bars, grocery, 2 pools, minibars, nightclubs, children's program, meeting rooms. AE, DC, MC, V. Closed Nov.–Apr.*

En Route   If you are bypassing the fingers that are the Kassandra and Sithonia peninsulas, the best route from Thessaloniki to Chalkidiki's easternmost peninsula is not, as it would seem, directly across the palm to Ouranopolis. This route from west to east involves much uphill driving, particularly frustrating if you get behind a bus or truck. Therefore, leave Thessaloniki at Platia Vardaris, take the E79 north toward Serres, then turn east onto the E90 toward Kavala. Continue past the long and beautiful lakes of **Koronia** and **Volvi** until you come to the forested turnoff for the coast, signposted to **Stavros** and **Olympiada**.

Between these charming little fishing villages (as yet relatively unravaged), you'll see some of the most spectacular landscape—rivaling Big Sur in California—as the road travels high above the coast through pine-scented forests. After Olympiada, a popular family and tourist spot for locals with its recently excavated old walls, an optional turnoff of about 10 km (6 mi) leads to Stagira, Aristotle's birthplace. A statue of the great philosopher stands on a wooded knoll as you approach the modern town. The mining town of **Stratoni** appears irresistible from above but is most depressing up close. You'll pass **Nea Roda,** near the site of Xerxes's Canal, dug by the Persian king in 480 BC to avoid having his ship hit the rocks in the violent storms around Mt. Athos. Today the canal is barely visible in the grassy marsh.

Ouranopolis

➋➐ *110 km (68½ mi) east of Thessaloniki.*

Known as "Heaven's City," Ouranopolis is a charming cul-de-sac on the final point of land that separates the secular world from the sacred walled-off sanctuaries of Mt. Athos. The village, noted for its rug and tapestry weaving, is particularly entrancing because of the bay's aquamarine waters.

Ouranopolis was settled by refugees from Asia Minor in 1922 and before that was occupied only by monks from Mt. Athos, who lived in the Byzantine **Tower of Proforion** (✉ On the point), built in the 12th century by Emperor Andronicus II. When the villagers arrived, the monks fled, and the tower subsequently became the abode of Joice and Sydney Loch, a couple who worked with Thessaloniki's noted American Farm School to help the refugees develop their rug-weaving industry. The tower has now been fully restored and is occasionally open for various exhibitions by local artists.

Floating on its turquoise waters are the **tiny emerald islands** and **atolls** of **Drenia** and **Amouliani,** which are reachable by a 15-minute caïque ride and by small outboard motorboats, which you can rent by the day. All have glorious white-sand beaches, and two—**Gaidoronisi** (part of the Drenia group) and the fishing hamlet of **Amouliani**—have places to eat.

Dining and Lodging

$$ ✕ **Kritikos.** The owner is a local fisherman, so everything is served catch-of-the-day at this simple restaurant. The family re-creates traditional

village recipes—but never gives away the secrets. Their lobster with pasta is haute cuisine on paper tablecloths. ⊠ *Town center, just north of village square (you may have to ask the way),* ☎ *0377/455760. No credit cards.*

$$ ✕ **Skites Restaurant.** On a terrace overlooking the sea, in the hotel of ★ the same name, this restaurant serves home-style meals that change from day to day, according to the season. ⊠ *Skites hotel, southeast of Ouranopolis,* ☎ *0377/71140. No credit cards.*

$$ ✕ **Sugar.** Despite its name, this restaurant-bistro serves filling fare. The pasta, drinks, and view of the marina and promenade leading to Mt. Athos are all worthy of a visit. ⊠ *Port,* ☎ *0377/71319. No credit cards.*

$$$ ⛺ **Xenia.** Tucked under tamarisk trees on the beach entering Ouranopolis, this hotel is definitely the best buy for the money. Its low-lying design makes it almost invisible from the village; likewise from within: The windows open to only the blue of the sea. A wood exterior and clean, functional furnishings make for a pleasantly unpretentious lodging. ⊠ *Ouranopolis 63075,* ☎ *0377/71202, 0377/71264, or 0377/71265. 22 rooms with bath, 20 bungalows. Restaurant, bar, air-conditioning. No credit cards.*

$$ ⛺ **Skites.** Set on a bluff 1 km (½ mi) outside Ouranopolis, this is the peachiest hotel in the area. All bungalow-style rooms are small, with separate entrances, flower gardens, and privacy. You'll enjoy views from the restaurant's terrace and the comforts of home: nostalgic cooking and a personal atmosphere. Note that there is no air-conditioning. ⊠ *Ouranopolis 63075,* ☎ *0377/71140. 17 bungalows with bath. Restaurant, bar. No credit cards.*

Mt. Athos

28 *120 km (74½ mi) southeast of Thessaloniki.*

One of the last great bastions of exclusivity, Mt. Athos isn't easy to enter, even for men (women must content themselves with shopping and sunning far from the boundaries of the holy settlements). Reservations, especially for summer and Easter, must be made months in advance. Booking in hand, you must then go in person to the Directorate of Political Affairs in Thessaloniki to obtain your visa (☞ Visitor Information *in* Northern Greece A to Z, *below*). Visas are issued only to adult males, and boys if they are accompanied by an adult, who must make a formal declaration that the purpose of the visit is a religious one. Stays for non-Greeks are limited to four days.

This third peninsula of Athos, an isolated landscape of virgin forest, valleys, and gorges, is called Ayion Oros (Holy Mountain) by the Greeks, although it does not become a mountain until its southernmost point, and there are no monasteries actually on its slopes. Its 6,670-ft height once prompted Alexander the Great's architect to suggest carving it into a replica of Alexander, a proposal that did not come to fruition.

The Virgin Mary, it is said, was brought here by accident from Ephesus, having been blown off-course by a storm. She found the spot to be a holy one and asked that it be venerated as her own very special place. This story has since become the rationale for keeping it off-limits to all women but the Virgin herself!

In the 5th–6th centuries the peninsula was occupied by only a few cave-dwelling hermits, and in 885 the Byzantine emperor Basil I decreed the area to be exclusively the province of hermits and monks. It was not until the 11th century that another decree specifically prohibited "smooth-faced persons" from entering: women, young boys, children, and eunuchs. Today, men do not have to grow a beard to visit.

In 963, the first organized monastic community (*lavra*) was established at the foot of the mountain. Called Great Lavra, it is still functioning today. Nineteen other communities followed (including some Orthodox Russians), the last in the 14th century. Since then, a number of hermitages and the separate dependencies called *skites* have been built, some precariously clinging to the rocky slopes. In 1926, Athos was formally united with Greece, but it still remains theoretically autonomous in its administration, similar to that of the Vatican. Hence the need for visas and a *diamonitirion* (official residence permit).

EXPLORING MT. ATHOS

A small boat leaves from the Ouranopolis dock daily at 9:45 AM. Before boarding, you go to the office near the dock with your visa to obtain the diamonitirion, which permits you to stay for the night. The boat then leaves you off at the tiny, somewhat disreputable-looking port of **Daphni**, a loading point for goods. From here, caïques take you to the monasteries along the western coast; otherwise, a rickety bus takes you up the steep promontory to the administrative center at **Karyes**, and you are on your own to walk or find a ride to the monastery of your choice. Be aware that most monasteries close for the night at sunset, about 9 PM in summer, and dinner is served at about 7.

An alternative excursion (women allowed here, thank you very much!) would be one of the **daily cruises** around the spectacular coast of the peninsula. Book either in Thessaloniki (☞ Contacts and Resources *in Northern Greece A to Z, below*) or Ouranopolis at any of various agencies. You can see many superb monasteries that are built at the water's edge or clinging to rocky outcroppings.

Kavala

㉙ *136 km (84½ mi) northeast of Thessaloniki.*

Exceptionally pretty for a commercial city, and blessed with natural riches, architectural treasures, and a thriving economy, Kavala is the main city of eastern Macedonia. When Philip II founded Philippi to protect the eastern route to the mineral riches of the Pangeon mountains, he made Kavala—in those days, Neapolis—its port. Today, besides being a major gateway for the islands in the northeast Aegean, it is the capital of Greece's tobacco industry. A combination of old and new, its buildings rise like tiers in an amphitheater up Mt. Simvolo. The aqueduct built in 1550 is the boundary between the modern, bustling town and the older section, with fragrant gardens spilling over walls, steep, cobbled alleyways under jutting, enclosed balconies, and squares with domed, 18th-century Turkish houses. The imposing eastern promontory is dominated by a **Byzantine castle** overlooking a harbor lined with brightly colored seafaring caïques and a number of fine seafood tavernas and clubs. Visiting the castle is free and can be done Tuesday to Sunday from 8:30 to 3.

It was at the site of the **archaeological museum,** on the west side of town, that the apostle Paul disembarked on his first trip to Greece in AD 49 en route to Philippi. Today you can see sculpture, jewelry, and terra-cotta finds from Amphipolis. ⊠ *17 Erythrou Stavrou,* ☎ *051/ 222335.* 🖼 *800 dr.* ☉ *Tues.–Sun. 8:30–3.*

Dining and Lodging

$$ ✕ **Beautiful Mytilini.** This extraordinary seafood taverna under the fortress promontory specializes in mussel pilaf and other *fruits de mer.* ⊠ *Eastern end of harbor,* ☎ *051/223034 or 051/221777. MC, V.*

$$ 🏠 **Egnatia Hotel.** Charming may not be the operative word, but the Egnatia is clean and well run. It's on the main road as you enter the city and is easily accessible—and there's a roof garden. Note the assorted shapes of the windows, like puzzle pieces, puzzling indeed. ⊠ *Evthono Meraxias 139, Kavala 65403,* ☎ *051/244891,* FAX *051/245396. 45 rooms with bath. Bar, dining room, minibars, meeting room, free parking. MC, V.*

$$ 🏨 **Galaxy Hotel.** This classic international-modern style hotel enjoys the most central location in the city, on the main drag on the port. It can be noisy at night, so request a back room if you don't care about watching the ferries come and go from the front balconies. ⊠ *Elefthirios Venezelou 27, 65403,* ☎ *051/224811,* FAX *051/226754. 150 rooms with bath. Bar, dining room, meeting rooms, free parking. MC, V.*

$$ 🏨 **Ocean View Beach Hotel.** Located in Nea Peramos, a 20-minute drive west of Kavala, this hotel delights with its beach location. If you like being on the water, you'll enjoy its laid-back island feel with its lawns, pretty pool, and white umbrellas set against the sea. Rooms have balconies to enjoy the breezes. ⊠ *Eleohorion, Nea Peramos 64007,* ☎ *0594/23059. 32 rooms with bath. Restaurant, bar, air-conditioning, minibars, health club, parking. MC, V.*

Philippi

③⓪ *150 km (93¼ mi) northeast of Thessaloniki, 14 km (8½ mi) west of Kavala.*

Phillipi is most famous for two historic reasons: In AD 42, the armies of Antony and Octavian caught up here with Caesar's assassins, Brutus and Cassius, and defeated them. Second, it was here that the apostle Paul first preached the gospel in Europe, later writing his famed Epistle to the Philippians. Just outside the west wall of Philippi on the banks of the river Gangitis he also performed the first baptisms on European soil. Noteworthy are an expansive **theater,** where ancient Greek plays are performed in summer, and the **Roman crypt** from which Paul was miraculously freed by an earthquake. ⊠ *Archaeological site:* ☎ *051/ 516470.* 🎫 *800 dr.* ☉ *Tues.–Sun. 8:30–3. Museum:* ☎ *051/516251.* 🎫 *800 dr.* ☉ *Tues.–Sun. 8:30–7. Closed in winter.*

Amphipolis, 60 km (42 mi) southwest of Philippi, once the most important Athenian colony in Northern Greece, and now a modern village, still offers up sections of its acropolis and tombs. Of special note is the **Lion of Amfipolis,** a 4th-century BC burial monument, beyond the bridge over the Strymon River. Ruins of early Christian basilicas with exceptional mosaic floors are also worth seeking out.

Thasos

③① *About a 75-minute ferry ride from Kavala, 45 minutes by hydrofoil.*

Land of the mythical Sirens, the ancient and lovely island of Thasos has a past whose significance far outweighs its relative obscurity to today's overseas travelers. Traces of life date back to 2,000 BC. Hercules was considered a guardian of the island, and Hippocrates, father of medicine, studied botany here. Tribes fought in the Trojan War, and the first Greek colonists, who received an oracle from the Temple of Apollo in Delphi, arrived in 700 BC.

Only 8 km (5 mi) from the northern Greek mainland, Thasos is known as "The Green Island" because of its thick pine-and-cypress forests and tracts of olive and fruit trees. It could just as well be called "Gold Island," for the precious metal mined here in the Pangeos mountains since the time of the Phoenicians, or "White Island," for its fine sand and local marble. The circular coastline is etched out in coves and beaches, and the island has two distinct sections: The north and east region is mountainous, with rocky cliffs and sandy bays; the south and west region is strung with traditional villages, set among low hills and olive groves.

Parts of its main harbor town of **Limenas** (also known as Thasos) are touristy, but wander off a bit and you will find ruins and sanctuaries scattered among the houses, and sections of old stone walls, still intact. The small, excellent **museum** holds traces of Greek, Roman, and early Christian artifacts. It's open daily 9–2; admission is 500 dr. **Classical ruins,** including an acropolis, temples to Dionysos, Poseidon, and Athena; an agora; and an **amphitheater** nestled in the forest above the town were built from local quarries.

The villages of Thasos are by and large rural and retain a quiet beauty. **Panagia,** east of the harbor of Limenas and overlooking Golden Beach, is named after the Virgin Mary. Whitewashed houses contrast with green pines and russet mountains, and the charming square, with its fountain and 700-year-old platanos tree, is an ideal place to snack on traditional walnuts or figs in syrup. Check out the nearby church, which houses elaborate altar carvings and a crusader's banner. Skala Panagia, the beach resort below, still has archaic walls, classical ruins, and a round watchtower from the 5th century BC. Tavernas are built into the cliffside.

To the west of Limenas, **Kazaviti** is divided by a stream—each section claims to be the real village, but locals distinguish them by using the prefixes "big" and "small." The more diminutive side is perched on the mountainside, with narrow lanes and courtyards draped with scented vines. Houses are built of stone, with wood-supported balconies; try to peek in to see the painted ceilings. The bigger side of the village has some shops and tavernas that serve simple fare and local wine, made from black grapes.

The ancient fishing village of **Skala Prinos** is still home to shipbuilders, and wooden boats are crafted in the small shipyard on the waterfront. Ferries leave for Kavala from here as well as from Limenas. Hard to find, and high in the center of the island, **Kastro** is the oldest village on Thasos. Ruins of a 15th-century Genoese wall and ruined houses are all around, but locals are starting to rebuild in the traditional style. The church has pretty hand-painted walls, a carved pulpit, and a harem section. To enter you have to ask for the heavy, hand-forged key.

The fishing port of **Limenaria,** now a commercial fishing port, was a major wine exporter in ancient times. Here you can still find Amelia, a local liquor of walnuts and honey, and Pergoula, a wine distilled from Thasian Georgina grapes. During the Byzantine period the village of **Theologos** was the mountain capital of Thasos and remained so during Turkish rule in the 19th century. A folklore museum in a Thasian-style house displaying costumes, household items, rugs, old flour mills, and antique olive presses is interesting for a brief stop. St. Dimitris church has wood carvings of religious themes that took a monk 18 years to complete. Small waterfalls are nearby.

Beaches

Thasos has dozens of good beaches, ranging from hidden coves to long sunny stretches. The largest have changing facilities and umbrellas; the most secluded are perfect for nude bathing; and all overlook a clear, turquoise sea. Ten minutes from the center of town is **Limenas Beach,** with views of the harbor, and a backdrop of the acropolis. Families might prefer **Makryammos Beach,** 10 minutes farther, with a children's playground. The traditional villages of **Panagia** and **Potamia** overlook Golden Beach, named after the color of its sand, a 20-minute drive away from the harbor. Brightly colored beehives dot the road, and indeed, the area is known for its delicate pineblossom honey.

Hiking

A walkers' guide is available at the tourist office near the dock at the harbor. Trails connect villages throughout the island, each of which has a distinct identity. Terrain varies from mountainous to flat, affording options for just about any walker or hiker. Even day-trippers can have a fascinating walk to the ancient ruins above the harbor town. One of the most challenging hikes is from Potamia, at the foot of Ipsarion, up the highest peak on Thasos (3,500 ft). Along the way, small, home-made ouzo distilleries are tempting, and, in the village itself, you can stroll through the museum housing the expressionistic works of the local sculptor Vargis. Everywhere, everyday scenes reflect life unchanged here for millennia: outdoor clay ovens and the scent of freshly baked bread; women on doorsteps, creating needlework; bags set in trees, straining whey for feta cheese; wood fires with bubbling cauldrons of figs and walnuts for Thassian sweets; donkeys laden with olive branches led by wizened villagers; herds of goats scattered over the roadside, foraging for anything within range. A walk in Thasos offers photo-ops around every turn.

Dining and Lodging

$ ★ **✗ Sirtaki.** Under tamarisk trees on the edge of a tiny beach at the far end of the harbor, dig into the fried squid or "sun-fried fish"—start with any salad. Vegetables are organically raised, and the loving care lavished on the food reflects the nature of the owners. Try the Thassian wine, dry, with a light aroma. (The area has been a major wine exporter since ancient times but today keeps most of it to itself.) Also good are Amelia, a liqueur made from local walnuts and honey, and fiery Tsipouro, similar to ouzo and just as potent. ⌧ *East end of town, past the harbor,* ☎ *0593/22651. No credit cards.*

$$$$ ★ **⊞ Makryammos Hotel.** Surrounded by a lush game preserve with strolling peacocks, this series of private bungalows on a curving, white-sand beach is a relaxing venue, especially for families. Guest rooms, while adequate, are not up to the surroundings. ⌧ *Limenas 64004,* ☎ *0593/22101 or 0593/22102,* FAX *0593/22761. 196 bungalows, 10 suites. Restaurant, bar, pool, 2 tennis courts, waterskiing, boating, children's program. AE, MC, V.*

$$$ **⊞ Hotel Amfipolis.** Behind an imposing iron gate, this converted mansion with a lush garden, one block inland from the harbor, is the most elegant place to stay in Limenas. Rooms are immaculate, wood-trimmed, with spare, local furnishings. Ben, the huge, rumply dog often slumbering by the reception desk, is a sweetheart who loves a nuzzle. ⌧ *Limenas 64004,* ☎ *0593/23101 through 0593/23104,* FAX *0593/22110. 42 rooms. Bar, dining room, outdoor café, pool. AE, MC, V.*

$$ **⊞ Alkyon.** Rooms in this in-town, family-run hotel are clean, airy, and adequate, but the reason to stay is the proprietor, Persephone, and her fabulous apple cake (she will happily recite the recipe, as well as talk philosophy and love). Rooms on the front side have balconies and views of the promenade; rear rooms are quieter and overlook a peach orchard and neighbors' houses. This hotel is 300 ft from the ferry terminal and 1,500 ft from the beach. ⌧ *Limenas Harbor 64004,* ☎ *0593/ 22138. 12 rooms. Café, tea shop. No credit cards. Closed in winter.*

$$ **⊞ Dionysos.** Spilling down a hill among pine forests, with splendid views of the Aegean, this group of blindingly white buildings outside a quiet, traditional village has locally inspired decor, and verandas from which to gaze and relax. It hugs the rugged terrain as if it has been there for years, but it was built in 1994. ⌧ *Panagia 64004,* ☎ *0593/61822, 33 rooms. Restaurant, bar, pool, meeting rooms. MC, V. Closed Nov.–Mar.*

$$ 🏨 **Timoleon.** The most convenient place to stay if you want to get around the island, this modest, functional hotel is owned by the president of the Hotel Association of Thasos. You can rely on getting info about sites and history. ⊠ *Harbor, facing central bus stop and next to tourist police, Limenas 64004,* ☎ *0593/22177 through 0593/22179,* FAX *0593/23277. 30 rooms with bath. Dining room. AE, MC, V.*

NORTHERN GREECE A TO Z

Arriving and Departing

By Bus

The trip from Athens takes about seven hours, with one rest stop. Buy tickets at least one day in advance (⊠ 100 Kifissou St., ☎ 01/5148856); one-way fare is 7,700 dr.

By Car

Driving to Greece from Europe through the former Yugoslavia is possible but often time-consuming owing to many border problems. You may prefer to drive through Italy and take a car ferry from Bari, Ancona, or Brindisi to Igoumenitsa on the west coast of Greece. This more beautiful route takes seven–eight hours, either by the northern route via Ioannina and Kozani, or via Ioannina, Kalambaka (and the famous Meteora monasteries), and Larissa. Both drives are spectacular, but the one to the south, used by regional buses, is much less treacherous and marginally faster. The Athens–Thessaloniki part of the National Road (500 km/310 mi), the best in Greece, takes five–seven hours.

By Plane

There are direct flights to Thessaloniki from London, Amsterdam, Brussels, Paris, Frankfurt, Stuttgart, Munich, Zurich, and Vienna, with good connections from the United States. You can also take an **Olympic Airways** flight to Thessaloniki from Athens. The airport is at Mikras (⊠ On the coast some 13 km/8 mi [20 minutes] southeast of the city center). A municipal bus to the airport (30 minutes; 200 dr. exact change) leaves at irregular intervals from the train station and makes a stop at Aristotelous Square opposite Electra Palace. Kavala also has an airport, with daily flights to Thessaloniki and Athens.

By Train

Three daily **express trains** connecting Athens and Thessaloniki take five–six hours; they are comfortable and air-conditioned. You can also take an **overnight train** with sleeping accommodations. Make reservations a few days in advance at the station or in Thessaloniki (⊠ 18 Leoforos Aristotelous, ☎ 031/517527 or 031/517517); express fare is 8,000 dr.; for other trains: first-class fare 5,580 dr., second class 3,750 dr.; sleeper surcharge from 2,500 dr. to 7,500 dr. Tickets can also be purchased at Zorpidis Travel (⊠ Egnatia 76, corner of Egnatia and Aristotelous).

Getting Around

By Bus

Intercity **KTEL** buses connect Thessaloniki with locations throughout Greece. There are small ticket office terminals (*praktorio*) for each line, usually located on the side of the city toward their destination. Ticket offices for departure to Athens (⊠ 67 Monastiriou, opposite the Thessaloniki train station, ☎ 031/51083 or 031/516104); Chalkidiki (⊠ 68 Karakasi St., in the southeastern suburb of Harilaou, ☎ 031/924444); Kavala (⊠ 59 Langada St., on the northwest side of Thessaloniki, ☎ 031/525530). For information about other offices contact the EOT (☞ *below*) or check the listings in the daily newspaper of all buses, trains, and airlines.

By Car

The roads in general are well maintained and constantly being improved and widened throughout the region. A good **four-lane highway** that begins in Athens (E90) goes to the border with Turkey (E84); beware, posted speed-limit speeds are exceedingly fast. Mobil gas stations sell excellent **road maps.** You can get information from the **Greek Automobile Touring Club** (ELPA; ✉ 230 Vasilis Olgas St., ☎ 031/420645). You can reserve space for yourself and your car on **ships** and **car ferries** traveling between ports throughout Greece at the **Plaris Travel Agency** (✉ 22 Pavlou Mela, ☎ 031/278613 or 031/232078, 🖷 031/286825) and **Zorpidis Travel** (✉ 76 Egnatius St., ☎ 031/286812 or 031/286825, 🖷 031/274422). In summer you should reserve a month in advance.

By Plane

Domestic carriers connect Thessaloniki with a number of cities and Mykonos, Santorini, Crete, Rhodes, Corfu, Limnos, Chios, and Lesbos. There are usually at least five daily flights to and from Athens, which take 40–45 minutes.

By Ship

Nomicos Lines ships connect Thessaloniki to Chios, Heraklion (Crete), Lesbos, Limnos, Mykonos, Paros, Santorini, Skiathos, Skiros, and Tinos. Buy tickets at the **Karaharissis Agency** (✉ N. Kountouriotous St., near Platia Eleftherios, ☎ 031/513005 or 031/524444).

By Train

The regional train service is not recommended; travel by bus is usually faster and always more dependable.

Contacts and Resources

Emergencies

Tourist Police (☎ 031/554871). **American Consulate** (☎ 031/242905). **Honorary British Consulate** (☎ 031/286696). **Honorary Canadian Consulate** (☎ 031/230456).

Guided Tours

Athos City Tours: Thessaloniki (✉ 5 Ayios Sofias, ☎ 031/264150); Chalkidiki (☎ 0377/71150, 🖷 0377/71399). **Doucas Tours** (☎ 031/269984). **Zorpidis Travel** (☎ 031/244400)..

Hiking and Climbing

ALMA eco-adventure tourism office (☎ 031/855629). **Chalkidiki Hotel Association** (✉ 33 G. Papandreou, Thessaloniki, ☎ 031/429020, 🖷 031/429021). **Hellenic Alpine Club** (✉ Thessaloniki, ☎ 031/278288 or 035/281944).

Pharmacies

Lists of late-night pharmacies are published in newspapers and posted in the windows of all pharmacies.

Visitor Information

The **Greek National Tourist Organization (GNTO or EOT)** regional office in Thessaloniki is open 8 AM–8 PM (✉ 8 Aristotelous Sq., ☎ 031/222935, 🖷 031/265504);airport (☎ 031/269984, ext. 215); **Kavala** (✉ 5 Filellinon St., ☎ 051/228762 or 051/222425, 🖷 051/223885).

American Educational Services (✉ 76 Egnatia, ☎ 031/264483).

Applications for bookings and visas can be made by writing to or visiting the **Ministry of Foreign Affairs** (✉ Department of Ecclesiastical Affairs, 3 Akadamias St., 6th floor, Athens 10671, ☎ 01/362–3144 or 01/362–3264); in Thessaloniki, write or go to the **Ministry of Macedonia and Thrace** (✉ Directorate of Political Affairs, Platia Dikasterion, Room 222, Ayiou Dimitriou St., Thessaloniki 54123, ☎ 031/270092). You should have a note attesting to the religious nature of your proposed visit from your consulate in Greece.

A easier way of doing this, particularly from abroad, is to contact Christos Sigoulis, manager of **Athos City Tours** (☞ *above*). He can do all of the paperwork for your visa and bookings prior to your arrival.

7 Corfu

Temperate, multihued Corfu—of emerald mountains; turquoise waters lapping rocky coves; ocher and pink buildings; shimmering silver olive leaves; puffed red, yellow, and orange parasails; scarlet roses, bougainvillea, and lavender wisteria and jacaranda spread over cottages—could have inspired Impressionism. The island has a history equally as colorful, reflecting the commingling of Corinthians, Romans, Goths, Normans, Venetians, French, Russians, and British. First stop, of course, is Corfu town—looking for all the world like a stage set for a Verdi opera.

THE IONIAN ISLANDS ARE ALL LUSH AND LOVELY, but Kerkyra, or Corfu, is the greenest and, quite possibly, the prettiest of all Greek islands. Homer's "well-watered gardens" and "beautiful and rich land" were Odysseus's last stop on his journey home. Corfu is also said to be the inspiration for Prospero's island in Shakespeare's *The Tempest*. This northernmost of the major Ionian Islands has, through the centuries, inspired other artists, as well as conquerors, royalty, and, of course, tourists. Today more than a million visitors a year—mainly English—enjoy and, in summer, crowd its evocative capital city. As a result, it is increasingly filled with stylish restaurants and resorts—but also package resorts and clogged roadways, blighting areas of its beauty. Still, the entire island has gracefully absorbed its many layers of history and combines neoclassical villas and ecosensitive resorts, horse drawn carriages and Jaguars—simplicity and sophistication—in an alluring mix.

By Lea Lane

Corfu lies strategically in the northern Ionian Sea at the entrance to the Adriatic, off the western edge of Greece. The lush, mountainous landscape seems more classic European than Greek, and indeed, this flower-filled island is only 72 km (45 mi) from Italy, and ⅔ km (1 mi) or so from Albania; some geologists believe it is the top of a submerged mountain range that broke off from the mainland. It is moderated by westerly winds, scored with fertile valleys, and punctuated by enormous, gnarled olive trees, planted over the course of 400 years by the Venetians. Figs, oranges, and grapes grow abundantly in the clear light and mild climate, and sunny beaches, traditional villages, and cosmopolitan atmosphere remain a potent mix here.

The Ionian islands' proximity to Europe and their sheltered position on the East–West trade routes made them prosperous; both their wealth and strategic position assured them a lively history of conquest and counter-conquest. The classical remains have suffered from this history and also from earthquakes; architecture from the centuries of Venetian, French, and British rule is most evident, leaving the towns with a pleasant combination of contrasting design elements.

In classical times, Corinth colonized the northern islands, but Corfu, growing powerful, revolted and allied itself with Athens, a fateful move that triggered the Peloponnesian War. Subjection followed: to the tyrants of Syracuse, the kings of Epirus and of Macedonia, and, in the 2nd century BC, to Rome. After the Byzantine Empire shattered, the islands fended for themselves against sporadic Germanic and Saracen invasions, and from the 11th to the 14th century were ruled by Norman and Angevin kings. Then came the Venetians, who protected Corfu from Turkish occupation and provided a 411-year period of peace for commercial development and the flowering of arts and letters. Venice also made Italian the official language, for a while, at least. Napoléon Bonaparte took the islands, which he called "the key to the Adriatic," after the fall of Venice. "The greatest misfortune which could befall me is the loss of Corfu," he wrote to Talleyrand, his foreign minister. Unfortunately for Bonaparte, he lost it within two years to a Russo-Turkish fleet, though, as the island was never occupied by the Turks, local culture continued to thrive here during the hated Turkish occupation of the rest of Greece.

For a short time the French regained and fortified Corfu from the Russians, and their occupation especially influenced the island's educational system, architecture, and cuisine. Theirs was a Greek-run republic—the first for modern Greece—which whetted local appetites for the independence that arrived later in the 19th century. But in 1814 the islands came under British protection; roads, schools, and hospitals were constructed, and commercialism developed. Corfu was ruled by a series of eccentric Lord High Commissioners, beginning with the much-hated Sir Thomas Maitland, and then by Sir Frederick Adam, who married a Corfiot lady with a heavy mustache. Nationalism finally prevailed, and the islands were ceded to Greece in 1864.

Corfu is the most developed of the Ionians, with a population of about 100,000. The island's northeast section has been heavily built up, although stony, inland farming villages seem undisturbed by civilizations that have come and gone, or even by today's events. Although it was bombed when the Italians and Nazis occupied it during World War II, the town of Corfu remains one of the loveliest in all of Greece and is a haven for travelers who return year after year. Desirability, of course, comes at a price: Corfu is expensive.

Pleasures and Pastimes

Boating
Calm waters in the coves and bays make boating a popular pastime. Sailors can moor boats at the new ports in Corfu town, at Gouvia Marina on the east coast, and at Paleokastritsa on the west coast. Motorboats and sailboats can be rented at the Old Port in Corfu town, in Paleokastritsa, Kondokali, and Kassiopi, and on the northeast coast. To charter a yacht or sailboat without a crew, you'll need a proficiency certificate from a certified yacht club. Corfu has customs and health authorities, passport control, supply facilities, and exchange services, and it is one of the few official entry-exit ports in Greece; from here you can sail throughout the islands.

Dining
The food, atmosphere, and prices at some Corfu town restaurants are as European as they are Greek, although inexpensive tavernas and typical Greek cuisine predominate throughout the island. As elsewhere in Greece, the demand for fresh fish often exceeds the supply. Be aware that lobster and seafood are often priced by the kilo, and injudicious ordering can easily produce an expensive meal in a moderate restaurant. To be sure, ask the price before ordering a dish, even if the waiter recommends it.

Greeks have been successfully storing grape juice in barrels for thousands of years, producing fine and interesting wines. Two great Greek whites are Hadjimichalis or Strofilia—but consistency can be a problem, especially with Corfu's Theotoki wines and other labels. Unfortunately, *hima* (barrel wine) isn't readily available in Corfu, as there are too few vineyards and too many tourists. Occasionally, restaurants serve barrel house wine with meals, and sometimes sell it by the bottle to go; try it—you'll rarely be disappointed. Bottled water can be bought everywhere, and you'll want to order it because Corfu's tap water is *not* one of its pleasures.

Corfiot specialties are served at most restaurants and tavernas. Those worth a try are *sofrito* (veal cooked in a sauce of vinegar, parsley, and plenty of garlic) served with rice or potatoes; *pastitsio* (beef cooked in a rich and spicy tomato sauce) served with spaghetti (always called "macaroni" in Greece); *bourdetto* (firm-fleshed fish stewed in tomato sauce with lots of hot red pepper); and *bianco* (whole fish stewed with potatoes, herbs, black pepper, and lemon juice).

If service has been satisfactory, it is customary to leave a tip of about 5% of the bill, since a service charge is included in the prices.

CATEGORY	COST*
$$$$	over 10,000 dr.
$$$	7,000 dr.–10,000 dr.
$$	3,000 dr.–7,000 dr.
$	under 3,000 dr.

for a three-course meal, including modest service charge and tax but excluding drinks

Golf

Corfu has one of the best golf courses on the Greek islands, near Ermones Bay in the Ropa Valley. The par-72, 18-hole course, with water hazards and well-kept fairways, is open to the public.

Lodging

Corfu has accommodations to satisfy every taste and budget, from in-town bed-and-breakfasts in renovated Venetian mansions to sleek resorts with children's camps and spas. If you're after peace and quiet, you can find it; but disco, drink, and crowds are readily available, too. Expect air-conditioning only in the $$$ or $$$$ categories. Larger accommodations have historically catered to groups, but the explosion of tourism in recent years has led to prepaid, low-priced package tours; these masses can get rowdy and overwhelm otherwise pleasant surroundings. You'll recognize the haunts of these beer-guzzling revelers, mainly in towns along the southeast coast.

Bargain hunters should go to the Greek National Tourist Organization (GNTO or EOT), which has a list of basic accommodations that are usually clean, comfortable, and inexpensive (☞ Visitor Information *in* Corfu A to Z, *below*). Rates can be negotiable, but a double room should cost around 5,000 dr.; Continental breakfast is often included, but you should ask. Telephones and radios are standard on the island, but hair dryers are not. Televisions are a rarity; it's noted below which places have them.

CATEGORY	COST*
$$$$	over 30,000 dr.
$$$	15,000 dr.–30,000 dr.
$$	10,000 dr.–15,000 dr.
$	under 10,000 dr.

All prices are for standard double rooms, usually including Continental breakfast but excluding tax.

Shopping

Prices are high here, but you can still find some bargains. Olive-wood bowls and carvings, hand embroidery, jewelry, silver, local wine and liqueurs, and dried herbs are a few of them. For the most picturesque picks, head to the shops that line the narrow streets of the Old Venetian Quarter in Corfu town.

Tennis

Courts and lessons are available in Corfu town, at the oldest tennis club in Greece. It's played in Kefalomandouko, where you can also take lessons. Most large hotels also have courts.

Water Sports

Fishing is unrestricted in Corfu's clear coastal waters. For a special pleasure, join local fishermen, who often will take groups out if you negotiate a fair deal. Sand and pebble beaches and coves edge the island, but the west coast has the widest sand beaches for sunning and swimming. Snorkeling and diving are best in the many rocky inlets and grottos on the northwest coast, and Paleokastritsa, Ermones, and Ipsos have diving schools where you can take lessons and rent equipment. The winds on the west coast are best for windsurfing, although the water on the east coast is calmer. Sailboards are available, and pedal and row-boats can be rented at many beaches. Waterskiing, water polo, para-sailing, jet-skiing, and other water-related activities sponsored by resorts are easily available.

Exploring Corfu

Corfu, about 64½ km (40 mi) long and up to 29 km (18 mi) wide with 201 km (125 mi) of sparkling, indented coastline, is small enough to cover completely in a few days. Roads vary from gently winding to spiraling, but they're generally well marked. The focus is Corfu town, but historic attractions are nearby, while valley farming villages are spread inland, and a series of coastal villages and towns are separated by mountains, coves, or beaches. Within a couple of turns the landscape can vary from flatland to rocky outcrop to mountains, but the green landscape and clear blue sea are constant.

Numbers in the text correspond to numbers in the margin and on the Corfu Town and Corfu maps.

Great Itineraries

Corfu must often be explored in a day by people off a cruise ship or ferry on a tour of the Greek islands. Two days allows enough time to visit Corfu town's nearby environs and most famous sites. For those with four days, time can be spent exploring the island's other historic sites and natural attractions along both coasts. And those with six days will get a closer look at the museums, churches, and forts, and some time to relax, perhaps even with a day trip to Albania.

IF YOU HAVE 2 DAYS

On the morning of the first day meander along the narrow, cobbled lanes of ⚏ **Corfu town** ①–㉓, have a bite at one of the cafés along the Liston, and then take in the view at the rooftop café of the Cavalieri hotel. If you can be torn away from the historic sector, spend the afternoon just south of Corfu town at the acropolis at nearby **Analipsis** ⑳, the ruins of the **Temple of Artemis** ㉑, and **Kanoni** ㉒, where you can see the most famous vista on Corfu—**Pontikonisi,** or **Mouse Island** ㉓. On the second morning drive to **Gastouri** ㉔ and the Achilleion, the 19th-century palace built for Empress Elizabeth of Austria. Then follow the inland road north from **Corfu town** to reach the beautiful northwest-coast resort area of ⚏ **Paleokastritsa** ㉕. You can pedal-boat into the grottoes, snorkel, dive, or relax on the beach. If you choose, return to **Corfu town** area for an overnight stay.

IF YOU HAVE 4 DAYS

Because Corfu is small, if you're driving, you can return to the same accommodations each night. Spend the first day the same way as in the two-day itinerary—but now you can relax, with more time to see Corfu town, before and after visiting other sites. On day two, start again at the Achilleion in **Gastouri** ㉔. In the afternoon, get to the beach resorts of **Ermones** ㉗ and/or ⚏ **Glyfada** ㉙. From ⚏ **Corfu town** ①–㉓, you hug the coast for a few miles with the mountains of Epirus a backdrop on your right; pass the bay at Gouvia, turn inland on Route 24, and explore the small farms in the fertile Ropa plain. On the third day go to ⚏ **Paleokastritsa** ㉕, and also see the ruins of Angelokastro in the mountains in **Lakones** ㉖. On the fourth day, take the coast road from **Corfu town** northeast around the bay, through a string of highly developed resort towns like ⚏ **Dassia, Ipsos, Pirgi,** and **Nissaki,** set among olive groves, beaches, hotels, and restaurants. The pretty coastal road now leads north to the most mountainous part of the island, to

Kouloura ㉛, historic **Kassiopi** ㉜, and the northern beaches of **Roda** ㉝ and **Sidari** ㉞.

IF YOU HAVE 6 DAYS

Follow the four-day itinerary above. ⛯ **Corfu town** ①–㉓ is worth a second or third visit to shop, sightsee, visit museums, and sit in the courtyards and absorb the pace of Corfian life. From **Kanoni** ㉒, you can take a boat trip to **Pontikonisi** ㉓. Those who don't mind tourist-filled towns can go farther south on the island, or head north to hike around **Mt. Pantokrator.** You might return to ⛯ **Glyfada** ㉙, where the beaches are the best on the island, or to ⛯ **Paleokastritsa** ㉕. Adventurers will take a day trip to Albania, only about 2 km (1 mi) away from the northern part of the island. Or just spend the extra days relaxing in the Corfian sun, or on one of the other Ionian islands—or even in Albania.

When to Tour

The best time to enjoy Corfu is April through June, and September through October, when the weather is at its finest, crowds are smallest, and sites, dining, and lodging are up and running. Unlike on most of the Greek Isles, winter months in Corfu can be rainy and cool, and although summers are not quite as hot as some of the more southern islands, overcrowding and humidity can make things uncomfortable.

Festivals are held throughout the year, especially around the Greek Orthodox holidays. Worth noting are Carnival, with a parade on the last Sunday before Lent; and Holy Week, including Easter Sunday, and the breaking of crockery on Holy Saturday. Bands accompany the processions carrying the remains of St. Spyridon, Corfu's patron saint, held four times a year: Palm Sunday, Holy Saturday, August 11, and the first Sunday in November. The Corfu Arts Festival is in September.

Visiting attractions and participating in activities early or late in the day will help you to avoid heat and long lines. Be sure to check on times and schedules before setting out, and watch out for the mid-afternoon closings. Greeks eat lunch and dinner quite late by American standards, so if you don't mind being unfashionable you can lunch at noon and dine at seven without having to battle for tables, saving precious time for seeing the sights or lazing around.

CORFU TOWN

16 km (10 mi) east of Glyfada, 26 km (16 mi) east of Paleokastritsa.

This lovely capital and cultural, historical, and recreational center is just off the middle of the island's east coast. All ships and planes lead to Corfu town, on a narrow strip of land hugged by the Ionian Sea. Though beguilingly Greek, much of Corfu's old town displays the architectural styles of many of its conquerors—molto of Italy's Venice, a soupçon of France, and more than a tad of England.

A Good Walk

This walk can take half a day or more, depending on how long you wander in the medieval section, and how far south you go along the bay. It encompasses the highlights of Corfu town, offers views beyond, and if you linger a bit here and there, observe daily life, and let yourself feel the slightly languid pace, you can get a real taste of the history and beauty of this famous town. If you arrive from mainland Greece by ferry, you will dock at the **Old Port** ① on the north side of town, just to the left of the **New Fortress** ②, with its British Citadel within. Just off the New Fortress Square is the **Museum of Sea Shells** ③, a short but charming stop to see what's under the Ionian sea.

Corfu Town

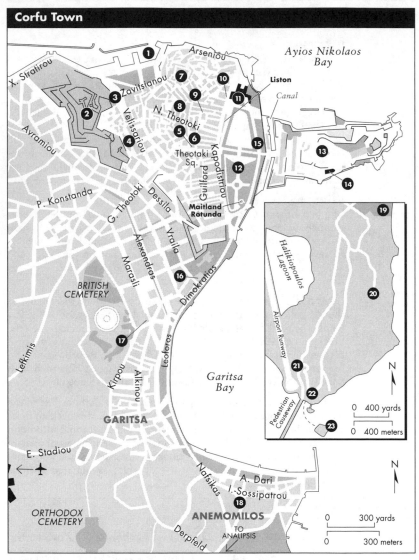

A five-minute walk from the museum has you crossing Tenedoy and continuing around the area of Velissariou, one of Corfu town's main streets, and the western edge of the historical center. Here is the former **Jewish Quarter** ④, with its old synagogue. From Velissariou, go southeast toward Voulgareos, turn left on Theotoki, and go left about 10 minutes to Theotoki Square (there are several Theotokis, with different first letters). Ahead is the ornate, marble, 17th-century **Town Hall** ⑤. Note the elaborate Venetian design, popular throughout the town. Adjacent is the neoclassical **Catholic Church of Ayios Iakovos,** ⑥, the Cathedral of San Giacomo. Go north on Theotoki to Filarmonikis, four blocks to the **Orthodox Cathedral** ⑦. This whole area, known as the medieval **Campiello** ⑧, is filled with narrow winding streets filled with artisans' shops, restaurants, and pretty squares.

From the cathedral, look up to see the nearby red bell tower of the **Church of St. Spyridon** ⑨, dedicated to the island's patron saint. The church is filled with silver treasures. If you keep the tower in sight you can wander as you wish without getting lost around this fascinating section. From the Church of St. Spyridon, continue northeast six blocks or so toward the water, enjoying the historic area as you go, and stopping whenever. At the north end of Kapodistriou is the historic **Corfu Reading Society** ⑩, with its grand outside staircase. From here go south two blocks to Ayios Ekaterinis. Just east is the colonnaded **Palace of St. Michael and St. George** ⑪. You are now at the north end of the **Esplanade** ⑫. You can stop at the arcaded Liston to shop or sit at a café and have a bite. Sunday cricket matches are played near here, and activity is always going on. Relax awhile, and then cross over the bridge to the **Old Fortress** ⑬ on the northeastern tip of Corfu town. In the southern section of the fort is the **Garrison Church of St. George** ⑭, with views of Albania.

On the walk back to the Esplanade along the central path is the **Statue of Count Schulenburg** ⑮, hero of the siege of 1716. The southern half of the Esplanade has a Victorian bandstand, Ionic Rotunda, and statue of Ioannis Kapodistrias, a Corfu resident and the first president of Greece. If you have the time and enjoy walking, go south along Leoforos Dimokratias along the water, about 10 minutes—longer if you stroll, which you may tend to do, enjoying the breeze. Just past the Corfu Palace hotel and the gardens of the Garitsa neighborhood on the right is the **Archaeological Museum** ⑯. The walk farther south along Garitsa Bay is pleasant, about 10 minutes to the **Tomb of Menekrates** ⑰, two blocks west on Menekratous. At the south end of Garitsa Bay, the suburb of Anemomilos (windmill) is crowned by the ruins of the Paleopolis church and the **Church of Ayios Iason and Ayios Sosipater** ⑱.

Sights to See

⑯ **Archaeological Museum.** This showcase exhibits finds from ongoing excavations. Note the Gorgon from the 56-ft-long pediment of the 6th-century BC Temple of Artemis (☞ *below*), from the ancient capital—one of the best-preserved pieces of archaic sculpture in Greece. This small museum is located just past the Corfu Palace Hotel. ⊠ *South of Esplanade along Leoforos Dimokratias,* ☏ *0661/30680.* ⬚ *800 dr.* ⊙ *Daily 9–4:30.*

⑧ **Campiello.** Narrow, winding streets and steep stairways make up the Campiello, the large, traffic-free medieval area of the town. Balconied Venetian buildings are mixed among multistory, neoclassical 19th-century ones built by the British, with laundry often hanging between them. Small cobbled squares centered with wells, high-belfried churches, and alleyways that lead nowhere and back, with artisans' shops along the way, add to an utterly lovely urban space. ⊠ *West of the Esplanade, between the 2 forts.*

⑥ Catholic Church of Ayios Iakovos. Built in 1588 and consecrated 50 years later, this elegant cathedral was erected to provide a grand place of worship for Corfu town's Catholic occupiers. If you use the Italian name, San Giacomo, locals will know it. Bombed by the Nazis in 1943, the cathedral's neoclassical facade of pediments, friezes, and columns was practically destroyed, but the bell tower remained intact. ⊠ *Next to the town hall.*

⑱ Church of Ayios Iason and Ayios Sosipater. The suburb of Anemomilos (windmill) is crowned by the ruins of the Paleopolis church and this 11th-century church. It is named after two of St. Paul's disciples, St. Jason and St. Sossipater, who brought Christianity to the island in the first century. The frescoes are faded, but its icons are beautiful, and the exterior, set in unspoiled greenery, is dramatic. This is one of only two Byzantine churches on the island; the other is in the northern coastal village of Ayios Markos. ⊠ *At the south end of Garitsa Bay.*

⑨ Church of St. Spyridon. Built in 1596, this church is the tallest on the island, thanks to its distinctive red-domed bell tower. The patron saint's internal remains—smuggled here after the fall of Constantinople and contained in a silver reliquary—are carried in procession four times a year, along with his mummified body, which can be seen through a glass panel; his slippered feet are actually exposed so that the faithful can kiss them. The saint was not a Corfian but originally a shepherd from Cyprus, who became a bishop before his death in AD 350. His miracles are said to have saved the island four times: once from famine, twice from the plague, and once from the hated Turks. During World War II, a bomb fell on this holiest place on the island but didn't explode. Maybe these events explain why it seems every other man on Corfu is named Spiros. ⊠ *In the center of the old town,* ☎ *0661/41350.* ⊠ *Free.*

⑩ Corfu Reading Society. The oldest cultural institution in modern Greece, the Corfu Reading Society was founded in 1836 and is filled with archives of the Ionian islands. Modeled after the Reading Society of Geneva, it is one of the loveliest buildings in Corfu and has a stunning exterior staircase leading up to a loggia. ⊠ *Kapodistriou,* ☎ *0661/39528.* ☉ *Daily 9–1, Thurs–Fri. 5–8.*

⑫ The Esplanade. Central to the life of the town, this huge, open parade ground on the land side of the canal is, many say, the most beautiful *spianada* (esplanade) in Greece. It is bordered on the west by a street lined with seven- and eight-storied Venetian and English Georgian houses, and arcades, called the **Liston** (modeled on the Parisian Rue de Rivoli, by the French architect Mathieu de Lesseps, under Napoleon's short occupation of Corfu). The name Liston refers to a list that the Venetians kept of lucky upperclass townspeople who were allowed to walk and linger here. Today, happily, its beauty can be enjoyed by all. Cafés spill out onto the passing scene, and Corfiot celebrations, games, and trysts occur in the sun and shadows. Sunday cricket matches, a holdover from British rule, are played on the northern half of the Esplanade, which was once a Venetian firing range. On the southern half of the Espanade are an ornate **Victorian bandstand**; a graffiti-covered **Ionic Rotunda,** built in honor of Sir Thomas Maitland, the not-much-loved first British Lord High Commissioner, appointed in 1814 when the island became a protectorate of Britain; and a **statue of Ioannis Kapodistrias,** a Corfu resident and the first president of Greece. He was also unfortunately, in 1831, the first Greek president to be assassinated. ⊠ *Between the Old Fortress and old town.*

⑭ Garrison Church of St. George. Landmarked by its distinctive Doric portico, this church was built in the mid-19th century. In summer there's folk dancing, and in August sound-and-light shows relate the Old Fortress's history. The views from here, east to the Albanian coast and west over the town, are splendid. ⊠ *In middle of Old Fortress.* ⊡ *Free.* ⊙ *Daily 8–7.*

➍ **Jewish Quarter.** This twist of streets was the home to 5,000 Jews from the 1600s until 1940. The community was decimated, sent to Auschwitz by the occupying Nazis. Fewer than 100 Jews survived. At the southern edge of the ghetto, a 300-year-old **synagogue** (☎ 0661/38802) with an interior in Sephardic style still proudly stands. ⊠ *South of the cathedral, 4th Parados, off Velissariou, 2 blocks from the new fort.*

➌ **Museum of Sea Shells.** An deep-sea collection considered the best in Europe is the treasure here, including shells, sponges, corals, sharks' jaws, snakes, and mysterious pickled creatures from throughout the world. ⊠ *Old Port on Solomou St. just off New Fortress Sq.,* ☎ *0661/28568.* ⊡ *500 dr.* ⊙ *Daily 10–7.*

➋ **New Fortress.** Built in 1577–78 by the Venetians three decades later than the "older" fortress, to strengthen defenses, the New Fortress was expanded by the French and the British to protect Corfu town from a possible Turkish invasion. The fort was a Greek naval base until 1992, when it was opened to the public. A classic **British citadel** stands at its heart. You can now wander through the maze of tunnels, moats, and fortifications, and the moat (dry now!) is the site of the town's marketplace. Note the best time to come here is early morning or late afternoon, out of the noonday sun. ⊠ *On a promontory northwest of the old fortress and medieval town,* ☎ *0661/22477.* ⊡ *800 dr.* ⊙ *Apr.– Oct., daily 9–9.*

⓭ **Old Fortress.** Originally, Corfu's population lived within the walls of the Old Fortress, or Citadel. Separated from the rest of the town by a moat once spanned by a movable wooden bridge, the fort is on the promontory mentioned by Thucydides. Its two heights, or *korypha* (bosom), gave the island its Western name. This striking landmark on the edge of the sea was built by the Venetians in 1546 on the site of a Byzantine castle. Most of the fortifications were blown up by the British when they left, but it's interesting to wander through the parts that remain. ⊠ *On northeastern point of Corfu Town peninsula.*

➊ **Old Port.** If you arrive from Igoumenitsa or Patras, on mainland Greece, your ferry will dock at the Old Port, on the north side of town, near the New Fortress.

➐ **Orthodox Cathedral.** This small, icon-filled cathedral was built in 1577. It is dedicated to St. Theodora, the island's second saint, whose headless body was brought to Corfu at the same time as St. Spyridon's remains. It now lies in a silver coffin by the altar; look for the shining gold icons, as well. Steps lead down to the harbor. ⊠ *In the southwest of the medieval quarter, east of St. Spyridon,* ☎ *0661/39409.*

⓫ **Palace of St. Michael and St. George.** This elegant, colonnaded 19th-century Regency structure was built as a residence for the Lord High Commissioner and headquarters for the order of St. Michael and St. George. The oldest official building in Greece, it was abandoned after the British left in 1864, and aptly renovated about a hundred years later by the British ambassador to Greece. The State Rooms were the setting for an EU summit meeting in June 1994. It contains a notable collection of Asian porcelains and bronzes and Byzantine relics, but these are due to be moved sometime in the future to another venue. ⊠ *At north end of Esplanade,* ☎ *0661/23124.* ⊡ *500 dr.* ⊙ *Tues.–Sat. 8:30– 3, Sun. 9:30–2:30.*

⑮ **Statue of Count Schulenburg.** This monument to the Austrian mercenary immortalizes the hero of the siege of 1716, which was the Turks' last (and failed) attempt to conquer Corfu. ⊠ *Along the central path of the Esplanade.*

⑰ **The Tomb of Menekrates.** Part of an ancient necropolis, the funerary items from this site are now exhibited in the Archaeological Museum (☞ *above*). ⊠ *South around Garitsa Bay, to the right of the obelisk dedicated to Sir Howard Douglas.*

⑤ **Town Hall.** The ornate marble, 17th-century Town Hall was built as a Venetian loggia and converted in 1720 into Greece's first modern theater—a far cry from the classic amphitheater pioneered in Epidaurus. A second story was added by the British before it became a grand town hall early in this century. ⊠ *Theotoki Sq.,* ☎ *0661/40401.* 🎟 *Free.* ☉ *Weekdays 9–1.*

Dining and Lodging

$$$$ ✕ **Albatros and Panorama Restaurants.** Both of these expensive restaurants in the Corfu Palace hotel (☞ *below*) have Swiss chefs and stylish service. The Albatross's terrace overlooks the pool, Garitsa Bay, and the gardens, and the Saturday night barbecue and buffet is a Corfu tradition; book well in advance. The Panorama is more luxurious but remains Corfu-comfortable. At both, local specialties are particularly good, and the international cuisine is exceptional. If you can't afford staying here, eating here will give you a taste of the very good life. ⊠ *Leoforos Democratias 2, Corfu Palace hotel,* ☎ *0661/39485. AE, DC, MC, V.*

$$$ ✕ **Aegli.** Right on the Liston, Aegli serves more than 100 different dishes, both local and international; the swordfish with red-pepper sauce is a treat. Tables in front, with comfortable armchairs and spotless tablecloths, overlook the nonstop parade on the promenade. For a more private meal, choose one of the 40 or so tables with white pine chairs inside, under the wood ceiling. The late-night cafeteria area serves beer, light snacks, sweets, and ice creams in more flavors than Baskin-Robbins. ⊠ *Liston,* ☎ *0661/31949. AE, DC, MC, V. Closed Dec.–Feb.*

$$$ ✕ **Quattro Stagioni.** Although hard to find in the twisting, narrow streets of the old town, this place has a bright and airy old-world feeling. The snails with butter and garlic sauce as well as the baked feta are great for starters. Try the typical local specialties, or, for a light alternative, the salads and pastas. Dessert might be yogurt and honey, or Black Forest gâteau. ⊠ *Maniarisi and Arlioti 16, Kaduni Bisi,* ☎ *0661/43956. AE, DC, MC, V. Closed Dec.–Feb.*

$$$ ✕ **Venetian Well.** On the most charming little square in the old town, with tables around a 17th-century well, this romantic restaurant—its staff tiptoes around lingering lovers—is as delicious as the food. The dining rooms in the handsome Venetian building are painted classic Greek blue, one with a satirical fresco painted by the owner's ex-wife. Greek and international specialties are served to operatic music. Creative entrées might include duck with kumquats or wild boar. ⊠ *Across from Church of the Panayia, Kremasti Sq.,* ☎ *0661/44761. AE, DC, MC, V.*

$$ ✕ **Fish Taverna Roula.** This is the place for bream, snapper, sardines, and whatever is fresh that day; you can even come early in the morning—and do during high season—to choose from the catch. When the fish runs out, Roula stops serving. Sit on the balcony under the enormous, ancient olive tree, and watch the boats on the bay. Follow the signs to the Kondokali Bay hotel (☞ *below*) and continue on, keeping your eyes open for the sign to Roula's. ⊠ *Kondokali,* ☎ *0661/91832. Reservations essential in high season. No credit cards.*

$$ ✕ **Rex Restaurant.** "We have air-conditioning," the waiter says, pointing up to a huge fan turning languidly, at this friendly Greek taverna

BONUS MILES MAKE GREATE SOUVENIRS.

```
MCI                    Calling Card

123 456 7891 2345
J.D. SMITH
                              WorldPhone
```

Earn Miles With Your MCI Card.

Take the MCI Card along on this trip and start earning miles for the next one. You'll earn frequent flyer miles on all your calls and save with the low rates you've come to expect from MCI. Before you know it, you'll be on your way to some other international destination.

Sign up for MCI by calling
1-800-FLY-FREE

Earn Frequent Flyer Miles.

AmericanAirlines
A'Advantage®

Continental Airlines
OnePass®

▲ Delta Air Lines
SkyMiles®

NORTHWEST
AIRLINES
WORLDPERKS®

MILEAGE PLUS.
United Airlines

US AIRWAYS
DIVIDEND MILES

Is this a great time, or what? :-)

MCI

Easy To Call Home.

1. To use your MCI Card, just dial the WorldPhone access number of the country you're calling from.
2. Dial or give the operator your MCI Card number.
3. Dial or give the number you're calling.

# Austria (CC) ♦	022-903-012
# Belarus (CC)	
From Brest, Vitebsk, Grodno, Minsk	8-800-103
From Gomel and Mogilev regions	8-10-800-103
# Belgium (CC) ♦	0800-10012
# Bulgaria	00800-0001
# Croatia (CC) ★	0800-22-0112
# Czech Republic (CC) ♦	00-42-000112
# Denmark (CC) ♦	8001-0022
# Finland (CC) ♦	08001-102-80
# France (CC) ♦	0-800-99-0019
# Germany (CC)	0800-888-8000
# Greece (CC) ♦	00-800-1211
# Hungary (CC) ♦	00▼800-01411
# Iceland (CC) ♦	800-9002
# Ireland (CC)	1-800-55-1001
# Italy (CC) ♦	172-1022
# Kazakhstan (CC)	8-800-131-4321
# Liechtenstein (CC) ♦	0800-89-0222
# Luxembourg	0800-0112
# Monaco (CC) ♦	800-90-019
# Netherlands (CC) ♦	0800-022-9122
# Norway (CC) ♦	800-19912
# Poland (CC) ÷	00-800-111-21-22
# Portugal (CC) ÷	05-017-1234
Romania (CC) ÷	01-800-1800
# Russia (CC) ÷ ♦	
To call using ROSTELCOM ■	747-3322
For a Russian-speaking operator	747-3320
To call using SOVINTEL ■	960-2222
# San Marino (CC) ♦	172-1022
# Slovak Republic (CC)	00-421-00112
# Slovenia	080-8808
# Spain (CC)	900-99-0014
# Sweden (CC) ♦	020-795-922
# Switzerland (CC) ♦	0800-89-0222
# Turkey (CC) ♦	00-8001-1177
# Ukraine (CC) ÷	8▼10-013
# United Kingdom (CC)	
To call using BT ■	0800-89-0222
To call using C&W ■	0500-89-0222
# Vatican City (CC)	172-1022

Flying to France on Friday? Get Francs from Chase on Thursday. Call Currency To Go at 935-9935 for overnight delivery.

r pounds for London. Or Deutschmarks for Düsseldorf. Or any of 75 foreign currencies. Call **Chase Currency To Go**[SM] at **935-9935** in area codes 212, 718, 914, 516 and Rochester, N.Y.; all other area codes call 1-800-935-9935. We'll deliver directly to your door.* Overnight. And there are no exchange fees. Let Chase make your trip an easier one.

CHASE. The right relationship is everything.[SM]

set within a 19th-century town house. Try the local specialties such as *stifado* (meat stewed with sweet onions, white wine, garlic, cinnamon, and spices) or the *lachano dolmades* (cabbage leaves stuffed with seasoned ground meat and rice). The *stamna* (lamb baked with potatoes, rice, beans, and cheese) is delicious. Outside tables are perfect for people-watching. ⊠ *Kapodistriou 66, just west of Liston,* ☎ *0661/39649. No credit cards. No dinner. Closed Sun.*

$ ✕ **O Yiannis.** South of town, this popular restaurant is unpretentious and full of locals. It's also cheap: You'll be hard-pressed to tally up 3,000 dr. on the barrel wine and wide variety of imaginative dishes, which you can check out in the kitchen. Try the stifado, the pork with Brussels sprouts, or the dolmades. For the bold, there's also *hordi* (intestines baked with a flavorful sauce). Order an ample supply of starters and hima, and eat in good company, while checking out the ancient photos of Corfu's old-timers. ⊠ *Sophia Kremona and Iassonos-Sossipatrou 30, Anemomilos,* ☎ *0661/31066. Reservations not accepted. No credit cards.*

$$$$ ▦ **Corfu Palace.** Overlooking the bay, 100 yards from the center of town, this elegant hotel is one of the most beautiful in Greece, filled with old-world grandeur. Spacious rooms, furnished in Louis XIV and Empire style, have TVs and wide balconies with splendid views of gardens and water. The bathrooms have hair dryers and telephones, and attention has been paid to every detail. Guests can play tennis at the nearby Corfu Tennis Club and use the facilities of the Corfu Yacht Club (☞ Outdoor Activities and Sports, *below*). ⊠ *Leoforos Democratias 2, 49100,* ☎ *0661/39485,* FAX *0661/31749. 103 rooms, 12 suites. 2 restaurants, 2 bars, minibars, room service, outdoor saltwater pool, indoor saltwater pool, health club, shops, baby-sitting, meeting rooms. AE, DC, MC, V.*

$$$$ ▦ **Imperial Palace.** On a 14-acre peninsula jutting into Komeno Bay in an upscale residential area, 10 km (6 mi) north of town, this deluxe resort complex run by top Greek chain Grecotel has luxury rooms and bungalows that focus on comfortable elegance, with balconies and sea views. This is a "green" hotel, respectful of the environment despite its extensive facilities. ⊠ *Komeno Bay, 49100,* ☎ *0661/91481,* FAX *0661/91881. 176 rooms, 124 bungalows. Restaurant, 2 bars, pool, beauty salon, 2 tennis courts, beach, waterskiing, boating, shops, dance club, laundry service. AE, DC, MC, V. Closed Nov.–Apr.*

$$$ ▦ **Cavalieri Hotel.** In this venerable, eight-story building near the arcade of the Liston, get a room on the fourth or fifth floor with a number ending in 2, 3, or 4 for a breathtaking view of the Old Fort. The building is swank, yet graceful and chock-full of history. Have a drink at the usually empty but delightful English-style wood-paneled bar. Best of all is the roof garden, which offers light meals and the most remarkable view in town. ⊠ *4 Kapodistriou, 49100,* ☎ *0661/39041,* FAX *0661/39283. 50 rooms. Restaurant, bar. AE, DC, MC, V.*

$$$ ▦ **Kontokali Bay.** When you tire of exploring the streets and museums in town, this hotel about 6½ km (4 mi) north of town is a fine place to relax. The pastel guest rooms, with modern wood appointments, are cheerful and sunlit, with safes, minibars, and balconies facing the sea, the mountains, or the lake. There's a buffet and grill restaurant that serves Greek and Italian cuisine. ⊠ *Kondokali Bay, 49100,* ☎ *0661/38736,* FAX *0661/91901. 152 rooms, 82 bungalows. 2 restaurants, bar, room service, pool, 2 lighted tennis courts, beach, dock, waterskiing, boating, dance club, children's program. AE, DC, MC, V. Closed Nov.–Mar.*

$$ ▦ **Hotel Bella Venezia.** This two-story Venetian building in the center of town was operated as a hotel as early as the 1800s. Though it's in a lower classification—and price range—because it lacks views and a restaurant, its large lobby with a marble floor and wood-paneled ceiling and its huge garden make it quite pretty and grand. The rooms are small but tastefully furnished, and they have radios, telephones, and

TVs. Breakfast is held on a patio. All in all, it's a good value for the money. It's just behind the Cavalieri Hotel (☞ *above*). ✉ *4 Zambelli, 49100,* ☎ *0661/46500,* FAX *0661/20708. 32 rooms. Lobby lounge, snack bar. AE, DC, MC, V.*

$ ⛫ **Hotel Cyprus.** Staying here will be an adventure, but the price is certainly right. The rooms at this hotel are clean, but the seemingly ancient building and the odds and ends of furniture—not to mention the masonry and walls—are in need of repair. Perhaps the Ministry of Culture is holding out on issuing a historic- building special repair permit. ✉ *13 Ayios Pateron, 49100,* ☎ *0661/30032. 16 rooms with shared bath. No credit cards.*

$ ⛫ **Hotel Konstantinoupoulis.** A hotel for more than 200 years, this can be most ambitiously called traditional. But rooms are reasonably clean and acceptable if you're on a budget. Long-distance phone calls can be made in the lobby, a rarity in low-cost hotels. It's opposite the dock for car ferries to the islands, with a great view of the old port. ✉ *Zavitsianou 11, Old Port, 49100,* ☎ *0661/39826. 44 rooms with shared bath. No credit cards.*

Nightlife and the Arts

BAR

For sunset views with your ouzo and mezedes, try the **Acteon Bar,** on the water just south of the Old Fort. For even better views, the rooftop bar at the Cavalieri Hotel (☞ *above*) can't be bettered. **Bill's Bar** (✉ On the main drag of the Commercial Center) has a quiet scene, with a definite trend toward music from the '60s, slower dancing, and even a taste of blues.

DISCOS AND NIGHTCLUBS

Just past the Commercial Center, 3 km (2 mi) west of town is a string of **discos** that really don't start swinging until after midnight. They have names like **Sax, Slik, Electron, Bora Bora, Slaze, Astral, Rondo, Mobile Club, Interview, Hippodrome,** and **LA Boom,** and they throb with all the latest international sounds and styles, from heavy metal to rap, techno, and fusion. Incredibly loud sound systems are just what the young T-shirted crowd needs for dancing into the wee hours of the morning. A drink costs about 1,000 dr., and most of the clubs charge 3,500 dr. to get in and for the first drink. Greek clubs come and go by the minute, so be sure to ask the concierge and locals for the current hot spots.

At **Ekati** (✉ Opposite the main junction) crowds are more sophisticated and older, but the volume of the live music is nevertheless high for the *skiladiko* (roughly, "dog party"). Chichi is the theme here, with excessive baubles and Paris collections; buy a whisky bottle for your table, carnations to throw at your favorite performer, and a plate or two to break if you're in the mood. Drinks cost 1,500 to 2,000 dr. It's at the end of the disco strip.

FILM

Corfu town has an indoor cinema showing undubbed American flicks at the **Pallas** (✉ North of Platia San Rocco). Go to the **outdoor theater** (✉ Halfway down Marasli, seaside, on the right) on especially nice evenings.

MUSIC

Corfiots love music, from traditional bouzouki to classical. Corfu town has more than a dozen **small orchestras,** a **choir,** and a **chamber music group.** Sunday concerts are held at the bandstand on the esplanade throughout the summer, and brass bands can often be heard throughout the town. For entertainment information in English, tune into Radio Rama: 96.3 FM, Monday–Saturday 3–5.

Outdoor Activities and Sports

SAILING

The **Corfu Yacht Club** (✉ Corfu town, ☎ 0661/25759) offers sailing training courses.

TENNIS

The **Corfu Tennis Club** (✉ Between I. Romanou and Kalosgourou Sts., west of the Corfu Palace hotel), founded in 1896, is the oldest in Greece. You may rent courts and take lessons.

SOUTH OF CORFU TOWN

Just south of Corfu town, near the suburb of Kanoni, are several of Corfu's most unforgettable sights, including the lovely vista of Pontikonisi—famed throughout the world as Mouse Island—and Empress Elizabeth of Austria's Achilleion, an amazing extravaganza of a palace. The villages south of Benitses have become overrun with raucous package-tour groups and have lost much of their original charm. Unless you seek a hard-drinking, late-night crowd, and beaches chockablock with activities and tanning bodies, opt for other parts of the island.

Mon Repos

4 km (2½ mi) mi south of Corfu town.

⑲ Along the road to Kanoni is the **palace of Mon Repos** (✉ Near the public beach of Mon Repos), surrounded by gardens. It was built in 1824 by Sir Frederic Adam for his wife, and it was later the summer residence of the Lord High Commissioners. Prince Philip, Duke of Edinburgh, was born here. The villa, which belongs to the former King Constantine of Greece, was expropriated by the Greek government in 1990; the king has appealed. Though closed to the public, the extensive grounds are open from April to October. Opposite Mon Repos are ruins of Ayia Kerkyra, the 5th-century church of the Old City.

Analipsis

⑳ *4 km (2½ mi) south of Corfu town, just south of Mon Repos.*

The village of Analipsis was built on the site of an acropolis, and a path leads to a spring where the Venetians gathered drinking water for their ships.

En Route Along the road to Kanoni, you'll pass through gardens and parks to
㉑ the ruins of the archaic **Temple of Artemis** and past the **lagoon of Halikiopoulou** down to the tip of the peninsula.

Kanoni

㉒ *5½ km (3½ mi) south of Corfu town. 1½ km (1 mi) south of Analipsis.*

At Kanoni, the site of the ancient capital, you may behold Corfu's most picturesque view, which looks out over two lovely islets. A French cannon once stood in this hilly landscape, which is now built up and often noisy because of the nearby airport.

From Kanoni, against the backdrop of the green slopes of Mount Ayia Deka, is the serene view of two tiny islets: One, **Moni Viahernes,** is
㉓ reached by causeway. The other islet, **Pontikonisi,** famed throughout the world as Mouse Island, has a white convent and, beyond, tall cypresses guarding the 13th-century chapel. Legend has it that the island is really Odysseus's ship, which Poseidon turned to stone here: the reason why Homer's much-traveled hero was shipwrecked on Phaeacia

Corfu

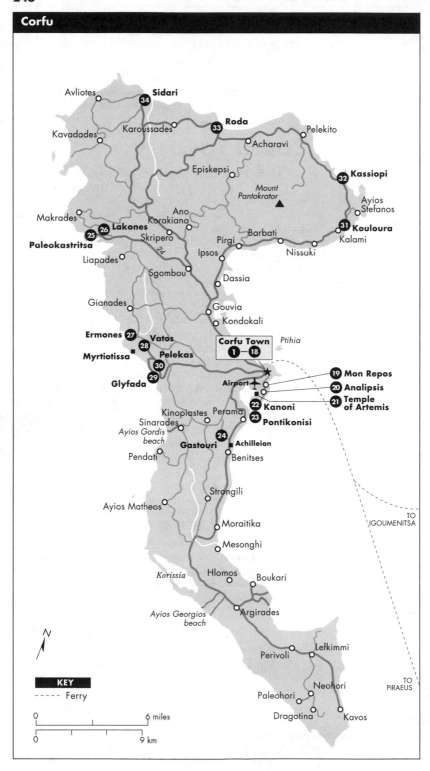

Avliotes

Sidari 34

Kavadades

Karoussades

Roda 33

Pelekito

Acharavi

Episkepsi

Mount Pantokrator

Kassiopi 32

Ayios Stefanos

Makrades

26 **Lakones**

25

Paleokastritsa

Ano Korakiana

Skripero

Pirgi

Barbati

31 **Kouloura**

Kalami

Liapades

Sgombou

Ipsos

Nissaki

Gianades

Dassia

Gouvia

Kondokali

Ermones 27

Vatos

28

Pelekas

30

Corfu Town
1 — 18

Ptihia

Myrtiotissa

29 **Glyfada**

Airport

19 **Mon Repos**

20 **Analipsis**

21 **Temple of Artemis**

22 **Kanoni**

23 **Pontikonisi**

Kinopiastes

Perama

Sinarades

Ayios Gordis beach

24

Gastouri

■ **Achilleion**

Pendati

Benitses

Strongili

Ayios Matheos

Moraitika

Mesonghi

Korissia

Hlomos

Boukari

Ayios Georgios beach

Argirades

TO IGOUMENITSA

Lefkimmi

Perivoli

TO PIRAEUS

Neohori

Paleohori

Dragotina

Kavos

KEY

----- Ferry

0   6 miles

0   9 km

(Corfu) in the *Odyssey*. In summer you can take a little launch or pedal boat to visit it—or even swim there.

Lodging

$$$$ ⊡ **Corfu Holiday Palace.** Don't get this big and busy group-oriented hotel confused with its more elegant, almost-namesake, the Corfu Palace. A sleek and curving former Hilton, it has extensive facilities, including the island's only casino. Modern wood-paneled rooms offer panoramic views. The less-expensive "lake view" rooms in back look over the lagoon and the nearby airport. ⊠ *On beach at Kanoni, 49100,* ☎ *0661/36540,* FAX *0661/36551. 205 rooms, 14 suites, 37 bungalows. 2 restaurants, bar, snack bar, room service, 2 saltwater pools, sauna, 2 tennis courts, golf privileges, bowling, health club, beach, boating, casino, meeting rooms. AE, DC, MC, V.*

Gastouri

㉔ *19 km (11¾ mi) southwest of Corfu town, 23 km (14¼ mi) southwest of Kanoni.*

The village of Gastouri, still lovely despite the summer onrush of day-trippers, is the site of the palace **Achilleion,** in remarkable bad taste (Lawrence Durrell called it "a monstrous building"), but redeemed by lovely gardens stretching to the sea. Built in the late-19th century by the Italian architect Rafael Carita for Empress Elizabeth of Austria, it was a retreat for her to nurse her health and her heartbreak over husband Franz Josef's numerous affairs. Elizabeth named the palace after her favorite hero, Achilles, whom she identified with her son. After she was assassinated, Kaiser Wilhelm II bought it and lived here until the outbreak of World War I, after which he still used it as a summer residence. After the armistice, the Greek government received it as a spoil of war.

The interior contains a **pseudo-Byzantine chapel, a pseudo-Pompeian room,** and a **pseudo-Renaissance dining hall,** culminating in a vulgar fresco called *Achilles in His Chariot.* One of the more interesting furnishings, as bizarre as the rest of the building, is Kaiser Wilhelm II's saddle seat, used at his desk. On the terrace, which commands a superb view over Kanoni and the town, is an Ionic peristyle, with a number of statues, in various degrees of undress. The best is *The Dying Achilles.* In 1962 the palace was restored and leased as a gambling casino and was the setting for the casino scene in the James Bond film *For Your Eyes Only.* The casino has since moved to the Corfu Holiday Palace (☞ *above*). A **museum** on the ground floor of Achellion contains mementos and portraits, and rooms are available for meetings. ⊠ *Past resort area of Perama,* ☎ *0661/56210.* 🖼 *700 dr.* ☾ *Daily 9–4:30 (winter 9–2).*

Dining and Lodging

$$$$ ✕ **Taverna Tripas.** Surrounded by dusty wine bottles, hanging meats, and sundry stuffed birds and animals, you are in for an experience at this most famous restaurant on Corfu, 13 km (8 mi) up the mountains southwest of Corfu town. It has now become terribly tourist-ridden, though you might recognize important politicians or well-known artists. You'll get an impressive array of *mezedakia* (delicious tidbits) and do try the fine barrel retsina. Live music and traditional Greek dances add to the festivity. ⊠ *Kinopiastes,* ☎ *0661/56333. Reservations essential in high season. AE, DC, MC, V.*

$$$$ ⊡ **San Stefano.** Close to the Achillion Palace and 900 ft from the beach, this modern hotel commands a hill overlooking the water in 35 acres of garden. Rooms have balconies to savor the coastline vistas. Families will find lots to do here, with a children's program and nightly entertainment, and the facilities are extensive enough to host big-deal

European conferences. ⊠ *Benitses 49084, 11 km (6½ mi) from Corfu town on the main road.* ☎ *0661/71112-18,* FAX *0661/71124. 238 rooms, 21 suites. 2 restaurants, 3 bars, pool, 2 tennis courts, boating, waterskiing, children's program. AE, DC, MC, V. Closed Dec.–Mar.*

THE WEST COAST

The agricultural Ropa Valley divides the sandy beaches and freshwater lagoon of the lower west coast from the dramatic mountains of the northwest. Hairpin bends take you through orange and olive groves, over the mountainous spine of the island to the rugged bays and promontories of the northwest coast. Here the road descends to the sea, where two headlands, 130 ft high and covered with trees and boulders, form a pair of natural harbors. This is an especially fine area for outdoor recreation.

Paleokastritsa

㉕ *25 km (15½ mi) northwest of Corfu town, 21 km (13 mi) northwest of Kanoni.*

Identified by archaeologists as the site of Homer's city of the Phaeacians, this area of grottoes and cliffs has a big rock called Kolovri, resembling the mythological ship that brought Ulysses home. The natural beauty and water sports of Paleo, as Corfiots call it, have brought hotels, tavernas, bars, and shops to the hillsides above the bays, and the beaches swarm with hordes of people on day trips from Corfu town. But this spectacular spot of three large coves, rock formations, and turquoise waters is definitely worth a visit.

A **17th-century monastery** is set on the site of an earlier one, among terraced gardens overlooking the Ionian Sea. Its treasure is a 12th-century icon of the Virgin Mary, and there's a small **museum** with some other early icons. On the ceiling, note the Tree of Life motif. Be sure to visit the **inner courtyard** (go through the church), built on the edge of the cliff, dappled white, green, and black by the sunlight on the stonework, vine leaves, and habits of the hospitable monks. Under a roof of shading vines you look precipitously down to the placid green cove and the torn coastline stretching south. ⊠ *On northern headland.* 🎫 *Free, but donation expected.* ☉ *Daily 7–1 and 3–8.*

En Route   Eight kilometers (5 miles) northeast of Corfu, just off the road to Paleo, is a re-creation of a 200-year-old Corfiot village, complete with people working at crafts, olive and wine presses, animals and shepherds in the fields, an agricultural museum, and an Orthodox church. **Danilia Village** (⊠ *2 km/1 mi outside Gouvia;* ☎ *0661/36833* reservations) condenses much of what can be found inland only if you have enough time to seek it. Cost is 12,000 dr. for everything including dinner, drinks, and transportation; it's open Monday–Saturday, closing midday and reopening for dinner. For day-trippers, kids, and fun-loving adults who don't mind faux-Williamsburgs and a virtual day in a frankly fake village, this is a fun tourist stop. At night, the taverna is filled with bouzouki and retsina and a crowd singing and dancing like Zorba.

㉖ The village of **Lakones** (⊠ *5 km/3 mi northeast of Paleokastritsa*) is on the steep mountain behind the monastery. Crested by the grim **ruins of Angelokastro**, it was built in the 13th century on an inaccessible pinnacle by a despot of Epirus during his brief rule over Corfu. It sheltered Corfiots in 1571 from attack by Turkish wanna-be conquerors. Look for the chapel and caves, which served as sanctuaries for hermits. The road to this spot was reputedly built by British troops in part to reach Lady Adam's favorite picnic place, the Bella Vista terrace. Kaiser Wilhelm also came here to enjoy the magnificent view of Paleokastritsa's coves.

NEED A
BREAK? Though it may be crowded, having a drink and savoring the view at the **Bella Vista Café** (⊠ On a bluff) is worth the wait.

Dining and Lodging

$$ ✕ **Chez George.** Overlooking the rock of the bay in Paleokastritsa, where Homer's wine-dark sea touches forest-green mountains, the view here is one of those Greek keys that explain all. As for the food, the pork chops are delicious and the *horiatiko* (village salad) is a tasty mix of carrot and onion with the hackneyed tomato, cucumber, feta, and olive combo. Some relevant thoughts: Order simply, don't buy the wine, and remember that moderate prices seldom go with gorgeous vistas. ⊠ *The rock, Paleokastritsa,* ☎ *0663/41233. MC, V.*

$$$ 🏨 **Akrotiri Beach Hotel.** Newly renovated and looking sparkling, this modern, five-story resort sits on a private little peninsula, and balconies in the stylish, well-equipped rooms overlook dreamy views of grottoes and turquoise water. This place is great for families, and for nature-lovers who desire the comforts of room service and minibars as well. ⊠ *Paleokastritsa 49100,* ☎ *0663/41237,* FAX *0663/ 41277. 127 rooms. 2 restaurants, 2 bars, 2 pools, tennis court, boating, snorkeling, mountain bikes, shops, playground, parking. AE, MC, V. Closed Nov.–June.*

$$ 🏨 **Fundana Villas.** On a hilltop in the mountains west of Corfu town, surrounded by gardens and olive and orange groves, this special complex comprises 10 villas built in and around a 17th-century stone-and-mortar Venetian storehouse, with walls almost a yard thick. The common room–bar still contains the huge olive press and an old stone mill. You can really imagine life hundreds of years ago and at the same time enjoy modern baths and kitchens. It's unique, and an ideal place for families interested in biking, exploring, and discovering history. The villas are a short drive from the Paleokastritsa beaches; you will need your own transportation. ⊠ *Spyros Spathas, Box 167, 49100,* ☎ *0663/22532,* FAX *0663/22453. 10 villas. Playground. No credit cards. Closed Nov.–Mar.*

Outdoor Activities and Sports

DIVING

The clear water is wonderful for underwater adventure, but it can get crowded in the shallows. Diving lessons and equipment are available at the **Barracuda Club** (⊠ On the water in Paleokastritsa, ☎ 0663/ 41211).

Ermones

㉗ *16 km (10 mi) west of Corfu town, 6 km (4 mi) south of Paleokastritsa.*

South of Paleokastritsa, across the fertile Ropa Valley, is the resort of Ermones, with good, pebbly sand beaches; heavily wooded cliffs; water with plentiful fish; large hotels; and a backdrop of green mountains. The Ropa River flows into the Ionian Sea here.

Beach

The little sheltered **beach at Kondo Yialo** (⊠ Just south of Ermones) is especially beautiful.

Outdoor Activities and Sports

GOLF

The island's only golf course is here, at the **Corfu Golf Club** (⊠ Ermones, ☎ 066/94220), linked to the beach by an elevator. Look forward to a par-72, 18-hole course, with water hazards, well-kept fairways, rentals, lessons, a pro shop, and a clubhouse with a restaurant and bar. It's open to the public, and reservations can be booked through hotels.

Vatos

28 *24 km (15 mi) west of Corfu town, 2 km (1 mi) west of Ermones.*

Vatos is an inland agricultural village, clinging to a hill and to the simplicity of the past. Its considerable charms can be discovered by sitting at one of the couple of tavernas with the locals and just observing details and everyday goings-on. Let your eyes roam and you might find balconies filled with pansies in terra-cotta pots, whitewashed cottages and rocky walls, farmers tilling fields in the cool of the evening, boys throwing olives into black nets, a skinny dog chasing an even skinnier cat, men playing cards and laughing, women all in black sitting on stoops, gossiping. This is the real world, far from the sophistication of Corfu town, but in its way just as special.

Glyfada

29 *16 km (10 mi) west of Corfu town, 6 km (4 mi) south of Ermones.*

The large, sandy Glyfada beach is packed with busloads of bathers and sun worshipers on day trips from Corfu town. The area is filled with hotels, condos, tavernas, and discos.

In the village of Sinarades on the west coast, there's a **folk art museum** (⊠ Sinarades, ☎ 0661/35673), exhibiting a private collection of local costumes, embroidery, furniture, and pottery. It's open Tuesday to Sunday 9:30 to 12:30.

Lodging

$$$ 🏨 **Louis Grand Hotel Glyfada.** Two patios with Japanese gardens redeem this otherwise overdone, quasi-Asian setting. The guest rooms are basic, and air-conditioning operates at the manager's whim. Buffets spotlight Greek specialties; the bar is done in a Viennese theme, a nod to the hotel's Germanic package tours. There's a children's program and a game room. The social staff keeps things jumping in summer, running courtesy cars to town and the golf course. The hotel is at the biggest, sunniest beach on the island. ⊠ *46 Diadochou Pavlou, Glyfada 49100,* ☎ *0661/94140–5,* 🖷 *0661/94146. 242 rooms. 2 restaurants, 2 bars, saltwater pool, 2 lighted tennis courts, boating, waterskiing, nightclub, children's program. AE, MC, V. Closed Nov.–Mar.*

Pelekas

30 *13 km (8 mi) west of Corfu town, 2 km (1 mi) north of Glyfada.*

Just inland from Glyfada is Pelekas, a hilltop village that overfills with tourists because of its much- touted lookout point called the **Kaiser's Throne,** where German Kaiser Willhelm II enjoyed the sunset when not relaxing at the Achilleion Palace. This rocky hilltop does deliver spectacular views of the entire island and sea beyond.

A 14th-century monastery on the west coast is the **Myrtiotissa** (⊠ Below Mt. Ayios Georgios), 3 km (2 mi) or a one-hour walk north of Pelekas, and a half-hour walk (2 km/1 mi) south of Vatos.

Beaches

The long, sandy **beach at Pelekas** is well known and popular with nudists. The isolated **beach at Myrtiotissa,** between sheer cliffs, is noted for its good snorkeling and nude sunbathing. Backed by olive and cypress trees, this sandy stretch was called by Lawrence Durrell in *Pros-*

pero's Cell (with debatable overenthusiasm) "perhaps the loveliest beach in the world." Alas, the statement has brought summer crowds.

Dining

$$ ✕ **The Nornberg.** Everybody in the area knows this restaurant as Mihali's in Livadi Ropa, about a mountainous 13 km (8 mi) west of Corfu town. It's a *psistaria* (grill taverna), and it's one of the best. First savor fried eggplant, *tzatziki* (yogurt, chopped cucumber, and garlic), fresh salad, and feta. Mihali Moumouris bastes the best local meat—maybe *paidakia* (lamb chops) or pork chops—with lemon juice and local olive oil, sprinkles it with salt and fresh oregano, and grills it over charcoal. And don't forget to order some of his homemade retsina. ✉ *Livadi Ropa,* ☎ *0661/51473. No credit cards.*

NORTH OF CORFU TOWN

The main roads along the northeast coast just above Corfu town are crowded with hotels, gas stations, and tourist cafés and shops. But head inland a bit and you'll find more peaceful settings—dusty villages where olives, herbs and home-brewed wine are the main products, with goats roaming the squares and chickens pecking at the roadsides. Steep Mt. Pantokrator (The Almighty), at 2,970 ft the highest peak on Corfu, forms the northeast lobe of the island. The northern coastal area is replete with pretty coves, and it has the longest sand beach in Corfu, curving around Roda to Archaravi.

Kouloura

③ *31 km (19¼ mi) northeast of Corfu town.*

This pretty harbor town is on a U-shape bay enclosed by cypress, eucalyptus, and palm trees and has a small shingle beach with close views of the Albanian coastline. This is the part of Corfu immortalized by Gerald Durrell in *My Family and Other Animals,* and by his brother Lawrence in *Prospero's Cell,* which was written in a taverna called the **White House** (✉ In Kalami). Donkeys still plod the roads, cafés serve local wine, and life here on the lower slopes of Mt. Pantokrator holds its sweet charm, even when besieged by tourists in July and August.

Lodging

$$$ 🏨 **Corfu Chandris and Dassia Chandris Hotels.** This huge two-hotel complex is set in 25 acres of gardens, with private chalets and bungalows for groups. The public areas feature scads of marble; the modern guest rooms are comfortable and basic, with large sea-view balconies, radios, and telephones. These two hotels are 11 km (7 mi) north of Corfu town and about the same distance south of Kouloura in an overbuilt stretch of roadway. ✉ *Dassia 49100,* ☎ *0661/33871 through 0661/33875,* 🖷 *0661/93458;* ✉ *Athens Chandris Hotel, 385 Syngrou, P. Faliron, Athens 17564* ☎ *01/941–4824 through 01/941–4826,* 🖷 *01/942–5055. 526 rooms. Restaurant, bar, lobby lounge, room service, pool, beauty salon, 4 tennis courts, golf privileges, beach, boating, parasailing, waterskiing, shops, playground, meeting rooms. AE, DC, MC, V. Closed Nov.–Mar.*

Kassiopi

③ *36 km (22½ mi) northeast of Corfu town, 7 km (4½ mi) north of Kouloura.*

Kassiopi, north around the mountain, occupies a promontory between two bays, where the wind blows hard during late summer. It was an important town during Roman times, with a shrine to Zeus that Nero and other emperors visited; Tiberius had a villa here. A **church** with a 17th-century icon and frescoes now occupies what was probably the site of Zeus's shrine, on the western side of the harbor.

During the Byzantine era this area rivaled Corfu town. But the town declined when Kassiopi's fortress, built by the Angevins, was destroyed by the Venetians. Now the fishing village has discovered the tourist trade and has become a busy resort; its harbor is lined with tavernas, shops, and bars catering to charter groups.

Dining and Lodging

$$ ✕ **Tria Adelphia.** A view of the pretty fishing harbor framed by a cypress-covered hill is a big bonus at this authentic restaurant, where the menu depends on the day's catch by fishermen (you can even watch them hauling in their nets from here). Grab an outdoor table; order a glass of local wine; stick to seafood, the Greek classics, or the owner's recommendations; and you won't go wrong. ⊠ *On the harbor,* ☎ *0663/91136. MC, V. Closed Nov.–Mar.*

$$ ⌂ **Apraos Bay Hotel.** On the northern tip of the island sits this small, Venetian-style hotel. Rooms are fresh and airy with light-filled balconies. It's 40 yards from a private beach, with a fantastic view of the sea and the Albanian coast: a perfect place to relax in a friendly atmosphere, far from noise. Though it's almost completely isolated, just 2 km (1 mi) away in the village of Kassiopi is all the action anyone could want; it's about 32 km (20 mi) from Corfu town. ⊠ *Loutses, 49100,* ☎ *0663/98331,* FAX *0663/98336. 16 rooms with bath. Restaurant, piano bar, beach. AE, DC, MC, V. Closed Dec.–Feb.*

Roda

㉝ *37 km (23 mi) north of Corfu town, 8 km (5 mi) northwest of Kassiopi.*

On the north coast, Roda, a growing resort community, has pebble beaches and plenty of tourists, and though some spots farther west are less crowded, the roads to them are not as passable. Its narrow beach, which adjoins the beach at tiny Acharavi, has especially calm and shallow waters and a campsite, so it's popular with local families. The **remains of a 5th-century Doric temple** have been found here.

Sidari

㉞ *36 km (22½ mi) north of Corfu town, 4 km (2½ mi) west of Roda.*

Sidari has archaeological remains dating back to 7000 BC but today is heavily touristed with families splashing in its calm waters. Just to the west, unique striated cliffs are constantly being eroded into tunnels and caves, notably the "tunnel of love." Think carefully: Legend has it that if you take a boat through this narrow channel, you will be able to marry whoever was in your thoughts at the time. A competing legend says that couples swimming through it will stay together forever; perhaps that is why this area is less crowded than nearby swimming areas.

CORFU A TO Z

Arriving and Departing

By Boat

Passenger ships stop at Corfu about twice a week, April to October, but schedules change frequently, so always check ahead. **Minoan Lines** (⊠ Piraeus, ☎ 01/463–5241–5, FAX 01/411–8631) runs the *Festos,* which connects Corfu with Ancona, Igoumenitsa, Heraklion, and Piraeus. The *Ariadne* connects Corfu with Kusadasi (Turkey), Samos, Paros, Kephallonia, and Ancona.

Ferries from Igoumenitsa on the mainland leave every hour in summer and every two hours off-season, landing in Corfu town (two hours) and in Lefkimmi, at the southern tip of Corfu (45 minutes).

By Bus

KTEL Corfu buses (☎ 0661/39985 or 0661/37186) leave Athens (☎ 01/512–9443) three or four times a day. The trip, via Patras and the ferry from Igoumenitsa, takes about nine hours. The fare is approximately 8,400 dr. each way.

By Car

The best route from Athens is the national road via Corinth to the Rion/Antirion ferry, then to Igoumenitsa (472 km/274 mi), where you take the ferry to Corfu. In winter, severe weather conditions often close the straits at Rion/Antirion, and the ferries from Igoumenitsa can also stop running. Call the **Touring Club of Greece** (☎ 104) for information.

By Plane

Olympic Airways (☎ 0661/34141) has three flights a day from Athens that land at Corfu's airport (⊠ Northwest of Kanoni, a few miles south of Corfu town). For a round-trip, the fare is 34,600 dr. each way; the one-way fare is 17,300 dr.

Getting Around

By Bus

Bus travel on Corfu is inexpensive, and the bus network covers the island. Buses tend to run fairly close to their schedules, and you can get timetables and information at the depots of the two bus companies and at many other places. Publications such as *Mythos Guide to Corfu,* the *Corfiot,* and the *Corfu Sun* all give good information.

The **Spilia** (⊠ Avramiou St., ☎ 0661/30627) bus company's terminal is at the New Port. Buses also run from the **San Rocco** (⊠ San Rocco Sq., ☎ 0661/31595) bus company's depot.

By Motorbike and Car

The gentle climate and rolling hills make Corfu ideal motorbike country, but you should drive very slowly until you feel comfortable. There is little or no system to Greek driving, and "depend on the other guy's brakes" best expounds the basic philosophy of many drivers. The road surfaces deteriorate as the tourist season progresses, and potholes abound. Helmets are rarely provided, and then only on request. Check the lights, brakes, and other mechanics before you accept a machine. Be warned and be careful.

By Taxi

Radio-controlled taxis (☎ 0661/33811) are available 24 hours a day, and rates, which are set by the government, are reasonable—when adhered to. Many drivers speak English and they know the island in a very special way. If you want to hire a cab and driver on an hourly or daily basis, you must negotiate the fee; ask for advice at your hotel's front desk. Always check the prices before you travel.

Contacts and Resources

Car and Motorbike Rental

A 50cc motorbike can be rented for about 4,000 dr. a day (100cc for 6,000 dr.), but you can bargain, especially if you want it for two or more days. Rentals are available in even the most remote villages. In Corfu town, try **George's Bikes** (✉ El. Venizelou 38, ☎ 0661/32727).

Car rental can be considerably more expensive, starting at about 10,000 dr. a day for a Fiat 127 (100 km/62 mi minimum) plus insurance, delivery, and so forth. A four-wheel-drive Jeep, with the extras, can run to 25,000 dr. a day. In Corfu town you can try **Olympus Rent-a-Car** (✉ 29 National Stadium, ☎ 0661/36147). Also in Corfu, try **Suncars, Ginargirou Brothers Ltd.** (✉ 40 Alexandras, ☎ 0661/31565).

Emergencies
Police (✉ Alexandras 19, ☎ 100).

Medical: hospital (✉ Polychroniou Kostanda, ☎ 0661/45811 through 0661/45815). **Polyclinik** (✉ Just outside town on the road to Paleokastritsa, ☎ 0661/22946).

Guided Tours
Many agencies run half-day tours of Old Corfu town, and tour buses go daily to all the sights on the island. Tickets and information are available at travel agencies all over town. **Vaba Travel** (✉ Ethnikis Antistaseos, New Port, ☎ 0661/44455, FAX 0661/22174) is reliable.

Most agencies offer an evening tour to **Danilia Village** (☎ 0661/91621, FAX 0661/91485), a fairly accurate reconstruction of an entire 17th-century Corfiot settlement in the countryside on the road to Paleo, 14 km (8 mi) from Corfu town.

The main tour operator to Albania is **Petrakis Shipping Company** (✉ Eleftheriou Venizelou 9, next to the Old Port, ☎ 0661/31649). The cost is around 7,000 dr., plus a small additional charge to cover port taxes and an entry permit to Albania.

Visitor Information
Greek National Tourist Organization (GNTO or EOT; ✉ 15 Zavitsianou, ☎ 0661/37520, 0661/37638, or 0661/37630, FAX 0661/30298).

Tourist Police (✉ Kapodistriou 1, ☎ 0661/30265).

8 Northern Peloponnese

Nauplion, Patras, and Olympia

The gods of ancient Greece blessed the Northern Peloponnese with natural beauty and the mysteries of forgotten civilizations. The ruined city of Mycenae, with giant tombs to the heroes of Homer's Iliad, *stands sentinel over the Argive plain, where warriors once assembled en route to Troy. In the rolling hills of Elis, Olympia plays host to the scattered remains of the ancient Olympic Games. And Nauplion, its ancient Greek, Venetian, and Turkish edifices jutting out into the Bay of Argos, is, to the Greeks, the embodiment of beauty.*

By Mark J.
Rose and Toula
Bogdanos

Updated by
Terrence
Moloney

HANGING LIKE A LARGE LEAF from the stem of the Corinthian Isthmus, the Peloponnese has also been called Morea, which means mulberry leaf. This slight botanical variance is nothing compared to the bewildering variety of imposing ruins, situated in equally varied and beautiful scenery—massive mountains covered with low evergreen oak and pines surround coastal valleys and loom above rocky shores and sandy beaches. Over the millennia this rugged terrain nourished kingdoms and empires and witnessed the birth of modern Greece. Traces of these lost realms—ruined Bronze Age citadels, Greek and Roman temples and theaters, and the fortresses and settlements of the Byzantines, Franks, Venetians, and Turks—attest to the richness of the land. No wonder visitors who spend less than a week here usually wind up asking themselves why they didn't allot more time to this fascinating area of Greece.

Named for Pelops, son of the mythical Tantalos, whose intolerantly tragic descendants dominate the half-legendary Mycenaean centuries, the Northern Peloponnese comprises the Argive peninsula, jutting into the Aegean, and runs westward past the isthmus and along the Gulf of Corinth to Patras and the Adriatic coast. The oldest region is the fertile Argive plain, the heart of Greece in the late Bronze Age and the home of the heroes of Homer's *Iliad*. A walk through the lion gate to Mycenae, the citadel of Agamemnon, brings the Homeric epic to life, and the massive walls of nearby Tiryns glorify the age of might. The thriving market town of Argos, the successor to Mycenae and Tiryns, engaged in a long rivalry with Sparta, generally gets the short end of the stick. Corinth, the economic superpower of the 7th and 6th centuries BC, dominated trade and established colonies abroad. Although eclipsed by Athens, Corinth earned a reputation for wealth and easy living. Today, modern Corinth is a bustling, if unremarkable, regional center. Not far from Corinth is Epidauros, the sanctuary of Asklepios, god of healing, where in summer Greek dramas are re-created in the ancient theater, one of the finest and most complete to survive. The main site lies far to the west: Olympia, the sanctuary of Zeus and site of that famous contest the Peloponnese gave mankind, the Olympic Games.

Four thousand years of history are more fully and comprehensively illustrated in this region than nearly anywhere else in Europe. A gap of a hundred years in the stately cavalcade of temples, palaces, churches, Crusader castles, and mosques is a rare exception (and is generally due to catastrophic barbarian invasions). By the 13th century, the armies of the Fourth Crusade (in part egged on by Venice) had conquered the Peloponnese after capturing Constantinople in 1204. But the dominion of the Franks was brief, and Byzantine authority was restored under the Palaiologos dynasty. Soon after Constantinople fell in 1453, the Turks, taking advantage of an internal rivalry, crushed the Palaiologoi and helped themselves to the Peloponnese. In the following centuries the struggle between the Venetians and the Ottoman Turks was played out in Greece. The two states alternately dominated the Northern Peloponnese until the Ottomans ultimately prevailed, as Venetian power declined in the early 1700s. The Turkish mosques and fountains and the Venetian fortifications of Nauplion recall this epic struggle. The Peloponnese played a key role in the Greek War of Independence, and from 1828 to 1834 Nauplion was the capital of Greece.

Today Patras is the modern hub and the third-largest city in Greece, while holiday resorts such as Porto Heli in the east and Killini in the west attract crowds seeking sand and sea. But knowing travelers venture to this region for far more than suntans. After all, the "cyclopean" walls at Tiryns, the Lion gate and beehive tombs at Mycenae, the theater in Epidauros, and the world-famous sculptures at Olympia are just some of the once-in-a-lifetime wonders to be seen and relished here.

Pleasures and Pastimes

Beaches

The beaches along the western coast of the Peloponnese are considered some of the best in Greece and are generally less crowded than other beaches in other areas. There are excellent beaches near Chlemoutsi castle. There are good beaches along the Gulf of Corinth, with spectacular views of the opposite shore, but some are of cobbles rather than sand. Xylokastro starts out cobbly but farther from town becomes sandy. The popular beaches are well equipped for water sports: Paddle boats can be hired, and you can arrange windsurfing lessons at small "beach-bum" operations at many beaches, such as Tolo. In some resorts, like Porto Heli, waterskiing and jet-skiing are making an appearance.

Dining

One of the simplest pleasures of Greece is enjoying a late dinner of traditional food with good Greek wine, preferably from the barrel. In the small towns here, any restaurant that pretends to offer more than this should be viewed with suspicion. Dress is always casual and reservations unnecessary, although you might have to wait for a table if you're dining with the majority at 10 PM or later. Keep freshness and the season in mind; if you order fish, have a look at it before it's cooked—there's no reason to eat something that has been frozen. Grape leaves are best early in the season, no later than early July, when they're young and tender. Ask to visit the kitchen; any chef worth his salt will tell you what's good and what's left over from lunch.

Greek vintners, faced with EU competition, are producing better wines than ever before. Look for red wines from the region around Nemea, between Corinth and Argos. Be sure to try Patras's sweet *mavrodaphne* (a heavy dessert wine, literally "black Daphne"), so called, because after the death of Daphne, Baron von Clauss's object of desire, he took his darkest grapes and made the sweet wine in her honor.

CATEGORY	COST*
$$$$	over 7,000 dr.
$$$	5,000 dr.–7,000 dr.
$$	2,500 dr.–5,000 dr.
$	under 2,500 dr.

for a three-course meal, including tax, service, and usually beer or a small carafe of wine

Hiking and Climbing

The mountainous terrain of the Northern Peloponnese is an ideal habitat for hikers and climbers. The **Greek Federation of Mountaineering Associations** in Athens operates several huts in the Peloponnese that are open to the public (☞ Contacts and Resources *in* Northern Peloponnese A to Z, *below*).

Lodging

Visitors accustomed to traveling in the United States and Europe should not expect to find such amenities as color televisions, much less VCRs, everywhere they go. Hotels in the $$$$ and $$$ categories have air-conditioning unless noted; it is only specified when it exists in hotels of $$ and $ rank. Breakfast is not included in the price unless noted.

CATEGORY	COST*
$$$$	over 39,000 dr.
$$$	22,000 dr.–39,000 dr.
$$	13,000 dr.–22,000 dr.
$	under 13,000 dr.

for a standard double room in high season, including tax and service

Shopping

Olympia has many shops specializing in big-ticket gold jewelry—some very nice, some very gaudy. Patras is the best bet for fashion, especially downtown around Korinthos and Maizonos streets. If you are traveling by car, be on the lookout for roadside stands selling the wonderful peaches and apricots—perfectly ripe and far superior to grocery-store fruit.

Exploring the Northern Peloponnese

The Northern Peloponnese comprises several distinct geographical areas; on the eastern side is the Argolid plain and the Corinthiad, where we find Mycenae, Tiryns, Epidauros, and Nauplion, and on the western side the provinces of Achaea and Elis, home of ancient Olympia and the bustling port city of Patras. We describe each of these regions in separate sections, below.

Numbers in the text correspond to numbers in the margin and on the Northern Peloponnese, Nauplion, Tiryns, Mycenae, and Ancient Olympia maps.

Great Itineraries

The eastern and western portions of the Northern Peloponnese are easily divided into two separate three- to four-day itineraries; a thorough exploration of both requires about eight or nine days. Those with less time should consider investigating either the eastern or western half only; for travelers entering Greece from Italy, Patras and Olympia are a must, and for those entering Greece through Athens, Nauplion and the Argolid are only a short hop away.

IF YOU HAVE 2 OR 3 DAYS

The wealth of interesting sites on either side of the Northern Peloponnese will keep the intrepid occupied for at least three days, but if your schedule allows for only two days consider a day trip to lovely ⛴ **Nauplion** ⑤–⑳ followed by a day spent exploring some of the highlights of the Argolid—**Mycenae** ㉜–㊷ and **Tiryns** ㉑–㉚, for example. A third day near **Nauplion** will allow a visit to the theater at **Epidauros** ② and perhaps the beaches at **Tolo** ④ or **Porto Heli** ③. For those entering Greece from Italy and with only a couple of days to spare, try spending a day in and around ⛴ **Patras** ㊾ followed by a day trip to ⛴ **Olympia** ㊿–. An extra day on the western side of the Northern Peloponnese could be spent either enjoying a train ride along the picturesque **Vouraikos Gorge** ㊻ en route to **Kalavrita** ㊼ or clambering over the parapets of the Frankish **Chlemoutsi Castle** ㊿.

IF YOU HAVE 6 DAYS

Six days will allow you to see most of the major sites of the Northern Peloponnese. Spend two or three days in ⛴ **Nauplion** ⑤–⑳ and use it as a base to explore the Argolid. You can get to **Nauplion** by boat, train, or car, and it is possible to rent transportation from there. After you have explored nearby **Mycenae** ㉜–㊷, **Tiryns** ㉑–㉚, **Epidauros** ②, and **Argos** ㉛, spend a day in ⛴ **Patras** ㊾, visiting **ancient Corinth** ㊹ on the way, or forested **Kalavrita** ㊼ if you need a rest from antiquities! A fifth and sixth day can be divided between **Patras** and ⛴ **Olympia** ㊿–. Remember that this trip can be easily reversed if you are coming from Italy and arriving in **Patras**.

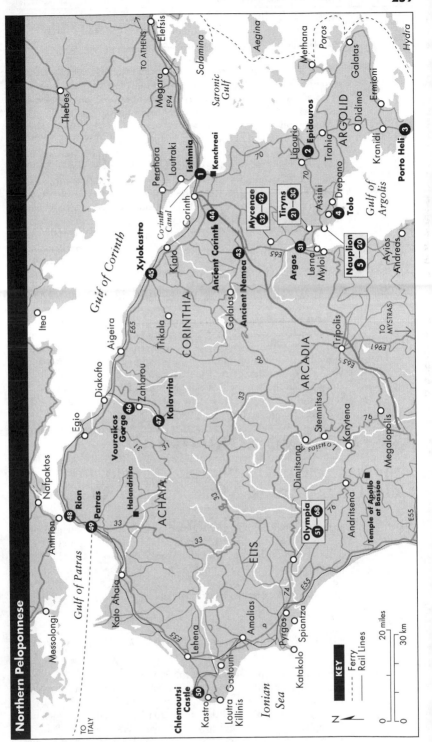

Northern Peloponnese

KEY
- - - Ferry
——— Rail Lines

20 miles

30 km

IF YOU HAVE 9 DAYS

Starting at the isthmus, journey south toward ⊞ **Nauplion** ⑤–⑳, visiting **Isthmia** ①, **Kenchreai**, and **Epidauros** ② en route. Spend your second day in ⊞ **Nauplion** ⑤–⑳, and perhaps visiting the beaches at nearby ⊞ **Tolo** ④ or ⊞ **Porto Heli** ③, both of which can be used as alternative bases for exploring the Argolid. The five major sites north of **Nauplion—Tiryns** ㉑–㉚, **Argos** ㉛, **Mycenae** ㉜–㊷, **ancient Nemea** ㊸, and **ancient Corinth** ㊹—could easily occupy two or even three days, using Nauplion as a base for daily excursions. ⊞ **Olympia** ㊳–㊽ beckons the Peloponnesian traveler sooner or later, but don't rush! There's plenty to see en route from the Argolid, including the beaches of **Xylokastro** ㊺, and the alluring beauty of the **Vouraikos Gorge** ㊻ near ⊞ **Kalavrita** ㊼, a sight best experienced from the train that winds its way up the **Vouraikos Gorge. Kalavrita** can be enjoyed as a side trip on the way to Patras, or as an overnight stay, followed by a quick hop to **Patras** ㊾, with fashionable shops, sophisticated cafés, and lots of energy. Stay in Patras for a couple of nights, exploring the city itself and the nearby sights, including the traditional village of **Halandritsa,** and the best-preserved Frankish castle in the Peloponnese, **Chlemoutsi Castle** ㊿. Finally, take a languid trip through the verdant province of Elis to awesome, ancient **Olympia** ㊳–㊽, where the Olympic Games were first held almost three millennia ago.

When to Tour

As in much of Greece, late spring provides the optimum conditions for exploration—this is when hotels, restaurants, and sites have begun to extend their hours of operation but the hordes of travelers have not yet arrived. In summer, morning and early evening activity will avoid the worst of the heat, which can be a formidable obstacle. Remember that on Mondays most state museums and sites are closed. On off-season Sundays, many are free.

ARGOLID AND CORINTHIAD

Isthmus, Epidauros, Nauplion, Tolo, Porto Heli, Tiryns, Argos, Mycenae, Nemea, Corinth

Most of the sites in this area are in the Argolid—Tiryns and Mycenae gaze over the plain of Argos, which dominates the Argolid, and nearby Epidauros hosts audiences from around the world who come to see drama performed in its classical theater. Argos lies in the center of the plain of the same name; behind the mountains that surround the plain on all sides (except the south) is the Corinthiad, a more hilly region, with ancient Corinth as its principal site.

Isthmus

75 km (46½ mi) southwest of Athens, 7 km (4½ mi) southeast of Corinth.

More of a pit stop than a town, the isthmus is where the Peloponnese begins. Were it not for this narrow neck of land less than 7 km (4½ mi) across, the waters of the Gulf of Corinth and the Saronic Gulf would meet and would make the Peloponnese an island; the name, in fact, means "Pelop's island." The tragic myths and legends surrounding Pelops and his family provided the grist for poets and playwrights from Homer to Aeschylus and enshroud many of the region's sites to this day.

For the ancient Greeks the isthmus was strategically important for both trade and defense; Corinth, with harbors on either side of the isthmus, grew wealthy on the lucrative east—west trade. Ships en route from Italy and the Adriatic to the Aegean had to go clear around the Peloponnese, so in the 7th century BC a paved roadway called the Diolkos was constructed across the isthmus, over which ships were hauled using rollers. You can still see remnants near the bridge at the western end of the canal. Nero was the first to begin cutting a canal, supposedly striking the first blow, with a golden pickax, in AD 67. But the canal project died with Nero the following year, and the roadway was used until the 13th century. The modern canal, built 1882–93, was cut through 285 ft of rock to sea level. The impressive sight is a fleeting one if you are traveling by bus, so keep a sharp lookout.

❶ Isthmia, an ancient sanctuary dedicated to Poseidon, scarcely a mile from the canal, isn't much to look at today, largely because its buildings were dismantled for stone to repair the Isthmian wall and to build a large fortress. Better preserved, not surprisingly, are the remains of the fortress, called the **Hexamilion,** and of the **wall** (east of the sanctuary is a stretch that rises more than 20 ft). Ancient Isthmia was an important place, the site, from 580 BC, of the Isthmian Games, biennial athletic and musical competitions on a par with those at Nemea, Delphi, and Olympia. ⊠ *1 km/½ mi west of isthmus,* ☎ *0741/37244.* ⊿ *500 dr.* ☉ *Tues.–Sun. 9–3.*

Dining
The chain of **rest-stop restaurants** at the isthmus may be a more effective defense against invasion than the walls ever were. Be wary of these restaurants: It might be better to enter the Peloponnese hungry than to eat the souvlaki served here.

Epidauros

❷ *41 km (25½ mi) east of Nauplion, 62 km (38½ mi) south of the isthmus. When heading south from the isthmus on Highway 70 you may find the names confusing. You first pass a sign for Nea Epidauros; 6½ km (4 mi) later there's a turnoff marked for Palaio Epidauros (don't take this either). After this seaside village the road turns inland and gradually the tall pines give way to scrubby vegetation. Keep going— the Epidauros you want is about 8 km (5 mi) farther, about 3 km (2 mi) southeast of Ligourio. If you are coming from another direction look for the signs that say "Ancient Theatre of Epidauros" which dot the highways.*

★ The Sanctuary of Asklepios remains world renowned for one thing: the **Theater at Epidauros,** the best-preserved Greek theater anywhere. Built in the 4th century BC with 14,000 seats, it was never remodeled in antiquity, and because it was rather remote, its stones were never quarried for secondary building use. Its extraordinary qualities were recognized even in the 2nd century AD. Pausanias of Lydia, an early traveler and geographer, wrote, "The Epidaurians have a theater in their sanctuary that seems to me particularly worth a visit. The Roman theaters have gone far beyond all the others in the world . . . but who can begin to rival Polykleitos for the beauty and composition of his architecture?"—or for the acoustics of his theater, which are so perfect that even from the last of the 55 tiers every word can be heard. Test this fact out during the **summer drama festival,** which, as Pausanias might say, is definitely "worth a visit." The quality of the theater, the setting, and the productions are outstanding, which cannot be said of any other festival in Greece. The rest of the site—the ancient shrine of the god of healing—does not match the standard set by the theater. The **temple of Asklepios** is not well preserved; some copies of its sculptures are in the **site museum,** but the originals are in the National Museum in Athens. An exhibit of ancient medical implements is of interest, as are models of the sanctuary. The **reconstruction of the tholos,** a circular building also possibly by Polykleitos, is noteworthy. Currently a large-scale restoration is taking place that includes reconstructions of the **abyton** and of the **temple of Hygeia.** ⊠ *Epidauros,* ☎ *0753/22009.* ⊠ *1,500 dr.* ⊙ *Daily 8–7 (winter 8–5).*

Dining and Lodging

$$ ✕ **Leonidas.** Rest your weary bones at this taverna, with liquid refreshment, excellent meals, and, in cold or wet weather, a blazing fire on the raised brick hearth. Theater actors often frequent Leonidas, as the theatrical decorations attest. ⊠ *Epidauros main road,* ☎ *0753/ 22115. No credit cards.*

$ ⊡ **Xenia.** At this functional if unexciting hotel, the principal attrac-
★   tion is the opportunity to linger amidst the pine-rich hills surrounding Epidauros. Being located within minutes of the site makes it a great place to stay if you want to explore the site in great detail, or use it as an alternative base for exploring the Argolid. However, its rooms will certainly not be featured in *Architectural Digest* and, as part of the state-run hotel chain, it can be lackadaisical in meeting travelers' needs. ⊠ *Epidauros, 26223,* ☎ *0753/22003,* ⓕⓧ *0753/22219. 24 rooms. Restaurant. No credit cards.*

The Arts

FESTIVAL

The **Festival of Ancient Drama** (⊠ Stadiou 4 arcade, ☎ 0753/22006 or 0752/22691) in the theater at Epidauros takes place July to August, weekends only, at 9 PM. Many productions are in English and are produced by companies from around the world. In fact, well-known English theater troupes, such as the Royal Shakespeare Company, will often premiere their ancient drama productions here. Tickets can be bought at the theater before performances or in advance from the **Athens Festival box office** (⊠ 4 Stadiou St., ☎ 01/322–1459), open Mondays–Saturdays 8:30–2 and 5–7, Sundays 10–1.

En Route   From Epidauros, head south toward the resort town of Porto Heli. After 16½ km (10 mi), just beyond the village of Trahia, the road divides. Follow the left fork as it swings east to the coast, with a beautiful view across the Saronic Gulf to Aegina. After 30 km (18½ mi), a left turn takes you to the peninsula known as Methana, where a spa (⊠ In the small port) of the same name will treat you for rheumatism and skin disorders with hot sulfurous water. Continuing past Methana on the main road brings you to Galatas, overlooking the island of Poros. The road sweeps around the end of the peninsula and runs west along the coast to Ermioni, opposite Hydra, then to the beach at Kosta, opposite Spetses, and finally to Porto Heli.

Porto Heli

❸ *81 km (50⅓ mi) southeast of Nauplion, 54 km (33½ mi) south of Epidauros.*

A booming summer resort, Porto Heli is well supplied with tavernas, restaurants, souvenir shops, and discos. If you're in search of traditional Greek culture, look elsewhere. On the south side of the bay are the submerged ruins of the ancient city of Halieis.

Beaches

The beach at **Kosta** (⊠ In the south of the Argolid, south of Porto Heli) is more pleasant and less crowded than those at Porto Heli.

Dining and Lodging

$$–$$$ ✕ **Papadias.** In a town of undistinguished dining options, this taverna near the church in the older part of Porto Heli stands out. Dishes include appetizers like shrimp or *midia saganaki* (mussels baked with cheese), rabbit *stifado* (a baked stew with meat, white wine, garlic, cinnamon, and spices) resplendent with onions, and grilled crayfish. The seafood is good, and in general fish is the high-water mark of Porto Heli cuisine. ⊠ *Beach Rd.,* ☎ *0754/52342. MC, V.*

$$$ ▥ **Porto Heli.** This lodging of the former Kymata Club, like the other resorts around the sheltered bay, offers more than just a room for the night: The nearby beach has a range of water sports, and buffet breakfast is included in the price. The reasonably large white-stucco rooms have phones, stone floors, and, as wall decorations, colorful Byzantine-style plates. ⊠ *Beach Rd., 21300,* ☎ *0754/51490 through 0754/ 51494. 210 rooms, 8 suites. Restaurant, pool, miniature golf, 2 tennis courts, windsurfing, playground. MC, V. Closed Oct.–Apr.*

$$ ▥ **La Cité.** The buildings climbing the hillside behind the beach here resemble gigantic, white stucco Lego blocks. Inside, wood-frame furniture fills the rooms, which, although clean and well kept, could be larger. They do have balconies overlooking the beautiful bay, and each comes with a fan. There are rental bicycles and mopeds at the beach opposite, just 65 ft away. Continental breakfast is included in the price. ⊠ *Beach Rd., 21300,* ☎ *0754/51485,* ℻ *0754/51265. 164 rooms. 2 restaurants, bar, pool, miniature golf, 2 tennis courts, beach, water sports. AE, DC, MC, V. Closed Nov.–Mar.*

$ ▥ **Rozos.** An alternative to the giant resorts, Rozos can be summed up in a few words: crafty on a budget. The rooms are clean and decorated with nautical photos. Some of the furniture in each room matches, and large ceiling fans, like salvaged propellers from B–29 bombers, ensure good air circulation. A saving grace for this establishment, if you deem one is needed, is the front terrace, shaded by grapevines, lemon trees, and olive trees. ⊠ *Kosta 7, 21300,* ☎ *0754/ 51416,* ℻ *0754/51415. 23 rooms. Restaurant. MC, V.*

Nightlife

DISCOS

Disco Thea has enraptured multiseason visitors. **Disco Pop Rebel** has managed to stay in tourists' good graces for more than a summer.

Outdoor Activities and Sports

WATER SPORTS

Although its beach is not as good as others in the vicinity, Porto Heli's circular bay offers sheltered water for windsurfing, waterskiing, and other aquatic sports, and a safe harbor for sailboats. Waterskiing lessons are given at the **Porto Heli** hotel (⊠ Beach Rd., ☎ 0754/51546; ☞ *above*).

Tolo

➍ *11 km (7 mi) southeast of Nauplion, 77 km (47¾ mi) northwest of Porto Heli.*

Tolo is a resort center close to Nauplion, and it can be used as a base for exploring the northeastern Peloponnese. There are boats to the islands of Hydra and Spetses, and a hydrofoil to Athens in the summer. Organized tours to Mycenae, Tiryns, and Olympia are readily available in the tourist season. It has many fines beaches strung along the coast's crystalline waters, discos, and seafood tavernas supplied by the local fleet, but little in the way of traditional Greek culture. There is frequent bus service from Nauplion's KTEL station to Tolo.

Beaches

Just before Tolo, at the Bronze Age and classical site of Asine, the road takes a sharp turn to a fine **beach** that's less crowded than Tolo's. Asine lies on a small peninsula that forms the left arm of the Bay of Tolo. At its very tip is a odd bit of military history: a shattered but still legible mosaic made by Italian soldiers during WWII and dedicated to Il Duce—Mussolini.

Dining and Lodging

$–$$ ✕ **Chryso Feggari (Golden Moon).** This seaside taverna, handed down from father George to son Dimitris, is one of Tolo's better restaurants, albeit that's no blue ribbon. Ask for *fagri* (sea bream), *barbounia* (red mullet), or a delicious local fish called *kotsomoura*. The taverna also serves Greek dishes such as *pastitsio* (a casserole of pasta, meat, and cheese with seasonings and cinnamon), moussaka, *keftedes* (oniony meat balls), as well as pizzas and grilled meats. ⊠ *Aktis 52, about 325 ft from harbor,* ☏ *0752/59323. No credit cards. Closed Nov.–Feb.*

$ ✕ **Akroyiali.** Matriarch Anastasia Moutzouris still cooks up good traditional Greek fare at this almost 40-year-old beach taverna. Appetizers include fried eggplant slices, tender broad beans, marinated octopus, and grilled squid. For a main course, there is fresh fish, as well as lamb and pork chops, souvlaki, and grilled chicken. The barrel wine (white and red) is light but potent; locals order it a kilo at a time. ⊠ *Aktis 10,* ☏ *0752/59789. No credit cards. Closed Dec.*

$$ ▦ **Aris.** A recent renovation has blessed the Aris with a new floor, ceilings, and furniture. The neat, clean rooms have mahogany furniture, the ubiquitous blue-and-white fabric scheme, and balconies; be sure to ask for one with a sea view. Breakfast is included in the price. ⊠ *Aktis 28, 21056,* ☏ *0752/59231,* FAX *0752/59510. 50 rooms. Restaurant, bar, air-conditioning, recreation room. MC, V. Closed Nov.–Mar.*

$$ ▦ **King Minos.** One of the town's newest—it opened in 1992—this hotel offers amenities usually found in more expensive establishments. Almost all the rose and light-green rooms with bamboo touches have color-TVs, hair dryers, air-conditioning, and balconies; many have sea views. A beautiful outdoor pool looks out over the bay. Buffet breakfast is included in the price. The hotel is not on the shoreline but up the hill, above the main road. ⊠ *Miaouli 56, 21056,* ☏ *0752/59902,* FAX *0752/ 59968. 57 rooms. Restaurant, 2 bars, air-conditioning, pool. AE, MC, V. Closed Nov.–Feb.*

$$ ▦ **Minoa.** Renovated last year, this pleasant hotel has a crisp, clean, new feel to it—rooms are relatively large, done in the signature blue-and-white scheme, and all feature radio, hair dryer, safe, and television. The hotel is near the end of the town, and though there is a beach in front, it's a little walk to the wide sandy beach for which Tolo is known. Happily, many rooms feature delightful sea views. Buffet breakfast is included in the price. ⊠ *Aktis 56, 21056,* ☏ *0752/59207,* FAX *0752/59707. 44 rooms. Bar, outdoor café, air-conditioning, in-room safes. AE, MC, V. Closed Nov.–Feb.*

$$ ▦ **Tolo and Tolo II.** These two hotels run by the Scalidis family are op-
★ posite each other on the town's main street. The rooms are straightforward in decor and well kept—nothing fancy. Tolo has the best views and immediate access to the nicest part of the beach. Buffet breakfast is included in the price. ⊠ *Bouboulinas 15, 21056,* ☏ *0752/ 59248 or 0752/59464,* FAX *0752/59689. 59 rooms. Restaurant, bar, air-conditioning. MC, V. Closed Nov.–Feb.*

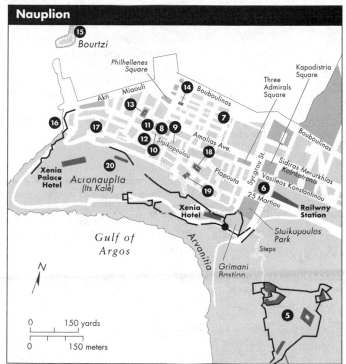

Nauplion

★ *65 km (40½ mi) south of Corinth, 11 km (7 mi) northwest of Tolo.*

Oraia (beautiful) is the word Greeks use to describe Nauplion. They say the word with assurance and enthusiasm, wanting to appreciate Nauplion's beauty while convinced that it is self-evident and that you share their recognition of it. The town's old section, on a peninsula jutting into the Gulf of Argos, mixes Greek, Venetian, and Turkish architecture; narrow streets, often just broad flights of stone stairs, climb the slopes beneath the walls of Acronauplia; statues honoring heroes preside over tree-shaded plazas surrounded by neoclassical buildings; and the Palamidi fortress—an elegant display of Venetian might from the early 1700s—draped over the high cliff guards the town. The Greeks are indeed right: Nauplion is beautiful. It deserves at least a leisurely day of your undivided attention.

Though it's hard to imagine anyone not liking Nauplion, Henry Miller, in the late 1930s, whined about it at length in *The Colossus of Maroussi.* "Nauplia," he wrote, "is dismal and deserted at night. It is a place which has lost caste. . . . There is a little military garrison, a fortress, a palace, a cathedral—and a few crazy monuments. There is also a mosque which has been converted into a cinema. By day it is all red tape, lawyers and judges everywhere, with all the despair and futility which follows in the train of these blood-sucking parasites. The fortress and the prison dominate the town. Warrior, jailer, priest—the eternal trinity which symbolizes our fear of life. I don't like Nauplia. I don't like provincial towns. I don't like jails, churches, fortresses, palaces, libraries, museums, or public statues to the dead." If you spend at least a day or two in Nauplion, your impression may be more positive.

Little is known about ancient Nauplion, although Paleolithic remains and Neolithic pottery have been found in the vicinity. It grew in importance in Byzantine times, and it was fought over by the Byzantines and the Frankish crusaders. It has been held by the Duke of Athens, the Venetians, and the Turks. In the War of Independence, the Greeks liberated the city, and it briefly became the capital. During World War II, German troops occupied Nauplion from April 1941 until September 1944. Today it is once again just a "provincial town," busy only in the tourist season and on weekends when Athenians arrive to get away from city pressures.

A Good Walk

Just wandering around Nauplion you'll quickly learn that this town is not merely picturesque, not merely beautifully situated—it's probably the prettiest in the Peloponnese and virtually seems to be designed for strolling. To get your bearings, you might start by climbing the hill of the **Palamidi,** the elegant Venetian fortress that sits atop its 700-ft peak (take a taxi up the road or tackle the 800-step climb skyward)—an on-a-clear-day-you-can-see-forever view of the Nauplion peninsula and the surrounding Argive plain will be your reward. Once you explore the fort—incidentally, the name Palamidi is taken from the son of Poseidon, Palamedes, who, legend has it, invented dice, arithmetic, and some of the Greek alphabet—head back down to relax at the foot of the fort in a pleasant series of tree-shaded parks and plateias, including **Kokokotronis Park, Kapodistria Square, Staikopolos Park,** and **Three Admiral Square.** As you head north along Syngrou Street, another park awaits, replete with statues including one of the famed heroine Bouboulina. Turn the corner on which Bouboulina's pedestal sits and walk one block from the harbor along Sophoni Street to the award-winning **Peloponnesian Folklore Foundation Museum.** Then walk south and turn right on Amalias or on Vasileos Konstantinou St. to reach **Syntagma (Constitution) Square,** the center of the old town. The latter street is more picturesque, with older buildings; the more commercial Amalias is lined with butcher shops and grocery stores. Immediately to the left as you enter Syntagma from Vasileos Konstantinou Street is the **old mosque** (turned movie theater) that Henry Miller took as an example of Nauplion's crassness. Walking from the cinémosque along the south side of Syntagma, continue past the "Mycenaean"-style **National Bank,** a fitting overture to your visit to the town's **Archaelogical Museum,** on the west side of Syntagma.

Westward you'll find the **Church of the Virgin Mary's Birth,** an elaborate post-Byzantine structure. Continuing north, you come to quayside and **Philhellenes Square** and the church of **St. Nicholas.** From St. Nicholas westward along the quayside (called Akti Miaouli) is an unbroken chain of restaurants, most just average, and, farther along, more successful patisseries. It is pleasant in the afternoon for postcard writing, an iced coffee or ouzo, and conversation. Sparrows looking for handouts will flit around your feet; the air is warm and the sky blue; and Argos's high acropolis is clearly visible across the smooth sea. Back at the quay, you can embark on a boat trip out to the miniature fortress of the **Bourtzi** in the harbor. Walk along the waterfront promenade to the **Five Brothers** bastion, and then follow the winding Kostouros Street up to the parking lot below the Xenia Palace hotel and explore **Psaromachalas,** the picturesque fishermen's quarter. Return to the Five Brothers to continue the promenade around the peninsula or, instead, go through the tunnel that looks like a James Bond movie set from the parking lot, and take the elevator to the Xenia Palace hotel and the top of the **Acronauplia** fortress. Repair to the Xenia Palace hotel bar for a sundowner.

Timing

A full exploration of this lovely town takes an entire day; a quick tour, with some omissions, could be done in three hours. While the above itinerary will show you all the main sights, you can get a good sample of Nauplion's distinctive ambience by just following your nose through its winding streets and charming squares.

Sights to See

㉟ Acronauplia. Potamianou Street, actually a flight of stone steps, ascends from St. Spyridon Square toward this imposing hill, which the Turks once called Its Kalé. Until the Venetian occupation, it had two castles: a Frankish one on the eastern end and a Byzantine one on the west. The Venetians added the massive Castello del Torrione (or Toro for short) at the eastern end around 1480. If you have trouble locating the Toro, look under the Xenia Hotel (not the Xenia Palace), which was built on part of it. During the second Venetian occupation, the gates were strengthened and the huge Grimani bastion was added (1706) below the Toro. The Acronauplia is only accessible from the elevator on the west side, or by the road from the east side, near the Xenia Palace hotel.

⑪ Archaeological Museum. This red stone building on the west side of Constitution Square was built in 1713 to serve as the storehouse for the Venetian fleet. To say that it is "well constructed" is an understatement; its arches and windows are remarkably well proportioned. It has housed the regional archaeological museum since 1930, and artifacts from such sites as Mycenae, Tiryns, Asine, and Dendra are exhibited here. Of special interest are a Mycenaean suit of armor, jewelry from Mycenaean tombs in the area, and 7th-century gorgon masks from Tiryns. ⊠ *West side of Constitution Sq.,* ☎ *0752/27502.* ▣ *500 dr.* ☉ *Tues.–Sun. 8:30–3.*

⑮ Bourtzi. If you like the view to distant Argos, the sight of the Bourtzi, Nauplion's pocket-size fortress, will captivate you. Built in 1471 by Antonio Gambello, one of those industrious Venetians, the Bourtzi (or Castelli) was at first a single tower, on a speck of land generously called St. Theodore's Island. Morosini is said to have massacred the Turkish garrison when he recaptured it for Venice in 1686. A tower and bastion were then added, giving it the shiplike appearance it has today. In 1822, after it was captured in the War of Independence, it was used to bombard the Turks defending the town. In the unsettled times after the revolution, the government retreated to the Bourtzi for a while; after 1865, it was the residence of the town executioners; and from 1930 until 1970 it was run as a hotel. During the day the Bourtzi is no longer menacing; a tree blooms bright red in its courtyard during spring. You can take a small boat out to it for spectacular views of the old part of Nauplion and the Palamidi. Illuminated by floodlights in summer, it is beautiful at dusk but becomes grimmer as darkness falls. Extending from the extreme end of the quay is a large breakwater, the west mole, built by the Turks as the anchor point for a large chain that could be drawn up between it and the Bourtzi, blocking the harbor completely. A **small café** operates on the Bourtzi, where you can take in the view and refuel; it's open daily from 4 PM to 1 AM, May to September. ⊠ *In the harbor.*

⑲ Catholic Church of the Transfiguration. King Otho returned this Venetian-built church to Nauplion's Catholics. It is best known for the wooden arch erected inside the doorway in 1841, with the names carved on it of Philhellenes who died during the War of Independence (Lord Byron is number 10). Note also the evidence of its use as a mosque by the Turks: the mihrab (Muslim prayer recess) behind the altar and the amputated stub of a minaret. The church boasts a small museum and an underground crypt in which can be found a recent sculptural work commemorating the defeat of the Turks at the hands of the Greeks and Philhellenes. ⊠ *2 blocks south [uphill] from St. Spyridon.*

Church of Ayios Georgios. On Plapouta Street you'll find a square whose showpiece is the Church of Ayios Georgios, a Byzantine-era monument set at an angle, with five domes dating from the beginning of the 16th century and a Venetian arcade and campanile. Inside is the throne of King Otho. Around the square are several high-quality **neoclassical houses**—the one opposite the church is exceptional. Note the fine palmette centered above the door, the pilasters on the third floor with Corinthian capitals, the running Greek-key entablature, and the end tiles along the roofline. This house is matched perhaps by the one at the intersection of Plapouta and Tertsetou streets, whose window treatments are especially ornate. Nauplion has many other fine neoclassical buildings; keep your eyes open and don't forget to look up once in a while. ⊠ *2 blocks west of Syngrou on Plapouta.*

🔞 **Church of the Virgin Mary's Birth.** The church rises next to an **ancient olive tree**, where, according to tradition, St. Anastasios, a Naupliote painter, was killed in 1655 by the Turks. Anastasios was supposedly engaged to a local girl, but he abandoned her because she was immoral. Becoming despondent as a result of spells cast over him by her relatives, he converted to Islam. Upon returning to his senses, he cried out, "I was a Christian, I am a Christian, and I shall die a Christian." A Turkish judge ordered that he be beheaded, but the mob, outraged by the insult to Islam, stabbed Anastasios to death. A local tradition holds that he was hanged on this olive tree and that it never again bore fruit. The church, a post-Byzantine three-aisle basilica, was the main Orthodox church during the Venetian occupation. It has an elaborate wooden reredos carved in 1870. ⊠ *West of Constitution Sq.*

🔞 **Five Brothers.** South of the Bourtzi is the bastion known as the Five Brothers, the only remaining part of the wall built around Nauplion in 1502. The name comes from the five guns placed here by the Venetians; there are five here today, all from around 1690 and all bearing the winged lion of St. Mark. ⊠ *Near promontory of the peninsula.*

NEED A BREAK?

A small taverna called the **Banieris** (⊠ Just south of Five Brothers) is a good place to sit with an ouzo and watch the sun set behind the mountains across the gulf. Keep an eye out for the arrival of the evening hydrofoil from Piraeus, as it comes up the gulf.

Kapodistria Square. Just west of Kolokotronis Park, this park is centered on a marble statue of the Corfiote diplomat and father of modern Greece. Standing statesmanlike, he's quite oblivious to the noise from the playground at his feet, the tavernas across the street, and the taxis and buses turning left onto Amalias Street. ⊠ *At Syngrou St. and Sidiras Merarkhias.*

Kolokotronis Park. The centerpiece of this park is a bronze equestrian statue surrounded by four small Venetian cannons, which commemorates the revolutionary hero. South of the street is the **old train station** with a steam engine and vintage freight and passenger cars. In front of the station is a new **statue of Bouboulina,** the heroine of the revolution, shown with an alarming hairstyle the sculptor must have adapted from the Bride of Frankenstein. The **bust of Bouboulina** (Bouboulina St.) is a much better, if more traditional, representation. ⊠ *On north side of pedestrian King Constantine St.*

Miniature triangular park. This contains, inevitably, a monument to **admiral Konstantinos Kanaris,** a revolutionary hero; across from its far end is the **bust of Laskarina Bouboulina.** Twice widowed by wealthy shipowners, she built her own frigate, the *Agamemnon.* Commanding it herself, along with three small ships captained by her sons, Bouboulina blockaded the beleaguered Turks by sea, cutting off their supplies. **Bouboulina's pedestal** sits on the corner. ⊠ *Syngrou, north of Three Admiral Sq.*

Nauplion Promenade. This promenade around the entire Nauplion peninsula, once a simple gravel pathway, is now paved with reddish flagstones and graced with an occasional ornate lamppost. Here and there a flight of steps goes down to the rocky shore below. (Be careful if you go swimming here, since the rocks are infested with sea urchins.) Just before you reach the very tip of the peninsula, marked by a ship's beacon, there is a little shrine at the foot of a path leading up toward the Acronauplia walls above. Little Virgin Mary, or **Ayia Panagitsa** (⊠ At end of promenade) hugs the cliff on a small terrace and is decorated with an array of icons. During the Turkish occupation it hid one of Greece's secret schools. Two other terraces, like garden sanctuaries, have a few rosebushes and the shade of olive and cedar trees. They are very restful places to sit and not much frequented. Along the south side of the peninsula, the promenade runs midway along the cliff—it's 100 ft up to Acronauplia, 50 ft down to the sea. All along there are magnificent views of the cliff on which the Palamidi sits and the slope below, known as the Arvanitia.

⑩ National Bank. This structure displays an amusing union of Mycenaean and modern Greek architectural elements with concrete. (The Mycenaeans covered their tholos tombs with mounds of dirt; the bank's ungainly appearance may explain why.) Take a look at the **sculptures** (⊠ On square next to National Bank) of a **winged lion of St. Mark** (which graced the main gate in the city's landward wall, long since demolished) and of Kalliope Papalexopoulou (a leader of the revolt against King Otho), whose house once stood in the vicinity. ⊠ *Just south of Constitution Sq.*

⑨ Old mosque. Immediately to the left as you enter Constitution Square from Vasileos Konstantinou Street is this venerable mosque—once used as a school, a courthouse, and for municipal offices, its current incarnation is as a dingy movie theater. ⊠ *Constitution Sq.*

NEED A BREAK?

Walking from the old mosque along the south side of Constitution Square, you pass a café and a store called **Odyssey** (⊠ Constitution Sq.), the best place in Nauplion for newspapers and books in English; the owners are very helpful if you need advice or directions.

⑥ Palace of Justice. If Henry Miller loathed Nauplion for its lawyers and public buildings, you have to believe that he must have spent much of his time staring at the Palace of Justice, a building whose ugliness is magnified by its large size. This monumentality makes it useful as a landmark, however, since the telephone company (OTE) office and pay phones are in the next building. Nearby, across Syngrou Street from the KTEL bus station, is a **square** with a statue honoring Nikitaras the Turk-Killer, who directed the siege of Nauplion. ⊠ *Syngrou, 2 blocks down from Kapodistria Sq.*

★ ⑤ Palamidi. Seen from the old part of Nauplion, this fortress, set on its 700-ft peak, is elegant, with the red stone bastions and flights of steps that zigzag down the cliff face. A modern road lets you drive up the less precipitous eastern slope, but if you are in reasonable shape and it isn't too hot, try climbing the stairs. Most guidebooks will tell you there are 999 of them, but 892 is closer to the mark. From the top you can see the entire Argive plain and look across the gulf to Argos or down its length to the Aegean.

Built in 1711–14, the Palamidi comprises three forts and a series of freestanding and connecting defensive walls. Sculpted in gray stone, the lion of St. Mark looks outward from the gates. The Palamidi fell to the Turks in 1715 after only eight days, and if you climbed those stairs, you'll be able to feel the desperation of the fleeing defenders racing down them with the Turks in hot pursuit. After the war, the fortress was used as a prison, its inmates including the revolutionary war hero Kolokotronis; a sign indicates his cell. On summer nights the Palamidi is illuminated with floodlights, a beautiful sight from below. ⊠ *Above town,* ☎ *0752/28036.* ✉ *800 dr.* ⊙ *Weekdays 8:30–7 (8:30–3 in winter), weekends 8:30–2:30.*

NEED A BREAK?

For a respite, head to a pleasant series of tree-shaded **Staikopoulos platias** (⊠ At foot of Palamidi). A tranquil café welcomes the weary, benches here are perfect for giving your less-than-bionic feet a time-out, while children will enjoy the playground, duck pond, and some small aviaries. At the west end of the park the Naupliotes have reconstructed the Venetian Gateway that originally guarded the entrance to the Palamidi and commemorates the Venetian recapture of the city in 1487. Standing amidst the detritus of earlier Byzantine and classical ruins, the gateway invites contemplation on the passage of time.

7 **Peloponnesian Folklore Foundation Museum.** An exemplary, small museum focusing on textiles, this won the EC's 1981 Museum of the Year award for its displays. Regrettably it is closed for renovation until some time in 1999. Its lovely gift shop has relocated to Vasilissis Olgas and Ferraou until the museum reopens. ⊠ *Vas. Alexandrou 1, on block immediately north of Amalias, going up Sofroni,* ☎ *0752/28379.* ✉ *500 dr.* ⊙ *Mar.–Jan., Wed.–Mon. 9–2:30.*

17 **Psaromachalas.** This is the fishermen's quarter, a small district of narrow, alleylike streets running between cramped little houses that huddle beneath the walls of Acronauplia. The old houses, painted in brownish yellow, green, and salmon, have had all sorts of additions and overhangs added. The walk is enjoyable, but it is a poor neighborhood, and it's easy to feel like a voyeur scrutinizing the private lives of the locals. The pretty, miniature whitewashed chapel of **Ayios Apostoli** (⊠ Just off the parking lot of Psarmochalas) has six small springlets that trickle out of the side of Acronauplia. ⊠ *Along Kostouros St.*

14 **St. Nicholas Church** Built in 1713 for the use of sailors by Augustine Sagredo, the prefect of the Venetian fleet, this church has a facade and belfry that are recent additions. Inside, the church is furnished with a Venetian reredos and pulpit, and a chandelier from Odessa. ⊠ *Off Philhellenes Sq.*

18 **St. Spyridon Church.** Just west of Ayios Georgios is this church, a one-aisle basilica with a dome (1702). It has a special place in Greek history, for it was at its doorway that the statesman Ioannis Kapodistrias was assassinated in 1831 by the Mavromichalis brothers from the Mani, the outcome of a long-running vendetta. The mark of the bullet can be seen next to the Venetian portal. On the south side of the square, opposite St. Spyridon, are two of the four Turkish fountains preserved in Nauplion. A third is a short distance east (away from St. Spyridon) on Kapodistria Street, at the steps that constitute the upper reaches of Tertsetou Street. ⊠ *Terzaki, St. Spirdonas Sq., Papanikolaou St.*

8 **Syntagma (Constitution) Square.** This is the center of the old town and one of Greece's prettiest platias. In summer, the restaurants and patisseries along the west and south sides of Constitution Square—a focal point of Naupliote life—are boisterous with the shouts and laughter of children and filled with diners well into the evening. ⊠ *Along Amalias and Vasileos Konstantinou Sts.*

12 **Turkish mosque.** Ironically now the *Vouleftiko* (Parliament), this mosque was where the Greek National Assembly held its first meetings. The mosque is well built of carefully dressed gray stones. Legend has it that the lintel stone from the Treasury of Atreus was used in the construction of its large square-domed prayer hall. The mosque recently served as a music school, and occasionally the sound of a Rossini overture played on a piano could be heard. Today it is undergoing restoration and is not open to the public. ⊠ *Next to Archaeological Museum and behind National Bank.*

OFF THE
BEATEN PATH

AYIA MONI – Before or after exploring Nauplion, drive out the Epidauros road and turn right after 1 km (½ mi) to visit the fine Byzantine convent and church of Ayia Moni, a place of Christian devotion with a pagan twist. It was built in 1149 by Leo, the Bishop of Argos and Nauplion, and an inscription on the west gate records his efforts in building it and hopefully expresses the possibility that the Virgin will reward him by absolving him of his sins. In the monastery garden is a fountain said to be the spring Kanathos, where Hera annually renewed her virginity. On the way back to town, be sure to stop and see the Bavarian Lion, a beast of more than life size carved from a rock outcrop in the Pronoia section, Nauplion's modern suburb. The sleeping lion, a memorial to the Bavarian troops who died of typhus while serving King Otho, is a sad symbol of mortality compared to the invincible Venetian lions on Nauplion's fortresses.

Beaches

In Nauplion, **Arvanitia Beach** (⊠ On south side of town nestled between Acronauplia and the Palomides) is rocky but nice for a plunge after a day of sightseeing, and it has convenient kiosks. If you want to make a day out of relaxing in the sun, you're better off heading for one of the beaches farther away from town. Close to Nauplion are **Kastraki** and **Plaka**. The closest is **Karathona**, favored by Greek families with children and picnic baskets and serviced by buses.

Dining and Lodging

With one or two exceptions you'll eat better for less at the restaurants on Constitution Square or just beyond on Staikopoulos Street than at the ones along the waterfront. After dining have a dessert at **Galaxia** (⊠ Constitution Sq.) or in one of the patisseries on the harbor.

$$ ✕ **Mermaid.** If you need to escape the relative bustle of Nauplion, and you have a car, take a ride down the Candia–Irion road about 12 km (8 mi) to this excellent fish taverna sitting right on the bay. Jimmy, the owner, speaks very good English and has been serving excellent fresh fish for 12 years. The type of fish served varies with the season, and although Jimmy recommends the flatfish *tsipouria* as a reliable favorite, try the snapper if it's available. No matter what fish you choose, it's easy to succumb to the friendliness of the staff and the serenity of the location. ⊠ *Vivari on the Candia–Irion road,* ☎ *0752/92421. No credit cards.*

$$ ✕ **Savouras.** Fresh seafood is served in this unpretentious taverna overlooking the bay; it is generally regarded as one of the best fish restaurants in the area, so don't let the modest interior fool you. Specialties are red mullet, pandora, and dorado. Good side dishes are the eggplant dip and the fava with onions. ⌧ *Bouboulinas 79,* ☎ *0752/27704. No credit cards.*

$–$$ ✕ **O Arapakos.** Settle in on the waterfront for excellent Greek cooking, starting with grilled octopus and moving on to specialties like *yiouvetsi ton arapi* (beef with potatoes, tomatoes, carrots, and eggplants cooked in a ceramic dish) or *arnaki exohiko* (lamb stuffed with feta and potatoes). You can also have fresh fish, such as sea bream cooked over charcoal, or *bakaliaro skordalia* (dried cod, fried and served with a dollop of garlic sauce), all complemented by the light barrel retsina. To further entice you, there's usually some pan dessert like *galaktobouriko* (a sinful custard pastry) or baklava. ⌧ *Bouboulinas 81,* ☎ *0752/27675. V.*

$ ✕ **Hellas.** This reliable restaurant is not Nauplion's finest, but it is probably the most inexpensive on Constitution Square. It's best to go here when you're simply too tired to venture farther and are looking for an inexpensive lunch and an opportunity to watch the comings and goings on the square. ⌧ *Constitution Sq., opposite archaeological museum,* ☎ *0752/27278. V.*

$ ✕ **Karamanlis.** Just far enough away from the tourist area to attract the locals but close enough to be within walking distance of everything "important," this simple taverna is an authentic treat. At lunch it gets crowded with civil servants from the nearby courthouse who come for its tasty though limited number of *magirefta* (precooked dishes). The light fish soup makes a good starter, followed by *yiouvarlakia* (meat-rice balls), oven-baked potatoes, wild greens, and barrel retsina. Fresh fish is also available at very reasonable prices. ⌧ *Bouboulinas 1,* ☎ *0752/27668. No credit cards.*

$ ✕ **Ta Fanaria.** This is one of the finest restaurants in Nauplion. Follow this advice and enjoy: Arrive late, sit at one of the tables in the narrow alley beside the restaurant, and ask what's best that night. It's known for its *ladera* (vegetables cooked in olive oil), but the charcoal-grilled lamb ribs, the *imam* (eggplant stuffed with onions), and the lamb baked with vegetables such as okra or green beans are equally delicious. ⌧ *Staikopoulos 13,* ☎ *0752/27141. V.*

$$$$ ▥ **Candia House.** Nineteen kilometers (12 miles) south of Nauplion on Kandia Beach, this beautifully decorated hotel is the creation of a Greek publisher, Hara Papadimitriou, who has flawlessly matched good taste with comfort. Fresh flowers, antiques, paintings by Greek artists, handcrafted mirrors, fireplaces—these are just a few of the embellishments in the suites. Each one is different in its decor, and their size ranges from palatial to truly enormous. The Presidential suite boasts glorious antique Greek furniture that has been in the family for generations. All have balconies, sitting rooms, televisions, and refrigerators, and buffet breakfast is included in the price. The hexagonal restaurant with large windows looking onto the sea specializes in healthy meals, and the hotel offers hydromassage and botanotherapy treatments. Hara's effusive and enthusiastic welcome is also complimentary. ⌧ *Kandia-Irion, 21100,* ☎ *0752/94060 through 0752/94063,* ⅁⅂ *0752/94480. 10 suites. Restaurant, pool, massage, exercise room, recreation room. AE, DC, MC, V.*

$$$$ ▥ **Xenia Palace.** The view of the picturesque Bourtzi from the rooms in the Xenia Palace is exceptional; it appears in Greek National Tourist Organization (GNTO or EOT) television advertisements, and the view is possible only because the hotel was built on the ruins of the Frankish fortification atop Acronauplia. Modern art adorns the lobby, the relatively spacious rooms have exposed stonework, and the marble bathrooms are, without qualification, among the best in Greece. Lighting in the rooms is dim, some of the furniture needs reupholstering, and half-board (included in the price) is mandatory. An elevator cut through the rock takes you to a tunnel leading straight into town, below. ⊠ *Acronauplia, 21100,* ☎ *0752/28981 through 0752/28985,* FAX *0752/28987. 48 rooms, 3 suites. Restaurant, bar, pool, dance club. AE, MC, V.*

$$ ⊡ **Byron.** Definitely one of Nauplion's more popular hotels—particu-
★ larly with the younger crowd—this place has simply but tastefully dec-
orated rooms, with Turkish carpets and the odd sloping ceiling. A light
pink decor predominates and a delightful outdoor patio set atop an
old Turkish Haram compensates for the dark and dingy breakfast
room. Little touches make the difference here: welcoming staff, an atmo-
sphere of intrepid adventure, and an absurd wooden phone at the front
desk. Breakfast is an additional 1,600 dr. Amenities such as televisions,
air-conditioners, and hair dryers are available in some rooms. ⊠ *Plateia
Kapodistriou, near Agiou Spiridona, 21100,* ☎ *0752/22351,* FAX *0752/
26338. 12 rooms. Breakfast room, air-conditioning. AE, V, MC.*

$$ ⊡ **Victoria.** Although it was built in the 1970s, the Victoria is well maintained by its friendly managers, the Zoubelakis. It is spotless, and the
pink-and-green wallpaper is as new as the furnishings. So what if the
bathrooms are on the small side; the location in the heart of old Nauplion is hard to beat, and from the balconies you can see either the neoclassical houses or Acronauplia. ⊠ *Spiliadou 3, 21100,* ☎ *0752/
27420,* FAX *0752/27517. 36 rooms. Bar, air-conditioning. V. Closed Nov.*

$ ⊡ **Epidauros.** This hotel, a former merchant prince's home, is simple
but delightful. The two buildings feature an assortment of room styles,
all with pine decor. This was one of Nauplion's first three hotels. The
owner brims with pride, but the staff can be a little indifferent. One cautionary note: The hotel stands amid a number of nightclubs, whose proximity may delight you if you're into clubbing but may also keep you
awake at night from all the noise. ⊠ *Kokkinou 2, 21100,* ☎ FAX *0752/
27541. 35 rooms, 25 with bath. Breakfast room, bar. No credit cards.*

Nightlife

BARS AND DISCOS

Though Naupliotes drive to Tolo for their evening revels, Nauplion enjoys (if that's the word) a strip of nightclubs that prosper along the
northwest coastal road to Argos. Two currently popular waterfront hot
spots of the minute are **Shiva Liquid** (☎ 0752/26542) and **Epiples.** Along
the road to Tolo are more clubs, including **Club Memory.**

Shopping

Many stores in Nauplion and Olympia have the reproductions of
bronzes, frescoes, and vase paintings, the T-shirts, and the worry beads
for which your family, friends, and coworkers have been hankering.
Nauplion is better for antiques, especially toward the end of Staikopoulos Street in the old part of town.

GIFTS AND JEWELRY

It's fun to poke around at **Ithaki** (⊠ 9 Farmaleopoulou, ☎ 0752/
22816 or 0752/22091). For good-looking jewelry of fine quality,
there's **Camara** (⊠ Spiliadou 11 and ⊠ Konstantinou 10, ☎ FAX 0752/
24093).

Tiryns

★ *5 km (3 mi) north of Nauplion.*

Partly obscured by citrus trees are the well-preserved ruins of the
Mycenaean acropolis of Tiryns. Some tours skip the site in their mad
dash to cover everything in a single day, but if you see this citadel, with
its massive walls and its palace, before touring Mycenae, you can understand those rambling ruins more easily. Homer describes Tiryns as
"the wall-girt city," the only ancient literary reference to it, and Henry

Miller was repelled by the place, as he records in *The Colossus of Maroussi:* "Tiryns is prehistoric in character. . . . Tiryns represents a relapse. . . . Tiryns smells of cruelty, barbarism, suspicion, isolation." Today the site seems harmless, home to a few lizards who timidly sun themselves on the Bronze Age stones and run for cover if you approach. Archaeological exploration of the site, which still continues, shows that the acropolis was occupied in Neolithic times.

The citadel makes use of a long, low outcrop, on which was set the circuit wall of gigantic limestone blocks (of the type called "cyclopean" because the ancients thought they could have been handled only by the giant cyclops—the largest block is estimated at more than 15 tons). ㉑ Via the **cyclopean ramp** it was entered on the east side, through a gate leading to a narrow passage between the outer and inner walls. One could then turn right, toward the residential section in the **lower citadel** (now usually closed to the public) or to the left toward the **upper citadel** ㉒ ㉓ and **palace.** The heavy **main gate** and **second gate** blocked the passage to the palace and trapped attackers caught between the walls. After ㉔ the second gate, the passage opens onto a rectangular **courtyard,** whose ㉕ massive left-hand wall is pierced by a **gallery of small vaulted chambers,** or casemates, opening off a **long narrow corridor** roofed by a **corbeled arch.** (They were possibly once used to stable horses, and the walls have been worn smooth by the countless generations of sheep and goats who have sheltered there.) This is one of the famous galleries of Tiryns; another such gallery at the southernmost end of the acropolis also connects a series of five casemates with sloping roofs.

An elaborate entranceway leads west from the court to the upper citadel and palace, sited at the highest point of the acropolis. The ㉖ ㉗ complex included a colonnaded **court;** the great *megaron* (main hall) opened onto it and held the royal throne. Surviving fragments suggest that the floors and the walls were decorated, the walls with frescoes (now in the National Archaeological Museum of Athens) depicting a boar hunt, women riding in chariots, and a procession of women. Beyond the megaron, a large **court** overlooks the houses in the lower citadel; ㉘ ㉙ from here, a long **stairway** descends to a small **postern gate** in the west wall. At the excavated part of the lower acropolis a significant discovery ㉚ was made; two parallel **tunnels,** roofed in the same way as the galleries on the east and south sides, start within the acropolis and extend under the walls, leading to **subterranean cisterns** that ensured a continuous water supply.

From the palace you can see how Tiryns dominated the flat, fertile land at the head of the Gulf of Argos. The view would have been different in the Late Bronze Age: The ancient shoreline was nearer to the citadel, and outside the walls there was an extensive settlement. Profitis Ilias, the prominent hill to the east, was the site of the Tiryns cemetery. ⊠ *On low hill just past suburbs of Nauplion,* ☎ *0752/22657.* ▦ *500 dr.* ☉ *Weekdays 8:30–7 (8:30–5 in winter), weekends 8:30–3.*

Argos

㉛ *12 km (7½ mi) northwest of Nauplion, 7 km (4½ mi) northwest of Tiryns.*

On the western edge of the Argive plain, amid citrus groves, is the city of Argos (population 21,000), the economic hub of the region. The fall of Mycenae and Tiryns at the close of the Late Bronze Age proved favorable for Argos. Under King Pheidon, Argos reached its greatest power in the 7th century BC, becoming the chief city in the Peloponnese. In the mid-5th century, it consolidated its hold on the Argive plain by eradicating Mycenae and Tiryns. But like Corinth, Argos was never pow-

In case you want to be welcomed there.

We're here to see that you're always welcomed at establishments everywhere. That's why millions of people carry the American Express® Card – for peace of mind, confidence, and security, around the world or just around the corner.

do more®

Cards

And just in case.

We're here with American Express® Travelers Cheques and Cheques *for Two*.® They're the safest way to carry money on your vacation and the surest way to get a refund, practically anywhere, anytime.

Another way we help you...

do more

Travelers Cheques

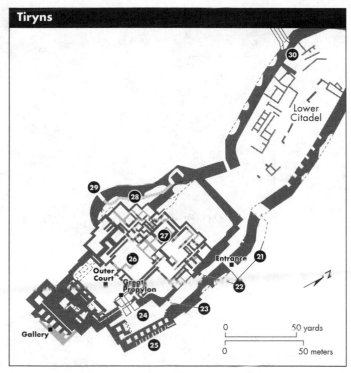

Tiryns

Lower
Citadel

Entrance

Outer
Court

Great
Propylon

Gallery

0   50 yards

0   50 meters

erful enough to set its own course, following in later years the leadership of Sparta, Athens, and the Macedonian kings. Twice in its history, women are said to have defended Argos: once in 494 BC when Telesilla the poetess (who may be mere legend) armed old men, boys, and women to hold the walls against the Spartans; and again in 272 BC when Pyrrhus, king of Epiros, who was taking the city street by street, was felled from above by an old woman armed with a tile. Remains of the classical city are scattered throughout the modern one, and along Tripoleos Street you can see in a small area the extensive **ruins of the Roman bath, theater, odeon,** and **agora.** ⊠ *Tripoleos St.* ▨ *Free* ☉ *Tues.–Sun. 8:30–3.*

The Kastro is a Byzantine and Frankish structure incorporating remnants of classical walls, and it was later expanded by the Turks and Venetians. It's quite a hike to get to, but your reward will be an unsurpassed view of the Argolid plain. Nestle yourself into a ruined castle wall to guard against the fierce wind and ponder the mysteries of the long-lost Mycenaean civilization. A small **archaeological museum** on the main platia, **Ayios Petros,** has well-displayed finds from Argos and nearby sites. ⊠ *Vasilissis Olgas,* ☎ *0751/28819.* ▨ *500 dr.* ☉ *Tues.–Sun. 8:30–3.*

Shopping
MARKET

On Saturday mornings, the platia is transformed into a huge open **household-merchandise and produce market** (dwarfing that at Nauplion). It's more fun than yet another tourist shop, and you can often find good souvenirs, such as wooden stamps used to impress designs on bread loaves, at prices that haven't been inflated. Argos is also well known throughout Greece for its ouzo.

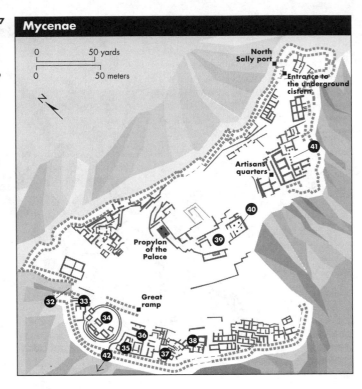

Mycenae

★ *21 km (13 mi) north of Nauplion, 9 km (5½ mi) north of Argos.*

The ancient citadel of Mycenae, which Homer describes as "rich in gold," stands on a low hill, wedged between sheer, lofty peaks but separated from them by two deep ravines. It is only 5 km (3 mi) from the Argos–Corinth highway to the gloomy, gray ruins, hardly distinguishable from the rock beneath. In their uncompromising severity they provide a fitting background to the horrors perpetrated by three generations of the hateful family of Atreus. The following saga seems more legend than history—but Hermann Schliemann's belief in Homer was triumphantly vindicated when he discovered the royal town of Mycenae, which became infamous as Agamemnon's realm.

Mycenae was founded by Perseus, son of Zeus and Danae, and the Perseid dynasty provided many of its rulers. After the last of them, Eurystheus (famous for the labors he imposed on Herakles), the Mycenaeans chose Atreus, son of Pelops and Hippodamia, as their ruler. But Atreus hated his brother, Thyestes, so much that he offered Thyestes his own children to eat, thereby incurring the wrath of the gods. Thyestes pronounced a fearful curse on Atreus and his progeny; Atreus's heir, the renowned and energetic Agamemnon, was murdered on his return from the Trojan War by his wife, Clytemnestra, and her lover, Aegisthus (Thyestes's surviving son). Orestes and his sister Electra, the children of Agamemnon, took revenge for this murder, and Orestes became king of Mycenae. During the rule of his son, Tisamenus, the descendants of Herakles returned and claimed their birthright by force, thus satisfying the wrath of the gods and the curse of Atreus.

In the 17th century BC, Mycenae began an extraordinary growth in wealth and power that was to influence all of the eastern Mediterranean.

The Mycenaean civilization, at first heavily influenced by that of Minoan Crete, spread throughout Greece, and by 1350 BC the Mycenaean culture was predominant, not only on the mainland and in the Aegean but also on Crete. Clay tablets inscribed with Mycenaean Greek writing (called Linear B) have provided us with information about the society. At its height, it centered on palaces, from which kings or princes governed feudally, holding sway over various bakers, bronze workers, textile and perfumed oil manufacturers, masons, potters, and shepherds. And there were merchants, priests and priestesses, possibly a military leader, the nobility, and, perhaps, slaves. The dwellings of the elite were decorated with wall paintings depicting processions of ladies, hunting scenes, ox-hide shields, heraldic griffins, and such religious activities as priestesses bearing stalks of grain.

From the list of deities who received offerings, it seems that the Mycenaeans worshiped familiar classical deities, but the bizarre figurines found in a shrine at Mycenae (now in the Nauplion archaeological museum)—along with models of coiled snakes—are scarcely human, let alone godlike in the style of classical statuary. Mycenaeans usually buried their dead in chamber tombs cut into the sides of hills, but rulers and their families were interred more grandly, in shaft graves at first and later in immense tholos tombs—circular vaults, a hallmark of Mycenaean architecture, made by overlapping successive courses of stones, while reducing the diameter of the opening, until it was closed with a single stone on top. The tholos was built into a hillside, like a chamber tomb, entered by a long passage, or *dromos,* and covered with a mound of earth. Doors at the end of the dromos allowed the tomb to be opened and reused—not a bad feature, since the average life expectancy of a Mycenaean was about 36 years.

Massive fortification walls and gateways, also Mycenaean specialties, were necessary defenses in a culture whose economy of agriculture and trade was supplemented by occasional raiding and intercity warfare. The Mycenaeans had widespread trade contacts—their fine pottery has been found in Cyprus, southern Italy, Egypt, and the Levant. Wrecks of trading ships apparently headed toward Greece have yielded ox-hide-shape bronze ingots, aromatic resin, logs of ebony and ivory, and blue glass for jewelry. But the heyday of the Mycenaeans did not last. Drought, earthquake, invasion, and economic collapse have all been suggested individually and in combination for their fall. Around 1250 BC, arrangements were made to secretly secure the water supplies at Mycenae itself as well as at Tiryns and Athens. Coincidence? Sometime around 1200 many sites, but not all, seem to have suffered some destruction. An uprising, invasion, or earthquake? Recovery and rebuilding took place, but it is likely that the palaces were no longer used, and it is certain that a major shift in political and economic administration was under way. By 1100 BC, when there may have been another round of destruction, Greece was heading into a Dark Age. Writing became a lost art, connections beyond the Aegean were nearly severed, and many sites were abandoned. Whatever the cause, or causes, the lights eventually went out.

In 1841, soon after the establishment of the Greek state, excavations of the **ancient citadel** by the Archaeological Society uncovered the parts of the Lion Gate that lay below the surface, and in 1874, Schliemann began to dig. Today you'll enter the citadel from the northwest through the famous **Lion Gate.** The triangle above the lintel depicts in relief two lions, whose heads, probably of steatite, are now missing. They stand facing each other, their forepaws resting on a high pedestal representing an altar, above which stands a pillar ending in a uniquely shaped capital and abacus. Above the abacus are four sculptured discs, interpreted as representing the ends of beams that supported a roof. The **gate** was closed by a double wooden door sheathed in bronze. The two halves were secured by a wooden bar, which rested in cuttings in the jambs, still visible. The holes for the pivots on which it swung can still be seen in both sill and lintel.

(33) Just inside on the right stands the **Granary,** so named for the many *pithoi* (clay storage vessels) that were found inside the building and held carbonized wheat grains. Between it and the Lion Gate a flight of steps used to lead to the top of the wall. Today you see a broad ramp leading steeply up to the palace; the staircase is modern. Beyond the gra-

(34) nary is the **Grave Circle A,** which contains six **royal shaft graves,** encircled by a row of upright **stone slabs** interrupted on its northern side by the entrance. Above each grave stood a vertical stone stele. The "grave goods" buried with the dead were an array of personal belongings including gold face masks, gold cups and jewelry, bronze swords with ivory hilts, and daggers with gold inlay, now in the National Archaeological Museum of Athens. South of the Grave Circle lie the remains

(35) (36) (37) of the **House of the Warrior Vase,** the **Ramp House,** the **Cult center,**
(38) and others; farther south is the **House of Tsountas** of Mycenae.

The palace complex covers the summit of the hill and occupies a series of **terraces;** one entered through a monumental gateway in the north-

(39) west side and, proceeding to the right, beyond it, came to the **Great Courtyard** of the palace. The ground was originally covered by a plaster coating above which was a layer of painted and decorated stucco.

(40) East of the Great Courtyard is the **Megaron** with a **porch, vestibule,** and the **throne room** itself, which had four columns supporting the roof (the bases are still visible) and a circular hearth in the center. Remains of an **archaic temple** and a **Hellenistic temple** can be seen north of the palace, and to the east on the right, on a lower level, are the **workshops** of the artists and craftsmen employed by the king. On the same

(41) level, adjoining the workshops to the east, is the **House of the Columns,** with a row of columns surrounding its central court. The remaining section of the east wall consists of an addition made in around 1250 BC to ensure free communication from the citadel with the subterranean reservoir cut at the same time. ⊠ *Site,* ☎ *0751/76585.* 🎫 *1,500 dr. (includes admission to Treasury of Atreus;* ☞ *below).* ☉ *Weekdays 8:30– 7 (8:30–5 in winter), weekends 8:30–3.*

On the hill of Panagitsa, on the left along the road that runs to the citadel, lies another Mycenaean settlement, with, close by, the most imposing

(42) example of Mycenaean architecture, the **Treasury of Atreus.** Its construction is placed around 1250 BC, contemporary with the Lion Gate and after Grave Circle A was no longer used for burials. Like the other tholos tombs, it consists of a passageway built of huge squared stones, which leads into a domed chamber. The facade of the entrance had applied decoration, but only small fragments have been preserved. Traces of bronze nails suggest that similar decoration once existed inside. The tomb was found empty, already robbed in antiquity, but it must at one time have contained rich and valuable grave goods. Pausanias tells us that the ancients considered it the Tomb of Agamemnon, its other name. ⊠ *Across from ancient citadel.* 🎫 *Fee for citadel includes this site; hang on to your ticket.* ☉ *Weekdays 8:30–7 (8:30–5 in winter).*

Ancient Nemea

(43) *18 km (11 mi) north of Mycenae.*

As the ancient storytellers once had it, *It was here that Herakles performed the first of the Twelve Labors set by the king of Argos in penance for killing his own children—he slew the ferocious Nemean lion living in a nearby cave.* Historians are interested in ancient Nemea as the site of a sanctuary of Zeus and the home of the biennial Nemean games, a Panhellenic competition like those at Isthmia, Delphi, and Olympia (today, there is a society dedicated to reviving the games and a modest competition was held at here in 1996).

The main monuments at the site are the **temple of Zeus** (built about 330 BC to replace a 6th-century BC structure), the **stadium,** and an **early Christian basilica** of the 5th–6th centuries. Three columns of the temple still stand, and efforts have begun to re-erect two more. An extraordinary feature of the stadium, which dates to the last quarter of the 4th century BC, is its vaulted tunnel and entranceway. The evidence indicates that the use of the arch in building may have been brought back from India with Alexander, though arches were previously believed to be a Roman invention. A spacious **museum** displays finds from the site, including pieces of athletic gear, and coins of various city-states and rulers. Around Nemea, keep an eye out for roadside stands where local growers sell the famous red Nemean wine of this region. ⊠ *In upland valley,* ☎ *0746/22739.* ✉ *500 dr.* ☉ *Tues.–Sun. 8–3.*

En Route As the road emerges from the hills onto the flatter terrain around Corinth, the massive rock of Acrocorinth peaks nearly 1,900 ft on the left. The ancient city sat at the foot of this imposing peak, its long walls reaching north to the harbor of Lechaion on the Gulf of Corinth.

Ancient Corinth

★ ㊹ *81 km (50½ mi) southwest of Athens, 35 km (21¾ mi) northeast of Nemea.*

West of the isthmus, the countryside opens up into a low-lying coastal plain around the head of the Gulf of Corinth. **Modern Corinth,** near the coast about 8 km (5 mi) north of the turnoff for the ancient town, is a regional center of some 23,000 inhabitants. Concrete pier-and-slab is the preferred architectural style, and the city seems to be under a seismic curse: Periodic earthquakes knock the buildings down before they have time to develop any character. It was founded in 1858 after one of these quakes leveled the old village at the ancient site; another flattened the new town in 1928; and a third in 1981 destroyed many of its buildings. Most tourists avoid the town altogether, visiting the ruins of ancient Corinth and moving on.

Ancient Corinth, at the base of the massive Acrocorinth peak (1,863 ft), was blessed: It governed the north–south land route over the isthmus and the east–west sea route. The fertile plain and hills around the city (where currants are grown, which are named for Corinth) are extensive, and the Acrocorinth afforded a virtually impregnable refuge. It had harbors at Lechaion on the Gulf of Corinth and at Kenchreai on the Saronic Gulf. Corinth was a wealthy city with a reputation for luxury and vice, including a Temple of Aphrodite with more than 1,000 sacred prostitutes. These facts are emphasized too often today, and amid the titillation the real story of Corinth is lost.

The city came to prominence in the 8th century BC, becoming a center of commerce and founding the colonies of Syracuse in Sicily and Kerkyra on Corfu. The 5th century BC saw the rise of Athens as the preeminent economic power in Greece, and Athenian "meddling" in the Gulf of Corinth and in relations between Corinth and her colonies helped bring about the Peloponnesian War. After the war, Corinth made common cause with Athens, Argos, and Boeotia against Sparta, later remaining neutral as Thebes and then Macedonia rose to power.

In the second half of the 4th century, Corinth became active once more; in 344 BC the city sent an army to rescue Syracuse, which was threatened by local tyrants allied with the Carthaginians. Timoleon, the aristocrat who led the army, was in self-imposed exile after killing his own brother, who had plotted to become tyrant of Corinth. Corinthian opinion was divided as to whether Timoleon was the savior of the city or merely a fratricide, so no one objected to Timoleon's appointment to this dangerous mission (he wasn't present at the time). The Corinthian statesman Teleclides understood the challenge facing Timoleon perfectly, saying, "We shall decide that he slew a tyrant if he is successful; that he slew his brother if he fails." The tyrants were suppressed and Carthaginian armies expelled from Sicily; Timoleon, declared a hero, retired to a small farm outside Syracuse, where he died two years later.

Corinth was conquered by Philip II of Macedon in 338 BC, but it was named the meeting place of Philip's new Hellenic confederacy. After Philip was assassinated, Alexander immediately swooped down on Corinth to meet with the confederacy, to confirm his leadership, and to forestall any thoughts of rebellion.

After the death of Alexander, the climate continued profitable for trade, and Corinth flourished. When the Roman general Flamininus defeated Macedonia in 198–196 BC, Corinth became the chief city of the Achaean confederacy, and in fact the chief city of Greece. Eventually the confederacy took up arms against Rome, attacking with more impetuosity than brains or training, and was crushed. The Romans under Lucius Mummius marched to Corinth and defeated a second Greek army, and Pausanias says: ". . . Two days after the battle he took possession in force and burnt Corinth. Most of the people who were left there were murdered by the Romans, and Mummius auctioned the women and children." Corinth was razed and its wealth sent back to Rome, and for nearly 100 years the site was abandoned. In 44 BC, Julius Caesar refounded the city, and under Pax Romana Corinth prospered as never before; its population (about 90,000 in 400 BC) was recorded as 300,000 plus 450,000 slaves.

The apostle Paul lived in Corinth for 18 months (AD 51–52), working as a tent maker or leather worker, making converts where he could. The city received imperial patronage from Hadrian, who constructed an aqueduct from Lake Stymfalia to the city, and Herodes Atticus made improvements to its civic buildings. Corinth survived invasions but was devastated by earthquakes and began a long decline with further invasions and plague. After 1204, when Constantinople fell to the Fourth Crusade, Corinth was a prize sought by all, but it eventually surrendered to Geoffrey de Villehardouin (the subsequent Prince of Achaea) and Otho de la Roche (soon to be Duke of Athens). Corinth was captured by the Turks in 1458, the Knights of Malta won it in 1612; the Venetians took a turn from 1687 until 1715, when the Turks returned; and it finally came into Greek hands in 1822.

The ancient city was huge. Excavations, which have gone on since 1896, have exposed ruins at several locations: on the height of Acrocorinth and on the slopes below, the center of the Roman city, and northward toward the coast. Most of the buildings that have been excavated are from the Roman era; only a few from before the sack of Corinth in 146 BC were rehabilitated when the city was refounded.

The **Glauke Fountain** is just past the parking lot on the left. According to Pausanias, "Jason's second wife, Glauke (also known as Creusa), threw herself into the water to obtain relief from a poisoned dress sent to her by Medea." Beyond the fountain is the **museum,** which displays examples of the pottery decorated with friezes of panthers, sphinxes, bulls, and such, for which Corinth was famous; some fine mosaics from the Roman period; and a variety of marble and terra-cotta sculptures. The remains of a temple (Temple E) adjoin the museum, and steps lead from there left toward the **Temple of Apollo.**

Seven of the original 38 columns of the Temple of Apollo are still standing, and it is by far the most striking of Corinth's ancient buildings, as well as being one of the oldest stone temples in Greece (mid-6th century BC). Beyond the temple are the remains of the **North Market,** a colonnaded square once surrounded by many small shops. South of the Temple of Apollo is the main Forum of ancient Corinth. A row of shops bounds the Forum at the far western end. East of the market is a series of small temples, and beyond is the Forum's main plaza. A long line of shops runs lengthwise through the Forum, dividing it into an **upper (southern)** and **lower (northern) terrace,** in the center of which is the bema (large podium), perhaps the very one where the Roman proconsul Gallio refused to act on accusations against St. Paul.

The southern boundary of the Forum was the **South Stoa,** a 4th-century building, perhaps erected by Philip II to house delegates to his Hellenic confederacy. There were originally 33 shops across the front, and the back was altered in Roman times to accommodate such civic offices as the council hall, or *bouleterion,* in the center. The road to Kenchreai began next to the bouleterion and headed south. Farther along the South Stoa were the entrance to the **South Basilica** and, at the far end, the **Southeast Building,** which probably was the city archive.

In the lower Forum, below the Southeast Building, was the **Julian Basilica,** a former law court; under the steps leading into it were found two starting lines (an earlier and a later one) for the course of a footrace from the Greek city. Continuing to the northeast corner of the Forum, we approach the facade of the **Fountain of Peirene.** Water from a spring was gathered into four reservoirs before flowing out through the arcadelike facade into a drawing basin in front. Frescoes of swimming fish from a 2nd-century refurbishment can still be seen. The Lechaion road heads out of the Forum to the north. A colonnaded courtyard, called the **Peribolos of Apollo,** is directly to the east of the Lechaion Road and beyond it lies a **public latrine,** with toilets in place, and the remains of a **Roman-era bath,** probably the Baths of Eurykles described by Pausanias as Corinth's best-known.

Along the west side of the Lechaion road is a large basilica entered from the Forum through the **Captives' Facade,** named for its sculptures of captive barbarians. West of the Captives' Facade the row of **Northwest Shops** completes the circuit.

Northwest of the parking lot is the **Odeon,** cut into a natural slope, which was built during the AD 1st century, but it burned down around 175. Around 225 it was renovated and used as an arena for combats between gladiators and wild beasts. Just north of the Odeon is the **Theater** (5th century BC), one of the few Greek buildings reused by the Romans, who filled in the original seats and set in new ones at a steeper angle. By the 3rd century they had adapted it for gladiatorial contests and finally for mock naval battles.

North of the Theater, just inside the city wall, are the **Fountain of Lerna** and the **Asklepieion,** the sanctuary of the god of healing with a small temple (4th century BC) set in a colonnaded courtyard and a series of dining rooms in a second courtyard. Terra-cotta votive offerings representing afflicted body parts (hands, legs, breasts, genitals, etc.) were found in the excavation of the Asklepieion, and many of them are displayed at the museum; similar votives of body parts can be purchased and blessed at some Orthodox churches in Greece today. A stone box for offerings, complete with copper coins, was found at the entrance to the sanctuary. Off the lower courtyard are the drawing basins of the Fountain of Lerna. ⊠ *5 km/3 mi west of Corinth,* ☎ *0741/31207.* 🎫 *1,200 dr.* ☉ *Daily 8:45–7 (8:45–3 in winter).*

On the slope of Acrocorinth is the **Sanctuary of Demeter,** a small stoa (long, narrow portico) and a series of dining rooms with couches. The climb up to Acrocorinth is worth the effort for both the medieval fortifications and the view, one of the best in Greece. The entrance is on the west, guarded by a moat and outer gate, middle gate, and inner gate. Most of the fortifications are Byzantine, Frankish, Venetian, and Turkish—but the right-hand tower of the innermost of the three gates is apparently a 4th-century BC original. There is no access to the site; it can only be viewed. ⊠ *Below road to Acrocorinth and on its lower slopes.*

Xylokastro

⑤ *34 km (21 mi) west of Corinth.*

Xylokastro, a pleasant little town, is perfect if you want to soak your feet after trudging around Corinth. The road just west of town that climbs up Sithas Valley also climbs up to Ano Trikala, an alpine landscape where the peak (second highest in the Peloponnese) stays covered with snow into June.

Beaches
A wide, paved promenade along the shore, with a beautiful view of the mountains across the gulf, leads to a good if somewhat pebbly **beach** (⊠ Beyond the east end of town).

ACHAEA AND ELIS
Vouraikos Gorge, Kalavrita, Rion, Patras, Chlemoutsi, Olympia

Achaea's wooded mountains guard the mountain steadfasts of Arcadia to the south and mirror the forbidding mountains of central Greece on the other side of the Corinthian Gulf. Those who venture into Achaea will inevitably find their way to Patras, a teeming port city, with all the flavor, color, and vices of port cities. Elis, farther to the south, is bucolic and peaceful. It is a land of rolling hills green with forests and vegetation, and it is not surprising that the Greeks chose this region as the place in which to hold the Olympic Games.

Vouraikos Gorge

⑥ *Diakofto, the coastal access point: 47 km (29¼ mi) west of Xylokastro; Kalavrita: 25 km (15½ mi) south of Diakofto.*

The *Kalavrita Express,* a narrow-gauge train starting at Diakofto, heads up into the mountains through the Vouraikos Gorge, a fantastic landscape of towering pinnacles and precipitous rock walls. The diminutive train, a cabless diesel engine sandwiched between two small passenger cars, crawls upward, clinging to the rails in the steeper sections with a rack and pinion. The *Kalavrita Express* makes the round-trip from Diakofto six times daily; the first trip is at 6:48 AM, and the last returns at 5:51 PM. 🎫 *Fare 1,000 dr. round-trip. Although the trip can be made from Athens (round-trip fare, Athens–Kalavrita: first-class*

4,000 dr., second-class 2,800 dr.), it is best enjoyed between Corinth and Patras.

A road goes directly from Diakofto to Kalavrita; the spectacular 25-km (15½ mi) drive negotiates the east side of the gorge. A cab from Diakofto to Kalavrita costs about 5,500 dr.

Forty-five minutes into the trip the train pauses at Zakhlorou, where you can hike up a steep path through evergreen oak, cypress, and fir to the monastery of **Mega Spileo** (altitude 3,117 ft). This 45-minute trek offers superb views of the Vouraikos valley and distant villages on the opposite side. The occasional sound of bells carries on the wind from flocks of goats grazing on the steep slopes above. The monastery, founded in the 4th century, sits at the base of a huge, curving cliff face and incorporates a large cavern (the monastery's name means "large cave"). You can tour the monastery to see an icon of the Virgin supposedly painted by St. Luke, vellum manuscripts of early gospels, and the heads of the founding monks. ⊠ *Start hike on path in Zakhlorou.* ⊗ *Daily 8–3.*

Beyond Zakhlorou, the gorge widens into a steep-sided green alpine valley for the last 11 km (7 mi) to Kalavrita (☞ *below*), a small town of about 2,000 nestled below snowcapped Mt. Helmos.

Kalavrita

㊌ *25 km (15½ mi) south of Diakofto.*

The ruins of a **Frankish castle, the Church of the Dormition,** and a **small museum** are worth seeing, but Greeks remember Kalavrita as the site of the Nazis' most heinous war crime on Greek soil. On December 13, 1943, the occupying forces rounded up and executed the town's entire male population over the age of 15, then locked women and children into the school and set it on fire. They escaped, but the Nazis later returned and burned the town to the ground. The clock on the church tower is stopped at 2:34 PM, marking the time of the execution.

Lodging

$$ 🏨 **Filoxenia.** This modern hotel caters largely to ski-season tours. All the rooms have balconies that look either to the gorge or the mountains of the Peloponnese. The decor appears to be a holdover from the '70s, but the friendliness of the staff allows you to overlook such lapses in taste. ⊠ *Kallimani, 25001,* ☎ *0692/22290 or 0692/22493,* 🗊 *0692/23009. 28 rooms. Restaurant, bar. AE, DC, MC, V.*

Outdoor Activities and Sports

HIKING AND CLIMBING

Diaselo Avgou on Mt. Helmos has a refuge for hikers, with a capacity of 12 to 16. Contact the Kalavrita Alpine Club (⊠ Top end of 25 Maritiou [25th of March St.], ☎ 0692/22611), open Mondays through Fridays from 7 to 3. The Athens travel agency **Trekking Hellas** runs a six-day "Mountains and Monasteries" hiking tour on Mts. Ziria and Helmos (☞ Contacts and Resources *in* Northern Peloponnese A to Z, *below*).

Rion

㊽ *5 km (3 mi) east of Patras, 49 km (30½ mi) west of Diakofto.*

Rion is distinguished by the **Castle of the Morea,** built by Sultan Bayazid II in 1499; it sits forlorn amid a field of oil storage tanks. Here, the Turks made their last stand in 1828, holding out for three weeks against the Anglo-French forces. Along with the **Castle of Roumeli** on Antirion's shore opposite, it guarded the narrows leading into the Gulf of Corinth. A half-hourly car ferry connects Rion with Antirion, linking the Peloponnese with central and northwestern Greece. Of the titanic bridge proposed during the first Papandreou administration, there is no trace, although officially the plan is still in the works.

Beaches
Try **Agios Vassilios** (✉ Near Rion), which received one of the highest cleanliness ratings from Perpa, Greece's ministry of the environment.

Patras

49 *135 km (84 mi) west of Corinth, 5 km (3 mi) west of Rion.*

Patras, the third-largest city in Greece, begins almost before Rion is passed. Like all respectable Greek cities, it has an ancient history. Off its harbor in 429 BC Corinthian and Athenian ships fought inconclusively, and in 279 BC the city helped defeat an invasion of Celtic Galatians. Its acropolis was fortified under Justinian in the 6th century, and Patras withstood an attack by Slavs and Saracens in 805. Silk production, begun in the 7th century, brought renewed prosperity, but control passed successively to the Franks, the Venetians, and the Turks, until the War of Independence. Thomas Palaiologos, the last Byzantine to leave Patras before the Turks took over in 1458, carried an unusual prize with him—the skull of the apostle St. Andrew, which he gave to Pius II in exchange for an annuity. St. Andrew had been crucified in Patras and had been made the city's patron saint. In 1964 Pope Paul VI returned the head to Patras (perhaps thinking that Pius II had gotten his money's worth, or that it had been a while since Thomas last collected his annuity). Today it graces St. Andrew's Cathedral, seat of the Bishop of Patras.

The major western port for freighters carrying the all-important currants, and for passenger and car ferries sailing to Italy, thoroughly modern Patras has the international, outward-looking feel common to port cities. The waterfront is pleasant enough, though not very interesting; you'll find lots of mediocre restaurants, a range of hotels, the bus and train stations, and numerous travel agents (caveat emptor). Back from the waterfront, the town gradually rises along arcaded streets, which provide welcome shade and rain protection but make some feel claustrophobic. Of the series of large platias, tree-shaded Queen Olga Square is the nicest. A good walk is to take Ayios Nikolaos Street upward through the city until it comes to the long flight of steps leading to the ruined castle overlooking the harbor.

The **Archaeological Museum**'s small rooms are choked with Mycenaean, Roman, and other ancient finds. It is a pleasant surprise to find some antiquities in a city not known for them. ✉ *Mezonos 42,* ☎ *061/275070.* ▣ *Free.* ◷ *Tues.–Sun. 8:30–3.*

Platia Olga (✉ 2 blocks uptown from Othonos Amalias, off Kolokotroni) is one of Patras's many popular squares—locals sip their ouzo and observe their fellow townspeople as they eat, drink, shop, and play in this quintessentially Greek meeting place. Other popular squares include **Platia 25 Martiou (25th of March Square)**, and **Platia Ypsila Alonia.**

In the evening the **Kastro** (✉ On hill uptown, southeast of train station) overlooking Patras draws many Greek couples seeking privacy and a spectacular view, and visitors are well advised to follow suit: The sight of the shimmering ships negotiating the harbor stirs even the most travel-weary. A word of advice: Going without a date can make you feel really out of place!

A **Roman odeon** (✉ Southwest of the Kastro, off 25th of March Sq.) remains in use in Patras, almost 2,000 years after it was first built. Today the productions of summer arts festivals are staged in the well-preserved theater, which was discovered in 1889 and heavily restored in 1960 (☞ Nightlife and the Arts, *below*).

NEED A
BREAK? Some wineries are now open for tours and tastings; among them is **Antonopoulos Winery** (✉ Tripolis, 19 km/11¾ mi south of Patras, ☎ 061/277723), open daily 9–4, with shorter hours in summer. **Achaia Clauss** (✉ 9 km/5½ mi east of Patras, ☎ 061/325051) operates tours daily 9–7:30 and in winter 9–5. Call ahead for tours and tastings.

Beaches
The closest decent beach to Patras is **Kalogria** (✉ About 32 km/20 mi west of Patras).

Dining and Lodging
Avoid the indifferent restaurants along much of Patras's waterfront. For lighter fare or after-dinner ice cream, coffee, and pastries, choose one of the cafés along upper Gerokostopoulou Street, which is closed to traffic.

$$ × **Kalypso.** One of the city's better restaurants, Kalypso serves grilled meats and *magirefta*. Star dishes include fresh grilled red mullet and dorado. Bacchus blesses the tables with several Patras vintages and barrel wine. ✉ *Posidonios 21, 9 km/5½ mi north of Patras,* ☎ *061/ 994739 or 061/994740. AE, DC, MC, V.*

$ × **Faros.** By day the owner is out hauling in his catch; by night he is serving it up to locals. Ambience does not reign here: This bare-bones place—without tablecloths or even a menu—is often quite noisy, but it serves the freshest fish at the lowest prices. Nobody speaks English, but all you have to do is point to the fish you want (you're charged by weight), order an accompanying Greek salad, sit back, and enjoy yourself. ✉ *Othonos-Amalias 101,* ☎ *061/336500. No credit cards. No lunch.*

$ × **Trikoyia.** Down by the port, the Trikoyia family cooks delicious food in its traditional taverna, where a typical menu features *kalofaga* (beef baked with ham), fresh grilled fish, and octopus with macaroni and oregano. Enjoy the ocean view while you complete your meal with a piece of baklava. ✉ *Othonos-Amalias 46,* ☎ *061/279421. AE, DC, MC, V.*

$$$ ⌂ **Astir.** Near the Patras waterfront, the genteel Astir is easily the fan-
★ ciest hotel in Patras, but discerning travelers will bemoan its rather complete absence of character. It is, however, very convenient and has a professional, courteous staff. The decor is nostalgic of the tacky mid-'60s and rundown—happily, the rooftop patio view over the quayside to the mountains on the other side of the gulf is a real winner. At night you can watch the brilliantly lighted ferries as they glide northwest toward Brindisi. The rooms are nice, some with TVs upon request, and there are plenty of public lounges. Continental breakfast is included in the price. ✉ *Ayios Andreou 16, 26223,* ☎ *061/277502,* FAX *061/271644. 120 rooms. Restaurant, bar, pool, sauna, meeting rooms. AE, DC, V.*

$$ ⌂ **Galaxia.** The Galaxia is dependable. Its wallpapered rooms have TVs and clean, gray-tile bathrooms with tubs, and there is no hokey decor. Near, but not on, the waterfront, this hotel will allow you a good night's sleep without frills or annoyances, and Continental breakfast is included in the price. ✉ *Ayios Nikolaos 9, 26221,* ☎ *061/275981 through 061/275983,* ☎ FAX *061/278815. 53 rooms. Air-conditioning. AE, DC, MC, V.*

$ ⌂ **Adonis.** The Adonis has, for its class, very good, well-kept rooms,
★ and they all have TVs, a balcony, and views in those facing the gulf and the Adriatic. On the down side, the bathrooms are closetlike, with showers of the curb-and-curtain variety. Adonis adjoins the bus terminal, and some rooms may be noisy during the day. Buffet breakfast

is included in the price. ✉ *Zaimi and Kapsali 9, 26221,* ☎ *061/ 224235, 061/224213, or 061/224257;* ℻ *061/226971. 56 rooms. Bar, air-conditioning, AE, MC, V.*

Nightlife and the Arts

BARS AND CAFÉS

For nightlife, in general it's best to ask around when you arrive. On the northern side of 25th of March Square are the steps at the head of **Gerokostopoulou Street,** below the odeon. Closed to traffic along its upper reaches, this street has myriad cafés and music bars that make it a relaxing place to spend an evening. It is the place to be for the young and hip of Patras.

FESTIVALS

Patras holds a lively **summer arts festival** (✉ Office: 104 Ayios Georgiou, ☎ 061/278206) with concerts and dance performances at the Roman odeon in the fortress. It usually runs from mid-June to early October. For more information, contact the festival hot line (☎ 061/ 272911) or the Patras EOT (☞ Visitor Information *in* Northern Peloponnese A to Z, *below*).

With a few successful vineyards in the area, Patras has also become the site of an annual **Wine Festival.** The festival aims at promoting Greek wines and usually runs during the first two weeks of September. Contact the organizers at ☎ 061/279866.

If you're lucky enough to be in Patras in late January to February, you're in for a treat: The **Carnival** (✉ Office: 104 Agios Georgiou, ☎ 061/ 279008), which lasts for several weeks, is celebrated with masquerade balls, fireworks, and the Sunday Grand Parade competition for the best costume. Be warned, however: Room rates can double or even triple during this time; tickets for seats (3,000 dr.) at the parade, which is held in front of the Municipal Theater at Platia Georgiou, are sold at the Carnival office.

NIGHTCLUBS

Worth a spin on the dance floor is the music club **Privé** (✉ Germanou 55, ☎ 061/274912). **Utopia Music Hall** (✉ Ayios Andreou 91, ☎ 061/ 222104) usually has a Greek bouzoukia variety program.

Outdoor Activities and Sports

HIKING AND CLIMBING

There is a hiking and climbing refuge at **Psarthi** on Mt. Panahaiko (capacity 50). Contact the **Patras Alpine Club** (✉ Pantanassis 29, ☎ 061/273912) for information.

TENNIS

Patras Tennis Club (☎ 061/226028) is open to the public.

Shopping

Patras is a major city and thus it is possible to buy fashionable clothing, jewelry, and other products. However, unlike most other Greek cities, Patras also has shops that sell handmade and machine-made Greek icons, which make beautiful decorations. At night in the small narrow streets surrounding the Kastro, one can find Greek craftsmen burning the midnight oil in their workshops and stores painting images of saints on wood and stone.

Chlemoutsi Castle

🔟 *56 km (34¾ mi) west of Patras.*

At the foot of Chlemoutsi Castle, the **Kastro** (✉ From Neokori 8 km/5 mi along the Loutra Killinis) is the best-preserved Frankish monument in the Peloponnese. Geoffrey I de Villehardouin, who built it from 1220 to 1223, named it Clairmont. The Venetians called it Castel Tornese, perhaps on account of the Frankish *tournoi* (coins) minted in nearby Glarentza, stamped with the facade of St. Martin's Church in Tours. The Byzantine despot Constantine Palaiologos captured it in 1427 and used it as a base from which to attack Patras, the last Frankish stronghold. The castle has a huge irregular hexagon keep, with vaulted galleries around an open court. After 1460 the Turks strengthened the gate and altered the galleries. It was captured by the Venetians in 1687, and shortly thereafter was ceded to the Turks. On the southwest side you can see a breach made by Ibrahim Pasha's cannon during the War of Independence. Basically untended, the castle is open for exploring at all hours.

Beaches

The coast south of Chlemoutsi Castle toward **Loutra Killinis** is a beach resort area, where its wide, sandy beach on the Adriatic is among the best in Greece. Farther south of the castle, near Gastouni and Pyrgos, are the fine beaches **Katakolo** and **Spiantza** (⊠ Off Hwy. 9).

Olympia

★ *112 km (69½ mi) south of Patras, 65 km (40½ mi) southeast of Chlemoutsi Castle.*

Ancient Olympia, the ancient Sanctuary of Zeus, is one of the most popular sites in Greece. Two hours is the minimum necessary to see the ruins and the fine museum, and three or four hours would be even better. Modern Olympia, of course, pales to its earlier namesake: The village is a one-street town (Praxitelous Kondilis Street, to be exact), consisting largely of hotels and tourist shops with a smattering of tavernas. It provides visitors to the ancient site with the services they need, and little else. For more of a stopover, soak up the surrounding pleasant hilly countryside, which is, for once in southern Greece, well watered and green.

Although the first Olympiad is thought to have been in 776 BC, bronze votive figures of the Geometric period (10th–8th centuries) reveal that the sanctuary was in use before that date. The festival took place every four years over a five-day period in the late summer during a sacred truce, observed by all Greek cities. Initially only native speakers of Greek (excepting slaves) could compete, but Romans were later admitted. Foreigners could watch, but married women, Greek or not, were barred from the sanctuary during the festival on pain of death. One woman caught watching was spared, however, since not only all her sons but her husband and father had won Olympic victories. The events included the footrace, boxing, chariot and horse racing, the pentathlon (combining running, jumping, wrestling, and both javelin and discus throwing), and the *pankration* (a no-holds-barred style of wrestling in which competitors could break their opponent's fingers and other body parts). By and large the Olympic festival was peaceful, though not without problems. The Spartans were banned in 420 BC for breaking the sacred truce; in 364 BC there was fighting in the Altis between the Eleans and the Pisans and Arcadians in front of the crowd who had come to watch the games; the Roman dictator Sulla carried off the treasure to finance his army and five years later held the games in Rome. The 211th festival was delayed for two years so that Nero could compete, and despite a fall from his chariot, he was awarded the victory.

The long decline of Olympia began after the reign of Hadrian. In AD 267, under threat of an invasion, many buildings were dismantled to construct a defensive wall; Christian decrees forbade the functioning of pagan sanctuaries and caused the demolition of the Altis. Earthquakes settled its fate, and flooding of the Alpheios and the Kladeos, together with landslides off the Kronion hill, buried the abandoned sanctuary.

Olympia's ruins are fairly compact, so it's easy to get a quick overview in an hour and then investigate specific buildings or head to the museum. The site is very pleasant, with plenty of trees providing shade. The ancient sanctuary occupies a compact, flat area at the base of the Kronion hill (on the north), where the Kladeos and Alpheios rivers join. It comprised the **sacred precinct,** or **Altis,** a large rectangular enclosure south of the Kronion, with **administrative buildings, baths, and workshops** on the west and south, and the **Stadium** and **Hippodrome** on the east. In 1829, a French expedition investigated the Temple of Zeus and brought a few metope fragments to the Louvre. The systematic excavation begun by the German Archaeological Institute in 1875 has continued intermittently to this day.

51 South of the entrance are the remains of a small **Roman bath** and the
52 **Gymnasion,** essentially a large open practice field surrounded by stoas.
53 The large complex opposite the Gymnasion was the **Prytaneion,** where the *prytaneis* (magistrates in charge of the games) feted the winners and where the Olympic flame burned on a sacred hearth. Just south is the gateway to the Altis, marked by two sets of four columns. Just
54 beyond is the **Philippeion,** a circular shrine started by Philip II and completed after his death by Alexander the Great.

Directly in front of the Philippeion is the large Doric temple of Hera,
55 the **Heraion** (circa 600 BC). It is well preserved, especially considering that it is constructed from the local coarse, porous shell limestone. At first it had wooden columns, which were replaced as needed, so although they are all Doric, the capitals don't exactly match. Three of the columns have been set back up. A colossal head of a goddess, possibly from the statue of Hera, was found at the temple and is now in the site museum. Just south of the Heraion are the remains of a **6th-cen-**
56 **tury BC pentagonal wall** built to enclose the **Pelopeion** (Shrine of Pelops) at the time an altar in a sacred grove. According to Pausanias, the **Altar of Olympian Zeus** was southeast of the temple of Hera, but no trace of it has been found. Some rocks mark its supposed location, the most sacred spot in the Altis, where daily blood sacrifices are said to have been made.

57 There is no doubt about the location of the **Nymphaion,** or Exedra, which brought water to Olympia from a spring to the east. A colonnade around the semicircular reservoir had statues of the family of
58 Herodes Atticus and his imperial patrons. The 4th-century **Metroon,** at the bottom of the Nymphaion terrace, was originally dedicated to Cybele, Mother of the Gods, and was taken over by the Roman imperial cult. Nearby, at the bottom of the steps leading to the Treasuries and outside the entrance of the Stadium, were **16 bronze statues of Zeus,** called the Zanes, bought with money from fines levied against those caught cheating at the games. Bribery seems to have been the most common offense (steroids not being available). Olympia also provides the earliest case of the sports-parent syndrome: In the 192nd Olympiad, Damonikos of Elis, whose son Polyktor was to wrestle Sosander of Smyrna, bribed the latter's father in an attempt to buy the victory for his son.

59 On the terrace itself are the city-state **Treasuries,** which look like small temples and were used to store valuables, such as equipment used in
60 rituals. Just off the northeast corner of the Altis is the **Stadium,** which at first ran along the terrace of the Treasuries and had no embankments

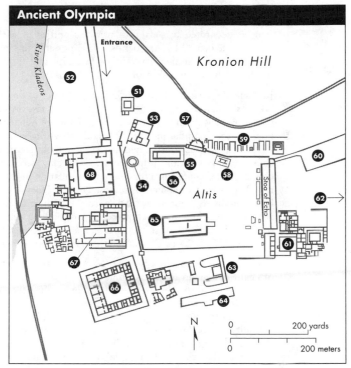

for the spectators to sit on; embankments were added later but were never given seats, and 40,000–50,000 spectators could be accommodated. The starting and finishing lines are still in place, 600 Olympic ft apart.

61 The **House of Nero,** a 1st-century villa off the southeastern corner of the Altis, was hurriedly built for his visit. Nearby was found a lead water pipe marked NER. AUG. Beyond this villa, running parallel to the **62** Stadium, was the **Hippodrome,** where horse and chariot races were held. It hasn't been excavated, and much has probably been eroded away by the Alpheios. Beyond the Altis's large southeastern gate, appended **63 64** to its southern wall, is the **Bouleuterion** and, just south of it, the **South Hall.** The Bouleuterion consisted of two rectangular halls on either side of a square building that housed the Altar of Zeus Horkios, where athletes and trainers swore to compete fairly.

65 In the southwestern corner of the Altis is the **Temple of Zeus.** Only a few column drums are in place, but the huge size of the temple platform is impressive. Designed by Libon, an Elean architect, it was built from about 470 to 456 BC. The magnificent **sculptures** from the pediments are on view in the museum at Olympia (☞ *below*). A gilded bronze statue of Nike (Victory) stood above the east pediment, matching a marble Nike (in the site museum) that stood on a pedestal in front of the temple. Both were the work of the sculptor Paionios. The cult statue inside the temple, made of gold and ivory, showed Zeus seated on a throne, holding a Nike in his open right hand and a scepter in his left. It was created in 430 BC by Pheidias, sculptor of the cult statue of Athena in the Parthenon, and was said to be seven times life size; it was one of the Seven Wonders of the Ancient World. It is said that Caligula wanted to move the statue to Rome and replace the head with one of his own, but the statue laughed out loud when his men approached it. It was removed to Constantinople and destroyed by fire in AD 475. Pausanias relates that behind the statue there was "a woolen curtain . . . decorated by Assyrian weavers and dyed with Phoenician crimson, dedicated by Antiochos." It is possible this was the veil of the Temple at Jerusalem (Antiochos IV Epiphanes forcibly converted the Temple to the worship of Zeus Olympias).

Just outside the gate at the southwestern corner of the Altis stood the **Leonidaion,** at first a guest house for important visitors and later a residence of the Roman governor of the province of Achaea. Immediately north of the Leonidaion was the **Pheidias' workshop,** where the cult statue of Zeus was constructed in a large hall of the same size and orientation as the interior of the temple. Tools, clay molds, and Pheidias's own cup (in the museum) make the identification of this building certain. It was later used as a Byzantine church. North of the workshop is the **Palaestra,** built in the 3rd century BC, for athletic training. The rooms around the square field were used for bathing and cleansing with oil, for teaching, and for socializing. ⊠ ½ km (¼ mi) outside of Olympia, ☎ 0624/22517. ☏ 1,200 dr. ☉ Weekdays 8–7, weekends 8:30–5.

The **"new" museum at Olympia** (⊠ Across from ancient Olympia), officially opened in 1982, has in its collections the sculptures from the Temple of Zeus and the Hermes of Praxiteles, discovered in the Temple of Hera in the place noted by Pausanias. The central gallery of the museum holds one of the greatest sculptural achievements of classical antiquity: the pedimental sculptures and metopes from the Temple of Zeus, depicting Herakles' Twelve Labors. The Hermes was buried under the fallen clay of the temple's upper walls and is one of the best-preserved classical statues. Unfortunately the famous Nike of Paionios is in the old museum, which is closed, so it can't be seen by visitors. There's also a notable terra-cotta group of Zeus and Ganymede; the head of the cult statue of Hera; sculptures of the family and imperial patrons of Herodes Atticus; and bronzes found at the site, including votive figurines, cauldrons, and armor. Of great historic interest are a helmet dedicated by Miltiades, the Athenian general who defeated the Persians at Marathon, and a cup owned by the sculptor Pheidias. ⊠ Southern end of main road, ☎ 0624/22529. ☏ 1,200 dr. ☉ Mon. noon– 7, Tues.–Fri. 8–7, weekends 8:30–3.

The **Museum of the Olympic Games** is just about the only tourist attraction in modern Olympia. Its impoverished collection is of some, if not great, interest. ⊠ Spiliopoulou St., ☎ 0624/22544. ☏ 500 dr. ☉ Weekdays 8–3:30, weekends 1–4:30.

Dining and Lodging

$ ✕ **Ambrosia.** Don't let the tour groups deter you; there's a reason why they flock here. You, too, should try the tasty dishes, like rabbit or lamb *ladorigani* (with olive oil and dried crushed oregano), beef yiouvetsi (meat baked in a clay pot with orzolike pasta), *briam* (a baked dish of potatoes, squash, and eggplant), fresh green beans, pastitsio, tart *dolmades* (stuffed vegetables, grape leaves, or fruit) in the traditional avgolemono sauce, and savory grilled meats. Save room for some homemade galaktobouriko for dessert. ⊠ Near train station (no street numbers outside the center), ☎ 0624/23414, ℻ 0624/22439. MC, V.

$ ✕ **Taverna Bacchus.** As in so much of Greece, the best restaurants are often in little villages outside the towns. Dimitris Zapantis' family-run taverna in the village of Miraka (just 3 km/2 mi outside of Olympia along the road to Lambia) is one such establishment and has been entertaining its guests for 20 years. Locals start to trickle in around 10:30, which is the standard dinner time for Greeks (indeed it's a little early!). Try the delectable chicken with oregano and enjoy an evening in a quaint Greek village. ⊠ *Miraka Village,* ☎ *0624/22498. No credit cards. Closed Dec.–Feb.*

$ ✕ **Taverna Praxitelous.** This taverna serves an array of mouthwatering appetizers; to sample them all, order the *pikilia* (variety) plate, which includes zucchini fritters, bourekakia, *tirolates* (ham and cheese fingers), *tzatziki* (yogurt-garlic dip), eggplant dip, and moussaka. Besides grilled meats, the typical magirefta like rabbit stifado and stuffed tomatoes go well with the barrel red or one of the local Achaea wines. In winter sit inside near the fireplace (the tables are always brightened with fresh flowers) and in summer sit out in the pedestrian zone. ⊠ *Spiliopoulou 7, near police station,* ☎ *0624/23570. V.*

$$$ 🏨 **Antonios.** This first-class hotel, set on a hill at town's edge, has fairly
★ spacious rooms with TVs and balconies. There's a swimming pool and barbecue patio, and the hotel operates the adjacent Touris [sic] Club, which has a restaurant, bar, disco, folk dance performances, and a pool. Buffet breakfast is included in the price. All rooms boast television with a satellite connection to U.S. channels. The rather worn furniture in the public areas is scheduled for replacement sometime in the "near" future. ⊠ *Road to Krestena, 27065,* ☎ *0624/22348 or 0624/22349,* FAX *0624/22112. 70 rooms. Restaurant, bar, pool. AE, MC, V.*

$$$ 🏨 **Europa (Best Western).** Olympia's best, the Europa combines white
★ stucco, pine, and red tiles in a traditional style, then mixes in high ceilings and large windows. The rooms have large beds, *flokati* (sheep wool) rugs, marble bathrooms, and small terraces. Most face the pool. Buffet breakfast is included in the price. An excellent gift shop inside the hotel specializes in high-quality Greek icons and jewelry. Set just a few minutes away from ancient and modern Olympia the Europa is surrounded by a small wood and offers a tranquil respite from the throngs of the tourist sites. ⊠ *Oikismou Drouba (off road to ancient Olympia), 27065,* ☎ *0624/22650 or 0624/22700,* FAX *0624/23166. 42 rooms. Restaurant, pool, tennis court, shop. AE, DC, MC, V.*

$ 🏨 **Apollon.** Although the rooms at the Apollon are not exceptional, the wood furnishings and white walls do create a cheerful beach-bungalow atmosphere. The owner manages to keep things in good shape, renovating bit by bit every year. Apollon is in the center of the modern town, convenient to both bus and train stations; buffet breakfast is included in the price. ⊠ *Douma 13, 27065,* ☎ *0624/22513 or 0624/22522,* FAX *0624/23068. 96 rooms. Restaurant, pool. AE, DC, MC, V.*

$ 🏨 **Kronion.** The rooms at the Kronion are uniform in many crucial respects: They're clean, and they have private baths, balconies, telephones, and high ceilings. Recent renovations have given the rooms an especially crisp, new look, though they're still basic. There are new tiles in the bathrooms and the overall decor is now a consistent yellow in the halls, and white in the rooms. The train station is close at hand. ⊠ *Tsoureka 1, 27065,* ☎ *0624/22188,* FAX *0624/22502. 33 rooms. Restaurant. AE, DC, MC, V.*

NORTHERN PELOPONNESE A TO Z

Arriving and Departing

By Bus

The regional **bus associations** (KTEL) provide frequent service at reasonable prices to Patras, Pyrgos (for Olympia), Corinth, Argos, Epidauros, Kranidi, Nauplion (for Mycenae), Sparta (for Mystras and Monemvassia), and Xylokastro. Some sample prices: Corinth (every 30 minutes, 1½ hours, 1,550 dr.), Patras (every 45 minutes, 3 hours, 3,350 dr.), Nauplion (hourly, 2½ hours, 2,450 dr.), Olympia (four buses daily, 5½ hours, 5,150 dr.), Tripolis (10 daily, 3½ hours, 3,000 dr.), Kalamata (12 daily, 4½ hours, 4,1000 dr.) Epidauros (two to three buses daily, 2½ hours, 2,000 dr.). Buses leave from Terminal A (✉ 100 Kifissou, ☎ 01/512–4910) on the outskirts of Athens (take Bus 51 at corner of Zinonos and Menandrou Sts. near Omonia Square). Pick up a bus schedule from the Athens EOT (☞ *below*) or call the following numbers for departure times or to reserve a seat: Corinth (☎ 01/512–9233); Sparta and Monemvassia, ☎ 01/512–4913; Patras (☎ 01/513–6185); Nauplion, Mycenae, and Epidauros, ☎ 01/513–4588.

By Car

Most people take the **toll highway** from Athens to the Isthmus of Corinth (84 km/52 mi, 1¼ hours) and on to Nauplion, Patras, and Olympia. Others take the **car ferry** between Patras and Italy (Ancona, Bari, or Brindisi). Car ferries for Brindisi or the Ionian islands leave from Patras's main terminal on the port; for Bari and Ancona, the pier is about 1 km (½ mi) west. An alternative route from Athens to Patras is via Delphi and the Rion–Antirion ferry.

By Ferry and Hydrofoil

Ceres (✉ Akti Miaouli 69, Piraeus, ☎ 01/459–1000) operates the Flying Dolphin hydrofoils (passengers only) from Zea Marina in Piraeus to ports on the east coast of the Peloponnese, sailing daily in summer to Porto Heli (1 hour 55 minutes, 3,375 dr.) and to Nauplion (3 hours, 4,040 dr.), and once or twice a day (3 hours 10 minutes, 5,541 dr.) to Monemvassia. In winter, there is a much-reduced schedule, especially because hydrofoils leave port only in the calmest weather. You may take your car only on the slower-moving ferryboats, which leave Athens a few times weekly for Monemvassia (car: 9,887 dr.–12,866 dr.; passenger: 2,897 dr.) and Porto Heli (car: 8,986 dr.–10,397 dr., passenger: 1,995 dr.). Call the Piraeus port authority (☎ 01/422–6000) or the Athens EOT (☞ *below*) for a ferry schedule.

Nauplion port authority (☎ 0752/27022) and Patras port authority (☎ 061/341002) can advise you about entry and exit in their ports for yachts. Patras's EOT (☞ *below*) is at the port.

By Plane

There is no plane service to the Northern Peloponnese.

By Train

Traveling by train is convenient for the Northern Peloponnese and is relatively inexpensive. Trains from Athens depart from the Peloponnissos station (✉ Sidirodromon); take Bus 057, which leaves every 10 minutes from Panepistimiou (fare 75 dr.). There are five departures daily to Nemea–Mykines–Argos–Nauplion (3 to 5 hours to Nauplion, 1,500 dr.); 13 trains daily to Corinth (2 hours, 780 dr.; on the IC, the Inter-City express, 1½ hours, 1,430 dr.); and eight daily to Patras (4½ hours, 1,580 dr.; IC 4 hours, 2,580 dr.). There is also a train line from Athens to Tripolis and Kalamata (7 hours, 2,200 dr.). Another line runs along the west coast connecting Kalamata with Patras (6 hours, 1,500 dr.). Going to Olympia by train isn't worth the trouble; the trip takes almost eight hours, with a change at Pyrgos. Note that continued rail service to the Peloponnese is in some doubt; the state-owned rail company recently recommending canceling all lines except to Patras because of aging equipment, but the government rejected the proposal. For schedule information call (☎ 01/513–1601 or 01/821–3882); some English is spoken.

Getting Around

By Bus

In addition to serving major centers, such as Nauplion, Argos, Corinth, and Patras, the coaches of the regional bus associations (KTEL) travel to virtually every village in the Northern Peloponnese. The bargain price and the extensive network makes bus travel a viable alternative to renting a car, although frequency decreases off the beaten track. Schedules are posted at local KTEL stations, usually on the main square or main street.

By Car

The roads are good in the Northern Peloponnese, and driving can be the most enjoyable (if not the most economical) way of seeing the region. The **Greek Automobile Touring Club (ELPA)** has an office in Patras (⊠ Patroon Athinon 18, ☎ 061/425411) and can assist with repairs and information. During the Epidauros Festival ELPA road-assistance vehicles patrol the roads around there.

By Train

Trains run from Athens to Corinth and then the route splits; you can go south to Argos and Nauplion or west along the coast to Patras and then south to Pyrgos and Kalamata. Alternatively you can go directly through the Peloponnese to Kalamata via Tripolis. On the western route the train stops at Kiato, Xylokastro, and Diakofto, where a wonderful narrow-gauge branch line heads inland to Kalavrita, and Aigion, before arriving in Patras. In high summer the trains between Patras and Athens can be crowded with young people arriving from or leaving for Italy on ferries from Patras. Branch lines leave the main line at Kavasila for Killini and at Pyrgos for Olympia. If you know you are returning by train, buy a round-trip ticket (good for a month); there is a substantial discount.

The *Kalavrita Express* train makes the round-trip from Diakofto–Kalavrita along the **Vouraikos Gorge** six times daily; the first trip is at 6:48 AM (leaving Diakofto), and the last returns at 5:51 PM. The fare is 1,000 dr. round-trip. Although the trip can be made from Athens (round-trip fare, Athens–Kalavrita: first-class 4,000 dr., second-class 2,800 dr.), it is best enjoyed between Corinth and Patras.

Contacts and Resources

Emergencies

Tourist Police: Patras (⊠ Patreos 53, ☎ 061/220902 or 061/220903); **Corinth** (⊠ Ermou 51, ☎ 0741/23282); **Nauplion** (⊠ 25 Martiou, ☎ 0752/28131); **Olympia** (⊠ Spiliopoulou 15, ☎ 0624/22550).

Guided Tours

Many companies offer bus tours from Athens to the major archaeological sites in the Northern Peloponnese, including half-board accommodations, guide, and entrance fees. **CHAT Tours** (⊠ Stadiou 4, ☎ 01/322–2886) and **Key Tours** (⊠ Kallirois 4, ☎ 01/923–3166) organize a two-day tour to Corinth, Mycenae, and Epidauros (25,000 dr.) and a six-day tour to all major sites in the Peloponnese, with accommodations at the best available hotels (120,000 dr.). Many local travel agents offer whirlwind day trips to sites, especially Epidauros (usually including the performance and stops at some combination of Nauplion, Mycenae, and Corinth) and Olympia. These basic, no-frills tours are for those who don't expect a lot of hand-holding and have trouble planning in advance. They can be booked at travel agencies and at larger hotels.

Hiking and Climbing

For information on hiking and mountain climbing in the Northern Peloponnese, contact the **Greek Federation of Mountaineering Associations** in Athens (⊠ Milioni 8, Athens, ☎ 01/363–6617 or 01/364–5904), which operates several huts, open to the public; a detailed brochure is available at their offices.

Pharmacies

Pharmacies, clearly identified by red-cross signs, take turns staying open late. A listing is published in the local newspaper; it is best to check at your hotel to find out not only which pharmacy is open but how to get there.

Travel Agency

Trekking Hellas (⊠ Fillelinon 7, Athens 10557, ☎ 01/315–0853 ord 01/325–0317).

Visitor Information

Greek National Tourist Organization (GNTO or EOT): Athens (⊠ Karageorgi Servias 2, ☎ 01/322–2545); **Nauplion** (⊠ 25th of March St., across from OTE, ☎ 0752/24444); **Olympia** (⊠ Praxitelous Kondili 75, ☎ 0624/23100); and **Patros** (⊠ Harbor, Terminal 6, Glyfada, ☎ 061/653358, FAX 061/423866). **Local tourist police** (☞ *above*).

9 Southern Peloponnese

Tripolis, Kalamata, Sparta, Mystras, and Monemvassia

From its ebullient ports to its ghostly Byzantine ruins, its sea of olive groves to its dizzying gorges and languorous beaches, the southern half of the Peloponnese is a land of extremes, its scenery unsubtle, almost theatrical. Cement-laden towns like Tripolis, Sparta, and Kalamata are sprawled across the region, their startling natural beauty juxtaposed with modern development. Despite the waves of invaders—Franks, Venetians, and Turks—this land is considered the distillation of all that is Greek: indulged idiosyncrasy, intractable autonomy, appreciation of simple pleasures.

By Toula
Bogdanos

Updated by
Terrence
Moloney

ANCIENT RUINS AND MEDIEVAL MONUMENTS pervade the landscape here more than in any other region of Greece. On a high plateau in the center of the Peloponnese, ungainly Tripolis contrasts sharply with the forgotten stone towns of Arcadia: Stemnitsa, Dimitsana, and medieval Karitena shield themselves beneath the Taygettus's massive range. Those who penetrate these forbidding mountains discover not only crumbling towns but also the remote Temple of Apollo in Bassae. Farther south the sandy cape of Messinia offers refuge for those escaping from earthquake-ravaged Kalamata, while Messene with its mammoth fortifications conjures up images of ancient civilizations. The Mycenaean ruins of Nestor's Palace are almost a millennium older than ancient Messene but only an hour away, as is Pylos, whose famous sea battle was immortalized in *The Guns of Navarone*.

Across the Taygettus lies Laconia, where the ancient Spartans practiced their famously disciplined armies and where Byzantium's final flourish has left us the astonishingly well preserved Mystras. The legend of Sparta still looms large, but the hour of Sparta's greatness was shorter than that of cultured Athens, and pleasure-loving Corinth outlasted both. Except for the foundations of Artemis's sanctuary and some fragments of Apollo's shrine at Amyclae, where hyacinths still bloom in spring from his lover Hyacinthus's drops of blood, nothing remains of ancient Sparta—fitting tribute perhaps to what was the first totalitarian state. Boys were taken from their parents at the age of seven and submitted to a training without parallel in history for ruthlessness; the kingdom's iron coinage was not accepted outside Sparta's borders, creating a contempt for wealth and luxury (and, in turn, rapacious kings and generals); Sparta's warrior castle subjugated the native Achaean inhabitants of the region. Today, all that remains of this realm founded on martial superiority is dust. As you move on, at the very tip of continental Europe dangles the Mani peninsula, from the charmingly dilapidated port of Gythion to the underground caves of Pirgos Dirou and to villages studded with tower houses, vestiges of the Mani's blood feuds and vendettas. Finally, on Laconia's southeast peninsula sits the inhabited medieval city of Monemvassia, known as Greece's Mont-Saint-Michel.

Pleasures and Pastimes

Dining
You won't find many fancy restaurants in the Southern Peloponnese, but the countless local tavernas and *estiatoria* (restaurants) serve memorable Greek home cooking and a great variety of fresh fish. Villages here in the south were the source of such international favorites as avgolemono soup and lamb fricassee. Don't go by looks; an underground hole-in-the-wall may serve the town's best meals, and what's available is what the butcher, fisherman, and grocer sold that day, despite what's printed on the menu. Local specialties to watch for: In the mountain villages near Tripolis, order *stifado* (beef with pearl onions), *arni souvla* (lamb on the spit), *kokoretsi* (entrails on the spit), and thick, creamy yogurt. In Sparta, look for *bardouniotiko* (a local dish of chicken stuffed with cheese, olives, and walnuts), and around Pylos, order fresh ocean fish (priced by the kilo). In the rest of Laconia, try *loukaniko xoriatiko* (village sausage), and in the Mani, ask for ham. As for wines, the light white from Mantinea is a favorite, and whenever possible, sample the *xima* (barrel wines), which range from light, dry whites to heavy, sleep-inducing reds. Except in some hotel dining

rooms, casual dress is always acceptable, and unless noted, reservations are unnecessary or not accepted.

CATEGORY	COSTS*
$$$$	over 6,000 dr.
$$$	3,500 dr.–6,000 dr.
$$	2,000 dr.–3,500 dr.
$	under 2,000 dr.

*for a three-course meal, including tax, service, and usually beer or a small carafe of wine

Fishing

The bays of the Southern Peloponnese offer fishermen a plentiful habitat of species. In Arcadia, the best place for boat fishing is south of Leonidion, off the headlands of Capes Bournia and Tourkoviglas to Fokianou bay; in April every four years, Leonidion bay fills with schools of bonito. In Messinia, try offshore Kalamata for rockfish, and southeast at Kardamili and Stoupa for blackfish, red mullet, octopus, and sea bream. The Mani coast around Kotronas (in Laconia province) has plentiful octopus, grouper, and lobster. Also in Laconia you can catch blackfish, sea bream, and lobster in the waters near Monemvassia, and rockfish, lobster, and red mullet at Neapolis, down to Cape Malea. The waters of Aia Pelagia and Kapsali, though full of fish, are difficult to negotiate because of currents.

Greek Dancing

If local folk musicians play where you are staying, go to watch the dancing, which might include the popular *kalamatianos* (a circular dance from Kalamata), or the *tsakonikos* (in which the dancers wheel tightly around each other and then swing into bizarre spirals), which resembles the sacred dance of Delos, first performed by Theseus to mime how he escaped from the Labyrinth; the *tsamikos*, from Roumeli in central Greece, is an exclusively male dance for showing off agility and derring-do.

Hiking

Throughout the Peloponnese there are many small trails or *kalderimi* (mule paths) to hike, as well as the international E4 European Rambler Trail, which starts in the Pyrenees, winds through Yugoslavia, and traverses Greece to Gythion. The southern half, from Delphi to Gythion, is considered less difficult than the northern section and can be walked most of the year; the best time is mid-May to early October. Pick up the southern section at Menalon Refuge, and continue through Vresthena, Sparta, Taygettus Refuge, and Panagia Yiatris monastery to Gythion. For more information, call the Tripolis Alpine Club, Sparta Alpine Club, or the Greek Federation of Mountaineering Associations; request a map from the Army's Geographical Service in Athens (☞ Contacts and Resources *in* Southern Peloponnese A to Z, *below for all*).

Lodging

Except for a few luxury complexes along the coast, most hotels are standard, with plain rooms and no air-conditioning, though the newer ones have more services and a bit more decorative flair. Bathrooms usually have showers instead of tubs. It's important to reserve ahead if you plan to travel in the high season (July and August), especially in coastal hotels that cater to groups. It's often cheaper to book the larger hotels through a travel agent in the town or in Athens, and in most hotels you can negotiate a lower-than-official rate off-season. If the hotels are full, you can always find private rooms, though often without a private bath. Ask the tourist police or a local travel agency for assistance.

CATEGORY	COST*
$$$$	over 25,000 dr.
$$$	10,000 dr.–25,000 dr.
$$	6,000 dr.–10,000 dr.
$	under 6,000 dr.

for a standard double room in high season, including tax and service

Nightlife

Beach towns always have their "in" bars, usually along the waterfront, and in more rural towns inland you may observe a curious ritual called the *nymphopazaro* (bride bazaar), in which groups of young marriageable women walk arm-in-arm past the main square several times a night in view of the young men sitting at the *kafenion* (traditional Greek coffeehouse) A more sophisticated version of this is the *volta* (a sort of Saturday night stroll), in which young people of both sexes, along with black-garbed grandmothers and couples with baby carriages, amble back and forth all evening in a popular spot.

If you want something faster-paced yet still traditionally Greek, try the ubiquitous *kentra* (the bouzoukia places that operate outdoors in summer). Be prepared for a lesson in decadence as dancers twirl in a frenzy, onlookers smash plates—though it's a no-no—and buy cases of champagne to toast the dancers, and singers wail away about forgotten love and remembered sins.

Water Sports

You can usually rent paddleboats and canoes on the beaches in front of major hotels; occasionally there are windsurfing and waterskiing instructors, though the rates are rather high. For example, waterskiing runs about 5,000 dr. for 15 minutes.

Sailing in Greece isn't restricted to the Aegean Islands. Many people prefer to sail to the islands near Methoni, with stops at Sapientsa, Skiza, and Venetiko. When you rent a sailboat or charter a yacht, the agency will usually indicate where to find water and fuel. The local port authority and the Naval Association can advise you on mooring information (☞ Contacts and Resources *in* Southern Peloponnese A to Z, *below*). You can moor at Gythion, which has water and fuel; in Kalamata repair service and moorings are usually available; for sailing around the Messinian cape, the port authority at Pylos can be of help.

Exploring the Southern Peloponnese

Politically, the Southern Peloponnese is divided into regions established by the ancients—Messinia in the southwest, Laconia in the southeast, and Arcadia to the north. Massive mountain ranges sweep down the fingers of the peninsula; the beaches are some of the finest and least developed in Greece. The area is considered somewhat isolated from the rest of Greece, especially politically, but its people are great respecters of *filoxenia* (hospitality). For the traveler, the regions are best divided into four: Arcadia, Messinia, Laconia, and a fourth, the Mani, part of which is administered by Messinia, and the other part by Laconia. We describe each of these regions in its own section, below.

Numbers in the text correspond to numbers in the margin and on the Southern Peloponnese map.

Great Itineraries

Though it may be less accessible, this part of the Peloponnese holds forth for the visitor a less hectic pace, and fewer crowds. The best moments come to those who stray beyond the familiar, who take time to have a coffee in the square of a village on Mt. Taygettus, a picnic at the ruins of Bassae, or a sunset swim beneath the brooding towers of a Maniote fishing hamlet. A short visit forces the traveler to make some difficult choices: Any of the four areas covered in this chapter can be explored in a few days, but not more than one. Arcadia is perhaps the most accessible from Athens. A longer stay will permit additions to the itinerary, and from Arcadia neither Messinia nor Laconia far. The Mani at the tip of the Taygettus mountain range awaits those wise enough to plan an extended stay in this outpost of Greece and Europe.

IF YOU HAVE 3 DAYS

Travelers who spend three days in the Southern Peloponnese would best be served with a visit to ☷ **Tripolis** ①, from where you can visit the Arcadian mountain village of **Andritsena** ⑤ and the **Temple of Apollo at Bassae** ⑥. These can be explored in one or even two days at a leisurely pace. On the second day, either head south to ☷ **Sparta** ⑳ and **Mystras** ㉑, or go southwest, over the forbidding Taygettus mountains to ☷ **Kalamata** ⑦. In Kalamata enjoy a seaside meal, a stroll along the long promenade by the sea, or a visit to the nearby ruins of **ancient Messene** ⑧. On the third day simply cross the famous and exquisitely beautiful Langada Pass, going east to Sparta if you're coming from Kalamata, or west to Kalamata if you're leaving Sparta.

IF YOU HAVE 6 DAYS

Begin by exploring Arcadia, basing yourself at ☷ **Tripolis** ①, from which you can visit the surrounding mountain villages of **Stemnitsa** ②, **Dimitsana** ③, **Karitena** ④, and **Andritsena** ⑤, and the Apollo **Temple at Bassae** ⑥. After two days make your way across the Taygettus to Messinia's major centers ☷ **Kalamata** ⑦. While in Messinia visit the ancient Mycenaean **Nestor's Palace** ⑩, and the port town of ☷ **Pylos** ⑪, for its archaeological museum, castles, and a beautiful bay. Finally, venture into the Mani and see **Kardamyli** ⑬; **Areopolis** ⑯, the sun-baked gateway to the Inner Mani; and the gloomy **Pirgos Dirou Caves** ⑰. If the Mani fills you with foreboding, or if you haven't seen your fill of fine Byzantine ruins, cross the Langada Pass from Kalamata to ☷ **Sparta** ⑳ where you can stomp about the Laconian Plain for a couple of days, seeing the last jewel in the Byzantine crown, **Mystras** ㉑, followed by a day's sojourn to the colorful, crumbling Laconian port of **Gythion** ⑲.

When to Tour

The Southern Peloponnese is not as popular a travel destination as the Northern Peloponnese, which means that those who choose to venture here will find many unspoiled and uncrowded sites, but they will also discover that services and resources are proportionally limited: Be prepared to endure a reduced selection of hotels and restaurants. As with the rest of Greece, on Mondays most state museums and sites are closed. On Sundays many have free admission.

ARCADIA

Tripolis, Stemnitsa, Dimitsana, Karitena, Andritsena, Bassae

Arcadia was named after Arcas, whom Zeus fathered with Callisto. Unfortunately, according to one version of the legend, Callisto's father chopped Arcas into bite-size pieces and served him to Zeus for dinner. Zeus managed to give his son new life as a bear, but in a fit of ingratitude, Arcas eventually had his wicked way with his mother. That's when Zeus decided to turn both mother and son into the constellations Ursa Major and Minor, the Big and Little Dipper.

Southern Peloponnese

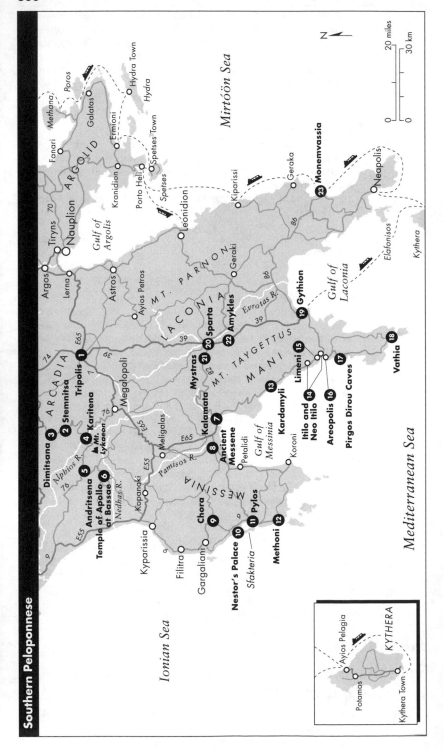

Mirtóön Sea

Mediterranean Sea

Ionian Sea

Gulf of Argolis

Gulf of Laconia

Gulf of Messinia

Methana
Poros
Hydra Town
Hydra
Fanari
ARGOLID
Galatas
Ermioni
Nauplion
Spetses Town
Kranidion
Spetses
Porto Heli
Tiryns
70
Argos
Lerna
Astros
Leonidion
Ayios Petros
Kiparissi
Geraka
Monemvassia **23**
Neapolis
Elafonisos
Kythera
MT. PARNON
LACONIA
Geraki
Sparta **20**
Amykles **22**
Evrotas R.
39
86
Gythion **19**
Tripolis **1**
E65
74
39
1
ARCADIA
Stemnitsa **2**
Dimitsana **3**
Karitena **4**
Mt. Lykaeon
Megalopoli
76
Mystras **21**
E65
82
MT. TAYGETTUS
MANI
Limeni **15**
Itilo and Neo Itilo **14**
Areopolis **16**
Pirgos Dirou Caves **17**
Vathia **18**
Kalamata **7**
Kardamyli **13**
Andritsena **5**
Temple of Apollo at Bassae **6**
Alphios R.
76
Nedhas R.
E55
Meligalas
E65
Ancient Messene **8**
Pamisos R.
Petalidi
Koroni
Kopanaki
MESSINIA
Kyparissia
Chora **9**
Gargaliani
Filitra
9
Nestor's Palace **10**
Sfakteria
Pylos **11**
Methoni **12**

N
20 miles
30 km

KYTHERA
Ayios Pelagia
Potamos
Kythera Town

No conqueror ever really dominated the Arcadians. Even when Tripolis was the Turks' administrative center, the mountain villagers lived much as they pleased, maintaining secret schools to preserve the rudiments of Greek language and religion, and harassing the Turks in roaming bands. In recent years, locals have abandoned their pastoral life to look for work in Athens; Arcadia now has no more people than Corinthia, a region half its size.

Tripolis

① *150 km (93¼ mi) southwest of Athens, 70 km (43½ mi) southwest of Corinth.*

Regardless of which direction you approach the southern half of the Peloponnese, history suggests you're sure to spend some time in Tripolis. In the days of the Ottoman Empire, this crossroads was the capital of the Turkish Pasha of the Peloponnese, and during the War of Independence it was the first target of Greek revolutionaries. They captured it in 1821 after a six-month siege, but the town went back and forth between the warring sides until 1827, when Ibrahim Pasha's retreating troops burned it to the ground. Tripolis is a dreary town; one of its few redeeming features is Platia Areos, one of the largest and most beautiful *platias* (central squares) in Greece—definitely the place to while away the time if marooned in Tripolis. Tripolis is also the ideal jumping-off point for exploring the surrounding mountain villages in an area nicknamed the Switzerland of Greece.

If you do have some extra time, visit Tripolis's small **archaeological museum** to see the artifacts from the nearby sites of Mantinea, Tegea, and elsewhere. There's some excellent inscriptions dating from the Achaean League as well as some beautiful early Christian funerary stele. ✉ *Euaggelistrias 8,* ☎ *071/242148.* ✉ *300 dr.* ☉ *Tues.–Sun. 8:30–3.*

Whether you're driving through Tripolis or are using it as a base for exploring the Arcadian mountains, catch an authentic Greek experience by visiting one of the **kafenions** on Plateia Agiou Vasiliou. Here Greek men smoke, play cards, and talk politics; women may feel a little uncomfortable but will be treated with great respect if they enter. You can also grab a quick and juicy (and very inexpensive) souvlaki at **E Gonia** in a corner of the plateia (*gonia* means "corner" in Greek).

Dining and Lodging

$$$ ✕ **Petit Trianon.** Locals no longer scowl at the gold statues and mini-
★ obelisks: they've discovered the decent prices and great cooking. Special dishes include *argitiko* (beef with pearl onions slow-cooked in a ceramic dish) and bacon-wrapped filet mignon with mouthwatering potatoes. Beware: Many appetizers and desserts are perilously heavenly. French and German wines are well matched. ✉ *Platia Areos 2 4,* ☎ *071/237413,* ℻ *071/241615. DC, MC, V.*

$$ ✕ **Café Kallisto.** Sit under the large white umbrellas of this café and order an exotic fruit tea; raisin crepes soaked in Grand Marnier; baklava; or the chef's special cake. Or savor drinks with a plate of *pikilia* (appetizers) such as meats, smoked trout, shrimp, olives, and cheese. The rosy pink interior with Hollywood prints is cozy, and a large evil-eye charm over the bar will protect you from jealous admirers. ✉ *Platia Areos 5,* ☎ *071/237019. No credit cards.*

$$ ✕ **Touristiko Periptero.** Pine trees and birdsong surround this refuge, nestled in a park—replete with a peacock and pheasant aviary—just outside of town. Try the wild chicory salad, chicken *rollo* (stuffed with ham, bacon, and cheese), *sofrito* (beef with parsley and garlic), or just a coffee. In a small hut nearby, **To Xayiati,** drinks only are served. ✉

Off Ethniki Antistasis in Agios Georgios township, look for small parking lot on the right, amidst the pines, ☎ *071/238433 or 071/222971. No credit cards.*

$$ ⊞ **Arcadia.** Tripolis's hotels aren't as distinguished as its restaurants. This six-story green cement box with ordinary rooms is the town's most comfortable and convenient; saving graces are the high ceilings, heavy dark furniture, and the roof garden. It looks like thousands of others throughout Greece—at least you'll know you're not in Kansas. ⊠ *Kolokotroni Sq. 1, 22100,* ☎ *071/225551 through 071/225553,* fax *071/222464. 45 rooms. Restaurant, bar. No credit cards.*

$ ⊞ **Menelaon.** When it opened in 1939, the Menelaon was the grandest hotel in town. It served as a hospital after the war, and thus began its denouement, although in 1960 King Constantine and his queen spent the night. It's no longer plush, but it's a good choice; spacious, clean rooms have balconies overlooking the main square. Rooms vary quite a bit; ask to see a selection. ⊠ *Platia Areos, 22100,* ☎ *071/222450, 071/224747, and 071/232740. 36 rooms. Restaurant, air-conditioning. No credit cards.*

Outdoor Activities and Sports

HIKING AND CLIMBING

The **Ostrakina Refuge** (⊠ On Mt. Menalon, ☎ 0796/22227), northwest of Tripolis, houses 26 hikers and climbers, with a kitchen, oil- and wood-burning stoves, tank water, and indoor toilets.

On Mt. Parnon at Arnomoussa, southeast of Tripolis, the **George Pierce Refuge** has accommodations for 40 people, a kitchen, oil stoves, spring water, a fireplace, and indoor toilets.

SKIING

Mt. Menalon ski center (☎ 071/22227) at Oropedio Ostrakina (4,310 ft) has five downhill runs and three tows; food and overnight accommodations are available. The center is 30 km (18½ mi) from Tripolis, with the last 3 km (2 mi) a dirt road. For information, call the Tripolis Alpine Club (☞ Contacts and Resources *in* Southern Peloponnese A to Z, *below*).

Stemnitsa

❷ *43 km (26¾ mi) northwest of Tripolis.*

The town, also called Ipsous, is wondrously perched 3,444 ft above sea level amid a forest of fir and chestnut trees. For centuries it was one of the Balkans' best-known metalworking centers, and today a minuscule school is still staffed by local artisans.

The unusual **folklore museum** devotes one floor to mock workshops for indigenous crafts such as candle making and bell casting; the other two floors house re-created traditional rooms and a haphazard collection of costumes, weapons, icons, and plates. ⊠ *Off main road,* ☎ *0795/81252.* ⊡ *Free.* ☉ *Weekdays 4–6; Wed. and Thurs. 11–1; Sat. 11–1 and 4–6; Sun. 11–1.*

Lodging

$ ⊞ **Trikoloneion.** This simple but welcoming hotel is the only accommodation of note in Stemnitsa. A wood decor dominates in an attempt to evoke the traditional Arcadian style. When the mountain air is cool and the sky begins to darken, the warm well-lit interior provides an enchanting refuge. As it is the only hotel in town it can get full on occasion, particularly if it has been booked by a tour. ⊠ *On main road, 22024,* ☎ *0795/81297,* fax *0795/81483. 20 rooms with bath. Restaurant, bar, lounge. No credit cards.*

Dimitsana

❸ *50 km (31 mi) northwest of Tripolis, 10 km (6 mi) north of Stemnitsa.*

Visit Dimitsana for a stunning view of the Arcadian mountains. Leave your car at the entrance to town and stroll the maze of narrow cobbled lanes. Archaeologists found ruins of a Cyclopean wall (irregular stones without mortar) and classical buildings near the town that belonged to the acropolis of Teuthis, the ancient city.

The **town library** displays manuscripts, rare books, and memorabilia from the Greek revolutionary period, when Dimitsana was a center for revolutionary activity against the Turks. Also explore the site of a **gunpowder mill** and the monk Hatzi Agapios's **School of Greek Letters,** which educated leaders such as Germanos, the bishop of Patras. ☒ *Main square,* ☎ *0775/31219.* ☒ *Free.* ☉ *Weekdays 8–2, Sat. 8–noon. Closed Nov.–Mar.*

Lodging

$$ ☷ **Hotel Dimitsana.** On the lamentably dull side, this roadside hotel dominates the Dimitsana hotel scene. Happily, the rooms are spotless and all feature balconies, the views from which—particularly those facing away from the road—offer delightful vistas of mountains and woods. ☒ *On main road between Stemnitsa and Dimitsana, 22007,* ☎ *0795/31518,* ℻ *071/239061. 24 rooms, 4 suites. Breakfast room. No credit cards.*

Karitena

❹ *54 km (33½ mi) west of Tripolis, 26 km (16 mi) south of Dimitsana.*

Karitena, a picturesque medieval village of stone houses topped by a Frankish castle, is depicted on the back of the 5,000 dr. bill. Now inhabited by fewer than 300 people, Karitena had a population of 20,000 during the Middle Ages. For a stunning view of the gorge and the town, walk over to the multiarched Frankish bridge that spans the Alpheios.

When the Franks took over from the Byzantines in 1209, they gave the town to Hugo de la Bruyères, who built the **Frankish castle** in 1245, then bequeathed it to his son Geoffrey, the only well-liked Frankish overlord, who was praised in *The Chronicle of Morea* for his chivalry. The castle was known as the Toledo of Greece because of its strategic position at the mouth of the Alpheios Gorge. Later, during the Revolution, the hero Theodore Kolokotronis again made use of its location, repairing the fortifications and building a house and a church within the walls as his base, out of reach of Ibrahim Pasha.

The 11th-century **Ayios Nikolaos** church has vivid and generally well preserved frescoes, though some of the faces were scratched out during the Ottoman Empire. Ask in the square for the caretaker, who has the keys. ☒ *Below the town square.*

En Route As you continue west toward Andritsena in the prefecture of Elis, you have views down into the gorge, and the road skirts narrow passes guarded by castles, known during the Middle Ages as the *Escorta.*

Andritsena

❺ *83 km (51½ mi) west of Tripolis, 29 km (18 mi) southwest of Karitena.*

Once a major hillside town, Andritsena today enjoys a claim to fame for its collection of 15th-century Venetian and Vatican first editions and documents relating to the War of Independence. A new **library** has been completed recently. ☒ *On main road, 100 yards after the square,* ☎ *0626/22242.* ☒ *Free.* ☉ *Weekdays 8:30–3.*

Temple of Apollo at Bassae

❻ *97 km (60¼ mi) southwest of Tripolis, 14 km (8½) south of Andritsena.*

The solitude of the Temple of Apollo Epikourios at Bassae, with its craggy, uncompromising scenery, may catch you unprepared: The building is elegant and spare, and untouched by vandalism or commercialism. Pausanias believed this temple was designed by Iktinos, the Parthenon's architect. Although this theory has recently been disputed, it is one of the best-preserved classical temples in Greece, superseded in its state of preservation only by the Hephaistion in Athens. The residents of nearby Phygalia built it atop an older temple in 420 BC to thank Apollo for delivering them from an epidemic; *epikourious* means "helper." The Bassae temple, made of local limestone, has some unusual details: exceptional length compared to its width; a north–south orientation rather than the usual east–west (probably because of the slope of the ground); and Ionic half-columns linked to the walls by flying buttresses. It had the first known Corinthian column sporting the characteristic acanthus leaves—only the base remains now—and the earliest example of interior sculptured friezes illustrating the battles between the Greeks and Amazons and the Centaurs and Lapiths. The friezes now hang in the British Museum.

Take the time to climb to the **summit** northwest of the temple for a view overlooking the Nedhas River, Mt. Lykaeon, and, on a clear day, the Ionian Sea. Despite its splendid setting, the temple has lost some of its impact, veiled as it is by a canopy to protect it from acid rain. ⊠ *14 km (8½ mi) south of Andritsena,* ☎ *0626/22254.* 🎫 *500 dr.* ☉ *Daily 8:30–3.*

MESSINIA
Kalamata, Pylos

Euripides called this region "a land of fair fruitage and watered by innumerable streams . . . neither very wintry in the blasts of winter, nor yet made too hot by the chariot of Hellos." Long, cool summers and mild winters may be Messinia's blessing, but nature was no ally in 1986 when an earthquake registering 6.2 on the Richter scale razed its capital, Kalamata. Though the port city started to rebuild immediately, jumbles of masonry and other reminders of the earthquake abound.

Kalamata

❼ *91 km (56½ mi) southwest of Tripolis.*

Though not Greece's finest city, Kalamata does have a pleasant mixture of sights, seaside restaurants, and beaches, and it makes an excellent base for exploring Messinia, one of Greece's most beautiful regions. Kalamata is built atop ancient Pharai, described by Homer as subject to the kingdom of Agamemnon. In the 8th century BC, Pharai was annexed as a province of Laconia, and like most other towns in the area, was not independent again until the Battle of Leuctra ended Spartan domination, prompting the Theban general Epaminondas to erect the great fortifications of Messene.

The small, well-organized **Benakeion museum** exhibits local stone tools, proto-Geometric and Geometric pottery, and a 1st-century AD Roman mosaic floor depicting Dionysos with a panther and a satyr. ⊠ *Benaki mansion, Benaki and Papazoglou Sts., near Platia 25 Martiou (25th of March Sq.),* ☎ *0721/26209.* 🎫 *Free.* ☉ *Tues.–Sat. 8–2:30, Sun. 8:30–3.*

The earthquake felled the keep of the city's **Kastro** (⊠ Hill overlooking town), but it's worth hiking the small hill for the view of the coast and the Messinian Plain. Only the theater area near the entrance is open.

In the early 13th century William de Champlitte divided the Peloponnese into 12 baronies, bestowing Kalamata on Geoffrey de Villehardouin, who built a winter **castle** (⊠ At the end of Ipapandis). Through the centuries, the castle was bitterly fought over by Franks, Slavs, and Byzantines, and today it's difficult to tell what of the remains is original. From 25th of March Square, walk up Ipapandis Street past the church and take the first left at the castle gates, which are always open.

The oldest church in Kalamata is the 13th-century **Ayii Apostoli** (Holy Apostles), a small Byzantine church dedicated to the Virgin of Kalamata (of the good eye), from whom the town may get its name. Restored after its devastation in 1986, it is one of Greece's curious double churches with two naves—one for the Roman Catholics and one for the Orthodox—that resulted from 13th- and 14th-century ecumenical efforts. The Revolution was formally declared here on March 23, 1821, when Kolokotronis captured Kalamata from the Turks. Unfortunately the church is almost always closed; your best chance of finding it open is to visit in the late afternoon (5–7). ⊠ *25th of March Sq.*

Beaches
West of Kalamata at Petalidi is the beginning of a long chain of sandy ☺ **beaches** that are ideal for children because of the shallow water. Closer to town are Verga (⊠ To the east) and the more crowded **Bouka** (⊠ 7 km/4½ mi to the west); both have showers and changing rooms.

Dining and Lodging
$$ ✗ **Selitsa.** Take in all of Kalamata and the Gulf of Messinia from the ★ tables at this hillside taverna. Wood, rock, and running water set the stage for hearty meats such as *katsiki tou fournou* (roasted goat) and roasted lamb. For a light snack, enjoy the special *paximadia* (rusks served with oregano and oil) while quaffing a glass of barrel white. Next door is a small castle, which in summer is a drinks-only bistro. ⊠ *Take main road out of Kalamata to Almiro; signs indicate where to turn for Selitsa village,* ☎ *0721/41331 or 0721/41020. No credit cards.*

$ ✗ **Kaloutas.** At this waterfront restaurant, watch the men laying out their nets to dry while you enjoy copious helpings of well-cooked Greek food: tender beef *kokkinisto* (stew) and *arni lemonato* (lamb cooked in a light lemon sauce). Mr. Kaloutas prides himself on his selection and, if he's not too busy, he takes requests. He also prepares large breakfasts with croissants, eggs, orange juice, and drip coffee instead of the drearily ubiquitous *nes* (boiled Nescafé). ⊠ *Navarinou 93,* ☎ *0721/29097. No credit cards.*

$ ✗ **Meltemi.** If you can't make it to this rustic taverna on the day they're serving a whole roast pig, you can still be smitten with the fresh fish, the *tsoutsoukakia* (rolls of spicy sausage), the *imam* (a Turkish version of moussaka), or the *exohiko* (grilled lamb). Standbys are pizza, pork chops, and the local retsina. Outdoor seating is on the harbor. ⊠ *Navarinou 25,* ☎ *0721/21260. No credit cards.*

$$$ ⌂ **Pharae Hotel.** This A-class hotel in downtown Kalamata is *the* ★ place to stay for those who can swing it. The lobby is handsome, with tasteful green furniture and marble floors. The restaurant patio overlooks the sea, as will a rooftop patio that is being built. Rooms are modern and immaculate, with all the amenities you would expect, such as TVs. ⊠ *Navarinou and Riga Fereou, 24100,* ☎ *0721/94421 through 0721/94424,* fax *0721/93969. 75 rooms, 1 suite. Restaurant, breakfast room, sauna, meeting room. AE, MC, V.*

$$ 🏨 **Haikos.** This modest beach hotel is a less expensive alternative to Kalamata's grand establishments, and it's meticulously run by the Haikos brothers. The cool blue bedrooms have ocean views, showers, and comfy sofas; a pebble-and-sand beach is just a few steps away. ✉ *Navarinou 115, 24100,* ☎ *0721/82886 or 0721/82888. 112 rooms with shower. No credit cards.*

Festivals

The annual **Independence Day celebration** is held on or around March 25, the national holiday date. Stick around for the festivities—dancing, local bands, and a spirited parade. Contact the Greek National Tourist Organization (GNTO or EOT) for information (☞ Visitor Information *in* Southern Peloponnese A to Z, *below*). In summer Kalamata holds a **theater festival**; contact the **festival office** (☎ 0721/29909) for further information.

Outdoor Activities and Sports

SWIMMING

Kalamata has public pools; call ☎ 0721/29717 for information.

Shopping

LOCAL SPECIALTIES

Kalamata is famous for its *pastelli* (sesame seed and honey candy), figs, fleshy black olives, olive oil, and the silk scarves handmade by nuns from the convent of the Virgin Ypapanti in the cathedral square.

Ancient Messene

❽ *75 km (46½ mi) southwest of Tripolis, 31 km (19¼ mi) north of Kalamata.*

The ruins of ancient Messene near Mavromati are set on the slopes of majestic Mt. Ithomi (also known as Voulkanos). Epaminondas built Messene in 370–369 BC to provide a citadel, further undermining Sparta's authority. The Messenians had battled Sparta in two Messenian Wars (743–724 BC and 650–620 BC). Even after they were defeated and reduced to helots the Messenians seized the opportunity of a severe earthquake in 464 BC to wall themselves up in the stronghold of Ithome, so that Sparta had to beg Athens to help them recapture the acropolis.

Its most striking ruin is the city's **circuit wall,** a feat of defensive architecture. Four gates remain; the best preserved is the north or **Arcadian Gate,** a double set of gates separated by a round courtyard. On the slabs of ancient paving stone below the arch, grooves worn by ancient chariot wheels are still visible. The heart of the walled city is now occupied by the village of **Mavromati,** but excavations have uncovered the most important public buildings, including a **theater,** whose seats have now been restored; the **Synedrion,** a **meeting hall** for representatives of independent Messene; the **Sebasteion,** dedicated to worship of a Roman emperor; the **sanctuary to the god Asklepios;** and a **temple to Artemis Orthia.** Outside the walls lie a **stadium** and a **cemetery.** The guard at the site usually has the key to the village's **small museum** if you want to examine the finds. ✉ *From modern town of Messene, turn north at intersection of road to Mavromati; from village, you must walk the last 2 km (1 mi),* ☎ *0724/51257.* 🎟 *Free.* ☉ *Daily 8:30–1.*

Chora

❾ *48 km (29¾ mi) west of Kalamata, 64 km (39¾ mi) west of ancient Messene.*

Stop in at Chora's **archaeological museum** to see the artifacts: golden cups and jewelry from the Mycenaean period; fragments of frescoes, including a warrior in a boar's-tusk helmet described by Homer; and plaster casts of the Linear B tablets—the originals are in the Archaeological Museum in Athens. ⊠ *Marinatou St. off town square,* ☎ *0763/ 31358.* ▣ *500 dr.* ☉ *Tues.–Sun. 8:30–3.*

⑩ **Nestor's Palace** belonged to the king of Pylos, commander, according to Homer, of the fleet of "ninety black ships" in the Trojan War. Nestor founded the town around 1300 BC—only Mycenae was larger— but the palace was burned a century later. It was here, the *Iliad* tells us, that Telemachus came to ask for news of his father, Odysseus, from Nestor, who welcomed the young man to a feast at the palace. Most of the palace rooms are clearly marked, but it's a good idea to buy the guidebook, available at the site, prepared by the University of Cincinnati, whose archaeologists excavated the site; the illustrations will help you imagine the palace in its original condition. Archaeologists believe the complex, excavated in 1952, was similar to those found in Crete and Mycenae, except that it was unfortified, an indication that surrounding towns had sworn strict allegiance to and depended economically on Pylos. In the **main building,** a simple **entrance gate** is flanked by a **guard chamber** and two **archives,** where 1,250 palm leaf–shape tablets were discovered on the first day of excavation. The tablets— records of taxes, armament expenses, and debts in Linear B script— were the first such unearthed on the Greek mainland, thus linking the Mycenaean and Minoan (Crete) civilizations, because the writing (like that in Knossos) was definitely Greek.

The entrance gate opens into a spacious **courtyard** with a balcony where spectators could watch the royal ceremonies. To the left are a **storeroom** that yielded thousands of tall-stemmed vases and a **waiting room** with built-in benches. Beyond the courtyard a **porch of the royal apartments** and a **vestibule** open onto a richly decorated **throne room.** In the middle of the room is a ceremonial **hearth** surrounded by four wooden columns (only the stone bases remain) that probably supported a shaft. Now completely destroyed, the throne once stood in the center of the wall to the right. Each **frescoed wall** depicted a different subject, like a griffin (possibly the royal emblem) or a minstrel strumming his lyre. Even the columns and the wooden ceiling were painted. Along the southern edge of the throne room were seven **storerooms** for oil, which together with the one on the floor immediately above fueled the fire that destroyed the palace.

Off a corridor to the right of the entrance are a **bathroom,** where the oldest known bathtub stands, along with jars used for collecting bathwater. Next to it are the **Queen's apartments:** In the largest room a hearth is adorned with a painted flame, the walls with hunting scenes of lions and panthers. Other rooms in the complex include the **throne room** from an earlier palace, a **shrine, workshops,** and a **conduit** that brought water from a nearby spring. Several **beehive tombs** were also found outside the palace. ⊠ *On the hwy. 4 km/2½ mi south of Chora,* ☎ *0763/ 31437.* ▣ *500 dr.* ☉ *Tues.–Sun. 8:30–3.*

Pylos

⑪ *52 km (32¼ mi) southwest of Kalamata, 22 km (13½ mi) south of Chora.*

Pylos, with its bougainvillea-swathed, pristine white houses fanning up Mt. Saint Nicholas, will remind you of an island. It was built according to a plan drawn by French engineers stationed here from 1828 to 1833 with General Maison's entourage. This port town was the site of a major naval battle in the War of Independence. Ibrahim Pasha had chosen Sfakteria, the islet that virtually blocks Pylos bay, from which to launch his attack on the mainland. For two years Greek forces flailed under Turkish firepower until in 1827, Britain, Russia, and France came in to support the Greek insurgents. They sent a fleet to persuade Turkey to sign a treaty, were accidentally fired upon, and found themselves retaliating. At the end of the battle, the allies had sunk 53 of 89 ships of the Turko-Egyptian fleet without a single loss among their 27 war vessels. The Sultan was forced to renegotiate, which paved the way for Greek independence. A column rising between a Turkish and a Venetian cannon in the town's main square, Platia Trion Navarchon (Three Admirals Square), commemorates the leaders of the fleets.

For a closer look of the bay, take an hour-long boat tour to the various monuments on **Sfakteria,** sunken Turkish ships, and the neighboring rock of **Tsichli-Baba,** which has a vast, much-photographed natural arch, nicknamed Tripito, a former pirate hideout with 144 steps. It's said that if a pregnant woman sails under this arch, she will have a boy. Boat rentals can cost up to 8,000 dr. (less expensive if you go with a group). They can also take you to the weed-infested 13th-century **Paleokastro,** one of the two fortresses guarding the channels on either side of Sfakteria, and make a stop also at **Nestor's cave.** Look for the many signs on the waterfront advertising captains' services. ⊠ *West of Pylos Port.*

For views of Pylos, the bay, and the Kamares Roman aqueduct, the **Neokastro,** the newer fortress that dominates the town, is unbeatable. It was built by the Turks in 1573 to control the southern—at that time, the only—entrance to the bay (an artificial embankment had drastically reduced the depth of the northern channel). Neokastro's well-preserved walls enclose a **church of the Transfiguration,** originally a mosque; cannons; and two anchors from the battle. The southwest wall, which could be attacked by sea, was especially strong. The highest point of the castle is guarded by a hexagonal fort flanked by towers. Until recently the fort was a prison, but unlike most Greek penitentiaries, which are fairly open, this was more secure, apparently to squelch feuds with the Mani prison, whose inmates were notoriously bellicose. ⊠ *Road to Methoni,* ☎ *0723/22897.* ☜ *800 dr.* ☉ *Daily 8–3.*

The small **archaeological museum** of Pylos has a collection of Hellenistic pottery, Roman bronze statues, engravings, battle memorabilia, gold pots, jewelry, and other objects of the Mycenaean period. ⊠ *Methonis 8,* ☎ *0723/22448.* ☜ *500 dr.* ☉ *Tues.–Sun. 8:30–3.*

Dining and Lodging

$$ ✕ **To Diethnes.** This rather nondescript restaurant serves solid Greek food. Especially good are the *briam* (a delicate mixture of potatoes and artichokes), *moschari psito* (roasted beef), and the squid. Look forward to an aromatic red barrel wine and a wide choice of Greek wines. Off-season, just the basics are served. ⊠ *Waterfront, next to police station,* ☎ *0723/22772. No credit cards.*

$ ✕ **Ta Pente Aderfia.** Blessed with perhaps the town's best sunset view, this unpretentious restaurant specializes in grilled meats, popular Greek *magirefta* (precooked dishes served at room temperature), and fresh seafood. Order the special dish called *navomaxia* (a seared fillet of beef) served in wine sauce; *psari macaronada* (an unusual combination of fish and pasta), which has to be ordered a day ahead; and the large mussels. After dinner, try the succulent local grapes or oranges. All in all, a meal here is a real treat. ⊠ *Waterfront,* ☎ *0723/22564. No credit cards.*

$$$ ☷ **Karalis Beach.** This '60s minimalist Greek hotel has typical rooms in pale shades—the ones in the front, however, have beautiful sea views, balconies, and bathtubs; those in back overlook greenery. Relax in the roof garden. A large breakfast is served buffet style. The geo-

graphic advantages are its beach locale and its four-minute walk to town center; the disadvantage is the tacky decor. ✉ *Paralia, 24001,* ☎ *0723/23021 or 0723/23022. 14 rooms. Bar. MC, V. Closed Nov.–Mar.*

$$ ⌨ **Karalis.** Probably the best value in Pylos, the Karalis has well-appointed rooms, with comfortable light-pink decor and TVs. Recent renovations include the addition of a spacious, high-ceiling restaurant. Various artistic knickknacks add a cluttered, homey feeling. The owners also run the Karalis Beach (☞ *above*), so inquiries about that hotel can be made here as well. ✉ *26 Kalamatis St., 24001,* ☎ *0723/22960 or 0723/22980. 35 rooms. Restaurant, bar, air-conditioning. MC, V.*

Methoni

⑫ *98 km (61 mi) southwest of Kalamata, 14 km (8½ mi) south of Pylos.*

Methoni, a resort at a cape south of Pylos, is so delightful, so tempting, it was one of the seven towns Agamemnon offered Achilles to appease him after his beloved Briseis was carried off. According to Homer, Pedasos, as it was called, was "rich in vines," and tradition says that the town got its modern name because *onoi* (donkeys) carrying the town's wine became *methoun* (intoxicated) from the aroma.

Methoni's principal attraction is its **Kastro.** After the Second Messenian War, the victorious Spartans gave Methoni to the Nauplians, who had been exiled from their homeland for their Spartan alliance. The town remained autonomous under Roman rule and finally came into its own during the Middle Ages as an important stop on trade routes between Europe and the East. The Venetians, who had long had designs on its fine natural harbor, took control of Methoni in 1209, building the impressive Kastro along the shoreline. If you're feeling ambitious, cross the stone bridge over the dry moat to this imposing, well-kept citadel; various coats of arms mark the walls, including that of Genoa and Venice's Lion of St. Mark. A second bridge joins the fortified town with the **Bourtzi,** an octagonal tower built on an islet during the Turkish occupation (after 1500) and now a favorite lovers' haunt. ✉ *By the coast,* ☎ *0731/25363. ▧ Free. ☉ Daily, winter 8:30–3, summer 8:30–7.*

Dining and Lodging

$$ ✕ **Louis's (formerly Kali Kardia).** Even though the owner's son Ilias
★ (Louis) has taken the reins, this place still serves the four-star food it has long been renowned for. In a neoclassical house, the restaurant's interior delights with checked tablecloths, lush plants, and family portraits. The swordfish, moschari psito flambée, and excellent desserts such as *ravani* (farina, almonds, and a heavy cognac-orange syrup) are all worthy of attention. Breakfast is also served. ✉ *Main road near castle,* ☎ *0723/31260. MC, V.*

$$ ✕ **Nikos's.** "The only time this kitchen closes is if I'm sick," says Nikos Vile, who insists on cooking everything from *mamboulas* (a moussaka made with tomatoes) to *maridakia* (lightly fried whitebait) each day. He also makes wonderful *fassolia* (beans) and *garides tsaganaki* (shrimp and cheese in a lemony red sauce). Or you may sip an aperitif at the bar or hide out in the secluded courtyard. ✉ *Miali road,* ☎ *0723/31282. No credit cards.*

$ ✕ **Rex.** Right on the beach, surrounded by large shady pines, Rex serves delicious food: hearty dolmades, pungent *tzatziki* (garlic-yogurt-cucumber dip), fresh fish such as sea bream, and for dessert, local grapes, honeydew melons, and fragrant peaches. Throughout the summer, a nearby playground entertains kids. ✉ *On beach below fortress,* ☎ *0723/31239. No credit cards. Closed Nov.–Mar.*

$$$ ☎ **Ulysses.** From the shady, well-manicured courtyard to the rooms' fresh-cut flowers, all aspects extend a welcome at this hotel. A room bonus is individual cooling and heating units. The breakfast spread includes 22 items, such as fresh orange juice, omelets, and yogurt with honey. The hotel also charters yachts; for every week's hotel stay, guests receive a free day of yacht use. ⊠ *Paralia, 24006,* ☎ *0723/31600. 12 rooms. Restaurant, bar. MC.*

$$ ☎ **Amalia.** Built in 1990, this modest hotel has basic rooms at very reasonable prices. All rooms have huge verandas that face the sea or town, both close by. The lush garden is the pride of the Kalligas family. ⊠ *Coastal road to Finikoundas, 24006,* ☎ *0723/31129 or 0723/ 31139,* FAX *0723/31195. 34 rooms with shower. Restaurant, bar. MC, V. Closed Nov.–Apr.*

Festival

On **Kathari Deftera** (Clean Monday), just before Lent, Methoni holds a mock Koutroulis village wedding at the town platia, a riotous annual performance, in which both the bride and groom are played by men.

MANI

Kardamyli, Itilo, Limeni, Areopolis, Vathia, Gythion

You now enter the Mani, which, on its western side, stretches from Kardamyli to Cape Tenaro, the mythical entrance to the underworld, and on its eastern side from Cape Tenaro up to Gythion. The western half is the Messinian Mani, while the eastern half is the Laconian Mani. Isolated and invincible, this was the land of bandits and blood feuds. The Dorians never reached this far south, Roman occupation was perfunctory, and Christianity was not established here until the 9th century. Neither the Venetians nor the Turks could quell the constant rebellions.

The Maniotes were thought to be descended from the ancient Spartans and to have been expelled from northern Laconia by invading Slavs in the 7th century. An aristocracy arose—the Nyklians—whose clans began building defensive tower houses (the oldest dates to the 15th century) and fighting for precious land in this barren landscape. The object in battle was to annihilate the enemy's tower house, as well as its entire male population. Feuds could last for years, with the women—who were safe from attack—bringing in supplies. Mani women were famous throughout Greece for their singing of the *moirologhi* (laments), like the ancient choruses in a Greek tragedy.

A truce had to be called in long-lasting feuds during the harvest, but a feud only ended with the complete destruction of a family or its surrender, called *psychiko* (a thing of the soul) in which losers filed out of their tower house one by one, kissing the hand of the enemy clan's parents. The victor then decided under what conditions the humbled family could remain in the village. When King Otto tried to tame this incorrigible bunch in 1833, his soldiers were ambushed, stripped naked, and held for ransom. Today, few people still live in the Mani. If you have the good luck to share a shot of fiery raki with a Maniote, you may notice a Cretan influence in his dress—older men still wear the baggy breeches, black headbands, and decorated jackets wrapped with heavy belts.

Kardamyli

⑬   *122 km (75¾ mi) southwest of Tripolis, 31 km (19¼ mi) southeast of Kalamata.*

Kardamyli is the gateway to the Mani on the Messinian side. It is considered part of the outer Mani, an area less bleak and stark than the inner Mani that begins at Areopolis. Here the foothills of Mt. Taygettus are still verdant and the sun is more forgiving. It has become a tourist destination for the more discerning traveler attracted to its remoteness and stark beauty, and it is particularly popular with the English. Kardamyli's most famous resident is Patrick Leigh-Fermor, an Anglo-Irish writer who has written extensively on Greece and on the Mani in particular.

Kardamyli is dotted with small clusters of **tower houses** that are being restored; some are occupied, but it is possible for the public to stroll through the paths that cut through the enclave. ⊠ *Northwest of modern town.*

Dining and Lodging

$$ ✕🏠 **Lela's Taverna Pension.** Mrs. Lela is famous here for her cooking;
★ the secret is probably in the fragrant homemade olive oil and the exceedingly fresh tomatoes and herbs. Try the chicken with rosemary, the light moussaka, and the fish soup—even if you don't like fish. Good local barrel wine is usually available. There are also three rooms and two apartments behind the taverna in an oleander-, cyclamen-, and mulberry bush–covered building. Inside, therapeutic prints of indigenous flowers hang on the walls. The rooms face the sea and are very quiet; it is a respite from busy Kalamata. ⊠ *Seaside, above a rocky beach near old soap factory,* ☎ 🖷 0721/73541. *3 rooms, 2 apartments. Restaurant. No credit cards.*

$ 🏠 **Castle Pension.** This informal pension in a restored castle rents pleasant studio rooms and apartments with cooking facilities. There is a small balcony for everyone's use, and the public areas are filled with miscellaneous paintings and sculptures—thankfully not for sale. ⊠ *Main road, 24022,* ☎ 0721/73226 or 0721/73396, 🖷 0721/73685. *10 rooms, 5 apartments. Breakfast room. No credit cards.*

Itilo and Neo Itilo

⑭ *68 km (42¼ mi) southwest of Kalamata, 37 km (23 mi) south of Kardamyli.*

Itilo and Neo Itilo are, respectively, the upper and lower parts of the same town. Neo Itilo is plunk on the curve of an enormous bay with a white pebble beach ideal for swimming; its uphill counterpart, Itilo, is nestled in a ravine amid slender cypresses. Formerly the capital of the Mani, verdant Itilo looks better from afar, with its red-tile roofs and bright blue window frames; up close, the houses are falling apart, neglected by a dwindling population. From the 16th to the 18th century, the harbor was infamous as a base for piracy and slave trading (Maniotes trading Turks to Venetians and vice versa, depending on who was in power).

Outraged by the piracy and hoping to control the pass to the north, the Turks built the nearby and deserted **Castle of Kelefa** (⊠ Across gorge from Itilo). You may walk or drive to Kelefa on a road that turns off to the right 4 km (2½ mi) before the Limeni junction.

Beach

Neo Itilo sits on a beautiful large bay with a **white pebble beach.** Enjoy a swim as you watch the fishermen fixing their nets, checking their ship hulls, and chattering amongst themselves amid the din of their portable radios.

Lodging

$$–$$$ 🏠 **Limeni Village.** Only five years old, the Limeni Village is perched on the edge of a cliff overlooking Limeni Bay. More than a dozen towers make up the "village," each with two rooms, except for two suites,

which have towers to themselves. All rooms come with balconies and overlook the sea. ⊠ *Seaside, on the road between Limeni and Areopolis, 23062,* ☎ *0733/51111 or 0733/51112,* ☏ *0733/51182. 33 rooms, 2 suites. Restaurant, pool, air-conditioning. No credit cards,*

Limeni

⑮ *70 km (43½ mi) southwest of Athens, 2 km (1 mi) south of Itilo and Neo Itilo.*

In Limeni the **restored tower** of Revolution hero Petrobey Mavromichaelis now guards little more than a string of cottages with their backs to the sea and a main street crammed with tiny shops. You may be mesmerized by the coastal scenery, but keep an eye out for donkeys, sheep, and flocks of goats that may suddenly trot into the road.

Areopolis

⑯ *74 km (46 mi) southwest of Kalamata, 4 km (2½ mi) south of Limeni.*

In Areopolis the typical Maniote tower houses began to appear in earnest, spooky sentinels in the harsh landscape. The town was renamed after the god of war Ares, because of its role in the Revolution: Mavromichaelis initiated the local uprising against the Turks here (his statue stands in the square). Areopolis now enjoys protection as a historical monument by the government, but although the town seems medieval, most of the tower houses were built in the early 1800s; the Taxiarchis (Archangels) church, though it looks like it has 12th-century reliefs over the doors, was actually built in 1798. Still, it's easy to slip vicariously into a time warp as you meander down Kapetan Matapan Street through the fields to the sea or along the dark cobblestone lanes past the tower houses with their enclosed courtyards and low-arched gateways.

Lodging

$$$ 🏠 **Londas Guest House.** The diverse influences of Hans and Jacobis, ★ Swiss and Greek respectively, have created a unique "hotel." The restored tower house—with only four rooms and two terraces—is splashed with a white-and-blue island theme. Jacobis—whose cooking has been featured in newspapers as far away as Paris—cooks upon request in the small dining room. ⊠ *Near Archangels church, 23062,* ☎ *0733/51360,* ☏ *0733/51012. 4 rooms, 2 with shared bath. No credit cards.*

$ 🏠 **Tsimova Tower.** A very unusual hotel, this is set in an old Maniote tower, complete with a narrow stone staircase and common areas cluttered with military memorabilia that the owner describes as his "museum." Despite its idiosyncracies, or perhaps because of them, the Tsimova is a good place to stay, and offers very clean rooms with TVs and excellent views. Breakfast is included. ⊠ *Near Archangels church, 23062,* ☎ *0733/51301. 7 rooms. No credit cards.*

Pirgos Dirou Caves

⑰ *84 km (52¼ mi) southwest of Kalamata, 10 km (6 mi) south of Areopolis.*

Smack-dab in the middle of nowhere appears one of Greece's natural wonders, the Pirgos Dirou caves. Carved out of the limestone by the slow-moving underground river Vlychada on its way to the sea, the **Alepotripia** and **Glyfada** caves were places of worship in Paleolithic and Neolithic times and hiding places millennia later for Resistance fighters during World War II. Even earlier, Pirgos Dirou became known throughout Greece when Maniote women beat off Ibrahim Pasha's men with scythes when they tried to take the town. Cave paintings, stone implements, evidence of pottery making, and skeletons were found in Alepotripia. The skeletons were of unburied dead, leading to speculation that an earthquake early in the Bronze Age had blocked the cave, trapping the inhabitants.

Alepotripia is closed for excavation, but visitors can see Glyfada's fantastical grottoes, with luminous pink, white, yellow, and red stalagmites and stalactites. The cave is believed to be at least 70 km (43 mi) long, with more than 2,800 waterways, perhaps extending as far as Sparta. In the **Great Ocean room,** the flowing water is nearly 100 ft deep. Visitors can take a half-hour guided boat tour for 2 km (1 mi) through nine large **chambers** full of surreal "buildings" and mythical beasts, with names like Dragon's Lair, Cathedral, and Hanging Beds of the Water Sprites. The close quarters in the passageways are not for the claustrophobic, and even in summer the caves are chilly. During the high season, you may wait up to two hours for a boat, so plan to arrive early. Next to the caves are a small bathing beach, snack bar, taverna, and small **archaeological museum** (⊠ Methonis 8), which houses the Neolithic finds from the caves. ⊠ *Along southern coast, 5 km (3 mi) west of Areopolis–Vathia Rd.,* ☎ *0733/52222 and 0733/52223.* ⊡ *3,500 dr.* ⊙ *Daily 8–2:45 in winter, 8–5 in summer.*

Vathia

⓲ *107 km (66½ mi) southwest of Kalamata, 33 km (20 ½ mi) south of Areopolis.*

Vathia's two- and three-story stone towers, clustered around the hilltop, have small windows and tiny openings over the doors through which boiling oil was poured on the unwelcome. Vathia is worth a visit simply because of the density of the tower houses and the pervasive feeling of emptiness. It is nearly a ghost town. Oddly enough, the **tower houses** are now guest houses, restored by the government to entice visitors to the village.

Lodging

$$ ⊞ **Traditional Settlements.** This is one of the government-restored tower houses, which loom over a square, a church, and abandoned domestic buildings. Rooms are simple, with regional handicrafts; the lobby, framed by heavy wooden beams and a stone floor, displays equipment from an olive press. The future of this hotel is uncertain; it may be closed or sold within a year or two, so call in advance. ⊠ *Vathia,* ☎ *0733/54244. 50 rooms. Restaurant. No credit cards.*

En Route On the way to Areopolis, about 54 km (33½ mi) from Gythion, you'll pass the fine sandy beach of Mavrovouni and the castle of Passava. It's challenging to get to the top, albeit with no regular path, but the view takes in two bays. Originally constructed in 1254 by French baron Jean de Neuilly, the castle was rebuilt by the Turks in the 18th century, then abandoned.

Gythion

⓳ *46 km (28½ mi) south of Sparta, 79 km (49 mi) north of Vathia.*

Gythion, at the foot of the Mt. Taygettus range, is a welcome sight. Graceful 19th-century pastel houses march up the steep hillside, and along the harbor, fruit-laden donkeys sidestep the peanut vendors and gypsies hawking strings of garlic. Laconia's main port, the town is the Laconian gateway to the Mani peninsula. It claims Hercules and Apollo as its founders, and survives today by exporting olives, oil, rice, and citrus fruits.

Gythion has a few rather insignificant ruins, including a well-preserved **Roman theater** (✉ Archaio Theatrou St.) with stone seats intact. Some remains of the ancient town (Laryssion) are visible on **Mt. Koumaros** (✉ 2 km/1 mi along the road), a settlement that in Roman times exported the murex shell for dyeing imperial togas purple.

It is on the tiny islet of **Marathonissi** (✉ Just east of Gythion), once called Kranae, that Paris and Helen (wife of Menelaos) consummated their love affair after escaping Sparta, provoking the Trojan War described in the *Iliad*. A causeway now joins Marathonissi to Gythion. Recently, the EOT restored a castle-house on the islet as an ethnological museum. The **Pyrgos Tzannetaki Tower** currently displays an exhibition on Mani traditional villages, which appears likely to remain in the tower indefinitely. ✉ *Marathonissi,* ☎ *0733/22676.* 🎟 *About 500 dr.* 🕙 *Daily 9–noon and 5–9.*

NEED A BREAK?	Take a late-afternoon break for grilled octopus and ouzo; Gythion is the octopus capital of Greece. The best place is **Nautilia** (✉ Southern end of waterfront, across from pier); look for the octopi dangling in the doorway.

Beaches
Near Gythion the best beaches (almost all are stony) are south on the coast between Mavrovouni and Skoutari; avoid the slightly littered public beach off the town waterfront.

Dining and Lodging
$$ ✕ **Poulikakos.** Word of mouth has made this small place a favorite for such traditional dishes as broiled stuffed peppers and *kotopoulo* (chicken) kokkinisto. Highlights are *soupies* (fresh cuttlefish) and octopus marinated in vinegar—excellent with ouzo. And sample the local barrel red if you're planning a beachside nap anyway. Heartwarming desserts, such as *rizogalo* (rice pudding with cinnamon), and a super breakfast are also served. ✉ *Platia Limani (harbor square),* ☎ *0733/ 22792. No credit cards.*

$ ✕ **Sinantisi.** Since its opening, this grill hasn't been closed for a day. The freshest seasonal local produce—artichokes in spring, squash and eggplant in summer, wild greens in winter—construct the *casserolas* (casserole-style dishes). You may also order fresh fish, appetizers such as tzatziki and *taramosalata* (pink fish-roe dip), and homemade sweets like clove-scented baklava. ✉ *On square in Mavrovouni village, about 2 km (1 mi) outside town,* ☎ *0733/22256. MC, V. No lunch.*

$$$ 🏨 **Lakonis.** For romance, choose these white bungalows set like an amphitheater on a cliff 3 km (2 mi) out of town. Brilliant red and pink ★   flowers dot the landscape, and the beach below is so popular the hotel drained the Olympic-size pool in defeat. Nestle up to the bar and fireplace at the lofty circular restaurant, enjoying the vistas through the plate-glass windows; in summer, the informal beach restaurant is great for lunch. ✉ *Skalas 3, 23200,* ☎ *0733/22666 or 0733/22667,* 🖷 *0733/ 23668. 100 rooms, 80 with bath. Restaurant, bar. No credit cards. Closed Nov.–Mar.*

$$ 🏨 **Aktaion.** This hotel is a pleasure. All rooms are squeaky clean and ★   modern, with subdued colors, seafaring balconies, and TVs. Lovely prints depict Maniote life. ✉ *39 Vassileos Pavlou, 23200,* ☎ *0733/23500 or 0733/23501,* 🖷 *0733/22294. 22 rooms. No credit cards. Breakfast room, air-conditioning.*

$ 🏨 **Githion.** This good town-center hotel is booked a year in advance, so call ahead. All the double and triple rooms are stark white with wood furniture, TVs, and sea views. Request a room with two balconies and, if you're traveling with children, two housekeeping apartments for an economical alternative. ✉ *Vassileos Pavlou 33, 23200,* ☎ *0733/22289 or 0733/22166,* 🖷 *0733/22284. 57 rooms. Dining room, air-conditioning. MC, V.*

Outdoor Activities and Sports

SWIMMING

Gythion is best for daydreaming on the waterfront or swimming off the rocks of Marathonissi.

LACONIA

Sparta, Mystras, Monemvassia

The Laconian Plain is surrounded on three sides by mountains and on one side by the sea. Perhaps it was the fear that enemies could descend those mountains at any time that drove the Spartans to make Laconia their training ground, where they developed the finest fighting force in ancient Greece. A mighty power that controlled three-fifths of the Peloponnese, Sparta contributed to the Greek victory in the second Persian War (5th century BC). Ultimately, its aggressiveness and its jealousy of Athens brought about the Peloponnesian War, which drained its resources but left it victorious. The Greek world found Sparta to be an even harsher master than Athens, and this fact may have led to its losses in the Boetian and Corinthian wars, at the Battle of Leuctra, and in 222–221 BC at the hands of the Achaean League, who liberated all areas Sparta had conquered. A second period of prosperity under the Romans ended with the barbarian invasions in the 3rd century, and Sparta declined rapidly.

Laconia can also claim two important medieval sites: Mystras and Monemvassia. Jewels in the Byzantine crown, the former is an intellectual and political center, the latter a sea fortress meant to ward off invaders from the east.

Sparta

㉑ *60 km (37¼ mi) south of Tripolis, 60 km (37¼ mi) east of Kalamata.*

For those who have read about ancient Sparta, the bellicose city-state that once dominated the Greek world, the modern city is a disappointment—it is all too spartan in its dreary angularity, unrelieved by the broad Eurotas River, which is screened by pleasant orchards. Given the area's earthquakes and the Spartans' no-frills approach—living more like an army camp than a city-state—no elaborate ruins remain, a fact that so disconcerted Otto, Greece's first king, that in 1835 he ordered the modern city built on the ancient site.

The Spartans' relentless militarism set them apart from other Greeks. They were expected to emerge victorious from a battle or not at all, and for most of its existence Sparta was without a wall, because according to Lykourgos, its leader, who wrote Sparta's constitution, "chests, not walls, make a city." From the 9th to the 4th century BC, Spartans trained for a life of war. From the age of seven, boys in the reigning warrior class submitted to a strict regimen, eating mostly herbs, roots, and the famous black broth. Rich foods were thought to stunt growth. Forbidden to work, they trained for combat and practiced stealing, an acceptable skill unless one was caught. One legend describes a Spartan youth who let a concealed fox chew off his arm rather than reveal his theft. Girls also trained rigorously in the belief they would bear healthier offspring; for the same reason, newlyweds were forbidden to make love frequently.

At the **Temple of Artemis Orthia** (⊠ Just outside of town on Tripolis Rd., down the path to the Evrotas River), the young Spartan men underwent *krypteia* (initiations) that entailed severe public floggings. The altar had to be splashed with blood before the goddess was satisfied. Traces of two such altars are among sparse vestiges of the 6th-century BC temple. The larger ruins are the remains of a grandstand built in the 3rd century AD by the Romans, who revived the flogging tradition as a public spectacle.

Ancient Sparta's **acropolis** (⊠ At north end of town) is now part archaeological site, part park. Locals can be seen here strolling, along with many young couples stealing a romantic moment amid the fallen limestone and shady trees. The ruins include a **theater,** a **stadium,** and a **sanctuary to Athena.**

Stop a moment and contemplate the stern **Statue of Leonidas** (⊠ At end of Konstantinou St.). During the Second Persian War, with 30,000 Persians advancing on his army of 8,000, Leonidas, ordered to surrender his weapons, jeered, "Come and get them." For two days he held off the enemy, until a traitor named Efialtes (the word has since come to mean "nightmare" in Greek) showed the Persians a way to attack from the rear. Leonidas ordered all but 300 Spartans and 700 Thespians to withdraw, and when forced to retreat to a wooded knoll, he is said to have commented, "So much the better, we will fight in the shade," before his entire troop was slaughtered.

Enjoy an hour in the city's **archaeological museum,** tucked into a cool park. Its eclectic collection reflects Laconia's turbulent history: Neolithic pottery; jewels and tools excavated from the Alepotrypa cave; Mycenaean tomb finds; bright 4th- and 5th-century Roman mosaics; and objects from Sparta, including an expressive clay woman's head, a Parian marble statue of Leonidas (490 BC), prizes given to the Spartan youths, and ritual dance masks. Most characteristic of Spartan art are the bas-reliefs with deities and heroes; note the one depicting a seated couple bearing gifts and framed by a snake (540 BC). ⊠ *Ayios Nikonos between Dafnou and Evangelistria,* ☎ *0731/28575.* 🎟 *500 dr.* ⊘ *Tues.–Sat. 8:30–3, Sun. 8:30–2:30.*

NEED A BREAK?	If you should find yourself waiting for a bus out of Sparta at dinnertime, cross the street to **Parthenon** (⊠ Vrasidou 106, ☎ 0731/23767) for the best gyro you may ever eat. The meat, which has a local reputation for being a cut above, is served in pita with just the right amount of chew and generous doses of onion, tomato, and tzatziki sauce.

Dining and Lodging

$$ ✕ **Diethnes.** Local vernacular claims this is one of Sparta's best restaurants. You'll be wowed by classic specialties that, here, translate into a special fish dish made with garlic, parsley, wine, oil, and rusks; bardouniotiko made with onions, *sfela* (a hard Kalamatan cheese), and red sauce; and occasionally delicacies such as sheep's heads cooked on a spit and kokoretsi. The summer courtyard rounds out a perfect meal. ⊠ *Paleologou 105,* ☎ *0731/28636. No credit cards.*

$$ ✕ **Stelakos.** Just outside of Sparta in the quaint village of Parori, this spot has been delighting locals and visitors with its excellent chicken dishes, which are its specialty. After enjoying the charming and rustic pleasures of this place, take a stroll outside for an unimpeded view of the Taygettus mountain range. ⊠ *Parori, 5 km (3 mi) south of Sparta on the road to Mystras,* ☎ *0731/83346. No credit cards. Closed Sun.*

$ **✕ Semiramis.** This underground restaurant, with fluorescent lighting
★ and a linoleum floor, is no visual treat, but the simple Greek dishes are
perfectly cooked. In spring, try the *anginares antidia* (wild artichokes
with red sauce) and in summer the stuffed squash. The barrel wine is
fragrant but deceivingly light. For dessert try the rich sheep yogurt with
honey before you stagger outdoors. ⊠ *Paleologou 48,* ☎ *0731/26640.*
No credit cards. No lunch alternate Sun.

$$$ **☷ Lida.** This hotel is pricey for its category, but it provides flawless
service. The owner's wife is an interior designer, as is evident in the
rooms and in the lobby with antique treadles, stones from flour mills
and olive presses, and lithographs of Greek revolutionary heroes. Ask
for a room above the third floor for views of Mt. Taygettus. ⊠ *Anan-
iou and Atreidon, 23100,* ☎ *0731/23601 and 0731/23602. 40 rooms.
Restaurant, bar. AE, MC, V. Closed mid-Nov.–Feb.*

$$ **☷ Hotel Maniatis.** It's hard to believe this hotel is so reasonably priced.
★ Though the color scheme is unfortunately reminiscent of Los Angeles
in the '80s, it is unusually well run, with attention to detail. Ask for a
room with a view, and, if you need a bathtub, a corner room. All the
rooms were renovated in 1997 and have a fairly classy sleek decor (which
contrasts sharply with the lobby)—the dark, rounded furniture provides a welcome break from the rectangular pine which is the usual
favorite of Greek hoteliers. Rooms now come with TVs, air-conditioning,
and wall-to-wall carpeting. The hotel's Dias restaurant is elegant, with
specialities such as *arni araxobitiko* (lamb with onions, cheese, red sauce,
and walnuts) and *bourekakia* pastries. ⊠ *Paleologou 72, 23100,* ☎
0731/22665, ℻ *0731/29994. 80 rooms. Restaurant, bar, lobby lounge,
air-conditioning. MC, V.*

$$ **☷ Menelaion.** Sparta's dowager hotel presides over the main strip. A
thorough renovation has left the Menelaion with that part of its past
which is delightful and eliminated those parts which were a nuisance.
There's still the old-fashioned high-ceiling lobby (check out the phone
booths), but the room now has new, very comfortable furniture. With
their dark furniture, the guest rooms are just the place to retire with a
dog-eared copy of *The Magus.* There's a TV lounge and even 24-hour
room service. ⊠ *Paleologou 91, 23100,* ☎ *0731/22161 through 0732/
22165,* ℻ *0731/26332. 48 rooms. Restaurant, bar, air-conditioning,
minibars, indoor pool. MC, V.*

Sports

SWIMMING

If you absolutely must have your daily swim, bring your goggles and
fins to the public pool run by the Sparta Municipal Center (☎ *0731/
24852*).

Mystras

★ ㉑ *64 km (39¾ mi) southwest of Tripolis, 4 km (2½ mi) west of Sparta.*

Ethereal Mystras, with its abandoned gold and stone palaces, churches,
and monasteries lining serpentine paths, is eerie. The scent of herbs and
wildflowers permeates the air, goat bells tinker yonder, and the silvery
olive trees glisten with the slightest breeze. An intellectual and cultural
center where philosophers like Chrysoloras, "the sage of Byzantium,"
held forth on the good and the beautiful, it seems an appropriate place
for the last hurrah of the Byzantine emperors in the 14th century.

In 1249 William de Villehardouin built the castle in Mystras in an at-
tempt to control Laconia and establish Frankish supremacy over the
Peloponnese. He held court here with his beautiful Greek wife, Anna
Comnena, surrounded by knights of Champagne, Burgundy, and Flan-
ders, but in 1259 he was defeated by the Byzantines. As the Byzantines

built a palace and numerous churches (whose frescoes exemplified several periods of painting), the town gradually grew down the slope.

At first the seat of the Byzantine governor, Mystras later became the capital of the Despotate of Morea. It was the despots who made Mystras a cultural phenomenon, and it was the despots—specifically Emperor Constantine's brother Demetrios Palaiologos—who surrendered the city to the Turks in 1460, signaling the beginning of the end. For a while the town survived because of its silk industry, but after repeated pillaging and burning by bands of Albanians, by Russians, and by Ibrahim Pasha's Egyptian troops, the inhabitants gave up and moved to modern Sparta.

In spring Mystras is resplendent with wildflowers and butterflies like brimstones and swallowtails, but it can be oppressively hot in summer, so get an early start. Bring water and sturdy shoes for the slippery rocks and the occasional snake.

Among the most important buildings in the lower town (Kato Chora) is **Ayios Demetrios,** the *mitropolis* (cathedral) founded in 1291. Set in its floor is a stone with the two-headed Byzantine eagle marking the spot where Constantine XII, the last emperor of Byzantium, was consecrated. The cathedral's brilliant frescoes include a vivid depiction of the *Virgin and Child* on the central apse and a wall painting in the narthex of the *Second Coming,* its two red-and-turquoise winged angels sorrowful as they open the records of Good and Evil. One wing of the church houses a **museum** that holds fragments of Byzantine sculptures, including an eagle seizing its prey (11th century), later Byzantine icons, jewels, decorative metalwork, and coins. ✉ *Lower town.* ▦ *1,200 dr. covers all Mystras sites.* ⊗ *Daily winter 8:30–3, summer 8–7.*

In the **Vrontokion monastery** are Ayios Theodoros (AD 1295), the oldest church in Mystras, and the 14th-century **Church of Panagia Odegetria,** or **Afendiko,** which is decorated with remarkable murals. These include, in the narthex, scenes of the miracles of Christ: *The Healing of the Blind Man, The Samaritan at the Well,* and *The Marriage of Cana.* The fluidity of the brush strokes, the subtle but complicated coloring, and the resonant expressions suggest the work of extremely skilled hands. ✉ *Lower town, along path to the right.* ▦ *1,200 dr. covers all Mystras sites.* ⊗ *Daily winter 8:30–3, summer 8–7.*

The **Pantanassa monastery** is a visual feast of intricate tiling, rosette-festooned loops mimicking frosting on a wedding cake, and myriad arches. It is the only inhabited building in Mystras; the hospitable nuns still produce embroidery for sale. Step out onto the east portico for a view of the Evrotas River valley below. ✉ *Lower town.* ▦ *1,200 dr. covers all Mystras sites.* ⊗ *Daily winter 8:30–3, summer 8–7.*

Every inch of the tiny **Perivleptos monastery,** meaning "attracting attention from all sides," is covered with exceptional 14th-century illustrations from the New Testament, including *The Birth of the Virgin*—in a lush palette of reds, yellows, and oranges—*The Dormition of the Virgin* above the entrance (with Christ holding his mother's soul represented as a baby), and immediately to the left of the entrance, the famous fresco of the *Divine Liturgy.* ✉ *Lower town, in the southernmost corner.* ▦ *1,200 dr. covers all Mystras sites.* ⊗ *Daily winter 8:30–3, summer 8–7.*

In the upper town (Ano Chora), where most aristocrats lived, stands a rare Byzantine civic building, the **Palace of Despots,** home of the last emperor. The older, northeastern wing contains a guardroom, a kitchen, and the residence. The three-story northwest wing contains an immense reception hall on its top floor, lit by eight Gothic windows and heated by eight huge chimneys; the throne probably stood in the shallow alcove that's in the center of a wall.

In the palace's **Ayia Sofia chapel,** the Italian wives of emperors Constantine and Theodore Palaiologos are buried. Note the polychromatic marble floor and the frescoes that were preserved for years under whitewash, applied by the Turks when they transformed this into a mosque. Climb to the **castle** and look down into the gullies of Mt. Taygettus, where it's said the Spartans, who hated weakness, hurled their malformed babies. ✉ *Ano Chora,* ☎ *0731/93377.* 🎫 *1,200 dr. covers all Mystras sites.* ☉ *Daily winter 8:30–3, summer 8–7.*

Outdoor Activities and Sports
HIKING AND CLIMBING

The Athens travel agency **Trekking Hellas** (☞ Contacts and Resources *in* Southern Peloponnese A to Z, *below*) arranges weekend hiking trips to Mystras and a six-day walk through the Taygettus foothills, with visits to the Mani and Mystras.

A mountain refuge, with a capacity of 24, is set up at **Varvara-Dereki** on Mt. Taygettus. It has a kitchen, an oil stove, a tank, spring water, and outdoor toilets. Contact the Sparta Alpine Club (☞ Contacts and Resources *in* Southern Peloponnese A to Z, *below*).

Shopping
EMBROIDERY

In Mystras the nuns at **Pantanassa** (✉ Lower town) monastery still make and sell their delicate embroidery.

Amykles

 67 km (41½ mi) south of Tripolis, 7 km (4½ mi) south of Mystras.

Achaean rulers made Amykles their capital, which was inhabited from the early Bronze Age on, and eventually one of Sparta's settlements.

The **Temple of Apollo** (✉ On the knoll) once housed a colossal statue of the god, which was engraved on coins of that period. Only a few traces of Amykles' **acropolis wall** (✉ On the knoll) remain, but the site is an excellent picnic spot. A *tholos* (Mycenaean beehive tomb; ✉ On a knoll at Vapheio) yielded important gold and silver artifacts, including two famous hammered gold cups depicting wild bulls savagely trampling a hunter, then peacefully grazing. The cups are now in Athens's Archaeological Museum.

Monemvassia

★ *96 km (59½ mi) southeast of Sparta, 89 km (55¼ mi) southeast of Amykles.*

The Byzantine town of Monemvassia clings to the side of the 1,148-ft rock that seems to blast out of the sea; in AD 375, it was separated from the mainland by an earthquake. Like Gibraltar, Monemvassia once controlled the sea lines from western Europe to the Levant. The name *moni emvasia* (single entrance) refers to the narrow passage to this walled community. If you come from Athens by ferry or hydrofoil, you'll get the most spectacular view; if you walk or take a taxi down the causeway from the adjoining town of Gefira, the rock looks uninhabited until you suddenly see castellated walls with an opening only wide enough for one person.

The town was first inhabited in the 6th century AD, when Laconians sought refuge after Arab and Slav raids. During its golden age in the

1400s under the Byzantines, Monemvassia was home to families made wealthy by their inland estates and the export of malmsey wine, a sweet variety of Madeira praised by Shakespeare. When the area fell to the Turks, Monemvassia ended up under the Pope's control and then came under sway of the Venetians, who built the citadel and most of the fortifications.

Well-to-do Greeks once again live on the rock in houses they have restored as vacation homes. Summer weekends are crowded, but off-season Monemvassia is nearly deserted. Empty houses are lined up along steep streets only wide enough for two people abreast, and remnants of another age—escutcheons, marble thrones, Byzantine icons—evoke the sense that time has stopped. It's worth a splurge to stay overnight here.

Christos Elkomenos (Christ in Chains; ⊠ Platia Tzamiou, along the main street) is reputed as the largest medieval church in southern Greece. The carved peacocks are symbolic of the Byzantine era; the detached bell tower—like those of Italian cathedrals—is a sign of Venetian rebuilding in the 17th century.

The 10th-century **Agios Pavlos** (⊠ Across from Platia Tzamiou), though converted into a mosque, was allowed to function as a church under the Ottoman occupation, an unusual indulgence.

For solitude and a dizzying view, pass through the upper town's wooden entrance gates, complete with the original iron reinforcement. Up the hill is a rare example of a domed octagonal church, **Agia Sofia** (⊠ At top of the mountain), founded in the 13th century by Emperor Andronicus II and patterned after Dafni monastery in Athens. Follow the path to the highest point on the rock for a breathtaking view of the coast.

Dining and Lodging

$$ ✕ **Marianthi.** You'll feel like you're dropping into someone's home at dinner here: Family photos of stern, mustachioed ancestors hang on the walls along with local memorabilia; someone's aunt is doing the cooking, and the service is just as homey. Order the wild mountain greens, any of the fish—especially the fresh red mullet—the addictive potato salad (you may have to order two plates), and the marinated octopus sprinkled with oregano. ⊠ *Old town,* ☏ *0732/61371. No credit cards.*

$$ ✕ **To Kanoni.** After you roll out of bed, wander over to the Kanoni, which serves breakfast on a terrace overlooking the square's *kanoni* (cannon). Choose from omelets, ham and eggs, bacon, or thick, creamy yogurt and honey. Inside you'll find red-and-white checked tablecloths, 19th-century prints of Greece, and a glorious sea view, accompanied by calming wave music. If you miss breakfast, you can always order a burger or beef *yiouvetsi* (meat baked in a clay pot with orzolike pasta). ⊠ *Old town,* ☏ *0732/61387. No credit cards.*

$$ ▥ **Byzantinon.** The Byzantinon is housed in an old building; the re-
★ quirement that owners get permission from the archaeological bureau before making any changes explains the rudimentary showers in some rooms. All the rooms are shaped differently, with beautiful decorations: a carved marble tile depicting a scale set in the floor; a Greek costume sketch adorning an alcove; sailors' lanterns for illumination. The best is Suite 1, a perfect hideout with an antique radio, marble bath, balcony, hidden kitchen, and large, cozy bed. ⊠ *Old town, 23070,* ☏ *0732/ 61351,* 𝔽𝔸𝕏 *0732/61562. 25 rooms with shower. MC, V.*

$$ ▥ **Malvasia.** Staying in this hotel is like living in a fairy tale; it is so
★ engaging you may prolong your stay. Rooms are tucked into nooks and crannies under cane-and-wood or vaulted brick ceilings. Each is decorated with bright patchwork rugs, embroidered tapestries, an-

tique marble, and dark antique wood furniture. The hotel is in three buildings; the best is the one on the main street. Many rooms have sea views, and some have fireplaces; suites are also available. The nonagenarian owner has plans to build an additional tower so keep your eyes open for even more options. ⊠ *Old town, 23070,* ☎ *0732/61323,* FAX *0732/61722. 32 rooms. Bar, breakfast room. AE, MC, V.*

$$ ⊞ **Ta Kellia.** Built in an old monastery (*kellia* means "cells"), this establishment is now run by the EOT. Though it's not glamorous like the competition, the rough-hewn rooms are a good alternative. Only a few rooms on the second floor have ocean views, and they can get quite hot in summer. ⊠ *Old town, on lower square opposite Church of Panagia Chrissafitissa, 23070,* ☎ *0732/61520. 11 rooms with shower. Breakfast room. No credit cards.*

$ ⚠ **Kapsis Paradise.** This simple site is arranged on terraces above a pebble beach, a paradise for beach-lovers. It's open year-round. ⊠ *Above beach, 4 km (2½ mi) south of Monemvassia,* ☎ *0732/61123. RV and tent sites. Grocery, common kitchen.*

SOUTHERN PELOPONNESE A TO Z

Arriving and Departing

By Boat

In both winter and summer the costly **Flying Dolphin hydrofoils** (☎ 01/4280001) make the trip to Monemvassia several times a week. They leave from Piraeus's Marina Zea Harbor for Leonidion, Monemvassia, and Neapolis.

In the Peloponnese, call the local **port authority** for the latest information on boat travel: Gythion (☎ 0733/22262); Kalamata (☎ 0721/22218); Pylos (☎ 0721/23100); and Monemvassia (☎ 0732/61266).

By Bus

Buses leave Athens several times daily for Gythion, Kalamata, and Tripolis, and once a day for Andritsena, Monemvassia, and Pylos. For departure times, call the **KTEL station office** that handles your destination: **Andritsena** (☎ 01/5134574), **Gythion** (☎ 01/5124913), **Kalamata** (☎ 01/5134293), **Monemvassia** (☎ 01/5124913), **Pylos** (☎ 01/ 5134293), **Sparta** (☎ 01/5124913), and **Tripolis** (☎ 01/5134575).

To get to the station at **Kifissou 100** on the outskirts of Athens, take Bus 051 (24 hours a day, every 10 minutes) from the corner of Vilara and Menandrou off Omonia square.

In the Peloponnese, you may buy tickets at the **local station: Andritsena** (⊠ Main square, ☎ 0626/22239); **Gythion** (⊠ Ebrikleous at north end of harbor, ☎ 0733/22228); **Kalamata** (⊠ Artemidos 50, ☎ 0721/ 22851); **Monemvassia** (⊠ Off main square, ☎ 0732/61432); **Pylos** (⊠ Platia Trion Navarchon, ☎ 0723/22230); **Sparta** (⊠ Vrasidou and Paleologou, ☎ 0731/26441); **Tripolis** (⊠ Platia Kolokotronis, ☎ 071/ 224314).

By Car

Even if **highways** have assigned numbers, no Greek knows them by any other than their informal names, usually linked to their destination. For those traveling on the E-92 from Athens to Tripolis, the new section of the highway (the Corinth–Tripolis road) now cuts travel time in half, to little more than two hours. From Olympia in the northwest Peloponnese, you may take a smaller local road (number 74, the Pirgos–Tripolis road). Both approaches have mountainous stretches that occasionally close in winter because of snow, but conditions are otherwise good. An accurate road map is essential: The Greek Motoring Association (ELPA) publishes one of the most detailed map books on Greece, available in most Athens bookstores (3,000 dr.).

By Plane

Olympic Airways offers daily one-hour flights from Athens to Kalamata's airport, 10½ km (6½ mi) outside of town near Messinia. Call the Athens reservations line (☎ 01/9616161) or Olympic Airways' office in **Kalamata** (✉ Sidirodromikou Stathmou 17, ☎ 0721/22376). For the latest flight information in Kalamata, contact the airport (☎ 0721/69442).

By Train

Train travel into the area costs half the price but is slower and much more limited than journeying by bus. Buy tickets before you leave; prices shoot up 50% when purchased on board. If traveling during a national holiday, when many Athenians head to the Peloponnese for their villages, it's worth paying the extra fee for first class to ensure a seat, especially in no-smoking compartments. Train food is dismal, so stock up if you're taking a long trip. A further warning: Trains in this area run at less than 10% capacity and the rail company is desperate to shut it down; it may be unavailable soon and the rail company claims that not all the lines are completely safe from a technical standpoint. Only politics have kept service running up until now.

Trains (lines 422, 424, 426, 428, and 436) run from Athens to Kalamata five times daily with stops in Corinth, Mycenae, and Tripolis, not to be confused with those traveling a second, longer route to Kalamata via Patras. Lines 421, 425, 427, 429, and 435 return from Kalamata to Athens. In Athens, the **Greek National Railway (OSE)** offices (✉ Fillelinon 17, ☎ 01/3236747; or ✉ Sina 6, ☎ 01/3624402) are the most convenient for visitors staying near Platia Syntagma (Constitution Square); otherwise purchase your ticket before departure at the **Peloponnese station** (✉ Peloponnesou 3, ☎ 01/5131601). You can reach the station by catching Trolley 1 in front of Parliament above Syntagma Square (5 AM–midnight, every 10 minutes).

In **Kalamata** depart from the station (✉ Sidirodromikou Stathmou, ☎ 0721/23904) and in **Tripolis** (✉ Grigoris Lambraki at Xeniou Dios, ☎ 071/222402).

Getting Around

By Boat

The **Martha** runs five times weekly in winter and daily in summer between Gythion, Neapolis, and Kythera. Call ticket offices in Gythion (☎ 0733/22996).

En route from Piraeus, **Flying Dolphin hydrofoils** stop once or twice a week in winter, depending on the weather, and almost daily in summer at Monemvassia (☎ 0732/61219 or 0732/61419) and Neapolis (☎ 0734/22214). For departure information, you may also call the local port authority (☞ *above*).

By Bus

The network of bus routes lets you move easily about most of the towns mentioned, even to more remote sites such as the Pirgos Dirou caves, the Arcadian mountain villages, and Nestor's Palace museum in Chora. Keep in mind that there are fewer buses in winter and on weekends. For short distances, you may buy tickets on board; otherwise purchase them in advance at the station.

If you have trouble reaching a site—for example, there is no public transportation to ancient Messene—just take a taxi from a town's main square, which is always near the bus station. In rural areas, drivers may not switch on the meter if the destination has a fixed price, but make sure you agree on the cost before getting in—remember that it's the same price whether you're alone or in a company of four. It's the mileage that counts. When leaving town limits, the driver may switch his meter to the higher rate (Tarifa 2). Don't panic: This is perfectly legal, as is starting the meter at 200 dr. The price also goes up after midnight. If you think you've been had, don't hesitate to argue or threaten to report the driver to the police.

By Car
Especially off-season when buses don't run regularly, it's most rewarding to explore this region by car. In some areas—like the Mani peninsula—it's difficult to get around if you rely on public transportation. Rent a car in Athens or in any of the Peloponnese's bigger towns, like Kalamata, Tripolis, Gythion, and Sparta, thus leaving the harrowing prospect of exiting Athens up to someone else.

By Train
Within the region, train travel is limited to the lines that run from Kalamata to Tripolis.

Contacts and Resources

Camping
There are several camping sites throughout the southern Peloponnese; contact the **EOT** (☞ *below*) for a free camping guide.

Car and Moped Rental Agencies
Gythion: **Motor Mani** (✉ On waterfront near causeway to Marathonissi, ☏ 0733/22853); Kalamata: **Maniatis** (✉ Iatropoulou 1, ☏ 0721/25300 or 0721/27694; ✉ 202 Faron, ☏ 0721/26025); **Stavrianos**: (✉ Nedontos 89, ☏ 0721/23041 or 0721/25370); Pylos: **Venus Rent-A-Car** (✉ Platia Trion Navarchon, ☏ 0723/22393); Sparta: **Kottaras Rent-A-Car** (✉ Menelaon 54, ☏ 0731/28966); Tripolis: **Stephany's Tours** (✉ Deligianni 23, ☏ 071/239577).

Emergencies
Police: Areopolis (☏ 0733/51209). **Gythion** (☏ 0733/22271 or 0733/22316). **Kalamata** (☏ 0721/25444). **Methoni** (☏ 0723/31203). **Monemvassia** (☏ 0732/61210). **Pylos** (☏ 0723/22316). **Sparta** (☏ 0731/28701 or 0731/26229). **Tripolis** (☏ 071/222411 or 071/222519).

Medical assistance: Areopolis: first aid (☏ 0733/51259), hospital (☏ 0733/22315). **Gythion**: clinic (☏ 0733/22001/3). **Kalamata**: hospital (☏ 0721/23561), first aid (☏ 0721/25555). **Methoni**: clinic (☏ 0723/31456). **Pylos**: hospital (☏ 0723/22315). **Sparta**: hospital (☏ 0731/28671 and 0731/28672). **Tripolis**: hospital (☏ 071/238542).

Guided Tours
Unlike in the Northern Peloponnese, the choice of **English-language tours** in the south is limited. If an agency does venture into the region, it's usually a detour through Tripolis and Sparta for a cursory visit to Mystras, as part of a package to the Northern Peloponnese. Both **G.O. Tours** (✉ Voulis 31, Athens, ☏ 01/322–5951 and 01/322–5955) and **CHAT Tours** (✉ Stadiou 4, Athens, ☏ 01/323–0827 or 01/322–2886) offer a five-day combination called the Archaeological Tour for 81,000 dr., covering Corinth, Mycenae, Epidauros, Nauplion, Mystras, Olympia, and Delphi. CHAT also offers a more extensive six-day Grand Tour of the Peloponnese that adds Tiryns, a drive through Gythion to the

Pirgos Dirou caves, Kalamata, Methoni, Nestor's Palace, and its museum at Chora, Bassae, and Patras for 150,000 dr. If you can't get to these tour companies, most travel agencies in Athens can book the tour as well.

Hiking and Climbing

Army's Geographical Service, (⊠ Evelpidou 4, Athens, ☎ 01/884–2811). **Sparta Alpine Club** (☎ 0731/22574 or 0731/24135). **Tripolis Alpine Club** (☎ 071/232243).

Greek Federation of Mountaineering Associations (⊠ Milioni 8, Athens, ☎ 01/363–6617 or 01/364–5904).

Road Assistance

The **Automobile and Touring Club of Greece** (ELPA) provides assistance for light repairs around the clock (☎ 104 anywhere in the country). There are also ELPA main offices in Kalamata (⊠ New Entrance, ☎ 0721/93366 or 0721/9393376) and Tripolis (⊠ Vassileos Pavlou 3, ☎ 071/224101).

Sailing

Naval Association (☎ 0721/23860). **Port authority** (☞ *above*).

Skiing

Mt. Menalon ski center (⊠ Oropedio Ostrakina, ☎ 071/22227); call the Tripolis Alpine Club (☞ *above*).

Travel Agency

Trekking Hellas (⊠ Fillelinon 7, Athens 10557, ☎ 01/315–0853 or 01/325–0317).

Visitor Information

Greek National Tourist Organization (GNTO or EOT): Kalamata (⊠ Marina, ☎ 0721/22059); Sparta (⊠ Platia Vassileos Georgios in the town hall, ☎ 0731/26517); Tripolis (⊠ Ethnikis Antistaseos 43, ☎ 071/231844). **Tourist police** often speak English and help you find accommodations: Gythion (☎ 0733/22236); Kalamata (☎ 0721/23187); Sparta (☎ 0731/28701).

10 The Cyclades

Andros, Tinos, Mykonos, Delos, Naxos, Paros, and Santorini

The magical words "Greek island" conjure up beguiling images of fantasy. If you long for sun and sea, blazing bare rock and mountains, olive trees and vineyards, white peasant architecture and ancient ruins, fresh fish and fruity oils, the Cyclades are isles of quintessential plenty, the ultimate Mediterranean archipelago. "The islands with their drinkable blue volcanoes," wrote Odysseus Elytis, winner of the Nobel Prize for poetry, musing on Santorini. That Homer—who loved these islands—is buried here is unverifiable but spiritually true.

By Melissa
Dailey

Updated by
Jeffrey Carson

THE SIX MAJOR STARS IN THIS CONSTELLATION of islands in the central Aegean Sea, Andros, Tinos,
Mykonos, Naxos, Paros, and Santorini, are the
archetype of the islands of Greece. Here, it always seems—at least in
summer—Zeus's sky is faultlessly azure, Poseidon's sea warm, and
Dionysus's nightlife swinging (especially in Mykonos's discos). The prevailing wind is the northern *vorias*; called *meltemi* in summer, it cools
the always sunny weather. In a magnificent fusion of sunlight, stone,
and sparkling aqua sea, the Cyclades offer both culture and hedonism:
ancient sites, Byzantine castles and museums, lively nightlife, shopping,
dining, and beaches plain and fancy.

These arid, mountainous islands are the peaks of a deep, submerged
plateau, and their composition is rocky, with few trees. They are volcanic in origin, and Santorini (Thera), southernmost of the group, actually sits on the rim of an ancient drowned volcano that exploded about
1500 BC. The dead texture of its rock is a great contrast to the living,
warm limestone of most Greek islands. Santorini's geological colors—
black, pink, brown, white, or pale green—are never beautiful; as you
arrive by boat little shows above the cliff tops but a string of white villages—like teeth on the vast lower jaw of some monster. Still, the island was called Kállisti, "the Loveliest," when it was first settled, and
today, hordes of visitors find its mixture of Cycladic architecture,
Venetian elegance, and stunning sunsets all but irresistible.

Thankfully, a more idyllic rhythm of life can still be found on many
of the other Cyclades (and, of course, in off-season Santorini). Well-
to-do Andros, where ship-owning families once lived, retains an air of
dignity, and its inhabitants go about their business largely indifferent
to visitors. It's a good place for adults in search of history, fine museums, and quiet evenings. Tinos has stayed authentically Greek, since
its heavy tourism is largely owing to its miracle-working icon and not
to its beautiful villages. In the town of Mykonos, the whitewashed houses
huddle together against the meltemi winds, and backpackers rub elbows with millionaires in the mazelike white-marble streets. The island's sophistication level is high, the beaches fine, the shopping varied
and upscale, and it's the jumping-off place for a mandatory visit to tiny,
deserted Delos. That windswept dot, birthplace of Apollo, still watched
over by a row of marble lions, was once the religious and commercial
center of the eastern Mediterranean.

Naxos, greenest of the Cyclades, makes cheese and wine, raises livestock, and produces potatoes, olives, and fruit. For centuries a Venetian
stronghold, it has a shrinking, aristocratic Roman Catholic population;
Venetian houses and fortifications; and Cycladic and Mycenaean sites.
Paros, a hub of the ferry system, has reasonable prices and is a good base
for trips to other islands. It's also good for lazing on long, white-sand beaches
and for visiting fishing villages. Of course, throughout the Cyclades,
there are countless classical sites, monasteries, churches, and villages to
be explored. The best reason to visit them may be the beauty of the walk,
the impressiveness of the location, and the hospitality you will likely find
off the beaten track. Despite its depredations, the automobile has brought
life back to Cycladic villages. Many shuttered houses are being authentically restored, and much traditional architecture can still be found in Ia
on Santorini, Kardiani on Tinos, and Apeiranthos on Naxos—villages
that are part of any deep experience of the islands. In the countryside,
many of the sites and buildings are often or permanently closed, though
the fencing around sites may have fallen, and monks and nuns may let
you in if you are polite and nicely dressed. And the gods are still out there.

Pleasures and Pastimes

Beaches and Water Sports

The best sport in the islands is swimming, and the islands gleam with beaches, from long blond stretches of sand to tiny pebbly coves. Waterskiing, parasailing, jet-skiing, scuba diving, and especially windsurfing have become ever more popular, though venues change from season to season. Anybody who invests in a mask, snorkel, and flippers has entry to intense, serene beauty.

Dining

Eating is a lively social activity in the Cyclades, and the friendliness of most taverna owners compensates for the lack of formal service. Unless you order intermittently, the food comes all at once. Reservations are not required unless otherwise noted, and casual dress is the rule.

Greek food, like English or indeed American, has a bad international reputation, and you can certainly find bad food in Greece. This is often a result of restaurants' trying to adapt to the tastes and wallets of the throngs of tourists. For example: When a tourist asks for less of the islands' culinary gem—fruity, expensive olive oil—in a dish, the essence is lost. Greece produces top-quality tomatoes, lamb chops, melons, olive oil, and farmer's cheese. When Greeks go out to eat, they expect good, simple food culled from these elements, as should you. A few things to watch out for: "fresh" fish on the menu when the weather has been stormy; store-bought eggplant salad; frozen potatoes. Pay attention, and you will dine with much pleasure.

Dishes are often wonderfully redolent of garlic and olive oil; as an alternative, order grilled seafood or meat—grilled octopus with ouzo is a treat. A typical island lunch is fresh fried calamari with a salad of tomatoes, peppers, onions, feta, and olives. Lamb on a skewer and *keftedes* (spicy meatballs) are also favorites.

The volcanic soil of Santorini is hospitable to the grape, and Greeks love the Santorini wines. Greek wines have tripled in quality in the last decade. Santorini and Paros now proudly produce officially recognized "origin" wines, which are sought throughout Greece. Barrel or farmer's wine is common, and except in late summer when it starts to taste a bit off, it's often good. Try to be on Santorini on July 20 for the celebration of St. Elias's name-day, when a traditional pea-and-onion soup is served, followed by walnut and honey desserts and folk dancing.

Restaurant schedules on the Cyclades vary; some places close for lunch, most close for siesta, and all are open late.

CATEGORY	COST (ALL ISLANDS)*
$$$$	over 7,000 dr.
$$$	4,000 dr.–7,000 dr.
$$	3,000 dr.–4,000 dr.
$	under 3,000 dr.

per person for three-course meal, including tax, service, and beer or barrel wine

Hiking

The Cyclades are justly famous for their hiking, with Andros and Naxos at the top of most Santa Claus lists. Ancient goat and donkey trails go everywhere—through fields, over mountains, along untrodden coasts. Rarely is the sea out of view, and almost never are you more than an hour's walk from a village. Since tourists tend to visit Greece for classical sites, for nightlife, and for the beach, walking is uncrowded even in July and August.

The Cyclades

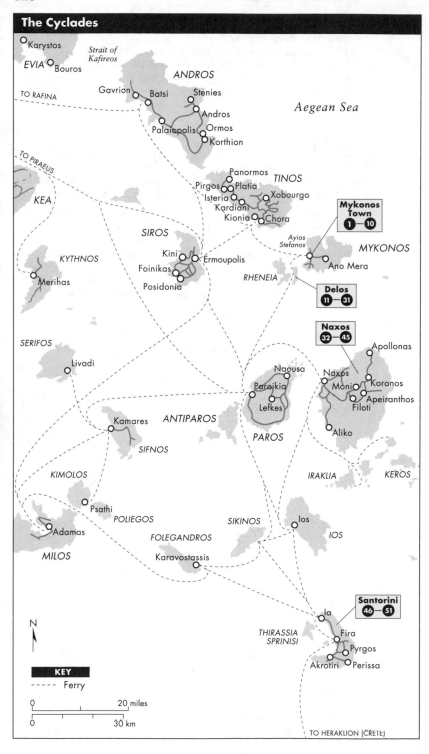

Karystos

Strait of Kafireos

EVIA Bouros

ANDROS

Gavrion Batsi Stenies

TO RAFINA

Aegean Sea

Andros

Palaiopolis Ormos

Korthion

TO PIRAEUS

Panormos TINOS

KEA

Pirgos Platia

Isteria Xobourgo

Kardiani

Kionia Chora

Mykonos Town 1 – 10

SIROS

Ayios Stefanos MYKONOS

Kini Ermoupolis

KYTHNOS

Foinikas

Posidonia Ano Mera

RHENEIA

Merihas

Delos 11 – 31

SERIFOS

Naxos 32 – 45

Apollonas

Livadi

Naousa Naxos

Paroikia Moni Koronos

Kamares ANTIPAROS

Lefkes Apeiranthos

Filoti

SIFNOS

PAROS

Aliko

KIMOLOS

IRAKLIA KEROS

Psathi

POLIEGOS SIKINOS

Adamas FOLEGANDROS Ios

MILOS

IOS

Karavostassis

N

Santorini 46 – 51

Ia

THIRASSIA Fira

SPRINISI Pyrgos

Akrotiri Perissa

KEY

- - - Ferry

0   20 miles

0   30 km

TO HERAKLION (CRETE)

Lodging

Rooms in the islands have proliferated at a truly amazing rate. Although the simple room with oil lamp and Grandmother's furniture is a charming memory, tasteful modern accommodations with amenities are everywhere. Managers—and quality—change year by year, but overall the already high quality is rising.

Island accommodations range from run-down pensions or an extra bedroom in a private house to first-class hotels. It is customary to leave your passport with the proprietor when you check in (for Greek tax records—and to ensure payment). Unless you're traveling at the very height of the season (July 15–August 30), you're unlikely to need advance reservations; often the easiest—and most recommended—way to find something on the spot is to head for a tourist office and describe your needs and price range. Rates, which are regulated by the Greek National Tourist Organization (GNTO or EOT), vary tremendously from month to month: In shoulder season you can pay 2,000 dr.–3,000 dr. less per room than you would in July or August. For budget travelers, room touts often meet the ferries with pictures advertising their properties: Check the location. Alternatively, walk around town and ask where you can rent a cheap room, but take a good look first, and check the bathroom before you commit. If there are extra beds in the room, clarify in advance that the amount agreed on is for the entire room—owners occasionally try to put another person in the same room.

The best rooms and service (and noticeably higher prices) are on Mykonos and Santorini, where luxury out-of-town resort hotels are mushrooming—and our recommendations hardly represent the only choices. To experience the Cyclades properly, you should not go seeking technological amenities; make a room with a view your priority—preferably one with a balcony that overlooks the sea. Avoid hotels on main roads or near all-night discos. And an evening dip in a freshwater pool after swimming in the sea is a luxury.

Often only expensive hotels provide hot water 24 hours a day; in some hotels you must turn on a thermostat for a half hour to heat water for a shower (don't forget to turn it off). Signs tell you that water is in short supply in the Cyclades, reminding you to conserve it. Fresh water is often shipped from the mainland, and though the tap water is potable, you should not drink from fountains or springs. Most people drink bottled water, available everywhere.

Hotels close from November through March unless otherwise noted. Most do not serve breakfast, unless a restaurant or breakfast room is noted, and it usually costs extra.

CATEGORY	COST (ALL ISLANDS)*
$$$$	over 39,000 dr.
$$$	22,000 dr.–39,000 dr.
$$	13,000 dr.–22,000 dr.
$	under 13,000 dr.

All prices are for a standard double room in high season, including taxes and service but excluding breakfast.

Nightlife

So many young backpackers and older holiday revelers pass through the islands in summer that lively all-night places have naturally cropped up. Greeks, too, like to stay out on balmy summer nights. All the major islands throb with bars, discos, and cafés; keep in mind that venues change in popularity week by week. Young women especially will enjoy the opportunity to go partying, unescorted, in utter safety.

Shopping

Mykonos, with Santorini taking a close second, is the best island in the Cyclades for shopping. You can buy anything from Greek folk items to Italian designer clothes, cowboy boots, and leather jackets from the United States. Although island prices are better than in the expensive shopping districts of Athens, there are many tourist traps in the resort towns, with high-pressure sales tactics and inflated prices for inferior goods. The Greeks have a word for naive American shoppers—*Americanaki.* It's a good sign if the owner of a shop selling traditional crafts or art lives on the island and is not a hotshot Athenian over for the summer to make a quick buck.

Each island has a unique pottery style that reflects its individuality. Santorini potters like the bright shades of the setting sun, though the best pottery islands are Paros and especially Siphnos. Island specialties are icons hand-painted after Byzantine originals; weavings and embroideries; local wines; and gold worked in ancient and Byzantine designs.

Don't be surprised when the stores close between 2 and 5:30 in the afternoon and reopen in the evenings; even on the chic islands everybody takes a siesta.

Traditional Festivals

Ano Approvato, a village south of Batsi on Andros, holds a *paneyiri* (festival) on August 15, for the Dormition of the Virgin Mary, with feasting and dancing along with the religious rites.

In Chora on Tinos the icon is paraded with much pomp on Annunciation Day, March 25, and especially Dormition Day, August 15. As it is carried on poles over the heads of the faithful, including thousands of bedecked gypsies who make Tinos seem a gigantic glittering encampment, cures are effected, and religious emotion runs high. On July 23, in honor of St. Pelagia, the icon is paraded from Kechrovouni Nunnery, and afterward the festivities continue long into the night, with music and fireworks.

Naxos town celebrates the Dionysia festival during the first week of August, with concerts, costumed folk dancers, and free food and wine in the square. At other times, feast days are honored with a paneyiri. For example, during Carnival, preceding Lent, "bell wearers" take to the streets in Apeiranthos and Filoti, running from house to house, making as much noise as possible with strings of bells tied around their waists. They're a disconcerting sight in their hooded cloaks, with scarves concealing their faces, as they ritually escort a man dressed as a woman from house to house to collect eggs. In Apeiranthos, villagers square off in rhyming-verse contests: On the last Sunday of Lent, the *paliomaskari,* their faces blackened, challenge each other in improvising *kotsakia* (satirical couplets). At the May Day Festival in Koronis, wildflower garlands are made, and there's lively dancing. On July 14, Ayios Nikodemos Day is celebrated in Chora with a procession of the patron saint's icon through town, but the Dormition of the Virgin on August 15 is, after Easter and Christmas, the festival most widely celebrated, especially in Sangri, Filoti (August 4), and Apeiranthos.

On Paros each year on August 23, Naousa celebrates the heroic naval battle against the Turks, with children dressed in native costume, great feasts, and traditional dancing. The day ends with 100 boats illuminated by torches converging on the harbor.

Exploring the Cyclades

Numbers in the text correspond to numbers in the margin and on the Cyclades, Mykonos Town, Delos, Naxos, and Santorini maps.

Great Itineraries

There is no bad itinerary for the Cyclades. The islands differ remarkably, and are all beautiful. It is possible to "see" any island in a day, for they are small and the "must-see" sights are few—Delos, Santorini's caldera, the Minoan site at Akrotiri, and Paros's Church of a Hundred Doors. So planning a trip depends on your sense of inclusiveness, your restlessness, your energy, *and* your ability to accommodate changing boat schedules.

IF YOU HAVE 2 OR 3 DAYS

For a three-day trip that promises shopping, nightlife, a serious summer beach scene, classical Greece, and traditional Greece, go directly to ⊞ **Mykonos** ①–⑩, the next morning visit **Delos** ⑪–㉛, and in the afternoon go to ⊞ **Tinos** for its landscape, villages, and church.

IF YOU HAVE 5 DAYS

If you want to see the two most popular islands in five days you can visit ⊞ **Mykonos** ①–⑩ (and **Delos** ⑪–㉛) and ⊞ **Santorini** ㊺–㊿①, with its volcanic bay, ancient site, and Greece's most-photographed village.

IF YOU HAVE 8 DAYS

If you want some hiking, Byzantine churches, and relaxation between Mykonos and Santorini, visit **Naxos** and **Paros** for an overfilled eight days. And if you have two weeks really to see the Cyclades, start the four-day itinerary in elegant, nontouristy ⊞ **Andros**; then go to ⊞ **Tinos,** ⊞ **Mykonos** ①–⑩ (and **Delos** ⑪–㉛), then ⊞ **Naxos** ㉜–㊺, ⊞ **Paros,** and ⊞ **Santorini** ㊻–㊿①. You may continue on to explore the other Cycladic islands—they are endless.

When to Tour

Most people come to Greece in the summer, but especially during August, Greece is crowded and less personal, and the penetrating sun bleaches hot afternoons. Walkers, nature lovers, and devotees of classical and Byzantine Greece would do better to come in the spring and fall, both being cooler and less tourist-riddled. Spring's islands burst with thousands of varieties of wildflowers, and sprightly crimson poppies dapple stern marble blocks, but the sea is cold. Autumn's days are short but the sea remains alluringly swimmable. This is the memorable time when zesty olives are gathered and bulging grapes are pressed.

ANDROS

The northernmost and second largest of the Cycladic islands, Andros is about 32 km by 16 km (nearly 20 mi by 10 mi), and its rugged, mountainous geography is best seen by foot, bike, or car. The highest peak, Mt. Kouvari, reaches 3,260 ft. A network of springs gives birth to streams, which whirl down from the mountaintops, feeding lush valleys; unlike the other Cyclades, Andros is green with pines, sycamores, mulberries, and oaks. In ancient times it was called Hydroussa, or "Well-Watered." The springs, streams, and falls have a cooling effect that, together with summer's northerlies (*meltemia*), ameliorate the Aegean heat. Spring's southerlies bring heat and sometimes jellyfish.

Foreign tourism is in an early stage on Andros, and most of the islanders are indifferent to it. Perhaps the reason for this snobbishness is that Andros has been a wealthy island since silk production began in the 12th century; today, Andros thrives on Greeks who own villas and bring their own cars on their two-hour journeys from Athens. The well-known Goulandris shipping family from Andros has founded two museums of modern art and the archaeological museum in Andros town, arguably the best in the Aegean. If Andros is considered an island for the cultured elite, prices are, surprisingly, still in line with the Greek economy, and restaurants and hotels cost less than in Mykonos or Santorini.

Across the entire landscape of Andros you will notice an interesting system of stone walls that mark the boundaries between the fields of different owners. In a building style unique to Andros, the walls are interrupted at regular intervals, and each gap is filled with a large, flat, upright slab. This saves stone and labor and allows herders to move the large slab for the passage of animals. Another common feature (also seen on Mykonos and especially Tinos) is the dovecotes: square towers whose pigeonholes form decorative geometric designs. The Venetians introduced them in the 13th century. Though many fell into disuse, when hard times struck the islands in this century, local farmers started breeding the pigeons and selling them abroad as a delicacy. Today only a few dovecotes are still maintained.

Gavrio

75 km (46½ mi) east of Rafina Port, 35 km (21¾ mi) northeast of Andros town.

Though recently spruced up, Gavrio, on the northwest coast, is Andros's dull little port town. Although there are some accommodations here, most people go south to Batsi, the island's only resort, or to Andros town, on the opposite side of the island. It's a good idea to buy a map.

Batsi

27 km (16¾ mi) northwest of Andros town.

Originally a small fishing village, Batsi has developed only over the last 10 years, and as a new resort town, many of the businesses have a friendly, nonhustling quality. On the hillside, a few lovely houses from a century ago look down to the promenade along the sea, where Athenian and foreign visitors stroll, patronizing the new restaurants and bars. Many people stay here because the social life is a bit more lively than in Andros town and because of the beach, where Windsurfers, paddleboats, and Jet Skis can be rented.

Beach

Batsi beach is sandy, accessible, and protected from the north wind. Just to the south are **Dellavoya beach** and **Ayia Marina beach,** both with tavernas and rooms. To the north, **Ayios Petros** is also lovely.

Dining and Lodging

$$ ✕ **Balcony of the Aegean.** Ask an Andriot what his favorite restau-
★ rant is, and he will inevitably name this one. Located in Ano Aprovato (6 km/4 mi up from Batsi; follow Greek signs), it has a spectacular sunset view and lovingly traditional food. Upon your arrival Socrates and Stella Kolitsas usually offer a raki, a grappalike drink (which some wags call homemade grapeskin firewater). Sip it with *dra,* a cheese made from freshly made butter, or with unaged *kopanisti,* a very sharp soft cheese. Stella is especially proud of her *fortalia* (homemade sausage omelet) and Socrates his finely toned meats, since he is a butcher who raises it all himself. With everything homemade or homegrown, this is what Greek food is supposed to taste like. The Kolitsases are open for dinner all year and for lunch in season. ✉ *Ano Aprovato,* ☎ *0282/41020. No credit cards.*

$$ ✕ **Stamatis.** Pity this high-class taverna has no sea view, but the food—
★   traditional Greek, since 1965—is better than at many other spots and
the place is open year-round. Outside, green chairs and tables are
crammed into the gleaming white alleys. Inside is homey and rustic,
with a fireplace and a wall displaying hunting relics (dinner's harbinger?).
Stamtis or son Yannis will invite you to have a look at the wonderful
dishes. Try the fresh stuffed roasted chicken or the tender lamb chops
with a special Andros stuffing; on Wednesdays, lamb "klephtiko" is
prepared. The good barrel wine is their own. For dessert, splurge on
the light crème caramel. ⊠ *One street up from the main quay,* ☎ *0282/
41283. MC, V.*

$$$–$$$$ ☷ **Epaminondas.** Looking something like a cross between a dovecote
★   and a monastery, the exterior of this quiet complex—all terra-cotta and
white plaster—climbs Batsi's northern hillside, about 15 minutes by foot
from the town center. If you have children, or even if you don't, this is
the place, as duplexes or triplexes vary in size, with space for two to
six people. The cool, spacious interiors are tasteful and relaxing, with
marble floors and traditionally embroidered curtains. Most rooms have
kitchenettes, and all have phones and huge balconies overlooking Batsi
Bay. The hotel's deep freshwater pool is lit all night. ⊠ *On road to lower
Batsi, on left, 84500,* ☎ *0282/41682 or 0282/41683,* ⅢX *0282/41681.
23 apartments. Kitchenettes, pool, parking. No credit cards.*

$$$ ☷ **Erato Apartments.** Three years old, these comfortable apartments are
right above Batsi's main seafront. All have seaview terraces, blue tile floors,
and island furnishings. Dimitris Vlamis makes you feel at home. ⊠ *Up
from main quay, 84500,* ☎ *0282/41682 and 0282/4141943–4683. 4
singles, 3 duplexes. Kitchenettes, parking. No credit cards.*

Nightlife

NIGHTCLUBS

Beware: Evenings at the **Titanium** (⊠ On perimeter road of Batsi)
nightclub can extend into the wee hours. It has Greek dancing to live
music in summer. There are several music bars on the Batsi waterfront
where the young congregate: Follow your ears.

Outdoor Activities and Sports

WATER SPORTS

Windsurfing equipment, Jet Skis, and pedal boats can be rented by the
hour at Batsi Beach. More adventurous travelers might want to try waterskiing or parasailing, tethered behind a motorboat (but the town
hopes to limit these activities, as they bother swimmers).

Palaiopolis

*18½ km (11½ mi) southwest of Andros town, 9 km (5½ mi) south of
Batsi.*

Unfortunately, most of Palaiopolis, the ancient capital of Andros, lies
beneath the sea, destroyed in the 4th century either by an earthquake
or a landslide. The town today is a quiet but gorgeous village that
stretches down the slope of Mt. Kouvari to the shore. The road cuts
through the **upper town,** where you'll find a café and an excellent roadside taverna. From the taverna you can look up to the hill and see the
site of an **ancient acropolis,** 984 ft above the sea, now occupied by a
small **Orthodox chapel;** some **waterfalls** are located a short climb up.
In 1832 a farmer turned up the famous **statue of Hermes** in this area,
which is now on display in the archaeological museum in Andros
town (☞ *below*). Opposite the café, 1,039 steps lead down through
the **lower village,** in the shade of flowering vines and trees heavy with
lemons. Scattered near the **beach** are marble remnants of early buildings and statues. Though it has not been systematically excavated, ar-

chaeologists did enough digging around here in 1956 to conjecture that the bits and pieces are remains from the ancient agora.

NEED A   Stop in **Menites** (⊠ ½ km/¼ mi off main road, halfway between the fork
BREAK?   in the road and Andros town) to see the sacred springs and have a
           glass of local wine and a bite to eat at one of two **shaded tavernas**; they
           both serve whole rooster—an Andriot specialty. Mineral spring water
           tumbles from a series of lion-head spouts along a stone wall, and hidden
           by greenery in the background is **Panayia tis Koumoulous**, an Orthodox
           church supposedly built on the site of a temple to Dionysos. According
           to legend, these are the very springs whose water turned to wine each
           year on the god's feast day.

Andros Town

27 km (16¾ mi) south of Batsi.

Andros town (Chora) has been the capital of the island since the Venetian occupation in the 13th century. The city is built on a long, narrow peninsula, at the end of which is a **small island** with the remains of a **Venetian castle** built about 1220.

Take a leisurely stroll down the center's **marble promenade** (⊠ Main St.), past the impressive 13th-century **Palatiani Church** and the interesting **gift shops** that sell the local pottery. Handsome 19th-century stone mansions line the streets, and over their doors are carved galleons, indicating that the original owners were shipowners or sea captains. The town is deliberately kept traditional, and its tidy appearance and the distinction of its neoclassical houses bear witness to its longstanding prosperity.

The main street leads to **Kairis Square** (⊠ At tip of peninsula), where in the center stands a bust of **Theophilos Kairis,** a local hero. Born in Andros town in 1784, Kairis was educated in Paris, and returned to Andros in 1821 to become one of the leaders in the War of Independence. A philosopher, scholar, and social reformer, he toured Europe to raise money for an orphanage and school, which he founded in 1835. The school became famous in Greece, and enrollment eventually rose to 600, but the Orthodox church closed it down and tried Kairis as a heretic for his individualistic religious beliefs. He died in a Syros prison in 1852.

The **Museum of Modern Art** is the first of the three museums on Andros funded by the Goulandris Foundation. It stages exhibitions of international and Greek artists of the 20th century. ⊠ *Andros town,* ☎ *0282/22650.* ⌑ *700 dr. (free Sun.).* ☉ *Sat.–Mon. 10–2.*

The **Museum of Sculpture** displays rotating exhibitions by Greece's best modern painters and a permanent collection of the works of sculptor Michael Tombros (1889–1974), whose parents were born on Andros. ⊠ *Andros town,* ☎ *0282/22444.* ⌑ *Free.* ☉ *Sat.–Mon. 10–2.*

The pride of Andros's **Archaeological Museum** is the life-size marble statue of Hermes discovered in Palaiopolis and thought to be a copy of a Praxiteles. The collections range from the Mycenaen through Roman eras. Upstairs is an extensive display on Zagora, the earliest known settlement in Andros, a town built during the Geometric Period on the southwest coast, on a promontory 529 ft above sea level, surrounded by jagged cliffs. It was the main settlement from 900 BC to 700 BC, before the rise of Palaiopolis. The site is not open, but the museum provides a model. ⊠ *Kairis Sq.,* ☎ ℻ *0282/23664.* ⌑ *500 dr.* ☉ *Tues.–Sun. 8:30–2:30.*

The Arts
Check the art museums for lectures, recitals, and opening nights.

Beaches
Nimborio Beach (✉ About 300 ft from the Andros town center) is on the edge of Andros town. About a mile north of Andros town is **Yialia beach** (✉ Stenies) with a taverna.

Dining and Lodging
$ ✕ **Parea.** This shaded taverna perched high above a windswept beach is a fine place to lunch on *fourtalia* (the island's oven-baked version of an omelet, packed with potatoes, cheese, sausage or bacon, a handful of broad beans, and herbs). Other favorites are veal in lemon sauce, and *kannelonia* (cannelloni) stuffed with mincemeat. For dessert go to one of the cafés next door for homemade fruit ices. ✉ *Kairis Sq., Chora,* ☎ *0282/23721. V.*

$$$ ☉ **Hotel Pighi Sariza.** This peaceful hotel is in a green mountain village near the Sariza mineral springs (be sure to buy a bottle) and is wonderful for a break from the summer heat. From here you can hike the many mountain trails nearby, view waterfalls, and—sigh—hear nightingales. Half the comfortable rooms have sea views and half have (just as good) mountain views. The spacious restaurant has an international menu. Nature-lovers will appreciate the fact the hotel is open year-round. ✉ *Apikia Rd., 3 km (2 mi) north of Andros town, 84500,* ☎ *0282/23799,* 𝖥𝖠𝖷 *0282/22476. 42 rooms. Restaurant, minibars, pool, sauna, recreation room. AE, DC, MC, V.*

$$$ ☉ **Irene's Villas.** These isolated blue-washed "villas," furnished with dark wood, floral prints, and tapestries, are in a dense green garden a short stroll up from the beach. All have balconies; many have phone, TV, and kitchenette; and the fireplaces mean it's open all year. ✉ *Above Nimborio beach, Andros town 84500,* ☎ *0282/23344,* 𝖥𝖠𝖷 *0282/24554. 10 apartments. No credit cards.*

$$ ☉ **Hotel Egli.** Sometimes a simple cheap hotel is all you want. This one, in a 100-year-old building and serving as a hotel since 1955, is right in the center of town and open all winter. Some rooms feature balconies and refrigerators. ✉ *Andros town, 84500,* ☎ *0282/22303 or 0282/ 22525,* 𝖥𝖠𝖷 *0282/22159. 15 rooms, 7 with bath. Bar, breakfast room, refrigerators. No credit cards.*

Outdoor Activities and Sports
BOATING
The **Andros Naval Club** (✉ Nimborio port, just north of Andros town) offers rowing and sailing.

HIKING
The mountainous geography and lush greenery make Andros a pleasant island for hiking, especially around Andros town and near Messaria (south), Apikia (west), and Stenies (north). The 5-km (3-mi) hike from the little village of Lamira to Andros town is popular. Andros Travel in Batsi organizes many hiking trips.

Shopping
GIFT SHOPS
A number of gift shops on the **main street** sell local pottery, embroidery, ship's models, and other handmade objects. Two of them are **Lasia** (✉ Main street, ☎ 0282/25095), which features mementos of Andros's great shipping days, and **Paraporti** (✉ Kairis Sq., ☎ 0282/23777), which features pottery.

SWEETS
Andros is noted for candies and sweetmeats, and there are several shops in Andros town that maintain the tradition. Perhaps the best, and most

old-fashioned, is **Konstantinos Laskaris** (✉ Main street, ☎ 0282/ 22305), where bitter almond taffy, rose petals in syrup, and *kalsounia* (walnut-honey sweetmeat) are among the once common, now exotic, things for sale.

TINOS

Perhaps the least-visited of the major Cyclades, Tinos (or, as archaeologists spell it, Tenos) is among the most beautiful and most fascinating. The third largest of the Cyclades after Naxos and Andros, with an area of 195 square km (121 square mi), it is home to nearly 10,000 people, many of whom still live the traditional life of farmers or craftsmen. Its long mountainous spine, rearing amid Andros, Mykonos, and Siros, makes it seem forbidding, and in a way it is. It is not popular among tourists for several reasons: The main village, Tinos town (Chora), lacks charm; the beaches are mediocre; there is no airport; and the prevailing north winds are the Aegean's fiercest (passing mariners used to sacrifice a calf to Poseidon—ancient Tinos's chief deity— in hopes of avoiding shipwreck). For Greeks, a visit to Tinos is essential: Its great Church of the Evangelistria is the Greek Lourdes, a holy place of pilgrimage and miraculous cures; 799 other churches adorn the countryside. Encroaching development here is to accommodate those in search of their religious elixir and not, as on the other islands, the beach-and-bar crowd.

Tinos is renowned for its 1,300 dovecotes which, unlike on Mykonos or Andros, are mostly well maintained; in fact, new ones are being built. Two stories high, with intricate stonework, carved-dove finials, and thin schist slabs arranged in intricate patterns resembling traditional stitchery, the dovecotes have been much written about—and are much visited by doves.

Tinos is dotted with possibly the loveliest villages in the Cyclades, which, for some welcome reason, are not being abandoned. The dark arcades of Arnados, the vine-shaded sea views of Isternia and Kardiani, the Venetian architecture of Loutra, the gleaming marble squares of Pirgos: These, finally, are what make Tinos unique. A map, available at kiosks or rental agencies, will make touring these villages by car or bike somewhat less confusing, as there are nearly 50 of them.

Tinos Town

55 km (34 mi) southeast of Andros's port.

Civilization on Tinos is a millennium older than **Tinos town,** or Chora, founded in the 5th century BC. On weekends and during festivals, Chora is thronged with Greeks attending church and with restaurants and hotels catering to them. As the well-known story goes: In 1822, a year after the War of Independence began (Tinos was the first of the islands to join in), the Virgin sent the nun Pelagia a dream about a buried icon of the Annunciation. On January 30, 1823, such an icon was unearthed amid the foundations of a Byzantine church, and it started to heal people immediately.

The Tiniots, hardly unaware of the icon's potential, immediately built the splendid **Panayia Evangelistria,** or Annunciate Virgin, on the site, using the most costly marble from Tinos, Paros, and (alas) Delos. The church's **marble courtyards** (note the green-veined Tiniot stone) are paved with pebble mosaics and surrounded by offices, chapels, a health station, and **seven museums.** Inside the **upper three-aisle church** dozens of beeswax candles and precious votives—don't miss the golden orange tree near the door donated by a blind man who was granted sight—dazzle the eye. You must often wait in line to see the little icon, which is encrusted with jewels, donated as thanks for cures. To beseech the icon's aid, a sick person sends a young female relative and a mother brings her sick infant. As the pilgrim descends from the boat, she falls to her knees, with traffic indifferently whizzing about her, and crawls painfully up the main street—1 km (½ mi)—to the church. In the church's courtyards, she and her family camp for several days, praying to the magical icon for a cure, which sometimes comes. This procedure is very similar to the ancient one observed in Tinos's temple of Poseidon. The **lower church,** called the Evresis, celebrates the finding of the icon; in one room a baptismal font is filled with silver and gold votives. The chapel to the left commemorates the torpedoing by the Italians, on Dormition Day, 1940, of the Greek ship *Helle*; in the early stages of the war, the roused Greeks amazingly overpowered the Italians. ⊠ *Chora, at end of Megalohari,* ☎ *0283/222.56.* ▱ *Free.* ☉ *Daily 8:30–3.*

On the main street, near the church, is the small **Archaeological Museum**; its collection includes a sundial by Andronicus of Cyrrhus, who in the 1st century BC also designed Athens's Tower of the Winds. Here, too, are Tinos's famous huge, red storage vases, from the 8th century BC. ⊠ *Megalohari,* ☎ *0283/226/0.* ▱ *500 dr.* ☉ *Tues.–Fri. 8–2.*

One and a half kilometers (¾ mile) from Chora you'll see a copse of pines shading a small parking lot, whence a path leads down to Stavros (Holy Cross) chapel; right on the water is the unmarked **Markos Velalopoulos's Ouzeri** (⊠ Under church, ☎ 0283/23276), which serves *strophia* (raki), ouzo, and traditional snacks like fried cheese or figs with sesame. This is Tinos's most romantic spot to watch the sunset. It is also good for swimming. Note that the sunken breakwater along the coastal road in Stavros Harbor is ancient.

Beaches

There is a series of beaches between Chora and Kionia (and beyond, for walkers). **Stavros** is the most romantic. **Ayios Yannis** (⊠ Near Porto) is long, sandy, and peaceful. **Pachia Ammos** (⊠ Past Porto, reached by a dirt road) is undeveloped and sparkling.

Dining and Lodging

$$ ✕ **Alonia.** In a terraced hotel (☞ *below*) with magnificent views of fields
★ and sea, you can savor home-style meals prepared by the owners. To begin, try homemade onion focaccia (which they call bread), eggplant-olive salad, or marinated raw saury fillets (recipe: debone sauries, salt well, drain 30 hours, rinse well, marinate in lemon juice two hours). Homespun entrées may be chicken breasts stuffed with bacon, cheese, and herbs; beef in cream sauce with mushrooms; and grilled treats—the menu changes. The wine is served from barrel or bottle. ⊠ *2 km (1 mi) from Chora toward Porto (Ayios Ioannis), Alonia Hotel,* ☎ *0283/23541 through 0283/23543,* ☒ *0283/23544. MC, V.*

$$ ✕ **Metaxi Mas.** On a narrow lane next to the Old Pallada, Euripides and Marigo Tatsionas's elegant new restaurant turns out to be no more expensive than a taverna. The name means "between us." The decor is traditional—white walls, wooden furniture, mirrors—the soft music is Greek, and the service is quick and friendly. From starters to desserts, the food is homemade, but with a haute-Athenian flair. For starters try Macedonian cabbage salad with red pepper, deep-fried sun-dried tomatoes, or hot eggplant slices wrapped around cheese, mint, and green pepper. For a main dish the lamb (or kid) casserole is especially succulent. With a fireplace in winter, and an air conditioner for summer, this place is open year-round. ⊠ *Kontogiorgi alley,* ☎ *0285/ 29545. MC, V.*

$$ ✕ **Old Pallada.** Choose this popular old taverna, near the busy center of things, over its neighbors—the locals do. The outdoor area, in a pedestrian's alley, is shaded by grapevines. Trusty starters are roasted peppers with garlic and parsley, and stuffed squid. The stuffed zucchini blossoms, when in season, are a treat. Chef's favorites are beef or lamb in lemon sauce and his homemade wine. It's open all year. ⌧ *Kontogiorgi alley, facing the square,* ☎ *0283/23516. No credit cards.*

$$$ ⊡ **Porto Tango.** This ambitiously up-to-date, popular resort-hotel strives for the best in decor and service. Greece's late prime minister, Andreas Papandreou, stayed here during his last visit to Tinos. Modular Cycladic architecture lends privacy; the lobby, where an art exhibition is usually on display, has a wooden ceiling, marble floors, and Tiniot furnishings, both modern and antique. Rooms are simple, white, and private, with wood furniture and TVs. *Cement road up hill, Porto 84200,* ☎ *0183/24411 through 0183/24415,* FAX *0283/24416. 62 rooms. Restaurant, bar, pool, sauna, exercise room. D, V.*

$$ ⊡ **Akti Aegeou.** The family that runs this little resort must know they are lucky to own such a valuable piece of property. Akti Aegeou, or "Aegean Coast," is right on the fine, uncrowded beach at Porto. All airy rooms come with balconies, marble floors, traditional rag rugs, and personal amenities, including minibus service. The restaurant, specializing in fresh fish, is very good. It must take a lot of water to keep the lawns so green under the blazing Aegean summer sun. ⌧ *Beach of Ayios Ioannis, Porto 84200,* ☎ *0283/24248,* FAX *0283/23523. 5 rooms, 6 apartments. Restaurant, bar, kitchenettes, pool. No credit cards.*

$$ ⊡ **Alonia Hotel.** This hotel is not exciting, aesthetically interesting, in
★   town, or near the beach (1 km/½ mi away). It is, however, Tinos's very best. Comfortable, family-run, and quietly efficient, it is for you if you dislike snazzy resorts and want to be out of hectic Chora. The fairly large rooms all have dazzling views (rooms overlooking the pool are best), telephones, and bathrooms *with* bathtubs. Tinos's largest freshwater pool is surrounded by lawns, trees, and gardens—not baking cement. And the superb restaurant is often frequented by Tiniots. An hourly minibus makes the run to Chora; the hotel is open in winter for groups. ⌧ *2 km (1 mi) from Chora toward Porto (Ayios Ioannis), 84200,* ☎ *0283/23541 through 0283/23543,* FAX *0283/23544. 34 rooms, 4 suites. Restaurant, bar, air-conditioning, café, pool. MC, V.*

$$ ⊡ **Leandros.** If you want to be in Chora, but also desire peace and quiet, this charming 11-room hotel, run by Jack and Anna Paravalos (he also runs the local tree farm), is the place. The lobby and breakfast room are of all wood, stone, and whitewash. Traditional Tiniot marble carvings are everywhere. A plant-filled outdoor stairway leads to the rooms, which have balconies. The whitewashed walls of the rooms are textured with traditional *sardeles* (sardines), stripes made with a trowel—Jack did much of the work himself. *Behind new dock, Chora 84200,* ☎ *0283/ 23545,* FAX *0283/24390. 11 rooms. Breakfast room. No credit cards.*

Nightlife

Tinos has fewer **bars** and **discos** than the other big islands, but there is plenty of late-night bar action just behind the waterfront on the way to the new dock.

Outdoor Activities and Sports

Of all the major islands, Tinos is the least developed for sports. The strong winds discourage water sports, and their concessions come and go.

Shopping

FARMERS AND FLEA MARKETS

Tinos is a rich farming island, and every day but Sunday farmers from all the far-flung villages fill the **square** (⌧ Between new and old docks) with vegetables, herbs, and flowers. In the next square closer to town, the local pelican (a rival to Mykonos's) can often be found cadging snacks from the **fish market.**

Tinos produces a lot of milk. A short way up from the harbor, on the right, is the little store of the **Enosis,** or Farmer's Cooperative (✉ Megalohari, up from harbor, ☎ 0283/23289), which sells milk, butter, and a variety of cheeses, including very sharp kopanisti, perfect with ouzo.

Evangelistria, the street parallel to the church, is closed to traffic and is a kind of **religious flea market,** lined with shops hawking immense candles, chunks of incense, tacky souvenirs, tin votives, and sweets. There are several good jewelers' shops on the market street where, as always on Tinos, the religious note is supreme.

JEWELRY

The selection at **Ostria** (✉ Evangelistria, ☎ 0283/23893) is especially good; in addition to delicate silver jewelry, it sells silver icon covers, silver plate, and 22-karat gold. **Anna Maria** (✉ Chora waterfront, on patio of Avra hotel, ☎ 0283/23456) sells traditional Greek silver jewelry amid much culture.

WEAVINGS

The 100-year-old weaving school, or **Biotechniki Scholi** (✉ Evangelistria, three-quarters of the way up from the sea), sells traditional weavings—aprons, towels, spreads—made by its students, local girls. The largest of its three high-ceiling, wooden-floored rooms is filled with looms and spindles.

OFF THE BEATEN PATH
MOUNTAIN VILLAGES ABOVE CHORA – At night the lights of the hill villages surrounding Tinos's highest mountain, Mt. Tsiknias—2,200 ft high and the ancient home of Boreas (the wind god)—glitter over Chora like fireworks. By day they are worth visiting. Take the good road that runs through Dio Horia and Monastiri, ascending and twisting around switchbacks, passing fertile fields and a few of Tinos's most fanciful old dovecotes. After 9 km (5½ mi) you reach **Kechrovouni,** or just Monastiri, which is a veritable city of nuns, founded in the 10th century. One cell contains the head of St. Pelagia in a wooden chest; another is a small icon museum. Though a nunnery, Kechrovouni is a lively place, since many of the church's pilgrims come here by bus. Out front, a nun sells huge garlic heads and braids to be used as charms against misfortune; the Greeks call these "California garlic." One kilometer (½ mile) farther on, Tinos's telecommunications towers spike the sky, marking the entrance to **Arnados,** a strange village 1,600 ft up, overlooking Chora. Most of the streets here are vaulted, and thus cool and shady, if a bit claustrophobic; no medieval pirate ever penetrated this warren. In one alley is the **Ecclesiastical Museum,** which displays icons from local churches. Another 1½ km (¾ mi) farther on are the **Dio Horia** (Two Villages), with a marble fountain house, unusual in Tinos. The spreading plane tree in front of it, according to the marble plaque, was planted in 1885. Now the road starts winding down again, to reach **Triandaros,** which has a good restaurant; many of the pretty houses in this misty place are owned by Germans. Yannis Kyparinis, who made the three-story bell tower in Dio Horia, has his workshop and showroom here.

Kionia

2½ km (1¼ mi) northwest of Tinos town.

The large, untended **Sanctuary of Poseidon** (✉ Northwest of Tinos town) is also dedicated to the bearded sea god's sea-nymph consort, Amphitrite.

The present remains are from the 4th century BC and later, though the sanctuary itself is much older. The sanctuary was a kind of hospital, where the ailing came to camp and solicit the god's help. The marble dolphins in the museum were discovered here. According to the Roman historian Pliny, Tinos was once infested with serpents (goddess symbols) and named Serpenttown (Ophiousa), until supermasculine Poseidon sent storks to clean them out. The sanctuary functioned well into Roman times.

Beaches

The Kiona road ends at a long sheltered **beach,** which is unfortunately being worn away by cars heading for the two pretty **coves** beyond, including the **Gastrion cave,** whose entrance bears Byzantine inscriptions.

Dining and Lodging

$$ ✕ **Tsambia.** Abutting the sanctuary of Poseidon, this multilevel taverna prepares homemade traditional fare. For starters try a mélange of indigenous specialties: *louza* (smoked peppered pork roll coated and preserved in wax), local Tiniot cheeses, and homegrown vegetables. Fresh fish is available, depending on the weather. Tried-and-true are *stifado* (rabbit stew), the strictly local meat, and the outstanding codfish croquettes in garlic sauce. To get here, follow signs for TRADITIONAL GREEK RESTAURANT just before the Sanctuary of Poseidon. ⊠ *Cement road, Kionia 84200,* ☏ *0283/23142. No credit cards.*

$$$ 🏨 **Tinos Beach.** Part of the government's all-too-successful sponsorship to promote tourism in the '70s, this is Tinos's most varied resort. In the large, cool lobby, featuring lots of wood and tiles, a pianist sometimes plays at night. Though the carpeted rooms show some signs of age, many rooms have splendid sea views, and there are suites and bungalows with marble floors that sleep four. *Tinos beach, at end (3 km/2 mi) of Kiona Rd., just past sanctuary to Poseidon, Kionia 84200,* ☏ *0283/22626 or 0283/22627,* ℻ *0283/23153. 80 rooms, 3 suites, 3 bungalows. Restaurant, bar, café, 2 pools, tennis courts, shops. MC, V.*

Outdoor Activities and Sports

HIKING

Ktikados village is a beautiful hour-long walk up into the panoramic mountains; 9th-century BC graves have been found in the settlement.

RACQUET SPORTS

Tennis and Ping-Pong are usually going on at **Tinos Beach Hotel** (⊠ Kionia, ☏ 0283/22626).

VOLLEYBALL

You can usually join—or organize—a pick-up game of volleyball at **Tinos Beach Hotel** (⊠ Kionia, ☏ 0283/22626).

Kardiani

21 km (13 mi) northwest of Tinos town.

The mountainside village of Kardiani is 4,000 years old; views here are spectacular and its elegant peasant architecture preserved.

Isternia

24 km (15 mi) northwest of Tinos town, 3 km (2 mi) north of Kardiani.

The village of Isternia (Cisterns) is verdant with lush gardens. Many of the marble plaques hung here over doorways—a specialty of Tinos—indicate the owner's profession, e.g., a sailing ship for a fisherman or sea captain. A long, paved road winds down to a little **port,** with a **beach** and two **fish tavernas;** a small boat ferries people to Chora in good weather.

Pirgos

32 km (20 mi) northwest of Tinos town, 8 km (5 mi) north of Isternia.

The village of Pirgos, second in importance to Chora, is inland from the little harbor of **Panormos.** Tinos is famous for its marble carving, and Pirgos, a prosperous town, is noted for its sculpture school (the town's highest building) and marble workshops, where craftsmen make fanlights, fountains, tomb monuments, small objects for tourists, plus whatever you wish to order. The village's **main square** is aptly crafted of all marble. In fact, the quarries for the green-veined marble are just north of here, reachable by car. The cemetery here is, appropriately, a showplace of marble sculpture.

The marble-working tradition of Tinos survives here from the last century and is going strong, as seen in the **Kardamites Museum,** which features the work of Pirgos's renowned sculptor, Iannoulis Chalepas. ✉ *1 block from bus stop.* 🎫 *300 dr.* ☉ *Daily 10–2.*

Beaches
The beaches next to Panormos are popular in summer.

Shopping
CARVINGS
A number of marble carvers are, appropriately, found in Pirgos. You may visit the shop of probably the best master carver, **Lambros Diamantopoulos** (✉ Near main square, ☎ 0283/31365), who accepts commissions for work to be done throughout Greece. He makes and sells traditional designs to other carvers and to visitors, who may bring a portable slab home to copy.

Panormos

35 km (21¾ mi) northwest of Tinos town, 3 km (2 mi) north of Pirgos.

Panormos, an unpretentious port, has several seafood restaurants and a good beach with a collapsed sea cave. More coves with secluded swimming are beyond, as is the islet of Panormos.

Dining
\$\$ ✕ **Ayia Thalassa.** This taverna is undoubtedly the best on the Panormos waterfront. The name means "Sacred Sea," and seafood is the specialty here; fresh fish is charged by weight. The caïques sell their gleaming catch right on the quay, attended by cats, gulls, and a quackery of ducks. The appetizers are good, too: try the chickpea salad. This spot may look unpretentious but it's popular—on August evenings reservations are a good idea. *In the middle of the Panormos waterfront,* ☎ *0283/31364. AE, MC, V.*

MYKONOS AND DELOS

Put firmly on the map by Jackie O, Mykonos has become one of the most popular of the Aegean islands. Although the dry, rugged island is one of the smallest of the Cyclades—it's only 16 km (10 mi) long and 11 km (7 mi) wide—travelers from all over the world are drawn to its many stretches of sandy beach, its thatched windmills, and its picturesque port town of Mykonos. Happily, the islanders seem to have been able to fit cosmopolitan New Yorkers or Londoners gracefully into their way of life. You may see, for example, an old island woman leading a donkey laden with vegetables through the town's narrow streets, greeting the suntanned vacationers walking by. The truth is Mykoniots regard a good tourist season as a fisherman looks at a good day's catch; for many, the money earned in July and August will support them for the rest of the year. Not long ago Mykoniots had to rely on what they could scratch out of the island's arid land for sustenance, and some remember suffering from starvation under Axis occupation during World War II. In the 1950s a few tourists began trickling into Mykonos on their way to see the ancient marvels on the nearby islet of Delos, the sacred isle.

For almost 1,000 years Delos was the religious and political center of the Aegean and host every four years to the Delian games, the region's greatest festival. The population of Delos actually reached 20,000 at the peak of its commercial period, and throughout antiquity Mykonos, eclipsed by its holy neighbor, depended on this proximity for income, as it partly does today. Visitors interested in antiquity should plan to spend a morning on Delos. Most travel offices in Mykonos town run guided tours that cost about 8,500 dr., including boat transportation and entry fee. Alternatively, take one of the caïques that visit Delos daily from the port: The round-trip costs about 2,000 dr., and entry to the site (with no guide) 1,500 dr. They leave between 8:30 AM and 1 PM and return 1–3.

Mykonos Town

16 km (10 mi) southeast of Tinos town.

For some, Mykonos Town remains the Saint-Tropez of the Greek islands. The setting is memorable, with its whitewashed streets, Little Venice, the Kato Myli ridge of windmills, Kastro—the town's medieval quarter—and its cubical two-story houses and churches with their red or blue doors and domes and wooden balconies, long celebrated as some of the best examples of classic Cycladic architecture. Pink oleander, scarlet hibiscus, and trailing green pepper trees form a contrast amid the dazzling whiteness—kept up by frequent renewal of whitewash. Any visitor who has the pleasure of getting lost in its narrow streets (made all the narrower by the many outdoor stone staircases, which maximized housing space in the crowded village) will appreciate the fact that its confusing layout was designed to foil attacking pirates. After Mykonos fell under Turkish rule in 1537, the Ottomans allowed the islanders to arm their vessels against pirates, which had a contradictory effect: Many of them found that raiding other islands was more profitable than tilling arid land. At the height of Aegean piracy, Mykonos was the principal headquarters of the corsair fleets—the place where pirates met their fellows, found willing women, and filled out their crews. Eventually the illicit activity evolved into a legitimate and thriving trade network.

❶ A bust of Mando Mavroyennis, the island heroine, stands on a pedestal in the **main square.** In the 1821 War of Independence the Mykoniots, known for their seafaring skills, volunteered an armada of 24 ships, and in 1822, when the Ottomans later landed a force on the island, Mando and her soldiers forced them back to their ships. After independence, a scandalous love affair caused her to be exiled to Paros, where she died.

The best time to visit the **central harbor** is in the cool of the evening, when the islanders promenade along the **esplanade** to meet friends and visit the numerous cafés. By the open-air fish market, Petros the Pelican preens and cadges eats, disdaining a group of ducks. In the 1950s a group of migrating pelicans passed over Mykonos, leaving behind a single exhausted bird; Vassilis the fisherman nursed it back to health, and locals say that the pelican in the harbor is the original Petros.

The main shopping street, **Matoyanni** (✉ Perpendicular to harbor), is lined with jewelry stores, clothing boutiques, chic cafés, and candy shops.

Aegean Maritime
Museum, **3**

Archaeological
museum, **2**

Church of
Paraportiani, **7**

Folk museum, **6**

Greek Orthodox
Cathedral, **8**

Little Venice, **4**

Main square, **1**

Monastery of the
Panayia Tourliani, **10**

Mykonos windmills, **5**

Roman Catholic
Cathedral, **9**

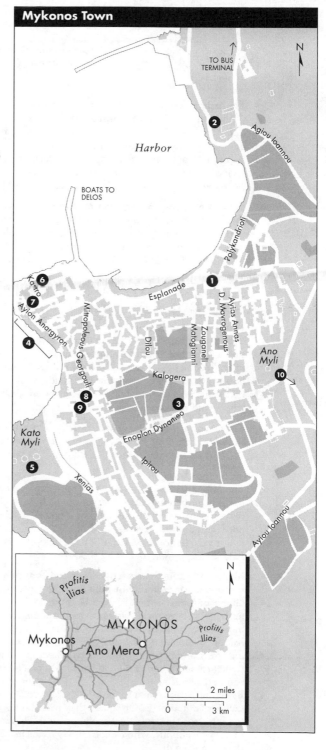

Mykonos Town

N

TO BUS
TERMINAL

Harbor

BOATS TO
DELOS

Esplanade

Agiou Ioannou

Polykandrioti

Ayias Annas

D. Mavrogenous

Zouganeli
Matogianni

*Ano
Myli*

Mitropoleous Georgouli

Dilou

Kalogera

Enoplon Dynameo

Ipirou

Xenias

*Kato
Myli*

Kano

Ayion Anargyron

Ayiou Ioannou

N

*Profitis
Ilias*

MYKONOS

*Profitis
Ilias*

Mykonos

Ano Mera

0   2 miles

0   3 km

The **Public Art Gallery** (⊠ Matoyanni, ☎ 0289/27190) is also here, with exhibitions changing weekly.

NEED A BREAK?   For homemade ice cream, stop at **Snowstorm** (⊠ In middle of shopping area, ☎ 0289/24995), which has been making its creamy product, in 40 flavors, for 17 years.

❷   The **archaeological museum** affords insight into the intriguing history of the Delos shrine. The museum houses Delian funerary sculptures discovered on the neighboring islet of Rhenea, many with scenes of mourning. The most significant work from Mykonos is a 7th-century BC *pithos* (storage jar), showing the Greeks in the Trojan horse and the sack of the city. ⊠ *Ayios Stefanos Rd., between boat dock and town,* ☎ *0289/22325.* ⊡ *500 dr.* ⊙ *Tues.–Sun. 8:30–2:30.*

❸   The charming **Aegean Maritime Museum** contains a collection of model ships, navigational instruments, old maps, prints, coins, and nautical memorabilia. The backyard garden displays some old anchors and ship wheels and a reconstructed 1890 lighthouse, once lit by oil. ⊠ *Enoplon Dynameon,* ☎ *0289/22700.* ⊡ *500 dr.* ⊙ *Daily 10:30–1 and 6:30–9.*

Take a peek into **Lena's House,** an accurate restoration of a middle-class Mykonos house from the last century. ⊠ *Enoplon Dynameon,* ☎ *0289/22591.* ⊡ *Free.* ⊙ *Apr.–Oct., daily 7 PM–9 PM.*

Many of the early ship's captains built distinguished houses directly on the sea here, with wooden balconies overlooking the water. Today,
★ **❹**   this neighborhood, at the southwest end of the port, is called **Little Venice** (⊠ Mitropoleos Georgouli). A few of the old houses have been turned into stylish bars, which are quite romantic at twilight. Overlooking them
❺   on the high hill are the famous **Mykonos windmills,** echoes of a time when wind power was used to grind the island's grain.

The **Mykonos Agricultural Museum** displays a 16th-century windmill, traditional outdoor oven, waterwheel, dovecote, and more. ⊠ *Petassos, at top of Mykonos town,* ☎ *0289/22591.* ⊡ *Free.* ⊙ *June–Sept., daily 4–6 PM.*

❻   The **folk museum,** housed in an 18th-century house, exhibits a bedroom furnished and decorated in the fashion of that period. On display are looms and lace-making devices, Cycladic costumes, old photographs, and Mykoniot musical instruments that are still played at festivals. ⊠ *South of boat dock,* ☎ *0289/22591 or 0289/22748.* ⊡ *Free.* ⊙ *Mon.–Sat. 4–8, Sun. 5:30–8.*

Mykoniots claim that exactly 365 churches and chapels dot their landscape, one for each day of the year. The most famous of these is the
❼   **Church of Paraportiani** (Postern Gate) (⊠ Ayion Anargyron, near folk museum). The sloping, whitewashed conglomeration of four chapels, mixing Byzantine and vernacular idioms, has been described as "a confectioner's dream gone mad," and its position on a promontory fac-
❽   ing the sea sets off the unique architecture. The **Greek Orthodox Cathedral of Mykonos** (⊠ On square that meets both Ayion Anargyron and Odos Mitropolis) has a number of old icons of the post-
❾   Byzantine period. Next to the Greek Orthodox Cathedral is the **Roman Catholic Cathedral** (⊠ On square that meets both Ayion Anargyron and Odos Mitropolis) from the Venetian period. The name and coat of arms of the Ghisi family, who took over Mykonos in 1207, are inscribed in the entrance hall.

Beaches

There is a beach for every taste in Mykonos. **Beaches near Mykonos town,** within walking distance, are Tourlos and Ayios Ioannis. **Ayios Stefanos,** about a 45-minute walk from Mykonos town, has a mini-golf course, water sports, restaurants, and umbrellas and lounge chairs for rent. The **south coast**'s Psarou, protected from wind by hills and surrounded by restaurants, offers a wide selection of water sports and is often called the finest beach. Nearby **Plati Yialos,** popular among families, is also lined with restaurants and dotted with umbrellas for rent. From here you can take a caïque to **Paranga, Paradise, Super Paradise,** and **Elia,** on all of which nudity is common. All have tavernas on the beach. At the easternmost end of the south shores is **Kalafatis,** known for package tours, and between Elia and Kalafatis there's a remote beach at **Kato Livadhi,** which can be reached by road. The great indentation on the **north coast** of the island, called **Panormos Bay,** has unprotected sandy beaches, which can get windy.

Dining and Lodging

$$$$ ✕ **Chez Cat'rine.** This restaurant is hidden, but the Greek and French
★ cuisine and formal hospitality are worth the search. The splendid interior mixes Cycladic arches and whitewash with a French feeling and a faded 16th century mural from Constantinople. Candles and classical music set the tone for baby squid stuffed with rice and Greek mountain spices, or soufflé, puffed to perfection and loaded with cheese, mussels, and prawns. For entrées, try grilled swordfish, leg of lamb, or tournedos langoustine (a beef fillet with lobster sauce, flamed with cognac). ⊠ *Ayios Gerasimos, Mykonos town,* ☎ *0289/22169. Reservations essential on weekends. AE, DC, MC, V.*

$$$$ ✕ **La Taverne.** Haute cuisine, in a tasteful room overlooking Mykonos Bay on one side and a pool on the other, makes for satisfying dining. Amidst graceful surroundings—dark wood-beam ceilings and white walls lined with art—start with *manouri* (cheese rolled in toasted almonds and cooked with red wine) or eggplant with seafood, Gorgonzola, and arugula. If you are not having fresh fish, try fillet of beef in puff pastry with Mavrodaphni wine sauce or tenderloin pork stuffed with feta cheese with manouri cheese sauce. Large portions make the best dessert, an invigorating espresso cream, unnecessary—but why not? The maître d', Christos Balaskas, loves to advise on quality Greek wines. ⊠ *Hotel Cavo Tagoo, 15 mins by foot north of Mykonos town on sea road,* ☎ *0289/23692 through 0289/23694. Reservations essential July–Aug. AE, DC, MC, V.*

$$$–$$$$ ✕ **Edem.** Prompt service and excellent food are well received at the cool white garden of Edem; some tables are also on a platform over the lighted pool. The extensive menu offers three lamb dishes; lamb wrapped in vine leaves with a wine sauce is especially good. Fresh fish and lobster are specialties. For appetizers, choose from dolmades, baked potatoes stuffed with spiced meat and cheese, and Edem shrimp cooked in a garlic, olive oil, and tomato sauce. ⊠ *At an alley end off Matogianni (follow signs) behind the Panachra church,* ☎ *0289/22855 or 0289/ 23355. AE, DC, MC, V.*

$$ ✕ **Phillipi.** This old, lovely restaurant features authentic Greek dishes in a beautiful garden. Fish-roe salad, eggplant salad, fried calamari, and many other traditional dishes have stayed nicely old-fashioned here. ⊠ *Just off Kaloyera,* ☎ *0289/22295,* 🖷 *0289/23382. No credit cards.*

$$ ✕ **Sesame Kitchen.** Dimitri and Violetta's little alley restaurant has a regular clientele who come here for the fresh-daily seafood and the stir-fried regional vegetables. From the large assortment of starters, the mixed-dips plate is a good way to get going. Then move on to the mixed seafood platter and seafood paella, both of which will quickly explain this

kitchen's popularity. The pineapple tart sends you away happy, but rarer fine Greek wines will keep you happy while there. ⊠ *Three Wells district,* ☎ *0289/24710. AE, V.*

$ ✕ **Kounelas.** This is the long-established fresh-fish taverna where many fishermen themselves eat, for no frills and solid food. The menu depends on the weather—low winds: lots of fish. ⊠ *Just off the port near Delos boats,* ☎ *no phone. No credit cards.*

$$$$ ⊞ **Cavo Tagoo.** This hotel seems to emerge from its cliff-side backdrop ★ and reach out to the sea 150 ft below. A prizewinner for its environmentally sensitive architecture in a competition sponsored by the EOT, this medley of cream-tone cubical suites features roof-level sunset terraces and an alluring saltwater pool. The reception area, restaurant, and guest rooms all have marble floors, dark beamed ceilings, and wood furniture. It's a 15-minute walk to town. ⊠ *Follow Polykandrioti, north of the port, Mykonos town 84600,* ☎ *0289/23692–5,* ℻ *0289/24923. 72 rooms. Restaurant, bar, snack bar, saltwater pool. AE, MC, V.*

$$$$ ⊞ **Kivotos Clubhotel.** Spyros Michopoulos's deluxe hotel is architec- ★ turally ambitious, in a richly decorative island style, with statues in niches and stone-mosaic work, and unexpected little courtyards with bright flowers. The rooms, most with sea views, display local crafts. A hotel minibus runs into town, about 3 km (2 mi) away, and to the airport. ⊠ *Ornos Bay, 2 km (1 mi) from Mykonos town, 84600,* ☎ *0289/25795 or 0289/25796,* ℻ *0289/22844. 30 rooms, 4 suites. 2 restaurants, bar, pool, hot tub, sauna, exercise room, beach. AE, DC, MC, V.*

$$$–$$$$ ⊞ **Petinos.** This casual resort community of four hotels on Plati Yialos beach is comfortable, convenient, and friendly, a favorite among extended vacationers and families. The wind-protected crowded beach, dotted with umbrellas and lounge chairs, is noisy with water sports, snack bars, and restaurants; a boat goes to five other beaches. In the seaside taverna, which comes to life two nights a week with Greek music and dancing, pink tablecloths and flower arrangements brighten the painted wooden tables. Fresh fish is good, or try the salad bar for 1,000 dr. Make reservations on weekends. Frequent port and airport buses (4 km/2½ mi) stop by the hotel. **Petinos Beach Hotel,** the most popular hotel, is yards away from the beach and has a saltwater pool. **Petinos Hotel,** a short walk up the street, has less-expensive, smaller rooms, with showers instead of bathtubs, and studios with kitchenettes upstairs. The elegant and pricier new **Palladium,** 500 yards up the road and so serenely quiet, is all cool colors and green marble. Farther down, the cheaper **Nissaki** completes the complex; top-floor rooms with a balcony are best. All the hotels have the standard wood beds with multicolor spreads, desks, and chairs. ⊠ *Plati Yialos Beach, 2 km (1 mi) from Mykonos town, 84600,* ☎ *0289/22913 or 0289/ 23903,* ℻ *0289/23680. 130 rooms. Restaurant, bar, snack bar, 2 pools, hot tub, exercise room, laundry service. AE, MC, V.*

$$$ ⊞ **Ilio Maris.** At this quality hotel, a five-minute walk from the main shopping area, enjoy extras such as stereos and phones in the white, squarish rooms, and suites with TVs. The stone-paved lobby has traditional furniture with striped fabric, wooden beams, and lots of whitewash. Here you'll find easy parking, and it's open all year (with central heating). ⊠ *Despotika area, 1 block out of town, 84600,* ☎ *0289/23755,* ℻ *0289/ 24309. 22 rooms with bath. Bar, breakfast room, pool. AE, V.*

$$ ⊞ **Myconian Inn.** One of the inexpensive, unpretentious, and practical hotels right in town is the Myconian Inn. The small rooms are tastefully furnished in island style and have TVs and balconies overlooking the port. Breakfast is included. The owner, George Ghikas, also runs Sunspots Travel (☞ Guided Tours *in* Cyclades A to Z, *below*). ⊠ *Petassos, edge of town, 84600,* ☎ *0289/22663 or 0289/23420,* ℻ *0289/ 27269. 13 rooms. Air-conditioning, refrigerators. No credit cards.*

Nightlife and the Arts

When the sun sets, Mykonos becomes an insomniac's paradise. Whether it's bouzouki music, breakbeat, or transvestite techno, Mykonos's nightlife beats to an obsessive rhythm until undetermined hours—little wonder some of Europe's gilded youth come here *just* to enjoy the night scene. After midnight, they often head to the techno bars along the Paradise and Super Paradise beaches. Some of Little Venice's nightclubs become gay in more than one sense of the word, while in the Kastro, convivial bars welcome all for tequila-sambukas during sunset. What is "the" place of the moment? The scene is everchanging—so you'll need to track the buzz once you arrive.

BARS AND DISCOS

Little Venice is a good place to begin an evening, and the **Diva** (⊠ Little Venice) is a cocktail bar with a view full of the romance of the neighborhood. **Montparnasse** (⊠ Little Venice, ☎ 0289/23719) has Toulouse-Lautrec posters and a superb sunset view, with live music; cabaret and musicals are featured. Leave your habit and robes behind when you go to **Thalami** (⊠ Near Paraportiani Church, ☎ 0289/ 23291), a small underground bar with Greek dancing in a cozy nightclub setting. As the night goes on you feel the heightened energy level, which continues to build as dawn approaches. Kostas Karatzas's longstanding **Kastro Bar** (⊠ Just behind Paraportiani, ☎ 0289/23872), with heavy beamed ceilings and island furnishings, creates an intimate environment for enjoying the evening sunset over the bay; classical music sets the tone. And at the famous gay **Pierro's** (⊠ Matoyanni), you can find late-night wild dancing to American and European rock. In summer, Greeks dance all night at **Cava Muses** (⊠ Ayios Stefanos), which is off the beaten path, but worth it.

PERFORMING ARTS

The **Anemo Theatre** (⊠ Steno Roharis, ☎ 0289/23944) is a nonprofit open-air center for the performing arts set in a unique olive garden in the center of town, where, between July and September, distinguished international artists present an eclectic array of concerts, performances, and seminars.

Outdoor Activities and Sports

DIVING

For exciting diving and certification, try **Lucky Scuba Divers** (⊠ Mykonos town, ☎ 0289/22813)or **Psarou Diving Center** (⊠ Mykonos town, ☎ 0289/24808).

HORSEBACK RIDING

Equestrians will find a horseback-riding program—for the novice or expert—at the huge and luxurious **Aphrodite Beach Hotel** (⊠ Kalafati Beach, ☎ 0289/71367), which includes beach access.

TENNIS

The **Kochyli Hotels** (⊠ On hill above Mykonos town, ☎ 0289/22929 or 0289/22107) has tennis courts. **Aphrodite Beach Hotel** (⊠ Kalafati Beach, ☎ 0289/71367, ℻ 0289/71525) also has courts.

WATER SPORTS

Aphrodite Beach Hotel (⊠ Kalafati Beach, ☎ 0289/71367, ℻ 0289/ 71525) has water sports. The windy **northern beaches on Ornos Bay** are best; you can rent surfboards and take lessons. There's windsurfing and waterskiing at **Ayios Stefanos, Plati Yialos,** and **Ornos.** The program at **Surfing Club Anna** (⊠ Agia Anna, ☎ 028971205) is well organized.

You can work out at the **Body Work Gym** (⊠ From taxi square go to Alexis Snack Bar and turn right), run by a Dutch couple.

Shopping

FASHION

Yiannis **Galatis** (⊠ Platia Manto, opposite LALAoUNIS, ☏ 0289/22255) has outfitted such famous women as Elizabeth Taylor, Ingrid Bergman, and Jackie Onassis. He will probably greet you personally and show you some of his coats and costumes, hostess gowns, and long dresses. He also has men's clothes. **Armonia** (⊠ Laka Sq., ☏ 0289/27022, FAX 0289/23930) carries a racier selection of men's and women's fashions by such designers as Versace, Moschino, Byblos, and Ozbek.

FINE AND DECORATIVE ART

Soula Papadakou's **Venetia** carries authentic copies of traditional handmade embroideries in clothing, tablecloths, curtains, and such, all in white; the women who work for her come from all over Greece, including a nunnery in Ioannina (⊠ Ag. Anargiron St. 16, Little Venice, ☏ 0289/24464). In **Nikoletta** (⊠ Little Venice, ☏ 0289/27503), Mykonos's last traditional weaving shop, Nikoletta Xidakis sells her skirts, shawls, and bedspreads made of local wool. The **Mykonos Antiques Centre** (⊠ In garden of the Edem restaurant off Matoyanni, ☏ 0289/27597) offers traditional antiques and other objets d'art in a gallerylike setting.

JEWELRY

Ilias LALAoUNIS (⊠ 14 Polykandrioti, near taxis., ☏ 0289/22444, FAX 0289/24409) is known internationally for jewelry based on classic ancient designs, especially Greek. The **Gold Store** (⊠ On waterfront) is Mykonos's oldest jewelry shop.

SWEETS

Since 1921, Nikolaos Skaropoulos and family have been making traditional almond biscuits and almond milk at **Skaropoulos** (⊠ Pano Matoyanni, ☏ 0289/24983); now a number of confection shops carry them. Nikolaos's grandson claims that their cookies were a favorite of Winston Churchill. You can also visit the **factory and shop** (⊠ A short way up past Ano Mera turnoff on left).

Ano Mera

8 km (5 mi) east of Mykonos town.

⑩ Monastery buffs should head to Ano Mera, a village in the central part of the island, where the **Monastery of the Panayia Tourliani,** founded in 1580 and dedicated to the protectress of Mykonos, stands in the central square. Its massive Baroque iconostasis (altar screen), made in 1775 by Florentine artists, has small icons carefully placed amid the wooden structure's painted green, red, and gold-leaf flowers. At the top are carved figures of the apostles and large icons depicting New Testament scenes. The hanging incense holders with silver molded dragons holding red eggs in their mouths show an eastern influence. In the hall of the monastery, an interesting **museum** displays embroideries, liturgical vestments, and wood carvings. ⊠ *On central square,* ☏ *0289/71249.* ⊙ *By appointment only; call in advance.*

Delos

25-minute caïque ride southwest from Mykonos.

Why did Delos, an islet with virtually no natural resources, become the religious and political center of the Aegean? One answer is that Delos, shielded on three sides by other islands, provided the safest anchorage

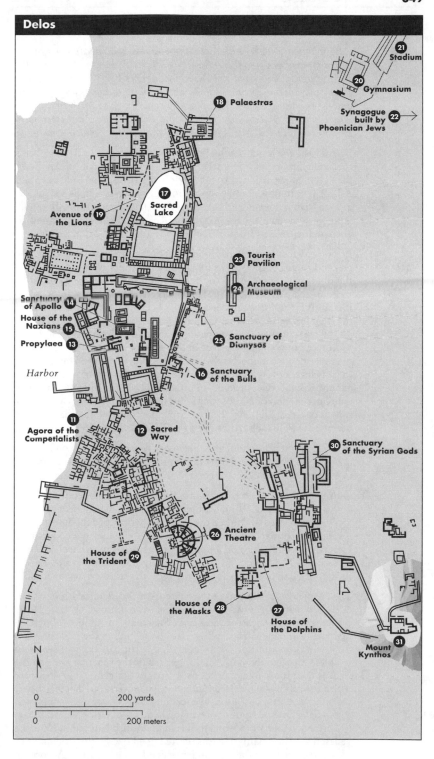

Delos

21 Stadium

20 Gymnasium

22 Synagogue built by Phoenician Jews →

18 Palaestras

17 Sacred Lake

19 Avenue of the Lions

23 Tourist Pavilion

24 Archaeological Museum

14 Sanctuary of Apollo

15 House of the Naxians

13 Propylaea

Harbor

16 Sanctuary of the Bulls

25 Sanctuary of Dionysos

11 Agora of the Competialists

12 Sacred Way

30 Sanctuary of the Syrian Gods

26 Ancient Theatre

29 House of the Trident

28 House of the Masks

27 House of the Dolphins

31 Mount Kynthos

N

0 ____ 200 yards

0 ____ 200 meters

for vessels sailing between the mainland and the shores of Asia. The saga begins back in the times of myth:

Zeus fell in love with gentle Leto, the Titaness, who became pregnant. When Hera discovered this infidelity, she forbade Mother Earth to give Leto refuge and ordered the Python to pursue her. Finally Poseidon, taking pity on her, anchored the floating island of Delos with four diamond columns to give her a place to rest. She gave birth first to the virgin huntress Artemis on Rhenea and then, clasping a sacred palm on a slope of Delos' Mt. Kynthos, to Apollo, god of music and light.

By 1,000 BC the Ionians, who inhabited the Cyclades, had made Delos their religious capital. Homeric Hymn 3 tells of the cult of Apollo in the 7th century BC. A difficult period began for the Delians when Athens rose to power and assumed Ionian leadership. In 543 BC an oracle at Delphi conveniently decreed that the Athenians purify the island by removing all the graves to Rhenea, a dictate designed to alienate the Delians from their past.

After the defeat of the Persians in 478 BC, the Athenians organized the Delian League, with its treasury and headquarters at Delos (in 454 BC the funds were transferred to the Acropolis in Athens). Delos had its most prosperous period in the late Hellenistic and Roman times, when it was declared a free port and quickly became the financial center of the Mediterranean, the focal point of trade, and a slave market, where 10,000 persons were said to be sold every day. Foreigners from as far as Rome, Syria, and Egypt lived in this cosmopolitan port, in complete tolerance of one another's religious beliefs, and each group built its various shrines. But in 88 BC Mithridates, the king of Pontus, in a revolt against Roman rule, ordered an attack on the unfortified island. The entire population of 20,000 was killed or sold into slavery. Delos never fully recovered, and later Roman attempts to revive the island failed because of pirate raids. After 70 BC the island was gradually abandoned.

In 1872, the French School of Archaeology began excavating on Delos—a massive project, considering that much of the island's 4 square km (1½ square mi) is covered in ruins. Their work continues today.

⓫ On the left from the harbor is the **Agora of the Competialists** (circa 150 BC), members of Roman guilds, mostly freedmen and slaves from Sicily who worked for Italian traders. They worshiped the *Lares Competales,* the Roman "crossroads" gods; in Greek they were known as Hermaistai, after the god Hermes, protector of merchants and the
⓬ crossroads. The **Sacred Way,** east of the Agora, was the route, during the holy Delian festival, of the procession to the sanctuary of Apollo.

⓭ The **Propylaea,** at the end of the Sacred Way, were once a monumental white marble gateway with three portals framed by four Doric
⓮ columns. Beyond the Propylaea is the **Sanctuary of Apollo;** though little remains today, when the Propylaea were built in the mid-2nd century BC, the sanctuary was crowded with altars, statues, and temples—three of them to Apollo. Just inside the sanctuary and to the
⓯ right is the **House of the Naxians,** a 7th- to 6th-century BC structure with a central colonnade. Dedications to Apollo were stored in this shrine. Outside the north wall a massive rectangular **pedestal** once supported a colossal statue of Apollo (one of the hands is in Delos's archaeological museum, and a piece of a foot is in the British Museum). Near the pedestal a bronze palm tree was erected in 417 BC by the Athenians to commemorate the palm tree under which Leto gave birth. According to Plutarch, the palm tree toppled in a storm and brought the statue of Apollo down with it.

⑯ Southeast of the Sanctuary of Apollo are the ruins of the **Sanctuary of the Bulls,** an extremely long and narrow structure built, it is thought, to display a trireme, an ancient boat with three banks of oars, dedicated to Apollo by a Hellenistic leader thankful for a naval victory. Maritime symbols were found in the decorative relief of the main halls, and the head and shoulders of a pair of bulls were part of the design of an interior entranceway. A short distance north of the Sanctuary of the **⑰** Bulls is an oval indentation in the earth where the **Sacred Lake** once sparkled. It is surrounded by a stone wall that reveals the original periphery. According to islanders, the lake was fed by the River Inopos from its source high on Mt. Kynthos until 1925, when the water stopped flowing and the lake dried up. Along the shores are two an- **⑱** cient **palaestras,** buildings for the practice of exercise and debate.

★ ⑲ One of most evocative sights of Delos is the 164-ft-long **Avenue of the Lions.** The five Naxian marble beasts crouch on their haunches, their forelegs stiffly upright, vigilant guardians of the Sacred Lake. They are the survivors of a line of at least nine lions, erected in the second half of the 7th century BC by the Naxians. One was removed in the 17th century and now guards the Arsenal of Venice. Northeast of the palaes- **⑳** tras is the **gymnasium,** a square courtyard nearly 131 ft long on each **㉑** side. The long, narrow structure farther northeast is the **stadium,** the site of the athletic events of the Delian Games. East of the stadium site, **㉒** by the seashore, are the remains of a **Synagogue built by Phoenician Jews** in the 2nd century BC.

㉓ A road south from the gymnasium leads to the **tourist pavilion,** which **㉔** has a meager restaurant and bar. The **Archaeological Museum** is also on the road south of the gymnasium; it contains most of the antiquities found in excavations on the island: monumental statues of young men and women, steles, reliefs, masks, and ancient jewelry. The museum, recently redone, keeps the same hours as the site.

㉕ Immediately to the right of the museum is a small **Sanctuary of Dionysos,** erected about 300 BC; outside it is one of the more boggling sights of ancient Greece: several monuments dedicated to Apollo by the winners of the choral competitions of the Delian festivals, each decorated with a huge phallus, emblematic of the orgiastic rites that took place during the Dionysian festivals. Around the base of one of them is carved a lighthearted representation of a bride being carried to her new husband's home. A marble phallic bird, symbol of the body's immortality, also adorns this corner of the sanctuary.

Beyond the path that leads to the southern part of the island is the **㉖** **ancient theater,** built in the early 3rd century BC in the elegant residential quarter inhabited by Roman bankers and Egyptian and Phoenician merchants. Their one- and two-story **houses** were typically built around a central courtyard, sometimes with columns on all sides, and their floors were covered with decorative mosaics, which channeled rainwater into cisterns below. The colorful mosaics show fantastical natural themes: panthers, birds, and dolphins; the best preserved can **㉗ ㉘** be seen in the **House of the Dolphins,** the **House of the Masks,** and **㉙** the **House of the Trident.** A dirt path leads east to the base of Mt. Kynthos, where there are remains from many **Middle Eastern shrines, ㉚** including the **Sanctuary of the Syrian Gods,** built in 100 BC. A flight **㉛** of steps goes up 368 ft to the summit of **Mt. Kynthos** (after which all Cynthias are named), on whose slope Apollo was born. ⊠ *Delos island and historic site, take a caïque from Mykonos town,* ☎ *0289/ 22259.* ▨ *1,500 dr.* ⊙ *Apr.–Oct., Tues.–Sun. 8:30–3.*

NAXOS

"Great sweetness and tranquillity" is how Nikos Kazantzakis, premier novelist of Greece, described Naxos, and indeed a tour of the island leaves you with an impression of abundance, prosperity, and serenity. The greenest, most fertile of the Cyclades, Naxos, with its many potato fields, its livestock and its thriving cheese industry, and its fruit and olive groves framed by the pyramid of Mt. Zas (3,295 ft, the Cyclades' highest), is practically self-sufficient. Inhabited for 6,000 years, the island offers today's visitor memorable landscapes—abrupt ravines, hidden valleys, long sandy beaches—and towns that vary from a Cretan mountain stronghold to the seaside capital, strongly evoking its Venetian past.

Naxos Town

 *Seven hours by ferry from Piraeus; 35 km (21¾ mi) east of Paros town.*

As your ferry chugs into the harbor, you see before you the white houses of Naxos town (Chora) on a hill crowned by the one remaining tower of the Venetian castle, reminding us that Naxos was once the beautiful capital of the Venetian duchy of the Aegean. The tiny church of **Our Lady of Myrtle** (⊠ Perched on a sea rock off the waterfront) watches over the local sailors, who built it for divine protection.

While the capital town is primarily beloved for its Venetian elegance and picturesque blind alleys, Naxos's most famous landmark is ancient: the **Portara** (⊠ At harbor's far edge), a massive doorway that leads to nowhere. The Portara stands on the islet of **Palatia,** which was once a hill (since antiquity the Mediterranean has risen quite a bit) and in the 3rd millennium BC was the acropolis for a nearby Cycladic settlement. The Portara, an entrance to an unfinished Temple of Apollo that faces exactly toward Delos, Apollo's birthplace, was begun about 530 BC by the tyrant Lygdamis, who said he would make Naxos's buildings the highest and most glorious in Greece. He was overthrown in 506 BC and the temple was never completed; by the 5th and 6th centuries AD it had been converted into a church; and under Venetian and Turkish rule it was slowly dismembered, so the marble could be used to build the castle. The gate, built with four blocks of marble, each 16 ft long and weighing 20 tons, was so large it couldn't be demolished, so it remains today, along with the temple floor. Palatia itself has come to be associated with the tragic myth of Ariadne, princess of Crete.

Ariadne, daughter of Crete's King Minos, helped Theseus thread the labyrinth of Knossos and slay the monstrous Minotaur. In exchange, he promised to marry her. Sailing for Athens, the couple stopped in Naxos, where Theseus abandoned her. Jilted Ariadne's curse made Theseus forget to change the ship's sails from black to white, and so his grieving father Aegeus, believing his son dead, plunged into the Aegean. Seeing her tears, smitten Dionysos descended in a leopard-drawn chariot to marry her, and set her bridal wreath, the Corona Borealis, in the sky, in eternal token of his love.

The myth inspired one of Titian's best-known paintings, as well as Strauss's opera *Ariadne auf Naxos.*

Old town (⊠ Along the quay, left at first big square) possesses a bewildering maze of twisting cobblestone streets, arched porticoes, and towering doorways, where you're plunged into cool darkness and then suddenly into pockets of dazzling sunshine. The old town is divided into the lower section, **Bourgos,** where the Greeks lived during Venetian times, and the upper part, called **Kastro** (castle), still inhabited by the Venetian Catholic nobility.

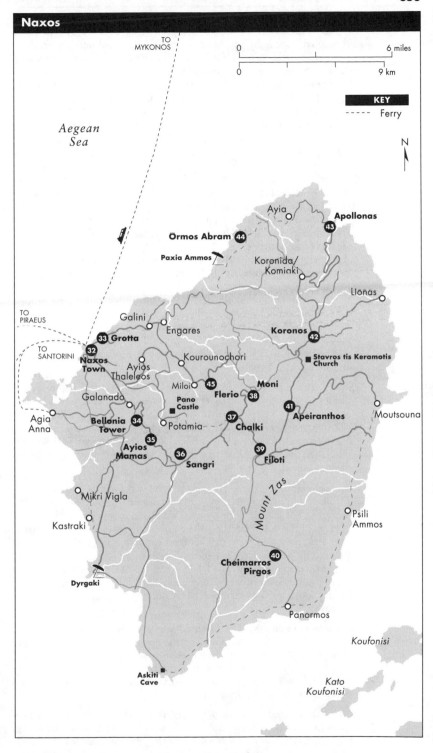

Naxos

TO
MYKONOS

0   6 miles

0   9 km

KEY
----- Ferry

N

*Aegean
Sea*

Ayia

Apollonas 43

Ormos Abram 44

Paxia Ammos

Koronida/
Komiaki

Llonas

TO
PIRAEUS

Galini

Engares

Koronos 42

33 **Grotta**

32 **Naxos
Town**

TO
SANTORINI

Kourounochori

■ **Stavros tis Keramotis
Church**

Ayios
Thaleleos

Miloi

45

Flerio 38

Moni

Galanado

**Pano
Castle** ■

41

Apeiranthos

Moutsouna

Agia
Anna

**Bellonia
Tower** 34

Potamia

37

Chalki

**Ayios
Mamas** 35

36

39

Filoti

Sangri

Mount Zas

Mikri Vigla

Psili
Ammos

Kastraki

40

**Cheimarros
Pirgos**

Dyrgaki

Panormos

Koufonisi

**Askiti
Cave** ■

*Kato
Koufonisi*

You won't miss the gates of the **castle** (⊠ Kastro). The south gate is called the **Paraporti** (side gate), but it's more interesting to enter through the northern gate, or **Trani** (strong), via Apollonos Street. Note the vertical incision in the gate's marble column—it is the Venetian yard against which drapers measured the bolts of cloth they brought to the noblewomen. Step through the Trani into the citadel and enter another age, where sedate Venetian houses still stand around silent courtyards, their exteriors emblazoned with coats of arms and bedecked with flowers, the only sign of present-day occupants the drying clothes fluttering occasionally from a balcony. The citadel was built in 1207 by Marco Sanudo, a Venetian who, three years after the fall of Constantinople, landed on Naxos as part of the Fourth Crusade. For two months he laid siege to the Byzantine castle at t'Apilarou and upon its downfall made Naxos the headquarters of his duchy. He divided the island into estates and distributed them to his officers, who built the *pirgi* (tower houses) that still dot the countryside. When in 1210 Venice refused to grant him independent status, Sanudo switched allegiance to the Latin emperor in Constantinople, becoming Duke of the Archipelago. Under the Byzantines, "archipelago" had meant "chief sea," but after Sanudo and his successors, it came to mean "group of islands," i.e., the Cyclades. For three centuries Naxos was held by Venetian families, who resisted pirate attacks, introduced Roman Catholicism, and later rebuilt the castle in its present form. In 1564 Naxos came under Turkish rule, but even then, the Venetians still ran the island, while the Turks only collected taxes. The rust-color **Glezos tower** was home to the last dukes; it displays the coat of arms: a pen and sword crossed under a crown.

Few Turks settled on Naxos, and inland villages developed to avoid pirates. When the War of Independence began in 1821, the only Turk remaining was a clerk who, at the war's first rumblings, sailed away. The only reminder of Turkish rule is a ruined fountain on the road from Naxos town to Engares; it was the lack of schools under Turkish rule that led to the founding of the Kastro's Ursuline convent and the commercial school.

The **cathedral** (⊠ At the Kastro's center) was built by Sanudo in the 13th century and restored by Catholic families in the 16th and 17th centuries. The marble floor is paved with tombstones bearing the coats of arms of the noble families. Venetian wealth is evident in the many gold and silver icon frames. The icons reflect a mix of Byzantine and Western influences: The one of the Virgin Mary is unusual because it shows a Byzantine Virgin and Child in the presence of a bishop, a cathedral benefactor. Another 17th-century icon shows the Virgin of the Rosary surrounded by members of the Sommaripa family, whose house is nearby.

The **convent and school of the Ursulines** (⊠ A few steps beyond cathedral) was begun in 1739. In a 1713 document, a General of the Jesuits, Francis Tarillon, mentions that the proposed girl's school should be simple; grandeur would expose it to the Turks' covetousness. Over the years, extensions were added, and the Greek state has now bought the building for cultural purposes.

Today the convent and school of the Ursulines houses the **archaeological museum,** best known for its Cycladic and Mycenaean finds. During the Early Cycladic period (3200 BC–2000 BC), there were settlements along Naxos's east coast and just outside Naxos town at Grotta. The finds are from these settlements and graveyards scattered around the island. Many of the vessels exhibited are from the Early Cycladic I period, hand-built of coarse-grained clay, sometimes decorated with a herringbone pattern.

Gradually, the variety of shapes and decoration increased—new forms appeared, such as candlesticks, wine pourers, and sauce boats with spiral patterns, fish, or the typical many-oared boat. One common shape is known as the "frying pan"; uncertain, some archaeologists believe it held water and served as a mirror, while others think that skins were stretched across it to make a drum for funeral processions.

Though the museum has too many items in its glass cases for a short visit, you should try not to miss the white marble Cycladic statuettes, which range from the early "violin" shapes to the more detailed female forms with their tilted flat heads, folded arms, and legs slightly bent at the knees. The male forms are simpler and often appear to be seated. The most common theory is that the female statuettes were both fertility and grave goddesses, and the males servant figures. ⊠ *Kastro*, ☎ *0285/22725*. ⊒ *500 dr., free Sun.* ☺ *Tues.–Sun. 8:30–3.*

The **French School of Commerce** is marked by an escutcheon bearing a fleur-de-lis surrounded by the collar of the Order of the Holy Spirit. The school was run in turn by Jesuits, Lazarists, and Salesians. Under the last it enjoyed its most distinguished period (1891–1927); the Cretan writer Nikos Kazantzakis attended the school for two years. Its library, archives, and opulent furnishings were destroyed during the German Italian occupation, but it's easy to imagine rows of schoolboys running to class as you enter its vast, cool halls.

The **Greek Orthodox cathedral** (⊠ Bourgos) was built in 1789 on the site of a church called Zoodochos Pigis (Life-giving Source). The cathedral was built from the materials of ancient temples: The solid granite pillars are said to be from the ruins of Delos. Amid the gold and the carved wood, there is a vividly colored iconostasis painted by a well-known iconographer of the Cretan school, Dimitrios Valvis, and the Gospel Book is believed to be a gift from Catherine the Great of Russia.

Excavations of the ruins of the **agora,** the center of the ancient city, have revealed a 167-ft by 156-ft square closed on three sides by Doric stoas, so that it looked like the letter "G." A shorter fourth stoa bordered the east side, leaving room at each end for an entrance. The *heroon* (shrine for a hero) and bases for statues stood in front of the stoas; the inscriptions recovered indicate Artemis was worshiped here.

Beaches

The southeast coast of Naxos, facing Paros and the sunset, offers the Cyclades' longest stretches of fine beaches. In order, heading south: **Ayios Georgios** is now part of town and very developed; **Ayios Prokopios** has a small leeward harbor and lagoons with waterfowl; **Ayia Anna,** partly nude, has a small harbor with connections to Paros; **Plaka,** ringed by sand dunes and bamboo groves, is about 8 km (5 mi) south of town and only now developing; **Mikri Vigla** is sandy and edged by cedar trees; **Kastraki** has white marble sand; **Pyrgaki** is the least developed, with idyllic crystalline water. All these have tavernas and rooms.

Dining and Lodging

$$$ ✕ **The Old Inn.** Dieter Ranizewski, a trained chef and instructor of chefs
★ from Berlin, has built his "dream place," and it is one of the Cyclades' very best restaurants. In a courtyard under a chinaberry tree, with rough whitewashed walls and bits of ancient marble, two of the old church's interior sides open into the wine cellar and gallery; on the fourth side, with beams and wood paneling, is a fireplace, handy for the winter months. The menu is extensive. For starters you might try smoked ham, jellied pork, or liver pâté—all homemade. For entrées, Berlin liver with apples and onions, and the fresh trout with almonds and parsleyed potatoes are especially good. For dessert the homemade red forest—

berry jelly with vanilla cream beckons voluptuously. Kids love both the small playground and the children's menu. ⊠ *Naxos town, up car road around the town, 2 alleys in on right from waterfront,* ☎ *0285/26093,* FAX *028923325. AE, V.*

$$ ✕ **Gorgona.** Dimitris and Koula Kapris's beachfront taverna is popular both with sunworshipers on Ayia Anna beach and locals from Chora, who come here winter and summer to get away, and sometimes to dance till late. The menu is extensive and fresh daily—the fresh fish comes from the caïques that pull up at the dock right in front every morning. Two good appetizers are *kakavia* (fish stew) and shrimp *saganaki*(with cooked cheese), while octopus in red wine is a fine entrée. The barrel wine is their own. They also have studio apartments for rent. ⊠ *Beach Rd. south into Ayia Anna from Chora,* ☎ *0285/41007. AE, MC, V.*

$$ ✕ **I Apothiki tou Ballidras/Kraemerladen.** Though the service may be slow, this taverna is worth the wait, as this place offers traditional and local specialties you don't usually find. After the fried zucchini appetizer, for instance, sample the *boxa* (lamb, mountain greens, and a lemon sauce cooked slowly in a ceramic pot) or the *kouneli krasato* (rabbit in red wine). Most dishes come with the island's delicious potatoes, lightly covered with olive oil and dill. I Apothiki also serves fresh fish, some non-Greek dishes, and several of the well-known local cheeses like the salty *kefalograviera* and a creamy, almost sweet *mizithra*—perfect after your meal. ⊠ *Naxos town waterfront,* ☎ *0285/24242. MC, V.*

$ ✕ **Meltemi.** Mihalis Mathiassos's restaurant is typically Greek, with fluorescent lighting and plastic-wrap tablecloths, but it is by the sea and set among vines. It's known locally as the place to go for inexpensive Greek staples like souvlaki, lamb *exohiko* (cooked in paper with vegetables), barbecued fillets of Mihalis's daily catch, and pans and pans of *gigantes* (giant white beans in olive oil) and *tsoutsoukakia* (meat patties made from spicy sausage). *Kaloyero* (eggplant with ham and béchamel) is a bit more unusual. The crème caramel is heavenly. The waiters are fast and efficient, even when the place is packed. ⊠ *Chora waterfront, at other end of dock,* ☎ *0285/22654. No credit cards.*

$$$ ▦ **Chateau Zevgoli.** If you stay in Chora, try to stay here. Each room
★ in Despina Kitini's fairy-tale pension, in a comfortable Venetian house, is distinct. The living room is filled with dark antique furniture, gilded mirrors, old family photographs, and locally woven curtains and tablecloths. One of the nicest bedrooms has a private bougainvillea-covered courtyard and pillows handmade by Despina's great-grandmother; the honeymoon suite has a canopy bed, a spacious balcony, and a view of the Portara. Rooms can sometimes be had off-season for half price. Despina also has roomy studios, called Pension Irene, in Chora's old town; you can get details at the EOT in the harbor (☞ Visitor Information *in* The Cyclades A to Z, *below*). ⊠ *Chora old town (follow signs stenciled on walls), 84300,* ☎ *0285/22993 or 0285/24358, 01/ 651–5885 in Athens;* FAX *0285/25200. 10 rooms with shower. Breakfast room. AE, MC, V.*

$$$ ▦ **Galaxy.** As you approach this hotel from a distance, it seems to shimmer—all whitewash and marble. Its three buildings rather resemble grand pueblos, except that they have wide stone arches; wooden doors in shades of green, purple, and turquoise; and balconies with grillwork depicting swans. Archways also span the large rooms, which have beamed ceilings and trim orange accessories, plus plants, kitchenettes, dining areas, telephones, and cable TV. Most rooms have ocean views (the beach is a minute away); all have balconies. Though mostly shadeless, the carefully tended grounds are a pleasure, with yellow roses and a fountain. ⊠ *Ayios Georgios Beach, 84300,* ☎ *0285/22422 or 0285/22423,* FAX *0285/22889. 54 rooms. Snack bar, pool, playground. AE, V.*

$$$ ▦ **Lianos Village.** Yannis Lianos, a Naxian, has just built an attractive resort that resembles the Cycladic-village style he grew up with. A 10-minute walk from Ayios Prokopios beach, it has island furnishings, very private rooms with magnificent sea views across the lagoons and straits to Paros, immaculate and unobtrusive service, and heavenly quiet. A restaurant is nearby. The bus stops here twice a day. ⊠ *Ayios Prokopios beach, 84300,* ☎ *0285/26366, 0285/23865, or 0285/ 26380,* FAX *0285/26362. 40 rooms. Bar, café, pool. MC, V.*

$$$ ▦ **Orkos Village Hotel.** When Norwegian doctor Kaare Oftedal first saw Orkos beach years ago, he fell in love with the almost isolated strand ringed by sand dunes and cedars. Today he returns from Norway every April to open his small, popular hotel, whose guests seem perfectly content never to leave their idyllic surroundings to go to town. The hotel's white cubist bungalows that stagger down the hillside to the sea's edge are simply furnished and decorated (dried flowers and blue wooden shutters just about covers it). They all have sea views and verandas, most have an additional sitting area. The stones by the walkways have been gathered from Naxian beaches. Guests love to hang around the friendly stone bar, where the doctor's Naxian wife, Katerina, leads dances and serves up classic Greek meals, and to ramble downhill to the idyllic beach (a pool would be profane here). The hotel shuttle bus is infrequent. ⊠ *Orkos beach between Plaka and Mikri Vigla, 84300,* ☎ *0285/75321,* FAX *0285/75320. 28 apartments. Restaurant, bar, kitchenettes. No credit cards.*

$$ ▦ **Iria Beach.** Maria Refene's hotel is right on the beach and echoes
★ Chora's old town with its stucco arches, peaceful nooks and crannies, sunlit courtyard, and bright red and blue shutters. The reception area is quite luxurious, with huge glass doors, cool marble floor, and brass details. The owners have eschewed the usual Greek hotel furniture for unlacquered wood with a gray wash, and an interior color scheme of light blue, gray, and white for the spacious one- and two-room apartments. Guests enjoy hanging out in the shady beach-bar and restaurant. ⊠ *Ayia Anna, 84300,* ☎ *0285/42600,1,* FAX *0285/42603. 17 rooms, 8 apartments. Restaurant, bar, kitchenettes. MC.*

Nightlife

BARS

Nightlife in Naxos is quieter than it is on Santorini or Mykonos, but there are several popular bars at the south end of Chora. **Veggera** (⊠ Chora waterfront near Ayios Georgios Beach, ☎ 0285/23567) has a garden that offers a respite from the rap and rock music inside. Next door to Veggera, in a small white house, **Ecstasis** (⊠ Chora waterfront near Ayios Georgios Beach) has a spacious bar, happy-hour specials, strong drinks, all kinds of music from surf to blues, and a terrace overlooking the sea. For Greek music try the **Greek Bar** (⊠ Chora waterfront, ☎ 0285/24675).

Outdoor Activities and Sports

SAILING

To rent a sailboat, contact the **Rental and Travel Center** (⊠ Chora, ☎ 0285/23395 or 0285/23396); call the port authority (☎ 0289/22300) for information about where to go in Chora for gas, water, and repairs.

WATER SPORTS

At **Ayios Prokopios** and **Ayia Anna** beaches the wind and water conditions are ideal for inexperienced windsurfers, and there are also waterskiing equipment rentals, and instruction for both sports. Jet Skis can also be rented at **Ayios Prokopios.** The Mikri Vigla hotel complex has a **windsurfing center** (⊠ South of Chora, ☎ 0285/75241 or 0285/ 75242), but experienced windsurfers prefer **Kastraki, Pyrgaki, Mout-**

souna, and **Agiassos beaches,** where wind speeds can reach 7 on the Beaufort scale.

Shopping

ANTIQUE COSTUMES AND JEWELRY

Kostas Koutelieris, the deskman at the Museum, also owns **Loom** (In Old Market, off main square, third street on the right, ☎ 0285/25531), which specializes in "handwoven items of Old Greece" (as his card says) and antique silver jewelry.

BOOKS

At Eleftherios Primikirios's **Zoom** (✉ Chora waterfront, ☎ 0285/23675 or 0285/23676) there's an excellent selection of English-language history and picture books about Naxos. Zoom also has another shop (✉ On cemetery square, ☎ 0285/24357).

FOOD, WINE, AND LIQUEUR

A large selection of the famous *kitro* (citron liqueur) and preserves, as well as Naxos wines and thyme honey, packed in attractive gift baskets, can be found at **Promponas Wines and Liquors** (✉ Chora waterfront, ☎ 0285/22258), which has been around since 1915. Free glasses of kitro are always offered.

JEWELRY

For a large selection of beautiful jewelry, try **Midas** (✉ Old Town, up the main street behind Pampronas on the Chora waterfront, ☎ 0285/24852); Midas also has a smaller store (✉ On waterfront, ☎ 0285/26291). The owner, Fotis Margaritis, creates talismans in different settings that feature a "Naxos eye," which is the operculum, or door, of a seashell with a spiral design that fishermen bring him. The workshop of **Nassos Papakonstantinou** (✉ Old Town, far left street of main square, ☎ FAX 0285/22607) sells one-of-a-kind pieces both sculptural and delicate. The shop is easy to find, although it is tiny and has no sign.

TRADITIONAL KNITS, JEWELS, AND LINENS

The embroidery and knitted items made by women in the mountain villages are known throughout Greece; they can occasionally be bought in a Chora tourist shop like **Old Market Naxos** (✉ Old Town, ☎ 0285/24767) or from villagers hawking their wares in front of tourist sites. For a wide selection of old designs for jewelry, linens, household items, and so forth, try **Techni** (✉ Near entrance to Chora's old town, ☎ 0285/24767 or 0285/25673).

En Route   On your way to Bellonia, on the main road from Naxos town, you'll go southeast past Galanado and drive through the reed beds, cacti, and plains of the Livadi Valley.

Grotta

㉝ *Just a few steps east of Naxos town.*

In Grotta you can sometimes see **underwater remains of Cycladic buildings** strewn along an area of about 130 ft, a series of large worked stones, perhaps the remains of the mole, and a few steps that locals say go to a tunnel leading to the islet of Palatia.

Bellonia Tower

㉞ *5 km (3 mi) south of Naxos town.*

The graceful **Bellonia tower** (Pirgos Bellonia) belonged to the area's ruling Venetian family, and like other fortified houses, it was built as a refuge from pirates and as part of the island's alarm system. The towers were located strategically throughout the island; if there was an attack, a large fire would be lit on the nearest tower's roof, setting off a chain reaction from tower to tower and alerting the islanders. Bellonia's thick stone walls, its Lion of St. Mark emblem, and flat roofs with zigzag chimneys are typical of these pirgi. The unusual 13th-century **"double church" of St. John** (⊠ In front of Bellonia tower) exemplifies Venetian tolerance. On the left side is the Catholic chapel, on the right the Orthodox church, separated only by a double arch. A family lives in the tower and the church is often open. From here, take a moment to gaze across the peaceful fields to Chora and imagine what the islanders must have felt when they saw pirate ships on the horizon.

Ayios Mamas

⑮ *8 km (5 mi) south of Naxos town, 3 km (2 mi) south of Bellonia Tower.*

A kilometer (½ mile) past a valley with unsurpassed views is one of the island's oldest churches (9th-century), Ayios Mamas. St. Mamas is the protector of shepherds and is regarded as a patron saint in Naxos, Cyprus, and Asia Minor. Built in the 8th century, the stone church was the island's cathedral under the Byzantines. Though it was converted into a Catholic church in 1207, it was neglected under the Venetians and is now falling apart. You can also get to it from the Potamia villages.

Sangri

⑯ *11 km (7 mi) south of Naxos town, 3 km (2 mi) south of Ayios Mamas.*

Sangri is the center of an area with so many monuments and ruins spanning the Archaic to the Venetian periods, it is sometimes called "little Mystras." The name Sangri is a corruption of Sainte Croix, which is what the French called the town's 16th-century monastery of **Timios Stavros** (Holy Cross). The town is actually three small villages spread across a plateau. During the Turkish occupation, the monastery served as an illegal school, where children met secretly to learn the Greek language and culture. Above the town, you can make out the **ruins of t'Apilarou** (⊠ On Mt. Profitis Ilias), the castle Sanudo first attacked.

Chalki

⑰ *17 km (10½ mi) southeast of Naxos town, 6 km (4 mi) northeast of Sangri.*

You are now entering the heart of the lush Tragaia Valley, where in spring the air is heavily scented with honeysuckle, roses, and lemon blossoms, and many tiny Byzantine churches hide in the dense olive groves.

Chalki is home to one of the most important of these Byzantine churches: the white, red-roof **Panayia Protothrone** (First Enthroned Virgin). Restoration work has uncovered frescoes ranging from the 6th through the 13th centuries, and the church has remained alive and functioning for 14 centuries. The oldest layers, in the apse, depict the Apostles. ⊠ *On main road.* ☉ *Mornings.*

Chalki itself is a pretty town, known for its neoclassical houses in shades of pink, yellow, and gray, which are oddly juxtaposed with the plain but stately 17th-century Venetian **Frangopoulos tower.** ⊠ *Main road, next to Panayia Protothrone.* ☉ *Sometimes in the morning.*

Moni

⑱ *23 km (14¼ mi) east of Naxos town, 6 km (4 mi) north of Chalki.*

At Moni is one of the Balkans' most important churches, **Panayia Drosiani,** which has faint, rare Byzantine frescoes from the 7th and 8th centuries. Its name means Our Lady of Refreshment, because once during a severe drought, when all the churches took their icons down to the sea to pray for rain, only the icon of this church got results. The frescoes are visible in layers: To the right when you enter are the oldest—one shows St. George the Dragon Slayer astride his horse, along with a small boy, an image one usually sees only in Cyprus and Crete. According to legend, the saint saved the child, who had fallen into a well, and there met and slew the giant dragon that had terrorized the town. Opposite him is St. Dimitrios, shown killing barbarians. The church is made up of three chapels—the middle one has a space for the faithful to worship at the altar rather than in the nave, as became common in later centuries. Next to that is a very small opening that housed a secret school during the revolution. Walk to the back of the church for a view of its odd configuration; the undulating curves are reminiscent of a Gaudi building. It is open mornings and again after siesta; in deserted winter, ring the bell if it is not open.

Filoti

39 *20 km (12½ mi) southeast of Naxos town, 6½ km (4¼ mi) south of Moni.*

Filoti, a peaceful village on the lower slopes of Mt. Zas, is the interior's largest. Nothing much seems to happen here, but if you're lucky, you may see a festive bridal procession. According to custom, the groom, accompanied by musicians, goes to the bride's house to collect her and her family, and then the party strolls through the village picking up well-wishers. A three-day festival celebrating the Dormition starts on August 14. In the center of town is another Venetian tower that belonged to the Barozzi, and the main church with its fine marble iconostasis and carved bell tower.

Hiking

Filoti is better known as the starting place for several walks in the countryside, for example, the climb up to **Zas Cave,** where obsidian tools and pottery fragments have been found; lots of bats live inside. Mt. Zas, or Zeus, is one of the god's birthplaces; on the path to the summit lies a block of unworked marble that reads *Oros Dios Milosiou,* or "boundary of the temple of Zeus Melosios." (Melosios, it is thought, is a word that has to do with sheep.) The islanders say that under the Turks the cave was used as a chapel, and two stalagmites are called the Priest, and the Priest's Wife, who are said to have been petrified by God to save them from arrest. It's best to ask directions for the start of the path (⊠ Southeast of town off a small dirt track).

40 For less-determined walkers and hikers, there is a more level 3½-hour walk with excellent views of the island, which culminates at the **Cheimarros Pirgos** (Tower of the Torrent), a cylindrical Hellenistic tower preserved up to 45 ft, with marble blocks perfectly aligned. The tower, which also served as a lookout post for pirates, is often celebrated in the island's poetry: "O, my heart is like a bower/And Cheimarros's lofty tower!" The bad dirt road (which really requires a four-wheel drive vehicle) begins from the main road to Apeiranthos, just outside Filoti.

Apeiranthos

41 *32 km (20 mi) southeast of Naxos town, 12 km (7½ mi) northeast of Filoti.*

Apeiranthos is very picturesque, with fine views and marble-paved streets running between the Venetian Bardani and Zevgoli towers. As you walk through the arcades and alleys, notice the unusual chimneys—no two are alike. The elders sit in their doorsteps chatting, while packs of children shout "Hello, hello" at any passerby who looks foreign.

A very small **archaeological museum,** established by a local mathematician, Michael Bardanis, displays Cycladic finds from the east coast. The most important of the artifacts are unique gray marble plaques from the 3rd millennium BC with roughly hammered scenes of daily life: hunters and farmers and sailors going about their business. If it's closed, ask in the square for the guard. ⊠ *Off main square.* ⌑ *Free.* ◷ *Daily 8:30–3.*

Koronos

㊷ *36 km (23⅓ mi) east of Naxos town, 4 km (2½ mi) north of Apeiranthos.*

The paved road from Apeiranthos, winding and narrow in places, passes through the lovely village of Koronos, which tumbles spectacularly down the green mountainside. On the right you come to the **Stavros tis Keramotis church,** the only point from which you can see both the east and west coasts of Naxos.

Apollonas

㊸ *54 km (33½ mi) northeast of Naxos town, 12 km (7½ mi) north of Koronos via road from Komaki.*

Apollonas is a small resort town on Naxos's northeast corner. Look for the steps leading to the unfinished 35-ft **kouros** of Apollonas, which lies in an ancient quarry. It's thought to represent Dionysos. Initially, the Greeks represented gods with small idols; later, they were seen as supermen and depicted by these giant, highly stylized statues. This early 6th-century kouros was probably abandoned because cracks developed in the marble while the work was in progress. It lies on its back, eroded by the winds, but still, somewhat eerily, in the shape of a bearded man. ⊠ *On main road past Apollonas, on the left.* ⌑ *Free.*

Beaches

In the far northeast, **Apollonas** is a spread-out beach with small white marble pebbles. Much more rewarding are the **bays** of **Abram, Ayias Mamas, Xilia Brisi,** and **Paxia Ammos,** small sand beaches to the west that are seldom crowded. Most of these can be reached by bus.

Dining and Lodging

$$$ ✕ **Apollon.** In Apollonas the pickings are slim, and this is the best of the tavernas encircling the harbor. Between frying potatoes and garnishing Greek salads, the sweet-faced grandmother-chef can often be found sitting down to chat (or gesture) with customers, or joining a table of local women stringing garlic in the corner. Her food is basic—fresh fish such as red mullet, *paidakia* (bite-size lamb chops) with oregano and dolmades. ⊠ *Apollonas waterfront,* ☎ *0285/81324. No credit cards.*

$–$$ ▥ **Flora's.** The apartments and rooms at Flora's, the best bet in Apollonas, overlook the owner's fields and the tiny bay below. To get to the hotel, you must cross the potato patch, fording irrigation rivulets, which can be a bit annoying. But the spacious apartments all have marble floors, comfortable beds, and pine furniture. Most have a bedroom and a sitting area and are large enough for a family of four, but no maid service is provided. ⊠ *Above waterfront, Apollonas 84300,* ☎ *0285/ 81270. 9 rooms. Kitchenettes, coin laundry. No credit cards.*

Ayia

2½ km (1¼ mi) west of Apollonas.

The partially unpaved coast road from Apollonas to Naxos town passes, in a lush valley, the **Ayia tower,** once a lookout post for northwestern Naxos. At the nearby church, during the feast of the Dormition (August 15), women who had taken a vow to the Virgin used to attend the service after walking barefoot from Apollonas along the rough paths.

Beaches

㊹ The road from Apollonas to Chora runs along steep cliffs, traversing inlets and secluded beaches; the most accessible is **Ormos Abram,** 5 km (3 mi) from Apollonas, which has a pension and taverna and is pleasant when the north winds aren't blowing.

Flerio

㊺ *12 km (7½ mi) east of Naxos town.*

The island's second famous **kouros** is at Flerio, in the Melanes Valley; though smaller (26 ft), it is more detailed and lies in a beautiful private orchard; it has become one of Naxos's more popular sights. The silent kouros, like Ozymandias, is a reminder of a once-glorious age. Archaeologists think the 6th-century statue was abandoned either because the artist made a mistake or because the client who commissioned it died. Also, when the tyrant Lygdamis came to power, he confiscated all the orders of the rich that were still in the quarries. When he couldn't find a way to dispose of some of the kouroi, he tried to sell them back to former owners. ⊠ *On right just before small white shack; through small gate.* ⊡ *Free.* ☉ *May–Oct., daily 8–sunset.*

NEED A BREAK? After seeing the kouros, relax in the **garden** (⊠ On right before small white shack), among bougainvillea and lilac, and order the local family's homemade kitro preserves or a shot of citron liqueur.

PAROS

In the golden age, the great sculptor Praxiteles prized the Parian marble that came from the quarries here; in the 19th century, Paros was beloved by Byron. Today, Paros is favored by people for its lower prices, golden sandy beaches, and charming fishing villages. It may lack the chic of Mykonos and has fewer top-class hotels, but at the height of the season it often gets Mykonos's overflow. The island is large enough to accommodate the traveler in search of peace and quiet, yet the lovely port towns of Parikia, the capital, and Naousa also have an active nightlife. Parikia is a focal point of the ferry network, and many people stay here for a night or two while waiting for a connection. It's particularly good for bars and discos, though Naousa has a more chic island atmosphere.

Paros Town

35 km (21¾ mi) west of Naxos town, 10 km (6 mi) southwest of Naousa.

One of your first impressions of Paros town will be the many travel agencies dispensing information on the waterfront and a multitude of car and motorbike rental agencies nearby. If you walk east on the harbor road you will see a lineup of bars, fast-food restaurants, and coffee shops—some owned by Athenians who come to Paros to capitalize on tourism during the summer. Past them are the bus stop, fishing-boat dock, ancient graveyard, and post office; then the beaches start. The better restaurants and the shopping district are in the town, where it is easy to get lost in the maze of narrow, stone-paved streets that intersect with the streets of the quiet residential areas. Though the tourist culture has not blended in as smoothly as it has on Mykonos, and Paros has looked neglected in the past, much restoration work, especially in the areas around the great church and along the watefront, has recently been undertaken.

The splendid square above the port, to the northwest, was built in 1996 to celebrate the church's 1,700th anniversary. From there you will see a white gate, the front of the former monastic quarters that surround the magnificent **Panayia Ekatontapyliani** (Hundred Doors) church, the earliest remaining Byzantine church in Greece. According to legend, 99 doors have been found in the church and the 100th will be discovered only after Constantinople is Greek again. Inside, the subdued light mixes with the dun, reddish, and green tufa. The columns are classical and their capitals Byzantine. At the corners of the dome are two fading Byzantine frescoes depicting six-winged seraphim. The 6th-century iconostasis (with ornate later additions) is divided into five frames by marble columns. One panel contains the just-restored 14th-century icon of the Virgin, with a silver covering from 1777. The Virgin is carried in procession on the church's crowded feast day, August 15, the Dormition. The adjacent **Baptistery** has a marble font and bits of mosaic floor.

In 326, St. Helen—the mother of Emperor Constantine the Great—took ship for the Holy Land to find the True Cross. Stopping on Paros, she had a vision of success and vowed to build a church there. She founded it but died before it was built. Her son built the church in 328 as a wooden-roof basilica. Two centuries later Justinian the Great, who ruled the Byzantine Empire in 527–565, had it splendidly rebuilt with a dome. He appointed Isidorus, one of the two architects of Constantinople's famed Ayia Sophia, to design it; Isidorus decided to send an apprentice, Ignatius, to Paros. Folk legends says that upon its completion, Isidorus arrived in Paros for an inspection and discovered the dome to be so magnificent that, consumed by jealousy, he pushed the young apprentice off the roof. Ignatius grasped his master's foot as he fell, and the two tumbled to their death together. Two folk sculptures near the toilets at the sanctuary's Baroque left portal portray them as two fat men, one pulling his beard with remorse and the other holding his cracked head. The church **museum**, at right, contains fine post-Byzantine icons. ⊠ *750 ft east of the dock,* ☎ *0284/21243.* ☜ *Free.* ☉ *Daily 8–1 and 4–9.*

The **Archaeological Museum** is another must-see site on Paros. It contains a fragment of the famed Parian chronicle, which recorded cultural events in Greece from about 1500 BC until 260 BC (a larger section is in Oxford's Ashmolean Museum). It interests scholars that the historian inscribed detailed information about artists, poets, and playwrights, completely ignoring wars and shifts in government. Some primitive pieces from the Aegean's oldest settlement, Saliagos (an islet between Paros and Antiparos), are exhibited in the same room, on the left. In the large room to the right rests a marble slab depicting the poet Archilochus in a banquet scene, lying on a couch, his weapons nearby. The ancients ranked Archilochus, who invented iambic meter and wrote the first signed love lyric, second only to Homer. When he died in battle against the Naxians, his conqueror was cursed by the oracle of Apollo for putting to rest one of the faithful servants of the muse. Also there are a monumental Nike and three superb just-found pieces: a waist-down kouros, a gorgon, and a dancing-girl relief. ⊠ *Behind Church of a Hundred Doors,* ☎ *0284/21231.* ☜ *500 dr.* ☉ *Tues.–Sun. 8:30–2:30.*

Beaches

From Parikia, boats leave throughout the day for beaches across the bay: to sandy **Krios** and the quieter **Kaminia. Livadia,** a 10-minute walk, is very developed but has shade.

Dining and Lodging

$$$ ✕ **Loulaki.** This restaurant is a bit hard to find, and therefore rarely crowded—happily so, for the Mediterranean food is good and the atmosphere romantic. Eggplant with three cheeses (a Syros dish) or potatoes in cream and bacon are good starters; follow it with chicken stuffed with white cheese in a delicate sauce of raki, grapes, and sage. For dessert treat yourself to bite-size *galactobureko* (custard pastry). If you go for lunch, take your bathing suit and go for a dip in the cove; if for dinner, take your lover, for the glittering view across Parikia bay. To get there, walk seven minutes from Parikia's Livadia beach along the sea, or drive around the bay and descend at the sign. ⊠ *Across Paros Bay, between Livadia and Krios,* ☎ *0284/22751. AE, MC, V.*

$$$ ✕ **Porphyra.** For the most civilized dining on Paros, Porphyra is unique
★   in the islands because the owner farms his own shellfish in Paros's and Lesbos's pellucid waters (his two tall sons fill in as both divers and waiters); the fresh oysters, shell of Venus, clams, and cockles are Aegean-sweet. His wife, Roula, cooks; her mussels Provençal is a great favorite. Fresh fish, fish salads, and local seasonal vegetables round out the menu. And where else can you taste sea-urchin salad or marinated ray? The inside, popular in winter, is simple and authentic. ⊠ *Paros town (along waterfront toward post office),* ☎ *0284/23410. AE, MC, V.*

$$$–$$$$ ▥ **Xenia Hotel.** If you want a good night's sleep away from the pulse of Paros town but you don't want to give up shopping, nightlife, restaurants, and cafés, the Xenia, built on a hill with a splendid view overlooking Paros Bay, is the best choice. The hotel's lobby looks like an enormous living room, with low, cushioned seats around circular wooden tables; a stone fireplace with antique keys; and a cozy bar. The veranda off the lobby is perfect for sunset-watching. The rooms are sparsely decorated, but most have balconies and all have sea views. ⊠ *On the hill at the southwest edge of Parikia; the seaside road goes to it, 21009,* ☎ *0284/21394; 01/360–5611in Athens,* ▣ *0284/23501. 24 rooms with bath or shower. Bar, breakfast room. AE, MC, V.*

Nightlife and the Arts

MUSIC AND BARS

Turn right along the waterfront from the port in Paros town to find the town's famous bars; then follow your ears. For a mellower alternative, head for **Evinos and Pebbles** (⊠ On the Kastro hill), which plays classical selections and overlooks the sunset. **Pirate** (⊠ Market St.) is partial to jazz and blues.

At the far end of the Paralia is the laser-light-and-disco section of town, which you may want to avoid. In the younger bars, cheap alcohol, as everywhere in tourist Greece, is often added to the more colorful drinks. The Parian young go late to **Myrobolos** (⊠ Seaside, next to ancient cemetery, 2nd floor) for live music, a restaurant, wine bar, and roof garden.

ARTS EVENTS

The **Aegean Center for the Fine Arts** (⊠ At end of Market St., Paros town, ☎ ▣ 0284/23287) periodically stages readings and exhibitions of students' work. It is run by John Pack, an American photographer who lives on the island with his family. Since 1966 the center has offered courses in writing, painting, and photography, among other disciplines; it even takes a study group to Tuscany.

The **Archilochos Cultural Society** (⊠ Near bus stop, behind Splash disco, ☎ 0284/23595) runs a film club in winter, stages art exhibitions during the summer, and offers a program of concerts and lectures throughout the year. Watch for posters.

Outdoor Activities and Sports

GYM

To stay in shape, Fotis Skiadas's well-appointed **Gymnasium** (⊠ Hotel Zanet, near Livadia beach, ☎ 0284/22233), for aerobics and body-building, is air-conditioned and has a sauna.

HORSEBACK RIDING

For riding along the coast, **Time Riding Center** (⊠ Livadi, Paros town, ☎ 0284/23408) has fine animals; the cost is 5,500 dr. for 1½ hours.

MOUNTAIN BIKING

For organized mountain-bike tours (one includes Naxos) and rentals, there's **Hellas Bike Travel** (☎ 0284/52010, ☒ 0284/51720).

WATER SPORTS

Many beaches offer water sports, especially windsurfing. Every summer the **F2 Windsurfing Center** (⊠ New Golden Beach, at Philoxenia Hotel, near Marpissa, ☎ 0284/41878) hosts the **International Windsurfing World Cup.**

Shopping

JEWELRY

Vangelis Skaramangas and Yannis Xenos have been making their own delicate, precious jewelry at **Jewelry Workshop** (⊠ Paros town, at the far end of Market St., ☎ 0284/21008) for 18 years.

TEAS, HERBS, AND SPICES

Teapot (⊠ On an alley off middle of Market St., ☎ 0282/21177) sells locally gleaned spices, teas, and herbs—the perfect lightweight gifts.

En Route   Halfway from Paros town to Naousa, on the right, the 17th-century **Monastery of Longovarda** shines on its mountainside; these days only six monks are in residence there. The monastic community farms the local land and makes honey, wine, and olive oil. Only men, dressed in conservative clothing, are allowed inside, where there are post-Byzantine icons, 17th-century frescoes depicting the Twelve Feasts in the Life of Christ, and a library of rare books; it is usually open mornings. ☎ *0284/21202.*

Naousa

10 km (6 mi) northeast of Paros town.

Naousa, impossibly pretty, long ago discovered the benefits of tourism. Its outskirts are mushrooming with villas and hotels that exploit it further. Along the harbor, red and navy-blue boats knock gently against one another as fishermen repair their nets and foreigners relax in the ouzeries—Barbarossa being the traditional favorite—by the water's edge. Navies of the ancient Persians, flotillas from medieval Venice, and the imperial Russian fleet have anchored in this harbor. The half-submerged ruins of the Venetian fortifications still remain; they are a pretty sight when lit up at night.

Beaches

A boat goes regularly to **Lageri** (⊠ North of Naousa), a long, sandy beach with dunes, and to **Santa Maria** (⊠ Northeastern shore of Paros), the windsurfers' beach. Another boats crosses the bay to **Kolimbithres** (⊠ Directly across the bay from Naousa), noted for its rock formations, water sports, a choice of tavernas, and several luxury hotels, and to **Ayios Ioannis** (⊠ Across from Naousa) for nude sunbathing.

Dining and Lodging

$$$ ✕ **Lalula.** The delicious Mediterranean cooking and fine service here
★ induce repeat visits. In the garden you'll be soothed by the mood music, sparkling gray walls, and flourishing vines. The menu changes regularly, but the chicken liver pâté with pink peppercorns and red onion confiture hors d'oeuvre and the butterfly shrimp fried in sesame sauce or lamb Provençal are unforgettable. For dessert, the charlotte with yogurt-lemon sauce is perfect. The daily fixed-price menu is a good deal. ⊠ *Naousa, opposite Minoa Hotel,* ☎ *0284/51547. Reservations essential in Aug. AE, V.*

$$$ ✕ **Taverna Christos.** Christos has been improving his place for 20
★ years—no wonder it's so good! In a spacious garden in the heart of Naousa, the place is bright and fresh, with gracious service and good Mediterranean cuisine. Excellent first courses include little shrimp pies in sour pineapple sauce and fresh vegetables in honey-lemon dressing. Among entrées, try pork fillet with dates and chicken breasts in dark rum, with ginger and corn. For dessert, the warm chocolate mousse cake is sinful. ⊠ *Naousa, up hill from central square,* ☎ *0284/51442. AE, V. Closed Oct.–May.*

$$$$ 🏠 **Astir of Paros.** Across the bay from Naousa twinkle the lights of this deluxe resort hotel, an elegant and expensive retreat, with green lawns, tall palm trees, lush gardens, and an art gallery. Rooms are pretty and spacious—perfect for romantic couples of taste—with antiques, artwork, and views of the sparkling Naousa Bay. Its Greek restaurant is excellent. ⊠ *Take Kolymbithres Rd. from Naousa, 84400,* ☎ *0284/51976 or 0284/51984,* ℻ *0284/51985. 50 rooms, 7 suites with bath. Restaurant, bar, refrigerators, pool, sauna, miniature golf, tennis court, exercise room, windsurfing, waterskiing, baby-sitting, laundry service. AE, DC, MC, V.*

$$$ 🏠 **Sovronos Bungalows.** These bungalow apartments always seem to be fully occupied. The friendly Sovronos family tends the lush garden, and the comfortable apartments and Cycladic whitewashed courtyards are decorated with antiques and objects from the host's extensive travels. This is convenient and quiet, with easy access to Naousa's lively shopping and nightlife. Breakfast is included. ⊠ *Behind big church, 1 block in from Santa Maria Rd., Naousa 84400,* ☎ *0284/51211 or 0284/51409,* ℻ *0284/52281. 19 apartments. Bar. No credit cards.*

Nightlife and the Arts

BARS
Leonardo's (⊠ Fishing harbor) is lively and is open into the wee hours. **Agosta** (⊠ Fishing harbor) is a pretty spot.

DANCE
The group **N.E.L.E.** (☎ 0284/51082 or 0284/51480), formed in 1988 to preserve the traditional dances and music of Paros, performs all summer long in Naousa in the costumes of the 16th century and has participated in dance competitions and festivals throughout Europe. Keep an eye out for posters.

Outdoor Activities and Sports

WATER SPORTS
Santa Maria Surf Club (⊠ Santa Maria beach, about 4 km/2½ mi north of Naousa) is popular, with windsurfing, jet-skiing, waterskiing, and diving. If you're traveling with children, **Aqua Paros Waterpark** (⊠ Koymbithres, next to Porto Paros Hotel, ☎ 0284/53271, ℻ 0284/

53264), with its 13 waterslides big and small, will cool a hot afternoon. Admission is 3,000 dr.

Shopping

LOCAL JEWELRY AND ART

Metaxas gallery (⊠ On second street from harbor toward main church, Naousa, ☎ 0284/52667) shows painting, photography, sculpture, and especially jewelry, all done by Paros residents. One of the jewelers, Gregory Altamirano, creates his elegant designs in his workshop (⊠ Near Monastery of Saint Andreas), with a splendid view overlooking Naousa Bay.

Marathi

10 km (6 mi) east of Paros town.

During the classical period the island of Paros had an estimated 150,000 residents, many of them slaves who worked the ancient marble quarries in Marathi. The island grew rich from the export of this white, granular marble known among ancient architects and sculptors for its ability to absorb light. They called it *lychnites* ("won by lamplight").

Marked by a sign, **three caverns** (⊠ A short walk from the main road) are bored into the hillside, the largest of them 300 ft deep. The most recent quarrying done in these mines was in 1844, when a French company cut marble here for Napoléon's tomb.

Shopping

LOCAL CRAFTS

At **Studio Yria** (⊠ 3 km/2 mi east of Marathi, above the road to Kostos village, ☎ 0284/29007, ℻ 0284/29024) master potters and other craftsmen can be seen at work. Marble carvers, metalsmiths, painters, and more all make for a true Renaissance workshop. Both the ceramic tableware and the works of art make use of Byzantine and Cycladic motifs in their designs, and some pieces incorporate Parian marble. Easily accessible by bus, taxi, and rental car, the studio is open 8–8.

Lefkes

10 km (6 mi) southeast of Paros town, 6 km (4 mi) south of Marathi.

Rampant piracy in the 17th century forced thousands of people to move inland from the coastal regions; thus for many years the scenic village of Lefkes, built on a hillside in the protective mountains, was the island's capital. It remains the largest village in the interior and has maintained a peaceful, island feeling, with narrow streets fragrant of jasmine and honeysuckle. Farming is the major source of income, as you can tell from the well-kept stone walls and olive groves.

Two **17th-century churches** of interest are **Ayia Varvara** (St. Barbara) and **Ayios Sotiris** (Holy Savior). The big 1830 neo-Renaissance **Ayia Triada** (Holy Trinity) is the pride of the village.

Beaches

Piso Livadi (⊠ On road past Lefkes) was the ancient port for the marble quarries and today is a small resort town convenient to many beaches.

Lodging

$$$ ⚑ **Lefkes Village.** All island-style rooms in this elegant new hotel have
★ magnificent views down the olive-tree valley and over the sea to Naxos. The lobby is tasteful and comfortably simple. The restaurant is noted for its traditional Greek food; the folk museum here is chockablock with interesting objects. ⊠ *Just east of Lefkes on the main road,*

84400, ☎ 🄵🄰🄷 *0284/41827 or 0284/42398. 20 rooms. Restaurant, bar, refrigerators, pool. AE, DC, MC, V.*

Shopping

On the way to the little main square, near the café with olive-wood tables, are several **weaving shops.**

In the little weaving shop named for her, **Anna Kritikou** (✉ In Lefkes, on the main street) has her loom set up and makes everything she sells by hand: elegant bedspreads, rag rugs, and donkey saddlebags, the first two most practical for gift ideas.

Petaloudes Park

4 km (2½ mi) south of Paros town.

A species of moth returns year after year to mate in Petaloudes (the Valley of the Butterflies), a lush oasis of greenery in the middle of this dry island. In May, June, and perhaps July, you can watch them as they lie dormant during the day, their chocolate-brown wings with yellow stripes still against the ivy leaves. In the evening they flutter upward to the cooler air, flashing the coral-red undersides of their wings as they rise. A notice at the entrance asks visitors not to disturb them by taking photographs or shaking the leaves. ✉ *Petaloudes.* 🄯 *300 dr.* ☉ *Mid-May–mid-Sept., daily 9–8. Closed Oct.–mid-May*

NEED A BREAK? | Even when the butterflies are not there, it is pleasant to have coffee in the small **kafenion** (✉ Inside entrance to park) and enjoy the shade of the cypress, olive, chestnut, mulberry, and lemon trees.

On the summit of a hill just beyond the garden reigns a lopped **Venetian tower.** Its founder's name, Iakovos Alisafis, and the date, 1626, are inscribed on it.

En Route A 15-minute walk back toward Paros town from the Valley of the Butterflies leads to the convent known as **Christos sto Dasos** (Christ of the Wood), from where there's a marvelous view of the Aegean. The convent contains the tomb of Ayios Arsenios (1800–77), who was a schoolteacher, an abbot, and a prophet. He was also a rainmaker whose prayers were believed to have ended a long drought, saving Paros from starvation. The nuns are a bit leery of tourists. If you want to go in, be sure to wear long pants or skirt and a shirt that covers your shoulders, or the sisters will either offer you makeshift black-and-white striped skirts that look like prison uniforms or turn you away.

Outdoor Activities and Sports

You can rent courts at the **Holiday Sun Hotel** (✉ Pounda, ☎ 0284/91284 or 0284/91285, 🄵🄰🄷 0284/91288), which also has an exercise room and sauna.

SANTORINI

Undoubtedly the most extraordinary island in the Aegean, crescent-shape Santorini will always be a must for most Cycladic visitors—even if they have to enjoy the sensational sunsets from Oia, the fascinating excavations, and the dazzling white towns with a million other travelers. Arriving by boat, you are met by one of the world's truly breathtaking sights, the **caldera:** a crescent of cliffs, striated in black, pink, brown, white, and pale green, rising 1,100 ft, with the white clusters of the towns of Fira and Ia perched along the top. The encircling cliffs

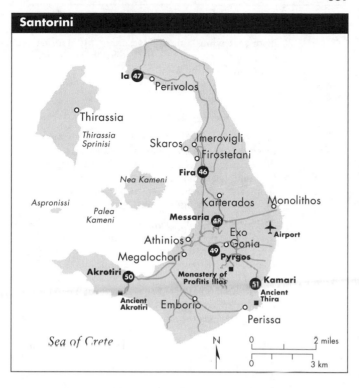

Santorini

Ia **47** ○
○ Perivolos

○ Thirassia

Thirassia
Sprinisi

Skaros ○ Imerovigli
○ Firostefani

Fira **46**

Nea Kameni

Aspronissi

Palea
Kameni

Karterados ○ ○ Monolithos

Messaria **48**

Athinios ○ Exo
○ Gonia ✈ Airport

Megalochori ○ **49** Pyrgos

Akrotiri **50**

Monastery of
Profitis Ilios ■ **51** **Kamari**

■ **Ancient**
Akrotiri Emborio

Ancient
Thira

Perissa

Sea of Crete

N

0 — 2 miles
0 — 3 km

are the ancient rim of a still-active volcano, and you are sailing east across its flooded caldera.

Santorini and its four neighboring islets are the fragmentary remains of a larger landmass that exploded about 1625 BC: The volcano's core blew sky high and the sea rushed into the abyss to create the great bay, which measures 10 km by 7 km (6 mi by 4 mi) and is 1,292 ft deep. The other pieces of the rim, which broke off in later eruptions, are Thirassia, home to a few hundred people, and deserted little Aspronissi ("White Isle"). In the center of the bay, black and uninhabited, are two still-smoldering cones, the "Burnt Isles" of Palea Kameni and Nea Kameni, which appeared between 1573 and 1925. The ancients called Santorini's island group Strongyle ("Round") and Kalliste ("Loveliest"); the island was named Thera, and it still officially is. Its medieval name of Santorini (a corruption of Sant' Irene) is more common.

There has been too much speculation about the identification of Santorini with the mythical Atlantis, mentioned in Egyptian papyri and by Plato (who says it's in the Atlantic), but myths are hard to pin down. This is not true of arguments about whether or not tidal waves from Santorini's cataclysmic explosion destroyed the Minoan civilization on Crete. The latest carbon-dating evidence clearly indicates that the Minoans outlasted the eruption by a couple of hundred years.

Since antiquity, Santorini has depended on rain collected in cisterns for drinking and irrigating—the well water is often brackish—and the serious shortage is alleviated by the importation of water. The fertile volcanic soil produces small, intense tomatoes with tough skins used for tomato paste; the famous Santorini fava beans, which have a light, fresh taste; barley; wheat; pistachio nuts; and white-skinned eggplants. The locals say that in Santorini there is more wine than water, and it may be true; wine is the island's largest export. The volcanic soil, high daytime temperatures, and humidity at night produce 36 varieties of grape, and these unique growing conditions are ideal for the production of a distinctive white wine that is gaining international recognition. Farmers twist the vines into a basketlike shape, in which the grapes grow, protected from the wind.

Fira

46 *10 km (6 mi) west of the airport, 14 km (8½ mi) southeast of Ia.*

Tourism, the island's major industry, adds more than 1 million visitors per year to its population of 7,000. As a result, Fira, the capital, midway along the west coast of the east rim, is no longer just a picturesque village but a major tourist center, overflowing with discos, shops, and restaurants. Many of its employees, young travelers extending their summer vacations, hardly speak Greek.

The modern Greek Orthodox cathedral of **Panayia Ypapantis** (⊠ Southern part of town) is a major landmark; the local priests, with somber faces, long beards, and black robes, look strangely out of place in summertime Fira. Along **Eikostis Pemptis Martiou** (25th of March St.) (⊠ East of Panayia Ypapantis) is where you'll find inexpensive restaurants and accommodations. The blocked-off Ypapantis Street (⊠ West of Panayia Ypapantis) leads to **Kato Fira** (Lower Fira), built into the cliff side overlooking the caldera, where prices are higher and the vista wonderful. For centuries the people of the island have been digging themselves rooms-with-a-view right in the cliff face—many bars and hotel rooms have actually been made out of caves—for posh atmosphere and constant temperature.

The **Ghyzis Palace,** Fira's cultural museum, is housed in a restored 17th-century mansion once owned by the Catholic church. The collection includes old maps, engravings, photographs, and paintings by 20th-century Greek artists. ⊠ *Stavrou and Ioannis Sts.,* ☎ *0286/22244 or 0286/22721.* 🎟 *500 dr.* ☉ *Daily 10:30–1:30 and 5–8.*

The **Archaeological Museum** displays pottery, statues, and grave artifacts found at excavations mostly from Ancient Thera and Akrotiri, from the Minoan through the Byzantine period. ⊠ *Stavrou and Nomikos Sts.,* ☎ *0286/22217.* 🎟 *800 dr.* ☉ *Tues.–Sun. 8:30–3.*

OFF THE BEATEN PATH　　**NEA KAMENI –** To peer into a live, smoldering volcano, join one of the popular excursions to Nea Kameni, the larger of the two Burnt Isles. After disembarking, you hike 430 ft to the top and walk around the edge of the crater, wondering if the volcano is ready for its fifth eruption this century—after all, it has been quite some time since the last, in 1956. Tours (about 4,500 drs.) are scheduled regularly (☞ Contacts and Resources *in* The Cyclades A to Z, *below*).

Dining and Lodging

$$$　✕ **Kastro.** The expansive outdoor dining area is usually packed and festive throughout the evening. European dishes reign: Danish or Russian caviar and prosciutto with melon can even be paired with Dom Perignon. You can have your filet mignon prepared in seven ways, and five scrumptious soufflés have been dreamed up. Grilled shrimp, lobster, and swordfish are sold by the kilo. Because of the caldera view, it is a good lunch and sunset café too. The upstairs cafeteria serves American breakfasts and fast food. ⊠ *Ayios Ioannis Walkway,* ☎ FAX *0286/22503. AE, DC, MC, V.*

$$$　✕ **Kukumavlos.** This fine restaurant has found a new location (it was for years in Ia), with an elegant vaulted room and 12-table patio over-

looking the caldera. The cuisine is "creative Mediterranean," prepared by Nikos Pouliasis, the owner. Nikos recommends starters such as calamari stuffed with chicken marinated in a basil sauce with saffron shrimp or fava with roasted almonds; for main dishes, veal fillet with fresh goat cheese, sun-dried tomatoes, and porcini-mushroom sauce, or shrimp sautéed in vin santo with sesame seeds. His pannacotta made with yogurt and drizzled with honey and sour-cherry syrup is unique and perfect. The menu is ever-changing, so expect other unheralded delights. ⊠ *Right below the Atlantis Hotel,* ☎ *02286/23807. AE, V.*

$$$ ✕ **Selene.** Since 1986, this has probably been Santorini's best place for quiet, elegant dining. The spacious terrace edged with flowers has a splendid caldera view and the food is splendid, too. The indoors is an old cliff house with traditional vaulted ceiling and dark wood furniture; the banquettes are the built-in benches intrinsic to traditional island houses. The menu is full of interesting dishes, such as mushrooms stuffed with crabmeat and cheese; a "brodero" with fish, squid, octopus, prawns, and fish in a clay pot; and squab stuffed with bulgur and apricots. For dessert, the custard with fig preserves and almonds is both rich and light. ⊠ *Cliff-side walkway 310 ft to the left of the Hotel Atlantis,* ☎ *0286/22449,* ☒ *0286/24395. AE, DC, MC, V.*

$$ ✕ **Nicholas.** This is Santorini's oldest taverna, where you'll find locals in winter. Island dishes are prepared well and served in a simple, attractive room. Try the yellow lentils and, for a delicious entrée, the lamb fricassee with an egg-lemon sauce. ⊠ *2 streets in from cliff side on Erythrou Stavrou, Fira,* ☎ *no phone. No credit cards.*

$$$$ ⊞ **Aigialos Houses/Villas.** This hotel is new (1995) but its renovated ★ buildings are old and comprise the most comfortable and discreetly luxurious—as well as the most poetic—place to stay in Fira. The one-, two-, and three-bedroom houses, with marble floors and beautiful furniture, also have terraces or balconies overlooking the caldera—no need to venture out at sunset. There's satellite TV, maid service twice daily, impeccable 24-hour service, and fresh flowers. ⊠ *South end of Ypapantis Walkway (left from Hotel Atlantis), Fira 84700,* ☎ *0286/25191–5,* ☒ *0286/22856. 16 villas. Bar, refrigerators, pool, spa. AE, DC, MC, V.*

$$$$ ⊞ **Hotel Aressana.** The only drawback to the Aressana is that the big Atlantis Hotel blocks its view of the caldera (though not of the sea). Its advantages are its large freshwater pool (with classical music piped in, no less), its spacious paneled lobby, and its location in central Fira. If you want a spanking-new room—some with patios by the pool— with white tile floors, a balcony, and a spotless bathroom, this is a good bet. ⊠ *South end of Ypapantis Walkway, Fira 84700,* ☎ *0286/23900 or 0286/23901,* ☒ *0286/23902. 50 rooms with bath. Bar, pool. AE, DC, MC, V.*

$$$ ⊞ **Panorama Hotel.** From the cliff side of Fira, this lofty white hotel provides a breathtaking view of the caldera from every room, each with a balcony. There's a great roof garden. A travel desk in the reception area can book tours and rent cars. ⊠ *Ypapantis Walkway, Fira 84700,* ☎ *0286/22481,* ☒ *0286/23179. 23 rooms. Café, travel services. AE, DC, MC, V.*

$$ ⊞ **Delphini II.** Owner-manager Vassilis Rousseas says he has "prices for everyone." Delphini II has spacious apartments, all different in architecture and decor, which once were village homes. (Ask to see the one with the old stove.) ⊠ *Down hill in front of Atlantis Hotel, Fira 84700,* ☎ *0286/24370,* ☎☒ *0286/22780. 3 studios and 4 apartments. Kitchenettes or refrigerators. No credit cards.*

$–$$ ⊞ **Delphini I.** Vassilis's (☞ *above*) other property, Delphini I, is less expensive and has no views. ⊠ *Near hospital, Fira 84700,* ☎ *0286/22371. 10 rooms. Refrigerators. No credit cards.*

Nightlife and the Arts

DANCING

Bar 33 (⊠ Fira, ☎ 0286/23065) has bouzouki music and a celebratory atmosphere. The **Koo Club** (⊠ Fira, ☎ 0286/22025) is Fira's most popular outdoor disco by far. **Ellenes** (⊠ Opposite Fira's Olympic Office) is for Greek dancing.

FESTIVAL

The **International Santorini Music Festival** (⊠ Estis Hall, ☎ 0286/22220) takes place in late August–early September. The performance schedule, including internationally known musicians, is announced during the summer and posted about town.

MUSIC

As the sun sets on the caldera, **Palia Kameni** (⊠ Fira, ☎ 0286/22430) is the place to go for well-selected jazz, classical, and passionate Greek music. Try a strawberry margarita or one of the other reasonably priced drinks. **Franco's Bar** (⊠ Fira), much written up, plays calm, classical music; it's flights down from the Ypapantis Walkway.

Outdoor Activities and Sports

SAILING

The **Santorini Sailing Center** (⊠ Merovigli, ☎ 0286/23058 or 0286/23059) arranges charters and runs weekly two- to three-day sailing trips around the Cyclades for groups up to 10.

TENNIS

The **Santorini Tennis Club** (⊠ Santorini Tennis Club Hotel, Kartaradoes, ☎ 0286/22122) has two concrete courts where two can play in high season for 2,000 drs. per hour; it's open April–October.

Shopping

JEWELRY

Kostas Antoniou Jewelry (⊠ Ayios Ioannou, ☎ 0286/22633). *Vogue* and *Marie Claire* have taken photographs of some of the Kostas's original pieces, many inspired by Ancient Thera. Imagine the magnificence of solid gold necklaces named Earth's Engravings, Ritual, and Motionless Yielding! Kostas also carries a selection of Van Cleef & Arpels watches from Paris. Fortunately, he takes plastic. *Opposite cable car,* ☎ ℻ *0286/22633. AE, MC, V.*

Ia

★ ㊼ *80 km (50 mi) southeast of Paros town (with a ferry connection on Ios), 14 km (8½ mi) northwest of Fira.*

At the tip of the northern horn of the island sits Ia (or Oia), Santorini's second-largest town and the Aegean's most-photographed village. More tasteful than Fira, Ia's cubical white houses stand out against the green, brown, and rust-color layers of rock, earth, and solid volcanic ash that rise from the sea. Every summer evening, travelers from all over the world congregate at the caldera's rim—sitting on whitewashed fences, staircases, beneath the town's windmill, on the old castle—each looking out to sea in anticipation of the performance: the Ia sunset. The two-hour rim-edge walk from Ia to Fira at this hour is unforgettable.

In the middle of the quiet caldera, the volcano smolders away eerily, adding an air of suspense to an already awe-inspiring scene. Its most recent eruption, in 1956, caused tremendous earthquakes (7.8 on the Richter scale) that left 48 people dead (thankfully, most residents were working outdoors at the time), hundreds injured, and toppled 2,000 houses. The island's west side—especially Ia, until then the largest town—was hard hit, and many residents decided to emigrate to Athens, Australia, and America. And although Fira, also damaged, rebuilt rapidly, Ia proceeded slowly, sticking to the traditional architectural style. The perfect example of that style is the restaurant 1800, a renovated ship captain's villa.

The **Naval Museum of Thera** is in an old mansion. It displays ships' figureheads, seamen's chests, maritime equipment, models, and more. ⊠ *Near telephone office,* ☎ *0286/71156.* 🎫 *500 dr.* ☉ *Tues.–Sun. 8:30–3.*

Beaches

There are no beautiful beaches close to Ia, but if you hike down Ia's cliff side, you can catch a bus to the small sand beach of **Baxedes** (⊠ Port of Armoudhi).

Dining and Lodging

$$$ ★ ✕ **1800.** The goal here is to revive the special homelike atmosphere of a captain's house. Indeed this historic Venetian-style building, with tall windows and a cathedral ceiling, was owned by a sea captain. It was abandoned after the 1956 earthquake until its purchase (with antique furniture intact) and restoration a few years ago. Try the zucchini pie with onions, eggs, and cheese, or the veal cooked in tomato sauce and served with smashed eggplant. ⊠ *Main St., central Ia,* ☎ *0286/ 71485. AE, DC, MC, V.*

$$$ ★ ✕ **Kuku.** Eleni Paliasi's tiny restaurant, whose eight outdoor tables (there is a tiny vaulted interior too) are filled every night, serves the best food in Ia. Start with large grilled mushrooms with local sun-dried tomatoes or cabbage leaves stuffed with lamb, wild rice, pine nuts, and raisins in a sour sauce of yogurt, Gorgonzola, and mint. Then have filleted monkfish in pastry with tomatoes, feta, thyme, and eggplant, or stuffed pork fillet with prunes, figs, and yogurt sauce. If you can still eat, the walnut cake with bitter chocolate and creamy ice cream will satisfy. Reservations are advised. ⊠ *Down from Main St., central Ia,* ☎ *0286/ 71413. AE, V. No lunch.*

$$$–$$$$ ★ 🏨 **Atlantis Villas.** Most of these "villas" are actually built into caves in Ia's cliff face, making this one of the most unusual and dramatic places to stay in Greece. The caves, linked into a small complex by steep walkways, are quiet, always cool, and furnished with traditional woven rugs and curtains. They all have private balconies or patios fitted with umbrellas, and a glorious view, 600 ft up, across the caldera. As you watch the sunset, you'll make your next year's reservation. ⊠ *Ia cliff face, just before main town, 84702,* ☎ *0286/71214 or 0286/71236,* 📠 *0286/71312. 17 apartments. Kitchenettes, refrigerators, saltwater pool, laundry service. AE, MC, V.*

$$$–$$$$ 🏨 **Lampetia Villas.** This EOT Traditional Settlement, 800 ft up the cliff from the sea, offers charm and comfort and friendliness. The owner, Tom Alafragis, has a charm all his own. Each of the eight accommodations—all have private balconies with a view—is different in size and furnishings. ⊠ *Nomikou St., Ia cliff face, down from main street, 84702,* ☎ 📠 *0286/71237. 8 houses. Kitchenettes, refrigerators, pool. No credit cards.*

$$$–$$$$ ★ 🏨 **La Perla.** These quintessential cliff-face villas are the domain of Kiki Moutsatsos, whose considerable claim to fame is that she was the private secretary to Aristotle and Jacqueline Onassis for many years and is reputedly the most charming person on the face of the earth (at least that's what *Condé Nast Traveler* reported). These villas, and not just Kiki, will bring a smile to your face, for they are authentic cave houses, with white rooms adorned with traditional island handicrafts, modern bathrooms, antique brass beds, private terraces, and fully stocked kitchenettes (you'll appreciate the fact you can keep fresh food at hand, since much of a Santorini day is spent relaxing on a terrace). Kiki may, in fact, arrive with your breakfast in the morning (or it may be her son Yianni or a staff member), but you won't need to bother her for stories about Ari and Jackie—she set them all down in a tome published by Putnam in 1998. Note that U.S. bookings (payment by personal check/money order only) are made through Ivy International Ventures. ⌷ *Ia cliff face, just before main town, 84702,* ☏ *For U.S. bookings: 415/885–6846,* ℻ *415/346–5084. Seven apartments. Kitchenettes, refrigerators, laundry service. AE, MC, V.*

$$$–$$$$ ⊡ **Oia's Sunset.** This modern hotel looks like a castle made from miniature Cycladic chapels. The rooms, decorated in traditional style, all have balconies. ⌷ *Near main square, Ia 84700,* ☏ *0268/71420 or 0268/71490,* ℻ *0286/71421. 8 rooms, 7 apartments. Pool. AE, DC, MC, V.*

Nightlife

BARS

In Ia, sophistication and architectural splendor are the selling points of the **1800** bar and restaurant (☞ *above*). Those in search of a happy-hour beer go to **Zorba's** (⌷ On the cliff side).

Shopping

Ia is the right place for finding locally crafted items. The inhabitants are sophisticated, and here you will find art galleries, "objets" shops, crafts shops, and icon stores.

ART

Art Gallery (⌷ Main shopping street, ☏ 0286/71448) sells large, three-dimensional representations of Santorini architecture by Bella Kokeenatou and Stavros Galanopoulos. Their lifelike depth invites the viewer to walk through a door or up a flight of stairs. **Art Gallery Oia** (⌷ Main shopping street, ☏ 0286/71463) is the place to find a watercolor to take home; painter Manolis Sivridakis captures the special light of Santorini with remarkable accuracy.

"OBJETS"

Meteor (⌷ Ia's main shopping street, ☏ ℻ 0286/71051) has a rich collection of objects and antiques culled from just about everywhere, from Greek houses to junk shops abroad. Kilims, ceramics, jewelry, and dresses all bespeak the owners' taste. Chara Kourti's **Loulaki** (Ia's main shopping street, ☏ 0286/71856) is similar except that her taste is distinctive and the antiques, odd pieces, jewelry, and art she features make exploring her shop a pleasure.

Messaria

★ ㊽ *3 km (2 mi) south of Fira, 9 km (5½ mi) south of Ia.*

Messaria's **Archontiko Argyrou Museum,** a splendid neoclassical house with painted walls and traditional furniture of the 19th century, is well worth a stop on the way to the Monastery of Profitis Ilias. ⌷ *Messaria,* ☏ *0286/31669,* ℻ *0286/33064.* ⛁ *1,000 dr.* ☉ *Hourly guided tours 11–7.*

Nightlife

MUSIC AND DANCING

You can see the best traditional Greek music and dancing at **Canava Roussos Winery** (⌷ Mesagonia, ☏ 0286/31276 reservations), the oldest on the island, founded in 1838, where professional and local dancers in costume perform nightly 8–midnight.

Pyrgos

★ **49** *5½ km (3¼ mi) south of Fira, 2½ km (1¼ mi) south of Messaria.*

Stop in Pyrgos to see its medieval houses, stacked on top of one another and back to back for protection against pirates. And you can also see the crumbling walls of the old Venetian castle here.

The **Monastery of Profitis Ilias** is at the highest point on Santorini, which spans to 1,856 ft at the summit. From here you can see the surrounding islands and, on a clear day, the mountains of Crete, more than 100 km (66 mi) away. You may also be able to spot Ancient Thira on the peak below Profitis Ilias (☞ Kamari, *below*). Unfortunately, radio towers and a NATO radar installation provide an ugly backdrop for the monastery's wonderful bell tower.

Founded in 1711 by two monks from Pyrgos, Profitis Ilias is cherished by islanders because here, in a secret school, the Greek language and culture were taught during the dark centuries of the Turkish occupation. A museum in the monastery contains a model of the secret school in a monk's cell, another model of a traditional carpentry and blacksmith shop, and a display of ecclesiastical items. The monastery's future is in doubt because there are so few monks left. ✉ *Pyrgos, at highest point on Santorini.* ⊙ *No visiting hrs; try to find a caretaker early in morning.*

NEED A
BREAK?
Heading south to Akrotiri, stop at **Antoniou Winery** (✉ Megalochori, ☎ FAX 0286/23557), and take a tour of the multileveled old facility—it's so beautiful local couples get married here. An oenologist leads a wine-tasting with snacks, and a slide show describes local wine production; it costs 1,000 dr.

Akrotiri

★ **50** *13 km (8 mi) south of Fira, 7 km (4½ mi) west of Pyrgos.*

★ If you visit only one archaeological site during your stay on Santorini, make sure it is **ancient Akrotiri,** near the tip of the southern horn of the island.

In the 1860s, in the course of quarrying tephra (volcanic ash) for use in the Suez Canal, workmen discovered the remains of an ancient town. The town was frozen in time by ash from an eruption 3,600 years ago, long before Pompeii's disaster. In 1967 Spyridon Marinatos of the University of Athens began excavations, which occasionally continue. It is thought that the 40 buildings that have been uncovered are only one-thirtieth of the huge site and that excavating the rest will probably take a century. You enter from the south, pass the ticket booth, and walk 100 yards or so up a stone-paved street to a vast metal shed that protects 2 acres of the site from wind and sun. A path punctuated by explanatory signs in English leads through the ancient town.

Marinatos's team discovered great numbers of extremely fine and well-preserved frescoes depicting many aspects of Akrotiri life, now displayed in the Archaeological Museum in Athens; Santorini wants them back. Meanwhile, postcard-size pictures of them are posted outside the houses where they were found. The antelopes, monkeys, and wildcats they portray suggest trade with Egypt. One notable example, apparently representing a festival, shows two ports: The left village has ordinary people in skins and tunics, and a symbolic lion runs overhead; and the other, probably Akrotiri, more aristocratic, has in its center a fleet of sailing ships at sea, with playful dolphins swimming alongside.

Culturally an outpost of Minoan Crete, Akrotiri was settled as early as 3000 BC and reached its colonized peak about 2000 BC, when it developed trade and agriculture and settled the present town. The inhabitants cultivated olive trees and grain, and their advanced architecture—three-story frescoed houses faced with fine masonry (some with balconies) and public buildings of sophisticated construction—is evidence of an elaborate lifestyle. Unlike at Pompeii, no human remains, gold, silver, or weapons were found here—probably tremors preceding the eruption warned the inhabitants to pack their valuables and flee. After the eruptions Santorini was uninhabited for about two centuries while the land cooled and plant and animal life regenerated. The site is accessible by public bus or guided tour. ⊠ *South of modern Akrotiri, near tip of southern horn,* ☎ *0286/81366.* 🖭 *1,200 dr.* ⊙ *Tues.–Sun. 8:30–3.*

Beaches
Red Beach (⊠ On southwest shore just below Akrotiri; sign on road) is quiet with a taverna.

Kamari

★ ⑤ *6 km (4 mi) south of Fira, 6½ km (4¼ mi) east of Akrotiri.*

Archaeology buffs will want to visit the site of **Ancient Thira.** There are relics of a Dorian city, with 9th-century BC tombs, an engraved phallus, Hellenistic houses, and traces of Byzantine fortifications and churches. At the sanctuary of Apollo, graffiti dating to the 8th century BC record the names of some of the boys who danced naked at the god's festival (Satie's famed musical compositions, the Gymnopedies, reimagine these). To get there, hike up from Perissa or Kamari or take a taxi up **Mesa Vouna.** On the summit are the scattered ruins, excavated by a German archaeology school around the turn of the century; there's a fine view. ⊠ *On a switchback up the mountain right before Kamai, 2,110 ft high,* ☎ *0286/31366.* 🖭 *1,200 dr.* ⊙ *Tues.–Sun. 8:30–3.*

Beaches
If you're a beach bum, it's better to stay at the long **black beaches** in **Kamari** or **Perissa** (Perissa's is volcanic sand, not rock). The black beaches are a natural treasure of Santorini and are consequently overdeveloped. Deck chairs and umbrellas can be rented at both beaches, and tavernas and refreshment stands abound.

Dining and Lodging
$$$–$$$$ ✕ **Camille Stéfani.** This fine restaurant, founded in 1977, in a garden
★ on the black beach of Kamari, serves superb international cuisine with the local stamp of approval (especially in winter). For an appetizer, you can't do better than the *poikilia* ("variety" of calamari, octopus, fried tomato balls, deep-fried eggplant, and zucchini). For an entrée, owner Ares especially recommends beef fillet with green peppercorns and Madeira. A variety of fresh fish is also usually available. For dessert, chocolate crepes with whipped cream are sure to satisfy. ⊠ *At end of coast road,* ☎ 𝖥𝖠𝖷 *0286/31716. AE, DC, MC, V.*

$–$$ 🏨 **Hotel Astro.** This hotel is a short walk to the black sandy beach and minutes away from the local nightlife. Rooms have phones, and those on the lower level have verandas; those on the second floor have balconies facing the mountains or the Aegean. After spending the day at the sea, it's great to take a dip in the freshwater pool in the evening. And it's not far from Camille Stéfani restaurant (☞ *above*), Kamari's best. ⊠ *Central Kamari 84700,* ☎ *0286/31366,* 𝖥𝖠𝖷 *0286/31732. 42 rooms. Breakfast room, coffee shop, air-conditioning, pool. MC, V.*

Nightlife

DISCO

In Kamari the younger set heads for the **Yellow Donkey** disco (⌧ Promenade, ☎ 0286/31462) and the other bars along the beach promenade.

THE CYCLADES A TO Z

Arriving and Departing

By Boat

Most visitors use the island's extensive ferry network, which has been much improved in recent years. Watching the islands, the sparkling Aegean, and occasional dolphins from the deck will let you know where you are. Ferries sail from Piraeus (Port Authority, ☎ 01/451–1311 or 01/415–1321) and from Rafina, 35 km (22 mi) northeast of Athens (Port Authority, ☎ 0294/22300). Leaving from Rafina cuts traveling time by an hour; buses leave for the one-hour trip from Rafina to Athens every 20 minutes 6 AM–10 PM. Traveling time from Piraeus to Mykonos is 6 hours; to Santorini, 8–11 hours. The new high-speed ferries are twice as expensive and twice as fast. Interisland catamarans and hydrofoils are fast, closed in, and dependent on weather.

Third-class boat tickets cost roughly one-quarter the airfare, and passengers are restricted to seats in the deck areas and often-crowded indoor seating areas. A first-class ticket, which sometimes buys a private cabin and better lounge, costs about half an airplane ticket. For information on interisland connections, contact the port authorities on the various islands (☞ *below*). High season is June through September; boats are less frequent in the off-season. Very advance schedules must be checked, as they change with the season, for major holidays and for weather.

ANDROS

For Andros, you must take a ferry from Rafina (not Piraeus); they leave at least three times a day in summer, and the trip takes about two hours. From Andros (⌧ Port Authority, ☎ 0282/22250) boats leave twice daily for Tinos and Mykonos. Boats leave three times weekly for Paros, Naxos, Ios, and Crete; they also leave once a week for Skiathos and Salonica. An excursion boat goes daily to Mykonos and Delos, returning in the late afternoon. Big boats dock at Gavrio and hydrofoils at Batsi.

TINOS

Tinos is served in summer by two boats a day from Piraeus and one from Rafina. There are daily connections with Andros and Mykonos; several boats a week for Paros, Naxos, and Santorini; and a weekly boat to Skiathos and Salonica. An excursion boat goes daily to nearby Delos, returning in the afternoon. The Port Authority in Chora gives information, but it's not more reliable than that given at the agencies clustered near the old harbor (☎ 0283/22348).

MYKONOS

In summer, there are two to three ferries daily to Mykonos from Piraeus and Rafina. From Mykonos (Port Authority: ⌧ Harbor, above National Bank, ☎ 0294/22218) there are daily departures to Paros, Tinos, and Andros and five to seven departures per week for Santorini, Naxos, Ios, and Crete.

NAXOS

In summer, ferries leave Piraeus for **Naxos** at least four times a day. (The trip takes about seven hours.) A boat goes daily from Naxos (Port

Authority, ☎ 0285/22300) to Mykonos, Ios, and Santorini. There are daily connections with Paros, Ios, and Santorini, and weekly trips to Skiathos and Salonica. Boats from Naxos serve the Little Cyclades, Iraklia, Schinousa, Koufonis, and Donousa.

PAROS

About four ferries leave Piraeus for **Paros** every day in summer. Paros (✉ Port Authority, ☎ 0284/21240) has daily ferry service to Santorini, Ios, Mykonos, and Naxos. There are also boats to Tinos, Andros, Crete, Rhodes, Kos, Siphnos, Anaphe, Samos, Skiathos, and Salonica. Cruise boats leave daily from Paros town and Naousa for excursions to Delos and Mykonos.

SANTORINI

Santorini is served at least twice daily from Piraeus; from Santorini, ferries make frequent connections to the other islands—daily to Paros, Naxos, and Ios, and usually once a week to Mykonos, Anaphe, Crete, Tinos, and Andros. Almost all ferries dock at Athinios port, where taxis and buses take passengers to Fira, Kamari, and Perissa Beach. Travelers bound for Ia take a bus to Fira and change there. Some boats stop first below Ia, whence small caïques transport passengers to waiting donkeys at the bottom of the cliff below the village. The port below Fira is used only by small steamers and cruise ships. Passengers disembarking here face a 45-minute hike or they can take the cable car (or ride up on the traditional donkeys, but spare the poor things). The port police (☎ 0286/22239) can give information on ferry schedules.

By Plane

There are no airports on **Andros** or **Tinos.**

MYKONOS

Some European countries now have charter flights to Mykonos. **Olympic Airways** (✉ Athens, ☎ 01/966–6666) is the only domestic carrier. It has seven flights daily to Mykonos (10 daily during peak tourist season); reservations are always a good idea. There are also summer flights between Mykonos and Santorini, Heraklion (on Crete), and Rhodes. The Olympic Airways **offices in Mykonos** are at the port (☎ 0289/22490 or 0289/22495) and at the airport (4 km/2½ mi southwest of Mykonos town, ☎ 0289/22327).

NAXOS

Olympic Airways has two flights daily between Athens and Naxos airport (✉ A few miles outside Naxos town, ☎ 0285/23292).

PAROS

Olympic Airways (✉ Paros town, ☎ 0284/21900) has five daily flights to the Paros airport (✉ Near Alyki village, 9 km/5½ mi south of Parikia, ☎ 0284/91257) from Athens and up to seven a day in high season.

SANTORINI

Olympic Airways (✉ Ayia Athanassiou, Fira, ☎ 0286/22493 or 0286/22793) flies six times daily to Santorini airport (✉ Monolithos, on east coast, 8 km/5 mi from Fira, ☎ 0286/31525) from Athens in peak season. In summer there are flights to Mykonos, Heraklion (Crete), and Rhodes about three times per week.

Getting Around

By Bus

ANDROS

About six buses a day from Andros town (✉ To right of marble walkway, ☎ 0282/22316) go to and from the harbor, in conjunction with the ferry schedule; all buses stop in Batsi. Daily buses also go to and return from Stenies, Apikia, Strapouries, Pitrofos, and Korthi.

TINOS

Buses run several times daily from the quay of Chora to nearly all the many villages in Tinos (☎ 0283/22440), and in summer buses are added for beaches.

MYKONOS

In Mykonos town the Ayios Loukas station near the Olympic Airways office is for buses to Ornos, Ayios Ioannis, Plati Yialos, Psarou, the airport, and Kalamopodi. Another station near the archaeological museum is for Ayios Stefanos, Tourlos, Ano Mera, Elia, Kalafatis, and Kalo Livadi. For bus information, dial ☎ 0289/23360.

NAXOS

The bus system is reliable and fairly extensive. Daily buses go from Chora (✉ Waterfront, ☎ 0285/22440) to Engares, Melanes, Sangri, Filoti, Apeiranthos, Koronida, and Apollonas. In summer there is added daily service to the beaches, including Ayia Anna, Pyrgaki, Ayiassos, Pachy Ammos, Ayios Mamas, and Abram. The bus office is near the dock.

PAROS

From the Paros town bus station (✉ 3 mins away from the town, east of the dock, ☎ 0284/21133) there is service every hour to Naousa and less-frequent service to Alyki, Pounda, and to the beaches at Piso Livadhi, Chrissi Akti, and Drios. Schedules are posted.

SANTORINI

Buses leave from the main station in central Fira (✉ Deorgala) for Perissa and Kamari beaches, Ia, Pyrgos, and other villages.

By Caïque

On all islands, caïques leave from the main port for the most popular beaches and interisland trips. You can also hire a caïque (and haggle over the price, of course) for your tour of choice. For popular routes, captains have posted signs showing their destinations and departure times.

By Car, Motorbike, and Bicycle

To take cars on ferries you must make reservations. All the major islands have car- and bike-rental agencies at the ports and in the business districts. Car rentals cost about 15,000 dr. per day, with unlimited mileage and third-party liability insurance. Full insurance costs about 2,000 dr. a day more. Motorbikes and scooters start at 3,000 dr. a day, including third-party liability coverage. Jeeps and dune buggies are also available in Santorini, Mykonos, Paros, Tinos, and Naxos. Choose a dealer that offers 24-hour service and a change of vehicle in case of a breakdown. Beware: Too many travelers end up in Athenian hospitals owing to poor roads, slipshod maintenance, and excessive partying.

ANDROS

Though there is bus service on this large and mountainous island, it is much more convenient to travel by car. Cars can be rented at **Rent a Car Tasos** (✉ Near the ferry-boat quay, ☎ 0282/71391 or 0282/71040). It's easiest to let Helena Prodromou of Andros Travel (Batsi opposite beach, ☎ 0282/41252 or 0282/41751, FAX 0282/41608) arrange your needs.

TINOS

Vidalis Rent-a-Car (✉ Zanaki Alavanou, ☎ 0283/23400) and **Dimitris Rental** (✉ Zanaki Alavanou, ☎ 0283/23585, FAX 0283/22744), almost next door to each other, are reliable.

MYKONOS

There are several agencies near the windmill bus stop; no cars are permitted in town. Or let George Ghikas of Sunspots Travel (☞ *below*) do it for you.

NAXOS

The roads don't go everywhere and are sometimes poor. Often it's easier just to take the bus, especially to places like Apollonas, where the road is steep and twisting. Still, if you drive carefully, you shouldn't have any problem. Car-rental outfits are concentrated in the Chora new town: Try **Jeep Rent-A-Car** (⊠ Chora new town, ☎ 0285/23396) or **Tourent A Car** (⊠ Chora new town, ☎ 0285/23330 or 0285/23331).

PAROS

It is a good idea to rent a vehicle here, because the island is large; there are many beaches to choose from, and taxis are in demand. Among the many agencies near the port, **Vintsi Travel** (⊠ A little past the bus stop, ☎ 0284/21830, FAX 0284/23666) is reliable; also there is a **Thrifty** car-rental desk in Polos Travel (By OTE office, ☎ 0284/21309) and at the airport.

SANTORINI

Extreme caution is advised on Santorini, the car- and bike-accident capital of the Cyclades; the narrow roads are extremely crowded with inexperienced (and often drunk) drivers. Cars can be rented at **Avis** (⊠ Fira, ☎ 0286/23742) or at **Hertz** (⊠ Fira, ☎ 0286/22221).

By Taxi

ANDROS

Taxi stands (⊠ Off main street, near bus station in Andros town; ⊠ in Batsi at the small quayside square beneath the Dolphins restaurant; ☎ 0282/22171 for both locations).

TINOS

Taxis wait on the quay (⊠ Near central boat dock, ☎ 0283/22470).

MYKONOS

Taxi stand (⊠ Harbor near Mando Mavroyennis statue, ☎ 0289/22400 or 0289/23700). Meters are not used; standard fares for each destination are posted on a notice bulletin board.

NAXOS

Taxi stand (⊠ Near the harbor, ☎ 0285/22444).

PAROS

Taxi stand (⊠ Across from windmill on the harbor, ☎ 0284/21500); in high season taxis are often busy.

SANTORINI

Taxi station (⊠ Near Fira's central square [25th of March St.], ☎ 0286/22555).

Contacts and Resources

Emergencies

ANDROS

Police (⊠ Gavrio ☎ 0282/71220; ⊠ Batsi, ☎ 0282/41204; ⊠ Andros town, ☎ 0282/22300). **Medical assistance** (⊠ Batsi, ☎ 0282/41326; ⊠ Gavrio, ☎ 0282/71210). **Health center** (⊠ Andros town, ☎ 0282/22222).

TINOS

Police (✉ Chora, ☎ 028322255; ✉ Pirgos, ☎ 0283/31371). **Medical assistance:** Health Center (✉ East end of town, ☎ 0283/22210; ✉ Isternia, ☎ 0283/31206).

MYKONOS

Police (☎ 0289/22235). **Medical assistance:** hospital (✉ Mykonos town, ☎ 0289/23994) has 24-hour emergency service with pathologists, surgeons, pediatricians, dentists, and X-ray technicians; first aid (✉ Ano Mera, ☎ 0289/71395).

NAXOS

Police (✉ Chora, ☎ 0285/22100 or 0285/23280; ✉ Filoti, ☎ 0285/31244). **Medical assistance:** health center (✉ Just outside Chora, ☎ 0285/23333 or 0285/23676) is open 24 hours a day; Medical Center of Naxos (✉ Quay, ☎ 0285/23234, FAX 0285/23576).

PAROS

Police (✉ Paros town, ☎ 0284/23333; ✉ Naousa, ☎ 0284/51202). **Medical Center:** Paros town health clinic (✉ Paros town, ☎ 0284/22500; ✉ Naousa, ☎ 0284/51216; ✉ Antiparos, ☎ 0284/61219).

SANTORINI

Police (✉ Fira, ☎ 0286/22649). **Medical assistance:** first aid (✉ Fira, ☎ 0286/22237; ✉ Ia, ☎ 0286/71227).

Guided Tours

ANDROS

Helena Prodromou's **Andros Travel** (✉ Batsi, ☎ 0282/412252 or 0282/41751, FAX 0282/441608) arranges coach tours and especially walking tours, from strolling to climbing. Helena, a British Cypriot, is friendly and very knowledgeable.

TINOS

Windmills Travel (✉ Above new dock behind playground, ☎ FAX 0283/23398) runs daily guided coach tours of the island for 2,000 dr., a variety of specialty tours by Jeep, and unguided Delos–Mykonos trips (4,000 dr.).

MYKONOS

Sunspots Travel (✉ Near airport bus stop, into town, on left, second floor, ☎ 0289/24196, FAX 0289/23790) takes a group every morning for a day tour of Delos (7,500 dr.). It has half-day guided tours of the Mykonos beach towns, with a stop in Ano Mera for the Panagia Tourliani Monastery. **Delos Tours** (✉ Fabrica Sq., ☎ 0289/26442) runs all-day excursions (about 7,500 dr.) to nearby Tinos to visit the marble studios, monasteries, and a Venetian ruin.

NAXOS

The **Tourist Information Center** (✉ Waterfront, ☎ 0285/22993), run by Despina Kitini of the Chateau Zevgoli (☞ Naxos *in* Exploring, *above*), offers round-the-island tours, and a weekly boat trip, Mykonos by Night, for 5,000 dr. **Zas Travel** (✉ Chora, ☎ 0285/23330 or 0285/23331, FAX 0285/23419; ✉ Ayios Prokopios, ☎ 0285/24780) runs two good one-day tours of the island sights with different itineraries, each costing about 4,000 dr., and one-day trips to Delos and Mykonos (7,500 dr.), and Santorini (8,000 dr.).

PAROS

A variety of trips by land and sea, such as around Antiparos, are arranged by Kostas Akalestos's **Paroikia Tours** (☎ 0284/22470 or 0284/22471, FAX 0284/22450). **Simitzi Tours** (✉ Naousa, ☎ 0284/51113, FAX

0284/51761) are good. Most agencies handle Delos–Mykonos trips for about 4,000 dr.

Bellonias Tours (✉ Fira, ☎ 0286/22469 or 0286/23604; ✉ Kamari, ☎ 0286/31721) runs coach tours that include Akrotiri, Ancient Thera, Ia, wine tastings, and churches; it also has daily boat trips to the volcano and Thirassia and arranges private tours. **X-Ray Kilo** (☎ 0286/22624 or 0286/23243) has tours to the same sights, and to the island's wineries and the Monastery of Profitis Elias.

Visitor Information

The **Greek National Tourist Organization (GNTO or EOT)** is housed in a converted dovecote (✉ Near Batsi Rd., ☎ 0282/71785). **Police station** (✉ Gavrio, across from ferry dock, ☎ 0282/71220) lists available accommodations. Your best bet is to ask **Andros Tavel** (Batsi waterfront, opposite the beach, ☎ 0282/41252, FAX 0282/41608).

From June to October, the Town Hall (✉ Evangelistria) runs a **Greek National Tourist Organization (GNTO or EOT)** (☎ 0283/22255). For all tourist services (schedules, room bookings, tours, happenings), see friendly Sharon Turner, manager of **Windmills Travel** (✉ Above new dock behind playground, ☎ FAX 0283/23398); she's a mine of information—there's nothing she doesn't know about her adopted island.

Tourist police (✉ Harbor, near departure point for Delos, ☎ 0289/22716). George Ghikas's **Sunspots Travel** (✉ Near airport bus stop, into town, on left, second floor, ☎ 0289/24196, FAX 0289/23790) is super-efficient, with a multitude of services.

The well-organized **Greek National Tourist Organization (GNTO or EOT)** (✉ Waterfront, ☎ 0285/24525, 0285/24358, and 0285/22993) has free booking service, bus and ferry schedules, international dialing, luggage storage, and foreign exchange at bank rates.

The **Greek National Tourist Organization (GNTO or EOT)** (✉ Paros town, in café across from dock, ☎ 0284/22079) is sometimes open. For efficient and friendly service—tickets, villa rentals for families, apartments, and quality hotel reservations—try Kostas Akalestos's **Paroikia Tours** (Market St., ☎ 0284/22470 or 0284/22471, FAX 0284/22450). Kostas, efficient and full of the Greek spirit, has many repeat customers. **Polos Tours** (Next to the dockside OTE office, ☎ 0284/22092, FAX 02284/21983), is big, inclusive, and efficient. **Simitzi Tours** (✉ Naousa, on main square, ☎ 0284/51113, FAX 0284/51761) is helpful.

There's no EOT on Santorini, but **Nomikos Travel** (☎ 0286/23660 or 0286/22660, FAX 0286/23666), which has offices in Fira and Perissa, can handle most needs.

11 Crete

To Greeks, Crete is the Megalonissi
(Great Island), a hub of sophisticated
ancient art and architecture, where
rebellion was endemic for centuries—
against Arab invaders, Venetian
colonists, Ottoman pashas, and
German occupiers in World War II.
Mountains, split with deep gorges and
honeycombed with caves, rise in sheer
walls from the sea. Snowcapped peaks
loom against sandy beaches, vineyards,
and olive groves. As spectacular as the
scenery is, it can't compare to Crete's
treasure of all treasures: the Palace of
Knossos—the incomparable monument
of ancient Minoan culture and one of
the cradles of civilization.

By Kerin Hope

Updated by
Stephen
Brewer

AROUND 1500 BC, WHILE THE REST OF EUROPE was
still in the grip of primitive barbarity, one of the
most brilliant and amazing civilizations the world
was ever to know approached its final climax. The sophisticated elegance of King Minos's court on the island of Crete was an appropriate manifestation of imperial power patiently built up over centuries.
In fact, the Minoans, prehistoric Cretans, had founded Europe's first
urban culture as far back as the third millennium BC, and the island's
rich legacy of art and architecture strongly influenced both mainland
Greece and the Aegean islands in the Bronze Age. From around 1900
BC the Minoan palaces at Knossos (near present-day Heraklion), Mallia,
Phaistos, and elsewhere were centers of political power, religious authority, and economic activity—all concentrated in one sprawling complex of buildings. Their administration seems to have had much in
common with contemporary cultures in Egypt and Mesopotamia.
What set the Minoans apart from the rest of the Bronze Age world was
their art. It was lively and naturalistic, and they excelled in miniature
techniques. From the scenes illustrated on their frescoes, stone vases,
seal-stones, and signet rings, it is possible to build a picture of a pro-
ductive, well-regulated society. Yet new research suggests that prehistoric Crete was not a peaceful place; there may have been years of warfare
before Knossos became the island's dominant power, in around 1600
BC. It is now thought that political upheaval, rather than the devastating volcanic eruption on the island of Santorini, triggered the violent downfall of the palace civilization around 1450 BC.

Vestiges of the Minoan civilization abound at Knossos, Phaistos, and
many other archaeological sites around the island. In addition to enjoying miles of beaches, evocative ruins, and fascinating towns and cities,
immersing oneself in the island's lifestyle can be an immense pleasure.
Even in the large cities Cretans remain family oriented, rooted in tradition and openly inviting to their visitors who want to experience the
real Greece.

Pleasures and Pastimes

Bicycling

Crete is rewarding biking country. Though the rugged White Mountains of the west are for hardened addicts, there is plenty of pleasant
riding in the gentler landscapes of eastern Crete on the agricultural plains
near the south central coast. Bicycle rentals are available in most Cretan towns. Mountain bikes for cycling in the uplands are now easier
to find, especially in Heraklion and Chania.

Bird-Watching

Bird-watchers have access to a huge variety of bird life, though most
species are not indigenous. There is a bird sanctuary east of Heraklion
at the Gouves estuary, which is a stopover for a large range of migra-
tory birds. Mt. Iuktas, south of Heraklion, is the place to spot vultures.

Dining

Crete cannot claim to be a center of gastronomy, but ingredients are
always fresh, and the family-run tavernas take pride in their cooking.
The island produces top-quality fruit and vegetables—cherries from
the Amari Valley in June, oranges from the groves around Hania in
winter, tomatoes and cucumbers all year round, and, increasingly, av-
ocados and bananas. The Cretans enjoy grilled meat, generally lamb
and pork, but there is also plenty of fresh fish. Cretan *graviera* cheese
is prized, along with *mizythra* (a creamy white variety). Cretan olive

oil is famous throughout Greece, though it's heavier than other varieties. The island's wines are improving fast: Look for Boutari Kritikos, a crisp white, and Minos Palace, a smooth red. Retsina is not part of the Cretan tradition, but it can be found in town restaurants.

In restaurants, *magirefta* (precooked dishes served at room temperature) are prepared in the morning and are best eaten at lunch. As a rule, it is hard to go hungry in Crete; in a village *kafenion* (traditional Greek coffeehouse), you can almost always order salad and an omelet or eggs fried with graviera cheese. Make sure you try the *tsikouthia* (also known as *raki*), the Cretan firewater, which is drunk at any hour, often accompanied by a dish of raisins, or walnuts drenched in honey. You will almost certainly eat better in a taverna or restaurant than at a hotel, where, unless you are staying at a first-class resort, the menu is usually of the bland "international" variety. Hotel desk clerks willingly recommend a choice of tavernas. Dress is invariably casual, though except in the most casual places shorts are not worn in the evening, and reservations are unnecessary unless noted. Credit cards are usually accepted only in more expensive restaurants.

CATEGORY	COST*
$$$$	over 8,000 dr.
$$$	5,000 dr.–8,000 dr.
$$	3,000 dr.–5,000 dr.
$	under 3,000 dr.

per person for a three-course meal, including tax and service but excluding drinks

Lodging

Crete has luxury resort hotels with sports and entertainment facilities that compare with those anywhere in the Mediterranean. For a more authentic way to experience Crete, opt for the simple whitewashed, cement-floor rooms in mountain and seaside villages. Unfortunately, Crete also has many undistinguished, concrete-block hotels, mostly along the north coast, that defile the landscape and have little character. Some of Greece's finest hotels line the shores of Elounda peninsula, just outside the town of Ayios Nikolaos. In the west especially, old houses, Venetian mansions, and 19th-century consulates are being sensitively restored as small hotels. Hania has several such hotels, and they are excellent.

Unless the months of closing are noted, all hotels are open year-round. Prices rise in July and come down again in mid-September, but even in high season you can often negotiate a discount at medium-price hotels if you are staying more than a night or two. Resort hotels sometimes require half-board (MAP); many will give substantial discounts at the beginning and end of the season. If you are staying in Hania or Heraklion in July or August, you may want to pay a little more for a room with air-conditioning. You should assume that hotels of $$$$ and $$$ rating will have air-conditioning; air-conditioning is noted when available at less-expensive establishments. Travel agencies, the local Greek National Tourist Organization (GNTO or EOT) offices, and the tourist police all will help you find accommodation at short notice. In villages, ask at the kafenion about rooms for rent. Standards of cleanliness are high in Crete and service is almost always friendly.

CATEGORY	COST*
$$$$	over 25,000 dr.
$$$	14,000 dr.–25,000 dr.
$$	9,000 dr.–14,000 dr.
$	under 9,000 dr.

All prices are for a standard double room including breakfast, service, and tax.

Nightlife and the Arts

An evening out in Crete is generally spent in a *kentron* (a taverna that features traditional Cretan music and dancing). The star performer is the *lyra* player, who can extract a surprisingly subtle sound from the small pear-shape instrument, held upright on the thigh and played with a bow. Cretan dances range from monotonous circling to astonishing displays of athletic agility, but much depends on the *kefi* (enthusiasm) of the participants. In winter, the kentron moves indoors and becomes a more typical bouzouki joint. Ask at your hotel where the best-known lyra players are performing. Throughout the warmer months, almost every town and village celebrates the feast of its patron saint with a *panayiria* (celebration), with food, drink, and traditional music and dancing usually lasting until dawn. If you are lucky, you may be invited to a *glendi* (local party), or even a traditional Cretan wedding, where the celebrations can last 24 hours.

Crete has few serious arts activities and events. Though the island attracts painters from all over Europe, they rarely exhibit locally. In Heraklion, Rethymnon, and, occasionally, Hania, however, local authorities sometimes organize concerts, theater, and folk dancing events during the summer. Athenian and even some foreign musical groups stage open-air performances in the Koules fort at Heraklion and the Fortessa at Rethymnon. Ask at the EOT offices for up-to-date booking information (☞ Visitor Information *in* Crete A to Z, *below*). In winter, both local and visiting choirs and chamber-music groups perform occasionally. The town hall will have information on times and bookings.

Shopping

Crete is a serendipitous place for the shopper. Little serious attempt has been made to adapt the island's traditional crafts to the demands of foreign customers, but by poking around the backstreets of Heraklion, Rethymnon, and Hania, you can find things both useful and exotic—and sometimes even beautiful. Crete was famous even in Minoan times for its weaving. You still occasionally come across the heavy scarlet-embroidered blankets and bedspreads that formed the basis of a traditional dowry chest. Woven wool rugs in plain geometric designs from the village of Axos on the slopes of Mt. Ida are attractive, as are heavy sweaters in natural oily wool. All the villages on the Lashiti plateau have shops selling embroidered linens, made in front of the stove during the long winter months when snow blocks roads in and out of the area. All over the island, local craftsmen produce attractive copies of Minoan jewelry in gold and silver, as well as some with original modern designs. A shepherd's kit, a striped woven haversack, and a staff are useful for the hiker. Boot makers in Heraklion and Hania will make you a pair of heavy Cretan leather knee boots to order. A Cretan knife, whether plain steel or with a decorated blade and handle, makes a handy kitchen or camping implement. In the village of Thrapsano, 20 km (12½ mi) southeast of Heraklion, at one of the potteries you can choose a new *pithos* (the tall Ali Baba–style jar used by the Minoans for storing wine and oil and still popular today, often as a flowerpot); have it air-freighted home.

Water Sports

Water-sports enthusiasts will find Windsurfers available for rent on any beach frequented by tourists. Scuba diving, snorkeling, dinghy sailing, and yachting are available at large resort hotels or can be arranged through local travel agencies. As is the case elsewhere in Greece, diving is strictly limited because of the presence of underwater antiquities; local tourist boards can provide details.

Exploring Crete

From the glossy beach resorts along the north coast—with the faint echoes of Minoan hedonism in their stunning settings—to the backpackers' haunts in the south, from frescoed Byzantine churches deep in the countryside to beaches reachable only by boat, there are destinations on Crete to suit every tourist's taste. English is spoken widely.

Crete is a long narrow island, and therefore as a matter of convenience most visitors tend to approach it in halves. Western Crete is especially rugged, with inland mountains and the equally craggy southern shoreline; some of the best beaches on the island are on the western coast, surrounding the town of Falasarna. Hania and Rethymnon, both lovely, mysterious old cities that trace their roots to the Arab and Venetian worlds, are here in the west. The east begins at Crete's largest town, Heraklion, and most important archaeological site, Knossos, and includes many of its most developed resorts. In both the east and the west of Crete, you'll find the most development on the north shore, while for the most part the southern coast remains blessedly unspoiled.

Numbers in the text correspond to numbers in the margin and on the Eastern Crete, Heraklion, Palace of Knossos, Palace of Mallia, Western Crete, and Palace of Phaistos maps.

Great Itineraries

Although Crete is a large island, in the north, at least, it is crossed by a good highway and serviced by a good bus system. Even on a one-day stopover you can see the greatest of the island's Minoan sights, though beware: You will be tempted to stay longer. A three-day tour allows you to taste the pleasures of Heraklion and the cities of western Crete, and seven days will allow time to see most of the major towns and sights on a circular tour of the island.

IF YOU HAVE 1 DAY

Many visitors stop off in Crete for only a day, often en route from Santorini to Rhodes. This stopover doesn't allow much time, but you can begin in ⊞ **Heraklion** ①–⑬ with a visit to the **archaeological museum** ⑬, with its stunning displays of Minoan culture, then move onto the island's largest and most well-preserved Minoan sight, the **Palace of Knossos** ⑭–㉔. In the afternoon, make the hour-long trip to the **Palace of Phaistos** ㊻–㊿, another great Minoan site overlooking the south coast, and before returning to **Heraklion** enjoy a drink or a meal in the pretty nearby resort of **Matala** ㊼.

IF YOU HAVE 3 DAYS

⊞ **Heraklion** ①–⑬ is the best starting point for a visit to the island. Spend one day visiting that city, its **archaeological museum** ⑬, and the **Palace of Knossos** ⑭–㉔. From there, follow the north coast west to the city of ⊞ **Rethymnon** ㊎, with its Venetian and Arab heritage, and later in the afternoon travel on to ⊞ **Hania** ㊵, one of the most beautiful cities in Greece and, with its gorgeous harbor and fascinating old town, a delightful place to spend an evening. En route back to **Heraklion,** drive south from **Rethymnon** to the Minoan **Palace of Phaistos** ㊻–㊿, returning for the night to **Heraklion** or staying in seaside ⊞ **Matala** ㊼ or, for a taste of rural Cretan life, one of the other nearby villages.

IF YOU HAVE 7 DAYS

A week allows time to see all of Crete, if not exactly at leisure, at least at an enjoyable pace. The place to begin is ⊞ **Heraklion** ①–⑬, where a stay of a day and a night allows enough time to see the city, the **archaeological museum** ⑬, and the **Palace of Knossos** ⑭–㉔. From there you can explore the island on a more or less circular tour. However, since there is no road directly across the south shore, you will return to the north shore frequently as you travel. As you head east from **Heraklion,** your first stop is the **Lasithi Plateau** ㉕, where you'll get a taste of one of the most scenic corners of rural Crete. After lunch there, you'll want to return to the north shore and, after a stop (via the 20-year-old north coast road still labeled NEW ROAD) at the Minoan ruins at the **Palace of Mallia** ㉗–㊱, continue on to **Ayios Nikolaos** ㊲. The nearby peninsula, ⊞ **Elounda** ㊳, with its fine hotels and wonderful views of the Gulf of Mirabello, is an excellent place to stay. The next day head south to the Minoan city of **Gournia** ㊹, and continue on to **Ierapetra** ㊺. After lunch and maybe a swim, it's back up to the north coast to ⊞ **Siteia** ㊽. The next morning you'll want an early start to the beautiful beach at **Vai** ㊿. The afternoon is devoted to driving, all the way to ⊞ **Rethymnon** ㊅ on the western side of the island—however, the distance is only a little more than 200 km (120 mi) and the highway along the north coast is wide and well paved. After an evening in **Rethymnon,** preferably staying in the charming old town, make the short trip on to ⊞ **Hania** ㊟. You may want to spend two nights here, allowing time to see the city and to explore the area. You might, for instance, want to take a day trip to the **Samaria Gorge,** to the beaches in the far west, or to the rugged southern coast around **Paleochora** or **Hora Sfakion** ㊏. From **Hania** take the long route back to **Heraklion,** making a loop south at **Rethymnon** to visit the Minoan **Palace at Phaistos** ㊐–㊑ then turning back to the north coast.

When to Tour

The best times for visiting Crete are April and May, when every outcrop of rock is ablaze with brilliant wildflowers, or October, when the sea is still warm and the light golden but piercingly clear. In July and August the main Minoan sites and the coastal towns come close to overflowing. Places like Mallia and Limin Hersonissos, hideously developed towns where bars and pizzerias fill up with heavy-drinking northern Europeans, should be avoided especially in summer and in any other season as well. Driving can be especially hazardous in July and August amid the profusion of buses, Jeeps, and motorbikes, not to mention the impatient Cretan drivers.

EASTERN CRETE

Eastern Crete includes the towns and cities of Heraklion, Ayios Nikolaos, Siteia, and Ierapetra, as well as the archaeological sites of Knossos and Gournia. Of course, many natural wonders lie between these man-made places, including the palm-fringed beach at Vai and the stunning Elounda Peninsula.

Heraklion

175 km (108¾ mi) south of Piraeus, 78 km (48½ mi) east of Rethymnon, 69 km (43 mi) west of Ayios Nikolaos.

The narrow, crowded alleys and thick stone ramparts of Heraklion, Crete's largest city and the fourth-largest city in Greece, recall the days when soldiers and merchants clung to the safety of a fortified port. In Minoan times, this was a harbor for Knossos, the largest palace and effective power center of prehistoric Crete. But the Bronze Age remains were built over long ago, and now Heraklion, with more than 120,000 inhabitants, stretches far beyond even the Venetian walls. In any event, any student interested in Minoan civilization and the Palace of Knossos makes this city an obligatory stop because of its renowned archaeological museum.

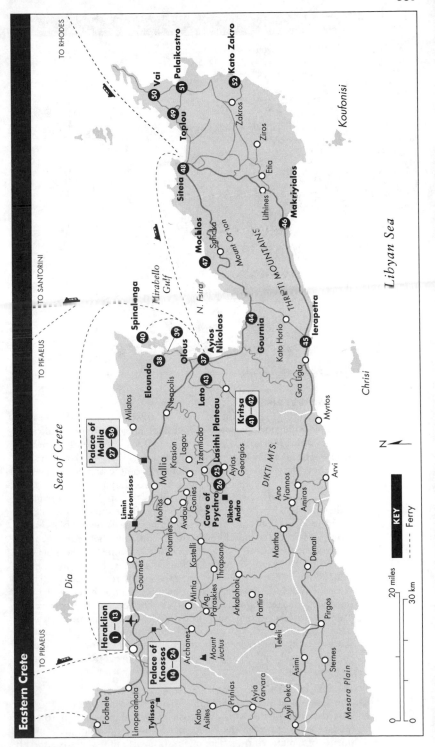

Eastern Crete

TO RHODES

TO PIRAEUS

TO SANTORINI

50 Vai
51 Palaikastro
52 Kato Zakro
Zakros
49 Toplou
Ziros
48 Siteia
Etia
Lithines
Makriyialos 46
THRIPTI MOUNTAINS
Mochlos 47
Sphaka
Mount Ornon
N. Psira

Koufonisi

Libyan Sea

Mirabello Gulf

Spinalenga
40
39 Olous
38 Elounda
37 Ayios Nikolaos
44 Gournia
Kato Horio
Gra Ligia
45 Ierapetra
Myrtos

Chrisi

Neapolis
43 Lato
41—42 Kritsa
Lasithi Plateau
Milatos

Palace of Mallia 27—36

Mallia
Krasion
Lagou
Tzermiado
26 25 Ayios Georgios
Cave of Psychro
Dikteo Andro
DIKTI MTS.
Ano Viannos
Arvi
Amiras
Demati

Limin Hersonissos
Mohos
Gones
Avdou
Potamies
Kastelli
Thrapsano
Martha

Gournes
Mirtia
Ag. Paraskies
Arkalohori
Partira
Pirgos
Tefeli
Sternes

Heraklion 1—13

Palace of Knossos 14—24

Archanes
Mount Juctus
Prinias
Ayia Varvara
Asimi
Ayii Deka
Mesara Plain

Fodhele
Linoperamata
Tylissos
Kato Asites

Sea of Crete

Dia

TO PIRAEUS

N

KEY
----- Ferry

20 miles
30 km

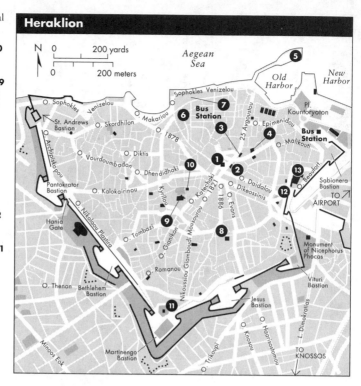

A Good Walk

You can nicely explore the compact old town in a walk of an hour or two, beginning at **Ta Leontaria** ① with its famous fountain and cathedral of **Ayios Markos** ②. As you follow Odos 1866 south from here, you will be in the heart of Heraklion's market—busy by day with shoppers, at night with residents who converge on the area for an evening stroll. The market ends in **Kornarou Square,** dominated by two fountains—one Turkish (which now actually is the site for a café) and the other Venetian. If you follow Vikela Street off the square, you will pass many of Heraklion's most famous churches: the cathedral of **Ayios Minas** ⑨, dedicated to Heraklion's patron saint, and the medieval church of the same name, then the church of **Ayia Aikaterina** ⑩, where El Greco is said to have studied. At Ayia Ekaterini you will come to Leoforos Kalokerinou, another major shopping thoroughfare; a left turn will bring you back to Ta Leontaria. If you now proceed north across the busy intersection, you will come to another remnant of Venetian occupation, the **Loggia** ③, then the church of **Ayios Titos** ④, named for the patron saint of Crete. You are now within sight of the fortifications known as the **Koules** ⑤ and the inner harbor. By following the old city walls, you will come to the famed **Archaeological Museum** ⑬ and the café-filled **Platia Eleftherias** ⑫.

Sights to See

★ ⑬ **Archaeological Museum.** Standing in a class of its own, this museum guards many of the Minoan treasures brought to light by the legendary excavations of the Palace of Knossos and other great monuments of Cretan culture. The civilization of 3,000 years is superbly illustrated by a unique collection of pottery and jewelry, including the famous seal-stones with Linear B script, which first attracted Sir Arthur Evans's attention. Yet it is the frescoes, restored fragments found in Knossos, that most catch the eye; delightfully sophisticated representations of broad-shouldered, slim-waisted youths, their large eyes fixed with an enigmatic expression on the Prince of the Lilies; ritual processions and scenes from the bullring, young men and maidens somersaulting over the back of a charging bull; and groups of bare-breasted court ladies, whose puffed sleeves and flounced skirts led a French archaeologist to exclaim in surprise, "des Parisiennes," a name still applied to this striking fresco.

The museum is best visited early in the morning before tourist buses start disgorging their passengers; happily, installation of air-conditioning has been recently completed, and all galleries are open. The Minoan collection compares to that in any of the great museums of western Europe. Even before the great palaces were built, around 1900 BC, the prehistoric Cretans excelled at metalworking and in carving stone vases, such as that seen in the box in Gallery I with a lid whose handle is in the shape of a lazing dog. They were also skilled at producing fine pottery, such as the eggshell-thin Kamares ware decorated in delicate abstract designs (in Gallery III), and miniature work like the superbly crafted jewelry (in Galleries VI and VII) and the colored seal-stones (in Gallery III) that are carved with lively scenes of people and animals.

Though naturalism and an air of informality distinguish much Minoan art from that of contemporary Bronze Age cultures elsewhere in the eastern Mediterranean, you will also see a number of heavy, rococo set pieces, such as the fruit stand with a toothed rim and the punch bowl with appliquéd flowers (both in Gallery III). The Linear B script, inscribed on clay tablets (Gallery V), is now recognized as an early form of Greek, but the earlier Linear A script (Gallery V) and that of the Phaistos Disk (Gallery III) have yet to be deciphered. The Minoans' talents at modeling in stone, ivory, and a kind of glass paste known to archaeologists as faience peaked in the later palace period (1700 BC–1450 BC). A famous rhyton (vase for pouring libations) carved from dark serpentine in the shape of a bull's head has eyes made of red jasper and clear rock crystal with horns of gilded wood (Gallery IV). An ivory acrobat—perhaps a bull-leaper—and two bare-breasted faience goddesses in flounced skirts holding wriggling snakes (both Gallery IV) were among a group of treasures hidden beneath the floor of a storeroom at Knossos. Bull-leaping, whether religious rite or a favorite sport, inspired some memorable Minoan art. Three vases of serpentine (probably covered originally in gold leaf) from Ayia Triada (Gallery VII) are carved with scenes of Minoan life thought to be rendered by artists from Knossos: boxing matches, a harvest-home ceremony, and a Minoan official taking delivery of a consignment of hides. The most stunning rhyton of all, from Zakro, is made of rock crystal (Gallery VIII). Commodities were stored in the palaces: An elephant tusk and bronze ingots (Gallery VIII) were found at Zakro and Ayia Triada. Make sure to save some time and energy for the fresco galleries upstairs. Dating from the later palace period, they show both the Minoans' preoccupation with religious ritual and enjoyment of their island's natural beauties. ⊠ *Platia Eleftherias,* ☎ *081/226092.* 💶 *1,500 dr.* ⊙ *Apr.–mid-Oct., Mon. 12:30–7, Tues.– Sun. 8–7; mid-Oct.–Mar., daily 8–5.*

❿ **Ayia Aikaterina.** Nestled in the shadow of the Ayios Minas cathedral, this is one of Crete's most attractive small churches. Built in 1555, it is now a **museum of icons** by Cretan artists, who traveled to Venice to study with Italian Renaissance painters. Look for six icons (Nos. 2, 5, 8, 9, 12, and 15) by Michael Damaskinos, who worked in both Byzantine and Renaissance styles in the 16th century. ⊠ *Kyrillou Loukareos.* 💶 *500 dr.* ⊙ *Mon. and Wed–Sat. 9:30–1.*

②   **Ayios Markos.** This 13th-century church (now an exhibition center) is named for Venice's patron saint, but, with its modern portico and narrow interior, it bears little resemblance to its grand namesake in Venice. ⊠ *Eleftheriou Venizelou.*

❾   **Ayios Minas.** This is a huge, lofty, but ultimately unprepossessing 19th-century cathedral. ⊠ *Kyrillou Loukareos, main road west from Platia Cornarou.*

④   **Ayios Titos.** As you head north toward the harbor, you'll pass this church, named for Crete's patron saint. A **chapel** to the left of the entrance contains the saint's skull, set in a silver-and-gilt reliquary. Ayios Titos is credited with converting the islanders to Christianity in the 1st century AD on the instructions of St. Paul. ⊠ *Set back from 25th of August St.*

❼   **Historical Museum of Crete.** Once known as the Historical and Ethnological Museum, this is housed in an imposing mansion and contains a varied collection of early Christian and Byzantine sculptures in the basement and several rooms filled with Venetian and Ottoman stonework. Look out for a splendid **lion of St. Mark,** with an inscription that says in Latin I PROTECT THE KINGDOM OF CRETE, and some striking tombstones of Ottoman officials, topped with stone turbans. Left of the entrance is a room stuffed with memorabilia from Crete's bloody revolutionary past: weapons, portraits of mustachioed warrior chieftains, and the flag of the short-lived independent Cretan state set up in 1898. The 19th-century banner in front of the staircase sums up the spirit of Cretan rebellion against the Turks: ELEFTHERIA I THANATOS (Freedom or Death). Upstairs, look in on a room arranged as the study of Crete's most famous writer, Nikos Kazantzakis, the author of *Zorba the Greek* and an epic poem, *The Odyssey, a Modern Sequel.* The top floor contains a stunning collection of **Cretan textiles,** including the brilliant scarlet weavings typical of the island's traditional handwork, and another room arranged as a comfortable domestic interior of the early 1900s. ⊠ *Odos Kalokorinou, off western coast road near the Xenia Hotel,* ☎ *081/283219.* 🖃 *1,000 dr.* ☉ *Weekdays 9–5, Sat. 9–2.*

❺   **Koules.** This Turkish-named miniature fortress dominates Heraklion's **inner harbor.** Fishing boats land their catch and yachts are now moored at what was once the city's Venetian port. To the right rise the tall vaulted tunnels of the arsenal; here, Venetian galleys were repaired and refitted and timber, cheeses, and sweet malmsey wine were loaded for the three-week voyage to Venice. The Koules was built by the Venetians, and three stone lions of St. Mark, symbol of Venetian imperialism, decorate the exterior. The view from its battlements takes in both the outer harbor, where freighters and passenger ferries drop anchor, and the sprawling labyrinth of concrete apartment blocks that is modern Heraklion. To the south rises Mt. Iuktas and to the west, the pointed peak of Mt. Stromboli. ⊠ *Inner harbor, end of 25th of August St.* 🖃 *500 dr.* ☉ *Tues.–Sun. 8:30–3.*

③   **Loggia.** A gathering place for the island's Venetian nobility, this loggia was built in the early 17th century by Francesco Basilicata, an Italian architect. Recently restored to its original Palladian elegance, it adjoins the old Venetian Armory, now the City Hall. ⊠ *25th of August St..*

NEED A
BREAK?

There are two ***bougatsa shops*** (⊠ Eleftheriou Venizelou), side by side, where you can stop for this envelope of flaky pastry stuffed with a sweet, creamy filling dusted with cinnamon and sugar, or with soft white cheese. A double portion served warm with Greek coffee is a nice change from a hotel breakfast, especially if you've just arrived off the ferry from Piraeus.

⑪ Martinengo Bastion. The largest of six bastions shaped like arrowheads jutting out from the well-preserved Venetian walls, the Martinengo was designed by Micheli Sanmicheli as one of the bastions built in the 16th century to keep out Barbary pirates and Turkish invaders. When the Turks finally overran Crete in 1648, the garrison at Heraklion held out for another 21 years in one of the longest sieges in European history. General Francesco Morosini finally surrendered the city to the Turkish Grand Vizier in September 1669. He was allowed to sail home to Venice with the city's archives and such precious relics as the skull of Ayios Titos—which was not returned until 1966. Literary pilgrims come to the Martinengo to visit the **burial place of Kazantzakis.** The grave is a plain stone slab marked by a weathered wooden cross. The inscription, from his writings, says: I FEAR NOTHING, I HOPE FOR NOTHING, I AM FREE. ⊠ *South of Kyrillou Loukareos on N. G. Mousourou.*

⑧ Platia Cornarou. This square is graced with a Venetian fountain and an elegant Turkish stone kiosk. Fruit and vegetable stalls alternate with butchers' displays of whole lambs and pigs' feet at the lively **open-air market** on Odos 1866. ⊠ *At top of Odos 1866, south of Ta Leontaria and across Kalokairinous.*

⑫ Platia Eleftherias. Sometimes called Treis Kamares, this is the city's biggest square. Daidalou, which follows the line of an early fortification wall, is now a pedestrian walkway lined with tavernas, boutiques, jewelers, and souvenir shops. ⊠ *At end of Daidalou St., 1 street east of Ta Leontaria, just south of Ayios Markos.*

⑥ St. Peter's church. Only a shell now remains of this medieval church, which was heavily damaged during World War II in the bombing before the German invasion in 1941. ⊠ *West of harbor along the seashore road.*

❶ Ta Leontaria. The centerpiece of Heraklion's town center—Eleftherious Venizelous Square, a triangular pedestrian zone filled with cafés—this stately marble Renaissance fountain, called "the Lions," remains a beloved town landmark. The square is named after the Cretan statesman who united the island with Greece in 1913. But for hundreds of years before then it had been the heart of the colony founded in the 13th century, when Venice bought Crete, and Heraklion became an important port of call on the trade routes to the Middle East. The city, and often the whole island, known then as Candia, was ruled by the Duke of Crete, a Venetian administrator. ⊠ *Eleftheriou Venizelou.*

Dining and Lodging

$$ ✕ Kyriakos. With its pink tablecloths and green chairs, this is no ordinary taverna. Just a short walk from the Galaxy Hotel (☞ *below*), Kyriakos offers a wide range of well-prepared salads, grills, and fish dishes. Watch for seasonal Cretan specialties, such as snail stew in summer and *volvi* (baked iris bulbs in olive oil and vinegar) in spring. There is a good wine list, with Cretan and mainland wines. ⊠ *Leoforos Dimokratias 43,* ☏ *081/224649. AE, DC, V.*

$ ✕ Terzakis. This unassuming establishment is one of Heraklion's most popular *mezedopolio* (a meze joint) in which you choose half a dozen or more dishes from a long list of fish, dips, and salads. Traditionally mezes are accompanied by ouzo, but beer or wine is equally acceptable. ⊠ *Loh. Marineli 17, behind Ayios Dimitrios church,* ☏ *081/ 221444. No credit cards. No dinner Sun.*

$ ✕ **Yacoumis.** This hole-in-the-wall is reputed to be the best of the small restaurants in the covered Meat Alley: Follow the aroma of roasting meat and clouds of steam wafting out between the stalls. Sizzling chunks of spit-roasted lamb and pork are sold by weight, accompanied by salads of roughly sliced tomatoes and onions, drenched in thick Cretan olive oil. ⊠ *Meat alley, leading off market. No credit cards. Closed Sun.*

$$$ 🏨 **Galaxy.** This modern hotel on the road to Knossos is efficiently run and popular with Greek businessmen, but its decoration and furnishings are on the drab side. However, there are two good reasons for making it your base—the swimming pool and the coffee shop, which offers the best patisserie in town. To avoid traffic noise, make sure you ask for an inside room on an upper floor. ⊠ *Leoforos Dimokratias 67, 71306,* ☎ *081/232157 or 081/238812,* 🖷 *081/211211. 120 rooms. Restaurant, coffee shop, air-conditioning, pool, sauna. DC, MC, V.*

$$ 🏨 **Astoria Capsis.** Conveniently located opposite the archaeological museum in the liveliest area of the city, this recently refurbished hotel has delightful, modern-style rooms decorated in cool shades and furnished with sleek blond wood; it has a rooftop swimming pool, as well as a delightful poolside bar, and it is fully air-conditioned. ⊠ *Platia Eleftherias, 71201,* ☎ *081/229002,* 🖷 *081/229078. 120 rooms. Restaurant, bar, coffee shop, air-conditioning, pool. AE, DC, MC, V.*

$ 🏨 **Daedalos.** On a pedestrian street in the city center, this small hotel is shabby but extremely friendly. The owner, Takis Stoumbidis, used to run an art gallery, and the rooms and corridors are lined with Cretan landscapes. The ground-floor bar is a local gathering place, where you may run into a distinguished archaeologist or folklorist downing a glass of tsikouthia. ⊠ *Daidalou 15, 71202,* ☎ *0897/244812,* 🖷 *081/244391. 58 rooms with shower. DC, MC, V.*

Outdoor Activities and Sports

BICYCLING

Bicycle rentals are available in all Cretan towns. Mountain bikes for cycling in the uplands are now easier to find. To rent a bike in Heraklion, ask at the **Creta Tours** (⊠ Epimenidou 20–22, ☎ 081/227002).

Shopping

BOOKSTORES

In Heraklion, you can find **English-language books** at **Kouvidis-Manouras** (⊠ Daidalou 6, ☎ 081/220135) or **Astrakianakis** (⊠ Eleftheriou Venizelou, ☎ 081/284248). **Newspapers and magazines** are available in Platia Venizelou.

Palace of Knossos

180 km (111¾ mi) south of Piraeus, 5 km (3 mi) south of Heraklion.

The palace of Knossos belonged to King Minos, who kept the Minotaur, a hybrid monster of man and bull, in an underground labyrinth.

★ Only the intuition of the great Hermann Schliemann, father of archaeology and discoverer of Troy, would have suspected that the huge mound hemmed in by low hills that once stood here covered one of the most amazing archaeological sites. Troy and Mycenae, Tiryns and Knossos—what a record of sensational finds, yet Turkish obstruction prevented Schliemann from exploring his last discovery. Cretan independence made it possible for Sir Arthur Evans to start excavations in 1899, and a forgotten and sublime civilization came again to light with the uncovering of the great Palace of Knossos. Its site had actually been occupied from Neolithic times, and the population spread to the surrounding land. Around 1900 BC, the hilltop was leveled and the first

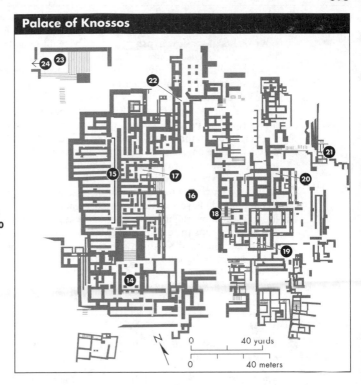

Palace of Knossos

palace constructed; around 1700 BC, after an earthquake destroyed it, the later palace was built, surrounded by houses and other buildings. Around 1450 BC, another widespread disaster occurred, perhaps an invasion: Palaces and country villas were razed by fire and abandoned, and though Knossos remained inhabited, the palace suffered some damage. But around 1380 BC the palace and its outlying buildings were destroyed by fire, and, at the end of the Bronze Age, the site was abandoned. Still later, Knossos became a Greek city-state. Fine houses with mosaic floors and statuary have been excavated. Evidence of the Minoan civilization was unearthed in the early 1900s, when Crete had just achieved independence after centuries of foreign rule by Venice and then by the Ottoman Turks.

You enter the palace from the west, passing a **bust of Sir Arthur Evans,** the British archaeologist who excavated at Knossos on and off for more than 20 years after 1900. Opinions vary about his concrete restorations and copies of the **frescoes.** But without his reconstructions of the wonderfully theatrical great staircase and the throne room, it would be impossible to experience, even at second hand, the ambience of a Minoan palace, with its long pillared halls, narrow corridors, deep stairways and light wells, and curious reverse-tapering columns. But the restorations themselves are in need of renovation; some areas of the palace are now closed off. A path leads you around to the monumental **south gateway;** the **west wing** encases lines of long, narrow storerooms where the true wealth of Knossos was kept in tall clay jars: oil, wine, grains, and honey. The **central court,** about 164 ft by 82 ft, lies before the cool, dark **throne room complex,** with its griffin fresco and tall, wavy-back gypsum throne. It is a spectacular sight to see the oldest throne in Europe, still standing on its original site.

⑱ The most spectacular piece of palace architecture is the **Grand Staircase,** on the east side of the court, leading to the domestic apartments. Four flights of shallow gypsum stairs survive, lit by a deep light well. Here you get a sense of how noble Minoans lived; rooms were divided by sets of double doors, giving privacy and warmth when closed, cool-

⑲ ness and communication when open. The **Queen's Megaron** (apartment) is decorated with copies of the colorful Dolphin fresco and furnished with stone benches. Beside it is a bathroom, complete with a clay tub, and next door a toilet, whose drainage system permitted flushing into a channel flowing into the Kairatos stream far below. The

⑳ east side of the palace also contained **workshops.** Beside the staircase
㉑ leading down to the **east bastion** is a stone water channel made up of parabolic curves and settling basins: a Minoan storm drain. Northwest

㉒ of the east bastion is the **north entrance,** guarded by a relief fresco of
㉓ a charging bull. Beyond is the **theatrical area,** shaded by pines and over-
㉔ looking a shallow flight of steps, which lead down to the **Royal Road.** This was perhaps the ceremonial entrance to the palace. In the end, a visit to the Palace of Knossos, resurrecting past splendor, can be one of the unforgettable experiences for all students of western civilization. ✉ *Site,* ☎ *081/231940.* ✉ *1,500 dr.* ☉ *Summer, daily 8–6; winter, daily 8:30–3. Bus 2 leaves every 15 mins from Odos Evans, close to the market.*

Lasithi Plateau

㉕ *52 km (32¼ mi) southeast of Heraklion, 47 km (29¼ mi) southeast of the Palace of Knossos.*

The Lasithi Plateau, 2,800 ft high and the biggest of the upland plains of Crete, lies behind a wall of barren mountains. Covered with mechanical windmills pumping water for fields of potatoes and the apple and almond orchards that are a pale haze of blossom in early spring, the Lasithi plateau is remote and breathtakingly beautiful. It is ringed by small villages that in winter are sometimes cut off from the outside world by heavy snowfalls. It appears that the villagers spend these long winter months weaving and doing embroidery, and their handicrafts are for sale at shops in almost every village on the plateau.

㉖ The **Cave of Psychro** is an impressive, stalactite-studded cavern that was once a Minoan sanctuary. It's where Zeus, the king of the gods, was supposedly born, and it is well worth a visit. ✉ *Descend slippery path near village of Psychro.* ✉ *800 dr.* ☉ *Daily 8–5.*

Dining and Lodging

$ ✕ **Kronio.** The promise of a meal in this cozy, family-run establishment is alone worth the trip up to the plateau. A delicious array of meat and vegetable pies and homemade casseroles and lamb dishes emerges from the kitchen, and the charming young proprietors, Vassilis and Christine, will encourage you to linger over your wine and raki. ✉ *Lasithi Plateau,* ☎ *0844/22375. No credit cards. Closed Nov.–Mar.*

Mallia

37 km (23 mi) east of Heraklion.

In its effort to serve mass tourism, Mallia has also submerged whatever character it might once have had. Its sandy beach, overlooked by the brooding Lasithi mountains, is backed by a solid line of hotels and vacation apartments. Mallia itself may not be worth a visit, but the Minoan **Palace of Mallia** on its outskirts definitely is. Like Knossos and Phaistos, it was built around 1900 BC, but it was less sophisticated both in architecture and decoration. The layout, however, is similar. Across

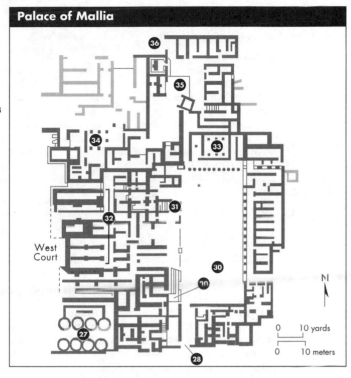

Palace of Mallia

the west court, along one of the paved raised walkways, is a double
㉗ row of **round granaries** sunk into the ground, which were almost cer-
㉘ tainly roofed. East of the granaries is the **south doorway,** from which
㉙ to see the large, circular limestone table, or *kernos* (on which were placed
offerings to a Minoan deity), with a large hollow at its center and 34
㉚ smaller ones around the edge. The **central court** has a shallow pit at
its center, perhaps the location of an altar. To the west of the central
㉛ court are the remains of an imposing **staircase** leading up to a second
floor, and a terrace, most likely used for religious ceremonies; behind
㉜ is a long corridor with **storerooms** to the side. In the north wing is a
㉝ ㉞ large **pillared hall,** part of a set of public rooms. The **domestic apartments** appear to have been in the northwest corner of the palace, entered through a narrow dogleg passage. They are connected by a
㉟ smaller **northern court,** through which you can leave the palace by the
㊱ **north entrance,** passing two giant *pithoi* (storage jars). Much excavation has been done nearby, but only a few of the sites are open. ⊠ *3
km (2 mi) northeast of Mallia,* ☎ *0841/22462.* 🖼 *800 dr.* ☉ *Daily
8:30–3.*

Ayios Nikolaos

★ **㊲** *69 km (43 mi) east of Heraklion, 32 km (20 mi) southeast of Mallia.*

Ayios Nikolaos, built just over a century ago by Cretans from the southwest of the island, is clustered around the **Gulf of Mirabello,** a dramatic
composition of bare mountains, islets, and deep blue sea. Behind the
crowded harbor lies a natural curiosity, tiny Lake Voulismeni, linked
to the sea by a narrow channel. The **archaeological museum** at Ayios
Nikolaos displays some unique finds, such as the *Goddess of Myrtos,*
an Early Minoan rhyton from a site on the southeast coast. The goddess is an appealing figure cradling a large jug in her spindly arms. There

are also fine examples of Late Minoan pottery in the naturalistic marine style, with lively octopus and shell designs. ⊠ *Odos Palaiologou,* ☎ *0841/24943.* 🖼 *800 dr.* ⊘ *Tues.–Sun. 8:30–3.*

Dining

$ ✕ **Itanos Restaurant.** This old-fashioned taverna, with a formal arrangement of palm trees at its center, is patronized by locals, as it offers much better value than the establishments on the seafront. The wine comes from a row of barrels in the kitchen. In summer you dine on a terrace with a view of the town's comings and goings in the square below. The *soutzoukakia* (oven-cooked meatballs) are tender and spicy, and vegetable dishes like braised artichokes or green beans with tomato are full of flavor. ⊠ *Platia Iroon,* ☎ *0841/25340. No credit cards.*

Elounda

38   *80 km (49¾ mi) east of Heraklion, 11 km (7 mi) north of Ayios Nikolaos.*

A narrow corniche road with spectacular sea views runs north from Ayios Nikolaos around the Gulf of Mirabello to Elounda. This is not an area renowned for beaches, which tend to be narrow and pebbly, but the water is crystal clear and sheltered from the *meltemi* (the fierce north wind that blows in summer). Elounda village is becoming a full-scale resort, serving the dozens of villas and apartment hotels dotting the surrounding hillsides. You can escape the crowds in Elounda by
39   following signs for **Olous,** 3 km (2 mi) east of Elounda, an ancient city whose sunken remains are still visible beneath the sea as you cross a causeway to Spinalonga.

Dining and Lodging

$$ ✕ **Marilena.** If the scenery alone doesn't lure you out to the village of Elounda, this delightful family-run restaurant might. In good weather, meals are served in the large rear garden, although you can also choose a table on a sidewalk terrace overlooking the harbor. The Gaitanos brothers serve an excellent selection of fresh grilled fish and a rich fish soup, and any meal should begin with a platter of assorted appetizers. ⊠ *Elounda Village,* ☎ 🖹 *0841/41322. MC, V.*

$$$$ 🏨 **Elounda Beach.** This is one of Greece's most renowned resort ho-
★   tels, set in 40 acres of gardens looking across the Mirabello Gulf. It has inspired imitations on a half dozen other Aegean islands. The architecture reflects Cretan tradition: whitewashed walls, shady porches, and cool flagstone floors. You can have a room in the central block or a bungalow at the edge of the sea; 11 of the suites have their own swimming pool. The hotel has two sandy beaches and a wide range of beach and water sports, including scuba diving. ⊠ *Elounda 72053,* ☎ *0841/41412,* 🖹 *0841/41373. 279 rooms. Pool, sauna, Turkish bath, miniature golf, 2 tennis courts, windsurfing, boating, parasailing, waterskiing, cinema. AE, DC, MC, V. Closed Nov.–Mar.*

$$$$ 🏨 **Elounda Mare.** If you plan to stay in one luxurious hotel in Crete,
★   make it this extraordinary Relais & Château property on the Mirabello Gulf, one of the finest hotels in Greece. More than half of the rooms, all bathed in cool marble and stunningly decorated in traditional but luxurious Greek furnishings, are in villas set in their own gardens with private pools. The service is what you would expect from the best European hotel, yet the atmosphere is relaxed and welcoming. Verdant gardens line the shore above a sandy beach and terraced waterside lounging areas, a stone's throw from the large pool. Menus in three restaurants, all with outdoor dining, range from Greek to Continental cuisine (note that readers' letters have complained about poor food). ⊠ *Elounda 72053,* ☎ *0841/41102 or 0841/41103,* 🖹 *0841/41307. 40*

rooms, 55 bungalows. 3 restaurants, pool, sauna, Turkish bath, 9-hole golf course, 2 tennis courts, windsurfing, boating, waterskiing. AE, DC, MC, V. Closed Nov.–Mar.

$ ⌂ **Akti Olous.** This friendly, unassuming hotel on the edge of the Mirabello Gulf is just a step away from a strip of sandy beach and a short swim from the sunken city of Olous—its remains are easy to spot while snorkeling. The rooftop bar, next to the swimming pool, has a stunning view across the gulf, especially at sunset, and there is a waterside taverna and beach. The rooms, decorated in a handsome, modern neoclassical style, all have balconies overlooking the sea. ⌧ Elounda 72053, ☎ 0841/41270, ℻ 0841/41425. 70 rooms with shower. Bar, pool, beach. No credit cards. Closed Nov.–Mar.

Spinalonga

㊵ 82 km (51 mi) east of Heraklion, 2 km (1 mi) east of Elounda.

Spinalonga, a small, narrow island in the center of the Mirabello Gulf, is a fascinating if somewhat macabre place to visit. The Venetians built a huge, forbidding fortress here in the 17th century, and in the early 1900s the island became a leper colony. To reach it you must take an excursion boat from Ayios Nikolaos. Ask at the harbor, there are two or three trips every day in summer, some including a midday beach barbecue and a swim on a deserted islet. As you cruise past the islet of Ayioi Pantes, look for the *agrimi* (the Cretan wild goat), with its impressive curling horns. The islet is a reserve for about 200 of this protected species.

Kritsa

㊶ 80 km (50 mi) east of Heraklion, 20 km (12½ mi) south of Elounda.

The village of Kritsa, 9 km (5½ mi) west of Ayios Nikolaos, is renowned for its weaving tradition. If you visit only one Byzantine church in Crete, **㊷** it should be the whitewashed **Panayia Kera.** It has an unusual shape, with three naves supported by heavy triangular buttresses. Built in the early years of Venetian occupation, it contains some of the liveliest and best-preserved medieval frescoes on the island, painted in the 13th century. ⌧ On main road just before town, Kritsa. ▨ 200 dr. ☉ Sat.–Thurs. 9–3.

㊸ One of the best views in Crete can be had at **Lato** (⌧ 1 km/½ mi beyond Kritsa's church of Panayia Kera; follow the dirt track), an ancient city built in a dip between two rocky peaks. Make your way over the ancient masonry to the far end of the site: On a clear day, you can see the island of Santorini, about 135 km (84 mi) across the Cretan Sea.

Gournia

㊹ 98½ km (61 mi) southeast of Heraklion, 18½ km (11½ mi) east of Kritsa.

The Minoan site of Gournia was excavated in 1904 by Harriet Boyd Hawes, the first woman archaeologist to work here, along with her team of Cretan workmen and a chaperon. Most of what you see dates from the later Palace period, though Gournia had only a small mansion set among dozens of small houses. Finds indicated that it was a fishing and weaving community, destroyed around 1400 BC and never resettled. ⌧ To right of main highway, on low hillside. ▨ Free. ☉ Mon.–Sat. 8:30–3, Sun. 9:30–2:30.

Ierapetra

45 *113½ (70¼ mi) southeast of Heraklion, about 15 km (9 mi) south of Gournia.*

From Gournia, a road branches to the right and crosses the narrowest part of the island to Ierapetra. The only major town on the south coast, Ierapetra is a flourishing agricultural center, its prosperity based on the plastic-covered greenhouses where early tomatoes and cucumbers are grown and exported all over Europe. The climate in this part of Crete is North African; you are nearer to Libya than to mainland Greece.

Beaches

Tourism is fast developing to the east of Ierapetra, where there are some **46** fine sandy beaches. At the village of **Makriyialos,** 28 km (17 mi) east of Ierapetra, you can take your pick; even in high summer you might have most of a cove to yourself.

Lodging

$$ ☷ **Astron.** Opened in 1992, all rooms at this comfortable hotel have a terrific vantage point, with balconies, of a quiet stretch of the town's waterfront. The beach is just a minute away. The coffee shop looks onto a pleasant interior courtyard with a fountain. ⊠ *Mihail Kothri 56, 72200,* ☎ *0842/25114,* ℻ *0842/25917. 66 rooms. Restaurant, coffee shop, snack bar, air-conditioning, minibars. V.*

Mochlos

47 *50 km (31 mi) east of Ayios Nikolaos, 35 km (21¾ mi) northeast of Ierapetra.*

If you feel like a swim, or a leisurely taverna meal, wind along the north-coast road between the base of the mountains and the sea to the island of Mochlos, separated from shore by a swimmable channel. On the island is a Minoan cemetery excavated early in this century, now being re-excavated by a team of American archaeologists. Mochlos is a good place for lazing in the hottest part of the day; there are several pleasant tavernas on the shore and, if you want to stay longer, rooms to rent.

Siteia

48 *73 km (45 mi) east of Ayios Nikolaos, 23 km (14¼ mi) east of Ierapetra.*

Like Ierapetra, Siteia is an unpretentious town where agriculture is at least as important as tourism: Raisins and, increasingly, bananas are the main crops. Siteia's waterfront, lined with cafés and tavernas, is lively in summer. From Siteia you can take a plane or ferry to Rhodes via the small islands of Kassos and Karpathos. A Venetian fort, the **Kazarma** (⊠ Follow road up from waterfront), overlooks Siteia from a height on the west: It offers a spectacular view across the bay. Siteia's
★ **archaeological museum** contains a unique find: a **Minoan ivory and gold statuette of a young man,** found at Palaikastro on the east coast. The figure dates from around 1500 BC and, though incomplete, is a masterpiece of Minoan carving. ⊠ *Museum: Outskirts of town.* ☷ *800 dr.* ☉ *Tues.–Sun. 9–3.*

49 The fortified monastery of **Toplou** (to the east of Siteia) is set among barren hills where the sparse trees are twisted into strange shapes by the fierce north winds that sweep this region. Only a few monks live here now, though the monastery is slowly being renovated. Inside the tall loggia gate, built in the 16th century, the cells are arranged around a cobbled courtyard with a 14th-century church at its center. It contains a famous icon, composed of 61 scenes, each inspired by a phrase from the Orthodox liturgy. ✉ *12½ km/8 mi east of Siteia on the road for Palaikastro and Zakro.* 🎫 *800 dr.* ⏲ *Daily 9–1 and 2–6.*

Beaches

A long, sandy beach stretches to the east of the waterfront.

Lodging

$ 🏨 **Hotel El Greco.** This friendly establishment on a narrow street several blocks above the waterfront is perfectly comfortable and not without charm. Many of the simple rooms have balconies overlooking the old town and the sea, and the manager, Jankov Marjan, goes out of his way to help guests. ✉ *G. Arkadiou, 72300,* ☎ FAX *0843/23133. 15 rooms with shower. MC, V. Closed Nov.–Apr.*

Vai, Palaikastro, and Kato Zakro Beaches

Vai is 170 km (105½ mi) east of Heraklion, 27 km (16¾ mi) east of Siteia.

★ (50) The palm grove of the renowned beach at **Vai** (✉ 7½ km/4½ mi northeast of Toplou) existed in classical Greek times; it is unique in Europe. The sandy beach with nearby islets set in clear turquoise water is one of the most attractive in Crete, but in summer it is very crowded.

(51) Follow a dirt track through olive groves to the sandy beach at **Palaikastro** (✉ 9 km/5½ mi south of Vai; follow sign for Marina Village). It is rarely crowded, and service is friendly at the waterside tavernas. The sprawling Minoan town, currently being excavated by British and American archaeologists, lies off to the right.

At Ano Zakro, 20 km (12 mi) south of Palaikastro village, a path leads down through a deep ravine past caves used for early Minoan burials ★ (52) to the Minoan palace site at **Kato Zakro** (✉ Ask at one of the cafés for directions to the start of the path). The walk down takes about one hour. You can also drive 9 km (5½ mi) down to the site by a circuitous but spectacular route. The village of Kato Zakro, on a fine beach, is a cluster of tavernas with a few rooms to rent. Kato Zakro's **Minoan palace,** smaller than those of Knossos, Phaistos, and Mallia, is surrounded by a terraced town with narrow cobbled streets, like Gournia. ✉ *Ascend paved Minoan Rd. from harbor, through once-covered gateway, reaching northeast court down stepped ramp,* ☎ *0841/22462.* 🎫 *500 dr.* ⏲ *Tues.–Sun. 8–3.*

WESTERN CRETE

Western Crete, with soaring mountains, deep gorges, and rolling green lowlands planted with olives and oranges, is much less affected by the growth of mass tourism than is the rest of the island. There are a wealth of interesting byways to be explored. This region is rich in Minoan sites, Byzantine churches, Venetian monasteries, and friendly upland villages. There are some outstanding beaches on the west and south coasts. South and west of Heraklion lies the traditional agricultural heartland of Crete: long, narrow valleys where olive groves alternate with vineyards growing sultana grapes for export. The outstanding site remains Phaistos, the great Minoan palace.

Western Crete

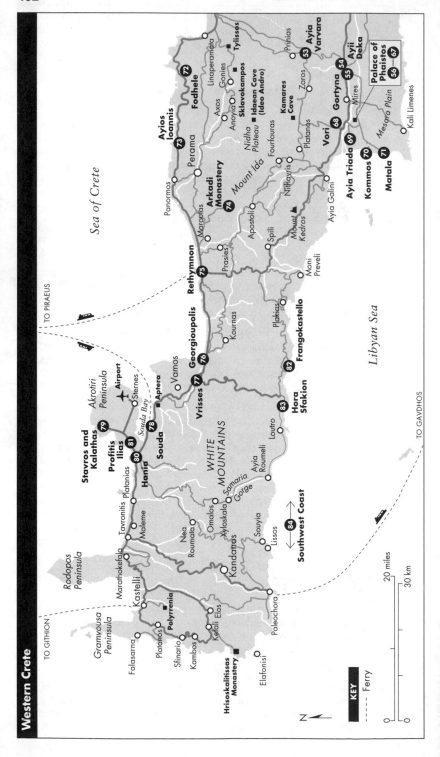

Sea of Crete

Libyan Sea

TO PIRAEUS

TO GITHION

TO GAVDHOS

Fodhele 72
Ayios Ioannis 73
Linoperamáta
Tylissos
Gonies
Axos
Anoyia
Sklavokampos
Idaean Cave (Ideo Andro)
Nidha Plateau
Fourfouras
Kamares Cave
Platanos
Zaros
Prinias
Ayia Varvara 53
Ayii Deka 54
Gortyna 55
Palace of Phaistos 56 — 67
Vori 68
Ayia Triada 69
Kommos 70
Matala 71
Mires
Mesara Plain
Kali Limenes

Perama
Panormos
Margarites
Prasies
Arkadi Monastery 74
Mount Ida
Apostoli
Spili
Mount Kedros
Ayia Galini
Nithavris
Moni Preveli
Rethymnon 75

Kournas
Georgioupolis 76
Plakias
Frangokastello 82
Vrisses 77
Vamos
Sternes
Airport
Aptera
Souda 78
Souda Bay
Stavros and Kalathas 79
Profitis Ilias 80
Hania 81
Akrotiri Peninsula
Hora Sfakion 83
Loutro
Ayia Roumeli
Samaria Gorge
Xyloskala
Omalos
WHITE MOUNTAINS
Souyia
Lissos
Southwest Coast 84
Platanias
Tavronitis
Maleme
Nea Roumata
Kandanos
Marathokefala
Kastelli
Polyrrenia
Platanos
Sfinario
Kefali Elos
Kambos
Hrisoskalitissas Monastery
Elafonisi
Paleochora
Falasarna
Gramvousa Peninsula
Rodopos Peninsula

N

KEY
--- Ferry

0   20 miles
0   30 km

Mesara Plain and Gortyna

Gortyna is 45 km (28 mi) south of Heraklion.

After climbing through a vine- and olive-clad valley, the narrow road south from Heraklion to Gortyna swings toward the Mesara plain. The plain, filled with silver-gray olives interspersed with plastic greenhouses for growing early tomatoes and cucumbers, rises again to the craggy **Asterousia Mountains**; beyond them is the Libyan Sea. In summer especially, the temperature rises sharply as you descend. The village of **Ayia Varvara,** with the whitewashed church of Profitis Ilias built high on a rock, said to mark the center of Crete, lies some 32½ km (20½ mi) south of Heraklion.

The village of **Ayii Deka** (14 km/8 mi south of Ayia Varvara) is home to the church of **Ayios Titos** (⊠ Follow signs from road), an early 6th-century Christian basilica, reputedly St. Titos's burial place.

Ayios Titos is at the entrance to the Greco-Roman city of **Gortyna,** a huge expanse of scattered ruins sliced through by the main road. At Gortyna, which was made a capital by the Romans in AD 67, sights include the **Odeion,** a small amphitheater where musical recitals were staged in the 1st century AD. In the brick building behind it the **Gortyna Law Code** is displayed. Inscribed on a set of stone blocks, this is Europe's earliest code, dating from the first half of the 5th century BC. In 600 lines it details the laws concerning marriage, divorce, inheritance, adoption, assault and rape, and the status of slaves. From the ruins of Gortyna, a path climbs a few hundred feet uphill to the **acropolis of Gortyna** (⊠ Above Gortyna), which has a fine view across the plain. Italian archaeologists, who have dug here since the 1880s, recently completed a detailed topographical survey. A plan is posted at several points around the site, enabling you to find your way through the olives to **several temples, a small theater,** and the **public baths.** Although it was destroyed by Arab raiders in the 7th century and never rebuilt, Gortyna did provide most of the building material for the town of Ayii Deka. Fragments of ancient sculpture and inscriptions can still be seen in the 13th-century village **church.**

Phaistos

★ *50 km (31 mi) south of Heraklion, 18 km (11 mi) west of Gortyna.*

Enjoying an incomparably more splendid setting than that of Knossos, Phaistos is the site of one of the greatest Minoan palaces. Today, the traveler heads to Mires, a flourishing market town, which lies some 5 km (3 mi) west of Gortyna. From here, a road crosses the Geropotamos River and climbs a hill to the Minoan **palace of Phaistos.** Like Knossos and Mallia, it was built around 1900 BC and rebuilt after a disastrous earthquake around 1650 BC. It was burned and abandoned in the wave of destruction that swept across the island around 1450 BC. You enter down a flight of steps leading into the **west court,** and climb a **grand staircase.** From here you pass through the **Propylon porch** into a light well and descend a **narrow staircase** into the **central court.** Much of the southern and eastern sections of the palace have eroded away. But there are large pithoi still in place in the old **storerooms.** On the north side of the court the recesses of an **elaborate doorway** bear a rare survival: red paint in a diamond pattern on a white ground. A passage from the doorway leads to the **north court** and the **northern domestic apartments,** now roofed and fenced off. The **Phaistos Disk** was found in 1903 in a chest made of mud brick at the northeast edge of the site. East of the central court are the **palace workshops,** with a metalworking furnace fenced off in the east court. South of the workshops lies a set of **southern domestic apartments,** in-

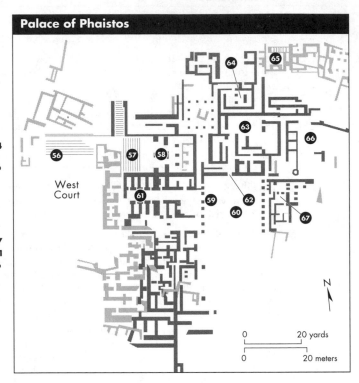

Palace of Phaistos

cluding a clay bath. They have a memorable view across the Mesara plain. ⊠ *From Gortyna, cross Geropotamos River and ascend hill,* ☎ *0892/22615.* ☞ *1,200 dr.* ☉ *Daily 8–7.*

Vori

68 *65 km (40½ mi) southwest of Heraklion, 5 km (3 mi) north of the palace of Phaistos.*

69 The site of **Ayia Triada** dates from the later Palace period and was destroyed at the same time as Phaistos. It was once believed to have been a summer palace for the rulers of Phaistos but now is thought to have been a group of villas and warehouse areas. There's another magnificent view toward the Paximadia islets in the Mesara Gulf. Rooms in the L-shape complex of buildings were paneled with gypsum slabs and decorated with frescoes: Two now in the Heraklion Museum show a woman in a garden and a cat hunting a pheasant. A road from the upper courtyard leads to the sea. ⊠ *Follow signs from main road,* ☎ *0892/91360.* ☞ *500 dr.* ☉ *Daily 8:30–3.*

Beaches

70 One of the best and least crowded beaches on the south coast lies just below the recently excavated Minoan harbor site of **Kommos** (⊠ 3 km/2 mi south of main road from Mires to Matala, near village of Pitsidia).

Matala

71 *70 km (42 mi) southwest of Heraklion, 10 km (6 mi) south of Vori.*

Renowned in the 1960s as a stopover on the hippie trail across the eastern Mediterranean, Matala is today a pleasant, low-key beach resort. The 2nd-century AD Roman tombs cut in the cliff side (where the hippies lived) are now fenced off but continue to attract day-trippers on coach tours from Heraklion, for whom Matala is a stop on the Phaistos–Ayia Triada circuit. Once the crowds leave (usually by the early afternoon), the town beach is delightful, and there is another excellent strand, the so-called Red Beach, accessible only by a 20-minute walk across a rocky promontory.

Tylissos

24 km (15 mi) southwest of Heraklion, 65 km (40½ mi) from Phaistos.

The road to the Minoan site at Tylissos, via the Heraklion–Rethymnon road turning at the town of Gazi, just west of Heraklion, winds uphill through vineyards. The pine-shaded complex reveals three later **Palace-period buildings**: workshops, living quarters, and storerooms. ⊠ *To left of road at the 14-km (9-mi) mark.* ☜ *800 dr.* ☉ *Daily 8:30–3.*

Fodhele

72 *12 km (7½ mi) west of Heraklion, 10 km (6 mi) northwest of Tylissos.*

The straggling village of Fodhele is said to be the birthplace of Domenico Theotokopoulos, the 16th-century Cretan painter known as El Greco.

73 The monastery of **Ayios Ioannis** (⊠ 23 km/14 mi west of Fodhele) is dedicated to John the Baptist. It is just above the highway, with a spectacular view from its terrace across the Cretan Sea. Inside is an historic small chapel, but there is rarely anyone around to let you in.

Arkadi Monastery

★ **74** *30 km (18½ mi) west of Heraklion, 18 km (11½ mi) from Fodhele.*

Running parallel to the coast highway, the old Heraklion–Hania road follows a gorge inland before emerging into the flat pastureland that is part of the holdings of the Arkadi Monastery. The monastery is a place of pilgrimage for Cretans and one of the most stunning pieces of Renaissance architecture on the island. Built in the 16th century, of honey-color local stone, it has an ornate facade decorated with Corinthian columns and an elegant belfry above. In 1866, the monastery was besieged during a major rebellion against the Turks, and Abbot Gabriel and several hundred rebels, together with their wives and children, refused to surrender. When the Turkish forces broke through the gate, the defenders set the gunpowder store afire, killing themselves together with hundreds of Turks. ⊠ *Just south of town of Perama.* ☜ *300 dr.* ☉ *Daily 8–5.*

Rethymnon

75 *78 km (48½ mi) west of Heraklion, 54 km (33½ mi) west of Arkadi Monastery.*

Rethymnon is Crete's third-largest town, after Heraklion and Hania. As the population (about 30,000) steadily increases, villagers move into new houses on the outskirts of town. The old Venetian quarter is being restored, and the port has been expanded, allowing Rethymnon to have its own ferry service to and from Piraeus. Unfortunately, a long strip of beach to the east of the old town has been tastelessly developed with large hotels and other resort facilities catering to tourists on package vacations, diminishing much of the charm that Rethymnon once had.

Thankfully, much of Rethymnon's remaining charm perseveres in the **old section** (⊠ Town center). Wandering through the narrow alleyways, you come across handsome carved-stone Renaissance doorways belonging to vanished mansions, fountains, archways, and wooden Turkish houses. One of the few surviving minarets in Greece is in the

Neratzes mosque (⊠ Old town), now a concert hall, and you can climb its 120 steps for a panoramic view. Don't miss the carefully restored **Venetian loggia** (⊠ Near center of town on Arkadiou St.), the clubhouse of the local Rethymnon nobility. Rethymnon's small **Venetian harbor,** with its restored 13th-century lighthouse, comes to life in summer, with restaurant tables cluttering the quayside.

Rethymnon is dominated by the huge Venetian castle known as the **Fortessa.** High, well-preserved walls enclose a large empty space occupied by a few scattered buildings and filled with wildflowers in spring. Forced labor from the town and surrounding villages built the fortress from 1573 to 1583, but it never fulfilled its purpose of keeping out the Turks: Rethymnon surrendered after a three-week siege. ⊠ *At village's western end.* ⊙ *Daily 8–8.*

The **archaeological museum** is in what used to be Rethymnon's Turkish prison. Look for the collection of beautifully made bone tools from a Neolithic site at Yerani, west of Rethymnon. An unfinished statue of Aphrodite, the goddess of love, is interesting: The ancient chisel marks show clearly. ⊠ *Western end, next to entrance of Fortessa,* ☎ *0831/ 29975.* ▨ *800 dr.* ⊙ *Tues.–Sun. 8:30–3.*

One of the town's most delightful attractions is the new **Historical and Folk Art Museum,** housed in a restored Venetian palazzo near the mosque. Rustic furnishings, tools and costumes provide a charming and vivid picture of what life on Crete was like until well into this century. ⊠ *Vernadou 28,* ☎ *0831/29975.* ▨ *400 dr.* ⊙ *Daily 9–1.*

Dining and Lodging

$$ ✗ **Cavo D'Oro.** This is the most stylish of the handful of fish restau-
★   rants around the tiny Venetian harbor, and one of the finest restaurants in Crete. Lobster and a wide range of innovative fresh fish dishes are always served. The high, wood-paneled dining room was once a medieval storeroom, and diners also sit on the old cobbled waterfront. ⊠ *Nearchou 42–43,* ☎ *0831/24446. DC, MC, V.*

$ ✗ **Castelvecchio George.** Just down from the Venetian Fortessa, this pleasant taverna just above the narrow streets of the old town catches a refreshing evening breeze in summer. George's specialties, among the traditional Greek and international dishes, are pepper steak and *stifado* (a rich stew made with lamb and sometimes with hare). George has also recently added four simple guest rooms to his establishment. ⊠ *Heimaras 29,* ☎ *0831/55163. No credit cards.*

$$$ ▥ **Hotel Fortessa.** This newer hotel has many of the advantages of the
★   larger hotels that have sprung up farther out of town on Rethymnon's charmless beach strip, yet it is only steps from the Fortessa, the old town, and the beach. The tile-floored rooms, with handsome traditional furnishings, are built around a marble atrium and sunny courtyard; many have balconies. The nicest rooms face the street, which is closed to vehicular traffic during tourist season, and the fortress. ⊠ *Melisinou 16, 74100,* ☎ *0831/23828 or 0831/55552,* ℻ *0831/54073. 54 rooms. Restaurant, snack bar, air-conditioning, pool, free parking. AE, DC, MC, V.*

$$$ ▥ **Palazzo Rimondi.** This all-suite hotel was formed from combining
★   several 15th-century houses in the heart of the old quarter. All of the tasteful, stylish rooms have sitting and sleeping areas and kitchenettes; many retain such architectural details as vaulted or paneled ceilings, fireplaces, and latticed Venetian windows. A courtyard with a tiny swimming pool offers a nice retreat from the tourist clamor. ⊠ *Xanthoudidou 21, 74100,* ☎ *0831/51289,* ℻ *0831/51013. 21 rooms. Bar, air-conditioning, pool. AE, DC, MC, V.*

$ ▦ **Liberty.** This quiet, friendly, family-owned hotel opposite a park has a roof garden with an attractive view up to the hills overlooking the town. The rooms are small but comfortable. ✉ *Themis Moatsou 8, 74100,* ☎ *0831/55851, 0831/55852, and 0831/55853,* ℻ *0831/ 55850. 24 rooms with shower. DC, MC, V.*

Outdoor Activities and Sports

BICYCLING

For bicycle rentals in Rethymnon, ask at the **Grecotel Rithymna Beach** hotel (✉ Rethymnon 74100, ☎ 0831/71002 or 0831/29491).

TREKKING

The **Happy Walker** (✉ Tombazi 56, Rethymnon 74100, ☎ 0831/ 52920) arranges walking tours in the surrounding mountains.

Shopping

BOOKS AND NEWSPAPERS

Several souvenir stores on the waterfront sell English-language books and newspapers, as does the **International Press Bookshop** (✉ Venizelou 26, Rethymnon).

Georgioupolis

76 *99½ km (61½ mi) west of Heraklion, 21½ km (13½ mi) west of Rethymnon.*

Georgioupolis was named for Prince George of Greece, the high commissioner of Crete from 1898 to 1906. Here, at the mouth of the Vrysanos River, where migrating birds gather, he built a shooting lodge, which is closed to the public. There are several good fish tavernas and many rooms to rent.

Vrisses

77 *30 km (18½ mi) west of Rethymnon, 5 km (3 mi) west of Georgioupolis.*

Vrisses is famous throughout Crete for its thick, creamy yogurt. Served in the cafés beneath the plane trees as you come into the village, it's best eaten with a large spoonful of honey on top.

Souda Bay and the Akrotiri Peninsula

71½ km (45 mi) west of Rethymnon, 20 km (12½ mi) northwest of Vrisses.

The road from Vrisses to Hania climbs across the Vamos peninsula and approaches Souda Bay. This deep inlet, considered the best harbor in the eastern Mediterranean, can shelter the entire U.S. Sixth Fleet. Taking photos is forbidden around Souda Bay, a regulation to be taken seriously: If you are caught doing so you may be charged with spying. At the top of **78** Souda bay is **Souda port,** where passenger ferries arrive from Piraeus dock.

Beaches

79 There are good beaches at **Stavros** and **Kalathas** on the Akrotiri peninsula.

Hania

80 *78 km (48½ mi) west of Rethymnon, 6½ km (4 mi) west of Souda.*

As you approach Hania—one of the most attractive towns in Greece— a long avenue lined with eucalyptus trees takes you to the outskirts, where signs lead you around the one-way system to the large, cross-shape covered market in the town center. Highlights include its well-
★ preserved **Venetian quarter** and harbor. It was here that the Greek flag

was raised in 1913 to mark unification with Greece, and until 1971 Hania was the island's capital.

On Sundays, Hania's time-honored flag-raising ceremony is repeated at the **Firka,** the old Turkish prison, now the naval museum. ⊠ *Waterfront, at far west end of port.* 🖾 *400 dr.* ☉ *June–Sept., Tues.–Sun. 10–2 and 5–7; Oct.–May, Tues.–Sun., 10–2 and 4–6.*

From Hania's market, work your way through a maze of narrow streets to the **waterfront,** which is a pedestrian zone in summer. Walk around Hania's **inner harbor,** where the fishing boats moor, and east past the **Venetian arsenals.** If you head around to the **old lighthouse,** you'll get a magnificent view of the town with the imposing White Mountains looming beyond. The **Janissaries mosque** (⊠ East side of harbor), now an information center, was built when the Turks captured the town in 1645 after a two-month siege. The **Kastelli hill** (⊠ Above harbor), where the Venetians first settled, remained the quarter of the local nobility, but it had been occupied much earlier; parts of what may be a Minoan palace have been excavated at its base. Both **Theotocopoulou and Zambeliou streets** (⊠ Behind outer harbor) lead you into the narrow alleyways with predominantly **Venetian and Turkish houses.** Look for an old **synagogue** (⊠ In Parodos Kondylaki, behind outer harbor), formerly the Venetian Church of St. Catherine and now a warehouse. The **archaeological museum** occupies the Venetian church of St. Francis. Finds on display come from all over western Crete: The painted Minoan clay coffins and elegant Late Minoan pottery indicate that the region was as wealthy as the center of the island in the Bronze Age, though no palace has yet been located. ⊠ *Venetian Church of St. Francis, Chalidron St.,* ☎ *0821/20334.* 🖾 *800 dr.* ☉ *Tues.–Fri. 8:30–3.*

⑧① **Profitis Ilias** (⊠ 4½ km/3 mi east of Hania in the Halepa suburb), the burial place of Eleftheriou Venizelou, Crete's great statesman, is lined with fine neoclassical mansions dating to the turn of the century, when Britain, France, Russia, and Italy were active in Cretan politics. A panoramic view from here takes in Hania and its surrounding villages, along with much of the northwest coast.

Dining and Lodging

An almost unbroken row of **tavernas** lines Hania's old harbor in summer. Their menus are nearly identical and almost all offer grills and fresh fish at reasonable prices. Among those frequented by Haniots are **Apostolis** (⊠ Inner harbor) and **Karnagio** (⊠ Outer harbor), with tasty Cretan specialties.

$$ ✕ **Well of the Turk.** Part of the adventure is finding this restaurant on a narrow alley near the minaret in the old Arab quarter, just behind the Venetian warehouses on the harbor; you will have to ask your way, but just about everyone in the neighborhood knows this place. The food ranges from simple Greek fare—a prerequisite is the wonderful appetizer platter, a meal in itself—to some Continental dishes, such as sautéed chicken in a wine sauce. ⊠ *Kalinikou Sarpaki 1–3 Splantiza,* ☎ *0821/54547. No credit cards.*

$$$$ 🏨 **Casa Delfino.** This small hotel, set in the heart of the old town, oc-
   ★   cupies a Venetian Renaissance palace. In the 1880s, it was home to Pedro Delfino, an Italian merchant, and now it belongs to two of his descendants. The cool pastel rooms, four of which are housed in an adjoining building of the same era, are located behind graceful stone archways surrounding a courtyard paved in pebble mosaic; most have stylish modern furniture and are on two levels. The view takes in the medieval harbor and the old town, but you are protected by thick stone walls from the noise of nearby bars and tavernas. ⊠ *Theofanous 9,*

Palio Limani, 73100, ☎ *0821/93098 or 0821/87400,* FAX *0821/96500. 16 rooms with bath. Minibars. AE, DC, MC, V.*

$$$ ⊞ **Doma.** This enchanting hotel occupies a converted 19th-century man-
★   sion facing the sea, on the outskirts of town, and feels like a private
house. As it turns out, it was once the Austrian consulate and later the
British vice-consulate, then the childhood home of proprietor Rena Va-
lyraki. Traditional Cretan-style furnishings grace the salons and guest
rooms. Bedrooms overlook the garden or the sea and are extremely
attractive with their simple, elegant Cretan-style furnishings; the rooftop
suites are especially charming, set in enormous terraces. The Doma is
one of the best places in town to dine; one of the owners prepares a
traditional dinner each evening, which nonguests also enjoy. Breakfast
features breads to be slathered with homemade jams, and yogurt comes
with a Turkish topping: a delicious mix of spices, quince preserves, and
honey. ⊠ *124 Eleftheriou Venizelou St., 73100,* ☎ *0821/51772 or 0821/
51773,* FAX *0821/41578. 22 rooms with shower, 3 suites. Restaurant.
DC, MC, V. Closed Nov.–Mar.*

$ ⊞ **Porto del Colombo.** Occupying a renovated Venetian house, this pleas-
ant hotel is full of architectural surprises: wooden ceilings, small deep-
set windows, two-floor rooms with loft areas. Furnishings are traditional
and comfortable. Weather permitting, breakfast is served on the nar-
row street out front. ⊠ *Old town, Theofanous and Moshon Sts.,
73100,* ☎ FAX *0821/70945. 10 rooms with shower. MC, V.*

Outdoor Activities and Sports

BICYCLING

You may arrange bike rentals through the **G & A Travel Agency** (⊠
Halidon 25, ☎ 0821/24965).

HIKING

Alpin Travel (⊠ Bonaili 11) offers many hiking tours throughout west-
ern Crete. The **Greek Federation of Mountaineering Associations** op-
erates refuges in the White Mountains (☎ 0821/24647) and on Mt.
Ida (☎ 081/267110). For more details on trekking from Hania, ask
at the EOT office (☞ Visitor Information *in* Crete A to Z, *below*).

Shopping

ANTIQUE BLANKETS AND RUGS

Exceptional finds may be had at **Top Hanas** (⊠ Odos Anghelou, No.
3), which sells a fine selection of antique blankets and rugs, most of
them made for dowries from homespun wool and natural dyes.

BOOKS AND NEWSPAPERS

One or two souvenir stores on the waterfront sell English-language books
and newspapers.

GOURMET GOODS

Take a stroll through Hania's **covered market** (⊠ Town center), where
local merchants sell rounds of Cretan cheese, jars of golden honey, lengths
of salami, salt fish, lentils, and other pulse from sacks.

JEWELERS AND CRAFTS

The silver jewelry and ceramics are especially striking at **Carmela** (⊠
Odos Anghelou, No. 7), which represents contemporary jewelers and
other craftspeople from Crete and throughout Greece.

En Route   To venture to the southern coast of Crete, backtrack east to Vrisses to
the turnoff for a spectacular drive traversing the Askyphou plain,
watched over by an Ottoman fort perched on a knob-shape hill, and
then descending to the Libyan Sea along the **Nimbros gorge.**

Hora Sfakion

62 km (38½ mi) southwest of Rethymnon, 36 km (22½ mi) south of Vrisses.

㉒ **Frangokastello,** 10 km (6 mi) east of Hora Skafion, is a medieval
㉓ Venetian fort (with rooms to rent), overlooking a fine sandy beach. **Hora
Sfakion** is the landing point for the boat trip from the mouth of the
Samaria Gorge, farther west. The gorge gets crowded with buses and
walkers in the early evening but is otherwise a tranquil place where
you can find a taverna.

㉔ In summer, a boat service operates along the **southwest coast** from Hora
Sfakion to Loutro, Ayia Roumeli, Souyia, Lissos, and Paleochora, the
main resort on the southwest coast. You can easily rent a room for the
night in these towns.

CRETE A TO Z

Arriving and Departing

By Boat
Heraklion and Souda Bay (5 km/3 mi east of Hania) are the island's
main ports. Two **Cretan shipping companies,** Anek (✉ 25th of August St. 33, Heraklion, ☎ 081/222481) and **Minoan Lines** (✉ 25th
of August St. 78, Heraklion, ☎ 081/7512356), have daily ferry service to both ports from Piraeus year-round. **Cretan Ferries-Rethym-
niaki** (✉ Arkadiou 250, Rethymnon, ☎ 0831/21518) has service
from Piraeus to Rethymnon three or four times a week. The overnight
crossing takes 10–12 hours. You can book a berth in a first-, second-
, or tourist-class cabin or an aircraft-style seat. Make reservations for
summer crossings through a travel agent several days in advance. At
other times of the year, you can buy a ticket from a dockside agency
in Piraeus an hour before the ship sails. Before buying, make sure your
cabin is air-conditioned. There are cafeterias in second and tourist classes
and a dining room in first class. All ferries take cars: A discount may
be available if you buy a round-trip ticket for the car. In summer, you
should make your return-trip reservation several days in advance at
the shipping company: Both Anek and Minoan Lines have offices in
all the main towns on the island. A one-way first-class fare (with accommodation) costs about 11,000 dr., second-class about 8,000 dr.,
and tourist class 6,000 dr., with little or no discount for round-trips.
Car fares are 16,000 dr. to 20,500 dr., one-way, depending on size.
Other **ferry services** change from year to year, but there are weekly
trips in summer from Piraeus to Siteia and to Kastelli Kissamou. A
small ferry links Siteia with the Dodecanese islands of Kassos,
Karpathos, and Rhodes, and both ferries and catamarans operate in
summer between Santorini and Heraklion. There is also a weekly sail
from Heraklion to Limassol in Cyprus, and to Haifa, Israel. Ferries
sometimes sail to Kusadasi, Turkey, and Alexandria, Egypt. Travel agents
can advise you on schedules.

By Plane
The principal arrival point on Crete is **Heraklion airport** (✉ Center of
island, 5 km/3 mi east of city, ☎ 081/2245644), where up to six flights
daily arrive from Athens, four flights arrive weekly from Rhodes, three
weekly from Thessaloniki, and two weekly from Mykonos. Heraklion
is also serviced directly by flights, many of them charters, from other
European cities. There are several daily flights from Athens to **Hania
airport** (✉ Western Crete, 15 km/10 mi east of town, ☎ 0821/58005).
There are flights two or three times weekly to **Siteia airport** (✉ East-

ern Crete, 2 km/1 mi west of the town, ☎ 0843/22270). Twice-weekly flights from Rhodes via Karpathos also land in Siteia.

A municipal **bus** outside Heraklion airport will take you to Platia Eleftherias (⊠ Town center), known locally as Treis Kamares. Tickets are sold from a kiosk next to the bus stop; the fare is 200 dr. From Hania and Siteia airports, Olympic Airways buses take you to the airline office in the town center. The fare is 400 dr. from Hania airport and 150 dr. from Siteia airport. **Cabs** are lined up outside Heraklion and Hania airports; the fare into town is 1,500 dr. from Heraklion and 1,800 dr. from Hania. Taxis usually turn up to meet flights into Siteia airport, but if there are none to be seen, ask the information desk to call one from town. The fare will be approximately 800 dr.

Getting Around

By Boat

To reach the island of **Spinalonga,** you must take an excursion boat from Ayios Nikolaos. Ask at the harbor; there are two or three trips every day in summer, some including a midday beach barbecue and a swim on a deserted islet.

In summer, a boat service around the **Samaria Gorge** operates along the southwest coast from Hora Sfakion to Loutro, Ayia Roumeli, Souyia, Lissos, and Paleochora, the main resort on the southwest coast.

For the boat timetable from **Paleochora to Ghavdos,** check with any travel agency in Paleochora or Sfakia, or try the **Paleochora Harbor Authority** (☎ 0823/41214) or **Sfakia Harbor Authority** (☎ 0825/91292).

By Bus

The **public bus companies (KTEL)** have regular, inexpensive service among the main towns. You can book seats in advance at whichever bus station is the terminus for the district of the island you're going to. The efficient village bus network operates similarly, from the bus station in each *komopolis,* or market town. In **Heraklion,** the bus station for western Crete (☎ 081/221765) is opposite the Historical Museum; the station for the south (☎ 081/283287) is just outside the Hania Gate to the right; and for the east (☎ 081/282637), the station is just east of the traffic circle at the end of Leoforos D. Bofor, close to the old harbor.

By Car

Roads on Crete are not congested but, apart from the north coast highway, tend to be winding and narrow. Most are now asphalt, but dirt tracks between villages are still found in mountainous regions. Most road signs are in Greek and English. Gas stations are not plentiful outside the big towns, and road maps are not always reliable, especially in the south. Driving in the main towns can be nerve-racking, especially during the lunchtime rush hour. Drive defensively wherever you are, as Cretan drivers are aggressive and liable to ignore the rules of the road. In summer, tourists on motor scooters can be a hazard. Sheep and goats frequently stray onto the roads, with or without their shepherd or sheepdog. Night driving is not advisable.

With Children

There is practically no provision made on Crete for the specific amusement of children, but people take them everywhere, and Cretans will welcome yours. Just remember that there is a limit to most children's tolerance for ruins, which can be greatly extended by frequent administrations of ice cream and cold drinks, and many dunks in the sea, a pleasure in itself.

Contacts and Resources

Bicycling
Hania: **G & A Travel** (✉ Halidon 25, ☎ 0821/24965). Heraklion: **Creta Tours** (✉ Epimenidou 20–22, ☎ 081/227002). Rethymnon: **Grecotel Rithymna Beach hotel** (✉ Rethymnon 74100, ☎ 0831/71002 or 0831/29491).

Bird-Watching
For Gouves estuary, contact the Grecotel group, which runs the **Creta Sun Hotel** (☎ 0831/71602).

Boating
Local travel agencies, large resort hotels, municipal information offices, or the **Greek National Tourist Organization (GNTO or EOT)** (☞ *below*) can help with information and arrangements for renting Windsurfers, dinghies, yachts.

Car Rentals
You can rent cars, Jeeps, and motorbikes in all the island's towns, or you can arrange beforehand with a major agency in the United States or in Athens to pick up a car on arrival in Crete. **Avis** (☎ 081/225421) and **Hertz** (☎ 081/229702) have offices at Heraklion airport as well as in the city. Other reliable companies, like **Hellascars** (☎ 081/223240), and many local agencies have cheaper rates; many agencies renting cars and motorbikes are located on 25th of August Street. A medium-size, four-door car costs about 15,000 dr.–30,000 dr. a day with 100 km (63 mi) of free mileage (extra mileage costs about 50 dr. per 1 km/½ mi), including insurance and taxes. Weekly prices are negotiable, but with unlimited mileage they start at about 60,000 dr.

Emergencies
Your hotel will call an **English-speaking doctor. Pharmacies** stay open late by turns, and a list of those open late is displayed in their windows.

Police: Ayios Nikolaos (☎ 0841/22251); Hania (☎ 0821/73333); Heraklion (☎ 081/28224); Ierapetra (☎ 0842/24200); Rethymnon (☎ 0831/22289); Siteia (☎ 0843/24200).

Hospitals: Aigos Nikolas (☎ 0841/25221); Hania (☎ 0821/27231); Heraklion (☎ 081/269463); Rethymnon (☎ 0831/27491).

Guided Tours
Resort hotels and large travel agents organize guided tours by air-conditioned bus to the main Minoan sites; excursions to spectacular beaches like Vai in the northeast and Elafonisi in the southwest; and trips to Santorini and to some islands like Gaidouronisi, south of Ierapetra, and Spinalonga, a former leper colony off Ayios Nikolaos.

Heraklion: Creta Travel (✉ Epimenidou 20–22, ☎ 081/227002).

Hania: Canea Travel (✉ Tzanakaki 28, ☎ 0821/28817); El Greco Tours (✉ Theotocopoulou 63, ☎ 0821/21829); G& A Travel (✉ Halidon 25, ☎ 0821/24965) organize hikes through the Samaria Gorge and other local excursions. For example: A tour of the Heraklion Museum and Knossos costs 4,500 dr.; a tour of Phaistos and Gortyna plus a swim at Matala costs 6,000 dr.; a trip to Omalos and the Samaria Gorge, returning to Sfakia by boat, costs about 9,000 dr. Travel agents can arrange for personal guides, whose fees are negotiable.

Hiking
The **Greek Federation of Mountaineering Associations** operates refuges in the White Mountains (☎ 0821/24647) and on Mt. Ida (☎ 081/289440). For details on trekking from Hania, ask at the EOT (☞ *below*).

Post Offices and Telephones
Post offices are open weekdays 8–8. You can sometimes buy stamps at a kiosk. **Hania** (⊠ Tzanakaki 3). **Heraklion** (⊠ Platia Daskaloyianni). **Rethymnon** post office and OTE (⊠ Koundourioti).

You can often make metered calls overseas from kiosks and kafenions, even in small villages. To avoid heavy surcharges imposed by hotels on long-distance calls, you can make them from offices of the Greek phone company, known as **OTE.** OTE office **Hania** (⊠ Tzanakaki 5); **Heraklion** (⊠ El Greco Park); **Rethymnon** post office and OTE (⊠ Koundourioti).

Visitor Information
The **Greek National Tourist Organization (GNTO or EOT):** Heraklion (⊠ Xanthoudıdou 1, ☎ 081/228225) and Hania (⊠ Odos Kriari 40, ☎ 0821/92943) are open 8 AM–2 and 3–8:30.

12 Rhodes and the Dodecanese

Kos, Patmos, and Symi

The Dodecanese (Twelve Islands), wrapped enticingly around the shores of Turkey and Asia Minor, are the easternmost holdings of Greece. Romans, Crusaders, Turks, and Venetians left their mark through a remarkable array of temples, castles, and fortresses in exotic towns of shady lanes and tall houses. In addition, what is likely to capture the visitor is the varied landscape—from the cypress-clad hillsides of Patmos to the craggy shoreline of Symi and lush fields of Kos—and the possibility of finding a way of life that, despite invasions of armies and sunseekers, remains essentially and delightfully Greek.

LYING AT THE EASTERN EDGE OF THE AEGEAN sea bordering the west coast of Asia Minor is the southernmost group of Greek Islands, the Dodecanese, sometimes known as the Southern Sporades. Of them, the largest by far is Rhodes, for many years one of the most popular vacation spots in the Mediterranean; best known of the others are Kos and Symi; while one other island, Patmos, remains a place of pilgrimage, as it was here that St. John the Divine wrote the Apocalypse. Here, at the top of a hill, is the Monastery of the Apocalypse, which enshrines the cave where St. John received the Revelation; the voice of God spoke through a threefold crack in the rock, and the saint dictated to his disciple Prochorus—a slope in the rock wall is shown as the desk where Prochorus wrote, and silver haloes are set on the stone that was the apostle's pillow. Today, the monastery's library contains magnificent illuminated manuscripts, the greatest artistic treasures of the Dodecanese.

By Catherine Vanderpool

Updated by Stephen Brewer

The dozen islands, plus additional tiny members of the archipelago, have long shared a common history and fate. Their landscapes, however, are sharply contrasting. Patmos, Karpathos, Symi, and Kassos, for example, resemble in some ways the Cycladic islands: rugged hills and mountains almost devoid of vegetation, with villages and towns clinging in picturesque disarray to craggy landscapes. Rhodes and Kos unfold in fertile splendor, creased with streams and dotted with large stretches of green; their major towns sit next to the sea on almost flat land, embracing exceptionally large and well-protected harbors facing the mainland of Asia Minor. Leros, perhaps the greenest, is seldom visited by foreigners; its splendid harbor is adorned with monumental examples of Italian fascist architecture constructed in the 1930s in expectation of a supremacy that never came. Kalymnos, home to what was once one of the major sponge-diving fleets of the Mediterranean, still shows traces of its former prosperity, and its native sons have done well by their island and their town, whose colorfully painted houses ornament the amphitheatrical harborside. At the very edge of the archipelago, connected only administratively, is Kastellorizo, a lonely outpost that has lost much of its population through emigration.

Pleasures and Pastimes

Beaches

On both the south and north coasts of Kos there are highly developed little resort towns with sandy beaches, equipped with showers, and umbrellas and sun beds for rent; the beach on the Gulf of Kefalos is a haven for those wishing to escape the tourist fray—broad, sandy, scenically magnificent, and for much if its length devoid of development, curving around an enchanting bay. In the morning, caïques make regular runs from Skala to the beaches of Patmos; some can be reached by car or bus and many delightfully empty strands are the reward for a short trek on foot. Most of Patmos's beaches are coarse shingle, but there are sand-and-pebble strips with cafés and tavernas nearby. Twenty-seven of the beaches in Rhodes have been awarded EU Blue Flags for cleanliness and infrastructure; and another 15 have received the *Golden Starfish* for outstanding natural beauty and limited number of bathers. Rhodes town and the more sheltered east coast have exquisite stretches of fine-sand beaches, while the west side, which is subject to prevailing on-shore winds, can be choppy.

Bicycling

Kos's north coast is especially good for bicycling: in a word, flat. You can rent bicycles just about anywhere in the Dodecanese, in towns and at the more popular resorts.

Dining

Although Dodecanese cooking doesn't differ greatly from that of the mainland, there are some restaurants with unique locations and imaginative preparations. Rhodes produces most of its own foodstuffs, so you can count on fresh fruit and vegetables and, of course, a variety of fish (as everywhere, very expensive). Kos, too, is a garden island with lush fields; fresh vegetables are easy for chefs to come by, and even simple salads can be delicious. Despite the fact that neither Patmos or Symi, with their barren landscapes, has much homegrown produce, tavernas and restaurants on both serve some excellent fare. Always check the food on display in the kitchen, and ask about the specialty of the day. Dress on all the islands is casual and reservations are not necessary unless specified.

CATEGORY	COST*
$$$$	over 9,000 dr.
$$$	6,000 dr.–9,000 dr.
$$	3,000 dr.–6,000 dr.
$	under 3,000 dr.

per person for an appetizer, main course, and dessert, including service and tax but excluding drinks.

Diving

Rhodes offers the most opportunities for divers. At Thermes Kallitheas, on the island of Rhodes, a company with customized boats provides 30-minute theory lessons to beginning divers. After practicing in shallow water, you'll descend to a moderate depth to explore the underwater world.

Lodging

Except for Athens, Rhodes probably has more hotels per capita than anywhere else in Greece. Almost all of them are resort or tourist hotels; a few of the more luxurious cater to conference and incentive business as well. Some of the most elaborate, at the edge of town, have sea views and easy access to the beaches, which are extremely crowded in high season. You may have difficulty finding a room in Rhodes; in high season, it is best to book through an agent. The hotels in Kos tend to be only a bit more modest in size and facilities, and fully equipped tourist accommodation is plentiful. On both Rhodes and Kos, however, travelers may find it challenging to find lodging that is refreshingly Greek rather than anonymously international in style; keep in mind, too, that both islands cater largely to package tours from northern Europe, so you may find yourself surrounded by non-Greek merrymakers who never budge from the beach. Symi and Patmos offer a greater number of small hotels with charm, since neither island has encouraged the development of mammoth caravansaries. Many hotels in Rhodes and throughout the Dodecanese are closed from November through April. Hotels in only the $$$ and $$$$ categories are air-conditioned unless noted otherwise.

CATEGORY	COST*
$$$$	over 39,000 dr.
$$$	22,000 dr.–39,000 dr.
$$	13,000 dr.–22,000 dr.
$	under 13,000 dr.

All prices are for a standard double room in high season, excluding breakfast, unless indicated.

Shopping

Although Rhodes is no longer a duty-free port, some people still consider shopping to be one of its major attractions. Upscale shops sell furs and jewelry as well as more affordable trinkets. The styling of the jewelry can be extremely attractive, but the prices are no better than in Athens and are often even higher. In both Rhodes town and in Lindos, you can buy good copies of Lindos ware, a fine pottery with green and red floral designs. Patmos, an upscale tourist island that caters largely to prosperous Athenians, has some elegant boutiques selling jewelry and crafts, including antiques mainly from the island. In Chora, you'll find a wide selection of traditional ceramics, icons, and silver jewelry.

Water Sports

The larger resort hotels and beach facilities in Rhodes and Kos offer windsurfing, waterskiing, and, in some cases, jet-skiing and parasailing. On Rhodes, windsurfing is best near Ixia and Ialyssos; waterskiing, on the sheltered east coast. It's also possible to rent boats on Rhodes for sailing and sculling.

Exploring Rhodes and the Dodecanese

Of the Dodecanese, we highlight four: Strategically located Rhodes has played by far the most important role in history; Kos comes in second, particularly in its vestiges of antiquity, when its famous Sanctuary of Asklepeios, a center of healing, drew people from all over the ancient world. Both islands are worth visiting for a couple of days each. Symi, easily accessible from Rhodes, is a virtual museum of 19th-century neoclassical architecture, and Patmos, where St. John wrote his Revelation, became a renowned monastic center during the Byzantine period and continues as a significant focal point of the Greek Orthodox faith. Patmos and Symi offer qualities that in large part have been lost on overdeveloped Rhodes and Kos—peace, quiet, and a way of life that remains essentially Greek.

Numbers in the text correspond to numbers in the margin and on the Rhodes and the Dodecanese map.

Great Itineraries

If you have at least two weeks, exploring the Dodecanese by boat makes for a marvelous holiday. Ferries and hydrofoils run frequently between the main islands. Boats to the less-visited islands are infrequent, however, especially in winter, and no boats sail if the weather is bad—so you have to allow time for getting stranded.

Even on a short visit, travelers can partake of the diverse pleasures of the Dodecanese by combining a visit to one of the busier islands with a retreat to a quieter place. You may want, for instance, to begin in Rhodes (which has excellent air connections to Athens), to visit the architectural wonders of Rhodes town and Lindos, then make the crossing to nearby, much quieter Symi, with its neoclassical architecture and striking, arid landscape. Or, you may want to begin in Kos for a visit to its ancient sites and mountain villages, as well as to get a taste of its tourist life, then move on to nearby Patmos, with its stunning beaches and hilly landscape that is as mystical as its famous monastery.

IF YOU HAVE 3 DAYS

Confine your visit to ⊡ **Rhodes** ①–⑧, where you can spend a day walking through the fascinating old town and visiting the Grand Palace of the Masters and other sights. You will definitely want to make a day trip to the old city of **Lindos** ②, where you can also enjoy a fine beach, and stop in **Petaloudes** ⑦, the Valley of the Butterflies, en route back to Rhodes town. By all means, though, make the day trip by boat to Symi, close to Rhodes but quiet and unspoiled.

IF YOU HAVE 5 DAYS

🎔 **Rhodes** ①–⑧ is the best place to begin a longer tour of the Dodecanese. You will want to spend several days there, following your own version of the itinerary above, then on the fourth day take the hydrofoil or slower ferry to 🎔 **Patmos.** Of course you'll want to visit the famous monastery and Chora, the charming village that sprung up around its walls, and leave a day to relax on your own stretch of beach.

IF YOU HAVE 7 DAYS

Again after exploring 🎔 **Rhodes** ①–⑧ and 🎔 **Symi,** where you should spend at least one night to enjoy the island once the day-trippers have returned to Rhodes, you will want to take a hydrofoil or ferry to 🎔 **Kos,** and spend a couple of days exploring this island with its Greek and Roman excavations, Venetian and Turkish architecture, and beautiful landscape that along the coast is flat enough to provide perfect biking terrain. After touring the mosque and narrow streets of 🎔 **Kos town,** which is also a good place to stay, make the trip just out of town to the archaeological site of Asklepieion; then venture farther afield to other archaeological sites and the island's excellent beaches. From 🎔 **Kos,** you can travel on to 🎔 **Patmos** by ferry or hydrofoil.

When to Tour

The best time to tour Rhodes and the Dodecanese is during high season, from about March or April to November, when all establishments are open and the weather is most agreeable.

RHODES

The island of Rhodes (1,400 sq km/540 sq mi) is, after Crete, Evia, and Lesbos, the largest Greek island and, along with Sicily and Cyprus, one of the great islands of the Mediterranean. Rhodes is a country unto itself, and in the years before tourism, it was easily self-sufficient. It lies almost exactly halfway between Piraeus and Cyprus, 18 km (11 mi) off the coast of Asia Minor, and it was long considered a bridge between Europe and the East. Geologically similar to the Turkish mainland, it was probably once a part of it, separated by one of the frequent volcanic upheavals this volatile region has experienced.

Rhodes saw successive waves of settlement, culminating with the arrival of the Dorian Greeks from Argos and Laconia sometime early in the first millennium BC. They settled in Ialyssos, Lindos, and Kameiros and together with Dorians from Kos, and from Knidos and Halicarnassos in Asia Minor, formed a kind of loose confederation, later known as the Hexapolis (Six Cities). From the 8th to the 6th century BC the three Rhodian cities established settlements in Italy, France, Spain, and Egypt and actively traded with mainland Greece, exporting pottery, oil, wine, and figs. By the end of the 6th century BC, the flourishing independence, creativity, and expansion came to an abrupt halt when the Persians took over the island, later forcing Rhodians to provide ships and men for King Xerxes's attack on the mainland in 480 BC. The Persian failure resulted in their final expulsion from the mainland and the creation of a league of city-states under Athenian leadership. In 408 BC the inhabitants of the three cities established the united city of Rhodes, on the site of the modern town; much of the populace moved there, and the earlier towns eventually became mainly religious centers.

The new city grew and flourished, and its political organization was the model for the city of Alexandria in Egypt. At the end of the 4th century BC the Rhodians commissioned the sculptor Chares, from Lindos, to create the famous Colossus, a huge bronze statue of the sun

Rhodes and the Dodecanese

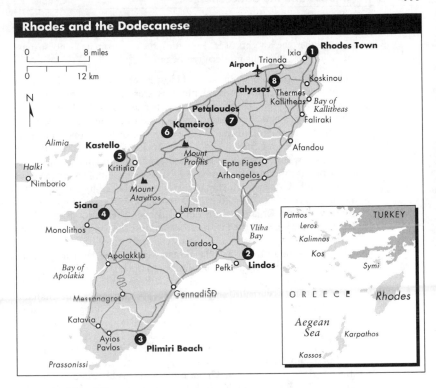

god, Helios, one of the Seven Wonders of the Ancient World. The next two centuries were prosperous for Rhodes's economy, thanks to its superb location on trade routes. In 227 BC, when an earthquake razed the city, help poured in from all quarters of the eastern Mediterranean, attesting to the city's importance. After the calamity the Delphic oracle advised the Rhodians to let the great Colossus lie where it had been toppled. So it lay, for some eight centuries, until AD 654, when it was sold as scrap metal and carted off to Syria allegedly by a caravan of 900 camels. After that, we know nothing of its fate.

In 42 BC, Rhodes came under the hegemony of Rome, and through the years of the empire, it was fabled as one of the most beautiful of cities, with parks and gardens and the straight streets that had been laid out in the 4th century BC. The roads were lined with porticoes, houses, and gardens, and according to Pliny, who described the city in the 1st century AD, it possessed some 2,000 statues, at least 100 of them of colossal scale. The sculptural school flourished through the Hellenistic period, and one of its most famous exemplars—probably executed in the 1st century BC—was the *Laocöon,* showing the Trojan priest who warned the Trojans to beware of Greeks bearing gifts, and his sons, in their death struggles with a giant serpent, a work that Pliny reports having seen in Rome in the 1st century AD. Excavations in Rome in 1506 uncovered the statue, which stands in the Vatican today. The intellectual life of Rhodes was also dazzling, attracting students and visitors from around the Mediterranean; its schools of rhetoric and philosophy found great favor among young Romans.

Today, there is almost nothing left of the ancient glory of Rhodes. The city was ravaged by Arab invaders in AD 654 and again in 807, and only with the expulsion of the Arabs, and the reconquest of Crete by the Byzantine emperors, did the city begin to revive. Rhodes was a crucial stop on the road to the Holy Land during the Crusades. It came briefly under Venetian influence, then Byzantine, then Genoese, but in 1309, when the Knights of St. John took the city from its Genoese masters, its most glorious modern era began.

The Knights of St. John, an order of Hospitalers organized in Jerusalem to protect and care for Christian pilgrims, were grouped into "tongues" by country of origin. Each tongue's inn, its place of assembly, was under the orders of a bailiff; the bailiffs were ruled by an elected Grand Master. By the beginning of the 12th century the order had become military in nature, and after the fall of Acre in 1291, the Knights fled from Palestine, withdrawing first to Cyprus and then to Rhodes. In 1312, the Knights inherited the immense wealth of the Templars (another religious military order, which had just been outlawed by the Pope) and used it to fortify the city. But for all their power and the strength of their walls, the Knights could not hold back the Turks. By the 16th century they manned the last bastions against the Turks in the eastern Mediterranean, as one by one the towns and cities of Byzantium fell. In preparation for the attack they knew would come, the Knights continually enlarged the moats and reinforced the sea walls, building new towers, fortifying gates, and installing artillery of all sizes. In 1522, the Ottoman Turks, with 300 ships and 100,000 men under Süleyman the Magnificent, began what was to be the final siege, taking the city after six months. During the Turkish occupation, Rhodes became a possession of the Grand Admiral, who collected taxes but left the Rhodians to pursue a generally peaceful and prosperous existence. They continued to build ships and to trade with Greece, Constantinople (later Istanbul), Syria, and Egypt. The Greek mainland was liberated by the War of 1821, but Rhodes and the Dodecanese remained part of the Ottoman Empire until 1912, when the Italians took over. After World War II, the Dodecanese were formally united with Greece in 1947.

Rhodes Town

★ ❶ *250 km (155 mi) east of Piraeus.*

Early travelers described Rhodes as a town of two parts: a castle or high town (Collachium) and a lower city. Today Rhodes town is still a city of two parts, but now the divisions are the **old town,** which incorporates the high town and lower city, and the **new town,** the modern metropolis that spreads away from the walls that encircle the old town. Old town contains numerous Orthodox and Catholic churches (a great number of which have disappeared), Turkish structures, and fine houses, some of which follow the ancient orthogonal plan. All the public buildings are similar in style, creating a harmonious whole, which has been enhanced in recent years by careful reconstruction. Staircases are on the outside, either on the facade or in the court; the facades are elegantly constructed of well-cut limestone from Lindos. Windows and doors are often outlined with strongly profiled moldings and surmounted by arched casements.

In the castle area, a city within a city, the Knights built most of their monuments. The **Palace of the Grand Masters,** at the highest spot of the medieval city, is the best place to begin a tour of Rhodes; here you can get oriented before wandering through the labyrinthine old town. Of great help is the permanent exhibition on the downstairs level, with extensive displays on the building, and maps and plans of the city. A large rectangular building with a broad central courtyard, the palace was so solidly built that it withstood unscathed the Turkish siege, but in 1856, an explosion of ammunition stored nearby in the cellars of the Church of St. John devastated the palace; the present buildings are

Italian reconstructions. Note the Hellenistic and Roman mosaic floors throughout, which came from the Italian excavations in Kos. ✉ *Castle, old town,* ☎ *0241/23359.* ☞ *1,200 dr.* ◷ *Tues.–Fri. 8:30–7 (8:30–3 in winter), weekends 8:30–3.*

The Knights of St. John were buried in the church that once stood at the site of the **Loggia of St. John** (✉ Old town, in front of court of Palace of the Grand Masters), which was also almost totally rebuilt by the Italians. From the Loggia, the **Street of the Knights** descends toward the **Commercial Port,** bordered on both sides by the **Inns of the Tongues,** where members supped and held their meetings.

The **Inn of France** (✉ About halfway down St. of the Knights from Loggia) was the largest of the Knights' gathering spots. The ground floor of this typically Rhodian building is occupied by vaulted utility areas opening onto the road; the first floor is reached by a stairway rising from the central courtyard. The facade is carved with flowers and heraldic patterns and bears an inscription that dates the building between 1492 and 1509.

The **Hospital** (✉ At end of St. of the Knights) was the largest of the Knights' public buildings. The imposing facade of this building, completed in 1489, opens into a courtyard, where cannonballs remain from the siege of 1522.

The main floor of the **Archaeological Museum** contains a collection of ancient pottery and sculpture, including two well-known representations of Aphrodite: the *Aphrodite of Rhodes,* who, while bathing, pushes aside her hair as if she's listening; and a standing figure, known as *Aphrodite Thalassia,* or "of the sea," as she was found in the water off the northern city beach. Other important works include the 6th-century kouroi found in Kameiros and the beautiful 5th-century BC funerary stele of Timarista bidding farewell to her mother, Crito. ✉ *Platia Mouseou (Museum Sq.), reached by wide staircase from Hospital,* ☎ *0241/27657.* ☞ *1,000 dr.* ◷ *Tues.—Sat. 8:30–6 (8:30–3 in winter), Sun. 8:30–3.*

The soaring vaults of **Our Lady of the Bourg** (✉ In ruins just inside remains of wall), the magnificent Gothic cathedral, are a startling reminder of Rhodes's Frankish past. The **Commercial Harbor** (✉ Just past St. Catherine's Gate) is Rhodes's largest, close to the cathedral.

The **Mosque of Süleyman** (✉ At top of Sokratous) was built soon after 1522 and rebuilt in 1808. The **Turkish Library** (✉ Sokratous, opposite mosque) dates to the late-18th century. Striking reminders of the Ottoman presence, the library and the mosque are still used by those members of Rhodes's Turkish community who stayed behind after the population exchange of 1922.

The **walls** of Rhodes in themselves are one of the great medieval monuments in the Mediterranean. Wonderfully preserved (even before the extensive Italian reconstruction), they illustrate the engineering capabilities as well as the financial and human resources available to the Knights. Each stretch of the wall was called a "curtain," and its defense was the responsibility of a tongue. For 200 years the Knights strengthened the walls by thickening them, up to 40 ft in places, and curving them so as to deflect cannonballs. The moat between the inner and outer walls never contained water; it was a device to prevent invaders from constructing siege towers. Part of the road that runs along the top for the entire 4 km (2½ mi) is accessible through municipal guided tours. ✉ *Old town,* ☎ *0241/21954.* ☞ *800 dr.* ◷ *Tours Tues. and Sat. 2:45 (arrive at least 15 mins early); departure from palace entrance.*

The medieval city of Rhodes is now completely surrounded by the **new city** (⊠ North of medieval walls, bordering small Mandraki Harbor); many of the city's official buildings are found here, their style heavily influenced by the Grand Masters' Palace and other medieval monuments and making abundant use of Lindos stone, crenellation, and Gothic architectural detail.

Rhodes's harbor is dominated by the **cathedral** (⊠ Harbor), modeled after the destroyed Church of St. John in the Collachium. The **Governor's Palace** (⊠ Harbor, next to cathedral) is constructed in an arcaded Venetian Gothic style. Other buildings in the vicinity include the **port authority** and **customs offices**, the **municipal buildings**, and a huge **open-air bazaar** now faced by fancy confectionery shops. The **main shopping areas** of new Rhodes are just behind these buildings.

To the west of Rhodes town rises **Mt. Smith**, its slopes still dotted with villas and gardens that in the early part of this century made Rhodes look like a miniature Italian Riviera. Many of them, unfortunately, have been torn down to make way for modern apartment buildings. The **acropolis** contains the remains of many ancient buildings, including a heavily restored **theater**, a **stadium**, the three restored columns of the **Temple of Apollo Pythios**, and scrappy remains of the **Temple of Athena Polias**. For a dramatic view, walk to the westernmost edge of Mt. Smith, which drops via a sharp and almost inaccessible cliff to the shore below, now lined with enormous hotels. ⊠ *At top of Mt. Smith,* ☎ *0241/21954.* ▭ *Free.*

Beaches

Elli beach (⊠ Modern town) has fine sand, an easy slope, chairs and umbrellas for rent, showers, pedal boats, and Windsurfers. All of the coast around Rhodes town is developed, so you can reach some of the best beaches only through the hotels that occupy them.

Dining and Lodging

$$$ ✗ **Alexis.** Carrying on the tradition begun by his father in 1957, Yiannis Katsimprakis spares nothing to bring his loyal clientele the very best
★ seafood, speaking passionately of eating fish as though it were a lost art. Don't bother with the menu; just look at the day's offerings, and if you're a neophyte, ask for suggestions. Whether it's beluga caviar, mussels in wine sauce and garlic, smoked eel, oysters, or sea urchins, you'll savor every bite. He even serves *porphyra* (murex), the mollusk yielding the famous purple dye for the Byzantine emperors. A side dish might be sautéed squash with local greens like *vlita* (notchweed) and *glistrida* (purslane). Yiannis also offers bountiful menus for two, which include champagne. Eat your meal on the quiet, shady terrace, perhaps with the new local dry white, Rodos 2400 (in honor of the city's 2,400th anniversary), and don't miss the house salad and the dessert called *hilli* (baklava with ice cream). ⊠ *Sokratous 18, old town,* ☎ *0241/29347. AE, V. Closed Nov. No lunch Sun. in summer.*

$$$ ✗ **Ta Kioupia.** Set just outside Rhodes town in a group of humble farm
★ buildings, Ta Kioupia is anything but modest. The white-stucco rooms with exposed ceiling beams are elegant: Antique farm tools are displayed, and there are linen tablecloths and napkins, fine china, and crystal. Regular customers get their own engraved plate and glass. Food is presented on large platters and you select what you fancy: pine-nut salad, *tiropita* (four-cheese pie), an eggplant dip that customers joke can't be beat, *bourekakia* (phyllo pastry stuffed with cheese and nuts), *korkorosouvlaki* (rooster kebab) . . . the list goes on—and the food is extraordinary in its variety and quality. ⊠ *Tris, about 7 km (4½ mi) west of Rhodes,* ☎ *0241/91824. AE, V. Closed Sun. Oct.–May. No lunch.*

$$ ✕ **Dinoris.** In a great hall built in 1530 as a stable for the Knights, Di-
★ noris has long specialized in fish. The food and service lure apprecia-
tive and demanding clients, from the mayor to hotel owners and
visiting VIPs. Rusticity prevails, with embroidered tablecloths, brightly
painted pottery, and thick, seemingly handwoven draperies on the
windows. For mezes, try the variety platter, which includes
psarokeftedakia (fish balls made from a secret recipe) as well as mus-
sels, shrimp, and lobster. Other special dishes are coquilles Jacques, grilled
prawns, and the sea urchin salad. ⊠ *Museum Sq. 14a, old town,* ☎
*0241/35530. Reservations essential for the garden and for weekends
in high season. AE, MC, V.*

$$ ✕ **Palia Istoria.** Never mind that this *mezedopolio* (meze joint) is a bit
★ out of the way in the new town. Gregarious former actor Haris Kera-
siotis has created a visual treat in the space ensconced in an old house
with high ceilings, beautiful floors, and genteel murals. Deciding among
the entrées can be tantalizing—*ameletes piperaki* (testicles in pepper
sauce), shrimp ouzo with orange juice, pork tenderloin in garlic and
wine sauce. The flambéed banana dessert wrapped in phyllo, followed
by the portlike Komantaria liqueur from Cyprus and an espresso will
complete this serendipitous meal. ⊠ *Mitropoleos 108 (about 800 dr.
by taxi from old town),* ☎ *0241/32121. Reservations essential. MC,
V. No lunch.*

$ ✕ **Kavo d'Oro.** This simple taverna is one of the few places in the old
town where you can get a good, inexpensive roast chicken, veal, and
lamb and grilled meat dishes. Especially good are the *papoutsakia*
(eggplant "shoes" stuffed with mincemeat). The decor is taverna style:
plain whitewashed walls, with the typical rush-seat, straight-back
chairs, and a vine-shaded courtyard at the back for warm-weather dining. The same management runs a second taverna by the same name
at Orfeous 40–42. ⊠ *Parodos Sokratous 41 (street behind Sokratous),
old town,* ☎ *0241/36181. Reservations not accepted. V. Closed Nov.–
Mar.*

$$$$ 🏨 **Rodos Park.** Rhodes's most luxurious hotel is also one of its most
★ quiet retreats, with more staff than guests. The large, marble-floored
guest rooms and suites have such amenities as Jacuzzis, satellite color
TVs, minibars, and direct-dial phones; many have stunning views over
the old town, which is just a few minutes' walk away. ⊠ *Odos Riga
Ferous 12, Rhodes town 85100,* ☎ *0241/24612,* ℻ *0241/24613. 30
rooms, 30 suites. Restaurant, bar, minibars, sauna, steam room, exercise room. AE, DC, MC, V.*

$$$ 🏨 **Grand Hotel Summer Palace.** A cut above other resort hotels in the
area, the Grand is actually in Rhodes, near the beach, the old town,
and the new town's nightlife scene. Though the hotel is not exceptional
from the outside, once you enter the name makes sense: The atrium
lobby is spacious, with giant plants and views onto the porticoed pool
and garden. The best rooms are in the newer wing, with pink marble
floors and pretty paintings of nymphs and goddesses. They feature sub-
dued blue and rose furnishings, trompe l'oeil touches, alcoved bath-
tubs, and key cards that automatically turn on the lights. Breakfast is
included. ⊠ *Akti Miaouli 1, new town, 85100,* ☎ *0241/26284, 01/
291–7027 in Athens;* ℻ *0241/35589. 362 rooms, 18 suites. Restau-
rant, bar, 1 indoor and 2 outdoor pools, sauna, tennis court, exercise
room, shops, casino, nightclub. AE, DC, MC, V.*

$$ 🏨 **S. Nikolis Hotel.** One of the finest accommodations in the old
town—and one of the most charming in Rhodes—occupies a restored
house. The small but tidy rooms are enlivened by arches and other architectural details, and many have balconies overlooking a lovely garden. Breakfast is served on the roof terrace. Excellent service, including
laundry, is caringly administered by Sotiris and Marianne Nikolis. ⊠

Odos Ippodamou 61, old town, 85100, ☎ 0241/34561, FAX 0241/32034. 10 rooms, 4 apartments. Breakfast room. AE, MC, V.

$ ⌐ **Pension Sofia.** The old town is full of rooms to rent, but budget-priced Sofia's, run by the same people that own Kavo d'Oro (☞ *above*), is bright, pleasant, and framed by trailing jasmine; each room has a little bath. ⊠ *Aristofanous 27, old town, 85100, ☎ 0241/36181. 10 rooms. No credit cards. Closed Dec.–Mar.*

Nightlife and the Arts

BARS AND DISCOS

It's claimed that Rhodes has more bars and discos per person than New York, Berlin, or Paris—most are in the new town and resort areas like Faliraki. They come and go, so it's best to check with your concierge or the free *Rodos News*, available at the Greek National Tourist Organization (GNTO or EOT) office (☞ Visitor Information *in* Rhodes and the Dodecanese A to Z, *below*).

CASINO

Rhodes's **casino** (⊠ Next to Grand Hotel Summer Palace, new town, ☎ 0241/28109) is open all year; you must show your passport to get in. The entry fee is 1,500 dr., and it is open from 8 PM to 2 AM.

GREEK DANCE

With performances since 1971, the **Nelly Dimoglou Folk Dance Theatre** (⊠ Andronikou 7, behind Turkish baths, old town, ☎ 0241/20157) keeps alive the tradition of Greek dance, with strict adherence to authentic detail in costume and performance. From May until September it can be seen weekdays at 9:20 PM for 2,800 dr. It also gives dance lessons.

SOUND-AND-LIGHT SHOW

From April through October the **Sound-and-Light Show** (⊠ Grounds of the Palace of the Grand Masters, ☎ 0241/21922) tells the story of the Turkish siege. English-language performances are Mondays and Tuesdays 8:15 PM; Wednesdays, Fridays, and Saturdays 9:15 PM; and Thursdays 10:15 PM. From mid-May to July performances start one hour later; the cost is 2,000 dr.

Outdoor Activities and Sports

DIVING

The **Dive Med Center** (⊠ Dragoumi 5, new town, ☎ 0241/33654) offers a "resort dive" (11,000 dr.) for first-time divers and for those who don't have a certificate. Customized boats will take you to Thermes Kallitheas, the only place where you can dive on the island. After a 30-minute theory lesson and practice in shallow water, you'll descend to a moderate depth to explore the underwater world. The center also offers courses leading to PADI or NAUI certification. Keep in mind that even if you are certified, it is illegal to dive on your own in Greece. The center is open from May to October.

FISHING

No license is required for trolling or line fishing in Rhodes. The best fishing is reputed to be off Kameiros Skala, Kallithea, Lindos, and Gennadi. Sometimes the commercial fishing boats that moor opposite St. Catherine's Gate will take visiting anglers out on trips.

GOLF

There is an 18-hole golf course in the village of **Afandou** (⊠ About 20 km/12 mi outside Rhodes town, ☎ 0241/51451). The course is open daily 8 to 8; a round costs 4,000 dr. and a weekly pass worth seven rounds costs 22,000 dr. Prices are lower off-season. The Rodos Open takes place here in October.

Information can be obtained on dinghy sailing and sculling from the **Rodos Yacht Club** (NOR) (⊠ Platia Kountouriotou 9, Rhodes new town, ☎ 0241/23287). To rent yachts, call the **Yacht Agency Rhodes Ltd.** (⊠ Amerikis 95, ☎ 0241/22927).

TENNIS

Several first-class and luxury hotels have courts, where equipment can be rented and where nonguests can usually play. The **Rhodes Tennis Club** (☎ 0241/25705) is open to nonmembers. Prices are 1,600 dr. per hour for two people.

WATER SPORTS

The larger resort hotels offer windsurfing, waterskiing, and, in some cases, jet-skiing and parasailing. Windsurfing is best near Ixia and Ialyssos; waterskiing, on the sheltered east coast.

Shopping

BOUTIQUES

The **old city's shopping center** (⊠ Intersection at Sokratous) is lined with boutiques selling furs, jewelry, and other high-ticket items. In Rhodes town you can also buy good copies of **Lindos ware,** a fine pottery decorated with green and red floral motifs.

AROUND THE ISLAND

The island's east coast, particularly the stretch between Rhodes town and Lindos, is blessed with white sandy beaches and dotted with copses of trees, interspersed with fertile valleys full of figs and olives. Unfortunately, its beauty has meant that long stretches of this country are now given over to vast resort hotels and holiday villages. Even so, there are still some wonderfully untrammeled sections of beach to be found all around the island, and the town of Lindos alone warrants an excursion from Rhodes town.

Faliraki

16 km (10 mi) south of Rhodes town.

As you leave Rhodes town and travel south along the East Coast, you approach a strange sight: **Thermes Kallitheas** (⊠ About 10 km/6 mi south of Rhodes town; 6 km/4 mi north of Faliraki), a group of buildings that look as if they've been transplanted from Morocco. In fact, this is a spa built in 1929 by the Italians, now much neglected. The great physician Hippocrates of Kos extolled these mineral springs in the early 2nd century BC for alleviating liver, kidney, and rheumatic ailments.

Beaches

Faliraki Beach (⊠ 6 km/4 mi south of Thermes Kallitheas) is a splendid strip of sandy beach now ringed by hotels. At **Afandou Beach** (⊠ About 7 km/4½ mi past Faliraki), you'll see on the right small tavernas spread out under grape arbors in the brilliant sun. Before or after your meal, you can run across the road to the beach for a dip.

Dining

$$ ✕ **Epta Piges.** If you've had enough of Afandou beach, take an easy, uphill walk through a pleasant ravine to a deeply shaded glen surrounding Epta Piges, or Seven Springs. Here an enterprising local shepherd began serving simple fare to visitors about 40 years ago, and his sideline turned into the busy taverna of today. He imported peacocks and turned them loose in the woods, where they pierce the silence with their scratchy shrieks and flaunt their bright plumage high up in the trees.

If you arrive before mealtime, you can have a glass of freshly squeezed orange juice. ⊠ *About 2 km (1 mi) from Afandou Beach via the footpath. No credit cards. Closed Oct.–Mar.*

Lindos

②   *60 km (37 mi) southeast of Rhodes town, 30 km (18 mi) southwest of Faliraki.*

Lindos, cradled between two harbors, had a particular importance in antiquity. Before the existence of Rhodes, it was the island's principal maritime center. Perhaps the poverty of Lindos's land forced the Lindians to turn outward from their fine harbor for survival and led to their maritime success. Lindos possessed a revered sanctuary, consecrated to Athena, whose cult probably succeeded that of a pre-Hellenic divinity named Lindia, and the sanctuary was dedicated to Athena Lindia. By the 6th century BC, an impressive temple dominated the settlement, and after the foundation of Rhodes, the Lindians set up a *propylaia* (monumental entrance gate) on the model of Athens's. In the mid-4th century BC, the temple was destroyed by fire and almost immediately rebuilt, with a new wooden statue of the goddess covered by gold leaf, and with arms, head, and legs of marble or ivory. In the Hellenistic period, the Acropolis was further adorned with a great portico at the foot of the steps to the propylaia. Lindos prospered into Roman times, during the Middle Ages, and under the Knights of St. John. Only at the beginning of the 19th century did the age-old shipping activity cease. The population decreased radically, reviving only with the 20th-century influx of foreigners.

For 1,000 dr., donkeys can be hired for the 15-minute climb from the modern town to the **Acropolis.** The winding path leads past a gauntlet of Lindian women who spread out their lace and embroidery over the rocks like fresh laundry. The final approach ascends a steep flight of stairs, past a marvelous 5th-century BC **relief** of the prow of a Lindian ship, carved into the rock; and through the main gate of the **Crusader castle.**

The **entrance** to the Acropolis, almost all of it undergoing restoration, takes you through the **medieval castle,** with the Byzantine **chapel of St. John** on the next level above. On the **upper terraces** are the remains of the elaborate **porticoes** and **stoas,** initially restored by the Italians. As is the case with Sounion (☞ Chapter 3), the site and temple command an immense sweep of sea, making a powerful statement on behalf of the deity and city to which they belonged; the lofty white columns on the summit must have presented a magnificent picture. The main portico had 42 Doric columns, at the center of which an opening led to the staircase up to the **propylaia.** The temple at the very top is surprisingly modest, given the drama of the approach. There is no encircling colonnade; instead, as was common in the 4th century BC, both the front and the rear are flanked by four Doric columns, like the Temple of Athena Nike on the Acropolis of Athens (☞ Chapter 2). Numerous inscribed statue bases were found all over the summit, attesting in many cases to the work of Lindian sculptors, who were clearly second to none. ⊠ *Acropolis of Lindos,* ☎ *0244/31258.* ☞ *1,000 dr.* ⊙ *Tues.–Sun. 8:30–2:45.*

Lindos town (⊠ On land side of Acropolis) is remarkably well preserved, and many 15th-century houses are still in use. Everywhere are examples of the Crusader architecture you saw in Rhodes town: substantial houses of finely cut grayish Lindos limestone with inner courtyards containing stairs to the upper level. The facades are pierced by doors and windows crowned with stone arches, often elaborately carved in the characteristic rope patterns. Many floors are paved with the typical Rhodian black-and-white pebble mosaics. Intermixed with these Crusader buildings are other houses of almost Cycladic appearance: White geometric shapes pierced by plain square windows framed with blue shutters nestle in gardens filled with bougainvillea and hibiscus. Many of the owners of these homes offer rooms for rent; the tourist office (⊠ Platia Eleftherias, ☎ 0244/31227), open May–October, daily 9–10, can arrange rentals, but rooms are often booked well in advance by tour operators.

Like Rhodes town, Lindos town is enchanting off-season and almost unbearably crowded otherwise, since pilgrims make the trek from Rhodes daily. The main street is lined with shops selling clothes and trinkets of all types; the streets are medieval in their narrowness and twisting course, so the passage slows to a snail's pace. Lindos town can be reached only on foot from the parking lot.

The **Church of the Panayia** (⊠ Just off main platia) is a graceful building with a fine bell tower, now in perilous condition. The body of the church probably antedates the Knights, although the bell tower bears their arms with the dates 1484–90. The interior has frescoes painted in 1779 by Gregory of Symi.

Gennadi and the South Coast

80 km (50 mi) south of Rhodes town, 20 km (12½ mi) south of Lindos.

The area south of Lindos is less traveled than the rest of the island. The land is not as attractive as in the north, the sandy beaches are fewer, and the soil is less fertile, so there is much less development. The village of Gennadi offers some inexpensive pensions and rooms for rent, as well as tavernas.

Beach

❸ There's a detour to **Plimiri Beach** (10 km/6 mi south of Gennadi), a good place for a swim to break the long drive. The ancient city of Kyrbe is believed to have stood in the hills behind the town until it was destroyed by a *plimiri* (flood); hence the name of the village.

En Route From Gennadi, turn inland on a road that leads west across the island, through a river valley dotted with curious hillocks, to the town of Apolakkia, where you bear right at the crossroads to begin your return trip north. The road to Siana climbs through spectacularly wooded hills.

Siana

❹ *60 km (37¼ mi) southwest of Rhodes town, 20 km (12 mi) northwest of Gennadi.*

The town of Siana perches above a vast, fertile valley and sits in the shadow of a rock outcropping crowned with the ruin of a castle.

Shopping

LOCAL SPECIALTIES

Siana is known for *souma* (a local liqueur distilled from grapes, resembling unflavored schnapps). Its renowned honey and walnuts can be obtained at **Tasia's Kafenion** (⊠ Just past town church on the main road) or any of the other **cafés** at which hordes of tourist buses occasionally stop.

En Route Beyond Siana, the road continues on a high ridge through thick pine forests, which carpet the precipitous slopes dropping toward the sea. To the right looms the bare, stony massif of **Mt. Ataviros**, Rhodes's highest peak, at 3,986 ft.

Kritinia

> *35 km (21¾ mi) southwest of Rhodes town, 12 km (7½ mi) northeast from Siana.*

❺ The **Kastello** (⊠ South of Kritinia), a fortress built by the Knights in the late-15th century, is an impressive ruin, situated high above the sea with fine views in every direction.

Kameiros

❻ *25 km (15½ mi) south of Rhodes town, 17 km (10½ mi) northeast of Kritinia.*

The site of ancient Kameiros is one of the three ancient cities of Rhodes. The apparently unfortified ruins, excavated by the Italians in 1929, lie on a slope above the sea. Most of what is visible today dates to the classical period and later, including impressive remains of the early Hellenistic period. ⊠ *Kameiros archaeological site,* ☎ *0241/41435.* 🎟 *500 dr.* ☉ *Tues.–Fri. 8:30–4:45 (8:30–2:45 in winter), weekends 8:30–2:45.*

Petaloudes

❼ *22 km (13½ mi) from Kameiros, 20 km (12½ mi) from Rhodes town.*

Petaloudes, the Valley of the Butterflies, lives up to its name, especially in July and August. In summer the *kalimorpha quadripunctaria,* actually a moth species, cluster by the thousands around the low bushes of the pungent storax plant, which grows all over the area. Don't agitate the butterflies. Over the years, unfortunately, their number has diminished, partly owing to busloads of tourists clapping hands to see them fly up in dense clouds, startled by the slightest sound. Access to the valley is through a main road and admission booth. ⊠ *Petaloudes.* 🎟 *600 dr.* ☉ *Butterfly season, May–Sept., 8–5.*

❽ Mt. Filerimos is capped by the site of **Ialyssos,** the third of the ancient Rhodian communities. There are some remains of an early Hellenistic Temple of Athena, as well as those of a Byzantine church. Because of its strategic position, Filerimos also was used by the Knights for a fortress, which stands above a monastery of Our Lady of Filerimos. ⊠ *Acropolis of Ialyssos; take turnoff, going on the coast road west from Petaloudes, at Trianda and head south for 5 km (3 mi),* ☎ *0241/92202.* 🎟 *800 dr.* ☉ *Tues.–Fri. 8:30–5 (8:30–3 in winter), weekends 8:30–3.*

SYMI

The island of Symi, 11 km (7 mi) north of Rhodes, is an enchanting place, with its star attraction being Chorio, a 19th-century town of fine neoclassical mansions. Fortunately, the island has few beaches (and even some of those are accessible only by boat) and almost no flat land, so it is not attractive to developers. As a result, quiet Symi provides a peaceful retreat for travelers, who tend to fall in love with the island on first visit and return year after year.

Nireus, the ancient king of Symi, who sailed with three vessels to assist the Greeks at Troy, is mentioned in Homer. Symi was later part of the Dorian Hexapolis dominated by Rhodes, and it remained under Rhodian dominance throughout the Roman and Byzantine periods. The island has good natural harbors, and the nearby coast of Asia Minor provided plentiful timber for the Symiotes, who were fine shipbuilders, fearless seafarers and sponge divers, and finally, rich and successful merchants. Under the Ottomans their harbor was proclaimed a free port and attracted the trade of the entire region. Witness to their prosperity are the fine neoclassical mansions that were fashionable elsewhere in Greece at the same time. The Symiotes' continuous travel and trade and their frequent contact with Europe led them to incorporate foreign elements in their furnishings, clothes, and cultural life. At first they lived in Chorio, high on the hillside above the port, and in the second half of the 19th century spread down to the seaside at Yialos. There were some 20,000 inhabitants at this acme, but under the Italian occupation at the end of the Italo-Turkish war in 1912, the island declined; the Symiotes lost their holdings in Asia Minor and were unable to convert their fleets to steam. Many emigrated to work elsewhere, and now there are just a few thousand inhabitants in Chorio and Yialos.

Yialos

11 km (7 mi) north of Rhodes, 452 km (281 mi) east of Piraeus.

As the boat from Rhodes to Symi rounds the last of many rocky barren spurs, the port of Yialos, at the back of a deep, narrow harbor, comes into view. The shoreside is lined with houses, and the ground floors of many of them have been converted to shops and restaurants with waterside terraces that provide the perfect locale in which to wile away lazy hours; the esplanade at the head of the harbor, once the site of shipyards, is now full of pleasant outdoor tavernas and cafés. The **Church of Ayhios Ioannis** (✉ Near center of Yialos village), built in 1838, incorporates in its walls fragments of ancient blocks from a temple that apparently stood on this site and is surrounded by a plaza paved in an intricate mosaic, fashioned from inlaid pebbles.

Dining and Lodging

$$ ✕ **Mylopetra.** This extraordinary restaurant is in the back streets of Yialos, just behind the church, and occupies an old flour mill, for which it is named. It is the creation of a German couple, Hans and Eva Sworoski, who painstakingly oversaw the delightful conversion and tend to the excellent cooking and gracious service. Dining is in the interior of the restored mill, where decorations include an ancient tomb embedded in glass beneath the floor, or on a candlelit terrace in front. The menu changes daily, though perpetual favorites include a wonderful lasagna with prawns and sea bream in a light mustard sauce. ✉ *Yialos,* ☎ *0241/72333. MC, V. Closed Nov.–Apr.*

$ ✕ **Trawlers.** This pleasant taverna in Yialos does simple cooking better than most places on the island, and it is reasonably priced. Weather permitting, dining is also offered in a pretty square just a few steps from the port. ✉ *Yialos. No credit cards.*

$$ 🏨 **Dorian Studios.** You can cook your own meals in these small effi-
★ ciency apartments that climb a terraced hillside just above the waterfront in Yialos. Most have a miniature living and dining room and a cozy loft-style bedroom, both with dark wood furniture; the best accommodations face one of the several patios. ✉ *Yialos 85600,* ☎ *0241/71181, 0241/71811, or 0241/71307. 2 rooms, 7 apartments. No credit cards. Closed Nov.–Mar.*

Chorio

1 km (½ mi) east of Yialos.

It's a 10-minute walk from the main harbor of Yialos up to Chorio, along a staircase of some 500 steps, known as **Kali Strata.** There is also a road that can be traveled in one of the island's few taxis or by bus (100 dr.), which makes an hourly circuit with stops at the harbor in Yialos, Chorio, and the little seaside community of Pedi. The Kali Strata is flanked by many elegant pastel stucco houses of neoclassical design, with fine, often classical stonework; lavish use of pediments; and intricate wrought-iron balconies. Just before the top of the stairs, to the left, a line of windmills crowns the hill of **Noulia.**

The collection at the **archaeological museum** displays Hellenistic and Roman sculptures and inscriptions as well as more recent carvings, icons, costumes, and handicrafts. ⊠ *Laikos Milos Sq., Chorio,* ☏ *0241/ 71114.* ☑ *Free.* ☉ *Mon.–Sat. 8:30–2.*

Most of Chorio's many churches date to the 18th and 19th centuries, and many are ornamented with richly decorated iconostases and ornate bell towers. The **Kastro** (⊠ At the top of the town, Chorio's ancient Acropolis) incorporates fragments of Symi's history in its walls. The view from here takes in the village of Pedhi (a yachting center), as well as both Chorio and Yialos.

Dining and Lodging

$ ✕ **Georgio's Taverna.** Meals at this simple Chorio taverna, which is as popular with locals as it is with tourists, are served in a high-ceilinged, whitewashed dining room or on a terrace that is partially shaded by a grape arbor and affords wonderful views over the sea and surrounding hills. Fish is a specialty, and simply prepared *mezedes,* such as roasted peppers topped with feta cheese and fried zucchini, can constitute a delicious meal in themselves. If you're lucky, one of the neighbors will stroll in with instrument in hand to provide an impromptu serenade. ⊠ *Chorio,* ☏ *0241/71665. No credit cards.*

$ ▨ **Hotel Fiona.** This bright, new hotel, run by a family who recently re-
★ turned to Symi after years in Australia, is perched on the hillside in Chorio, affording splendid views over the island and sea. Just about all of the large rooms, with spotless white-tile floors and attractive blue-painted furnishings and pastel fabrics, have a sea-facing balcony. A full breakfast, with yogurt, homemade cakes, and marmalade, is served in the breezy, attractive lobby lounge. ⊠ *Chorio 85600,* ☏ *0241/72088,* 🖷 *0241/ 72088. 14 rooms. Lobby lounge. No credit cards. Closed Nov.–Mar.*

$ ▨ **Village Hotel.** On a small lane just off the main square of Chorio,
★ the Village Hotel is set in a traditional neoclassical mansion that has been enlarged and was nattily restored in 1992. The hotel has good views in all directions . . . and a steep climb home after you've had a morning coffee in the port. All the rooms open onto a balcony or terrace and surround an attractive garden. ⊠ *Symi 85600,* ☏ *0241/ 71800,* 🖷 *0241/71802. 17 rooms. Breakfast room. No credit cards. Closed Nov.–Mar.*

Southern Area

Monastery is 7 km (4½ mi) south of Chorio.

The main reason to venture to the atypically green, pine-covered hills surrounding the little gulf of Panormitis is to visit the **Monastery of Taxiarchis Michael Panormiti,** Symi's patron saint, and also the protector of sailors. The entrance to the site is surmounted by an elaborate **bell tower,** of the multilevel wedding-cake variety already seen in Yialos and Chorio. In the **courtyard,** which is surrounded by a vaulted stoa, the floor is adorned with a black-and-white pebble mosaic. The **interior** of the church, entirely frescoed in the 18th century, contains a marvelously ornate wooden iconostasis, flanked by a heroic-size 18th-century representation of Michael, completely covered with silver. Note also the collection of votives, including ship models, gifts brought from all over, and a number of bottles with money in them, which, according to local lore, traveled to Symi on their own after having been thrown into the sea. Some rooms are available for lodging, and any trip to the monastery should be accompanied by a refreshing swim in the harbor. **Symi Tours** (⌑ In a distinctive stone house at the end of the harbor, Yialos, ☎ 0241/71307, ⟨FAX⟩ 0241/72292) offers excursions to the monastery that combines a truck trip over the most difficult terrain, a three-hour trek the rest of the way to the monastery, then a barbecue lunch and time for a swim, with return by boat. The company also arranges other boat trips and walking excursions around the island, as well as recommended lodgings on the island. ⌑ *Symi's south side, at harbor,* ☎ *0241/71581.* ⌑ *Free.* ☉ *Daily.*

Beaches

Symi does have some excellent pebble beaches, though you may have to go to a little effort to reach them. The only beach near Yialos is a little strip beyond the harbor—just follow the road past the bell tower and the Aliki Hotel and you'll come to a seaside taverna that offers umbrellas and beach chairs. If you continue walking on the same road for about 3 km (2 mi) you'll come to the pine-shaded beach at **Nibrios Bay,** where there is another taverna; swimming off the rocks along the way is excellent. From Pedhi, a little yacht harbor about 1 km (½ mi) beneath Chorio (a bus makes an hourly run from both Yialos and Chorio, 100 dr.), you can hire a boat (about 1,500 dr. a person) for an excursion to two of the island's best beaches: **Nanou Bay,** nestled beneath an imposing cliff, then on to **Marathounda Bay,** where you can enjoy a swim and a refreshing meal at a little taverna while your boatman waits.

Dining and Lodging

Symi Tours (☞ *above*) arranges lodging around the island, in accommodations that range from rooms in private homes to villas.

$$ ✕ **Manos Fish Restaurant.** Many people think this outdoor, harborside eatery serves the best fish on Symi, and you will probably agree as you try the succulent mussels steamed in white wine, followed by a mixed grill of octopus, squid, prawns, and locally caught fish. Manos, an enterprising young man from Athens who married a local woman, is on hand to provide tips about what to see and do on his adopted island. ⌑ *Yialos harborfront, Symi,* ☎ *0241/72429. MC, V. Closed Nov.–Apr.*

KOS

The island of Kos, the third-largest in the Dodecanese, is certainly one of the most beautiful, with verdant fields and tree-clad mountains, surrounded by miles of sandy beach. Its highest peak, part of a small mountain range in the northeast, is less than 3,280 ft. All this beauty has not gone unnoticed, of course, and Kos undeniably suffers from the effects of mass tourism: Its beaches are often crowded, most of its seaside towns have been recklessly overdeveloped, and the main town is noisy and busy between June and September.

In Mycenaean times and during the Archaic period, the island prospered. In the 6th century BC it was conquered by the Persians but later joined the Delian League, supporting Athens against Sparta in the Peloponnesian War. Kos was invaded and destroyed by the Spartan fleet, ruled by Alexander and various of his successors, and has twice been devastated by earthquakes. Nevertheless the city and the economy flourished, as did the arts and sciences. The painter Apelles, the Michelangelo of his time, came from Kos, as did Hippocrates, father of modern medicine. Under the Roman Empire, the island's Asklepieion and its renowned healing center drew emperors and ordinary citizens alike. The Knights of St. John arrived in 1315 and ruled for the next two centuries, until they were replaced by the Ottomans. In 1912 the Italians took over, and in 1947 the island was united with Greece.

Kos Town

370 km (230 mi) east of Piraeus, 92 km (57 mi) north of Rhodes.

The modern town lies on a flat plain encircling a spacious harbor called Mandraki and is a pleasant assemblage of low-lying buildings and shady lanes. The fortress, which crowns its west side, where Hippocrates is supposed to have taught in the shade of a large plane tree, is a good place to begin your exploration of Kos town.

On one side of Platia Platanou, the little square named after the tree, stands the graceful Loggia (⊠ Platia Platanou), actually a mosque, built in 1786.

The **Castle of the Knights,** built mostly in the 15th century and full of ancient blocks from its Greek and Roman predecessors, is a repository of fragments of ancient inscriptions, funerary monuments, and other sculptural material. A walk around the walls affords fine views over the town, whose flat skyline is pierced by a few remaining minarets and many palm trees. ⊠ *Over bridge from Platia Platanou,* ☎ *0242/ 28326.* ⊡ *500 dr., free on Sun.* ⊙ *Tues.–Sun. 8:30–3.*

Excavations have uncovered the **Roman agora and harbor** (⊠ Over bridge from Platia Platanou, just behind Castle of the Knights), as well as portions of 4th-century BC and Hellenistic buildings. The **ruins,** which are not fenced, blend charmingly into the fabric of the modern city; it's a shortcut for people on their way to work, a place to sit and chat, an outdoor playroom for children. The ruins are now overgrown, and in spring they're covered with brightly colored flowers, which nicely frame the ancient gray-and-white marble blocks tumbled in every direction.

★   Kos town's **archaeological museum** contains extremely important examples of Hellenistic and Roman sculpture by Koan artists. Among the treasures is a group of sculptures from various Roman phases, all found in the House of the Europa Mosaic, and a remarkable series of Hellenistic draped female statues mainly from the Sanctuary of Demeter at Kyparissi and the Odeion. ⊠ *Platia Eleftherias, west of agora through gate leading to main square,* ☎ *0242/28326.* ⊡ *500 dr., free on Sun.* ⊙ *Tues.–Sun. 8:30–3.*

The **West Excavations** (⊠ Just below ancient Acropolis) have uncovered a portion of one of the main Roman streets with many houses, including the **House of the Europa Mosaic.** Part of the **Roman baths** (⊠ Near main Roman street), it has been converted into a basilica. The **gymnasium,** distinguished by its partly reconstructed colonnade, and the so-called **Nymphaion,** a lavish public latrine that has been restored, are also of interest. These excavations are always open with free access.

Beaches

Kardamena (⊠ On south coast of Kos) and **Tingaki** (⊠ On north coast of Kos), are both highly developed little resort towns with sandy beaches, and showers, plus umbrellas and sun beds for rent. At **Mastichari** (⊠ On north coast, farther from Kos town), another resort, there's a wide sand beach, tavernas, rooms for rent, and a pier where boats sail on day trips to the uncrowded islet of Pserimos. The pebble beach at **Empros Thermes** (⊠ On north coast east of Kos town) has the added attraction of a bubbling, seaside hot springs. **Paradise Beach** (⊠ On southeast coast) has plenty of parking, and thus crowds, but the broad, sandy beach is magnificent and gives its name to a long stretch of sand that curves around the enchanting Gulf of Kefalos and, at its northern end, is undeveloped, almost deserted, and popular with nude bathers. If you must get wet but can't leave **Kos town,** try the **narrow pebbly strip** (✉ Just south of main harbor).

Lodging

$$$ ⊞ **Ramira Beach.** This is one of the better resort hotels for family holidays, just outside Kos town. Most of the white and blue rooms, most with balconies and many situated in pleasant bungalows set amid gardens, have sea views. ✉ *Psalidi Beach, Kos town 85300,* ☎ *0242/22891 through 0242/22894. 268 rooms. Restaurant, bar, pool, 2 tennis courts. AE, DC, MC, V. Closed Nov.–Mar.*

$$ ⊞ **Titania Hotel.** This in-town hotel, right on the sea, delivers good quality at an easy price. Modern outside and in, its rooms are plain but comfortable. Because it's on the main road, the rooms may be noisy in high season, but offsetting this, you are within walking distance of town, and there's a little strip of beach right across the street. ✉ *6b Vasileos Georgiou, Kos town 85300,* ☎ *0242/22556. 108 rooms. Bar, lobby lounge, beach. No credit cards. Closed Nov.–Apr.*

Asklepieion

4 km (2½ mi) west of Kos town.

One of the great healing centers of antiquity is framed by a thick grove of cypress trees and laid out on several **broad terraces** connected by a monumental staircase. The lower terrace probably held the Asklepieian Festivals. On the middle terrace is an **Ionic temple,** once decorated with paintings by Apelles, including the renowned depiction of Aphrodite often written about in antiquity and eventually removed to Rome by the emperor Augustus. On the uppermost terrace is the **Doric Temple of Asklepeios,** once surrounded by colonnaded porticoes. ✉ *Asklepieion,* ☎ *0242/28763.* ▦ *750 dr., free on Sun.* ☉ *Daily 8:30–3.*

OFF THE BEATEN PATH	Leaving the main road southwest of Asklepieion (turnoff is at Zipari, 9 km/5½ mi southwest of Kos Town), you can explore an enchanting landscape of cypress and pine tree on a route that climbs to three lovely, whitewashed rural villages that cling to the craggy slopes of the island's central mountains: **Asfendiou, Zia,** and **Lagoudi.** The busiest of them is Zia, with an appealing smattering of churches; crafts shops selling local honey, weavings, and handmade soaps; and open-air tavernas where you can enjoy the views over the surrounding forests and fields toward the sea.

Dining

$$ ✕ **Taverna Ampavris.** The setting and the food are both delightful at this
★ charming, rustic taverna, just outside Kos town on a lane leading to the village of Platani. Meals are served in the courtyard of an old farmhouse, and the kitchen's emphasis is on local country food—including wonderful stews and grilled meats, accompanied by vegetables from nearby gardens. ✉ *Platani La., Kos town,* ☎ *0242/25696. No credit cards.*

$ ✕ **Aklipios.** A memorable meal can be had at this little restaurant near
★ the Asklepieion, in the village of Platani. Sit in the shade of an ancient laurel tree and try the exquisite selection of mezedes: home-prepared *dolmadakia* (stuffed vine leaves), bourekakia, *imam bayaldi* (baked eggplant). Even the boiled cauliflower is perfect. ✉ *Platani,* ☎ *0242/25264. No credit cards.*

Bay of Kamares

35 km (21¾ mi) southwest of Kos town, 10 km (6 mi) south of the Castle of Antimacheia.

Close to shore here is a little rock formation holding a **chapel to St. Nicholas,** and opposite are the ruins of a magnificent 5th-century **Christian basilica** (⊠ On mainland, edge of public beach). The little beach community of Kamares is pleasant and much less frantic than the island's other seaside resorts, and perched on a summit above is the lovely old town of Kefalos, a pleasant place to wander just to enjoy its views and quintessential Greekness.

Dining and Lodging

$$ ✗ **Faros.** It's not too surprising that fish rules the menu at this seaside
★   taverna at the very end of the beach in Kamari, which is the beach town of Kefalos. In fact, some patrons arrive by dinghies from their yachts anchored just offshore. The friendly staff will take you into the kitchen and show you the fresh catch of the day, then grill or bake it to your liking. ⊠ *Kamari, Kefalos,* ☎ *0242/71240. MC,V.*

$ 🏨 **Hotel Eleni.** This new, family-run hotel is in the little community of the Kamari, just about the only seaside town on Kos not to have succumbed lock, stock, and barrel to tourism. Surrounded by gardens and fields, the Eleni is absolutely delightful; rooms are large and much better furnished and decorated than those in most hotels in this price range, and all have shuttered doors that opened to large terraces with views of the sea. ⊠ *Kamari, Kefalos 85300,* ☎ *0242/71267. 32 rooms. Bar, breakfast room. MC, V.*

Beach

A chunk of the public beach (⊠ Mainland) is now occupied by a Club Méditerranée, though the rest is given over to beach clubs renting umbrellas and chairs and offering activities that include waterskiing and jet-skiing; the northern stretch, though, is undeveloped, providing miles of deserted sand backed by pine forests and dunes.

Outdoor Activities and Sports

BICYCLING

The flat island of Kos, particularly the area around the town, is good for bicycle riding. Ride to the **Asklepieion** for a picnic, or visit the **Castle of Antimacheia.** Note: Be aware of hazards such as cistern openings; very few have security fences around them. You can rent bicycles everywhere—in Kos town and at the more popular resorts. Try the many shops along Eleftheriou Venizelou Street in town. Renting a bike costs about 600 dr. per day; scooter rentals begin at about 2,000 dr.

PATMOS

Rocky and barren, the small island of Patmos, northwest of Kos, is the site of the famed Monastery of St. John the Theologian. Most of the island's approximately 2,500 people live in three villages: Skala, medieval Chora, and the small rural settlement of Kambos.

There is scattered evidence of Mycenaean presence on Patmos, and walls of the classical period indicate the existence of a town near Skala. In AD 95, during the emperor Domitian's persecution of Christians, St. John was banished to Patmos, where he lived until his reprieve two years later. He writes that it was on Patmos that he "heard . . . a great voice, as of a trumpet," commanding him to write a book and "send it unto the seven churches." Patmos was virtually abandoned after the 6th century and reemerges in history at the end of the 11th century with the arrival of Hosios Christodoulos, a man of education, energy, devotion, and vision who built the Theotokos Monastery in Kos and came to Patmos in 1088 to set up the island's now-famous monastery.

The island, which is popular among the faithful making pilgrimages to the monastery as well as with vacationing Athenians and a wealthy international set who have bought homes in Chora, has carefully contained development. As a result, Patmos retains its charm and natural beauty and even in the busy month of August is a delightfully sedate, unspoiled retreat.

Skala

302 km (187½ mi) east of Piraeus, 161 km (100 mi) north of Kos.

Skala, the island's main port, is also its commercial center and the location now of almost all the hotels and restaurants. It's a popular port of call for cruise ships, and in summer, huge liners often loom over town. There is not much to see in the town, but it is lively and very attractive, since strict building codes have been enforced and even new buildings have traditional architectural detail.

Beaches

While most of Patmos's beaches, which tend to be coarse shingle, are accessible by land, many sun worshipers choose to sail to them on the caïques that make regular runs from Skala, leaving in the morning; prices vary with the number of people making the trip (or with the boat). Ask for several "bids" to find out the going rate and the time of return, and don't be shy about negotiating. **Melloi Beach,** a 20-minute walk north of Skala or a quick caïque ride, is a sand-and-pebble strip with cafés and tavernas nearby. The beach at **Kambos Bay,** a 15- to 20-minute caïque ride or 10 minutes by car or bus from Skala, and mostly fine pebble and sand, is the most popular on the island, with nearby tavernas, windsurfing, waterskiing, and pedal boats. (The island bus network serves both beaches.) Both **Psiliamo** and **Little Psiliamo** (✉ On south shore) have fine sand, but they're hard to get to: a 45-minute caïque ride or a 20-minute walk from the taverna near the end of the road to the south end of the island. **Kakoskalo and Livadi** (✉ Beyond Kambos on the northern end of the island) are both easily accessible by road, are a combination of sand and pebbles, and are backed by shade-providing pine trees. The Livadi Beach Restaurant (✉ Take turnoff along the narrow road that follows the coast from Kambos toward Kakoskalo and Livadi beaches, ☎ 0247/32046) sits just above the beach and serves simple food, including delicious zucchini pancakes, and is an excellent place to retreat from the heat of the day and enjoy a beverage.

Dining and Lodging

$$ ✕ **Benetos.** Benetos Matthaiou, a native Patmian, and his American wife, Susan, recently opened this lovely restaurant, which is on the harborside road between Skala and the little community of Grikos. Dining is on a flowery terrace surrounded by a seaside garden that supplies the kitchen with fresh herbs and vegetables. These ingredients find their way into a selection of Mediterranean-style dishes that include phyllo parcels stuffed with spinach and cheese, the island's freshest Greek salad, and fresh seafood pastas, accompanied by an excellent wine list and gracious, friendly service. ✉ *Sapsila,* ☎ *0247/33089. MC, V. Closed Nov.–Apr.*

$$ ✕ **To Kima.** To say this excellent fish restaurant is "on the water" is an understatement—waves practically lap right onto the lovely sea-level dining terrace, while a covered terrace above suffices in bad weather. The menu changes daily, depending on what the local boats bring in. You will need to take a taxi or drive, since the restaurant is in the tiny community of Aspri at the end of a narrow track near Meloi Beach, about 10 minutes by car from Skala. ✉ *Aspri,* ☎ *0247/31192. No credit cards. Closed Nov.–Apr.*

$ ✕ **Grigoris.** This old favorite near the ferry landing is a good place to wait for the night boat to Athens. You can have grilled fish and meat, or a selection from the *magirefta* (precooked dishes). The interior is carefully decorated in rustic taverna style, and the tables under the spreading laurel tree are an especially pleasant place to take in the passing (and noisy) scene. ⊠ *Skala,* ☎ *0247/31515. No credit cards. Closed Nov.–Mar.*

$$$ ⊡ **Porto Scoutari.** It seems only fitting that Patmos should have a hotel
★   that reflects the architectural beauty of the island while providing luxurious accommodations, and this newly built, Mediterranean-style inn just outside Skala fits the bill. Guest rooms, which are enormous and have sitting and sleeping areas as well as kitchenettes, all have large terraces and face the sea and a verdant garden with a swimming pool. Furnishings differ from room to room and include brass beds and reproduction Greek antiques, while the lobby and breakfast rooms are also exquisitely decorated with traditional pieces. The gracious owner, Elina Scoutari, who lived in Washington, D.C., for many years, is on hand to see to the needs of her guests. ⊠ *Meloi 85500,* ☎ *0247/ 33123,* ⒻⒶⓍ *0241/33175. 35 rooms. Bar, breakfast room, kitchenettes, pool. AE, DC, MC, V.*

$ ⊡ **Blue Bay Hotel.** An enterprising Greek-Australian family has returned
★   to open this hotel, which is just outside Skala but within a 10-minute walk of everything. Its location, with a view over the open sea (shared by all but two of the rooms), is one of its great charms, as are the neatly decorated, immaculate rooms, all with terraces or balconies. ⊠ *Skala 85500,* ☎ *0247/31165,* ⒻⒶⓍ *0247/32303. 22 rooms. Breakfast room. No credit cards. Closed Nov.–Mar.*

$ ⊡ **Captain's House.** One of the very special places to stay in Patmos, largely because the owners are so pleasant, the Captain's House faces the sea at the edge of Skala. The feel of old Patmos has been re-created with stone arches accenting the multilevel lobby, while the white-painted rooms with their simple wood furniture are spotless and breezy, all with balconies that face either the harbor or the shady garden. ⊠ *Skala 85500,* ☎ *0247/31793,* ⒻⒶⓍ *0247/32277. 14 rooms. Breakfast room. AE, DC, MC, V. Closed mid-Oct.–Mar.*

Chora

2½ km (1½ mi) south, and above, Skala.

The village of Chora, clustered around the walls of the Monastery of St. John the Theologian, has become a preserve of international wealth; many of the houses, now exquisitely restored, are owned by Athenians and foreigners who discovered the settlement some years ago. Though the short distance from Skala may make walking seem attractive, the heat and steep incline can make this a challenging mode of transport. A taxi ride is not expensive, about 2,000 dr., and there is frequent bus service from Skala and other points on the island (240 dr.).

According to tradition, St. John wrote the text of Revelation in the little cave, the Sacred Grotto, now built into the **Monastery of the Apocalypse.** It is decorated with wall paintings of the 12th century and icons of the 16th. The monastery, constructed in the 17th century from architectural fragments of earlier buildings, and further embellished in later years, also contains chapels to St. Artemios and St. Nicholas. ⊠ *2 km/1 mi along the cobbled road from Skala heading to Chora,* ☎ *0241/31234.* 🎫 *Free, including lecture in English.* ☉ *Daily, usually 8–noon and 4–6 (hrs vary).*

★   The **Monastery of St. John the Theologian,** high above Skala, is one of the finest extant examples of a fortified medieval monastic complex.

From its inception, it attracted monks of education and social standing, who made sure that it was ornamented with the best sculpture, carvings, and paintings. It was an intellectual center, with a rich library and a tradition of teaching, and by the end of the 12th century it owned land on Leros, Limnos, Crete, and Asia Minor, as well as ships, which carried on trade exempt from taxes. A broad staircase leads to the entrance, which was fortified by towers and buttresses. The complex consists of buildings from a number of periods: In front of the entrance is the 17th-century **Chapel of the Holy Apostles;** the **main church** dates from the time of Christodoulos; the **chapel of the Virgin, refectory, kitchen,** and some of the **cells** are 12th century.

The monastery contains three of the most important cultural treasures of the Orthodox Church. The **library** (closed to the public), with a wonderful series of illuminated manuscripts, approximately 1,000 codices, and more than 3,000 printed volumes, was first catalogued in 1200; of the 267 works of that time, the library still has 111. Later catalogues make it possible to reconstruct the library's history and the monastery's intellectual life. The oldest codices, dating to the early 6th and the 8th centuries, contain parts of the Gospel of St. Mark and the Book of Job.

The documents in the archives (not open to the public) preserve a near-continuous record, down to the present, of the history of the monastery as well as the political and economic history of the region. The **treasury** contains a wide range of relics, icons, silver, and vestments, most dating from 1600 to 1800. Many of the objects are votives dedicated by the clerics, nobles, and wealthy individuals; one of the most beautiful is an 11th-century icon of St. Nicholas, executed in the finest mosaicwork, in an exquisitely chased silver frame. The more than 600 vestments are of luxurious fabrics, elaborately embroidered with gold, silver, and multicolored silks. ⊠ *Along cobbled road from Skala to Chora,* ☎ *0241/21954.* 🎫 *Monastery free, treasury 100 dr.* ☉ *Daily, usually 8:30–noon and 4–6 (hrs vary).*

Dining

$ ✕ **Vangelis.** This pleasant taverna is on the main square of Chora, and you can choose between a table there or in the back garden, where a raised terrace affords stunning views of the sea. Fresh grilled fish and lamb are the specialties, and simple dishes such as fried eggplant and tsatziki are excellent. The management is happy to help find rooms in private homes in Chora, which is otherwise devoid of tourist accommodation. ⊠ *Chora,* ☎ *0247/31967. No credit cards.*

Shopping

Patmos has some elegant boutiques selling jewelry and crafts, including antiques, mainly from the island. **Katoi** (⊠ On the main road to monastery, Chora, ☎ 0247/31487 or 0247/32107) has a wide selection of ceramics, icons, and silver jewelry of traditional design.

RHODES/THE DODECANESE A TO Z

Arriving and Departing

By Boat

Of the several ferry lines serving the Dodecanese, the **Dane Sea Line** (⊠ Akti Miaouli 33, Piraeus, ☎ 01/429–3240) and **G and A Ferries** (⊠ Etolikou 2, Piraeus, ☎ 01/419–9100) have the largest boats and the most frequent service, both sailing daily out of Piraeus. Travel agencies throughout Athens and on all the islands represent these and other lines serving the Dodecanese. The Athens–Dodecanese ferry schedule changes seasonally, so call the **Piraeus port authority** (☎ 01/422–

6000), any Athens EOT (☎ 01/322–2545), or a travel agency before booking.

If traveling to **Rhodes** by ferry, book one of the few ferries that go direct (like the *Rodos*); most stop first at Patmos, Leros, Kalymnos, and Kos. Fares from Athens to Rhodes are about 6,500 dr.–12,000 dr. (the top range includes berth), cars 14,000 dr.–17,500 dr., not including taxes. Ferry fares from Athens to **Patmos** are 3,405 dr.–5,828 dr., cars 13,500 dr.–17,500 dr.

By Car

If you drive to Greece, you may take your car to the Dodecanese on one of the large ferries that sail daily from Piraeus to Rhodes and less frequently to the smaller islands.

By Plane

There are at least four flights per day to Rhodes from Athens, and extra flights are added during high season. The flight, via **Olympic Airways** (✉ Ierou Lochou 9, Rhodes, ☎ 0241/24555, 01/966–6666 in Athens; FAX 01/966–6111), takes less than an hour and costs 22,800 dr. one-way. You can also fly to Rhodes from Heraklion four to five times a week (45 mins; 18,800 dr.) and from Thessaloniki usually twice weekly (75 mins; 26,800 dr.). It is possible to fly directly to Rhodes from a number of European capitals, especially on charters.

Rhodes airport (☎ 0241/92839) is about 20 minutes from Rhodes town, and it's best to take a taxi (about 1,600 dr.). Though private vehicles must have permits to enter the old town, a taxi may enter if carrying luggage, no matter what a reluctant driver tells you. In Kos, the **Olympic Airways office** is in Kos town (✉ 22 Vasileos Pavlou, ☎ 0242/28331 or 0242/28332) and a bus runs between the office and the **Kos airport** (☎ 0242/51229), about 45 minutes away, to meet the twice-daily flights from Athens. The smaller islands of **Leros, Karpathos, Kassos,** and **Kastellorizo** also have airports with less frequent service.

Getting Around

By Boat

There are frequent local boats, and in summer, hydrofoils connect the Dodecanese with one another. For information, contact any travel agency or local tourist office (☞ *below*).

By Bus

There is a good bus network on all the islands. Buses from Rhodes town leave from the bus stop (✉ Alexander Papagou, near Platia Rimini, ☎ 0241/27706) for points on the east side of the island, and from Averoff Street (✉ Beside new market, ☎ 0241/26300) for the west side.

By Car and Bicycle

On **Rhodes,** the roads are good, there are not many of them, and good maps are available. It is possible to tour the island in one day if you rent a car. Traffic is likely to be heavy only from Rhodes town to Lindos, and again as you near Kameiros. You can rent bicycles, including mountain bikes, in Rhodes town from **Mike's Motor Club** (✉ Kazouli 23, ☎ 0241/37420). In **Kos,** a car is advisable only if you are very pressed for time; most of what you want to see in Kos can by reached by bicycle or public transportation. Bicycle shops are plentiful. In **Patmos,** a car or motorbike makes it easy to tour the island, though most other sights and outlying restaurants are easily reached by bus or taxi and beaches can be reached either by bus or boat. There are no roads suitable for cars on **Symi,** where exploration is done on foot or by boat. The other Dodecanese islands are also best visited by public transportation.

By Plane
Olympic Airways (☞ *above*) runs five flights a week from Rhodes to Kos (30 minutes, 9,000 dr.) and other flights to the less-visited islands of Karpathos (8,800 dr.), Kassos (8,800 dr.), and Kastellorizo (7,000 dr.); the latter two are not served directly from Athens. You can also hook up with the Cycladic islands by flying to Mykonos (weekly flight, 15,000 dr.) or Santorini (three times weekly, 15,000 dr.). Schedules are reduced in winter.

By Taxi
Taxis are available throughout the island of **Rhodes,** with ranks in most resorts—cars can be flagged down anywhere. The central rank is in Rhodes town (⊠ Off Platia Rimini). If you call a radio taxi (☎ 0241/64712), the pick-up charge is an extra 200 dr. Typical fares from Rhodes town are as follows: to Ixia, 600 dr.; to Ialyssos/Trianda, 900 dr.; to Faliraki, 1,600 dr.; and to Lindos, 5,000 dr. Fares almost double between midnight and 6 AM.

Contacts and Resources

Car Rental
RHODES

Interrent-EuropCar (⊠ 28th of October St. 18, ☎ 0241/21958; ⊠ Airport, ☎ 0241/93105; ⊠ Lindos, ☎ 0244/31132). **Roderent** (⊠ A. Diakou 64, ☎ 0241/31831).

KOS

Helen's (⊠ Hotel Ramira, Psaldi, ☎ 0242/28882, FAX 0242/21013).

PATMOS

Tassos (⊠ Skala, ☎ 0247/31753, FAX 0247/32452).

Emergencies
As elsewhere in Greece, **pharmacies** in the Dodecanese post in their windows a list showing which locations are open 24 hours and on which days.

RHODES

Hospital (☎ 166 or 0241/25555). **Police** (⊠ Ethelondon Dodekanissou 45, new town, ☎ 100). **Tourist police** (⊠ On Museum Sq., old town, ☎ 0241/27423).

KOS

Police (☎ 0242/22100). **Tourist police** (☎ 0242/28277).

PATMOS

Hospital (☎ 0247/31211). **Police** (☎ 0247/31303).

SYMI

Police (☎ 0247/7111).

Guided Tours

A wide variety of local boat and land tours offered in Rhodes, Kos, Patmos, and Symi will take you to the usual sites (which you can probably reach by yourself anyway) and will give you a day picnicking on a remote beach, or even visiting the shores of Turkey.

RHODES

From April to October **Triton Holidays** (⊠ Plastira 9, ☎ 0241/21690, FAX 0241/31625), for example, organizes a visit to Lindos by boat; a caïque leaves Mandraki Harbor in Rhodes in the morning, deposits you in Lindos for a day of sightseeing and beachgoing, and returns you to Rhodes in the evening (3,500 dr.–4,500 dr.). Triton also offers day cruises down the east coast of Rhodes (3,500 dr.), to Symi (3,500 dr.), Kos (10,000 dr.), and Marmaris, Turkey (17,000 dr.), as well as a half-day inland hike (5,000 dr.); a half-day tour of Kameiros, Filerimos, and Petaloudes (5,000 dr.); and a scuba diving trip (9,000 dr.).

KOS

Aeolos Travel (⊠ 8 Annetas Laoumzi, ☎ 0242/26203, FAX 0242/25948) organizes one-day cruises to other islands.

PATMOS

Apollon Travel (⊠ Skala Harbor, ☎ 0247/31724, FAX 0247/31819). **Astoria Travel** (⊠ Skala Harbor, ☎ 0247/31205 or 0247/31208, FAX 0247/31975).

SYMI

Symi Tours (⊠ Symi Harbor, ☎ 0241/71307, FAX 0241/72292) will take you on a boat trip to the magical islet of Seklia (with a barbecue) for about 6,000 dr., or on a round-the-island trip for 6,000 dr.

Visitor Information

RHODES

The **Greek National Tourist Organization (GNTO or EOT)** (⊠ Archbishop Makarios and Papagou, in the new city, close to the medieval walls, ☎ 0241/23655, 0241/23255, or 0241/27466) has brochures and bus schedules.

The centrally located **Rhodes Municipal Tourism Office** on the east side of Platia Rimini near the bus station (☎ 0241/35945), open May–October, weekdays 8–7 and Saturday 8–6, is helpful with information and can exchange money for a 2% commission.

KOS

EOT (⊠ Akti Miaouli, ☎ 0242/29200).

PATMOS

EOT (⊠ Skala, ☎ 0247/31666).

13 The Northern Islands

Chios, Lesbos, Limnos, and Samos

Flung like puzzle pieces into the Aegean, each of these green and gold islands is distinct: Though ravaged by fire, Chios retains an eerie beauty and fortified villages, old mansions, Byzantine monasteries, and stenciled-wall houses; Lesbos, Greece's third-largest island and birthplace of legendary artists and writers, is dense with gnarled olive groves and dappled with mineral springs; Limnos is imprinted with mournful volcanic outcroppings, sand dunes, and ancient ruins; and lush, mountainous Samos, land of wine and honey, whispers of the classical wonders of antiquity.

By Lea Lane
and Toula
Bogdanos

QUIRKY, SEDUCTIVE, FERTILE, sensual, faded, sunny, worldly, ravishing, long-suffering, hedonistic, luscious, mysterious, legendary—these adjectives only begin to describe the northeastern Aegean islands of Limnos, Lesbos, Chios, and Samos. Closer to Turkey's coast than to Greece's—and quite separate from one another—they zigzag from north to south, respectively. Other islands most often considered a part of this startling and rather arbitrary archipelago are Ikaria, Samothraki, and Thasos—and four islets: Fourni, southeast of Ikaria; Psara and Inousses, flanking Chios to the west and east; and Agios Efstratios, south of Limnos.

Despite the Northern Islands' proximity to Asia Minor, they are the essence of Greece, the result of 4,000 years of Hellenic influence that lasted until 1923. Although Limnos, Lesbos, Chios, and Samos fell into obscurity in later centuries, especially under the Ottoman Empire, in the ancient world they prospered gloriously as important commercial and religious centers. They also were cultural hothouses, producing geniuses like Pythagoras, Sappho, and probably Homer.

Whether or not they once again become centers of art and culture, these islands are becoming popular travel destinations for Europeans, despite a military presence (most visible in Limnos), and the vestiges of bitterness about their mainland neighbors (and former conquerers) a few miles east. Despite the rhetoric—mostly instigated by the two governments—islanders don't hesitate to shuttle people back and forth to Turkey. And why not, when tourism has at last arrived?

Hilly, sometimes mountainous, with uncrowded beaches, natural attractions, noteworthy architecture, and historic sites, these are Greek islands to one-up your well-traveled friends with; they probably haven't even heard of most of them. They are not "party" islands, but towns and villages operating on a year-round schedule, much as the Cyclades may have been 50 years ago. People here go about their business as they have for centuries, with a gratifying Greek temperament of generosity, humor, open-mindedness, and optimism.

Pleasures and Pastimes

Beaches
From golden sand to black and red pebbles, from isolated turquoise coves to long sweeps of sunny coastline, beaches here are varied and often excellent. The relative lack of tourism often results in deserted stretches, rare in the more popular Greek islands. Many beaches allow topless sunbathing, unless they're part of the town's waterfront, but there is almost always a designated non-nude stretch where families congregate. Nude bathers should use discretion; in general, if you choose your spot carefully, you should have no problem with local people or the law.

Dining
Dine as the Greeks do on these islands, nursing an ouzo, observing the world, chatting with the service staff (even if you don't speak the same language, a smile and some hand motions will work wonders). Hospitality and good, fresh food abound. Although waterfront restaurants in the touristed areas can be mediocre, you will most often find delightful meals, especially in the villages. Unless noted, reservations are unnecessary, and casual dress is always acceptable. Go to the kitchen and point to what you want, or be adventurous and let the waiter choose for you (although you may wind up with enough food to feed a village). Ex-

cept for smaller catch, fish is relatively expensive and usually sold by the kilo. Remember that Greek lobster is often not the same sweet, succulent crustacean Americans enjoy now and then. Most Greek restaurants feature "lobster"—*astakos*—but this is really a sort of salt-water crayfish (its smaller cousin is called *karavides*). Shrimp is usually frozen, but most fish is fresh, except for the dried cod used in *bakaliaro* (fried cod with garlic sauce). If you can find it, try *kakavia* (a fishermen's soup with small catch, stewed with onions and tomatoes).

In Limnos, specialties include halvah, often served hot with lemon squeezed over it to cut the sweetness. Limnos is also the place for octopus grilled over embers and sweet *trahanas* (wheat kernels boiled in milk and dried). Besides being recognized for its mastic products, Chios is known for tangerines, eaten fresh or preserved in *gliko koutaliou* (a thick sugar syrup). In Lesbos, try the *keskek* (a special meat mixed with wheat served most often at festivals), and Kalloni bay sardines, the fleshiest in the Mediterranean; eat them with lemon and oil. Octopus simmered in wine, another island dish, goes perfectly with the famous island ouzo, most of which is made in Plomari. Fresh figs, almonds, and raisins are delicious; a local dessert is *baleze* (almond pudding). Samos is known for its thyme-scented honey; its wines, both pale dry white and Samian *moskhato* (sweet dessert wine); *yiorti* (the local version of keskek); and *revithokeftedes* (garbanzo patties).

CATEGORY	COST*
$$$$	over 10,000 dr.
$$$	7,000 dr.–10,000 dr.
$$	3,000 dr.–7,000 dr.
$	under 3,000 dr.

per person, for a three-course meal, including appetizer, entrée, and dessert (usually fruit), service, and tax but exluding drinks

Fishing

Fish thrive in these cool, clear Aegean waters. In Chios, locals usually fish the bays of Komi, Kardamila, and Limnia. In Lesbos you can catch sea bream, horse mackerel, dorado, and blackfish everywhere. Most fishing in Limnos is in Plateos Bay and off Cape Moudros. In Samos, sea bream, dorado, red mullet, and blackfish are plentiful in Marathokambos and Kerveli bays.

Hiking

Mountains and deep valleys, deserted towns, and craggy coasts provide for great walking or hiking. Be it while walking along flat coastal areas or trekking to summits, hikers can cover a variety of terrains and, through the seasons, a plethora of wildflowers, birds, and butterflies.

Lodging

Restored mansions, village houses, sophisticated resorts, budget hotels are all in place, and with the exception of summer you'll have little trouble finding accommodations. Local tourist boards will help, and cooperatives have been established in some villages, such as Mesta and Pirgi in Chios, which offer private rooms for rent. So in off-season here you might want to take a chance and wait till you get to town, to seek the best match, in person. Also, bargaining a bit is easier that way. Most hotel rooms are basic, with simple pine furniture and sparse furnishings often created by local craftspeople. These islands are still less costly than most, but prices are starting to go up and deluxe resorts are expensive.

Reserve early for better-category hotels, especially in Pythagorio on Samos and Molyvos on Lesbos. Off-season you can usually bargain over the official prices and avoid paying for a compulsory breakfast. Hotels are not air-conditioned unless noted, and, even in those that are, you must sometimes insist that it be turned on. Islanders are extremely friendly hosts, and although they may get a little irritable when the hordes descend in August, they still consider you a guest rather than a billfold. Unless noted otherwise, all hotels are open year-round.

CATEGORY	COST*
$$$$	over 30,000 dr.
$$$	15,000 dr.–30,000 dr.
$$	10,000 dr.–15,000 dr.
$	under 10,000 dr.

Prices are official rate for a standard double room with bath in high season, including tax and service and excluding breakfast. For those hotels in which half-board is compulsory, meals (one is breakfast) for two are included in price.

Monasteries

Aglow in jewel-toned marble and golden icons, fragrant with incense, some of Greece's best-preserved Byzantine monasteries are scattered throughout these islands, especially on Chios, Lesbos, and Samos. Sometimes they are in marvelous villages that are also filled with Byzantine treasures; often they are set high in the hills, so you can hike and enjoy the scenery and views as well. The bearded, ponytailed monks in their long black robes present dramatic visages and are often friendly and informative, happy to enlighten you on Greek Orthodox rituals and history. Be sure to cover your skin as much as possible, and show respect for the sanctity of the premises.

Nightlife and the Arts

Nightlife is expanding, especially in harbor towns such as Chios. Outdoor movie theaters are popular summer entertainment for islanders and tourists alike. They can be found in Mytilini, Molyvos, Eressos, Limnos, Kokkari, and Karlovassi. Check the billboards in the town square for showings. Every summer brings a new wave of trendy bars and discos, usually clustered on the beach. They come and go, so ask what's new when you arrive.

Island municipalities often organize cultural events that range from philosophy conferences to evenings of folk music. Chios usually is host to the summer conference of the International Society of Homeric Studies. In summer on Limnos, the Kehayiades folklore association presents island festivities. The best-known celebration is the **Molyvos Theater Festival** (☎ 0253/71323 tickets; 0253/71347 tourist office) held July–August in Lesbos. On Samos, the **Art School of the Aegean** (☎ 0941/351–5597), an American-based group, offers 2½-week courses in applied arts, with optional add-on tours.

Sailing

The islands' ragged coastlines, calm and uncrowded waters, strong winds, and deserted beaches make sailing a particular pleasure. Boat rentals are available on all the islands; repair services, fuel, and water are available at many of the larger ports on the islands, and moors are available at some. Your charter agency can usually give basic details about where to find fuel and water.

Shopping

Unique products, hard to find in Athens—and on other Greek islands—make interesting and original gifts. Snatch up the Samian wine, honey, and ceramics. The wine comes in several varieties: Samena is a dry white with a tinge of green; Fokianos is a rosé; Nectar and Dux are two familiar names for the sweet dessert wines favored by locals. On Lesbos, olive oil, chestnuts, local liquors, and local fabrics and pottery are popular. On Chios look for the unique mastic products, preserved fruits, ceramics, handwoven fabrics, and ouzo. Limnos is known for its honey, pistachios, ouzo, white wine, dried figs, and blue-black plums.

Traditional Festivals

As is true throughout this ancient country, festivals offer the visitor a wonderful view into age-old traditions—and lots of fun. Samos is filled with celebrations year-round. A wine festival in late-summer to early fall pleases with Panhellenic dances. In the height of summer, a fisherman's festival centers on the harbor at Pythagorio. Swimming races in Pythagorio commemorate the battle of Cavo Fonias on August 6, a day of celebration for the entire island. On Samos, on September 7 and 8 at Vourliotes village and the nearby Vrondiani monastery, there's dancing in the square and a distribution to the faithful of yiorti to celebrate the birthday of the Virgin. On September 14, the Timiou Stavrou monastery on Samos celebrates its feast day with a service followed by a *paniyiri* (feast), with music, firecrackers, booths of coconut candy, plastic toys, and *loukoumades* (honey-soaked dumplings). In October, Platanos, on Samos, throws a big bash when the new batch of wine and raki is ready. The firewater flows freely, served with *mezedes* (appetizers) and fruit macerated in alcohol.

One of Limnos's biggest festivals takes place September 7 at Ayios Sozon monastery, at the southern tip of the island, with island dances and songs. On Lesbos on the archangel Ayios Charalambos's feast day, usually the third weekend after Easter, you may observe an ancient, probably pagan, custom. A bull and several sheep decorated with flowers are sacrificed in the monastery's courtyard. The faithful dip handkerchiefs into the blood and mark their foreheads to protect themselves from sickness. The next day everyone feasts on keskek. Bull roasts and horse races also take place. The same occurs at Ayia Paraskevi, where horse races are held after the distribution of the meat. On August 15 the islanders of Lesbos flock to Agiassos to celebrate the Feast of the Assumption of the Virgin with dancing, drinking, and eating. On Clean Monday, at the end of Carnival in February, costumed islanders take part in a custom known as *vallia* (an improvised exchange of satirical verse). On Chios, festivities are held the last Sunday in Lent in Mostra Thymianon. In Thimiana, on Chios, on the last Sunday of Carnival (late February), islanders reenact the expulsion of the pirates in the Festival of Mostras; youths wave swords and dance the vigorous *talimi*. On Chios in Pirgi on August 15 and August 23 villagers perform local dances to commemorate the passing of the Virgin, the second most important religious holiday of the Greek Orthodox Church. On Chios on Easter Saturday night the effigy of Judas is burned in Mesta. Olympoi, southeast of Mesta, is host to festivities on the first Monday of Lent.

Turkish Jaunts

All within a few miles of the Turkish coast, the islands are good springboards for day trips (and longer) to ports such as Bodrum, Izmir, and Kuşadasi in Turkey. Ferry schedules can be checked at individual ports on the islands and at travel agencies. Day-trippers must carry passports.

Water Sports

The northern Aegean is relatively cold, except in summer and early fall, so most activity is on or next to the water rather than in it throughout much of the year. Snorkeling is not especially popular here, but if you bring your own equipment you can find calm coves on all the islands. Most resort hotels provide water sports on their beaches, and thanks to strong winds, windsurfing is especially popular. Scuba diving is prohibited in most areas because of underwater antiquities.

Exploring the Northern Islands

These unspoiled islands offer commodities that are valued in the ever-growing tourist business—a sense of discovery and a dose of reality. Here you'll get a chance to hang out with the locals and be treated more as a new friend than a tourist. Visitors to Limnos, Lesbos, Chios, and Samos tend to be Greeks or Europeans who have previously traveled to other Greek islands. Charters are limited because of lack of major airports, and English is not spoken as frequently as it is in more touristed areas. Trendy nightlife-seekers should stick to Mykonosynos; here the pleasures are quiet charms and great people. Each of these islands is worth a visit, even if it only a quick one.

Numbers in the text correspond to numbers in the margin and on the Limnos and Lesbos and Chios and Samos maps.

Great Itineraries

Seeing all four islands without having to rush—or hang around terminals—will take some preparation, as interisland transportation may not be as frequent as it is on the more touristed islands. Check ahead for transportation schedules. Whenever possible, take hydrofoils rather than ferries; they are more costly, but they can cut time in half. Lesbos has daily air service from Athens and Salonica and daily ferry service from Piraeus; it makes a good base from which to start exploring.

The packed four-day itinerary will give you a brief overview of each island; more relaxed travelers can pick and choose among the islands. The 7- and 10-day itineraries will allow you to explore each island in greater depth, pursuing what strikes your fancy. In general, it is best to arrive on Lesbos and head north to Limnos; the two are connected by ferry, hydrofoil, and daily air service. Then head back to tour Lesbos. Take the ferry or hydrofoil to nearby Chios and then to Samos, the most southerly island of the four. You can go on from Samos to other Greek islands, the Turkish coast, or back to Athens or Piraeus, as connections are good by sea and sometimes by air.

IF YOU HAVE 4 DAYS

This is a real challenge, but you can at least manage an overview of each island. You will need to rent vehicles to get around, and you must make sure that the ferry from ⊞ **Lesbos** ⑫–㉘ to ⊞ **Limnos** ①–⑪ is running on the day you start out. Day one starts with a quick tour of **Limnos,** encompassing **Myrina** ① port and the **Cabiri** and prehistoric **Poliochni** sites (only for archaeological diehards). Return to **Myrina,** where you can catch the ferry or fly to **Lesbos.** On day two move from the capital, **Mytilini** ⑫, to northern villages like **Petra** ⑳ and dreamy **Molyvos** ⑲, to Sappho's birthplace in **Eressos,** to Agiassos hill village and **Plomari,** a fishing hamlet that's also a resort. Day three begins on ⊞ **Chios** ㉙–㊵ in the Ottoman quarter of **Chios town** ㉙. It continues to **Nea Moni monastery** ㉞, with its fine mosaics and tragic history. From hilltop Avgonima, head west down to the coast road; then travel via **Lithi** and **Vessa** to the southern mastic villages of stenciled **Pirgi** ㊱ and labyrinthine **Mesta** ㊳. Day four circles ⊞ **Samos** ㊶–㊿, including **Pythagorio** ㊶ and the **Temple of Heraion** ㊷, one of the Seven Wonders of the Ancient World. Then travel through mountain villages such as **Pirgos** ㊹ to the tiny harbor of **Ormos Marathokambou** ㊻ and the fishing village of **Kokkari** ㊿, ending at **Samos town** ⑸, the capital.

IF YOU HAVE 7 DAYS

Enhance the four-day schedule, exploring your interests in greater depth. Depending on how you add the time, for the three extra nights you could remain in one favorite place to cut down on traveling. You might add another day on ⊞ **Chios** ㉙–㊵, traveling north from the capital to **Daskalopetra** ㉚ (Teacher's Rock), where Homer is said to have taught, visiting the Byzantine village there, and the isolated beaches of the north. You could spend more time in **Pirgi** ㊱ and **Mesta** ㊳, with time for shopping, and relaxing at the volcanic beach at **Emborio** ㊲, near the mastic villages. On ⌘ **Lesbos** ⑫–㉘, you could visit the hot springs around **Eftelo,** east of Mithymna. Or on ⌘ **Samos** ㊶–㊾, meander on the trails around the picturesque hill villages between **Kokkari** ㊿ and **Kondeika.**

IF YOU HAVE 10 DAYS

Stick to the seven-day schedule, adding three extra days wherever they fit best, on the islands of your choice, for relaxing and recreation—hiking, enjoying water sports, shopping, or just lazing on an Aegean beach. You might bird-watch on ⌘ **Samos** ㊶–㊾, study ancient ruins on ⌘ **Lesbos** ⑫–㉘, or just veg out in one of the new deluxe beach resorts on ⌘ **Limnos** ①–⑪. You could visit the other nearby north-Aegean islands and islets, or take a ferry to ⌘ **Turkey** from Chios or Samos.

When to Tour

Ask locals and they'll usually say May. But also April, June, and September through October are especially lovely periods—the weather is ideal, wildflowers and shrubs are in bloom, and the crowds have thinned. Since these four islands are not yet overrun with tourists even in summer, you will find isolated nooks where you can enjoy the therapeutic sounds of the wind, the birds, and the lapping water.

When booking, keep in mind the enlightening cultural events and religious festivals called *paniyiri,* which usually take place on a saint's day or patriotic holiday. Easter, in April, comes later than the time celebrated at home. On Lesbos a cultural week of drama, dance, and music exhibitions occurs each May. On Chios, festivities take place during Lent and summer.

LIMNOS

Low and gently rolling on the Aegean, near Turkey and the Dardenelle straits separating Europe and Asia, Limnos is essentially an agricultural and garrison island guarding the entrance to the Black Sea. On the route less traveled, for years the island attracted few visitors except for Greek families who came for the beaches; German windsurfers; and British subjects on cruise ships who wanted to see Moudros Bay, an important site of the Gallipoli campaign. But today, resort development and a new jetport to be completed before the turn of the century are slowly turning Limnos into a sun-and-fun hideaway for European charter groups.

The island is divided into west and east by deeply indented Moudros Bay on the south and Pournias Bay on the north. Tiny villages of stone houses punctuate a checkerboard of hay and grain fields decorated with gaudy scarecrows; calm plains give way to dark volcanic rocks and remote sandy beaches. Once well wooded, the island's interior is now so barren that, when giving directions, villagers might tell you to turn at "the tree." Green enough in spring, the island becomes crackling brown in summer, and villages often shut off water in the evenings to conserve. Dirt roads cover much of the island, and the southern part is filled with sand dunes, unusual for Greece, and dubbed rather grandly "The Sahara of Limnos."

Archaeological sites scattered throughout the island and artifacts collected in the museum in the port town of Myrina attest to four ancient cities. Civilizations here had contact with the Trojans across the straits. Limnos sided with Athens during the Peloponnesian Wars, and in AD 395, with the Roman Empire split, it became an important outpost of Byzantium. The Genoese ruled Lesbos starting in 1462, and the Turks conquered it in 1478 and ruled until 1912 during which time it prospered in shipping and trade. Pirate attacks through the centuries resulted in many inland villages, established for protection. These villages maintain an atmosphere of calmness and timelessness, reflected in the gentle landscape as well.

Myrina

❶ *25 km (15½ mi) west of Moudros.*

Myrina, the capital on the west end, was a flourishing town during antiquity; according to legend, it was named after the wife of the first king. Cobblestone streets and a bazaar remind you of its past. Today, deluxe resorts are making the area prosperous again, and young sailors fill the town with good cheer and a rather casual military presence in an altogether peaceful setting.

A 12th-century **Genoese-Turkish fortress** melds with the rust-brown rock formations cleaving the bay in two. Of all the north Aegean kastros (forts), this one looms most dramatically. The castle was begun by Byzantium, then fell to the Venetians, the Genoese, and finally in 1479 to the Turks. It's a short hike to the top, and although not much is there except some cisterns, at sunset on a clear day distant Mt. Athos seems to rise, shimmering out of the western sea. ✉ *Above town.* ✆ *Free.*

Backing up to the castle are wind-buffetted white houses with wood balconies, many of them mariners' homes, interspersed with the occasional Ottoman stone mansion. The **Romeikos Yalos,** or "Roman Beach" (✉ On waterfront below fortress), is the best place to stroll, especially in the fading purple twilight. Sophocles referred to this area in the one line saved from his tragedy "Limneades"; roughly translated: "Athos overshadows the back of Lemnian cow." Mt. Athos in northern Greece can indeed be seen still, and in antiquity there was a record of a stone or bronze cow standing here in this promenade area.

The exceptionally good provincial **archaeological museum** in a 19th-century mansion near the water chronicles the island's history with finds from Poliochni, Hephaestia, the Cabirion sanctuary (☞ *below*), and ancient Myrina. Gold jewelry and bronze cheese graters share space in a room of metal objects. Presentation is chronological and better arranged than at many larger museums. In fact, in 1996 it was named by the European Council of Culture as the fifth-best small museum in Europe. ✉ *Romaikos Gialos beach,* ✆ *0254/22990.* ✆ *500 dr.* ◷ *Tues.– Sun. 9–3.*

On the other side of the harbor is the **Turkish Quarter,** with its colorful bazaar, but scant remnants of the Ottoman occupation. Among them, the ruins of a hamam, a former bathhouse, now serve as an impressive entrance to a store, and a fountain built in 1771 still spills potable water. Its inscription in calligraphy, perhaps an unknowing portent of cruise business to come, states: "Every living thing comes out of water."

Beaches

Although the Limnean coasts are rocky, sand beaches are common throughout the island. The closest beach to town is **Avlonas,** past Akti Myrina. Just southeast of Myrina are two lovely, quiet beaches. The **❷** beach at **Plati** village, down the road about 2 km (1 mi), is long and **❸** sandy, with sheep grazing below. The sandy beach near **Thanos** village,

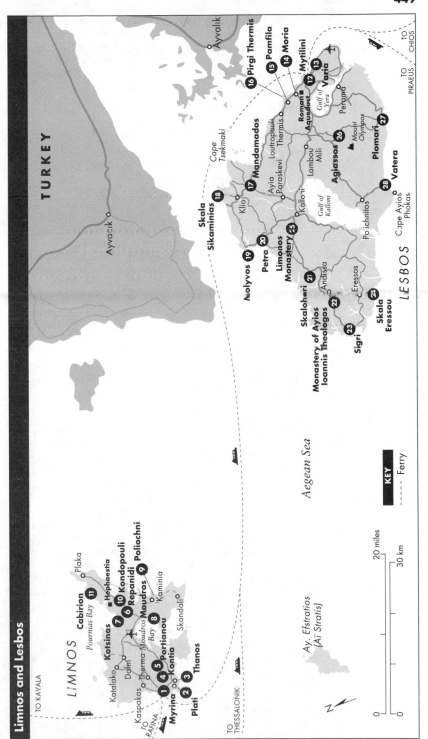

Limnos and Lesbos

with its ruined 14th-century church, 4 km (2½ mi) south of Myrina and easily reached by car or moped, is huge and set between volcanic crags—reputed to be the best on Limnos. **Ayios Pavlos** is a nearly 1-km-long (½-mi-long) stretch of beach near Kondias, a traditional village with stone houses.

Dining and Lodging

$$ ✕ **Zimbabwe.** The food at this café-ouzeri, with seating under a huge jujube tree, belies its humble appearance and is quite popular among locals. Grills—such as octopus, sausage, or chops, or mezedes like *melitsanosalata*, or beets—are tasty and carefully prepared but not inexpensive. As the name suggests, the friendly English-speaking chef and his wife spent 30 years in southern Africa (as many Limnians seem to). Go early to be sure of a table. ⊠ *Plati village, off main square,* ☎ *0254/ 24954. No credit cards.*

$ ✕ **Avra.** Although the service may be slow (who's in a rush?), this excellent taverna serves substantial portions of *magirefta* (here, casseroles) and grilled items in the evenings. Try the spit-roasted chicken basted with lemon-oregano sauce, moussaka, and the *tzoutzoukakia* (sausage meatballs). ⊠ *Next to Myrina port authority, on harbor square,* ☎ *0254/22523. No credit cards.*

$ ✕ **O Platanos.** This family-style taverna sits in a charming square among old houses and two huge plane trees planted a century ago. The owner has a limited menu of traditional dishes: *kokkinisto* (stewed meat) with okra, spinach, or peas; *makaronada* (pasta); *stifado* (a traditional dish of stewed rabbit in tomatoes, wine, and onions); *horiatiki* (large Greek salads); and *lakhano* dolmades (grape leaves stuffed with cabbage and rice). The barrel wine is a hefty red from the village of Ayia Sofia. ⊠ *Odos Kyda, main bazaar street, Myrina,* ☎ *0254/22070. No credit cards.*

$$$$ 🏨 **Portomyrina Palace.** Opened in 1995 with white angled architecture and scads of cool white marble within, this understated resort is now the best in town, built around a tiny archaeological site incorporated into the landscaped property. White umbrellas crisply line a shimmering Olympic-size pool with mosaic tiles the color of the sea beyond. Rooms have balconies, and some are set up for guests with disabilities, an uncommon accommodation at Greek hotels. For fun, check out the astoundingly lush Akti Myrina Bungalows, a five-minute walk away. This well-known rustic resort is now a private club for Italians but worth a walk through for the flowers alone. ⊠ *Myrina 81400,* ☎ *0254/ 24805 or 0254/24806,* ℻ *0254/24858. 140 rooms, 12 bungalows. 2 restaurants, 3 bars, in-room safes, 1 indoor and 1 outdoor pool, 3 tennis courts, shops, conference room. AE, MC, V. Closed Apr.–Nov.*

$$$ 🏨 **Villa Afroditi.** Panayiotis Papasotiriou, Afroditi, his wife, and son George provide energetic multilingual service at this hotel and the Afroditi Apartments in Myrina (☞ *below*). The garden hotel has careful landscaping, generous buffet breakfasts, and an enduringly popular pool flanked by a bar and restaurant. Giant *kioupia* (ceramic urns) salvaged from an old olive oil mill dot the lawn, and live guitar music is a bonus after dinner in summer. ⊠ *150 yards inland from Plati beach, 81400,* ☎ *0254/24795,* ℻ *0254/25031. 20 rooms, 2 suites. Restaurant, bar, air-conditioning. No credit cards.*

$$ 🏨 **Afroditi Apartments.** The owners run this hilltop hotel with cheerful efficiency, and it could easily belong to a higher price category. Just a few yards from Romaikos, this complex is surrounded by geraniums, roses, petunias, and fruit trees. Besides the housekeeping apartments, five rooms are on the roof. The spic-and-span rooms are sprightly, with cane-and-bamboo furniture and orthopedic-quality mattresses. Guests can go for a spin on the speedboat or rent the hotel caïque—prices are

negotiable. ⊠ *Riha Nera area, across from Ayios Pandelimon, Myrina 81400,* ☎ *0254/23489, 01/964–1910 in Athens;* FAX *0254/25031. 5 rooms, 16 apartments. Kitchenettes, minibars. AE, DC, MC, V. Closed Nov.–Mar.*

The Arts

The **Kehayiades folklore association** presents island dances in costume, accompanied by the local version of a Cretan lyre; contact the Myrina tourist office (☞ Visitor Information *in* The Northern Islands A to Z, *below*).

Nightlife

Bars and music spots that appeal as much to soldiers stationed on the island as to tourists are clustered by the harbor and north of the kastro. A typical club with pop music is **Disco Avlonas Club** (⊠ 2 km/1 mi outside town on the Thanos road, ☎ 0254/23885).

Outdoor Activities and Sports

SAILING

Ports at both Myrina (☞ *above*) and Moudros (☞ *below*) have fuel, water, and repair services.

WATER SPORTS

You can usually rent paddleboats and canoes on **Romaikos Gialos beach** (⊠ East of Kastro) in Limnos.

Shopping

Even in ancient times, Limnos produced estimable agricultural products. Until the 1960s, its cotton, ginned in a stone building in Myrina, was considered second only to Egyptian. During the Byzantine period, Limnos was the granary for Constantinople and known for its fine wheat; it is no longer exporting it. You can still find special products. Pottery and woodcarvings are popular and traditional. Like its sister island Samos, Limnos is known for its wine: red, rosé, a dry white (a favorite of Aristotle's), and sweet Moschato. It also produces exceptional thyme-scented honey, jewel-tone syruped sweets made from local fruits such as cherries and black plums, and a rich-tasting white sheep cheese called Kalathi, prepared in small baskets.

En Route   At **Therma** (⊠ 5 km/3 mi east, between Myrina and the airport), medicinal waters have been soothing tired muscles and bones since the 15th century. You can spend an hour or even overnight at this former Turkish bath now named Sirens—newly renovated into a comfortable, modern environment with roses in front, private rooms and baths, and a café; cost is 1,000 dr. for bath, 5,000 dr. for overnight. Five minutes away is an orchard that sells sublime syruped fruits and sweets, packaged to go, in a small roadside storefront. Samples are happily provided. Ask at the spa for directions.

Kontia

④   *8 km (5 mi) east of Myrina.*

Set between volcanic outcroppings, this is one of the most traditional villages in Limnos, with tree-lined streets and stone houses once owned by shipowners. The many plane trees and eucalyptus in the area are unusual on this island, and the pine forest is the only one on Limnos.

Portianou

⑤   *3 km (2 mi) northeast of Kontia.*

The island's only folk museum containing costumes and handicrafts is on the main street here but is often closed. Ask a local for the hours. In 1915, a young Winston Churchill installed his headquarters in this village while organizing the Allied powers for the Gallipoli campaign of World War I. The mansion he once lived in was being renovated at press time. A nearby cemetery, smaller than the one in Moudras across the bay, holds the graves of 348 English-speaking servicemen killed in the battle.

Repanidi

6   *26 km (16 mi) east of Myrina.*

On your way to Moudros you can take the side road to this farming village, set in the remains of an oak forest; acorns were once valued as trade goods and locals owned the ships to transport them. This was the site of one of the first schools on the island, in an old mill, in 1824. Two huge jars dug in volcanic stone are at the edge of the village, used

7   for storing grain and wine. From here you can turn off for **Kotsinas,** a village and the ruins of a Byzantine city, with its castle overlooking Pournias Bay. A statue on a hill commemorates a local woman named Mauroula who became a heroine when she died in a battle against the Turks in 1478. A few steps away is a tiny sanctuary, and an older one, in a cave, can be reached by steep steps.

Music
Locals say that this area is where to go for the real thing—live Greek music of all sorts. Ask around when you get here.

Moudros

8   *25 km (15½) mi east of Myrina.*

Moudros is the island's second-largest town. In 1915, the Allies launched an attack on the Dardanelles from this large, protected harbor. Casualties were evacuated back here to the hospital, or were laid to rest. A thousand or so Allied war graves are in the **East Moudros Military Cemetery** (⊠ 1 km/½ mi out of town on Roussopoli Rd.), the largest Commonwealth cemetery in Greece. Here in 1918 the Turks surrendered to the British a few days before the Germans sued for peace.

Poliochni

9   *32 km (20 mi) east of Myrina, 20 km (12½ mi) south of Cabirion.*

Poliochni, on a bluff overlooking a rocky beach, predates Troy across the Aegean on the Turkish Coast. Italian archaeologists, sometimes working on-site, may offer their expertise on this complicated archaeological site. They have uncovered four layers of settlements, the oldest predating the Minoan kingdoms in Crete. In 2100 BC an earthquake destroyed the settlement, and discoveries from that time, such as gold jewelry, were sent to Athens for display. The only architectural remnants—an extremely thick wall and house foundations—come from the second-oldest level, the 2000 BC city where the oldest baths in the Aegean were found. The third dates to the Late Bronze Age, and the last settlement is a contemporary of Mycenae, a close contact of Poliochni in ancient times (1500 BC–1100 BC). ⊠ *On bluff overlooking rocky beach.* 🎟 *Free.* ☉ *Daily 9:30–5:30.*

Kondopouli

10   *26 km (16 mi) northeast of Myrina, 9 km (5½ mi) northeast of Moudros.*

Archaeology buffs should watch for signs to the ruins of ancient **Hephaestia** (sometimes called Paliopoli), inhabited since prehistory. Located on Tigani Bay, from classical times to the Byzantine era, it was the prin-

ciple city on Limnos, honoring the patron diety. Excavations have so
far uncovered traces of houses, a 6th-century BC sanctuary, a cemetery,
and a Roman theater. This and Cabirion (☞ *below*) are informal
sites—they will be disappointing for those expecting grand ruins. The
treasures found here in the graves are in the museum in Myrina. ✉
On dirt road on rocky promontory. 💺 *Free.* ⊙ *Daily 9:30–3:30.*

Shopping
The **Weaving Cooperative** here contains the island's best examples of
local folk art, including woven goods, pottery and wood carvings.

Chloe

*30 km (18½ mi) northeast of Myrina, 3 km (2 mi) northeast of Kon-
dopouli.*

In a dramatic setting overlooking the water near the village of Chloe,
⑪ Cabirion is the ruins of one of the oldest sanctuaries of the Cabiri cult,
which worshiped the underworld gods. Archaeologists found a large
stoa with 11 columns and many inscriptions giving clues to early
Limnian life. According to legend, Cabirion is also the site of the famous cave of Philoctetes, the hero of the Trojan War who supposedly
hid here with a gangrenous leg and whose story has been dramatized
by Sophocles. The steep walk down to the cave by the sea is bordered
by wildflowers. Wear comfortable shoes, hold on to the rope as you
descend, and enjoy the view. ✉ *Across silted-up bay from Hephaestia,
reached via a separate road toward Plaka.* 💺 *Free.* ⊙ *Daily 9:30–3:30.*

LESBOS

This third-largest island in Greece is filled with beauty, but its real treasures are the creative artists and thinkers it has produced and inspired
though the ages. Lesbos was once a major cultural center, known for
its Philosophical Academy, where Epicurus and Aristotle taught; it was
the birthplace of the philosopher Theophrastus, who presided over the
Academy in Athens; of the great lyric poet Sappho; of Terpander, the
"father of Greek music"; and of Arion, who influenced the later playwrights Sophocles and Alcaeus, inventors of the dithyramb (a short poem
with an erratic strain). Even in modernity, artists emerged from Lesbos: Theophilos, a poor villager who earned his ouzo by painting
some of the finest naive art modern Greece has produced; novelists Stratis
Myrivilis and Argyris Eftaliotis; and, more recently, the latest Greek
Nobel Prize winner, poet Odysseus Elytis.

The island's history stretches back to the 6th century BC, when its two
mightiest cities, Mytilini and Mithymna, settled their squabbles under
the tyrant Pittahos, considered one of Greece's Seven Sages. Thus
began the creative era, but later times brought forth the same pillaging and conquest that overturned other Greek islands. In 527 BC the
Persians conquered Lesbos, and the Athenians, Romans, Byzantines,
Venetians, Genoese, and Turks took their turns adding their influences. After the Turkish conquest, from 1462 to 1912, much of the
population was sent to Turkey and traces of past civilizations that weren't
already destroyed by earthquakes were wiped out by the conquerors.

Lesbos has more inhabitants than either Corfu or Rhodes, with only
a fraction of the tourists, so here you'll get a good idea of real island
life in Greece. It looks like a giant jigsaw-puzzle piece, carved by two
large sandy bays, the gulfs of Yera and Kalloni. The Turks called Lesbos the "garden of the empire" for its fertility: In the east and center
of the island, about 12 million olive trees line the hills in seemingly

endless undulating groves, reputedly producing Greek's finest oil. The western lansdscape is filled with oak trees, sheep pastures, rocky outcrops, and mountains. Wildflowers and grain cover the valleys, while the higher peaks are wreathed in dark green pines. Marshes, beaches, springs, desert, even a pertified forest—Lesbos terrain provides a little something for everyone.

Mytilini

⑫ *42 km (26 mi) northeast of Plomari.*

This busy main town and port, with stretches of grand waterfront mansions and an interesting old bazaar area, was once the scene of a dramatic moment in Greek history. Early in the Peloponnesian War, it revolted against Athens, but surrendered in 428 BC. As punishment, the Athens assembly decided to kill all men in Lesbos and enslave all women and children, and a boat was dispatched to carry out the order. The next day a less vengeful mood prevailed and the assembly repealed its decision and sent a second ship after the first. The second ship pulled into the harbor just as the commander of the first finished reading the death sentence. Just in time, Mytilini was saved.

Mytilini (so important through history that many call Lesbos by the port's name alone) is set on the ruins of an ancient city and sprawls across two bays like an amphitheater. The intervening pine-covered headland—a nice spot for a picnic—supports a **stone fortress,** its intact walls seeming to protect the town even today. Built by the Byzantines on a 600 BC temple of Apollo, it was repaired with available material (note the ancient pillars crammed between the stones) by Francesco Gateluzzi of the famous Genoese family. Look above the gates for the two-headed eagle of the Palaiologos emperors, the horseshoe arms of the Gateluzzi family, and inscriptions made by Turks, who enlarged it; today it is a **military bastion.** Inside the castle there's only a crumbling **prison** and a **Roman cistern,** but you should make the visit for the fine view. ⊠ *On pine-covered hill,* ☎ *0251/27297.* ☞ *400 dr.* ☉ *Daily sunrise–sunset.*

The only vestige of ancient Mytilini is a **Hellenistic theater** (⊠ In pine forest northeast of town), one of the largest in ancient Greece. Pompey admired it so much that he copied it for his theater in Rome; it is currently under excavation.

The bustling waterfront just south of the headland is where most of the town's sights are clustered. Stroll the main bazaar street of the former Turkish quarter, **Ermou,** past the fish market on the southern end, where men haul in their sardines, mullet, and octopi. Narrow lanes are filled with antiques shops and grand old mansions. The enormous post-Baroque church of **St. Therapon,** built in the 19th century, is reminiscent of some styles in Italy. It has an ornate interior, a frescoed dome, and, in its courtyard, a **Byzantine museum** filled with icons. ⊠ *Southern waterfront,* ☎ *0251/28916.* ☞ *200 dr.* ☉ *Mon–Sat. 10–1.*

In front of the cathedral of **Ayios Athanasios,** there is a **traditional Lesbos house,** restored and furnished in 19th-century style. Call owner Marika Vlachou to arrange a visit. ⊠ *Mitropoleos 6,* ☎ *0251/28550.* ☞ *Free.* ☉ *By appointment only.*

The **archaeological museum,** in a neoclassical mansion, will help you imagine Lesbos's past. Among its treasures are finds from prehistoric Thermi, mosaics from Hellenistic houses, and reliefs of comic scenes from the 3rd-century Roman House of Menander. A garden in the back holds an annex and some grave stelae. Note that a new wing of the museum is nearby at the corner of Noemvriou and Melinas Merkouri.

✉ *Argiri Eftaliotis 7, behind the ferry dock.* ☎ *0251/28032.* ⊡ *500 dr.* ⊙ *Tues.–Sun. 8:30–3.*

Dining and Lodging

$$ ✕ **Dimitrakis.** As many as 10 types of decidedly fresh fish are available at this restaurant, which locals call the "little boat grill" because of its nautical decor. Start your meal with *bourekakia* (ham and *kasseri*-cheese pie); favorites are the simple grilled fish and the bakaliaro. This restaurant is hopping, but you can enjoy dinner outside, lulled by the sounds of rocking boats. ✉ *Hristouyennon 1944 Rd., Fanari quay of Mytilini,* ☎ *0251/23818. No credit cards.*

$ ✕ **Asteria.** This Mytilini institution offers seven or eight magirefta nightly and a complete grill selection, including thick, juicy beef patties and *exohiko* (meat baked in a pot with vegetables). Among the specialties are eggplant with artichokes and *yiouvetsaki politiko* (beef cooked in a clay pot with aromatic sweet spices). In summer, you sit at tables facing the harbor. ✉ *Koundourioti 56, Mytilini,* ☎ *0251/22689. No credit cards.*

$$$ ⛆ **Laureate Hotel.** Encompassing an 1880 stone mansion with friezes, cornices, pedestals, and other architectural delights, this hotel lets you live like well-off islanders have here for a century. Located on the beach, the modern complex has most of the rooms and facilities; the mansion building contains seven of the suites. All units have kitchenettes, balconies, and phones in the bathrooms, and rooms are available for disabled guests. Locals say this is the best in town. ✉ *Varia, 2 km (1 mi) from Mytilini, 81100,* ☎ *0251/43111,* FAX *0251/41629. 76 rooms, 10 suites. 2 restaurants, 2 bars, kitchenettes, pool, meeting rooms. AE, MC, V.*

$$$ ⛆ **Mytilana Village.** Several buildings circling a pool on 14 acres make up this hotel on a predominantly pebbled beach in the Gulf of Yera. The rooms have blond pine furniture and balconies. The half-board option, which includes two meals, is convenient, since most restaurants are a taxi drive away. The taverna by the seaside is especially lovely. A local bus makes the round-trip into town once a day. ✉ *Ethniki Odos, 6 km (4 mi) outside Mytilini toward Kalloni, 81107,* ☎ *0251/20653, 0251/20654, or 0251/29655,* FAX *0251/26572. 62 rooms. Restaurant, bar, minibars, pool. AE, DC, V. Closed Nov.–Mar.*

$$ ⛆ **Rex.** This peaceful hotel, in one of the town's well-heeled neighborhoods, is covered with such glorious bougainvillea that tourists often stop to photograph the entrance; but the facade may be its best feature. Mirrors and high ceilings in the rooms create a spacious feeling despite the dark carved furniture. ✉ *Katsakouli 3, behind archaeological museum, Mytilini 81100,* ☎ *0251/28523. 16 rooms, 7 with bath. No credit cards.*

$$ ⛆ **Villa 1900.** This renovated neoclassical house, in a fairly quiet lo-
★ cation near the stadium, is a real treat, with stonework, a lush garden, and old-fashioned details such as iron beds, family photographs, and, in a few rooms, ceilings painted with women and flowers. The best rooms are the three in the converted garret. Guests sit in the garden for breakfast, which includes fresh juice from the hotel's own fruit trees. ✉ *Vostani 24, Mytilini 81100,* ☎ *0251/23448 or 0251/43437,* FAX *0251/ 28034. 9 rooms. Breakfast room. No credit cards. Closed Nov.–Mar.*

Nightlife

BARS

Action is at both ends of the harbor, with lots of variety. Packed on summer nights is **To Musio** (The Museum) (✉ *Vournazi 21, Mytilini,* ☎ *0251/42140*), so called because it's ensconced in a neoclassical house with traditional furnishings.

A popular music bar for a youngish crowd is the **Music Cafe** (⊠ Corner of Mitropoleos and Vernardaki), with jazz, blues, and classical tapes and live jazz. It opens at 7:30 PM and stragglers can stay until 2.

Outdoor Activities and Sports

WATER SPORTS

You can moor at most large coastal villages in Lesbos, including Mytilini, Molyvos, Skala Sikaminias, Sigri, Plomari, and Skala Eressou, for fuel and water. Paddleboats, canoes, and sailboarding equipment are available on Lesbos at Sigri, Molyvos, Petra, Vatera, and Skala Eressou.

Varia

⑬ *4 km (2½ mi) southeast of Mytilini.*

This suburb is a cultural center, the home village of early 20th-century painter Theophilos. Crammed sometimes to the ceiling in the **Theophilos museum** are 80 of his imaginative works—great washes of color detailing the everyday life of local folk such as fishermen and farmers, and fantasies of another age. Theophilos lived in poverty but painted airplanes and exotic cities—which he had never seen. His work is also displayed in the folk museum in Athens. ⊠ *Near the sea,* ☎ *0251/28179.* 🖅 *500 dr.* 🕑 *Tues.–Sun. 10–1 and 4:30–8.*

The **Museum of Modern Art** was the home of Stratis Eleftheriadis, better known by his French name, Thériade. This artist and critic helped publicize Theophilos and rose to fame as the foremost publisher of graphic art in Paris. The museum exhibit includes his publications—*Minotaure* and *Verve* magazines—and his colorful collection of works (mostly lithographs) done exclusively for the avant-garde publisher by Picasso, Matisse, Chagall, Roualt, Giacometti, and Miró. The display is surprisingly joyous and, combined with a visit to the Theophilos museum (☞ *above*), is a must for art lovers who enjoy originality, whimsy, and new works by favorites. ⊠ *Next to Teriade Library,* ☎ *0251/23372.* 🖅 *600 dr.* 🕑 *Tues.–Sun. 9–2 and 3–5.*

Moria

⑭ *6 km (4 mi) northwest of Mytilini, 7 km (4½ mi) northwest of Varia.*

Moria's **Roman aqueduct** dates back to the 2nd century. It was in Lesbos that Julius Caesar first made his mark. Sent to Bythinia to drum up a fleet, he hung around so long at King Nicodemus's court that he was rumored to be having an affair with the king, but he finally distinguished himself by saving a soldier's life.

Pamfila

⑮ *8 km (5 mi) north of Mytilini, 4 km (2½ mi) north of Moria.*

In the 19th century, Pamfila's traditional tower mansions were used by wealthy families as summer homes. The views across the straits to Turkey are wonderful.

Pirgi Thermis

⑯ *8 km (5 mi) northwest of Mytilini, 2 km (1 mi) east of Pamfila.*

Pirgi Thermis is known for its tower mansions and for its 12th-century church, **Panayia Tourloti** (⊠ Near the outskirts).

The village of **Loutropouli Thermis,** about 3 km (2 mi) northwest of Pirgi Thermis, is aptly named for its *loutra* (hot springs). These sulphur baths are dramatically enclosed with vaulted arches. A settlement existed here, centered on the spa's curative properties, from before 3000 BC until Mycenaean times. In all, remnants of five cities have been excavated at this site.

Lodging

$$$ ☑ **Lesbos Inn.** This small, well-managed hotel sits smack on a sandy beach, framed by a backdrop of green-dappled hills. Built in 1996 in sleek international style, each well-equipped, air-conditioned room offers a curving balcony from which to view the Aegean. A minibus shuttles you around if you care to have lunch at the town taverna, or you can just stay put and enjoy the alluring comforts of minibars, room service, and chaises by the pool. ☒ *Pirigi Thermis, 81100,* ☎ *0251/ 71781–4,* ℻ *0251/71711. 26 rooms. 2 restaurants, bar, air-conditioning, minibars, room service, pool, sauna, tennis court, exercise room, meeting rooms, parking. AE, MC, V.*

Mandamados

🄗 *36 km (22½ mi) northwest of Mytilini, 7 km (4½ mi) northwest of Pirgi Thermis.*

Mandamados is a pretty village of stone houses, wood carvings, and the ruins of a medieval castle. It is famous for its pottery, *koumari* urns (they keep water cool even in scorching heat), and for its black icon of Archangel Michael in the 17th-century monastery dedicated to the island's patron saint, **Taxiarchis Michail** (☒ Just north of village). Legend has it that the icon was carved by a monk who used mud and the blood of his comrades, slain in an Ottoman attack, to darken it. Visitors used to make a wish and press a coin to the archangel's forehead; if it stuck, the wish would be granted. Owing to wear and tear on the icon, the practice is now forbidden. In another ceremonial mode, on the third Sunday after Easter a bull is slaughtered here, and the celebrants dine on the stewed meat.

Skala Sikaminias

★ 🄘 *35 km (21¾ mi) northwest of Mytilini, 5 km (3 mi) north of Mandamados.*

At the northernmost point of Lesbos, past Pelopi (the ancestral village of 1988 presidential candidate Michael Dukakis), is the exceptionally lovely fishing port of Skala Sikaminias, If you crave pictureque harbor towns you'll flip over this miniature gem—serene, quaint, real, with several good fish tavernas on the edge of the dock where you can eat, relax, and soak up the atmosphere. The novelist Stratis Myrivilis used it as the setting for *The Mermaid Madonna.* If you've read the book, you'll recognize the tiny chapel at the base of the jetty. The author's birthplace and childhood home is in Sikaminia, a corkscrew road above, overlooking the Turkish coast.

En Route To get to Molyvos, most people take the main road a bit inland from Sikaminia. But there is a little-trafficked coastal route rimming the water between from Skala Sikaminias, unpaved for much of the way. To drive on this narrow path takes about 20 minutes, to walk about an hour, and there are hotels at which to refresh. You are amply rewarded along the way with close-up views of passing fishing boats and fresh sea breezes.

Dining

$$$ ✕ **Sykiminia.** The scene: you at a table under a mulberry tree sipping a glass of ouzo from nearby Plomari, watching the boats bob and the fishermen hauling in sardines, anchovies, squid, and bigger catch, practically at your feet. Then squeezing lemon on your own grilled fish, perhaps with some squash blossoms, or cucumbers and tomatos tossed with local olive oil. This oldest taverna on the tiny harbor can provide a memorable experience, so leave some time. ⊠ *Skala Sykaminias, on the waterfront,* ☎ *0253/55319. MC, V.*

Molyvos

★ ⑲ *61 km (38 mi) west of Mytilini, 17 km (10½ mi) southwest of Skala Sikaminias.*

Molyvos, also known as Mithimna, is a place people have been wanting to visit since antiquity. Legend says that Achilles beseiged the town until the king's daughter fell for him and opened the gates; then, in a surprising act, or acting out of she-loves-me, she-loves-me-not, he killed her. Before 1923 the Turks made up about a third of the population, living in many of the best stone houses. Today these balconied buildings with center staircases are weighed down by roses and geraniums; the red-tile roofs are required by law, and the street cobbles are mandatory. As proof of the town's visual charms, many artists live here. Although new hotels have been banned in the old town, Molyvos swells with tour groups in summer and its edges are getting a bit touristy; you may want to stay overnight in nearby Petra.

Come before high season and ascend to the **Byzantine-Genoese castle** for a hypnotic view down the tiers of red-tile roofs to the glittering sea. At dawn the sky begins to light up from behind the mountains of Asia Minor, casting silver streaks through the placid water as weary night fishermen come in. The grapevine-sheltered lane that descends from the castle passes numerous Turkish fountains, some still in use. ⊠ *Above town,* ☎ *0253/71803.* ▢ *Free.* ☼ *Tues.–Sun., dawn–sunset.*

Dining and Lodging

$$ ✗ **Gatos.** Gaze at the island and the harbor from the veranda, or sit inside and watch the cooks chop and grind in the open kitchen. Fish plates are limited; a better bet is the kokkinisto with garlic and savory onion. The beef fillet is tender, the lamb chops nicely grilled. Breakfast is also served. ⊠ *Main pedestrian street, Molyvos,* ☎ *0253/71661. No credit cards. Closed Nov.–Mar.*

$$ ✗ **Medusa.** In a traditional stone house on the wharf, this restaurant
★   offers some interesting specialties, including *pita thalassinon* (seafood pie), *mydia akhnista* (steamed mussels), and *kalamarakia yemista* (squid stuffed with rice). The owners provide flawless service and quality at low prices. ⊠ *Molyvos Harbor, across from Ayios Nikolaos chapel,* ☎ *0253/72080. MC, V. Closed Nov.–Apr.*

$$ ⊞ **Aeolis.** This cluster of beach bungalows offers all the comforts of a resort complex. From the raised pool area with its eye-popping purple umbrellas (preferable to the mediocre beach), guests have a great view of the sea as well as of Molyvos castle. Most of the bungalows have two or three beds, thick armchairs that fold out, and French doors opening onto a veranda. Kick back in the lounge's deep-seated sofas near the fireplace and potted plants. A hotel shuttle service runs up to town, as does the local bus. ⊠ *Outside Molyvos on road to Eftalou, 81108,* ☎ *0253/71772,* ᶠᴬˣ *0253/71773. 52 rooms. 2 restaurants, 2 bars, pool. MC, V. Closed Nov.–Mar.*

The Arts

FESTIVAL

The best-known celebration on the islands is the **Molyvos Theater Festival,** held July through August. With the castle as backdrop, artists from all over Europe stage entertainments that range from a Dario Fo play to contemporary music concerts. For tickets call ☎ 0253/71323; for information call the Molyvos tourist office (☞ Visitor Information *in* The Northern Islands A to Z, *below*).

Outdoor Activities and Sports

TENNIS

Hotels near Molyvos with courts to reserve include **Sun Rise Bunga-lows** (⊠ Efthalou, ☎ 0253/71713), **Alkeos** (⊠ Mithimna, ☎ 0253/71002), **Aphrodite** (⊠ Mithmna, ☎ 0253/71725), **Delfinia I Hotel and Bungalows** (⊠ Mithimna, ☎ 0253/71373), and **Olive Press** (⊠ Mithimna, ☎ 0253/71246).

Shopping

FINE ARTS

In Molyvos, the **Athens School of Fine Arts** (⊠ In Krallis Mansion near town center, ☎ 01/361–6930 in Athens) occasionally holds sales of its paintings.

Petra

㉑ *55 km (34 mi) northwest of Mytilini, 5 km (3 mi) south of Molyvos.*

Petra stretches along the shore of a large sandy bay fringed by tamarisk trees. Tavernas line the harborside, tempting the tourists with Greek versions of fast-food. Its oldest section still retains traditional stone houses with overhanging balconies, which the government now protects. Atop a giant monolith (*petra* means "rock" in Greek) is the 18th-century church Panayia Glikofiloussa (Virgin of Tenderness), reached by climbing 114 steps. The less ambitious may want to stroll the **beach,** visit **Ayios Nikolaos** church (⊠ Off the square) with its 16th-century frescoes, or tour the intricate **Vareltzidaina mansion** (⊠ Near marketplace).

Lodging

$$$ 🏨 **Clara.** A superior hotel of its class, completed in 1991, the Clara
★ has a striking contemporary reception area done in cool whites, pastel pinks, and gray. The bungalows all have spacious verandas with simultaneous views of Petra, Molyvos, and the sea, and with their comfortable gray beds, steel-blue covers, and pink curtains, they are a cut above the usual. Guests (mostly German package groups) can hop the shuttle bus to explore Petra, float in the large L-shape pool, or play a few sets of tennis. A buffet breakfast is served out on the terrace. ⊠ *Avlaki, south of Petra, 81109,* ☎ *0253/41522 through 41524,* FAX *0253/41535. 41 rooms. 2 restaurants, 2 bars, pool, tennis court, wading pool. AE, MC, V.*

Skalohori

㉒ *58 km (36 mi) west of Mytilini, 3 km (2 mi) south of Petra.*

Skalohori is set beautifully in a valley, with tiered houses facing west toward the Aegean sunsets. Until recently the volcanic northwestern part of Lesbos around Skalohori and Andissa was home to wild horses, believed to be the last link with the horse-breeding culture of the Troad, mentioned by Homer.

㉓ The **monastery of Ayios Ioannis Theologos,** or Moni Ipsilou, was founded in 800 and rebuilt in the 12th century. Of special note are the small collection of 12th-century manuscripts, icons, and textiles; the tiles embedded in the facade; and the outstanding wood-lattice ceiling. ⊠ *On summit of extinct volcano.*

Sigri

 93 km (57¾ mi) west of Mytilini, 4 km (2½ mi) south of Skalohori.

Sigri is built around a lovely cove; at water's edge is a small but impressive **Turkish castle** (⊠ Waterfront) with the sultan's monogram over the gate. A much-touted **petrified forest** (⊠ Between Sigri and Eressos) consists of conifer trees fossilized by volcanic ash up to 20 million years ago. If you expect a thick woods resembling the redwoods of California, this seemingly barren site at first appears like a bunch of stumps leaning every which way among shrubs and rock and even sea. But a closer look reveals delicate colors and a stark, strange beauty. You can also study the specimens in **Sigri's Square,** or at **Ipsilou** (⊠ Below monastery), a large monastery on the highest peak in this wild, volcanic landscape, overlooking western Lesbos and Asia Minor across the Aegean.

Beaches
Throughout the island beach composition varies from pebble to sand. Some of the most spectacular sandy beaches and coves are in the southwest. Exceptional dark-sand beaches stretch from **Sigri** to **Skala Eressou.**

Skala Eressou

 89 km (55¼ mi) west of Mytilini, 15 km (9¼ mi) southeast of Sigri.

On the acropolis of ancient Eressos (⊠ 1 km/½ mi north of Skala Eressou) overlooking the coastal area and beach are **remains of pre-Hellenic walls, castle ruins,** and the 5th-century church, **Ayios Andreas.** The church has a mosaic floor (currently covered over) and a tiny adjacent **museum** housing local finds from tombs in the ancient cemetery.

The poet Sappho was born here in the 7th century BC. Dubbed the Tenth Muse by Plato because of her sensual lyric poetry and new poetic meter, she ran a school for young women. Though she was married and had a daughter, she is reputed to have been homosexual because her surviving poetry is dedicated to her students. Sappho's works were burned, and only fragments of her books survive. Despite its erotic reputation, Sapphic meter was in great favor in the medieval ages and used in hymns, especially by Gregory the Great. Today, besides European and Greek tourists, many lesbians come here to visit her birthplace. (The word "lesbian" derives from Lesbos.)

The modern town of **Eressos** (⊠ 11 km/7 mi inland), separated from the coast by a large plain, developed to protect its inhabitants from pirate raids. Along the mulberry tree-line road leading from the beach you might encounter a villager wearing a traditional head scarf (mandila), plodding by on his donkey. This charming village of two-story, 19th-century stone and shingle houses is filled with superb architectural details. Note the huge wooden doors decorated with nails and elaborate door knockers, loop-hole windows in thick stone walls, elegant pediments topping imposing mansions, and fountains spilling under Gothic arches.

Beaches
Some of the island's best beaches are in the vicinity of Skala Eressou. Especially popular is the **town's dark-sand beach,** long and wide and lined with tamarisk trees. A small island is within swimming distance, and northerly winds lure windsurfers as well as swimmers and sunbathers.

Dining
$$ ✕ **Bennetts'.** Max and Jackie Bennett's place has seating on elevated wooden platforms, near the illuminated resort. This British-run es-

tablishment offers an unusually full menu of Greek and Western meat and vegetarian specialties. When listless from Greek food, you'll appreciate such novelties as lasagna, mushrooms in garlic sauce, and apple crumble smothered in cream. ☒ *At east end of beach, Skala Eressou,* ☎ *0253/53624. No credit cards. Closed Nov.–Apr.*

Kalloni

40 km (24¾ mi) west of Mytilini, 4 km (2½ mi) northeast of Skala Eressou.

Known for the anchovies in its gulf, this agricultural market town in the center of Lesbos is rather quiet, but 5 km (3 mi) northwest of Kalloni **㉕** is the sprawling 16th-century **Limonos monastery,** filled with frescoes and patrolled by peacocks and the tenants of the sanitarium here. Three stories of cells ring the courtyard. A bishop has collected a jumble of plates and doodads in a sort of **folk-art museum** upstairs, but more interesting is the ground-floor **treasury** of 450 Byzantine manuscripts. Women are not allowed inside the main church. ☒ *On northern outskirts of village.* 🎟 *Museum/treasury: 100 dr.* ☉ *Daily 9– 1 and 5–7:30.*

Agiassos

★ **㉖** *28 km (17½ mi) southwest of Mytilini, 10 km (6 mi) northeast of Kalloni.*

Agiassos village, the prettiest hill town on Lesbos, sits in an isolated wooded valley near the middle of the island at the foot of Mt. Olympus, the highest peak. (In case you're confused, there are 19 mountains in the Mediterranean named Olympus, almost all of them peaks sacred to the local sky god, who eventually became associated with Zeus.) Exempted from taxes by the Turks, the town thrived. Despite its recent discovery by tourists and the spread of tacky souvenir shops, Agiassos remains a special settlement with gray stone houses, cobblestone lanes, a medieval castle, and worthwhile local handicrafts, particularly pottery and wood crafts. The church of **Panayia Vrefokratousa** was founded in the 12th century to house an icon believed to be the work of St. Luke. Built into its foundation are shops whose revenues support the church, as they have through the ages. This has always been a pilgrimage site and even today celebrates festivals in an especially lively style.

NEED A BREAK? Stop at one of several cafés in the winding streets of the old bazaar area past the church of Panayia Vrefokratousa. On weekend afternoons sip an ouzo and listen to a santoúri band, featuring hammered dulcimer, accompanied by clarinet, drum, and violin. As the locals dance, rather haphazardly, on the cobblestones, you might be tempted to join in the merriment.

Dining

$ ✕ **Dagieles.** If nothing else, you must stop here for a coffee made by ★ owner Stavritsa. And you might try the *kolokitholouloudo* (stuffed squash blossoms) and the dishes that entice the local police throughout the winter: *kritharaki* (barley-shape pasta), kokkinisto, and *varkoules* ("little boats" of eggplant slices with minced meat). For a few short weeks in spring the air is laden with the scent of overhanging wisteria. ☒ *Agiassos near bus stop,* ☎ *0252/22241. No credit cards.*

Plomari

㉗ *42 km (26 mi) southwest of Mytilini, 20 km (12½ mi) south of Agiassos.*

Plomari, the second-largest town on Lesbos, is dramatically set in a cliff face overlooking a wide harbor and Aegean sunsets. This was once a major maritime area but today is a cheerful mix of package resort and quiet fishing village with narrow, cobbled lanes and houses spilling down to the sea. Known for its potent ouzo and its happy Scandinavian crowd, there's a lively night scene on the harbor, where tourists gather after a long day at the beach.

Lodging

$$ ☎ **Aegean Sun.** Right on the beach of Agios Isidoros, centered on a small pool, this new hotel has the feel of a traditional seaside village, with two-story, tile-roof bungalow units; iron balconies; and flowers spilling over stairways. All rooms have Aegean views and TVs. Lots of charm and comfort are here indeed. ⊠ *Plomari, on the water, 81200,* ☎ *0252/31830–33,* 𝔽𝔸𝕏 *0252/31829. 43 rooms with bath. Restaurant, bar, pool. MC, V. Closed Nov.–Mar.*

Vatera

㉘ *53 km (33 mi) east of Mytilini, 6 km (4 mi) west of Plomari.*

The village of Vatera is all about its 9 km-long (5½-mi-long) sandy strip of sparkling water, lined with tamarisk trees and framed by green hills. Local families favor the relaxed atmosphere and the mineral springs nearby. You can sit and enjoy the view of the cape of Ayios Fokas, with its newly excavated temple of Dionysus. As is often the case in succeeding cultures, the temple's marble fragments were recycled, built into the center aisle of a Christian basilica.

Beaches

The **town beach,** with its curving, southern exposure, is idyllic. In the southeast, there is a good sand-and-pebble beach at **Ayios Isidoros** (⊠ Near Plomari). A sandy beach southeast in **Gera Bay** (⊠ Just south of Skala Polihnitos) is another good choice.

Lodging

$$ ☎ **Vatera Beach.** This low-key but well-designed hotel has all the makings of a higher-category lodging. Rooms in the four white-and-blue buildings have their own entrances, balconies, and a sea view. Small groups can visit in winter, when a fireplace and central heating make it a treat. Most of the food for the hotel's restaurant, served under tamarisk trees on a terrace with an Aegean view, is raised or grown organically: fruits, vegetables, rabbits, and even pigs. ⊠ *Vatera beach, 81300,* ☎ *0252/61212,* 𝔽𝔸𝕏 *0252/61164. 24 rooms, 16 with shower. Restaurant. No credit cards. Closed Nov.–Apr.*

CHIOS

Chios could use better press. "Craggy Hios" is what local boy Homer, its first publicist so to speak, called this starkly beautiful island, which almost touches Turkey's coast and shares its topography. It may not seem to offer much charm when you first see its modernized capital, but consider its misfortunes: the bloody Turkish massacre of 1822 in its fight for Greek independence; major earthquakes, including one in 1881 that killed almost 6,000 Chiotes; severe fires, which in the 1980s burned two-thirds of its pine trees; and, through the ages, the steady stripping of forests to ax-wielding boatbuilders. But look a bit deeper and Chios will surprise you. Within are rare mosaics and villages so unique that even one of them would make this island worth a special stop.

The name Chios comes from the Phoenician word for mastic, the resin of the *Pistacia lentisca,* evergreen shrubs that with few exceptions thrive only here, in the southern part of the island. Every August incisions are made in the bark of the shrubs; the sap leaks out, permeating the air with a sweet fragrance, and in September it is harvested. This aromatic resin, which brought huge revenues until the introduction of petroleum products, was used in varnishes, waxes, cosmetics, and in the chewing gum used by odalisques in the Ottoman harems. Today we may not use the mastic, but you will be enchanted by the *mastikhohoria* (the villages where mastic is produced and processed) (☞ Pirgi and Mesta, *below*).

Until charter tourism began in the late 1980s, Chios prospered through the centuries from medicinal brews, turpentine, wine, silk production, and mainly from its mastic export. It is also home to the elite families that control Greece's private shipping empires: Livanos, Karas, Chandris; even Onassis came here from Smyrna. The island did not seem to need tourists, nor to draw them. Yet Chios intrigues, with its deep valleys, uncrowded sand and black-pebble beaches, fields of wild tulips, Byzantine monasteries, and haunting villages—remnants of a poignant history. It is both demanding and giving, memorable even among these special islands.

Chios Town

㉙ *24 km (15 mi) northeast of Pirgi.*

The main port and capital, Chios town, or Chora (which means "town"), is a busy commercial settlement on the east coast, across from Turkey. Since most of the buildings were constructed after the 1881 earthquake, and the modern waterfront is crowded with private yachts, its charm is limited. But in the evening when the lights twinkle on the water and the scene is softened by a mingling of blues, the many cafés begin to overflow with ouzo and good cheer, and locals proudly promenade along the bay side.

The capital is crowded with half the island's population, but its fascinating heart is the **bazaar district** (⊠ Sprawling south and east of Platia Vounakiou, main square). Merchants hawk everything from local gum and fresh dark bread to screeching monkeys.

The **old quarter** (⊠ On northern highlands) is found inside the **kastro** (castle), built in the 9th century by the Byzantines. Later, under Turkish rule, the Greeks lived outside the wall; the gate was closed daily at sundown. A deep dry moat remains on the western side. Note the old wood-and-plaster houses on the narrow backstreets, typically decorated with latticework and jutting balconies, on which you might find a woman in black smoking a thin cigar. This old Muslim and Jewish neighborhood, full of decaying monuments, fountains, baths, and mosques, wears an air of mystery.

The **Giustiani museum,** inside a 15th-century mansion, has religious art and has wood carvings, mosaics, and airy rooms hung with frescoes from Nea Moni and Panayia Krina church (☞ *below*). ⊠ *Just inside old quarter in Giustiani mansion,* ☏ *0271/22819.* 🎫 *Free.* ☉ *Tues.–Sun. 9–3.*

In **Platia Frouriou** (⊠ In the fort's small square), look for the **Turkish cemetery** and the large **marble tomb** (with the fringed hat) of Kara Ali, chief of the Turkish flagship in 1822. Along the **main street** are elegant **Ayios Georgios** church (closed most of the time), which has icons from Asia Minor; houses from the Genoese period; and the **remains of Turkish baths** (⊠ North corner of fort).

NEED A
BREAK? Try a Chiote snack of rice pudding or sheep's-milk yogurt and thick honey. The food is fresh and authentic at the unnamed **little dairy shop** (⊠ Corner of Roihou and Veneizelou, behind Appolonio lodgings).

In 1822, in the tiny **prison** (⊠ Just inside main gate), 75 leading Chiotes were jailed as hostages before they were hanged by the Turks, part of the worst massacre committed during the War of Independence. The Turks, who drove out the Genoese in 1566, had been fond of the island for its mastic, which they chewed in the company of their harems to sweeten their breath in the days before packaged mints. But Chios, spurred by Samians who had fled to the island, joined the rest of Greece in rebellion. The revolt failed, and the Sultan retaliated: The Turks killed 30,000 Chiotes and enslaved 45,000, an event written about by Victor Hugo and depicted by Delacroix in *The Massacres of Chios*. The painting shocked Western Europe and led indirectly to support for Greek independence. Copies of the Delacroix hang in many places here, including the dusty **post-Byzantine museum,** filled with odds and ends and housed in the only intact mosque, complete with a slender minaret, in this part of the Aegean. Note the *tugra* (the swirling monogram of the sultan that shows royal possession). Although the tugra is common in Istanbul, it is rarely seen elsewhere, and its presence indicated the favor Chios enjoyed under the sultan. But more poignant are the Jewish, Turkish, and Armenian gravestones leaning with age in the courtyard, a silent reminder of past suffering. ⊠ *Platia Vounakiou,* ☎ *0271/26866.* ▣ *Free.* ☉ *Tues.–Sat. 10–1, Sun. 10–3.*

The **archaeological museum** collection ranges from proto-Helladic pottery dug up in Emborio to a letter from Alexander the Great addressed to the Chiotes dated 332 BC. ⊠ *Michalon 5,* ☎ *0271/26664.* ▣ *500 dr.* ☉ *Tues.–Sun. 9–3.*

The **Philip Argenti Museum** is the most interesting collection in town, housed on the top floor of the **Korais Library,** one of Greece's largest. It holds self-serving portraits of the aristocratic family that endowed it, and more copies of the Delacroix painting, but also some fascinating costumes, embroideries, implements, and engravings evocative of earlier times. ⊠ *Koraii 2, near cathedral,* ☎ *0271/23462.* ▣ *Free.* ☉ *Mon.–Thurs. 8–2, Fri. 8–2 and 5–7:30, Sat. 8–12:30.*

Beaches
Karfas beach (⊠ 8 km/5 mi south of Chios town) fronts a shallow sandy bay. Tavernas are in the area, and in summer, there's transportation to town. Farther south, Komi has a fine, sandy beach.

Dining and Lodging
$$ ✕ **Bel Air.** With its black-lacquer chairs, rows of potted plants, piano, and wall of mirrors, the faux-deco decor is a step up (or down, as your taste runs) from that of most tavernas. It's open 24 hours a day. The menu changes often: Look for *soupies me sevgola* (cuttlefish stuffed with mountain greens) and *soupa petropsaris* (rockfish soup). The schnitzel is stuffed with Edam and topped with onion-mushroom sauce. ⊠ *Aegeou 118, near Chandris Hotel, Chios town,* ☎ *0271/29947. MC, V.*

$$ ✕ **Karatzas.** At a table by the water, you'll savor the fresh grilled seafood at this informal taverna, where locals congregate to enjoy simple pleasures. Enjoy lots of fresh Chiote vegetables and local fruits as well as classic Greek dishes such as moussaka, which are always a tasty backup. This is a place where you can sit nursing a coffee and you won't be disturbed. ⊠ *Karfas, on the waterfront,* ☎ *0271/3122. MC, V.*

$$ ✕ **O Hotzas.** This spacious taverna, reputed to be the capital's best, ★ has a medieval interior with a beamed ceiling, brass implements, and family portraits. Most dishes are deep-fried, but you may also nosh on succulent lamb with lemon sauce, and many vegetable dishes. The squid is always reliable, and it's delicious with the homemade retsina or ouzo. For dessert, order yogurt with homemade cherry or quince preserves. ✉ *Yioryiou Kondili 3, Chios,* ☎ *0271/23117. No credit cards. Closed Sun. No lunch.*

$$$ 🏨 **Chios Chandris.** On the water, midway between the port and the beach, this big, bustling, and boxy member of the Greek hotel and ship chain is considered one of the capital's best. The pool and stone terrace by the sea, lunch buffets, disco, and friendly social staff make for a resortlike atmosphere, but with in-town convenience. Rooms are basic but comfortable in shades of Aegean blue, but best are the balconies, with views of the mountains or of the caïques and fishing boats plying the harbor. ✉ *Prokymea, between port and beach, 82100,* ☎ *0271/25761 or 02/1/25765,* 🖷 *0271/25768. 141 rooms, 16 suites. Restaurant, 2 bars, pool, meeting rooms. AE, MC, V.*

$$–$$$ 🏨 **Fedra.** From the moment you enter this neoclassical former mansion, painted ocher and planted with jubilant flowers, you feel at home. A pension run by a playwright, it is an appealing, inexpensive choice. All the rooms have baths, air-conditioning, and heating. The summer outdoor bar generates some noise, so ask for a back room. Off-season, a piano bar warms up the place. ✉ *M. Livanou 13, Chios 82100,* ☎ *0271/41129 or 0271/41130. 10 rooms. Bar, café, air-conditioning. MC.*

$$–$$$ 🏨 **Kyma.** Begun in 1917 for a shipping magnate, this neoclassical villa was completed in 1922, when it served as General Plastiras's headquarters after the Greek defeat in Asia Minor. From here he ordered the deposition of the king and the court martial of six cabinet ministers. A modern cement addition only slightly mars the stone facade and grillwork. Some rooms have whirlpool baths. The only problem is noise from the street below. With the great breakfast, waking up won't be so bad once you taste the fresh Chios tangerine juice. ✉ *Chandris 1, Chios 82100,* ☎ *0271/44500,* 🖷 *0271/44600. 59 rooms. Air-conditioning, hot tubs. No credit cards.*

The Arts

Chios usually is host to a summer conference at the **International Society of Homeric Studies** (✉ 5 Heroon Polytechneiou St., ☎ 0271/44391).

Nightlife

Chios has a surprising number of restaurants, clubs, and stylish nightspots along the harbor. The look is more sophisticated than in most of the other northern Aegean islands, and most of the clubs are filled with well-off young tourists and locals. You can just walk along, listen to the music and size up the crowd; most of the clubs are open to the harborside and dramatically lit.

Outdoor Activities and Sports

SAILING

In Chios you can moor in Kardamila, Limnia, and Chios town. In Chios town call ☎ 0271/27286 for fuel; call ☎ 0271/27377 for water; repairs are available in the harbor. A new yacht marina is near completion at Vrondados.

Shopping

LOCAL CRAFTS

It's no surprise that gum is a best buy here; the brand is Elma. It makes a fun stocking stuffer and conversation piece. You can also find an unusual mastic liquor called *mastíha,* and gliko koutaliou, the sugary goo added to water on a spoon—a favorite with children.

Chios and Samos

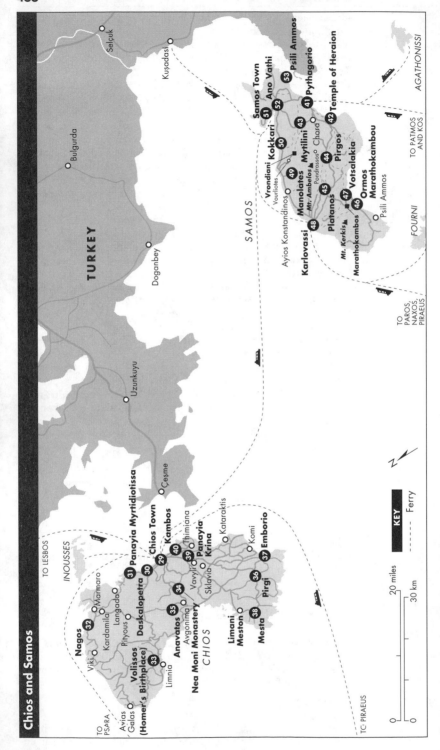

KEY

----- Ferry

20 miles

30 km

Vrontados

4 km (2½ mi) north of Chios town.

③⓪ **Daskalopetra** (Teacher's Rock), where Homer is said to have taught his pupils, is just above the port of Vrontados, a haven for sailors. Archaeologists believe this weathered lectern on a rocky outcrop above the sea to be actually part of an ancient altar, but today you can sit on it and muse about how the blind storyteller might have spoken here of the fall of Troy and the voyage of Odysseus in the *Iliad* and *Odyssey*.

③① North of Teacher's Rock are several sites of historic interest. The 19th-century monastery of **Panayia Myrtidiotissa** (Our Lady of the Myrtle; ⊠ On shoreline) overlooks the Aegean past the villages of Pandoukios. **Langada** (⊠ At nearby Delphinion) is where a 5th-century BC Athenian naval base was unearthed. **Kardamila** (⊠ 28 km/17½ mi north of Chios town), a former shipowner enclave, actually has two villages, ③② upper and lower. **Nagos** harbor, a swampy area, is the site where a ruined temple of Poseidon was found early this century. Its ancient church gives the town its name.

Beaches

In these parts try Yiosonas and wooded Nagos beaches. Many of the northern pebble beaches are windy and deserted.

Volissos

③③ *42 km (26 mi) northwest of Chios town, 4 km (2½ mi) west of Vrontados.*

Homer's birthplace is thought to be here at Volissos, though Smyrna, Colophon, Salamis, Rhodes, Argos, and Athens also claim this honor. Once a bustling market town, this pretty, narrow-laned northern village is today half empty, with only a few hundred inhabitants. Solid stone houses march up the mountainside to the Genoese fort, where Byzantine nobles were once exiled. Atop the hill is the place for sunset lovers.

Beaches

Some of the best beaches on the island are in the vicinity, including **Limia** (⊠ 2 km/1 mi south of Volissos).

Lodging

$$ ☶ **Village Houses.** Since 1987, energetic Stella Tsakiri has overseen the meticulous restoration of 11 medium-size houses, preserving where possible such vernacular touches as unworked tree trunks supporting a sleeping loft. Yet all modern conveniences are present, and each unit, designed for two to five people, has a fully equipped kitchen and a terrace with sweeping views—you're just under the half-ruined Byzantine castle. It's ideal for families on a get-away-from-it-all holiday. ⊠ *Volissos village, Chios 82100,* ☎ *0274/21421,* 𝔽𝔸𝕏 *0274/21521. 11 units. Air-conditioning, kitchenettes. No credit cards.*

The Arts

In summer, arts events are held in historic Vrontados, during the annual **"Homeria."**

Nea Moni

17 km (10½ mi) west of Chios town, 59 km (36½ mi) southeast of Volissos.

Almost hidden among the olive groves, the island's most important monument—and one of the finest examples of mosaic art anywhere—is the ★ ③④ 11th-century **Nea Moni monastery** (⊠ High in mountains of Nea

Moni). Emperor Constantine Monomachos VIII ordered it built where three monks found an icon of the Virgin in a myrtle bush. The octagonal *katholikon* (medieval church) created by architects and painters from Constantinople exemplifies the artistic ideas prevailing during the 11th century in that city. Its distinctive three-part vaulted sanctuary has two narthexes, with no buttresses supporting the dome. This design, a single square space covered by a dome, is rarely seen in Greece. Aged, but still blazing with color, the church's interior gleams with marble slabs and mosaics of Christ's life, austere yet sumptuous, with azure blue, ruby red, velvet green, and skillful applications of gold. The saints' expressiveness comes from their vigorous poses and severe gazes, with heavy shadows under the eyes. On the iconostasis hangs the icon—a small Virgin and Child facing left. Also inside the grounds are an **ancient refectory, a vaulted cistern, a chapel** filled with bones of Turkish massacre victims, and a large **clock** still keeping Byzantine time, with the sunrise reckoned as 12 o'clock. ⊠ *In mountains.* ⊙ *Daily 8–1 and 4–8.*

En Route   Heading toward Anavatos via the Nea Moni side-road junction, the main road turns southwest to **Avgonima,** one of the many distinctive villages on the island and from which there is an expansive view of the west coast. Its name means "clutch of eggs," perhaps because its buildings seem to touch each other like eggs in a basket. Many Greek-Americans have bought ancestral homes here, lovingly restoring them to their original beauty and using them for vacation and retirement. To return here for their own wedding is a goal of many expatriates.

Anavatos

★   *16 km (10 mi) west of Chios town, 5 km (3 mi) northwest of Nea Moni.*

The haunting, mud-color village of Anavatos blends into its hillside like a chameleon, built that way to hide from pirates. About 50 crumbling houses still stand. Climbing the steep paths and gazing into tumbled houses filled with rubble and wildflowers is a good half-hour workout each way but is a walk you won't forget. In this once heavily fortified town, where seven people—give or take a few—live year-round, the biggest sign of life is the farmers who come to gather pistachios that grow in the untended orchards below. In 1822, during the revolution, 400 women and children threw themselves over the cliff here rather than surrender to the Turks, and their presence can be felt if you stand at the summit and observe a minute of silence.

NEED A   A tiny café is at the base of Anavatos, where you park your car. Try the
BREAK?   fresh-made spoonsweets made of local figs or pistachios in syrup.
           Washed down with a cold bottle of water it seems a perfect ending to
           the climb.

Pirgi

★   *24 km (15 mi) south of Chios town, 22 km (13½ mi) southeast of Anavatos.*

From the 14th century, the Genoese founded 20 or so inland, fortified villages in southern Chios, which got the name Pirgi from the lucrative gum product in the region. They shared a defensive design with double thick walls, a maze of narrow streets, and a square tower in the middle—a last resort to hold the residents in case of pirate attack. The villages prospered on the sales of mastic gum and were spared by the Turks because of it. Today they depend on tangerines, apricots, olives—and tourists.

Pirgi is the largest of these mastic villages, and in many ways the most wondrous. It could be a graphic designer's model or a set from a mad moviemaker, or a town from another planet. Many of the buildings along the tiny arched streets are adorned with *xysta* (like Italian sgraffito). They are coated with a mix of cement and volcanic sand from nearby beaches, then whitewashed and stenciled, often top to bottom, in traditional patterns of animals, flowers, and geometric designs. The effect is both delicate and dazzling. Especially lavish are xystra on buildings near the main square, including the **Kimisis tis Theotokou** church (Dormition of the Virgin) (⊠ Near main square), built in 1694.

This exuberant village has more than 50 churches (successful people afraid of attack tend to pray for a continuation of life). Check out the fresco-embellished 12th-century church **Ayii Apostoli,** a very small replica of the earlier Nea Moni katholikon. The 17th-century frescoes that completely mask the interior, the work of a Cretan artist, have a distinct folk-art leaning. To get in, ask at the main square for the current doorkeeper. ⊠ *In town, northwest of square.* ◷ *Tues.–Thurs. and Sat. 10–1.*

About 50 people named Kolomvos live in Pirgi, claiming kinship with Christopher Columbus, known to have been from Genoa, the power that built the mastikhohoria (some renegade historians claim Columbus, like Homer, was really born on Chios).

Lodging

$–$$ ☷ **Women's Agricultural Tourist Cooperative of Chios.** This local agency can find you a room in the town or the area, perhaps even on a farm. These may be basic digs, some without private baths, but if in doubt, check out the lodgings first. If you choose to, you may get the added experience of harvesting mastic or cooking local dishes with inevitably congenial Greek hosts. This is an especially wonderful opportunity for families. ⊠ *Pirgi, near the center square, 82102,* ☎ *0271/72496.*

Beaches

From Pirgi it's 8 km (5 mi) southeast to the glittering **black volcanic beach** near **Emborio.** Known by locals as Mavra Volia ("black pebbles"), the cove is backed by jutting volcanic cliffs, the calm water's dark-blue color created by the deeply tinted seabed. Here perhaps was an inspiration for the "wine-dark sea" that Homer writes about.

Shopping

CERAMICS

In the small mastic village of **Armolia,** 20 km (12½ mi) south of Chios town, pottery is a specialty. In fact, *armolousis* ("man from Armola") is synonymous with potter.

Mesta

★ ❸ *28 km (17½ mi) southwest of Chios town, 11 km (7 mi) west of Pirgi.*

Pirgi is the most unusual of the mastic villages, but Mesta is the island's best preserved, a labyrinth of twisting vaulted streets linking two-story stone-and-mortar houses, which are supported by buttresses against earthquakes. The striking, somber village sits inside a system of 3-ft-thick walls, and the outer row of houses also doubles as protection. Most of the narrow streets lead to blind alleys; the rest lead to the six gates; the one in the northeast still has an iron grate.

One of the largest and wealthiest churches in Greece, the 18th-century **Megas Taxiarchis** commands the main square, its vernacular Baroque and rococo features combined in the late-folk-art style of Chios. It was built on the ruins of the central refuge tower. Ask at the main square for Elias, the gentle old man in the village who is the keeper of the keys.

As you head out of town, on the way to Chios town, near Vavili, is the
39 12th-century **Panayia Krina** (Our Lady of the Source) (⊠ On road to
left marked TO SKLAVIA), where three layers of frescoes spanning six periods were discovered. The very earliest period is represented by portraits of the saints facing the entrance; most of the restored frescoes hang
in the Giustiani mansion in Chios town (☞ *above*). The church is rarely
open, but the finely worked exterior makes the trip worthwhile.

Beaches

Escape to the string of **secluded coves** (⊠ Between Elatas and Trahil-
iou bays) with good swimming; a **nudist beach** (⊠ About 2 km/1 mi
north of Lithi) with fine white pebbles is among them.

Dining and Lodging

$$ ✕ **O Moreas sta Mesta.** The proprietor spends winter and spring gath-
★ ering herbs and greens from nearby hills and seashores. Typical are *kri-
tama,* to give salads a tang, and *horta* (greens like Swiss chard and
dandelion sautéed with lemon and oil) for his excellent *hortopita* (a
pie made with horta). Unusual for a taverna, there's excellent brown
bread, and a potent, semisweet red wine made from raisins. The goat
fricassee must be ordered in advance, and *ksifias* souvlaki (swordfish
chunks on a spit), *domotokeftedes* (fried tomato patties), and *hirino
krasato* (pork simmered in wine) are usually available. ⊠ *Mesta Sq.,
Mesta, Chios,* ☎ *0271/76400. No credit cards.*

$ ✕ **Limani Meston.** This taverna has something for every budget: mostly
magirefta in summer, with a few inexpensive fish. Meats include home-
made sausage, whole roasted piglets (order ahead), and lamb or beef
on the spit. You can sit outside among the ivy and blossoms, where
Mesta's working harbor unfolds before you; or on colder days, enjoy
the fireplace with the locals. ⊠ *Mesta Harbor, 3 km (2 mi) from Mesta
village,* ☎ *0271/76367 or 0271/76265. No credit cards.*

$$ ▥ **Rooms to Let.** This group of houses with charming, authentic, and
well-maintained rental properties in Mesta and the nearby harbor of
Limenas is the largest cooperative here. Stone, wood, stucco, antiques,
verandas filled with geraniums, and balconies overlooking labyrinthian
lanes or the Aegean sea make these properties special indeed. Most have
kitchens and two or more bedrooms. Each house has individual phones,
but you can fax for general information or a brochure. ⊠ *Mesta, built
into maze; Limenas, by the harbor, 82102,* ☎ *0271/76290. 19 houses,
6 with shower. No credit cards.*

Nightlife

BAR
Karnayio (⊠ Leoforos Stenoseos, outside town on road to airport) is
a popular spot for dancing.

Shopping

Artists hang out in this area. Ilias Likourinas, an icon painter who will
paint to order, has a workshop on the main street in Mesta. Sergias Paten-
tas, whose shop is on the road between Mesta and the harbor of Limenas (⊠ 3 km/2 mi north of Mesta), sculpts fantasies based on mythology
and history. He is currently setting up a history museum in Mesta.

Kambos

★ 40 *4 km (2½ mi) south of Chios town, about 29 km (18 mi) northeast of
Mesta.*

Mastodon bones were found here in the Kambos region, a fertile plain
of tangerine, lemon, and orange groves, which is perfect for cycling. Since
medieval times, wealthy Genoese and Greek merchants built ornate, earth-
color, three-story mansions. Behind forbidding stone walls adorned

with coats of arms, each is a world of its own, with multicolored sandstone patterns, arched doorways, and pebble-mosaic courtyards. **Manganos** (waterwheels), a part of most mansion courtyards, were once powered by donkeys to draw water and irrigate the orchards; they are used now for decorations and pools filled with carp and waterlilies. Some houses are crumbled and some still stand, reminders of the wealth, power, and eventual downfall of an earlier time. These suburbs of Chios town are exceptional but the unmarked lanes can be confusing, so leave time to get lost and to peek behind the walls into another world.

Lodging

$$$ ☎ **Pension Perivoli.** Behind an ornate pediment-topped gate and across from the (closed) Villa Argentiko, this grand yet informal two-story 18th-century mansion is set in an orange orchard (think fresh-squeezed at breakfast in the large garden). Fireplaces, a massive outdoor staircase of native stone, a *mangonos* (an exterior waterwheel, once driven by donkey power, now usually just a showpiece), and local furnishings and antiques combine for an evocative ambience. The rooms are spare, but the grounds sing. ⊠ *9–11 Argenti St., Kambos district, 82100,* ☏ *0271/31513,* ℻ *0271/32042. 15 rooms with bath. Restaurant, bar, patio. No credit cards.*

SAMOS

The southernmost of this group of four north-Aegean islands, Samos is the closest to Turkey of any Greek island, separated by only 3 km (2 mi). It was, in fact, a part of Asia Minor until it split off during the Ice Age. Samos means "high" in Phoeneician, and its abrupt volcanic mountains soaring dramatically like huge hunched shoulders from the rock surface of the island are among the tallest in the Aegean, geologically part of the great spur that runs across western Turkey. Approaching from the west, Mt. Kerkis seems to spin out of the sea, while in the distance Mt. Ambelos guards the terraced vineyards that produce the famous Samian wine. The felicitous landscape has surprising twists with lacy coasts and mountain villages perched on ravines carpeted in pink oleander, red poppy, and purple sage.

When Athens was young, in the 7th century BC, Samos was already a naval power. In the next century during Polykrates' reign, it was noted for its arts and sciences and the expanded site of the vast Temple of Hera, one of the wonders of the ancient world. Herotodus wrote extensively of Samos, and Plutarch wrote that in Roman times Anthony and Cleopatra took a long holiday here; "giving themselves over to the feasting," that artists came from afar to entertain them, and kings vied to send the grandest gifts.

Small though it may be, Samos has a formidable list of great Samians stretching through the ages. It was home to fabled Aesop, to the philosopher Epicurus, and to Aristarchos (first in history to place the sun at the center of our solar system). The mathematician Pythagoras was born in Samos's ancient capital in 580 BC; it was renamed Pythagorio in AD 1955 (it only took a couple of millennia).

Pirates controlled this deserted island after the fall of the Byzantine empire, but in 1562 an Ottoman admiral repopulated Samos with expatriates and Orthodox believers. It languished under the sun for hundreds of years until tobacco and shipping revived the economy in the 19th century. Although in the last decade Samos has become packed with European charter tourists in July and August, its curving terrain allows you to escape the crowds easily and feel as if you are still in an undiscovered Eden.

Pythagorio

41   *14 km (8¾ mi) southwest of Samos town.*

Samos had been a democratic state, but in 535 BC the town now called Pythagorio (formerly Tigani, or "frying pan") fell to the tyrant Polycrates (540 BC–522 BC), who used his fleet of 100 ships to make profitable raids around the Aegean, until he was caught by the Persians and crucified in 522 BC. His rule produced what Herodotus described as "three of the greatest building and engineering feats in the Greek world." One is the Heraion (☞ *below*), west of Pythagorio, the largest temple ever built in Greece and one of the Seven Wonders of the Ancient World. Another is the ancient mole protecting the harbor on the southeast coast, on which the present 1,400-ft jetty rests. The third is the Efpalinio tunnel, built to guarantee that water flowing from mountain streams would be available even to besieged Samians.

An underground aqueduct, the **Efpalinio tunnel,** was finished in 524 BC with primitive tools and without measuring instruments. Efpalinos of Megara, a hydraulics engineer, set perhaps a thousand slaves into two teams, one digging on each side of Mt. Kastri. Fifteen years later, they met in the middle with just a tiny difference in the elevation between the two halves. The tunnel was used during the Middle Ages as a hideout from pirate raids. More than a mile of (long gone) ceramic water pipe once filled the space. Today the tunnel is exclusively a tourist site, and though some spaces are tight and slippery, you can walk the first 1,000 ft; it's fenced, thankfully. Although it is electrically lit, you might want to bring a flashlight to note the chisel marks of human effort on the walls. ⊠ *Just north of town,* ☎ *0273/61400.* 🖭 *500 dr.* ☉ *Tues.–Sun. 9–2* PM.

Among acres of excavations, little else remains from the **ancient city** (⊠ Bordering small harbor and hill) except a few pieces of the **Policrates wall** and the **ancient theater** a few hundred yards above the tunnel.

Pythagoria's quiet cobblestone streets are lined with mansions and filled with fragrant orange blossoms. At one corner sits a crumbling **fortress** (⊠ East corner), probably on top of the ruins of the acropolis. Revolutionary hero Lycourgos Logothetis built this 19th-century edifice; his statue is in the **courtyard** of the church built to honor the victory, next door. He held back the Turks on Transfiguration Day, and a sign on the church announces in Greek: CHRIST SAVED SAMOS 6 AUGUST, 1824. At night the villagers light votive candles in the church cemetery, a moving sight with the ghostly silhouette of the fortress and the moonlit sea in the background.

The small **Pythagorio Museum** contains local finds, including headless statues, grave markers with epigrams to the dead, and portraits of Roman emperors. ⊠ *Platia Pythagora, in municipal building,* ☎ *0273/61400.* 🖭 *500 dr.* ☉ *Apr.–Oct., Tues.–Sun. approximately 9–2.*

Pythagorio remains a picturesque little port, with red-tiled roof houses and a curving harbor filled with fishing boats. To the west of town are remains of **Roman Baths,** their doorways still standing (☎ 0273/61400); they're open Tuesday–Saturday 11–2. A bit west of that are the remains of the ancient Aegean harbor, long ago bustling with the mighty naval fleets of samains, ships with five tiers of oarsmen. That harbor is now a silted-in lake and the ships a mere memory.

Dining and Lodging

$$ ✕ **Lito.** One of the only true restaurants lining Pythagorio's esplanade, Lito has such interesting dishes as the addictive *kolokithakia* yemista (zucchini stuffed with feta and bacon). Besides the usual grilled meats, you may savor a mixed grill with beef patties, souvlaki, liver, and Mexican chicken in Madeira sauce. Late risers can have breakfast all day. Look for the mustard-color awning and gray-and-blue chairs. ✉ *Pythagorio Harbor,* ☎ *0273/61101. No credit cards. Closed Nov.–Mar.*

$ ✕ **Maritsa.** This simple fish taverna, on a quiet, tree-lined side street, opened in 1992 and quickly established a regular Pythagorio clientele. In the garden courtyard, you can try grilled flying fish (!), red mullet, octopus, and squid garnished with garlicky *skordalia* (a thick lemony sauce with pureed potatoes, vinegar, and parsley). The usual appetizers include a sharp *tzatziki* (tangy lemon-yogurt dip) and a large horiatiki salad, piled high with tomatoes, olives, and feta cheese. ✉ *Last street on right off Lykourgou Logotheti as you descend to harbor,* ☎ *0273/61957. No credit cards.*

$$$$ 🏨 **Doryssa Bay Hotel and Village.** Overlooking Glyfada Lake, the
★   body of water by the Aegean that was the site of the ancient naval port, this pseudo-village has pastel houses (containing housekeeping apartments) with a small church, a square, *kafenion* (traditional Greek coffeehouse), and shops. The hotel is modern and is centered on a large pool. Half-board is mandatory, but the food at the hotel's Taverna Asterias is unusually good—sample it at Tuesday's pricey Greek night, which entails lavish spreads and traditional dancers. ✉ *Outside Pythagorio on main road to Chora, 83103,* ☎ *0273/61360,* 🖷 *0273/ 61463. 172 rooms, 125 bungalows, 5 suites. 3 restaurants, 2 bars, air-conditioning, pool, tennis court, beach, boating, fishing, waterskiing. AE, DC, MC, V. Closed Nov.–Mar.*

$$$ 🏨 **Hydrele Beach.** On one of the longest and most beautiful beaches in Samos, this two-story hotel behind a gate and lush garden is built in local style. Rooms have balconies overlooking the huge, meandering pool, with the sea and brown hills beyond. There is a wide array of water sports available. ✉ *Pototaki, a 15-min walk from Pythagorio, 83103,* ☎ *0273/61702,* 🖷 *0273/61602. 12 rooms. Restaurant, 2 bars. No credit cards.*

$$ 🏨 **Galini.** You won't pay dearly for comfort at this hotel. Reached only by steps and with no cars passing in front, Galini (meaning tranquillity) is aptly quiet. The large marble-adorned rooms face the town or the sea. Each floor has a refrigerator. The friendly Kanatas family serves breakfast in the garden or the dining room. ✉ *Aesopos, off Platia Irinis, Pythagorio 83103,* ☎ *0273/92331,* 🖷 *0273/28039. 9 rooms. Dining room, lobby lounge, in-room safes. No credit cards. Closed Nov.– late Mar.*

Outdoor Activities and Sports

SAILING

On Samos, **Pythagorio, Karlovassi, Ormos Marathokambou,** and **Samos town** have fuel, water, and repair services.

Sun Yachting (✉ 9 Dosmani St., Athens, ☎ 01/983–7312) in Athens specializes in charter rentals to Samos; you can pick up the boat in Piraeus or Pythagorio for one- and two-week rentals.

TENNIS

Near Pythagorio the **Doryssa Bay** (✉ Outside Pythagorio on main road to Chora, ☎ 0273/61360), **Apollon** (✉ Outside Pythagorio on main road to Chora, ☎ 0273/61683), and **Princessa** hotels (✉ Outside Pythagorio on main road to Chora, ☎ 0273/61698) have courts to rent.

WATER SPORTS

On Samos many beaches have windsurfing rentals, including **Heraion, Karlovassi, Mykali, Potokaki, Tsamadou,** and **Votsalakia.**

Heraion

8 km (5 mi) southwest of Samos town, 6½ km (4 mi) southwest of Pythagorio.

★ ㊷ The early Samians worshiped Hera, believing she was born here near the stream Imbrassos and that there she also lay with Zeus. Several temples were built on the site, the last by Polycrates, who rebuilt the **Temple of Heraion,** enlarging it and lining it with two rows of columns, 133 in all. The huge temple, four times larger than the Parthenon, and the largest Greek temple ever conceived, was damaged by fire in 525 BC and never completed, owing to Polycrates' untimely death. In the intervening years, masons recycled the stones to create other buildings, including a basilica (foundations remain at the site) to another highly worshiped woman, the Virgin Mary. Today, we can only imagine the Heraion's massive glory; of its forest of columns only one remains standing amid acres of marble remnants in marshy ground thick with poppies.

At the semiannual celebrations to honor Hera, the faithful approached from the sea along the **Sacred Way,** which is still visible at the site's northeast corner. Nearby are replicas of a 6th-century BC sculpture depicting an aristocratic family, whose chiseled signature reads "Genelaos made me." The originals and the world's largest kouros, also found here, are in the Samos archaeological museum (☞ *below*). ⊠ *Near Imvisos River,* ☎ *0273/95277.* ☒ *800 dr.* ☉ *Tues.–Sun. 8:30–3.*

Mytilini

㊸ *12 km (7½ mi) west of Samos town, 9 km (5½ mi) north of Heraion.*

Mytilini, an inland village with a pretty market square, has a **paleontological museum** exhibiting local animal fossils dating back 15 million years. The prize exhibit, among the bones of ancient hippos, rhinos, and evolving three-toed horses, is a 13-million-year-old fossilized horse brain. ⊠ *City Hall,* ☎ *0273/52055.* ☒ *500 dr.* ☉ *Apr.–Oct., weekdays 9–3.*

Dining

$ ✕ **Dionyssos.** When you tire of eating on Pythagorio's waterfront, where food is often overpriced and monotonous, take a taxi to Mytilini and this taverna (there's no sign: just say the name to the first Greeks you'll encounter—pronounce it Dee-u-*neye*-sis—and chances are they will accompany you there) for inexpensive, well-cooked chops; *kotopoulo* krasato (chicken in wine); lemon chicken; and the seldom-seen chicken breast on a spit. The good appetizers go well with the chilled barrel retsina, which may prepare you for the random Gypsy vendor who parks his van next to your table and pulls out stereo speakers to foist upon you. ⊠ *Mytilini Sq. (Platia Kalymniou),* ☎ *0273/51820. No credit cards.*

Music

Clubs throughout Greece are named after everybody's favorite lusty Greek, and here on the road to Samos town is **Zorba's,** for bouzouki music (bring your own plates if, inspired by the movie, you want to smash any).

Pirgos

㊹ *30 km (18½ mi) west of Samos town, 14 km (8¾ mi) west of Mytilini.*

This area produces distinctive honey, with a hint of herbs the Samian bees buzz around. The landscape here still shows the charred signs of a 1990 fire that destroyed acres of pine forest. Hilltop **Timiou Stavrou**

monastery, 14 km (8½ mi) northeast of Pirgos, is considered Samos's most important monastery and is worth a stop to enjoy the icons, carved wooden iconostasis, and the bishop's throne.

Shopping
CERAMICS

Aesthetic ceramics are a specialty in the villages of **Koumaradei** and **Mauratzei.** The most popular item is the "Pythagoras" cup, which leaks when it's more than half full. It was invented by Pythagoras to ensure that his students didn't imbibe during lessons.

Platanos

45 *27 (16¾ mi) west of Samos town, 11 km (7 mi) northwest of Pirgos.*

Mt. Kerkis, the second-highest peak in the Aegean (after Sao on Samothraki), hangs in the distance and the island's undeveloped west coast plummets below as you follow the curve around the western side of the island. Platanos is a typical hillside village, where, except for during "Greek nights" staged by travel agencies in summer, very little changes from year to year.

Marathokambos

40 km (25 mi) west of Samos town, 8 km (5 mi) west of Platanos.

The village of Marathokambos stretches like an amphitheater across the lower flanks of Mt. Kerkis. In the afternoons, when the haze clears, the view down to the Bay of Marathokambos and the southern beaches is dazzling, with the island of Patmos looming on the horizon. Nearby caves are fun for spelunkers to explore.

Ormos Marathokambou

46 *40 km (25 mi) west of Samos town, 5 km (3 mi) south of Marathokambos.*

Ormos Marathokambou, on the bay, still has a small caïque-building industry, and these boats make daily trips to Fourni with its one fishing village and empty beaches, and the islet of Samiopoula. A few tavernas serve Samian wine, and strollers enjoy the quay, which is closed to traffic. But the port's unique attraction is at its western end: a lone traffic light.

Beaches

47 Ormos Marathkambou has a narrow pebble beach favored by windsurfers, but Samos's longest beach, **Votsalakia** (⊠ 2 km/1 mi west of Ormos Marathkambou), is a pine-shaded strip of sand backed by a growing, low-rise family resort. Several tavernas serve up informal food and drink. Mt. Kerkis looms dramatically above it all. Scant crowds and lots of rays reign at **Psili Ammos** beach, 15 km (9¼ mi) southwest of Votsalakia.

Outdoor Activities and Sports
HIKING

From Votsalakia beach (☞ *above*) you can climb **Mt. Kerkis** on a path that runs past a convent and, once above the tree line, embrace some grand views. The round-trip, including rest stops, will take most of the day. If you want to drive part of the way, a paved road goes past villages west of the summit. You can hike to caves that once housed religious hermits (and now, who knows?). Two isolated monasteries are also in the area.

Karlovassi

48 *33 km (20½ mi) northwest of Samos Town, 16 km (10 mi) north of Ormos Marathokambou.*

Karlovassi, Samos's second-largest harbor, is a good base for exploring the western beaches. It seems grim until you take a closer look at its neighborhoods. The area called Paleo spreads across a ravine above the harbor area of Limani; it is surprisingly pretty. Above it is a hilltop church, visible from the sea. Below the main square, richly decorated churches and elaborate neoclassical mansions, padlocked and slightly dilapidated, hint of at time when Karlovassi was a center of leather production. Note the empty tanneries as you drive through the coastal suburbs toward the ferry port and Potami.

OFF THE BEATEN PATH

MIKRO SEITANI AND MEGALO SEITANI – Beach lovers can easily travel from Karlovassi, first by bus and then on foot, to two delightfully secluded coves: Mikro Seitani (pebble) and Megalo Seitani (sand). No food stands are around, and often no people, so bring your own picnic. From the port, walk or take the bus west to tree-rimmed Potami beach (☞ *below*), where the asphalt ends. After about 10 minutes you'll come to a dirt path that veers right. Ignore it. Two minutes later, turn off at the second path going right, marked by a stone pile. The trail is steep, and it's marked with blue and white paint dots all the way to the cove. After a small farm, it winds through olive trees, giving eyefuls of the turquoise sea below. After another 15 minutes, another path bears left, but continue straight, and some 40 minutes out of Potami you'll come upon the limpid cove of Mikro Seitani. If you can manage to tear yourself away, continue on, along a path that has good views of Mt. Kerkis and, in spring, winds through masses of wildflowers; after about 30 minutes you'll see a path going up to the left; continue straight and you will reach Megalo Seitani in another 15 minutes. Seitani Bay on this north coast is a marine preserve for the monk seal, an endangered mammal also found off Alonnisos, in the Sporades islands.

Beaches

Along the north coast near Karlovassi are some of the island's best beaches. Two kilometers (1 mile) west of Karlovassi is **Potami,** a wide pebble-and-sand beach (☒ About 45 mins by foot on the coast road from Limani, or an hour's drive on the scenic road from Paleo). It has shady bushes under which people camp, pine trees overhead, and interesting rock formations. Hidden in a reedy area halfway along the beach is a small **white house** where a local family serves lunch amid greenery and under the scrutiny of the family donkey. A short walk inland is an isolated medieval settlement just waiting to be explored, with a Byzantine castle and an 11th-century church, the island's oldest.

Dining and Lodging

$$ ✕ **Steve's.** The owner has lived in South Africa, but the cuisine is all Samos, and his restaurant has earned a reputation for some of the best food on the island. Generous portions of standard Greek fare such as *fasolakia freska* (snap peas or green beans) and pastitsio are executed impeccably. The splendid homemade cheesecake will make you tap your shoes. ☒ *Karlovassi Harbor quay, easternmost establishment on harbor,* ☎ *0273/33434. MC. Closed Dec.–Mar.*

$ ✕ **Psarades.** It's worth a detour to find this family-run taverna, where occasional kittens may nip at your heels, but good, inexpensive fish is served on a terrace overlooking the waves. In spring or autumn there are trays of fresh saddled bream and grouper, and you can also order *fassolada* (bean stew), *yiouvarlakia* (rice-and-meat balls in white sauce), and pungent tzatziki and skordalia dips. ⊠ *About 100 yards east of Ayios Dimitrios you'll come to a sign for the taverna; turn left down paved driveway and continue to end, Ayios Nikolaos, 5 km (3 mi) outside Karlovassi,* ☎ *0273/32489. No credit cards.*

$$$ 🏨 **Samina Bay.** Without a doubt the best hotel in Karlovassi, the Samina Bay is convenient to the ferry. The hotel is spacious, with framed embroideries adding a homey touch in the reception and bar area; guest rooms have white lacquer furniture, the suites, bamboo. The polite young staff is fluent in several languages. A breakfast buffet is served on the veranda, and you can usually arrange for other meals, too. Potami beach is a 15-minute walk away. ⊠ *Main road, near harbor, Karlovassi 83200,* ☎ *0273/34004-7,* 🗎 *0273/34008. 75 rooms. Restaurant, bar, air-conditioning, pool, sauna, playground. MC, V. Closed Nov.–Apr.*

$$ 🏨 **Merope.** Though not much to look at, this four-story '70s hotel strives for high standards at reasonable rates. Each floor has a lounge; the simple rooms have the usual pine furniture and balconies, with fantastic views above the second floor. A local bus runs to Potami beach; otherwise lounge by the pool or stroll down the street to see some of Karlovassi's fine old tobacco warehouses, some of them deserted. If you get hungry, the kitchen always has some well-prepared magirefta on hand. ⊠ *Main road in Pefkakia area, by the post office, Karlovassi 83200,* ☎ *0273/32650 or 0273/32651,* 🗎 *0273/32652. 80 rooms with shower. Bar, pool. No credit cards. Closed Nov.–Mar.*

Manolates

㊾ *15 km (9⅓ mi) northwest of Samos town, 5 km (3 mi) east of Ayios Konstandinos through steep vineyards up Mt. Ambelos.*

The delightful village of Manolates is surrounded by forest. Squares are lined with balconied stone houses with tile roofs, and cats prowl narrow streets whitewashed with floral designs. Most hikers set out from here to gawk at coastal panoramas or to watch for birds. Steep vineyards on these lower slopes of Mt. Ambelos offer wide-ranging views and produce wines in white and rosé. But it is the dark, sweet moskhato grape about which Lord Byron wrote, "Dash down yon cup of Samian wine."

Kokkari

㊿ *27 km (16¼ mi) southeast of Karlovassi, 9 km (5½ mi) northeast of Manolates.*

Beyond the popular beaches of Tsabou, Tsamadou, and Lemonakia, the spectacular stretch of coast road with olive groves and vineyards ends suitably in the fishing village of Kokkari, one of the most appealing spots on the island. Until 1980, there was not much here except for a few dozen houses between two headlands, and tracts of onion fields, which gave the town its name. Though now there are a score of hotels, and many German tourists, you can still traipse along the rocky, windswept beach and spy fishermen mending trawling nets on the paved quay. Cross the spit to the eastern side of the headland and watch the moon rise over the lights of Vathi in the next bay.

Beaches
Acclaimed **coves of the north coast** are the partly nudist **Tsamadou, Lemonakia,** and **Tsabou;** all are just a few minutes from one another, and they're to be avoided when the *meltemi* (northern winds) blow, unless you're a professional windsurfer.

Dining and Lodging
$$ ✕ **Avgo tou Kokkora.** The name comes from the Greek tale of a woman who invited her son-in-law to dinner, promising such variety

that there'd even be an *avgo tou kokkora* (rooster's egg). That is still the key here: Besides fresh fish and the usuals, the seaside restaurant offers *kokkoras* (rooster), *flambé bastounia tou sef* (a fried ham-and-cheese appetizer), and *glosses tis petheras* ("mother-in-law's tongue," made from beef tongue). It stays open until 3 AM. If this won't do, head for the adjacent Porto Picolo for Italian fare or Barino for a nightcap (same management). ⊠ *Kokkari promenade,* ☎ *0273/92113. DC, MC, V. Closed Nov.–Apr.*

$$ ✕ **Kariatida.** Here you teeter on the water's edge, and the waiters can always squeeze in another table. The fresh-fish menu features sea bream and various incarnations of shrimp and swordfish. House specialties also include rabbit stew, and *pikilia* (a medley of mixed starters). The wine list is long and well chosen. ⊠ *Kokkari promenade,* ☎ *0273/92103. MC, V. Closed Nov.–Apr.*

$$ ▦ **Olympia Beach/Olympic Village.** At this bright-white hotel with traditional marble and wood interiors, you can stroll into Kokkari for a movie yet avoid the bustle. The immaculate rooms are spare but have balconies overlooking the sea and are decorated with flowery Samian ceramics. The same owners run the nearby Olympia Village, whose apartments, incluuding bedroom, living room, two baths, and a kitchen, are ideal for families. You can walk to Tsamadou cove, favored for its shallow water, pine trees, and secluded setting. ⊠ *Northwest Beach Rd., near Kokkari, 83100,* ☎ *0273/92353,* 𝔽𝔸𝕏 *0273/92457. 22 rooms. Restaurant, bar. No credit cards. Closed Nov.–Apr.*

$$ ▦ **Venus (Afroditi).** Your first impression is of potted plants, red marble, and wood trim—a modern interior in an unremarkable building about 100 yards from the beach. The reasonably priced rooms have wood ceilings and balconies that survey the vineyards. Breakfast is Continental or "American," which means yogurt, eggs, juice, cereal, and coffee. ⊠ *In-town road, Kokkari 83100,* ☎ *0273/92230,* 𝔽𝔸𝕏 *0273/ 92305. 46 rooms with shower. Pool, sauna, beauty salon. AE, DC, MC, V. Closed Nov.–Apr.*

En Route After Kokkari you pass through Malagari, the winery where farmers hawk their harvested grapes every September, hoping for a knockout vintage.

Samos Town

51 *33 km (20½ mi) southeast of Karlovassi, 6 km (4 mi) southeast of Kokkari.*

On the northeast coast at the head of the island's deepest bay is the capital, Samos town, also known as Vathi. Red-tiled roofs swirled in a semicircle seem to reach toward the top of red-earth hills. In the morning at the sheltered harbor, fishermen are still grappling with their nets, spreading them to dry in the sun, and in the early afternoon everything shuts down. Tourism does not alter this centuries-old schedule.

The stepped streets ascend from the **shopping thoroughfare,** which meanders from the port to the city park next to the **archaeological museum,** the town's most important sight. The museum's older wing has a collection of pottery and cast-bronze griffin heads (the symbol of Samos). Samian sculptures from past millennia were considered among the best in Greece, and examples here show why. An exceptional collection of tributary gifts from ancient cities far and wide, including bronzes and ivory miniatures, affirms the importance of the shrine to

★ Hera. The newest wing holds the impressive **kouros from Heraion,** a votive offering to the goddess and the largest freestanding sculpture surviving from ancient Greece, dating from 580 BC. It stands alone in the room, massive, with an inscrutable smile, the enigma of ancient

Samos. It's so large (16 ½ ft tall) that the wing had to be rebuilt specifically to house it. ⊠ *Platia Dimarhiou*, ☎ *0273/27469.* 🖭 *800 dr.* ☉ *Tues.–Sun. 8:30–3.*

❷ In the quaint 17th-century village of **Ano Vathi** (⊠ Beyond museum, to the right), wood-and-plaster houses with pastel facades and red-tile roofs are jammed together, their balconies protruding into cobbled paths so narrow that the water channel takes up most of the space. From here you have a view of the gulf.

OFF THE
BEATEN PATH

From Samos town (and Pythagerio) you can easily ferry to Turkey. Once there, it's a short drive from the Kusadasi on the Turkish coast, where the boats dock, to Ephesus, one of the great archaeological sites and a major city of the ancient world. (Note that the Temple of Artemis in Ephesus is a copy of the Temple of Hera, destroyed in Heraion, so you can see it in Turkey, sort of.) A guided round-trip full-day tour costs about 25,000 dr. Many travel agencies run this popular trip, which can be lengthened and customized. You leave your passport with the agency and it is returned when you come back from Turkey.

Beaches

❸ One of the island's best beaches is sandy **Psili Ammos** (⊠ Southeast of Samos Town near Mesokambos). Closer to Samos town is **Mykali beach** (⊠ On coast east of Samos town), with a stunning view of Turkey and Mykali peak. From here you might fantasize about swimming the straits to Turkey, about 2 km (1 mi) across the sea.

Dining and Lodging

$$ ✕ **Apanemia.** The name of this ouzieri on the shore of Vathy bay means "the lee spot," and it's rather ambitious on choppy days, though the garden seating is pleasant. The Athenian proprietor-chef brings years of experience to the panoply of dishes—familiar Western favorites like stroganoff and cannelloni as well as Greek specialties. Among the latter choose *kopanisti* (spicy cheese puree), *pastourmas* (pastrami), and mussels saganaki or *ahnista* (steamed in wine). ⊠ *Themistokleous Sofouli 26, Vathy,* ☎ *0273/28147. No credit cards. Closed Nov.–Apr. No lunch.*

$$ ✕ **La Calma.** Everybody always seems to be having a good time here. Maybe it's the setting, on a waterfront terrace, or maybe it's the large selection, from grilled fresh fish to traditional meat dishes. For dessert, go for the caramel custard or a glass of sweet Samian moskhato. ⊠ *Kefalopoulou 5, Vathi,* ☎ *0273/22654. No credit cards. Closed Nov.–Apr.*

$$ ✕ **The Steps.** Climb the steps and enter a courtyard draped with ivy and flowers in an atmosphere of candlelight, crisp white linen, and soft music. One of the chef's specialties is the mixed plate, which gives you a chance to try the souvlaki, lamb, village sausage, and meatball. Lamb is roasted on a spit, sliced, and served with gravy. The Krissakis family also serve exohiko, swordfish grilled with lemon-oil sauce, and sole breaded like schnitzel. To reach the Steps, turn left off the Samos waterfront, then left between the Dionyssos and Souda restaurants. ⊠ *Near Samos Harbor,* ☎ *0273/28649. No credit cards. Closed Nov.–Apr. No lunch.*

$$ 🛏 **Galaxy.** Off the harbor in a quiet neighborhood, this greenery-fringed hotel is a cheerful respite from the waterfront. Once in the courtyard, you see the pool shimmering and hear laughter from the bar area. The simply furnished rooms all have balconies overlooking the pool, the baby palm–sprouted lawn, or the adjacent grove. ⊠ *Angeou 1, behind the Fourth Primary School, Samos 83100,* ☎ *0273/22268,* 🖷 *0273/27679. 42 rooms. Bar, pool. V. Closed Nov.–Feb.*

$$ 🛏 **Paradise.** Simple but elegant, this hotel is a cut above the rest, with cushy details: marble, dark wood, and bird-of-paradise flower arrangements. Avoid the six front rooms; others overlook the garden and

the orchards of Perivoli district, so you're treated to evening birdsong. This hotel is convenient to the bus station and within walking distance of the harbor. ⊠ *Kanari 21, Samos 83100,* ☎ *0271/23911 through 0271/23913,* FAX *0271/28754. 51 rooms. Snack bar, pool. MC, V. Closed Nov.–Mar.*

Nightlife

The port area, as on most of the Greek islands, is the surest bet for clubs and action. If you seek smaller places, check out the adjoining streets, or ask if there's a strip, as bars tend to congregate, just as patrons do. Since the scene changes rapidly, it's always best to ask the locals.

THE NORTHERN ISLANDS A TO Z

Arriving and Departing

By Plane

Even if they have the time, most people avoid the 10- to 12-hour ferry ride from Athens and start their island-hopping trip by air. Most flights are one hour or less. **Olympic Airways** (☎ 01/926–9111) has at least a dozen flights a week from Athens to each of the islands in summer. Watch out for overbooking problems; if you have a reservation, you should be entitled to a free flight if you get bumped.

LIMNOS

Call the **Olympic Airways** office in Myrina (⊠ Garofalidi 6, ☎ 0254/22214 or 0254/22078) or at the airport (☎ 0254/31204). The **airport** (☎ 0254/31294 or 0254/31202) is near Moudros Bay, 22 km (14 mi) from Myrina.

LESBOS

Olympic Airways offices are in Mytilini (⊠ 44 Kavetsou, ☎ 0251/28660) and at the airport (☎ 0251/61490). The **airport** (☎ 0251/61212) is 7 km (4½ mi) from Mytilini.

CHIOS

Olympic Airways has offices in the port town of Chios (⊠ Prokymeia midport, ☎ 0271/20359) and at the airport (☎ 0271/23998). The **airport** is 4½ km (3 mi) from town (☎ 0271/24515 for airport information).

SAMOS

Olympic Airways offices are in Vathi (⊠ Kanari 5, ☎ 0273/27237), in Pythagorio (⊠ Logothetou 90, ☎ 0273/61300), and at the airport (☎ 0273/61219). The busiest **airport** (☎ 0273/61219 flight information) is here, 17 km (10½ mi) from Vathi. More than 40 international charters arrive every week in midsummer.

By Boat

If you can't get on a flight (☞ *below*), there's always the extensive **ferry network,** offering the consolation that you'll travel for a third of the airfare. Car ferries vary a bit, but most offer clean and comfortable overnight service between destinations. Newer ones offer buffet and sit-down meals, entertainment, and the carpeted, brass, and glass glitz of a small cruise ship. The Greek National Tourist Organization (GNTO or EOT) office in Athens distributes weekly ferry schedules. For last-minute departure times, call the Athens port authority (☎ 01/451–1311).

CHIOS

Boats arrive daily from Piraeus. The **Chios port authority** (☎ 0271/44433) can be of assistance.

LESBOS

There are at least four boats per week from Piraeus and three per week from Thessaloniki. The **port authority** (☎ 0251/28888) is in Mytilini.

LIMNOS

Arrivals port daily in summer from Piraeus, Rafina, or Kavala. On Limnos, call the **port authority** (☎ 0254/22225) for information.

SAMOS

Ferries arrive four to nine times per week from Athens, stopping at Paros and Naxos; and most of the year two or three ferries weekly serve Pythagorio from Kos and Patmos. Ferries and hydrofoils to Kusdasi on the Turkish coast leave from Vathi. Samos has **port authority offices** in Vathi (☎ 0273/27318), Karlovassi (☎ 0273/32343), and Pythagorio (☎ 0273/61225).

Getting Around

By Boat and Hydrofoil

Hydrofoil service via Flying Dolphin is available for travel among the local islands only; it is also more expensive than ferry travel, but it's quicker. Even in low season there are several connections weekly among Samos, Chios, and Lesbos. From Limnos a boat goes two to four times a week to Lesbos and back. In summer, scheduling can be more frequent. Check ahead.

By Bus

LIMNOS

On Limnos the few buses from Myrina (✉ Platia Venizelou, ☎ 0254/22464) depart early and occasionally don't return the same day. You can, however, go from Myrina to Moudros and all points in between quite easily.

LESBOS

Lesbos's **KTEL bus system** (✉ Platia Konstantinopoleos, ☎ 0251/28873) is relatively expensive and infrequent, though there are several buses a day from Mytilini to Molyvos via Kalloni, and you can also get to Mandamados, Agiassos Plomari, Eressos, and Sigri.

CHIOS

Buses leave the town of Chios several times per day for Mesta and Pirgi, and three leave daily for Volissos. For information call the **KTEL station** (✉ Vlatarias 13, ☎ 0271/27507).

SAMOS

Samos has excellent **KTEL bus service** (✉ Ioannou Lekati and Kanari, near Olympic Airways office, ☎ 0273/27262), with frequent trips between Pythagorio, Samos town, Kokkari, and Karlovassi. Buses also travel at least twice daily to Ireon, Pirgos, Marathokambos, and Votsalakia beach.

By Car and Moped

A car is handiest on Lesbos and Chios, the bigger islands, but costs about $75 a day. Mopeds (about $20 a day) are the ideal way to see Samos or Limnos. You won't have any trouble finding rentals.

By Plane

Other than daily summer flights between Limnos and Lesbos, and two weekly between Lesbos and Chios, there are no direct flights between these northern islands; it's best to count on going by ferry or hydrofoil.

Guided Tours

LIMNOS

El Travel (✉ Xristodoulidou 10, Myrina, ☎ 0254/24988, ℻ 0254/22697) gives English tours to the archaeological museum and to various villages and interesting sites such as the islet of Aï Stratis.

LESBOS

Aeolic Cruises, with branches in Mytilini (✉ Prokimea, ☎ 0251/23960 or 0251/23266, ℻ 0251/43694) and Plomari (✉ Ayios Isidoros, ☎ 0251/32009), offers a variety of island tours. In Molyvos, **Panatella Tours** (✉ Possidonion at town entrance, ☎ 0253/71520, 0253/71643, and 0253/71644, ℻ 0253/71680) has two tours that take in villages, monasteries, and other sights.

CHIOS

Ionia Touristiki (✉ Rodokanaki 17, ☎ 0271/41047 or 0271/22034, ℻ 0271/41122) organizes excursions to the mastikhohoria and other sights (one is a four-wheel-drive tour).

SAMOS

Most of the branches of **Samina** (Main office: Themistokleous Sofouli 67, Vathi, ☎ 0273/28841; 0273/28842 to find closest branch) run an island tour, a one-day trip to Patmos, and a picnic cruise.

Contacts and Resources

Emergencies

Police (☎ 100). **Ambulance** (☎ 166). **Fire** (☎ 199).

Visitor Information

LIMNOS

Tourist police, (✉ 66 Garrufalidi, ☎ 0254/22200). **Myrina tourist office** (✉ Near port, in municipal building, ☎ 0254/24110).

LESBOS

Information offices are in Eressos (✉ Main square, ☎ 0253/53214), Molyvos (✉ Possidonios near bus stop, ☎ 0253/71347), Mytilini (✉ Harbor, ☎ 0251/28199; ✉ Airport, ☎ 0251/61279), and Plomari (✉ Harbor, ☎ 0252/32535). **Tourist police** (✉ Harbor, Mytilini, ☎ 0251/22776). The **Women's Agricultural Tourist Collective** (✉ Petra, ☎ 0253/41238) finds rooms with farming families.

CHIOS

Greek National Tourist Organization (EOT; ✉ 18 Kanari, Chios, ☎ 0271/44389 or 0271/20324). **Tourist police** (✉ 37 Neoriou, Chios, ☎ 0271/44344 or 0271/44427). The **Women's Agricultural Tourist Collective** (✉ Main square, Pirgi, ☎ 0271/72496) finds rooms with local families, as will **Mesta's tourist information office** (✉ Main square, ☎ 0271/76319).

SAMOS

EOT: Vathi (✉ Ikostipemptis Martiou 4, ☎ 0273/28–582), Pythagorio (✉ Logothetou, 1 block up waterfront, ☎ 0273/61100), Kokkari (✉ Across from OTE, ☎ 0273/62274), **Tourist police** (✉ Vathi harbor, ☎ 0273/27980).

14 Portraits of Greece

Greece at a Glance: A Chronology

A Word About Greek Architecture

Books and Videos

GREECE AT A GLANCE: A CHRONOLOGY

ca. 6000 BC Beginning of Neolithic period in Greece with introduction of domesticated plants and animals from Anatolia.

ca. 3000 BC Development of early Bronze Age cultures: on Crete called "Minoan" after the legendary monarch, Minos, and on the mainland known as "Helladic"

ca. 1900 BC Rise of important settlement at Mycenae

1900 BC– Height of Minoan culture. On Crete the Palace of Minos at Knossos
1400 BC is built, which includes indoor plumbing. Its mazelike complexity gives rise to the legend of the labyrinth

1400 BC– Height of Mycenaean power: Crete is taken, and the city of Troy in
1200 BC Asia Minor is sacked. At Mycenae and Pylos impressive tombs mark this warrior culture

1200 BC– Mycenaean civilization falls, as Bronze Age civilizations of the
1100 BC Eastern Mediterranean collapse

1100 BC– The "dark ages": writing disappears. The legendary poet Homer
750 BC narrates a history of the Trojan War and describes an aristocratic society; this oral tradition is later written down as the *Iliad* and the *Odyssey*

ca. 750 BC Establishment of the *polis,* or city-state, as the characteristic form of political and civic organization in Greece

ca. 725 BC The poet Hesiod describes rural life in *Works and Days* and establishes the pantheon of Greek gods in *Theogony.* The Olympic Games are established as a Panhellenic event, during which peace prevailed

700 BC– Colonization builds Greek city-states throughout the Mediterranean.
500 BC Meanwhile, social pressures at home lead to the rule of tyrants

621 BC Dracon publishes a notoriously severe legal code in Athens

ca. 600 BC The legendary ruler Lykourgos establishes the Spartan system of a highly controlled, militaristic society. Thales of Miletus, the first Greek philosopher, starts wondering about the world

594 BC Solon is given extraordinary powers to reform the Athenian government and constitution

ca. 550 BC Establishment of the Peloponnesian League, a military alliance of city-states dominated by Sparta. The philosopher Pythagoras propounds a famous theorem and sets up a monastic colony in southern Italy; the poet Sappho of Lesbos describes a particular kind of love

508 BC– Clisthenes establishes Athenian democracy
501 BC

The Classical Era

499 BC– Persian wars: Athens leads Greek states against Kings Darius and
479 BC Xerxes. 490 BC: Battle of Marathon is a critical victory for Athens. 480 BC: Xerxes invades Greece; the Greek League, which includes Athens and Sparta, defeats him in a series of battles at Thermopylae, Salamis, and Plataea

478 BC– Founding of Delian League of city-states under Athenian hegemony;
477 BC it will evolve into an empire

ca. 475 BC– 400 BC Golden age of classical Greek culture, centered at Athens. Aeschylus (525 BC–456 BC), Sophocles (ca. 496 BC–406 BC), and Euripides (ca. 485 BC–402 BC) form the great triumvirate of classical drama; the comedies of Aristophanes (ca. 450 BC–385 BC) satirize contemporary mores. Socrates (469 BC–399 BC) and his disciple Plato (ca. 429 BC–347 BC) debate the fundamental questions of knowledge and meaning. Herodotus (ca. 484 BC–420 BC) and Thucydides (471 BC–402 BC) invent historical writing. The Acropolis epitomizes the harmony and precision of classical architecture and sculpture

462 BC Pericles (ca. 495 BC–429 BC) rises to the leadership of Athens and leads the city to its cultural height

460 BC– 445 BC First Peloponnesian War between Athens and Sparta ends with the "Thirty Years' Peace" and recognition of the Athenian Empire. At the height of his power, Pericles rebuilds Athens

432 BC The Second, or Great, Peloponnesian War begins when Sparta declares war on Athens

429 BC A disastrous plague kills more than one-third of the Athenian population, including Pericles

415 BC– 413 BC Athens's disastrous invasion of Sicily reopens the war and sets the stage for its downfall

404 BC Athens falls to Sparta and its walls are dismantled, ending an era

398 BC– 360 BC Rule of Agesilaus at Sparta, whose aggressive policies lead to its ruin

394 BC Spartan fleet destroyed by Persians

386 BC Plato founds the Academy in Athens, a school of philosophy that trains statesmen

384 BC Birth of Aristotle, the greatest ancient philosopher and scientist (died 322 BC)

378 BC Second Athenian Confederation marks the resurgence of Athens

362 BC Death of Epaminondas at the battle of Mantinea ends Theban dominance, documented by Xenophon (ca. 434 BC–355 BC)

355 BC Second Athenian Confederation collapses, leaving Greece in chaos

The Hellenistic Era

351 BC Demosthenes (384 BC–332 BC) delivers the First Philippic, warning Athens of the dangers of Macedonian power

342 BC Aristotle becomes tutor to a young Macedonian prince named Alexander (356 BC–323 BC)

338 BC Alexander's father, Philip of Macedon (382 BC–336 BC) defeats the Greek forces at Chaeronea and establishes Macedonian hegemony

336 BC Philip is assassinated, leaving his empire to his son Alexander, soon to be known as "the Great." Aristotle founds his school, the Lyceum, at Athens

323 BC Having conquered the known world and opened it to Greek culture, Alexander dies of a fever in Babylon

ca. 330 BC– 200 BC Hellenistic culture blends Greek and other influences in a cosmopolitan style. Epicureanism, Stoicism, and Cynicism enter philosophy; Hellenistic sculpture blends emotion and realism. At the new city of

Alexandria in Egypt, Greek science and mathematics flourish with Euclid (300 BC) and Archimedes (ca. 287 BC–212 BC); Aristarchus (ca. 310 BC–230 BC) asserts that the earth revolves around the sun

The Roman Era

215 BC The outbreak of the First Macedonian War signals Rome's rise in the Mediterranean

146 BC Rome annexes Greece and Macedonia as provinces. Roman culture becomes increasingly Hellenized

49 BC–31 BC Greece is a battleground for control of Rome's empire: 48 BC: Julius Caesar defeats Pompey at Pharsalus; 42 BC: Caesar's heir Octavian defeats Brutus at Philippi; 31 BC: Octavian defeats Mark Antony at Actium and becomes, as Augustus, the first Roman Emperor

125 The guidebook of Pausanias makes Greece a favored tourist stop; the emperor Hadrian undertakes the renovation of ancient monuments

394 The emperor Theodosius declares Christianity the official religion of the Roman Empire and bans pagan cults, suppressing the Olympic Games and closing the oracle at Delphi

The Medieval Era

476 The fall of Rome leaves Greece open to waves of invaders, though it remains nominally under the hegemony of the Byzantine emperors at Constantinople

529 The Byzantine emperor Justinian closes Plato's Academy in Athens

1054 The Great Schism divides the Christian church into Greek and Roman orthodoxies

1204–61 Greece briefly reenters the sphere of western influence with the Latin capture of Constantinople in the Fourth Crusade

1453 The fall of Constantinople to the Ottoman Turks leads to nearly four centuries of Turkish rule

The Modern Era

1770 The Russian prince Orloff attempts but fails to establish a Greek principality

1814 The *Philike Hetairia,* a "friendly society" established by Greek merchants at Odessa (Russia), is instrumental in the growth of Greek nationalism

1821–29 The Greek War of Independence. 1821: The Greek Patriarch, Archbishop Germanos, declares Greek independence, and war with the Turks breaks out. Among those aiding Greece in her struggle is the English poet Lord Byron. 1826: A Greek defeat at Missolonghi stirs European sympathy. 1827: The Triple Alliance of Great Britain, France, and Russia intervene against the Turks and their Egyptian allies. 1829: The Turks are defeated and Greece is declared an independent state, guaranteed by the Triple Alliance

1832 Prince Otho of Bavaria is offered the Greek throne by the Triple Alliance

1834 King Otho chooses Athens as his capital

1844 Greece adopts a constitution that establishes a constitutional monarchy

1863 As a result of Otho's pro-Russian policies during the Crimean War, he is forced to abdicate and is replaced on the throne by Prince George of Denmark

1909–10 The Military League, a group of young army officers, leads a peaceful revolt and installs as prime minister Eleutherios Venizelos, who enacts a series of reforms

1912–13 Greece gains Macedonia, Epirus, and Crete as a result of the Balkan Wars

1917–18 Greece fights on the Allied side in World War I

1924 Greece is declared a republic

1935 Monarchy is restored; in the next year, King George II allows General Joannes Metaxas to establish a military dictatorship

1940 Italy invades Greece, leading to four years of Axis occupation

1946 Greece becomes a charter member of the United Nations

1946–49 Communist rebellion is defeated with U.S. help

1952 Women are given the right to vote

1963 George Seferis wins the Nobel Prize for Literature

1967 A military coup ousts King Constantine II

1974 In the wake of the Cyprus crisis, the military government collapses and the first elections in 10 years are held. Constantine Karamanlis is named prime minister. The republic is confirmed by popular vote

1980 Odysseus Elytis becomes the second Greek to win the Nobel Prize for Literature

1981 Greece joins the European Economic Community

1993 Andreas Papandreou returns to power

1994 Minister of Culture Melina Mercouri dies

1996 Former prime minister Andreas Papandreou dies; Costas Simitis becomes leader and wins a vote of confidence shortly after Papandreou's death, when he was elected to the position of PASOK party president, a position that Papandreou never relinquished

A WORD ABOUT GREEK ARCHITECTURE

ALTHOUGH TODAY we are able to study the remains of a great variety of ancient Greek buildings, the mental picture formed at the sound of the words "Greek architecture" is likely to be that of a temple, and a Doric one at that. Though no city in classical times (500 BC–355 BC) was deemed complete without its agora (or city-center), its defensible acropolis (acro = high; polis = city), its theater, gymnasium, and stadium, it was the temple of the city's patron god or goddess that was commonly given the dominant position and the greatest honor. The chief temple often stood at the highest point of the acropolis, the nucleus around which the city grew in safety, itself enclosed by fortification.

In Mycenaean Greece, 1,000 years before the classical period, the chief building of a citadel was the king's palace, as seen at Mycenae, Tiryns, and Pylos. In these palace complexes the central feature is the *megaron*—a large rectangular room with the long walls extended to form the sides of an open porch, the roof of which was supported by columns. A single large doorway gives access to the megaron. In the center is a large hearth, the focus of the room: Around it, in a square plan, are four columns supporting the roof; in the right a raised platform for the royal throne. There are forecourts to these megara, and pillared gateways—copied from the Minoan palaces of Crete and replicated throughout Greek history. The Propylaea of the Acropolis at Athens (and of 20 other sites) derives from the Minoan gateway.

Clustered around the megaron and its forecourt are archive rooms, offices, oil-press rooms, workshops, potteries, shrines, corridors, armories, and storerooms for wine and oil and wheat—the whole forming an irregular complex of buildings quite unlike the precise, clear-cut arrangement that is later the hallmark of building in the classical period. This irregularity, characteristic of the Minoan palaces at Knossos, Mallia, and Phaistos on Crete, was one of the influences of that earlier and foreign culture on the Mycenaeans of the mainland.

But the megaron is Greek. The king's megaron, indeed a "great room," was essentially only the ordinary man's house built large; in some ordinary houses, as at Priene, the same megaron is found. And when the shrine ceased to be a mere house-chapel in a corner of the palace complex, as at Knossos, and the god was given a house of his own, his temple had the ground plan of that porched megaron. In its full development there is a porch, or maybe a room, also at the rear, and around it all runs a peristyle of columns. Thus the Greek temple is literally the god's house, intended not for the assembly of worshipers, but as a great room to contain the statue of the god.

The early temple builders found that sun-baked brick strengthened by horizontal and vertical timbers, if set on a stone footing, was a suitable material even for large buildings. This construction is seen at Knossos (circa 1900 BC) and at the Temple of Hera at Olympia 1,000 years later. The columns of the early temples were made of wood, and, later, when marble began to be used, constructional features appropriate to the use of timber were copied as decoration in the new material. It seems likely that the triglyph, the three-part stone slab set above the column and also above the space between columns in the Doric order, originates from a decorative wood slab that protected the beam ends of the ceiling from rain and rot—particularly when one looks at the six stone *guttae* always fixed below it, which seem to represent the six wood tre-nails, or pegs, that kept the slab in position. And the fluting of the Doric column is reminiscent of the grooves that the long strokes of the adze would make as the woodworker cut away the bark of a tree trunk before erecting it as the column.

If the origins of the Doric order are a matter of guesswork, this much is clear: that the Greeks used an elementary formula of vertical and horizontal lines of stone, so refined with skill and taste, with strict rules of proportion, that the total effect is one of balance, symmetry, and power. At the highest development, they added a series of optical corrections to ensure that the human eye, easily misled by the effect of light and shade in alternation, saw the whole as an apparent pattern of truly horizontal and vertical lines. In fact, with the application of these optical corrections, the entire building is made up of subtly curving or inclined surfaces. These refinements called for mathematical ability of a high order in the design and for extreme skill on the part of the masons.

In the Parthenon (5th century BC), the slight swell (*entasis*) and inward slant of the columns makes them seem straight-sided and vertical (which they are not); actual straightness would cause the eye to see them as waisted, and if vertical they would seem to be inclining outward. Also, without its slight upward curve, the steps of the platform (*stylobate*) would seem to sag under the line of standing columns. In short, the Greek mind took the simple idea of the upright and the crossbar, the child's building-block technique and, in developing it to its zenith in the Parthenon, produced a masterpiece that still informs us about those ingredients in a building that make for serenity combined with power, repose with majesty.

Marble was the perfect material for buildings in which sharp edges, clear-cut outline, precision, and the beauty of uncluttered wall surfaces were desired, so that each part, functional and decorative (the sculptured metopes and pediment), might do its work, and the horizontal members could lie without stress or mortar upon the supporting verticals.

The Doric order continued in use in Hellenistic (350 BC–215 BC) and Roman times, but it is easy to distinguish Greek from Roman Dorica. The later architects dared a wider space, enough for three triglyphs, between columns; they used a base for their columns, whereas a Greek Doric column rests directly on the stylobate; they economized often by omitting the fluting in the lower part of a column (where damage most often occurred); and they re-

duced the size of the capital most meanly. All these Hellenistic and Roman "improvements" are seen in Delos.

The Ionic order came to mainland Greece almost certainly from Asia Minor and the islands, when the Doric order was well established both there and in the colonies of Magna Graecia (southern Italy). Ionic columns have bases; the flutes have no sharp edges to them but are separated by a substantial fillet; the columns are more tall and slender; the capitals with their beautiful spiral volutes decorative; the architrave has lost its alternating triglyphs and metopes and, in Greece proper, has a frieze of plain or sculptured stone, in Asia Minor a string of dentils to suggest the beam ends of the ceiling. If the feeling of the heavier, more austere Doric order can be described as masculine, then the Ionic is certainly feminine (and very lovely), especially suitable for such smaller buildings as the Erectheum and the Temple of Nike on the Acropolis of Athens.

The Corinthian order came later. Its first appearances were in the temple at Bassae (circa 430 BC) and in the circular building (*tholos*) at Epidauros (360 BC), where one of the perfectly preserved capitals can be seen in the museum. It is decorative and graceful, and one may contrast the simplicity of its sculptured acanthus leaves and their slender tendrils with the complications bestowed on the Corinthian capital by later Hellenistic and Roman architects, in their constant striving for magnificence.

The classical Greeks rarely departed from the straight line and the rectangular plan; only a few circular buildings have survived—for instance, the Tholos at Delphi, the "folly" of the family of Philip of Macedon at Olympia, a temple at Samothrace built by Queen Arsinoe, and in the Agora at Athens, the building where the executive of the day lived.

— Guy Pentreath

BOOKS AND VIDEOS

Books

A. R. Burn's *The Pelican History of Greece* takes the reader from the Neolithic pioneers to the splendors of Athens to the last dark days when the philosophic schools were closed, capturing the culture of an amazing people. Extremely fluid, it is written for those who are not experts in classical literature. Just as erudite and enthusiastic is the *Oxford History of Greece and the Hellenistic World,* edited by John Boardman, Jasper Griffin, and Oswyn Murray, a comprehensive but never boring view of the ancient Greek world and its achievements. A late convert to classic Greece, Peter France will engage even the laziest reader in his *Greek as a Treat* (Penguin Books); theme by theme, with a sharp wit, he introduces readers to the greats—Homer, Pythagoras, Aeschylus, Socrates, and Plato—demonstrating how they still can enrich our 20th-century lives. C. M. Woodhouse's *Modern Greece: A Short History* (Faber and Faber) succinctly covers the ensuing development of Greece, from the fall of the Byzantine Empire to the War of Independence and the monarchy to the ongoing struggle between the socialist PASOK party and the conservative New Democracy party. *The Greeks: The Land and People Since the War* (Penguin), by James Pettifer, takes readers behind the postcard imagery of lazy beaches and sun-kissed villages to modern Greece's contradictions as he examines the far-reaching effects of the country's recent troubled past, including civil war and dictatorship.

John Julius Norwich's three-volume *Byzantium* (available through Penguin) is a good introduction to the medieval Byzantine empire. Timothy Ware's *The Orthodox Church* introduces the Westerner to the religion of the Greek people, while Paul Hetherington's *Byzantine and Medieval Greece, Churches, Castles, and Art* provides a useful introduction to Byzantine and Frankish mainland Greece.

Unearthing Atlantis, by Charles Pellegrino, is a fascinating book about Santorini. The idyllic youth of naturalist Gerald Durrell on the island of Corfu is recalled in many of his books, such as *My Family and Other Animals,* which are written with an unpretentious, precise style in a slightly humorous vein and are underrated as works of literature. Henry Miller's *The Colossus of Maroussi,* an enjoyable seize-the-day-as-the-Greeks-do paean that veers from the profound to the superficial—sometimes verging on hysteria—is the product of a trip Miller took to Greece, during which he experienced an epiphany.

Greece's premier writer Nikos Kazantzakis captures the strengths and weaknesses and the color of traditional Greek culture in his wonderful *Zorba the Greek*; he also wrote the classics *Christ Recrucified* and *The Odyssey.* Other modern Greek fiction will immerse readers in the joys and woes of Greece today: Kedros Books has an excellent series, *Modern Greek Writers* (✉ Gennadiou 3, Athens 10678, ☎ 01/360–9712; distributed in the United Kingdom by Forest Books), which includes *Farewell Anatolia,* by Dido Sotiriou, chronicling the traumatic end of Greek life in Asia Minor, and *Fool's Gold* by Maro Douka, about an aristocratic young woman who becomes enamored of and then disillusioned with the resistance movement to the junta. Noted for his translations of Kazantzakis, the late Kimon Friar demonstrated exquisite taste in his superb translations of modern Greek verse, including works by C. P. Cavafy, and the Nobel Laureates George Seferis and Odysseus Elytis. Friar's *Modern Greek Poetry* is published by the Efstathiadis Group in Athens. Overseas readers may have less difficulty finding Edmund Keeley and Philip Sherrard's *Voices of Modern Greek Poetry* (Princeton University Press).

Some people like to go back to the classics while in Greece. Try either Robert Fitzgerald's or Richmond Lattimore's translations of the *Iliad* and *Odyssey* of Homer, done in verse, unlike the clumsy prose translations you probably read in school. Take the *Iliad* as a pacifist work exposing the uselessness of warfare; read the *Odyssey* keeping in mind the relationships between men and women as illustrated by Odysseus and Penelope, Circe, and Calypso. Lattimore also translated

Greece's early lyric poets, Sappho and her lesser-known contemporaries, in a collection titled *Greek Lyric Poetry*. Aristophanes' play *The Wasps* is one of the funniest pieces of literature ever written. Although it isn't light reading, Thucydides' *Peloponnesian War* details the long struggle of Athens and Sparta, fought openly and through third parties, for and against democracy and autocracy. The events of the past 50 years and those of 2,500 years ago aren't so different.

Videos

A determination to live for the moment coupled with lingering fatalism still pervades Greek society. No film better captures this than Michael Cacoyannis's *Zorba the Greek* (1964; in English), starring the inimitable Anthony Quinn, Alan Bates, and Irene Pappas. Graced with the music of Mikis Theodorakis (the score won an Oscar even though Theodorakis's music was banned at the time in Greece), the film juxtaposes this zest for life with the harsh realities of traditional village society.

In perhaps the second-best-known film about Greece, Hellenic joie de vivre meets American pragmatism in *Never on Sunday* (1960; in English), directed by Jules Dassin. The late Melina Mercouri, a national icon, plays a Greek hooker, who in her simple but wise ways takes on the American who has come to reform her and teaches him that life isn't always about getting ahead.

The epic musical drama *Rembetiko* (1983; English subtitles), directed by Costas Ferris and awarded the Silver Bear in 1984, follows 40 years in the life of a rembetiko (Greek blues) singer, played by smoldering, throaty-voiced Sotiria Leonardou. The film, notable for its authenticity and the music's raw energy, spans the turbulent political history of Greece and the development of *rembetika* blues, which flourished from the 1920s until the '40s as 1.5 million Greeks were displaced from Asia Minor. They brought with them their haunting minor-key laments, as well as the Anatolian custom of smoking hashish; today rembetika is enjoying a resurgence with young Greeks.

Mediterraneo (1991; English subtitles) is a nostalgic, humorous depiction of life on a tiny, distant Greek island, occupied by Italian solders during World War II. The soldiers become inextricably involved with the island's vivid personalities—to the point that some refuse to leave when finally informed that the war has long been over. The movie, which won an Oscar for Best Foreign Film, features Vanna Barba, a popular Greek actress whose lusty yet stern gaze captivates the lead role.

One of Greece's leading directors, Theodoros Angelopoulos, has made several internationally acclaimed films, including *Journey to Kythera* (1984; English subtitles), which won for Best Screenplay in the 1984 Cannes festival. Considerably shorter than most of his films, it blends the mythical with the contemporary, detailing the life of a Greek civil war fighter who returns from the Soviet Union to reunite with his son in an adventure that leaves him and his wife on a raft bound for Kythera island. Manos Katrakis, considered one of Greece's finest stage actors, performs superbly (he died soon after), and the music and striking cinematography evoke Cavafy's famous poem, "Journey to Ithaki," familiar to all Greeks: "But do not hurry the voyage at all. It is better to let it last for long years; and even to anchor at the isle when you are old, rich with all that you have gained on the way."

A recent film that portrays life in Greece since tourism hit in the late '60s is *Shirley Valentine* (1989; in English). Set amid marvelous island scenes, the story is a cautionary tale about a bored British housewife who leaves her stultifying life to vacation in Greece. Here, she regains her identity through a liberating romance with the local flirt (Tom Conti speaking abominable Greek). In England, apparently, an unusually high number of women signed up for Greek language lessons after viewing the film. Although a bit dated, since the "kamaki" (men who prey on foreign women) is no longer in full force given the increased independence of Greek women, the movie is full of humor, sharp dialogue, and dazzling shots of the Aegean.

GREEK PLACE-NAMES

Abram	Αμπράμι
Achaea	Αχαία
Acronauplia	Ακροναυπλία
Aegina, Aigina, Egina	Αίγινα
Aigaleo	Αιγάλεω
Aigion	Αίγιο
Akrotiri	Ακρωτήρι
Amfissa	Άμφισσα
Amphiareion	Αμφιαρείον
Anavatos	Ανάβατος
Andritsena, Andritsaina	Ανδρίτσαινα
Andros Town (Chora)	Άνδρος (Χώρα)
Anilio	Ανήλιο
Ano Mera	Άνω Μερά
Anoyia	Ανώγεια
Anthochori	Ανθοχώρι
Antissa	Άντισσα
Apeiranthos, Apiranthos	Απείραθος
Apollonas	Απόλλωνας
Argolic Gulf, Argolikos Kolpos	Αργολικός Κόλπος
Argolid	Αργολίδα
Argos	Άργος
Arkadi Monastery	Μοναστίρι Αρκαδίου
Armolia	Αρμόλια
Arvanitis	Αρβανίτης
Askyphou plain	Οροπέδιο Ασκύφου
Aspropyrgos	Ασπρόπυργος
Avgonima, Avgonyma	Αυγώνυμα
Avlakia	Αυλάκια
Ayassos	Αγιάσος
Ayia Marina	Αγία Μαρίνα
Ayia Paraskevi	Αγία Παρασκευή
Ayia Roumeli	Αγία Ρούμελη
Ayia Sofia	Αγιά Σοφία
Ayia Triada	Αγία Τριάδα
Ayia Varvara	Αγία Βαρβάρα
Ayii Deka	Άγιοι Δέκα
Ayii Theodori	Άγιοι Θεοδώροι
Ayioi Anargyroi	Άγιοι Ανάργυροι
Ayioi Pantes.	Άγιοι Πάντες
Ayios Ioannis	Άγιος Ιωάννης
Ayios Nikolaos	Άγιος Νικόλαος
Ayios Nikolaos Anapafsas	Άγιος Νικόλαος Αναπαυσάς
Ayios Stephanos	Άγιος Στέφανος
Ayios Titos	Άγιος Τίτος
Ayos Ermogenis	Άγιος Ερμογένης
Ayos Isidoros	Άγιος Ισίδωρος
Ayos Konstantinos	Άγιος Κωνσταντίνος
Ayos Pavlos	Άγιος Παύλος
Bassae	Βασσές
Batsi	Μπατσί
Bay of Korthion	Όρμος Κορθίου
Brauron	Βραυρώνα

Cabirion	Καβείριο
Cave of Psychro, Psikro	Ψυχρο
Chalki, Chalkio	Χαλκί, Χαλκείο
Cheimaros tower, Chimarou	Πύργος Χειμάρρου
Chios, Hios	Χίος
Chlemoutsi Castle, Hlemoutsi	Κάστρο Χλεμούτσι
Chora, Hora	Χώρα
Chrisovitsa	Χρυσοβίτσα
Christos Elkomenos	Ελκόμενου Χριστού
Corfu	Κέρκυρα
Corinth, Korinthos	Κόρινθος
Cyclades	Κυκλάδες
Daskalopetra	Δασκαλοπέτρα
Dervenakia	Δερβενάκια
Diakofto	Διακοφτό
Didima	Δίδυμα
Dodecanese	Δωδεκάνησα
Dodona, Dodoni	Δωδώνα, Δωδώνη
Drepano	Δρέπανο
Egina, Aegina, Aigina	Αίγινα
Ekali	Εκάλη
Elafonisi	Ελαφονήσι
Elefsina	Ελευσίνα
Eleusis	Ελεύσις
Elis	Ηλεία
Elounda	Ελούντα
Emborio	Εμπόρειο
Engares	Εγγαρές
Epidauros, Epidavros	Επίδαυρος
Epiros, Epirus	'Ηπειρος
Eressos	Ερεσός
Ermioni	Ερμιόνη
Evia, Euboia, Euboea	Εύβοια
Falasarna	Φαλάσαρνα
Filoti	Φιλότι
Flerio	Φλέριο
Fodhele, Fodele	Φόδελε
Fourni	Φούρνοι
Frangokastello	Φραγκοκάστελλο
Gaidouronisi	Γαϊδουρόνησι
Galanado	Γαλανάδο
Galatas	Γαλατάς
Gavrion	Γαύριο
Gefira, New Monemvassia	Γέφυρα, Νέα Μονεμβασιά
Georgioupolis, Yioryioupoli	Γεωργιούπολη
Geropotamos river	Γέρω Ποταμός
Glifa	Γλύφα
Glyfada	Γλυφάδα
Gortyna, Gortys	Γόρτηνα, Γόρτυς
Gournes	Γούρνες
Gournia	Γουρνιά
Grotta	Γρόττα, Γκρότα
Gulf of Yera	Κόλπος Γεράς
Hania, Chania	Χανιά

Hephaistia	*Ηφαιστεία*
Heraion, Ireon	*Ηραίο*
Heraklion, Iraklio	*Ηράκλειο*
Hora Sfakia	*Χώρα Σφακίων*
Hydra	*Ύδρα*
Hymettos	*Υμηττός*
Idean Cave, Ideo Andro	*Ιδαίον Άντρον*
Ierapetra	*Ιεράπετρα*
Ikaria	*Ικαρία*
Ioannina	*Ιωάννινα*
Iria	*Ίρια*
Isthmia	*Ισθμία*
Kaisariani	*Καισαριανή*
Kalamata	*Καλαμάτα*
Kalambaka	*Καλαμπάκα*
Kalathas	*Καλαθάς*
Kalavrita	*Καλάβρυτα*
Kalloni	*Καλλονή*
Kaloritisa	*Καλορίτισσα*
Kamares Cave	*Σπήλαιο Καμαρών*
Kambia	*Καμπιά*
Kambos, Kampos	*Κάμπος*
Kaminia	*Καμίνια*
Kandia, Kantia	*Κάντια*
Kardamila, Kardamyla	*Καρδάμυλα*
Karlovassi	*Καρλόβασι*
Kastelli	*Καστέλλι*
Kastelli Kissamou	*Καστέλλι Κισσάμου*
Kastraki	*Καστράκι*
Katara	*Κατάρα*
Kato Zakro	*Κάτω Ζάκρος*
Kavala	*Καβάλα*
Kavasilas	*Καβάσιλας*
Keratea	*Κερατέα*
Kiato	*Κιάτο*
Kithairon, Kitheron	*Κιθαιρών*
Knossos	*Κνωσός*
Kokkari	*Κοκκάρι*
Kommos	*Κομμός*
Komotini	*Κομοτηνή*
Korfes	*Κορφές*
Koronos	*Κώρονας*
Koropi	*Κοροπί*
Kosta	*Κόστα*
Koutsi	*Κούτσι*
Kranidi	*Κρανίδι*
Kritsa	*Κριτσά*
Kyllini, Kilini, Killene	*Κυλλήνη*
Labou Mili, Lampou Myli	*Λάμπου Μύλοι*
Laconia	*Λακωνία*
Lake Voulismeni	*Λίμνι Βουλισμένη*
Langada	*Λαγκάδα*
Larissa	*Λάρισα*
Lasithi, Lasithio	*Λασίθι*

Lato	Λάτω
Lechaion	Λεχαίον
Legrena	Λεγρενά
Lesbos	Λέσβος
Libyan Sea	Λιβυκόν Πελαγός
Ligourio	Λυγουριό
Limin Hersonissos, Chersonissos	Λίμην Χερσονήσου
Limnopoula	Λιμνοπούλα
Limnos, Lemnos	Λήμνος
Limonas monastery	Μονή Λιμώνας
Lissos	Λισσός
Livadi Valley	Λιβαδιά
Loutra Killinis	Λουτρά Κυλλήνης
Loutro	Λουτρό
Makriyialos, Makrigialos	Μακρύγιαλος
Makronissos	Μακρόνησος
Malagari	Μαλαγκάρι
Mallia, Malia	Μάλια
Mandamados, Mantamados	Μανταμάδος
Manolates	Μανολάτες
Marathokambos	Μαραθόκαμπος
Marathon	Μαραθώνας
Marina Village	Αγία Μαρίνα
Markopoulos	Μαρκόπουλο
Maroussi, Amaroussion	Μαρούσι, Αμαρούσιον
Matala	Μάταλα
Megali Vrissi	Μεγάλη Βρύση
Megalo Meteoro, Metamorphosis	Το Μεγάλο Μετέωρο/ Μεταμόρφωση
Megara	Μέγαρα
Menites	Μένητες
Mesara	Μεσαρά
Mesogeion	Μεσογείων
Mesta	Μεστά
Meteora	Τα Μετέωρα
Metsovo	Μέτσοβο
Methana	Μέθανα
Mikri Vigla	Μικρή Βίγλα
Milia	Μηλιά
Miloi	Μυλοι
Mirabello Gulf, Kolpos Mirambellou	Κόλπος Μράμπελο
Mires	Μοίρες
Mochlos, Mohlos	Μοχλός
Molyvos, Mithimna, Methimna	Μόλυβος, Μήθυμνα
Monemvassia, Monemvasia	Μονεμβασιά
Moni	Μονη
Moria	Μόρια
Moudras	Μούδρας
Mt. Helmos	Χελμός Όρος
Mt. Kynthos	Όρος Κύνθος
Mt. Lykaeon	Όρος Λύκαιον
Mt. Minthis	Όρος Μίνθη

Mt. Mitsikelis	*Μιτσικέλι*
Mt. Ornon	*Όρος Ορνόν*
Mt. Panahaiko, Panakhaikon	*Όρος Παναχαϊκόν*
Mt. Parnis, Parnitha	*Ορος Πάρνης, Πάρνηθα*
Mt. Profitis Ilias	*Όρος Προφήτης Ιλίας*
Mt. Taygettus, Taygettos	*Όρος Ταύγετος*
Mt. Tomaros	*Τομάρος*
Mt. Zas	*Όρος Ζάς, Ζεύς*
Mt. Ziria, Z´npia, Mt. Killini	*Ζηρια, Όρος Κυλλήνης*
Mycenae, Mikine, Mikines	*Μυκήνες*
Myrina, Mirina, Kastro	*Μύρινα, Κάστρο*
Mystras	*Μυστράς*
Mytilinii	*Μυτιλήνη*
Nagos	*Ναγός*
Nauplion, Nafplio	*Ναύπλιο*
Naxos	*Νάξος*
Nea Epidauros	*Νέα Επίδαυρος*
Nea Makri	*Νέα Μάκρη*
Nea Moni	*Νέα Μονή*
Nemea	*Νεμέα*
Nida Plateau	*Κάμπος Νίδας*
Nimbros Gorge, Imbros Gorge	*Φαράγγι Νίμπρου,* *Φαράγγι Ίμπρου*
Olous	*Ολούς*
Olympia	*Ολυμπία*
Omalos Plain	*Οροπέδιο Ομαλός*
Ormos Marathokambos	*Όρμος Μαραθόκαμπου*
Paiania	*Παιανία*
Palaia Epidauros, Palea Epidaupus	*Παλαιά Επίδαυρος*
Palatia	*Παλάτια*
Paleochora; Paleohora	*Παλαιοχώρα*
Paleokastro, Palekastro, Palaikastro	*Παλαικάστρο*
Paleopolis	*Παλαιόπολη*
Pallini	*Παλλήνη*
Pamfila	*Πάμφιλα*
Panagitsa	*Παναγίτσα*
Panagia Hrisafitissa	*Παναγία Χρυσαφίτισσα*
Pandrossos, Pandroson	*Πάνδροσο*
Pantanassa monastery	*Μονή Παντάνασσας*
Pantoukios	*Παντουκιός*
Paros	*Πάρος*
Pastra	*Πάστρα*
Pateras	*Πατέρας*
Patmos	*Πάτμος*
Patras, Patra	*Πάτρα*
Patroklou	*Πάτροκλου*
Paximadia	*Παξιμάδια*
Peloponnesos	*Πελοπόννησος*
Pendeli	*Πεντέλη*
Penius River	*Πήνειος*
Perama, Perama Cave	*Πέραμα, Το Σπηλαίο τον* *Περάματος*
Perivleptos monastery	*Μονή Περιβλέπτου*

Perivoli	*Μονή Περιβόλη*
Petra	*Πέτρα*
Phaistos, Festos, Phaestos	*Φαίστος*
Phyle	*Φύλη*
Pikermi	*Πικέρμι*
Pindos	*Πίνδος*
Piraeus	*Πειραιάς*
Pirgos, Pyrgos	*Πύργος*
Pirgi Thermis	*Πύργοι Θερμής*
Pitsidia	*Πιτσίδια*
Plaka	*Πλάκα*
Platanos	*Πλάτανος*
Plataia	*Πλαταίες*
Platanakia	*Πλατανάκια*
Plati	*Πλατύ*
Plomari	*Πλωμάρι*
Polichnitos	*Πολιχνίτος*
Poliochni	*Πολιόχνη*
Poros	*Πόρος*
Portes	*Πόρτες*
Porto Heli, Porto Cheli, Portoheli	*Πόρτο Χέλι*
Potamia	*Ποταμιά*
Potamies, Potamos	*Ποταμιές, Ποταμός*
Pournias Bay	*Κόλπος Πουρνιάς*
Profitis Ilias	*Προφήτης Ηλίας*
Pseira	*Ψείρα*
Psili Ammos	*Ψιλή Άμμος*
Psiloritis, Ida, Idhi	*Ψηλορείτης, Ίδη*
Pyrgi	*Πυργί*
Pyrgos, Pirgos	*Πύργος*
Pythagorio	*Πυθαγόρειο*
Rafina	*Ραφήνα*
Repanidi	*Ρεπανίδι*
Rethymnon, Rethimno	*Ρεθυμνό*
Rhamnous	*Ραμνούς*
Rhodes	*Ρόδος*
Roussanou, Ayia Barbara	*Μονή Ρουσάνου, Μονή Άγιας Βαρβαράς*
Sacred Lake	*Ιερή Λίμνη*
Salamis, Salamina	*Σαλαμίς, Σαλαμίνα*
Salamis, straits of	*Στενόν Σαλαμών*
Samaria Gorge	*Φαράγγι Σαμαριάς*
Samos	*Σάμος*
Sangri	*Σαγκρί*
Sarakiniki Sarakina	*Σαρακήνα*
Saronic Gulf, Saronikos Kolpos	*Σαρωνικός Κόλπος*
Septsae, Spetses	*Σπέτσες*
Sigri	*Σίγρι*
Siteia, Sitia	*Σητεία*
Skala Eressou	*Σκάλα Ερεσού*
Sklavia	*Σκλαβιά*
Sklavokampos	*Σκλαβοκάμπος*
Souda Bay, O. Soudas	*Ορμός Σούδας*
Sougia, Souyia	*Σουγιά*

Sounion	*Σούνιο*
Sparta	*Σπάρτη*
Spetses	*Σπέτσες*
Sphaka	*Σφάκα*
Spinalonga	*Σπιναλόγκα*
Stavros	*Σταυρός*
t'Apilarou castle	*Κάστρο Απαλυρού*
Tatoi	*Τατόι*
Thanos	*Θάνος*
Thessaloniki	*Θεσσαλονίκη*
Thessaly	*Θεσσαλία*
Thimiana, Thymiana	*Θυμιανά*
Thorikos	*Θορικό*
Thripti	*Θρυπτή*
Timios Stavrou, Timiou Stavrou	*Τίμιου Σταυρού*
Tiryns, Tirinthos	*Τίρυνς, Τίρυνθος*
Tolo	*Τολό*
To Nissaki	*Το Νησάκι*
Toplou monastery	*Μονή Τοπλού*
Tragaia Valley	*Τραγαία*
Trahia	*Τραχειά*
Trikala	*Τρίκαλα*
Tripolis, Tripoli	*Τρίπολη*
Troezen	*Τροιζήν*
Tsabou	*Τσαμπού*
Tsamadou	*Τσαμαδού*
Tylissos	*Τύλισος*
Tzermiado	*Τζερμιάδο*
Vai	*Βάι*
Varia	*Βαρειά*
Varkiza	*Βάρκιζα*
Varlaam	*Μονή Βαρλαάμ*
Varybobi	*Βαρυμπόμπη*
Vatera	*Βατερά*
Vathi	*Βαθυ*
Vavili	*Βαβίλοι*
Virgin Odegetria Church	*Παναγία Οδηγήτρια*
Volissos	*Βολισσός*
Voni	*Βόνη*
Votsalakia	*Βοτσαλάκια*
Voula	*Βούλα*
Vouliagmeni	*Βουλιαγμένη*
Vouraikos Gorge	*Φαράγγι Βουραίκος*
Vranas	*Βρανάς*
Vrisses	*Βρύσες*
Vrondiani monastery, Moni Yronda	*Βρονδιανή, Μονή Βροντά*
Vrontados	*Βροντάδος*
Xylokastro	*Ξυλόκαστρο*
Za Cave	*Σπήλαιο Ζά, Ζεύς*
Zagora	*Ζαγορά*
Zakhlorou	*Ζαχλωρού*
Zakro, Zakros	*Ζάκρος*
Zoumberi	*Ζούμπερι*

GREEK VOCABULARY

The phonetic spelling used in English differs somewhat from the internationalized form of Greek place names. There are no long and short vowels in Greek; the pronunciation never changes. Note, also, that the accent is a stress mark, showing where the stress is placed in pronunciation.

Basics

Do you speak English?	Miláte angliká?
Yes, no	Málista *or* Né, óchi
Impossible	Adínato
Good morning, Good day	Kaliméra
Good evening, Good night	Kalispéra, Kaliníchta
Goodbye	Yá sas
Mister, Madam, Miss	Kírie, kiría, despiní
Please	Parakaló
Excuse me	Me sinchórite *or* signómi
How are you?	Ti kánete *or* pós íste
How do you do (Pleased to meet you)	Chéro polí
I don't understand.	Dén katalavéno.
To your health!	Giá sas!
Thank you	Efcharistó

Numbers

one	éna
two	dío
three	tría
four	téssera
five	pénde
six	éxi
seven	eptá
eight	októ
nine	enéa
ten	déka
twenty	íkossi
thirty	triánda
forty	saránda
fifty	penínda
sixty	exínda
seventy	evdomínda
eighty	ogdónda
ninety	enenínda
one hundred	ekató
two hundred	diakóssia
three hundred	triakóssia
one thousand	hília
two thousand	dió hiliádes
three thousand	trís hiliádes

Days of the Week

Monday	Deftéra
Tuesday	Tríti
Wednesday	Tetárti
Thursday	Pémpti
Friday	Paraskeví
Saturday	Sávato
Sunday	Kyriakí

Months

January	Ianouários
February	Fevrouários
March	Mártios
April	Aprílios
May	Maíos
June	Ióunios
July	Ióulios
August	Ávgoustos
September	Septémvrios
October	Októvrios
November	Noémvrios
December	Dekémvrios

Traveling

I am traveling by car . . . train . . . plane . . . boat.	Taxidévo mé aftokínito . . . me tréno . . . me aeropláno . . . me vapóri.
Taxi, to the station . . . harbor . . . airport	Taxí, stó stathmó . . . limáni . . . aerodrómio
Porter, take the luggage.	Akthofóre, pare aftá tá prámata.
Where is the filling station?	Pou íne tó vensinádiko?
When does the train leave for . . . ?	Tí óra thá fíyi to tréno ya . . . ?
Which is the train for . . . ?	Pío íne to tréno gía . . . ?
Which is the road to . . . ?	Piós íne o drómos giá . . . ?
A first-class ticket	Éna isitírio prótis táxis
Smoking is forbidden.	Apagorévete to kápnisma.
Where is the toilet?	Póu íne í toaléta?
Ladies, men	Ginekón, andrón
Where? When?	Póu? Póte?
Sleeping car, dining car	Wagonlí, wagonrestorán
Compartment	Vagóni
Entrance, exit	Íssodos, éxodos
Nothing to declare	Den écho típota na dilósso
I am coming for my vacation.	Érchome giá tis diakopés mou.
Nothing	Típota
Personal use	Prossopikí chríssi
How much?	Pósso?

I want to eat, to drink, to sleep.	Thélo na fáo, na pió, na kimithó.
Sunrise, sunset	Anatolí, díssi
Sun, moon	Ílios, fengári
Day, night	Méra, níchta
Morning, afternoon	Proí, mesiméri, *or* apóyevma
The weather is good, bad.	Ó kerós íne kalós, kakós.

On the Road

Straight ahead	Kat efthían
To the right, to the left	Dexiá, aristerá
Show me the way to . . . please.	Díxte mou to drómo . . . parakaló.
Where is . . . ?	Pou íne . . . ?
Crossroad	Diastávrosi
Danger	Kíndinos
Drive slowly!	Sigá!
Look out for the train (railroad crossing).	Prosséxte to tréno.

In Town

Will you lead me? take me?	Thélete na me odigíste? Me pérnete mazí sas?
Street, square	Drómos, platía
Where is the bank?	Pou íne i trápeza?
Far	Makriá
Police station	Astinomikó tmíma
Consulate (American, British)	Proxenío (Amerikániko, Anglikó)
Theater, cinema	Théatro, cinemá
At what time does the film start?	Tí óra archízi ee tenía?
Where is the travel office?	Pou íne to touristikó grafío?
Where are the tourist police?	Pou íne i touristikí astinomía?

Shopping

I would like to buy	Tha íthela na agorásso
Show me, please.	Díxte mou, parakaló.
May I look around?	Boró na ríxo miá matyá?
How much is it?	Pósso káni? (*or* kostízi)
It is too expensive.	Íne polí akrivó.
Have you any sandals?	Échete pédila?
Have you foreign newspapers?	Échete xénes efimerídes?
Show me that blouse, please.	Díxte mou aftí tí blouza.
Show me that suitcase.	Díxte mou aftí tí valítza.
Envelopes, writing paper	Fakélous, hartí íli
Roll of film	Film
Map of the city	Hárti tis póleos
Something handmade	Hiropíito

Wrap it up, please.	Tilixteto, parakaló.
Cigarettes, matches, please.	Tsigára, spírta, parakaló.
Ham	Zambón
Sausage, salami	Loukániko, salámi
Sugar, salt, pepper	Záchari, aláti, pipéri
Grapes, cherries	Stafília, kerássia
Apple, pear, orange	Mílo, achládi, portokáli
Bread, butter	Psomí, voútiro
Peach, figs	Rodákino, síka

At the Hotel

A good hotel	Éna kaló xenodochío
Have you a room?	Échete domátio?
Where can I find a furnished room?	Pou boró na vró epiploméno domátio?
A single room, double room	Éna monóklino, éna díklino
With bathroom	Me bánio
How much is it per day?	Pósso kostízi tin iméra?
A room overlooking the sea	Éna domátio prós ti thálassa
For one day, for two days	Giá miá méra, giá dió méres
For a week	Giá miá evdomáda
My name is. . . .	Onomázome. . . .
My passport	Tó diavatirió mou
What is the number of my room?	Piós íne o arithmós tou domatíou mou?
The key, please.	To klidí, parakaló.
Breakfast, lunch, supper	Proinó, messimergianó, vradinó
The bill, please.	To logariasmó, parakaló.
I am leaving tomorrow.	Févgo ávrio.

At the Restaurant

Waiter	Garsón
Where is the restaurant?	Pou íne to estiatório?
I would like to eat.	Tha íthela na fáo.
The menu, please.	To katálogo, parakaló.
Fixed-price menu	Menú
Soup	Soúpa
Bread	Psomí
Hors d'oeuvre	Mezédes, orektiká
Ham omelet	Omelétta zambón
Chicken	Kotópoulo
Roast pork	Psitó hirinó
Beef	Moschári
Potatoes (fried)	Patátes (tiganités)
Tomato salad	Domatosaláta

Vegetables	Lachaniká
Watermelon, melon	Karpoúzi, pepóni
Desserts, pastry	Gliká *or* pástes
Fruit, cheese, ice cream	Fróuta, tirí, pagotó
Fish, eggs	Psári, avgá
Serve me on the terrace.	Na mou servírete sti tarátza.
Where can I wash my hands?	Pou boró na plíno ta héria mou?
Red wine, white wine	Kokivó krasí, áspro krasí
Unresinated wine	Krasí aretsínato
Beer, soda water, water, milk	Bíra, sóda, neró, gála
Greek (formerly Turkish) coffee	Ellenikó kafé
Coffee with milk, without sugar, medium, sweet	Kafé gallikó me, gála skéto, métrio, glikó

At the Bank, at the Post Office

Where is the bank? . . . post office?	Pou íne i trápeza? . . . to tachidromío?
I would like to cash a check.	Thélo ná xargiróso mía epitagí.
I would like to change some money.	Théol na aláxo hrímata.
Stamps	Grammatóssima
By airmail	Aëroporikós
Postcard, letter	Kárta, grámma
Letterbox	Tachidromikó koutí
I would like to telephone.	Thélo na tilephonísso.

At the Garage

Garage, gas (petrol)	Garáz, venzíni
Oil	Ládi
Change the oil.	Aláksete to ládi.
Look at the tires.	Rixte mia matiá sta lástika.
Wash the car.	Plínete to aftokínito.
Breakdown	Vlávi
Tow the car.	Rimúlkiste tó aftokínito.
Spark plugs	Buzí
Brakes	Fréna
Gearbox	Kivótio tachitíton
Carburetor	Karbiratér
Headlight	Provoléfs
Starter	Míza
Axle	Áksonas
Shock absorber	Amortisér
Spare part	Antalaktikó

INDEX

WHEREVER
YOU TRAVEL,
*ℋ*ELP IS NEVER
FAR AWAY.

From planning your trip to providing travel assistance along the way, American Express® Travel Service Offices are always there to help you do more.

Greece

Athens
American Express Travel Service
2 Hermou Street
Syntagma Square
(30)(1) 32244976/7/8/9

Corfu Town
Greek Skies Travel (R)
20A Capodistria Street
(30)(661) 33410/32469

Fira Town
X-Ray Kilo (R)
15 Steps to Old Port
(30)(286) 23401/23601

Heraklion
Adamis Tours (R)
23, 25th August Street
(30)(81) 246202/223203

Igoumenitsa
Jolly Travel (R)
14 Ethn Antistaseos Street
(30)(665) 22406/24333

Myconos Town
Delia Travel Ltd. (R)
At the Quay
(30)(289) 22322/24300

Patras
Albatros Travel (R)
48 Othonos Amalias Street
(30)(61) 220127/224609

Rhodes Town
Rhodos Tours Ltd. (R)
29 Ammochostou Street
(30)(241) 21010

Salonica
Memphis Travel Service (R)
23 Nikis Avenue
(30)(31) 281217/222796/222745

Skiathos Town
Mare Nostrum Holidays Ltd. (R)
21 Papadiamanti Street
(30)(427) 21463/4

do more AMERICAN EXPRESS

Travel

www.americanexpress.com/travel